May 23–25, 2018
Chicago, IL, USA

Association for
Computing Machinery

Advancing Computing as a Science & Profession

GLSVLSI'18

Proceedings of the 2018

Great Lakes Symposium on VLSI

Sponsored by:

ACM SIGDA & IEEE CEDA

Supported by:

DEEPHi, Cādence, & ECE Illinois

Association for
Computing Machinery

Advancing Computing as a Science & Profession

The Association for Computing Machinery
2 Penn Plaza, Suite 701
New York, New York 10121-0701

ISBN: 978-1-4503-5724-1 (Digital)

ISBN: 978-1-4503-6149-1 (Print)

Additional copies may be ordered prepaid from:

ACM Order Department
PO Box 30777
New York, NY 10087-0777, USA

Phone: 1-800-342-6626 (USA and Canada)
+1-212-626-0500 (Global)
Fax: +1-212-944-1318
E-mail: acmhelp@acm.org
Hours of Operation: 8:30 am – 4:30 pm ET

Chairs' Welcome

Welcome to the 28th edition of the *Great Lakes Symposium on VLSI (GLSVLSI) 2018,* held at Chicago, IL. GLSVLSI is a premier venue for the dissemination of manuscripts of the highest quality in all areas related to VLSI, devices, and system-level design. The location of this year's GLSVLSI is Chicago, returning to the "Great Lakes" region of the USA. Conference will be held at Marriott Marquis Chicago located in downtown Chicago close to Lake Michigan and South Loop.

Chicago is the home of Willis Tower, Cloud Gate and Millennium Park, Navy Pier, Art Institute of Chicago, Field Museum of Natural History, Magnificent Mile, and Wrigley Field. The conference this year will host a social event aboard Chicago's First Lady Cruises for "Chicago Architecture Foundation River Cruise".

This year's central theme for GLSVLSI is *IoT Hardware and Heterogeneous Computing for Artificial Intelligence.* The conference will showcase a program highlighted by five keynote speeches related to the central theme by the following academic, industrial, and governmental leaders:

1. Matthew Casto, Chief, Air Force Research Lab, delivering the keynote entitled "Hardware Assurance: Trojans, Counterfeits, and Security in an Interconnected World".
2. Nikil Dutt, Chancellor's Professor, UC-Irvine, delivering the keynote entitled "Self-Awareness for Heterogeneous MPSoCs: A Case Study using Adaptive, Reflective Middleware".
3. Sharon Hu, Associate Dean, University of Notre Dame, delivering keynote entitled "A Cross-Layer Perspective for Energy Efficient Processing -- From Beyond-CMOS Devices to Deep Learning".
4. David Pellerin, Head of Global Business Development, Infotech/Semiconductor, Amazon Web Services, delivering keynote entitled "Connected Devices, AI, and Scale -- Trends Driving Semiconductor Innovation".
5. Wade Shen, Program Manager, DARPA, delivering keynote entitled "DARPA's Data Driven Discovery of Models (D3M) and Software Defined Hardware (SDH) programs".

Complementing the keynotes are six special sessions on:

1. Powering Heterogeneous IoT Systems: Design for Efficiency, Security, and Sustainability.
2. Emergence of Silicon Photonics in High-Performance Computing: How can the VLSI Community Contribute?
3. Artificial Intelligence at the Edge.
4. Implementing and Benchmarking Post-Quantum Cryptography in Hardware.
5. Stochastic and Approximate Computing for Emerging Learning and Communication Systems.
6. Circuits and Systems for Autonomous IoT Devices.

For the first time in 2018, GLSVLSI program is featuring panels. Panel chairs Ioannis Savidis and Avesta Sasan will be moderating panels on the timely topics of security and machine learning, respectively:

1. Securing the Systems of the Future -- Techniques for a Shifting Attack Space.
2. Low Power & Trusted Machine Learning.

Most importantly, GLSVLSI 2018 will continue the strong tradition of featuring a stellar technical program focusing on VLSI, devices and systems. The technical program is shaped by the strong representation of high-quality papers in the standard tracks in VLSI Design; VLSI Circuits and Power Aware Design; Computer-Aided Design; Testing, Reliability, Fault Tolerance; Emerging Computing and Post-CMOS Technologies; and Hardware Security. GLSVLSI 2018 adds a new track in "Machine Learning and Artificial Intelligence" to capture the increasing interest and demonstrated competence of our community in the emerging field that also helps shape the central theme of GLSVLSI 2018. There were 161 papers submitted to GLSVLSI 2018 from 22 countries. Thanks to tireless service of the track chairs, program committee members and anonymous reviewers, 97% of the submitted papers received 4+ reviews and more than 60% of the papers received 5+ reviews, for an average of 4.6 reviews per paper. The acceptance rate for the conference is 28.6%, with a program featuring 46 papers. Including the papers presented as posters, a total of 72 papers will be included in the proceedings. Special sessions add another ~20 invited papers on various exciting topics to the symposium organized by Yanjing Li, who has done an excellent job.

Our thanks go out to the organizing committee members Weisheng Zhao, Qi Zhu, Robert Wille, Yuan-Hao Chang, Miao Hu, Yi-Chung Chen and Kyle Rupnow for administering the various aspects of the conference that made this meeting possible. The track chairs (Massimo Poncino, Sudeep Pashricha, Sumeet Gupta, Ann Gordon-Ross, Bei Yu, Yanzhi Wang, Giorgio Di Natale, Ian G. Harris, Fadi Kurdahi, Sorin Cotofana, Gang Qu, Ramesh Karri, Philip Brisk, Yu Wang) have done an outstanding job in soliciting submissions, overseeing the review process and establishing the program sessions that showcase the best submissions at the conference. For the first time in 2018, the outstanding service of a few program committee members in each track is recognized. The process is centered around the nomination of track chairs based on quality of reviews and participation in the track discussions in the paper selection process. The selection for this award was very hard due to the outstanding service of so many of our PC members. The recipients of these inaugural awards of Best PC members are: Luca Cassano (Testing, Reliability and Fault Tolerance track), Ioannis Savidis (VLSI Circuits, and Power Aware Design track) and Benjamin Schafer (CAD track). In the inspiring light of this recognition, we would like to thank the track chairs, each PC member, and the anonymous reviewers, for their service, and hope to continue the tradition of best PC member recognitions for the GLSVLSI community.

We trust that you will find GLSVLSI 2018 highly rewarding and exciting in terms of the technical quality, networking opportunities, as well as content and diversity of the whole program.

Deming Chen	**Houman Homayoun and Baris Taskin**
General Chair	*Program Chairs*

Table of Contents

Session 3: Interconnects and Manycore Management

Session 4: Low Power Variation Aware Circuit Design

Session Chair: Inna Partin-Vaisband *(University of Illinois at Chicago)*

Session 5: The World of Neural Networks

Session Chair: Amlan Ganguly *(Rochester Institute of Technology)*

Session 6: New Solutions for Classic IP Protection Challenges

Session 7: Machine Learning and HW Accelerators

Session Chair: Fatemeh Tehranipoor *(San Francisco State University)*

Session 8: Scalable Simulation: Parallel and Approximate Computing

Session 9: Test and Fault Tolerance

Special Session 2: Emergence of Silicon Photonics in High-Performance Computing: How can the VLSI Community Contribute

Session Chair: Mahdi Nikdast *(Colorado State University)*

Special Session 3: Circuits and Systems for Autonomous IoT Devices

Session Chair: Emre Salman & Milutin Stanacevic *(Stony Brook University)*

Special Session 4: Implementing & Benchmarking Post-Quantum Cryptography in Hardware

Session Chair: Kris Gaj *(George Mason University)*

Special Session 5: Artificial Intelligence at the Edge

Session Chair: Cory Merkel *(Air Force Research Lab)* & Dhireesha Kudithipudi *(Rochester Institute of Technology)*

Special Session 6: Stochastic and Approximate Computing for Emerging Learning and Communication Systems

Session Chair: Jie Han & Yue Zhang *(University of Alberta & Beihang University)*

Poster Session 1

Poster Session 2

Panels

GLSVLSI 2018 Symposium Organization

General Chair:	Deming Chen (University of Illinois, USA)
Program Chairs:	Houman Homayoun (George Mason University, USA) Baris Taskin (Drexel University, USA)
Panels Chairs:	Avesta Sasan (George Mason University, USA) Ioannis Savidis (Drexel University, USA)
Proceedings Chair:	Kyle Rupnow (Inspirit IoT, Inc., USA)
Finance Chair	Weisheng Zhao (Beihang University, China)
Local Chair:	Qi Zhu (Northwestern University, USA)
Publicity Chair:	Yuan-Hao Chang (Academia Sinica, Taiwan) Miao Hu (Binghamton University, USA) Robert Wille (Johannes Kepler University, Austria)
Special Sessions Chair:	Yanjing Li (University of Chicago, USA)
Web & Registration Chair:	Yi-Chung Chen (SUNY at New Paltz, USA)
Steering Committee:	Jose Ayala (Univ. Complutense Madrid, Spain) Iris Bahar (Brown University, USA) Sanjukta Bhanja (University of South Florida, USA) Erik Brunvand (University of Utah, USA) Yehea Ismail (America University Cairo, Egypt) Alex K. Jones (University of Pittsburgh, USA) Fabrizio Lombardi (Northeastern University, USA) Hai (Helen) Li (Duke University, USA) Enrico Macii (Politecnico di Torino, Italy) Martin Margala (University of Massachusetts, USA) Ken Stevens (University of Utah, USA) Gang Qu (University of Maryland, USA) Yuan Xie (University of California Santa Barbara, USA) Zhiyuan Yan (Lehigh University, USA) Hai Zhou (Northwestern University, USA)

Program Committee (continued):

Jennifer Blain Christen (Arizona State University)
Jayita Das (Intel)
Jianwei Dai (Intel)
Jishen Zhao (University of California Santa Cruz)
Song Chen (University of Science and Technology of China)
Yasuhiro Takashima (University of Kitakyushu)
Donghwa Shin (Yeungnam University)
Daniel Grosse (University of Bremen & DFKI)
Hamed Tabkhi (Northeastern University)
Xiang Chen (George Mason University)
Weichen Liu (Nanyang Technological University)
Evangeline Young (The Chinese University of Hong Kong)
Wei Zhang (The Hong Kong University of Science and Technology)
Subhendu Roy (Cadence Design Systems)
Yukihide Kohira (The University of Aizu)
Hung-Ming Chen (National Chiao Tung University)
Bing Li (Technical University of Munich)
Wujie Wen (Florida International University)
Rickard Ewetz (University of Central Florida)
Benjamin Carrion Schafer (University of Texas Dallas)
Luca Cassano (Politecnico di Milano)
Alberto Bosio (LIRMM)
Christopher Harris (Auburn University)
Stefano Di Carlo (Politecnico di Torino)
Dimitris Gizopoulos (University of Athens)
Ramon Canal (Universitat Politècnica de Catalunya)
Wenjing Rao (University of Illinois Chicago)
Yanjing Li (University of Chicago)
Martin Margala (University of Massachusetts Lowell)
Sule Ozev (Arizona State University)
Spyros Tragoudas (Southern Illinois University)
Masahiro Fujita (University of Tokyo)
Andreas Veneris (University of Toronto)
Elena Ioana Vatajelu (TIMA Laboratory, France)
Peilin Song (IBM)
Zeljko Zilic (McGill University)
Samah Saeed (University of Washington, Tacoma)
Alex Orailoglu (University of California San Diego)
Ioannis Karafyllidis (Democritus University of Thrace)
Mayur Bubna (Synopsys, Inc.)
Anup Das (Drexel University)
Mathias Soeken (Ecole Polytechnique Fédérale de Lausanne)
Antonio Rubio (Universitat Politècnica de Catalunya)
Emanuel Popovici (University College Cork)
Georgios Ch. Sirakoulis (Democritus University of Thrace)

Program Committee (continued):

Anca Molnos (CEA LETI)
Amir Rahmani (UC Irvine, USA and TU Wien, Austria)
Dimin Niu (Samsung Semiconductor, Inc.)
Miao Hu (Binghamton University)
Lan Wei (University of Waterloo)
Dhireesha Kudithipudi (Rochester Institute of Technology)
Wujie Wen (Florida International University)
Amir Gholamipour (Western Digital)
Khaled Salama (King Abdullah University of Science & Technology)
Mohammed Zidan (University of Michigan Ann Arbor)
Baker Mohammad (Khalifa University)
Fabian Oboril (Karlsruhe Institute of Technology)
Amro Awad (University of Central Florida)
Fatemeh Tehranipoor (San Francisco State University)
Domenic Forte (University of Florida)
Mehran Mozaffari Kermani (University of South Florida)
Hassan Salmani (Howard University)
Guru Venkataramani (George Washington University)
Naghmeh Karimi (University of Maryland Baltimore County)
Yier Jin (University of Florida)
Avesta Sasan (George Mason University)
Jeyavijayan Rajendran (Texas A&M University)
Seyed-Abdollah Sohrab Aftabjahani (Intel)
Qiaoyan Yu (University of New Hampshire)
Kevin Kornegay (Morgan State University)
Ioannis Savidis (Drexel University)
Farinaz Koushanfar (University of California San Diego)
Yousef Iskander (Cisco Systems, Inc.)
Chengmo Yang (University of Delaware)
Michael Ferdman (Stony Brook University)
Anup Das (Drexel University)
Ying Wang (Chinese Academy of Sciences)
Amey Kulkarni (Velodyne LiDAR)
Sai Manoj Pudukotai Dinakarrao (Vienna University of Technology)
Xue Lin (Northeastern University)
Yang Yi (Virginia Tech)
Dimitrios Soudris (National Technical University of Athens)
Andrew Putnam (Microsoft)
Jing Li (University of Wisconsin-Madison)
Tinoosh Mohsenin (University of Maryland Baltimore County)
Tony Givargis (University of California Irvine)
Paul Bogdan (University of Southern California)
Sri Parameswaran (University of New South Wales)
Iris Bahar (Brown University)

Sponsors and Supporters

Technical Sponsors

Gold Corporate Contributors

Supporters

DARPA's Data Driven Discovery of Models (D3M) and Software Defined Hardware (SDH) Programs.

Wade Shen
DARPA
Arlington, VA
wade.shen@darpa.mil

BIOGRAPHY

Mr. Wade Shen joined DARPA in 2014 as a program manager. His research interests include machine learning, machine translation, speech recognition and data analytics for improved human/computer interaction.

Mr. Shen joined DARPA from the Massachusetts Institute of Technology, Lincoln Laboratory where he was an associate group leader in the Human Language Technology Group. Mr. Shen's area of research involved machine translation; speech; speaker and language recognition; information extraction and prosodic modeling for both small- and large-scale applications. Prior to joining MIT Lincoln Laboratory, Wade helped found and served as chief technology officer for Vocentric Corporation, a company specializing in speech technologies for resource-constrained and embedded applications.

Mr. Shen has served as the chair of Lincoln Laboratory's Advanced Concept Committee, on DARPA's Information Science and Technology (ISAT) study group and as the US technical representative for NATO's IST-078 and IST-102 speech/language processing study groups.

Mr. Shen received his master's degree in computer science from the University of Maryland, College Park and his bachelor's degree in electrical engineering and computer science from the University of California, Berkeley.

GLSVLSI '18, May 23–25, 2018, Chicago, IL, USA

ACM ISBN 978-1-4503-5724-1/18/05.
https://doi.org/10.1145/3194554.3200206

Self-Awareness for Heterogeneous MPSoCs: A Case Study using Adaptive, Reflective Middleware

Nikil Dutt
Department of Computer Science
University of California, Irvine
Irvine, CA 92697-3435, USA
Email: dutt@uci.edu
http://www.ics.uci.edu/~dutt

ABSTRACT

Self-awareness has a long history in biology, psychology, medicine, engineering and (more recently) computing. In the past decade this has inspired new self-aware strategies for emerging computing substrates (e.g., complex heterogeneous MPSoCs) that must cope with the (often conflicting) challenges of resiliency, energy, heat, cost, performance, security, etc. in the face of highly dynamic operational behaviors and environmental conditions. Earlier we had championed the concept of CyberPhysical-Systems-on-Chip (CPSoC), a new class of sensor-actuator rich many-core computing platforms that intrinsically couples on-chip and cross-layer sensing and actuation to enable self-awareness. Unlike traditional MPSoCs, CPSoC is distinguished by an intelligent co-design of the control, communication, and computing (C3) system that interacts with the physical environment in real-time in order to modify the system's behavior so as to adaptively achieve desired objectives and Quality-of-Service (QoS). The CPSoC design paradigm enables self-awareness (i.e., the ability of the system to observe its own internal and external behaviors such that it is capable of making judicious decision) and (opportunistic) adaptation using the concept of cross-layer physical and virtual sensing and actuations applied across different layers of the hardware/software system stack. The closed loop control used for adaptation to dynamic variation -- commonly known as the observe-decide-act (ODA) loop -- is implemented using an adaptive, reflective middleware layer.

In this talk I will present a case study of this adaptive, reflective middleware layer using a holistic approach for performing resource allocation decisions and power management by leveraging concepts from reflective software. Reflection enables dynamic adaptation based on both external feedback and introspection (i.e., self-assessment). In our context, this translates into performing resource management actuation considering both sensing information (e.g., readings from performance counters, power sensors, etc.) to assess the current system state, as well as models to predict the behavior of other system components before performing an action.

GLSVLSI'18, May 23-25, 2018, Chicago, IL, USA.

ACM ISBN 978-1-4503-5724-1/18/05.
DOI: https://doi.org/10.1145/3194554.3200203

BIOGRAPHY

Nikil Dutt is a Chancellor's Professor of CS, Cognitive Sciences, and EECS at the University of California, Irvine. He received a PhD from the University of Illinois at Urbana-Champaign (1989). His research interests are in embedded systems, EDA, computer architecture and compilers, distributed systems, and brain-inspired architectures and computing. He has received numerous best paper awards and is coauthor of 7 books. Professor Dutt has served as EiC of ACM TODAES and AE for ACM TECS and IEEE TVLSI. He is on the steering, organizing, and program committees of several premier EDA and Embedded System Design conferences and workshops, and has also been on the advisory boards of ACM SIGBED, ACM SIGDA, ACM TECS and IEEE ESL. He is an ACM Fellow, IEEE Fellow, and recipient of the IFIP Silver Core Award.

Hardware Assurance: Trojans, Counterfeits, and Security in an Interconnected World

Matthew Casto
Air Force Research Laboratory,
Sensor's Directorate, Trusted
Electronics Branch, USA
Matthew.Casto@us.af.mil

BIOGRAPGY

Dr. Matthew Casto is Chief of the Air Force Research Laboratory, Sensor's Directorate, Trusted Electronics Branch. He is the Air Force's Hardware Assurance technical lead for the Department of Defense (DoD) Joint Federated Assurance Center, and the Science and Technology technical execution lead for the DoD Trusted and Assured Microelectronics Initiative. Dr. Casto is a Senior Electronics Engineer with a BSEE and MSEE degree from Wright State University, and a PhD from The Ohio State University Electro-science Laboratory. Matt is a member of the IEEE and has authored numerous publications and patents in the areas of non-linear and electro-thermal device modeling, advanced mixed-signal integrated circuit, system on a chip, design and characterization, and the design and analysis of secure, trustworthy microelectronics.

GLSVLSI '18, May 23–25, 2018, Chicago, IL, USA

ACM ISBN 978-1-4503-5724-1/18/05.
https://doi.org/10.1145/3194554.3194555

A Cross-Layer Perspective for Energy Efficient Processing - From beyond-CMOS Devices to Deep Learning

X. Sharon Hu
University of Notre Dame
Notre Dame, Indiana, USA
shu@nd.edu

ABSTRACT

As Moore's Law based device scaling and accompanying performance scaling trends are slowing down, there is increasing interest in new technologies and computational models for fast and more energy-efficient information processing. Meanwhile, there is growing evidence that, with respect to traditional Boolean circuits and von Neumann processors, it will be challenging for beyond-CMOS devices to compete with the CMOS technology. Nevertheless, some beyond-CMOS devices demonstrate other unique characteristics such as ambipolarity, negative differential resistance, hysteresis, and oscillatory behavior. Exploiting such unique characteristics, especially in the context of alternative circuit and architectural paradigms, has the potential to offer orders of magnitude improvement in terms of power, performance and capability.

In order to take full advantage of beyond-CMOS devices, however, it is no longer sufficient to develop algorithms, architectures and circuits independent of one another. Cross-layer efforts spanning from devices to circuits to architectures to algorithms are indispensable. This talk will examine energy-efficient neural network accelerators for embedded applications in this context. Several deep neural network accelerator designs based on cross-layer efforts spanning from alternative device technologies, circuit styles and architectures will be highlighted. A comprehensive application-level benchmarking study for the MNIST dataset will be presented. The discussions will demonstrate that cross-layer efforts indeed can lead to orders of magnitude gain towards achieving extreme scale energy-efficient processing.

CCS Concepts/ACM Classifiers

• Emerging technologies, architectures, neural networks

Author Keywords

Beyond-CMOS devices; computing with emerging technologies; neural network accelerators; cellular neural networks

BIOGRAPHY

X. Sharon Hu is a professor in the department of Computer Science and Engineering at the University of Notre Dame, USA. Her research interests include low-power system design, circuit and architecture design with emerging technologies, hardware/software co-design and real-time embedded systems. She has published more than 300 papers in these areas. Some of her recognitions include the Best Paper Award from the Design Automation Conference and from the IEEE Symposium on Nanoscale Architectures, and the NSF CAREER award. She has participated in several large government and industry sponsored center-level projects and is a theme leader in an NSF/SRC E2CDA project. She is the General Chair of Design Automation Conference (DAC) in 2018, was the TPC chair of DAC in 2015, and was a member of TPC and Executive Committees of a number of other conferences. She also served as Associate Editor for IEEE Transactions on VLSI, ACM Transactions on Design Automation of Electronic Systems, etc. and is an Associate Editor of ACM Transactions on Cyber-Physical Systems. X. Sharon Hu is a Fellow of the IEEE.

GLSVLSI'18, May 23-25, 2018, Chicago, IL, USA.

ACM ISBN 978-1-4503-5724-1/18/05.
DOI: https://doi.org/10.1145/3194554.3200204

Logic-Encrypted Synthesis for Energy-Harvesting-Powered Spintronic-Embedded Datapath Design

Arman Roohi, Ramtin Zand, and Ronald F. DeMara
Department of Electrical and Computer Engineering, University of Central Florida, Orlando, Florida, 32816

ABSTRACT

The objectives of advancing secure, intermittency-tolerant, and energy-aware logic datapaths are addressed herein by developing a spin-based design methodology and its corresponding synthesis steps. The approach selectively-inserts Non-Volatile (NV) Polymorphic Gates (PGs) to realize datapaths which are suitable for intrinsic operation in Energy-Harvesting-Powered (EHP) devices. Spin Hall Effect (SHE)-based Magnetic Tunnel (MTJs) are utilized to design NV-PGs, which are combined within a Flip-Flop (FF) circuit to develop a PG-FF realizing Boolean logic functions with inherent state-holding capability. The reconfigurability of PGs is leveraged for logic-encryption to enhance the security of the developed intermittency-resilient circuits, which are applied to ISCAS-89, MCNS, and ITC-99 benchmarks. The results obtained indicate that the PG-FF based design can achieve up to 7.1% and 13.6% improvements in terms of area and Power Delay Product (PDP), respectively, compared to NV-FF based methodologies that replace the CMOS-based FFs with NV-FFs. Further PDP improvements are achieved by using low-energy barrier SHE-MTJ devices within the PG-FF circuit. SHE-MTJs with 30kT energy exhibit 40.5% reduction in PDP at the cost of lower retention times in the range of minutes, which is still sufficient to achieve forward progress in EHP devices having more than hundreds of power-on and power-off cycles per minute.

ACM Reference Format:
Arman Roohi, Ramtin Zand, and Ronald F. DeMara. 2018. Logic-Encrypted Synthesis for Energy-Harvesting-Powered Spintronic-Embedded Datapath Design. In *GLSVLSI '18: 2018 Great Lakes Symposium on VLSI, May 23–25, 2018, Chicago, IL, USA.* ACM, New York, NY, USA, Article 4, 6 pages. https://doi.org/10.1145/3194554.3194557

1 INTRODUCTION

Energy-harvesting-powered computing offers intriguing and vast opportunities to dramatically transform the landscape of IoT devices and wireless sensor networks [9]. These devices require drastically-reduced energy consumption such that they are able to operate using only ambient sources of light, kinetic, and electromagnetic energy [4] as a means to achieve battery-free computing [13]. Thus, energy-harvesting-powered devices could enable a sustainable computing platform for future medical, aerospace, and IoT applications. energy-harvesting-powered devices are characterized by intermittent behavior, which can result in disturbances in execution of programs, data loss, glitch conditions, and lack of execution progress that may lead to irregular and unpredictable results [11].

To implement intermittent-resilient computing architectures, Non-Volatile Flip-Flops (NV-FFs) fulfill essential roles as a hardware-based approach. Various techniques are proposed to address the intermittency challenge facing energy-harvesting-powered designs. In [7, 17], a traditional checkpointing approach is utilized to ensure the accurate forward progress of computation, whereby any volatile execution context is proactively preserved in Non-Volatile Memory (NVM) prior to anticipated periods of power failure. A checkpointing approach may suffer from internal and external inconsistencies after each power loss. Internal inconsistency occurs when the execution context is partially-retained in NVM, while external inconsistency arises when the power failure occurs between two checkpoints [16]. DINO [10] innovated a checkpointing-based approach that utilizes non-volatile versioning to retain the memory consistency. Duty Cycling with Scheduling [3] offers another approach for tolerating intermittence. In this method, critical states of the processor will be partially-retained before the power failure, then the device will enter an extremely-low power mode. However, this results in full availability of the device only when power interruption is unlikely, which can incur relatively long sleeping periods due to the inevitable power outages in many energy harvesting-powered systems. Chain [5] is another model for programming intermittent devices, in which forward-progress is ensured at the task granularity level. It utilizes idempotent processing concepts to make tasks restartable, whereas they never incur discrepancies and thus act to keep NVM coherent. In [12], a Non-Volatile MIPS Processor (NVP) is introduced in which specific blocks, such as register files and pipeline registers, were replaced by non-volatile elements. NVP uses a checkpointing approach to retain the processor volatile states, which may result in the mentioned internal and external inconsistencies in non-volatile elements. Additionally, the mentioned approaches require an extra supporting circuitry such as capacitor arrays and voltage detection systems that impose large area consumption, which is a critical challenge for area-constrained IoT devices since conventional NV-FF register-based designs cannot detect power failure to store and to retain checkpoints without these additional circuits.

Moreover, the ever-increasing growth in the usage of energy-harvesting powered devices amplifies their hardware security issues. Hardware security threats in the integrated circuit (IC) supply chain, including hardware counterfeiting and Trojans, reverse engineering and IP piracy cost the US economy more than $200 billion annually [6]. Logic encryption/locking [14, 20] techniques are developed as highly-used countermeasures for reverse engineering, injecting hardware Trojan and tampering with IP privacy [15].

GLSVLSI '18, May 23–25, 2018, Chicago, IL, USA

ACM ISBN 978-1-4503-5724-1/18/05...$15.00
https://doi.org/10.1145/3194554.3194557

In [15, 20], XOR-XNOR key gates are inserted to hide designs' logic functionalities. Roy et al. in [20], randomly inserted XOR-XNOR gates to make a design resilient in presence of physical tampering. Alasad et al. [1] inserted MUXs instead of XOR-XNOR gates in a way that maximizes the hamming distance between the correct and incorrect outputs. These techniques are susceptible to most critical reverse engineering attacks, such as sensitization [14] and Boolean Satisfiability (SAT) based attacks [22]. So, several techniques as countermeasures for SAT attacks such as Anti SAT [24], which is vulnerable to SPS attacks, and SARLock [25], which is vulnerable to DDIP. Since implementing this technique requires reconfigurability, conventional CMOS-based implementation leads to increase in area/power consumption and complexity. Therefore, emerging technologies, such as Spintronics [2], are being studied.

In this paper, we propose a new approach to eliminate the need for checkpointing while reducing data movement via intrinsic pipelining capabilities of non-volatile elements in the datapath. In particular, non-volatile datapaths will be researched by designing spin-based polymorphic gates which embed non-volatility within the logic elements themselves. The designed polymorphic gates provide limited reconfigurability, which is leveraged to increase hardware security features via logic encryption.

2 PROPOSED APPROACH

2.1 Secure intermittent-robust PG-based design

2.1.1 Spin-based polymorphic gate (PG). Polymorphic electronics were introduced in [21], whereby a PG would be an AND gate or OR gate depending if VDD is 3.3V or 1.5V, respectively. Various CMOS-based polymorphic gates have employed mechanisms such as gradations in VDD and signaling levels, or temperature to achieve reconfigurability. Meanwhile, the spin-based devices can naturally function as polymorphic threshold gates since their computational mechanism is accumulation-mode operation that realizes reconfigurable logic functions with inherent security attributes. Figure 1(a) shows the schematic of 3-input Non-Volatile Polymorphic Gates (NV-PGs), which is designed using spin-Hall Effect (SHE)-based Magnetic Tunnel Junction (MTJ) devices [18, 19]. A pre-charge sense amplifier (PCSA) [26] is utilized to sense the state of the SHE-MTJs. Reference MTJ dimensions are designed such that its resistance value in parallel configuration is between low resistance, R_{Low}, and high resistance, R_{High}, of the PG cells. The minimum current required for switching the state of the SHE-MTJ devices is called the critical current (I_C), which is relative to the dimensions of the device. In an n-input NV-PG, the device is designed such that at least (n-1)/2 of the input transistors should be ON to produce a switching current amplitude greater than the critical current. For instance, by affixing one of the three input transistors in ON or OFF states upon demand during the circuit operation, then a 2-input OR gate or a 2-input AND gate can be realized, respectively.

The functionality of the proposed 2-input OR, NOR, AND, and NAND gates implemented by SHE-MTJ based PGs have been validated by SPICE circuit simulator using parameters listed in Table 1, as shown in Fig. 1(b). Figure 1(c) shows the proposed 3-input and 5-input PGs containing two and three control bits, respectively, which can determine the functional modes of the gates. For instance,

Table 1: Simulation Parameters of SHE-based PGs.

Parameter	Description	Value
3-PG	HM Volume (L×W×T)	100×60×3 nm^3
	MTJ Area (L×W)	60×30×π/4 nm^2
5-PG	HM Volume (L×W×T)	150×80×3 nm^3
	MTJ Area (L×W)	80×40×π/4 nm^2
$I_{C\text{-}3\text{-}PG}$	SHE1 Critical Current	108 μA
$I_{C\text{-}5\text{-}PG}$	SHE2 Critical Current	139 μA
θ_{SHE}	Spin Hall Angle	0.3
ρ_{HM}	Resistivity	200 $\mu\Omega.cm$
ϕ	Potential Barrier Height	0.4 V
t_{ox}	Thickness of oxide barrier	1.2 nm
α	Gilbert Damping factor	0.08
M_s	Saturation magnetization	10e5 A.m^{-1}

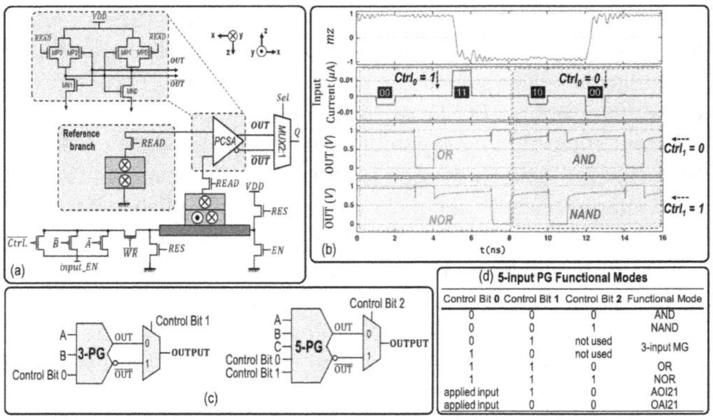

Figure 1: (a) SH-MTJ based 3-input PG, (b) 2-input OR, NOR, AND and NAND logic using 3-input PG, (c) 3-input and 5-input SHE-MTJ based PGs, (d) 5-input PG Functional Modes.

various functional modes of a 5-input PG are shown in Fig. 1(d). The PGs utilize intra-gate control to provide a functionally-complete set of Boolean logic expressions.

2.1.2 PG-based flip-flop (PG-FF) design. The PG-FF circuit is composed of an NV-PG based master latch using SHE-MTJ devices, as well as a CMOS-based slave latch, as shown in Fig. 2(a). In A PG-FF, a targeted Boolean logic can be implemented and stored in non-volatile (NV) PG within the master latch, where data can be held during the power OFF interval due to the non-volatility feature of SHE-MTJs. While, the stored data in NV-PG can be read and moved to the slave latch when the power is ON again. The proposed PG-FF circuit can intrinsically compute the primary Boolean expressions, in addition to storing a value with near-zero standby power, resulting in area, complexity, and power reductions. Moreover, utilization of PG-FFs in large scale designs reduces the duration of signal propagation between two NV elements in which data will be lost if a power failure occurs. Without non-volatility, then upon power resumption, pipeline flushing would be required along with a sufficient checkpointing mechanism in hardware and/or middleware. Those may be too costly or prohibitive in lightwieght energy-harvesting circuits.

PG-FF functionality is verified by SPICE circuit simulation using the SHE-MTJ model developed by Kazemi et al. [8], as depicted in Fig. 2(b). The SHE-MTJ is initially in the Parallel (P) configuration, which denotes binary "0". The applied inputs ABC = 001 produces

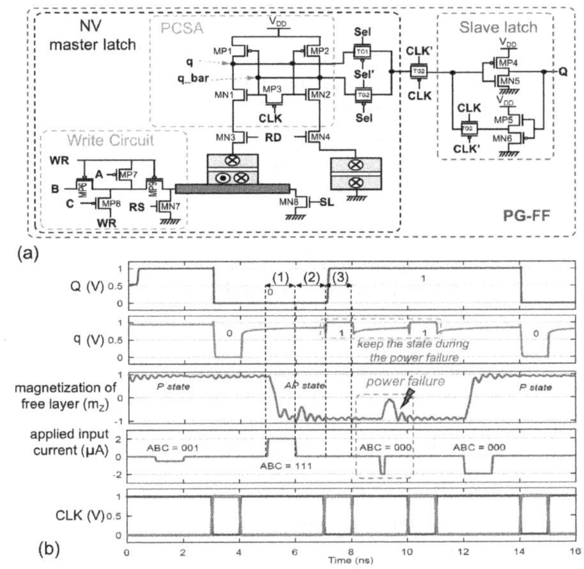

Figure 2: (a) Schematic of PG-FF circuit, and (b) functionality of PG-FF in presence of power failure.

an input charge current of |-56| μA, which is smaller than SHE-MTJ critical current, i.e., I_C=108 μA. Thus, the SHE-MTJ state is not changed and remains in the P state, which in the next cycle denotes binary 0 as an output of the slave latch. Then, the input is set to ABC = 111 generating a 196 μA charge current that changes the SHE-MTJ's state from P to an anti-parallel (AP), hence the slave latch outputs one in the next cycle. The third and fourth cycles show its functionality in presence of power failure and power-up situations, respectively. Due to the non-volatility feature of SHE-MTJ devices, its state remains unchanged during the power-off, which verifies the desired forward progress of the design's operation while supporting intermittent operation. In order to design optimized NV architectures using the proposed PG-FF, we will develop a systematic methodology, which incorporates all PG-FF features to design power-failure tolerant architectures. The proposed approach leverages the maximum capability of PG-FFs in terms of replacement and implementation steps.

2.1.3 Low-energy barrier PG-FF design. Energy-harvesting- powered devices are characterized by having charge/discharge cycles, which may occur hundreds of times per minute due to the capacity limitation of power supplies. Although NV-FF and PG-FF implementations provide power failure tolerant designs, the write energy consumption of NV elements remains an issue, which can lead to an increase in the number of charge/discharge cycles. On the other hand, since the power-off periods are normally less than a second in energy-harvesting-powered devices, the NV elements in PG-FFs are required to retain the stored data for only a few seconds to ensure the forward progress. Thus, in this paper the thermal barrier properties of the nanomagnet are leveraged to achieve the required retention time, i.e. the average time period before the magnetization of the nanomagnet flips due to thermal noise, while reducing the write energy consumption.

The NV attributes of SHE-MTJ devices can be tuned to meet these goals. The energy barrier and retention time are related by the following expression [23], $\tau = \tau_0 exp(\Delta/kT)$, where Δ represents the thermal barrier of the nanomagnet and it is related to the uniaxial anisotropy (H_K), saturation magnetization (M_s) and the volume of a nanomagnet (Vol.) through $\Delta = (H_K)(M_s)(Vol.)/2$. τ_0 is a material dependent quantity that can range from 1 ps to 1 ns [23]. For most memory-centric applications, the retention time τ is arranged to be 10-15 years by choosing a Δ between 40-60 kT. On the other hand, the critical spin-current is linearly proportional to the thermal barrier, Δ [23]. Thus, for applications that do not require retention times of years, the thermal barrier of nanomagnets can be reduced by lowering their volume, uniaxial anisotropy or their saturation magnetization. This ultimately reduces the charge currents that are required for write operation, which can result in significant energy improvement due to the quadratic relationship between the Ohmic (I^2R) losses and the input write currents. In this paper, PG-FFs using SHE-MTJ devices with 30kT energy barriers are investigated that can achieve retention times ranging from minutes to hours, while providing at least 50% energy reduction.

2.1.4 Secure PG-FF design. The reconfigurability characteristic of SHE-MTJ based PGs is achieved by means of the multiplexer (MUX) and control bits existing in their structure. Despite the area and performance overheads imposed to the design by using PGs, they can be utilized for logic encryption in addition to enabling intermittent computing, which can provide the hardware with increased security capabilities. In the proposed approach, each PG and its corresponding MUX can be leveraged as the encryption key gates, which increases the key bit space. It means to retain the correct operation of the design, the appropriate key bits of both PGs and MUXs should be applied. The length of the key is determined by the number of inserted PG-FFs, which is normally greater than or equal to the number of output bits. While, in the previous MUX-based logic encryption methods [1, 15], the key length is limited to the number of outputs in a design. The vulnerability of PG-FF based circuits is similar to that of the designs that are secured by the random insertion of XOR/XNOR gates [15, 20]. In the proposed approach, the PGs will be inserted to the logic circuits based on a methodology that is designed to enable intermittent computing. Therefore, the main focus of the methodology is on intermittency-resilient and the logic encryption is the secondary objective. Thus, the inserted PGs and MUXs may not enable the intermittent-robust design to achieve the optimum Hamming distance (HD) of ~50%, which is a security metric defined based on the number of bit positions at which a correct and faulty output are different. In order to minimize the memory overhead, the configuration bits of PGs and MUXs, which are considered as key bits should be stored in an external non-volatile memory. To implement and synthesize an optimized, secure, and intermittent-resilient logic circuit using PG-FFs, a systematic methodology is developed that is described in the next section.

2.2 PG insertion methodology

To design optimized NV architectures using the proposed PG-FF, we develop a methodology that incorporates all PG-FF features to design partially-secure power-failure tolerant architectures. This approach leverages the maximum capability of PG-FFs in terms of replacement and implementation steps, which incorporates various criteria to design a tolerant circuit in the presence of power failure with minimum PDP overhead.

The proposed algorithm, which is developed in Python consists of two main procedures: (1) `intermittency()`, and (2) `logic encryption()`. The PG insertion methodology takes a Hardware Description Language (HDL) representation of a datapath and PG-based gate modules as its inputs and produces an optimized NV-enhanced datapath. The proposed methodology is described in Algorithm 1, which first explores the HDL of the logic circuit and finds the gates and pipeline registers that can be combined and replaced by spin-based PG-FF circuits, and the remainder of the pipeline registers will be replaced by NV-FFs. Next, the optimized intermittent-robust design is investigated to encrypt the datapath and generate a key based on Hamming distance (HD) calculations as a security metric. In particular, the algorithm first finds all of the FFs in the design, and then checks the cone of logic gates connected to the inputs of the FFs. If each cone of gates meets the circuit-level criteria mentioned below, then the cone and its corresponding FF can be replaced by an PG-FF cell. The three primary criteria regarding the intermittency issue are:

Criterion #1: it should be possible to implement the cone of gates with a single PG. Since each PG-FF operates in one clock cycle, the cone of combinational logic gates that are merged with a master latch should operate within one clock cycle to ensure the correct functionality. Hence, use of more than one PGs for complex functions could increase propagation delay, which might lead to timing violations.

Criterion #2: fan-out of every gates in the cone should not exceed one. This is mainly because in the process of PG-insertion a multiple logic gates can be implemented by a single PG that exists in the structure of the PG-FF's master latch. Therefore, the logic gates existing in the cone will not have separate outputs to drive other logic gates, and there will be only one output for the PG showing the combined logic of the merged gates.

Criterion #3: none of the gates in the cone should be connected to the output of another FF. This will cause the selected cone to include two FFs requiring two clock cycles for operation, while based on the developed algorithm the cone will be replaced by a single PG-FF resulting in a timing violation. Therefore, due to the timing considerations, each of the cones can include only a single FF and multiple logic gates.

If all of the aforementioned conditions are satisfied, then the cone of gates and their corresponding FF will be replaced by a single PG-FF. Otherwise, only the FF is replaced by a simple NV-FF. Herein, the primary objective of the algorithm is implementation of intermittent-robust datapaths. The secondary objective is enhancing hardware security through logic encryption using the inserted PGs. In order to reduce the overhead of logic encryption, the proposed algorithm follows a recursive process to find the minimum key length required to achieve a desired security, which is directly related to the number of inserted PGs utilized for encryption. In particular, first the logic-encryption procedure takes the intermittent-resilient datapath from the intermittency procedure, and starts with using only one PG to generate the key and calculates the HD between the correct and wrong output bits. Then, the procedure checks the below criteria (4) and (5), and if they are achieved it will stop. Otherwise it will increment the number

Algorithm 1 PG-insertion Methodology

1: **Input:** Hardware Description Language (HDL) code
2: **Output:** Logic-encrypted intermittent-robust HDL code
3: **procedure** **`intermittency()`**
4: *gate_list* ← all FFs in a netlist
5: **for** i ← 1 to length(*gate_list*) **do**
6: *input_list* ← inputs of connected gate to gate$_i$
7: **for** item in *input_list* **do**
8: **`check`** (criterion #3)
9: **`update`** (*input_list*)
10: **`check`** (criterion #1 and criterion #2)
11: **`update`** (*gates_cone*)
12: **go to** 6 until one of each criterion is violated.
13: **end for**
14: **`replace`** (*gates_cone* by PG_FF) **if** size (*gates_cone*) > 2 **else** **`replace`** (*gates_cone* by NV_FF)
15: **`update`** HDL code
16: **end for**
17: **end procedure**
18: **procedure** **`logic encryption()`**
19: **for** n ← 1 to #inserted PG-FFs **do**
20: *key_size* ← $2^{3n_1+2n_2}$ ▷ n ← n_1(#5-PG-FFs) + n_2(#3-PG-FFs)
21: **`compute`** $HD_{(n)}$ based on *key_size*
22: **`store`** (key bits in NVM) **if** (criterion #4 or criterion #5) **else** (HD_list ← $HD_{(n)}$)
23: **end for**
24: **end procedure**

of PGs utilized for producing the key and repeats this process until one of the below criteria are met:

Criterion #4: roughly 50% HD is achieved. To maximize the security of a PG-inserted design, the correlation between the wrong output and the correct output should be minimized to achieve better encryption. Thus, the measured HD value needs to be approximately 50% to demonstrate a highly-encrypted implementation.

Criterion #5: increasing the key length has less than 1% effect on the calculated HD values. This means that if increasing the number of PGs used for logic-encryption is not significantly improving the HD values, then the procedure stops and outputs the key. In particular, every time that the key length is incremented, the following expression $HD_{(n)} \simeq \frac{1}{m}\sum_{i=n-m-1}^{n-1} HD\_list[i]$ is used to compare the current HD value with the average of last m measured HDs, where m is defined by user based on the security demands, and n is the total number of inserted 3- and 5- input PG-FFs. Finally, the key bits that satisfy the security metrics with the minimum overhead, are stored in an external NVM, and the encrypted intermittent-resilient datapath is generated.

3 SIMULATION RESULTS

In this section, we have utilized ISCAS-89, ITC-99, and MCNC benchmark circuits to evaluate the performance of our proposed PG-insertion methodology. For instance, third row in Table 2 lists the gate counts of various ISCAS-89 benchmark circuits when the FFs are simply replaced by NV-FF, while the fourth row shows the decreased number of logic gates when the PG-insertion methodology is applied. Moreover, the last three columns illustrate the investigated security metrics including key length, HD, and logic key that is the maximum number of PG-FFs used within the datapath. The key length is directly proportional to the number of

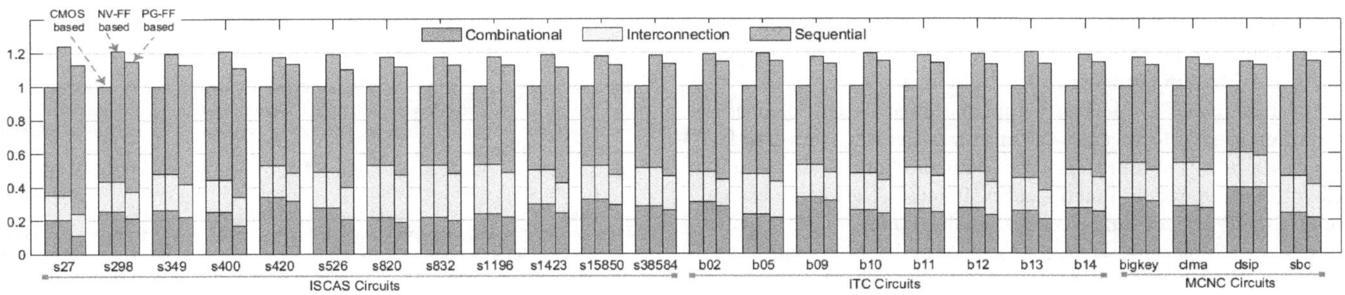

Figure 3: Normalized area consumption compared to CMOS-based implementations for ISCAS, ITC, and MCNC benchmarks.

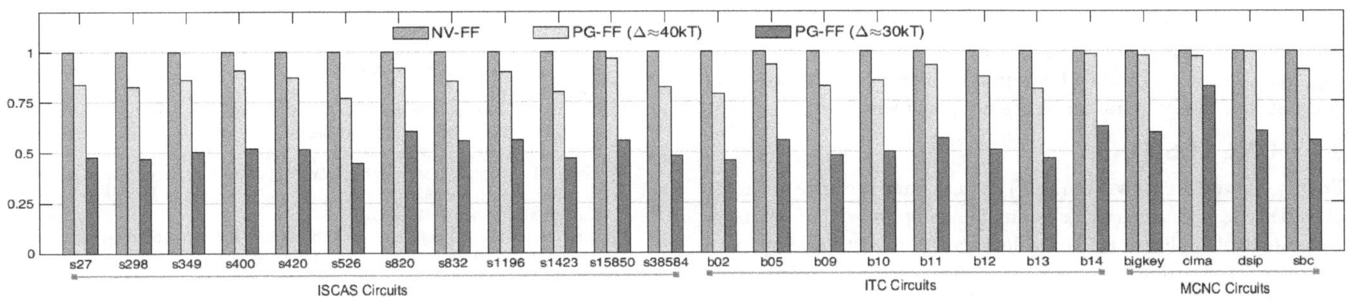

Figure 4: Normalized PDP compared to NV-FF based implementations for ISCAS, ITC, and MCNC benchmarks.

Table 2: PG-insertion results for ISCAS benchmarks.

ISCAS 89	Circuit Function	Gate-Equivalent NV-FF	Gate-Equivalent PG-FF	#Logic Key	#Key bits	Best HD
s27	Logic	10	8	2	4	0.142
s298	PLD	119	49	11	24	0.125
s349	4-bit Mult.	161	102	7	14	0.063
s400	TLC	164	144	22	49	0.229
s420	Frac. Mult.	218	152	6	12	0.057
s526	TLC	193	83	22	50	0.196
s820	PLD	289	259	10	20	0.035
s838	Frac. Mult.	446	329	14	28	0.061
s1196	Logic	529	459	8	20	0.015
s1423	Logic	657	396	54	116	0.135
s15850	Logic	9772	8942	207	423*	0.092
s38584	Logic	19253	12504	303	675*	0.037

*Using 128-length key bit, obtains 0.028 and 0.007 HD, respectively.

3-input and 5-input PGs inserted into the design. The best HD values are achieved when all of the PG-FFs are considered as logic keys. However, in larger designs, the obtained HD values are relatively low since the ratio of inserted PGs to total number of gates existing in the design is small. This is mainly because the primary goal of the proposed PG-insertion methodology is to support intermittent-computing, while various alternative methods proposed in [14, 15] can be leveraged to further fortify the security of the design.

3.1 Area Analysis

Figure 3 compares the area consumption between CMOS, NV-FF, and PG-FF based implementations using various ISCAS-89, ITC-99, and MCNC benchmarks. The results obtained are normalized to the area consumption of conventional CMOS-based circuits. In all of the investigated designs the interconnection area remains relatively unchanged, since replacing FFs does not significantly affect the interconnection circuitry. In the NV-FF based design, the combinational logic remains unchanged compared to CMOS-based design, while the area of the sequential logic is increased since the NV-FF includes more transistors in their structure than CMOS-based FF circuit due to the additional write and read circuitry. The proposed PG-insertion methodology leverages PGs to implement portions of the combinational logic within the PG-FFs without adding overhead to the sequential logic. Thus, the combinational logic in PG-FF based datapaths is smaller than CMOS and NV-FF based designs. For instance, benchmark circuit *s1423* originally has 657 gates, which is reduced to approximately 60% of the original number of gates, i.e. 396 gates, after the PG-insertion algorithm is applied. This improvement leads to a reduction in area consumption, as well as routing complexity. Since the spintronic devices can be vertically fabricated on top of CMOS transistors, their corresponding area overhead is negligible. The results shown in Fig. 3 exhibit that the proposed PG-insertion methodology can achieve an average of 7.1%, 4.2%, and 3.4% improvements in terms of area consumption for ISCAS-89, ITC-99, and MCNC benchmark circuits, respectively, compared to NV-FF based implementations.

3.2 Power-Delay Analysis

Figure 4 shows the power-delay-product (PDP) values for NV-FF, PG-FF, and low-energy barrier PG-FF based implementations using various ISCAS-89, ITC-99, and MCNC benchmark circuits. The results exhibit an average of 13.6%, 12.3%, and 3.5% PDP improvements, respectively, for PG-FF based designs compared to NV-FF based implementations, in which the CMOS-based FFs are simply replaced by NV-FFs. This improvement is mainly achieved through reducing the combinational logic in the PG-inserted designs as explained in previous section, while the PDP values for interconnection and sequential logic remain unchanged. As shown in Fig. 4, further PDP improvements can be achieved by using low energy barrier SHE-MTJ devices within PG-FFs at the cost of smaller retention times. However, in the energy-harvesting-powered IoT devices, a retention time in range of days and hours could be sufficient to achieve proper functionality. Therefore, the energy barrier of SHE-MTJ devices can be reduced to 30kT, realizing 25% reduction in switching critical current ($I_C \propto \Delta$) and approximately 44% decrease in write energy consumption ($E \propto I^2$), while providing non-volatility for a few hours. Thus, leveraging SHE-MTJ devices with 30kT energy barrier provides up to 48.5% and 40.5% average PDP improvements compared to NV-FF based designs and PG-FF based implementations with SHE-MTJ devices having $\Delta = 40kT$, respectively, without incurring any area overhead. It is worth noting, that the results provided herein are obtained at the gate level and physical design parameters are not considered.

4 CONCLUSIONS

Energy-harvesting-powered (EHP) devices have recently attracted considerable attentions as a sustainable computing platform for a wide range of applications. These devices are characterized by intermittent operation due to unpredictable energy failures. In this paper, we have developed a systematic methodology to realize middleware-transparent intermittent computing through insertion of NV-PGs within the logic datapath. The developed PG-insertion methodology takes the HDL representation of a datapath and generates an NV-enhanced datapath using SHE-MTJ based PG-FF circuits, which are used as state-holding elements also realizing basic Boolean logic functions. Therefore, a portion of the combinational logic is implemented within the sequential blocks, leading to area and energy savings compared to the conventional intermittent computing circuits where all of the registers are replaced with NV-FFs. Moreover, the power consumed by the sequential logic can be reduced by using SHE-MTJ devices with lower energy barriers, which can significantly reduce their write operation at the cost of shorter retention times that can be tolerated in EHP devices due to frequent refresh of devices on the datapath, while imparting the intrinsic provision of power outage resilience in energy-harvesting. Finally, PGs can be used for logic encryption due to their reconfigurability characteristic. Therefore, the logic encryption is defined as secondary objective of our proposed methodology, according to which a logic key will be generated based on Hamming distance calculations as a security metric. We applied the proposed algorithm to various benchmark circuits, including ISCAS-89, ITC-99, and MCNC, to evaluate the performance of our methodology in comparison with NV-FF based implementations. Results obtained exhibit that PG-FF based implementations using SHE-MTJ devices with 30kT energy barrier achieve up to 48.5% and 7.1% reductions in terms of average PDP and area consumption, respectively. While SHE-MTJ devices are utilized herein, any other emerging resistive devices could be leveraged without loss of generality, which can also result in further energy consumption improvements.

REFERENCES

[1] Qutaiba Alasad, Yu Bi, and Jiann-Shuin Yuan. 2017. E2LEMI: Energy-Efficient Logic Encryption Using Multiplexer Insertion. *Electronics* 6, 1 (2017), 16.

[2] Qutaiba Alasad, Jiann Yuan, and Deliang Fan. 2017. Leveraging All-Spin Logic to Improve Hardware Security. In *Proceedings of the on Great Lakes Symposium on VLSI 2017*. ACM, 491–494.

[3] Domenico Balsamo, Alex S Weddell, Geoff V Merrett, Bashir M Al-Hashimi, Davide Brunelli, and Luca Benini. 2015. Hibernus: Sustaining computation during intermittent supply for energy-harvesting systems. *IEEE Embedded Systems Letters* 7, 1 (2015), 15–18.

[4] Saurav Bandyopadhyay and Anantha P Chandrakasan. 2012. Platform architecture for solar, thermal, and vibration energy combining with MPPT and single inductor. *IEEE Journal of Solid-State Circuits* 47, 9 (2012), 2199–2215.

[5] Alexei Colin and Brandon Lucia. 2016. Chain: tasks and channels for reliable intermittent programs. In *Proceedings of the 2016 ACM SIGPLAN International Conference on Object-Oriented Programming, Systems, Languages, and Applications*. ACM, 514–530.

[6] Frontier Economics. 2011. Estimating the global economic and social impacts of counterfeiting and piracy. *A report commissioned by business action to stop counterfeiting and piracy (BASCAP), An ICC Initiative* (2011).

[7] Hrishikesh Jayakumar, Arnab Raha, and Vijay Raghunathan. 2014. QuickRecall: A low overhead HW/SW approach for enabling computations across power cycles in transiently powered computers. In *VLSI Design and 2014 13th International Conference on Embedded Systems, 2014 27th International Conference on*. IEEE, 330–335.

[8] Mohammad Kazemi, Graham E Rowlands, Engin Ipek, Robert A Buhrman, and Eby G Friedman. 2016. Compact model for spin–orbit magnetic tunnel junctions. *IEEE Transactions on Electron Devices* 63, 2 (2016), 848–855.

[9] Mihai T Lazarescu. 2013. Design of a WSN platform for long-term environmental monitoring for IoT applications. *IEEE Journal on Emerging and Selected Topics in Circuits and Systems* 3, 1 (2013), 45–54.

[10] Brandon Lucia and Benjamin Ransford. 2015. A simpler, safer programming and execution model for intermittent systems. *ACM SIGPLAN Notices* 50, 6 (2015), 575–585.

[11] Andrew Ma and Ada SY Poon. 2015. Midfield wireless power transfer for bioelectronics. *IEEE Circuits and Systems Magazine* 15, 2 (2015), 54–60.

[12] Kaisheng Ma, Yang Zheng, Shuangchen Li, Karthik Swaminathan, Xueqing Li, Yongpan Liu, Jack Sampson, Yuan Xie, and Vijaykrishnan Narayanan. 2015. Architecture exploration for ambient energy harvesting nonvolatile processors. In *High Performance Computer Architecture (HPCA), 2015 IEEE 21st International Symposium on*. IEEE, 526–537.

[13] Matthai Philipose, Joshua R Smith, Bing Jiang, Alexander Mamishev, Sumit Roy, and Kishore Sundara-Rajan. 2005. Battery-free wireless identification and sensing. *IEEE Pervasive computing* 4, 1 (2005), 37–45.

[14] Jeyavijayan Rajendran, Youngok Pino, Ozgur Sinanoglu, and Ramesh Karri. 2012. Security analysis of logic obfuscation. In *Proceedings of the 49th Annual Design Automation Conference*. ACM, 83–89.

[15] Jeyavijayan Rajendran, Huan Zhang, Chi Zhang, Garrett S Rose, Youngok Pino, Ozgur Sinanoglu, and Ramesh Karri. 2015. Fault analysis-based logic encryption. *IEEE Transactions on computers* 64, 2 (2015), 410–424.

[16] Benjamin Ransford and Brandon Lucia. 2014. Nonvolatile memory is a broken time machine. In *Proceedings of the workshop on Memory Systems Performance and Correctness*. ACM, 5.

[17] Benjamin Ransford, Jacob Sorber, and Kevin Fu. 2012. Mementos: System support for long-running computation on RFID-scale devices. *Acm Sigplan Notices* 47, 4 (2012), 159–170.

[18] Arman Roohi and Ronald F DeMara. 2018. NV-Clustering: Normally-Off Computing Using Non-Volatile Datapaths. *IEEE Trans. Comput.* PP, 99 (2018), 1–1. https://doi.org/10.1109/TC.2018.2795601

[19] A. Roohi, R. Zand, D. Fan, and R. F. DeMara. 2017. Voltage-Based Concatenatable Full Adder Using Spin Hall Effect Switching. *IEEE Transactions on Computer-Aided Design of Integrated Circuits and Systems* 36, 12 (Dec 2017), 2134–2138. https://doi.org/10.1109/TCAD.2017.2661800

[20] Jarrod A Roy, Farinaz Koushanfar, and Igor L Markov. 2010. EPIC: Ending piracy of integrated circuits. *Computer* 43, 10 (2010), 30–38.

[21] Adrian Stoica, Ricardo Zebulum, and Didier Keymeulen. 2001. Polymorphic electronics. *Evolvable Systems: From Biology to Hardware* (2001), 291–302.

[22] Pramod Subramanyan, Sayak Ray, and Sharad Malik. 2015. Evaluating the security of logic encryption algorithms. In *Hardware Oriented Security and Trust (HOST), 2015 IEEE International Symposium on*. IEEE, 137–143.

[23] Jonathan Z Sun. 2000. Spin-current interaction with a monodomain magnetic body: A model study. *Physical Review B* 62, 1 (2000), 570.

[24] Yang Xie and Ankur Srivastava. 2016. Mitigating sat attack on logic locking. In *International Conference on Cryptographic Hardware and Embedded Systems*. Springer, 127–146.

[25] Muhammad Yasin, Bodhisatwa Mazumdar, Jeyavijayan JV Rajendran, and Ozgur Sinanoglu. 2016. Sarlock: Sat attack resistant logic locking. In *Hardware Oriented Security and Trust (HOST), 2016 IEEE International Symposium on*. IEEE, 236–241.

[26] Weisheng Zhao, Claude Chappert, Virgile Javerliac, and Jean-Pierre Noziere. 2009. High speed, high stability and low power sensing amplifier for MTJ/CMOS hybrid logic circuits. *IEEE Transactions on Magnetics* 45, 10 (2009), 3784–3787.

Low-Energy Deep Belief Networks Using Intrinsic Sigmoidal Spintronic-based Probabilistic Neurons

Ramtin Zand[1], Kerem Yunus Camsari[2], Steven D. Pyle[1], Ibrahim Ahmed[3], Chris H. Kim[3], and Ronald F. DeMara[1]

[1]Department of Electrical and Computer Engineering, University of Central Florida, Orlando, FL, 32816 USA

[2]Department of Electrical and Computer Engineering, Purdue University, West Lafayette, IN, 47906 USA

[3]Department of Electrical and Computer Engineering, University of Minnesota, Minneapolis, MN 55455 USA

ABSTRACT

A low-energy hardware implementation of deep belief network (DBN) architecture is developed using near-zero energy barrier probabilistic spin logic devices (p-bits), which are modeled to realize an intrinsic sigmoidal activation function. A CMOS/spin based weighted array structure is designed to implement a restricted Boltzmann machine (RBM). Device-level simulations based on precise physics relations are used to validate the sigmoidal relation between the output probability of a p-bit and its input currents. Characteristics of the resistive networks and p-bits are modeled in SPICE to perform a circuit-level simulation investigating the performance, area, and power consumption tradeoffs of the weighted array. In the application-level simulation, a DBN is implemented in MATLAB for digit recognition using the extracted device and circuit behavioral models. The MNIST data set is used to assess the accuracy of the DBN using 5,000 training images for five distinct network topologies. The results indicate that a baseline error rate of 36.8% for a 784×10 DBN trained by 100 samples can be reduced to only 3.7% using a 784×800×800×10 DBN trained by 5,000 input samples. Finally, Power dissipation and accuracy tradeoffs for probabilistic computing mechanisms using resistive devices are identified.

ACM Reference Format:

Ramtin Zand[1], Kerem Yunus Camsari[2], Steven D. Pyle[1], Ibrahim Ahmed[3], Chris H. Kim[3], and Ronald F. DeMara[1]. 2018. Low-Energy Deep Belief Networks Using Intrinsic Sigmoidal Spintronic-based Probabilistic Neurons. In *GLSVLSI '18: 2018 Great Lakes Symposium on VLSI, May 23–25, 2018, Chicago, IL, USA.* ACM, New York, NY, USA, Article 4, 6 pages.

1 INTRODUCTION

The interrelated fields of machine learning (ML), and artificial neural networks (ANN) have grown significantly in previous decades due to the availability of powerful computing systems to train and simulate large scale ANNs within reasonable time-scales, as well as the abundance of data available to train such networks in recent years. The resulting research has realized a bevy of ANN architectures that have performed incredible feats including a wide range of classification problems, and various recognition tasks.

GLSVLSI '18, May 23–25, 2018, Chicago, IL, USA

ACM ISBN 978-1-4503-5724-1/18/05...$15.00

https://doi.org/10.1145/3194554.3194558

Most ML techniques in-use today rely on supervised learning, where the systems are trained on patterns with a known desired output, or label. However, intelligent biological systems exhibit unsupervised learning whereby statistically correlated input modalities are associated within an internal model used for probabilistic inference and decision making [5]. One interesting class of unsupervised learning approaches that has been extensively researched is the Restricted Boltzmann machine (RBM) [11]. RBMs can be hierarchically organized to realize deep belief networks (DBNs) that have demonstrated unsupervised learning abilities, such as natural language understanding [17]. Most RBM and DBN research has focused on software implementations, which provides flexibility, but requires significant execution time and energy due to large matrix multiplications that are relatively inefficient when implemented on standard Von-Neumann architectures due to the memory-processor bandwidth bottleneck when compared to hardware-based in-memory computing approaches [16]. Thus, research into hardware-based RBM designs has recently sought to alleviate these constraints.

Previous hardware-based RBM implementations have aimed to overcome software limitations by utilizing FPGAs [12, 15] and stochastic CMOS [2]. In recent years, emerging technologies such as resistive RAM (RRAM) [4, 21] and phase change memory (PCM) [9] are proposed to be leveraged within the DBN architecture as weighted connections interconnecting building blocks in RBMs. While most of the previous hybrid Memristor/CMOS designs focus on improving the synapse behaviors, the work presented herein overcomes many of the preceding challenges by utilizing a novel spintronic p-bit device that leverages intrinsic thermal noise within low energy barrier nanomagnets to provide a natural building block for RBMs within a compact and low-energy package. The contribution of this paper is go to beyond using low-energy barrier magnetic tunnel junctions (MTJs), as has been previously introduced for a neuron in spiking neuromorphic systems [19, 20]. To the best of our knowledge this paper is the first effort to use MTJs with near-zero energy barriers as neurons within an RBM implementation. Additionally, various parameters of a hybrid CMOS/spin weight array structure are investigated for metrics of power dissipation, and error rate using the MNIST digit recognition benchmarks.

2 FUNDAMENTALS OF RBM

Boltzmann Machines (BM) are a class of recurrent stochastic ANNs with binary nodes whereby each possible state of the network, v, has an energy determined by the undirected connection weights between nodes and the node bias as described by (1), where s_i^v is the state of node i in v, b_i is the bias, or intrinsic excitability of node

i, and w_{ij} is the connection weight between nodes i and j [1].

$$E(v) = -\sum_i s_i^v b_i - \sum_{i<j} s_i^v s_j^v w_{ij} \quad (1)$$

$$P(s_i = 1) = \sigma(b_i + \sum_j w_{ij} s_j) \quad (2)$$

Each node in a BM has a probability to be in state 1 according to (2), where σ is the logistic sigmoid function. BMs, when given enough time, will reach a Boltzmann distribution where the probability of the system being in state $\boldsymbol{v}$ is found by $P(v) = \frac{e^{-E(v)}}{\sum_u e^{-E(u)}}$, where $\boldsymbol{u}$ could be any possible state of the system. Thus, the system is most likely to be found in states that have the lowest associated energy. Restricted Boltzmann machines (RBMs) are BMs constrained to two fully-connected non-recurrent layers called the *visible layer*, where salient inputs clamp nodes to output levels of either zero or one, and the *hidden layer*, where associations between input vectors are learned. By enforcing the conditional independence of the visible and hidden layers, unbiased samples from the input can be obtained in one time-step, which enhances the learning process.

The most widely used method for training RBMs is contrastive divergence (CD), which is an approximate gradient descent procedure using Gibbs sampling [8]. CD operates in three phases: *(1) Positive Phase:* A training input vector, v, is applied to the visible layer by clamping the nodes to either 1 or 0 levels, and the hidden layer is sampled, h. *(2) Negative Phase:* by clamping the hidden layer to h, the reconstructed input layer is sampled, v'. Then, clamp the visible layer to v' and sample the hidden layer to obtain h'. *(3)* Update the weights according to $\Delta W = \eta(vh^T - v'h'^T)$, where η is the learning rate and W is the weight matrix.

DBNs are realized when additional hidden layers are stacked on top of an RBM, and can be trained in a very similar way to RBMs. Essentially, training a DBN involves performing CD on the visible layer and the first hidden layer for as many steps as desired, then fixing those weights and moving up a hierarchy as follows. The first hidden layer is now viewed as a visible layer, while the second hidden layer acts as a hidden layer with respect to the CD procedure identified above. Next, another set of CD steps are performed, and then the process is repeated for each additional layer of the DBN.

3 SPIN-BASED BUILDING BLOCK FOR RBM

In this section, we provide a detailed description of the p-bit that provides the building block for our proposed spin-based BM architecture. Individual building blocks are interconnected by networks of memristive devices whose resistances can be programmed to provide the desired weights. For instance, in this paper, we will assume that the memristive devices are implemented using the three terminal spin-orbit torque (SOT)-driven domain wall motion (DWM) device proposed in [18].

The activation function is achieved by a spintronic building block that has been used in the design of probabilistic spin logic devices (p-bits) for a wide variety of Boolean and non-Boolean problems [3, 6, 10, 22]. The basic functionality of the p-bit shown in Fig. 1 [6] is to produce a stochastic output whose steady-state probability is modulated by an input current to generate a sigmoidal activation function. For instance, a high positive input current produces a stochastic output with a high probability of "0", and vice versa. In the absence of any input current, the device generates either 0 or VDD outputs with roughly equal probability of 0.5, as shown in Fig. 2. This device consists of a 3-terminal, spin-Hall driven MTJ [14] that uses a circular, unstable nanomagnet ($\Delta \ll 40kT$), whereby its output is amplified by CMOS inverters as shown in Fig. 1. This MTJ with an unstable free layer can be fabricated using standard technology such that the surface anisotropy to achieve perpendicular magnetic anisotropy (PMA) that is not strong enough to overcome the demagnetizing field. Thus, the magnetization stochastically rotates in the plane, due to the presence of thermal fluctuations.

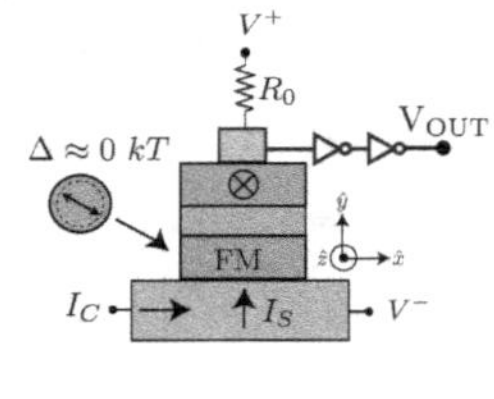

Figure 1: Structure of a p-bit.

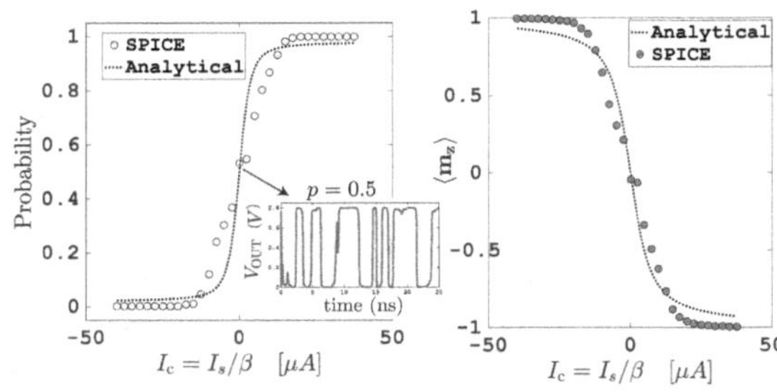

Figure 2: Time-averaged results over 100 ns for p-bit.

The charge current that is injected to the spin-Hall layer creates a spin-current flowing into the circular FM (in the +y direction), which does not have an axis with any preferential geometry. The spin-polarization of this spin-current is in the ($\pm z$) direction, and pins the magnetization in the (+z) or (-z) direction depending on the direction of the charge current, through the spin-torque mechanism [22]. The inherent physics of the spin-current driven low-barrier nanomagnet provides a natural sigmoidal function when a long time average of magnetization is taken. Through the tunneling magnetoresistance effect, a charge current flowing through the MTJ with a stable fixed layer detects the modulated magnetization as a voltage change. To achieve this, a small read voltage V_R is applied between the $V+$ and $V-$ terminals through a reference resistance R_0, adjusted to the average conductance of the MTJ ($R_0^{-}1 = GP + GAP/2$) where GP and GAP represented conductance in parallel (P) and anti-parallel (AP) states, respectively. This voltage becomes an input to the CMOS inverters that are biased at the middle point of their DC operating point, creating a stochastic output whose probability can be tuned by the input charge current.

Each component of the device is represented by an independent spin-circuit based on experimentally-benchmarked models that have been established in [7] and simulated as a spin-circuit in a SPICE-like platform. Here, we obtain an analytical approximation to the time-averaged behavior of the output characteristics. We

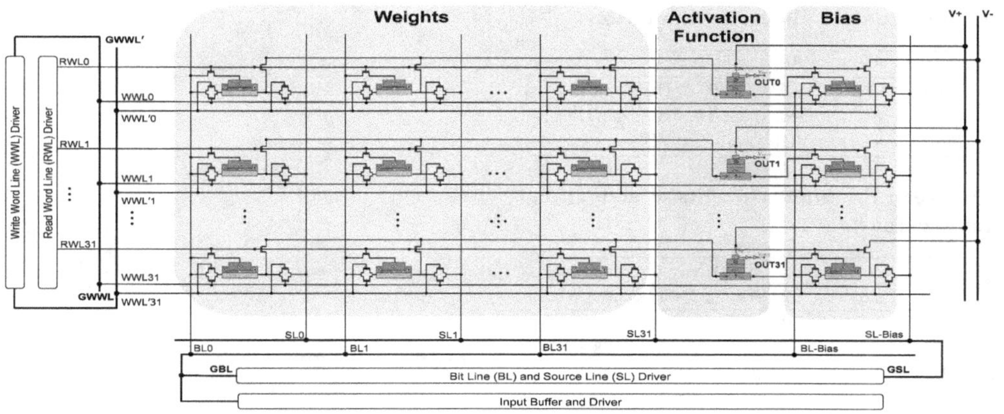

Figure 3: Proposed 32×32 **hybrid CMOS/spin-based weighted array structure for RBM implementation.**

Table 1: Parameters for p-bit Based Activation Function.

Parameter	Description	Value
Circular FM		
ϕ	Diameter	$100nm$
t	Thickness	$2nm$
α	Damping coefficient	0.01
MTJ		
$G0$	Conductance	$150e^{-6}S$
P	Spin Polarization	0.52
Giant Spin Hall Layer(GSHE)		
λ	Spin-diffusion length	$2.1nm$
θ	Spin Hall Angle	0.5
$Volume$	$l \times w \times t$	$100nm \times 100nm \times 3.15nm$

start by relating the charge current flowing in the spin Hall layer to the spin-current absorbed by the magnet, assuming short-circuit conditions for simplicity, i.e. 100% spin absorption by the FM:

$$I_s/I_c = \beta = \frac{L}{t}(\theta)(1 - sech(\frac{t}{\lambda})) \tag{3}$$

where I_s is the spin-current, I_c is the charge current, θ is the spin-Hall angle, L, t, λ are the length, thickness and spin diffusion lengths for the spin-Hall layer. The length and width of the GSHE layer are assumed to be the same as the circular nanomagnet. With a suitable choice of the L and t, the spin-current generated can be greater in magnitude than the charge current generating "gain." For the parameters used in this paper, which are listed in Table 1, the gain factor β is $\sim$ 10. Next, we approximate the behavior of the magnetization as a function of an input spin-current, polarized in the ($\pm z$) direction. For a magnet with only a PMA in the $\pm z$ direction, a distribution function at steady state can be written analytically as below, as long as the spin-current is also fully in the $\pm z$ direction:

$$\rho(m_z) = \frac{1}{Z}exp(\Delta m_z^2 + 2i_s m_z) \tag{4}$$

where Z is a normalization constant, m_z is the magnetization along $+z$, is the thermal barrier of the nanomagnet, and i_s is a normalization quantity for the spin-current such that $i_s = I_s/(4q/\hbar\alpha kT)$, α being the damping coefficient of the magnet, q the electron charge and $\hbar$ the reduced Planck constant. It is possible to use (4) to obtain an average magnetization $< m_z >= \int_{-1}^{+1} dm_z m_z \rho(m_z) / \int_{-1}^{+1} dm_z \rho(m_z)$. Assuming $\Delta \ll kT$, $< m_z >$ can be evaluated to give the Langevin function, $< m_z >= L(i_s)$ where $L(x) = \frac{1}{x} - coth\frac{1}{x}$, which is an exact description for the average magnetization in the presence of a z-directed spin-current for a low barrier PMA magnet.

In the present case, however, the nanomagnet has a circular shape with a strong in-plane anisotropy and no simple analytical formula can be derived, thus We use the Langevin function with a fitting parameter that adjusts the normalization current by a factor η, so that the modified normalization constant becomes $(4q/\hbar\alpha kT)(\eta)$. This factor increases with elevating the shape anisotropy ($H_d \sim 4\pi M_s$) and becomes exactly one when there is no shape anisotropy. Once the magnetization and charge currents are related, we can approximate the output probability of the CMOS inverters by a phenomenological equation along with fitting parameter χ as follows, $p = \frac{V_{OUT}}{VDD} \approx \frac{1}{2}[1 - tanh(\chi < m_z >)]$, which allows us to relate the input charge current to the output probability, with physical parameters. Fig. 2 shows the comparison of the full SPICE-model with respect to aforementioned equations showing good agreement with two fitting parameters η and χ, which fit the magnetization and CMOS components, respectively.

4 PROPOSED WEIGHTED ARRAY DESIGN

Figure 3 shows the structure of the weighted array proposed herein to implement the RBM architecture including the SOT-DWM based weighted connections and biases, as well as the p-bit based activation functions. Transmission gates (TGs) are utilized in write circuits within the bit cells of the weighted connection to adjust weights by moving the DW position. As investigated in [24], TGs can provide energy-efficient and symmetric switching operation for SOT-based devices, which are desirable during the training phase. Table 2 lists the required signaling for controlling the training and read operations in the weighted array structure. Herein, a chain of inverters are considered to drive signal lines, in which each successive inverter is twice as large as the previous one.

During the read operation, write word line (WWL) is connected to ground (GND) and the source line (SL) is in high impedance

Table 2: Signaling to Control The Array Operations.

Operation	WWL	RWL	BL	SL	V+	V-
Increase Weight	VPULSE	GND	VDD	GND	Hi-Z	Hi-Z
Decrease Weight	VPULSE	GND	GND	GND	Hi-Z	Hi-Z
Read	GND	VDD	VIN	Hi-Z	VDD	VDD/2

Table 3: Relation between the input currents of activation functions and array size for $R_P = 1M\Omega$.

Features	Array Size			
	8×8	16×16	32×32	64×64
Max. Positive Current (μA)	2.71	5.14	10.79	21.46
Max. Negative Current (μA)	3.57	7.14	14.23	28.28
Max. output "0" Probability	0.77	0.88	0.95	0.97
Min. output "0" Probability	0.175	0.08	0.038	0.026

(Hi-Z) state, which disconnects the write path. The read word line (RWL) for each row is connected to VDD, which turns ON the read transistors in the weighted connection bit cell. The bit line (BL) will be connected to the input signal (VIN), which results in producing a current that affects the output probability of the p-bit device. The direction of the generated current relies on the VIN signal. In particular, since V- is supplied by a voltage source equal to VDD/2, if VIN is connected to VDD the injected current to the p-bit based activation function will have positive value, and if VIN is zero the input current will be negative. The amplitude of the generated current depends on the resistance of the weighted connection which is defined by the position of the DW in the SOT-DWM device.

During the training operation, the RWL is connected to GND, which turns OFF the read transistors and disconnects the read path. The WWL is connected to an input pulse (VPULSE) signal which activates the write path for a short period of time. The duration of the VPULSE should be designed in a manner such that it can provide the desired learning rate, η, to the training circuit. For instance, a high VPULSE duration results in a significant change in the DW position in each training iteration, which effectively reduces the number of different resistive states that can be realized by the SOT-DWM device. Resistance of the weighted connections can be adjusted by the BL and SL signals, as listed in Table 2. A higher resistance leads to a smaller current injected to the p-bit device. Therefore, the input signal connected to the weighted connection will have lower impact on the output probability of the p-bit device, which means the input signal exhibits a lower weight. The bias nodes can also be adjusted similar to the weighted connection.

5 SIMULATION RESULTS AND DISCUSSION

To analyze the RBM implementation using the proposed p-bit device and the weighted array structure, we have utilized a hierarchical simulation framework including circuit-level and application-level simulations. In circuit level simulation, the behavioral models of the p-bit and SOT-DWM devices were leveraged in SPICE circuit simulations using 20nm CMOS technology with 0.9V nominal voltage to validate the functionality of the designed weighted array circuit. In application-level simulation, the results obtained from device-level and circuit-level simulations are used to implement a DBN architecture and analyze its behavior in MATLAB.

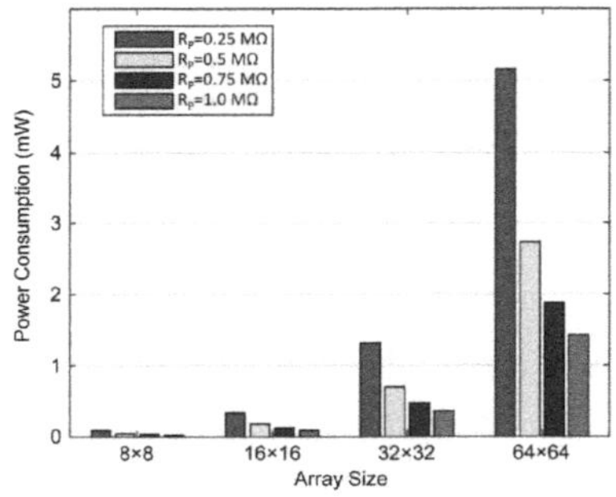

Figure 4: Weighted array power consumption versus the resistance of the weighted connections and array size.

Table 4: Relation between the input currents of activation functions and R_P in a 32×32 array.

Features	$R_P(M\Omega)$			
	0.25	0.5	0.75	1
Max. Positive Current (μA)	36.56	20.02	13.97	10.79
Max. Negative Current (μA)	54.95	28.12	18.9	14.23
Max. output "0" Probability	0.98	0.965	0.96	0.95
Min. output "0" Probability	0.01	0.026	0.032	0.038

5.1 Circuit-level simulation

The device-level simulations shown in Fig. 2 verified a sigmoidal relation between the input current of the p-bit based activation function and its output probability. The shape of the activation on function is one of the major factors affecting the performance of the RBM. Therefore, we have provided comprehensive analyses on the impacts of weighted connection resistance and weighted array dimensions on the input currents of the p-bit based activation functions, and the power consumption of the weighted array.

Table 3 lists the range of the activation function input currents for various weighted array dimensions, while the resistance of the SOT-DWM device in parallel state (RP) is constant and equals $1M\Omega$. The experimental results provided in [19, 28] exhibit that an MTJ resistance in the $M\Omega$ range can be obtained by increasing the oxide thickness in an MTJ structure. The highest positive and negative currents can be achieved while the weighted connections are in parallel state, i.e. lowest resistance, and all of the input voltages (VIN) are equal to VDD and GND, respectively. The difference between the amplitude of positive and negative currents in a given array size with constant RP is caused by the different pull-down and pull-up strengths in NMOS read transistors. The maximum and minimum output-level "0" probabilities are listed in Table 3, which can be obtained according to the measured input currents and the sigmoidal activation function shown in Fig. 2.

Moreover, Table 4 illustrates the relation between the R_P values and input currents of the activation functions, and their corresponding output probabilities, for a given 32×32 weighted array. The lower RP resistance and higher array size provides a wider range of output probabilities which can increase the RBM performance. However, this is achieved at the cost of higher area and power consumption. The trade-offs between the array size, weighted connection resistance, and average power consumption in a single read operation is shown in Fig. 4. The lowest power consumption of

Table 5: Comparison between various RBM implementations with an emphasis on activation function structure.

Design	[12]	[15]	[2]	[21]	[4]	[9]	Proposed Herein
Weighted Connection	Embedded multipliers	Embedded multipliers	- LFSR - AND/OR gates	RRAM memristor	RRAM	PCM	SOT-DWM
Activation Function	CMOS-based LUTs	-2-kB BRAM - Picewise Linear Interpolator - Random number Generator	- LFSR - Bit-wise AND - tree adder - FSM-based tanh unit	Off-chip	- 64×16 LUTs - Pseudo Random Number Generator - Comparator	Off-chip	- near-zero energy barrier probabilistic spin logic device
Energy per neuron	N/A	$\sim 10 - 100nJ$	$\sim 10 - 100pJ$	N/A	$\sim 1 - 10nJ$	N/A	$\sim 1 - 10fJ$
Normalized area per neuron	N/A	$\sim 3000\times$	$\sim 90\times$	N/A	$\sim 1250\times$	N/A	$\sim 1\times$

22.6 μW is realized by an 8×8 array with $R_P = 1M\Omega$. However, this array provides the narrowest range of the output probabilities, which significantly reduces the performance of the DBN.

5.2 Application-level simulation

In the application-level simulation, we have leveraged the obtained device and circuit behavioral models to simulate a DBN architecture for digit recognition. In particular, learning rate and the shape of the sigmoid activation function is extracted by the SOT-DWM and p-bit device-level simulations, respectively, while the circuit-level simulations defines the range of the output probabilities. To evaluate the performance of the system, we have modified a MATLAB implementation of DBN by Tanaka and Okutomi [23] and used the MNIST data set [13] including 60,000 and 10,000 sample images with 28×28 pixels for training and testing operations, respectively. We have used Error rate (ERR) metric to evaluate the performance of the DBN, as expressed by $ERR = N_F/N$, where, N is the number of input data, N_F is the number of false inference [23].

The simplest model of the DBN that can be implemented for MNIST digit recognition consists 784 nodes in visible layer to handle 28×28 pixels of the input images, and 10 nodes in hidden layer representing the output classes. Fig. 5 shows the relation between the performance of various DBN topologies, and the number of input training samples ranging from 100 to 5,000, which is obtained using 1,000 test samples. The ERR and RMSE metrics can be improved by enlarging the DBN structure through increasing the number of hidden layers, as well as the number of nodes in each layer. This improvement is realized at the cost of larger area and power consumptions. Increasing the input training samples can improve the DBN performance as well, however it will quickly converge due to the limited weight values that can be provided by SOT-DWM based weighted connections. As shown in Fig. 5, some random behaviors are observed for networks with smaller sizes that are trained by lower number of training samples, which will be significantly reduced by increasing the number of training samples.

The simulation results exhibit the highest error rate of 36.8% for a 784×10 DBN that is trained by 100 training samples. Meanwhile, the lowest error rate of 3.7% was achieved using a $784\times800\times800\times10$ DBN trained by 5,000 input training samples. This illustrates that the recognition error rate can be decreased by increasing the number of hidden layers, and training samples, which is also realized at the cost of higher area and power overheads.

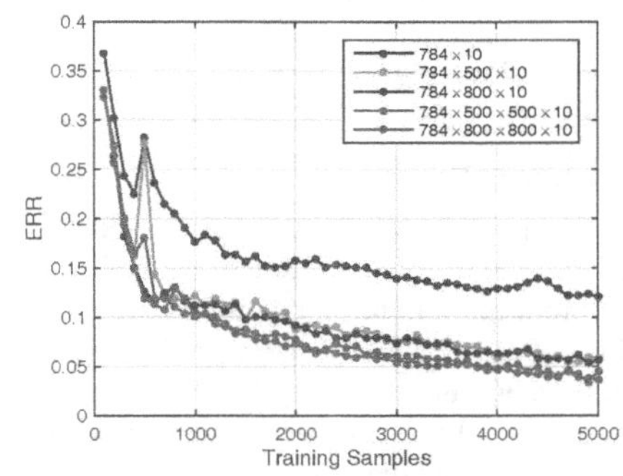

Figure 5: ERR for various DBN topologies.

5.3 Disucussion

Table 5 lists previous hardware-based RBM implementations, which have aimed to overcome software limitations by utilizing FPGAs [12, 15], stochastic CMOS [2], and hybrid memristor-CMOS designs [4, 9, 21]. FPGA implementations demonstrated RBM speedups of 25-145 over software implementations [12, 15], but had significant constraints such as only realizing a single 128×128 RBM per FPGA chip, routing congestion, and clock frequencies limited to 100MHz [15]. The stochastic CMOS-based RBM implementation proposed in [2] leveraged the low-complexity of stochastic CMOS arithmetic to save area and power. However, the need for extremely long bit-stream lengths negate energy savings and lead to very long latencies. Additionally, a significant amount of Linear Feedback Shift Registers (LFSRs) were required to produce the uncorrelated input and weight bit-streams. In both the FPGA and stochastic CMOS designs, improvements were achieved by implementing parallel Boolean circuits such as multipliers and pseudo-random number generators for probabilistic behavior, which has significant area and energy overheads compared to leveraging the physical behaviors of emerging devices to perform the computation intrinsically. Bojnordi et al. [4] leveraged resistive RAM (RRAM) devices to implement efficient matrix multiplication for weighted products within Boltzmann machine applications, and demonstrated significant speedup of up to 100-fold over single-threaded cores and energy savings of over 10-fold. Similarly, Sheri et al. [21] and Eryilmaz et al. [9] utilized RRAM and PCM devices to implement matrix multiplication, while the corresponding activation function circuitry is still based on the CMOS technology, which suffers from the aforementioned area and power consumption overheads.

While most of the previous hybrid Memristor/CMOS designs focus on improving the performance of weighted connections, the work presented herein overcomes many of the preceding challenges of generating sigmoidal probabilistic activation functions by utilizing a novel p-bit device that leverages intrinsic thermal noise within low energy barrier nanomagnets to provide a natural building block for RBMs within a compact and low-energy package. As listed in Table V, the proposed design can achieve approximately three orders of magnitude improvement in term of energy consumption compared to the most energy-efficient designs, while realizing at least 90X device count reduction for considerable area savings. Note that these calculations do not take into account the weighted connections, since the main focus of this paper is on the activation function. While SOT-DWM devices are utilized herein for the weighted connections, any other memristive devices could be utilized without loss of generality.

6 CONCLUSION

Herein, we developed a hybrid CMOS/spin-based DBN implementation using p-bit based activation functions modeled to produce a probabilistic output that can be modulated by an input current. The device-level simulations exhibited a sigmoid relation between the input currents and output probability. The SPICE model of the p-bit is used to design a weighted array structure to implement RBM. The circuit simulations showed that the performance of the array can be improved by enlarging the array size, as well as reducing the resistance of the weighted connections. However, these improvements are achieved at the cost of increased area and power consumption. For instance, the lowest power dissipation among the examined designs belongs to an 8×8 array with the maximum resistance of $1M\Omega$ for weighted connections. However, this structure can only provide the output probabilities ranging from 0.175 to 0.77, which is the narrowest range among the examined designs resulting in a DBN implementation with lowest accuracy.

Next, we simulated a DBN for digit recognition application in MATLAB using the device and circuit-level behavioral models. Trade-offs include the relations between the recognition accuracy of the DBN and the number of training samples, which are comparable to conventional hardware implementations. The recognition error rate decreased substantially for the first thousand training samples, regardless of the size of the array, while benefits continue through several thousand inputs. However, at least two hidden layers are desirable to achieve suitable error rates. Finally, we have provided a comparison between previous hardware-based RBM implementations and our design with an emphasis on the probabilistic activation function within the neuron structure. The results exhibited that the p-bit based activation function can achieve roughly three orders of magnitude energy improvement, while realizing at least 90X reduction in terms of device count, compared to the previous most energy-efficient designs. The research directions herein enable several intriguing possibilities for future work, including: (1) implementing the entire network in SPICE to obtain more robust results; 2) investigating the effect of process variation and noise on the accuracy of proposed architecture; 3) studying alternative devices with lower susceptibility to thermal noise; and 4) studying the scalability challenges of DBNs using larger datasets, e.g. CIFAR.

7 ACKNOWLEDGEMENTS

This work was supported in part by the Center for Probabilistic Spin Logic for Low-Energy Boolean and Non-Boolean Computing (CAPSL), one of the Nanoelectronic Computing Research (nCORE) Centers as task 2759.006, a Semiconductor Research Corporation (SRC) program sponsored by the NSF through CCF 1739635.

REFERENCES

[1] David H Ackley, Geoffrey E Hinton, and Terrence J Sejnowski. 1985. A learning algorithm for Boltzmann machines. *Cognitive science* 9, 1 (1985), 147–169.

[2] A. Ardakani, F. Leduc-Primeau, N. Onizawa, T. Hanyu, and W. J. Gross. 2017. VLSI Implementation of Deep Neural Network Using Integral Stochastic Computing. *IEEE Transactions on Very Large Scale Integration (VLSI) Systems* 25, 10 (2017).

[3] Behtash Behin-Aein, Vinh Diep, and Supriyo Datta. 2016. A building block for hardware belief networks. *Scientific reports* 6 (2016).

[4] M. N. Bojnordi and E. Ipek. 2016. Memristive Boltzmann machine: A hardware accelerator for combinatorial optimization and deep learning. In *2016 IEEE International Symposium on High Performance Computer Architecture (HPCA)*.

[5] Lars Buesing, Johannes Bill, Bernhard Nessler, and Wolfgang Maass. 2011. Neural dynamics as sampling: a model for stochastic computation in recurrent networks of spiking neurons. *PLoS computational biology* 7, 11 (2011), e1002211.

[6] Kerem Yunus Camsari, Rafatul Faria, Brian M. Sutton, and Supriyo Datta. 2017. Stochastic p-Bits for Invertible Logic. *Phys. Rev. X* 7 (Jul 2017), 031014. Issue 3.

[7] Kerem Yunus Camsari, Samiran Ganguly, and Supriyo Datta. 2015. Modular approach to spintronics. *Scientific reports* 5 (2015).

[8] Miguel A Carreira-Perpinan and Geoffrey E Hinton. 2005. On contrastive divergence learning.. In *Aistats*, Vol. 10. 33–40.

[9] S. B. Eryilmaz, E. Neftci, S. Joshi, S. Kim, M. BrightSky, H. L. Lung, C. Lam, G. Cauwenberghs, and H. S. P. Wong. 2016. Training a Probabilistic Graphical Model With Resistive Switching Electronic Synapses. *IEEE Transactions on Electron Devices* 63, 12 (Dec 2016), 5004–5011.

[10] R. Faria, K. Y. Camsari, and S. Datta. 2017. Low-Barrier Nanomagnets as p-Bits for Spin Logic. *IEEE Magnetics Letters* 8 (2017), 1–5.

[11] Geoffrey E Hinton, Simon Osindero, and Yee-Whye Teh. 2006. A fast learning algorithm for deep belief nets. *Neural computation* 18, 7 (2006), 1527–1554.

[12] S. K. Kim, P. L. McMahon, and K. Olukotun. 2010. A Large-Scale Architecture for Restricted Boltzmann Machines. In *2010 18th IEEE Annual International Symposium on Field-Programmable Custom Computing Machines*. 201–208.

[13] Y. Lecun, L. Bottou, Y. Bengio, and P. Haffner. 1998. Gradient-based learning applied to document recognition. *Proc. IEEE* 86, 11 (Nov 1998), 2278–2324.

[14] Luqiao Liu, Chi-Feng Pai, Y. Li, H. W. Tseng, D. C. Ralph, and R. A. Buhrman. 2012. Spin-Torque Switching with the Giant Spin Hall Effect of Tantalum. *Science* 336, 6081 (2012), 555–558.

[15] D. L. Ly and P. Chow. 2010. High-Performance Reconfigurable Hardware Architecture for Restricted Boltzmann Machines. *IEEE Transactions on Neural Networks* 21, 11 (Nov 2010), 1780–1792.

[16] Paul A Merolla, John V Arthur, Rodrigo Alvarez-Icaza, Andrew S Cassidy, Jun Sawada, Filipp Akopyan, Bryan L Jackson, Nabil Imam, Chen Guo, Yutaka Nakamura, et al. 2014. A million spiking-neuron integrated circuit with a scalable communication network and interface. *Science* 345, 6197 (2014), 668–673.

[17] Ruhi Sarikaya, Geoffrey E. Hinton, and Anoop Deoras. 2014. Application of Deep Belief Networks for Natural Language Understanding. *IEEE/ACM Trans. Audio, Speech and Lang. Proc.* 22, 4 (April 2014), 778–784.

[18] Abhronil Sengupta, Aparajita Banerjee, and Kaushik Roy. 2016. Hybrid Spintronic-CMOS Spiking Neural Network with On-Chip Learning: Devices, Circuits, and Systems. *Phys. Rev. Applied* 6 (Dec 2016), 064003. Issue 6.

[19] Abhronil Sengupta, Priyadarshini Panda, Parami Wijesinghe, Yusung Kim, and Kaushik Roy. 2016. Magnetic tunnel junction mimics stochastic cortical spiking neurons. *Scientific reports* 6 (2016), 30039.

[20] A. Sengupta, M. Parsa, B. Han, and K. Roy. 2016. Probabilistic Deep Spiking Neural Systems Enabled by Magnetic Tunnel Junction. *IEEE Transactions on Electron Devices* 63, 7 (July 2016), 2963–2970.

[21] Ahmad Muqeem Sheri, Aasim Rafique, Witold Pedrycz, and Moongu Jeon. 2015. Contrastive divergence for memristor-based restricted Boltzmann machine. *Engineering Applications of Artificial Intelligence* 37 (2015), 336 – 342.

[22] Brian Sutton, Kerem Yunus Camsari, Behtash Behin-Aein, and Supriyo Datta. 2017. Intrinsic optimization using stochastic nanomagnets. *Scientific Reports* 7 (2017).

[23] M. Tanaka and M. Okutomi. 2014. A Novel Inference of a Restricted Boltzmann Machine. In *2014 22nd International Conference on Pattern Recognition*. 1526–1531.

[24] R. Zand, A. Roohi, and R. F. DeMara. 2017. Energy-Efficient and Process-Variation-Resilient Write Circuit Schemes for Spin Hall Effect MRAM Device. *IEEE Transactions on Very Large Scale Integration (VLSI) Systems* 25, 9 (2017), 2394–2401.

Maxflow: Minimizing Latency in Hybrid Stochastic-Binary Systems

Paishun Ting
Department of Electrical Engineering and Computer Science
University of Michigan
Ann Arbor, MI 48109 USA
paishun@umich.edu

John P. Hayes
Department of Electrical Engineering and Computer Science
University of Michigan
Ann Arbor, MI 48109 USA
jhayes@umich.edu

ABSTRACT

Stochastic computing (SC) is an alternative way to design arithmetic circuits that have lower area and power than circuits employing conventional binary (base-2) computing (BC). Large SC-based systems like neural networks (NNs) or vision systems usually resort to BC, either explicitly or implicitly, for tasks requiring higher accuracy, such as data storage, control functions, or complex arithmetic operations. The resulting hybrid SC-BC features often incorporate unsatisfactory tradeoffs between system latency and accuracy. For example, they may require many costly SC-BC data format converters, which interrupt bit-stream flow and cause significant delay overhead. While improving accuracy has been a major research goal in SC, less attention has been paid to reducing latency. We present a novel design methodology called Maxflow that minimizes the latency of SC operations without reducing accuracy or interrupting data flow more than necessary. Maxflow supports delay-accuracy tradeoffs with little hardware modification. Its effectiveness is demonstrated for a deep NN, where it reduces overall latency substantially with no loss of accuracy compared to previous designs.

KEYWORDS

Stochastic circuits; hybrid systems; latency minimization; artificial neural networks

ACM Reference format:

P. Ting and J.P. Hayes. 2018. Maxflow: Minimizing Latency in Hybrid Stochastic-Binary Systems. In *Proceedings of ACM Great Lakes Symposium on VLSI, Chicago, Illinois USA, May 2018 (GLSVLSI'18)*, 6 pages. https://doi.org/10.1145/3194554.3194586

1 INTRODUCTION

Unlike conventional "binary" computing (BC) that computes with deterministic base-2 numbers, stochastic computing (SC) encodes data in randomized bit-streams called stochastic numbers (SNs). The value of a (unipolar) SN **X** in signal line x is defined as $X = p(x = 1)$, the probability that a 1 appears anywhere in **X**. For example, 01, 0101, 011010 all denote an SN of value 0.5, since half the bits in each SN are 1s. While their data are very different, BC and SC are compatible in that both use conventional logic circuits, so they can readily be combined into a single hybrid system.

GLSVLSI '18, May 23–25, 2018, Chicago, IL, USA

ACM ISBN 978-1-4503-5724-1/18/05...$15.00
https://doi.org/10.1145/3194554.3194586

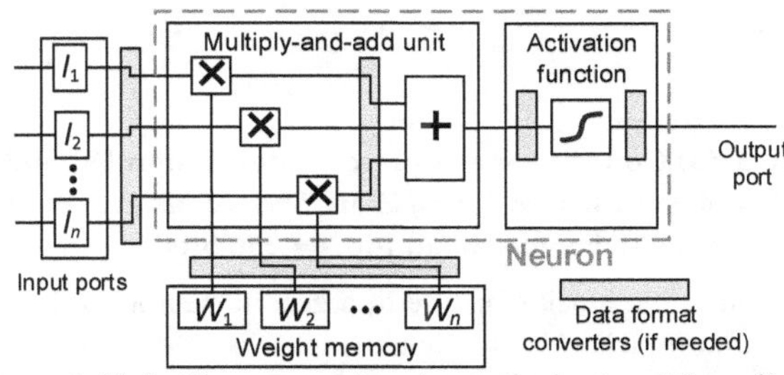

Figure 1. Hybrid neuron circuitry employing SC and/or BC components that are integrated via data format converters.

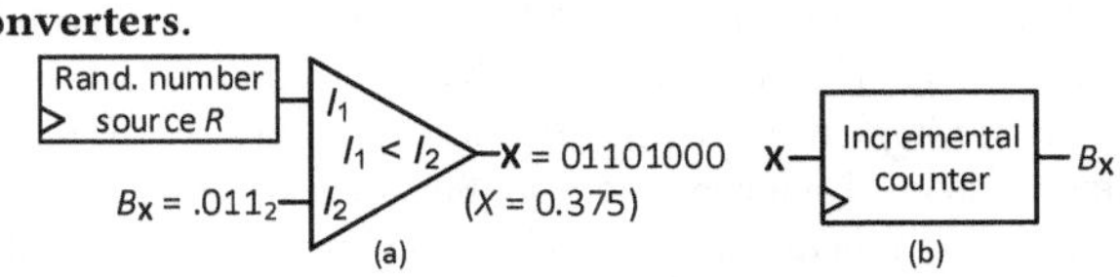

Figure 2. Data converters: (a) BC to SC, and (b) SC to BC.

The main advantages of SC are small area, low power and soft-error tolerance. An AND gate with inputs x, y and output z realizes stochastic multiplication, since $p(z = 1) = p(x = 1)p(y = 1)$, given **X** and **Y** being statistically independent. SC's drawbacks include long latency, low accuracy and complex behavior. The capabilities of SC can be expanded by various means. Examples include bipolar SC, which extends the SN range from [0, 1] to [–1, 1] via the mapping $X = 2p(x = 1) - 1$ [9], multiline SC which employs several bit-lines per SN [7], and low-discrepancy codes which improve accuracy [1]. Applications such as vision chips [2][16] and neural networks (NNs) [4][7][10][14][15][19], can take advantage of the massive parallelism enabled by SC.

SC is best suited to specialized arithmetic tasks that do not need high precision and benefit from SC's low cost and error tolerance. It is less well suited to data storage, control functions, and some complex arithmetic operations that are often better implemented with BC [18]. Thus, most so-called "SC-based" systems are in fact a hybrid combination of SC and BC features. For instance, many NN designs use BC for implementing activation functions [5][14][19] and for weight storage [7][10]; see Fig. 1. Hybrid SC-BC systems usually need many costly data converters to integrate their SC and BC parts; see Fig. 2. The converters themselves can be seen as hybrid sequential circuits [22]. Data converters are also used extensively to restore accuracy by regenerating correlation-corrupted SNs [8]. This is done by SC-to-BC conversion followed by BC-to-SC conversion with a new random number source.

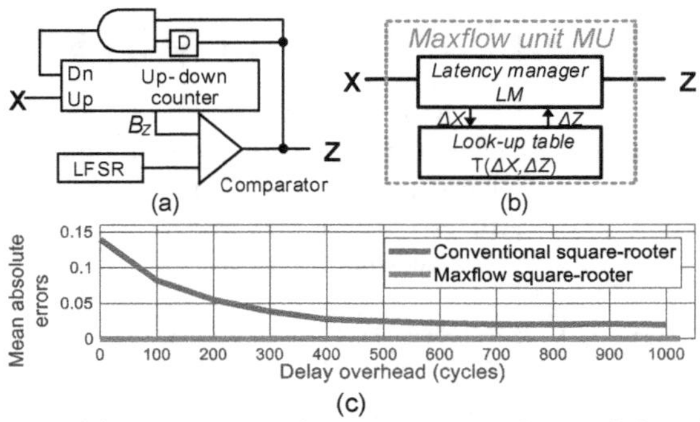

Figure 3. (a) Conventional square-rooter design [3] and (b) Maxflow design where X and Z are SNs. (c) Comparison of errors against delay overhead for N = 256 bits.

Fig. 1 shows the block structure of a generic neuron of the kind found in most NNs [7]. The figure emphasizes the hybrid nature of such systems. Each block processes SC- and/or BC-formatted data, so data converters (shaded) must be placed at the SC-BC interfaces. For example, the NN architecture proposed by Braendler et al. [5] is mainly based on SC, but its activation functions are implemented with BC via lookup tables (LUTs) for accuracy reasons. Data converters are thus placed before and after each activation function block to allow communication with other SC units. Lee et al. propose a hybrid NN [14] that only utilizes SC in the input layer; the remaining layers use BC. Sim and Lee describe an SC-based multiplication accelerator for deep NNs, which requires data converters at its inputs and outputs [19].

The impact of data converters on system latency is substantial, as Fig. 1 suggests. For example, a typical SC-to-BC converter (Fig. 2*b*) produces its BC output B_X by counting the 1s in the N-bit input SN **X**. This requires observing and accumulating all bits of **X**, a task that imposes a delay overhead of about N clock cycles. In a system with many processing stages, this kind of overhead contributes significantly to the system latency. Sometimes the BC parts of a hybrid design are implicit, so their impact on latency may be overlooked, as the following example illustrates.

Example 1: *Square-rooter.* The usual stochastic circuit to compute $Z(X) = \sqrt{X}$ was first described in the 1960s [9]. It is a multicycle sequential design built around an up-down counter. Fig. 3*a* shows a recent incarnation used in a power-supply monitoring system [3]. The output SN **Z** is fed back in such a way that the counter's state S converges toward $\sqrt{X}$. This is an implicit hybrid structure, since S is a binary number B_Z, and the BC-to-SC converter of Fig. 2*b* with an LFSR as its random number source, is required to convert B_Z to **Z**. The overall latency and accuracy of this circuit are hard to predict as they depend on complex circuit dynamics like warm-up time, convergence rate, LFSR quality, etc. and could be several times N. A significant factor contributing to this design's low accuracy is that, while it explicitly uses BC format for internal data representation, the main processing circuitry (a squarer comprising a delay flip flop and an AND gate) uses SC. As described in Sec. 2, Maxflow introduced in this paper yields a square-rooter with very low latency—just 2 clock cycles for N = 8—combined with high accuracy. Fig. 3*c* compares the error rates of the conventional and Maxflow square-rooters for N

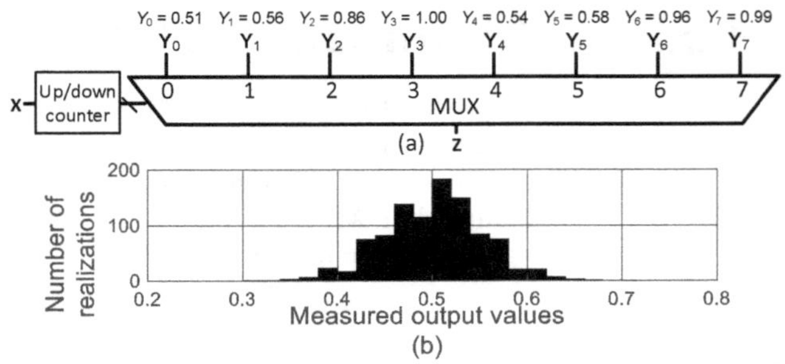

Figure 4. (a) Stochastic circuit C_{SIG} for Z = *sigmoid*(4X) generated using the sequential SC synthesizer in [17]. (b) Histogram of Z for 1,000 bipolar input SNs of value X = 0.0.

= 256 bits. The ground truth is the best possible SC approximation of $\sqrt{X}$ with N = 256. The delay overhead shown in Fig. 3*c* is the number of cycles that must elapse before the full output SN value is measured. The conventional square-rooter requires a long warm-up time to produce a reasonably accurate output, while the Maxflow design attains an accurate result after just 64 cycles. Further, with a delay less than 64 cycles, Maxflow still does not present significant errors. This shows another advantage of Maxflow: it can trade accuracy for shorter latency. □

In a nutshell, Maxflow exploits the fact that each bit in **X** provides partial information about **Z**, making it possible to start generating **Z** using early bits of **X**. Maxflow does this in a way that minimizes the latency of computing $Z(X)$ without compromising accuracy. This in turn tends to maximize data flow in complex all-SC or hybrid structures. Maxflow replaces a design like that of Fig. 3*a* along with associated data converters by the generic *MU* structure of Fig. 3*b*. *MU* has two parts: a LUT storing a table T(ΔX,ΔZ) that indirectly defines Z, and a small controller called the latency manager *LM*. Here ΔX denotes a parameter combining the current bit of **X** and the number of 1s and 0s from **X** received so far. From ΔX, *LM* incrementally computes a lower bound on the number of 1s in **Z**, and ΔZ symbolizes a change in this lower bound. Using ΔZ, *LM* identifies and buffers bits of **Z** which it outputs at the earliest cycle possible. Roughly speaking, as *LM* receives sufficient bits from **X**, it accumulates a precise number of 1s (0s) for later release into **Z**. Note that Maxflow can be seen as a type of hybrid design. It only stores the function definition in binary form, but it does not explicitly process **X** and **Z** in binary format. The hardware needed by Maxflow depends on $Z(X)$ and N.

In Fig. 3, the conventional design contains about $2\lceil \log_2 N \rceil$ flip-flops. The Maxflow design has a similar number of flip-flops in *LM,* while its LUT is of size $\lceil \log_2 N \rceil \times k$, where $k \le N$. As N increases, k grows at a rate of about $\log_2 \sqrt{N}$. For example, with N = 8, k = 2, while with N = 4,096, k = 6.

The paper is organized as follows. Sec. 2 briefly reviews the relevant aspects of SC and describes Maxflow in detail. Sec. 3 presents and analyzes an NN implementation based on Maxflow, while Sec. 4 draws some conclusions.

2 OPTIMIZING DELAY

This section first reviews relevant aspects of SC, and then describes in detail the Maxflow mechanism.

2.1 Accuracy and Latency in SC

Much research has been devoted to improving the accuracy of combinational stochastic circuits by using such techniques as deterministic bit-streams [5][11][19][23], low-discrepancy codes [1], non-standard SC designs [14][21], etc. However, little is known about how to design complex stochastic circuits with guaranteed levels of accuracy, especially when they employ sequential components which have complex behavior and high inherent latency [6][22].

Fig. 4*a* shows a sequential stochastic circuit C_{SIG} synthesized using the "linear FSM" architecture proposed by Li et al. [17] to implement the sigmoid function $sigmoid(4X) = 1/(1 + e^{-4X})$. The input **X** updates the state of the counter which indirectly determines **Z** at each clock cycle. C_{SIG}'s accuracy is affected by several factors like the bit-pattern of **X** and the warm-up time required for the counter to reach steady state [22]. These factors cause **Z** to fluctuate a lot as Fig. 4*b* shows. This is a histogram of the output values obtained by feeding C_{SIG} 1,000 independently generated bipolar SNs, each 256 bits long and containing exactly 128 1s, hence encoding the bipolar number zero exactly. The bit-patterns of the SNs, i.e., the locations of their 1s, vary widely. As Fig. 4*b* indicates, while the output values concentrate around the expected value $sigmoid(0) = 0.5$, they are widely dispersed. This highlights the design's lack of accuracy control.

Previous SC systems with stringent accuracy constraints alleviate the preceding problem by resorting to hybrid SC-BC designs that convert SC signals to BC signals, and process them with highly accurate BC components [5][14]. We will henceforth refer to these designs collectively as "Hybrid." The major drawback of Hybrid is the large delay overhead for data conversion. The Maxflow approach, on the other hand, uses **X**'s initial bits to provide fast estimation of the **Z**'s value, thereby allowing early but accurate generation of the output bit-stream. It does this in a manner reminiscent of interval arithmetic [12] by placing $N_{1,Z}$, the number of 1s in **Z**, in an integer interval $I(i) = [L_{1,Z}(i), U_{1,Z}(i)]$, where $L_{1,Z}(i)$ and $U_{1,Z}(i)$ are lower and upper bounds, respectively, on $N_{1,Z}$. The interval $I(i)$ represents the uncertainty about **Z**'s value, and reflects the number of 1s and 0s that are known or identified in **Z** at cycle i. Specifically, the least number of 1s and 0s that **Z** must contain at cycle i are $L_{1,Z}(i)$ and $N - U_{1,Z}(i)$, resp. A sequence of gradually shrinking intervals $I(0)$, $I(1)$, ..., $I(N)$ is generated as **X** streams into *MU* until eventually $L_{1,Z}(i)$ and $U_{1,Z}(i)$ coincide. Maxflow's accuracy can be attributed to the fact that it only includes identified bits in the output.

Example 1: *Square-rooter (contd.)* Consider implementing $Z = \sqrt{X}$ with $N = 8$ using Maxflow. (In practice, $N = 2^8$ is likely.) Here X can only have nine values of the form $N_{1,X}/N$, where $N_{1,X} \in \{0, 1, ..., 8\}$. The blue curve in Fig. 5*a* shows $Z(X)$, and the red dots mark the values of $N_{1,Z}$ for the nine possible values of $N_{1,X}$. For example, when $N_{1,X} = 6$, $Z(X) = 0.87$ and $N_{1,Z} = 7$. Figs. 5*b* tabulates $Z(X)$, while Fig. 5*c* shows an "N-table" $T(N_{1,X},N_{1,Z})$ that maps $N_{1,X}$ to $N_{1,Z}$. The values of $N_{1,X}$ and $N_{1,Z}$ in Fig. 5*c* are exact in that they represent the best possible approximation to $\sqrt{X}$ given the unavoidable quantization errors of 8-bit SNs. Maxflow accurately predicts $N_{1,Z}$, the number of 1s in **Z**, by inspecting **X**

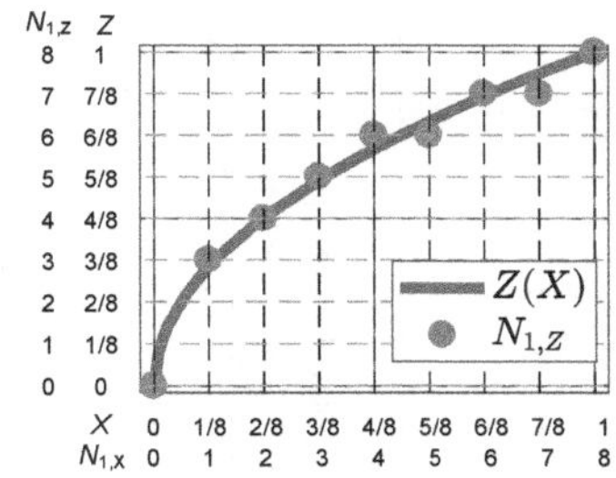

(a)

X	$Z(X)$
0	0
1/8	0.35
2/8	0.50
3/8	0.61
4/8	0.71
5/8	0.79
6/8	0.87
7/8	0.94
1	1

(b)

$N_{1,X}$	$N_{1,Z}$
0	0
1	3
2	4
3	5
4	6
5	6
6	7
7	7
8	8

(c)

Figure 5. (a) Plot of $Z(X) = \sqrt{X}$ for $N = 8$; red dots mark $N_{1,Z}$. (b) Tabulated $Z(X)$ values. (c) N-table mapping $N_{1,X}$ to $N_{1,Z}$.

Clock cycle	1	2	3	4	5	6	7	8	9	10
X	0	0	0	0	1	0	0	1		
Q = Number of identified 1s/0s	0/1	0/1	0/2	0/2	3/2	3/3	3/4	4/4	4/4	4/4
S = Number of outputted 1s/0s	0/0	0/0	0/1	0/2	1/2	2/2	2/3	3/3	3/4	4/4
Q – S	0/1	0/1	0/1	0/0	2/0	1/1	1/1	1/1	1/0	0/0
Z	←d_{MIN}→		0	0	1	1	0	1	0	1

Figure 6. Computation of $Z(X) = \sqrt{X}$ by a Maxflow square-rooter when X = 00001001.

bit by bit. Before computation starts, nothing is known about X and Z, and we can only say that $N_{1,Z}$ lies in the interval $I(0) = [0, 8]$. Suppose the first bit of **X** is $\mathbf{X}(1) = 1$. Fig. 5*c* indicates that with $N_{1,X} \geq 1$, $N_{1,Z}$ must be larger or equal to 3, i.e., **Z** must contain at least three 1s, so now we can place $N_{1,Z}$ in $I(1) = [3, 8]$. If $\mathbf{X}(2)$ is also 1, the interval containing $N_{1,Z}$ shrinks to $I(2) = [4,8]$. On the other hand, if $\mathbf{X}(2) = 0$, then $I(2) = [3,7]$, meaning that **Z** must have at least one 0. Continuing in this fashion, the interval shrinks monotonically until it reaches $I(N) = [N_{1,Z}, N_{1,Z}]$ and the exact value Z is known.

Suppose now **X** = 00001001 with time flowing from left to right. The latency manager *LM* computes the sequence of 9 intervals:

$$[0,8], [0,7], [0,7], [0,6], [0,6], [3,6], [3,5], [3,4], [4,4] \qquad (1)$$

where $I(i) = [L_{1,Z}(i), U_{1,Z}(i)]$, and the numbers of identified 1s and 0s are $L_{1,Z}(i)$ and $N - U_{1,Z}(i)$, resp. *LM* uses the interval sequence to gradually identify bits in **Z**. Fig. 6 tabulates the numbers of identified bits for this particular **X**. It shows that if we insert a delay of $d_{MIN} = 2$ cycles and start generating **Z** at cycle 3, enough identified output bits are always available and *LM* can output one of them. The SN **Z** in Fig. 6 contains the expected four 1s and four 0s, and its bit-pattern reflects the randomness of **X**'s bit-pattern. Thus, the Maxflow design computes accurately with a minimal delay $d_{MIN} = 2$ for the given **X**. In general, d_{MIN} must be set to cover all possible 8-bit input SNs. (We present an algorithm MIND to determine d_{MIN} in Sec. 2.2.) It turns out that $d_{MIN} = 2$ works for all possible **X**'s in this example. Therefore, Maxflow reduces the latency to 2 cycles; in contrast, the minimum delay overhead of a hybrid design is at least 7 (and probably much more.) As we show later, d_{MIN} scales linearly with N for a target function. Hence, Maxflow can reduce the latency to a fixed fraction of N. □

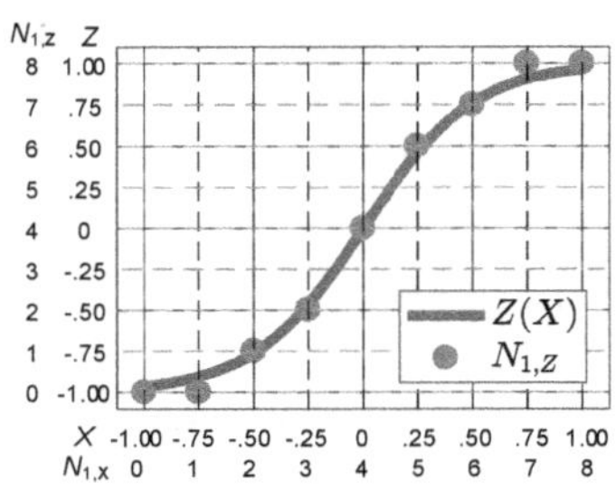

(a)

X	$Z(X)$
-1.00	-0.96
-0.75	-0.91
-0.50	-0.76
-0.25	-0.46
0.00	0
0.25	0.46
0.50	0.76
0.75	0.91
1.00	0.96

(b)

$N_{1,X}$	$N_{1,Z}$
0	0
1	0
2	1
3	2
4	4
5	6
6	7
7	8
8	8

(c)

Figure 7. Computation of $Z(X)$ = $tanh(2X)$. (a) Plot of $Z(X)$ with red dots marking $N_{1,Z}$. (b) SN values for $Z(X)$, and (c) the corresponding N-table T($N_{1,X}$, $N_{1,Z}$).

	$\mathbf{X}^{(3)}$	$N_{1,\mathbf{X}^{(3)}}$	$I(3)$	$q(3, N_{1,\mathbf{X}^{(3)}})$
Case I	000	0	[0,6]	2
Case II	001, 010, 100	1	[0,7]	1
Case III	011, 101, 110	2	[1,8]	1
Case IV	111	3	[2,8]	2

Figure 8. Initial 3-bit segments of X considered by MIND.

2.2 Determining Delay Overhead

This section details the algorithm MIND that computes d_{MIN} for a given Maxflow design. The hardware implementation of Maxflow is discussed in Sec 2.3.

To illustrate how MIND works, consider finding d_{MIN} for a hyperbolic tangent function, a common activation function in NNs. Fig. 7 plots $Z = tanh(2X)$ with $N = 8$, where **X** and **Z** are in bipolar format. d_{MIN} must be set so that the Maxflow unit always has enough bits to output, regardless of **X**'s pattern. Suppose the initial 3-bit segment $\mathbf{X}^{(3)}$ of **X** has been received. There are four possible cases defined by $N_{1,\mathbf{X}^{(3)}}$, the number of 1s in $\mathbf{X}^{(3)}$; see Fig. 8. For example, in Case III, $\mathbf{X}^{(3)}$ has two 1s and the corresponding output interval is $I(3) = [1,8]$, meaning that **Z** contains at least one 1. Let $q(i, N_{1,\mathbf{X}^{(i)}}) = L_{1,Z}(i) + (N - U_{1,Z}(i))$ denote the number of identified output bits on receiving an $\mathbf{X}^{(i)}$ that has $N_{1,\mathbf{X}^{(i)}}$ 1s. For instance, $q(3, 2) = 1 + (8 - 8) = 1$, since $I(3) = [1,8]$ when $N_{1,\mathbf{X}^{(3)}} = 2$. From Fig. 8, it is clear that regardless of $\mathbf{X}^{(3)}$'s bit-pattern, there is always at least $u^{(3)} = 1$ identified bit at clock cycle 3, where:

$$u^{(i)} = min\ q(i\,,\, N_{1,\mathbf{X}^{(i)}}) \quad (2)$$

and the *min* operation is over all possible $N_{1,\mathbf{X}^{(i)}}$'s for each cycle i. Note that $u^{(i)}$ increases monotonically with i, because we can identify additional bits in **Z** as we receive more bits of **X**. Recall that Maxflow guarantees accuracy by not outputting more bits than it has identified at each cycle. That implies that $u^{(i)}$ must be greater than or equal to the number of outputted bits for all i's under consideration. This translates to the set of inequalities:

$$u^{(i)} \geq i - d, \text{ for } i = 1 + d, 2 + d, \ldots, N \quad (3)$$

To gain further insight into the constraint set (3), we define two functions $H(i) = u^{(i)}$ and $G(i, d) = i - d$. $H(i)$ is the least number of bits that must have been identified at cycle i, while $G(i, d)$ is the number of bits that have been outputted at cycle i, which can be adjusted by controlling the delay overhead d. When satisfied, (3) guarantees that never will fewer bits be identified than are outputted at any clock cycle. MIND finds d_{MIN} by scanning for the smallest feasible d that satisfies the constraint set (3). Fig. 9 summarizes MIND.

Input: N-table T($N_{1,X}$, $N_{1,Z}$) for the target function $Z(X)$; Bit-stream length N
Output: Minimal delay overhead d_{MIN}
Step 1 **for** $i = 1, 2, \ldots, N$
  for $N_{1,\mathbf{X}^{(i)}} = 1, 2, \ldots, i$:
    Compute $I(i) = [L_{1,Z}(i), U_{1,Z}(i)]$ associated with $N_{1,\mathbf{X}^{(i)}}$ via T($N_{1,X}$, $N_{1,Z}$).
    Set $q(i, N_{1,\mathbf{X}^{(i)}}) = L_{1,Z}(i) + N - U_{1,Z}(i)$.
  Set $u^{(i)} = min\ q(i\,,\, N_{1,\mathbf{X}^{(i)}})$.
Step 2 **for** $d = 0, 1, \ldots, N - 1$:
  if $u^{(i)} \geq i - d$, for $i = 1 + d, 2 + d, \ldots, N$
    Set $d_{MIN} = d$, break, and output d_{MIN}

Figure 9. Pseudo-code of algorithm MIND to calculate the minimum latency overhead d_{MIN} for a Maxflow design.

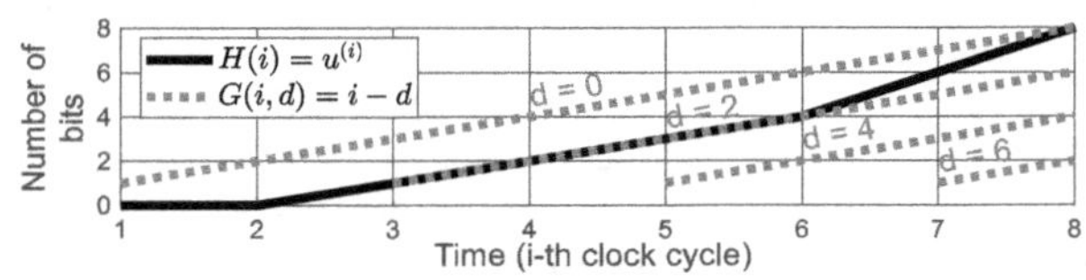

Figure 10. The black line plots the number of bits identified against time for $Z(X)$ = $tanh(2X)$. The red dashed lines plot the number of outputted bits against time for various delay values d.

Example 2: $tanh(2X)$. To find d_{MIN} for $tanh(2X)$ with $N = 8$, MIND first computes $I(i)$ for $\mathbf{X}^{(i)}$ and $N_{1,\mathbf{X}^{(i)}}$ for $i = 1, 2, \ldots, 8$. For instance, with $\mathbf{X}^{(5)} = 01001$, $N_{1,\mathbf{X}^{(5)}} = 2$, and the corresponding $I(5) = [1, 6]$, as can be inferred from Fig. 7*c*; $q(i, N_{1,\mathbf{X}^{(i)}})$ can then be computed from the corresponding $I(i)$. For instance, with $I(5) = [L_{1,Z}(5), U_{1,Z}(5)] = [1, 6]$, $q(5, 2) = L_{1,Z}(5) + (N - U_{1,Z}(5)) = 3$. Next, MIND calculates $u^{(i)}$ for $i = 1, 2, \ldots, 8$ via Eq. (2), resulting in:

$$\boldsymbol{u} = [u^{(1)}\ u^{(2)} \ldots u^{(8)}] = [0\ 0\ 1\ 2\ 3\ 4\ 6\ 8]$$

To visualize this, the black line in Fig. 10 plots $H(i) = u^{(i)}$ against time $i = 1, 2, \ldots, 8$. The red (dashed) lines plot $G(i, d) = i - d$ against time for various d's. Satisfying Eq. (2) requires red lines not to be above the black line. Finding d_{MIN} can thus be seen as finding the red line that touches, but does not lie above, the black line. This process is reflected in Step 2 of MIND (Fig. 9). In the present example, d_{MIN} is 2, implying that a delay of 2 cycles is needed to ensure accurate computation for $Z(X) = tanh(2X)$. □

2.3 Implementation and Performance Analysis

Rather than storing the N-table for the target function, it is more efficient to store a Δ-table which provides the incremental change of $N_{1,Z}$, and can be easily pre-computed from the corresponding N-table. In general, a Δ-table has an address consisting of $N_{0,X}(i\text{-}1)$, $N_{1,X}(i\text{-}1)$ and $\mathbf{X}(i)$. However, for monotonically increasing functions, including square-root, *tanh* and *sigmoid*, $N_{1,X}(i\text{-}1)$ and $\mathbf{X}(i)$ suffice as the address of the Δ-table, as we illustrate in this section.

Fig. 11 shows both the N-table and the Δ-table (for the part with $\mathbf{X}(i) = 1$ only) for $tanh(2X)$ with $N = 8$. Recall that an N-table maps the number of 1s in **X** to the number of 1s in **Z**. A Δ-table, on the other hand, stores the change in the number of 1s of **Z** on receiving a new bit from **X**. For example, in Fig. 11*a*, when $N_{1,X} = 3$, $N_{1,Z} = 2$. Also, when $N_{1,X} = 4$, $N_{1,Z} = 4$. This implies that if $N_{1,X}$ changes from 3 to 4, $N_{1,Z}$ will increase by 2, since it changes from

$N_{1,}$x	0	1	2	3	4	5	6	7	8
$N_{1,}$z	0	0	1	2	4	6	7	8	8

(a)

$N_{1,}$x(i-1)	0	1	2	3	4	5	6	7
ΔZ	0	1	1	2	2	1	1	0

(b)

Figure 11. (a) *N*-table for *Z*(*X*) = *tanh*(2*X*), and (b) the corresponding Δ-table with X(*i*) = 1.

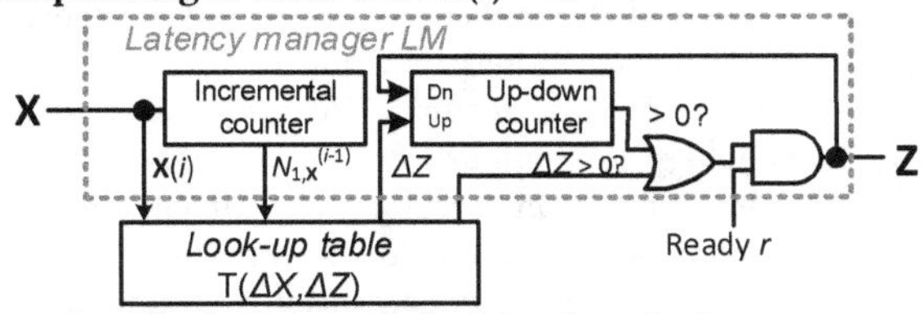

Figure 12. Block diagram of a Maxflow design

2 to 4. This is exactly the information stored in the Δ-table. Fig. 11*b* shows the Δ-table when the current bit **X**(i) = 1. We omit the part for **X**(i) = 0, since for a monotonically increasing function, **X**(i) = 0 implies no change in $N_{1,}$z . Observe that when $N_{1,}$x(i-1) = 3, ΔZ = 2. This is because given that **X**(i) = 1, and that we previously received three 1s from **X**, i.e. $N_{1,}$x = 3, the increment of $N_{1,}$z is 2, as discussed previously.

Fig. 12 shows a Maxflow unit (Fig. 3) in more detail. The Δ-table maps **X**(i) and $N_{1,}$x($i-1$) to ΔZ, the increment of newly identified 1s, which is then buffered by the up/down counter. The output is set to 1, if the buffer is larger than 0 or if there are newly identified 1s (ΔZ > 0). Further, if the current output is 1, the buffer will decrease by 1. Note that the buffer is initialized to the minimum value of $N_{1,}$z for the target function, which is the least number of 1s **Z** must contain. The ready bit r is set to 1 after d_{MIN} cycles, where d_{MIN} has been computed in advance using MIND.

Comparing the Maxflow and Hybrid designs, we see that they are similar in terms of memory size. Maxflow has two counters requiring approximately $\lceil \log_2(N) \rceil$ flip flops each. Hybrid uses $\lceil \log_2(N) \rceil$ flip flops for its SC-BC converter, and another $\lceil \log_2(N) \rceil$ flip flops for an LFSR random source. Both Maxflow and Hybrid may use LUTs of a comparable size to store the target function's definition. However, the Maxflow design guarantees minimum delay, while Hybrid imposes the worst-case delay of approximately N cycles.

Fig. 13 compares the delay overhead of Hybrid and Maxflow designs for some representative functions. Hybrid always imposes the worst-case delay overhead, since it requires about N clock cycles for data conversion, regardless of the function being implemented. Maxflow usually has much smaller delay than the worst case. The delay overhead d_{MIN} for all cases increases linearly w.r.t. the bit-stream length N. Note that for functions like *tanh*(*X*) and *sigmoid*(*X*), Maxflow can always compute accurately with no added delay. This is because these functions have sufficiently steep slopes when the input value is near −1 and 1, implying that a few initial bits from the input can quickly identify many bits for the output SN. Also, the minimum value of *sigmoid*(*X*) is 0, implying that there must be at least half bits in the output SN are 1. This further allows Maxflow to identify some output bits even before the computation starts.

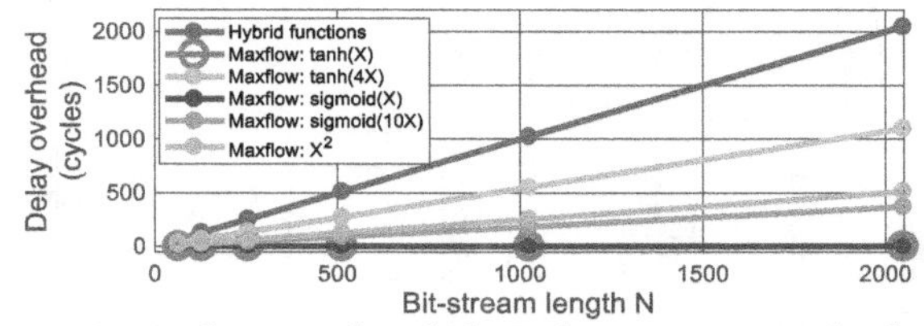

Figure 13. Delay overhead d_{MIN} for various Hybrid and Maxflow designs for some representative functions.

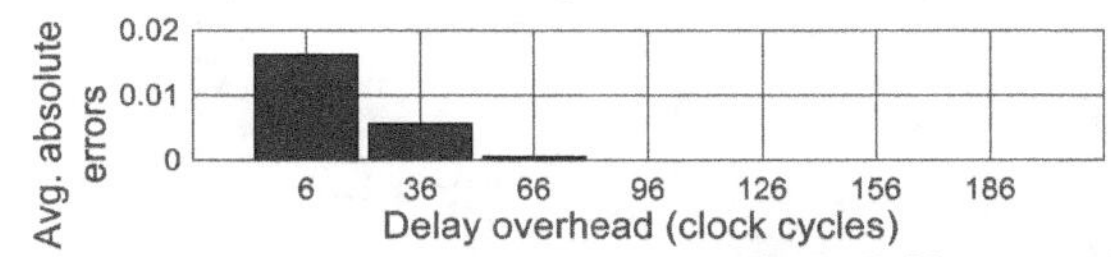

Figure 14. Error comparison under different delay conditions for Z = *sigmoid*(10X) implemented by Maxflow.

Maxflow can easily trade accuracy for shorter delay by setting the ready bit to 1 earlier. Ignoring the d_{MIN} constraint may result in insufficient identified bits of **Z**, in which case Maxflow must randomly output a 1 or a 0. In this experiment, we let Maxflow always output a 0 when there are not enough identified bits. Surprisingly, many stochastic functions seem very tolerant of aggressive delay-trading when they are implemented with Maxflow. Fig. 14 plots the absolute errors against delay overhead for a Maxflow implementation of *sigmoid*(10*X*), where the results are averaged over 10,000 random inputs of 1,024 bits. The required d_{MIN} in this case is 186 bits. However, even aggressively halving d_{MIN} does not produce significant errors. This favorable accuracy-delay tradeoff can be explained as follows. The delay constraint guarantees that the output will always be accurate, regardless of the input bit-patterns. However, our experiments show that for many functions, only a small fraction of the input patterns are "difficult" in the sense that they result in slow identification of the output bits. The probability of encountering difficult patterns is low, so even aggressively shortening the delay should not introduce significant errors.

3 CASE STUDY: NEURAL NETWORKS

We demonstrate Maxflow's effectiveness for a deep NN, which achieves a very low misclassification rate for the well-known MNIST [13] dataset of handwritten digits. The NN's topology is shown in Fig. 15, and is architecturally similar to the LeNet-5 family [13][14]. It has two convolution layers, two averaging pooling layers, a densely connected layer, a soft-max layer for training (omitted in Fig. 15), and achieves a software-based test accuracy of around 99%. For hardware-based NNs, Maxflow can be extended and applied to several SC variants like those using accumulative parallel counters (APCs) to improve multiply-and-add accuracy [4][15]. For clarity, we demonstrate Maxflow here for an NN employing conventional single-line SC with bipolar SNs to account for negative numerical weights. Multiplication of two SNs is thus implemented by a single XNOR gate. Scaled addition is realized by a highly accurate design proposed recently [14] and demonstrated to have optimal accuracy [21]. This new adder replaces the standard MUX-based adder by a sequential circuit that accurately averages all input patterns.

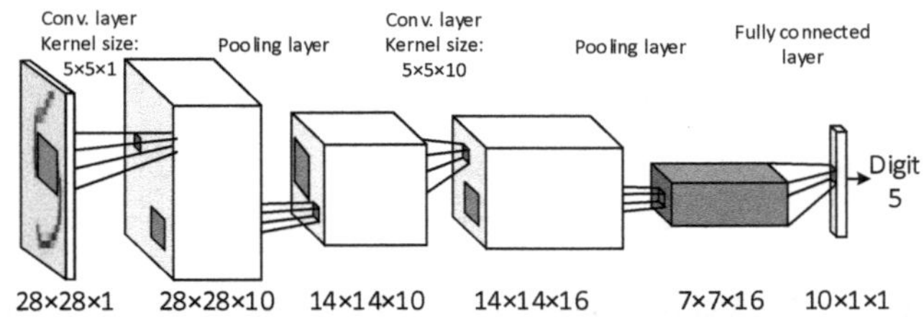

Figure 15. Deep NN trained for the MNIST dataset [13].

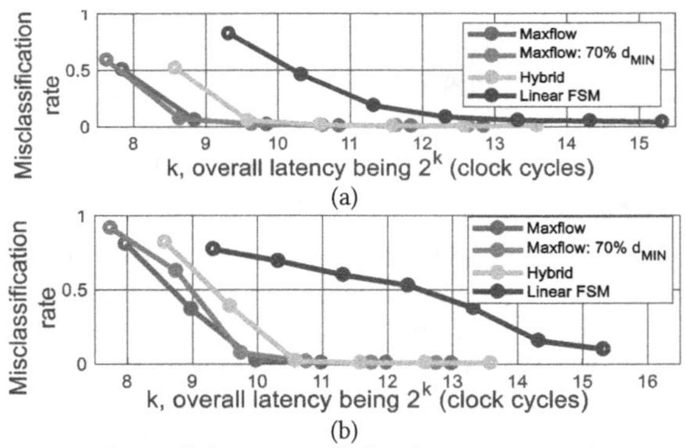

Figure 16. Overall latency of the deep NN in Fig. 15 with several versions of (a) *sigmoid*, and (b) ReLU as the activation function.

Further, the synaptic weights in our NN are represented by evenly distributed low-discrepancy SNs, as used in [5][19]. We tested the NN with various choices of activation functions, including *sigmoid* and ReLU. We define ReLU(X) = $min(max(0, X), 1)$, with the value capped at 1 due to SN range limitations. All the NN designs presented in this section were trained offline on images with pixels in the range [−1 1], and simulated at the gate level to test their inference performance using C++/CUDA.

We compared the performance of three deep NN types with activation functions implemented by (1) Maxflow, (2) a Hybrid design with an accurate binary LUT like that in [5], and (3) a sequential stochastic circuit with a linear FSM architecture [17], respectively. Increasing the number of states for a linear FSM generally improves its ability to approximate a function, but at the cost of a long warm-up period during which the accuracy can be very low [22]. We chose 128-state linear FSMs to strike a balance between the number of states and accuracy. Further, to provide the randomness required by the FSMs, we place a re-randomizer before each of them. Similar to the Edge Memory proposed in [20], the re-randomizer used here is an M-bit shift register that stores an SN and randomly selects a bit from the SN to output. Here M is set to $N/8$, where N is the SN length. We also configured Maxflow to trade accuracy for speed by reducing d_{MIN} by 30%. Fig. 16 plots the resulting misclassification rate against latency for the foregoing designs, where latency is defined as the cycle count from the beginning of the computation until the classification result appears. Fig. 16*a* shows the results for *sigmoid* functions., The aggressive Maxflow design reduces the latency to about half of that of Hybrid with the same accuracy. Specifically, for misclassification rate of about 2%, Hybrid has a latency of about 1,530 cycles, while the aggressive Maxflow design requires about 780 cycles, which is around 49% reduction in latency. The linear-FSM NN, on the other hand, requires about 2^{13} cycles to achieve an error rate of about 5% due to its lack of accuracy guarantees. As shown in Fig. 16*b*, ReLU functions yield similar results as those for *sigmoid*.

4 CONCLUSIONS

We have investigated the problem of excessively long delay in complex SC systems, noting that much of this delay is attributable to hybrid SC-BC features. We introduced Maxflow, a design methodology to minimize delay overhead in a hybrid system without compromising accuracy. Experimental results for a deep NN demonstrated that Maxflow significantly reduces the NN's overall latency without reducing its classification rate.

REFERENCES

[1] Alaghi, A. and Hayes, J.P. "Fast and accurate computation using stochastic circuits." *Proc. DATE*, pp. 1-4, 2014.

[2] Alaghi, A. et al. "Stochastic circuits for real-time image-processing applications." *Proc. DAC*, Art.136, 2013.

[3] Ananth, R.S. "Programmable supervisory circuit and applications thereof," US Patent no. 6,618,711, Sept. 9, 2003.

[4] Ardakani, A. et al. "VLSI implementation of deep neural networks using integral stochastic computing." *Proc. ISTC*, pp. 216-220, 2016.

[5] Braendler, D. et al. "Deterministic bit-stream digital neurons." *IEEE Trans. Neural Nets.*, 13, pp. 1514-1525, 2002.

[6] Brown, B.D. and Card, H. "Stochastic neural computation I: computational elements." *IEEE Trans. Computers*, 50, pp.891-905, 2001.

[7] Canals, V. et al. "A new stochastic computing methodology for efficient neural network implementation." *IEEE Trans. Neural Nets. & Learning Sys*, 27(3), pp. 551-564, 2016.

[8] Chen, T.-H. and Hayes, J.P. "Analyzing and controlling accuracy in stochastic circuits." *Proc. ICCD*, pp.367-373, 2014.

[9] Gaines, B.R. "Stochastic computing systems." *Advances in Info. Sys. Sci.*, 2, pp. 37-172, 1969.

[10] Hikawa, H. "A digital hardware pulse-mode neuron with piecewise linear activation function." *IEEE Trans. Neural Nets.*, 14, pp. 1028-1037, 2003.

[11] Jenson, D. and Riedel, M. "A deterministic approach to stochastic computation." *Proc. ICCAD*, pp. 1-8, 2016.

[12] Kearfott, R.B. "Interval computations: Introduction, uses, and resources." *Euromath Bulletin*, 2(1), pp. 95-112, 1996.

[13] LeCun, Y. et at. "Gradient-based learning applied to document recognition." *Proc. the IEEE*, 86(11), pp. 2278-2324, 1998.

[14] Lee, V. T. et al. "Energy-efficient hybrid stochastic-binary neural networks for near-sensor computing." *Proc. DATE*, pp. 13-18, 2017.

[15] Li, J. et al. "Hardware-driven nonlinear activation for stochastic computing based deep convolutional neural networks." *Proc. IJCNN*, pp. 1230-1236, 2017.

[16] Li, P. and Lilja, D.J. "Using stochastic computing to implement digital image processing algorithms." *Proc. ICCD*, pp. 154-161, 2011.

[17] Li. P. et at., "The synthesis of linear finite state machine-based stochastic computational elements." *Proc. ASPDAC*, pp. 757-762, 2012.

[18] Manohar, R. "Comparing stochastic and deterministic computing." *IEEE Comp. Arch. Letters*, 14(2), pp. 119-122, 2015.

[19] Sim, H. and Lee, J. "A new stochastic computing multiplier with application to deep convolutional neural networks." *Proc. DAC*, pp. 1-6, 2017.

[20] Tehrani, S. et al. "Stochastic decoding of LDPC codes." *IEEE Communications Letters*, 10(10), pp. 716-718, 2006.

[21] Ting, P. and Hayes, J.P. "Eliminating a hidden error source in stochastic circuits." *Proc. DFT*, pp. 44-49, 2017.

[22] Ting, P. and Hayes, J.P. "On the role of sequential circuits in stochastic computing." *Proc. GLSVLSI*, pp. 475-478, 2017.

[23] Vahapoglu, E. and Altun, M. "Accurate synthesis of arithmetic operations with stochastic logic."*Proc. ISVLSI*, pp.415-420, 2016.

Methodology to Capture Statistical Effect of Process Imperfections on Glitch Suppression in CNFET Circuits and to Improve by Using Approximate Circuits

Kaship Sheikh
Department of Electrical and Computer Engineering
University of Waterloo, Waterloo, ON, Canada
k3sheikh@uwaterloo.ca

Lan Wei
Department of Electrical and Computer Engineering
University of Waterloo, Waterloo, ON, Canada
lan.wei@uwaterloo.ca

ABSTRACT

Carbon nanotube field effect transistor (CNFET) technology has shown tremendous potential, and thus extensively studied among the emerging materials-based technologies to replace Si for the post-Si era. However, emerging technologies including CNFET technology suffer from immature, poor process quality, leading to process imperfections, which in turn degrade circuit performance. This paper presents a methodology to evaluate circuit level impact and design solution related with imperfect process. Monte Carlo simulation is applied to consider the statistical nature of the process imperfections. With a specific study on glitch tolerance (important circuit-level performance metric in advanced technology nodes) in CNFET circuits, our simulation framework provides the link between degradation in glitch tolerance with poor process quality. Moreover, we have proposed that approximate circuits can significantly improve glitch tolerance in comparison to precise counterparts, due to lesser nodes, reduced stacked configurations, and reduced number of connections at some nodes because of simpler topologies. With examples of 4-bit adder and 4-bit multiplier circuits, we have demonstrated that approximate circuits are able to lower the glitch vulnerability to an acceptable level, with a tolerable logic error. Moreover, approximate circuits would also relax the requirement on process quality to keep process-induced failures below certain target.

Keywords

Carbon nanotube field effect transistor, low dimensional material, process imperfections, Monte Carlo, approximate circuit, glitch tolerance.

ACM Reference format:

K. Sheikh and L. Wei. 2018. Methodology to Capture Statistical Effect of Process Imperfections on Glitch Suppression in CNFET Circuits and to Improve by Using Approximate Circuits. In *Proceedings of the Great Lakes Symposium on VLSI 2018, Chicago, IL, USA, May 2018* (*GLSVLSI '18*), 6 pages.
DOI: https://doi.org/10.1145/3194554.3194587.

GLSVLSI '18, May 23–25, 2018, Chicago, IL, USA

ACM ISBN 978-1-4503-5724-1/18/05...$15.00
DOI: https://doi.org/10.1145/3194554.3194587

1. INTRODUCTION

Despite tremendous investment in Si transistor scaling to continue Moore's law, further Si transistor scaling is showing diminishing returns, hence active research is currently being pursued to explore new materials, which could replace Si in future technology nodes [1,2]. Preliminary results with the low dimensional materials (LDMs) including transition metal dichalcogenides (TMD) [3], black phosphorous [4], graphene [5], carbon nanotubes (CNT) [6, 7] have shown potentials to replace Si as channel material. However, none of LDMs have been close to high-volume manufacturing because of their immature and poor process quality, hence with the current projection it seems they might not be able to replace Si in the mainstream technology for general purpose computing in the nearby future.

In the recent years, approximate computing in applications like image and video processing has gained traction, because of its benefits of speed, power, area [8, 9]. Such applications are ideally suited for the emerging low dimensional materials because they can tolerate errors to some degree during computation thus relaxing the need to have very high yield and precise circuitry. Hence, by introduction of low dimensional materials in such applications, one can further benefit in terms of speed/power, even with an immature, relatively poor process quality. In most cases, approximate circuits have clear advantages of fewer nodes along a path and fewer nodes in the entire circuit in comparison to their precise counterparts, which results in lower chances of getting affected by process induced failures. Moreover, approximate circuits have reduced stacked transistor configurations, reduced number of connections at some nodes, which both improve glitch tolerance.

Considering the statistical nature of process imperfections of CNT process, we propose a methodology to conduct Monte Carlo (MC) simulations on circuits based on carbon nanotube field effect transistor (CNFET). Additionally, we apply the methodology to a few adder and multiplier topologies (precise and approximate designs) to quantify the benefits of having approximate designs in dealing with process imperfection while still having reasonable logic accuracy. We have taken CNFET as an example of low dimensional material (LDM) for our study, as CNT was the first LDM introduced in 90's [10] and has arguably the most matured process for large volume manufacturing among the LDMs [6, 7, 11]. Moreover, a brain-inspired computing system consisting of CNFETs has been recently fabricated and utilized for language recognition task. Simulation results (after place and route) for such nanosystem have shown significant EDP advantage (~ 35x) compared to silicon-based design at 28 nm technology node [12].

2. CNFET PROCESS

Among the existing processes aimed at growing large-scale aligned CNT array, the recently reported ion-exchange process of placement of solution based CNTs [13] has gained popularity because of its potential to achieve high density, high semiconducting purity (percentage of semiconducting tubes > 99.9%) [6, 14]. The process first separates metallic tubes from semiconducting tubes in the solution, and then place the semiconducting tubes into pre-patterned trenches using ion-exchange process to form semiconducting channels connecting source and drain of CNFETs [6, 13].

There can be two kinds of imperfections, which can arise from the ion-exchange separation and placement process. First, the metallic tubes, which are still present after the separation step, lead to "short CNTs", which do not turn off during "off" state. Recently, the "short CNTs" has been reported by various groups to be < 0.1% [6, 14] and is less of an issue in performance degradation. Second, the trenches which are left empty after the placement step, lead to "open CNTs", which do not conduct current even in the on state. The open CNTs are by far the dominant factor for CNFET performance degradation. For HfO2 trench width of 50nm, up to 30% of designed channels are uncovered [7]. If trench width is scaled further, the "open CNTs" are expected to go beyond 30%. For the rest of the paper, we focus on the imperfection due to "open CNTs".

3. METHODOLOGY

In this section, we explain the methodology to set up MC simulation for glitch analysis of CNFET circuits suffering from process open trenches imperfection.

3.1 Capturing Effect of Process Opens for HSPICE Simulation

We have used Stanford VSCNFET model [15] for simulation of CNFET based circuits in HSPICE. By adjusting the spacing parameter "s", the number of CNTs for a given width can be varied, thus capturing the effect of open CNTs in a CNFET device without affecting the parasitic capacitance. Fig. 1 shows the schematic of a CNFET device suffering from process imperfections. We define N as the total number of open trenches to be covered by CNTs in ideal case and N_{open} as the number of open trench due to imperfect process. In the given example, N=6, N_{open}=1 meaning the driving current is reduced by 1/6. The main impact of the open CNT is the reduction of current.

3.2 Capturing Effect of Process Opens for MC Seed Generation

We use the term seed for each trial or sample of the MC run. The generation of seeds for the MC run is done in two steps:

1) Generation of *Space File*
2) Assignment of space values to spacing parameter "s" of transistors in the HSPICE netlist.

We define term *Space File* as a file-containing list of spacing parameter values at a particular $PCNT_{open}$ (percentage of open CNTs). The generation of *Space File* at a particular $PCNT_{open}$ involves mapping of uniform random numbers (between 0 to 1) on to the cumulative probability distribution (given by equations below), followed by storing the corresponding spacing parameter values in *Space File* (Fig. 2)

$$P_{N_{open}} = C_N^{N_{open}} . PCNT_{open}^{N_{open}} . \left(1 - PCNT_{open}\right)^{N-N_{open}} \quad (1)$$

$$C_K = \sum_{i=0}^{K} P_{N_{open}=i} \quad (2)$$

where P_{Nopen} is the probability of N_{open} among N total trenches and C_k represents the cumulative probability distribution for $N_{open} \le k$ (k = 0, 1, 2, ..., N-1).

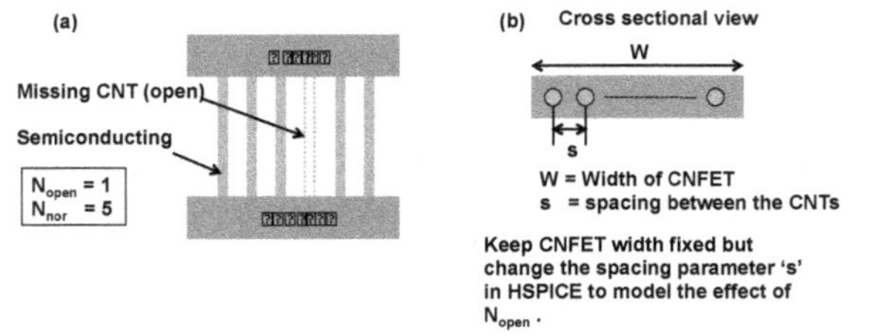

Figure 1: (From Left to Right) (a) Schematic showing CNFET with process imperfections with N = 6, N_{nor} = 5, N_{open} = 1. (b) Shows the cross-sectional view of the CNFET with W as width and s as spacing between CNTs. To consider N_{open} in HSPICE, the spacing is increased while the width of the CNFET is kept fixed. Keeping the width as fixed would ensure that the parasitic capacitance of CNFET remains nearly the same among the cases where number of semiconducting tubes might be different. [Adopted from [16]]

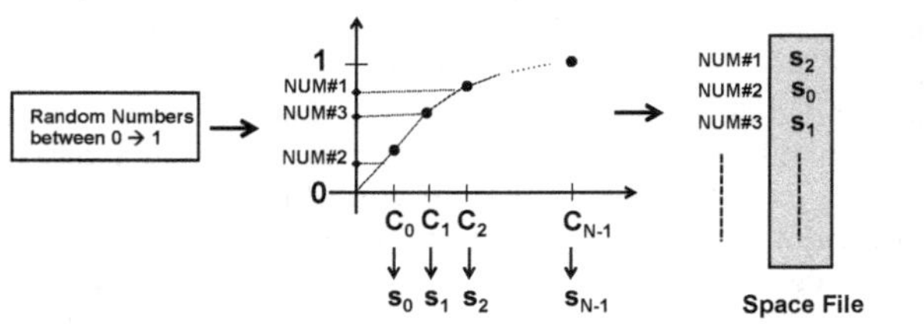

Figure 2: Show the generation of *Space File* (containing list of spacing parameter values) at a particular $PCNT_{open}$ involves the mapping of random numbers with uniform distribution on to the cumulative distribution and finding the corresponding spacing values. Each of the random number generated is mapped to the y-axis of the cumulative distribution and the next highest cumulative distribution point is chosen corresponding to the number. e.g. The first number generated *NUM#1* is closest to point C_2 which maps to space value s_2. In a similar manner, *NUM#2*, *NUM#3* correspond to space values s_0, s_1 respectively. s_0, s_1, s_2, ..., s_{N-1} in the figure are the spacing values corresponding to cumulative distribution points C_0, C_1, C_2, ..., C_{N-1} respectively.

Once the *Space File* at each $PCNT_{open}$ is obtained, the next step is the seed generation for the MC run. The spacing parameter "s" of each transistor in the netlist is parameterized for acquiring values from *Space File* for seed generation. For a given $PCNT_{open}$, the values from the *Space File* are then used for the generation of separate copies of the netlist, which might differ in the spacing values assigned to each transistor. Each of the obtained netlist is the seed for MC run. The number of values in *Space File* ≥ *#seeds*#transistors*, where *#seeds* and *#transistors* are number of seeds for the MC run and number of transistors in the circuit respectively. In this paper, we have conducted MC simulations for 100 seeds.

3.3 Effect of Process Opens on Glitch Handling in CNFET Circuits

As explained earlier, the presence of open CNTs would reduce the driving current of a stage, leading to several negative impacts at the circuit level such as speed degradation and vulnerability to noise. In particular it may reduce the ability of a driver to suppress the glitches occurring at its otherwise stable output node, which is proven to be one of the major sources of circuit level failures due to process imperfection in CNFET circuits [16]. Fig 3. shows an example of glitches at the nodes of the circuit due to coupling from the aggressors. In the absence of the aggressors, the nodes n1 and n2 in Fig. 3, would have voltages close to VDD, GND respectively for the given input vector combination of [00]. For our glitch analysis we create a scenario, wherein each internal/output node of the circuit is being evaluated for glitch tolerance. We assume that the glitches are induced from the external circuit, and the primary inputs of the victim circuit are invariant (i.e. in DC condition) when glitches happen. We also assume that, an aggressor of similar drive strength is attacking each internal and output node of the circuit. Practically, the aggressor and the coupling capacitor from an aggressor to a node depend on the actual layout. In general, the more number of gates connected to output of victim driver, the greater can be the value of coupling capacitor from aggressor to that victim node. Without the loss in generality, we assume the coupling capacitance at a victim node to be ~ 0.5 fF/um. If the layout is known, the information can be easily obtained and included in the HSPICE netlist, in the proposed framework. It should be noted that the glitch magnitude at the output of victim driver also depends on the input vector combination to victim driver, hence to observe the glitch tolerance of the circuit, the analysis should be carried under worst case input vector conditions (the input vector combinations which result in least driving current to suppress the glitch at the output of victim driver).

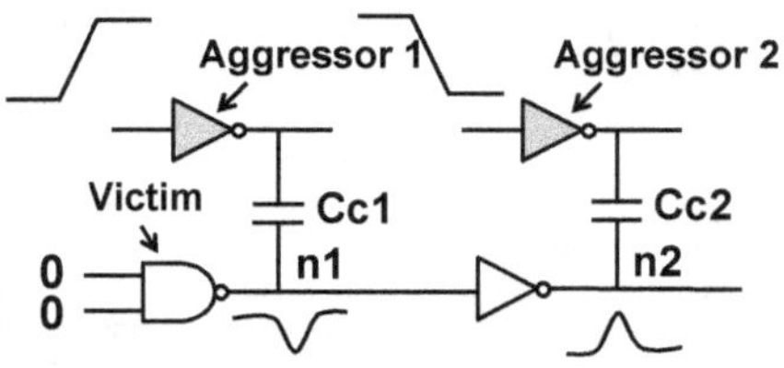

Figure 3: Schematic shows the induction of glitches at the nodes n1 and n2 of the circuit by aggressors (grey shading). In the absence of aggressors, the node voltage at n1, n2 would be close to VDD, GND respectively. But with the given transitions at the input of the aggressors, both n1 and n2 would experience glitches and their corresponding voltages would go below VDD, above GND respectively.

3.3.1 Glitch Simulation MC Setup

In this sub-section, we present the steps to capture the effect of process imperfection ($PCNT_{open}$) on the peak glitch magnitude for each victim (internal/output) node of the circuit for different seeds of MC run at the worst-case input vector combination (discussed in 2nd paragraph of 3.3). The glitch simulation is carried in two phases (Fig. 4):

1. **DC Sim Phase**: This step provides the type of transition (rise/fall) to be applied at the input of each aggressor during Glitch Sim Phase, for injecting the glitch to its corresponding victim node according to the input vector combination of victim driver. E.g. for the input vector combination 00 to NAND2 (Fig. 3), the node n1 would be VDD, hence, rising input transition is applied at Aggressor1 to induce falling glitch at node n1 during Glitch Sim phase. Similarly, falling input transition is required for Aggressor 2.
2. **Glitch Sim Phase**: In this step, the spacing parameters of the circuit netlist are assigned space values from the Space File (at given $PCNT_{open}$), to generate multiple netlist files (equal to number of seeds for MC run). After the transient HSPICE simulation, the peak glitch magnitude for each victim node of the circuit is stored for each seed. The results are then evaluated using Figures of Merit introduced in next sub-section.

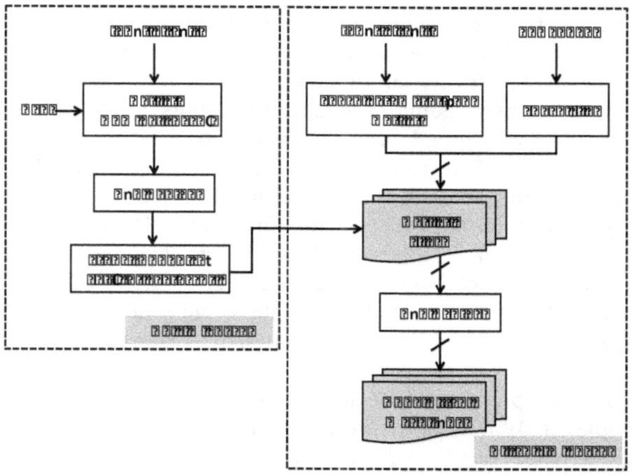

Figure 4: Steps to obtain peak glitch magnitude for each internal/output node of the circuit at a particular $PCNT_{open}$.

3.3.2 Figures of Merit

Fig. 5 shows one instance of simulation output from the MC run (100 seeds) for a victim node of an example circuit (4-bit adder). For each such victim node in the circuit, we capture the peak glitch for each seed.

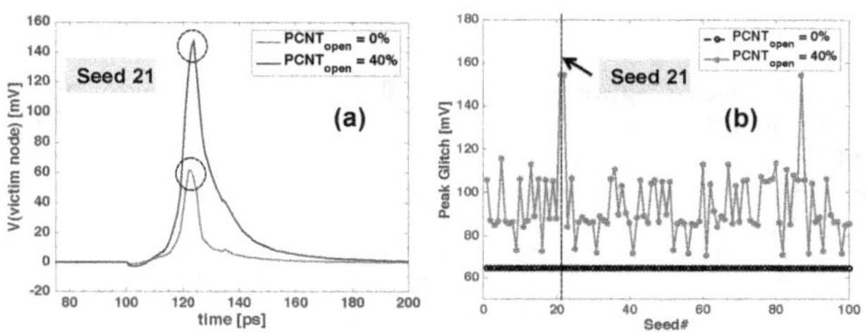

Figure 5: (a) Transient simulation showing glitch at the victim node of an example circuit for $PCNT_{open}$ = 0% and 40% for Seed 21. (b) Peak glitches at the victim node for 100 seeds (Seed #0 to Seed #100). At $PCNT_{open}$=0%, across the seeds there will be single value for the spacing parameter, hence the peak glitch magnitude does not vary across the seeds. However, at $PCNT_{open}$ = 40%, the peak glitch magnitude vary between ~ 70mV to ~ 154 mV across the seeds for this particular node.

For our analysis, we set a criterion for maximum allowable glitch of 175 mV (= 0.25*VDD*). If peak glitch magnitude at a certain node exceeds this value, we say that particular node is failing glitch criteria and thus vulnerable to noise. To compare different CNFET circuits in terms of their glitch tolerance, we define few more terms: 1) *Mean Fail Nodes$_{PATH}$* as the number of nodes (primary input nodes excluded) along a path to the output of circuit, failing glitch criteria, averaged over the total number of seeds. 2) *Mean Fail Nodes$_{CKT}$* as the total number of nodes in the circuit, failing glitch criteria, averaged over the total number of seeds.

$$Mean\,Fail\,Nodes_{PATH} = \frac{1}{M}\sum_{i=1}^{M} \#\,Fail\,Nodes_{PATH}(Seed_i) \quad (3)$$

$$Mean\,Fail\,Nodes_{CKT} = \frac{1}{M}\sum_{i=1}^{M} \#\,Fail\,Nodes_{CKT}(Seed_i) \quad (4)$$

where M is total number of Seeds (M = 100 for this study), *#Fail Nodes$_{PATH}$*, *#Fail Nodes$_{CKT}$* are the total number of failing nodes along the path and in the circuit respectively.

The term *Mean Fail Nodes*$_{CKT}$ provides an estimate of the average number of nodes in the circuit failing glitch criteria. This serves as an easy indicator for circuit comparison in terms of their glitch tolerance without going into specific details of where in the circuit or on which path towards the output the nodes are failing glitch criteria. The term *Mean Fail Nodes*$_{PATH}$ provides the estimate of the average number of nodes failing glitch criteria along a particular path. This holds significance for cases wherein the output of the path can directly act as data input to a sequential element e.g. flop. If a glitch of significant size is transferred to the output, wrong data value will be captured in the flop and correct data value cannot be restored till the next clock cycle.

Fig. 6 shows procedure to calculate *#Fail Nodes*$_{PATH}$ by taking an example of 4-bit Ripple Carry Adder (RCA). At a given seed, internal nodes (*Co0b, A1b, B1b, Co1, Co2, A3b, B3b, Cout*) and node S_3 can all contribute to the *#Fail Nodes*$_{PATH}$ for S_3. In a similar manner, *#Fail Nodes*$_{PATH}$ can be calculated for paths towards other output nodes S_0, S_1, S_2, *Cout*.

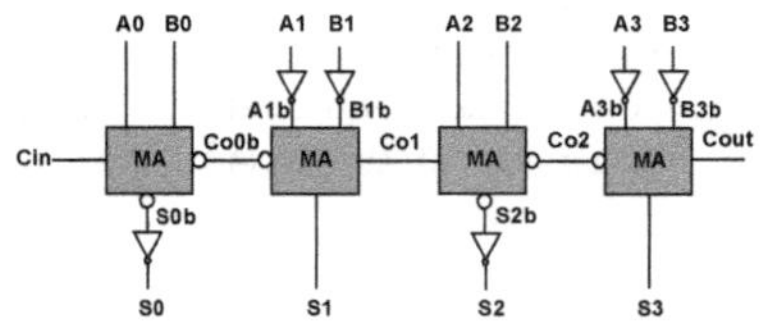

Figure 6: Block diagram shows 4-bit RCA with all (primary, internal, output) nodes. Output node *S3* has the maximum number of nodes on its path from the primary inputs.

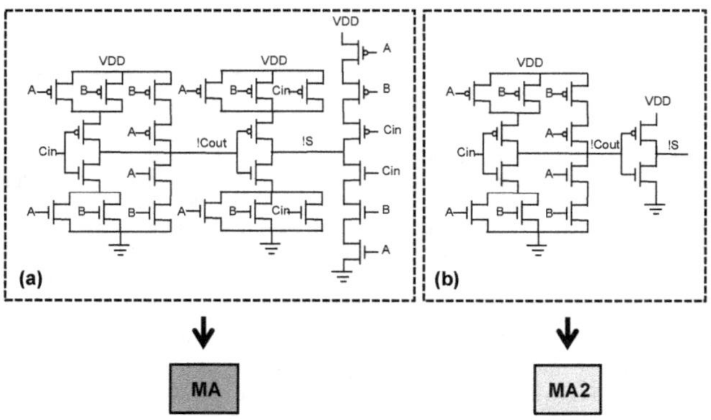

Figure 7: (From Left to Right) (a) Precise Mirror Adder 'MA'. (b) Approximate Mirror Adder schematic 'MA2' taken from [17]. 'MA2' has the accurate circuitry for carry (*!Cout*), however, the sum (*!S*) is approximated. Both circuits 'MA', 'MA2' would be represented by their box symbol or by letters 'MA', 'MA2' for rest of the paper.

4. USING APPROXIMATE CIRCUITS FOR 4-BIT CNFET ADDER AND MULTIPLIER

As briefly discussed before, comparing with precise circuits, using approximate circuits is an effective way to reduce number of glitches exceeding glitch criteria due to process imperfections because of fewer nodes, fewer stacked transistors, and fewer connections at some nodes. We have used 4-bit Ripple Carry Adder (RCA) and 4-bit Wallace Multiplier (WM) as case study for testing our methodology. 4-bit Ripple Carry Adder (RCA) is a simpler and small circuit (in total 14 internal/output nodes), which can help to easily correlate the result to the circuit design. Moreover, considering 4-bit Wallace Multiplier (WM) would show the applicability of the methodology to slightly complex circuits (> 50 internal/output nodes). Further in this section, we will introduce different approximate designs for 4-bit Adder and 4-bit multiplier, which utilize the blocks in Fig. 7. This comes with a penalty of logic accuracy. However, the significant reduction in number of nodes failing glitch criteria, justifies the logic accuracy degradation in particular for high $PCNT_{open}$ (> 10%). Moreover, given the other performance benefits such as delay, power, the improvement in glitch vulnerability to a tolerable level enables the emerging technology to be actually used for circuit design targeting error resilient applications. To account for the logic error in approximate designs, we define the term $\%Error_{Logic}$ in a standard way,

$$\%Error_{Logic} = mean\left(\left|\frac{S_{approx} - S_{orig}}{S_{orig}}\right| * 100\right) \tag{5}$$

where S_{orig} is the original sum/multiplier value based on input vector combination, S_{approx} is the sum/multiplier value computed based on output of the adder/multiplier. The term 'mean' refers to the average over all possible input vector combination for the 4-bit adder/multiplier.

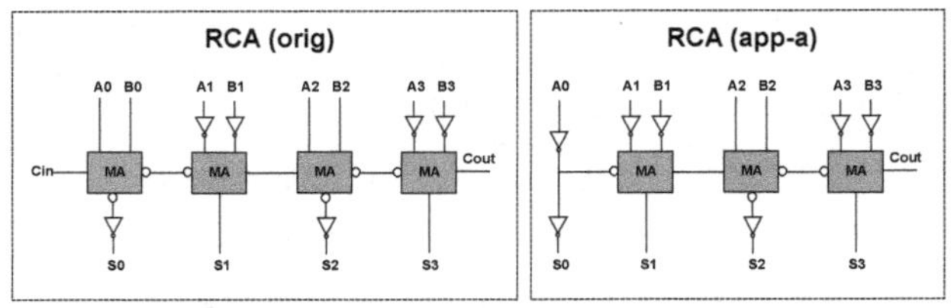

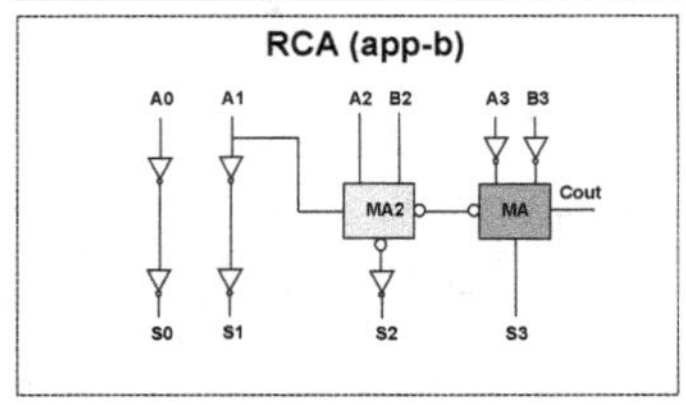

CKT	$\%Error_{Logic}$	Norm. Area
RCA (orig)	0%	1X
RCA (app-a)	9.02%	0.78X
RCA (app-b)	17.45%	0.39X

Figure 8: Shows the schematic of 4-bit precise RCA 'RCA (orig)', 4-bit approximate adders 'RCA (app-a)', 'RCA (app-b)'. *%Error*$_{Logic}$ is computed over all the possible 512 input vectors. The area of RCA (app-a) and RCA (app-b) are 0.78X and 0.39X that of the precise adder RCA (orig) respectively.

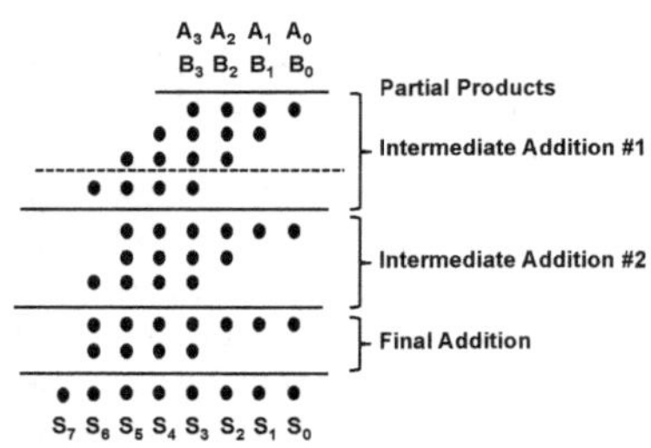

Figure 9: Schematic shows different stages of precise 4-bit Wallace Multiplier.

4.1 4-bit CNFET RCA Precise/Approximate Circuits

We have constructed 2 approximate 4-bit Adder circuits using combination of (MA, MA2 introduced in Fig. 7) and buffer circuits (Fig. 8). The idea of using MA2, buffer circuits is taken from [17], which explains the advantage of using them over the precise MA counterpart in terms of speed, power, area, with some compromise in logic accuracy. The 2 approximate adder circuits represented as [RCA (app-a), RCA (app-b)] differ in logic accuracy and area (Fig. 8). The introduction of MA2 in place of MA replaces the two stacked branches by single transistor in each

PU/PD at sum (!S) node (Fig. 7). This helps to improve glitch tolerance by couple of reasons. 1) The single transistor provides required driving current with a smaller size instead of stacked transistors in MA which need increased sizes to provide the drive current, more number of transistors connected to node !S, and thus suffers from increased coupling capacitor at the node !S in comparison to MA2. 2) In MA2, there are fewer transistors connected to each input *A, B, Cin* in comparison to MA, this reduces the number of connections and thus results in reduction in coupling capacitor for nodes driving each of the input *A, B, Cin* of MA2. So, both the node !S and nodes driving *A, B, Cin* benefits from reduced coupling capacitor and thus become more glitch tolerant for MA2 in place of MA. Similar explanation can be applied for buffer circuits where both carry (*!Cout*) and !S are approximated, and the benefits are even more in terms of glitch tolerance. Additional benefit with approximate circuits is reduced number of internal/output nodes. In comparison to 14 internal/output nodes of precise RCA (orig), approximate circuits RCA (app-a), RCA (app-b) have 13, 11 internal/output nodes respectively.

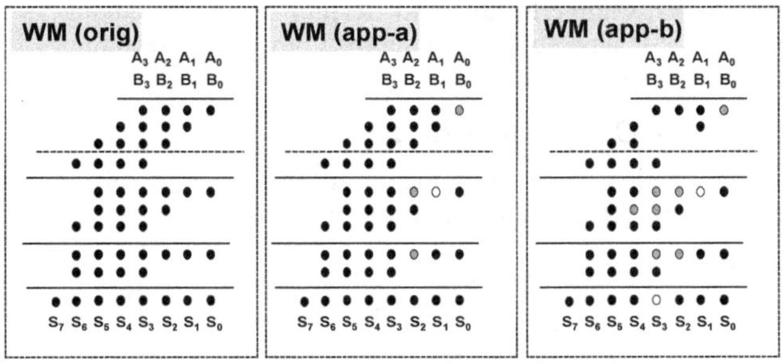

CKT	$\%Error_{Logic}$	Norm.Area
WM (orig)	0%	1X
WM (app-a)	8.78%	0.90X
WM (app-b)	21.42%	0.69X

Figure 10: (Starting from left) shows the schematic of 4-bit precise Wallace multiplier 'WM (orig)', 4-bit approximate multiplier 'WM (app-a)', 'WM (app-b)'. $\%Error_{Logic}$ is computed over all the possible 256 input vectors. The area of WM (app-a) and WM (app-b) are 0.90X and 0.69X that of the precise multiplier WM (orig) respectively.

4.2 4-bit CNFET Wallace Multiplier Precise/Approximate Circuits

Wallace Multiplier (WM) is commonly used for the purpose of fast multiplication. Fig. 9 shows the schematic of precise 4-bit Wallace multiplier. The partial products in the first stage are followed by intermediate addition stages consisting of full adder and half adder blocks, followed by 4-bit adder in the final stage. The full adder blocks can be approximated using MA2, buffer circuits (as discussed in previous section). We have proposed 2 approximate 4-bit multiplier circuits using MA2, buffer circuits for full adder blocks (Fig. 10). The 2 approximate multiplier circuits represented as [WM (app-a), WM (app-b)] differ in logic accuracy and area (Fig. 10). Gray dots in 'WM (app-a)' and 'WM (app-b)' (Fig. 10) represent the approximate sum (!S)/carry (*!Cout*) signals from MA2 or buffer circuits. White dots represent approximate sum signal of half adder where NAND2/NOR2 gates are used instead of XOR2 gates (this simplification also reduces number of nodes). Some of the partial products are not required as part of the approximation approach and hence omitted in 'WM (app-b)'. As explained in section 4.1, the overall effect of the simplifications in approximate circuits would be enhancement of glitch tolerance at some nodes and also the reduction in number of nodes. In comparison to 56 internal/output nodes of precise WM (orig), approximate circuits WM (app-a), WM (app-b) have 52, 48 internal/output nodes respectively.

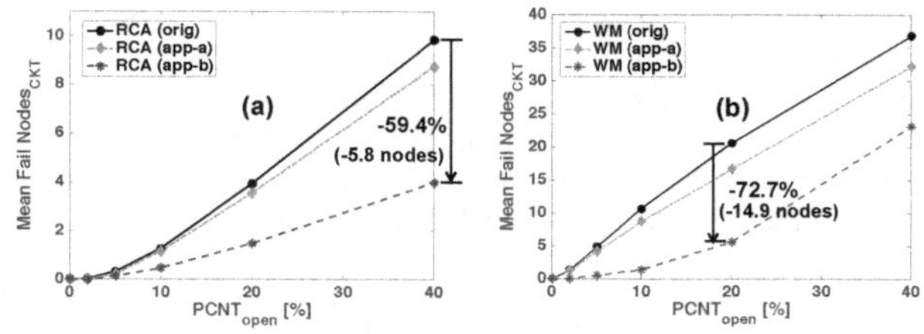

Figure 11: *Mean Fail Nodes$_{CKT}$* for different precise and approximate circuits of (a) 4-bit adder, (b) 4-bit multiplier. Using approximate circuits significantly reduces the number of vulnerable nodes which fail the glitch criteria.

5. RESULTS AND DISCUSSION

5.1 Fail Nodes in the Whole Circuit

Mean Fail Nodes$_{CKT}$ provides average estimate of total number of failing nodes of a circuit at given $PCNT_{open}$. Fig. 11(a) show that *Mean Fail Nodes$_{CKT}$* for precise and all approximate 4-bit RCA is quite small (< 2) for $PCNT_{open} \leq 10\%$. However, for higher $PCNT_{open}$ range *Mean Fail Nodes$_{CKT}$* for RCA (orig) cannot be ignored. At $PCNT_{open}$ = 40%, *Mean Fail Nodes$_{CKT}$* for RCA (orig) becomes a significant percentage (70.2%) of its total number of nodes (9.8 out of 14 nodes). However, with RCA (app-b) the *Mean Fail Nodes$_{CKT}$* at $PCNT_{open}$ = 40% is lower by 59.4% down to 4.0 nodes in comparison to precise RCA (orig). Similarly in Fig. 11(b), approximate 4-bit multiplier WM (app-b) has significantly lower *Mean Fail Nodes$_{CKT}$* over its precise WM (orig) counterpart for $PCNT_{open} \geq 5\%$. At $PCNT_{open}$ = 20%, with WM (app-b) the *Mean Fail Nodes$_{CKT}$* is only 5.6 compared with 20.6 of WM (orig) (lower by 72.7%) (Fig. 11(b)). For a circuit with about 50 nodes, that is a significant reduction in the number of vulnerable nodes, hence a prominent improvement in glitch tolerance. The reasons for the improvement in glitch tolerance in both RCA (app-b) and WM (app-b) in comparison to their precise counterparts are the reduction in number of nodes and improvement in glitch tolerance of some of the nodes (explained in section 4.1 and 4.2).

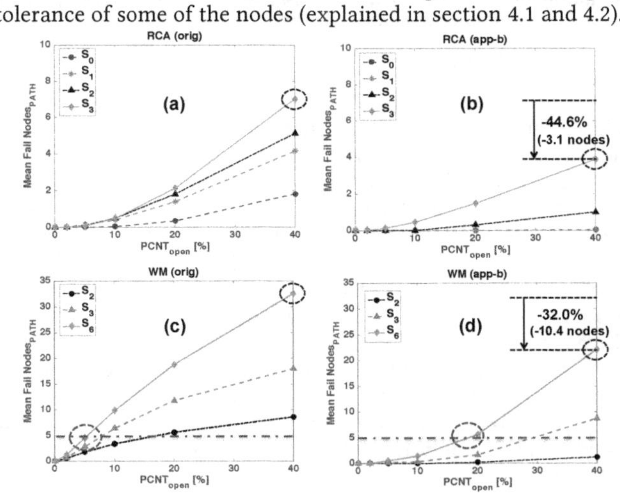

Figure 12: *Mean Fail Nodes$_{PATH}$* for (a) RCA (orig). (b) RCA (app-b), (c) WM (orig), (d) WM (app-b). Black dotted circle indicate the critical output (worst *Mean Fail Nodes$_{PATH}$*) at $PCNT_{open}$ =40%. Highlighted blue line and blue dotted circle indicate that using WM (app-b) instead of WM (orig), the requirement of $PCNT_{open}$ is largely reduced to achieve *Mean Fail Nodes$_{PATH}$* below certain target value (5 in this case).

5.2 Fail Nodes Along a Path

Fig. 12(a), (b) show that *Mean Fail Nodes*$_{PATH}$ for both precise and approximate 4-bit RCA is negligible for outputs S_0, S_1, S_2, S_3 for $PCNT_{open} \leq 10\%$. S_3 with highest number of internal nodes connected to its path from the primary inputs, has the expected worst *Mean Fail Nodes*$_{PATH}$ over the entire $PCNT_{open}$ range for both RCA (orig) and RCA (app-b) (Fig. 12 (a), (b)). As towards the most significant bit, S_3 is considered as a critical output for both RCA (orig) and RCA (app-b). At $PCNT_{open}$ = 40%, using RCA (app-b) *Mean Fail Nodes*$_{PATH}$ of S_3 is only 3.8 compared with 7 of RCA (orig) (lower by 44.6%). For both WM (orig) and WM (app-b), S_6 is the critical output with highest *Mean Fail Nodes*$_{PATH}$ over the entire $PCNT_{open}$ range. At $PCNT_{open}$ = 40%, S_6 of WM (app-b) is 22.1 compared with 32.5 of WM (orig) (lower by 32.0%) (Fig. 12 (c), (d)). Assuming a design target of *Mean Fail Nodes*$_{PATH}$ < 5 is set for this application, we can observe that using WM (app-b) can largely relax the requirement of $PCNT_{open}$ (from ~ 5% to ~ 20%) in comparison to WM (orig) (Fig. 12 (c), (d)).

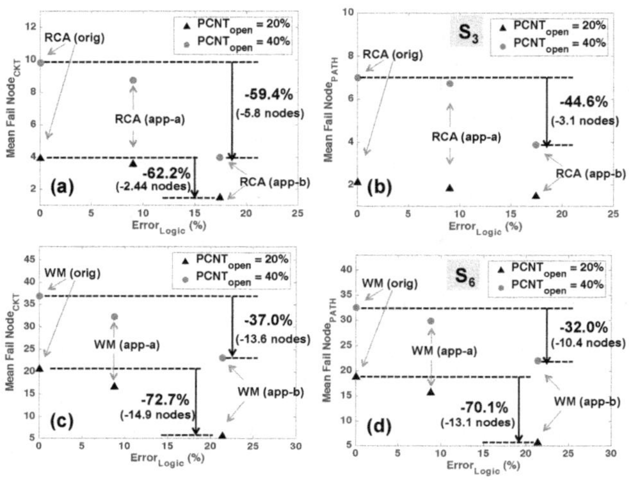

Figure 13: Plot for 4-bit adder between (a) *Mean Fail Nodes*$_{CKT}$ and *%Error*$_{Logic}$, (b) *Mean Fail Nodes*$_{PATH}$ for S_3 and *%Error*$_{Logic}$. Plot for 4-bit multiplier between (c) *Mean Fail Nodes*$_{CKT}$ and *%Error*$_{Logic}$, (d) *Mean Fail Nodes*$_{PATH}$ for S_6 and *%Error*$_{Logic}$.

5.3 Choosing Optimum Circuit

The improvement of glitch tolerance, and imperfect process induced failure in general, by using approximate circuits, comes with the penalty of logic inaccuracy. Tradeoff between the two must be considered. Fig. 13(a) show that at $PCNT_{open}$= 40%, *Mean Fail Nodes*$_{CKT}$ with RCA (app-b) reduces by 5.8 nodes (59.4%) in comparison to its precise counterpart RCA (orig) with a penalty of logic error 17%. However, this reduction of 5.8 nodes is significant considering the fact that RCA (orig) in total has only 14 internal/output nodes. Similar trend is observed in Fig. 13(b), where *Mean Fail Nodes*$_{PATH}$ of S_3 with RCA (app-b) are reduced by 44.6% at $PCNT_{open}$= 40% in comparison to RCA (orig). In comparison to RCA (app-b), RCA (app-a) has lesser logic error of 9% but the reduction in *Mean Fail Nodes*$_{CKT}$ and *Mean Fail Nodes*$_{PATH}$ of S_3 is only 1.1 and 0.2 nodes respectively compared to RCA (orig) at $PCNT_{open}$= 40%. Hence, RCA (app-b) is considered as a better option at $PCNT_{open}$= 40%.

Fig. 13(c) show that in comparison to WM (orig) *Mean Fail Nodes*$_{CKT}$ with WM (app-b) is reduced by 14.9 nodes and 13.6 nodes at $PCNT_{open}$= 20%/$PCNT_{open}$= 40% respectively, with a tolerable logic error of 21%. Fig. 13(d) show a similar trend for *Mean Fail Nodes*$_{PATH}$ for S_6, wherein using WM (app-b) reduces the *Mean Fail Nodes*$_{PATH}$ by 13.1 nodes and 10.4 nodes at $PCNT_{open}$= 20%/$PCNT_{open}$= 40% respectively. With WM (app-a), the reduction in *Mean Fail Nodes*$_{CKT}$ in comparison to WM (orig) is 3.9 nodes and 4.6 nodes at $PCNT_{open}$= 20%/$PCNT_{open}$= 40% respectively (Fig. 13(c)), which is much lesser compared to improvement seen with WM (app-b). So, for applications where we want to reduce logic error below 10%, WM (app-a) will be considered in place of WM (app-b). However, for error resilient applications, WM (app-b) will be the optimum choice.

6. CONCLUSIONS

In this paper, we have proposed a methodology to conduct MC simulation on CNFET circuits, considering the statistical nature of the imperfections encountered with CNFET process. We have also provided a framework to evaluate glitch tolerance in CNFET circuits, and the degradation in glitch tolerance with decrease in process quality. With the example of various approximate designs of 4-bit adder and multiplier circuits, we have demonstrated that using approximate designs have the potential to counter process-induced degradation, with tolerable logic error. The methodology links process imperfection with its impact at the circuit level, which facilitates applying imperfect emerging technology to error-resilient applications.

7. ACKNOWLEDGMENTS

The authors would like to thank Dr. Shu-Jen Han for valuable discussions. This work is supported by NSERC Discovery Grant.

8. REFERENCES

[1] M. M. Waldrop. 2016. The chips are down for Moore's law. *Nature*, vol. 530, no. 7589 (Feb. 2016), 144-147.

[2] C. Qiu et al. 2017. Scaling carbon nanotube complementary transistors to 5-nm gate lengths. *Science*, vol. 355, no. 6322 (Jan. 2017), 271-276.

[3] B. Radisavljevic et al. 2011. Single-layer MoS2 transistors. *Nature nanotechnology*, vol. 6 (Jan. 2011), 147-150.

[4] L. Li et al. 2016. High-performance p-type black phosphorus transistor with scandium contact. *ACS nano*, vol. 10, no. 4 (Mar. 2016), 4672-4677.

[5] S.-J. Han et al. 2014. Graphene radio frequency receiver integrated circuit. *Nature communications*, vol. 5 (Jan. 2014), 3086.

[6] S.-J. Han et al. 2017. High-speed logic integrated circuits with solution-processed self-assembled carbon nanotubes. *Nature nanotechnology*, vol. 12, no. 9 (July 2017), 861-865.

[7] B. Kumar et al. 2017. Spatially Selective, High-Density Placement of Polyfluorene-Sorted Semiconducting Carbon Nanotubes in Organic Solvents. *ACS nano*, vol. 11, no. 8 (July 2017), 7697-7701.

[8] J. Han and M. Orshansky. 2013. Approximate computing: An emerging paradigm for energy-efficient design. In *18th IEEE European Test Symposium (ETS), May 2013*, 1-6.

[9] Q. Xu et al. 2016. Approximate Computing: A Survey. *IEEE Design and Test*, vol. 33, no. 1 (Feb. 2016), 8-22.

[10] S. Iijima. 1991. Helical microtubules of graphitic carbon. *Nature*, vol. 354, no. 6348 (Nov. 1991), 56-58.

[11] G. S. Tulevski et al. 2014. Toward High-Performance Digital Logic Technology with Carbon Nanotubes. *ACS nano*, vol. 8, no. 9 (Aug. 2014), 8730-8745.

[12] T. F. Wu et al. 2018. Brain-inspired computing exploiting carbon nanotube FETs and resistive RAM: Hyperdimensional computing case study. In *2018 IEEE International Solid-State Circuits Conference Digest of Technical Papers, Feb. 2018*, 492-493.

[13] H. Park et al. 2012. High-density integration of carbon nanotubes via chemical self-assembly. *Nature nanotechnology*, vol. 7, no. 12 (Oct. 2012), 787-791.

[14] D. Zhong et al. 2017. Solution-Processed Carbon Nanotubes based Transistors with Current Density of 1.7 mA/μm and Peak Transconductance of 0.8 mS/μm. In *2017 IEEE International Electron Devices Meeting, Dec. 2017*, 5.6.1-5.6.4.

[15] C-S. Lee and H.-S. P. Wong. 2015. Stanford Virtual-Source Carbon Nanotube Field-Effect Transistors Model (2015).

[16] K. Sheikh and L. Wei. 2018. Using Approximate Circuits to Counter Process Imperfections in CNFET based Circuits. In *2018 International Symposium on VLSI Design, Automation, and Test.*

[17] V. Gupta et al. 2013. Low-Power Digital Signal Processing Using Approximate Adders. *IEEE Transactions on Computer-Aided Design of Integrated Circuits and Systems*, vol. 32, no. 1 (Jan. 2013), 124-137.

Performance and Energy Enhancement through an Online Single/Multi Level Mode Switching Cache Architecture

Ramin Rezaeizadeh Rookerd
Department of Electrical and Computer Engineering
School of Engineering Colleges, University of Tehran
Tehran, Iran
Rookerdyramin@ut.ac.ir

Somayeh Sadeghi-Kohan
Department of Electrical and Computer Engineering
School of Engineering Colleges, University of Tehran
Tehran, Iran
Sm.sadeghi@ut.ac.ir

Zainalabedin Navabi
Department of Electrical and Computer Engineering
School of Engineering Colleges, University of Tehran
Tehran, Iran
Navabi@ut.ac.ir

ABSTRACT

STT-RAM cells can be considered as an alternative or a hybrid addition to today's SRAM-based cache memories. This is mostly because of their scalability and low leakage power. Moreover, their data storing mechanism (storing the value as resistance) makes them very suitable and applicable for multi-value cache architectures. This feature results in system performance enhancement without any area overhead. On the other hand, the required two-step read/write procedure in multi-level cells results in a non-uniform time access and energy and power overhead on the system. In this paper, we propose a new architecture to dynamically swap data between soft (fast read access) and hard (slow read access) bits in ML cell. Moreover, by reconfiguring cache block size, the proposed architecture can switch between ML and SL modes at runtime. In other words, the swapping method places the hot part of each cache block into soft-bits and the less accessed part into the hard-bits. The SL/ML switching method benefits from the low latency and energy of SL mode and the high storing capacity of ML mode at the same time. Although experimental results show that our proposed method slightly increases the miss rate compared with the conventional ML caches, the performance and energy are improved by 4.9% and 6.5%, respectively. Also, the storage overhead of our method is about 1% that is negligible.

KEYWORDS

Non-volatile memories, STT-RAM, ML mode, SL mode, Soft-bit, Hard-bit

1 INTRODUCTION

In the next generation of large-scale computing, workloads are very data intensive [1, 2]. This makes the cache size a very important factor in today's digital systems that directly affects the performance of the system. On the other hand, by further scaling down of transistor dimensions in chip fabrication, traditional cache structures such as SRAM suffer from large leakage power and low reliability. The experiments in [3] show that in an SRAM cache, up to 80% of consumed power of Last Level Cache (LLC) belongs to the standby time (static power). In order to overcome these issues (power consumption and reliability) in the traditional cache structures, use of the non-volatile memories has been proposed in today's digital systems. There are different types of non-volatile memories such as: Phase Change Memory (PCM), Magnetic RAM (MRAM), Resistive RAM (ReRAM), and Spin-Torque Transfer RAM (STT-RAM) technologies. Among these technologies, STT-RAM and ReRAM are the most promising candidates for taking the place of SRAM in cache structures, despite their drawbacks. ReRAM memories are more compatible with the CMOS technology, but, STT-RAM memories have higher cell endurance than ReRAM (about 1012 writes [4, 5]) and higher density (about four times of SRAM density [6]). One of the main problems of non-volatile memories is their low endurance that limits the number of possible writes to a cell. Some works such as [7] and [8] propose specific architectures and algorithms that can increase the lifetime of non-volatile memories. The main idea in these works is uniformity of read and write accesses in all cache lines.

Performance and energy are other important factors that are critical for cache memories and should be considered when non-volatile memories are used. Using non-volatile memory with multi-level capability is a simple idea for improving the performance of embedded caches in a digital system [9], [10]. A multi-level cell structure providing two bits in one cell divides the resistive range of the cell into four regions. Extracting each bit is performed by a binary search that results in a non-uniform data access [11, 12]. The stored data in the first level ("soft-bit") and the second level ("hard-bit") of the cell are extracted respectively. Therefore, access to bits of different levels is not identical. This non-uniform access latency degrades the performance of the system that uses cells only in multi-level mode. For example, in case of spread cache accesses, miss rate grows, which makes the use of cells at only one level preferable over multi-level due to low latency of soft-bit access. In order to exploit benefits of both multi-level and single level uses, one can use cells in two operation mode and switch between them at the runtime to achieve better performance. The idea of using both single level (SL) and multi-level (ML) modes and switching between them has been introduced first in [13] and [14]. In [13], their proposed algorithm for switching between ML and SL modes sacrifices the cache associativity. The proposed architecture in [14] solves the associativity problem, but it does not support hard and soft-bits swapping in the ML mode, which can degrade the performance in some scenarios. Suppose that the cache is in the ML mode, when

GLSVLSI '18, May 23–25, 2018, Chicago, IL, USA

ISBN 978-1-4503-5724-1/18/05...$15.00
DOI: https://doi.org/10.1145/3194554.3194599.

most accesses are related to the hard-bits, results in performance degradation. Moreover, their proposed switching method has a relatively high storage overhead without achieving a significant performance enhancement. In this paper, we propose a new architecture that can reconfigure cache block size by switching between SL and ML modes of it cells at runtime. Also, we propose a new efficient algorithm for switching the cache mode that supports soft and hard-bit swapping.

The main contributions of this paper are: 1) Introducing a new low storage overhead architecture that supports switching between ML and SL modes. 2) Proposing a novel and efficient algorithm for switching between ML and SL modes. 3) Using a Global Swapper beside the conventional Local Swappers.

The rest of this paper is organized as follows. Section 2 is a brief review on non-volatile memories and ML mode of a cache line. In Section 3, we propose a new architecture for switching between modes and swapping between hard and soft-bits. Section 4 illustrates the experimental results, and Section 5 concludes the paper.

2 BACKGROUND

The STT-RAM memory is a class in the magneto-resistive RAMs category. An STT-RAM cell uses Magnetic Tunneling Junctions (MTJs) to store data as shown in Fig. 1(a). An MTJ has two ferromagnetic layers that are referred to as "reference" and "free" layer with an oxide barrier in between. The magnetization direction of the reference layer is fixed while it can be changed for the free layer by a spin-polarized current [5]. If the magnetization direction of these two layers are in the same direction, the MTJ resistance becomes low and represents '0' and vice versa.

A multi-level STT-RAM cell is developed by utilizing two MTJs in a single cell. Serial ML cells (Fig. 1(b)) are formed by stacking two MTJs. This ML cell structure is more feasible and acceptable than other STT-RAM ML cell structures [10].

Write and read actions in an ML cell are performed in two steps shown in Fig. 2. To write, a high current pulse (IWH > IC,Hard) is applied to the cell to change the state of hard and soft-bit. Then, a smaller current (IC,Hard > IWS > IC,Soft) is used to change only the soft-bit (Fig. 2(a)). For reading the ML cell a binary search algorithm is performed. First, a reference voltage (Ref1) is applied to detect the soft-bit value. Then, based on the result, the second reference voltage is applied in the next step to determine the value of the hard-bit (Ref2 or Ref3) [14] and [15] (Fig. 2(b)). It should be noted that reading the soft-bit is just like SL cell, while determining the hard-bit requires more time.

3 PROPOSED METHOD

In addition to the standard set-associative cache hardware for finding ways, lines, and the replacement methods, our cache hardware includes several switches and swappers. Each cache set has a mode switcher that keeps history of the set accesses used to switch between SL and ML modes. In addition, each line has a Local Swapper (LS) that in case of using ML mode, decides on swapping the data between hard and soft bits. There is also a Global Swapper that determines the initial arrangement of data for all cache lines. In sections 3.1 to 3.3 this cache architecture and its hardware components are discussed. Section 3.4, 3.5, and 3.6, discuss the operation detail of the proposed cache. We consider a 4MB cache with 8K sets and 64-byte cache line size. For storing data in ML lines, interleaved mapping shown in Fig. 3

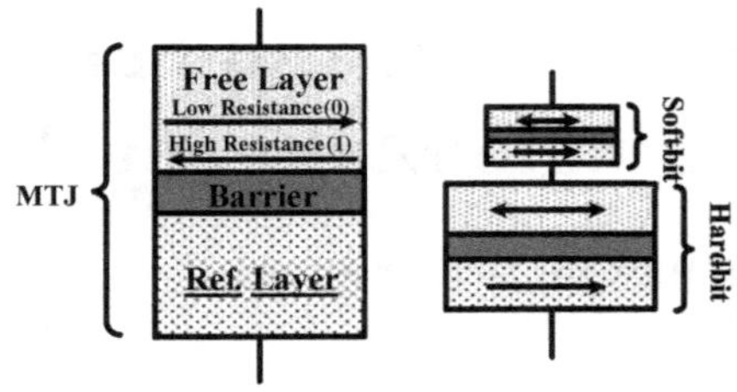

Figure 1: (a) MTJ structure. (b) The serial structure of ML STT-RAM cell

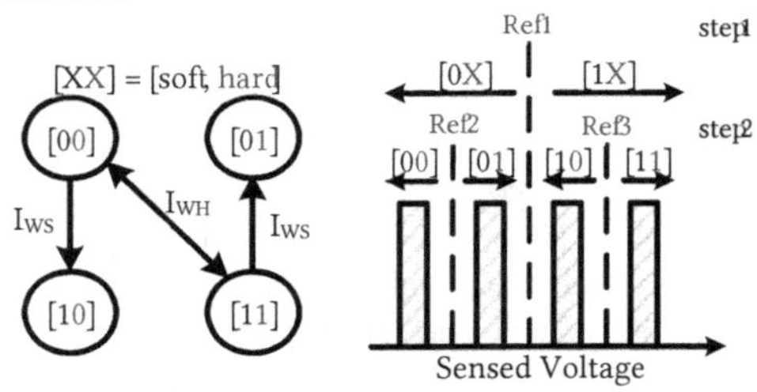

Figure 2: (a) 2-bit ML write operation (b) 2-bit ML read operation [14, 15]

Cell #	#0		#1		#2		...	#255	
Bit #	0	256	1	257	2	258		255	511

Figure 3: Interleaved mapping for 512-bit (64-byte) cache block size

is used which is common in the literature. In this mapping one data is stored in the soft part (0-255) and the next data is stored in the hard part (256-511). The overview of the proposed architecture is shown in Fig. 4.

Before starting the details of the proposed structure, some definitions used in the rest of the paper are explained below:

- **Valid-Hard:** A valid bit that indicates whether the data in the hard part of the cache line is valid (1) or not (0).
- **Valid-Soft:** A valid bit that indicates whether the data in the soft part of the cache line is valid (1) or not (0).
- **LSB-CMP:** A 1-bit comparator that compares Least Significant Bit (LSB) of input address-tag and LSB of the stored–tag in the cache way.
- **Hit-LSB:** This term is used for the output of LSB-CMP, if two inputs of LSB-CMP are equal, Hit-LSB will be '1', otherwise will be '0'.
- **Line-CMP:** Line-CMP is a comparator in our proposed structure that compares address-tag bits (except for LSB) with stored-tag bits (except for LSB) in the cache way.
- **Hit-Line:** This term is used for the output of Line-CMP, if two inputs of the comparator are equal, Hit-Line will be '1', otherwise it will be '0'.
- **Even-Part:** Part of data that the LSB of its tag is '0'.
- **Odd-Part:** Part of data that the LSB of its tag is '1'.
- **O-MSB:** This flag specifies where the requested data stored (soft part: 0, hard part: 1).

3.1 Cache line structure

Two valid bits (Valid-Soft (VS) and Valid-Hard (VH)) are added in the structure of each cache line shown in Fig 5 instead of the single valid bit of the conventional structures.

The LSB of a tag plays an important role in our swapping method in the ML mode. The '0' value indicates storing data with even tag in the soft part, and '1' shows the place of data with odd and even tags are changed and swapped. As shown in Fig 5, a Local Swapper is also used in the cache line structure that will be explained in detail in 3.5.

3.2 Address mapping

To support SL and ML modes in the cache structure, we change the address mapping unit. The proposed address mapping for a 4MB cache with 8K sets is illustrated in Fig. 6. The offset is 6-bit long which the five least significant bits of it come from five least significant bits of the address. Most Significant Bit (MSB) of the offset comes from the Hit/Miss Detector unit which is used for placement of the requested data (soft-bits or hard-bits). The sixth bit of address goes to the LSB of Tag and the next 13 bits construct the set number and the remaining bits are used for defining Tag.

3.3 Hit/Miss Detector

The proposed cache structure utilizes both SL/ML switching and soft/hard part swapping. For handling these features, the Hit/Miss Detector is modified to handle both SL and ML modes. In this architecture, when the accessed set is determined, Line-CMP is activated and determines the Hit-Line value. Simultaneously, the LSB of the address-tag is compared to its corresponding stored-tag bit using LSB-CMP, and Hit-LSB will be determined.

Hit/Miss cases according to Valid-Hard, Valid-Soft, Hit-LSB and Hit-Line are shown in Table 1. Once, Hit becomes '1' when Hit-Line and Hit-LSB are '1'. In this case, the incoming address must be fetched from soft part. Therefore, if Valid-Soft is '1', Hit signal is issued for the corresponding way. Hit also becomes '1' when Hit-Line is '1' and Hit-LSB is '0'. In this case, the incoming address must be fetched from hard part. Therefore, if Valid-Hard is '1', Hit signal is issued for the corresponding way. In other cases, Hit is '0' and cache miss occurs.

The proposed Hit/Miss Detector has another output (O-MSB) that determines the offset address MSB of the selected cache line. State 2 of Table 1 expresses the case that the requested signal is in hard part and O-MSB will be '1'. In other cases, it is '0'.

Since Valid-Hard is '0' in SL mode, O-MSB is '0' all the time. So, Hit/Miss Detector can simply handle this mode.

3.4 SL/ML Mode Switch

The proposed architecture simplifies handling the SL/ML switching method. We use some policy factors to switch between the ML and SL modes at the best point of the runtime. We employ an algorithm that statistically determines the distribution of runtime cache accesses which are centralized or distributed. The pseudo code of the proposed switching algorithm is shown in Algorithm. 1. It performs during online execution and decides the SL or ML mode of each cache set. The main idea behind this algorithm is to specify local miss rate in the ML mode and local hit rate in the SL mode. In the SL mode, in addition to hit rate, miss rate is also considered and should not exceed a predefined threshold (SC becomes all '1').

In the proposed structure, a number of saturating counters that are called Switch-Counters (SC) are embedded in each cache set. In the ML mode, this counter is initialized with maximum value (all 1's). While, in the SL mode, it is initialized with half its maximum value. Initialization is done when a new data is placed

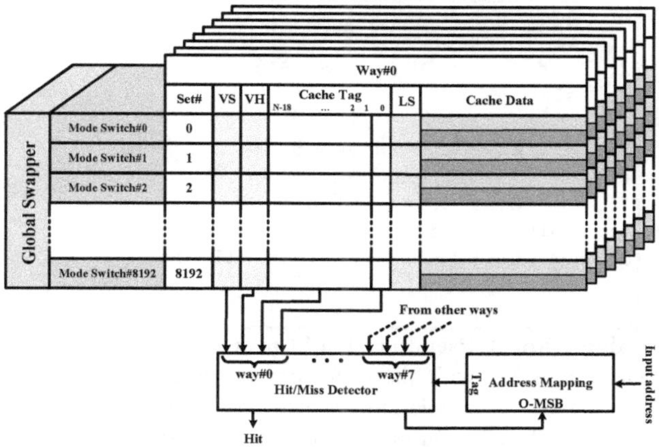

Figure 4: Overall view of the proposed structure

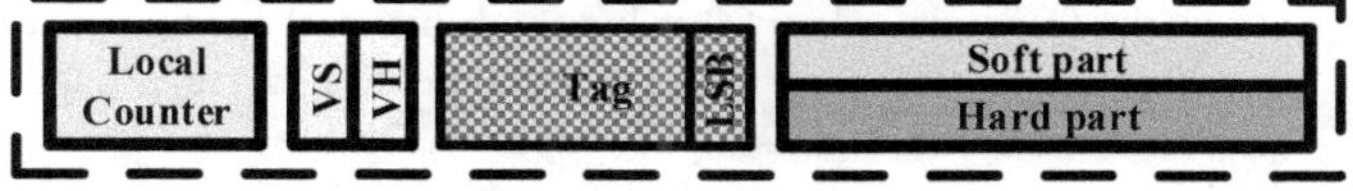

Figure 5: Cache line structure

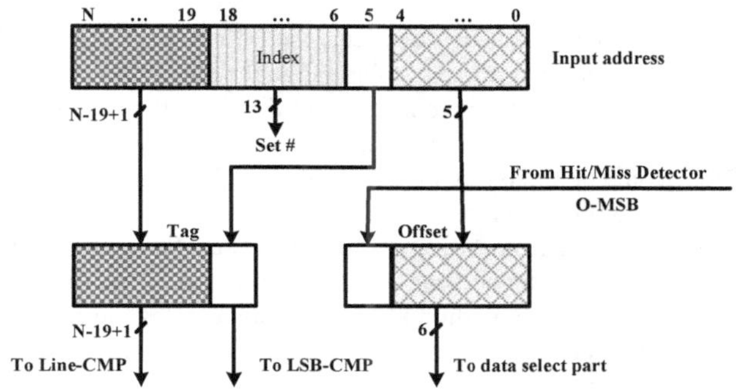

Figure 6: Address mapping

Table 1: Hit/Miss states

State	Hit-Line	Hit-LSB	Valid-Soft	Valid-Hard	Hit
1	1	1	1	-*	1
2	1	0	-*	1	1
-	Other conditions				0

* *Don't care value*

into the cache or during the switching between different modes. The mechanism of switching is as follows:

For each hit access in a set, its corresponding SC counts down (line 2). However, any time a miss occurs, Mode Switch makes a decision based on the current mode and the SC value. Since the number of misses is usually much lower than the number of hits, each time a miss occurs, the algorithm determines the accumulated amount of hits. Indeed, a high SC value (more than TH) shows a low number of hits. Since ML mode has higher overall latency with a low number of hits, its higher capacity is not utilized. Therefore, to achieve a better performance, cache switches to the SL mode. Otherwise, if the SC value is lower than TH, the cache stays at ML mode and because of low probability of miss in comparison with the probability of hit, the SC value will be increased by "W1" to balance the effect of a high number of hits versus misses on the SC value. By increasing the SC value, it is possible to track the number of hits in the future. "W1" is a fixed

```
Mode Switch (){
  if (cache hit)
    if (SC > 0) SC = SC -1;
  else
    if (in ML mode)
      if (SC > TH and SC != all one)
        Switch to SL;
      else SC = SC + W1;
    else if (in SL mode)
      if (SC < TH or SC == all one)
        Switch to ML;
      else SC = SC + W2;}
```

Algorithm. 1: Pseudo code of the switching algorithm

value that is set with the difference between all 1's and TH according to our simulation results. This selection statistically proves that the effect of unbalanced hit and miss accesses can be relaxed. So, the measured miss rate is more realistic.

In the SL mode, a low SC value (high hit rate) specifies data localization. In this case, being in ML mode leads to a better performance because of its higher capacity. On the other hand, a high miss rate (SC reaches to all 1's) is probably due to small cache size. So, cache switches to ML mode that virtually extend the cache size.

If the above cases do not occur, the SC remains between TH and all 1's, which is an acceptable range for the SL mode. So, the cache set stays in the current mode. In this case, the SC increases by "W2" that is equal to the difference of initial value and TH. "W2" would be smaller than "W1" due to the low sensitivity of the SL mode to the miss rate.

In switching from ML to SL, all Valid-Hard bits of the line in the related cache set become '0'. On the other hand, for switching from SL to ML, the method in [14] that invalidates the odd tags, re-fetches data and stores them in the hard part of the related lines and set is used.

3.5 Local Swapper

In the proposed architecture, we also use a Local Swapper unit beside each cache line that its structure is shown in Fig. 7. At first, the counter will be initialized with the half its maximum value. At the beginning of the operation, the data with the even/odd tag is stored in the soft/hard part. In this state, if the access is an even/odd tag, the counter counts up/down. If the counter reaches '0', it is the time for swapping. Zero value in the counter shows that the hard part is more accessed than the soft part. To obtain a higher performance, it is better to store odd tags in soft-bits. So, they will be accessed in one step (faster) in the future.

When the counter reaches '0', the T flip-flop toggles and its value becomes '1' and the counter presets to half value. The '1' value in T flip-flop represents the place of data for odd and even tags. When swapping occurs, the counter condition for counting up and down are changed.

At the swapping time, two approaches are considered [15]: 1) Write and swap, 2) Read and swap. In the first one, when a write to hard part occurs and T flip-flop becomes '1', the write circuit, first reads the soft part and then merges and swaps it with incoming data and writes them back. In the second one, during a read access to the hard part, if T flip-flop becomes '1', the read circuit, first reads the soft part and then hard part. After the reading operation, the cache controller has enough time to write this line in the reverse order of soft and hard parts. It is

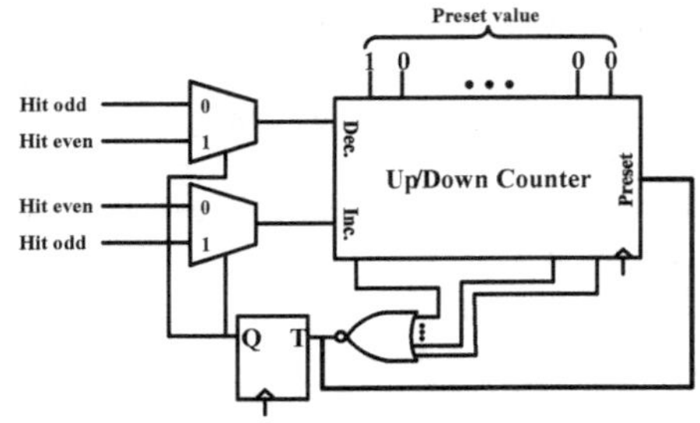

Figure 7: Structure of the Local/Global Swapper counter

noteworthy that according to the structure of the Local Swapper, the last access which can cause T flip-flop to become '1', is a read or write to the hard part.

3.6 Global Swapper

In addition to the Local Swapper, there is also a Global Swapper in our proposed structure. The Global Swapper is a counter for the whole cache structure with the same structure of Fig. 7. The Global Swapper initially checks all incoming addresses and if their tags are even/odd (access to soft/hard part), the counter counts up/down. If the counter reaches '0', it specifies that the hard parts of the cache are more accessed than the soft parts. Therefore, hereafter when a miss or a writeback from upper level occurs, the new data will be stored in the opposite form. It means storing even/odd tags in hard/soft part.

4 EXPERIMENTAL RESULTS

This section evaluates the efficacy of the proposed method. We evaluate the performance and energy enhancement, and the storage overhead of our proposed method and then compare experimental results with the previous works.

4.1 System configuration

To evaluate the proposed architecture, gem5 full system simulator [16] is modified to support it. We use nine multithread PARSEC benchmarks for evaluating design effectiveness. In the architecture there are several parameters that their exact values should be specified. Such as the size of Local and Global Swapper counters, TH value, and the size of SC in Mode Switch. In this section, proper values are obtained.

Table 2 shows the simulation system parameters. The parameters that are used for the LLC (shown in Table 3) are the same as what reported in [14].

4.2 Obtaining the optimal parameters

In the architecture there are several parameters that their exact values should be specified. Such as the size of Local and Global Swapper counters, TH value, and the size of SC in Mode Switch. In this section, proper values are obtained.

4.2.1 Swapping counters bit-width. It is obvious that, the bit-width of swapping counters can directly affect the area, performance, and energy consumption of the proposed structure. In this experiment, we find the most efficient bit-width of counters by sweeping their width. Fig. 8 illustrates the average normalized Instruction Per Cycle (IPC) of the system for different bit-width of the Global and Local Swapper's counter respectively. According to these experiments, we select a 6-bit counter for Global Swapper and 3-bit counters for the Local Swapper.

4.2.2 SC bit-width and TH parameter. The other two parameters that can affect performance are bit-width of SC and threshold of

Table 2: Configuration details of the simulated system

Simulated system parameters	
Cores	4 cores, ISA-ALPHA, 3GHz
L1 I/D cache	32KB/ 32KB, 4-way, 32-byte block, 2 cycle latency, LRU, SRAM
Coherency	MOESI
Last Level Cache	8K sets, maximum capacity 4MB, LRU, ML STT-RAM
Main Memory	4GB, 290-cycle latency

Table 3: LLC latency and energy numbers [14].

Last Level Cache Parameters		
Set operating mode	ML	SL
Set configuration	8-way, 64-byte block	8-way, 32-byte block
Read latency (cycle)	10	7
Write latency(cycle)	44	23
Miss latency (cycle)	4	
Read energy (nJ)	0.543	0.419
Write energy (nJ)	1.562	0.756
Miss energy (nJ)	0.056	

switching between SLC and MLC. To find the proper value for these two parameters, we simultaneously sweep the SC bit-width and TH in all nine PARSEC benchmark executions and measure the average normalized IPC for each configuration. Fig. 9 illustrates results of sweeping these two parameters. The appropriate number of bit-width for SC is 5 and the proper value for TH is 8. Note that we do not consider non-practical configurations. For example, for bit-width of 5, the TH of 32 is not possible.

4.3 Miss rate overhead

Miss rate is one of the most important parameters affecting the cache performance. This section examines the miss rate of our proposed method versus the Mixed Block Size (MBS) method in [14]. As shown in Fig. 10 the proposed method has lower miss rate than the MBS method because of two main features: first, it switches faster between modes, which is caused by the lower threshold value of switching and higher sensitivity to increase of hit rate in the SLC mode and miss rate in the MLC mode. Second, considers increase of miss rate in the SLC mode that, controls the miss rate by switching to MLC mode to achieve better performance.

The first mentioned feature affects some benchmarks such as *bodytrack*, *facesim*, *freqmine*, and *rtview*. In these benchmarks, MBS method usually has fewer SLC sets compared to our method. So, it experiences lower miss rate in the SLC mode. In addition, because of the higher sensitivity of our method and its lower TH, the proposed method has more sets in the SLC mode which results in higher miss rate. On the other hand, since the number of sets in MLC decrease, the cache has lower miss rate in the MLC mode. As illustrated in Fig.10, in these benchmarks the overall miss rate of two methods are almost equal.

However, in the rest of the benchmarks, the second feature of algorithm is prominent. In these benchmarks, MBS method has high miss rate in the SLC mode. In this case, our method changes the mode to MLC since it has control on high miss rate of the SLC mode. As a result, miss rate decreases in these benchmarks.

Experiments show that on average there is about 4% miss rate reduction rather than MBS. It should be noted that our proposed method has higher miss rate than the conventional MLC STT-RAM. This phenomenon is obvious since the conventional MLC

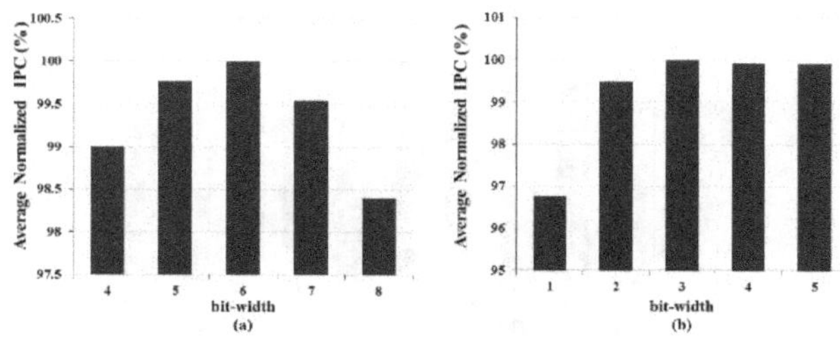

Figure 8: The average normalized IPC of the proposed method for (a) Different bit-widths of the global counter (b) Different bit-widths of the local counters

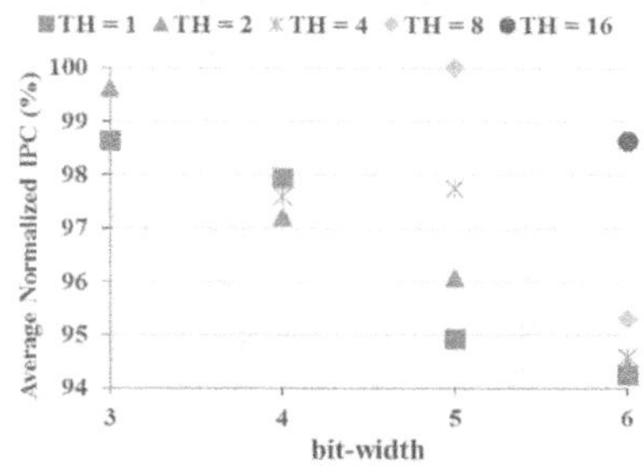

Figure 9: The average normalized IPC for different SC bit-widths and TH

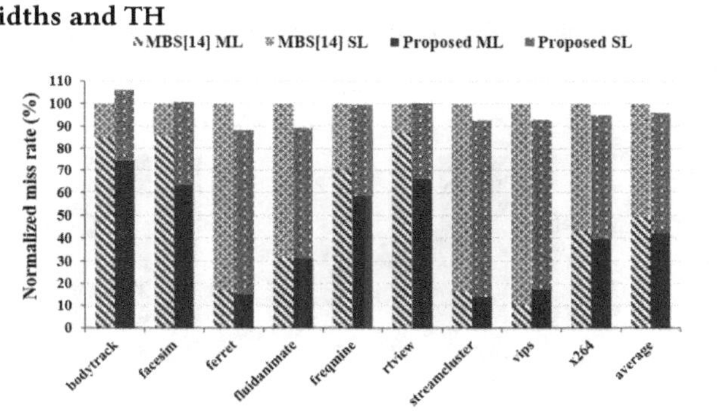

Figure 10: The miss rate for different structures and workloads

cache is always in the MLC mode. So, the cache size is virtually higher than our method and [14].

4.4 Performance evaluation

In the first evaluation, hit accesses (soft or hard) of the proposed cache structure are compared with the conventional MLC baseline cache structure. Fig. 11 shows the normalized amount of hit accesses to soft and hard-bits for each benchmark. As figure demonstrates, the proposed method causes an average of more than 75% hit in soft-bits. This leads to the performance and energy enhancement of the cache.

For the benchmarks with cache sets often in the MLC mode, swapping causes migration of cache accesses to the soft-bits. On the other hand, for the benchmarks that their cache sets are usually in the SLC mode, switching algorithm is the main reason of access migration to the soft-bits.

Second experiment compares IPC of the proposed method with the MBS method. Therefore, both swapping and switching methods are applied in the cache structure and the results are compared with the MBS structure. Fig. 12 demonstrates the normalized IPC of this method. The results show that our

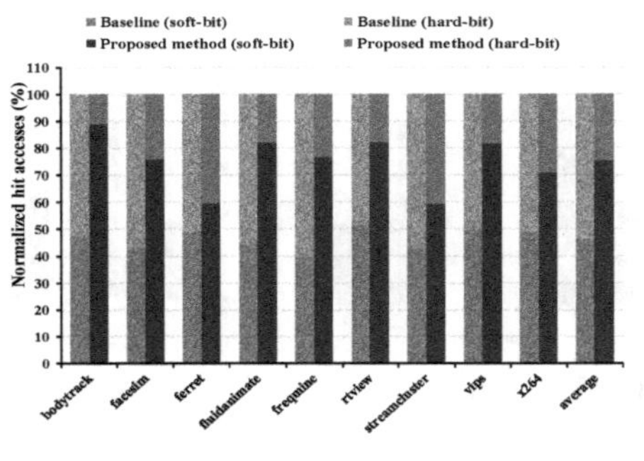

Figure 11: Normalized hit accesses in different methods

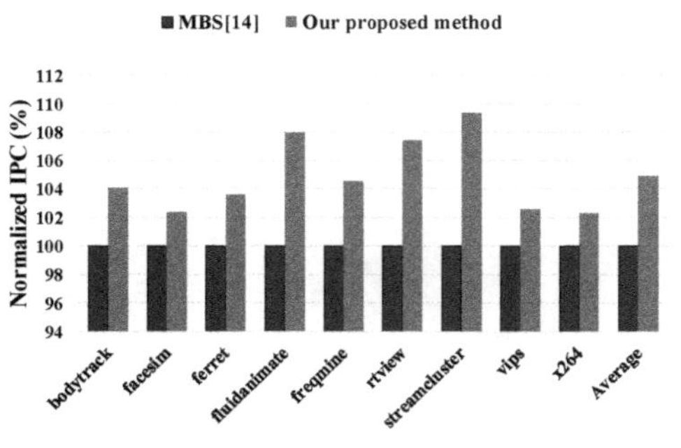

Figure 12: Normalized IPC comparison of the proposed method with MBS

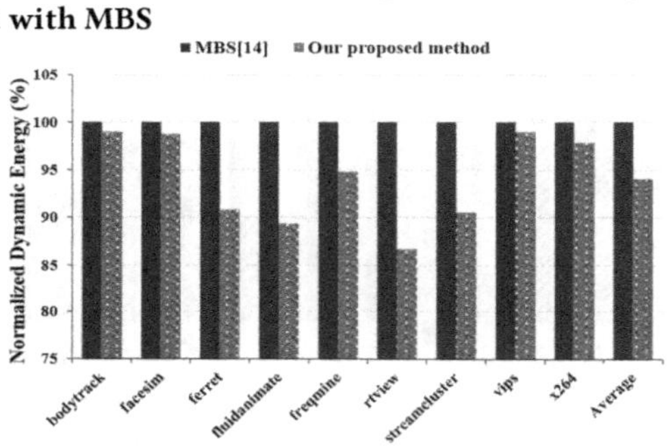

Figure 13: Normalized dynamic energy of our method in comparison with MBS

proposed method on average increases the IPC factor about 4.9%. In some benchmarks such as *fluidanimate*, *rtview*, and *streamcluster*, cache sets are in the MLC mode most of the time. Therefore, our swapping method has a better performance than the MBS method. In contrast to MBS, our method does not need to determine hot half lines and switch to SLC mode for these lines. In fact, our proposed method automatically transfers the hot half lines to the soft part by utilizing the swapping method that consequently leads to a better IPC. Our experimental results show about 9.5% improvement in the IPC factor compared to the conventional MLC STT-RAM structure.

4.5 Dynamic energy consumption

The static energy consumption of non-volatile memories is very low [7]. Therefore, in this section, we only consider the dynamic power and evaluate the dynamic energy consumption of the proposed structure. Fig. 13 illustrates the normalized dynamic energy of our method in comparison to MBS method. The results show that the dynamic energy is about 6.5% lower than the MBS. Our experiments also show about 30% energy saving in comparison to the conventional MLC STT-RAM.

Table 4: Storage overhead of the proposed structure

Module	Storage	Module	Storage
Local Swapper counter	3*65536 bits	Global Swapper counter	6 bits
Extra valid bit	1*65536 bits	Mode Switch counter	5*8192 bits

4.6 Storage overhead

Table 4 represents the storage overhead of the proposed method for an 8-way 4MB cache with 8K sets. In the proposed structure, we have a 3-bit local swapper counter and an extra valid bit for each cache line. Also, a 5-bit mode switch counter is employed for every cache set and a 6-bit Global Swapper counter for the whole cache structure. In total, about 37KB storage is needed. The storage overhead is lower than 1% and it is negligible. The storage overhead of the MBS method is about 32KB. The 5KB overhead is the cost of supporting swap between soft and hard parts.

5 CONCLUSIONS

In this paper, the performance and energy consumption of the MLC STT-RAM cache is improved by a new architecture that can support switching between the MLC and SLC modes at the online operation of the system. It also swaps hot and cold parts of a cache line in order to improve performance by migrating cache accesses to soft-bits. We achieved 4.9% enhancement in the performance and decreased the energy consumption by 6.5%. Our proposed method has about 1% storage overhead compared to the baseline system.

REFERENCES

[1] Desmet, L. et al. 2007. Enlarging instruction streams. IEEE Transactions on Computers. 56, 10 (2007).

[2] Tözün, P. et al. 2013. From A to E: analyzing TPC's OLTP benchmarks: the obsolete, the ubiquitous, the unexplored. Proceedings of the 16th International Conference on Extending Database Technology (2013).

[3] Kim, C.H. et al. 2003. A forward body-biased-low-leakage SRAM cache: Device and architecture considerations. Low Power Electronics and Design, 2003. ISLPED'03. Proceedings of the 2003 International Symposium on (2003), 6–9.

[4] Huai, Y. 2008. Spin-transfer torque MRAM (STT-MRAM): Challenges and prospects. AAPPS Bulletin. 18, 6 (2008), 33–40.

[5] Hosomi, M. et al. 2005. A novel nonvolatile memory with spin torque transfer magnetization switching: Spin-RAM. Electron Devices Meeting, 2005. IEDM Technical Digest. IEEE International (2005), 459–462.

[6] Dong, X. et al. 2008. Circuit and microarchitecture evaluation of 3D stacking magnetic RAM (MRAM) as a universal memory replacement. Design Automation Conference, 2008. DAC 2008. 45th ACM/IEEE (2008), 554–559.

[7] Jokar, M.R. et al. 2016. Sequoia: A high-endurance NVM-based cache architecture. IEEE Transactions on Very Large Scale Integration (VLSI) Systems. 24, 3 (2016), 954–967.

[8] Soltani, M. et al. 2016. Prolonging lifetime of non-volatile last level caches with cluster mapping. Proceedings of the 26th edition on Great Lakes Symposium on VLSI (2016), 329–334.

[9] Chen, Y. et al. 2011. Processor caches with multi-level spin-transfer torque ram cells. Proceedings of the 17th IEEE/ACM international symposium on Low-power electronics and design (2011), 73–78.

[10] Ishigaki, T. et al. 2010. A multi-level-cell spin-transfer torque memory with series-stacked magnetotunnel junctions. VLSI Technology (VLSIT), 2010 Symposium on (2010), 47–48.

[11] Chen, X. et al. 2016. AOS: adaptive overwrite scheme for energy-efficient MLC STT-RAM cache. Proceedings of the 53rd Annual Design Automation Conference (2016), 170.

[12] Chen, Y. et al. 2010. Access scheme of multi-level cell spin-transfer torque random access memory and its optimization. Circuits and Systems (MWSCAS), 2010 53rd IEEE International Midwest Symposium on (2010), 1109–1112.

[13] Bi, X. et al. 2013. Unleashing the potential of MLC STT-RAM caches. Computer-Aided Design (ICCAD), 2013 IEEE/ACM International Conference on (2013), 429–436.

[14] Wang, J. et al. 2014. Optimizing mlc-based stt-ram caches by dynamic block size reconfiguration. Computer Design (ICCD), 2014 32nd IEEE International Conference on (2014), 133–138.

[15] Bi, X. et al. 2017. Cross-Layer Optimization for Multilevel Cell STT-RAM Caches. IEEE Transactions on Very Large Scale Integration (VLSI) Systems. 25, 6 (2017), 1807–1820.

[16] Binkert, N. et al. 2011. The gem5 simulator. ACM SIGARCH Computer Architecture News. 39, 2 (2011), 1–7.

SEPUFSoC: Using PUFs for Memory Integrity andAuthentication in Multi-Processors System-on-Chip

Johanna Sepulveda, Felix Wilgerodt, Michael Pehl
Institute for Security in Information Technology, Technical University of Munich
Munich, Germany
{johanna.sepulveda,m.pehl}@tum.de

ABSTRACT

A persistent problem for modern Multi-Processors System-on-Chip (MPSoCs) is their vulnerability to code injection attacks. By tampering with the memory content, attackers are able to extract secrets from the MPSoC and to modify or deny the MPSoC's operation. This work proposes SEPUFSoC (Secure PUF-based SoC), a novel flexible, secure, and fast architecture able to be integrated into any MPSoC. SEPUFSoC prevents execution of unauthorized code as well as data manipulation by ensuring memory integrity and authentication. SEPUFSoC achieves: i) efficiency, through the integration of a fast and lightweight hash function for Message Authentication Code (MAC) generation and integrity verification of the memory lines at runtime; and ii) lightweight security, through the use of a Physical Unclonable Function (PUF) to securely generate and store the cryptographic keys that are used for the authentication of each application. We discuss the security and performance of SEPUFSoC for single core and multi-core systems. Results show that the SEPUFSoC is a secure, fast, and low overhead solution for MPSoCs.

ACM Reference Format:

Johanna Sepulveda, Felix Wilgerodt, Michael Pehl. 2018. SEPUFSoC: Using PUFs for Memory Integrity andAuthentication in Multi-Processors System-on-Chip. In *GLSVLSI '18: 2018 Great Lakes Symposium on VLSI, May 16–18, 2018, Chicago, IL, USA.* ACM, New York, NY, USA, 6 pages. https://doi.org/10.1145/3194554.3194562

1 INTRODUCTION

Multi-Processors System-on-Chip (MPSoCs) are considered a driving force behind the technology development in many critical applications and key industrial markets. MPSoCs integrate a set of heterogeneous IP hardware cores (e.g. single processor, hardware accelerators, peripherals or memory) which communicate through a bus. In order to increase the efficiency and flexibility of those systems, memory hierarchies up to L3 caches and DRAMs are integrated as well. This architecture is compliant with current state of the art market MPSoCs such as Tile-Mx100 from Tilera, MPPA from Kalray, or SCC from Intel [14]. The comprehensive use of MPSoCs in the Internet-of-Things (IoT) will be the driver of digitization in all domains, like industry automation, automotive, avionics, and health care. But the widespread use of MPSoCs in critical applications and key markets has turned them into targets of attacks. E.g., a compromised MPSoC may jeopardize the entire IoT environment. Thus, a major requirement for all critical domains is security.

GLSVLSI '18, May 16–18, 2018, Chicago, IL, USA

ACM ISBN 978-1-4503-5724-1/18/05...$15.00
https://doi.org/10.1145/3194554.3194562

But, code and data of MPSoCs are stored in non-volatile memories which are prone to malicious modifications. So a common attack to MPSoCs is code injection, i.e. an adversary stores malicious code in the MPSoC memory and executes it. Such an attack can have severe impact and give complete or partial control of the system to the attacker. In this way the attacker can compromise sensitive code and data or install new firmware. To avoid this kind of attacks, authenticity and integrity of all code and data on a secure MPSoC must be continuously verified along the operation.

Previous works have proposed different memory protection schemes for SoC [3, 6, 8, 9, 12, 16]. But they have two main limitations: i) Cryptographic keys are stored in on-chip non-volatile memory (NVM). Even if design flaws are avoided, no side-channel attack is possible, and the chip is protected by appropriate countermeasures during operation, an attacker can still try to read out the key using an invasive attack if the system is turned off. But protecting a chip while it is not operating is expensive, since it requires, e.g., battery-backed countermeasures [15]. ii) The suggested solutions are deeply embedded into the processor micro-architecture. So they prevent the use of general purpose CPU architectures (i.e., ARM and X86). This limits their widespread adoption.

In this work, we propose SEPUFSoC, an architecture for memory authentication and integrity verification of MPSoCs based on Physical Unclonable Functions (PUFs). SEPUFSoC is a secure, flexible, and efficient architecture. It uses SipHash as a fast and lightweight hash function integrated into an interface between the CPUs and the communication structure of the MPSoCs. SipHash is used in SEPUFSoC to verify code and data authenticity and integrity. In contrast to previous work, SEPUFSoC has three main advantages: i) security services are integrated into the SoC as a wrapper to the IP cores. This makes SEPUFSoC re-usable in different MPSoC architectures which are based on a wide range of different general purpose CPU architectures; ii) the keys for code and data authentication are generated and stored by a PUF. Since the PUF can store the key securely, SEPUFSoC can be used even if no secured NVM is available. iii) The performance of SEPUFSoC overcomes previous solutions. In summary, the contributions of the paper are:

- SEPUFSoC, a PUF-based architecture for code and data authentication and integrity verification for MPSoCs. It can be integrated on any general purpose CPU to prevent execution and use of manipulated code or data;
- SEPUFSoC implementation and performance/cost impact evaluation for an MPSoC. Synthesis is done for a 65nm technology;
- Discussion of security requirements of SEPUFSoC.

The rest of the paper is organized as follows: Section 2 presents previous work on memory authentication and integrity verification. Section 3 describes the MPSoC and the special requirements in terms of security. Section 4 provides our threat model. Section 5 presents the architecture and functionality of SEPUFSoC. Evaluation and results are shown in Section 6, before the paper concludes in Section 7.

2 RELATED WORKS

In order to provide security of the code and data executed on a System-on-Chip (SoC), encryption of application code/data, stored in an off-chip memory, is widely used [3, 8, 9, 12, 16]. However, this technique does not prevent code injection attacks completely. The lack of authentication and integrity verification allows an attacker to relocate code or perform replay attacks to modifying the program flow or execution state of an application.

In [9, 10] XOM (eXecute Only Memory) is proposed. It uses AES-256 to encrypt memory regions through multiple application-specific keys (*master* and *session keys*). All memory lines are encrypted together with a MAC to additionally provide authentication. Application-specific session keys are stored off-chip, encrypted by the master key. The master key is stored on chip. The main drawbacks of XOM are the vulnerability to replay attacks, allowing the attacker to store authorized code for executing it later and the high performance impact, due the encryption/decryption and authentication of each line by AES. XOM has a high memory access latency, turning it prohibitive for applications with high cache miss rates. Also, XOM requires secured NVM to store the master key on chip. The off-chip key storage forces the integration of memory encryption/decryption at the XOM.

In [16, 17, 19, 20] AEGIS (Architecture for Tamper-Evident and Tamper-Resistant Processing) is proposed. It integrates a One-Time-Pad (OTP) AES-128 encryption and a delay-based ring oscillator PUF for MAC generation to allow the verification of authenticity and integrity of code and data. AEGIS provides different levels of protection and security modes for different applications by including a secure operating system. This increases flexibility and performance when compared to XOM. The main drawbacks of AEGIS are that i) AEGIS requires extensive changes in the architecture, compiler and operating systems of the SoC; ii) it allows the execution of some part of the malicious code before an integrity violation is detected since verification is done while the code is executed. iii) it has low throughput due to the use of AES for MAC generation and impacts the execution of an application by at least 30% when compared to the unprotected execution.

CSHIA (Computer Security by Hardware-Intrinsic Authentication) [6] is an SRAM PUF-based architecture. The proposed CPU architecture uses an authentication tree, PUFs, and MACs to perform code and data verification similar to AEGIS. Each line of code and data that is stored in off-chip memory is tagged by a MAC. The MACs can be loaded and stored in parallel to the main memory, by integrating an additional memory for MAC storage and a private data bus for accessing the MACs. This decreases the impact on the performance of the execution of applications. However, it also requires deep SoC and CPU modifications, which turns integration of CSHIA into existing CPU architectures unfeasible. Also, similar to AEGIS, some unverified instructions can be executed before an interrupt is generated. Since CSHIA was not implemented, performance and cost cannot be quantified.

All of the proposed memory protection schemes do not support MPSoCs. Although, for authentication and integrity code and data verification the same principles can be applied, MPSoCs have special requirements. They require parallel execution in multiple and heterogeneous IP cores, high performance, and simultaneous execution of untrusted and sensitive applications on the same platform. SEPUFSoC offers a flexible, secure and high performance PUF-based architecture able to be integrated to any general purpose CPU architectures. It offers a solution suitable for MPSoCs and overcomes drawbacks of previous works. Table 1 compares key features of previous work with SEPUFSoC.

Table 1: Sumary of related work and SEPUFSoC

Approach	Authent. & Integrity Check before exec.	PUF	Imple-mented	MPSoC
XOM	No	No	FPGA	No
AEGIS	No	Yes (RO)	FPGA	No
CSHIA	No	Yes (SRAM)	-	No
SEPUFSoC	**Yes**	**Yes (k-SUM)**	**FPGA**	**Yes**

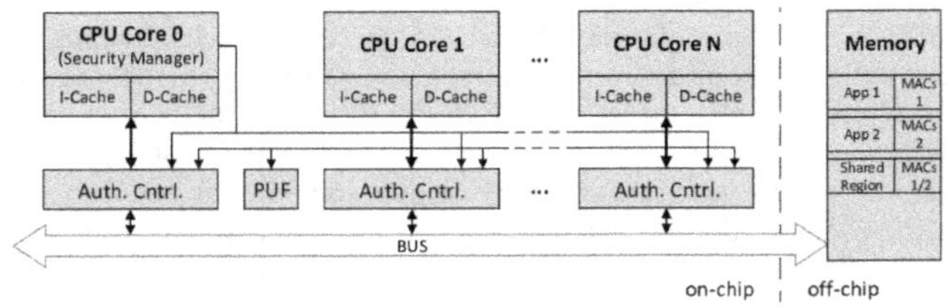

Figure 1: SEPUFSOC integrated into a MPSoC.

3 MPSOC DESCRIPTION

MPSoCs are tile-based structures which are able to meet a variety of application demands. As shown in Fig. 1, each MPSoC tile is either composed of a single IP core or a cluster of IP cores, which communicate through a communication structure. MPSoCs integrate heterogeneous general purpose CPUs, storage components, peripherals, hardware accelerators, and other IP hardware cores. In order to increase the performance, current SoCs implement memory hierarchies, where several levels of cache (e.g. L1 to L3) and a set of DRAMs are integrated. In case of a cache miss, all cache levels of a processing core are queried until the requested data is found. If no level contains the data, the cache coherency mechanism initiates an access to other distant cores or eventually to off-chip memories.

MPSoCs are able to support several applications, usually being executed simultaneously. For performance enhancement two approaches are used in MPSoCs: i) memory hierarchies, which use the spatial and timing locality principles; and ii) resource sharing, which allows to split applications into small pieces of code (tasks), which are mapped to different MPSoC resources. Code and data of the applications are normally stored into off-chip memories. Thus, avoiding code injection attacks is a serious security concern for MPSoCs.

4 THREAT MODEL

A SoC/MPSoC (Fig. 1) is composed of on-chip and off-chip components. On-chip components include the CPU and data and instruction caches. Off-chip components include the external memory to store application code/data, peripherals, and the memory bus, which interconnects the SoC/MPSoC and the external memory. Elements inside the chip are considered trusted and secure. So it is possible to download new trusted code to the device by using code signing techniques and subsequently storing the code to external memory. But off-chip components can be attacked. Therefore, we assume that an adversary can read from and write to any address in the external memory at any time, e.g. by probing the memory bus. Due to the performance overhead of code signing it is not feasible to use this to protect the transmitted code during operation.

For the on-chip components we assume for this work that an attacker can temper with the device as long as it is powered off.

Especially, he can read out and reprogram non-secured NVM on-chip. However, we assume that appropriate countermeasures are used to prevent invasive and semi-invasive physical attacks to on-chip components during operation, especially we assume that probing of wires and registers as well as observations of photon emissions of switching transistors is not feasible. Note, that this scenario would allow an attacker to modify unencrypted certificates for code-signing, if they are stored in non-secured NVM. Also, an attacker might be able to extract a key from, e.g. eFuses. Denial-of-service attacks, by deliberately inserting invalid memory lines are not considered in our threat model.

The security goal of the SEPUFSoC is to provide runtime security through memory integrity and authentication to multiprocessor systems to prevent code injection and memory modification attacks. It includes spoofing, reallocation and replay attacks to the off-chip components. Also, it can be used to prevent tampering with certificates which are used for code signing but this is not presented in this work.

5 SEPUFSOC

SEPUFSoC is a PUF-based architecture that provides memory integrity and authentication in order to avoid code injection attacks. Security services are implemented as interfaces which wrap the IP hardware cores of the system. SEPUFSoC has three main advantages. i) Flexibility: It has an interface-like and highly parameterizable architecture. Different PUF types can be used. Bit length and security (number of SipHash rounds) can be adapted to meet performance requirements and area/power constraints of the SoC/MPSoC. ii) Independence: The integration of SEPUFSoC is independent of the SoC architecture (processor architecture, memory hierarchy, communication structure) and IP characteristics (number of ports, communication protocol). iii) Low cost and high performance: The integration of security primitives are designed for high throughput applications. The PUF provides a low cost solution for secure key storage since it does not require additional manufacturing steps but prevents from reading out the secret while the chip is not operating.

The integration of SEPUFSoC into a general MPSoC is shown in Fig. 1. It is composed by N general purpose CPU IP cores (*CPU Core 0* to *CPU Core N*). Each includes instruction and data caches (I-Cache and D-Cache). CPU cores are linked to the bus through the Authentication Controller component (*Auth. Cntrl*). A single PUF is used to store keys for all Authentication Controllers. Instructions and data of the applications are stored in the off-chip memory. SEPUFSoC has two main elements: Authentication controller and PUF.

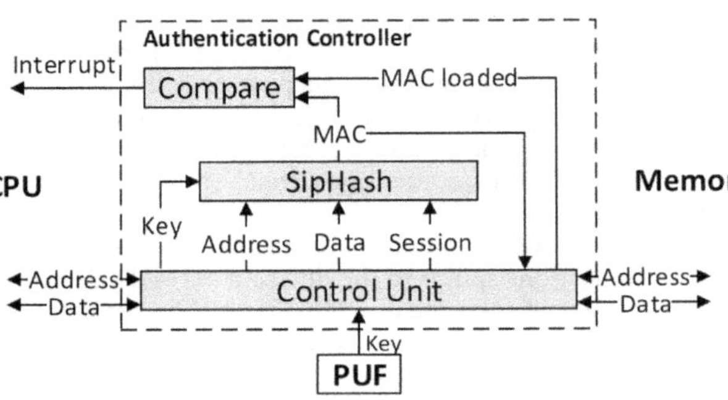

Figure 2: Controller architecture.

5.1 Authentication controller

The authentication controller is an interface to verify and to authenticate all data communicated from memory or other IP cores to a CPU core. By computing the MAC for each accessed cache line and matching it with the MAC stored in the cache line, the authentication controller validates the code. If the MAC is correct, data communication to the CPU is enabled, otherwise it is blocked. As shown in Fig. 2, the architecture of the Authentication Controller consist of: i) A SipHash, which is a keyed pseudorandom function able to generate 64-bit MACs for inputs of arbitrary length. ii) The compare module, which compares the 64-bit MAC stored in external memory and the MAC computed by the SipHash. iii) A control unit, to manage the communication between CPU and memory as well as the operation of SipHash and compare module.

SipHash. SipHash [1] is a fast and lightweight technique for MAC generation of short messages. It generates 64-bit MACs for input messages of arbitrary size using a 128-bit key. Message blocks of 128 bits and the key are split into 64-bit chunks (m_0, m_1 and k_0, k_1), as shown in Fig. 3. SipHash uses four 64-bit initialization values. Intermediate states (v_0 to v_3) are represented as 64-bit arrays which are iteratively processed over 8 SipRounds. Each round consists of 5 additions, 6 rotations and 3 XOR (ARX) operations. SipHash is divided into a compression stage (first 4 SipRounds), wherein m_0 and m_1, key, and initial values are processed, and a finalization, in which intermediate value v_2 is bit-wise inverted (XOR with 0xFF) before performing the last 4 SipRounds. Finally, the SipHash output (MAC) is obtained by XORing all intermediate values.

The security of SipHash depends on the number of SipRounds. It has been proven in [1] that an attacker is not able to retrieve any information about the secret key, even if multiple input/output pairs of the MAC function are revealed. Moreover, SipHash generates strong MACs and has low probability for collision.

SipHash is used in SEPUFSoC to generate a 64-bit MAC for each memory line based on memory address, data of the cache line, and a session token. Usage of address and data prevents spoofing and relocation attacks. The session token provides temporal information to reduce the feasibility of replay attacks. The MAC is embodied into each line as a tag (T). The secret key for the SipHash is provided by a PUF in our scenario.

Compare. This module matches the computed MAC of the memory line (MAC) with the MAC stored in memory (MAC_{loaded}). If

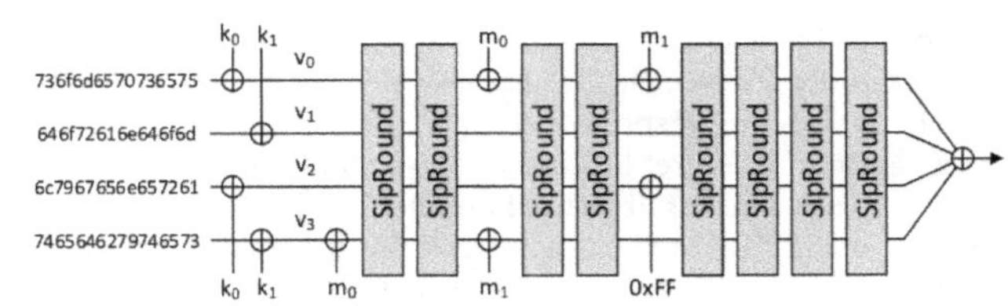

Figure 3: SipHash architecture.

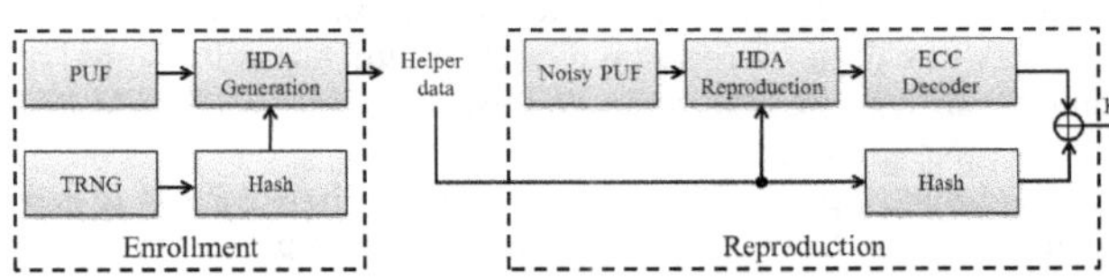

Figure 4: Key enrollment and reproduction using a PUF

the MACs do not match, an interrupted is triggered to alert the processor to the lack of code or data authenticity and integrity. As a consequence, the processing of untrusted code or data on the CPU IP core is prevented.

Control Unit. This unit manages the operation of the Authentication Controller. It loads address and data values from a memory line to the SipHash and Compare modules. Also, it requests loading the key (extracted from a PUF) and session token information.

5.2 PUF

The physical behaviour of every circuit is influenced by unpredictable variations during the manufacturing process. These are unique for every device. PUFs measure the variations to extract a device unique secret. In SEPUFSoC the secret derived from the PUF is used to store application individual keys for the authentication controller. Compared to classical secured NVM the key extracted from the PUF is only available during operation of the chip. So it is not necessary to use expensive countermeasures which need to detect attacks while the chip is turned off. Also, the PUF does not require any additional manufacturing or programming steps: It can be build from standard logic gates and the key in our scenario can be generated by the device on its own, e.g. during the first boot up.

Key storage is realized in this work using a Fuzzy Commitment scheme [7]. During an enrollment phase (see Fig. 4), a random number is generated for each application. The random number is encoded to the codeword of an error correcting code (ECC). Helper data are computed from the codeword and the PUF response by a Helper Data Algorithm (HDA). They describe the mapping from the PUF response to the codeword. Note that for good helper data algorithms and good PUFs, the helper data do not leak information about the secret [13]. So helper data can be stored in publicly available NVM.

To retrieve the key in a reproduction phase (right in Fig. 4), the HDA is used to map helper data and PUF response to the required codeword. Since the PUF response is noisy, also the resulting codeword contains errors and must be corrected to get the correct random number. To prevent helper data manipulation attacks, a SPONGENT hash function is used in our setting which hashes the helper data and XORs the result to the random number to get the final key.

To generate individual keys per application, a single, central PUF unit is suggested in SEPUFSoC. This PUF can be realized by a single-response (SR) PUF, e.g. an SRAM PUF or RO PUF, or a multi-response (MR) PUF, e.g. an Arbiter, Bistable Ring, or SUM PUF. If a sufficiently strong MR PUF is implemented, several thousand to millions of secret response bits can be extracted from it. Such a huge amount of secret bits, allows to generate keys for a large number of applications. If a small number of PUF response bits is sufficient, an SR PUF can be used. Especially, the start up behaviour of regular SRAM, which is typically available on every chip, can be used to extract a secret, e.g. [21]. If the number of keys extracted in this way does not fit the number of application keys, we suggested to modify SEPUFSoC: A single key stored by the PUF can be used as a master key. The application keys can than be encrypted by the master key to be stored as public data which are decrypted on demand. This can be recommended together with an SRAM PUF for IC implementations of SEPUFSoC.

Our sample implementation is on FPGA where SRAM is typically initialized but RO-based PUFs can be well implemented. Since RO-PUFs require a large area per bit, we selected a k-SUM PUF for our proof-of-concept implementation. It is reused to generate required random numbers using the approach in [11]. The encoding and decoding of the PUF is done by Differential Sequence Coding (DSC) and a Viterbi decoder [5], which is very efficient with respect to area and required helper data per key. The error correction is designed for a PUF with bit error probability of 15% and a key error probability of 10^{-6}. Note that any other PUF can be used in SEPUFSoC. The actual PUF implementation was not in the focus of this research.

5.3 SEPUFSoC functionality

The functionality of SEPUFSoC can be divided into three stages: i) Key generation; ii) MAC initialization and application installation; and iii) operation.

i) Key generation. During application installation, a key for each application is derived. For this purpose, an unused random challenge for the k-SUM PUF and a random number for the key are generated. These are used to compute the helper data for generation and reconstruction of the key. Application identifier, PUF challenge, and helper data are used by the Authentication Controller to trigger the regeneration of a certain, application-specific key which is required for MAC initialization during application installation as well as during the SoC/MPSoC operation. To reduce the performance impact of the PUF key regeneration, all keys are only regenerated once, after each reboot, and stored in a dedicated volatile on-chip memory.

ii) MAC Initialization and Application Installation. Before starting the normal system operation, MACs for all applications that are going to be executed on the SoC/MPSoC need to be computed and stored in the off-chip memory. Application MACs are based on the application code/data, identifier and a session token. This initialization and installation stage runs only once in a controlled environment and it is composed by three steps: i) Disable the compare module of the Authentication Controller, to avoid the generation of interruptions; ii) load code/data application on-chip, to quantify the MAC and write back code/data and MACs into the off-chip memory; and iii) enable compare modules and resume the SoC/MPSoC normal operation. This process is repeated until the whole application has been initialized with SEPUFSoC MACs.

iii) Operation. During SoC/MPSoC operation, code/data may be migrated to another IP core or write back to the main memory. In such situations, MACs are computed in the Authentication Controller and stored in the off-chip memory. During a read access, the loaded data is used to recompute the MAC, which is then compared with the MAC previously stored in memory. For an authentic and integral memory line the computed MAC matches to the MAC stored in memory. Thus, data is communicated to the CPU. Otherwise, the memory access is discarded and an interrupt is generated. During operation, the session tokens used to quantify the MACs are updated (to avoid reply attacks). Updating is performed during idle periods or booting time. This process is triggered using pre-programmed update-awake timing or activation by a trusted on-chip component. When the session token is updated, new MACs must be generated, thus, presenting a trade-off between security and performance.

SEPUFSoC allows the parallel and multi-threaded execution of multiple applications split into the different cores. Each application (mapped on a single core or multiple cores) has its individual key. Data exchange/modification among applications is possible by creating a shared PUF-based group key. Then, the authentication controller can use the shared PUF-based group key for memory accesses of shared regions and the individual application key for memory accesses of private regions.

Table 2: FPGA Resources utilization

Component	FFs	LUTs	DSPs	BRAM
Baseline System	9421	10919	6	75
SEPUFSoC (Total)	12523	14800	6	76
Authentication Controller	1796	1934	0	0
PUF	1306	1947	0	1

6 EVALUATION OF SEPUFSOC

The SoC/MPSoC based SEPUFSoCs shown in Fig. 1 are implemented on the Nexys4 DDR FPGA with Vivado 2015.3 Design suite from Xilinx. It is composed of 5 IP cores: i) single or multiple 5-pipeline deep Microblaze 9.5 running single or multiple testbenches; ii) private instruction and data caches characterized by 8 KB, 128 bit width and 4 words per line; iii) AXI bus with round-robin arbitration and 32 bit width; iv) Authentication Controller; and v) k-Sum PUF. Moreover, external 128 MB DDR and BRAM (integrated into the FPGA board) are used to store the application code/data and MACs, respectively. For sake of high performance and security, different buses are used to connect the Authentication Controller with the off-chip memory and to the memory which stores the MACs. It improves the SEPUFSoC performance, by allowing simultaneously code/data and MAC accesses. AXI4-Lite protocol is employed to perform the read/write transactions. For expediting the repeatability, all IP cores used inside the SoC are included in Vivado 2015.3. The PUF is connected directly to the Authentication Controller. The CPU cores of the MPSoC share the same program and MAC memory. However, each CPU core has its own private authentication controller. A single PUF can be shared by both cores. Different keys are derived using different PUF responses and corresponding helper data.

To generate the 128-bit PUF-based key, a k-Sum PUF is build from 64 Ring Oscillator (RO) pairs. The module can be triggered to generate a new key and public data for key reconstruction or to regenerate a key from this stored data and the PUF. To reduce performance overhead through the PUF, the regeneration of a key is done only once after reboot. We assume that 50% of the program memory has security requirements and must be protected through the 64-bit MACs. Data gathered from the execution of the benchmark on the SoC/MPSoC is transmitted to the PC through the UART interface (AXI Uartlite). In our implementation, a MAC per cache line is computed (PTAG). The fine grained security offers flexibility in the data management, but increases the performance overhead. Further exploration in the MAC granularity computation is part of future work.

6.1 SEPUFSoC Cost

The summary of the SEPUFSoC overhead when compared to the baseline system is presented in Table 2. Results show the reasonable low overhead of SEPUFSoC. Area and power results of SEPUFSoC Authentication Controller are obtained with the Cadence Encounter RTL Compiler RC12.24 tool. The synthesis targets the 65nm process technology at 100 MHz operating frequency and 25°C. Results are shown in Table 3.

6.2 SEPUFSoC Performance

SEPUFSoC memory access latency is higher than the baseline implementation (without security) due to the additional computations performed by the authentication controller. Fig. 5 shows the timing diagrams for each SEPUFSoC access: cache line read, write and word write. The MAC computation, bottleneck of SEPUFSoC, requires 14 cycles: 10 cycles for the SipHash computation (a SipRound is executed each cycle) and 4 additional cycles due AXI4 bus protocol. Cache line read and write just require a single MAC computation. In contrast, the word write transaction is performed into 3 steps: i) fetches and verifies the integrity of the target memory line; ii) computes the new MAC; and iii) writes the data back. To evaluate SEPUFSoC performance, eight different benchmarks were employed: CoreMark, Dhrystone and a six MiBench applications (Basicmath, Bitcount, Qsort, Dijkstra, FFT, Stringsearch). Such benchmarks are widely used in the SoC/MPSoC evaluation [4]. They were compiled using the Xilinx Microblaze GNU toolchain in Xilinx SDK 2015.3 with the compiler optimization -O3. Fig. 6 shows the normalized results for the different benchmarks for different first-level cache memory sizes.

Table 4 presents the performance results of SEPUFSoC and the baseline MPSoC (without security). Results are expressed as CoreMark iterations per second (CM), Dhrystone Million Instructions per Second (DMIPS) and instructions per second (I/sec). Higher

Table 3: SEPUFSoC Authentication Controller - 65nm

Component	Area (um^2)	Leakage Power (nW)	Dynamic Power (nW)
Authentication Controller (Total)	27797	558	4624079
SipHash	19264	261	2506971
SipRound	8533	102	905346

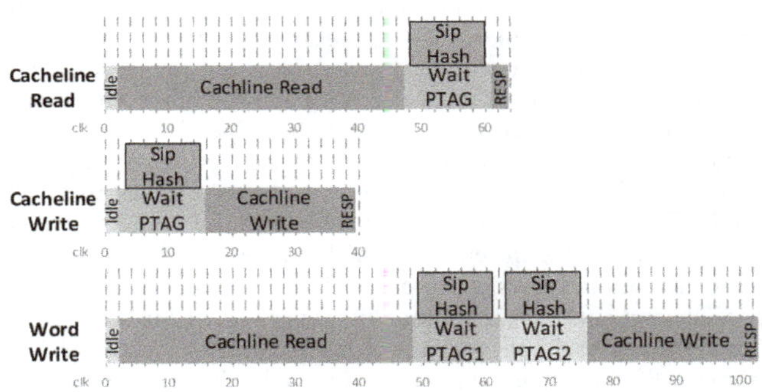

Figure 5: Performance figures of SEPUFSoC single transactions.

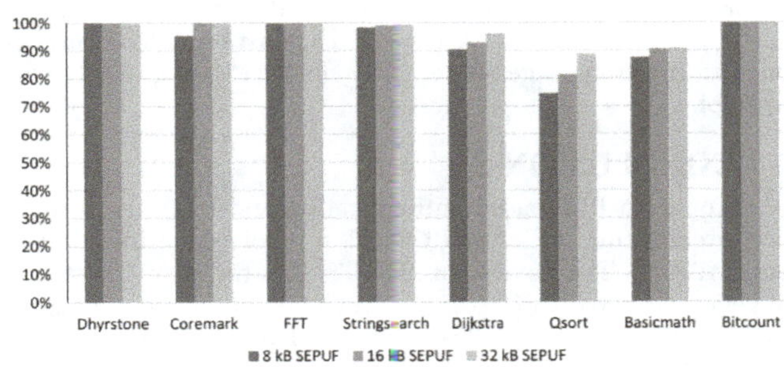

Figure 6: SEPUFSoC performance results.

Table 4: Summary of Performance Evaluation

Benchmark	Units	Baseline	SEPUFSoC	Degradation
CoreMark	CM	186.1	177.8	4.4%
Drystone	DMIPS	140.8	140.8	0%
Basicmath	I/sec	0.4	0.3	12.5%
Bitcount	I/sec	18.5	18.5	0.1%
Dijkstra	I/sec	0.2	0.2	0.2%
FFT	I/sec	1.5	1.5	0.2%
Qsort	I/sec	273.9	204.2	25.4%
Stringsearch	I/sec	39.3	38.6	1.6%

scores indicates a better system performance. Results show in general a small degradation of the performance due to the additional features of SEPUFSoC. These values depend on the number of byte writes of each benchmark. For instance Basicmath and Qsort demand a huge amount of byte writes, thus, forcing SEPUFSoC to constantly update the MACs.

6.3 Security requirements of SEPUFSoC

The main goal of the SEPUFSoC is to prevent illegitimate and unauthorized modifications of code/data applications. SEPUFSoC is able to successfully prevent spoofing and relocation attacks, due to the inclusion of memory address and data for the MAC computation. Moreover, updating session tokens avoids replay attacks.

Security of SEPUFSoC strongly depends on the security of the PUF, i.e. its type, implementation, and error correction codes. To ensure a high level of security, there must not exist correlations between the derived secrets for different keys.

While the strength of an MR PUF can be increased, e.g. by XORing the response from multiple PUF instances [18], for the error correction a reasonable choice is required: On the one side, this building block must not leak information about the reliability of an MR PUF to prevent the attack in [2]. On the other side, it also must not leak key information through the helper data and must be robust against helper data manipulation attacks. Provided such a reasonable choice for the error correction, the secret generated from the PUF can be considered secure as long as the number of used bits does not exceed the entropy which can be provided by the PUF implementation. For single response PUFs machine learning is not possible. But since the amount of bits is very limited in such a case, it is suggested to derive only one or few master keys for SEPUFSoC from the PUF and to encrypt application individual keys with these secrets. Note, that the security of our proof-of-concept implementation is weak regarding the selected PUF-implementation, since it was not in the focus of the work but was used only to provide a realistic PUF behaviour. Thus, the security of the PUF in our actual implementation is not further discussed. Regarding the MAC security, SEPUFSoC MACs are protected against brute-force attacks, once an interrupt is generated after the first wrong MAC guess attempt.

7 CONCLUSION

We propose a PUF-based authentication and integrity verification architecture, called SEPUFSoC, to avoid code injection in SoC/MPSoCs. The novelty of SEPUFSoC is the easy integration to general purpose CPUs and the protection of the different applications in MPSoCs. SEPUFSoC was implemented and evaluated under several MPSoC benchmarks. We show that SEPUFSoC is a flexible structure, which present good security and low impact on the MPSoC performance. As future work, we aim to implement different PUFs and hash techniques. As well as to further increase the security of our system against replay attacks.

Acknowledgments. This work was partly funded by the German Federal Ministry of Education and Research (BMBF), grant number 01IS160253 (ARAMiS II) and the Fraunhofer High Performance Center for Secure Connected Systems of Munich.

REFERENCES

[1] Jean-Philippe Aumasson and Daniel J. Bernstein. 2012. *SipHash: A Fast Short-Input PRF.* Springer Berlin Heidelberg, Berlin, Heidelberg.

[2] Georg T Becker, Alexander Wild, and Tim Güneysu. 2015. Security analysis of index-based syndrome coding for PUF-based key generation. In *Hardware Oriented Security and Trust (HOST), 2015 IEEE International Symposium on.* IEEE.

[3] Christopher W. Fletcher, Marten van Dijk, and Srinivas Devadas. 2012. A Secure Processor Architecture for Encrypted Computation on Untrusted Programs. In *Proceedings of the Seventh ACM Workshop on Scalable Trusted Computing (STC '12).* ACM, New York, NY, USA, 6.

[4] M. R. Guthaus, J. S. Ringenberg, D. Ernst, T. M. Austin, T. Mudge, and R. B. Brown. 2001. MiBench: A free, commercially representative embedded benchmark suite. In *Proceedings of the Fourth Annual IEEE International Workshop on Workload Characterization.*

[5] Matthias Hiller, Meng-Day (Mandel) Yu, and Georg Sigl. 2016. Cherry-Picking Reliable PUF Bits with Differential Sequence Coding. In *IEEE Trans. Inf. Forensics Security.* IEEE.

[6] C. Hoffman, M. Cortes, D. F. Aranha, and G. Araujo. 2015. Computer security by hardware-intrinsic authentication. In *2015 International Conference on Hardware/Software Codesign and System Synthesis (CODES+ISSS).*

[7] Ari Juels and Martin Wattenberg. 1999. A fuzzy commitment scheme. In *ACM Conference on Computer and Communications Security (CCS).* ACM.

[8] Stephan Kleber, Florian Unterstein, Matthias Matousek, Frank Kargl, Frank Slomka, and Matthias Hiller. 2015. Secure Execution Architecture based on PUF-driven Instruction Level Code Encryption. Cryptology ePrint Archive, Report 2015/651. (2015). http://eprint.iacr.org/2015/651.

[9] David Lie, Chandramohan Thekkath, Mark Mitchell, Patrick Lincoln, Dan Boneh, John Mitchell, and Mark Horowitz. 2000. Architectural Support for Copy and Tamper Resistant Software. *SIGPLAN Not.* 35, 11 (Nov. 2000), 10.

[10] David Lie, Chandramohan A. Thekkath, and Mark Horowitz. 2003. Implementing an Untrusted Operating System on Trusted Hardware. *SIGOPS Oper. Syst. Rev.* 37, 5 (Oct. 2003), 15.

[11] Abhranil Maiti, Raghunandan Nagesh, Anand Reddy, and Patrick Schaumont. 2009. Physical unclonable function and true random number generator: a compact and scalable implementation. In *ACM Great Lakes Symposium on VLSI.*

[12] Emmanuel Owusu, Jorge Guajardo, Jonathan McCune, Jim Newsome, Adrian Perrig, and Amit Vasudevan. 2013. OASIS: On Achieving a Sanctuary for Integrity and Secrecy on Untrusted Platforms. In *Proceedings of the 2013 ACM SIGSAC Conference on Computer & Communications Security (CCS '13).* ACM, New York, NY, USA, 12.

[13] Michael Pehl, Matthias Hiller, and Georg Sigl. 2017. *Information Theoretic Security and Privacy of Information Systems.* Cambridge University Press, Chapter Secret Key Generation and Authentication.

[14] Johanna Sepulveda, Mathieu Gross, Andreas Zankl, and Georg Sigl. 2017. Exploiting Bus Communication to Improve Cache Attacks on Systems-on-Chips. In *IEEE Computer Society Annual Symposium on VLSI (ISVLSI '17).*

[15] Sergei Petrovich Skorobogatov. 2005. *Semi-invasive attacks: a new approach to hardware security analysis.* Ph.D. Dissertation. University of Cambridge.

[16] G. Edward Suh. 2005. *AEGIS: A Single-Chip Secure Processor.* Ph.D. Dissertation. Massachusetts Institute of Technology.

[17] G. Edward Suh, Dwaine Clarke, Blaise Gassend, Marten van Dijk, and Srinivas Devadas. 2003. AEGIS: Architecture for Tamper-evident and Tamper-resistant Processing. In *Proceedings of the 17th Annual International Conference on Supercomputing (ICS '03).* ACM, New York, NY, USA, 12.

[18] G. Edward Suh and Srinivas Devadas. 2007. Physical Unclonable Functions for Device Authentication and Secret Key Generation. In *Proceedings of the 44th Annual Design Automation Conference (DAC '07).* ACM, New York, NY, USA, 6.

[19] G. E. Suh, C. W. O'Donnell, and S. Devadas. 2007. Aegis: A Single-Chip Secure Processor. *IEEE Design Test of Computers* 24, 6 (Nov 2007).

[20] G. E. Suh, C. W. O'Donnell, Ishan Sachdev, and Srinivas Devadas. 2005. Design and implementation of the AEGIS single-chip secure processor using physical random functions. In *32nd International Symposium on Computer Architecture (ISCA'05).*

[21] Florian Wilde. 2017. Large Scale Characterization of SRAM on Infineon XMC Microcontrollers as PUF. In *4th Workshop on Cryptography and Security in Computing Systems (CS2 2017) HIPEAC17.* Stockholm, Sweden.

Protecting Communication in Many-Core Systems against Active Attackers

Sadia Moriam
Center for Advancing Electronics Dresden, Technische Universität Dresden
sadia.moriam@tu-dresden.de

Elke Franz
Chair of Privacy and Data Security, Technische Universität Dresden
elke.franz@tu-dresden.de

Paul Walther
Chair of Privacy and Data Security, Technische Universität Dresden
paul.walther@tu-dresden.de

Akash Kumar
Center for Advancing Electronics Dresden, Technische Universität Dresden
akash.kumar@tu-dresden.de

Thorsten Strufe
Center for Advancing Electronics Dresden, Technische Universität Dresden
thorsten.strufe@tu-dresden.de

Gerhard P. Fettweis
Center for Advancing Electronics Dresden, Technische Universität Dresden
gerhard.fettweis@tu-dresden.de

ABSTRACT

The advent of hardware Trojans is posing an increasing threat on complex integrated circuits. Network-on-Chip, the established communication infrastructure for many core systems-on-chip, are growing in complexity. Integration of third-party components, which are increasingly becoming valuable targets, exposes the surface for attacks through the injection of hardware Trojans. In this paper, we address active attacks on NoCs, and focus on the integrity of transmitted data.

Basically, we use network coding for the transmission of data in order to increase efficiency and robustness. We introduce solutions that allow detection of active attacks under the consideration of the constraints in NoCs. The efficiency of these solutions is investigated by means of cycle-accurate simulations. Further, we develop an analytic approach for faster and more flexible but accurate evaluation. We finally analyze the area overhead using a state-of-the-art MPSoC and demonstrate that we can protect the integrity of data with reasonable effort.

KEYWORDS

Hardware trojans, integrity, availability

ACM Reference Format:

Sadia Moriam, Elke Franz, Paul Walther, Akash Kumar, Thorsten Strufe, and Gerhard P. Fettweis. 2018. Protecting Communication in Many-Core Systems against Active Attackers. In *Proceedings of 2018 Great Lakes Symposium on VLSI (GLSVLSI '18)*. ACM, New York, NY, USA, Article 4, 6 pages. https://doi.org/10.1145/3194554.3194582

1 INTRODUCTION

The rising power consumption and reduced performance of single core processors has led to increasing developments towards multi-processor systems-on-chip (MPSoCs) [7]. With potentially thousands of cores on a chip, it is crucial to have a scalable and efficient communication backbone. Packet-switched Network-on-Chip (NoC) has been established as the promising solution to the interconnection problem [4, 9, 15], replacing bus-based systems over the last decade.

The growing complexity of the systems implies a higher susceptibility to errors [24]. It also causes the design process to increasingly rely on the integration of components from third parties, potentially also from untrusted sources [25]. Even tools used for design and development may be compromised, and hence pose a tangible threat to MPSoCs. Such threats can be realized by inserting hardware Trojans (HT), as reported, e.g., in [3, 5, 10, 12, 25]. Designing NoCs, it hence becomes vital to ensure reliability to errors, but increasingly also security.

Considering HTs, an adversarial router may directly drop or alter the forwarded traffic, thus threatening the availability or integrity of the communication. With local or remote access to the device, the adversary may also eavesdrop on the communication. As attacks on the confidentiality additionally require a hidden channel to the attacker, we consider achieving availability and integrity of communication the more pressing goals. Particularly, we focus on active attackers who may modify or drop flits transmitted in the NoC.

In this paper, we make the following *contributions*: we (1) devise methods to ensure integrity and increase availability in NoCs, we subsequently (2) validate our results in extensive simulations, (3) develop an analytic model for faster and more flexible evaluation, and (4) estimate the actual area overhead of the schemes. The results demonstrate that our schemes can guarantee integrity at very reasonable overhead. Our schemes rely on lightweight message authentication codes (MACs) to guarantee detection of modification by adverse routers in the NoC. The use of network coding [1] generally allows to increase efficiency and robustness of transmission. Network coding achieves these benefits by computing and sending linear combinations of data packets instead of just forwarding them.

The paper is structured as follows. In Section 2, we review existing work on security for NoC communication. In Section 3, we summarize our system assumptions. Section 4 introduces the suggested solutions for the protection of integrity. In Section 5, we propose the analytic model and present evaluation results of this model and simulation runs as well as a discussion of area overhead. Section 6 concludes and gives an outlook.

This work is partly supported by the German Research Foundation (DFG) in the CRC 912 "Highly Adaptive Energy-Efficient Computing" and within the Cluster of Excellence EXC 1056 "Center for Advancing Electronics Dresden" and by Center for Information Services and High Performance Computing (ZIH) at TU Dresden.

GLSVLSI '18, May 23–25, 2018, Chicago, IL, USA

ACM ISBN 978-1-4503-5724-1/18/05...$15.00
https://doi.org/10.1145/3194554.3194582

2 RELATED WORK AND STATE OF THE ART

One major attack vector for MPSoCs is the incorporation of HTs (e.g. [2, 16]). Attacks on the communication channels hence are becoming a relevant threat, and effective countermeasures are required. Ancajas et al. reported on the problem of HTs in NoCs and presented the initial foundation of mitigation strategies: scramble lower layer data, certify packets, and implement process migration to obfuscate the destination applications [3]. The suggested methods aim at preventing an attacker to trigger an HT and an eavesdropping NoC component is disabled from identifying logical data streams. Setumadhavan et al. [25] also aim to prevent the activation of HTs by preventing their trigger events. However, the suggested measures require a significant overhead and, hence, influence the performance of the system.

Another strategy to reduce the potential risks implied by HTs is to detect and eliminate them. One direction is to focus on the design process, e.g., by conducting static analysis for backdoor during the design/build process and applying security orientated development procedures [19, 25]. Frey and Yu [12] focus on detecting HTs at runtime by means of finite state machine controllers that supervises the component's execution path. The drawback of the proposed solution is the implied computation and storage overhead. In [13], they subsequently designed a system for detecting HTs which changes the flits, especially control information like type and destination. The countermeasures are integrated into the router, implying overhead for each router.

However, HTs are an attack vector that cannot be mitigated completely. Therefore, other strategies aim to diminish the exposed risk by securing the communication during attacks. For example, Boraten and Kodi [5] propose the use of algebraic manipulation detection codes for the detection of modifications of flits. The authors claim a minimal performance impact of 1% compared to NoCs. But they provide no security measure. Kapoor et al. proposed to protect the communication by means of authenticated encryption [17]. However, the chosen cryptographic primitive, AES-128 in GCM mode, is heavy-weight regarding efficiency and area overhead and, therefore, it is an infeasible solution for NoCs [10].

The presented security measures all target the objectives of integrity and confidentiality, but neglect availability. In the seldom works considering all three objectives, then in turn efficiency and area considerations are neglected. Hence, our proposed solution aims at increasing integrity and availability under the constraints of restricted size and tight latency requirements. Additionally, our approach is completely orthogonal to the application.

3 ASSUMPTIONS ABOUT THE SYSTEM

3.1 System Model and Attacker Model

As underlying topology of the NoC, we assume a 2D mesh network with $n \times n$ nodes. Each node consists of a processing element (PE), a NoC interface (NI), and a router. Flits are in the order of 150 bits. They are processed in a FIFO manner by the forwarders. Since we additionally assume XY routing, the order of flits is not changed during transmission.

Within this paper, we use a spatial uniform traffic distribution with a constant injection rate per module. We assume transmission of single flits. The injection rate of flits into the network depends on the communication scheme, e.g., due to the addition of redundant flits because of network coding. Hence, the creation rate of flits at the module level is adapted so that the resulting injection rate into the network is equivalent for all schemes (on average 0.2 flits/module/cycle). Further, we assume retransmission buffers in the NI are of sufficient size to prevent flit loss (Sect. 5).

There is a 64-bit interface between a module and a router. To be able to refer to a flit in case of a retransmission, a 24-bit flit identifier (corresponding to network coded transmission, Sect. 3.2) is included. The 64-bit data field, the flit ID, the mode (4 bit) that specifies the flit type, and an address (32 bit) for memory accesses constitute the payload of a flit. The header of a flit contains x and y coordinates of source and target module as well as a bit for indicating burst mode (burst mode will be considered in future work). To support a 2D mesh of up to 16×16 modules, we assume 4 bits for each coordinate. Thus, the length of a flit is 141 bits.

We assume that only routers may be corrupted. Routers have a deterministic functionality and, therefore, are fit for outsourcing (making them susceptible for attacks), whereas PEs and NIs often bear business logic and, thus, are rather developed in house and under control.

We focus here on the attack scenarios that a corrupted router may modify a flit with a certain modification probability p_m or drop it with a drop probability p_d. Security measures are placed in the NI that is assumed to be trustworthy.

Designing the protection has to consider network performance and area as special requirements of MPSoCs. Securing the communication must not incur high penalties on the performance. Additionally, MPSoCs are restricted regarding available area and power consumption. Therefore, the proposed solution must be small with respect to the area needed.

3.2 Communication Model

We consider two approaches: uncoded (UC) and network coded (NC) transmission according to [8]. For NC, data to be sent is split into blocks $x_i = (x_{i,1}, x_{i,2}, \ldots, x_{i,n}) \in \mathbb{F}_q^n$ with $q = 2^m$. Blocks are organized in matrices (generations) of size G and amended with a unit vector $(\beta_{i,1}, \beta_{i,2}, \ldots, \beta_{i,G}) \in \mathbb{F}_q^G$ representing the global encoding vector (GEV). The coefficients for the computation of linear combinations are selected at random and applied to all elements of the amended blocks. Hence, the GEVs reflect all linear operations and enable the receiver to decode the original data. All operations are done in the underlying finite field $\mathbb{F}_q$. Since combinations are computed only from blocks of one generation, all blocks are tagged with a generation identifier *gid*. In our case, network coding is applied to flits. We use a generation size of $G = 2$ in order to achieve average latencies comparable to an uncoded transmission [21]. For each generation, the sender computes C linear combinations. Altogether, we considered three communication scenarios:

UC: uncoded transmission,
G2C3: network coded transmission with $G = 2, C = 3$,
G2C4: network coded transmission with $G = 2, C = 4$.

Hence, a generation always consists of two flits $\vec{f_1}, \vec{f_2}$:

$$\begin{pmatrix} \vec{f_1} \\ \vec{f_2} \end{pmatrix} = \begin{pmatrix} \beta_{1,1} & \beta_{1,2} & x_{1,1} & x_{1,2} & \cdots & x_{1,n} \\ \beta_{2,1} & \beta_{2,2} & x_{2,1} & x_{2,2} & \cdots & x_{2,n} \end{pmatrix} \quad (1)$$

Only the sender computes linear combinations. He selects at random encoding coefficients $\alpha_{i,j} \in \mathbb{F}_q, i = 1, 2, \ldots, C; j = 1, 2$ for the computation of linear combinations $\vec{c}_k, k = 1, 2, \ldots, C$.

The receiver needs $G = 2$ linear independent combinations to be able to decode by multiplying the matrix of these two combined flits with the inverse of the 2×2 matrix A of their corresponding encoding coefficients. Invertibility of A ensures invertibility of the matrix of combined flits and depends both on the size of A (given by G) and on the size of the finite field q [23]. For a 2×2 matrix A, the field GF(2^4) already provides an inverting probability of 0.93384 (Tab. I in [23]) which is sufficient, especially under the consideration that only the sender randomly selects encoding coefficients. Hence, we assume a symbol size of 4 bits. Since the receiver needs to know which flits belong to a generation, we also have to transmit the generation identifier *gid*. Altogether, a flit has a length of 149 bits. Uncoded flits contains the same fields except the GEV; the *gid* is reused as flit ID.

The *gid* should be unique to prevent an injection of a formerly intercepted flit into a transmission (replay attack). If the receiver included such an injected flit, a successful decoding would be prevented since that flit does not belong to the current generation. Due to the small data field of only 64 bits, there may be a large number of flits to be sent. Hence, we require that the *gid* in combination with the meta data fields (all other fields except the data field) is unique. A size of 24 bits allows 2^{24} different combinations of the *gid* even if exactly the same meta data are used which seems to be sufficient.

4 CONCEPT FOR AUTHENTICATION

4.1 Possible Approaches

Integrity is commonly achieved either via asymmetric cryptography (digital signatures) or via symmetric cryptography (Message Authentication Codes, MACs). Asymmetric cryptography implies a high computational effort and, furthermore, the resulting signatures are too long to be included in a flit. Hence, only MACs are suited for authentication of flits. Symmetric schemes require a secure key exchange, however, this is out of scope of this paper.

Considering the special requirements with respect to delay and area overhead, a lightweight cryptographic method optimized for hardware implementations should be chosen. AES, e.g., is not suited because it requires 1,032 cycles per block encryption [11]. As a promising algorithm for authentication in NoCs, we selected mCrypton [20] that needs only 13 cycles per block encryption and has an area of 2,681 gate equivalents only [11].

Authentication aims at preventing undetected modifications of transmitted data and meta data. If the receiver detects a modification and is not able to compensate this, he issues an ARQ to initiate a retransmission of the affected flits.

Since we assume that only senders compute linear combinations in case of NC, it is not necessary to use homomorphic MACs. To prevent computational overhead for routers, we further assume an end-to-end authentication, i.e., the sender computes a MAC and the receiver checks the validity of received flits by means of this MAC.

In general, there are two different possibilities for authentication in case of network coding: (1) authentication of original flits, or (2) authentication of linear combinations. The first approach allows to compute only a single MAC for a whole generation. There is a low communication overhead if there are no modifications. However, the receiver cannot check the validity of flits before decoding. In case of a modification, retransmission of the whole generation is necessary since the receiver cannot find out which of the flits was modified. Hence, we focus on the second approach where the receiver does not start decoding before a successful verification of the received combinations. Moreover, only single flits need to be retransmitted in case of a modification. Again, there are different possibilities for the authentication of linear combinations:

- Solution 1 (S1): send the MAC in a separate flit, or
- Solution 2 (S2): include both data and MAC in a flit.

4.2 S1: Send the MAC in a Separate Flit

We consider the use of the symmetric block cipher mCrypton in cipher block chaining (CBC) mode [22]. The size of the MAC depends on the block size of the underlying cipher; the block size of mCrypton of 64 bits fits into the data field of a flit. Hence, for each flit delivered by the PE, two corresponding flits are injected into the network: a data flit and a MAC flit. The only difference between these flits is that the MAC flit contains the MAC in the data field.

For NC, the sender first computes C linear combinations from G flits. Afterwards, he computes a MAC for each combination and puts the resulting $2 \cdot C$ flits into the transmission buffer. Flits of a generation are sent consecutively. If the receiver gets a data flit, he can immediately start with the computation of the MAC. After a successful verification of at least G combined flits, decoding can start.

If the receiver recognizes a loss, he issues an ARQ. In case of UC, the receiver starts a timer when he receives a data flit. If there is a time-out, he issues an ARQ. If the receiver gets first a MAC flit, he can directly issue an ARQ since the order of flits is not changed during transmission (Sect. 3.1). In case of NC, the receiver starts a timer when a flit of a generation arrives. If verification fails, the receiver issues an ARQ for both data and MAC flit since he cannot decide which of these two flits was modified. The sender buffers data and MAC flits so that it is not necessary to compute the MAC again. For NC, it is not necessary to issue an ARQ immediately. For example, if 2 of 4 received combinations failed verification, decoding is possible if the remaining 2 combinations are unmodified. After successful verification and, in case of NC, decoding, the flits are delivered to the module.

Input for the computation of the MAC is the whole data flit of 141 bits or 149 bits. Given the block length of 64 bits, there are three input blocks for mCrypton. Hence, the computation of the MAC implies a delay of $3 \cdot 13 = 39$ cycles for both sender and receiver. Since the injection rate of flits is much higher, it is necessary to consider a reasonable number of crypto modules for each NI in the NoC (Sect. 5.4).

4.3 S2: Include Data and MAC in One Flit

S2 has the advantage that the receiver does not need two corresponding flits to be able to verify the integrity. However, the size of the MAC is a problem if we do not want to extend the size of the flit. Just adding a 64-bit MAC to the flit would increase the flit size by 45.4% for UC and by 42.9% for NC. On the other hand, the block size must not be too small.

Hence, we consider as an alternative the use of an Authentication Code [26] that requires two key bits for the authentication of a single message bit (Tab. 1). If an attacker observes a flit with message bits and MAC bits, two keys remain possible for each message bit so that he can guess only with probability 0.5 the correct key bits and undetectably modify the data bit. For authentication of x message bits, we can simply use a stream of $2x$ key bits. Hence, if we use 32 bits of the data field for the actual data and 32 bits for the MAC bits, we need 64 key bits.

Table 1: Example for the authentication of one bit.

key bits		00	01	10	11
message bit	0	0	0	1	1
	1	0	1	0	1

The receiver must be able to generate the same key bits for each flit as the sender, even if previous flits are lost. Hence, key bits are generated pseudo randomly by encrypting the meta data of a flit. In case of UC, the size of the input for the block cipher is

77 bits, i.e., there are two input blocks. For NC, there is an input of 85 bits including the GEV, i.e., there are also two input blocks. Encryption of two blocks with mCrypton requires $2 \cdot 13 = 26$ cycles. The resulting block of 64 bits provides the required pseudo random key bits. The actual computation of the MAC bits can be done by a simple look up in the small table with negligible effort.

The sender splits the 64-bit data blocks into two flits containing only 32 bits. In case of NC, he than computes G linear combinations. After that, he computes the pseudo random key bits and the MAC, and, finally, sends the resulting flits to the receiver. The receiver can immediately start with the verification when a flit arrives. Since the sender splits a data block into two flits, the receiver needs both flits in case of UC to successfully deliver the 64-bit data block to the module. In case of NC, the sender needs G correct flits to be able to decode them to 2 flits that deliver the 64-bit data block.

For the recognition of loss, timers are used as well. If the receiver recognizes a modification, he also issues an ARQ but in contrast to S1, only a retransmission of one flit is necessary.

5 EVALUATION

5.1 Parameters and Performance Metrics

Parameters and their respective value ranges are summarized in Table 2. The flit generation rate has to be adapted wrt. the communication scheme used to achieve the mentioned injection rate. For UC, the desired network injection rate needs to be halved (since in both cases one original data flit becomes two transmitted flits). For NC, this rate needs to be further divided by the number of combinations. The resulting flit creation rates are 0.067 for G2C3 and 0.05 for G2C4.

Table 2: Overview of simulation parameters.

Topology	2D mesh of size 8 × 8
Routing	Deterministic, dimension-ordered XY
Arbitration	Round-robin
Injection rate	$\lambda = 0.2$
Communication model	S1/{UC,G2C3,G2C4}, S2/{UC,G2C3,G2C4}
Rogue routers	8 (randomly selected)
Modification probability	$p_m = 0.005 \cdot i, i = 0, 1, \ldots, 20$
Drop probability	$p_d = 0.005 \cdot i, i = 0, 1, \ldots, 20$
Simulation run time	50000 cycles

The maximum number of retransmissions (and therefore ARQs) is limited to 1 with respect to the logical transmission unit. For UC, one unit is a pair of flits (either a pair of one data and one MAC flit or a pair of combined data/MAC flits); for NC, one unit is a single generation. The current limitation of a single retransmission is in place to keep the error control mechanism both functional and simple. We assume correct transmission between routers. Finally, it was assumed that ARQs are prone to dropping attacks, but not to modification. At present, ARQs are not authenticated. A modified ARQ would result in the retransmission of wrong flits, which could not be associated with its logical transmission unit. Hence, it would behave exactly as a lost ARQ.

The following performance metrics were considered:

- **Acceptance rate (A):** The average number of flits received by a single router at each clock cycle; A indicates the network load. It is given by the total number of flits injected per cycle per node, including redundant flits, ARQs, and retransmissions.
- **Information rate (I):** The quotient of information transmitted and the total number of flits. Thus, it is the proportion of data flits to all transmitted flits (including retransmissions, ARQs, and MAC flits).
- **Residual error probability (ϵ):** The percentage of flits not transmitted successfully within the maximally allowed number of ARQs and retransmissions.

5.2 Simulation

To evaluate the performance of the proposed authentication schemes, the solutions were simulated by a cycle-accurate C++ framework for NoCs developed by our group. The existing framework was extended with the functionality of network coding and cryptographic primitives.

The values of p_m and p_d were kept equal for single runs. For simplicity, we will refer to their sum as attack probability. The efficiency of the communication models was determined in dependence on the attack probability. To eliminate the influence of attacker positions, results for each point were calculated by averaging outcomes of 1000 simulation runs with randomly selected positions of the 8 rogue routers.

Fig. 1 presents results of the simulation runs. For an attack rate of 0.0, the **acceptance rate** equals the network injection rate of 0.2 (Fig. 1a). With increasing attack probability, losses and modifications occur. The resulting ARQs and retransmissions imply an increase of the acceptance rate. UC schemes induce significantly more transmissions. Since there is no redundancy, each modification or loss of a flit implies an ARQ and a retransmission. The robustness of the NC schemes is clearly visible – the higher the redundancy, the lower the acceptance rate. Fig. 1a also shows that S1 performs worse than S2: S1 requires a retransmission of both flits, since the receiver cannot decide whether data or MAC flit was corrupted.

With an attack probability of 0.0, the **information rate** is determined only by the given communication schemes (Fig. 1b). The following decrease again reflects the required ARQs and retransmissions. The relative differences between S1 and S2 once more depict the different robustness of the schemes.

Since transmission errors were neglected, the **residual error probability** starts at 0 for all solutions (Fig. 1c). The different progression profiles are mainly determined by the probability that a logical transmission unit cannot be transmitted successfully considering the maximum allowed retransmissions. NC schemes benefit from the redundancy. However, S1 requires two successful retransmission in case of an ARQ, i.e., there is a bigger attack surface. The tradeoff between increased resilience and exposure to possible attacks is clearly visible at the course of S1/G2C3 compared to the UC schemes. Although S1/G2C3 starts with a lower residual error than the UC schemes, its error probability increases faster and becomes greater than the UC schemes at 11% and 17% attack probability. The results for S1/G2C4 show that an increased redundancy can effectively counteract this increased error growth. Nevertheless, S2 achieves best results. For the highest attack rate, S2/G2C4 provides the lowest error probability of ≈ 1.36%.

5.3 Analytical Model

An accurate analytic model allows for a flexible and faster approach analyzing performance in varying scenarios e.g. different traffic schemes or topologies or larger NoC sizes, instead of using time-consuming cycle-accurate simulations. Moreover, it provides a deeper insight into the system behavior.In the following, we only describe S2 due to space limitations. A short overview of further parameters used in the analytic model is given in Tab. 3.

The total flit loss or modification probability between a source-destination pair is determined by the number of rogue routers encountered in the XY route between them:

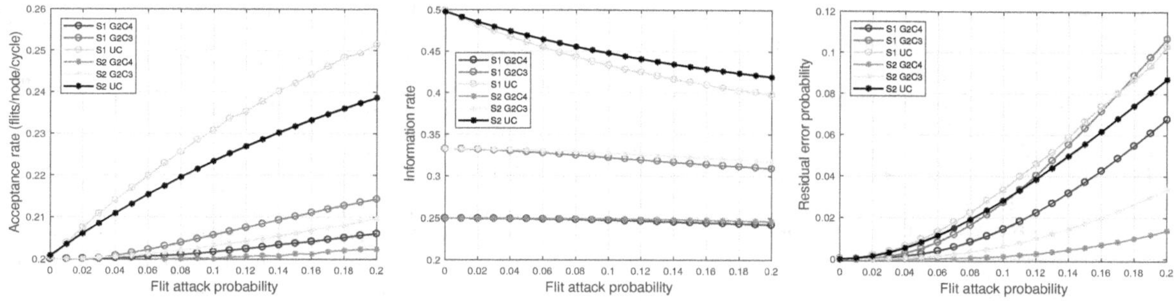

(a) Acceptance Rate (b) Information Rate (c) Residual error probability

Figure 1: Simulation results for 8x8 2D mesh with 8 attacking routers.

Table 3: Analytic model parameter symbols

Symbol	Description
M	Total number of modules or nodes
$\lambda_{x,y}$	Flit injection rate from x to y
$\lambda'_{x,y}$	Total flit injection rate from x to y including ARQs and retransmission
$N_{x,y}$	Total number of rogue routers in the XY route from x to y
$d_{x,y}$	Total flit drop probability from x to y
$d'_{x,y}$	Probability of no drop from x to y
$m_{x,y}$	Total flit modification probability from x to y
$m'_{x,y}$	Probability of no modification from x to y

$$d_{x,y} = 1 - (1 - p_d)^{N_{x,y}} \tag{2}$$

$$m_{x,y} = 1 - (1 - p_m)^{N_{x,y}} \tag{3}$$

A retransmission fails if the ARQ is lost or the retransmission is lost or modified. The expression $R_{x,y}$ denotes this probability:

$$R_{x,y} = 1 - d'_{y,x} d'_{x,y} m'_{x,y}. \tag{4}$$

Network Coded Transmission: A residual error happens if no flits of a generation are received or if with $G-1$ received flits, the retransmission fails or any of the received flits is modified (since no more ARQs are allowed):

$$p_1 = \binom{C}{G-1} {d'_{x,y}}^{G-1} {d_{x,y}}^{C-G+1} \tag{5}$$

$$p_2 = \sum_{i=0}^{C-G} \binom{C}{G+i} {d'_{x,y}}^{G+i} {d_{x,y}}^{C-G-i} \tag{6}$$

$$\bar{\epsilon} = \frac{1}{M(M-1)} \sum_{x=1}^{M} \sum_{\substack{y=1 \\ y \neq x}}^{M} \Bigg[{d_{x,y}}^{C} + p_1 \cdot ({m'_{x,y}}^{G-1} \cdot R_{x,y} + 1 - {m'_{x,y}}^{G-1}) + p_2 \cdot \Bigg\{ \binom{G+i}{1} m'_{x,y} {m_{x,y}}^{G+i-1} \cdot R_{x,y} + \sum_{k=2}^{G+i} \binom{G+i}{k} {m'_{x,y}}^{k} {m_{x,y}}^{G+i-k} \Bigg\} \Bigg] \tag{7}$$

The module flit acceptance rate $\lambda'_{x,y}$ is a sum of the normally injected flits ($\lambda_{x,y}$) and the ARQs ($\lambda_{arq\_x,y}$) and retransmissions ($\lambda_{retr\_x,y}$), which are directly related to the error cases from above. The acceptance rate A is computed by averaging $\lambda'_{x,y}$ over all modules. The rates of ARQ and retransmission are given by:

$$\lambda_{arq\_x,y} = \frac{\lambda_{y,x}}{C} \cdot \left[p_{1yx} + p_{2yx} \cdot \sum_{k=1}^{G+i} \binom{G+i}{k} {m'_{y,x}}^{k} {m_{y,x}}^{G+i-k} \right] \tag{8}$$

$$\lambda_{retr\_x,y} = d'_{y,x} \cdot \lambda_{arq\_y,x} \tag{9}$$

Due to the splitting over two flits, a factor of $\frac{1}{2}$ needs to be included for the computation of the information rate:

$$I_{NC} = \frac{G/C}{2} \cdot \frac{\sum_{x=1}^{M} \sum_{\substack{y=1 \\ y \neq x}}^{M} \lambda_{x,y}}{\sum_{x=1}^{M} \sum_{\substack{y=1 \\ y \neq x}}^{M} \lambda'_{x,y}}. \tag{10}$$

Uncoded Transmission: The expressions for the residual error probability and the flit acceptance and information rates are very similar to that in the coded case. The main difference is that, when a flit is modified, the ARQ asks for the retransmission of this flit only:

$$\bar{\epsilon} = \frac{1}{M(M-1)} \sum_{x=1}^{M} \sum_{\substack{y=1 \\ y \neq x}}^{M} {d_{x,y}}^2 + \binom{2}{1} d_{x,y} d'_{x,y} \cdot (m'_{x,y} R_{x,y} + m_{x,y}) + {d'_{x,y}}^2 (\binom{2}{1} m'_{x,y} m_{x,y} R_{x,y} + {m_{x,y}}^2) \tag{11}$$

$$\lambda_{arq\_x,y} = \frac{\lambda_{y,x}}{2} \cdot \left[\binom{2}{1} d_{y,x} d'_{x,y} + {d'_{y,x}}^2 (1 - {m'_{y,x}}^2) \right] \tag{12}$$

The analytical model was applied to the same scenarios as the simulation. The difference between the model and simulation results for all the estimated parameters were all less than 5% except for of S1 G2C4, where the residual error rate values had a difference of average of 7% (Tab. 4).

Table 4: Relative error between analytical model and simulation.

	S1			S2		
	UC	G2C3	G2C4	UC	G2C3	G2C4
Error probability	2.8%	5%	7%	1%	1.5%	1%
Information rate	< 1%	< 1%	< 1%	< 1%	< 1%	< 1%
Acceptance rate	< 1%	< 1%	< 1%	< 1%	< 1%	< 1%

5.4 Area Overhead

The area overhead of the solutions is given in Tab. 5. The main area overhead results from the mCrypton modules[20]. MACs must be generated at both the sender and receiver, requiring 39 and 26 cycles per flit, according to S1 and S2. The sender and receiver side of the NI share the crypto modules.With a flit injection rate of 0.2 flits/node/cycle, the total average rate of flits queuing up for MAC generation is 0.4 and 0.2 flits/node/cycle for S2 and S1, respectively. According to [18], the flit queuing rate, λ_q should be lower than the processing rate of the crypto modules, μ (1/39 or 1/26) to prevent buffer overflow and long queuing delays. For the case of m parallel servers (in this case crypto modules), the queue utilization rate, $\rho = \frac{\lambda_q}{m \cdot \mu}$. Aiming to have zero queuing delay, we estimated a total number of 18 crypto modules necessary, so that $\rho = 0.5778$ for S2 and 0.4333 for S1. Since the solutions protect the communication of the complete MPSoC, it is justified to compute the area overhead for the total area of an MPSoC. Considering, e.g., the state-of-the-art MPSoC in [14] with a total area of 24.43 M GEs and 10 NoCIFs, the area overhead is only $\approx 1.98\%$.

Table 5: Overview of area overhead.

Unit	Area per NI
Crypto modules	18 × 2681 = 48258 GEs
Retransmission buffer (depth=10)	19 × 10 = 190 bytes
LUTs (for network coding)	7080 GEs (G2C3) or 16992 GEs (G2C4)

The retransmission buffers in the NI also contribute to the area overhead. Flits of a generation are transmitted consecutively, so that they arrive at the receiver one cycle after the other since congestion delay is almost absent due to the low injection rate. An ARQ is sent when there is a gap greater than 8 cycles between consecutive flits of a generation. Assuming a retransmission buffer size of N_b flits, each flit will be in the buffer for $5 \cdot N_b$ cycles on average before it is overwritten (injection rate of 0.2 flits/node/cycle). Considering the farthest apart node pair (separated by 15 hops, 2 cycles/hop), the ARQ will reach the sender after a round trip delay of 60 + 8 cycles which should be less than $5 \cdot N_b$. Thus, with $N_b = \frac{68}{5}$ or $\sim$14, the original flit can be found. Flit modification is detected after 26 or 39 cycles after receiving the flit and then an ARQ is sent so that N_b $\sim$18 or 20 flits deep. Thus, a very small sized retransmission buffer is needed at each NI. In our reference MPSoC, the highest inter-module distance is 3 hops, so that an even smaller retransmission buffer of depth 10 flits is needed in order to recover the original flit when the ARQ reaches the sender.

Network coding implies further area overhead due to the matrix multiplications (Sec. 3.2) in the GF domain. To reduce complexity, we propose to use look-up tables (LUTs) storing all possible product values over GF(2^4). The LUT was implemented in Verilog HDL and synthesized in 65nm CMOS technology and found to have an area of 118 GEs. For generating one combination for S1, 36 table look ups are needed along with the addition (or XOR in GF). S2 requires only 20 look ups. Therefore, to create all the combinations in parallel in one cycle we need a maximum of 144 LUTs (for S1/G2C4) in each NI. Comparing to our reference MPSoC, this is an overhead of 0.7% only. For the decoding of the generation, we need the inverse of a 2×2 matrix containing the coding coefficients, which can be easily achieved using the determinant method. Since fewer multiplications are required for decoding, we do not need more LUTs.

6 SUMMARY AND OUTLOOK

In this paper, we presented and evaluated authentication schemes which protect the communication in a NoC against active attackers. This protection consists of a combination of creating MACs and applying network coding for increased efficiency and robustness. The use of mCrypton as lightweight cryptographic primitive allows for an efficient solution. Computation and verification of a MAC requires 26 or 39 cycles for sender and receiver; the overall area overhead is 2.7% in comparison to the total area of a state-of-the-art MPSoC. The redundancy of the NC schemes implies a lower information rate but significantly decreases acceptance rate (up to 19,6%) and residual error probability (up to 80%).

There are still several open research questions. One topic of future work is an efficient key management for the symmetric block ciphers. Additionally, the proposed solutions may be further examined regarding the used cryptographic primitive, e.g. PRINCE [6] in order to reduce latency, since it requires only 1 cycle per block. This would also be favorable in the reduced number of cryptographic modules. The increased performance of PRINCE would come at the cost of a bigger chip area (8260 GEs). Nevertheless, as fewer cryptographic units are needed, this could lead to a comparable or even lower area demand. Further, the applied communication scheme could be adapted. Thus, it seems to be interesting to investigate the performance of the mentioned authentication of a whole generation and to find out which solution should be preferred in dependence on the attack rate. A further topic of future work is multipath routing that also helps to improve robustness against attackers. Finally, the ARQ scheme could be revised, e.g., to allow additionally the use of acknowledgments.

REFERENCES

[1] R. Ahlswede, N. Cai, S.-Y. R. Li, and R. W. Yeung. 2000. Network information flow. *IEEE Trans. on Inf. Theory* 46, 4 (July 2000), 1204–1216.

[2] Y. Alkabani and F. Koushanfar. 2008. Extended abstract: Designer #x2019;s hardware Trojan horse. In *IEEE HOST.* 82–83. https://doi.org/10.1109/HST.2008.4559059

[3] Dean Michael Ancajas, Koushik Chakraborty, and Sanghamitra Roy. 2014. Fort-NoCs: Mitigating the Threat of a Compromised NoC. In *Proc. of DAC.* 158:1–158:6.

[4] L Benini and G De Micheli. 2002. Networks on chips: a new SoC paradigm. *Computer* 35, 1 (Jan. 2002), 70–78.

[5] Travis Boraten and Avinash Karanth Kodi. 2016. Packet Security with Path Sensitization for NoCs. In *Proc. of DATE.* 1136–1139.

[6] Julia Borghoff et al. 2012. *PRINCE - A Low-latency Block Cipher for Pervasive Computing Applications.* Technical Report. 208–225 pages.

[7] Shekhar Borkar. 2007. Thousand Core Chips: A Technology Perspective. In *Proc. of DAC.* 746–749.

[8] Philip A. Chou, Yunnan Wu, and Kamal Jain. 2003. Practical Network Coding. In *Proc. Annual Allerton Conf. on Comm., Control, and Computing.*

[9] W.J. Dally and B. Towles. 2001. Route packets, not wires: on-chip interconnection networks. In *Proc. of DAC.* 684–689.

[10] Samuel Evain and Jean-Philippe Diguet. 2005. From NoC Security Analysis to Design Solutions. In *Proc. of IEEE SiPS.*

[11] Samuel Evain and Jean-Philippe Diguet. 2005. From NoC Security Analysis to Design Solutions. *Proc. of IEEE SiPS* 1 (2005).

[12] J. Frey and Qiaoyan Yu. 2015. Exploiting State Obfuscation to Detect Hardware Trojans in NoC Network Interfaces. In *Proc. of IEEE MWSCAS.* 1–4.

[13] Jonathan Frey and Qiaoyan Yu. 2016. A hardened network-on-chip design using runtime hardware Trojan mitigation methods. *Integration, the VLSI journal* 56 (2016), 15 – 31.

[14] S. Haas et al. 2017. A heterogeneous SDR MPSoC in 28nmCMOS for low-latency wireless applications. In *Proc. of DAC.*

[15] Axel Jantsch and Hannu Tenhunen. 2004. Will Networks on Chip Close the Productivity Gap? In *Networks on Chip,* Axel Jantsch and Hannu Tenhunen (Eds.). Springer US, 3–18.

[16] Y. Jin, N. Kupp, and Y. Makris. 2009. Experiences in Hardware Trojan design and implementation. In *IEEE HOST.* 50–57. https://doi.org/10.1109/HST.2009.5224971

[17] Hemangee K. Kapoor et al. 2013. A Security Framework for NoC Using Authenticated Encryption and Session Keys. *Circuits, Systems, and Signal Processing* 32, 6 (2013), 2605–2622.

[18] Leonard Kleinrock. 1975. *Queueing systems - 1 : Theory.* Wiley, New York.

[19] Paul Kocher et al. 2004. Security as a New Dimension in Embedded System Design. In *Proc. of DAC.* 753–760.

[20] Chae Hoon Lim and Tymur Korishko. 2006. mCrypton – A Lightweight Block Cipher for Security of Low-Cost RFID Tags and Sensors. In *WISA 2005.*

[21] Sadia Moriam et al. 2015. Resilient and Efficient Communication in Many-Core Systems using Network Coding. In *Proc. of IEEE IPCCC.*

[22] NIST Special Publication 800-38A. 2001. Recommendation for Block Cipher Modes of Operation – Methods and Techniques. U.S. DoC/NIST. (December 2001).

[23] Stefan Pfennig and Elke Franz. 2017. Security Aspects of Confidential Network Coding. In *Proc. of IEEE ICC CISS.*

[24] M. Radetzki et al. 2013. Methods of Fault Tolerance in Networks-on-Chip. *Comput. Surveys* 46, 1 (Oct 2013).

[25] Simha Sethumadhavan et al. 2015. Trustworthy Hardware from Untrusted Components. *Comm. of the ACM* 58, 9 (Aug. 2015), 60–71.

[26] Gustavus J. Simmons (Ed.). 1991. *Contemporary Cryptography – The Science of Information Integrity.* IEEE Press.

A Homomorphic Encryption Scheme Based on Affine Transforms

Kyle Loyka
Texas A&M University
Department of Electrical & Computer Engineering
kyleloyka@tamu.edu

He Zhou
Texas A&M University
Department of Electrical & Computer Engineering
zhouhe@tamu.edu

Sunil P. Khatri
Texas A&M University
Department of Electrical & Computer Engineering
sunilkhatri@tamu.edu

ABSTRACT

As more businesses and consumers move their information storage to the cloud, the need to protect sensitive data is higher than ever. Using encryption, data access can be restricted to only authorized users. However, with standard encryption schemes, modifying an encrypted file in the cloud requires a complete file download, decryption, modification, and upload. This is cumbersome and time-consuming. Recently, the concept of homomorphic computing has been proposed as a solution to this problem. Using homomorphic computation, operations may be performed directly on encrypted files without decryption, hence avoiding exposure of any sensitive user information in the cloud. This also conserves bandwidth and reduces processing time. In this paper, we present a homomorphic computation scheme that utilizes the affine cipher applied to the ASCII representation of data. To the best of the authors' knowledge, this is the first use of affine ciphers in homomorphic computing. Our scheme supports both string operations (encrypted string search and concatenation), as well as arithmetic operations (encrypted integer addition and subtraction). A design goal of our proposed homomorphism is that string data and integer data are treated identically, in order to enhance security.

CCS CONCEPTS

• **Security and privacy → Public key encryption**;

KEYWORDS

homomorphic encryption, affine cipher, cloud, security

ACM Reference Format:

Kyle Loyka, He Zhou, and Sunil P. Khatri. 2018. A Homomorphic Encryption Scheme Based on Affine Transforms. In *GLSVLSI '18: 2018 Great Lakes Symposium on VLSI, May 23–25, 2018, Chicago, IL, USA.* ACM, New York, NY, USA, 6 pages. https://doi.org/10.1145/3194554.3194585

1 INTRODUCTION

With the rapid adoption of Internet-based services, the amount of information stored in the cloud is continuously rising. As a result, individuals and corporations have more incentive than ever to protect their data. Suppose a user (who has access to the encryption key) wanted to perform a binary operation (denoted as *op*) on two encrypted files stored in the cloud. Assume the two files are A and B, and their encrypted versions are *E(A)* and *E(B)* respectively. The user would have to download *E(A)* and *E(B)*, decrypt them, perform the operation *op* on the decrypted files, encrypt the result, and upload the result to the cloud as shown in Fig. 1(a). This process is inefficient, since a large amount of time and computation is spent on encryption, decryption and network communications. In addition, this process is insecure, since the key might be exposed or leaked during the decryption.

Homomorphic encryption [9] aims to solve these problems. Using homomorphic encryption, operations can be performed directly on encrypted files without decryption. Suppose two encrypted operands reside in the cloud. A user would simply send an instruction/operation request to the cloud. The operation would then be directly performed on *E(A)* and *E(B)*. During this process, the encrypted files *E(A)* and *E(B)* are never decrypted, so the process is secure and efficient. Fig. 1(b) shows how a homomorphic encryption scheme could be used to modify encrypted data stored in the cloud. In general, the operation *op* can be defined on strings or numerical values.

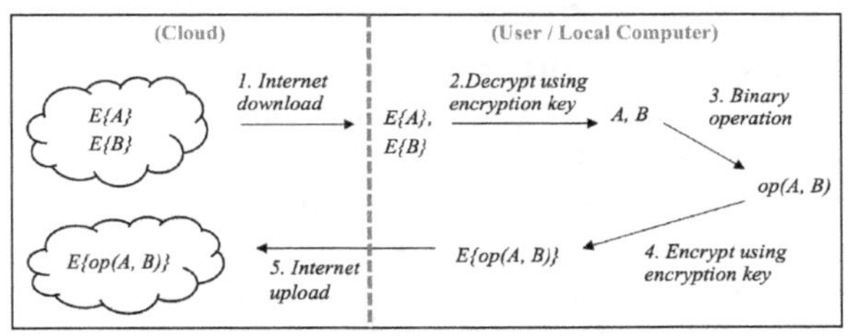

(a) A standard encryption scheme

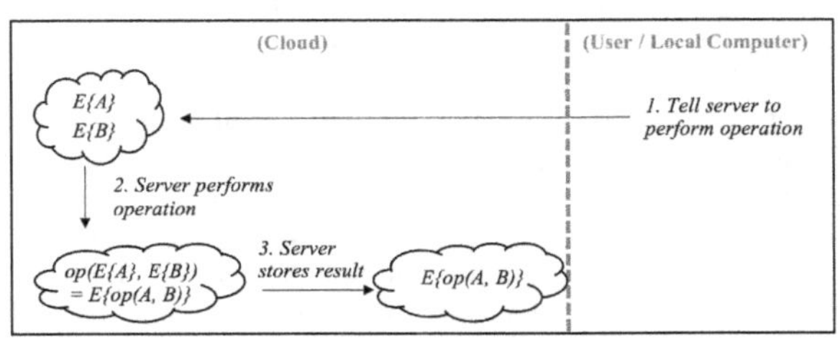

(b) A homomorphic encryption scheme

Figure 1: Example of an operation on cloud storage

Although homomorphic encryption enhances both security and efficiency, it may have a high inherent computation complexity and a correspondingly high communication cost, depending on the homomorphic encryption scheme that is deployed. For example, this is true for [13], which employs a complicated bit-by-bit encryption scheme. Therefore, for a practical homomorphic scheme, the computation and communication required by the encryption scheme needs to be simple. The affine cipher is a well known monoalphabetic substitution cipher [11]. Its encryption and decryption are

GLSVLSI '18, May 23–25, 2018, Chicago, IL, USA

ACM ISBN 978-1-4503-5724-1/18/05...$15.00
https://doi.org/10.1145/3194554.3194585

arithmetic and simple, including only modular arithmetic, multiplication, and addition operations. Besides, the affine cipher produces only one numerical output for a given input, limiting the store overhead. Therefore, we design our homomorphic encryption and decryption schemes based on the affine cipher.

However, the affine cipher has its own limitations. First, the affine encryption scheme cannot natively perform numerical homomorphic addition or subtraction. To overcome this obstacle, we modify the encryption algorithm and design a custom data structure including both the encrypted data and a counter. Secondly the security of the affine cipher is weak when applied to a single ASCII character, due to the the fact that the encryption is invertible and the lack of variety of the cipher keys [12]. To address this issue, we combine several ASCII characters together during encryption, which enlarges the input and output space. By choosing the number of ASCII characters to combine, we can make it arbitrarily hard for our scheme to be hacked by frequency analysis. Additionally, we use an identical scheme for both strings and integers, so that even the data type can be hidden from the third party.

The key contribution of this paper is that we have developed a homomorphic encryption scheme based on the affine cipher. To enhance the security, we use an identical scheme for both strings and integers. We group ASCII characters together during the encryption to gain more varieties of possible mappings from input to output, thereby making our scheme arbitrarily hard to defeat. Our scheme supports concatenation and search when applied to strings, and supports addition and subtraction when applied to integers. Our method scales elegantly both in runtime as well as storage requirements.

2 PREVIOUS WORK

2.1 Homomorphic Encryption

An encryption scheme E is homomorphic with respect to an operation op if E satisfies the following equation:

$$E(op(A, B)) = op(E(A), E(B)). \quad (1)$$

Here A, B are data objects. In order to apply homomorphic encryption on real world problems, Equation 1 should be valid for as many ops and as many data types as possible.

The field of homomorphic encryption was first introduced in the late 70s [9], after which it received very little attention until a few years ago [4] [1] [8]. Among the existing homomorphic schemes, Partially Homomorphic Encryption (PHE) schemes such as RSA [10] and Goldwasser-Micali [6] only supports either homomorphic addition or multiplication, which limits their application. On the other hand, Fully Homomorphic Encryption (FHE) supports an unlimited number of arbitrary operations on the encrypted data. The work of [4] proposes a promising lattice-based FHE scheme. However, it suffers from a high computation complexity, which limits its application in practice. Ring Learning with Error (RLWE) [1] and N-th degree truncated polynomial ring (NTRU) [8] based FHE schemes are able to achieve a better performance on efficiency, but still have an expensive computation cost.

Our affine cipher based scheme is designed with the goal of providing user-defined security level, with scalable runtime and storage requirements for string as well as arithmetic operations.

2.2 Affine Cipher

An affine cipher is usually used as a substitution cipher, which maps an element in the plain text to a unique element in the cipher text [7]. Equation 2 shows a generic affine cipher encryption definition.

$$\epsilon = (\alpha\lambda + \beta) \% \rho \quad (2)$$

The values of α, β and ρ are collectively considered as the encryption key. The resulting number ϵ represents the encrypted version of the input λ. It is important to note that for the affine cipher, $gcd(\alpha, \rho)$ must equal 1. This is due to the properties of modular reduction and ensures that every input results in a unique output. If this condition is not met, it is possible that the output may not be unique. The encrypted output can be decrypted by using the inverse of Equation 2, as shown in Equation 3. This inverse is also known as the affine cipher decryption equation.

$$\lambda = (\alpha^{-1}(\epsilon - \beta)) \% \rho \quad (3)$$

Here α^{-1} is the modular-inverse of α. By definition, the modular inverse, α^{-1}, is the value which satisfies Equation 4.

$$(\alpha\alpha^{-1}) \equiv 1 \; mod \; \rho \quad (4)$$

In Equation 3, the value $\alpha^{-1}(\epsilon - \beta)$ undergoes modulo reduction by ρ to yield λ.

In Equation 2, the $mod\ \rho$ operation limits the number of unique outputs to ρ possible values, ranging from 0 to $(\rho - 1)$. Hence there can be only ρ possible input values that each results in a unique output value. It is important to preserve this injective mapping between inputs and outputs, to ensure that ϵ can be decrypted. This effectively limits the number of unique inputs and outputs of the affine cipher to ρ possible values. As mentioned earlier, our approach encrypts groups of ASCII characters at a time, effectively ensuring an arbitrary, user-defined security level without affecting the decryption ability, and retaining runtime and storage efficiency.

3 OUR APPROACH

Our homomorphic encryption scheme is based on ASCII text encoding and the affine cipher [7] function. Together, they allow for the searching and concatenation of encrypted text, as well as addition and subtraction operations on encrypted integers. This approach treats strings the same way as integers, which makes encrypted string data indistinguishable from encrypted integer data. Suppose we are interested in performing a homomorphic string operation op_s on two encrypted strings $E(A)$ and $E(B)$. In practice, we would issue op_s along with an arithmetic operation op_a on $E(A)$ and $E(B)$, thereby obscuring the operation as well as the data types. In our design, encrypted data is stored in a data structure that contains two members: the encrypted data, and a counter (to count the number of arithmetic operations that were performed on the data). The procedure for handling string and integer data, as well as the reason why this data structure is needed, will be described in the following sections. In the rest of this section, we describe how to incorporate the affine cipher with homomorphic operations on both strings and integers (in Section 3.1 and 3.2 respectively). In Section 3.3, we will discuss the security properties of our homomorphic scheme.

3.1 Homomorphic Operations on Strings

In this section, we explain how our homomorphic scheme encrypts and decrypts string data, as well as how encrypted string searches are performed.

3.1.1 Encrypting Strings. Using the ASCII encoding of text characters yields integers which can be encrypted using the affine cipher defined in Equation 2. For each character in a text file, the character's numerical ASCII code would be inputted into the affine cipher. This results in an encrypted number, which is then appended to the encrypted file. The encrypted numbers are stored as a list of integers. To concatenate two encrypted strings, we simply append the list of integers corresponding to one encrypted string onto the end of the list of integers corresponding to the other encrypted string. The resulting list of integers represents the encrypted version of the concatenation of the two strings. In other words:

$$E(X_1 \cdot X_2) = E(X_1) \cdot E(X_2) \tag{5}$$

where "·" is the concatenation operator, $E()$ is the affine encryption operator, and X_1, X_2 are two strings. Note that Equation 5 indicates that affine encryption on string possesses the homomorphism property[1].

Since there are 256 ASCII characters, there are only 256 possible inputs to the affine cipher, and therefore the modulus, ρ, must be equal to at least 256. To increase the security of the encryption scheme, the input and output range could be increased. By increasing ρ, the affine cipher would have a larger range of unique input and output values. To utilize the larger input space, the number of characters encrypted at a time could be increased. Instead of encrypting one character at a time (which results in 256 possible input values), one could encrypt K characters at a time, resulting in 256^K unique values for the inputs as well as the outputs. This means that the modulus, ρ, must be equal to at least 256^K. Increasing the input and output ranges substantially increases the number of ways in which data can be encrypted and the number of possible encryption keys, thus making the scheme more secure. In Section 3.3, we show that by varying K, an arbitrary level of security can be achieved.

To encrypt K characters at a time, their individual ASCII encoding is looked-up and converted to an 8-bit binary string. These binary strings are then concatenated in the order in which their corresponding characters appear in the plain text file. This results in a single $8 \times K$ bit binary string. This binary string is then cast back to an integer, which is unique for a certain set of K ASCII characters. This number is then encrypted using the affine cipher expression of Equation 2, setting $\rho = 256^K$ or larger, to ensure the injective mapping from input to output.

With $K = 1$, our scheme is susceptible to frequency analysis attacks. An attacker could analyze the frequency with which certain encrypted values occur within an encrypted file, and correlate this with the frequency with which characters appear in the English language (or other language). This gives the attacker useful hints to decrypt an encrypted file. By grouping $K > 1$ characters together, such a frequency analysis is much harder since there are exponentially more possible inputs and outputs. This does not fully mitigate the threat, but does make the attack much more difficult. The threat is an artifact of the fact that characters (or groups thereof) have an inherent occurrence frequency which is a property of natural languages.

3.1.2 Decrypting Strings. During decryption, an encrypted value, ϵ, is first loaded from the encrypted file or encrypted list. It is decrypted according to Equation 3. The resulting integer value is cast into an $8 \times K$ bit binary string. This binary string is then split into K 8-bit blocks. Each 8-bit block is cast into an ASCII value, which yields a character that is appended to a new unencrypted file (or list) based on the order in which they appeared in the $8 \times K$ bit binary string.

[1]This is because $E(op(A, B)) = op(E(A), E(B))$ where "op" ≡ concatenation, A and B are unencrypted strings, and $E()$ is the affine cipher encryption operator.

3.1.3 Encrypted String Search. Our homomorphic encryption scheme for strings also supports search operations on strings. To search for text in an affine encrypted file, the user must encrypt the string they would like to search for (this will subsequently be denoted as the *query-string*). It is important that the *query-string* must be encrypted using the same parameters (K, α, β, and ρ) that were used to encrypt the file being searched. The encrypted *query-string* exists within the encrypted file, if the *query-string* exists within the unencrypted file, due to the uniqueness property of our homomorphic affine cipher-based encryption scheme. The location of the matched encrypted *query-string* in the encrypted file is then returned to the user if found. This process is straightforward for the case of $K = 1$.

In cases where $K > 1$, the search process becomes more complex. As K increases, the number of possible groupings in which a substring can be encrypted also increases. Since the file was encrypted

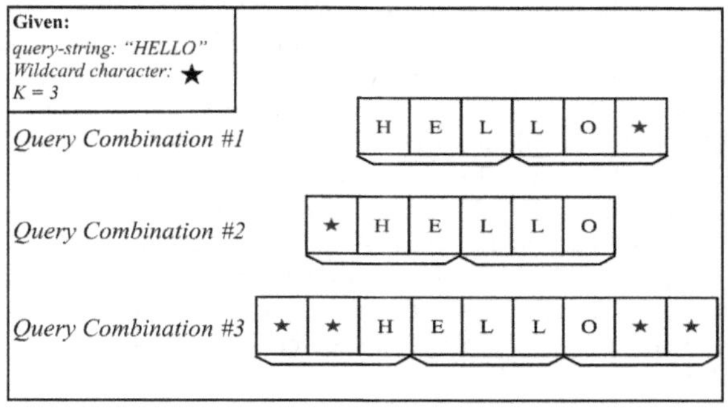

Figure 2: Number of ways a query-string can be grouped

in K-character blocks, it is possible that the encrypted *query-string* being searched exists in the encrypted file, but uses a different grouping of K-character blocks. If the *query-string* is "HELLO" as shown in Fig. 2, with $K = 3$. Here ★ can be any possible character. In order to search for "HELLO" in the encrypted file, for each query combination, we first search the block that doesn't include ★. For example, we first search if "ELL" exists in the encrypted file (Query Combination #3 in Fig. 2). Once the position of "ELL" is located in the encrypted file, then we can check if the block before "ELL" in the encrypted file has an "H" as its tail character, and the block after "ELL" in the encrypted file has an "O" as its head character. For Query Combination #1, we would first search for "HEL". Similarly, for Query Combination #2, we would first search for "LLO".

For this search to work, the length of the searched string must be greater than or equal to $2 \times K - 1$. This is because for each search, there must be at least one block that contains no ★. Search queries that are $2 \times K - 1$ characters long (or longer) are guaranteed to have at least one block with no ★s for each possible grouping of K-character blocks.

THEOREM 3.1. *To ensure that there is at least one full block in each query combination, the minimum length of the search query is larger than or equal to* $2 \times K - 1$.

PROOF. Consider a query of length $2 \times K - 2$. We will show that it is the largest search query with at least one non-full block, and thereby claim the result. A query of length $2 \times K - 2$ can be split down the middle, yielding 2 blocks of length $K - 1$ each. This is the only query combination with no full blocks. If the query length is increased by 1, to $2 \times K - 1$, then every query combination has at least one full block, yielding the result. □

3.2 Homomorphic Operations on Integers

One key feature of our encryption scheme is that integer data and string data are treated uniformly. To encrypt an integer, it is first cast into a string. The string is then encrypted using the same process as described in Section 3.1.1.

To support addition and subtraction, a special data structure is needed. As described at the beginning of Section 3, this data structure contains two members: a list of numbers (representing the encrypted string/integer) and a counter variable. This structure is used to represent both string data and numerical data. The counter is necessary when decrypting data that are the results of encrypted addition or encrypted subtraction. This is because when adding affine encrypted values, the number of β terms increments with each addition (see Equation 2). For subtraction, the number of β values decreases with each subtraction operation (there can be negative multiples of β values if multiple subtractions are performed). By keeping track of the number of additions and subtractions, the extra β values can be accounted for in the decryption process. The counter is initially set to zero and is incremented for every addition and decremented for every subtraction. The counter is also useful for interpreting the unencrypted output. This is illustrated in a small example. Consider two digits λ_1 and λ_2 which are being added. The encrypted versions of these digits are $\epsilon_1 = (\alpha\lambda_1 + \beta) \% \rho$ and $\epsilon_2 = (\alpha\lambda_2 + \beta) \% \rho$. When these are added, we get $\epsilon_1 + \epsilon_2 = (\alpha(\lambda_1 + \lambda_2) + 2\beta) \% \rho$. Note that if one β is subtracted from the RHS, the result is of the form of Equation 2, and can be decrypted to yield $(\lambda_1 + \lambda_2)$, the correct result of homomorphic addition.

Due to the way digits $(0, 1, 2, \ldots, 9)$ are encoded in ASCII, the value of an integer can be determined by subtracting 48 from any ASCII encoded numeric character. When adding or subtracting two ASCII values, this ASCII offset value (48) accumulates in the same way as β. While decrypting, the accumulation of 48s can be removed as discussed in the previous paragraph, to reveal the integer result of addition or subtraction. If the resulting integer is greater than nine, any digits in the tens, hundreds, thousands (etc.) places act as carry values into the next significant digit when interpreting the decrypted value. The maximum unencrypted representation for each element is limited by ρ. Specifically, the highest value for each element (that has been decrypted) is $\rho/2 - 1$, and the lowest is $-\rho/2$. If the value of an element exceeds $\rho/2 - 1$ then its value "rolls-over" into the negative interpretation. If the value of an element is less than $-\rho/2$, then it's value "rolls-under" into the positive interpretation. This behavior is based on the behavior of bitwise two's complement.

To add two operands, we add the corresponding elements of each operand. The results are stored in a new list. The counters for each operand are added together and incremented by one. The result of the list and counter additions are stored in a new instance of the data structure. Fig. 3 illustrates this process. Subtraction works in a similar way as addition, except that the corresponding elements of each list are subtracted and the counter values are subtracted and decremented by one.

Addition and subtraction are only supported for $K = 1$ due to a limitation of the encryption process and the ASCII encoding scheme. $K = 1$ works for arithmetic since each character's bits are not concatenated with anything else, as is the case for $K > 1$. Every element in any operand represents only one character value, and therefore all the bits in that element are known to represent a single character. An overflow or underflow does not disrupt other encrypted neighboring elements, since each element in the list is independent of the elements surrounding it. With $K > 1$, the independence property among groups is lost, making decryption impossible. Note that

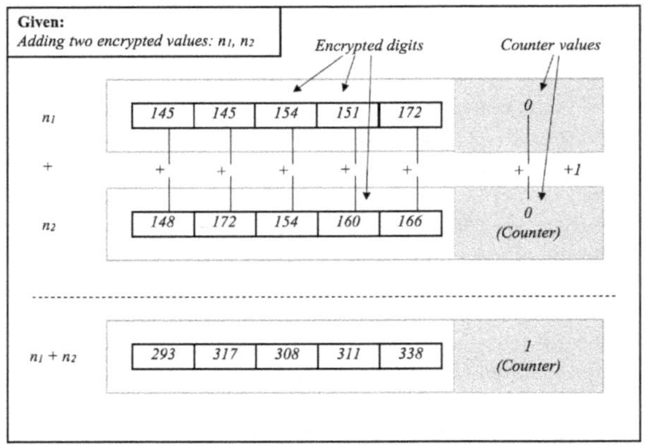

Figure 3: Addition of two encrypted values

it would be possible to "add" two non-numeric ASCII characters together. A user could encrypt "q" and encrypt "r" and add the two encrypted values, to obtain a result that would be indistinguishable from an encrypted integer result. Of course, when decrypting, the result would yield garbage data. This property is beneficial though, because a user could instruct the cloud computing platform to add two operands that were encrypted data strings (treating them as if they were encrypted integers) together, but the cloud would not be able to tell between what was garbage and what was a meaningful addition/subtraction operation, providing a further layer of security. In general, for any pair of encrypted integers (or strings) we would issue a string and an arithmetic operation, and disregard the string (or integer) results, thus enhancing security.

3.3 Security of Our Homomorphic Scheme

To study the asymptotic security of our homomorphic scheme based on the affine cipher, we assume that the lower bound of the difficulty to break our scheme is $\mathcal{D}_K$, when we group K characters together. A larger $\mathcal{D}_K$ indicates more effort is required to break the scheme. As discussed in Section 3.1, the security of our homomorphic scheme is significantly enhanced by grouping K characters together during encryption. The following analysis quantifies the security of our scheme by analyzing the relationship between $\mathcal{D}_K$ and K.

Suppose that the mapping from input λ to output ϵ is extracted by frequency analysis. The probability for a given mapping to be correct is $\mathcal{P}$, and when $K = 1$, let $\mathcal{P} = p$. When $K > 1$, $\mathcal{P} = p^K$ based on joint probability. To break the scheme (i.e. to find α, β and ρ), two equations with two correct mappings are needed:

$$\epsilon_1 = (\alpha\lambda_1 + \beta) \% \rho \quad (6)$$

$$\epsilon_2 = (\alpha\lambda_2 + \beta) \% \rho \quad (7)$$

To analysis the lower bound of $\mathcal{D}_K$, we assume that $\alpha\lambda + \beta < \rho$ for both λ_1 and λ_2. Therefore, if we subtract Equation 7 with Equation 6, we can eliminate β to get:

$$\epsilon_1 - \epsilon_2 = (\alpha(\lambda_1 - \lambda_2)) \% \rho \quad (8)$$

Since the output space is sparse, and K is hidden from the hacker, the value of ρ is not obvious. Assume that the number of possible ρ is $|\rho|$, and the the number of possible α is $|\alpha|$. Then to solve Equation 8, a total number of $|\rho| \times |\alpha|$ combinations of different ρ

and α need to be tested. Therefore, $\mathcal{D}$ can be estimated as following:

$$\mathcal{D} \propto |\rho| \times |\alpha| \times \frac{1}{p} \quad (9)$$

If we group K characters together, we get:

$$\mathcal{D}_K \propto |\rho| \times |\alpha| \times \frac{1}{p^K} \quad (10)$$

Based on Equation 10, $\mathcal{D}_K$ increases exponentially when K increases. Hence, by grouping K characters together, the minimal effort needed to break the scheme grows exponentially in K, which shows that our homomorphic scheme can be made arbitrarily "hard" to break with increasing K. In the next section, we study the computational consequences of increasing K.

4 EXPERIMENT RESULTS

In this section, we present the results of several experiments. We conducted to validate the runtime and memory performance of our scheme. We show and discuss the effect of varying different parameters in our scheme on the runtime and memory performance for both strings and integers in Section 4.1 and 4.2 respectively. It is impossible for us to compare our approach with the (few) existing homomorphic schemes for two reasons -- a) some of the existing schemes [3] [2] are theoretical in nature, with no experiment results and b) others [5] [14] present only absolute encryption results for their scheme without comparing the scheme with a baseline. Also, the problem they apply their techniques to are encryption of images, without performing operations on the result. Our focus, is different, on the other hand, since we focus on homomorphic encryption as well as operations on the encrypted results (for strings and integers instead of images).

Our code was written in the Python (2.7) programming language and tested on a system with a 2.7 GHz Intel i7 processor with 6MB L3 cache and 16GB RAM.In all our experiments, unless mentioned specifically, we set $\alpha = 12302342342342341231$ and $\beta = 71041$. The unit of the time results is millisecond (*ms*), and the unit of the size results is Megabyte (*MB*). Table 1 shows the summary of the notations we use in the result tables.

Table 1: Summary of Notations Used From Table 2 to Table 5

Symbol	Meaning
T_e	Encryption time
T_d	Decryption time
S_u	The size of unencrypted file
S_e	The size of encrypted file
T_{es}	The time of performing string search operations on the encrypted file
T_{us}	The time of performing string search operations on the unencrypted file
T_{eop}	The time of performing integer operations on the encrypted file
T_{uop}	The time of performing integer operations on the unencrypted file
N_{op}	The number of integer operations (add or subtract)
N_{dig}	The number of digits in each unencrypted number

4.1 Experiments on Strings

The following experiments will demonstrate features of our homomorphic scheme when it is applied to string manipulation tasks. In all these tests, the unencrypted search time was calculated by performing a *grep* on the plain text file and is used as a reference.

We first change α and β in Equation 2. According to Equation 2, α and β only provide a linear transform on the input. Therefore the encryption time, decryption time and the size of the encrypted file are not affected by changing α and β.

Table 2 shows the results when ρ is varied. As ρ increases, the range of possible output values also increases, which mean more bits are needed to store the output. Therefore the size of the encrypted file increases proportionally to the number of bits needed to represent ρ. When $K = 1$, each block in the encrypted file represents one character, so the number of encrypted blocks remained constant. Search time is only proportional to the number of encrypted blocks when $K = 1$, therefore search times for encrypted files was effectively constant.

Table 2: Varying ρ with $K = 1$

ρ	T_e	T_d	S_u	S_e	$\frac{S_e}{S_u}$	T_{es}	T_{us}	$\frac{T_{es}}{T_{us}}$
2^8	3567.828	5117.220	1.24	1.24	1.0	608.065	24.161	25.3
2^{16}	3545.013	5121.104	1.24	2.48	2.0	608.289	25.328	24.3
2^{32}	3635.781	5069.406	1.24	4.96	4.0	610.958	24.689	25.4
2^{64}	3534.376	5084.582	1.24	9.91	8.0	612.763	24.496	25.5
2^{128}	3437.900	5144.918	1.24	19.83	16.0	604.506	24.210	25.2

Table 3 reports the results for an experiment where the value of K is varied. This table shows how varying K influences encryption time, decryption time, file size, and search time. As K increases, the time to encrypt and decrypt the file decreases. This is because less affine cipher calculations need to be performed as more characters are grouped together. For the first 8 rows in the table, $\rho = 2^{64}$. With $K = 1$ and $\rho = 64$, one character is represented by a 64-bit number; hence the encrypted file was approximately 8 times larger than the unencrypted file as shown in Column 7. Note that each ASCII character is represented by 8 bits. When $K = 8$, and $\rho = 2^{64}$, 8 ASCII characters where represented in 64 bits. This is a full usage of the 64 bits (8 characters * 8 bits), which results in an encrypted file size that is equal to the unencrypted file size (see Column 7). As K increases with a fixed ρ, the size of the encrypted file decreases until it approaches the size of the unencrypted file as shown in Column 7 from rows 1 through 8. In general, the most spatially optimal configuration is when the unencrypted group size (in bits) is the same as $log_2(\rho)$. When this occurs, the encrypted file size is the same as the unencrypted file size. The search time T_{es} decreases as K increases. The reason can be explained by a complexity analysis. The number of ways a *query-string* can be grouped is K. The total number of blocks for N characters in plain text is N/K. The number of blocks in the *query-string* of n characters is n/K. Therefore, the overall complexity for searching is $(K * N/K * n/K) = O(1/K)$, assuming n and N are constant. Therefore, when K increases, T_{es} decreases, which shows that our homomorphic scheme scales very well on strings. Three trials are also done using $\rho = 2^{128}$ and $K = 8, 12, 16$ to show that the implementation does scale to larger values of K and ρ. The trends of decreasing encryption/decryption time, and search time continue, and the principle of optimized spatial use is still evident for these three trials.

Tables 2 and Tables 3 show that increasing ρ causes file sizes to increase with no effect on encryption/decryption or search times. Increasing K reduces these times as well as file sizes. Together, these tables illustrate that our scheme scales very elegantly.

Table 3: Varying K and ρ

K	ρ	T_e	T_d	S_u	S_e	$\frac{S_e}{S_u}$	T_{es}	T_{us}	$\frac{T_{es}}{T_{us}}$
1	2^{64}	3674.304	5138.524	1.24	9.91	8.0	727.690	30.596	24.2
2	2^{64}	2341.483	3045.651	1.24	4.96	4.0	491.524	30.440	16.4
3	2^{64}	1951.883	2311.462	1.24	3.30	2.7	403.495	30.371	13.4
4	2^{64}	1741.121	1971.933	1.24	2.48	2.0	426.807	30.426	14.2
5	2^{64}	1627.717	1845.920	1.24	1.98	1.6	366.105	28.937	13.1
6	2^{64}	1527.357	1703.331	1.24	1.65	1.3	325.850	30.265	10.8
7	2^{64}	1468.187	1611.892	1.24	1.42	1.2	405.795	29.978	14.0
8	2^{64}	1425.874	1516.756	1.24	1.24	1.0	274.211	29.547	9.4
8	2^{128}	1427.778	1572.157	1.24	2.48	2.0	287.074	29.912	9.9
12	2^{128}	1368.854	1414.978	1.24	1.65	1.3	238.417	28.895	8.5
16	2^{128}	1312.519	1306.293	1.24	1.24	1.0	213.739	29.897	7.3

4.2 Experiments on Integers

Table 4 shows how the number of encrypted integer operations N_{op} influences the performance of our encryption scheme. N_{op} doesn't have a major impact on encryption or decryption time (Column 3 and 4). However, as the number of operations increases, the size of the encrypted file S_e also increases. This is because as encrypted values are repeatedly added or subtracted, the magnitude of the value increases (when subtracting, values can go negative). As these magnitudes increase, more space is needed to store their values. In this case, S_e is measured by iterating through the encrypted array and summing the minimum number of bytes it would take to store each element including the counter member. Note that from Table 4, the units of S_u and S_e are Byte (B).

Table 4: Varying N_{op} with $K = 1$, $\rho = 2^{32}$, and $N_{dig} = 1$

Op.	N_{op}	T_e	T_d	T_{eop}	T_{uop}	$\frac{T_{eop}}{T_{uop}}$	S_u	S_e	$\frac{S_e}{S_u}$
add	2^1	0.015	0.028	0.015	0.002	7.600	5.0	1.0	5.0
add	2^2	0.024	0.020	0.026	0.003	10.440	5.0	1.0	5.0
add	2^8	0.017	0.017	1.178	0.048	24.540	7.0	2.0	3.5
add	2^{16}	0.016	0.029	279.892	12.084	23.163	9.0	3.0	3.0
add	2^{20}	0.026	0.028	4408.540	190.454	23.148	9.0	3.0	3.0
sub	2^1	0.026	0.026	0.016	0.002	7.524	5.0	1.0	5.0
sub	2^2	0.014	0.021	0.023	0.003	7.667	5.0	1.0	5.0
sub	2^8	0.018	0.019	1.171	0.051	22.961	7.0	2.0	3.5
sub	2^{16}	0.015	0.031	279.330	11.803	23.666	9.0	3.0	3.0
sub	2^{20}	0.022	0.030	4449.754	195.439	22.768	9.0	3.0	3.0

We also studied the effect of varying the ρ value for encrypted numbers with a large (2^{20}) number of operations performed on them. Similar to the results for strings, we find that the encryption, decryption and operation times are essentially constant as ρ varies. The $\frac{S_e}{S_u}$ ratio increases slightly as the number of bits of ρ increases.

Table 5 shows how varying the number of digits N_{dig} in the unencrypted number impacts the scheme's performance. The results from this test show how encryption and decryption times (T_e and T_d respectively) increase as N_{dig} increases. Since $K = 1$, N_{dig} is equal to the number of affine encryptions that occur. This means it takes longer to encrypt the entire number. This also means that as N_{dig} increases, the length of the encrypted result grows, which increases the encrypted file size S_e, and the operation time T_{eop} and $\frac{T_{eop}}{T_{uop}}$ both increase as well. As a result of all these observations

Table 5: Varying N_{dig} with $K = 1$, $N_{op} = 2^{20}$, and $\rho = 2^{32}$

Op.	N_{dig}	T_e	T_d	T_{eop}	T_{uop}	$\frac{T_{eop}}{T_{uop}}$	S_u	S_e	$\frac{S_e}{S_u}$
add	1	0.017	0.033	4900.348	204.147	24.004	9.0	3.0	3.0
add	2	0.031	0.037	5889.808	203.979	28.875	15.0	3.0	5.0
add	3	0.036	0.046	6848.432	207.804	32.956	21.0	3.0	7.0
add	4	0.038	0.048	7806.896	204.266	38.219	27.0	3.0	9.0
sub	1	0.030	0.033	4908.887	205.043	23.941	9.0	3.0	3.0
sub	2	0.032	0.037	5931.079	201.218	29.476	15.0	3.0	5.0
sub	3	0.043	0.045	6773.765	201.137	33.677	21.0	3.0	7.0
sub	4	0.040	0.048	7690.135	207.497	37.061	27.0	3.0	9.0

on both strings and integers, we recommend using larger values of ρ and K, with $\rho \approx 2^{8*K}$, to achieve a better security, as well as an optimal spatial use.

5 CONCLUSION

In this paper, we present an encryption scheme which has some powerful properties. First, it is homomorphic with respect to string operations (search and concatenation), and integer operations (addition and subtraction). Second, our homomorphic scheme is the first to be based on the affine cipher, with improvements made to increase security. We group K characters together to increase the input and output space in order to make hacking based on frequency analysis harder. We treat string and integer data identically, to avoid leaking information as to whether encrypted objects are of string or an integer type. Third, since the affine cipher is computationally light, our scheme is efficient and scales with the parameters of the scheme, especially for strings.

REFERENCES

[1] Zvika Brakerski and Vinod Vaikuntanathan. 2011. Fully homomorphic encryption from ring-LWE and security for key dependent messages. In *Annual cryptology conference*. Springer, 505–524.

[2] Craig Gentry. 2009. *A Fully Homomorphic Encryption Scheme*. Ph.D. Dissertation. Stanford, CA, USA. Advisor(s) Boneh, Dan.

[3] Craig Gentry. 2010. Computing arbitrary functions of encrypted data. *Commun. ACM* 53, 3 (2010), 97–105.

[4] Craig Gentry et al. 2009. Fully homomorphic encryption using ideal lattices.. In *STOC*, Vol. 9. 169–178.

[5] Ran Gilad-Bachrach, Nathan Dowlin, Kim Laine, Kristin Lauter, Michael Naehrig, and John Wernsing. 2016. Cryptonets: Applying neural networks to encrypted data with high throughput and accuracy. In *International Conference on Machine Learning*. 201–210.

[6] Shafi Goldwasser and Silvio Micali. 1982. Probabilistic encryption & how to play mental poker keeping secret all partial information. In *Proceedings of the fourteenth annual ACM symposium on Theory of computing*. 365–377.

[7] James S Kraft and Lawrence C Washington. 2016. *An introduction to number theory with cryptography*. CRC Press.

[8] Adriana López-Alt, Eran Tromer, and Vinod Vaikuntanathan. 2012. On-the-fly multiparty computation on the cloud via multikey fully homomorphic encryption. In *Proceedings of the forty-fourth annual ACM symposium on Theory of computing*. ACM, 1219–1234.

[9] Ronald L Rivest, Len Adleman, and Michael L Dertouzos. 1978. On data banks and privacy homomorphisms. *Foundations of secure computation* 4, 11 (1978), 169–180.

[10] Ronald L Rivest, Adi Shamir, and Leonard Adleman. 1978. A method for obtaining digital signatures and public-key cryptosystems. *Commun. ACM* 21, 2 (1978), 120–126.

[11] David Salomon. 2003. Introduction. In *Data Privacy and Security*. Springer, 1–17.

[12] Douglas R Stinson. 2005. *Cryptography: theory and practice*. CRC press.

[13] Marten Van Dijk, Craig Gentry, Shai Halevi, and Vinod Vaikuntanathan. 2010. Fully homomorphic encryption over the integers. In *Annual International Conference on the Theory and Applications of Cryptographic Techniques*. 24–43.

[14] Pan Yang, Xiaolin Gui, Jian An, and Feng Tian. 2017. An Efficient Secret Key Homomorphic Encryption Used in Image Processing Service. *Security and Communication Networks* 2017 (2017).

Resilient AES Against Side-Channel Attack Using All-Spin Logic

Qutaiba Alasad, Jiann Yuan, and Jie Lin
Department of Electrical & Computer Engineering, University of Central Florida, Orlando, FL 32816 USA
qutaibaeng@knights.ucf.edu,yuanj@ece.ucf.edu,ljie@Knights.ucf.edu

ABSTRACT

The new generation of spintronic devices, Hybrid Spintronic-CMOS devices including Magnetic Tunnel Junction (MTJ), have been utilized to overcome Moore's law limitation as well as preserve higher performance with lower cost. However, implementing these devices as a hardware cryptosystem is vulnerable to side channel attacks (SCAs) due to the differential power at the output of the Hybrid Spintronic-CMOS device and asymmetric read/write operations in MTJ. One of the most severe SCAs is the power analysis attack (PAA), in which an attacker can observe the output current of the device and extract the secret key. In this paper, we employ the All Spin Logic Device (ASLD) to implement protected AES cryptography for the first time. More precisely, we realize that in additional to ASLD features, such as small area, non-volatile memory, high density and low operating voltage, this device has another unique feature: identical power dissipation through the switching operations. Such properties can be effectively leveraged to prevent SCA.

ACM Reference Format:
Qutaiba Alasad, Jiann Yuan, and Jie Lin. 2018. Resilient AES Against Side-Channel Attack Using All-Spin Logic. In *GLSVLSI '18: 2018 Great Lakes Symposium on VLSI, May 23–25, 2018, Chicago, IL, USA.* ACM, New York, NY, USA, 6 pages.

1 INTRODUCTION

1.1 Motivation

Nowadays, the widespread apportionment of the Internet of Things (IoT) becomes widely used and requires a lot of components including hardware implementations of wireless sensor network devices and cryptographic algorithm [1], such as Advanced Encryption Standard (AES), which is one of the most important components in IoT to protect the transceived data among the devices in the entire system. AES consumes lower power and smaller area compared with others (e.g. Rivest-Shamir-Adleman (RSA)). The hardware implementation of AES cryptography is very important in order to accelerate the system, however, it also leads to the concern of protection of AES from side channel attacks (SCA) [2].

While CMOS scaled down reaches to the end due to the physics limitations on semiconductor, spintronic devices have been presented as an alternative. These devices can provide high-speed switching, zero leakage current, high-density, non-volatile storing element, and compatibility with CMOS. To further improve the performance of the spintronic devices and mitigate the consuming power when the device is off, CMOS-transistors are added to the nano-magnet instead of directly connecting the nano-magnet to the VDD supply [3]. This could be called Hybrid Spintronic-CMOS. Spintronic devices are good for in-memory computing applications, such as implementing a lightweight cryptography and image detection and processing [4]. Each memory cell should have Magnetic Tunnel Junction (MTJ) to store data and transistors to write and read the data. Using MTJ and transistor is good to implement efficient cryptography, but differences between the read and write currents are generated, which increases the possibility of SCA.

GLSVLSI '18, May 23–25, 2018, Chicago, IL, USA

ACM ISBN 978-1-4503-5724-1/18/05...$15.00

1.2 SCA: Attack and Defense Techniques

The secret key in a smart device can be revealed by SCA through observing the power dissipation, electromagnetic emissions, or time analysis [5]. Power analysis attack (PAA) is more popular and powerful than others. The first PAA was presented by Kocher et al. [2]. There are three types of PAA; simple power analysis (the data are directly taken from the power dissipation), differential power analysis (the related information is obtained from large number power traces, and then statistical analysis is used to identify the differences in these traces), and correlation power analysis (CPA) (the real power is correlated with the predicted power model to get the leakage data). CPA is more advanced and faster than others [6].

In CMOS technology, the PAA can reveal the secret key of a cryptography via measuring and analyzing the power consumption of the data dependence (intermediate data at specific operations) during the voltage transitions. For instance, the device consumes power from VDD supply only when its output switches from 0 to 1, and the capacitance at the output is discharged during the transition from 1 to 0. While during the two other degenerated transitions (0 to 0 or 1 to 1), no power is required [7].

In the spintronic devices, the operations of write-to and read-from in MTJ are asymmetric. For instance, if the previous stored data in the MTJ is '0' and the new data is '1', the write current will go from low to high. In contrast, when the previous stored data is '1' and the new data is '0', the write current will go from high to low. For the two other states ('0' to '0' and '1' to '1'), the current will be constant [8]. Note that the read current from MTJ cannot be increased since the stored data in MTJ might be changed accidentally, while reducing the write current will not guarantee storing the new data correctly. These differences between the two-write and two-read currents make the device vulnerable to PAA. Furthermore, adding transistor on the top of the nanomagnet reduces the power dissipation, however, this increases the device vulnerability to PAA since the power dissipation at the output of the device will be different.

There are many PAA countermeasures, but the most two popular ones are the masking [9] and hiding [10] techniques. Masking method targets to randomly mask the intermediate values, which

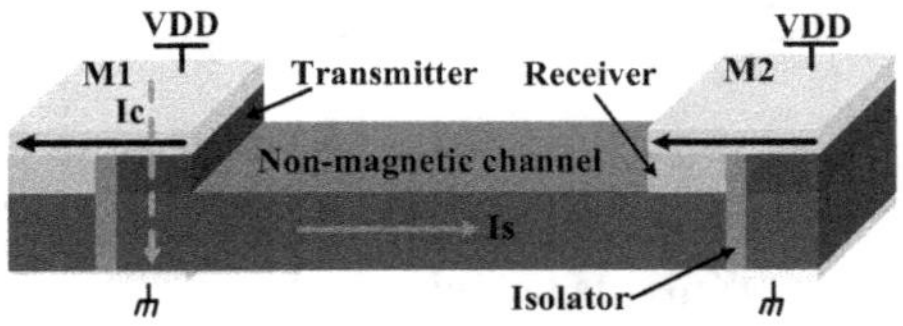

Figure 1: ASL devices function as a buffer or an inverter.

requires additional hardware resources, where large overhead requires for masking complex operations. For hiding method, even though the performance penalty is not that much large for different types of operations, there is a trade-off between the security and power dissipation. Increasing the noise power leads to increase the protection of the design, however, the signal to noise ratio will be reduced since the noise will control the power [1]. Employing a Sensing Amplifier Based Logic (SABL) [7] is more empirical technique to prevent PAA. A protected design, namely Current Mode Logic (CML), is employed to produce approximately a constant power dissipation at the output and thus PAA cannot identify the correct key. The above-mentioned techniques require large overhead for high protection level, which is not good for IoT applications since most of IoT devices are powered by battery.

1.3 Our Contribution

In short, the different powers during the transitions at specific internal operations in a device implemented using CMOS or Hybrid Spintronic-CMOS (including MTJ and transistor) make the device vulnerable to PAA. Preventing such attacks from exposing the secret key can be achieved by adding extra hardware resources. However, the performance penalty will significantly increase for a high PAA resilience. In this paper, we extract a new unique feature of All Spin Logic Device (ASLD), in which the power dissipation of all read/write operations from/to nano-magnet unit are constant. We also implement different kinds of logic gates with different input-sizes in order to implement resilient ASLD-based AES for the first time. Moreover, since the ASLD consumes large energy for high performance, we use the pipeline technique, where buffers are inserted in necessary locations through the design. The new feature of ASLD with the pipeline strategy enables us to implement resilient AES against PAA with small performance penalty. To evaluate the strength of the proposed technique, we attack the first round in AES since the original key is directly XORed with the plaintext in this round. Then, a correlation power analysis is executed to guess secret key information. Finally, this work is compared with other previous works in terms of energy and area.

2 EVALUATIONS AND ANALYSES OF ASLD

2.1 ASLD as Logic Gates and Data Storage

Emerging devices have been leveraged to help improve hardware security, e.g. silicon nanowire field effect transistors [11, 12] and all spin logic device (ASLD) [13]. ASLD is an improvement on the fabricated spin-based logic [14] to switch the direction of the nanomagnet without additional resources [15]. The ASLD model contains four main components; nanomagnetic (ferromagnetic) unit, interface element, isolator, and non-magnetic channel. The nanomagnet is used as a storing element. The interface element between the nanomagnetic unit and non-magnetic channel is used to improve the injected spin from the nanomagnet to the non-magnetic channel. The isolator is important to separate the input and output ports. To connect several ASL devices and transfer the signal from one to another, a non-magnetic channel should be added, which is made from copper or nickel. The purpose of this connection is to implement different logic gates. For instance, by connecting two ASL devices, the design can work as a buffer or an inverter, as shown in Figure 1.

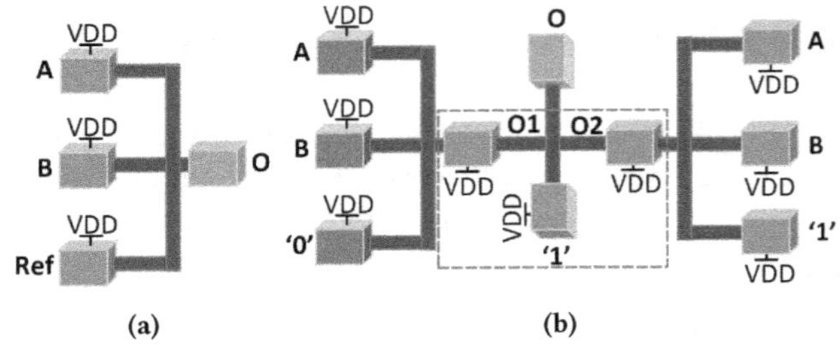

Figure 2: ASLD-based Logic gates: (a) AND, NAND, OR, and NOR gates; (b) XOR and XNOR gates.

The spin current flows from the nanomagnet to the channel through applying a voltage. When the supply voltage is positive, the charge current will flow from VDD to GND and the electrons will move from the GND to the first magnetic unit (M1). Spins with opposite orientation to M1 will accumulate in the channel while spins with same orientation will pass through M1. This happens because M1 output (transmitter) has high polarization and M2 input (receiver) has low polarization. Therefore, the accumulated spins in the channel will move through the channel to switch the orientation of the second magnet (M2). Hence, the design functions as an inverter. On the other hand, when the supply voltage is negative, the charge current will flow from GND to VDD and the electrons will move from VDD to GND. Only spins with same orientation to M1 will pass through the channel to M2, and the M2 orientation will not be switched since the orientation of M1 and M2 is the same. Thus, the design functions as a buffer. Note that the Landau-Lifshitz-Gilbert (LLG) should be applied at the output of each implemented ASLD to model the magnetic field of the output magnetics.

We also implement other logic gates, such as AND, NAND, OR, NOR, XOR, and XNOR by connecting more ASL devices, as shown in figure 2. Where A, B, and Ref are input nanomagnets and O is the output nanomagnet. In Figure 2 (a), when the VDD value is positive and reference (Ref) value is '0' or '1', the design performs as AND or OR gate, respectively; while when the VDD value is negative and the Ref value is '0' or '1', the circuit functions as NAND or NOR gate. This operation is called majority gate (MG). Two 3-input MGs with another ASLD are connected to produce an XOR gate. The first MG is implemented as an AND gate and the second is implemented as a NOR gate. Then, the outputs of these two MGs are connected with one more ASLD to produce two-input XOR gate, as shown in Figure 2 (b), where a positive and negative voltages are supplied on the green-magnet and blue-magnet, respectively. If a positive voltage is applied at the intermediate magnets (denoted inside a dot red-rectangle in Figure 2 (b)), the same design will function as XNOR gate. To implement the normal basis LUT, we first design the decoder with the logic gate that we designed. Then the output of the decoder is AND-ed with the data bits of the LUT to generate the output of the LUT. The ASLD is nonvolatile, consequently the shift register can be realized by connecting multiple nanomagentes in series. Using the same topology introduced by Yuhao Wang et al. [4], we add redundant bits shift to perform circularly shifting. More details regarding the implementation of AES using ASLD is provided in the next section.

2.2 PAA Prevention Using ASLD

In traditional CMOS, different input data to the same operations consume different powers due to the switching statement ('0' to '1' or '1' to '0'), while the MTJ-based spintronic logic unit produces four power differences in the current values. These values make the design vulnerable to PAA attacks. Interestingly enough, the principle operation of ASLD is based on the magnetization direction of the spin current (Is) in order to flip or not the orientation of the magnet at the target, which always consumes constant power. More specifically, the ASL device always consumes approximately the same power whether the supply voltage is positive or negative according to the targeted flipping of the magnet. This could be considered as a unique property in hardware security applications. A designer can implement a very resilient lightweight cryptographic algorithm, such as AES, DES, PRESENT, ECC, etc, using ASLD with high performance (small area with low switching power) against PAA without the need to add additional hardware resources. The PAA cannot figure out the correct secret key of an implemented cryptography designed using ASLD since the switching of the magnetization direction at each output stage depends on the direction of the generated spin current during the operation, as mentioned in the previous subsection. The spin current value that is required to switch the magnet is exactly the same for both directions.

To verify the above-mentioned theory analysis, the Current-In-Plane (CIP) non-local spin valve model [16] is adopted to characterize ASLD. A simple two-input XOR logic gate, as illustrated in Figure 2 (b), is designed using the HSPICE simulator. We supply 10 mV positive voltage (as a clock) with two sequences of input data (input A and input B normalized moments) to the design. The sequence of the output data response (output normalized moment) with the output current value is observed and reported, as shown in Figure 3. The simulation results of the design emphasize that the value of the output current has not changed during the four possible switching transient statements ('0' to '1', '1' to '0', '0' to '0', and '1' to '1') at the output of the XOR gate. This could provide a highly resilient design against PAA. Note that the output current waveform in Figure 3 shows some spikes, which are generated due to the coupling noise, that is because ALSD does not have capacitor at the output as in CMOS technology.

The ASLD has two limitations; first, the spin current cannot be transferred to a long distance or distributed to many paths or outputs (fan-out) since the value of the spin current is very small. Second, the ASLD is slow compared to CMOS. The switching delay can be reduced via increasing the supplied voltage; however, the power consumption will be increased as well. In other words, the energy dissipation will be large. Since we are looking to design resilient AES with lower power and smaller area, we keep the small supplied voltage to 10 mV and utilize the pipeline technique to improve the energy of the design. In the next section, we provide some techniques to overcome these two limitations based on the work in [17].

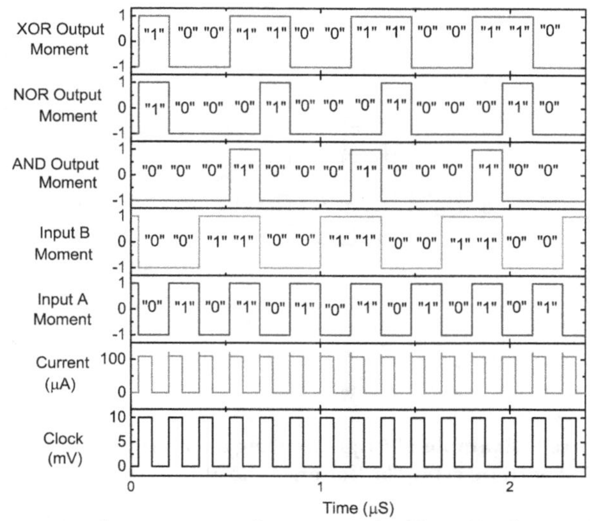

Figure 3: The ASLD simulation results show unchangeable output current during the switching of the XOR gate.

3 AES CRYPTOGRAPHY IMPLEMENTATION

3.1 AES Overview and Its Vulnerability to PAA

AES is one of the symmetric key algorithms, where both the encrypted and decrypted data are done using the same key. It encrypts a 128-bit plaintext (PT) with different key-sizes, 128, 196, and 256 bits in 10, 12, and 14 rounds, respectively [18]. AES with 128 key-bits is explained and considered in this work. AES with other key-sizes (196 and 256 bits) can also be addressed in the same manner. Figure 4 describes the implementation steps of AES-128 bits. The PT is 16 bytes (organized as 4X4 matrix) and XORed with the original key only at the initial round. Each round of AES after the initial one has four operations; SubstituteByte (SSB), ShiftRow (SR), MixColumn

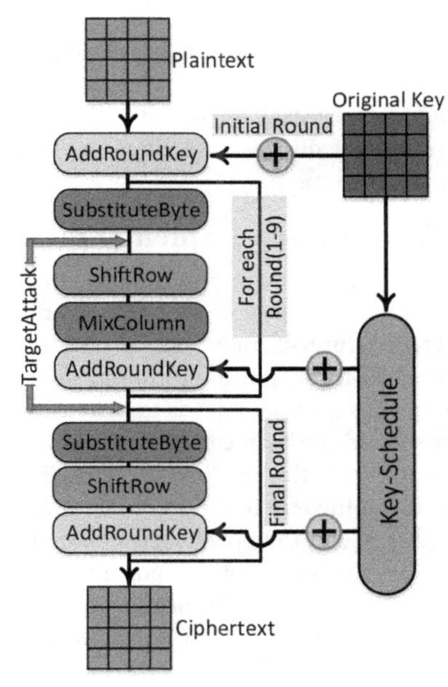

Figure 4: Block diagram of the AES with two points of SCA.

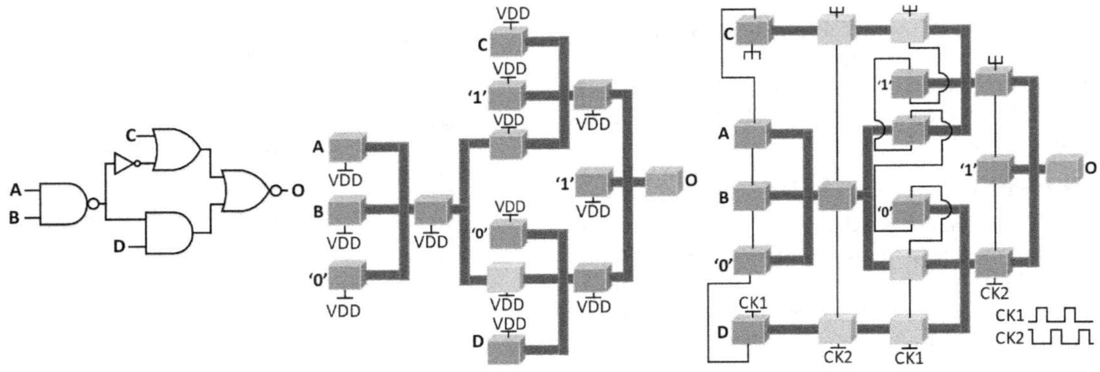

(a) (b) (c)

Figure 5: Example of implementing a circuit using ASLD (a) original circuit in CMOS (b) implementation of the circuit using ASLD with inserting buffer once the output has many fanout (c) incorporating two phase-clocks and applying the pipeline.

(MC), and AddRoundKey (ARK), except the last round which consists of only three steps (without MC). In the SSB, each byte of the XORed output result undergoes through a Look-Up Table (S-BOX) and is updated via non-linear transformation function. Then, two linear operations are performed on the data state in both SR and MC. The data state in each round, except the initial one, is XORed with a generated key round at the AddRoundKey. The generated key rounds are derived from the key-schedule block.

There are two vulnerable locations in AES to PAA [5]; one is at the last round (LR) and the second is at the first round (FR), as signified in Figure 4 as "targetAttack". The attacker at the LR can calculate the ciphertext as SR(SSB_LR) ⊕ KL and then recover the original key via reversing the key-schedule routine. The more critical place to be attacked is at the FR since the original key is directly XOR-ed with the PT, and the target data can be computed as: SSB_FR(K0⊕PT). Where KL is the generated round key at LR, and K0 is the original key. Therefore, we assume during our evaluation on ASLD-based AES that the point of the PAA is at the FR. The PT, SSB, and K0 are 16 bytes. Measuring the whole 16 bytes one time to recover the key will be very time consuming; however, if one byte of SSB_FR and K0 is revealed, the rest of the bytes can be recovered accordingly using the divide and conquer method, in which one byte is observed at a time.

3.2 ASLD-based AES Implementation

The pipeline technique is commonly wide used in many applications to speed up the design, especially in modern computer system and architecture. In traditional CMOS design, the pipeline can be achieved by incorporating flip-flops or registers between the stages in the design, which leads to increasing the power and area overhead significantly since each D flip-flop requires at least 12 transistors. In ASLD, the pipeline can be done by inserting ASL buffer-gates only at the required paths in the stages, which incurs a very small increase in the power and area penalties since each added ASL buffer-gate is very small compared to D flip-flop. Therefore, leveraging the pipeline will speed up a design implemented using ASLD with low overhead. Furthermore, the charge current (IC) in ASLD flows from VDD to GND (or GND to VDD based on the supply voltage) and its value does not decrease during the switching operation because the resistor value of the magnet is very small (few Ω). Consequently, the end terminal of the device can be used to connect all ASL devices in the same stage with one power supply. Since not all of the pipeline stages function at the same time (e.g. the output of a certain ALSD is input to the next stage), two clock phases are added, in which odd stages are performed first and then even stages sequentially. Furthermore, since the spin current is very small, it cannot be transferred to a long distance or drive in many paths (fanout). Therefore, ASL buffer-gates are added on the long path or at each output path.

Figure 5 gives an example to summarize the aforementioned improvements on circuit designed using ASLD. A simple logic circuit designed using CMOS is shown in Figure 5 (a). The circuit has four different logic gates (AND, NAND, OR, NOR gates) with an inverter. This circuit can be implemented using ASLD as demonstrated in Figure 5 (b). The output of the ASL NAND-gate is connected to two paths. The upper path has an inverter, which neglects the need of adding a buffer. In the second path, a buffer is inserted before the ASL AND-gate to enhance the spin current (the inserted ASL buffer-gate is donated in an orange color in Figure 5 (b)). To apply the pipeline technique, the end terminals of all devices in each stage are connected to one clock-phase, and buffers are inserted in the required locations, as illustrated in Figure 5 (c), where all of the necessary inserted buffers are donated in the orange color. For each odd stage, clock-phase1 (CK1) is employed while for each even stage clock-phase2 (CK2) is added. Such optimized strategy will help speed up the design with small performance penalty.

The main requirements of implementing AES are XOR-gate and shift register operations and LUT. These components are already elucidated in details in subsection 2.1. The flow-chart in Figure 6 shows the steps of implementing efficient AES against PAA. The first step is to add both AES with 128 bit key-size designed using Verilog language and the ASLD library as inputs to the Synopsys Design Compiler. The ASLD library has different logic gates (e.g. inverter, buffer, AND, NAND, OR, NOR, XOR, XNOR gates), each gate has different input-sizes and is implemented with single or multiple stages majority gates (MGs). Afterwards, buffers are inserted between the stages of the MGs. A buffer should be inserted once the distance between the sender and the receiver ASLD is

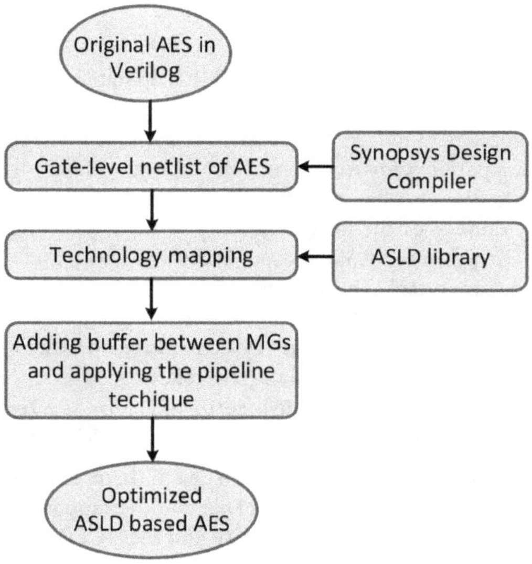

Figure 6: Efficient AES via applying ASLD-optimizations.

longer than the Spin-flip length of the channel (λ_{sf}) [17], or the output signal goes to more than two paths. To apply the pipeline with the generated multi-phase clock, the gates at each level in the design have been specified. Then, a two-phase-clock is generated at each stage (level), and buffers are inserted in different necessary locations, as shown in Fig. 5. The two-phase-clock generation is implemented based on the global optimization algorithm [19].

4 PERFORMANCE AND SECURITY EVALUATIONS

In this section, we provide the results of implementing efficient and resilient ASLD-based AES against PAA. A compression between our work and other related works is also performed in terms of the required area, energy dissipation, and number of cycles for the entire design.

4.1 Simulation Setup

The non-local lateral spin valve modular based CIP is leveraged to design different logic gates (inverter, buffer, AND, NAND, OR, NOR, XOR, and XNOR) with different input-sizes, the shift register, and the LUT. All these components are simulated and characterized using Synopsys HSPICE simulator. Synopsys Design Compiler is used to synthesize the Verilog code of the AES with 128 key-size. We develop an in house modified ASL library to perform technology mapping with the technology parameter in [20].

4.2 ASL-Parameters and AES-Performance

Even though the required voltage to switch the magnetization direction of ASLD (or other spintronic devices) is very small, the switching time is typically higher than CMOS. The switching time can be reduced by increasing the supply voltage, but the power dissipation will also increase accordingly. Therefore, the metrics to evaluate a design implemented using spintronic device are based on the energy (Power delay produce (PDP)) and the area. To accelerate the proposed AES and enhance the energy performance without increasing the supply voltage, we employ the pipeline technique. The required PDP, number of cycles, and area for the proposed

Table 1: Comparison of implementation AES-128 bits.

Publication	(PDP) Energy (nJ)	# of cycles	Area
[21]GPP	460	2309	$2.5e^6$
[22]ASIC	6.6	336	4400
[23]CMOL	10.3	470	320
This work	4.1	474	50.6

Table 2: Simulation parameters of ASLD

Parameter	setup value
Effective damping Alpha (α)	0.01
Spin-flip length of the channel (λ)	500 nm
Interconnection resistivity (ρ_N)	7 Ω-nm
Nano-magnet area (A)	30X10 nm^2
Interconnection element	Cu
Anisotropy field H_K	12.2 KOe
Saturation magnetization (M_S)	800 emu/cm^3
Magnet volume (V)	45X15X1 nm^2
Spin polarization ratio (P)	0.1/0.90

ASLD based AES 128-bit are evaluated and compared with other previous works, as shown in Table 1. It is worthwhile to mention that the previous works [21–23] have proposed to implement AES without taking into consideration the vulnerability of the design against PAA. Preventing such attacks requires a large surcharge for a high protection level of AES designed using only CMOS technology. Meanwhile, implementing resilient AES against PAA using hybrid Spintronic-CMOS devices including MTJ has not been presented yet. The throughput of the proposed AES is 204.8 Mbps, and it could be increased by increasing the supply voltage at the penalty of increasing the power consumption. The setup parameters of the ASLD based physics framework are shown in Table 2.

4.3 Security Analysis of ASLD-Based AES

We test our proposal using the CPA since it is more accurate and requires less number of traces to figure out the correct key. The simulation results of the ASL XOR-gate are not enough to prove that the proposal can prevent PAA. To further evaluate the resilience of our technique, we target the intermediate data in the SBOX at the first round since it is the only part that directly treats with the original secret key, as shown in Fig. 4. We assume that the attacker can get access to the primary inputs of the proposed AES, supply the input data (PT), and observe the power dissipation. We select one byte from the output result of the SBOX as a point of attack.

The power model can be created using either the hamming weight (HW); (it is a simple model to calculate the estimated power dissipation for each set-bits (count the number of set-bits in the data word)), or the hamming distance (HD); it is the relationship between the previous and the new data in the data set (the data set before and after the SBOX). Each of these power models have different properties. For stronger evaluation, we test the proposed AES against PAA using both the HW and HD models. Each model is built based on the work in [24], where 1% Additive White Gaussian Noise (AWGN) has been included. We apply each of the possible PT values each with the all possible combinational key values to create the two hypothetical power models. Afterwards, we apply

$$Corr(p * c) = \frac{\sum_{k=1}^{256} (t_{k,p,c} - \overline{t_{p,c}}).(h_{k,p,c} - \overline{h_{p,c}})}{\sqrt{\sum_{k=1}^{256} (t_{k,p,c} - \overline{t_{p,c}})^2 . \sum_{k=1}^{256} (h_{k,p,c} - \overline{h_{p,c}})^2}} \quad (1)$$

Where:

- $p * c$: number of PT (256) * number of traces (17).
- k: number of guess key (256).
- t: real power.
- h: hypothetical power model.

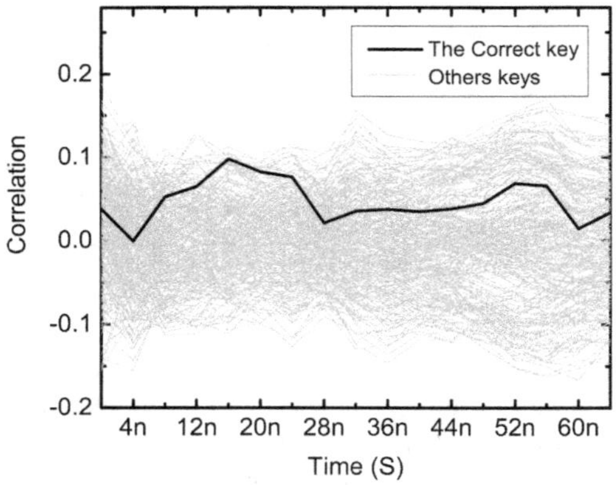

(a)

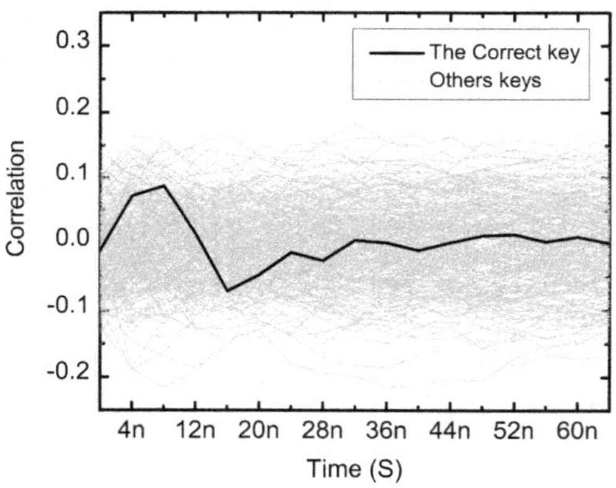

(b)

Figure 7: CPA attack vs the execution time: (a) correlation based on the HW (b) based on the HD.

the correct key of AES and measure the real power consumption. We sample the real power with 4ns sampling period. The power models are compared with the real power. Then we calculate the correlation between the sampled power and the two generated hypothetical models utilizing Equation 1. The highest resilient AES against PAA can be achieved if the correct key trace is mixed with the incorrect key traces while it is considered very weak if the correct key is stepped away from the incorrect keys. Figure 7 (a) shows the correlation outcomes of applying the correct key and incorrect keys on the proposed AES using the HW, while Figure 7 (b) shows the outcome results based on the HD. Implementing ASLD-based AES with different key-sizes will not affect on the PAA-resilient AES.

5 CONCLUSION

In this paper, ASLD has been leveraged to help implement resilient AES. We extract the unique features of ASLD, which can be utilized to implement different logic gates and provide unchangeable power dissipation without external resources during the transient statements. We also leverage the pipeline technique to improve the performance of the design, instead of increasing the power supply. The proposed ASLD-based AES is also evaluated against power analysis attack. Our analyses, supported by the evaluation results, emphasize that ASLD can provide a highly secure design with smaller area and lower energy compared to others. In our design, an attacker cannot learn the secret key based on the leakage information, as evidenced by the security analysis. As a result, the proposed technique could be a good candidate for IoT applications.

Acknowledgement: Q. Alasad wishes to thank his colleagues at Tikrit University for discussion. This work is supported in part by the Florida Center of Cybersecurity and the HCED in Iraq.

REFERENCES

[1] X. Li *et al.*, "Energy-efficient side-channel attack countermeasure with awareness and hybrid configuration based on it," *IEEE Transactions on VLSI Systems*, 2017.
[2] P. Kocher, "Design and validation strategies for obtaining assurance in countermeasures to power analysis and related," in *NIST Physical Security*, 2005.
[3] A. Jaiswal, I. Chakraborty, and K. Roy, "Energy-efficient memory using magneto-electric switching of ferromagnets," *IEEE Magnetics Letters*, vol. 8, pp. 1–5, 2017.
[4] Y. Wang, L. Ni, C. H. Chang, and H. Yu, "Dw-aes: A domain-wall nanowire-based aes for high throughput and energy-efficient data encryption in non-volatile memory," *IEEE Transactions on Information Forensics and Security*, 2016.
[5] K. J. Smith, "Methodologies for power analysis attacks on hardware implementations of aes," *Thesis. Rochester Institute of Technology.*, 2009.
[6] F. Zhang and Z. J. Shi, "Differential and correlation power analysis attacks on hmac-whirlpool," in *2011 8th ITNG*, 2011.
[7] K. Tiri *et al.*, "A dynamic and differential cmos logic with signal independent power consumption to withstand differential power analysis on smart cards," in *Solid-State Circuits Conference*, 2002.
[8] M. Khan *et al.*, "Side-channel attack on sttram based cache for cryptographic application," in *IEEE International Conference on Computer Design (ICCD)*, 2017.
[9] A. Moradi *et al.*, *Pushing the Limits: A Very Compact and a Threshold Implementation of AES.* Berlin, Heidelberg: Springer Berlin Heidelberg, 2011.
[10] P. Liu *et al.*, "A low overhead dpa countermeasure circuit based on ring oscillators," *IEEE Transactions on Circuits and Systems II: Express Briefs*, 2010.
[11] Q. Alasad, J.-S. Yuan, and Y. Bi, "Logic locking using hybrid cmos and emerging sinw fets," *Electronics*, vol. 6, 2017.
[12] Q. Alasad and J. Yuan, "Logic obfuscation against ic reverse engineering attacks using plgs," in *IEEE International Conference on Computer Design (ICCD)*, 2017.
[13] Q. Alasad, J. Yuan, and D. Fan, "Leveraging all-spin logic to improve hardware security," in *Proceedings of the on GLSVLSI '17*, 2017.
[14] H. Dery, P. Dalal, L. Cywinski, and L. J. Sham, "Spin-based logic in semiconductors for reconfigurable large-scale circuits," *Nature*, 2007.
[15] B. Behin-Aein, D. Datta, S. Salahuddin, and S. Datta, "Proposal for an all-spin logic device with built-in memory," *Nature*, vol. 5, 2010.
[16] K. Y. Camsari, S. Ganguly, and S. Datta, "Modular approach to spintronics," in *2015 Scientific Reports*, vol. 5.
[17] Z. Pajouhi *et al.*, "Exploring spin-transfer-torque devices for logic applications," *IEEE Transactions on CAD*, 2015.
[18] V. Rijmen *et al.*, "Advanced encryption standard," *Proceedings of Federal Information Processing Standards Publications, NIST*, 2001.
[19] J. M. Renders *et al.*, "Hybridizing genetic algorithms with hill-climbing methods for global optimization: two possible ways," in *IEEE Proceedings on EC*, 1994.
[20] M. G. Mankalale and S. S. Sapatnekar, "Optimized standard cells for all-spin logic," *J. Emerg. Technol. Comput. Syst.*, vol. 13, no. 2, pp. 21:1–21:22, Nov. 2016.
[21] K. Malbrain, "Byte-oriented-aes: A public domain byteoriented implementation of aes in c," *Available: " https://code.google.com/p/byte-oriented-aes/"*, 2009.
[22] S. Mathew *et al.*, "340mV–1.1V, 289Gbps/W, 2090-gate NanoAES hardware accelerator with area-optimized encrypt/decrypt GF(2^4)^2 polynomials in 22nm tri-gate cmos," in *Symposium on VLSI Circuits Digest of Technical Papers*, 2014.
[23] Z. Abid *et al.*, "Efficient cmol gate designs for cryptography applications," *IEEE Transactions on Nanotechnology*, 2009.
[24] Q. Tian and S. A. Huss, "Power amount analysis: Another way to understand power traces in side channel attacks," in *2nd ICDIPC*, July 2012.

DeEPeR: Enhancing Performance and Reliability in Chip-Scale Optical Interconnection Networks

Mahdi Nikdast[1], Gabriela Nicolescu[2], Jelena Trajkovic[3], and Odile Liboiron-Ladouceur[4]
[1]Colorado State University, CO, USA [2]Polytechnique Montréal, QC, Canada
[3]Concordia University, QC, Canada [4]McGill University, QC, Canada
Mahdi.Nikdast@colostate.edu

ABSTRACT

This paper presents an efficient device-level design method to enhance the performance and reliability (DeEPeR) in optical interconnection networks (OINs) under fabrication process variations (PV). Considering different range of variations, DeEPeR explores the design space of fundamental optical components in OINs (e.g., microresonators (MRs)) to improve the overall system performance and reliability. Our study also includes the design and fabrication of several MRs to experimentally validate our proposed method. Moreover, as a system-level case study, we apply DeEPeR to a general passive OIN under PV. Results indicate that DeEPeR considerably improves the optical signal-to-noise ratio (OSNR) in optical interconnection networks.

CCS CONCEPTS

• **Hardware → Photonic and optical interconnect; Process variations; Hardware reliability;**

KEYWORDS

Silicon Photonic Interconnects; MPSoCs; Process Variations; Reliability

ACM Reference Format:
Mahdi Nikdast[1], Gabriela Nicolescu[2], Jelena Trajkovic[3], and Odile Liboiron-Ladouceur[4]. 2018. DeEPeR: Enhancing Performance and Reliability in Chip-Scale Optical Interconnection Networks. In *GLSVLSI '18: 2018 Great Lakes Symposium on VLSI, May 23–25, 2018, Chicago, IL, USA.* ACM, New York, NY, USA, 6 pages. https://doi.org/10.1145/3194554.3194566

1 INTRODUCTION

Multiprocessor systems-on-chip (MPSoCs) are continuously scaling to support new applications demands, such as higher computation and communication bandwidth required for emerging big data applications. The inter- and intra-chip communication in MPSoCs need to keep pace with such rapidly growing requirements. Compared with conventional metallic interconnects, optical interconnection networks (OINs) can outperform MPSoCs through realizing an ultra-high bandwidth and low-latency communication with a low power consumption [1]. The bandwidth performance in OINs can be further improved through employing wavelength-division multiplexing (WDM), which allows simultaneous transmission of multiple optical wavelengths in a single waveguide.

Several WDM-based OINs have been proposed for MPSoCs [15], in which hundreds and thousands of microresonators (MRs) are integrated. These fundamental components, however, are considerably sensitive to fabrication process variations (PV) [6]. Particularly, while different MRs need to be precisely matched in terms of their central wavelengths (e.g., the resonant wavelength in MRs) to achieve a reliable communication in OINs, PV deviate MRs resonant wavelengths, resulting in performance and reliability degradation in OINs. Silicon-on-insulator (SOI) thickness and waveguide width variations, considered in this work, are the major concerns in silicon photonics fabrication [3, 6]. PV stem from optical lithography imperfection and are inevitable in OINs, necessitating developing efficient design methods to compensate for such variations.

Fabrication process variations have been studied in OINs at both device-level [3, 6] and system-level [9, 13, 14]. Several methods have been proposed to compensate for PV, and specifically to restore the resonant wavelength of MRs. Thefi rst type of solutions is to use high-energy particles, such as UV light, to adjust the refractive index of waveguides, and hence the resonant wavelength of MRs [8]. However, this technique is not applicable to systems consisting of a large number of MRs due to its complexity, and it degrades the quality factor (i.e., Q) of MRs. The second type of solutions (a.k.a. trimming) is to use thermal tuning to increase the wavelength (i.e., red shift), and current injection to decrease the wavelength (i.e., blue shift). Thermal tuning, however, is power hungry, while current injection has a limited correction range and imposes an extra power loss. Nevertheless, trimming is required to compensate for thermal variations and when using active devices and OINs.

Some efforts have been also made to develop different system-level design methods to compensate for PV in OINs. A reliability designfl ow to outperform OINs under process and thermal variations was proposed in [12], which is based on using thermal tuning and MR channel remapping. In [5], a framework was proposed to alleviate the impact of crosstalk noise in physically trimmed OINs under PV, improving the performance in such networks, but at a cost of a high power overhead (i.e., 50% on average).

The novel contribution of this paper is in developing an efficient device-level design method to enhance the performance and reliability (DeEPeR) in OINs under fabrication process variations. Considering different range of variations, DeEPeR explores the design space of MRs to study how employing different design parameters in such components impacts the performance and reliability at the device- and system-level. We consider strip waveguides, which are used for routing in OINs and passive devices (e.g., MRs,filters)

GLSVLSI '18, May 23–25, 2018, Chicago, IL, USA

ACM ISBN 978-1-4503-5724-1/18/05...$15.00
https://doi.org/10.1145/3194554.3194566

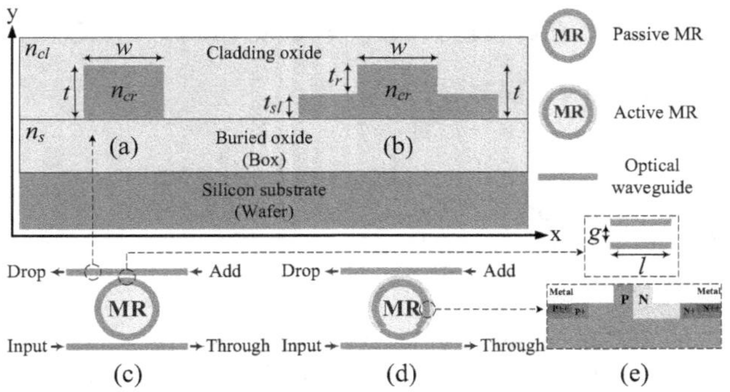

Figure 1: (a) and (b): Cross sections of a strip and a ridge waveguide; (c) and (d): an overview of a passive and an active MR; and (e): a P-N junction.

and networks, as well as ridge waveguides, which are employed in active devices (e.g., MR modulators) and OINs.

At the device-level, considering waveguides with various design parameters, DeEPeR comprehensively studies the impact of different variations on the resonant wavelength of passive and active MRs. Also, our study includes the design and fabrication of several MRs using DeEPeR to experimentally validate the proposed method, as well as demonstrating the efficiency of DeEPeR when it is employed in a device fabrication. Indicating the impact of DeEPeR at the system-level, we apply our method to a case study of a general passive WDM-based OIN, which can be applied to any specific passive OIN, under random PV. Results indicate that DeEPeR considerably improves the optical signal-to-noise ratio (OSNR) in the system (almost 6 dB improvement in the OSNR on average). The OSNR denotes the received optical signal quality and it impacts the bit error rate (BER) in a system, hence determining the performance and reliability. This paper does not consider thermal variations.

The rest of the paper is organized as follows. In Section 2, we present the fundamental concepts and the theory of strip and ridge waveguides as well as MR-based devices. Section 3 presents our proposed method, DeEPeR, and includes our fabrication details and results. The case study of the general passive OIN architecture and its results are presented in Section 4. Finally, we draw conclusions in Section 5.

2 OPTICAL WAVEGUIDES AND MRs

This section reviews some fundamental concepts in waveguides and MRs. In general, optical devices can be classified as passive or active (see Fig. 1). Strip waveguides are used in passive devices and OINs (i.e., optical signal transmits passively), while ridge waveguides are widely employed in electro-optic devices (i.e., active devices) as they allow for electrical connections to be made to the waveguides (see Figs. 1(d) and 1(e)). This paper considers the variations in the SOI thickness and waveguide width, and doping variations related to active devices are not considered.

2.1 Strip and Ridge Waveguides

Figs. 1(a) and 1(b) indicate cross sections of a strip and a ridge waveguide, respectively. As can be seen, the waveguide core, with a refractive index of n_{cr}, is buried in a cladding oxide layer at the top, with a refractive index of n_{cl}, and a substrate oxide layer at

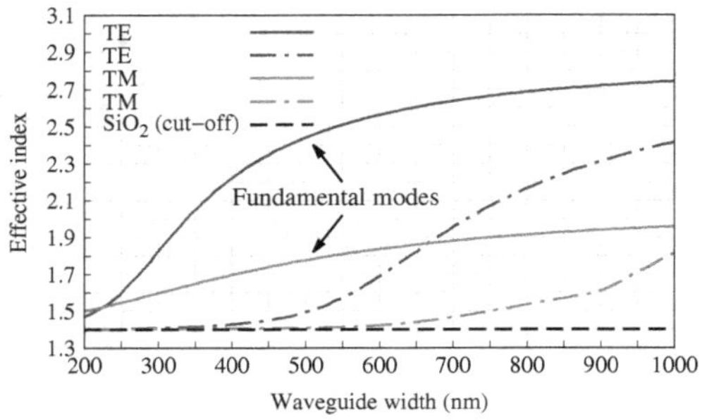

Figure 2: Effective indices of different waveguide modes in a strip waveguide for a SOI thickness of 220 nm (t = 220 nm and λ = 1550 nm).

the bottom, whose refractive index is n_s. Note that $n_{cr} > n_{cl,s}$, and hence the optical signal is confined in the waveguide core. In this work, we consider symmetric waveguides in which $n_{cl} = n_s$. Also, the waveguide core is from silicon (Si) while the cladding and substrate are from silicon dioxide (SiO_2). According to Fig. 1(a), the strip waveguide has a width of w and a thickness of t. Similarly, the ridge waveguide, indicated in Fig. 1(b), has a slab with a thickness of t_{sl}, as well as a ridge with a width of w and a thickness of t_r on the top (i.e., $t = t_{sl} + t_r$ and $t_r > t_{sl}$). Note that the etching depth and the SOI thickness determine t_r (and hence t_{sl}) and t, respectively.

One of the major parameters that determines different characteristics of optical waveguides is the effective index. The effective index quantifies the overall phase delay per unit length in a waveguide, relative to the phase delay in vacuum [7]. It highly depends on the optical wavelength and the dimensions of the waveguide. Given the original dimensions of an optical waveguide (w and t in Fig. 1), the effective index can be calculated as:

$$n_{eff}(\lambda, w, t) = \frac{\beta(\lambda, w, t)\lambda}{2\pi}, \quad (1)$$

in which λ is the optical wavelength. Also, β is the propagation constant of the optical mode, which we define shortly, in the waveguide that determines how the amplitude and phase of the light varies along the propagation direction. Numerical solutions of β in strip and ridge waveguides can be obtained using various numerical methods.

The effective index in waveguides also depends on the waveguide mode in which the light propagates. A waveguide mode is a transversefi eld pattern that propagates along the waveguide without changing amplitude and polarization profiles [7]. For instance, based on (1) and employing MODE [10], which is a commercial-grade simulator eigenmode solver and propagator, Fig. 2 indicates the effective indices of different waveguide modes in a strip waveguide when the optical wavelength (λ) is 1550 nm, 200 nm $\leq w \leq$ 1000 nm, and t = 220 nm. As can be seen, two types of optical modes exist in the waveguide, including transverse electric (TE) and traverse magnetic (TM) modes. When the effective index of a mode is larger than the refractive index of the cladding/substrate (i.e., SiO_2 in Fig. 2), then the mode is guided (i.e., it propagates in the waveguide along its longitudinal direction). Based on Fig. 2, strip waveguides with $w <\approx$ 450 nm and t = 220 nm only supports a single mode (i.e., one TE and one TM mode, which are called the fundamental modes). Also, as the waveguide width increases (i.e., $w >\approx$ 450 nm), more optical modes are being excited in the waveguide (i.e., multi-mode waveguides). Similar trends can be observed for different optical modes in ridge waveguides.

2.2 MR-Based Add-Drop Filters and Switches

Strip waveguides can form passive MR-based add-dropfi lters, as shown in Fig. 1(c). Similarly, as depicted in Fig. 1(d), active MR-based switches can be constructed using ridge waveguides. Such devices canfi lter/switch an optical signal based on the resonant wavelength of the MR, λ_{MR}, and the wavelength of the input optical signal, λ: when $\lambda = \lambda_{MR}$, the optical signal is dropped from the input port towards the drop port (i.e., the MR is on resonance), while it propagates towards the through port when $\lambda \neq \lambda_{MR}$ (i.e., the MR is off resonance). It is worth mentioning that the optical characteristics of active MRs (e.g., the resonant wavelength) can be dynamically altered by changing their effective indices through the thermo-optic or electro-optic effects. For example, Fig. 1(e) indicates a P-N junction based structure doped on a ridge waveguide that can be used to apply a reverse biased voltage to change the resonant wavelength of the MR. We detail some of the common properties of passive and active MRs in the following.

An MR is on resonance when the wavelength of the input optical signal (λ) matches a whole number of times inside the optical length of the MR [4]:

$$\lambda_{MR}(\lambda, w, t) = \frac{n_{eff}(\lambda, w, t,).(2\pi r + 2l)}{m}, \quad (2)$$

in which λ_{MR} is the resonant wavelength, m is an integer number that denotes the order of the resonant mode, r is the MR radius, and l is the coupler length (see Fig. 1(c)). Process variations change the width, and hence the radius, as well as the thickness of MRs, and consequently, shift the resonant wavelength in such devices. We assume that the variations on the input waveguide and the MR are the same. Considering thefi rst order approximation of the waveguide dispersion [4], the resonant wavelength shift ($\Delta\lambda_{MR}$) in an MR under PV can be calculated as:

$$\Delta\lambda_{MR}(\lambda, w', t') = \frac{\Delta_{v_{w,t}} n_{eff}.\lambda}{n_{eff}(\lambda, w, t) - \lambda.\frac{\partial n_{eff}(\lambda, w, t)}{\partial \lambda}}. \quad (3)$$

Here, $w' = w \pm v_w$ and $t' = t \pm v_t$, where v_w and v_t are the variations in the waveguide width and thickness, respectively. Also, $\Delta_{v_{w,t}} n_{eff}$ denotes the effective index changes due to the waveguide width and thickness variations.

3 DeEPeR: ENHANCING PERFORMANCE AND RELIABILITY IN OINs

This section studies the design space of MRs under PV, and presents different design guidelines required to apply DeEPeR to OINs. Also, we experimentally validate DeEPeR using fabrication results in this section.

3.1 DeEPeR: MRs Design Space

DeEPeR studies the impact of the different design parameters in waveguides (i.e., w and t) on the resonant wavelength shift in MRs. As SOI wafers have a standard thickness (e.g., t = 220 or 300 nm [16]), t cannot be freely altered during the design, and $t_{r,sl}$ depends on the available etching depths in the fabrication. Nevertheless, the waveguide width can be determined during the design process. Based on (3), the resonant wavelength shift in MRs depends on the waveguide width (w). Therefore, DeEPeR explores how altering w impacts the resonant wavelength shift in MRs. Firstly, DeEPeR studies and distinguishes between the impacts of the waveguide width and the thickness variations on the resonant wavelength (i.e., resonant wavelength shift slopes in (4)). Secondly, considering these impacts altogether, DeEPeR evaluates the total resonant wavelength shift in MRs at different waveguide widths (see (5)).

Employing (3), we found out that the resonant wavelength in MRs changes almost linearly with the variations in the waveguide width and thickness. As a result, the resonant wavelength shift slope, when the waveguide width varies for example (i.e., $\frac{\partial\lambda_{MR}}{\partial w}$), can be approximated as:

$$\frac{\partial\lambda_{MR}}{\partial w} = \left|\frac{\Delta\lambda_{MR}(\lambda, w + v_w, t) - \Delta\lambda_{MR}(\lambda, w - v_w, t)}{2v_w}\right|. \quad (4)$$

Similarly, we can define $\frac{\partial\lambda_{MR}}{\partial t_{r,t}}$, which are the resonant wavelength shift slopes with respect to the variations in the ridge (v_{t_r}) and waveguide thickness (v_t). Note that v_{t_r} is related to the etching depth variations in the case of active MRs. Considering $\frac{\partial\lambda_{MR}}{\partial w, t_r, t}$, the total resonant wavelength shift ($\Delta^T\lambda_{MR}$), due to the variations in the width as well as ridge and waveguide thickness altogether, is defined as:

$$\Delta^T\lambda_{MRp/a}(\lambda, w', t') = \sigma_t\left(\frac{\partial\lambda_{MR}}{\partial w}\alpha_{p/a} + \frac{\partial\lambda_{MR}}{\partial t_r}\alpha_a + \frac{\partial\lambda_{MR}}{\partial t}\right). \quad (5)$$

Here, the subscripts p and a denote the use of passive and active MRs, respectively. Moreover, $\alpha_p = \frac{\sigma_w}{\sigma_t}$ is the ratio between the standard deviation associated with the waveguide width (i.e., σ_w) and thickness (i.e., σ_t) variations. Also, when using active MRs, we have $\alpha_a = \frac{\overline{\sigma}_{w,t_r}}{\sigma_t}$, in which $\overline{\sigma}_{w,t_r}$ is the arithmetic mean between σ_w and σ_{t_r}. Note that $\sigma_{w,t_r,t}$ can denote within-die, within-wafer, or wafer-to-wafer variations, and can be quantified through different fabrications or obtained from the fabrication vendor.

Employing (4) and MODE [10], we quantitatively simulate the resonant wavelength shift slopes for passive and active MRs in Figs. 3(a) and 3(b), respectively. Results are indicated for the fundamental TE mode (see Fig. 2). Also, we consider different waveguide widths (x-axis in thefi gures) while t = 220 nm, t_{sl} = 90 nm, and λ = 1550 nm. As can be seen, the impacts of waveguide width and thickness variations on the resonant wavelength shift in MRs are different. For example, passive MRs with $w >\approx 360$ nm (see Fig. 3(a)) are more tolerant against width variations compared with thickness variations. The fundamental mode confines better in the waveguide core as the waveguide width increases. As a result, the variations in the waveguide width have less impact on the TE mode distribution in wider waveguides, in which the impact of thickness variations is higher and dominant. Similar trends can be noticed in the case of active MRs, while such MRs are also sensitive to the variations in the ridge thickness (see $\frac{\partial\lambda_{MR}}{\partial t_r}$ in Fig. 3(b)).

Using (5), Fig. 3(c) indicates the total resonant wavelength shift ($\Delta^T\lambda_{MR}$) in passive and active MRs. Note that the z-axis denotes

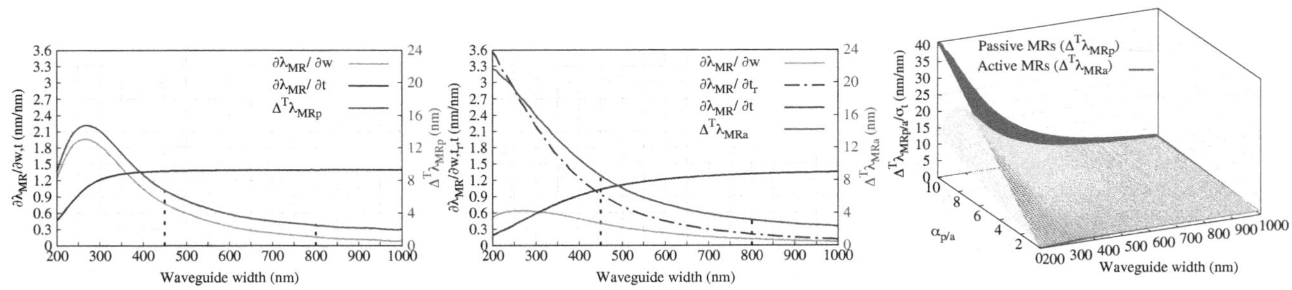

(a) $\Delta\lambda_{MR}$ slope in passive MRs (b) $\Delta\lambda_{MR}$ slope in active MRs (c) Total resonance shift ($\Delta^T\lambda_{MR}$)

Figure 3: (a) and (b): Resonant wavelength shift ($\Delta\lambda_{MR}$) slopes; and (c): the total resonant wavelength shift ($\Delta^T\lambda_{MR}$) in passive and active MRs for different waveguide widths (t = 220 nm, t_{sl} = 90 nm, and λ = 1550 nm).

$\frac{\Delta^T\lambda_{MR}}{\sigma_t}$. As can be seen, $\Delta^T\lambda_{MRp/a}$ highly depends on the MR waveguide width as well as $\alpha_{p/a}$. Given an $\alpha_{p/a}$, the total resonant wavelength shift decreases with an increase in the waveguide width due to the better confinement of the fundamental mode. For example, Figs. 3(a) and 3(b) depict the total resonant wavelength shift (green lines) in, respectively, passive ($\Delta^T\lambda_{MRp}$) and active ($\Delta^T\lambda_{MRa}$) MRs when σ_w = 7 nm, σ_{t_r} = 5 nm, and σ_t = 1 nm [16], and hence α_p = 7 and α_a = 6. As can be seen, $\Delta^T\lambda_{MRp/a}$ drops as the waveguide width increases, and this reduction is significant when 200 nm $\leq w <$ 450 nm and it further improves for $w >$ 450 nm (the waveguide transits from single-mode to multimode when $w >\approx$ 450 nm). Given a waveguide width in Fig. 3(c), $\Delta^T\lambda_{MRp/a}$ rises with an increase in $\alpha_{p/a}$. When $\alpha_{p/a}$ increases, more variations are introduced to the MRs, resulting in a higher total resonant wavelength shift. A wider waveguide can be employed to compensate for such higher variations.

3.2 DeEPeR: Design Guidelines

This section summarizes different steps required to apply DeEPeR to OINs. Based on Fig. 3, the impact of waveguide width variations is negligible when the waveguides are wide enough. Moreover, thickness variations, which become steady as w increases (see Figs. 3(a) and 3(b)), are the dominant contributor to the resonant wavelength shift. Also, the total resonant wavelength shift is higher for $w <\approx$ 450 nm and its improvement is negligible when $w >\approx$ 800 nm (i.e., increasing the waveguide width barely affects the resonant wavelength shift). Therefore, depending on the expected range of variations ($\alpha_{p/a}$ in Fig. 3(c)), designers can employ DeEPeR to optimize MRs design, minimizing $\Delta^T\lambda_{MR}$ based on 450 nm $\leq w \leq$ 800 nm (when t = 220 nm), and $\kappa \geq \kappa'$, where κ' is a minimum coupling required in the MR under design (step 1). Note that the cross-over coupling (κ) can be improved considering different gaps and coupler lengths in the MR (g and l in Fig. 1).

Waveguides with $w >\approx$ 450 nm support multiple optical modes (see Fig. 2). While multi-mode waveguides could be used for mode-division multiplexing (MDM) in OINs, WDM-based OINs are very often designed for a single mode operation. Avoiding the excitation of higher order modes when using DeEPeR, we propose employing waveguide tapers (see Fig. 5) when applying DeEPeR to OINs (step 2). Using a waveguide taper to connect two waveguides with different widths of w_1 and w_2, where $w_2 > w_1$, the taper length, L_t, should be long enough to avoid sudden changes in the waveguide width, and hence avoid exciting higher-order modes in the wider waveguide. We numerically simulated waveguides of different widths in MODE [10], and found out that considering L_t(in μm)= $\lfloor \frac{w_2-w_1}{100\ nm} \rfloor \times 10\ \mu$m can safely avoid exciting higher-order modes when connecting waveguides of different widths. Moreover, waveguide tapers are required when entering and exiting waveguide bendings (higher-order modes can be excited in wide waveguides as they bend). Also, MR structures can be engineered to mitigate the impact of higher-order modes [11]. Finally, when using DeEPeR, designers need to leave enough space for routing as well as for electrical contacts (for active MRs).

3.3 DeEPeR: Fabrication and Validation

We designed two passive MR-based add-dropfi lters to experimentally validate DeEPeR and demonstrate its efficiency. Ten identical copies of the designed layout, shown in Fig. 4(a), were placed on a 1.2×0.8 mm^2 chip fabricated by the Electron Beam (EBeam) Lithography facility at Applied NanoTools Incorporation. Each device is connected to three grating couplers designed for 1550 nm TE operation. Conventional 500 nm×220 nm strip waveguides are used for routing. According to step 1, we assess the impact of DeEPeR on $\Delta^T\lambda_{MR}$ at the proposed w range lower and upper bounds. As a result, in MR1 (without DeEPeR) indicated in Fig. 4(a), we consider 220 nm thick SOI strip waveguides with a 400 nm width connected to a TE polarization MR with a 6.1 μm radius, and a coupler length and gap (l and g in Fig. 1(c)) of 2 μm and 200 nm, respectively. Considering MR2 (with DeEPeR) in Fig. 4(a), the waveguide width increases to 800 nm, and the coupler length and the gap in the MR change to, respectively, 6 μm and 100 nm, in order to improve the coupling between the input waveguide and the MR. Both MRs have a free-spectral range (FSR), which is the spacing between two consecutive resonances, of 12 nm, and are designed to resonate at 1550 nm. The MRs are placed as close as possible on the chip (i.e., 3 μm, the minimum distance allowed in the fabrication) to make sure they experience similar variations. Several waveguide tapers are considered in the layout to avoid exciting higher-order modes as well as terminating optical waveguides.

We carefully tested all the MRs (ten identical copies per each MR) and the measured through and drop port responses around 1550 nm are indicated in Fig. 4(b) for MR1 and MR2. The resonant peaks (ten per each MR) are specified as circles in Fig. 4(b). During

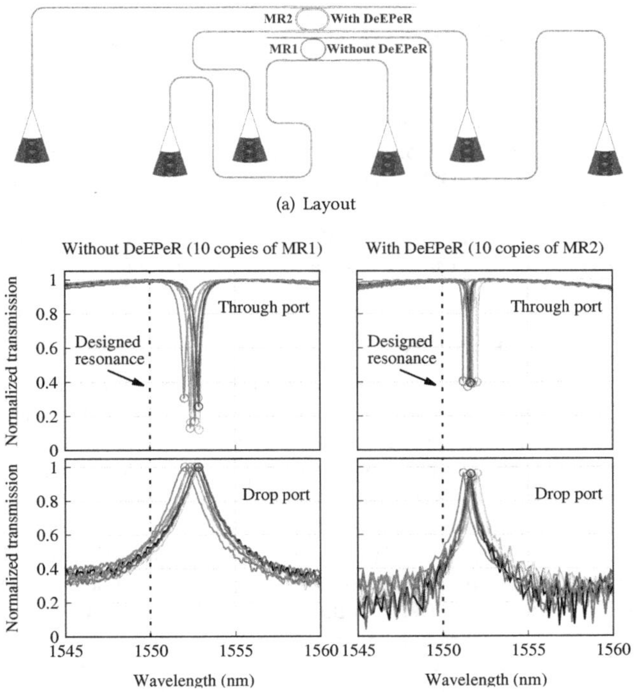

(a) Layout

(b) Measured through and drop port responses

Figure 4: (a) Layout of the fabricated MRs; and (b): measured through and drop port responses of the fabricated MRs without and with using DeEPeR.

the test, the chip was located on a thermal heater to eliminate thermal variations. As can be seen, the resonant peaks are much closer to the designed resonance (i.e., 1550 nm) in case of using DeEPeR. On average, the total resonant wavelength shift without using DeEPeR (MR1) is 2.6 nm, and it reduces to 1.6 nm when DeEPeR is applied (MR2). In the best-case, the shift is only 1 nm when DeEPeR is employed, while it is as worse as 3 nm without using DeEPeR, indicating the advantage of using DeEPeR. Note that the measured drop port response in MR2 is slightly noisier due to a weaker coupling between the input waveguide and MR2, which can be further improved by using a longer (smaller) coupler (gap) in MR2. Nevertheless, a good Lorentzian response is captured. The data from the fabrication vendor indicates that the within-wafer σ_t and σ_w are 10 nm and 5 nm, respectively (i.e., $\alpha_p = 0.5 < 1$). Based on Fig. 3(c), when $\alpha_p < 1$, $\Delta^T \lambda_{MRp}$ slightly improves when w increases from 400 nm (in MR1) to 800 nm (in MR2). It is worth mentioning that the fabrication cost is related to the chip exposure area in mm^2, and hence employing DeEPeR to partially increase the waveguides widths (i.e., a few hundred nms) has a negligible impact on the fabrication cost.

4 CASE STUDY AND RESULTS

This section explores the impact of DeEPeR on OINs at the system-level. We consider a case study of a general passive WDM-based OIN in MPSoCs, shown in Fig. 5, supporting n different wavelengths, and hence n processing cores. The case study represents an interconnect with several wavelength-selective optical switches ($n \times m$ in our model) and photodetectors (PDs, n PDs in our model) between two arbitrary processing cores in any passive WDM-based OIN. For simplicity, we explore the impact of PV on passive devices, and similar studies can be performed for the case of active devices. In Fig. 5, the source processing core P_a is communicating with the destination processing core P_b through the optical wavelength λ_i. The electrical-optical (E-O) interface is responsible for modulating the optical signal. When the optical signal on the wavelength λ_i matches the resonant wavelength of MR_i (i.e., $\lambda_i = \lambda_{MRi}$ in Fig. 5), it couples to that MR and proceeds to the next switching stage (m switching stages in total), while it passes the MRs whose resonant wavelengths are different. Ultimately, it is detected at the PDs located at the end of the communication line in the optical-electrical (O-E) interface.

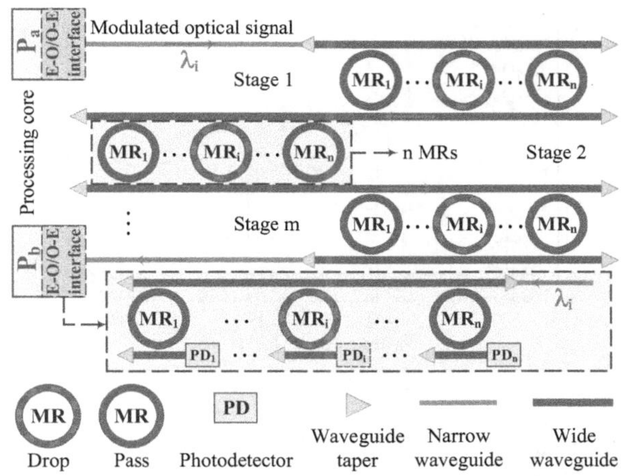

Figure 5: An overview of the general passive WDM-based OIN supporting n optical wavelengths and employing DeEPeR.

When optical signals are passing MRs, they suffer from some power loss and some crosstalk noise can be accumulated on the desired optical signal as well [2]. Also, PV shift the resonant wavelengths of the MRs, resulting in extra power loss and, most importantly, extra crosstalk noise. MRs with shifted resonant wavelengths drop fractions of the desired optical signal power, all of which can be accumulated at the PDs as crosstalk. In this paper, we consider thefi rst-order in-band coherent crosstalk that cannot befi ltered. Considering the desired optical signal power and the interfering crosstalk noise power received at the PDs (before detection), the OSNR associated with the optical wavelength λ_i can be defined as (in dB):

$$OSNR(\lambda_i, w', t') = 10 \log_{10} \frac{S_p(\lambda_i, w', t')}{N_p(\lambda_i, w', t')}, \quad (6)$$

where S_p and N_p are, respectively, the desired optical signal power and the crosstalk noise power received at the PD_i. We study the impact of DeEPeR on the OSNR as it determines the received optical signal quality and also the BER in a system, and hence the performance and reliability.

We consider $n = m = 4$ (see Fig. 5) with passive MRs of radii 5 μm and couplers with a length of 2 μm, and hence an FSR of 15 nm. Each MR's radius is slightly different to cover the whole wavelength range. Furthermore, $\lambda = 1550$ nm and $g = 200$ nm (see Fig. 1(c)).

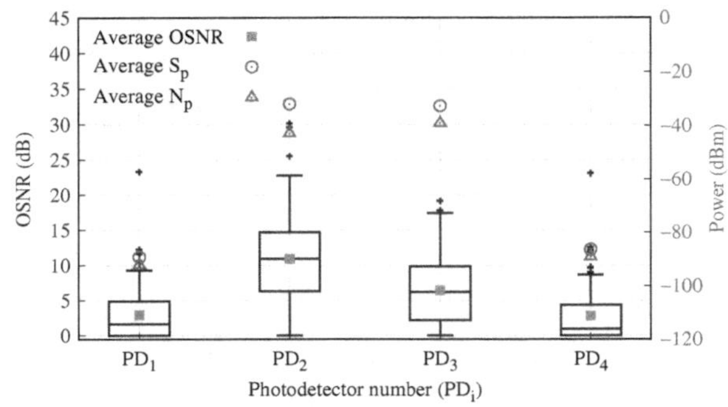

(a) Without DeEPeR (w = 400 nm)

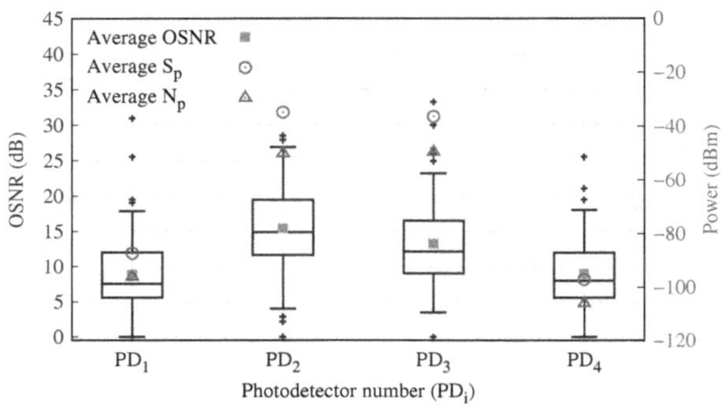

(b) With DeEPeR (w = 800 nm)

Figure 6: The OSNR as well as the average desired signal and crosstalk noise power calculated at different PDs in the general passive WDM-based OIN in Fig. 5 without and with using DeEPeR (t = 220 nm).

A channel spacing of 4 nm is assumed: $\lambda_1 = \lambda_{MR1} = 1550$ nm and $\lambda_4 = \lambda_{MR4} = 1562$ nm. The laser output optical power in the E-O interface is 0 dBm, and the chip size is 1 cm^2 (for propagation loss analysis). Also, an average propagation loss of 2 dB/cm is considered when using narrow and wide waveguides. Considering $\sigma_w = 7$ nm and $\sigma_t = 1$ nm [16] (see Section 3.1), and based on a normal distribution, we randomly generate 100 PV maps, each of which has 20 points ($n = 4 \times m = 4$ and four MRs connected to the PDs), and apply them to the OIN in Fig. 5. DeEPeR is implemented in our in-house simulator, which is also used to calculate the resonant wavelength shift in the MRs and also S_p and N_p (see(6)) received at each PD (before detection).

Fig. 6 depicts the OSNR (box-plots) at each photodetector (x-axis) in the OIN without and with employing DeEPeR when t = 220 nm. Similar to the fabrication, we consider w = 400 nm and w = 800 nm in Figs. 6(a) and 6(b), respectively. As can be seen, the OSNR at each PD increases when using DeEPeR: the average OSNR over all the PDs equals 5.8 dB without using DeEPeR, and it increases to 11.7 dB when DeEPeR is applied (i.e., almost 6 dB improvement). When using DeEPeR, the resonant wavelength shifts in the MRs at different stages are smaller, resulting in a lower crosstalk being accumulated on the desired optical signal, and hence a higher OSNR (see (6)). Considering Figs. 6(a) and 6(b), the average crosstalk power (N_p) is reduced by 9.8 dB when using DeEPeR. Also, when using DeEPeR, the average optical signal power (S_p) calculated at different PDs decreases, indicating some power penalty in the system (i.e., 3.9 dB average power loss when using DeEPeR). This power loss is due to a reduction in the dropped power in the MRs when using DeEPeR, which can be mitigated through further optimizing the MRs design (e.g., employing a longer (smaller) coupler (gap)). Note that the average power loss without considering PD_4 in Fig. 6 is only 1.5 dB. The results in this section indicate that employing DeEPeR considerably improves the OSNR in OINs, and hence their performance and reliability under PV. Also, DeEPeR helps reduce the tuning power required for correcting faulty MRs as their resonant wavelengths are closer to the designed resonances when DeEPeR is employed (see Fig. 4(b)).

5 CONCLUSION

We present DeEPeR, an efficient device-level design method that explores the design space of MRs to improve the performance and reliability in optical interconnects. The analytical models as well as the design guidelines required to apply DeEPeR to OINs are proposed. DeEPeR is experimentally evaluated through fabricating several MRs, in which the resonant wavelength shifts are reduced when using DeEPeR. As a system-level case study, we apply DeEPeR to a general passive WDM-based OIN, and we indicate that it considerably improves the OSNR in the system (almost 6 dB on average). Results of this work help system designers better understand the impact of MRs design space on realizing high-performance and reliable OINs for MPSoCs.

ACKNOWLEDGMENT

The authors acknowledge NSERC, and the Silicon Electronic-Photonic Integrated Circuits (Si-EPIC) program for the fabrication and automated measurements.

REFERENCES

[1] Y. Arakawa et al. 2013. Silicon Photonics for Next Generation System Integration Platform. *IEEE Communications Magazine* 51, 3 (2013), 72–77.
[2] M. Bahadori et al. 2016. Crosstalk Penalty in Microring-Based Silicon Photonic Interconnect Systems. *IEEE JLT* 34, 17 (2016), 4043–4052.
[3] R. G. Beausoleil et al. 2011. Devices and Architectures for Large-Scale Integrated Silicon Photonics Circuits. *Proceeding of SPIE* 7942 (2011), 794204–1–794204–6.
[4] W. Bogaerts et al. 2012. Silicon Microring Resonators. *Laser and Photonics Reviews* 6, 1 (2012), 47–73.
[5] S. V. R. Chittamuru et al. 2016. PICO: Mitigating Heterodyne Crosstalk Due to Process Variations and Intermodulation Effects in Photonic NoCs. In *DAC*. 1–6.
[6] L. Chrostowski et al. 2014. Impact of Fabrication Non-Uniformity on Chip-Scale Silicon Photonic Integrated Circuits. In *OFC*. Th2A.37.
[7] L. Chrostowski et al. 2015. *Silicon Photonics Design from Devices to Systems*. Cambridge University Press.
[8] Y. Kokubun et al. 2010. UV Trimming of Polarization-Independent Microring Resonator by Internal Stress and Temperature Control. *Optical Express* 18, 2 (2010), 906–916.
[9] Z. Li et al. 2012. Reliability Modeling and Management of Nanophotonic On-Chip Networks. *IEEE TVLSI* 20, 1 (2012), 98–111.
[10] Lumerical Solutions Inc. 2017. Lumerical MODE. (2017). http://www.lumerical.com/tcad-products/mode/
[11] Y. Luo et al. 2016. A Process-Tolerant Ring Modulator Based on Multi-Mode Waveguides. *IEEE Photonics Technology Letters* 28, 13 (2016), 1391–1394.
[12] M. Mohamed et al. 2014. Reliability-Aware Design Flow for Silicon Photonics On-Chip Interconnect. *IEEE TVLSI* 22, 8 (2014), 1763–1776.
[13] M. Nikdast et al. 2016. Chip-Scale Silicon Photonic Interconnects: A Formal Study on Fabrication Non-Uniformity. *IEEE JLT* 34, 16 (2016), 3682–3695.
[14] M. Nikdast et al. 2016. Modeling Fabrication Non-Uniformity in Chip-Scale Silicon Photonic Interconnects. In *DATE*. 115–120.
[15] X. Wu et al. 2014. SUOR: Sectioned Undirectional Optical Ring for Chip Multiprocessor. *ACM J. Emerg. Technol. Comput. Syst.* 10, 4 (2014), 29:1–29:25.
[16] D. X. Xu et al. 2014. Silicon Photonic Integration Platform - Have We Found the Sweet Spot? *IEEE J. Sel. Topics Quantum Electron.* 20, 4 (2014), 189–205.

A 0.24pJ/bit, 16Gbps OOK Transmitter Circuit in 45-nm CMOS for Inter and Intra-Chip Wireless Interconnects

Tanmay Shinde
Rochester Institute of Technology
NY – 14623 USA
tvs6972@rit.edu

Suryanarayanan Subramaniam
Rochester Institute of Technology
NY – 14623 USA
ss4050@rit.edu

Padmanabh Deshmukh
Rochester Institute of Technology
NY – 14623 USA
psd9321@rit.edu

M Meraj Ahmed
Rochester Institute of Technology
NY – 14623 USA
ma9205@rit.edu

Mark Indovina
Rochester Institute of Technology
NY – 14623 USA
maieee@rit.edu

Amlan Ganguly
Rochester Institute of Technology
NY – 14623 USA
axgeec@rit.edu

ABSTRACT

Research in recent years has demonstrated that intra and inter-chip wireless interconnects are capable of establishing energy-efficient data communications within as well as between multiple chips. This paper presents a circuit level design of an energy-efficient millimeter wave (mm-wave) on-off keying (OOK) transmitter suitable for such wireless interconnects in 45-nm CMOS process. The transmitter consists of an NMOS cross-coupled VCO, an OOK modulator and a power amplifier. The transmitter is able to achieve maximum modulation data rate of 16Gb/s at 60GHz with the output power of -3dBm consuming a total power of 3.9mW, which translates to a bit-energy efficiency of 0.24pJ/bit.

KEYWORDS

Wireless interconnect, mm-wave, transmitter, VCO, OOK modulator, power amplifier, transformer neutralization

ACM Reference Format:
T. Shinde, S. Subramaniam, P. Deshmukh, M. M. Ahmed, M. Indovina and A. Ganguly. 2018. A 0.24pJ/bit, 16Gbps OOK Transmitter Circuit in 45-nm CMOS for Inter and Intra-Chip Wireless Interconnects. In *GLSVLSI '18: 2018 Great Lakes Symposium on VLSI*, May 23–25, 2018, Chicago, IL, USA. ACM, NY, NY, USA, 6 pages. https://doi.org/10.1145/3194554.3194575

1 INTRODUCTION

To keep up with the demands in computation and communication of platform based computing devices like micro-servers or embedded systems with multiple multicore chips both on-chip and chip-to-chip communication infrastructures have been evolving at a rapid pace. However, recent trends according to the International Technology Roadmap for Semiconductors (ITRS) predict that the pitch of the I/O interconnects in ICs is not scaling as fast as the gate lengths or pitch of on-chip interconnects. This implies a gap in density and performance of traditional I/O systems relative to on-chip interconnections [1]. The wiring complexity of both intra and inter-chip interconnects poses design challenges, crosstalk and signal integrity issues. This has led to the exploration of novel interconnect technologies like photonic interconnect [2] and wireless interconnects [3] as an energy efficient solution for inter and intra-chip data communication. Long-range wireless transmitters and receivers (transceivers) operating in the millimeter-wave (mm-wave) frequencies [4] do not require laying out of physical interconnects making them suitable for a variety of application domains such as embedded system platforms, servers, wearable or flexible electronic devices as well as IoT devices. In addition, such mm-wave transceivers and antennas are designed in CMOS-compatible processes, solutions to the wired interconnect problem. Research in recent years has demonstrated that on-chip and off-chip wireless interconnects are capable of establishing radio communications within a chip as well as between multiple chips and are shown to improve system-level energy efficiency and bandwidth of inter and intra-chip data communications by avoiding or eliminating data communication over long multihop wired paths [3].

For computing platforms with multiple chips, an energy efficient, high bandwidth interconnect fabric is desirable. A multi-gigabit wireless channel has the potential to provide such high performance with high energy efficiency [5]. However, the constant need for lower energy expenditure in data transfer between chips motivates newer designs. Moreover, to be compatible for integration with current and future technology nodes the transceivers need to be designed in advanced technology nodes. This poses a problem to the design of power-efficient circuits as advanced technologies operate in low rail

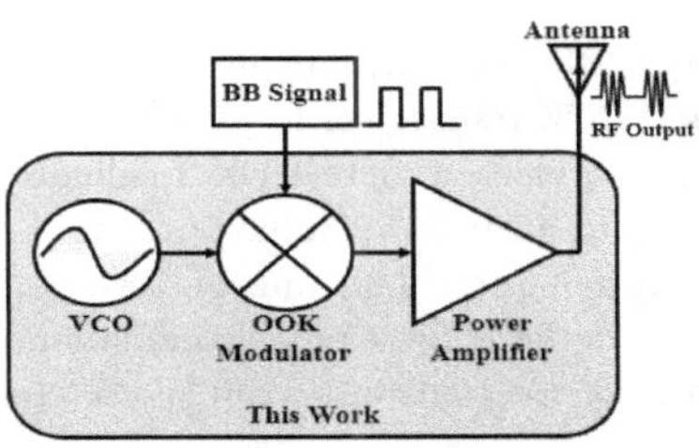

Figure 1: Proposed block diagram of the OOK

GLSVLSI '18, May 16–18, 2018, Chicago, IL, USA

ACM ISBN 978-1-4503-5724-1/18/05...$15.00
https://doi.org/10.1145/3194554.3194575

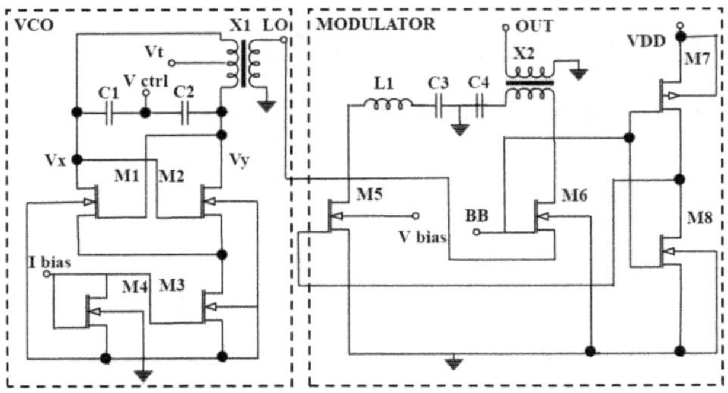

X1, X2	M1n, M2n	M3n	M4n	M5n, M6n
1:1, 1:1.5	6um/65nm	60um/65nm	1um/65nm	2.25um/45nm
M7p	**M8n**	**C1, C2**	**C3, C4**	**L1**
480nm/45nm	450nm/45nm	10fF	20.1fF	350pH

Figure 2: Schematic and component values of the proposed OOK modulator with NMOS cross-coupled

voltages which makes achieving high voltage swings at the output of the transmitter challenging. Therefore in our work we present the circuit design of an ultra-low power CMOS compatible 16Gbps mm-wave transmitter at 60GHz in 45nm technology node for inter and intra-chip wireless communication. We adopt On-Off Keying (OOK) as the modulation mechanism for its simplicity and low power consumption although it has the lowest bandwidth efficiency. The transmitter proposed in this work consists of 60GHz Voltage Controlled Oscillator (VCO), an OOK modulator and a power amplifier (PA) as shown in Fig. 1.

2 RELATED WORK

In [5], a 60GHz OOK transmitter that employed a five stage CS power amplifier have been proposed. Though the transmitter provided high amplification gain, it came with a cost of increased power dissipation and overall noise due to higher number of components. An energy dissipation of 114pJ/bit along with low data rate of 2.5Gbps over a 40mm communication range made the transmitter inefficient for future low power high performance intra and inter-chip communication. A 9.5pJ/bit, 6Gbps ASK transmitter operating at 43GHz was proposed in [6]. However, the use of Si-Ge process makes the integration of this transceiver circuit with a standard CMOS chip challenging. In [7] a data rate of 11Gbps with 10^{-11} Bit Error Rate (BER) was achieved with a cost of 6.4pJ/bit energy efficiency for the transmitter designed in 40nm node. However, the transmitter communication was limited to 14mm and therefore cannot be used for energy efficient chip-to-chip communication. In [8], author proposed OOK transceiver for on-chip communication as the transmitter provides 60GHz OOK modulation at 3.5Gbps maximum data rate. In [9], the author proposed a multi modal transmitter with a highest data rate of 20Gbps for free space communication. As the highest reliable communication distance was limited to 5mm, the transmitter can be used only for on-chip communication. The work proposed in [10] demonstrated a transmitter suitable for a maximum communicating distance of 100mm at 10.7Gbps data rate with 3.45pJ/bit efficiency. However the transmitter design was faced with the challenge of integrating the on-board Yagi-Uda antenna on a non-silicon substrate. An OOK transmitter capable of communicating within a range of 20mm with a BER of 10^{-15} and having an energy efficiency of 1.2pj/bit and 16Gbps data rate has been proposed in [11] as a solution for on-chip communication. However, its performance for chip-to-chip communication is not evaluated. In this work, we present the design of an OOK transmitter circuit for intra-chip as well as long range inter-chip communication for future high performance multichip computing platforms.

3 OOK TRANSMITTER

The scenario of inter-chip and intra-chip wireless mm-wave links requires extremely low energy consumption to be competitive with high-speed serial I/O and other emerging technologies like photonic interconnects. Therefore, an OOK transmitter is preferred for its energy-efficiency. Fig. 1 shows the block diagram of proposed OOK transmitter consisting of a VCO, modulator and PA. In this section we discuss the design approaches for these components of the 60GHz OOK transmitter.

3.1 Voltage Controlled Oscillator

The VCO is responsible for generating the 60GHz RF carrier wave for the OOK modulator. The maximum single-ended voltage swing with minimum phase noise can be achieved by an NMOS cross-coupled VCO as it has comparatively less phase noise compared to the other oscillators such as ring or LC oscillator [12]. Moreover, it takes less active area compared to Colpitts oscillator. In addition to providing a higher output swing, this design also supports wide tuning range. In the cross coupled NMOS oscillator shown in Fig 2, the positive feedback is given via the M1, M2 transistors and the LC tank circuit. Each of the transistors creates a 180° phase shift at its output. The control voltage i.e. V_{ctrl} is set at 100mV and given to both the capacitors as shown in Fig. 2. Current biasing is used for the VCO and the required current is generated via a simple NMOS current mirror for a reference input of 10uA. The startup time is a critical part in the oscillator design. To avoid the startup time from limiting the data rate we do not use the VCO as a modulator. Therefore, the output of the VCO, the Local Oscillator (LO) signal, is coupled to a separate OOK modulator input via a transformer, X1 with a 1:1 turns ratio to ensure symmetrical swing at the input of the modulator. We adopt transformer matching technique as it reduces overall power consumption by eliminating buffers or coupling capacitors. The two transistors of the VCO, M1 and M2, form a differential pair where only one of them is on at a given time degrading the trans-conductance of the pair. Therefore, we increase the width of the transistors M1 and M2 sufficiently, to provide high trans-conductance and drive the OOK modulator.

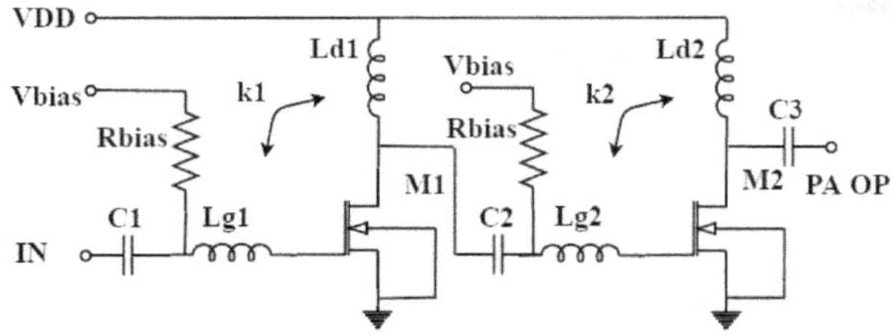

M1n, M2n	Ld1	Ld2	Lg1
10um/90nm	350pH	420pH	600pH
Lg2	**C1**	**C2, C3**	**k1, k2**
350pH	1pF	14fF	0.088, 0.128

Figure 3: Schematic and component values of the proposed power amplifier.

3.2 OOK Modulator

The design of a modulator for high speed inter and intra-chip communication poses a significant challenge on the energy efficiency of the transmitter as power consumption increases with data rate. In the proposed modulator shown in Fig. 2, the modulating M6 NMOS transistor is driven by the Base Band signal (BB). The BB signal turns on and off M6 by charging up the gate terminals above the threshold voltage V_{th} of the NMOS transistor. For logic HIGH at BB, NMOS M6 gets switched on and it passes the LO signal connected to the source of M6 towards its drain and the primary winding of the transformer X2. Effectively, M6 works a pass transistor, passing the carrier signal from its source to drain when the BB signal is logic HIGH and blocking it when the BB signal is logic LOW. When BB signal has a logic LOW value, all charge across primary side of X2 needs to be discharged. This charge gets discharged through NMOS transistor M5. Similar to the transformer X1 coupling the VCO to the modulator, another 1:1.5 transformer, X2 is designed to obtain single ended output from the modulator and for impedance matching of the modulator output with the input of the PA. The primary side of transformer X2 is connected to ground through capacitor C4. Capacitor C4 and C3 cancels the effect of the imaginary part of the impedance due to the inductor coil of the transformer. The body biasing technique is used with NMOS M5 for adjusting the threshold voltage to get symmetrical signal across 0V at the secondary coil of X2.

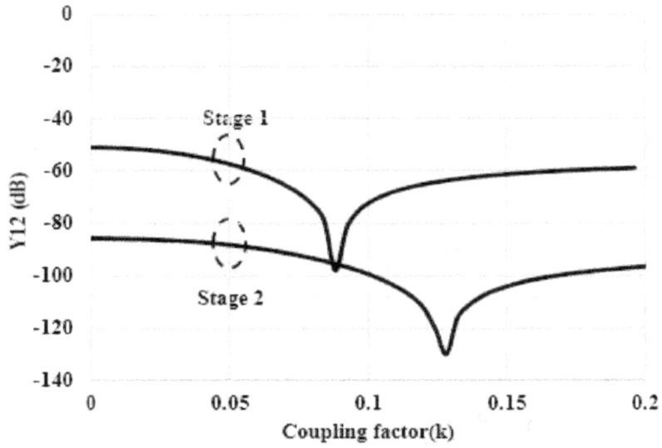

Figure 4: Simulated Y_{12} for PA versus coupling factor,

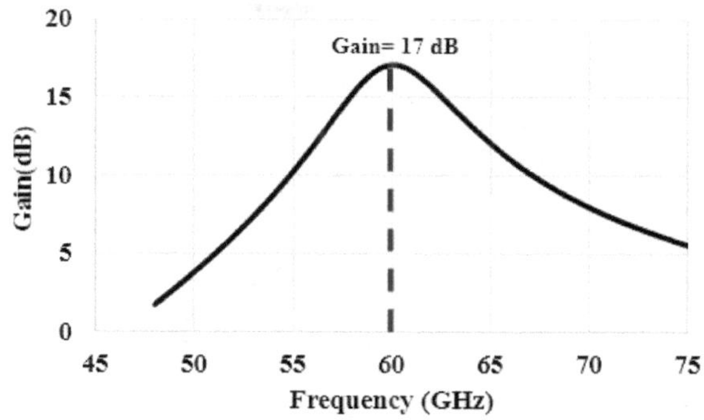

Figure 5: Simulated VCO gain.

3.3 Two Stage PA

In the transmitter, power amplifier is one of the power-hungry blocks that affects the overall efficiency of the transmitter. Cascode structures, which are commonly used to obtain high gains at lower frequencies, are not suitable for high frequency applications as the parasitic capacitances become dominant and the stacking of transistors reduces the voltage headroom in advanced technology nodes operating at low rail voltages [13]. Therefore, in our design, a two-stage Common Source (CS) topology is used as shown in Fig. 3 as it provides high frequency response and larger voltage swing compared to cascode designs. At high frequency of operation, degradation in the performance of power amplifier is caused by the drain-to-gate parasitic capacitor C_{gd}, which introduces a direct signal path between output and input. This drain-to-gate feedback degrades reverse isolation and can directly lead to instability of the amplifier. Moreover, as any change in output impedance affects the input impedance through C_{gd}, it significantly affects frequency response and output impedance matching of the transmitter. The two-stage PA proposed in this work uses a CS topology with drain-to-gate transformer-feedback neutralization technique which creates an additional signal path that neutralizes the current flow through C_{gd} [11] . The transformers are formed using inductors at the gate and drain terminals of M1 (Lg1 & Ld1) and M2 (Lg2 & Ld2) as shown in Fig. 3 with coupling factors, k1 and k2 respectively. The values of the coupling factors are chosen such that they minimize the reverse transformation of the two stages of the amplifier, $Y_{12} = \frac{I_{gs}}{V_{ds}}\Big|V_{in} = 0$. Fig. 4 plots the Y_{12} for the two CS stages of the PA and shows that the optimal values of the coupling factors, k1 and k2 are 0.088 and 0.128 respectively. The inductors Ld1 and Ld2 at the drain of the transistors M1 and M2 resonate with the drain capacitances. This increases the overall gain and bandwidth at the center frequency. Transistor M1 and M2 are biased using a voltage divider based biasing circuit. To complete the biasing, the DC blocking capacitor C1 and C2 are placed to prevent the upsetting of the gate to source bias of M1 and M2. The value of C1 is chosen to be 1pF. C2 and C3 cancels imaginary impedance effect of drain inductors Ld1 and Ld2 on the output side of both stages. Hence, it has negligible reactance at the center frequency. The output of the power amplifier is matched with 50Ohms by using L match impedance matching technique.

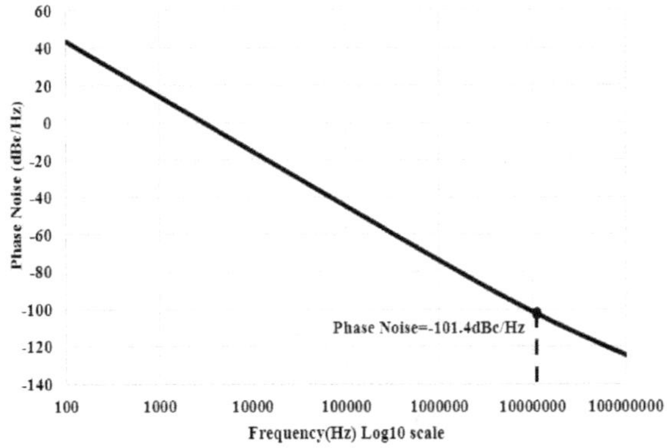

Figure 6: Simulated phase noise of VCO.

4 RESULTS AND SIMULATION

The proposed transmitter is designed in 45nm CMOS technology and the simulation is carried out using Cadence Virtuoso Analog Design Environment (ADE). In this section we present the characterization of the VCO, the modulator, the PA and the overall OOK transmitter.

4.1 Characterization of the VCO

In this section, we characterize the VCO for frequency response and phase noise. We consider the frequency range from 45GHz to 75GHz for the characterization of the VCO. Fig. 5 shows the frequency response of the VCO. From the figure, it can be observed that a peak-gain of 17dB is achieved for the VCO centered at 60GHz signifying a carrier frequency of 60GHz. Since the oscillator needs to be triggered initially for its proper functionality in the simulation environment, one of the tank capacitors was initialized with 1nV.

The frequency stability is an important concern for the VCO and ideally, it should be immune to the random frequency fluctuations. The measure of these fluctuations is characterized by the phase noise. Phase noise is defined as the ratio of power in one phase modulation sideband per Hz bandwidth, at an offset of f Hz away from the carrier, to the total signal power. The

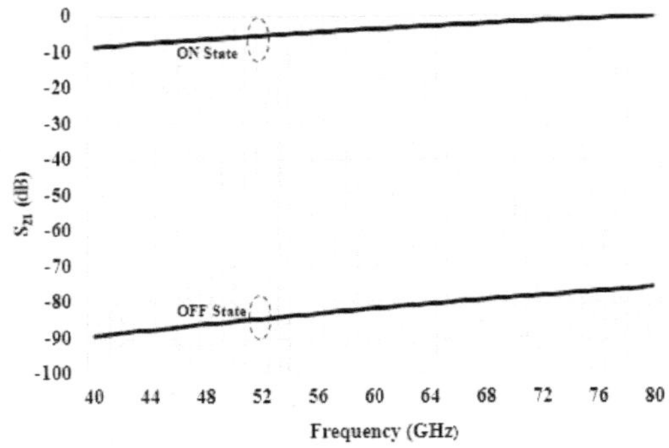

Figure 7: Simulated On-Off gain of the OOK

phase noise evaluated at an offset of 10MHz is -101.4dBc/Hz as shown in Fig. 6. The VCO consumes a maximum steady-state current of 1.1mA from a 1V supply.

4.2 Characterization of the OOK Modulator

An ideal OOK modulator should not have any output power in the off-state (when the BB input is logic LOW). However, due to non-ideal effects such as leakage, the output power is not completely zero in the off-state. Therefore, a high on-off gain is desirable for reliable detection at an OOK receiver. Here, we characterize our OOK modulator in terms of the on-off steady-state gain. The on-off steady-state gain can be defined as the difference between the steady-state gains of the modulator for the two valid logic levels of the BB input. At 60GHz the modulator has an "on" and "off" state gain of -3.6dB and -81.6dB respectively as shown in Fig. 7. Therefore, the on-off steady state gain is above 78dB for the frequency ranges from 45GHz to 75GHz. With this gain the valid logic levels can be detected with a transmitter output power penalty of less than 1dB [11].

4.3 Characterization of the PA

In this section, we characterize the PA in the OOK transmitter in terms of S-parameters, and Power Added Efficiency (PAE). First, we extract the S-parameter of the PA. At high frequencies i.e.

Table 1: Performance Comparison of mm-wave OOK Transmitter

References	This Work	[11] *	[7] *	[6] *	[10] *	[5] *	[8] *
Technology node	45-nm CMOS	65-nm CMOS	40-nm CMOS	180-nm SiGe	90-nm CMOS	90nm CMOS	90nm CMOS
Carrier Frequency	60GHz	60GHz	57GHz	43GHz	60GHz	60GHz	60GHz
Modulation	OOK	OOK	ASK	ASK	OOK	OOK	OOK
Maximum Data Rate	16Gb/s	16Gb/s	11Gb/s	6Gb/s	10.7Gb/s	2.5Gb/s	3.5Gb/s
Power Consumption	3.9mW	19mW	29mW	57mW	31.mW	183mW	156mW
Supply Voltage	1V	1V	1.1V	1.6V	0.8/1.8V	1.2V	N/A
RF output P1dB	-3dBm	1.5dBm	-2dBm	-1.5dBm	5.1dBm	5dBm	2dBm
Bit-Energy Efficiency	0.24pJ/bit	1.2pJ/bit	2.6pJ/bit	9.5pJ/bit	2.9pJ/bit	73.2pJ/bit	44.6pJ/bit
Active-Foot Print	N/A	0.077mm^2	0.06mm^2	0.25mm^2	0.15mm^2	0.43mm^2	N/A
FoM	2.055	1.19	0.24	0.07	1.12	0.04	0.04

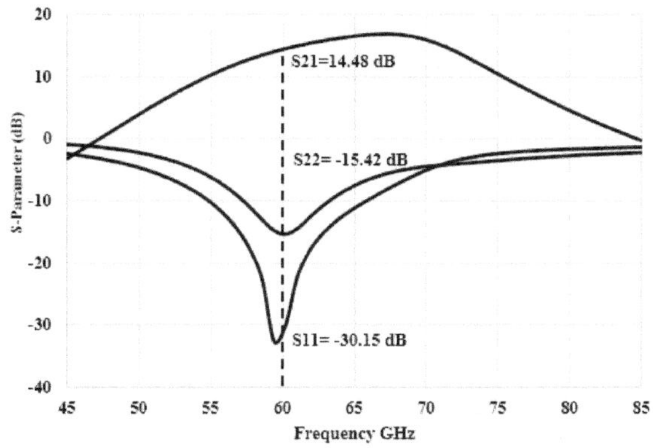

Figure 8: Simulated S-parameters of PA.

60GHz, it is important to consider the S-parameters of the circuit as it describes the input-output relationship between the terminals of the circuit. A two-port network is setup for the S-parameter extraction. Both the input and output ports are matched to 50Ohm impedance to extract the S-parameters. Fig. 8 shows the S_{11}, S_{22}, and S_{21} for the proposed PA. The S_{11} is the ratio of reflected power to the incident power at the input port and is known as reflection coefficient or return loss. For the proposed PA design the value of reflection coefficient, S_{11} is found to be −30.15dB at 60GHz. Therefore, we conclude that the input is matched well with the 50Ohm antenna impedance and hence we find negligible reflections at the input at 60GHz. Similarly, S_{22} is the ratio of reflected power to the incident power on the output port and it is found to be -15.42dB at 60GHz. S_{21} is the ratio of output power to the input power and represents the power gain for a well-matched PA. From Fig. 8 S_{21} is found to be 14.48dB.

The power added efficiency (PAE) is defined as the percentage ratio of difference between output and input power over total DC power. Hence it signifies the amplification factor of the PA. Fig. 9 shows the simulated PAE versus input power of the PA at 60GHz. It shows the output power at 1dB compression point is -3dBm. Maximum simulated PAE is found to be 17% at −3dBm of output power. Overall, the PA draws 2.2mA from a 1V supply.

4.4 Characterization of the Overall Transmitter

Here, we characterize whole OOK transmitter in terms of data rate, total DC power consumption and transmitted power and bit

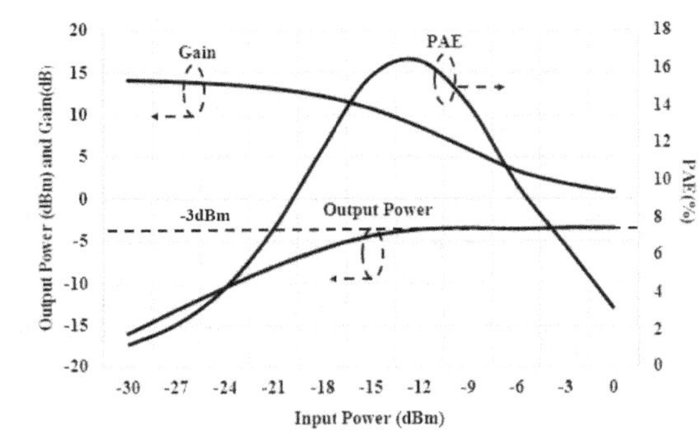

Figure 9: Simulated gain, output power and PAE of the PA versus input power at 60 GHz.

energy-efficiency. To characterize the OOK transmitter the input and output impedances of PA are matched with the output impedance of OOK modulator and that of a standard antenna impedance of 50Ohms respectively.

The waveform shown in Fig. 10 (a) shows the amplified OOK modulated signal at the output of PA with a pseudo-random sequence of logic 0s and 1s at baseband signal input. As demonstrated 10 bits (1110101001) are modulated between 1ns and 1.625ns indicating a data rate of 16Gbps. From Fig. 10(a) the output waveform indicates a 450mVpp which translates to -3dBm output power and is achieved with a total DC power consumption of 3.9mW. This implies a bit energy efficiency of 0.24pJ/bit at 16Gbps. The designed OOK transmitter is compared with other existing designs in comparable technology nodes. For a comprehensive comparison, we use Figure-of-Merit (FoM), which is given by

$$FoM(mW.\frac{bit}{pJ}) = \frac{Data\ Rate\ (Gbps).OP_{1dB}(mW)}{P_{DC}(mW)}. \quad (1)$$

Where P_{DC} is the power consumption and OP_{1dB} is the 1-dB compression point at the output of the transmitter. In Table 1 we compare our OOK transmitter with other transmitters designed for similar applications with respect to important performance metrics. While our design outperforms all the existing works it is to be noted that all the other works are post-layout or post-fabrication results while ours is circuit-level characterization.

4.5 Corner Analysis

The corner analysis is performed to obtain the performance of the transmitter over different operating voltages and temperatures. The analysis is performed for SS, TT, FF corners over 0.9, 1, 1.1 V and 125, 25, 0°C operation voltages and temperatures respectively. The

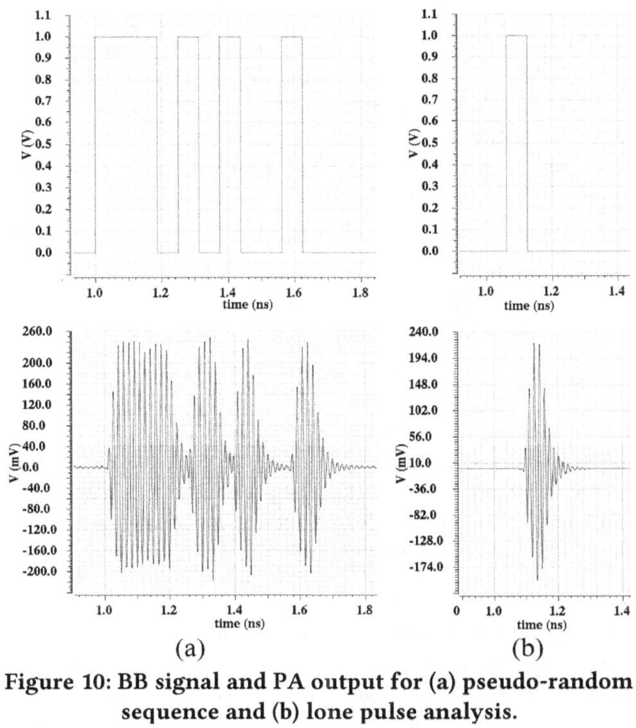

Figure 10: BB signal and PA output for (a) pseudo-random sequence and (b) lone pulse analysis.

Table 2: Performance of Transmitter at different corners

Corners	Voltage (V)	Temp.(C)	Speed (Gbps)	Power (mW)	R_{OOK} (dB)
SS	0.9	125	16	1.399	15.24
TT	1	25	16	2.064	16.54
FF	1.1	0	16	2.903	18.15

characterization of OOK transmitter at the various corner cases is shown in Table 2 with respect to total power consumption and on-off ratio of the overall OOK transmitter, R_{OOK} while operating at a data rate of 16Gbps.

4.6 Link Budget Analysis

In [11] the path loss for a 20mm intra-chip link is shown to be around 26dB. In [3] it is shown that the longest distance for an inter-chip link is 59mm resulting in a path loss of about 35dB. Here, we evaluate the BER corresponding to typical intra and inter-chip communication distances. The received signal power is

$$P_R = P_T - PL. \quad (2)$$

Here, P_R and P_T are the received and transmitted power respectively and *PL* is the path loss. We assume a non-coherent OOK receiver as these are most power efficient. LNAs used in typical non-coherent OOK receivers have a noise figure, *NF* of 10dB or less [11]. The Noise Floor, N_{Floor} of such a receiver is,

$$N_{Floor} = 10\log(kT) + 10\log(BW) + NF. \quad (3)$$

Where, k is the Boltzmann constant, T is the absolute temperature and BW is the bandwidth. Therefore, from (3) the N_{Floor} of the receiver is -67.8dBm at 300K for a *BW* of 16GHz. However, in addition to thermal AWGN, Inter-symbol Interference (ISI) due to bandwidth limitation of the transmitter can add interference noise. As can be seen from the lone-pulse analysis in Fig. 10(b) the transmitter output is 450mVpp and 67mVpp when it is transmitting a '1' and a '0' respectively when measured at the center of the pulses. Therefore, the on-off ratio of overall OOK transmitter, R_{OOK} is 16.54dB. The value of ISI noise, N_{ISI} is dependent on path loss and is given by,

$$N_{ISI} = P_T - R_{OOK} - PL. \quad (4)$$

The received Signal to Interference and Noise Ratio (SINR) is,

$$SINR = P_R - N_{Floor} - N_{ISI}. \quad (5)$$

For non-coherent OOK demodulation, the BER is given by,

$$BER_{OOK} = \frac{1}{2}\exp\left(-\frac{1}{2}SINR\right) + \frac{1}{4}erfc\left(\sqrt{\frac{1}{2}SINR}\right). \quad (6)$$

Where, *erfc*(.) is the complimentary error function. Fig. 11 shows the BER achieved with this transmitter for various values of path loss with and without ISI (for comparison). For a path loss of 35dB corresponding to a 59mm inter-chip link [3], the BER is dominated by the ISI and is around 10^{-10}.

5 CONCLUSIONS

In this paper we present the circuit-level design of a 60GHz mm-wave OOK transmitter for inter and intra-chip communications. A bit energy-efficiency of 0.24pJ/bit at 16Gbps is obtained at a low BER of 10^{-10} for typical transmission distances. This energy-efficiency

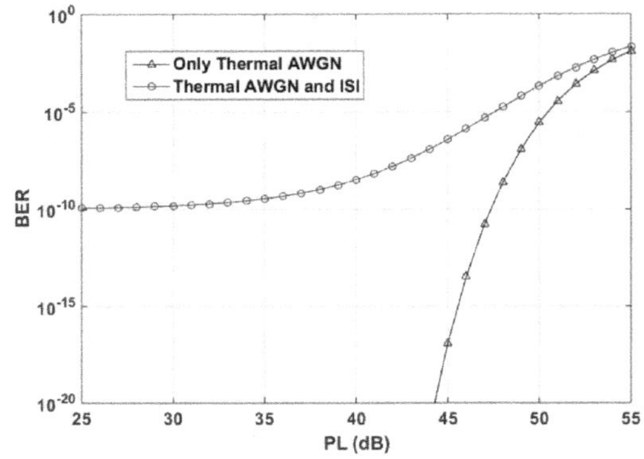

Figure 11: Variation of BER with Path Loss.

makes the mm-wave wireless interconnect competitive with other emerging technologies such as photonic interconnects.

ACKNOWLEDGMENTS

This work was supported in part by the US National Science Foundation (NSF) CAREER grant CNS-1553264. The authors would also like to thank Avijit Chakraborty, Intel Corp, for his valuable suggestions.

REFERENCES

[1] J.E. Jaussi, M. Leddige, B. Horine, F. O'Mahony and B. Casper. 2010. Multi-Gbit I/O and interconnect co-design for power efficient links. Electrical Performance of Electronic Packaging and Systems (EPEPS) 2010 IEEE 19th Conference, (October 2010), vol., no., pp.1,4.

[2] X. Wu et al. 2104. A Unified Inter/Intrachip Optical Network for Chip Multiprocessors. IEEE TVLSI, (May 2014), vol.22, no.5, pp.1082-1095.

[3] M. S. Shamim, N. Mansoor, R. S. Narde, V. Kothandapani, A. Ganguly and J. Venkataraman. 2017. A Wireless Interconnection Framework for Seamless Inter and Intra-Chip Communication in Multichip Systems. IEEE Transactions on Computers, (March 2017), 66, 3, pp. 389-402.

[4] S. Deb, A. Ganguly, P. P. Pande, B. Belzer, and D. Heo. 2012. Wireless NoC as Interconnection Backbone for Multicore Chips: Promises and Challenges. IEEE JESTCS, (June 2012) vol. 2, no. 2, pp. 228-239.

[5] J. Lee, Y. Huang, Y. Chen, H. Lu, and C. Chang. 2009. A low-power fully integrated 60 GHz transceiver system with OOK modulation and on-board antenna assembly. IEEE Int. Solid-State Circuits Conf. Tech. Dig, (February 2009) pp. 316–317.

[6] W. Chen et al. 2009. A 6-Gb/s wireless inter-chip data link using 43-GHz transceiver and bond-wire antennas. IEEE J. Solid-State Circuits, (October 2009). vol. 44, no. 10, pp. 2711–2721.

[7] K. Kawasaki et al. 2010. A millimeter-wave intra-connect solution. IEEE J. Solid-State Circuits, (December 2010). vol. 45, no. 12, pp. 2655–2666.

[8] E. Juntunen et al. 2010. A 60-GHz 38-pJ/b 3.5-Gb/s 90 nm CMOS OOK digital radio. IEEE Trans. Microw. Theory Techn., (February 2010). vol. 58, no. 2, pp. 348–355.

[9] Y. Tanaka et al. 2012. A versatile multi-modality serial link. IEEE Int. Solid-State Circuits Conf. Tech. Dig., (February 2012). pp. 332–333.

[10] C. W. Byeon, C. H. Yoon and C. S. Park. 2013. A 67-mW 10.7-Gb/s 60-GHz OOK CMOS transceiver for short-range wireless communications. IEEE Trans. Microwave Theory Techniques, (September 2013). vol. 61, no. 9, pp. 3391–3401.

[11] X. Yu, et al. 2014. A 1.2-pJ/bit 16-Gb/s 60-GHz OOK Transmitter in 65-nm CMOS for Wireless Network-On-Chip. IEEE Transactions on Microwave Theory and Techniques, (2014). vol. 62, no. 10, pp. 2357-2369.

[12] T. Dellsperger. 2002. Design of a 5 GHz VCO in CMOS. Technical report. Swiss Federal Institute of Technology Zurich, Zurich, Switzerland.

[13] A. Mineyama, et al. 2011. A millimeter-wave CMOS low noise amplifier using transformer neutralization techniques. Proc. Asia-Pacific Microwave Conference, (December 2011). pp. 223–226.

TaSaT: Thermal-Aware Scheduling and Tuning Algorithm for Heterogeneous and Configurable Embedded Systems

Mohamad Hammam Alsafrjalani
Department of Electrical and Computer Engineering,
University of Miami, Coral Gables, FL, USA
alsafrjalani@miami.edu

Tosiron Adegbija
Department of Electrical and Computer Engineering,
The University of Arizona, Tucson, AZ, USA
tosiron@email.arizona.edu

ABSTRACT

Heterogeneous and configurable systems (HaCS) have been widely used to meet stringent runtime performance and energy constraints in embedded systems. However, no prior work has addressed the emerging runtime thermal constraints in these systems. To leverage HaCS' capabilities to meet thermal constraints, in addition to performance and energy constraints, we propose *TaSaT, a Thermal-aware Scheduling and Tuning* algorithm for HaCS. TaSaT reduces HaCS temperature while meeting performance and energy constraints during runtime, without a priori knowledge of applications.

ACM Reference Format:

Mohamad Hammam Alsafrjalani and Tosiron Adegbija. 2018. TaSaT: Thermal-Aware Scheduling and Tuning Algorithm for Heterogeneous and Configurable Embedded Systems In *GLSVLSI '18: 2018 Great Lakes Symposium on VLSI,* May 23–25, 2018, Chicago, IL, USA. ACM, NY, NY, USA, 6 pages. https://doi.org/10.1145/3194554.3194576

1 INTRODUCTION

The ubiquitous nature of embedded systems has placed stringent and disparate constraints, including energy, performance, and temperature on these systems. Whereas energy and performance have traditionally been the predominant constraints, temperature is a growing concern in embedded systems due to the systems stringent resource constraints. Due to the small size, limited availability of cooling mechanisms (e.g., on-board fans), and cost of system real estate, keeping an embedded system's temperature within thermal constraints, in addition to necessary performance and energy optimizations, is a major challenge for system designers.

Several microprocessor optimizations exist to enable adherence to potentially competing performance and energy constraints. For example, heterogeneous multiprocessors—such as the ARM big.LITTLE [5], ARM Juno [6]—offer fixed, disparate configurations to provide coarse-grained adaptation to different applications' execution requirements. To enhance this adaptation, configurable systems with tunable components (e.g., cache, pipeline depth, issue window, etc.) can be tuned/adjusted to meet specific, fine-grained application requirements [10][19][23]. Furthermore, heterogeneous and configurable systems (HaCS) [3][4] provide larger design spaces that enable both coarse-grained and fine-grained adaptation to applications' runtime needs.

To address increasingly critical thermal challenges, several thermal-aware optimizations have been employed to reduce the core temperature. Dynamic thermal management (DTM) [8] leverages the temperature-performance tradeoff of dynamic voltage and frequency scaling (DVFS), decode throttling, speculation control and instruction cache toggling to reduce the core temperature. Complementing DTM, activity migration [13] and temperature-aware scheduling [22] reduce core temperature by executing the applications on the core(s) that will result in the lowest average system temperature. Furthermore, phase-based tuning [1] has been used to determine Pareto optimal configurations in configurable systems for fine-grained execution time, energy, and temperature.

Whereas prior thermal-aware optimizations addressed thermal issues in homogenous and configurable systems, to the best of our knowledge, no work has addressed thermal constraints in HaCS, which is particularly challenging due to the coarse- and fine-grained adherence to constraints in HaCS. We have identified three main challenges of thermal management in HaCS: (1) considering HaCS' typically large design spaces, the heterogeneous and configurable parameters that offer the best coarse- and fine-grained performance and temperature tradeoffs must be determined; (2) HaCS thermal optimization must be scalable to applications that are unknown at design time; and (3) given a multicore HaCS, a thermal-aware low-overhead scheduling and tuning algorithm that leverages HaCS' flexibility to satisfy performance and temperature constraints must be designed.

In this paper, we address the aforementioned challenges by evaluating design choices for a multicore heterogeneous and configurable system (HaCS) where the executing applications are unknown a priori. To enable thermal management in HaCS, while simultaneously satisfying performance and energy needs, we propose a novel thermal-aware scheduling and tuning (TaSaT) algorithm for HaCS that requires no a priori knowledge, or offline profiling of the applications. Due to the cache's significant impact on overall system performance and energy, we focus on cache optimization in this work, and show that a heterogeneous, configurable cache offers substantial advantages for thermal-aware runtime optimizations. We design our TaSaT algorithm as part of a hardware cache tuner that can hold scheduling and tuning information of an arbitrary number of applications using a least recently used (LRU) replacement policy.

Our results reveal that TaSaT reduces the system's temperature, execution time, and energy by 16.53%, 10.74%, and 22.87% respectively, as compared to a base commercial off-the-shelf (COTS) system. Additionally, TaSaT reduced the system temperature by 4.70%, as compared to prior work, and imposed a tuning-time performance overhead of 7.77% as compared to an

ACM ISBN 978-1-4503-5724-1/18/05...$15.00
https://doi.org/10.1145/3194554.3194576

ideal system with a priori knowledge of applications' best performance configurations.

2 RELATED WORK

Much prior work contributed novel heterogeneous systems (e.g., [5][16][17]), configurable systems (e.g., [10][11][19][23]), heterogeneous and configurable (e.g., [3][4]systems), and associated scheduling (e.g., [14][15][21]) , tuning (e.g., [1][11]), and scheduling and tuning algorithms (e.g., [3][4]). Given these expansive research areas, for brevity, we only discuss the most related works on heterogeneous and configurable systems (HaCS) and associated runtime scheduling and tuning algorithms.

2.1 Heterogeneous and Configurable Systems (HaCS)

To achieve coarse- and fine-grained adherence to energy, Alsafrjalani et al. [4] designed a quad-core heterogeneous and configurable system (HaCS). The cores featured fixed, heterogeneous cache sizes, and enabled coarse-grained adherence to performance constraints. The cores also featured configurable cache line size and associativities, and enabled fine-grained adherence to performance constraints. The authors designed a scheduling and tuning algorithm that dynamically profiled and mapped the applications to cores that consumed the lowest energy. Once the applications were scheduled, a tuner adjusted the core's cache line size and associativity to best match the application's cache requirements. However, the authors did not evaluate the thermal impacts of their proposed work.

Adegbija et al. [1] considered the thermal impact while optimizing the performance and energy of configurable systems. The authors used an evolutionary algorithm to determine Pareto optimal cache configurations and clock frequencies for different application phases. However, the proposed technique required the executing applications to be profiled and classified offline, at design time, which limited the technique from being applied to general purpose applications where the executing applications are unknown a priori. Furthermore, the proposed technique only considered a single-core system, and did not take into account application-to-core scheduling.

2.2 Scheduling and Tuning Algorithms

Yeo et al. [22] contributed a thermal-aware scheduler based on a thermal prediction model. The prediction model used the applications' runtime execution characteristics and classification derived from offline thermal profiling to predict the applications' thermal behaviors. Using this prediction information and a core-based thermal model, a thermal-aware scheduler migrates the application to a core that would take the longest to reach the temperature threshold. Although this approach is applicable to multicore systems, the work was evaluated on homogeneous multicore systems, which have much less variation in resource constraints as compared to heterogeneous systems. Furthermore, since this approach required offline application profiling, it is not scalable to applications that are unknown during design time.

To extend scheduling to unknown applications, Alsafrjalani et al. used a dynamic scheduling and tuning algorithm for a HaCS [4]. The algorithm profiled the applications dynamically, enabling the system to scale to an arbitrary number of applications. When the applications best (lowest) energy core was determined, the algorithm scheduled the application to that core and tuned the core's cache line and associativity. However, if the best core was not available the algorithm attempted to utilize a not-best, however idle, core, such that the total static and dynamic energy was minimized. However, the algorithm did not account for performance loss if applications needed to halt until the best, or near-best core was available.

To address performance bottleneck, Alsafrjalani et al. [3], developed a performance/quality aware scheduling and tuning algorithm for HaCS. To discover low energy core and configuration while maintaining performance, the algorithm profiled the application on the cores, and explored tunable configurations, using performance ordering. The algorithm explored cores/configurations that had the highest performance expectation and continued until a core/configuration degraded the application's performance below a predefined performance threshold. Even though the proposed approach was applicable to any HaCS and arbitrary number of applications, the approach did not consider temperature gain/loss as a byproduct of determining the best configurations for energy or performance.

In this paper, we present the first—to the best of our knowledge—dynamic thermal-aware scheduling and tuning (TaSaT) algorithm for heterogeneous and configurable systems (HaCS). TaSaT requires no a priori knowledge of executing applications, and determines system configurations that can optimize temperature, energy, or performance, while incurring minimal, tuning-time overhead.

3 Thermal-Aware HaCS Hardware Design

Given the expansive design space (available configuration options) to construct a thermal-aware HaCS, this section details the steps of determining the heterogeneous parameters, configurable parameters, and our hardware architecture and the tuner hardware requirements.

3.1 Heterogeneous and Configurable Parameters

To design a HaCS system that adheres to performance and energy constraints, and to evaluate and compare our system to prior work [4], we used configurable caches with configurations that have high impact on performance and energy [23]. To gain insight into coarse- and fine-grained performance-energy tradeoff, we used a design space of 729 configurations, comprising different cache sizes, line sizes, and associativities. The design space comprises the cross product of instruction and data caches with the following parameters: size of 32, 16, and 8KB, line sizes of 64, 32, and 16B, and associativities of 4, 2, and 1.

Since our goal is to reduce temperature while adhering to

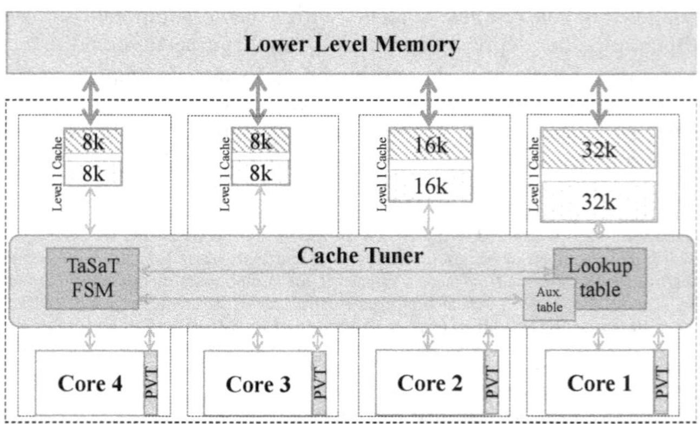

Figure 1. Thermal-aware HaCS with the hardware cache tuner

performance constraints, our system must feature configurations that simultaneously achieve both temperature and performance optimization goals. For coarse-grained performance optimization, we designed each core in our HaCS system with a fixed, different cache size. To complement coarse-grained optimization with fine-grained optimization, each core features configurable line size and associativity. As a first step, we explored the cache parameters that provided the best performance-temperature tradeoffs by exhaustively searching our design space, using a set of embedded applications [9].

Our exhaustive evaluation revealed that the different configurations had substantially different, and potentially conflicting, impacts on performance, energy, and temperature. However, since our approach features an online scheduling and tuning algorithm, exploring 729 configurations can impose significant performance and energy overhead, due to extreme configurations that significantly degrade performance, energy, and/or temperature. For example, our exhaustive search showed 48% and 49% performance and energy overheads, respectively.

Furthermore, using the exhaustive evaluation, we were able to narrow down the best cache configurations for performance, energy, and temperature. We observed that a wide range of configurations with sizes from 8KB to 32KB achieved the best

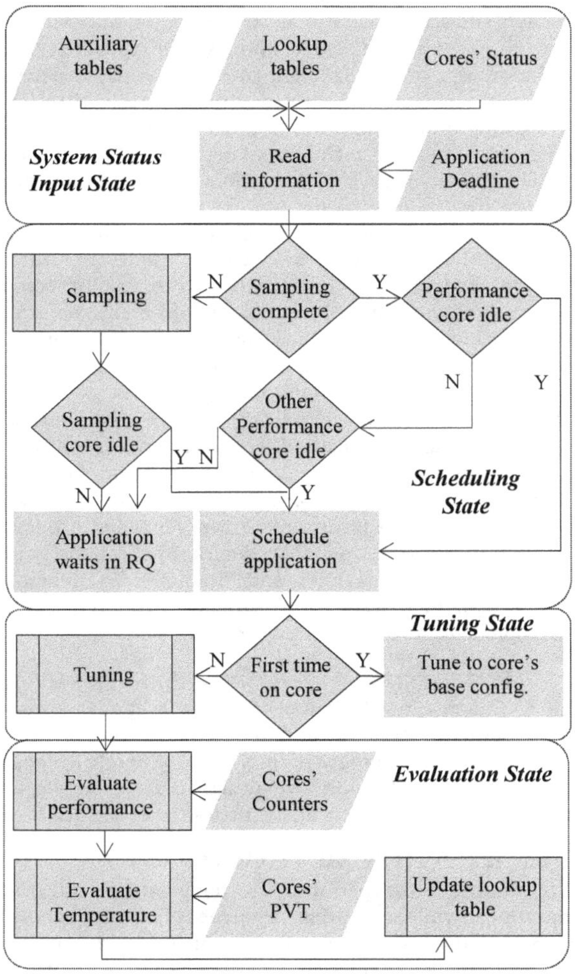

Algorithm 1 Thermal-aware Scheduling and Tuning (TaSaT) Algorithm

performance and energy for the different applications in our experiments (the experimental setup is detailed in Section 6). However, the best configurations for temperature optimization only included the 8KB cache. Based on these observations, our HaCS system features cores with 8, 16, and 32KB cache sizes, as shown in Figure 1. We empirically determined that the 8KB was the most likely to minimize temperature, at the expense of performance or energy. Thus, since our work targets temperature optimization, we designated two cores (out of four) as 8KB to provide more opportunities for scheduling to the lowest-temperature core. The 16KB and 32KB caches allow temperature optimization to be traded off, when necessary, in favor of performance or energy.

3.2 Hardware Tuner Requirements

To enable dynamic tuning, we use a low-overhead hardware cache tuner featuring dedicated buses connected to the cores' power, voltage, and thermal (PVT) sensors [6]. The tuner also implements TaSaT algorithm's finite state machine (Section 4), and a lookup table to store tuning information (e.g., explored configurations, applications' best configurations). The tuner imposes 322 cycles time overhead [2], an insignificant overhead compared to the number of cycles required for our tuning interval of 1 million instructions [3]. During each tuning interval, the tuner measures/calculates an application's energy, performance, and/or temperature, in order to determine which configuration to explore during the next interval. This interval is long enough to warm up and stabilize the caches [3].

The number of bits m required to store scheduling and tuning information per application is given by:

$$m = s + (e + p + t + f) * \lceil log_2(c) \rceil \quad (1)$$

where e, p, and t are 32-bit values that store the energy, clock cycles, and temperature information, s is a 1-bit *stop-tuning* flag, f is a 2-bit *performance and temperature* flag, and c is the number of configurations in the design space. Furthermore, the number of bits n required for an auxiliary table to store the applications' best configurations is given by:

$$n = a * \lceil log_2(c) \rceil \quad (2)$$

where a is an 8-bit value that stores the best configuration information for up to 256 simultaneously applications. If more space is needed for additional applications, the tuner uses LRU policy to update the lookup and/or auxiliary table(s).

Thus, the lookup and auxiliary tables require $m * n$ bits (728 bits in our case), which is insignificant, as compared to the level 1 cache sizes of 8KB to 32KB. Prior work [2] revealed that a hardware cache tuner with more storage requirements than our design (e.g., per-configuration energy consumption was also stored) imposed only a 4.7% area overhead in a very small MIPS M4K processor; our tuner's area overhead will be significantly less.

4 TaSaT FOR THERMAL AWARE HaCS

4.1 Overview

Algorithm 1 depicts our thermal-aware scheduling and tuning (TaSaT) algorithm's flow chart. The algorithm has four states: System Status Input, Scheduling, Tuning, and Evaluation states. For each application in the ready queue, the algorithm determines the core with the best cache size to schedule the application to, tunes the core's cache line size and associativity, evaluates the performance and temperature impact of this execution, and finally updates the lookup tables.

4.2 TaSaT Algorithm States

4.2.1 System Status Input State. When an application is placed in the ready queue to be executed, TaSaT starts/resumes the scheduling and tuning process based on the information in the system status input state. TaSaT checks the auxiliary table for information about the application's best core, cache size, and associativity. If the auxiliary table contains this information, TaSaT attempts to schedule the application to the best core and directly tune the core cache line size and associativity to the best configuration. Otherwise, TaSaT uses the cores' status information (e.g., idle, busy), application deadline information, which may be designer-specified or implicitly specified by the executing application due to input data stream processing requirements, and the application's tuning information from the lookup table, and transitions to the scheduling state.

4.2.2 Scheduling State. In the scheduling state, the algorithm determines which performance core to schedule the application to. A performance core is a core that does not violate an application's deadline constraint. If sampling is complete, the performance core(s)—there may be more than one for each application—are known, and the algorithm attempts to schedule the application to an idle performance cores. If no performance core is available, the application remains in the ready queue. If sampling is not complete, the algorithm uses a sampling sub-process to sample the application on all/remaining cores.

Since cache size has the highest impact on performance [3][23], the sampling sub-process starts with the core with the largest cache size. The application is executed for one tuning interval on each core in descending order of cache sizes and with the base line size and associativity. If the core does not violate the deadline, the algorithm flags the core as a performance core. When the algorithm schedules an application to a core, the algorithm transitions to the tuning state.

4.2.3 Tuning State. Using the information from the lookup table, the algorithm tunes the core's cache line size and associativity. If there is no tuning information in the lookup table (i.e., the application is executing on the core for the first time), the algorithm starts tuning from the largest line size and associativity, since these values are likely to not degrade performance [3]. For subsequent tuning intervals, the algorithm calls a tuning process that explores other cache line sizes and associativities, in a descending performance ordering (i.e., explores all line sizes first).

The tuning process employs a pseudo hill-climbing heuristic to explore the cache line size and associativity values. To avoid local performance degradation, the process uses a predetermined threshold value, *w*, that tracks the number of times the tuning resulted in degraded performance. The process tunes to a lower cache size and associativity for one tuning interval. Each time the application is scheduled to a core, the tuning process explores a lower cache line size and associativity, as long as the number of performance degradations has not exceeded *w*. Once the cache line size and associativity are determined, the algorithm begins the evaluation state.

4.2.4 Evaluation State. To evaluate the core/configuration performance, in the evaluation state, the algorithm uses an evaluate performance sub-process. The process reads in the core counters to measure the time elapsed for the application to execute and compares that time to the application deadline. If the application exceeded the deadline, the algorithm updates the performance flag bit, f_0, of that configuration to 1 (marked as a sub-performance configuration). Using the information from the lookup table, the process also determines the number of sub-performance configurations explored thus far. If this number exceeds *w* then the process sets the stop tuning flag, *s*, to 1 for the application.

Similarly, to evaluate the temperature reduction, the algorithm calls an evaluate temperature sub-process. The process reads in the cores' PVT and compares these values to the values of previously explored configurations. If the temperature value is lower than of the previously explored configuration(s), the process sets the temperature-saving flag, f_1, of that configuration for the application.

Using the results from the performance and temperature evaluation, the algorithm determines if the currently explored configuration results in acceptable performance and temperature reduction. The algorithm then update/store this information in the lookup table for the algorithm to use in subsequent executions.

5 EXPERIMENT SETUP

To evaluate our system, we used a quad-core HaCS architecture (Section 3), and ran seventeen applications that represent common embedded systems applications [9]. The quad-core HaCS features cores with separate level one (L1) instruction and data caches of fixed sizes 8, 16, and 32KB. The caches' line sizes and associativities are tunable to any combination of 8, 16, and 32B, and 1-, 2- and 4-way, respectively. We modeled our quad-core system similar to the ARM Cortex A9, consisting of a 4-width out-of-order issue processor with 8 pipeline stages, 45 nm technology, and a clock frequency of 2GHz. The PVT are modeled after ARM's Juno Development SoC [6].

We used the EEMBC [9] Automotive benchmarks and six MiBench [12] benchmarks selected to represent different application domains. The benchmarks were specific compute kernels performing specific tasks in different application domains, including networking, image processing, security, etc. To obtain performance results, we executed the application on gem5 simulator [7], to obtain energy results, we fed the simulation results output McPAT [18], and we used Hotspot 5.0 [20] as the thermal modeling tool. To model fan-less systems, we designed our system with a heat sink of 1mm and spreader 0.1 mm thickness, and we set the convection resistance to 4K/W.

To simulate a load environment, we generated a queue of 5000 applications from our benchmark applications with a designated ready/arrival time and deadline. To generate a realistic arrival rate, we used a Gamma distribution centered around a predetermined execution time

$$X = \frac{\sum_{i=1}^{A}\sum_{j=1}^{c} x(i,j)}{A*C*c} \qquad (3)$$

where *A*, *C*, and *c*, are the numbers of applications, cores, and configurations, respectively, and *x(i,j)* is the execution time of application *i* using configuration *j*. To generate a realistic deadline for an application, we designated the application's average execution time using all configuration as the deadline.

6 EVALUATION METHODOLOGY

We evaluated the performance, temperature, and energy optimizations while executing a queue of 5000 applications (Section 5) using six systems, all of which featured quad-core processors. However, to evaluate the system tradeoffs, and scheduling and tuning overhead, the systems differed in the

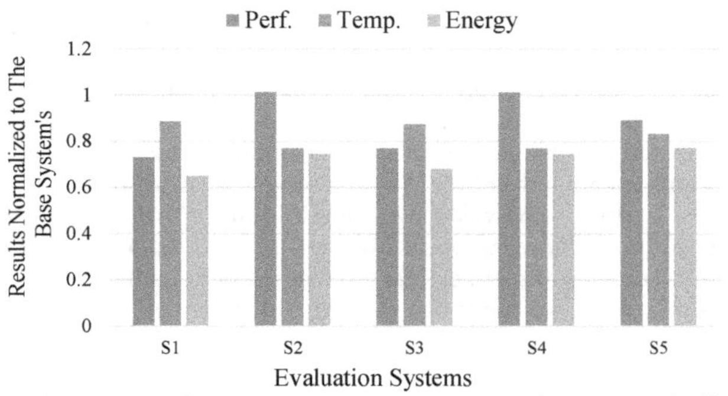

Figure 2. Performance, Temperature, and Energy of all systems, normalized to the Base System's

number of cache configurations, scheduling algorithms, and a priori knowledge of applications.

Table 1 depicts the six systems, including the cache configurations, a priori knowledge of applications (and the applications' deadlines), and the scheduling and tuning algorithms used in each system. The base system represents a commercial of-the-shelf (COTS) system with fixed 32KB-4W-64B cache and a first-come first-served (FCFS) scheduling. The configuration column represents the cache configurations featured in the system. S1 and S2 caches comprised the complete design space of 729 configurations, while S3-S5 comprised the same subset of 81 cache configurations (Section 3.1). All systems, except S5, had a priori knowledge of the applications' best performance and/or temperature configuration; i.e., we assumed there is no scheduling and tuning overhead. S1—S4 scheduled the applications using FCFS to the core with the best performance (P) or temperature (T) configuration, whereas S5 used our TaSaT algorithm to make scheduling and tuning decisions.

We compared systems S1, S2, S3, S4, and S5 to the base system for performance, temperature, and energy optimizations. We also compared S1 to S3 and S2 to S4 to measure performance and temperature degradation, respectively, when a configuration subset is used instead of the complete design space. Since S1—S4 assume a priori knowledge of executing applications, there is no scheduling and tuning overhead; the overhead results from using configuration subsets rather than the full design space.

Table 1: Evaluation Systems

System\Setup	$Config.	A Priori	Sched. Al.
Base	32-4-64	yes	FCFS
S1	complete	yes	FCFS-P
S2	complete	yes	FCFS-T
S3	subset	yes	FCFS-P
S4	subset	yes	FCFS-T
S5	subset	no	TaSaT

To obtain S5's performance and temperature tradeoffs with respect to an optimal system with a priori knowledge of application we compared S5 to S1 and S2, respectively. We also evaluated the S5's scheduling and tuning overhead by comparing S5's optimization potential to S3 and S4. Furthermore, since S3 comprised a subset of configurations, the systems represent prior work [3][4] in which performance is prioritized. We compared the temperature and energy savings of S5 to S3 to obtain tradeoffs as compared to prior work, when temperature is prioritized.

7 RESULTS AND ANALYSIS

This section presents the performance, temperature, and energy results and analysis based on our experiment setup and evaluation methodology.

7.1 Performance

Figure 2 depicts the average performance, temperature, and energy improvements of S1, S2, S3, S4, and S5 normalized to the base system. Values below one correspond to less time, temperature, and energy, as compared to the base system. S1, S3, and S5 resulted in 27.09%, 23.07%, and 10.74% better performance, as compared to the base system, since these systems prioritized performance optimization during scheduling. However, S2, and S4, degraded the performance by 1.33% and 1.30%, respectively, since these systems used FCFS-T, which prioritized lower temperature over better performance. Since S2 and S4 had a priori knowledge of the applications' best temperature configurations, the applications were scheduled to the best-temperature cores, which resulted in performance degradation. Furthermore, even though S2 had all the cache configurations, while S4 had a subset of configurations, both systems achieved similar performance for the applications; thus, the eliminated configurations in S4 did not affect the system's performance.

To extend our performance analysis, we recorded how much time the systems' scheduling and tuning decisions took. Figure 3 depicts the average number of deadline misses that occurred while executing the applications. The applications missed the deadline 25% of the time in the base system, since the base system scheduled the applications to first available cores, and all cores offered the same configuration. Our analysis revealed that although the base system's caches featured the largest cache size, and the best average case performance, the base configuration was not the best for all of the applications. Executing some of the applications (e.g., basefp) on the base configuration degraded performance; as a result, other applications were prevented from meeting their deadlines. In S1 and S3, no applications missed their deadlines, since both systems offered the complete design space and prior knowledge of the best configurations.

Since S1 and S3 offered the complete and subsetted design space, respectively, the subsetted design space contained enough best and near-best performance configurations. However, S3, S4 and S5 incurred deadline misses while executing the applications, since S3 and S4 prioritized temperature and S5 explored the design space during runtime and accrued runtime overhead. Since S2 and S4 offered the complete and subsetted design space, respectively, the subsetted design space contained the same best and near best performance configurations, while providing best temperature configurations. This result also suggests that even though execution times on S2 and S4 were similar (Figure 2), S2 and S4 may impact the performance of a hard real-time performance system differently (Figure 3).

Finally, the applications in S5, which represent our HaCS with TaSaT algorithm, missed the deadline on average of 7.77%. Since S5 had no a priori knowledge of the applications, the scheduling and tuning overhead accounted for the deadline misses of some of the applications. The 7.77% tuning time overhead will amortize over time and is acceptable in soft real-time systems [3]. Furthermore, as compared to prior work that

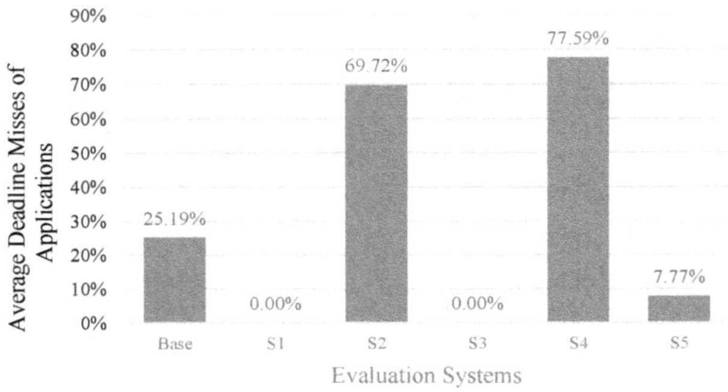

Figure 3. The average number of applications' executions that exceeded the deadline for all the application's in the queue

prioritized performance *and* had prior knowledge of the applications' best configurations (S3), S5 decreased performance by 16.03%, since S5 used multiple performance cores for an application. Although S5 degraded the performance, that did not necessarily translate to a substantial increase in applications missing deadlines and is then within 7.77% of an ideal system while saving 4.70% temperature (Section 7.2), as compared to S3.

7.2 Temperature

Systems S1, S2, S3, S4, and S5 reduced the temperature by 11.34%, 23.01%, 12.42%, 23.07%, and 16.53%, respectively, as compared to the base system, which had an average temperature of 89.55° C. Since S2 and S4 prioritized temperature, these two systems resulted in the highest temperature savings among the five systems. Also, S1 and S3 resulted in less temperature savings than S2 and S4, since S1 and S3 systems used FCFS-P, which prioritized higher performance over better temperature. Since S1 and S3 had a priori knowledge of the application's best performance configurations, the applications were scheduled to the best-performance core, which resulted in increased average temperatures as compared to S2 and S4. Moreover, we observed that even though S2 and S4 offered the complete and subsetted design space, respectively, there was no impact on the temperature; both systems' temperature savings were similar.

Furthermore, we observed that S5's temperature savings of 16.53% was less than that of S2 and S4, since S5's balanced between temperature reduction and performance, while S2 and S4 prioritized temperature only. Additionally, compared to an ideal system that prioritizes temperature (S4), S5, traded off 8.64% in temperature savings for 11.90% performance improvement, and 90.65% fewer missed deadlines.

7.3 Energy

Systems S1, S2, S3, S4, and S5 resulted in 35.10%, 25.52%, 31.90%, 25.53%, and 22.87% energy savings, respectively, as compared to the base system. Although S1 and S3 prioritized performance, the systems reduced the execution time substantially, with a less substantial power increase, which resulted in an overall energy reduction. Overall, our approach did not incur any energy overheads as compared to the base system.

8 CONCLUSION AND FUTURE WORK

In this work we presented a thermal-aware scheduling and tuning (TaSaT) algorithm for reduced temperature in heterogeneous and configurable systems (HaCS). Our algorithm required no a priori knowledge of applications and can be scaled to any HaCS and applications. TaSaT explored the design space using performance order configurations and obtained 16.53% and 22.87% temperature and energy reduction, respectively, as compared to a base system. The algorithm imposed tuning-time performance overhead of 7.77%, as compared to an ideal system with a priori knowledge of applications. Furthermore, our algorithm reduced temperature by 4.67% compared to prior work. Future work will extend our algorithm to multi-level cache optimization and multi-objective optimization of temperature, performance, energy, and energy-delay product (EDP).

REFERENCES

[1] Adegbija, T.; Gordon-Ross, A., *"Thermal-aware phase-based tuning of embedded systems,"* Great Lakes Symposium on VLSI (GLSVLSI), 2014

[2] Adegbija, T.; Gordon-Ross, A.; Rawlins, M., *"Analysis of cache tuner architectural layouts for multicore embedded systems,"* Int. Con. on Performance Computing and Communications, 2014.

[3] Alsafrjalani, M., H.; Gordon-Ross, A., *"Quality of service-aware, scalable cache tuning algorithm in consumer-based embedded devices,"* International Great Lakes Symposium on VLSI (GLSVLSI), 2016

[4] Alsafrjalani, M., H.; Gordon-Ross, A., *"Dynamic Scheduling for Reduced Energy in Configuration-Subsetted Heterogeneous Multicore Systems,"* Int. Con. on Embedded and Ubiquitous Computing, 2014

[5] ARM Ltd., big.LITTLE Technology, White Paper: http://www.arm.com/files/pdf/big_LITTLE_Technology_the_Futue_of_Mobile.pdf

[6] ARM Ltd., https://developer.arm.com/products/architecture/a-profile/docs/100113/latest/hardware-description/juno-arm-development-platform-soc

[7] Binkert, N.; et al., *"The gem5 simulator,"* Computer Architecture News, 2011

[8] Donald, J.; Martonosi, M., *"Techniques for Multicore Thermal Management: Classification and New Exploration,"* International Symposium in Computer Architecture (ISCA), 2006.

[9] EEMBC. The Embedded Microprocessor Benchmark Consortium http://www.eembc.org/benchmark/automotive _sl.php, Sept. 2013

[10] Folegnani, D.; Gonzalez, A., *"Energy-effective issue logic,"* Int. Symp. on Computer Architecture (ISCA), 2001

[11] Gordon-Ross, A.; Vahid, F., *"A Self-Tuning Configurable Cache,"* IEEE Design Automation Conference (DAC), 2007

[12] Guthausch, M., R.; et al., *"Mibench: a free, commercially representative embedded benchmark suite,"* IEEE Workshop on Workload Characterization, 2001.

[13] Heo, S.; Barr, K.; Asanovic, K., *"Reducing Power Density through Activity Migration,"* Int. Symp. on Low Power Electronics & Design (ISLPED), 2003

[14] Joao, José A., Aater Suleman, M., Mutlu, O., Patt, N., *"Utility-based acceleration of multithreaded applications on asymmetric CMPs. SIGARCH,"* Computer Architecture News, 2013

[15] Kim, K.; Kim, D.; Park, C.; *"Real-time scheduling in heterogeneous dual-core architectures,"* International Conference on Parallel and Distributed Systems, 2006

[16] Kumar, R.; et al., *"Single-ISA heterogeneous multi-core architectures: the potential for processor power reduction,"* 36th Int. Symp. on Microarchitecture, 2003

[17] Kumar, R.; Tullsen, D.; N. Jouppi, N.; Ranganathan, P., *"Heterogeneous chip multiprocessors,"* IEEE Computer, vol. 38, Nov. 2005

[18] Li, S.; et al., *"McPAT: an integrated power, area, and timing modeling framework for multicore and manycore architectures,"* Int. Symp. on Microarchitecture, 2009

[19] Malik, A.; Moyer, B.; Cermak, D., *"A low power unified cache architecture providing power and performance flexibility,"* Int. Symp. on Low Power Electronics and Design (ISLPED), 2000

[20] Skadron, K.; et al., *"Temperature-aware microarchitecture: modeling and implementation,"* Transactions on Architecture and Code Optimization, 2004.

[21] Van Craeynest, K.; Jaleel, A.; Eeckhout, L.; Narvaez, P.; Emer, J.; *"Scheduling heterogeneous multi-cores through performance impact estimation (PIE),"* 39th Int. Symp. on Computer Architecture (ISCA), 2012

[22] Yeo, I.; Kim, E.; J., *"Temperature-aware scheduler based on thermal behavior grouping in multicore systems,"* Conference on Design, Automation and Test in Europe (DATE), 2009

[23] Zhang, C.; Vahid, F.; Najjar, W.; *"A highly configurable cache architecture for embedded systems,"* Int. Sym. on Computer Architecture (ISCA), 2003

Interfacing 3D-stacked Electronic and Optical NoCs with Mixed CMOS-ECL Bridges: a Realistic Preliminary Assessment

Mahdi Tala[1], Oliver Schrape[2], Milos Krstic[2,3] and Davide Bertozzi[1]

(1) Engineering Department, University of Ferrara (Italy)
(2) IHP-Microelectronics, Frankfurt Oder (Germany)
(3) University of Potsdam, Potsdam (Germany)
(mahdi.tala,davide.bertozzi)@unife.it
(schrape,krstic)@ihp-microelectronics.com

ABSTRACT

The combination of optical networks-on-chip and 3D stacking represents the most promising system integration framework to overcome the communication bottleneck of future many-core processors. From an architecture viewpoint, the availability of an energy-efficient, low-latency bridge connecting the electronic network-on-chip with the optical one is as important as the maturity of the optical interconnect technology. The key design challenge consists of overcoming the inherent serial nature of optical communications, which is typically pursued by increasing either the data rate or the bit-level parallelism, or by a combination thereof. This paper explores an hybrid CMOS-ECL technology platform for bridge implementation by means of a complete logic synthesis effort. By spanning the wider configuration space of the hybrid bridge with respect to fully-CMOS realizations, the paper identifies the most energy-efficient configurations and provides a comparative assessment of achievable quality metrics. Derived results represent a solid and realistic starting point for future optimizations and for the refinement into an actual layout.

CCS CONCEPTS

• **Hardware → Emerging technologies; Network on chip; 3D integrated circuits; Photonic and optical interconnect; Logic synthesis;**

KEYWORDS

Optical network-on-chip; heterogeneous technology integration; bridge; emitter-coupled logic; serializer

ACM Reference Format:

Mahdi Tala[1], Oliver Schrape[2], Milos Krstic[2,3] and Davide Bertozzi[1]. 2018. Interfacing 3D-stacked Electronic and Optical NoCs with Mixed CMOS-ECL Bridges: a Realistic Preliminary Assessment. In *GLSVLSI '18: 2018 Great Lakes Symposium on VLSI, May 23–25, 2018, Chicago, IL, USA.* ACM, New York, NY, USA, 7 pages. https://doi.org/10.1145/3194554.3194593

1 INTRODUCTION

Two disruptive technologies are gaining momentum as ideal candidates to overcome the interconnect bottleneck in future many-core systems: optical networks-on-chip (ONoCs) and 3D stacking. Quality metrics of photonically-integrated three-dimensional systems have been extensively investigated in literature, demonstrating the potential of this system integration framework [26]. However, research in the field suffers from a large existing gap between technology- and device-level research and system-level analysis. The latter is typically performed by back-annotating some physical parameters into high-level functional models, most of the time taken from different sources. A closer link between technology developers and system-level designers can be established only through an investment on vertical as well as horizontal integration techniques. Vertical integration consists of populating the intermediate abstraction layers with design methods and tools. Hence, it has to do with the evolution of design automation beyond its electronic roots [20]. Horizontal integration instead addresses the integration of emerging technologies with electronics [25].

This paper contributes to the advance of horizontal integration methods through the experimental assessment of the bridge architecture connecting the electronic network-on-chip (ENoC) with the optical one in a photonically-integrated 3D-stacked parallel processor. This bridge is typically overlooked in system-level analysis, where it is generally abstracted as an E/O and O/E conversion stage with annotated conversion costs. In practice, it is a quite complex block taking care of challenging functional tasks for architecture correct operation, and built on top of a multi-technology (serialization, synchronization, flow control, etc.) platform supporting GHz-range signaling rates.

A key architectural concern addressed by the bridge is the inherent serial nature of optical transmissions, which may offset the performance speed-up of this emerging technology and introduce a significant power overhead for serialization and deserialization. There are two ways to overcome this limitation: increasing the signaling rate of optical channels or the bit-level parallelism (through spatial- or wavelength-division multiplexing) or a combination thereof. The configuration space of the architecture can be covered by changing these parameters, which requires modifications of the (de-)serializer structure. Thus, the latter ends up playing a critical role in determining the performance-power trade-off spanned by each bridge configuration.

The main goal of this paper is to explore the configuration space of the bridge by characterizing overall energy-per-bit and serialization latency as a function of transmission data rate and bit-level parallelism. In order to explore a design space representative of the opportunities provided by actual technology, we rely on a mix of technologies to stretch the data rate beyond what is affordable with a standard bulk CMOS process alone. In particular, we couple an ultra-low power 40nm CMOS process with Emitter Coupled Logic (ECL) implemented on top of a high-performance SiGe 130nm BiCMOS technology from IHP [9]. Analysis accuracy is pursued by detailed microarchitectural design of a reconfigurable (de-)serializer structure and by synthesizing the whole bridge on the target multi-technology platform with a commercial synthesis tool.

GLSVLSI '18, May 23–25, 2018, Chicago, IL, USA

ACM ISBN 978-1-4503-5724-1/18/05...$15.00
https://doi.org/10.1145/3194554.3194593

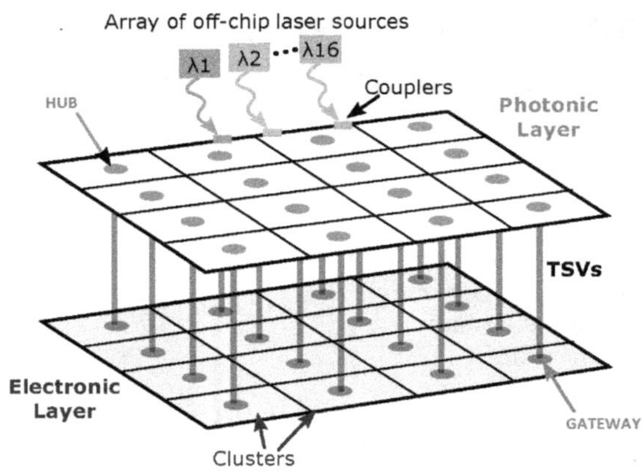

Figure 1: Target 3D-stacked architecture.

The main contributions of the paper are indicated as follows, together with the main findings:

- We characterize the performance limits of fully CMOS bridges, and quantify the extended scalability range enabled by ECL. We find that upper bounds on the data rate are not only ECL technology-specific, but also depend on the performance of the CMOS process through the interdependencies imposed by the serializer architecture. Overall, the hybrid bridge extends the feasible data rate by more than 3x when compared with the fully CMOS bridge.
- We investigate the best performing configuration of a bridge mapped onto the mixed CMOS-ECL technology platform, and whether this physical design solution makes sense from an energy efficiency viewpoint. We find that at its maximum speed of 8 Gbit/s, the fully CMOS realization incurs 8.7pJ/bit. The hybrid solution incurs a 2x overhead at the same speed, but at 25 Gbit/s a better energy-per-bit is achieved: 6.8pJ/bit.
- We derive realistic energy-per-bit and latency numbers for going through the hybrid bridge (both transmitter and receiver sides) as its architectural configuration changes, hence capitalizing on the flexibility of the proposed serializer architecture.

The analysis of this paper is preliminary in the sense that no thorough optimization was performed on the bridge architecture to improve its energy efficiency and/or performance. In fact, the assessment of technology-aware global quality metrics of this typically overlooked building block for heterogeneous technology integration is a milestone in itself, and the key novelty of this paper.

2 RELATED WORK

Integration aspects of photonic functions with electronic circuits are constantly investigated. A lot of previous work addresses this issue from the viewpoint of technology or physical design aspects [2, 18, 21, 27].

However, as ONoCs strive to become an interconnect solution of practical relevance, the focus is being quickly extended to the architectural layer. One simple idea is to use electrical links for short distances and optical ones for long distances [25]. Hybrid topology solutions are also proposed in [3, 19]. In many cases, heterogeneous technology integration is implemented through the composition of two subnetworks (an electronic NoC and an optical one) [4, 5, 12, 17, 24]. The solution is often custom-tailored for a 3D environment [16]. In this scenario, the problem addressed by this paper (efficient bridge architecture between ENoC and ONoC) arises. However, the complexity and the overhead introduced by the bridge are most of the times overlooked, although early works demonstrate that the overhead could be comparable with that of the optical network itself [11].

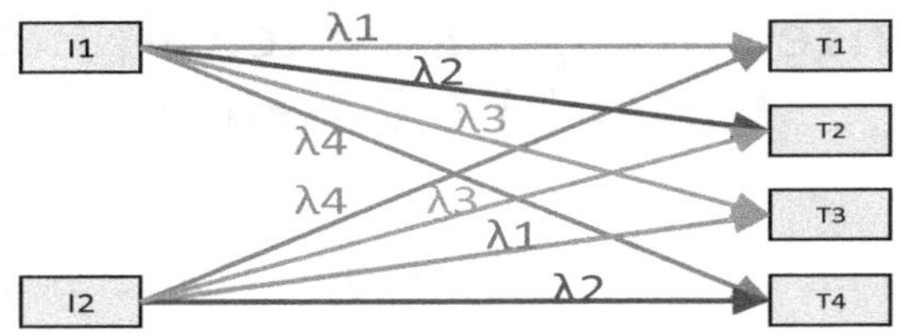

Figure 2: Wavelength-selective routing principle in a 4 × 4 ONoC.

The building blocks needed for the design of an entire bridge are highlighted in [22]. That work aims at architecture completeness, cycle-accurate simulation and functional correctness. With respect to that contribution, this paper makes a relevant step forward: here the focus is on implementation aspects and on post-synthesis characterization results. At this level, the technology library at hand plays a dominant role in determining bridge quality metrics. For the first time, latency and energy-per-bit achievable by a mixed CMOS-ECL technology are demonstrated.

Many advanced ONoC design solutions can only be enabled by a proper support in the network interface [6, 8, 10, 19]. The additional features can be implemented on top of the proposed bridge architecture, which is therefore a complementary yet enabling research effort for this prior work.

3 TARGET 3D ARCHITECTURE

The target architecture is a 3D-stacked system consisting of an optical layer vertically stacked on top of an electronic parallel processing layer (see Fig.1). Processing cores are grouped into 16 computation clusters and interconnected through an electronic network-on-chip (ENoC). Each cluster has a unique, shared gateway to the optical layer, and has a corresponding hub on it. Gateways and hubs are interconnected by through-silicon vias (TSVs).

A 16x16 ONoC is laid out on the optical plane. In this paper, we assume a wavelength-routed optical NoC, which has been showed in [23] to be a competitive solution for up to 16 hubs. With wavelength routing, each initiator sends optical packets to each target on different wavelengths, and targets receive packets from different iniators on different wavelengths. The global all-to-all conflict-free communication paradigm does not require any routing and arbitration stage. The principle is pictorially illustrated in Fig. 2.

This paper goes into the detail of gateway design. The latter does not only consist of opto-electronic circuits for domain conversion, but also of a connecting **bridge architecture** between ENoC and ONoC. The latter has to deal with high-level tasks such as:

i) Adaptation of ENoC clock rate and bit-level parallelism to ONoC modulation rate and transmission parallelism (via spatial- or wavelength-division multiplexing).

ii) Management of backpressure (flow control) across physical domains.

iii) Resynchronization: when an optical signal is converted back into the electronic domain, its alignment with the local clock is unknown.

iv) Deadlock avoidance: although routing-related deadlock cannot take place in the ONoC because of its bufferless nature, message-dependent deadlock [1] may still occur, as a result of the interactions and dependencies created at network endpoints between different message types (e.g., between requests and responses).

The bridge architecture will be discussed in section 5. In principle, the bridge can be entirely implemented on a bulk CMOS process, which will serve as our baseline solution. In this case, we assume that while the bridge resides on the electronic layer, opto-electronic components are placed on the optical layer. Different assumptions will be made for hybrid solutions (see section 4). For our synthesis experiments, we select an available ultra-low power 40nm industrial technology library, and project implications when using more scaled process nodes. While such technology is ideal for use in high-end embedded computing platforms, early roadmapping studies have advocated the use of ultra-low power technologies even for high-performance computing [14].

4 TARGET TECHNOLOGY

In static power dominated technologies like silicon photonics, operation at high transmission rates (even beyond the limits of standard CMOS processes) may become a high priority in order to cut down on energy-per-bit. Therefore, it may be convenient to implement a growing share of bridge devices with better-performing technologies than CMOS, thus giving rise to a new partitioning problem and to a wider configuration space of the bridge. Clearly, designers should engineer the bridge in such a way that the communication performance speedup is not overtaken by the power overhead.

Thus, until the performance requirement is not violated, the more complex components with higher logic depth could be mapped to CMOS logic. On the other hand, faster high-speed parts could be realized in an alternative technology using faster HBT (Heterojunction Bipolar Transistor) devices.

For the high-performance parts of the bridge architecture introduced in section 5, IHP's high performance 0.13 μm SiGe BiCMOS process is selected [9]. This process has five thin and two thick metal layers, fast HBT devices with an f_T/f_{MAX} = 250 GHz/340 GHz, and offers 3.3 V compatible and 1.2 V low voltage MOS devices. Additional important modules for 3D integration such as TSV (Through Silicon Via) and LBE (Localized Backside Etching) are also offered.

The target logic family for corresponding implementation in this BiCMOS process is a 2.5 V compatible positive Emitter Coupled Logic (ECL), a high performance current mode logic using HBTs, load resistors and NMOS current sources. A cell library provides common standard cell gates, such as MUX, NOR, XOR, latches, flip-flops and clock buffers and operates either in fully differential or in hybrid single-ended mode, in which for instance some complementary input pins are tied to the common mode voltage. The cells are designed with a larger voltage swing of 400 mV in order to (i) guarantee a proper operation under all conditions and (ii) to benefit from the wired-or functionality for single-ended cells. This allows to design more complex cells such as NOR16 or multiple-bit NAND/OR combinatorial gates. With these gates, high-speed blocks such as multiplexers, clock dividers or shift registers can be designed, thus meeting the performance requirements of electrical interfaces directly exposed to high-speed optical layers.

However, static ECL gates have high leakage currents up to several mA depending on the load resistance, the number of tail currents, and the defined voltage swing. Thus, the cells need to be carefully selected by speed class (load resistance, current consumption), cell functionality and their operating mode in order to achieve the desired trade-off between performance and power/silicon area overhead.

By default, HSS (High-Speed SerDes) components in the multi-GHz range are designed in analog manner, that is by-hand drawn circuit schematics, time consuming analog simulation runs, and individual device placement and wire routing at layout level. In order to reduce the design effort and simulation run time during the bridge configuration space exploration targeted by this paper, we have followed the previously published approach in [13] and enabled the gate-level synthesis step of the digital design flow for ECL. Candidate bridge architectural sections for speedup are thus described in hardware description language (HDL) and compiled with commercially available HDL compilers. We use Synopsys Design Compiler.

Similar BiCMOS processes to that used in this paper, even from the same foundry, have shown that the tight opto-electronic integration on the same chiplet is possible [7]. Thus, it is reasonable to envision that in the future the ECL section of the bridge might be implemented on the optical layer, together with the analog, domain conversion and optical components. This would give rise to an efficient, tightly-coupled and modular realization of photonically-integrated 3D-stacked systems. This is the assumption we make in this paper for the hybrid bridge.

5 BRIDGE ARCHITECTURE

In this section we present the complete bridge architecture proposed for wavelength-routed ONoCs (Fig.3). It is a modified version of the early interface concept in [22], with a completely new focus on the serialization archiecture and on cross-layer design and implementation issues of the bridge as a whole.

5.1 Front-End Architecture

Our bridge is divided into two parts, transmission part (Fig.3-top) and receiver part (Fig.3-bottom), since every gateway can be both initiator and target. In order to avoid message-dependent deadlock, we associate different buffering resources (virtual channels (**VCs**)) to different message classes. In this implementation, we use two VCs: one for requests and one for responses.

This should be combined with the distinctive requirement of wavelength routing: each initiator needs an output buffer for each possible target, and each target needs an input buffer for each initiator in order to enable concurrent contention-free communication. As a result, each target interface comes with 2 VC FIFOs for each potential source. The initiator interface can be instead optimized, since the same 2 VC buffers can be shared for all possible destinations, and packets can be routed afterwards to dedicated transmitters. For each replicated transmission path we use a separate arbiter solving VC contention issues.

All the FIFOs in the architecture must be dual-clock FIFOs (DC-FIFOs), to move data between the ENoC frequency domain *f0* (we assume 1 GHz) and the one used inside the bridge. We call it *network interface (NI) frequency*. We assume a depth of 8 slots for VC FIFOs.

After flits (i.e., the smallest packet chunks handled by the flow control mechanism) are sent to the appropriate path depending on their destination, they must go through different stages of serialization, to be then transmitted through the optical NoC at the target modulation rate (e.g., 10 Gbit/sec). The serializer and de-serializer architectures will be explained in detail in the next section. In Fig.3, we show a configuration with five-stage serializer and de-serializer and a bit-level parallelism of one.

Without lack of generality, in our architecture we assume to have one PLL in each transmitter, which is responsible for generating the clock that drives the last stage of the serializer. As will become clear in the next section, the transmission frequency (hence the data rate) is twice the frequency generated by the PLL. This clock is also fed to a chain of $N - 1$ clock dividers that halve the input clock frequency, where N is the number of the serializer stages. We exploit the clock generated by the last divider for driving the components at the front-end (e.g. Arbiters, DC-FIFOs, etc.). The remaining clock input of DC-FIFOs is the synthesized 1 GHz ENoC clock.

In this paper we assume source-synchronous communication, which implies that each point-to-point communication requires a strobe signal to be transmitted along with the data on a separate

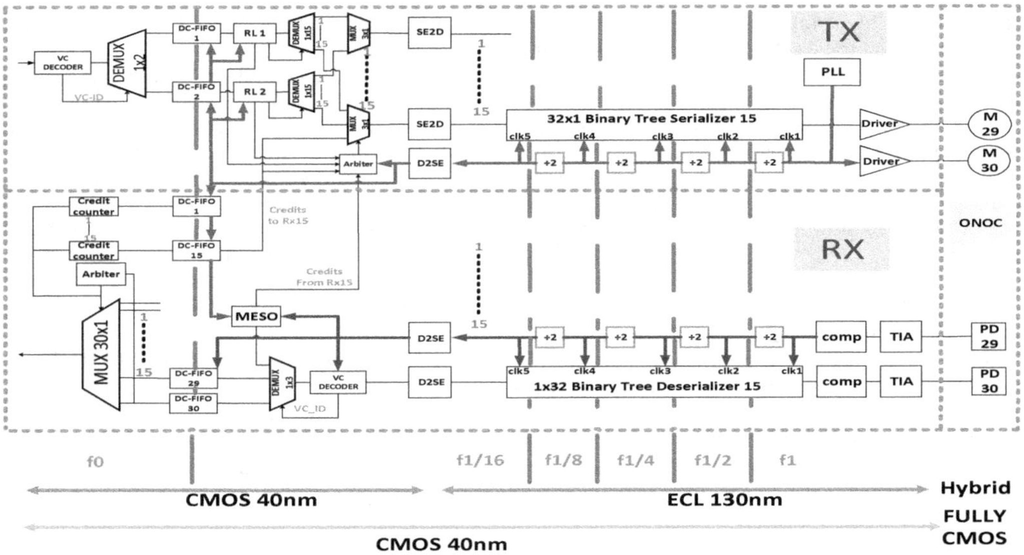

Figure 3: Bridge architecture for wavelength-routed ONoCs. It supports communications among 16 nodes without self-communication. Flit width is 32 bits. Each section runs at the frequency indicated at the bottom.

wavelength. The received source-synchronous clock at the receiver side of the bridge is then used to drive the de-serializers and, after a chain of clock dividers, the front-end of the DC-FIFOs.

As a backpressure mechanism, we opt for credit-based flow control, since credit tokens can reuse the existing data paths while taking advantage of the low dynamic power in optics. In order to synchronize credits between different frequency domains at the receiver side, we use again small DC-FIFOs. Unlike the ones adopted for VC implementation, here we assume a FIFO depth of 2 slots only, because the credit counter can meanwhile accumulate all credits until the credit packet goes through the FIFO. The credit packet arrives at destination and is then delivered to the interested arbiter in the transmission path. In this case, the clocks of the two domains run at the same frequency but with unknown phase offset. Therefore, a mesochronous synchronizer is required.

5.2 Serializer/De-serializer Architecture

Fig.4 shows the block diagram of a 16:1 serializer and its main building block: the 2:1 MUX cell. This cell has two input ports and one output port, and is composed of 3 latches and one standard cell multiplexer. In particular, when the clock (enable pulse) is low, latches of the first stage are transparent, thus the data can propagate. Conversely, when the clock goes high, the multiplexer opens the way for the upper data path. At the same time, the second latch on the lower data path is transparent and lets data flow through. When the clock goes again low, the lower data path is selected, where data has meanwhile become stable. This way, we are preventing data loss, and ensure transmission of stable data.

As shown in Fig.4, these building blocks are connected together in a perfect binary tree structure to construct a 16:1 MUX, which is the complete serializer architecture. In particular, the serializer is divided into M stages where $M = log_2 N$. In Fig.4, $N = 16$, then $M = 4$. The architecture can be easily scaled up to 32:1 by just adding one more stage to the left. The last stage, which provides the output signal, works at full rate (i.e., the modulation rate), which is twice the input clock frequency, while the other ones work at halved speed

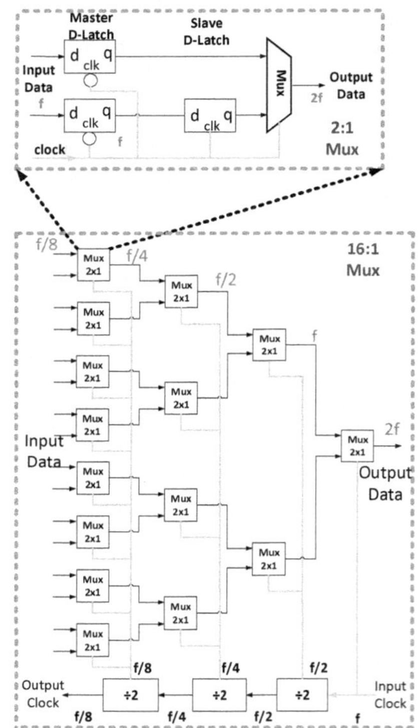

Figure 4: Serializer architecture and its main building blocks.

with respect to one another. Therefore, for an $N : 1$ MUX we need $M - 1$ dividers.

The main reasons for choosing this serialization structure are:

- This structure has different stages and each stage works at a different operating frequency. This means that not all the serializer components should work at the final (overly high)

transmission frequency. In addition, the number of basic building blocks in a stage is inversely proportional to the operating frequency of the stage, which leads to energy savings.
- As mentioned, the transmission frequency is twice the input clock frequency, which translates into lower clock frequency requirements for the PLL.
- This structure does not need additional selectors to enable the multiplexers, since they are enabled by the 2 levels of the clock.
- This structure is very flexible. In fact, the bit-level parallelism can be increased by a power of 2 by just removing stages from the serializer/de-serializer starting from highest-speed stages toward lower-speed ones. In practice, if we want an optical flit width of 2, we just need to remove the last serializer stage and one clock divider, and then add as many drivers, modulators, photodetectors and transimpedance amplifiers (TIAs) as the intended number of concurrent optical bits. Therefore, our flexible architecture can easily span a wide bridge configuration space.

The de-serializer works in a complementary way with respect to the serializer, and is omitted for lack of space.

6 EXPERIMENTAL RESULTS

We provide post-synthesis results of the entire bridge in Fig.3. We consider two extreme configurations, namely Fully-CMOS and Hybrid, with technology partitioning indicated at the bottom of Fig.3.

For the energy-per-bit calculation, we excluded the power consumption of the optical devices and of their transceiver circuits (e.g., off-chip laser, thermal tuning, modulators, photo-detectors, modulator Drivers, TIA), so to focus on the bridge contribution. Moreover, these components would deserve dedicated studies to custom-tailor them for the system at hand and get realistic cost estimates. This is left for future work.

We nonetheless approximate the power consumption of the PLL, since it is a part of the serializer. We assume a value of 270 mW, which is estimated from [15] while keeping technology homogeneity. In our target 16x16 wavelength-routed ONoC, we assume to have one PLL in each transmitter, and we share the divider chains among the 15 serializers to save power. At the receiver side, this cannot be done because each de-serializer receives its optical clock from a dedicated transmitter, then even the divider chains should be replicated 15 times. For the experiments that follow, we assume a flit size of 32 bits.

6.1 Energy-per-bit

We next compute energy-per-bit (E/b) for the complete path from source to destination, hence accounting for transmitter and receiver sides of the bridge. We initally assume 1-bit parallelism. Fig. 5 shows results as a function of the target bit rate.

For the hybrid bridge, we achieved a maximum transmission frequency of 25 GHz. This upper bound is not limited by the speed of the BiCMOS process, but rather by the maximum achievable NI frequency with the CMOS process in the bridge front-end: 1 GHz. In fact, the front-end and back-end frequencies are related by the serialization stages and by the clock dividers. We project that a scaled and/or higher performance CMOS process would allow to push ECL-enabled transmission frequency further ahead.

From Fig. 5, when the bit rate increases, the E/b decreases. In fact, the E/b of the Hybrid solution scales from 29.1 pJ/bit at a bit rate of 5 Gbit/s down to 6.8 pJ/bit at the upper bound bit rate of 25 Gbit/s. This trend is true also for the Fully-CMOS solution, where the E/b scales from 10.3 pJ/bit at a bit rate of 5 Gbit/s down to 8.7 pJ/bit at

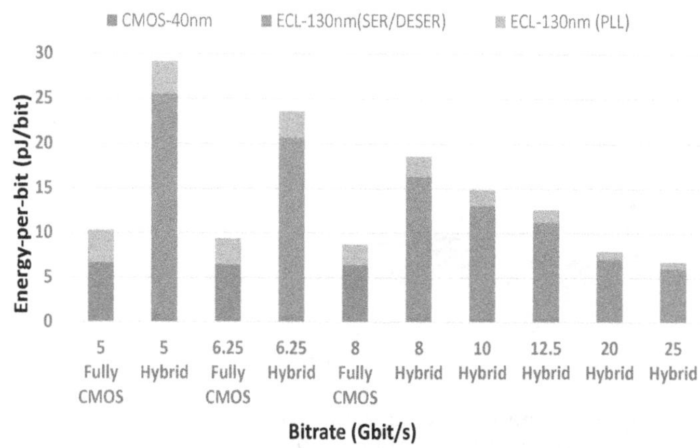

Figure 5: Energy-per-bit to go through the bridge (transmitter plus receiver sides).

the highest achievable bit rate of 8 Gbit/s. As can be noticed, the E/b of the Hybrid solution is more sensitive to the bit rate than the Fully CMOS one. In fact, power consumption of the ECL cells is dominated by their static power, then E/b clearly exhibits a higher sensitivity to the bit rate, since the infrastructure better amortizes the static power cost.

If we look at trend of the Fully-CMOS solution, the E/b decreases mainly due to the reduced contribution of the PLL. Instead, the contribution of the bridging components decreases only slightly. On the one hand, they are resynthesized for higher operating frequencies (enabling the higher bit rate) and dynamic power increases as well. On the other hand, the bit rate increases, thus cutting-down on E/b. Overall, the two effects tend to offset each other.

The fully-CMOS solution results more energy efficient than the Hybrid one for bit rates less than or equal to 8 Gbit/s. Beyond 8 Gbit/s, the Fully CMOS solution is not feasible, while the Hybrid solution continues to improve its energy-per-bit until it reaches 6.8 pJ/bit at the upper bound bit rate of 25 Gbit/s.

It is worth noting that higher bitrate leads to lower Serializer Latency, which means higher NI operating frequency. Indeed, the Fully CMOS solution can achieve in the best case a serializer latency of 4 ns, which leads to NI operating frequency of 0.25 GHz. In contrast, the Hybrid solution can achieve a serializer latency of 1.28 ns, which corresponds to an NI frequency of 0.78 GHz, close to the upper bound of 1 GHz. Therefore, the Hybrid solution achieves three goals at the same time, namely higher bit rate (25 Gbit/s vs. 8Gbit/s), lower serializer latency (1.28 vs. 4ns) and lower energy-per-bit (6.8 pJ/bit vs. 8.7 pJ) compared to the Fully CMOS solution.

6.2 Bit-Level Parallelism

Fig. 6 shows how the energy-per-bit changes when increasing the transmission frequency **and** the bit-level parallelism. At a fixed transmission frequency, the E/b of both solutions (Hybrid and Fully CMOS) decreases with a higher bit-level parallelism. This is due to the higher bit rate achieved at the same operating frequency and the lower number of stages in the (de-)serializers. When the transmission frequency increases, only the E/b of the Hybrid solution decreases. This confirms the outcome of the previous 1-bit energy-per-bit analysis.

Another outcome of Fig. 6 is that, in order to achieve a target throughput, using higher bit-level parallelism and lower transmission frequency is not significantly more energy efficient than using a higher frequency with lower parallelism. This holds for both schemes

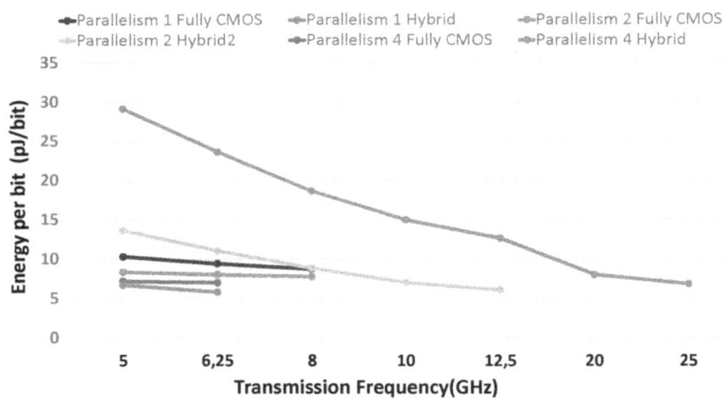

Figure 6: Energy-per-bit of the bridge at different transmition frequencies and bit-level parallelism (1, 2, 4).

under test. For example, a bit rate of 25 Gbit/s can be normally achieved with a transmission frequency of 25GHz and a bit-level parallelism of one, but also at 12.5 GHz with 2-bit parallelism, as well as at 6.25 GHz with 4-bit parallelism. In all these cases, the E/b is comparable. This is a bit counterintuitive, since a lower transmission frequency implies a lower operating frequency, hence a lower power consumption. In practice though, we are removing the last stages of the serializers running at high speed, which are however the simplest ones in terms of allocated resources. Therefore, the E/b variation is not significant. In addition to that, it is worth recalling that an increase of bit-level parallelism requires the replication of components whose cost is not considered in this analysis, such as optical modulator drivers, TIAs, modulators, photo-detectors, etc. Thus, our results indicate that a bit-level parallelism of one turns out to be the most energy efficient configuration for the hybrid platform in order to extract the maximum data rate from it.

7 CONCLUSIONS

This paper has investigated a mixed CMOS-ECL realization of a bridge between an electronic NoC and an optical one in a 3D-stacked parallel processor. The key take-away is that the most promising configuration for this multi-technology solution consists of a low bit-level parallelism while maximizing transmission frequency. Interestingly, such maximum speed is not dictated by the ECL technology but rather by the CMOS logic, when considering the detailed microarchitecture of the serializer and the cross-technology dependencies it imposes. Nonetheless, the Hybrid implementation not only extends the range of achievable transmission rates with respect to the fully CMOS solution (which was expected), but also yields lower energy-per-bit at 20 Gbit/sec and beyond. Microarchitectural simulation also reveals that such transmission rates cut down on the serialization latency, which approaches 1ns (thus keeping up with the typical clock period for ENoCs in low-power manycores). In future work, we will optimize the architecture for energy efficiency, and extend the analysis to the analog and optical components.

ACKNOWLEDGMENTS

This work is completely supported by IUSS-Ferrara (Istituto Universitario degli Studi Superiori a Ferrara), under the abroad mobility program for PhD students at University of Ferrara (Italy).

REFERENCES

[1] A.Hansson, K.Goossens, and A.Radulescu. 2007. Avoiding Message-Dependent Deadlock in Network-based Systems-on-Chip. *VLSI Design* (2007).
[2] L. Alloatti. 2017. High-Speed Photonics for Side-by-Side Integration With Billion Transistor Circuits in Unmodified CMOS Processes. J. Lightwave Technol. 35, 6 (2017), 1168–1173.
[3] S. Bahirat and S. Pasricha. 2014. METEOR: Hybrid Photonic Ring-mesh Network-on-Chip for Multicore Architectures. *ACM Trans. Embed. Comput. Syst.* 13, 3 (2014), 116:1–116:33.
[4] J. Chan, G. Hendry, A. Biberman, and K. Bergman. 2010. Architectural Exploration of Chip-Scale Photonic Interconnection Network Designs Using Physical-Layer Analysis. *Journal of Lightwave Technology* 28, 9 (2010), 1305–1315.
[5] D. Dang, B. Patra, and R. Mahapatra. 2015. A Multilayered Design Approach for Efficient Hybrid 3D Photonics Network-on-Chip. In *Proceedings of the 25th Edition on Great Lakes Symposium on VLSI.* 121–126.
[6] C. Killian et al. 2017. Energy and Performance Trade-off in Nanophotonic Interconnects Using Coding Techniques. In *2017 54th ACM/EDAC/IEEE Design Automation Conference (DAC).* 1–6.
[7] D. Petousi et al. 2016. High-Speed Monolithically Integrated Silicon Photonic Transmitters in 0.25 um BiCMOS Platforms. In *ECOC 2016; 42nd European Conference on Optical Communication.* 1–3.
[8] G. Thakkar et al. 2017. Improving the Reliability and Energy-Efficiency of High-Bandwidth Photonic NoC Architectures with Multilevel Signaling. In *Proceedings of the Eleventh IEEE/ACM International Symposium on Networks-on-Chip.* 4:1–4:8.
[9] H. Rucker et al. 2010. A 0.13 um SiGe BiCMOS Technology Featuring fT/fmax of 240/330 GHz and Gate Delays Below 3 ps. *IEEE Journal of Solid-State Circuits* 45, 9 (2010), 1678–1686.
[10] J. Sepulveda et al. 2015. Communication Aware Design Method for Optical Network-on-Chip. In *2015 IEEE 9th International Symposium on Embedded Multicore/Manycore Systems-on-Chip.* 243–250.
[11] L. Ramini et al. 2014. Assessing the Energy Break-Even Point Between an Optical NoC Architecture and an Aggressive Electronic Baseline. In *2014 Design, Automation Test in Europe Conference Exhibition (DATE).* 1–6.
[12] M. Nikdast et al. 2012. A Torus-Based Hierarchical Optical-Electronic Network-on-Chip for Multiprocessor System-on-Chip. J. *Emerg. Technol. Comput. Syst.* 8, 1 (2012), 5:1–5:26.
[13] O. Schrape et al. 2017. Routing Approach for Digital, Differential Bipolar Designs Using Virtual Fat-Wire Boundary Pins. In *2017 IEEE 20th International Symposium on Design and Diagnostics of Electronic Circuits Systems (DDECS).* 122–126.
[14] P.Kogge et al. 2008. ExaScale Computing Study: Technology Challenges in Achieving Exascale Systems. (2008).
[15] P. Ostrovsky et al. 2017. A Single Chip 16 GS/s Arbitrary Waveform Generator in 0.13 um BiCMOS Technology. In *2017 IEEE Nordic Circuits and Systems Conference (NORCAS): NORCHIP and International Symposium of System-on-Chip (SoC).* 1–4.
[16] R. Morris et al. 2014. Three-Dimensional Stacked Nanophotonic Network-on-Chip Architecture with Minimal Reconfiguration. *IEEE Trans. Computers* 63, 1 (2014), 243–255.
[17] W. Zhang et al. 2010. A Hierarchical Hybrid Optical-Electronic Network-on-Chip. In *2010 IEEE Computer Society Annual Symposium on VLSI.* 327–332.
[18] L. Fulbert and J. M. Fedeli. 2011. Electronics Integration on CMOS. In *2011 Proceedings of the ESSCIRC (ESSCIRC).* 13–18.
[19] E. Fusella and A. Cilardo. 2017. H2ONoC: A Hybrid Optical-Electronic NoC Based on Hybrid Topology. *IEEE Transactions on Very Large Scale Integration (VLSI) Systems* 25, 1 (2017), 330–343.
[20] A. B. Kahng and F. Koushanfar. 2015. Evolving EDA Beyond its E-Roots: An Overview. In *2015 IEEE/ACM International Conference on Computer-Aided Design (ICCAD).* 247–254.
[21] P. Munoz. 2016. *Photonic Integrated Circuits Using Generic Technologies. IEEE Photonics Society News* 30, 15.
[22] M. Ortìn, L. Ramini, V. Viñals, and D. Bertozzi. 2014. Capturing the Sensitivity of Optical Network Quality Metrics to its Network Interface Parameters. *Concurrency and Computation: Practice and Experience* 26, 15 (2014), 2504–2517.
[23] L. Ramini, M. Tala, and D. Bertozzi. 2014. Exploring Communication Protocols for Optical Networks-on-Chip based on Ring Topologies. In *Asia Communications and Photonics Conference 2014.* ATh3A.165.
[24] A. Shacham, K. Bergman, and L. P. Carloni. 2008. Photonic Networks-on-Chip for Future Generations of Chip Multiprocessors. *IEEE Trans. Comput.* 57, 9 (2008), 1246-1260.
[25] S. Werner, J. Navaridas, and M. Luján. 2017. Designing Low-Power, Low-Latency Networks-on-Chip by Optimally Combining Electrical and Optical Links. In *2017 IEEE International Symposium on High Performance Computer Architecture (HPCA).* 265–276.
[26] S. Werner, J. Navaridas, and M. Luján. 2018. A Survey on Optical Network-on-Chip Architectures. *Comput. Surveys* 50, 6 (2018).
[27] Kevin A. Williams. 2017. Prospects for Electronic-Photonic Integration. In *Advanced Photonics 2017 (IPR, NOMA, Sensors, Networks, SPPCom, PS).* IW3A.1.

A Framework Exploiting Process Variability to Improve Energy Efficiency in FPGA Applications

Konstantinos Maragos, George Lentaris, Ioannis Stratakos, Dimitrios Soudris
National Technical University of Athens, School of ECE
(komaragos,glentaris,istratak,dsoudris)@microlab.ntua.gr

ABSTRACT

As technology node scales-down and process variability increases, the vendors impose even more conservative guard-bands to prevent potential malfunction of their microchips. However, this approach introduces considerable amounts of unexploited performance to individual chips, which can be harvested by developing novel customization tools. In the current work, we focus on the exploitation of process variability in modern FPGA chips to provide more energy efficient solutions. We propose a framework that i) generates variability maps characterizing the energy efficiency of commercial chips and ii) combines voltage and frequency scaling to limit the power dissipation of any given design for a given set of performance constraints. Experimental results on Zynq XC7Z020 28nm FPGAs show that the developed framework achieves up to 28.3% power reduction while maintaining the performance and functional integrity of realistic benchmarks. Moreover, by selecting the most efficient chip, we achieve up to 5.1% additional power savings.

ACM Reference Format:

Konstantinos Maragos, George Lentaris, Ioannis Stratakos, Dimitrios Soudris. 2018. A Framework Exploiting Process Variability to Improve Energy Efficiency in FPGA Applications. In *Proceedings of 2018 Great Lakes Symposium on VLSI (GLSVLSI '18)*. ACM, New York, NY, USA, 6 pages. https://doi.org/10.1145/3194554.3194569

1 INTRODUCTION

Nowadays, in an aggressive trend, the industry focuses on the development of low-power processing systems able to deliver high performance per Watt solutions. On one hand, the chip vendors design diverse platforms allowing optimal adaptation to a variety of application-specific requirements, e.g., via sophisticated heterogeneous devices integrating more than one type of processors and accelerators. On the other hand, the vendors continue to rely on technology node downscaling to produce more energy efficient computers. This downscaling is followed by technological (e.g., equipment inaccuracy) and physical challenges (e.g., leakage currents), which result in increased process variability and smaller fabrication yield [6]. To preserve functional integrity, more conservative guard-bands are imposed on the manufactured chips to ensure that they will collectively meet their specifications in the field. However, this well-established worst-case scenario approach fails to utilize the full capabilities of individual chips, especially of those possessing higher quality electrical characteristics.

In-the-field exploitation of process variability via custom tools is an attractive alternative for improving the overall performance of digital systems. Indicatively, today, the performance variation among multiple identical 28nm chips can reach 17% in terms of speed, while the actual operating frequency of certain applications can increase by up to 87% compared to static timing analysis with conservative guard-bands [5]. In the future, such variability-induced degradation is expected to worsen due to the process downscaling (e.g., the total failure probability for SRAM writes is evaluated around 3% at 32nm and grows beyond 10% for 16nm technology [8]). Thus, process variability becomes of particular interest when targeting energy efficient solutions, i.e., when we seek to maintain the speed/throughput under lower voltage supply. By exploiting the unique electrical characteristics of each available chip, such customized solutions can, a) improve the energy savings, b) tackle the over-growing power demands of modern embedded devices (e.g., smart-phones, wearables and IoT), and c) expand the lifespan of the system by slowing down the silicon aging phenomenon (e.g., a V_{dd} increase from 1.2V to 2.2V accelerates aging by ~50x [10]).

In this direction, the current work presents a framework to exploit process variability in modern commercial Field-Programmable Gate Arrays (FPGAs). We begin by exploring the variability of energy efficiency over the fabric of the chips and we continue by developing an automatic tool to customize accordingly the frequency/voltage of the given designs. We focus on FPGA chips because, among all processing platforms, they provide increased flexibility for post-fabrication mitigation; FPGAs allow run-time reconfiguration and very low level programming –almost at gate level– on a uniform architecture distributing identical resources over the entire fabric. Such a combination enables the mapping of the design to the most efficient part of the manufactured chip(s), which in turn can be fine-tuned to the most suitable electrical configuration, e.g., voltage and/or frequency. Overall, the main contributions of the paper are:

- The evaluation of process variability in commercial off-the-shelf 28nm FPGAs with respect to supply voltage.
- The introduction of custom spatial maps to characterize each FPGA device with respect to its energy efficiency.
- A framework to exploit the underlying variability for improving the power consumption of the FPGA while meeting the application's performance requirements, without using extra equipment or modifying the vendor's tool or user's IP.

To validate the proposed method for power-wise optimization, we use a set of XC7Z020 Zynq FPGAs and realistic benchmark applications. The experimental results show 28.3% power reduction while

GLSVLSI '18, May 23–25, 2018, Chicago, IL, USA

ACM ISBN 978-1-4503-5724-1/18/05...$15.00
https://doi.org/10.1145/3194554.3194569

maintaining the performance and functional correctness. Moreover, 5.1% additional power savings are obtained through the selection of the most efficient device.

The paper is organized as follows: Section 2 includes the related work. Section 3 explores the performance and power variabilities in 28nm FPGAs. Section 4 presents the proposed framework. Section 5 provides experimental results using realistic benchmarks. Section 6 draws the conclusions.

2 RELATED WORK

There is a continuous research interest on establishing new approaches for reduced power consumption in FPGAs. At architecture level, the authors in [9] propose a low-swing dual V_{dd} global interconnect consuming 22x less energy than a conventional FPGA at nominal V_{dd} with a 5x delay penalty. In [2], the authors propose a technique to lower the capacitance of routing wires in FPGAs leading up to 15.5% dynamic power reduction of the interconnect, with only 1% performance degradation and 2.1% area overhead.

At CAD level, the authors in [3] present the combination of clock-aware placement techniques to achieve up to 5% more energy efficient solutions than conventional placers. The experiments were performed in academic tools (VPR) by using a set of synthetic benchmarks. In another direction, the authors in [1] developed a tool that initially generates a calibration bitstream which is used to identify the actual maximum operating frequency of the application's critical paths under various voltage-temperature conditions. Then, the derived results are stored in proper configuration tables which are used to calibrate the operation of the FPGA (with original application bitstream) through dynamic voltage scaling according to the operating conditions. Experimental results on a 60-nm Cyclone IV FPGA exhibit 33% power savings. However, the main drawback of this approach is that is not adaptable to aging effects (new configuration tables should be generated).

At netlist level, the authors in [4] present the deployment of online detectors to measure the actual timing slack of the application's critical paths. To do so, for each critical register they place an additional shadow register to latch the exact same input with a variable clock phase offset. By sweeping the phase offset and measuring the output mismatches between the registers (shadow and critical), they build a discrepancy profile indicating the corresponding timing slack. Based on that information, they perform dynamic voltage and frequency scaling to improve power and throughput (33.5% power reduction on a 60-nm Cyclone IV). On the same principle, in [7] a library of soft-macro flip-flops (in-situ detectors), augmented with detection logic, is introduced to replace original critical flip-flops. Power and energy savings (68% energy reduction on a 65-nm Virtex-5 FPGA) are achieved through adaptive voltage scaling by considering the detected timing violations. However, such techniques suffer from increased resource overhead, rendering them impractical for large-scale designs.

In comparison to the aforementioned works, we introduce a framework for optimizing energy at a higher level of abstraction, i.e., at function level, where no modification is required in the vendor's CAD tool or the design's netlist. Moreover, with a limited resource overhead, the proposed framework combines two different types of tools, i.e., the variability map generation and the frequency/voltage scaling. Adaptation to silicon aging can also be realized via systematic tuning of the FPGA.

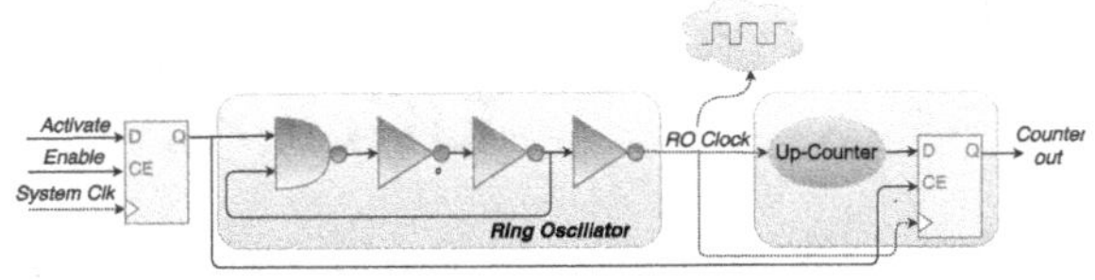

Figure 1: Structure of our ring oscillator sensor.

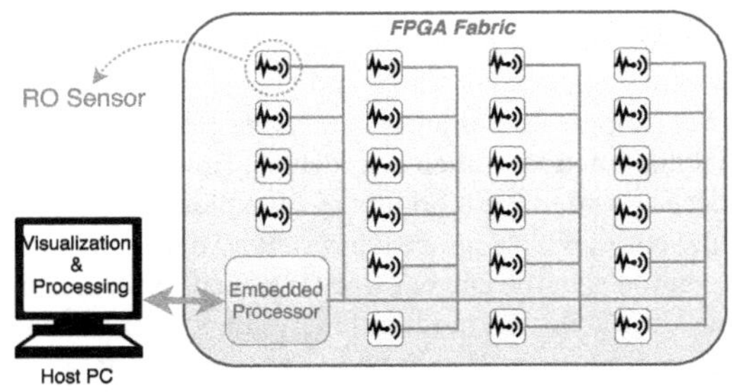

Figure 2: Sensing infrastructure for variability evaluation.

3 PERFORMANCE AND POWER VARIABILITY

In this section, we describe the evaluation of performance and energy efficiency in widely-used 28nm SoC FPGAs with respect to process variability. We employ two Xilinx Zynq XC7Z020 FPGA devices (hosted on identical ZC702 evaluation boards) including the Processing System (PS) with a dual-core ARM Cortex A9 processor and a variety of peripherals, as well as the Programmable Logic (PL) with the actual FPGA resources under investigation.

3.1 Sensing Infrastructure

To evaluate process variability, we rely on the ring oscillator (RO) structure shown in Fig. 1 and detailed in [5]. We deploy a network of uniformly placed RO sensors in the fabric of the FPGA (Fig. 2, also detailed in [5]) to measure the local performance (speed) of the various regions in the chip. The performance comparison among the different regions provides an assessment of the intra-chip variability. Similarly, the comparison among multiple identical chips provides an assessment of the inter-chip variability. On top of our sensing network, we employ the embedded ARM processor to supervise the operation of the RO's, collect their local data and forward the collected results to a host PC (e.g., via serial port) for further analysis.

The employed RO sensor consist of a chain of three inverters forming an asynchronous loop as shown in the middle box of Fig. 1. When the number of gates is odd and the RO is fed with a constant signal, its output oscillates to provide a square wave signal driving a 16-bit counter. Essentially, the counter measures the frequency of the signal generated from the RO, which depends only on the delay of the RO's asynchronous path, i.e., on the number and electrical characteristics of the transistors composing the loop. Upon initialization, the counter resets and the 1-bit input register holds an activation signal for a predefined time period T. During T, the RO

Table 1: Performance and intra-chip variability results.

Devices	Mean RO Freq. (MHz)	Intra-Chip Variability Metrics (MHz)		
		range = max − min	*range/min*	σ
Device 1	385.16	27.53	6.87%	4.16
Device 2	425.59	25.69	6.66%	4.74

oscillates and the counter increments continuously measuring the number of positive edges of the generated signal. At the end of T, the 16-bit output register holds the final outcome c_{ro} of the counter. The ARM processor can retrieve c_{ro} by having access to the 16-bit register and calculate the RO's frequency as $f_{ro} = c_{ro}/T$. To ensure same implementation and fair comparison among all employed RO sensors, we carefully develop with VHDL and constraints a detailed description of the sensor, which results in a robust macro-block being replicated within the FPGA and utilizing the exact same relative resources (only four CLBs, 0.06% of XC7Z020 device) and routing.

3.2 Variability Maps

By using our infrastructure with 408 ROs (sufficient coverage), we generate two distinct variability maps, one per FPGA device (Fig. 3a, 3b); each map represents the area of the chip divided in 408 small cells (top-left is the location of PS, not considered in this work), with each cell colored according to the frequency of its corresponding RO. The frequency of each RO is averaged over 10 runs (the standard deviation is negligible, i.e., 0.4 MHz). The color scale is common for both maps and ranges from 370 MHz to 445 MHz. Even with the limited sample of two devices, we observe a considerable variation in performance inside and between the devices. The frequencies vary rather smoothly in each map and reveal some homogeneous regions with respect to variability. We note that the variability maps were generated under the same environmental conditions: 24°C ambient temperature and 35°-37°C junction temperature according to the integrated monitor system of the chip (XADC block).

Table 1 reports more details regarding the measured performance of the ROs including various intra-chip variability related statistics (*range* and *standard deviation*). Considering the *range/min* metric, the intra-chip variability is calculated at 6.9% and 6.7% for device 1 and device 2 respectively. Furthermore, inter-chip variability is calculated at 10.5% in a similar way considering the maximum and the minimum mean RO frequency of both devices. Notice that, when we compare the fastest RO to the slowest RO in both devices, we get a variability of 18%.

3.3 Variability Evaluation Under Voltage Scaling

One step further, we explore the performance variation as a function of PL's supply voltage V_{PL} for logic resources. We perform voltage scaling and generate multiple new variability maps for each device and each V_{PL} level. We employ the power controller chip (UCD9248PFC, hosted on the ZC702 board) and we use the ARM and the I2C interface of PS to access the voltage rail driving the Zynq's PL subsystem. The communication with the controller is based on the PMBus protocol and a custom developed SW program, which implements all the necessary functions to set the user-defined V_{PL}.

For each device we generate 15 distinct variability maps where V_{PL} ranges in the area of 0.86-1V with step of 0.01V (below 0.86V

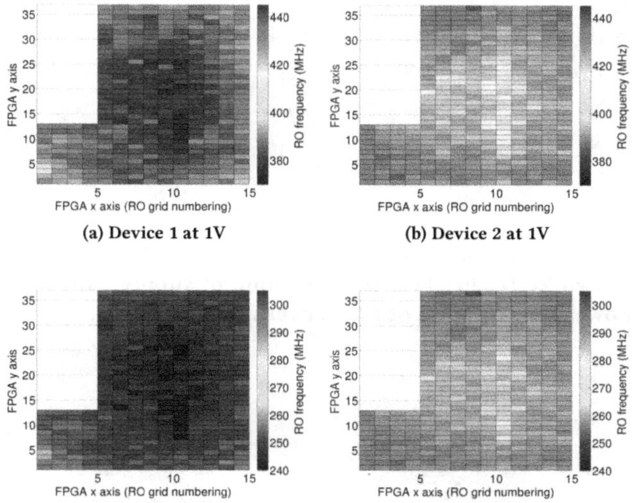

(a) Device 1 at 1V (b) Device 2 at 1V (c) Device 1 at 0.86V (d) Device 2 at 0.86V

Figure 3: Performance variability maps of 2 XC7Z020T FPGAs with supply voltage at 1V (a,b) and 0.86V (c,d).

the FPGA hardware becomes non-functional). As V_{PL} decreases, the performance of the chips degrades in a uniform fashion. Our analysis shows that for both devices, each new variability map is highly correlated to each other: 0.92-1 for device 1 and 0.98-1 for device 2 according to Pearson linear correlation. As representatives, Fig. 3c, 3d illustrate the variability maps of the two devices for V_{PL} = 0.86. Compared to the maps of Fig. 3a, 3b at nominal conditions ($V_{PL} = 1V$), the performance (mean RO frequency) is decreased by 35.4% and 32.1% for device 1 and device 2, respectively. Intra-chip variability increased slightly to 8% and 7.4% for device 1 and 2, whereas inter-chip variability increased considerably to 16.2%. Fig. 4a shows the scaling of inter-chip variability in function of V_{PL}. The results indicate that inter-chip variability tends to increase as V_{PL} decreases.

3.4 Energy Efficiency Characterization

Next, we evaluate the variability regarding energy efficiency in the FPGA devices and generate relevant, specialized maps. Initially, we measure the total power consumption of the RO network for various V_{PL} levels (0.86−1V). The power measurement is performed by using the ARM processor and the power controller as described above. According to the derived results (Fig. 4b), device 2 consumes more power, which is reasonable considering that for the same V_{PL} the ROs of device 2 operate at higher frequency compared to device 1 (Fig. 3). However, since the RO frequency is not fixed, we can not yet determine the most energy efficient device (consuming less power given a fixed operating frequency). To tackle this issue, we propose new maps, where each cell denotes the voltage required by the corresponding RO to achieve a given frequency, e.g., 373MHz. To calculate these values, we perform linear interpolation to the 15×1 matrix storing the performance of each RO for the 15 distinct V_{PL} levels (measured above). Based on the interpolation,

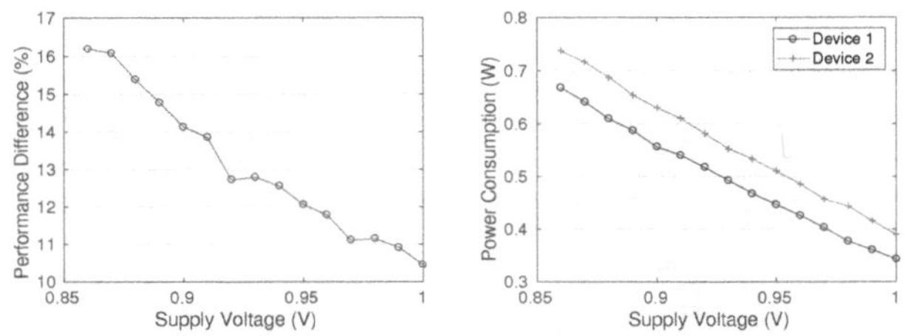

(a) (b)

Figure 4: (a) Performance difference (mean RO frequency) of two XC7Z020T FPGAs in function of supply voltage, (b) Power consumption of RO network in operation.

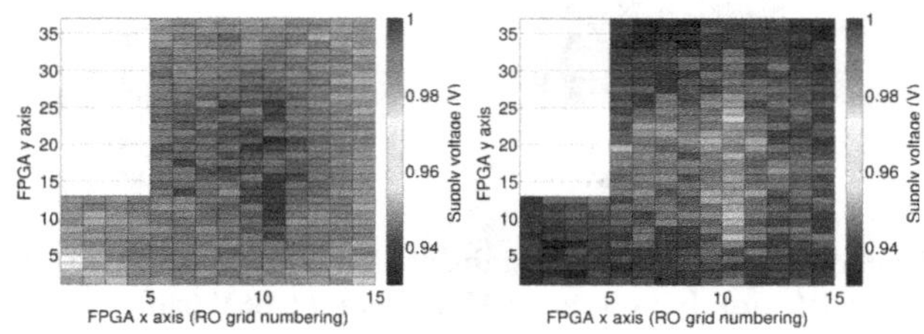

(a) Device 1 (b) Device 2

Figure 5: Energy efficiency variability of 2 XC7Z020T FPGAs.

we can determine in fine-grain the appropriate voltage for each RO to achieve a target frequency (arbitrarily selected a priori). By repeating the procedure for all 408 ROs, separately, we generate the voltage variability map of each chip, as depicted in Fig. 5 for $f = 373$ MHz (minimum RO frequency at nominal conditions). For both devices, the intra-chip variation is calculated at 2.8%. The inter-chip variation reveals that, on average, device 2 requires 4.6% lower V_{PL} than device 1 to achieve a certain performance, which translates to better energy efficiency. We note that a 4.6% voltage decrease can lead to more than 10% reduction of power in real-world designs as will be shown in Section 5. Furthermore, it is worth-mentioning that the voltage variability maps of Fig. 5 are highly correlated with the performance variability maps depicted in Fig. 3a, 3b (almost -1 for both devices) and Fig. 3c, 3d (-0.93 for device 1 and -0.99 for device 2), with negative coefficients implying that the inherently fast ROs require lower voltage to achieve a fixed frequency. These results show that, by having knowledge of the variability in an FPGA, we can be aware of its energy efficiency as well.

4 PROPOSED FRAMEWORK

Motivated by the aforementioned analysis showing considerable variation in terms of performance and energy efficiency in FPGAs, we propose a customization framework for decreasing power when given a user application with certain performance specifications.

The proposed framework is depicted in Fig. 6. It consists of two complementary phases: i) the generation of variability maps and ii) the design space exploration via frequency and voltage scaling. In particular, the framework's inputs are:

- *FPGAs*: The model and number of the employed FPGAs.

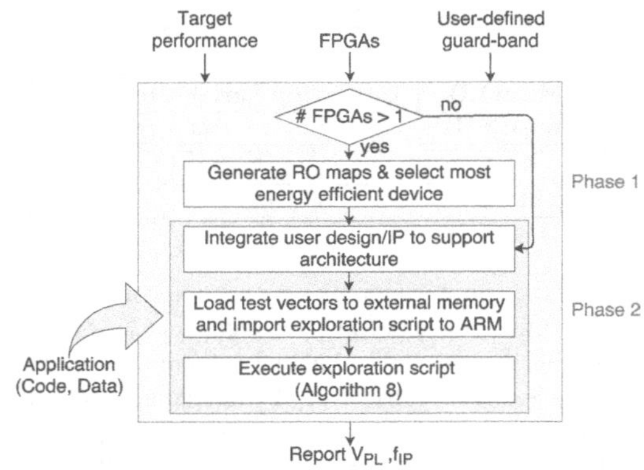

Figure 6: Proposed framework.

- *Target performance*: Specification of the application's operating frequency f_{IP}.
- *User-defined guard-band*: Imposed by the user for safety reasons (e.g., aging, environmental conditions). It is expressed as a percentage of the f_{IP}. For instance, 20% guard-band implies that the application should operate correctly at $f_g = 1.2 \cdot f_{IP}$.

The first phase of our framework involves the generation of variability maps for the employed FPGA(s). Depending on the FPGA model, a custom library provides the corresponding bitstream for the deployment of the RO network together with the SW program (hosted in ARM) for the generation of the variability maps. The generation requires less than 2sec when 10 consecutive runs are being averaged. Then, according to the generated maps, the user is able to select the most energy-efficient device (in case more than one are considered, e.g., in datacenters). Essentially, phase 1 constitutes a pruning stage in our exploration allowing for energy savings from the very start and avoiding the need to test each device separately.

The second phase of our framework consists of three steps. In the first step, the user integrates the application IP to a tailor-made support architecture described next (Fig. 7). In the second step, the user loads a tailor-made exploration script (Alg. 1) to the embedded ARM and stores the test vectors to the external memory (vectors can also be generated randomly). In the third step, the user executes the exploration script to automatically tune the FPGA for energy efficiency with respect to the performance specification inputs.

Towards providing a generic interface for the user to deploy his/her own application, we developed an architecture containing all the necessary units to support our framework. This support architecture (Fig. 7) expands the work of [5] to involve voltage scaling in the optimization procedure. It provides a Phase-Locked-Loop unit (PLL, bottom), which can be configured at run-time by the processor (PS, left) through the AXI-lite port. The PLL drives the clock of the user IP (top right), which is placed within a dedicated clock domain. Besides PLL, the IP is connected to 2 dual-clock FIFOs serving as synchronizers for clock domain crossing and correct transferring of the I/O data from the IP to the DMA controller (DMA, center). The DMA controller communicates with the PS, which includes the ARM processor executing the SW part of the application and the SW part of our framework. The DMA is used to implement AXI-stream PS-PL communication (the framework

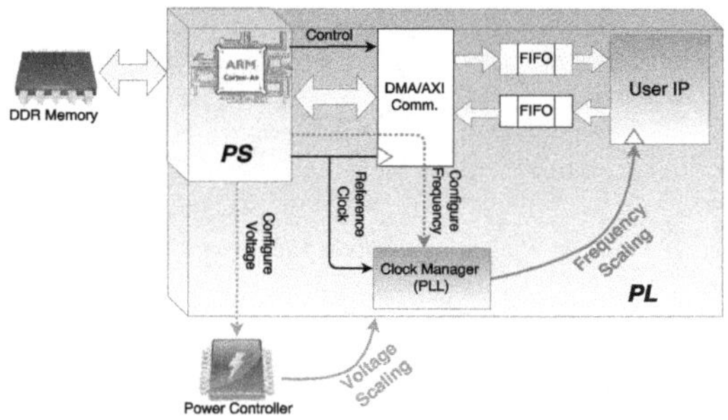

Figure 7: Support architecture of the proposed framework.

can adapt to any PS-PL communication in the user's application). The DMA and PLL operate in their own clock domain at 100 MHz (configurable up to 250 MHz), whereas the ARM processor operates at 667 MHz. The PS is connected to the power controller to enable the configuration of V_{PL}, as well as to the external DDR memory which, among others, holds the I/O data of the application. The resource utilization of the support architecture (with DMA for faster communication) is 4.7K LUTs and 6.5K DFFs (8.9% of the XC7Z020, but less than 2% for bigger devices, e.g., XC7Z100). Overall, the architecture is generic enough to be deployed either in SoC or standalone FPGAs (e.g., with Microblaze soft processor) and can be used as a baseline for even more complex systems.

Regarding the exploration script (framework's last step), the automatic tuning process is described by Algorithm 1. Initially, to produce the correct output (golden data), the application is executed at nominal conditions ($V_{PL} = 1V$, $f = f_{STA}$ rated by static analysis) and the output is stored in DDR memory. Then, the target frequency f_{IP} (with guard-banding) is tested to verify the functional correctness of the application. In case of malfunction, an iterative frequency scaling process is executed to search for the closest achievable error-free frequency $f_{IP'}$. Then, an iterative voltage scaling process follows, which gradually decreases the supply voltage V_{PL} to determine the lowest level allowing the IP to remain functional. At the end, the set of tuned $f_{IP'}$ and V_{PL} are reported. The total tuning time depends on the application delay, the SW/HW communication, and the number of test vectors. Indicatively, for the employed benchmarks of Section 5, the required time to perform the execution with 2M test vectors, retrieve the results and perform the comparison with the golden data stored in DDR memory was measured at 0.8-2 sec. The reconfiguration time of the clock's frequency was measured at 27-30 μsec, while the configuration of V_{PL} at 1.2 msec. We note that the tuning process can be applied also in a periodic fashion in-between the operation of the application to account for aging effects during the lifetime of the chip.

5 EXPERIMENTAL RESULTS

The current section uses realistic benchmarks to provide results with a twofold purpose. First, it presents a preparatory analysis regarding more generic performance and power figures, which validate the rationale of our framework. Second, it presents the final outcome of the framework including a representative exploration of the power-performance solution space for the selected benchmark applications.

Algorithm 1: Voltage/frequency exploration script

Input: Target performance f_{IP}, user-defined guard-band m
Output: Supply voltage V_{PL}, achieved performance $f_{IP'}$

$f = f_{STA}, f_{step} = 1MHz$ // f_{STA} reported by static analysis
$V_{PL} = 1V, V_{step} = 0.01V$
$D_c = execute(IP, f_{STA})$ // retrieve correct results D_c
$f = f_{IP} \cdot (1 + m)$ // include guard-band m
while *true* **do** // find error-free frequency f
  $D_n = execute(IP, f)$ // retrieve new results D_n
  if ($D_c \neq D_n$) **then**
    $f = f - f_{step}$
  else
    $f_{IP'} = f/(1 + m)$ // safe frequency $f_{IP'}$
    break
  end
end
$V_{PL} = V_{PL} - V_{step}$
while *true* **do** // find error-free voltage V_{PL}
  $D_n = execute(IP, f_{IP'})$
  if ($D_c == D_n$) **then**
    $V_{PL} = V_{PL} - V_{step}$
  else
    $V_{PL} = V_{PL} + V_{step}$
    return $V_{PL}, f_{IP'}$ // finish
  end
end

We employ two very popular DSP benchmarks/IPs: a 128-tap FIR filter (10.7K LUTs, 13.6 DFFs) operating nominally at 140 MHz and a 1024-size FFT (7.2K LUTs, 9.2K DFFs) operating nominally at 240 MHz, implemented with Xilinx Vivado 2017.1 on 2 Zynq XC7Z020 FPGAs. The IP's were integrated in our support architecture (Section 4, Fig. 7). For validation, we generate a 2-Msample random set of test vectors. All the experiments were conducted under the same environmental conditions (i.e., 24°C ambient temperature).

5.1 Performance and Power Analysis with realistic benchmarks

Fig. 8 presents the maximum achieved frequency (error-free operation) for various V_{PL} levels. At nominal $V_{PL} = 1V$, device 1 achieves 56.4% and 92.5% higher frequency than the tool rated f_{STA}, for FIR and FFT respectively. Device 2 provides even higher gain, i.e., 63.6% and 103.3%. The performance decreases gracefully with V_{PL}, i.e., a 36.4% for device 1 and 34.6% for device 2 degradation (on average, for both benchmarks) measured for a 14% decrease of V_{PL}. Considering all V_{PL} levels, device 2 is faster than device 1 by 6.7% (FIR) and 8.8% (FFT), on average, which is in accordance with the variability maps (Fig. 3). For distinct V_{PL}, the difference increases up to 10.3% (FIR) and 13.1% (FFT). Similar correlation between the variability map and chip performance has been presented in [5], for more than two Zynq devices, which indicates the validity of our maps and enables the use of a lower number of devices in the current work (limited availability of evaluation boards with power controllers).

To analyze power, we perform two experiments: 1) we measure power consumption with respect to frequency scaling for fixed V_{PL}, and 2) we measure power consumption with respect to V_{PL} for fixed frequency. Firstly, we set $V_{PL} = 1V$ and plot the derived results in Fig. 9a. For the FIR, an average reduction of 28.2% in power consumption is observed for 41.7% frequency decrease. Similarly, FFT shows a reduction of 34% in power consumption for 45.5% frequency decrease. We note that, although the measured power refers to the entire fabric of the FPGA, the frequency scaling impacts only a part of PL (the benchmarking domain, while

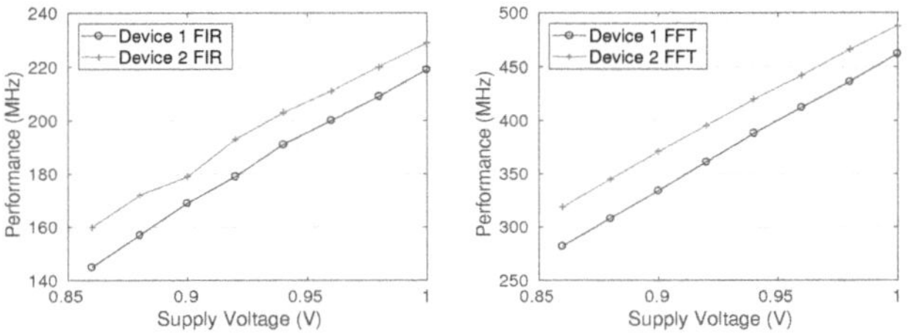

(a) FIR benchmark (b) FFT benchmark

Figure 8: Achieved performance as a function of V_{PL}.

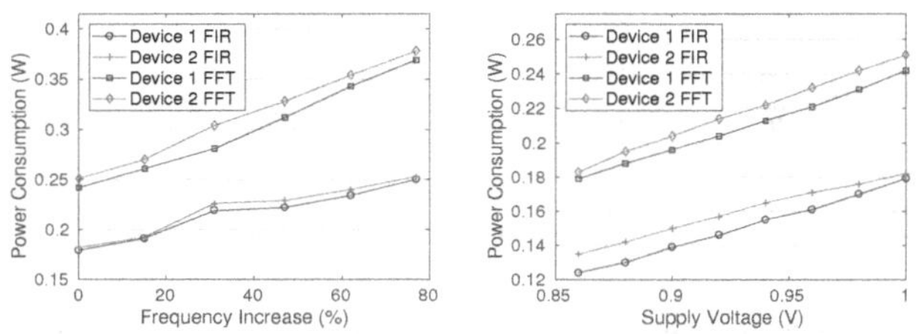

(a) (b)

Figure 9: Power consumption for (a) fixed V_{PL} and varying frequency, (b) fixed frequency and varying V_{PL}.

the support architecture, AXI communication, etc., use constant frequencies); that is, the FIR corresponds to the 69.1% of the total PL resource utilization, while the FFT to the 60%. By comparing the two FPGAs, we calculate that for both benchmarks device 1 consumes on average 3.2% less power than device 2.

Secondly, we fix the operating frequency to the 140 MHz for FIR and 240 MHz for FFT. We perform voltage scaling and we measure the power consumption for each distinct V_{PL}. On average, the FIR results plotted in Fig. 9b show 28.3% power reduction for 14% reduction of V_{PL}. The FFT power was reduced by 26.6%. Again, we observe that device 1 consumes less power than device 2, i.e., 4.7% on average for both benchmarks.

Overall, these experiments reveal that, for identical voltage/frequency conditions, device 2 is more power hungry than device 1 by around 4%. This is clearly an effect of variability in FPGAs and not in power controller chips, because reading out the corresponding voltage rails and comparing the V_{PL} values between the boards indicates negligible supply error (0.15%).

5.2 Energy efficiency and framework outcome

To measure and compare the actual performance per Watt of the applications, i.e., the amount of power consumed to achieve the target frequency, we generate the plots in Fig.10. The values are calculated based on the results of Fig. 8 having registered power consumption and on linear interpolation with 1MHz granularity. The plots show that device 2 provides better Perf./Watt than device 1: on average, it requires 2.7% (FIR) and 3.2% (FFT) less power to achieve the same throughput with device 1. The difference between the two FPGAs increases up to 5.1% for certain f_{IP}. These results are fully correlated with the analysis of the variability maps, which can

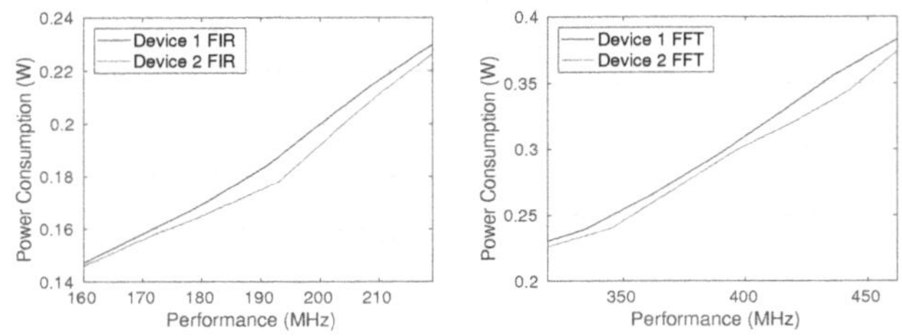

(a) FIR benchmark (b) FFT benchmark

Figure 10: Performance per Watt for 2 distinct benchmarks.

thus be used to successfully predict the energy efficiency difference between FPGAs, regardless of benchmark.

The plots of Fig.10 can be derived by the user executing the developed framework for various input frequencies f_{IP}. The user can explore the solution space or, e.g., can request directly the nominal frequency (supposedly, his/her initial goal) to gain 28.3% power decrease for FIR with minimal guard-band, or 18.7% power decrease for FFT with 50% guard-band.

6 CONCLUSIONS

The current paper evaluated in practice the performance and energy efficiency variations occurring in commercial 28nm FPGAs due to process variability. Motivated by variations up to 18% in frequency and 5% in required voltage, as well as typical guard-band losses of almost 30% in terms of power, the paper introduced a framework to adapt any given design with certain performance specifications to the individual characteristics of the user's available FPGA(s). Based on auto-generated variability maps and voltage/frequency scaling, the framework improved the power consumption of realistic benchmarks by up to 28.3% when comparing to the default implementation. Up to 5.1% power reduction was additionally gained when choosing among distinct chips. In future, we will advance the framework to exploit intra-chip variability for further gains and we will investigate even deeper sub-micron nodes (16/14nm).

REFERENCES

[1] Ibrahim Ahmed, Shuze Zhao, Olivier Trescases, and Vaughn Betz. 2016. Measure twice and cut once: Robust dynamic voltage scaling for FPGAs. In *FPL*. IEEE, 1–11.
[2] Safeen Huda, Jason Anderson, and Hirotaka Tamura. 2014. Optimizing effective interconnect capacitance for FPGA power reduction. In *FPGA*. ACM, 11–20.
[3] Julien Lamoureux and Steven JE Wilton. 2007. Clock-aware placement for FPGAs. In *FPL*. IEEE, 124–131.
[4] Joshua M Levine, Edward Stott, and Peter YK Cheung. 2014. Dynamic voltage & frequency scaling with online slack measurement. In *FPGA*. ACM, 65–74.
[5] Konstantinos Maragos, George Lentaris, Dimitrios Soudris, Kostas Siozios, and Vasilis F Pavlidis. 2017. Application performance improvement by exploiting process variability on FPGA devices. In *DATE*. IEEE, 452–457.
[6] Gustavo Neuberger, Gilson Wirth, and Ricardo Reis. 2014. *Protecting chips against hold time violations due to variability*. Springer.
[7] Jose Luis Nunez-Yanez. 2015. Adaptive voltage scaling with in-situ detectors in commercial FPGAs. *IEEE Trans. Comput.* 64, 1 (2015), 45–53.
[8] Vijay Janapa Reddi, David Z Pan, Sani R Nassif, and Keith A Bowman. 2012. Robust and resilient designs from the bottom-up: Technology, CAD, circuit, and system issues. In *ASP-DAC*. IEEE, 7–16.
[9] Joseph F Ryan and Benton H Calhoun. 2010. A sub-threshold FPGA with low-swing dual-VDD interconnect in 90nm CMOS. In *CICC*. IEEE, 1–4.
[10] Edward A Stott, Justin SJ Wong, Pete Sedcole, and Peter YK Cheung. 2010. Degradation in FPGAs: measurement and modelling. In *FPGA*. ACM, 229–238.

Assessing the Impact of Temperature and Supply Voltage Variations in Near-threshold Circuits using an Analytical Model

Sneh Saurabh
IIIT, Delhi
sneh@iiitd.ac.in

Vishav Vikash
IIIT, Delhi
vishav15117@iiitd.ac.in

ABSTRACT

In this paper, we develop an analytical model based on Enz Krummenacher Vittoz (EKV) current equations to assess the impact of temperature and supply voltage (V_{DD}) variations in circuits operating in near-threshold voltage (NTV) regime. Using the proposed model, we derive parameters that can be optimized to reduce the impact of these variations on devices operating in the NTV regime and highlight the dominant role of the inversion coefficient of the EKV equations. Further, we show that, instead of operating circuits such as a CMOS inverter very close to the threshold voltage (V_{TH}), it is beneficial to operate these circuits $3-4kT/q$ above the V_{TH}. At these voltages, the impact of the temperature variations on the delay is minimized and the impact of V_{DD} variations on delay is 0.7x lower than when operated at $V_{DD} = V_{TH}$. Additionally, compared to the super-threshold operation, the power consumption reduces by 5x and the delay increases by 5x. The results presented in this paper can be employed in estimating the increase in the time margins required when a circuit is migrated from the super-threshold operation to the near-threshold operation.

KEYWORDS

Current sensitivity; EKV model; near-threshold computing; PVT variations; timing margin

ACM Reference Format:
Sneh Saurabh and Vishav Vikash. 2018. Assessing the Impact of Temperature and Supply Voltage Variations in Near-threshold Circuits using an Analytical Model. In *Proceedings of Great Lakes Symposium on VLSI 2018 (GLSVLSI'18).* ACM, New York, NY, USA, 6 pages. https://doi.org/10.1145/3194554.3194589

1 INTRODUCTION

With the advancement in technologies and the failure to continue with Dennard's scaling law, power constraints have led to challenges such as dark silicon [1]. One of the techniques to tackle this challenge is to boost the energy-efficiency by employing near-threshold voltage (NTV) computing or operating circuits with supply voltage (V_{DD}) slightly above the threshold voltage (V_{TH}) of the transistors [1, 2]. NTV operation allows obtaining 10× decrease in the energy consumed per operation [2–4]. However, NTV operation is accompanied by degradation in performance and is more susceptible to process, voltage and temperature (PVT) variations [2–5].

The stronger impact of PVT variations on the performance of the circuits originates due to the exponential dependence of the MOSFET ON-state current (I_{ON}) in the NTV region on the V_{TH}, V_{DD} and the temperature [2, 6–8]. The increased impact of the PVT variations requires additional timing margins in the design flows and reduces operating clock frequency [2, 4, 9]. Moreover, the higher impact of the PVT variations in the NTV region can have adverse effect on the functionality and the reliability of the circuits such as SRAM [2, 10]. Therefore, it becomes necessary to thoroughly investigate the impact of PVT variations in the circuits operating in the NTV regime.

Many studies have been carried out to understand the temperature variations in the CMOS technology for different regions of operation [11–13]. There are a few studies on understanding and minimizing the impact of PVT variations in the near/sub-threshold circuits [4, 5, 14]. However, to the best knowledge of the authors, analytical models for assessing the impact of temperature and V_{DD} variations in the NTV regime, are not reported in the literature. An analytical sensitivity model is important in developing an intuitive understanding of the impact of temperature and V_{DD} variations and finding parameters that can be optimized to reduce these sensitivities. A sensitivity model can also be used in back-of-the-envelope calculations in designing of NTV circuits that have a dominant impact of these variations.

In this work, we develop an analytical model for the sensitivities of the I_{ON} of a MOSFET with respect to temperature and V_{DD}. Using the analytical model, we draw important conclusions regarding the dominant parameters that affect the temperature and V_{DD} sensitivities. Further, using these models, we examine the impact of these variations on a CMOS inverter and a ring oscillator and discover important trade-offs involved in circuits operating in the NTV regime.

In this work, we have developed two separate sensitivity models for MOSFET operating in super-threshold regime and sub-threshold regime. Though the focus of this paper is to investigate NTV operation, we have reported results for super-threshold operation for comparing the two regimes of operation. We have used Enz Krummenacher Vittoz (EKV) current equations for the sub/near-threshold regime. We have examined the accuracy of the proposed model by comparing the results obtained using SPICE simulations at 65 nm technology node with nominal $V_{DD} = 1.2V$. It is worthy to note that we have carried out simulations at 65 nm technology node due to infrastructure limitations. However, we expect that the inferences made in this study will be relevant at advanced processes also, since the EKV equations employed by the proposed model are reported to be sufficiently accurate at advanced processes [15, 16].

GLSVLSI'18, May 23–25, 2018, Chicago, IL, USA

ACM ISBN 978-1-4503-5724-1/18/05...$15.00
https://doi.org/10.1145/3194554.3194589

The rest of the paper is organized as follows. In section II and III, we derive analytical model for the temperature and V_{DD} sensitivities of the I_{ON} in the MOSFET, respectively. In Section IV, using the proposed model, we investigate the impact of temperature and V_{DD} variations on some digital circuits operating in the NTV region and conclude in Section V.

2 MODELING OF TEMPERATURE SENSITIVITY OF ON-STATE CURRENT

The performance of MOSFET based digital circuits is strongly dependent on the I_{ON} of the device. Therefore, it is important to assess the impact of the temperature and V_{DD} on the I_{ON} of the MOSFET. To develop an accurate sensitivity model, it is critical to accurately capture the dependency of the I_{ON} on temperature and V_{DD}. Therefore, we first ascertain that the model of the I_{ON} used in this study is accurate enough to capture the temperature and V_{DD} dependency.

2.1 ON-state current in MOSFET

The I_{ON} in a MOSFET is defined as the drain current when $V_{GS} = V_{DS} = V_{DD}$, where V_{GS} is the gate to source voltage and V_{DS} is the drain to source voltage. As the V_{DD} is reduced from super-threshold level to near/sub-threshold level, the mechanism of current transport changes. Therefore, we use different current equations for the I_{ON} in the sub-threshold regime and the super-threshold regime. It is worthy to note that, though we have described only n-type MOSFET in this work, p-type MOSFETs can easily be taken into account by appropriate changes in majority carriers and polarity of terminal voltages.

For sub/near-threshold region, the current model based on EKV equations, as shown below, is used [17]:

$$I_{ON} = 2n\mu_n C_{ox}(W/L).\phi^2[ln(e^{\frac{((1+D)V_{DD}-V_{TH})}{2n\phi}} + 1)]^2 \quad (1)$$

where n is the subthreshold slope factor, μ_n is the mobility of electrons, C_{ox} is the oxide capacitance, D is the drain-induced barrier lowering (DIBL) factor, ϕ is the thermal voltage given as kT/q with k=Boltzmann constant, q=charge of an electron, W, L are the width and length of the NMOS, respectively. The term in square brackets is known as inversion coefficient and indicates the degree of inversion of the channel in the transistor.

The V_{TH} of the transistor depends on the temperature and V_{DD} as follows:

$$V_{TH}(T) = V_{TH0} + \alpha_t.(T - T_o) - D.(V_{DD} - V_0) \quad (2)$$

where, V_{TH0} denotes the threshold voltage at the ambient temperature T_o and the drain biased in linear region with $V_{DS} = V_0$. The α_t is temperature coefficient of threshold voltage and is typically a negative quantity.

The mobility can be modeled as a function of temperature and V_{DD} as follows:

$$\mu_n(T) = \frac{\mu_{n0}.(T/T_o)^{\alpha_\mu}}{(1 + \gamma.V_{DD}^m)^{1/m}} \quad (3)$$

where, α_μ is the temperature coefficient of mobility, μ_{n0} denotes the mobility of electrons at ambient temperature T_o and when no electric field is applied, γ and m are fitting parameters. It should be noted that the coefficient α_μ is typically negative, i.e. mobility is expected to decrease with increase in temperature. However, with a decrease of μ_n, the I_{ON} is expected to decrease linearly, while with a decrease of V_{TH}, the I_{ON} is expected to increase.

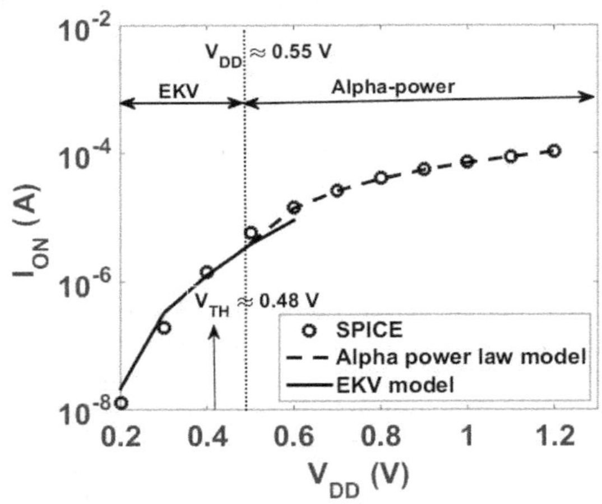

Figure 1: Comparison of I_{ON} computed using current models and measured using SPICE (T = 300K)

For the super-threshold region, current model based on alpha-power law, as shown below, is used [18]:

$$I_{ON} = (W/L)P_C(V_{DD} - V_{TH})^\alpha \quad (4)$$

where P_C is a fitting parameter and α is the velocity saturation index. In this work, we have taken P_C as a function of temperature as follows:

$$P_C(T) = P_{C0}.(T/T_0)^\beta \quad (5)$$

where β and P_{C0} are the fitting parameters. Intuitively, the above equation captures the effect of temperature on mobility in the super-threshold region.

The I_{ON} computed using eq. (1)-(5) were compared with SPICE simulations to assess their accuracy, as shown in Fig. 1. It is evident that EKV model is accurate up to $V_{DD} \leq 0.55V$, while for $V_{DD} > 0.55V$ the alpha-power law model is more accurate.

2.2 Temperature sensitivity of the ON-state current

The sensitivity of the I_{ON} with respect to temperature, denoted as S_T^I, can be defined as:

$$S_T^I = \left[\frac{1}{I_{ON}}\frac{\partial I_{ON}}{\partial T} \times 100\right]\% \quad (6)$$

The S_T^I is computed by summing up the sensitivities of the temperature-dependent terms in the expressions of I_{ON}. For the sub/near-threshold regime ($V_{DD} \leq 0.55V$), using eq. (1), S_T^I can be computed as:

$$S_T^I = \left[\frac{1}{\mu}\frac{\partial \mu}{\partial T} + \frac{2}{\phi}\frac{\partial \phi}{\partial T} + \frac{2}{\ln[\exp(\frac{(1+D)V_{DD}-V_{TH}}{2n\phi})+1]} \times \frac{1}{2n\phi}\cdot\frac{\exp(\frac{(1+D)V_{DD}-V_{TH}}{2n\phi})}{\exp(\frac{(1+D)V_{DD}-V_{TH}}{2n\phi})+1} \times \left(\frac{\partial V_{TH}}{\partial T} - \frac{((1+D)V_{DD}-V_{TH})}{nT}\right)\right] \times 100\% \quad (7)$$

In near/super-threshold regime ($V_{DD} > 0.55V$), using eq. (4), S_T^I can be computed as follows:

$$S_T^I = \left[\frac{\beta}{T} - \frac{\alpha.\alpha_t}{(V_{DD}-V_{TH})}\right] \times 100\% \quad (8)$$

The sensitivity S_T^I modeled using equations (7) and (8) was compared with SPICE simulations, as shown in Fig. 2. The proposed model is reasonably accurate compared to SPICE simulations. Following points are noteworthy for the S_T^I model:

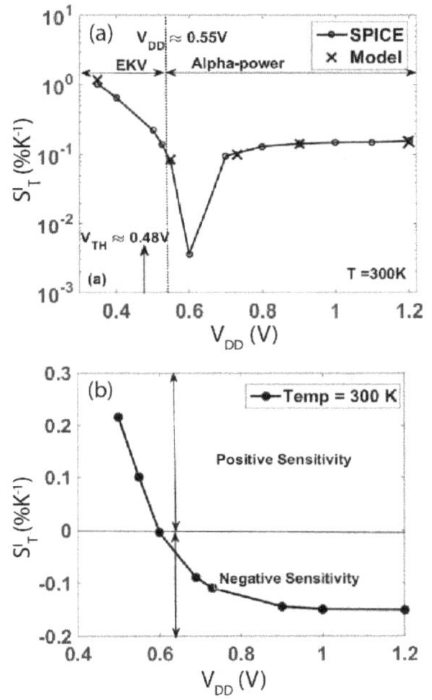

Figure 2: S_T^I obtained using the proposed model and SPICE simulations at different V_{DD} (a) in logarithmic scale (b) in linear scale showing reversal in the sign of S_T^I.

(1) In eq. (7), it can be seen that there are three terms that effect S_T^I: mobility, thermal voltage and inversion coefficient. The sensitivity model reveals that the term due to the mobility is very small compared to the inversion coefficient term. For instance, at $T = 300K$ and $V_{DD} = 0.35V$, the mobility term contributes only 2%, the thermal voltage term contributes around 46% and the inversion coefficient term contributes around 52%. This indicates that to reduce the S_T^I in the sub/near-threshold region, the variations due to inversion coefficient must be targeted.

(2) From Fig. 2(a) and 2(b), we can infer that the sensitivity of the I_{ON} decreases gradually with the decrease in V_{DD} and reaches a minima around $3-4kT/q$ above V_{TH}. The minimum sensitivity point can be computed using the proposed model. The existence of the minima can be explained by the mutual compensation of the thermal effects of μ_n and the V_{TH} [12, 13].

(3) In Fig. 2(b) we can note that there is a sign reversal in S_T^I in the sub/near-threshold region and super-threshold region. This is due to opposite effect of temperature on the I_{ON} in the sub/near-threshold regime and in the super-threshold regime.
In the sub/near-threshold region the increase in temperature results in an increase in the I_{ON}. Physically, it can be understood from the mechanism of current transport in the sub/near-threshold region. In this region, electrons with high thermal energy (or lying in the Boltzmann tail of Fermi Distribution Function) are able to overcome the potential barrier provided by the gate voltage. Thus, with an increase in temperature, the concentration of high energy electrons increases and it results in an increase in the sub/near-threshold current. This results in a positive S_T^I and can be inferred using eq. (7). For instance, at $V_{DD} = 0.35\ V$ and $T = 300K$, the S_T^I is computed to $1.19\%K^{-1}$.
In the super-threshold region, the I_{ON} decreases with the increase in temperature due to the dominant effect of the reduced mobility of electrons with increasing temperature. This can easily be inferred using eq. (8). For instance, at $V_{DD} = 0.90\ V$ and $T = 300K$, the S_T^I is computed to $-0.16\%K^{-1}$.

(4) Using the model, it was found that with an increase in temperature, S_T^I decreases. It can be understood using eq. (8), in which the first term (β/T) is found to be dominant compared to other terms. For instance, at $V_{DD} = 0.90V$ and $T = 300K$, the (β/T) term contributes around 140% in contrast to −40% from the other term.

(5) The model reveals that S_T^I decreases with a decrease in V_{TH}. The S_T^I also decreases when the subthreshold slope factor n increases.

3 MODELING OF SUPPLY VOLTAGE SENSITIVITY OF ON-STATE CURRENT

The sensitivity of I_{ON} with respect to the V_{DD}, denoted as $S_{V_{DD}}^I$, can be defined as:

$$S_{V_{DD}}^I = \left[\frac{1}{I_D}\frac{\partial I_D}{\partial V_{DD}} \times 100\right]\% \quad (9)$$

For the sub/near-threshold regime ($V_{DD} \leq 0.55V$), using eq. (1),

$S^I_{V_{DD}}$ can be computed as:

$$S^I_{V_{DD}} = \left[\frac{1}{\mu}\frac{\partial \mu}{\partial V_{DD}} + \frac{2}{\ln[\exp(\frac{(1+D)V_{DD}-V_{TH}}{2n\phi})+1]}\times \frac{\exp(\frac{(1+D)V_{DD}-V_{TH}}{2n\phi})}{1+\exp(\frac{(1+D)V_{DD}-V_{TH}}{2n\phi})} \times \frac{1}{2n\phi}.\left((1+D)-\frac{\partial V_{TH}}{\partial V_{DD}}\right)\right]\times 100\% \quad (10)$$

For the super-threshold regime ($V_{DD} > 0.55V$), using eq. (4), $S^I_{V_{DD}}$ can be computed as follows:

$$S^I_{V_{DD}} = \left[\frac{1.035\times\alpha}{V_{DD}-V_{TH}}\right]\times 100\% \quad (11)$$

The $S^I_{V_{DD}}$ is measured using SPICE simulations and computed using eq. (10) and (11), at different V_{DD} and temperatures, as shown in Fig. 3. The results demonstrate a fair accuracy of the proposed model.

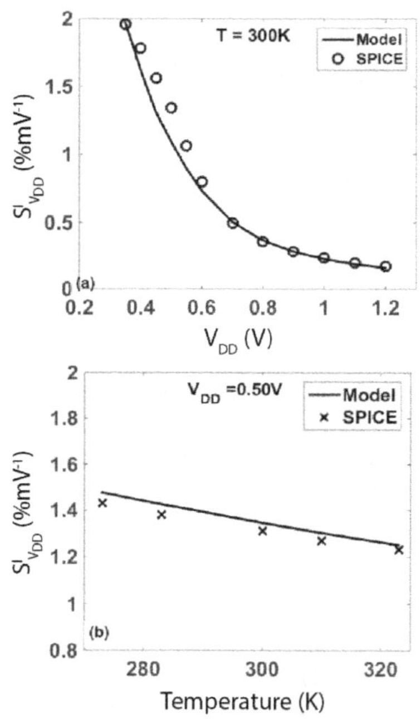

Figure 3: $S^I_{V_{DD}}$ obtained using proposed model and SPICE simulations (a) at different V_{DD} (b) at different temperatures

Following points are noteworthy for the $S^I_{V_{DD}}$ model:

(1) From eq. (10), it can be seen that there are two terms that contribute to $S^I_{V_{DD}}$: mobility and inversion coefficient. The sensitivity model (10) reveals that the term due to the mobility is very small compared to the inversion coefficient term. For instance, at $T = 300K$ and $V_{DD} = 0.50V$, the mobility term contributes only 1% to $S^I_{V_{DD}}$ in contrast to the inversion coefficient term that contributes 99% to $S^I_{V_{DD}}$. This indicates that to reduce $S^I_{V_{DD}}$ in the sub/near-threshold region, the variations due to the inversion coefficient must be reduced.

(2) As per eq. (10), V_{TH} of the device impacts $S^I_{V_{DD}}$ in a complicated manner. Our study reveals that in the NTV regime, if the V_{TH} is reduced then the first term in the inversion coefficient decreases, resulting in a decrease in $S^I_{V_{DD}}$. For example, at $V_{DD} = 0.50V$ and $T = 300K$, when the V_{TH} is reduced to $0.50V$, $0.43V$ and $0.40V$, the first term in the inversion coefficient changes to 2.52, 1.59 and 1.31, respectively. As a result, $S^I_{V_{DD}}$ decreases to 1.36, 1.13 and 1.02, respectively.

(3) From Fig. 3(a), it can be observed that $S^I_{V_{DD}}$ is high in the sub/near-threshold regime as compared to super-threshold regime. This can be understood physically from the mechanism of current transport. In sub/near-threshold region, the concentration of electrons in the channel is exponentially related to the gate voltage. This is manifested as a high $S^I_{V_{DD}}$ in sub/near-threshold regime.

(4) The proposed model reveals that the slope factor n has a large effect on $S^I_{V_{DD}}$. It is found that $S^I_{V_{DD}}$ decreases with an increase in n. The slope factor depends strongly on the length of the channel in a Fully Depleted Silicon On Insulator (FD-SOI) FETs and FinFETs: in general, it increases with the decrease in the channel length [15]. Therefore, $S^I_{V_{DD}}$ is expected to decrease at smaller channel lengths and it provides an additional motivation to use small channel devices in the NTV regime.

(5) From Fig. 3(b) it can be observed that the $S^I_{V_{DD}}$ decreases with temperature in sub/near-threshold regime. The dominant effect of the term $(1/2n\phi)$ is responsible for this.

4 SENSITIVITY OF SOME CIRCUITS IN NTV REGIME

4.1 Delay of a CMOS inverter

In this section, we assess the impact of temperature and V_{DD} on the delay (τ) of a CMOS inverter operating in the NTV regime. For simplicity, we have considered a CMOS inverter comprised of PMOS ($W/L = 2$), NMOS ($W/L = 1$) and a load capacitor ($C = 50fF$). The high-to-low delay (τ_{HL}) of the inverter can be approximated as follows:

$$\tau_{HL} = k\frac{C\times V_{DD}}{I_{ON}} \quad (12)$$

where, I_{ON} is the ON-state current through the NMOS in the inverter and k is some constant. The sensitivity of τ_{HL} with respect to temperature can be defined as:

$$S^{\tau}_{T} = \frac{1}{\tau_{HL}}\frac{\partial \tau_{HL}}{\partial T}\times 100\% \quad (13)$$

Using equation (12),

$$\frac{1}{\tau_{HL}}\frac{\partial \tau_{HL}}{\partial T} = \frac{1}{\tau_{HL}}\left(-\frac{k.CV_{DD}}{I^2_{ON}}\right)\left(\frac{\partial I_{ON}}{\partial T}\right) \quad (14)$$

$$\implies \left|\frac{1}{\tau_{HL}}\frac{\partial \tau_{HL}}{\partial T} \times 100\right|\% = \left|\frac{1}{I_{ON}}\frac{\partial I_{ON}}{\partial T} \times 100\right|\% \quad (15)$$

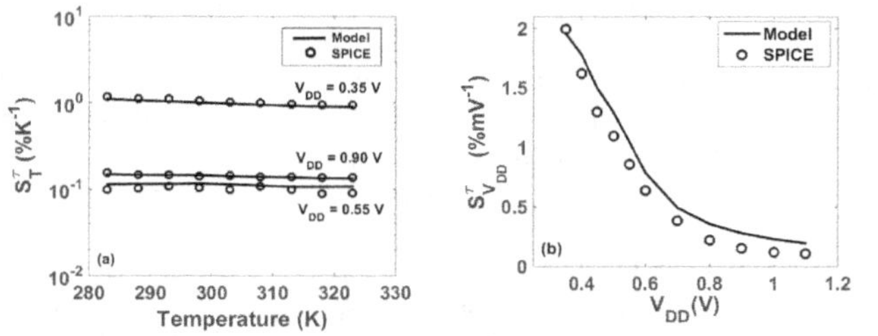

Figure 4: For the CMOS inverter (a)S_T^τ at different V_{DD} and temperatures (b) $S_{V_{DD}}^\tau$ at $T = 300K$

Therefore, the sensitivity of the delay of a CMOS inverter is directly related to the sensitivity of the I_{ON} in the constituent transistors. Similarly, the sensitivity of τ_{HL} on V_{DD} can be defined as:

$$S_{V_{DD}}^\tau = \frac{1}{\tau_{HL}}\frac{\partial \tau_{HL}}{\partial V_{DD}} \times 100\% \quad (16)$$

Using (12), the delay sensitivity can be expressed as below:

$$S_{V_{DD}}^\tau = \left(\frac{1}{V_{DD}} - \frac{1}{I_{ON}}\frac{\partial I_{ON}}{\partial V_{DD}}\right) \times 100\% \quad (17)$$

Fig. 4(a) and 4(b) shows the S_T^τ and $S_{V_{DD}}^\tau$, respectively, extracted using SPICE simulations and computed with the proposed model. These figures demonstrate a fair accuracy of the proposed sensitivity model for the CMOS inverter.

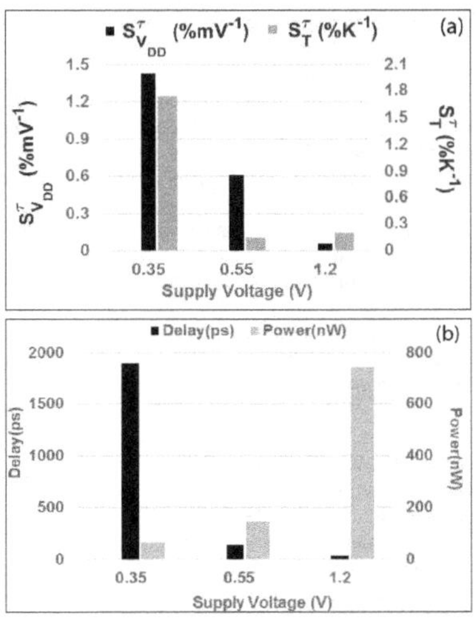

Figure 5: Figure of merit of the CMOS inverter in different regions of operation at $T = 300K$ (a) Temperature sensitivity and voltage sensitivity (b) Delay and power

The sensitivities of the CMOS inverter in three different regions of operations are summarized in Fig. 5(a) and the delay and power attributes are summarized in in Fig. 5(b). We can make the following observations:

(1) The temperature and V_{DD} sensitivities become more prominent in circuits operating in sub/near-threshold regime. Moreover, $S_{V_{DD}}^\tau$ becomes higher compared to S_T^τ in sub/near-threshold regime, in contrast to super-threshold regime. Therefore, dealing with V_{DD} variations becomes more important in circuits operating in the NTV regime.

(2) Fig. 5(a) shows that by operating the inverter in the NTV region (0.55 V) temperature sensitivity decreases by 0.8× as compared to normal operation (1.2 V) and the voltage sensitivity increases by 12×, while in the sub-threshold region (0.35 V) the temperature sensitivity increases by 9× compared to normal operation (1.2 V) and the voltage sensitivity increases by 29×. Moreover, Fig. 5(b) suggests that by operating the inverter in the NTV region (0.55 V) rather than normal operation (1.2 V), the power consumption is reduced by 5×, and therefore, the biggest merit of NTV regime is retained. However, as expected, NTV operation is also accompanied by an increase in delay by 5× compared to normal operation. On the other hand, in the sub-threshold region the power consumption is decreased by 12× compared to normal operation and is accompanied by an increase in delay by 75×, which could be unacceptable for most applications. Similarly, when the inverter is operated at $V_{DD} = V_{TH}$, the S_T^τ increases by 3× compared to normal operation, the $S_{V_{DD}}^\tau$ increases by 16×, power consumption reduces by 6× and delay increases by 11×.
Therefore, it would be practical to operate circuits $3 - 4kT/q$ above the V_{TH}, where the impact of the the temperature variations is greatly suppressed and the impact of V_{DD} variations is lower compared to when $V_{DD} = V_{TH}$. Moreover, when operated $3 - 4kT/q$ above the V_{TH}, there is still a substantial saving in power consumption and increase in delay is not as high as when operated at $V_{DD} = V_{TH}$.

(3) In order to account for PVT variations in digital design flows, a popular technique is to use extra margin for static timing analysis (STA). Due to the greater impact of temperature and V_{DD} variations in NTV circuits, a larger margin will be required in NTV circuits during STA. The results of Fig. 5 can be used to estimate the extra margin required in an NTV circuit.
As an illustration, assume that a circuit operates in a temperature range of $-10°C$ to $40°C$ and a variation of ±5% in V_{DD} is expected. Using S_T^τ and τ from Fig. 5, the expected variations in the delay of the inverter is computed to be around $0.8\ ps$ at $V_{DD} = 1.2\ V$ and around $3\ ps$ at $V_{DD} = 0.55\ V$. Similarly, the expected variations in the delay due to V_{DD} variations are computed to be around $0.5\ ps$ at $V_{DD} = 1.2\ V$ and around $13\ ps$ at $V_{DD} = 0.55\ V$. The relative increase in the delay variations in the NTV operation compared to the super-threshold operation can be used to estimate the extra margin required in STA when the circuit is migrated from the super-threshold operation to the NTV operation. Thus, if it is assumed that in the super-threshold circuit the timing margin due to temperature and V_{DD} variations was

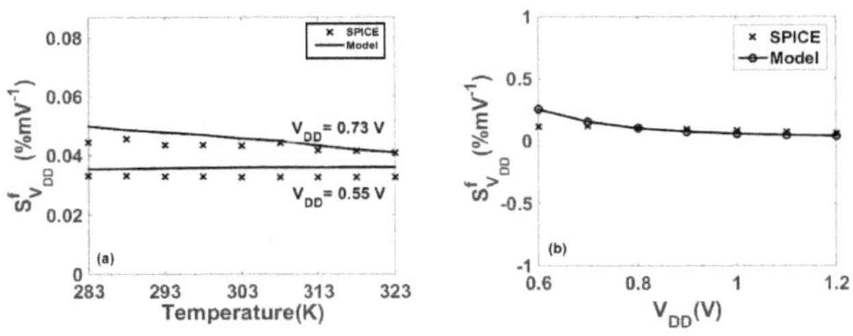

Figure 6: For the five stage ring oscillator (a) S_T^f (b) $S_{V_{DD}}^f$ at $T = 300\ K$

taken as 5 ps, then the corresponding timing margin in the NTV circuit would be $5 \times (3 + 13)/(0.8 + 0.5) = 62\ ps$. It is evident that a large timing margin is required in an NTV circuit and would pose another challenge in meeting the timing requirements of the circuit.

4.2 Frequency of a ring oscillator

Further, using the proposed model, we investigate the impact of temperature and V_{DD} variations on the frequency of a ring oscillator consisting of five stages of inverter. For simplicity, we have taken the pull-up network of the inverters used in the oscillator as a resistance of $5K\Omega$. The frequency of the oscillator depends on the delay of a single inverter as shown below:

$$f = \frac{1}{2N(\tau_{rise} + \tau_{fall})}$$

where, N represents the number of inverter stages. The rise time of the inverter depends on the pull-up network and is independent of temperature, assuming that the resistance is not changing with temperature. The pull-down network is composed of the NMOS transistor and the delay of the inverter depends on the current flowing through NMOS. It makes the frequency of the oscillator dependent on temperature and V_{DD}. The sensitivities on temperature (S_T^f) and supply voltage ($S_{V_{DD}}^f$) can be computed as follows:

$$S_T^f = \left|\frac{1}{f}\frac{\partial f}{\partial T}\right| \times 100\% = \frac{\tau_{fall}}{\tau_{rise} + \tau_{fall}}\left|\frac{1}{I_{ON}}\frac{\partial I_{ON}}{\partial T}\right| \times 100\% \quad (18)$$

$$S_{V_{DD}}^f = \frac{\tau_{fall}}{\tau_{rise} + \tau_{fall}}\left[\frac{1}{V_{DD}} - \frac{1}{I_{ON}}\frac{\partial I_{ON}}{\partial V_{DD}}\right] \times 100\% \quad (19)$$

The sensitivities measured using SPICE simulations and computed using the proposed sensitivity model are shown in Fig. 6, demonstrating a fair accuracy of the proposed model. Further, our model shows that when the ring oscillator is operated in the NTV regime ($3 - 4kT/q$ above the V_{TH}), S_T^f increases by around 4× and $S_{V_{DD}}^f$ increases by around 12×. Additionally, by operating the oscillator in the NTV region, the power consumption decreases by 4× and the frequency decreases by around 1.6×. Thus, NTV regime could be a practical operating point for energy-efficient circuits. However, the impact of temperature and V_{DD} variations should be considered carefully.

5 CONCLUSION

This paper highlighted the crucial role of temperature and V_{DD} sensitivities in NTV circuits. It also pointed out various factors that influence these sensitivities. Additionally, it demonstrated that while considering the trade-offs of power and delay in NTV circuits, it is important to consider the impact of temperature and V_{DD} variations. From this perspective, operating NTV circuits $3 - 4kT/q$ above V_{TH} could be a practical trade-off point. A natural extension of this work will be to verify the results on fabricated circuits, especially at advanced technology nodes.

REFERENCES

[1] Hadi Esmaeilzadeh, Emily Blem, Renee St Amant, Karthikeyan Sankaralingam, and Doug Burger. Dark silicon and the end of multicore scaling. In *ACM SIGARCH Computer Architecture News*, volume 39, pages 365–376. ACM, 2011.

[2] Ronald G Dreslinski, Michael Wieckowski, David Blaauw, Dennis Sylvester, and Trevor Mudge. Near-threshold computing: Reclaiming Moore's law through energy efficient integrated circuits. *Proceedings of the IEEE*, 98(2):253–266, 2010.

[3] Trevor Mudge and Urs Holzle. Challenges and opportunities for extremely energy-efficient processors. *IEEE micro*, 30(4):20–24, 2010.

[4] Saman Kiamehr, Mojtaba Ebrahimi, Mohammad Saber Golanbari, and Mehdi B Tahoori. Temperature-aware dynamic voltage scaling to improve energy efficiency of near-threshold computing. *IEEE Transactions on Very Large Scale Integration (VLSI) Systems*, 2017.

[5] Sheng Wang, Chen Chen, Xiao-Yan Xiang, and Jian-Yi Meng. A variation-tolerant near-threshold processor with instruction-level error correction. *IEEE Transactions on Very Large Scale Integration (VLSI) Systems*, 2017.

[6] Didac Gomez, Milosz Sroka, and José Luis González Jiménez. Process and temperature compensation for RF low-noise amplifiers and mixers. *IEEE Transactions on Circuits and Systems I: Regular Papers*, 57(6):1204–1211, 2010.

[7] Ronald Dreslinski, Michael Wieckowski, D Sylvester Blaauw, and T Mudge. Near threshold computing: Overcoming performance degradation from aggressive voltage scaling. In *Proc. Workshop Energy-Efficient Design*, pages 44–49, 2009.

[8] Dejan Markovic, Cheng C Wang, Louis P Alarcon, Tsung-Te Liu, and Jan M Rabaey. Ultralow-power design in near-threshold region. *Proceedings of the IEEE*, 98(2):237–252, 2010.

[9] Nathaniel Pinckney, Ronald G Dreslinski, Korey Sewell, David Fick, Trevor Mudge, Dennis Sylvester, and David Blaauw. Limits of parallelism and boosting in dim silicon. *IEEE Micro*, 33(5):30–37, 2013.

[10] T Manku and Y Wang. Temperature-independent output voltage generated by threshold voltage of an NMOS transistor. *Electronics Letters*, 31(12):935–936, 1995.

[11] Wei-Bin Yang, Zheng-Yi Huang, Ching-Tsan Cheng, and Yu-Lung Lo. Temperature insensitive current reference for the 6.27 MHz oscillator. In *Integrated Circuits (ISIC), 2011 13th International Symposium on*, pages 559–562. IEEE, 2011.

[12] IM Filanovsky and Ahmed Allam. Mutual compensation of mobility and threshold voltage temperature effects with applications in CMOS circuits. *IEEE Transactions on Circuits and Systems I: Fundamental Theory and Applications*, 48(7):876–884, 2001.

[13] Ranjith Kumar and Volkan Kursun. Impact of temperature fluctuations on circuit characteristics in 180nm and 65nm CMOS technologies. In *Circuits and Systems, 2006. ISCAS 2006. Proceedings. 2006 IEEE International Symposium on*, pages 4–pp. IEEE, 2006.

[14] Ken Ueno, Tetsuya Hirose, Tetsuya Asai, and Yoshihito Amemiya. A 300 nW, 15 $ppm/^{\circ}C$, 20 ppm/V CMOS voltage reference circuit consisting of subthreshold MOSFETs. *IEEE Journal of solid-state circuits*, 44(7):2047–2054, 2009.

[15] C. Enz, F. Chicco, and A. Pezzotta. Nanoscale MOSFET modeling: Part 1: The simplified EKV model for the design of low-power analog circuits. *IEEE Solid-State Circuits Magazine*, 9(3):26–35, Summer 2017.

[16] Christian C Enz. A short story of the EKV MOS transistor model. *IEEE Solid-State Circuits Society Newsletter*, 13(3):24–30, 2008.

[17] Christian C Enz, François Krummenacher, and Eric A Vittoz. An analytical MOS transistor model valid in all regions of operation and dedicated to low-voltage and low-current applications. *Analog integrated circuits and signal processing*, 8(1):83–114, 1995.

[18] Takayasu Sakurai and A Richard Newton. Alpha-power law MOSFET model and its applications to CMOS inverter delay and other formulas. *IEEE Journal of solid-state circuits*, 25(2):584–594, 1990.

Impolite High Speed Interfaces with Asynchronous Pulse Logic

Merritt Miller
ECE Department, UCSB
Santa Barbara, California
merrittmiller@ece.ucsb.edu

Carrie Segal
ECE Department, UCSB
Santa Barbara, California
chsegal@umail.ucsb.edu

David Mc Carthy
ECE Department, UCSB
Santa Barbara, California
davidmc@ece.ucsb.edu

Aditya Dalakoti
ECE Department, UCSB
Santa Barbara, California
adityadalakoti@ucsb.edu

Prashansa Mukim
ECE Department, UCSB
Santa Barbara, California
prashansa_mukim@umail.ucsb.edu

Forrest Brewer
ECE Department, UCSB
Santa Barbara, California
forrest@ece.ucsb.edu

Abstract

We present a design solution that allows design of higher-than-core rate operation with techniques that avoid PLL/DLL blocks to provide higher speed timing. Many modern integrated circuits (ICs) have high speed interfaces which operate at higher cycle rates than the core of the IC. As a result of the higher-than-core rate, these interfaces are not directly representable in the core sequential logic. Asynchronous pulse logic offers an alternative design method for high speed interfaces with similar performance, simpler circuitry and without resorting to high-power logic cells such as emitter coupled logic. Formal and practical considerations for constructing high-speed interfaces are described. Gate designs and timing information for example cases are presented. These cases suggest that 80% improvements on rate compared traditional clocked logic are possible.

ACM Reference Format:
Merritt Miller, Carrie Segal, David Mc Carthy, Aditya Dalakoti, Prashansa Mukim, and Forrest Brewer. 2018. Impolite High Speed Interfaces with Asynchronous Pulse Logic. In *Proceedings of 2018 Great Lakes Symposium onVLSI (GLSVLSI '18).* ACM, New York, NY, USA, 6 pages. https://doi.org/10.1145/3194554.3194592

1 Introduction

This paper presents a design methodology for creating asynchronous pulse circuits. The design style uses circuits that do not rely on hand-shakes, hence we call them impolite. This methodology offers a practical approach to energy-efficient, high-performance design. The approach not only allows interfaces to run faster than core logic but also easily enables interfaces between structurally different sources. Timed asynchronous automata can use high-frequency signals without the overhead of high-performance clock distribution and recovery. The methodology is an adaptation of existing asynchronous design approaches. It is targeted to the production of high-rate circuits embedded in slower fabrics. Circuits with such a rate disparity are not only common in data link and high-speed communication systems, but are especially useful in neuromorphic systems, distributed IOT sensor networks, and other applications with data primarily in bursts. This methodology promises to ease the design and extend the capability of such systems.

Interfacing between high and low speed clocking regimes is a common design problem in integrated circuits where serial interface and communication speeds frequently exceed core clock rates. Complex communication link circuits involve operating a metal wire near the rate where substantial amplitude loss and symbol timing jitter are serious issues. Correction of symbol-dependent timing errors are difficult to mitigate.

Synchronous circuits have limited capacity to handle timing issues. Specifically, time domain synchronization is difficult, and is commonly relegated to specialized blocks, such as DLLs, PLLs, and skew compensators, whose behaviors are outside of the synchronous domain.

The presented design implements asynchronous logic blocks with a style to handle the slow-parallel to fast-serial domain interface independent on the behavior of a PLL or timing circuit. Timed asynchronous logic increases tolerance of timing variance. Fully unconstrained asynchronous design has high design and verification complexity. In this work, a set of composition rules and a variety of pulse-logic gates are presented that allow a limited set of classical timing constraints to close both the low-speed and high-speed design behaviors.

Unlike existing asynchronous systems, the proposed "Impolite" scheme primarily uses feed-forward construction, meaning performance with picosecond timing resolution is possible. Feed-forward logic does come at a cost: the timing of the system needs to be verified as part of the construction procedure. One of the novel contributions of our methodology to the research community is the means to limit the complexity of the timing verification.

1.1 Related Asynchronous Design Paradigms

Existing asynchronous design paradigms fail to meet the intended performance requirements of interfaces operating at least 2X faster than core speed. In particular, classical feed-back based delay independent techniques are problematic. In the case of physically long transmission media (starting at the mm scale for multi-GHz signals) time of flight for the electromagnetic wave carrying the signals adds substantially to the system delay, reducing performance. On-die

GLSVLSI '18, May 23–25, 2018, Chicago, IL, USA

ACM ISBN 978-1-4503-5724-1/18/05...$15.00
https://doi.org/10.1145/3194554.3194592

scale structures (100μ scale) have substantial propagation delay and at lengths of 1mm have signal integrity issues. These considerations defeat design styles based on feed-back such as GasP[1] and Null Convention Logic[2].

Instead, the circuits presented here are a limited sub-class of self-resetting CMOS circuits – a design style that has a reset circuit assigned to small clusters of domino-like logic. SRCMOS circuits work in an inherently pulsed manner but have the down side that SRCMOS circuits require pulses to arrive nearly simultaneously for proper function[3]. Timing analysis for SRCMOS is presented in [4, 5]. SRCMOS circuits have seen application in asynchronous circuits in [6, 7] but use is commonly restricted to systems that have feed-back (polite handshakes) to confirm correct behavior.

2 ON-CHIP SIGNALING: PULSE VS. EDGE

A key feature of this work is that pulses (as opposed to edge based signals) are used for communicating timing critical events. The one-at-a-time pulse model makes the event timing check the dual of the SRCMOS timing check, *pulses must not overlap* for correct behavior. Since the use of a pulse is critical for the presented methodology to be successful, we now make the case that signaling with self resetting buffers permits an event cycle rate as fast or faster than edge event rates.

Jitter and propagation behavior of pulses and edges are nearly identical for practical interconnect cases. Pulsed signals, with a single characteristic width, allow the use of pulse gates, such as in [6, 8–10] and similar to [1]. These gates are known to maintain stable, narrow pulse widths, whereas logic without feedback would accumulate edge-to-edge uncertainty, widening the minimum pulse width.

In edge-based signaling, a rising edge must be followed by a falling edge, requiring separate types of event detection. Since different devices are involved, systems relying on edge-based signaling have inherently higher sensitivity to process variance but have been used successfully (e.g.) [11].

Since edge-based communication has a theoretical advantage in both power and bandwidth, it is important to demonstrate that pulsed signaling does not come at a high cost relative to edges in practical on-chip design. A case study using a 130nm process node interconnect wire is used to demonstrate, because it is in this process node where wire dimensions became a limiting factor[12] in signaling rate.

2.1 Case Study 5mm wire 130nm process node

A 5mm wire in a metal layer of a 130nm process is used to compare pulsed and edge encoding for an event signal. For this metal a conductor thickness of $.3\mu m$ and a inter-layer dielectric thickness of $.3\mu m$ is typical. The wire width and spacing is chosen to optimize the cost function of $delay \times wire\ pitch$ giving a wire width of $.55\mu$ and a wire spacing of $.38\mu$. This configuration gives a fringing capacitance of $100fF/mm$, a side coupling capacitance of $31fF/mm$, and, assuming a copper conductor, a resistance of $133\Omega/mm$.

With an inverter size of 26μ NMOS, minimal worst-case delay (with an even number of stages) occurs with 4 internal repeaters (5, 1mm long wire segments). The single-stage worst-case delay time constant in this configuration is 68.4ps.

Table 1: Propagation times for edge and pulse.

	(100ps rise) Edge		(165ps width) Pulse	
Coupling noise	Average	σ	Average	σ
No coupling	251.3 ± 1.0	8.6 ± 0.7	239.5 ± 0.9	7.7 ± 0.7
Fastest	215.6 ± 0.9	7.5 ± 0.7	208.5 ± 0.8	6.9 ± 0.5
Slowest	285.9 ± 1.1	9.5 ± 0.7	276.7 ± 1.0	8.7 ± 0.6

All values shown with 95% confidence interval marked.

2.2 Edge-communicated signal

Arrival jitter is approximated by Monte-Carlo simulation consisting of 1k runs, sufficient to gain 95% confidence values for most measures. Process variation is taken from a vendor (IBM) model for the 130nm process. Power variation is estimated to have a global, correlated variation of 30mV power to ground, modeling power regulator noise and a local, uncorrelated variation of 30mV is added to each power and ground node, modeling IR noise internal to the IC.

When there is a single fast edge (<100ps) of a slow signal ($f < 200MHz$) the average propagation time is projected to be $251.3 \pm 1.0ps$, close to the value that $\#stages \times stage\ delay \times ln(\frac{1}{2})$ predicts. The sample standard deviation (σ) of the arrival time in this experiment is $8.6 \pm .7ps$. Assuming a Gaussian distribution, a 5σ interval gives a delay between 203.5ps to 298.5ps for a 5mm wire.

Due to the high coupling capacitance (~38% of the total) the impact of neighbor wires must be considered. The worst-case jitter occurs when both neighbors are correlated in the same or opposing direction as the main signal. Same direction switching has delay $215.6 \pm .9ps$ with a sample σ of $7.5 \pm .7ps$. The 5σ fast arrival time under these circumstances is 173ps. Opposite direction switching delay is $285.9 \pm 1.1ps$ with $\sigma \approx 9.5 \pm .7ps$, giving a 5σ slow case of 338ps. This is a range of 165ps of environmental jitter that an ideal latching strategy cannot compensate for. A more common single clock phasing strategy would need a flip-flop with $\tau_{su} + \tau_{clk-Q} < 162ps$ to run at 2GHz.

2.3 Pulse-communicated signal

Table 1 compares the propagation times for edges and pulses. Using 165ps as the full-width, half-maximum measure of the pulse, propagation times are similar to edges. The minimum pulse period is twice the pulse width – 330ps, marginally faster than the non-skew-compensated rate of edges.

Using self-resetting gates to create a regenerative buffer, improves performance. Self-resetting gates protect pulse widths, and thus jitter cannot destroy a pulse. For systems using self-resetting buffers, two conditions must be met: First, the pulse width and its reset time must be obeyed. Second, the pulses must arrive in order. The pulse width is set locally within the buffer since it is self-timed. Native self-resetting pulse width in 130nm was determined to be 64ps with $\sigma \approx 4ps$, giving 84ps for a maximum pulse width, and 168ps for a safe pulse interval. Jitter for the self-timed buffer case is slightly higher than for the inverter buffer case at an estimated total jitter (5σ+pattern dependence) of 188ps. This extra jitter, as compared to the inverter buffer case, is due to the extra logic required in a self-resetting buffer. This extra logic extends maximum propagation time, in this case to $405ps$. The arrival order uncertainty limit of $188ps$ is the dominant of the two restrictions.

2.4 Pulse vs. edge for marking an event

The relative propagation timing of pulses and edges are very similar, even when the width of the pulse is small. Jitter dominates gain/bandwidth in limiting performance, and a pulse because it is atomic and unambiguous in its arrival, need not be correlated to any other signal. Thus pulse-based event detection can operate as fast or faster than edge event detection correlated to another signal or state.

Table 2: Event detection times for various signaling methods

Method	Period	Notes
Handshake	597p	Interleaving forward & backward wires (minimizes worst-case propagation)
Clocked Edge	338p	No Phase compensation
Edge with DLL or PLL	223p	Requires DLL/PLL of ~20mW (assumes 15ps RMS jitter ≈ -112dBc/Hz phase noise)
Pulse	*330p*	*Not using self-reseting buffers*
Pulse	*188p*	*With self-reseting buffers*

Table 2 shows a number of cases, and the associated minimum period of operation for a BER of 6×10^{-7} (corresponding to $\pm 5\sigma$ variance). For the purposes of comparison, the minimum latch timing is left out of the presented period. In a clocked system, the latch sample interval adds 50-200ps. In asynchronous systems, both pulsed and handshake, latch sampling time need not add to the minimum period, as both techniques have sampling times built into their respective operating mechanisms.

3 Composition Rules

The following construction techniques give rise to a class of systems that are delay sensitive, and are easier to verify than a system completely free in timing specification.

The lack of delay insensitivity means timing verification is required for behavioral closure. The construction only admits designs that can be verified with static timing. Static timing analysis is a common part of verifying clocked systems and numerous extensions, such as yield estimation, have been formulated[13]. This method uses a constraint system with the same analytic methodology, similar to clocked SRCMOS[5].

3.1 Basic Rules

There are a handful of rules to enable simple, closed examination of these event-driven circuits. The circuit can be specified hierarchically, where each level of the hierarchy obeys these rules. For the purposes of discussion a *Block* is a functional component at one level of the hierarchy, while a *Gate* is specifically at the lowest level. The rules for blocks are as follows

(1) There is a strong typing of *Event* and *Data* signals. A signal will be of exactly one of those two classes.
(2) Specification, and verification occurs within a time *Frame*. The time frame is marked by a start event and a finish event.
(3) Within a *Frame*, Data values will update at most once.
(4) For any *Block*, and most *Gates* only a single Event can occur at a time.
(5) When an event occurs, Data cannot be in transition.
(6) The *Consensus* gate is exempt from rule # 4. The behavior of this gate is handled as a special case.

The Frame requirement from these rules enforces a data-path check that is similar to traditional clocked logic. The model fits well with a system matching high-rate and low-rate regimes – the low-rate timing can easily provide the Frame.

3.2 Timing Check Complexity

For this acyclic-within-frame logic, the complexity of the static timing check is simply bound by the number of delays along the path and thus scales as $O(n)$ given n delay bearing nodes including latches. For a circuit with m unconstrained events $m!$ constraints are needed in worst case although this is practically limited by gate fan-in. The basic rules are placed on gates to ensure predictable (inertial) delays apply and have complexity $O(m^2 \cdot n)$. This has the consequence that some kinds of circuits fall outside of the constraints.

However, circuits including near-miss arbiters and all circuits necessary for communication links are permitted.

3.3 Logical Constraints on Construction

Signals are partitioned into two classes or types: Events and Data. The Event class serves to mark time, and is analogous to a clock. The state of a gate can only change with an event, communicated by a pulse of fixed width. The other class, Data informs state updates in the presence of an event. Data is communicated as traditional digital levels.

This leads to the first constraint, *the value of a Data signal must be stable between the setup and hold time* for each gate relative to the arrival of an updating event.

The second constraint is that a block interface may have only *one active event at a time.* One-at-a-time events prevent complex timing issues from arising within the relative timing check. In order for two events to be processed simultaneously they must act on separable parts of the system, or be passed into a Consensus gate for processing.

For two events to inform interacting parts of the system they must have a fixed timing relation. The relationship can be confirmed by verification, and event re-timing can be part of the construction. The designer should describe any two-event behavior as a set of one-at-a-time actions. Fair arbitration is not a feature of the methodology, instead the designer must describe the arbitration method. This can be aided by a Separating Arbiter gate, that while it cannot perform ideal arbitration, it can separate vanishingly-close (1ps) pulse interactions.

Because of these interaction rules the timing can be checked in $O(m^2 n)$ time complexity, involving two different timing checks limited by this complexity class. The timing checks are of *Event* $\rightarrow$ *Event* relationships, and *Event* $\rightarrow$ *Data* $\rightarrow$ *Event* relationships,

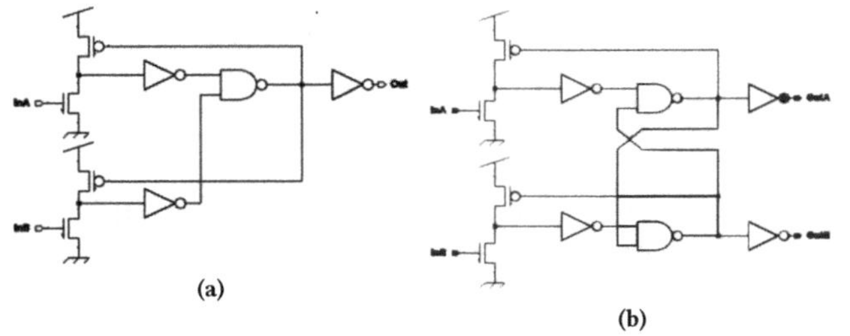

Figure 1: (a) Pulse Consensus gate. Gate fires output out once at least one pulse arrives on each input (since the last firing). (b) Separating Arbiter gate. Gate recreates input pulse sequence with restored separation.

since no more complex relation can exist. The Event simultaneity check needs to be performed at each gate to confirm that no two events arrive simultaneously; This allows the event-as-a-clock equivalent model. Then data timing is checked on *Event* $\rightarrow$ *Data* $\rightarrow$ *Event* sequences, similar to a clocked system where the sequence is *Clock* $\rightarrow$ *Data* $\rightarrow$ *Clock*. Since events are one-at-a-time, event-data and event-event checks are orthogonal.

In practice, the timing check is further simplified by the limited number of events used and the limited fan-in and fan-out of practical designs.

3.4 Event timing

The one-at-a-time pulse model makes the event timing check the dual of the SRCMOS timing check, *pulses must not overlap* for correct behavior. Pulse Gating is done with a self-resetting gate structure and data latching utilizes a Set-Reset latch style. The pulse arriving at the gate serves as the sampling aperture for the pull-down network; this sets the data hold window to the actual pulse width of an event. The minimum pulse-width is thus set by the need to reliably sample, and is a trade-off with the complexity of the pull-down network.

There is a special case to the non-overlap verification: the Arbiter circuit. An arbiter circuit is allowed, logically, to have two events occur at its inputs as long as the events are of known order and avoid exact overlap. This non-overlap constraint is of practical importance, as arbitration circuits near meta-stability have ill-defined behavior and can take an infinite time to resolve[14]. In the contexts of these checks, arbitration is reduced to describing near-miss cases.

4 Gate construction

The strict classification of signals is crucial for timing analysis and simplifies design of the gates. This structure allows a gate to act on a given event given a set of data guard values since the data is known to be stable on event arrival. Logic functions are incorporated into the front-ends of Latches and pulse Gates, giving fast, small designs.

There are two classes of gate in this construction paradigm, pulse *Gates* and *Latches*. Pulse Gates, Figure 2a, have a pulsed output, and thus are used to create Events, while Latches, Figure 2b, have a level output creating Data signals. Pulse Gates use a self-resetting logic to (re)-create the event pulse.

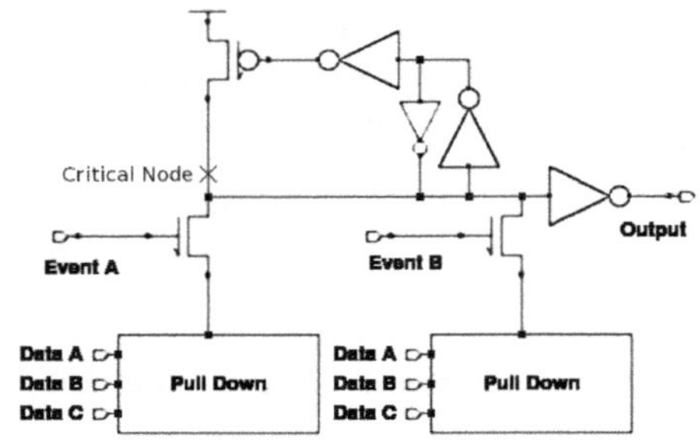

(a) The pulse-gate, outputs a pulse given a condition

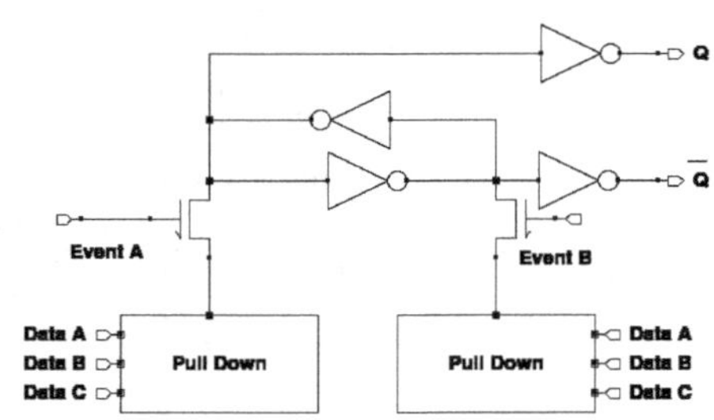

(b) Pulse-Triggered SR Data-Latch - outputs a data level that changes on a pulse given a condition

Figure 2: Pulse Gates and Latches

4.1 Pull-down network timing

The structure of the pull-down network, combined with the typing rules for Events and Data, create a timing constraint set for each pull-down network. The behavior of these networks are similar for pulse gates and latches, and the analysis holds for both. Correct functioning of the pull-down network determines the values for the timing constraints in the composition rules (Section 3). The prohibition on event overlap ensures that the action due to any event is not preempted by another event, a critical requirement for timing verification to not be forced to check all event combinations. Consider the timing of as SR latch, like the one shown in Figure 2b. Event A triggers setting this latch, while event B triggers reset. In both cases, the action is contingent on the logic of Data A, B, and C encoded into the respective pull-down networks. Electrically, the pull-down network is assumed conducting or non-conducting when the associated event pulse arrives. In the case of the SR latch, the set condition must be stable for the set pulse and the reset condition must be stable for the reset pulse.

4.2 Drive and Feed-back network

The characteristic pulse width of a self-resetting gate is set by the propagation delay through the feedback path. The output amplitude is dependent on both the output driver and its load. Pulse detection requires that the delay of the feedback path must match or exceed the amount prescribed by driver and load environment.

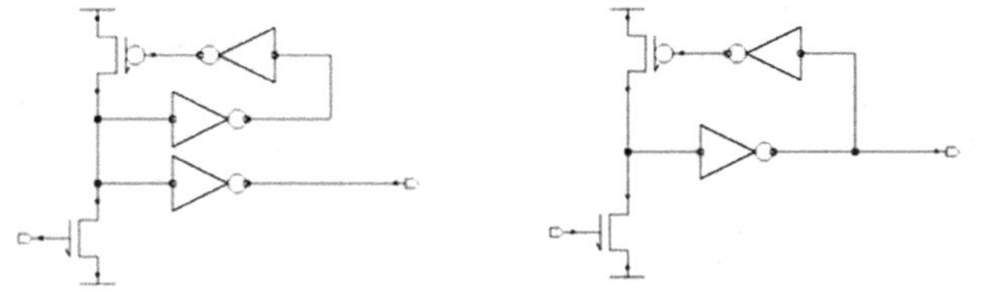

(a) Load isolated feed-back gate. (b) Load sensitive feed-back gate.

Figure 3: Two self-reset feed-back network options.

The feed-back network for a pulse gate can either be connected or isolated from its load as shown in Figure 3. The isolated-load model (Figure 3a) is faster than the load sensitive feedback and has more reliable timing. This feed-back network is well suited when the gate load is either constant, so that a correct pulse width can be selected, or for cases with small fan-out where pulse attenuation is not a concern. Load sensitive feedback (Figure 3b) is useful in a production environment where more universal cells are desired. The load sensitive gate's pulse-width and timing are derived from an estimate of pulse detectability. For reasonable levels of output loading, the feedback increases driver on-time until the local detectability threshold is met. This model keeps the impolite fire-and-forget model, by approximating detectability, rather than using a handshake. To illustrate the difference, we consider two different cases that arose in real designs executed in the 130nm process node. First with $7fF/\mu_{driver}$of load capacitance – a typical value for timing-critical, local wires. In this case, the two feedback networks perform similarly. In the second a load of $50fF/\mu_{driver}$ represents a typical drive configuration for moderate-distance interconnect or a heavily loaded reset signal. In this case, load-sensitive feedback produces a slower, longer, pulse. This results in a pulse that is nearly 4x as detectable.

4.3 Two-Pulse Gates

Gates where two pulses arrive with the potential of overlap are special cases. There are two types of these gates: The *Consensus* gate, which produces an event after seeing two events is shown in Figure 1a and the *Arbiter*, shown in Figure 1b can resolve pulses that are near complete event overlap (<5ps timing difference).

The Charlie diagram, a visualization of output timing vs input timing[15, 16], for these two gates is shown in Fig 4. It is important to note the unstable behavior of the arbiter circuit near complete event overlap (<5ps timing difference). This establishes the limiting constraint for event-event timing checks. Two architectural solutions exist for cases when operating in this regime. First, is to insert arbitration up-stream to correct order. Second is to design a system that is tolerant of this hard-to-arbitrate condition, for example creating a parallel data-path dependent on the consensus gate that will time-out an ambiguous arbitration.

4.4 Pulse Gate Timing Stability

Pulse gates have a higher timing stability when compared to standard CMOS gates. This phenomenon can be be seen in the high timing stability of ring oscillators made form pulse gates[17]. The

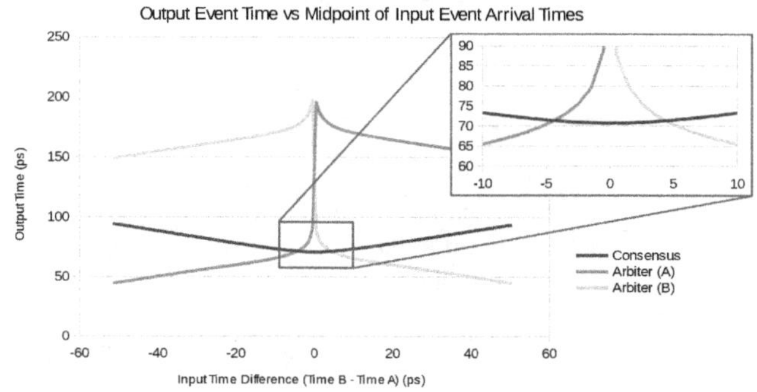

Figure 4: Consensus and Arbiter gates

stability of the timing may be due to lowered noise in MOS transistors for inputs in some state transitions[18]. In the case of pulse logic decisions are made by NMOS transistors turning on for all decision cases. To confirm the applicability of these results to the case of logic cells, timing is confirmed for the well-characterized 130nm process node, using noise models that take bias-condition into account. Figure 5 shows the timing stability of post-layout performance of pulse logic as compared to foundry-provided cells – in this case a buffer cell for driving a long wire.

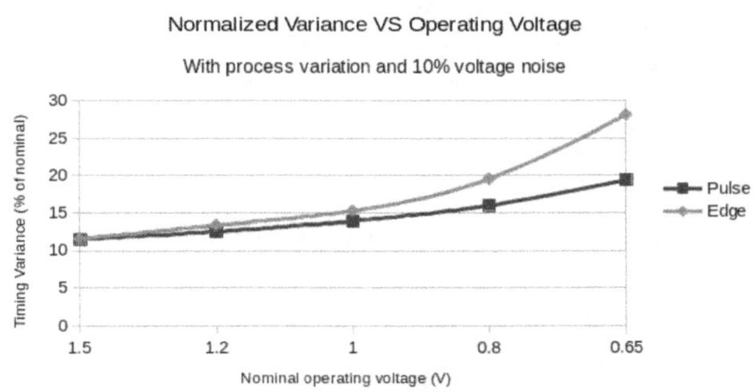

Figure 5: Variance of Pulse Gates, CMOS gates. Pulse gates have much lower variance at low operating voltage

4.5 Pulse Gate Library

Table 3 shows timing from a number of pulse gates. Computed from post-layout extracted designs. The gate set is an equivalent of a standard cell set for pulse-logic, and is used to build the designs of Section 5.The pull-down networks are sized for equal on current. The gate measured by simulation is triggered by a gate with similar drive (Fanout of 1) and loaded with a 4x pulse-repeater load (Fanout of 4, FO4). The decision threshold for measurement is set at VDD/3, an approximation of the pulse-gate decision threshold.

5 Data Link Performance Estimation

A hypothetical 4-bit serializer(SER) and deserializer(DES) are analyzed to demonstrate the verification procedure and construction

Table 3: Pulse Gate Timing in 130nm process

Gate	FO4 Delay	Delay Std. Dev.
Pulse Repeater	29.9ps	2.2ps
Or of two pulses	31.9ps	2.7ps
Pulse Single-condition	31.5ps	2.7ps
Pulse 2-Condition AND	29.4ps	2.6ps
Pulse 2-Condition OR	29.1ps	2.3ps
Or of 2 pulses, w/conditions	33.3ps	3.5ps
SR Latch	37.0ps	3.3ps

methodology For a high-speed interface. The 2-line encoding of [8, 9] is used. The SER uses 4 delayed copies of the data valid signal, which need not be locked to any other circuit. The DES produces 1 data vector per packet and a single data valid pulse. Given these constraints the timing results computed are shown in Table 4.

Table 4: Performance Estimates for 4-bit SER/DES system

	130nm	65nm	45nm
Trigger Time (Pulse Width)	93.8ps	52.1ps	23.0ps
Max Bit-Bit Time	187.6ps	104.2ps	46.0ps
Minimum DDR Clock Period	592MHz	960MHz	2.17GHz
Max Data Rate	4.74Gbps	7.68Gbps	17.4Gbps
Comparable Max Data Rate	2Gbps[19]	4.8Gbps[20]	10.5Gbps[21] [1]

5.1 Static Timing Analysis Complexity

For the serializer(SER) and deserializer(DES) from Section 5 there are 9 blocks in the DES and 13 blocks in the SER. For the SER there are 16 events, while the DES has 10 events. The composition rules require checking events at each block. A simplistic algorithm can verify timing with only 4228 path sums. This check not only allows verification with much less computation than a mixed-signal simulation, but also allows designers to use asymmetric or varying components without resorting to an exponential number of cases that need to be checked. The rules and verification become an enabling technology for systems checked in $O(m^2n)$ time, compared to free-for-all asynchronous systems bound by $O(m!n)$.

6 Conclusion

Since the "Impolite" methodology permits the exploration of a design space containing a much larger number of events, it is practical to consider what those sorts of systems could be developed to solve. The most obvious use is the embedding of simple mathematical functions in communications.

The Internet of things and the growing influence of practical artificial intelligence offers a platform where localized computational models can be of great benefit. The communications between these many diverse systems will require many channels variable, and burst data rates as well as unique light-weight interfaces. The logic family presented here shows promise for creating unique, and possibly asymmetric solutions that remain easy to verify.

Additionally, this composition style can implement Race Logic, which shows promise as a new computational model[22]. The required temporal functions (MIN, MAX, and COMPARE) are permissible using the composition rules discussed in Section 3.

In short, Impolite Asynchronous Pulse Logic enables verifiable construction of high-timing-performance circuits from small cells and simple composition rules. The fire-and-forget model, as well as timing rules enable static-logic style checking at decision rates typically reserved for mixed-signal style design. The resulting circuits maintain precise timing and have good idle behavior.

[1]Design uses even and odd channels, and when combined are limited at 21Gbps

References

[1] I. Sutherland and S. Fairbanks. Gasp: a minimal fifo control. In *ASYNC 2001*, pages 46–53, 2001.

[2] K.M. Fant and S.A. Brandt. Null convention logictm: a complete and consistent logic for asynchronous digital circuit synthesis. In *ASAP 1996*, pages 261–273, Aug 1996.

[3] Gunok Jung, V.A. Sundarajan, and G.E. Sobelman. A robust self-resetting cmos 32-bit parallel adder. In *ISCAS 2002*.

[4] Ayoob E Dooply and Kenneth Y Yun. Optimal clocking and enhanced testability for high-performance self-resetting domino pipelines. In *Advanced Research in VLSI, 1999. Proceedings. 20th Anniversary Conference on*, pages 200–214. IEEE, 1999.

[5] Vinod Narayanan, Barbara A Chappell, and Bruce M Fleischer. Static timing analysis for self resetting circuits. In *ICCAD 1996*.

[6] Mika Nyström and Alain J Martin. *Asynchronous pulse logic*. Springer, 2002.

[7] T. Säntti and J. Isoaho. Modified srcmos cell for high-throughput wave-pipelined arithmetic units. In *ISCAS 2001*, volume 4, pages 194–197 vol. 4, May 2001.

[8] Brian D Winters and Mark R Greenstreet. A negative-overhead, self-timed pipeline. In *ASYNC 2002*, pages 37–46. IEEE, 2002.

[9] Mark R Greenstreet and Jihong Ren. Surfing interconnect. In *ASYNC 2006*.

[10] Merritt Miller, Greg Hoover, and Forrest Brewer. Pulse-mode link for robust, high speed communications. In *ISCAS 2008*.

[11] Ivan E. Sutherland. Micropipelines. *Communications of the ACM*, 32(6):720–738, 1989.

[12] Ron Ho, Kenneth W Mai, and Mark A Horowitz. The future of wires. *Proceedings of the IEEE*, 89(4):490–504, 2001.

[13] Anirudh Devgan and Chandramouli Kashyap. Block-based static timing analysis with uncertainty. In *ICCAD 2003*, page 607. IEEE Computer Society, 2003.

[14] Thomas J Chaney and Charles E Molnar. Anomalous behavior of synchronizer and arbiter circuits. *IEEE Transactions on computers*, 22(4):421–422, 1973.

[15] Jo C Ebergen, Scott Fairbanks, and Ivan E Sutherland. Predicting performance of micropipelines using charlie diagrams. In *ASYNC 1998*.

[16] Anthony Winstanley and Mark Greenstreet. Temporal properties of self-timed rings. In *Advanced Research Working Conference on Correct Hardware Design and Verification Methods*, pages 140–154. Springer, 2001.

[17] Aditya Dalakoti, Merritt Miller, and Forrest Brewer. Pulse ring oscillator tuning via pulse dynamics. In *2017 IEEE 35th International Conference on Computer Design (ICCD)*, pages 469–472. IEEE, 2017.

[18] I Bloom and Y Nemirovsky. 1/f noise reduction of metal-oxide-semiconductor transistors by cycling from inversion to accumulation. *Applied Physics Letters*, 58(15):1664–1666, 1991.

[19] Rashed Zafar Bhatti, Monty Denneau, and Jeff Draper. 2 gbps serdes design based on ibm cu-11 (130nm) standard cell technology. In *Proceedings of the 16th ACM Great Lakes symposium on VLSI*, pages 198–203. ACM, 2006.

[20] Peng Wang, Ziqiang Wang, Chun Zhang, and Zhihua Wang. Data lane design for transmitter of 4.8 gbps serdes in 65nm cmos. In *Electron Devices and Solid-State Circuits (EDSSC), 2014 IEEE International Conference on*, pages 1–2. IEEE, 2014.

[21] Jonathan E Proesel and Timothy O Dickson. A 20-gb/s, 0.66-pj/bit serial receiver with 2-stage continuous-time linear equalizer and 1-tap decision feedback equalizer in 45nm soi cmos. In *VLSI Circuits (VLSIC), 2011 Symposium on*, pages 206–207. IEEE, 2011.

[22] Advait Madhavan, Timothy Sherwood, and Dmitri Strukov. Race Logic: A hardware acceleration for dynamic programming algorithms. *ISCA 2014*, pages 517–528, 2014.

Short-path Padding Method for Timing Error Resilient Circuits based on Transmission Gates Insertion

Wentao Dai
Southeast University
Nanjing, Jiangsu 210096 China
waes1313@163.com

Peiye Liu
Beijing University of Posts and Telecommunications
Beijing 100000 China
liupeiye@bupt.edu.cn

Weiwei Shan
Southeast University
Nanjing, Jiangsu 210096 China
wwshan@seu.edu.cn

ABSTRACT

Resilient circuits based on timing error detection and correction can mitigate the timing margin effectively, but usually at a cost of extra area overhead. One of the major sources of area overhead is short-path padding (hold time fix), which is much severer than in traditional IC design for near-threshold operation. Therefore, we propose an insertion methodology by using transmission gates to extend short-paths, which decreases area overhead than traditional resilient methods. Because the clock-controlled transmission gate (CTG) can extend all the short paths by half a clock when working as a transparent-low latch, the short-paths problem is solved. Besides, as the transmission gates synchronize the multiple short paths, it decreases the invalid flipping of combinational logic, which reduces the glitch power. Applied on a SHA-256 algorithm circuit in a 28nm CMOS process with 0.55V supply, the proposed technique reduces the area overhead a lot compared to the conventional short-path padding techniques. For combinational circuit, its area reduces from 153.34% to 4.43%, and for sequential circuit area, it reduces from 124.33% to 19.33%.

ACM Reference Format:

[1] Wentao Dai, Peiye Liu and Weiwei Shan. 2018. Short-path Padding Method for Timing Error Resilient Circuits based on Transmission Gates Insertion In *GLSVLSI '18: 2018 Great Lakes Symposium on VLSI*, May 23–25, 2018, Chicago, IL, USA. ACM, NY, NY, USA, 6 pages. https://doi.org/10.1145/3194554.3194600

1 INTRODUCTION

With the increasing complexity of SoC design, the demand of low power consumption also grows. However, due to process, voltage, and temperature (PVT) variations [1-3], conservative timing or voltage margin need to be reserved to ensure correct operation under the worst-case PVT conditions during IC design time. Such margin can severely limit the performance and energy efficiency of the ICs when they operate under nominal or best conditions.

Although eliminating the reserved margin can reduce the power consumption or increase the performance of a circuit, removing an excessive margin will cause failure. Thus, resilient designs based on timing error detection and correction (EDAC) [4-8] with dynamic voltage frequency scaling (DVFS) have been proposed to eliminate such margins while still ensuring correct operation across PVT variations. In these techniques, the endpoint registers in most critical paths are replaced by special error-detecting registers to detect the timing information. Then the monitored information is used to control DVFS system to adaptively tune the supply voltage or frequency, in order to make the circuits operate on the edge of failure. Thus, they can effectively eliminate the reserved timing.

However, the existing resilient designs [4, 5] severely suffer from the area overhead caused by short-path padding. Short-path problem refers to the situation that the signals propagate through short paths can also arrive in their speculation window, causing false error detection. Here the speculation window is defined as the time during which errors are detected. It is usually set as the positive phase of a clock period or a small part of it. Short-path padding is similar to hold time fix, but it is much severer in resilient circuits. In order to remove those signals arriving through short paths from actual timing errors, a large number of delay elements (e.g., buffers and inverters) are typically inserted in short paths to ensure their delay longer than that of the speculation window.

To avoid padding so many delay elements, Push-pull [6] focuses on the padding problem with a global view, utilize spare cells and a dummy metal to achieve further the derived padding values at physical implementation. Razor-lite [9] utilized initial self-calibration and run time calibration of the duty-cycle adjustment mechanism to correct the global clock, which can reduce the chances of short-path data falling within the speculation window. However, the corrected global clock had varied degrees of pulse width deformation and amplitude attenuation when it arrives at the leaf registers, which increased the complexity of timing closure. In addition, since the duty-cycle correcting circuit was composed of the delay chain, the pulse width of the clock was limited by the number of delay cells, thus it is not suited for large-scale circuits. iRazor [10] solved the problem of clock pulse width distortion and amplitude

GLSVLSI '18, May 23–25, 2018, Chicago, IL, USA

ACM ISBN 978-1-4503-5724-1/18/05...$15.00
https://doi.org/10.1145/3194554.3194600

attenuation by using the local pulse generator, but it also need a large amount of padding cells across various PVT conditions. Bubble Razor based on two-phase latch was proposed [11]. By using the consecutive opposite-clock-controlled latch, the short-path problem could be mitigated, but the area overhead of sequential logic could not be neglected. Then, S. Kim in [12] reduced the sequential overhead by sparse insertion of the error-detecting register.

Thus, in this paper, we propose a novel insertion mechanism of clock-controlled transmission gate (CTG) to solve this short-path problem. As the CTG can extend all the short paths by half a cycle clock phase when working as a transparent-low latch, the short-path problem is solved. By scaling the unnecessary width of the speculation window, reasonable positions for inserting CTGs are selected, which can reduce the amount of insertion.

Our main contributions are as follows:

1) Instead of inserting a padding unit of delay cells, we solve the short-path problem by inserting CTGs, which can easily extend the short paths by half cycle to reduce the area overhead of logic cell.

2) To optimize the number of CTGs, we investigate the utilization rate of the speculation window in the traditional resilient circuits, and explore the relationship between the speculation window and the insertion position of CTG.

3) We develop a selection and insertion mechanism for the CTG, and customize an automated design flow to make it suitable for large-scale circuits.

To evaluate the robustness and effectiveness of the proposed method, experiments are conducted on a small circuit of an 8th-order filter (with 25-FO4 delay of the inverter chain) and a larger circuit of SHA-256 encryption circuit. Experiment results show that our method can clean all short-path violations with a very small area overhead. Applied on the SHA-256 algorithm circuit in 28nm CMOS process when operating at 0.55V, compared to 153.34% (combinational) and 124.33% (sequential) area overhead of the conventional techniques, the overhead is reduced to 4.43% and 19.33% respectively. In addition, the invalid flip of combinational logic has been reduced, which decreases 46.06% glitch power.

This paper is organized as follows. In Section 2, we analyze the area overhead for existing EDAC designs. Next, in Section 3, we introduce the basics of our resilient circuit and its specific design flow. Then, in Section 4, we investigate the utilization rate of the speculation window in the traditional resilient designs, and based on the required speculation window, we design the selection and insertion mechanism for the transmission gate. We also compare the area power cost with the existing methods in Section 5. Finally, we conclude our study in Section 6.

2 OVERHEAR ANALYSIS OF THE EXSISTING TIMING ERROR RESILIENT CIRCUIT

2.1 Flop based Error Detection

The most classic flop based resilient technique [4] replaces the registers of critical paths by special error-detecting registers to detect the timing information (the RFF shown in Fig. 1 (a)). The error-detecting register is mainly composed of a flip-flop, a shadow latch and an XOR, etc. This technique severely suffers from the area overhead caused by short path padding because of the shadow latch. In this technique, any data arriving in the speculation window are regarded as timing errors. Thus, padding cells (e.g., buffers and inverters) are typically inserted to ensure the delay of short paths longer than that of the speculation window.

Short paths must be longer than the speculation window even under the worst-case PVT condition. This makes the overhead of short-path padding increase at lower VDD where delay variability becomes severer. In our previously designed resilient circuit [13], we applied our EDAC method on an 8th-order filter. Here it is taken as an experimental IC to study short-path padding. It is synthesized in a 28nm CMOS. As shown in Fig. 2, short paths become worse when VDD decreases to near-threshold voltage (NTV), for example, when VDD is 0.4V, paths need to be padded should be longer than 58% of TCK when considering 3σ delay variation incurred by local process variations. As a result, compared to the baseline without error detection, a large amount of delay buffers or inverters have to be inserted, causing 1.4× area increase of combinational logic.

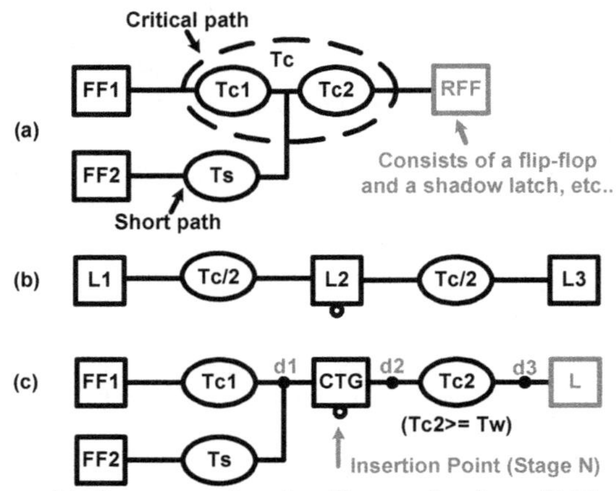

Figure 1: (a) The conventional resilient technology. (b) The two-phase latch technology. (c) The proposed CTG insertion mechanism.

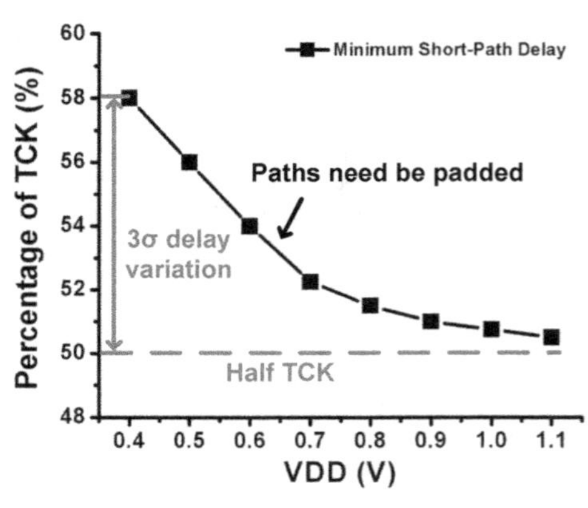

Figure 2: The minimum delays of short-path need to be padded across a wide VDD from 0.4V to 1.1V.

Typically, the delays of critical and near-critical paths are estimated under the worst-case dynamic variations. Those flip-flops that receive data from critical paths which have the potential to cause timing violation are replaced with error-detecting registers. In NTV regime, more paths are likely to cause violations due to severer sensitivity to dynamic variations. We investigate the amount of critical and near-critical paths requiring error detection on the 8th-order filter test circuit. As shown in Fig. 3, registers replacement ratio increases greatly when VDD decreases, which makes the number of padding cells also increases drastically in order to fix short-paths.

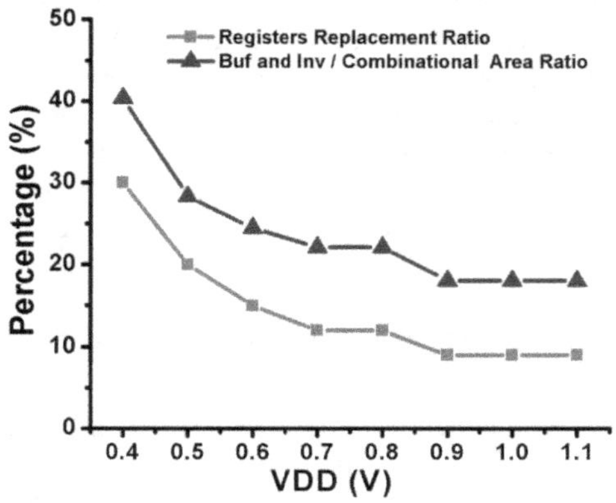

Figure 3: Registers replacement ratio and padding cells to combinational area ratio of padding cell across a wide VDD from 0.4V to 1.1V, for an 8th order filter circuit.

2.2 Two-Phase Latch based Error Detection

A resilient technique based on two-phase latch was proposed as Bubble Razor [11]. Its advantage is that it can overcome the short-path problem by using the consecutive opposite-latch (as shown in Fig. 1 (b)) since each consecutive latch stage becomes transparent at an opposite clock phase.

However, in our experiment, converting a flop-based design to a latch-based design will increase sequential overhead a lot. As the total number of latches is more than twice of flops and a pair of latch has larger area than a single flop, such transformation performed on an 8th-order filter test circuit increases the sequential area by 2.3×. In addition, applying latch-based design with the resilient technique can significantly increase the ratio of registers replacement. This is because the latch-based design has more sequential logic than a flop-based design. In addition, the delay of one latch stage is shorter (close to half of that of one flop stage), which can aggravate the impact of local variations.

3 OUR RESILIENT CIRCUIT AND ITS DESIGN FLOW

Since the flop based error detection has the advantage of lower replacement ratio and fewer sequential overhead, and the two-phase latch-based technique overcomes the problem of short-path. This work combines the advantage of both flop-based and two-phase latch-based technology. On the one hand, we replace the registers of critical paths by latches with error detectors to reduce the replacement ratio in two-phase latch-based design. On the other hand, we solve the short-path problem by inserting the CTG near the endpoints of critical paths. So we can obtain the ability of error-detection without any delay elements for short-path padding.

Fig. 4 shows the special design flow of our resilient circuit. After logic synthesis and timing analysis, those critical and near-critical paths are picked out. Next, the endpoint registers are replaced by resilient circuit in RTL, and followed by synthesis again. After the replacement, placement and routing are applied, ECO will be performed because of the potential variability of critical paths. Finally, since short-paths may exist in a placed and routed resilient design, short-path padding is performed.

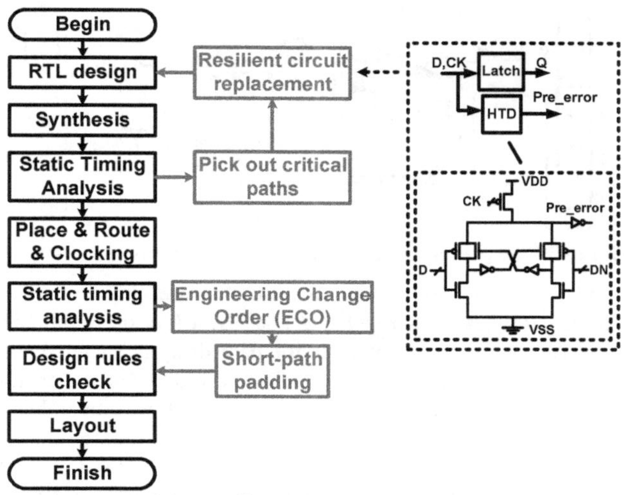

Figure 4: Special design flow of resilient circuits.

4 TRANSMISSION GATE INSERTION METHODOLOGY

4.1 Concept

For the resilient design, data transmission and timing error are all conducted among speculation window. While most of the resilient techniques often provide the speculation window of 50% of a clock period [10, 11], we find that more than half of the speculation window is not utilized even under the worst-case situation. Razor-lite [9] reduced the short-path padding by reducing the clock duty cycle of the global clock. For most resilient designs, rather than using 50% of the clock period as the speculation window, the positive clock phase can be reduced to just enough to cover the fast variations in order to mitigate the short-path problem.

In the proposed insertion mechanism of CTG, we reduce the waste of speculation window and combine the advantage of two-phase latch by inserting CTGs near the endpoints of critical paths. As shown in Fig. 5, Tw is the value that is equal to the width of the speculation window. The stage is defined as the minimum cell number between the current point to the endpoint latch (e.g., the stage of the input pins of U1 is 3 in Fig. 5). We analyse the topology of all logic cells of the circuit and set up a collection of the logic stages. By comparing the accumulated delay of each stage to the endpoint latch with Tw, the target stage N could be found if its delay to endpoint FF is just larger than Tw. Then we insert CTGs before all the target stage. The CTG works as a transparent-low latch, which means it turns off at positive clock and turns on at negative clock. Thus, all the short paths (e.g., SP1 and SP2) can be extended to negative clock phase to avoid the short-path problem.

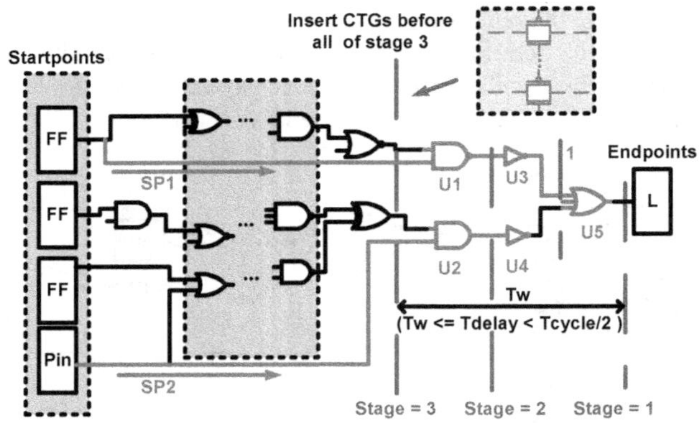

Figure 5: The principle of CTG insertion mechanism.

On the other hand, although the CTGs are also inserted in critical paths (as shown in Fig. 5 and Fig. 1 (c)), the setup time constraint can still be met since the path delay is longer than a half cycle when the CTG is turned on. The delay of the critical path extends only the cell delay of CTG, which is comparable to that of an inverter. In addition, as shown in the Fig. 6 and Fig. 1(c), by scaling the supply voltage, even if the data of stage N (d1) is influenced by a fast variation to make it arrive at the point between d1 and d3 actually (d1'), the final data to the endpoint latch (d3') can still be propagated correctly by the time-borrowing characteristic of latch. Thus, we can eliminate all the timing margin.

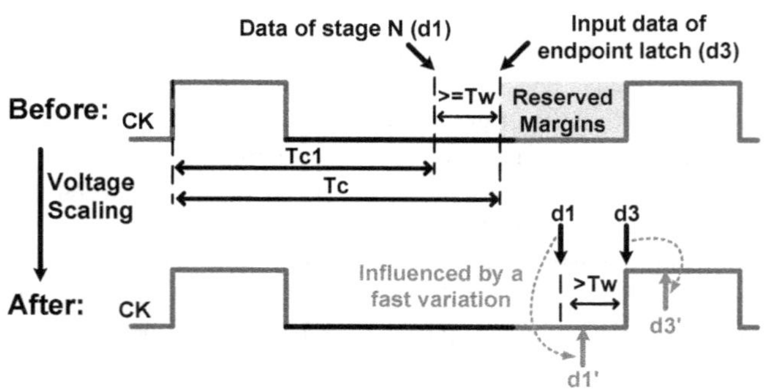

Figure 6: Timing diagram of a critical path with a fast variation before and after voltage scaling.

Compared to the traditional latch, the main problems of CTG are the stability and leakage when working as a latch. Thus, we adjusted the size of the CTG to fit for a wide-voltage-range operating. Then, both the function and stability of the CTG have been verified by 10^5 Monte-Carlo simulations in each voltage.

Differed from the two-phase latch technology, the proposed method replaces some paths with latches partially, it simplifies the design complexity and leads to the reduction of the area overhead. A significant benefit is the reduced invalid flip of combinational logic as the transmission gates synchronize the multiple short paths, which decreases the glitch power.

4.2 Speculation Window Design

In this paper, the 5% voltage drop of worst-case delay variability is used to account for all the dynamic variations. The sources of dynamic variation include IR-droop [14], clock jitters, capacitive coupling [15, 16], and temperature hot (or cold) spots [17]. In NTV operation, a smaller amount of driving current and relatively slow clock frequency can reduce the concern on inductive noise. In addition, device current has a positive temperature coefficient, i.e., current increases with higher temperature, in NTV regimes, which can relieve the concern for temperature hot spots. To precisely estimate the amount of dynamic variations is a design-specific task and beyond the scope of this paper.

4.3 Insertion Stage Selection in Inverter Chain

We perform SPICE-level simulations using 8th-order filter test circuit where each critical path has a 25-F04 long inverter chain. First, we analyze the relationship between the required speculation window and supply voltage. According to the setting of the speculation window in Section 4.2, Tw is obtained by Monte-Carlo simulation of multiple critical paths, with results shown in Fig. 7.

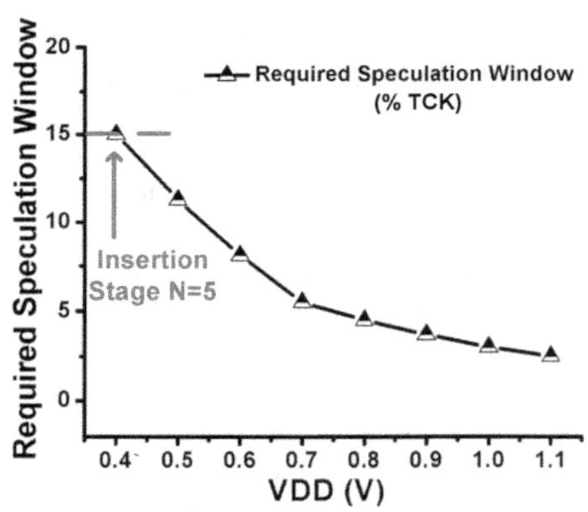

Figure 7: The required speculation window across a wide VDD.

The required speculation window is only 2.5% of the clock cycle when operating at 1.1V. As the decreasing of the supply voltage, the required window increases. The results also show that even at 0.4V, the window of 15 % of TCK is sufficient for the worst-case fast variations, making the remaining window of 35% of TCK redundant. The value of speculation window can be converted to the target insertion stage N (described in Section 4.1). In this work, it is sufficient when N is set as 5.

We also investigate the required N with the F04 length (most critical path) from 10 to 100 at 0.4V, as shown in Fig. 8. Since the delay variability can become worse in fine-grained inverter chain, it demands wider speculation window. The results show that 12-stage is enough even with 100 FO4 delays.

Then, we analyze the relationship between the insertion stage N and the number of CTG. As shown in the Table. 1, as the number of stages increases, the CTG increases correspondingly. When N is 14, the speculation window reaches 50% of TCK and the number of CTG becomes 122 at this point.

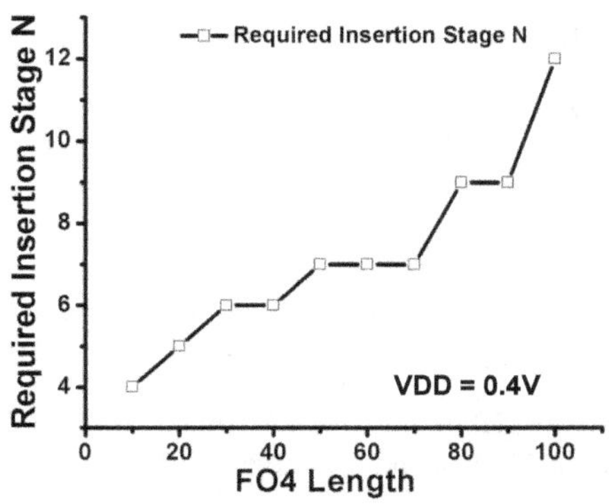

Figure 8: The required insertion stage N with the FO4 length across from 10 to 100.

Table 1: Required CTG number for various N

Insertion Stage (N)	Register replacement ratio (%)	TCK	Tw (% TCK)	Required CTG
1	15	25FO4	4	15
5	15	25FO4	15	47
7	15	25FO4	30	75
10	15	25FO4	40	98
14	15	25FO4	50	122

4.4 Insertion Stage Selection in General Circuit

In large-scale circuit designs, it is not necessary to do the search for the insertion stage N as we did for inverter chains in Section 4.3. We only need to analyze those critical paths. They can be found using commercial tools such as static timing analysis (STA). For the found critical paths, we run Monte-Carlo simulation with 5% voltage drop to obtain the delay distribution. Converted to the number of FO4 delay, the target insertion stages N can be obtained.

4.5 Insertion Points Selection Algorithm

The algorithm aims to find the reasonable insertion points for CTGs. First, we should calculate the Tw to defend the fast variation. Next, the Tw is converted to the target insertion stage N, which is the collection of the minimum cell number between the current point to the endpoint latch. Thus, the problem is converted to find out those points with stages equal to N.

The basic algorithm is depicted as follows:

Step 1: Find the stage N for this circuit as we discussed in Section 4.3 and 4.4.

Step 2: Create the endpoints collection L = {li}. Find all the paths to each endpoint by STA. Pick out the cell information by the customized script, so as to generate the collection of the topology between all the cells to each endpoint M = {Mij} and collection of the stage H = {Hij}. In addition, pick out all duplicated node collection D = {Dij}.

Step 3: Judge whether the **minimum** stage of all duplicated nodes in {Dij} equals to N. If not, insert a buffer between the nodes and its endpoint, and repeat Step 2 and Step 3. If yes, perform Step 4.

Step 4: Judge whether the **maximum** stage of all duplicated nodes in {Dij} equals to N. If not, insert a buffer between the nodes and its endpoint, and repeat Step 2 to Step 4. If yes, perform Step 5.

Step 5: Pick out all the nodes if their stages equal to N and delete the buffers inserted in Step 3 and Step 4.

5 APPLICATION AND COMPARISON

We apply our proposed method to a larger VLSI circuit SHA-256 circuit: which is an encryption circuit with over 6,000 registers and more than 30,000 logic cells. The target operating voltage is 0.55V and the clock cycle is 30 FO4 delays. The critical paths whose endpoint registers need to be replaced by latches are selected by the commercial EDA tool of STA. We also design a selection and insertion mechanism for the transmission gate.

Now we replace some of the flops with the latches. On the one hand, we select the insertion points for CTG, and then insert CTG. On the other hand, we fix the short-paths by padding cells (e.g., buffers and inverters). The comparison results are shown in the Table. 2. As the number of replacement registers increases, a large number of padding buffers are needed while the number of CTG remains roughly around 3× over the latches. It is worth noting that as the number of replacements reaches more than 500, the hold constraint can no longer be satisfied. To avoid this problem, the duty cycle of clock or the replacements ratio has to be adjusted.

Table 2: Comparison between CTG and delay cells

Register replacement number	NO. of CTGs	NO. of padding cells
1	4	10
10	39	187
50	185	843
100	359	2716
500	1774	18371
1000	3312	36297

Finally, according to the selected critical paths, 607 endpoint registers need to be replaced. We compare four design approaches: I. No resilient technique, II. Conventional resilient technique with the flop-based sequencing logic Razor [4], III. Conventional error detection technique with two-phase latch-based sequencing logic [11], and IV. Our proposed transmission gate insertion technique. For the technique II, we use the well-known Razor register circuits [4]. For the techniques III and IV, we use the error-detecting register which has a main latch, a shadow latch with an opposite phase, and an XOR gate [11]. As shown in Fig. 9 (a), technique II can incur more than 1.5× area overhead for combinational logic due to the excessive amount of short-path padding requirement. The technique III and IV have solved the short path problem thus need much less combinational logic than II.

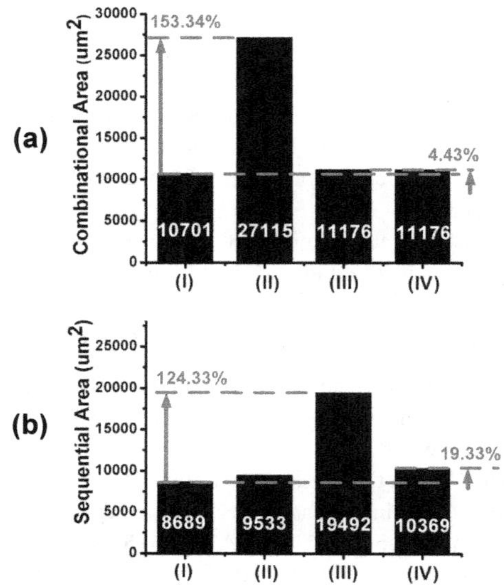

Figure 9: Comparisons of conventional methods with our method, (a) combinational area, (b) sequential area. (Abbreviation: I. baseline without EDAC ability, II. flop-based resilient circuit, III. two-phase latch-based resilient circuit, IV. Our method.

As Fig. 9 (b) shows, the sequential area of technique II is increased by 9.7%. The two-phase latch technique has to replace all the registers by latches, and needs more shadow latches than technique II and IV. Therefore, the area overhead increases to 124.33%. The proposed technique IV just replaces some registers by latches, thus the overhead of the sequential circuit is smaller.

As shown in Fig. 10, as the transmission gates are controlled by clocks, they synchronize multiple short paths, which decreases the invalid flip of combinational logic. Compared with the baseline circuit without using CTGs, it brings more than 46.06% glitch power saving when 1000 CTSs are used in the circuit.

6 CONCLUSIONS

In this paper, aim to solve the short path problem that exists in traditional resilient circuits, we proposed a novel insertion mechanism for transmission gate. By reducing the waste of the speculation window, analyzing and quantifying the node topology of the critical path, the reasonable insertion positions for clock-controlled transmission gates are picked out. Applied on a SHA-256 algorithm circuit in 28nm CMOS process, compared to the conventional techniques, the proposed method can reduce the combinational or sequential area overhead from 153.34% and 124.33% to 4.43% and 19.33%. It can also avoid the problem of high design complexity. In addition, the invalid flip of combinational logic has been decreased by the CTG, which brings 46.06% glitch power saving. We also customize a fully automated script which can be well-suited for large-scale circuit.

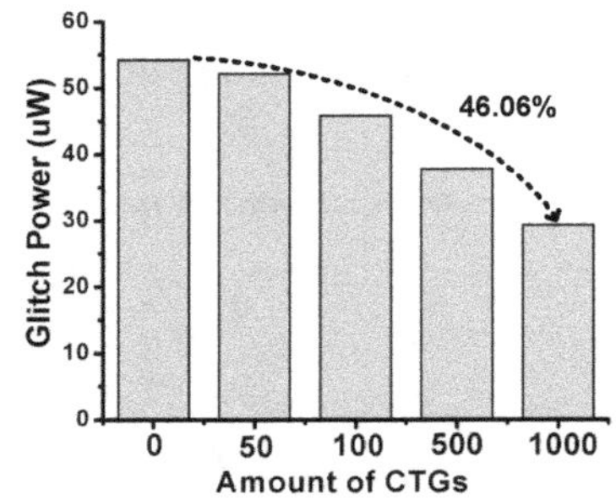

Figure 10: Glitch power savings with various amount of CTGs.

ACKNOWLEDGMENTS

Supported by the National Natural Science Foundation of China (61574033 and 61774038) and 863 Program (2015AA016601).

REFERENCES

[1] K. Bowman et al., "Impact of die-to-die and within-die parameter fluctuations on the maximum clock frequency distribution for gigascale integration," Solid-State Circuits, IEEE Journal of, vol. 37, no.2, pp. 183-190, 2002.

[2] S. Borkar et al., "Parameter variations and impact on circuits and microarchitecture," in DAC, 2012.

[3] M. Seok et al., "CAS-FEST 2010: Mitigating variability in near-threshold computing," Emerging and Selected Topics in Circuits and Systems, IEEE Journal of, vol. 1, no. 1, pp.42-49, 2011.

[4] D. Ernst et al., "Razor: A low-power pipeline based on circuitlevel timing speculation," in MICRO, 2003.

[5] D. Bull et al., "A power-efficient 32 bit ARM processor using timing-error detection and correction for transient-error tolerance and adaptation to PVT variation," Solid-State Circuits, IEEE Journal of, vol. 46, no. 1, pp. 18–31, 2011.

[6] Y. Yang et al. "PushPull: Short-path padding for timing error resilient circuits." Computer-Aided Design of Integrated Circuits and Systems, IEEE Transactions on, 33(4), VOL. 33, NO. 4, pp. 558-570, 2014.

[7] C. Wang et al., "Near-Threshold Energy and Area Efficient Reconfigurable DWPT/DWT Processor for Healthcare Monitoring Applications," Circuits and Systems Part II (TCAS-II), IEEE Transactions on, vol. 62, no. 1, pp. 70-74, 2015.

[8] J. Zhou et al., "HEPP: A new in-situ timing-error prediction and prevention technique for variation-tolerant ultra-low-voltage designs," in A-SSCC, 2013.

[9] S. Kim et al., "Razor-lite: A side-channel error-detection register for timing-margin recovery in 45nm SOI CMOS," in ISSCC, 2013.

[10] Y. Zhang et al., "iRazor: 3-transistor current-based error detection and correction in an ARM Cortex-R4 processor," in ISSCC, 2016.

[11] M. Fojtik et al., "Bubble Razor: An architecture-independent approach to timing-error detection and correction," in ISSCC, 2013.

[12] S. Kim, "Variation-tolerant, ultra-low-voltage microprocessor with a low-overhead, within-a-cycle in-situ timing-error detection and correction technique", Solid-State Circuits, IEEE Journal of, 50(6), 1478-1490, 2015.

[13] W. Dai et al., "HTD: A Light-Weight Holosymmetrical Transition Detector Based In-situ Timing Monitoring Technique for Wide-Voltage-Range in 40nm CMOS" in A-SSCC, 2017.

[14] K. Bowman et al., "Dynamic variation monitor for measuring the impact of voltage droops on microprocessor clock frequency," in CICC, 2010.

[15] Mingoo Seok, "Decoupling capacitor design strategy for minimizing supply noise of ultra low voltage circuits," in DAC, 2012.

[16] H. Fuketa et al., "Increase of crosstalk noise due to imbalanced threshold voltage between nMOS and pMOS in subthreshold logic circuits," Solid-State Circuits, IEEE Journal of, vol. 48, no. 8, pp. 1986–1994, 2013.

[17] S. Murali et al., "Temperature control of high-performance multi-core platforms using convex optimization," in DATE, 2008.

Energy and Performance Efficient Computation Offloading for Deep Neural Networks in a Mobile Cloud Computing Environment

Amir Erfan Eshratifar
Dept. of Electrical Engineering
University of Southern California
Los Angeles, California
eshratif@usc.edu

Massoud Pedram
Dept. of Electrical Engineering
University of Southern California
Los Angeles, California
pedram@usc.edu

ABSTRACT

In today's computing technology scene, mobile devices are considered to be computationally weak, while large cloud servers are capable of handling expensive workloads, therefore, intensive computing tasks are typically offloaded to the cloud. Recent advances in learning techniques have enabled Deep Neural Networks (DNNs) to be deployed in a wide range of applications. Commercial speech based intelligent personal assistants (IPA) like Apple's Siri, which employs DNN as its recognition model, operate solely over the cloud. The cloud-only approach may require a large amount of data transfer between the cloud and the mobile device. The mobile-only approach may lack performance efficiency. In addition, the cloud server may be slow at times due to the congestion and limited subscription and mobile devices may have battery usage constraints. In this paper, we investigate the efficiency of offloading only some parts of the computations in DNNs to the cloud. We have formulated an optimal computation offloading framework for forward propagation in DNNs, which adapts to battery usage constraints on the mobile side and limited available resources on the cloud. Our simulation results show that our framework can achieve 1.42× on average and up to 3.07× speedup in the execution time on the mobile device. In addition, it results in 2.11× on average and up to 4.26× reduction in mobile energy consumption.

KEYWORDS

computation offloading, mobile cloud computing, deep neural networks, energy efficient computing, high performance computing

ACM Reference Format:

Amir Erfan Eshratifar and Massoud Pedram. 2018. Energy and Performance Efficient Computation Offloading for Deep Neural Networks in a Mobile Cloud Computing Environment. In *GLSVLSI '18: 2018 Great Lakes Symposium on VLSI, May 23–25, 2018, Chicago, IL, USA.* ACM, New York, NY, USA, 6 pages. https://doi.org/10.1145/3194554.3194565

GLSVLSI '18, May 23–25, 2018, Chicago, IL, USA

ACM ISBN 978-1-4503-5724-1/18/05...$15.00
https://doi.org/10.1145/3194554.3194565

1 INTRODUCTION

With the exponential growth of deep learning techniques and digital raw data, a wide range of applications, that were previously intractable, are enjoying scalable and easy-to-train models. Deep learning has shown extremely promising results in Computer Vision[1][2], Speech Recognition[3], and Natural Language Processing [4]. Even though, DNNs outperform many other machine learning models, they often require a great amount of computational resources. Mobile devices like smart-phones and robots are often considered limited in terms of processing resources and energy budget compared to the cloud server, therefore, DNN workloads are often entirely offloaded to the cloud. However, as the computational resources in the mobile devices are becoming more powerful and energy efficient, we could possibly push some parts of the computations toward the mobile edge. Basically, there are following methods during neural networks inferences in mobile cloud computing context:

Cloud-only approach: In this method, when the user makes a query, all the input data will be uploaded to the cloud server, afterwards the cloud server does the inference and sends the output back to the mobile. The main drawback of this method is the communication overheads of uploading large inputs (e.g., images, audios, videos), which includes latency and energy costs or downloading large outputs in case of generative models, where the output of the network could be a multimedia file (e.g., image in [7]). The latency and energy costs of several benchmarks over three different wireless networks (Wi-Fi, 3G, LTE) are studied comprehensively in section (3). This approach also compromises user's privacy.

Mobile-only approach: In this method, all the computations are performed locally in either CPU or GPU depending on the available hardware and software architectures. There is an active research in empowering mobile devices for DNNs by designing accelerators[34][33]. Recently, Apple has unveiled a new machine learning framework API for developers named Core ML, enabling on-device processing[8]. They have also included a customized GPU specialized for machine learning tasks in their new smartphone[26]. In addition, by using this approach, no data will leave the device, which provides more privacy for the user.

Mobile-cloud collaborative approach: In this method, we seek to develop an optimal scheduling algorithm for collaboratively computation of feed forward neural networks. We break down the computations at layer granularity and decide upon which layers should be computed on mobile and which on the cloud server to achieve maximum performance and energy efficiency. Prior arts in this area often require to transfer the whole process state, which could have potentially large amount of variables to be offloaded, that is not taken into account[29]. Some rule-based offloading frameworks offload a function, when it is exceeding a pre-defined time ignoring the amount of data to be offloaded[31][30]. In addition, statistical prediction of the execution time and energy of functions used in [28] are prone to large errors especially in case of DNNs (Section 2). Our main contribution in this work is formulating optimal computation offloading in DNNs at layer granularity, where the optimality comes from solving an integer linear programming (ILP) setup.

There are three approaches in estimating the performance and energy consumption of inference with neural networks:

1. Statistical modeling by varying the configurable parameters of each layer and measuring the latency and energy consumption for each set of input parameters. A regression model can be used to fit over these profiles so as to estimate the latency and energy of the layer based on its configuration[27]. In section 2, we show that the complexities in latency and energy estimation of the conventional layers in deep neural networks are quite high so that it is not feasible to use statistical modeling, because we need exponential number of profiling measurements.

2. Analytical modeling by considering hardware and software specifications. State-of-the-art work in latency modeling of deep neural networks [5] fails to estimate fine-grained layer-level latency within an acceptable error bound. For instance, the latency of 6th layer in VGG-16, which is a fully connected layer with 4096 neurons, is underestimated by around 900 percent. Because of the fact that manufacturers do not reveal the detailed hardware architecture specifications in addition to the proprietary parallel computing architectures like CUDA, analytical approach could be quite challenging[6].

3. Application-specific profiling approach only requires to profile the latency and energy of the target neural networks. Because of the limited number of applications, which requires neural networks in user's mobile, this method seems more practical and leads to more accurate results.

In summary, the main contribution of this work is providing a framework to query DNNs efficiently on mobile devices collaborating with cloud server in the presence of battery usage constraints and cloud server limited resources.

2 EXECUTION TIME AND ENERGY PROFILING

In this section we elaborate upon the challenges in execution time and energy profiling. We performed four sets of experiments with the convolution operator, which is generally the most expensive operator in neural networks, on our mobile platform using Tensorflow™1.0.1[9]. The convolution takes a batch of images of width *img_w*, height *img_h*, and with *img_c* input channels. The image is convolved with a filter of width *f_w*, height *f_h*, and *f_c* output channels with a pre-defined stride in x and y directions. The input sizes in our experiments are listed in table 1. As depicted in Figure 1, at some points, increasing the input size decreases the execution time, which is caused by the heuristic selection of different convolution algorithms available in cuDNN[10]. For instance, for

Table 1: Convolution inputs size

	batches	img_w	img_h	img_c	f_w	f_h	f_c
Case1	16	64	64	Var	3	3	256
Case2	16	64	64	Var	9	9	256
Case3	16	64	64	3	Var	Var	256
Case4	16	64	64	128	Var	Var	256

small filter sizes, the convolution is calculated using General Matrix Multiplication (GEMM), while for large filter sizes an algorithm which uses Fast Fourier Transform (FFT) is chosen. Another source of non-linearity is when the GPU is under-utilized and increasing the input size would not affect the execution time. Moreover, as

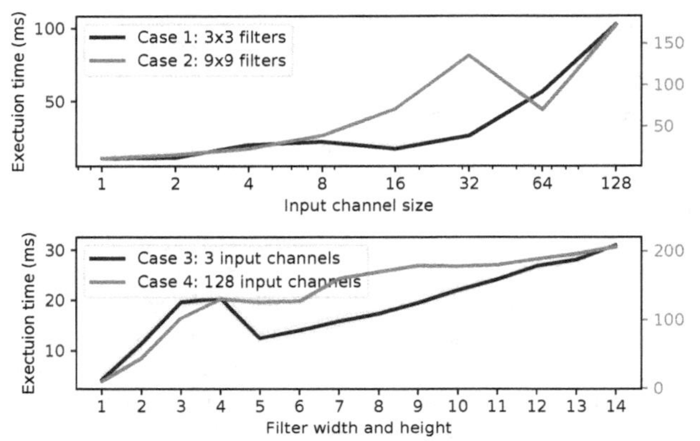

Figure 1: Non-linear execution time of convolutions w.r.t. inputs size. The execution time decreases even when the input size increases because of the heuristic selection of convolution algorithms.

depicted in Figure 2, layer-wise profiling is prone to large amount of errors in estimation. The reason is the accelerations done by hardware and software frameworks for the consecutive operations. For instance, the latency of two consecutive convolution $A * A * x$ is generally less than the sum of each convolution. The main reason is that the order of grouping of the operators affects the latency. In other words, the latency of $(A * A) * x$ and $A * (A * x)$ are not the same. In a nutshell, the execution time of two consecutive layers may not even be close to the sum of the execution times of the individual layers. This fact is depicted in Figure 2 for AlexNet[1]. Therefore, for a statistical model we need to profile not only each layer type with different input sizes but also the combination of various layers, which makes the act of profiling and regression very time-consuming and impractical. As a result, we decide to perform application-specific profiling. The level of granularity we are considering in our profiling step, is the following list of the layer types: convolution, deconvolution, pooling, fully connected, and activation functions.

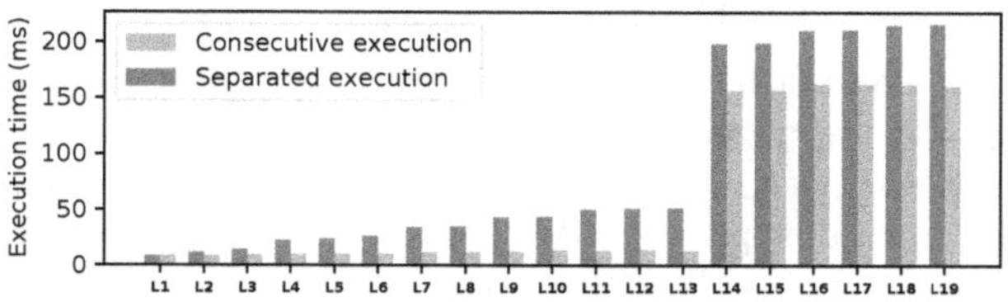

Figure 2: Non-linearity in the execution time of consecutive layers in AlexNet[1]. Each bar represents the execution time up to that layer.

3 COMPUTATION-OFFLOADING MODEL FOR DNN

3.1 Performance Efficient Computation Offloading Setup

As a parallel work [32] shows, mobile cloud computing scheduling of different tasks with constraints is a NP-hard problem. Therefore, we formulated this problem as an ILP with tractable number of variables. In our method, first we profile the latency and energy consumption of consecutive layers of size $m \in \{1, 2, \ldots, num\_layers\}$. We define the number of layers to be n consistently throughout this paper. Thus, we will have

$$n + (n-1) + \ldots + 1 = n(n+1)/2 \tag{1}$$

number of different profiling values for latency and energy. Considering ith layer to jth layer are computed either on the mobile edge or cloud server, we assign two binary variables $m_{i,j}$ and $c_{i,j}$ respectively. Download and upload communication latencies needs to be added to the execution time, while switching to/from cloud from/to mobile respectively.

$$T_{computation} = \sum_{i=1}^{n}\sum_{j=i}^{n}(m_{i,j}.T_{mobile_{L_{i,j}}} + c_{ij}.T_{cloud_{L_{i,j}}}) \tag{2}$$

$$\begin{aligned} T_{communication} = &\sum_{i=1}^{n}\sum_{j=i}^{n}\sum_{k=j+1}^{n} m_{i,j}.c_{j+1,k}.T_{upload_{L_j}} \\ &+ \sum_{i=1}^{n}\sum_{j=i}^{n}\sum_{k=j+1}^{n} c_{i,j}.m_{j+1,k}.T_{download_{L_j}} \\ &+ \sum_{i=1}^{n} c_{1,i}.T_{upload_{L_i}} \\ &+ \sum_{i=1}^{n} c_{i,n}.T_{download_{L_n}} \end{aligned} \tag{3}$$

$$T_{total} = T_{computation} + T_{communication} \tag{4}$$

$T_{mobile_{L_{i,j}}}$ and $T_{cloud_{L_{i,j}}}$ represent the execution time of ith layer to jth layer on the mobile and cloud respectively. $T_{download_{L_i}}$ and $T_{upload_{L_i}}$ represent the latency of downloading and uploading the output of ith layer respectively. Considering each set of consecutive layers, whenever $m_{i,j}$ and one of $\{c_{j+1,k}\}_{k=j+1:n}$ are one, output of jth is uploaded to the cloud. The same argument works for download. We also note that the last two terms in (3) represent the condition, when last layer is computed on the cloud and we need to download the output to the mobile edge and first layer is computed on the cloud and we need to upload the input to the cloud respectively. Because each set of consecutive layers should be computed either on mobile or cloud or none, we define the following set of constraints:

$$\forall i \in 1:n, \forall j \in i:n : m_{i,j} + c_{i,j} \leq 1 \tag{5}$$

Besides, we have to make sure that all layers are being computed exactly once. Therefore, we need to add the following constraints:

$$\forall m \in 1:n : \sum_{i=1}^{m}\sum_{j=m}^{n}(m_{i,j} + c_{i,j}) = 1 \tag{6}$$

Because of the non-linearity of multiplication, an additional step is needed to transform (3) to the standard form of ILP. We define two sets of new variables:

$$\begin{aligned} u_{i,j} &= m_{i,j}. \sum_{k=j+1}^{n} c_{j+1,k} \\ d_{i,j} &= c_{i,j}. \sum_{k=j+1}^{n} m_{j+1,k} \end{aligned} \tag{7}$$

with the following constraints:

$$\begin{aligned} &u_{i,j} \leq m_{i,j} \\ &u_{i,j} \leq \sum_{k=j+1}^{n} c_{j+1,k} \\ &m_{i,j} + \sum_{k=j+1}^{n} c_{j+1,k} - u_{i,j} \leq 1 \\ &d_{i,j} \leq c_{i,j} \\ &d_{i,j} \leq \sum_{k=j+1}^{n} m_{j+1,k} \\ &c_{i,j} + \sum_{k=j+1}^{n} m_{j+1,k} - d_{i,j} \leq 1 \end{aligned} \tag{8}$$

The first two constraints ensure that $u_{i,j}$ will be zero if either $m_{i,j}$ or $\sum_{l=j+1}^{n} c_{j+1,l}$ are zero. The third inequality guarantees that $u_{i,j}$ will take value one if both binary variables, $m_{i,j}$ and $\sum_{l=j+1}^{n} c_{j+1,l}$, are set to one. The same reasoning works for $d_{i,j}$. In summary, the total number of variables in our ILP formulation will be $4n(n+1)/2$, where n is total number of layers in the network.

3.2 Energy Efficient Computation Offloading Setup

Because of the nature of the application, we only care about the energy consumption on the mobile side. We formulate ILP as follows:

$$E_{computation} = \sum_{i=1}^{n}\sum_{j=i}^{n} m_{i,j}.E_{mobile_{L_{i,j}}} \tag{9}$$

$$E_{communication} = \sum_{i=2}^{n}\sum_{j=i}^{n} m_{i,j}.E_{download_{L_i}} + \sum_{i=1}^{n}\sum_{j=i}^{n-1} m_{i,j}.E_{upload_{L_j}} + (\sum_{i=1}^{n}(1-m_{1,i})-(n-1)).E_{upload_{L_1}} + (\sum_{i=1}^{n}(1-m_{i,n})-(n-1)).E_{download_{L_n}} \quad (10)$$

$$E_{total} = E_{computation} + E_{communication} \quad (11)$$

$E_{mobile_{L_{i,j}}}$ and $E_{cloud_{L_{i,j}}}$ represent the amount of energy required to compute ith layer to jth layer on the mobile and cloud respectively. $E_{download_{L_i}}$ and $E_{upload_{L_i}}$ represent the amount of energy required to download and upload the output of ith layer respectively. Likewise for performance efficient ILP constraints, we need to make sure that each layer get executed exactly once:

$$\forall m \in 1:n: \sum_{i=1}^{m}\sum_{j=m}^{n} m_{i,j} \leq 1 \quad (12)$$

The ILP problem can be solved for different set of parameters (e.g. different uplink and download speeds), and then the scheduling results can be stored as a look-up table in the mobile device. Moreover because the number of variables in this setup is tractable solving ILP is quick. For instance, solving ILP for AlexNet takes around 0.045 seconds on Intel(R) Core(TM) i7-3770 CPU with MATLAB®'s intlinprog() function using primal simplex algorithm.

3.3 Scenarios

- **Performance Efficient Computation:** In this case, all we need to do is to solve the ILP formulation for performance efficient computation offloading.
- **Energy Efficient Computation:** In this case, all we need to do is to solve the ILP formulation for energy efficient computation offloading.
- **Battery Budget Limitation:** In this case, according to the available battery, the operating system can decide to dedicate a specific amount of energy usage to each application. By adding the following constraint to the performance efficient ILP formulation, our framework would adapt to battery limitations:

$$E_{computation} + E_{communication} \leq E_{ubound} \quad (13)$$

- **Cloud Limited Resources:** There are situations in which the cloud server is busy or the subscription of the user is limited so that a limit of execution time could be applied to each application to alleviate the server load:

$$\sum_{i=1}^{n}\sum_{j=i}^{n} c_{i,j}.T_{cloud_{L_{i,j}}} \leq T_{ubound} \quad (14)$$

This constraint could be applied to both energy and performance efficient ILP formulations.

4 CASE STUDIES

4.1 Experimental Setup

We use Jetson TX2 board developed by NVIDIA[16], which fairly represents the computing power of mobile devices. Our server platform is equipped with NVIDIA®Tesla ™K40C[15], which has 11.25x more computing resources than our mobile platform. We measure the GPU power on our mobile platform using INA226 power monitoring sensor with sampling rate of 500kHz[19]. In our experiment, we use Tensorflow™[9], which is an open source software library equipped with cuDNN[10], a GPU-accelerated library of primitives for deep neural networks. Average download and upload speed of mobile networks in the U.S. are considered in this experiment[11][12]. We also use the power models of [14] for mobile networks with error less than 6%. The power level for uplink is $P_u = \alpha_u t_u + \beta$ and for downlink is $P_d = \alpha_d t_d + \beta$, where t_u and t_d are uplink and downlink throughputs respectively. The values for our power model paramters are as the following table:

Table 2: Power model parameters

Network	α_u (mW/Mpbs)	α_d (mW/Mpbs)	β (mW)
3G	868.98	122.12	817.88
4G	438.39	51.97	1288.04
Wi-Fi	283.17	137.01	132.86

Table 3: Average download and upload speed of mobile networks in U.S.

Network	Download speed (Mpbs)	Upload speed (Mbps)
3G	2.0275	1.1
4G	13.76	5.85
Wi-Fi	54.97	18.88

4.2 Benchmarks

Since the architecture of neural networks depends on the type of the application, we have chosen three common applications of DNNs:

(1) Discriminative neural networks are a class of models in machine learning for modeling the conditional probability distribution $P(y|x)$. This essentially is used in classification and regression tasks. AlexNet[1], OverFeat[21], VGG16[22] and NiN[20] are the discriminative models we use as benchmarks in this experiment.
(2) Generative neural networks model the joint probability distribtion $P(x, y)$, which allows for generating new samples. They have applications in computer vision[17] and robotics [13], which can be deployed on a mobile device. Chair[23] is a generative model we use as benchmark.
(3) Autoencoders are a class of neural networks, which are used to learn a representation for a data set. Their application is in image reconstruction, image to image translation, and denoising to name a few. Mobile robots can be equipped with autoencoders for their computer vision tasks.

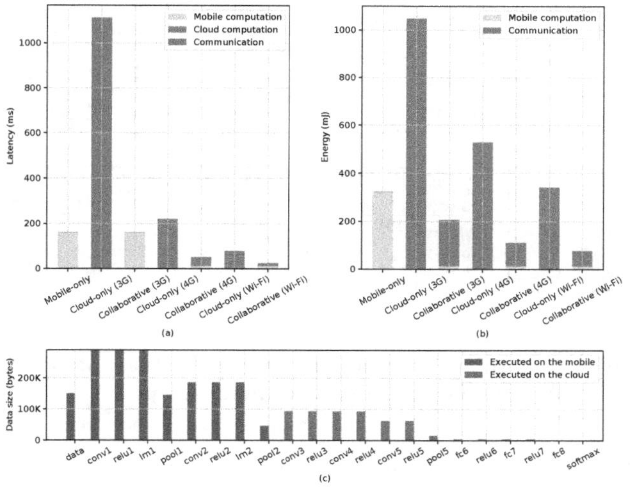

Figure 3: Execution time of AlexNet optimized for performance (a) Mobile energy consumption of AlexNet optimized for energy (b) Data size of the layers in AlexNet and the scheduled computation, where the first seven layers are being computed on the mobile and the rest on the cloud, which is optimal w.r.t. both performance and energy (c).

We use Pix2Pix[23], which has a similar architecture to autoencoders, as our benchmark.

Table 4: Benchmark Specifications

Type	Model	Layers
Discriminative	AlexNet	21
	OverFeat	14
	VGG16	37
	NiN	29
Generative	Chair	10
Autoencoder	Pix2Pix	32

4.3 Results

Execution time and energy breakdown for AlexNet, which is noted as a representative for the state-of-the-art models deployed in cloud servers[25], is depicted in Figure 3. Not only is the cloud-only approach dominated by the communication costs but also the collaborative one. As demonstrated in Figure 3, 99%, 93% and 81% of the total execution time is used for communication in case of 3G, 4G, and Wi-Fi. This relative portion also applies to energy consumption. Comparing the latency and energy of the communication to those of mobile-only approach, we figure out that mobile-only approach for AlexNet is better than the cloud-only approach in all the mobile networks.

Figure 4 shows the execution time and energy improvements for 6 different benchmarks. We have considered the best case of cloud-only and mobile-only as our baseline. We have also depicted the schedule of computations in this figure. As we can see, the cloud-only and mobile-only approaches are optimal for VGG16 and NiN respectively, while optimizing for mobile energy consumption. Our proposed framework can achieve 1.42X on average and up to 3.07X (OverFeat, 3G) speedup when optimizing for performance. Mobile energy consumption can be reduced 2.11X on average and up to 4.26X (OverFeat, 3G), while optimizing for energy consumption. The improvements in the execution time of deep neural networks benefits not only the mobile users but also the cloud providers, which essentially means that they could save more resources or have more users. Another key observation is the scheduling pattern of the computations in different types of neural networks. Generally, in discriminative networks, the input size is often large and the output size is small, which implies that it is better to compute the first layers on the mobile to avoid uploading large inputs to the cloud. On the other hand, in generative networks, output size is often large, which implies that it is better to compute the last layers on the mobile to avoid downloading large outputs from the cloud. In autoencoders, both the input and output data sizes are often large, therefore, it is better to compute the first and last layers on the mobile and offload the computations in the middle layers to the cloud.

4.4 Cloud Limited Available Resources Experiment

The cloud resource management may decide to allow a process to be executed for a limited amount of time. The reason could be the user's limited subscription or congestion in the cloud server. In this scenario, we have set up a experiment in which the cloud allows up to 50% of the execution time of the whole neural network on the cloud over Wi-Fi network setup. As we have shown in the Figure 5, multiple data transfer points may occur, whose maximum is four in case of OverFeat.

CONCLUSION AND ROADMAP

In this work, we demonstrated that cloud-only or mobile-only approaches are not necessarily optimal with regard to performance and energy. We formulated the problem with ILP setup, which is solved only once by the cloud server. The reason that we are using ILP is the fact that the number of data transfer points strongly depends on the network architecture and resource constraints applied by the cloud and mobile. It is possible to limit the number of data transfer points and solve the problem by a polynomial algorithm, but it is not guaranteed to be optimal for all kinds of network architecture and constraints. The output data size of generative models, are generally large so the last layers are expected to be computed on the mobile in the optimal case to avoid downloading large data. On the other hand, classification networks have smaller output data size, therefore last layers are expected to be computed on the cloud. Autoencoders have large input and output data sizes, which implies that the first and last layers are expected to be computed on the mobile. With these insights, the computation scheduling of deep neural networks can possibly have different patterns depending on the model architecture. The proposed framework in this paper can be extended to any data flow computational graphs with the granularity of primitive operators like multiplication.

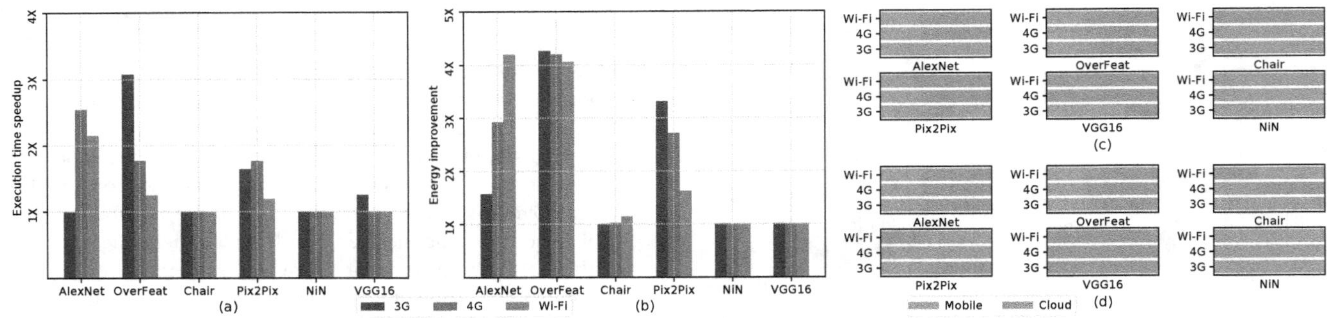

Figure 4: Execution time speed up (a) and energy improvement (b) using our proposed framework over the best case of mobile-only and cloud-only approaches. Scheduling patterns in performance efficient (c) and energy efficient (d) setups.

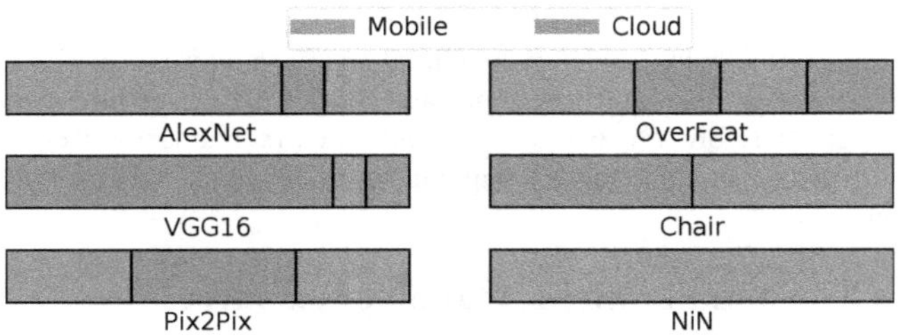

Figure 5: Computation scheduling patterns under execution time constraint of the cloud over Wi-Fi network setup

REFERENCES

[1] Krizhevsky et al., Imagenet classification with deep convolutional neural networks, NIPS, 2012.

[2] Karen Simonyan and Andrew Zisserman. Very deep convolutional networks for large-scale image recognition. preprint arXiv:1409.1556, 2014.

[3] Hinton, G. et al. Deep neural networks for acoustic modeling in speech recognition. IEEE Signal Processing Magazine 29, 2012.

[4] Collobert, R., et al. Natural language processing (almost) from scratch. J. Mach. Learn. Res. 12, 2493âĂŞ2537, 2011.

[5] Hang Qi, Evan R. Sparks, and Ameet Talwalkar. Paleo: A Performance Model for Deep Neural Networks. International Conference on Learning Representations, 2017.

[6] Sunpyo Hong and Hyesoon Kim. An integrated GPU power and performance model. In Proceedings of the 37th annual international symposium on Computer architecture, 2010.

[7] Alec Radford, Luke Metz, Soumith Chintala: Unsupervised Representation Learning with Deep Convolutional Generative Adversarial Networks. CoRR abs/1511.06434, 2015.

[8] Apple announces new machine learning API to make mobile AI faster https://www.theverge.com/2017/6/5/15725994/apple-mobile-ai-chip-announced-wwdc-2017

[9] M. Abadi, A. Agarwal et al., Tensorflow: Large-scale machine learning on heterogeneous distributed systems, arXiv:1603.04467, 2016.

[10] NVIDIA cuDNN https://developer.nvidia.com/cudnn

[11] State of Mobile Networks: USA - OpenSignal https://opensignal.com/reports/2017/08/usa/state-of-the-mobile-network

[12] 2017 United States Speedtest Market Report http://www.speedtest.net/reports/united-states/

[13] Finn, C. and Levine, S. Deep visual foresight for planning robot motion. arXiv preprint arXiv:1610.00696, 2016.

[14] Junxian Huang, Feng Qian, Alexandre Gerber, Z. Morley Mao, Subhabrata Sen, and Oliver Spatscheck. A close examination of performance and power characteristics of 4G LTE networks. In Proceedings of the 10th international conference on Mobile systems, applications, and services, 2012.

[15] Tesla GPU Accelerators for Servershttp://www.nvidia.com/object/tesla-servers.html

[16] Jetson TX2 Module https://developer.nvidia.com/embedded/buy/jetson-tx2

[17] Ian J. Goodfellow, Jean Pouget-Abadie et al., âĂIJGenerative Adversarial Networks,âĂİ arXiv:1406.2661, 2014.

[18] Vinod Nair and Geoffrey E. Hinton. Rectified linear units improve restricted boltzmann machines. In Proceedings of the 27th International Conference on International Conference on Machine Learning, 2010.

[19] INA226 http://www.ti.com/product/INA226

[20] Min Lin, Qiang Chen, Shuicheng Yan, Network In Network. arXiv preprint arXiv:1312.4400, 2014.

[21] Pierre Sermanet et al., OverFeat: Integrated Recognition, Localization and Detection using Convolutional Networks. arXiv:1312.6229, 2014.

[22] Karen Simonyan, Andrew Zisserman, Very Deep Convolutional Networks for Large-Scale Image Recognition. arXiv:1409.1556, 2014.

[23] Alexey Dosovitskiy et al., Learning to Generate Chairs, Tables and Cars with Convolutional Networks. arXiv:1411.5928, 2017.

[24] Phillip Isola, Jun-Yan Zhu, Tinghui Zhou, Alexei A. Efros, Image-to-Image Translation with Conditional Adversarial Networks. arXiv:1611.07004, 2016.

[25] Adam Coates, Brody Huval, Tao Wang, David J. Wu, Andrew Y. Ng, and Bryan Catanzaro. Deep learning with COTS HPC systems. In Proceedings of the 30th International Conference on International Conference on Machine Learning, 2013.

[26] The new iPhone 8 has a custom GPU designed by Apple with its new A11 Bionic chip https://techcrunch.com/2017/09/12/the-new-iphone-8-has-a-custom-gpu-designed-by-apple-with-its-new-a11-bionic-chip/

[27] Yiping Kang, Johann Hauswald, Cao Gao, Austin Rovinski, Trevor Mudge, Jason Mars, and Lingjia Tang. Neurosurgeon: Collaborative Intelligence Between the Cloud and Mobile Edge. SIGARCH Comput. Archit, 2017.

[28] Eduardo Cuervo et al., Maui: making smartphones last longer with code offload. In Proceedings of the 8th international conference on Mobile systems, applications, and services, ACM, 2010.

[29] Roelof Kemp Nicholas Palmer Thilo KielmannHenri Bal, Cuckoo: A Computation Offloading Framework for Smartphones, International Conference on Mobile Computing, Applications, and Services, 2010.

[30] Mark S Gordon, Davoud Anoushe Jamshidi, Scott A Mahlke, Zhuoqing Morley Mao, and Xu Chen. Comet: Code offload by migrating execution transparently, 2012.

[31] Byung-Gon Chun, Sunghwan Ihm, Petros Maniatis, Mayur Naik, and Ashwin Patti. CloneCloud: elastic execution between mobile device and cloud. In Proceedings of the sixth conference on Computer systems, 2011.

[32] Amir Erfan Eshratifar, M. S. Abrishami, and M. Pedram, JointDNN: an efficient training and inference engine for intelligent mobile cloud computing services, arXiv preprint arXiv:1801.08618, 2018.

[33] Mahdi Nazemi, Amir Erfan Eshratifar, and Massoud Pedram. 2018. A Hardware-Friendly Algorithm for Scalable Training and Deployment of Dimensionality Reduction Models on FPGA. In Proceedings of the 19th IEEE International Symposium on Quality Electronic Design.

[34] Kaiyuan Guo, Shulin Zeng, Jincheng Yu, Yu Wang, Huazhong Yang, A Survey of FPGA Based Neural Network Accelerator, arXiv preprint arXiv:1712.08934, 2018.

Adapting Convolutional Neural Networks for Indoor Localization with Smart Mobile Devices

Ayush Mittal, Saideep Tiku, Sudeep Pasricha
Department of Electrical and Computer Engineering
Colorado State University, Fort Collins, CO, U.S.A.
ayusmittal@gmail.com, {saideep, sudeep}@colostate.edu

ABSTRACT

Indoor localization is emerging as an important application domain for enhanced navigation (or tracking) of people and assets in indoor locales such as buildings, malls, and underground mines. Most indoor localization solutions proposed in prior work do not deliver good accuracy without expensive infrastructure (and even then, the results may lack consistency). Ambient wireless received signal strength indication (RSSI) based fingerprinting using smart mobile devices is a low-cost approach to the problem. However, creating an accurate 'fingerprinting-only' solution remains a challenge. This paper presents a novel approach to transform Wi-Fi signatures into images, to create a scalable fingerprinting framework based on Convolutional Neural Networks (CNNs). Our proposed CNN based indoor localization framework (*CNN-LOC*) is validated across several indoor environments and shows improvements over the best known prior works, with an average localization error of < 2 meters.

KEYWORDS

Indoor localization; convolutional neural networks, (CNN), mobile devices; Wi-Fi fingerprinting; deep learning

ACM Reference Format:

Ayush Mittal, Saideep Tiku, Sudeep Pasricha. 2018. Adapting Convolutional Neural Networks for Indoor Localization with Smart Mobile Devices. In GLSVLSI '18: 2018 Great Lakes Symposium on VLSI, May 23–25, 2018, Chicago, IL, USA. ACM, NY, NY, USA, 6 pages. http://dx.doi.org/10.1145/3194554.3194594

1. INTRODUCTION

Existing outdoor location based services have transformed how people navigate, travel, and interact with the world around them. Now, indoor localization techniques are emerging that have the potential to extend this outdoor experience across indoor locales. Industry is beginning to provide indoor location-based services to improve customer experience. For instance, Google can suggest products to its users through targeted indoor location based advertisements [1]. Stores such as Target in the USA are beginning to provide indoor localization solutions to help customers locate products in a store and find their way to these products [2]. Services provided by these companies combine GPS, cell towers, and Wi-Fi data to estimate the user's location. However, in the indoor environment where GPS signals cannot penetrate building walls, the accuracy of these geo-location services can be in the range of tens of meters, which is insufficient in many cases [3].

GLSVLSI '18, May 23–25, 2018, Chicago, IL, USA

ACM ISBN 978-1-4503-5724-1/18/05...$15.00
https://doi.org/10.1145/3194554.3194594

Many of the latest indoor localization techniques exploit radio signals, such as Bluetooth, UWB (Ultra-Wide Band) [4], RFID (Radio Frequency Identification) [5], [6], or other customized radios. The key idea is to use characteristics of radio signals (e.g., signal strength or triangulation) to estimate user location relative to a radio beacon (wireless access point). But these techniques suffer from multipath effects, signal attenuation, and noise-induced interference [8]. Also, as these techniques require specialized wireless radio beacons to be installed in indoor locales, they are costly and thus lack scalability for wide-scale deployment.

Wi-Fi based fingerprinting is perhaps the most popular radio-signal based indoor localization technique being explored today. Wi-Fi is an ideal radio signal source for indoor localization as most public or private buildings are pre-equipped with Wi-Fi access points (APs). Lightweight middleware-based fingerprinting frameworks have been shown to run in the background to deliver location based updates on smartphones [29]. Fingerprinting with Wi-Fi works by first recording the strength of Wi-Fi radio signals in an indoor environment at different locations. Then, a user with a smartphone can capture Wi-Fi received signal strength indication (RSSI) data in real-time and compare it to previously recorded (stored) values to estimate their location in that environment. Fingerprinting techniques can deliver an accuracy of 6 to 8 meters [28], with accuracy improving as the density of APs increases. However, in many indoor environments, noise and interference in the wireless spectrum (e.g., due to other electronic equipment, movement of people, operating machinery, etc.) can reduce this accuracy. Combining fingerprinting-based frameworks with dead reckoning can improve this accuracy somewhat [8]. Dead reckoning refers to a class of techniques where inertial sensor data (e.g., from accelerometer, gyroscope) is used along with the previously known position data to determine the current location. But dead reckoning is known to suffer from error accumulation (in inertial sensors) over time. Also, these techniques are not effective for people using wheelchairs or moving walkways.

The intelligent use of machine learning (ML) techniques can help to overcome noise and uncertainty during fingerprinting-based localization [8]. While traditional ML techniques work well at approximating simpler input-output functions, computationally intensive deep learning models are capable of dealing with more complex input-output mappings and can deliver better accuracy. Middleware-based offloading [30] and energy enhancement frameworks [31], [32] may be a route to explore for computation and energy-intensive indoor localization services on smartphones. Furthermore, with the increase in the available computational power on mobile devices, it is now possible to deploy deep learning techniques such as Convolutional Neural Networks (CNNs) on smartphones. A CNN is a special type of Deep Neural Network (DNN) that is geared towards image matching and recognition. The most popular aspect of CNN is that it can automatically identify essential input features that make the most impact towards the correctness of the final output. This process is known as feature learning. Prior to deep learning, feature learning was an expensive and time intensive process that had to be conducted manually. CNN has been extremely successful in complex image classification problems and is finding applications in many emerging domains, e.g., self-driving cars [27].

In this paper, we propose a new and efficient framework that uses CNN-based Wi-Fi fingerprinting to deliver a superior level of indoor localization accuracy to a user with a smartphone. Our approach utilizes widely available Wi-Fi APs without requiring any customized/expensive infrastructure deployments. The framework works on a user's smartphone, within the computational capabilities of the device, and utilizes the radio interfaces for efficient fingerprinting-based localization. The main novel contributions of this paper can be summarized as follows:

- We developed a new technique to extract images out of location fingerprints, which are then used to train a CNN designed to improve indoor localization robustness and accuracy;
- We implemented a hierarchical architecture to scale the CNN, so that our framework can be used in the real world where buildings can have large numbers of floors and corridors;
- We performed extensive testing of our algorithms with the state-of-the-art across different buildings and indoor paths, to demonstrate the effectiveness of our proposed framework.

2. RELATED WORK

Several efforts aim to address the challenges in the domain of indoor localization. Here we summarize some of the key efforts.

Several RFID [5], [6] based indoor localization solutions that use proximity-based estimation techniques have been proposed. But the hardware expenses of these efforts increase dramatically with increasing accuracy requirements. Also, these approaches cannot be used with smartphones and require the use of specialized hardware. Indoor localization systems that use UWB [4] and ultrasound [10] have similar requirements for additional (costly) infrastructure, and a lack of compatibility for use with commodity smartphones.

Triangulation based methods, such as [11], use multiple antennas to locate a person or object. But these techniques require several antennas and regular upkeep of the associated hardware. Most techniques therefore favor using the more lightweight fingerprinting approach, often with Wi-Fi signals. UJIIndoorLoc [7] describes a technique to create a Wi-Fi fingerprint database and employs a KNN (K-Nearest Neighbor) based model to predict location. Their average accuracy using KNN is 7.9 meters. Dead reckoning techniques use the accelerometer to estimate the number of steps, a gyroscope for orientation, and a magnetometer to determine the heading direction. Such techniques have been employed in [12] and [26], but have shown to deliver poor localization accuracy results when used alone.

Radar [12] and Indoor Atlas [26] proposed using hybrid indoor localization techniques. Radar [12] combines inertial sensors (dead reckoning) with Wi-Fi signal propagation models, whereas Indoor Atlas [26] combines information from several sensors such as magnetic, inertial, and camera sensors, for localization. LearnLoc [8] combines non-deep ML models, dead reckoning techniques, and Wi-Fi fingerprinting to trade-off indoor localization accuracy and energy efficiency during localization on smartphones.

A few efforts have begun to consider deep learning to assist with indoor localization. The work in [13] presents an approach that uses DNNs with Wi-Fi fingerprinting. The accuracy of the DNN is improved by using a Hidden Markov Model (HMM). The HMM takes temporal coherence into account and maintains a smooth transition between adjacent locations. But our analysis shows that the fine location prediction with the HMM fails in cases such as when moving back on the same path or taking a sharp turn. HMM predictions are also based on the previous position acquired through the DNN and hence, can be prone to error accumulation. DeepFi [14] and ConFi [15] propose approaches that use the Channel State Information (CSI) of Wi-Fi signals to create fingerprints. But the CSI information in these approaches was obtained through the use of specialized hardware attached to a laptop. None of the mobile devices available today have the ability to capture CSI data. Due to this limitation, it is not feasible to implement these techniques on smartphones. Deep Belief Networks (DBN) [16] have also been used for indoor localization, but the technology is based on custom UWB beacons that lead to very high implementation cost.

In summary, most of the above-mentioned frameworks either require additional costly infrastructure or cannot be deployed on smart mobile devices. Our implementation-based analysis shows that these frameworks can become slow and resource intensive if used for large buildings with multiple floors and corridors.

Our proposed framework in this paper, *CNN-LOC*, overcomes the shortcomings of these state-of-the-art indoor localization approaches. *CNN-LOC* creates input images by using RSSI of Wi-Fi signals that are then used to train a CNN model, without requiring any specialized hardware/infrastructure. *CNN-LOC* is easily deployable on current smartphones. The framework also integrates a hierarchical scheme to enable scalability for large buildings with multiple floors and corridors/aisles.

3. CONVOLUTIONAL NEURAL NETWORKS

Convolutional Neural Networks (CNNs) are specialized DNNs with a focus on image classification. They are highly resilient to noise in the input data and have shown to deliver excellent results for complex image classification tasks. The smallest unit of any neural network (NN) is a perceptron and is inspired by the biological neuron present in the human brain. A perceptron is defined by the following equation:

$$y = \sum_{i=1}^{n} w_i x_i + w_0 \tag{1}$$

Here y is the output, which is a weighted sum of the inputs x_i, with a weighted bias (w_0). NNs have inter-connected layers, and in each layer, there are several perceptrons, each with its own tunable weights and biases. Each layer receives some input, executes a dot product and passes it to the output layer or the hidden layer in front of it [17]. This output is often applied to an activation function that gives an input-output mapping defined by logistic regression. The most common activation functions used are *sigmoid* and *tanh* functions. The goal of an NN is to approximate a functional relationship between a set of inputs and outputs (training phase). The resulting NN then represents the approximated function that is used to make predictions for any given input (testing phase).

While an NN often contains a small number of hidden layers sandwiched between the input and output layer, a Deep Neural Network (DNN) has a very large number of hidden layers. DNNs have a much higher computational complexity but in turn are also able to deliver very high accuracy. CNNs are a type of DNN that include several specialized NN layers, where each layer may serve a unique function. CNN classifiers are used to map input data to a finite set of output classes. For instance, given different animal pictures, a CNN model can be trained to categorize them into different classes such as cats, dogs, etc. CNNs also make use of Rectified Linear Units (ReLUs) as their activation function, which allows them to handle non-linearity in the data.

In the training phase, our CNN model uses a feed forward deep learning algorithm. To update the weights during the training phase, a Stochastic Gradient Descent (SGD) algorithm is used. Adam [18], an optimized version of SGD, is used to optimize the learning process. The algorithm is designed to take advantage of two well-known techniques: RMSprop [19] and AdaGrad [20]. SGD maintains a constant learning rate for every weight update in the network. In contrast, Adam employs an adaptive learning rate for each network weight; with the learning rate being adapted as the training progresses. RMSprop uses the mean (first-order moment) of past squared gradients and adjusts the weights based on how fast the gradient changes. Adam, to optimize the process, uses the variance (second-order moment) of past gradients and adjusts the weights accordingly.

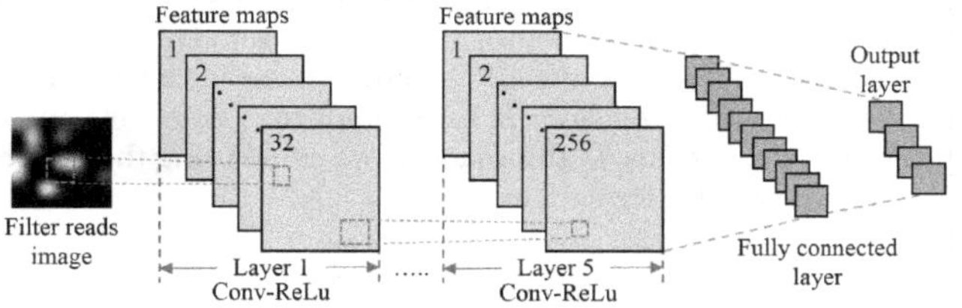

Figure 1: CNN architecture

The structure of the CNN in *CNN-LOC* is inspired from the well-known CNN architectures, LeNet [21] and AlexNet [22]. Our CNN architecture is shown in figure 1. The first hidden layer is partially connected to the input layer. This hidden layer only looks at a specific region of the input image at a time, and this region is known as a filter. The filter is shown by a rectangle (red-dotted lines). Each layer performs a convolution of a small region of the input image with the filter and feeds the result to the ReLu activation function. Therefore, we refer to each layer as [Conv-ReLu]. To capture more details from the input image we can use a larger number of filters. For each filter, we get a feature map. For the first layer of [Conv-ReLU], we used 32 filters to create a set of 32 feature maps. We used five hidden layers of [Conv-ReLU], but only two are shown for brevity. The number of filters and layers are derived through empirical analysis as discussed in section 4.4. A 'stride' parameter determines the quantity of pixels that a filter will shift, to arrive at a new region of the input image to process. The stride and other 'hyperparameters' of our CNN are further discussed in section 4.4. In the end, a fully connected layer helps in identifying the individual class scores (in our case each class is a unique location). The class with the highest score is selected as the output. In this layer, all the neurons are connected to the neurons in the previous layer (green-dotted-lines).

In a conventional CNN, a pooling layer is used to down-sample the image when the size of the input image is too big. In our case, the input image is small and therefore we do not need this step. We want our CNN to learn all the features from the entire image.

4. *CNN-LOC* FRAMEWORK: OVERVIEW

4.1 Overview

An overview of our *CNN-LOC* indoor localization framework is shown in figure 2. In the framework, we utilize the available Wi-Fi access points (APs) in an indoor environment to create an RSSI fingerprint database. Our framework is divided into two phases. The first phase involves RSSI data collection, cleaning, and pre-processing. This pre-processed data is used to create a database of images. Each image represents a Wi-Fi RSSI based signature that is unique to a location (i.e., x-y co-ordinate). This database of images is used to train a CNN model. The trained model is deployed on a smartphone. In the second phase, real time AP data is converted into an image and then fed to the trained CNN model to predict the location of the user. The CNN model predicts the closest block that was sampled as the users' location. A detailed description of the pre-processing is described in the next section.

4.2 Pre-processing of RSSI Data

The process of image database creation begins with the collection of RSSI fingerprints as shown in the top half of figure 2. The RSSI for various APs are captured along with the corresponding x and y coordinates at the training locations. We only maintain information for known Wi-Fi APs and hence clean the captured data. This ensures that our trained model is not polluted by unstable Wi-Fi APs. On the RSSI scale, values typically range between -95 dB (lowest) to -0 dB (highest). We normalize the RSSI values on a scale from 0 and 100, where 0 represents the weak or null signal, and 100 represents the strongest signal.

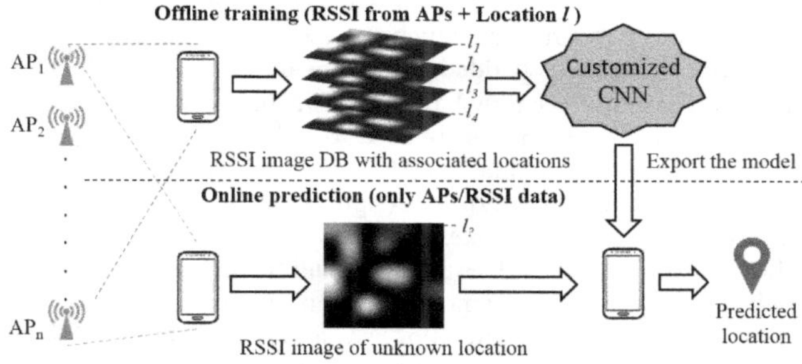

Figure 2: An overview of the *CNN-LOC* framework

Assume that while fingerprinting an indoor location, a total of K APs are discovered at N unique locations. These combine to form a two-dimensional matrix of size $N \times K$. Then the normalized RSSI fingerprint at the Nth location, denoted as l_N, is given by a row vector $[r_1, r_2, ..., r_K]$, denoted by R_N. Therefore, each column vector, $[w_1, w_2, ..., w_N]$ would represent the normalized RSSI values of the Kth AP at all N locations, denoted by W_K. We calculate the Pearson Correlation Coefficient (PCC) [23] between each column vector W_K and the location vector $[l_1, l_2, ..., l_N]$. The result is a vector of correlation values denoted as C. PCC is useful in identifying the most significant APs in the database that impact localization accuracy. The coefficient values range across a scale of -1 to +1. If the relationship is -1, it represents a strong negative relationship, whereas +1 represents a strong positive relationship, and 0 implies that the input and output have no relationship.

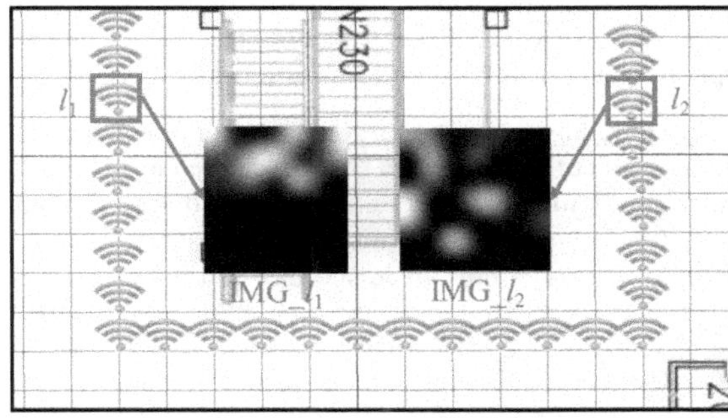

Figure 3: Unique images created for locations l_1 and l_2. The green icons represent locations that are fingerprinted along an indoor path. The two locations shown are 10 meters apart.

We only consider the magnitude of the correlation as we are only concerned with the strength of the relationship. APs with very low correlation with the output coordinates are not useful for the purpose of indoor localization. Therefore, we can remove APs whose correlation to the output coordinates is below a certain threshold ($|PCC| < 0.3$). This removes inconsequential APs from the collected Wi-Fi data and helps reduce the computational workload of the framework. The normalized RSSI data from the remaining high-correlation APs is used to create an RSSI image database, as explained in the next section.

4.3 RSSI Image Database

In this section, we present our approach to convert RSSI data for a given location into a greyscale image. A collection of these images for all fingerprinted locations forms the RSSI Image Database. To form greyscale images, a Hadamard Product (*HP*) [24] is calculated for each *R* and *C*. HP is defined as an element wise multiplication of two arrays or vectors:

$$HP = \sum_{i=1}^{N} R_i \circ C \tag{2}$$

The dimension of each *HP* is $1 \times K$. Then, the *HP* matrix is reshaped into a $p \times p$ matrix, which represents a 2D image as shown in figure 3. The HP is padded with zeros in the case that *K* is less than p^2. Therefore, we now have a set of *N* images of size $p \times p$ in our database. These images are used to train the CNNs.

Figure 3 shows two images (*IMG_l₁ and IMG_l₂*) of size 7×7 created for two unique fingerprints (signatures) associated with two different locations. Each pixel value is scaled on a scale of 0 to 255. The patterns in each of these images will be unique to a location and change slightly as we move along an indoor path.

In equation (2), the product of PCC and normalized RSSI value for each AP is used to form a matrix. Its purpose is to promote the impact of the APs that are highly correlated to fingerprinted locations. Even though there may be attenuation of Wi-Fi signals due to multipath fading effects, the image may fade but will likely still have the pattern information retained. These patterns that are unique to every location can be easily learned by a CNN. The hyperparameters and their use in *CNN-LOC* is discussed next.

4.4 Hyperparameters

The accuracy of the CNN model depends on the optimization of the hyperparameters that control its architecture which is the most important factor in the performance of CNN. A smaller network may not perform well and a larger network may be slow and prone to overfitting. There are no defined rules in deep learning that help in estimating the appropriate hyperparameters. Identifying the optimal values for the CNN hyperparameters is an empirical process and requires several iterations of experimentation and analysis. The estimated values are also highly dependent on the input dataset. Below, we discuss results of our analysis of CNN hyperparameters for our indoor localization problem domain.

- Number of hidden layers: A large number of hidden layers lead to longer execution times and conversely, fewer hidden layers may produce inaccurate results. We found that 5 layers of [Conv-ReLU] works best for our domain.
- Size of filter: This defines the image area that the filter considers at a time, before moving to the next region of the image. A large filter size might aggregate a large chunk of information in one pass. The optimum filter size in our case was found to be 2×2.
- Stride size: The amount of pixels a filter moves by is dictated by the stride size. We set it to 1 because the size of our image is very small and we do not wish to lose any information.
- Number of filters: Each filter extracts a distinct set of features from the input to construct different feature maps. Each feature map holds unique information about the input image. The best results were obtained if we started with a lower number of filters and increased them in the successive layers to capture greater uniqueness in the patterns. There were 32 filters in the first layer and were doubled for each subsequent layer up to 256 filters such that both the fourth and fifth layer had 256 filters.

4.5 Integrating Hierarchy for Scalability

Our *CNN-LOC* framework is designed to scale up to larger problem sizes than that handled by most prior efforts. For this purpose, we enhanced *CNN-LOC* by integrating a hierarchical classifier. The resulting hierarchical classifier employs a combination of smaller CNN modules, which work together to deliver a location prediction. Figure 4 shows the hierarchical decision structure of the framework. Each CNN module has a label that starts with C. The CNN in the first layer (C1) classifies the floor numbers, and then in the next layer, C20 or C21 identify the corridor on that floor. Once the corridor is located, one of the CNNs from the third layer (C30 – C35) will predict the fine-grain location of the user. It is important to note that the CNN models in the third layer actually represent two models each, i.e., C30 includes both CNN models for the x and y axis. In this manner, we avoid using the hierarchal classifier twice for each axis.

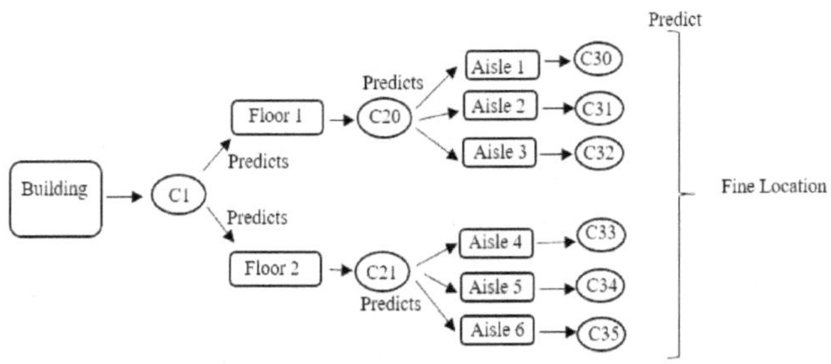

Figure 4: A general architecture for the hierarchical classifier

5. EXPERIMENTS

5.1 Experimental Setup

This section describes the *CNN-LOC* implementation and experimental results. The experiments were conducted on 3 separate indoor paths as described in Table 1. The corridors on the path are divided into a grid and labelled sequentially from 1 to *N*. Each square in the grid has an area of 1 m² and represents a "class". This allows us to treat indoor localization as a classification problem for CNN. Figure 5 shows an example of a path covered in the library building with labeled squares. Each label further translates into an x-y coordinate. Five Wi-Fi scans were conducted at each square during the fingerprinting (training) phase.

Table 1: Indoor paths used in experiments

Building	Path Length (m)	Shape
Library	30	U shape
Clark A	35	Semi-octagonal
Physics	28	Square shape

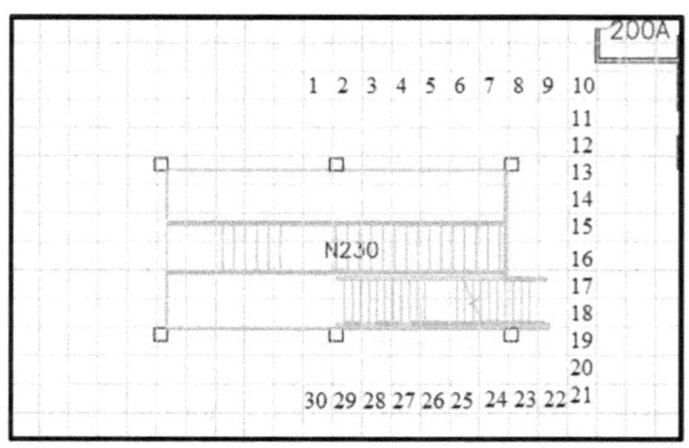

Figure 5: Library building path divided into a grid, with squares along the path labeled sequentially from 1 to 30

5.2 Smartphone Implementation

An Android application was built to collect Wi-Fi fingerprints (i.e., RSSI samples from multiple APs at each location) and for testing. The application is compatible with Android 6.0 and was tested on a Samsung Galaxy S6. After fingerprint data collection, the data was pre-processed as described in the previous section for the CNN model. The entire data set is split into training and testing samples, so we can check how well our models perform. We used $1/5^{th}$ of the total samples for testing and $4/5^{th}$ of the samples were used for training. Also, we implemented different CNN models for location estimation along different axes. Thus, we use a dedicated CNN model to predict the x coordinate of a location. Similarly, a separate CNN model predicts the y coordinates. The output from these models is combined to get the final results.

5.3 Experimental Results

We compared our *CNN-LOC* indoor localization framework with three other indoor localization frameworks from prior work. The first work we implemented is based on the approach in [25] and employs Support Vector Regression (SVR). The approach forms one or more hyperplanes in a multidimensional space segregating similar data points, which are then used for regression. The second work is based on the KNN technique from [8], which is a non-parametric approach that is based on the idea that similar input will have similar outputs. Lastly, we compare our work against a DNN based approach [13] that improves upon conventional NNs by incorporating a very large number of hidden layers. All of these techniques supplement the Wi-Fi fingerprinting approach with a machine learning model to provide robustness against noise and interference effects. Our experiments in the rest of this section first discusses the localization accuracy results for the techniques. Subsequently, we also discuss results for the scalability of our framework using a hierarchical classification enhancement approach. Lastly, we contrast the accuracy of *CNN-LOC* with that reported by other indoor localization techniques.

5.3.1 Indoor Localization Accuracy Comparison

Figure 6 shows the paths predicted by the four techniques, for the indoor path in the Clark building. The green dots along the path represent the points where Wi-Fi RSSI fingerprint samples were taken to create the training dataset. The distance between each of the green dots is 1 meter. In the training dataset, each green dot is converted into an image. The testing phase consists of the user walking along this path, and the red lines in Figure 6 show the paths predicted by the four techniques. It is observed that KNN [8] and SVR [25] stray off the actual path the most, whereas DNN and *CNN-LOC* perform much better. This is likely because KNN and SVR are both regression based techniques where the prediction is impacted by neighboring data points. In cases where the sampled points are very close to each other, there may not be enough variation across neighboring samples for the regression-based techniques to work properly. The transition from one location to another is smoother for CNN as it is able to distinguish between closely spaced sampling locations due to our RSSI-to-image conversion technique. From figure 6, it is evident that *CNN-LOC* produces stable predictions for the Clark path.

Figure 7 shows a bar graph that summarizes the average location estimation error for the various techniques on the three different indoor paths considered. We found that the KNN approach is the least reliable among all techniques with a mean error of 5.5 meters and large variations across the paths. The SVR-based approach has a similar mean error as the KNN approach. The DNN based approach shows lower error across all of the paths. But, it does not perform consistently across all of the paths and the mean error is always higher than that for *CNN-LOC*. This may be due to the fact that the filters in CNN are set up to focus on the image with a much finer granularity than the DNN approach is capable of. We also observe that all techniques perform the worst in the Physics department. This is due to the fact that the path in the Physics department is near the entrance of the building and has a lower density of Wi-Fi APs as compared to the other paths. The Library and Clark paths have a higher density of Wi-Fi APs present; hence, better accuracy can be achieved. Our proposed *CNN-LOC* framework is the most reliable framework with the lowest mean error of less than 2 meters.

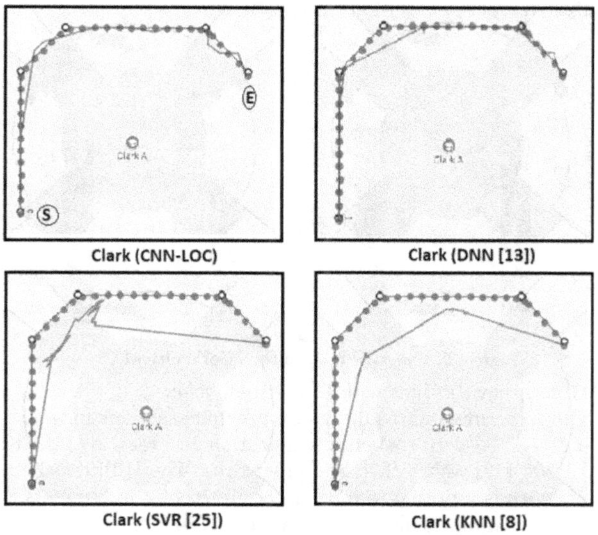

Figure 6: Path traced using different techniques

5.3.2 CNN-LOC Scalability Analysis

We discuss results for the hierarchal *CNN-LOC* (Section 4.5) here. We consider a scenario when *CNN-LOC* is required to predict a location inside a building with two floors and with three corridors on each floor. The length of each corridor is approximately 30 meters. We combined several small CNNs (in our case 9 small CNNs), such that a smaller number of weights are associated with each layer in the network than if a single larger CNN was used.

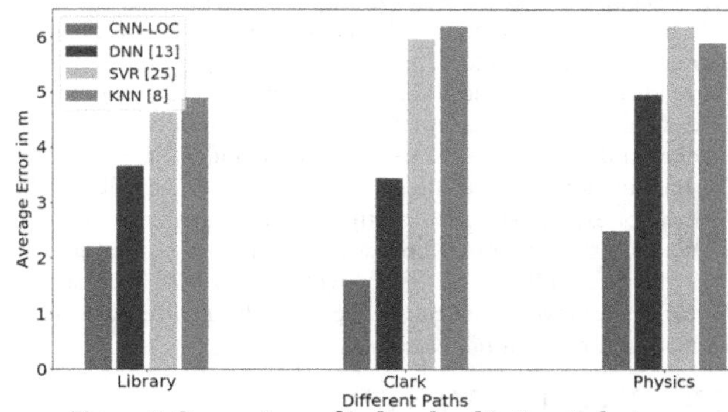

Figure 7: Comparison of indoor localization techniques

We first analyzed the accuracy of predictions, for our *CNN-LOC* framework with and without the hierarchical classifier. For the first and second layer of the hierarchical classifier (shown in Figure 4), the accuracy is determined by the number of times the system predicts the correct floor and corridor. We found that floors and corridors were accurately predicted 99.67% and 98.36% of times, respectively. For the final layer, we found that there was no difference in accuracy between the hierarchal and the non-hierarchal approach. This is because in the last level both the approaches use the same model.

Figure 8 shows the benefits in terms of time taken to generate a prediction with the hierarchical versus the non-hierarchical *CNN-LOC* framework. We performed our experiment for four walking scenarios ("runs") in the indoor environment (building with two floors and with three corridors on each floor). We found that the hierarchical *CNN-LOC* model only takes 2.42ms to make a prediction on average, whereas the non-hierarchical *CNN-LOC* takes longer (3.4ms). Thus, the hierarchical classifier represents a promising approach to reduce prediction time due to the fewer number of weights in the CNN layers in the hierarchical approach, which leads to fewer computations in real-time.

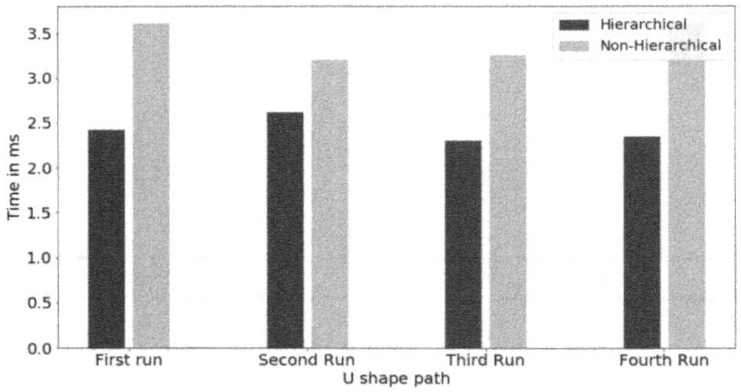

Figure 8: Execution time for Hierarchical CNN

5.3.3 Accuracy Analysis with Other Approaches

Our experimental results in the previous sections have shown that *CNN-LOC* delivers better localization accuracy over the KNN [8], DNN [13] and SVR [25] frameworks. The UJIIndoorLoc [7] framework is reported to have an accuracy of 4 to 7 meters. Our average accuracy is also almost twice that of RADAR [12]. If we consider frameworks that used CSI (DeepFi [14] and ConFi [15]), our accuracy is very close to both at just under 2 meters. However, [14] and [15] use special equipment to capture CSI and cannot be used with mobile devices. In contrast, our proposed *CNN-LOC* framework is easy to deploy on today's smartphones, does not require any specialized infrastructure (e.g., custom beacons), and can be used in buildings wherever Wi-Fi infrastructure pre-exists.

6. CONCLUSIONS

In this paper, we presented the *CNN-LOC* framework that uses Wi-Fi fingerprints and convolutional neural networks (CNNs) for accurate and robust indoor localization. We compared our work against three different state-of-the-art indoor localization frameworks from prior work. Our framework outperforms these approaches and delivers localization accuracy under 2 meters. *CNN-LOC* has the advantage of being easily implemented without the overhead of expensive infrastructure and is smartphone compatible. We also demonstrated how a hierarchical classifier can improve the scalability of this framework. *CNN-LOC* represents a promising framework that can deliver reliable and accurate indoor localization for smartphone users.

ACKNOWLEDGEMENTS

This research was supported by the National Science Foundation (NSF) under grant number ECCS-1646562, and endowments from the Monfort foundation and Rockwell-Anderson foundation.

REFERENCES

[1] "How Google Maps Makes Money", 2017 [Online] https://www.investopedia.com/articles/investing/061115/how-does-google-maps-makes-money.asp [Accessed: 1 Dec 2017]

[2] "Target and Retailers Using Hybrid Indoor Location Tech to Enable New Customer Experiences" [online] http://www.indoorlbs.com/new-blog-1/2015/11/30/target-and-other-retailers-using-indoor-location-tech [Accessed: 3 Dec 2017]

[3] "Case Study: Accuracy & Precision of Google Analytics Geolocation" 2017 [Online] Available at: https://radical-analytics.com/case-study-accuracy-precision-of-google-analytics-geolocation-4264510612c0 [Accessed: 1 Dec 2017]

[4] "Ubisense Research Network" [Online] Available: http://www.ubisense.net/ [Accessed: 1 Dec 2017]

[5] G. Jin, X. Lu, and M. Park, "An indoor localization mechanism using active RFID tag," SNUTC, 2006.

[6] Z. Chen, and C. Wang, "Modeling RFID signal distribution based on neural network combined with continuous ant colony optimization," Neurocomputing, vol. 123, pp. 354-361, 2014.

[7] J. Torres-Sospedra et al., "UJIIndoorLoc: A new multi-building and multi-floor database for WLAN fingerprint-based indoor localization problems," IPIN, 2014.

[8] S. Pasricha, V. Ugave, Q. Han and C. Anderson, "LearnLoc: A framework for smart indoor localization with embedded mobile devices," CODES+ISSS, 2015.

[9] L. Deng, "A tutorial survey of architectures, algorithms, and applications for deep learning," APSIPA, 2013.

[10] G. Borriello et al., "Walrus: wireless acoustic location with room-level resolution using ultrasound," Mobisys, 2005.

[11] C. Yang, and H. R. Shao, "WiFi-based indoor positioning," in IEEE Communications Magazine, vol. 53, no. 3, pp. 150-157, 2015.

[12] P. Bahl, and V. Padmanabhan, "RADAR: An in-building RFbased user location and tracking system," INFOCOM, 2000.

[13] W. Zhang et al., "Deep Neural Networks for wireless localization in indoor and outdoor environments," Neurocomputing, vol. 194, pp. 279-287, 2016.

[14] X. Wang et al., "DeepFi: Deep learning for indoor fingerprinting using channel state information," WCNC, 2015.

[15] H. Chen et al., "ConFi: Convolutional Neural Networks Based Indoor Wi-Fi Localization Using Channel State Information," IEEE Access, pp. 18066 – 18074, vol. 5, 2017.

[16] Y. Hua, et al., "Deep Belief Networks and deep learning," ICIT, 2015.

[17] "Stanford CNN tutorial" [Online] Available: http://cs231n.github.io/convolutional-networks [Accessed: 1 Dec 2017]

[18] D. P. Kingma et al., "Adam: a Method for Stochastic Optimization", ICLR, 2015.

[19] "RMSProp", [Online] http://www.cs.toronto.edu/~tijmen/csc321/slides/lecture_slides_lec6.pdf/ [Accessed: 1 Dec 2017]

[20] J. Duchi et al., "Adaptive Subgradient Methods for Online Learning and Stochastic Optimization", JMLR, vol. 12, pp. 2121–2159, 2011.

[21] Y. LeCun et al., "Gradient-based learning applied to document recognition," Proc. IEEE, vol. 86, no. 11, pp. 2278–2324, Nov. 1998.

[22] A. Krizhevsky et al., "ImageNet classification with deep convolutional neural networks", NIPS, 2012.

[23] J. Benesty, J. Chen, Y. Huang, I. Cohen, "Pearson Correlation Coefficient", in Topics in Signal Processing, Springer, vol. 2, 2009.

[24] G. Styan, "Hadamard products and multivariate statistical analysis", In Linear Algebra and its Apps., Elsevier, vol. 6, pp. 217-240, 1973.

[25] Y. K.Cheng, H. J. Chou and R. Y. Chang, "Machine-Learning Indoor Localization with Access Point Selection and Signal Strength Reconstruction", VTC, 2016.

[26] "IndoorAtlas" [Online] http://www.indooratlas.com/ [Accessed: 1 Dec 2017]

[27] V. Rausch, et al., "Learning a deep neural net policy for end-to-end control of autonomous vehicles," ACC, 2017.

[28] C. Langlois, S. Tiku, S. Pasricha, "Indoor localization with smartphones", CE, 2017.

[29] S. Tiku, S. Pasricha, "Energy-Efficient and Robust Middleware Prototyping for Smart Mobile Computing", RSP, 2017.

[30] A. Khune, S. Pasricha, "Mobile Network-Aware Middleware Framework for Energy-Efficient Cloud Offloading of Smartphone Applications" CE, 2017.

[31] B. Donohoo, C. Ohlsen, S. Pasricha, "A Middleware Framework for Application-aware and User-specific Energy Optimization in Smart Mobile Devices", Journal of Pervasive and Mob. Comp., vol. 20, pp. 47-63, 2015.

[32] B. Donohoo, C. Ohlsen, S. Pasricha, C. Anderson, Y. Xiang, "Context-Aware Energy Enhancements for Smart Mobile Devices", IEEE Trans. on Mob. Comp. (TMC), Vol 13, No. 8, pp. 1720-1732, 2014.

Face Recognition with Hybrid Efficient Convolution Algorithms on FPGAs

Chuanhao Zhuge[1], Xinheng Liu[1,3], Xiaofan Zhang[1], Sudeep Gummadi[1], Jinjun Xiong[2], Deming Chen[1,3]
[1]University of Illinois Urbana-Champaign, [2]IBM T. J. Watson Research Center,[3]Inspirit IoT, Inc.
{zhuge2, xliu79, xiaofan3, sgummad2, dchen}@illinois.edu, *jinjun*@us.ibm.com

ABSTRACT

Deep Convolutional Neural Networks (CNN) have become a Swiss knife in solving critical artificial intelligence tasks. However, deploying deep CNN models for latency-critical tasks remains to be challenging because of the complex nature of CNNs. Recently, FPGA has become a favorable device to accelerate deep CNNs thanks to its high parallel processing capability and energy efficiency. In this work, we explore different fast convolution algorithms including Winograd and Fast Fourier Transform (FFT), and find an optimal strategy to apply them together on different types of convolutions. We also propose an optimization scheme to exploit parallelism on novel CNN architectures such as Inception modules in GoogLeNet. We implement a configurable IP-based face recognition acceleration system based on FaceNet using High-Level Synthesis. Our implementation on a Xilinx Ultrascale device achieves 3.75x latency speedup compared to a high-end NVIDIA GPU and surpasses previous FPGA results significantly.

ACM Reference Format:
Chuanhao Zhuge[1], Xinheng Liu[1,3], Xiaofan Zhang[1], Sudeep Gummadi[1], Jinjun Xiong[2], Deming Chen[1,3] . 2018. Face Recognition with Hybrid Efficient Convolution Algorithms on FPGAs. In *GLSVLSI '18: 2018 Great Lakes Symposium on VLSI, May 23–25, 2018, Chicago, IL, USA.* ACM, New York, NY, USA, 6 pages. https://doi.org/10.1145/3194554.3194597

1 INTRODUCTION

Deep Convolutional Neural Networks (CNN) have demonstrated great success in various machine intelligence areas and enabled new advancement for applications such as video content understanding [1], face recognition [2], and crowd flow monitering [3]. To overcome the overwhelming computing pressure of these deep models, researchers have developed custom hardware accelerators including ASICs and FPGAs. FPGAs have already been proven to be an efficient device for implementing traditional computer vision algorithms [4–6]. More recently, they also gained popularity in deep neural network accelerations mainly because of their flexibility and high energy-efficiency. And with the help of High-Level Synthesis (HLS) tools, we are able to rapidly map and optimize the emerging deep neural network architectures on FPGAs.

GLSVLSI '18, May 23–25, 2018, Chicago, IL, USA

ACM ISBN 978-1-4503-5724-1/18/05...$15.00
https://doi.org/10.1145/3194554.3194597

Prior FPGA works [7] mostly focus on optimizing general convolution (CONV) layers. However, recent trend shows that state-of-the-art neural network architectures [8] tend to contain the topology of parallel branches, which are then merged through filter concatenation or summation. It is noticed that jointly optimizing a single acceleration engine for all layers of the deep networks leads to dynamic underutilization of resources [9]. This effect is especially acute on these advanced CNN structures with branches, since each branch would most likely carry different sizes and dimensions of convolutions. To overcome this problem, one solution is to implement multiple CONV engines that are specifically designed for each or subsets of layers. To achieve minimum overall latency, a resource partition solution has been proposed [10]. We extend such resource allocation strategy to exploit the intra-module parallelism of the multi-branch topology to attain better latency.

Besides hardware-specific tricks, researchers also look into algorithmic improvements to accelerate convolution computation. Researchers [11] exploit the equivalency between convolutions in spatial domain and element-wise multiplications in frequency domain. This method allows us to mathematically reduce the computation complexity with FFT-based convolution. More recently, the Winograd minimal-filter based convolution algorithm has been introduced [12], and it is suitable for small kernel sizes and strides. Although works have been done to adopt the FFT-based [13] and Winograd-based [14] algorithms to accelerate convolution on FPGAs, to the best of our knowledge, there is no work on combining the two fast algorithms to adapt to different sizes of convolutions so as to obtain better performance. In our work, we analyze and explore the properties of both FFT and Winograd-based convolution algorithms, and propose a heuristic methodology to design a hybrid accelerator for different convolutions. To summarize, this work highlights the following contributions:

- We analyze and find the suitable sizes and depths for applying FFT and Winograd convolution algorithms. The analysis is incorporated in a general methodology to design a hybrid convolution algorithm for FPGAs.
- We propose a novel resource allocation scheme that considers the intra-module parallelism of the recently invented CNN topology with branches, and minimize the overall system latency. We implement an algorithm to quickly find optimal resource partition parameters on HLS tools.
- We implement a face recognition system with a template based reconfigurable HLS IP for the Inception module [8]. We achieve better performance and energy-efficiency compared to GPUs and previous implementation of GoogLeNet on FPGAs [13].

2 BACKGROUND

2.1 Inception Module

In recent years, we have seen the booming of highly effective CNN architectures. One trend is that many networks apply the idea of splitting convolution layers into several branches, which may contain different sizes and depths of convolution kernels. These branches are often merged through concatenation or summation. Such a topology enhances the model's expressivity and enables the network to be several times deeper. The Inception module is the first architecture that employs such a forking mechanism. One inception module contains a composition of pooling, 1×1, 3×3, 5×5 convolutions. At the top, the results of different convolution branches are concatenated together. The Inception module is illustrated in Figure 1. The GoogLeNet (Inception V1) comprises nine Inception modules, making it the best performing CNN architecture in ImageNet competition 2014.

The FaceNet face recognition system [2] is based on Inception

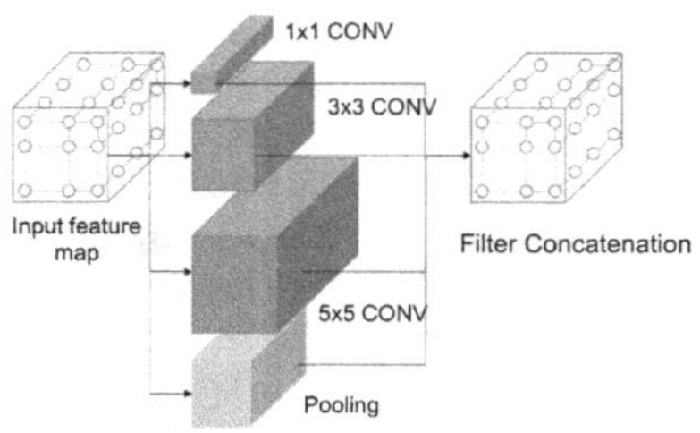

Figure 1: Inception module topology.

V2, which is an improvement of V1 with batch normalization. The model is designed to output a 128-d embedding vector. The model is trained using the triplet loss function, such that embeddings of two images of the same person have a small distance between them, while embeddings of different persons have a large distance.

2.2 Convolution in Frequency Domain

The well known convolution theorem states that spatial convolutions are equivalent to pair-wise multiplications in the frequency domain. Assuming the convolution input is a $L \times M \times M$ feature map, there are K kernels with size $L \times Q \times Q$. The spatial convolution's computation complexity is then $C_{spatial} = (KLQ^2M^2)$. 2D real-number FFT has logaritmic complexity. During inference, weights are usually only loaded once, therefore the FFT for weights (CONV kernels) can be done offline. Thus, the computation complexity for FFT-based convolution during inference consists of three parts: 2D FFT for feature map, pair-wise complex number multiplication, and inverse-FFT for the result. The overall computation complexity is given by:

$$C_{fft\_conv\_inference} = LM^2logM^2 + KL4M^2 + KM^2logM^2 \quad (1)$$

And the theoretical speed up is presented as:

$$SU = \frac{KLQ^2}{(K+L)logM^2 + 4KL} \approx \frac{1}{4}Q^2 \quad (2)$$

when number of feature maps (L) and number of kernels (K) are both large. The feature map size (M) is on log scale thus the impact is minimal. According to Equation 2, larger kernel size leads to more significant speed up.

2.3 Winograd Minimal Filtering Convolution

Another fast convolution is based on the Winograd minimal filtering algorithm[15]. The algorithm reduces the number of multiplications with the expense of additional addition and constant multiplication. Take $F(2,3)$ as an example. The standard convolution consumes $2 \times 3 = 6$ multiplications. The Winograd algorithm uses 4 multiplications. It uses 9 more constant multiplications, but they can be implemented as bit-shifts and additions, thus are much cheaper. The 2D Winograd algorithm is implemented from nesting the minimal 1D algorithm. In general, a 2D Winograd algorithm $F(m \times m, r \times r)$ can be represented by the following equations.

$$U = GgG^T, V = B^T dB, Y = F(m \times m, r \times r) = A^T(U \odot V)A, \quad (3)$$

where g, d refer to the original weight tile and feature map tile respectively, G, B, and A are transform matrices, generated by Cook-Toom algorithm, and U, V are the transformed weight tile and feature map tile. For example, $F(2 \times 2, 3 \times 3)$ consumes 16 multiplications, at the expense of additional 84 operations, yielding 2.25x reduction compared to 36 multiplications with standard convolution.

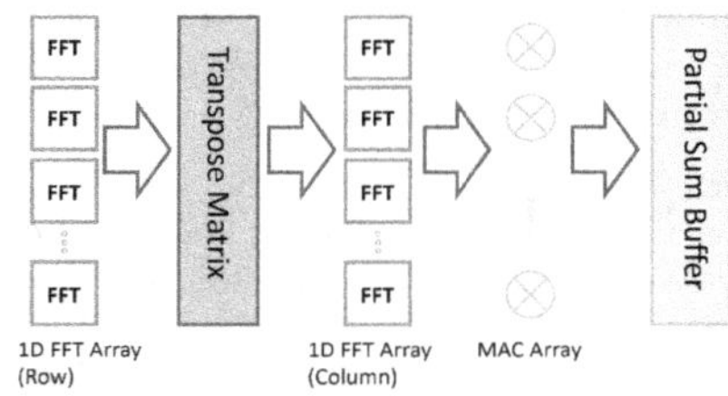

Figure 2: 2D FFT engine constructed from multiple 1D FFT cores.

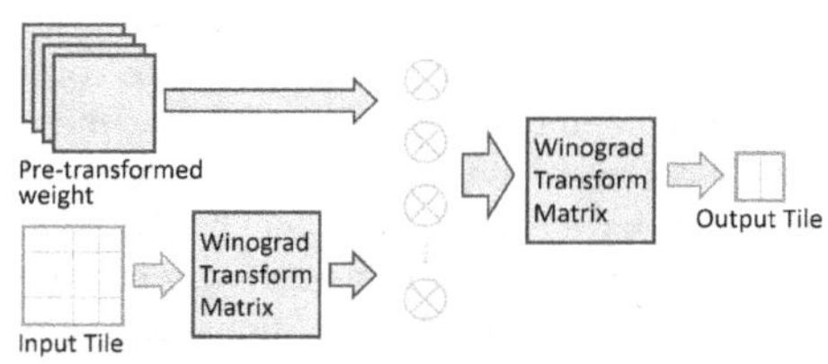

Figure 3: Winograd processing engine that exploits parallelism and data reuse.

3 SYSTEMIC CHARACTERIZATION FOR FAST CONVOLUTION ALGORITHMS

The two fast algorithms deliver remarkable speed compared to conventional convolution, but theoretical analysis and previous experiments [11, 12] have shown that these two algorithms have different optimal design points. FFT-based method in theory provides greater speed up when kernel size is larger. On the other hand, study claims that the Winograd algorithm's improvement on speed winds down quickly when kernel size becomes large because the transformation overhead increases quadratically, offsetting the savings in the multiplications.

Recent deep CNN structures contain multiple parallel branches with different kinds of convolutions. Therefore, a single efficient algorithm cannot provide the best optimization. Consequently, we come up with an innovative heuristic to design a hybrid accelerator that incorporates both fast algorithms to cover different workloads for better performance. In order to find a good strategy of using different algorithms, we systematically conduct studies for different implementations of FFT and Winograd CONV with different design parameters, and use latency cycle count as our performance metric. In our experiments we consider kernel sizes, feature map sizes, and input/output dimensions shown in Table 1. The empirical latency model obtained from the study can be used as a guidance to choose different algorithms for different network architectures.

For Winograd-based convolution with larger kernels, we evaluate $F(2 \times 2, 5 \times 5)$, and $F(2 \times 2, 7 \times 7)$. For our implementation of FFT-based convolution, since the Radix-2 FFT inputs must be of size of powers of 2, we choose the padding to make up size 8, 16, and 32, for input size 6, 12, and 24 respectively.

One observation is that the kernel size does not affect FFT's absolute performance in general because kernel and input need to be zero-padded to be the same size. There is one exception when input size is 6×6 and kernel size is 5×5 and 7×7. For these particular parameter combinations, we pad it to 16 instead of 8×8, to retain higher numerical precision as observed in our experiment. The padding overhead is significant, leading to similar performance as 12×12 input, thus less speed up compared to other algorithms.

We use Vivado HLS to implement the algorithms on the Xilinx VU9P FPGA. The implementations of FFT and Winograd CONV engines are illustrated in Figure 2 and 3. For each engine, they have respective transformation matrices, followed by MAC arrays for computing pair-wise multiplication. Our goal here is to evaluate the algorithmic impact, so we aim to eliminate the hardware resource usage difference as much as we can. We notice that both fast algorithms exhibit similar transform-compute-transform computation pattern, and each transformed feature map can be reused to do multiple pair-wise multiplication with pre-transformed kernels, to generate multiple partial results in parallel. Thus, one easier way to control resource usage is to designate the feature map reuse factor through *HLS UNROLL*. We try to keep the same reuse factor so that different algorithms uses similar amount of resource for fair comparison. However, as shown in Figure 4, which demonstrates the normalized resource usage, we observe that different algorithms have different preferences of resources. For example, for FFT-based algorithm, it uses 60% of the DSPs, but consumes as much as 2.2x of LUTs, compared to the baseline, which is implemented using a conventional loop-optimization method [10]. Also, BRAM usage is affected by the number of output channels, since it buffers the

Table 1: Design parameters for FFT-based and Winograd-based convolutions

Dimensions	Sizes evaluated
kernel sizes	3, 5, 7
feature map sizes	6, 12, 24
input/output dimensions	16, 32, 64, 128 (combinations)

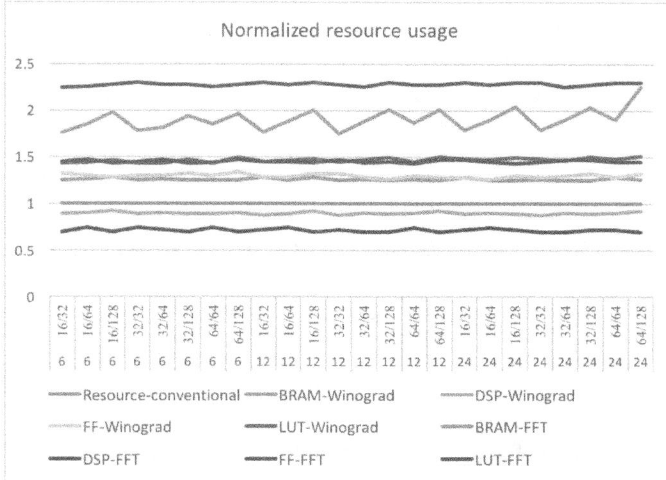

Figure 4: Normalized resource usage for different experiment setup.

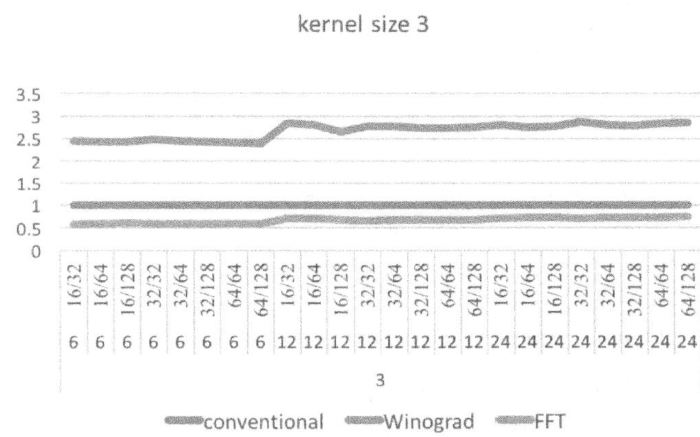

Figure 5: Speed up comparison when kernel size is 3×3.

intermediate results to prevent unnecessary IFFTs. In general, the fast algorithms prefer using LUTs to implement transformation operations, and save DSP usage due to reduced number of multiplications.

The result is shown in Figure 5, 6, and 7. The X-axis shows the input/output channel sizes, and 2D feature map sizes (6 denotes 6×6, etc.) of the convolution, and the Y-axis shows the normalized performance of each convolution method, measured in terms of simulation cycle count. Across the three figures, orange curves represent Winograd-based convolution's speed up against the baseline, and grey curves represent FFT-based method's speed up compared to the baseline. From the figure we learn that in small kernels, Winograd's algorithm dominates the performance. For larger kernel sizes, FFT-based convolution starts to catch up in speed, because the expense of Winograd transformation starts to overwhelm. Starting from kernel size 5×5 and feature map size 24×24, FFT starts to gain advantage over Winograd. When kernel size is 7×7 and input/output depth is large, FFT method outperforms Winograd's

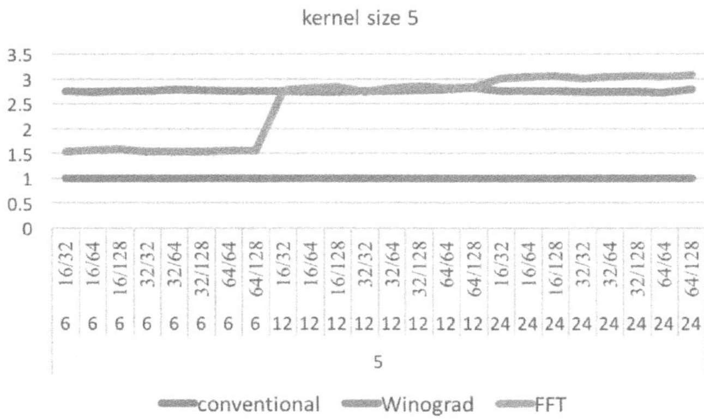

Figure 6: Speed up comparison when kernel size is 5×5**.**

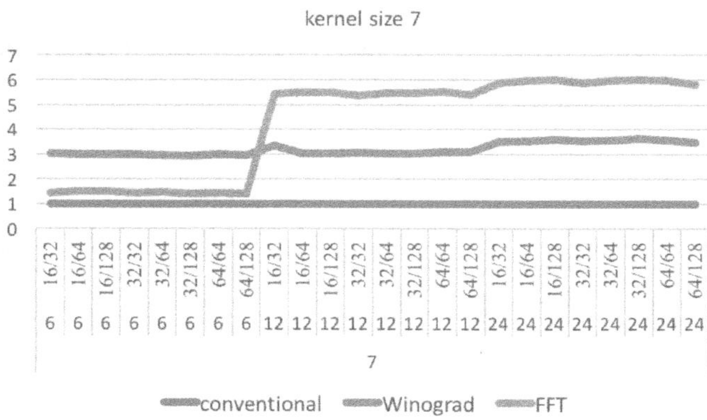

Figure 7: Speed up comparison when kernel size is 7×7**.**

method by a maximum of 2x margin. Considering that FFT generally has higher resource usage overhead with same unroll factor, it would be wise to apply FFT when kernel size is at least 5×5 and input size larger than 12.

4 RESOURCE ALLOCATION FOR MINIMAL LATENCY CONSIDERING INTRA-MODULE PARALLELISM

With the empirical model, we further develop a judicious resource partition algorithm, which is critical to achieve minimal latency for mapping the entire network onto FPGAs. Zhang's work [10] uses Cauchy inequations to prove that in order to optimize the overall latency for an entire network, we should partition the resources according to the equation $\frac{R_i}{R_j} = \frac{\sqrt{C_i}}{\sqrt{C_j}}$, where $\sqrt{C_i}$ and $\sqrt{C_j}$ represent the computation complexity of layer i and j, and R_i and R_j is the calculated ideal resource allocation for layer i and j. Applying such equation with the constraint $R_{total} = \sum_i R_i$, one is able to find the optimal resource partition between layers to achieve minimum latency.

However, such framework does not consider the properties of Inception like CNN structures with parallel branches, and does not provide us a solution on intra-module resource allocation. In such structure, latency is constrained by the longest branch. We appreciate the fact that each branch in such topology has no dependency and thus executes concurrently. In order to minimize the latency, we prorate the resource according to computation complexities of each branch: $\frac{R_{Bi}}{R_{Bj}} = \frac{C_{Bi}}{C_{Bj}}$, where Bi and Bj indicate different branches.

To quickly find out the most appropriate parallel factors for branched structures, we put forward a resource allocation scheme explorer, as shown in Algorithm 1. We first calculate the ideal allocation solution for each module as R_{ideal_i} by solving $\frac{R_i}{R_j} = \frac{\sqrt{C_i}}{\sqrt{C_j}}$ for each layer in the whole network model, then for each layer, we solve $\frac{R_{Bi}}{R_{Bj}} = \frac{C_{Bi}}{C_{Bj}}$ for each branch. In FPGA implementations, to utilize resource more efficiently, a common way is to specify parallel factors to launch multiple computing engines (Winograd or FFT-conv engines in our case) concurrently. To avoid on-chip memory port contention, arrays must be partitioned proportionally to the parallel factors. We designate our parallel factor to follow the power of two, such as 4, 8, and 16. This intends to boost the computing efficiency in hardware and avoid the misaligned parallelism between neighbouring layers (in HLS implementation, array partition factors should be consistent between adjacent layers). The proposed algorithm generates resource allocation scheme for different branch i to approach the theoretical optimum. The algorithm is depicted in Algorithm 1. By analyzing the computation demands of the branches, we have the normalized computation complexity (line 1 to 3) and then generate the ideal resource allocation scheme for branch i: R_{ideal_Bi}. Since hardware implementation is more

Algorithm 1 Resource Allocation for Intra-layer Branches

1: Calculate computation complexity of each concurrent branch: $C_{B1}, C_{B2}, ..., C_{Bn}$
2: Normalize the computation complexity: $C_{norm\_Bi} = \frac{C_{Bi}}{min(C_{B1}, C_{B2}, ..., C_{Bn})}$
3: Sum up normalized computation complexity: $C_{norm} = \sum_i \frac{C_{Bi}}{min(C_{B1}, C_{B2}, ..., C_{Bn})}$
4: Calculate the ideal resource allocation for branch i: $R_{ideal\_Bi} = R_{total} * \frac{C_{norm\_Bi}}{C_{norm}}$
5: **set** $R_{ideal\_sum} = \sum R_{ideal\_Bi}$
6: **set** $R_{Bi} = 2^{\lfloor \log 2(R_{ideal\_Bi}) \rfloor}$, $R_{sum} = \sum R_{Bi}$
7: **While** $R_{sum} < R_{ideal\_sum}$:
8: Form queue Q based on the utilization gap D_{Bi}: $D_{Bi} = R_{ideal\_Bi} - R_i$
9: Find the largest gap and allocate more resource $D_{max} = max(D_{Bi})$, $sel = i$
10: **if** $R_{sum} + R_{sel} <= R_{ideal\_sum}$,
11: $R_{sel} *= 2$, Continue
12: **Endif**
13: Delete branch sel in Q;
14: **if** Length(Q) = 0
15: Break
16: **Endif**
17: **Endwhile**

favorable to the power of two, we truncate the ideal scheme to use a more realistic option: R_{Bi}. From line 7 to 17, we use a while loop to fine-tune the resource allocated to each branch. If the gap between ideal and realistic resource allocation for a branch is non-zero and more resource is still available, we double the current resource utilization (line 10, 11) for the branch to remove this gap starting with the largest gap first to fulfill the computation demand for this critical branch.

5 INCEPTION MODULE IP

We use Vivado HLS to implement a C++ template based reconfigurable Inception module IP, which includes all the techniques of optimizations discussed in the above sections. Using the Inception engine, a face recognition network, based on Inception V2, is mapped onto a Xilinx VU9P FPGA development board. The Inception module IP is implemented as a template function, with the *cccp* (1 × 1 CONV), *conv*3, *conv*5, and *pool* sub-functions that represent the parallel branches in the Inception module. Although there are no data read/write dependencies between each sub-function, by default, Vivado HLS won't schedule sub-functions to execute concurrently if sub-functions read from or write to the same array (even when they are writing to different location of the array). To solve this problem, we have to explicitly implement *split_input* and *combine_output* functions to copy the input feature maps to different buffers, and write to isolated buffers for different sub-functions, and then concatenate the result at the end. Algorithm 2 describes the implementation, where *CONFIG* stands for an ensemble of multiple reconfigurable variables such as array sizes, flags for existence of sub-modules, and unroll factors etc. When Vivado HLS reads the code, it instantiates sub-modules according to the flags in the **if** statements. With the Inception module IP, we instantiate Inception modules that fit different input/output and CONV sizes by passing template parameters and construct the entire FaceNet system.

6 SYSTEM IMPLEMENTATION AND EVALUATION

6.1 Data Quantization and Numerical accuracy

In recent years researchers have shown that neural networks are exceptionally robust to low precision computation [16]. In this work, we explore both 16-bit fixed point and 8-bit fixed point. We

Algorithm 2 Inception Module IP

```
template <typename T0, config_t CONFIG>
void inception(T bottom, T top, T weights, T bias) {
    T bottom_conv3, bottom_conv5, bottom_cccp;
    T top_conv3, top_conv5, top_cccp; // buffers
    split_input<CONFIG>(bottom, bottom_conv3, ...);
    if(CONFIG.CONV3==1) conv3<CONFIG>(...);
    if(CONFIG.CONV5==1) conv5<CONFIG>(...);
    if(CONFIG.POOL==1) pool<CONFIG>(...);
    if(CONFIG.CCCP==1) cccp<CONFIG<(...);
    combine_output<CONFIG>(top, conv3_top, ...);
}
```

Table 2: Numerical analysis on Inception 3a

FIX16 L2 error regular CONV	FIX8 L2 error regular CONV	FIX16 L2 error fast CONV	FIX8 L2 error fast CONV
7.024e-5	9.989e-2	1.232e-4	2.031e-1

Table 3: Inception V2 (GoogLeNet-BN) detailed implementation

Inception #	3 × 3	5 × 5
Inception 2	Winograd $F(4 \times 4, 3 \times 3)$	-
Inception 3a	Winograd $F(4 \times 4, 3 \times 3)$	conventional
Inception 3b	Winograd $F(4 \times 4, 3 \times 3)$	FFT-based
Inception 3c	conventional	conventional
Inception 4a	Winograd $F(2 \times 2, 3 \times 3)$	FFT-based
Inception 4e	conventional	conventional
Inception 5a	Winograd $F(2 \times 2, 3 \times 3)$	-
Inception 5b	Winograd $F(2 \times 2, 3 \times 3)$	-

measure the numerical error of the network with regular convolutions, and fast algorithms, whose implementation configuration is listed on Table 3. We set the float-point embedding as the ground truth, and measure l_2 squared distance between the output with quantized data and float-point data, since this metric is used in the FaceNet system to measure if faces are from the same identity or not. Results are shown on Table 2. First we discover that 8-bit fixed-point weights are adequate to not lose too much accuracy compared with floating-point results. The network with fast algorithms and fixed 16-bit and fixed 8-bit values generate distance error at 10^{-4} and 10^{-1} magnitude compared to the floating-point version, which is tolerable in terms of face verification accuracy (threshold for same identity is set to 1). In our experiment of 100 face pairs at size 112 × 112, 12 pairs are classified differently compared to the float-point result with 8-bit fast algorithms, and only one mismatched pair with 16-bit fast algorithm. We believe that if we were to run re-training, accuracy can be further restored, as shown in previous works [17, 18].

6.2 Implementation

We implement our design targeting a Xilinx VU9P FPGA. The detailed implementation scheme of our Inception modules with hybrid algorithms is presented in Table 3, where "-" means the sub-branch does not exist in the module.

We start with the conventional 6-loop unoptimized convolution as our baseline. In optimization, we use Algorithm 1 to iteratively optimize the sub-branch and apply fast algorithms when possible. We implement Winograd $F(4 \times 4, 3 \times 3)$ in earlier modules and Winograd $F(2 \times 2, 3 \times 3)$ for later modules because although theoretically the former Winograd setup gives more performance gain, but in later modules, the input feature map sizes become so small that using $F(4 \times 4, 3 \times 3)$ results in lots of sampling of padded zeros, impairing both the accuracy and performance. We adopt FFT-based for **inception 3b** and **inception 4a** because the 5 × 5 branch becomes critical path after 3 × 3 branch is well optimized. CONVs in **inception 3c** and **inception 4e** have stride 2, which the fast methods don't support, so we optimize them with conventional methods [10].

Table 4: Inception V2 resource consumption

	BRAM	DSP	FF	LUT
Our work	3067	2041	539422	938159
	71%	32%	23%	79%

Table 5: Inception V2 performance comparison with previous implementations

	latency per image	latency speedup	power	energy efficiency
GPU	89.0 ms	2.16X	109.1 W	9.780 J/pic/s
FPT16 [19]	192.3 ms	1X (baseline)	N/A	N/A
FPGA17 [13]	83.6 ms	2.30X	13.2 W	1.175 J/pic/s
Our work	23.7 ms	8.11X	10.6 W	0.251 J/pic/s

Our implementation use 16-bit fixed point for both weight and feature map, and the operating frequency is 200 MHz. The resource consumption and simulation performance results are shown in Table 4 and Table 5.

We implement our design with Vivado HLS 2017.1 and find that our implementation tends to use more LUTs. This situation is due to the following reasons. First, both FFT and Winograd transformation comsume LUTs because multiplications are reduced to either additions or constant multiplications, which is implemented using LUTs. Second, the control logic in the Inception engine IP is more complicated compared to conventional convolution implementation, thus taking up more LUTs.

6.3 Evaluation

We first compare our implementation on FPGA with GPU result. We use a cutting-edge Pascal-based NVidia GTX 1080 GPU, which has a 8.9 TFLOPS peak performance. The GPU implmentation is on Torch, with CUDA 8.0. We also compare our work with the results reported in Zhang's work (FPGA2017) [13], and DiCecco's work (FPT2016) [19] which are works that evaluated GoogLeNet (Inception V1). These two works also implement fast convolution algorithms. FPGA2017 implements Overlap-Add FFT convolver on a CPU + FPGA system, and FPT2016 implements Winograd convolution on a Xilinx Virtex7 board. Our implementation is in fact Inception V2, which is the original Inception added with batch normalization layer after each CONV layer, thus has slightly more computations. The result is shown in Table 5. We use inference latency as the evaluation metric, since facial recognition/verification is a latency critical task. For works that don't report latency, we calculate single image latency by dividing the entire network computation operations with the reported GOPS. Our result shows that, compared with GPU, we achieve 3.75x latency improvement. For FPGA works, we achieve superior results, with 3.53x and 8.11x latency speed up compared to the FPGA2017 and FPT2016, respectively. We also achieve 4.68x better energy efficiency compared to FPGA2017.

7 CONCLUSIONS

In this paper, we explore different fast convolution algorithms including Winograd's minimum filter algorithm and FFT-based algorithm, and find the best strategy to apply them on different types of convolutions. We implement a configurable IP-based end-to-end CNN accelerator targeting FaceNet (Inception V2) using C-based HLS. Our solution surpasses both NVIDIA GTX 1080 GPU and previous FPGA results. We envision that such face recognition system can be paired with multiple low-power video capture systems, with the FPGA deployed in a central server and close to database, for fast real-time multi-face recognition and verification, to satisfy the need for security, border control, and other related applications.

ACKNOWLEDGMENTS

This work is supported by IBM-Illinois Center for Cognitive Computing Systems Research (C^3SR), a research collaboration as part of the IBM AI Horizons Network. We also thank Kyle Rupnow of Inspirit IoT Inc. for helpful discussions.

REFERENCES

[1] Jeffrey Donahue, Lisa Anne Hendricks, Sergio Guadarrama, Marcus Rohrbach, Subhashini Venugopalan, Kate Saenko, and Trevor Darrell. Long-term recurrent convolutional networks for visual recognition and description. In *CVPR*, 2015.
[2] Florian Schroff, Dmitry Kalenichenko, and James Philbin. FaceNet: A unified embedding for face recognition and clustering. In *CVPR*, 2015.
[3] Yuhong Li, Xiaofan Zhang, and Deming Chen. CSRNet: Dilated convolutional neural networks for understanding the highly congested scenes. *CVPR*, 2018.
[4] Su Liu, Alexandros Papakonstantinou, Hongjun Wang, and Deming Chen. Real-time object tracking system on FPGAs. In *SAAHPC 2011*.
[5] Kyle Rupnow, Yun Liang, Yinan Li, Dongbo Min, Minh Do, and Deming Chen. High level synthesis of stereo matching: productivity, performance, and software constraints. In *FPT 2011*.
[6] Chun He, Alexandros Papakonstantinou, and Deming Chen. A novel SoC architecture on FPGA for ultra fast face detection. In *ICCD 2009*.
[7] Chen Zhang, Peng Li, Guangyu Sun, Yijin Guan, Bingjun Xiao, and Jason Cong. Optimizing FPGA-based accelerator design for deep convolutional neural networks. In *FPGA*, 2015.
[8] Christian Szegedy, Wei Liu, Yangqing Jia, Pierre Sermanet, Scott Reed, Dragomir Anguelov, Dumitru Erhan, Vincent Vanhoucke, and Andrew Rabinovich. Going deeper with convolutions. In *CVPR*, 2015.
[9] Yongming Shen, Michael Ferdman, and Peter Milder. Overcoming resource underutilization in spatial cnn accelerators. In *FPGA*, 2016.
[10] Xiaofan Zhang, Xinheng Liu, Anand Ramachandran, Chuanhao Zhuge, Shibin Tang, Peng Ouyang, Zuofu Cheng, Kyle Rupnow, and Deming Chen. High-performance video content recognition with long-term recurrent convolutional network for FPGA. In *FPL*, 2017.
[11] Nicolas Vasilache, Jeff Johnson, Michael Mathieu, Soumith Chintala, Serkan Piantino, and Yann LeCun. Fast convolutional nets with fbfft: A GPU performance evaluation. *arXiv preprint arXiv:1412.7580*, 2014.
[12] Andrew Lavin and Scott Gray. Fast algorithms for convolutional neural networks. In *CVPR*, 2016.
[13] Chi Zhang and Viktor K Prasanna. Frequency domain acceleration of convolutional neural networks on CPU-FPGA shared memory system. In *FPGA*, 2017.
[14] Utku Aydonat, Shane O'Connell, Davor Capalija, Andrew C Ling, and Gordon R Chiu. An OpenCL (tm) deep learning accelerator on arria 10. *arXiv preprint arXiv:1701.03534*, 2017.
[15] Shmuel Winograd. Arithmetic complexity of computations, cbms-nsf regional conference series in applied mathematics. *SIAM*, 1980.
[16] Philipp Gysel, Mohammad Motamedi, and Soheil Ghiasi. Hardware-oriented approximation of convolutional neural networks. *arXiv:1604.03168*, 2016.
[17] Song Han, Huizi Mao, and William J Dally. Deep compression: Compressing deep neural networks with pruning, trained quantization and huffman coding. *arXiv preprint arXiv:1510.00149*, 2015.
[18] Xiaofan Zhang, Anand Ramachandran, Chuanhao Zhuge, Di He, Wei Zuo, Zuofu Cheng, Kyle Rupnow, and Deming Chen. Machine learning on FPGAs to face the IoT revolution. In *ICCAD, 2017*. IEEE, 2017.
[19] Roberto DiCecco, Griffin Lacey, Jasmina Vasiljevic, Paul Chow, Graham Taylor, and Shawki Areibi. Caffeinated FPGAs: FPGA framework for convolutional neural networks. In *FPT 2016*. IEEE.

SCALENet: A SCalable Low power AccELerator for Real-time Embedded Deep Neural Networks

Colin Shea
University of Maryland, Baltimore County
Baltimore, MD
cshea3@umbc.edu

Adam Page
University of Maryland, Baltimore County
Baltimore, MD
apage2@umbc.edu

Tinoosh Mohsenin
University of Maryland, Baltimore County
Baltimore, MD
tinoosh@umbc.edu

ABSTRACT

As deep learning networks mature and improve classification performance, a significant challenge is their deployment in embedded settings. Modern network typologies, such as convolutional neural networks, can be very deep and impose considerable complexity that is often not feasible in resource bound, real-time systems. Processing of these networks requires high levels of parallelization, maximizing data throughput, and support for different network types, while minimizing power and resource consumption. In response to these requirements, in this paper, we present a low power FPGA based neural network accelerator named SCALENet: a SCalable Low power AccELerator for real-time deep neural Networks. Key features include optimization for power with coarse and fine grain scheduler, implementation flexibility with hardware only or hardware/software co-design, and acceleration for both fully connected and convolutional layers. The experimental results evaluate SCALENet against two different neural network applications: image processing, and biomedical seizure detection. The image processing networks, implemented on SCALENet, trained on the CIFAR-10 and ImageNet datasets with eight different networks, are implemented on an Arty A7 and Zedboard™ FPGA platforms. The highest improvement came with the Inception network on an ImageNet dataset with a throughput of 22x and decrease in energy consumption of 13x compared to the ARM processor implementation. We then implement SCALENet for time series EEG seizure detection using both a Direct Convolution and FFT Convolution method to show its design versatility with a 99.7% reduction in execution time and a 97.9% improvement in energy consumption compared to the ARM. Finally, we demonstrate the ability to achieve parity with or exceed the energy efficiency of NVIDIA GPUs when evaluated against Jetson TK1 with embedded GPU System on Chip (SoC) and with a 4x power savings in a power envelope of 2.07 Watts.

CCS CONCEPTS

• **Computing methodologies** → *Neural networks*; • **Computer systems organization** → *Embedded hardware*; *Real-time system architecture*; • **Hardware** → *Hardware-software codesign*;

GLSVLSI'18, May 23–25, 2018, Chicago, IL, USA

ACM ISBN 978-1-4503-5724-1/18/05...$15.00
https://doi.org/10.1145/3194554.3194601

KEYWORDS

Low power;programmable hardware accelerator; convolutional neural network; machine learning; FPGA; scalable; embedded systems.

ACM Reference Format:
Colin Shea, Adam Page, and Tinoosh Mohsenin. 2018. SCALENet: A SCalable Low power AccELerator for Real-time Embedded Deep Neural Networks. In *Proceedings of Great Lakes Symposium on VLSI 2018 (GLSVLSI'18)*. ACM, New York, NY, USA, 6 pages. https://doi.org/10.1145/3194554.3194601

1 INTRODUCTION

Convolutional neural networks (CNN) have become the baseline implementation for computer vision and related fields with the ability to obtain an order of magnitude improvement over conventional techniques. As this area of deep learning matures, the challenge to efficiently deploy such networks in embedded settings for a variety of applications. Deployment requires an efficient network architecture implementation that meets the accuracy, power, and latency requirement of a targeted application. Graphics processing units (GPUs), predominately by NVIDIA, have shown the ability to significantly boost efficiency, especially during training, by exploiting the underlying data-level and task-level parallelism that exists within neural networks (NN). While massively outperforming their CPU counterparts, GPUs, including mobile GPUs, have a power envelop that is still too high for a large variety of low-power embedded settings. Current literature has started focusing on developing custom FPGA and ASIC accelerators suited for efficiently deploying pre-trained convolutional neural networks in resource-limited, real-time embedded systems. This work focuses on an architecture that addresses the challenges and characteristics of deploying a variety of Deep Neural Networks (DNN) in the embedded space. Here we propose SCALENet: a SCalable Low power AccELerator for real-time deep neural Networks. The main contributions of this paper include:

- Optimizing for power with coarse and fine grain scheduling of hardware configuration at compilation and runtime.
- Dedicated Hardware Acceleration of Fully Connected (FC) and two different methods, Direct and FFT, to Convolutional Neural Network.
- Implementation flexibility and scalability with hardware or hardware/software co-design.
- Testing SCALENet with a variety of applications.

2 RELATED WORK

In recent years, some publications on CNN accelerators for low-power embedded settings have been proposed. [4] describes a 168 16-bit fixed point processing element (PE) array ASIC with a configurable filter size and filter count. This work provides a series of optimizations for memory compression, data reuse, and clock gating. For data reuse, the authors approach the problem set with a spatial architecture for parallelization optimization where a filter row and an image row are mapped to a PE. [10] offers a Xilinx High-Level Synthesis defined Deep Neural Network (DNN) accelerator for fully connected layers. The accelerator is based on parameter encoding of weights and a reduction of the number of multipliers. The design targets 32-bit floating point operations and a unique encoding scheme by finding the mean of the positive and negative weights and representing them with a 1-bit substitution and storing them off. In [11] an energy-efficient CNN processor is proposed with an optimized CNN neuron processing engine, a dual-range multiply-accumulate block for low-power convolution operations and an on-chip memory architecture with the scheme to reduce off-chip memory accesses. The chip is fabricated in 65nm 1P8M CMOS technology. In [16], an analytical design scheme using a roofline model is proposed for CNNs. In their work, CNN's computation and memory access are optimized. Then, all possible designs in the roofline model are compared, and the best design for each layer is determined. The CNN accelerator is implemented on a Xilinx Virtex-7 (VX485T) FPGA using Vivado HLS. The authors in [13] also highlight the data-level and task-level parallelism that exists within CNN and how best to exploit the attributes. The authors of [14] evaluate different methodologies for detection of epileptic seizures in EEG signals. These methods include traditional variance-based detection and nonlinear time series analysis such as logistic regression and time-frequency distributions. Their conclusion was that time variance-based analysis, with a fixed threshold, still had the highest overall accuracy. While the work performed in [3], developed a 13-layer deep CNN algorithm to detect normal, preictal, and seizure classes. The customized CNN contained five convolution and max-pooling layers and three fully connected layers. Their results had an accuracy of 88.67%. Most of these previous works have focused on HLS for custom single purpose designs or creating custom application specific integrated circuits (ASIC) with specialized accelerator cores targeted for particular fixed network types. These previous works do not address power, area and the ability to efficiently process different network types without requiring a complete redesign.

3 PROPOSED HARDWARE ACCELERATOR

The high-level diagram of the SCALENet accelerator is depicted in Figure 1. SCALENet's design, as either an all hardware accelerator, or a hardware/software co-design implementation, uses layers as the basic building blocks of neural networks. These layers contain the bulk of the complexity, and this accelerator is designed to operate on a supplied layer configurations. Part of the design, a host application or the accelerator engine, decodes the run-time configuration and is tasked with serializing and dispatching a predefined network topology layer by layer.

Deployment of deep neural networks requires the accelerator to achieve satisfactory throughput while being efficient as possible regarding power and area. To do so, it requires an innovative design that exploits critical requirements of deploying a network architecture including network flexibility, resource consumption, and power minimization. In SCALENet, these design aspects are mapped to two main architectural choices in the design: the scheduler, and a customizable design feature set.

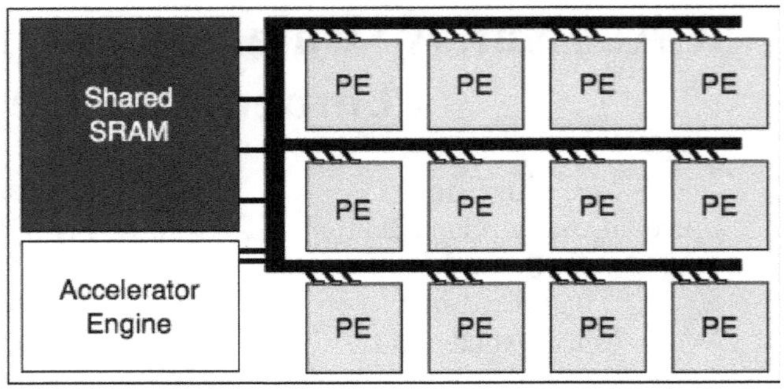

Figure 1: The high-level block diagram of the SCALENet accelerator. The processing engines (PEs) are arranged in a grid configuration with a unified network interface. The network provides two sets of buses that are unidirectional and contain two 16-bit channels. The accelerator engine is used to configure the PEs and perform all of the data marshaling. A shared on-chip memory is used to cache the current layers feature channels along with layer parameters.

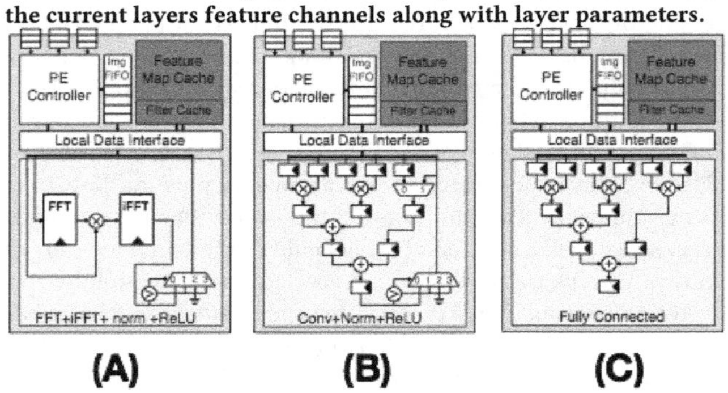

Figure 2: The PEs are instantiated in one of 3 forms, Fast Fourier Transform (FFT) Convolution (A), Direct Convolution (B), or Fully Connected (C), dependent on the coarse scheduler at compilation. In each PE there is a memory dedicated to filter and image caching, a clock enable, and a simple controller for dispatching configuration.

3.1 Scheduler

The SCALENet scheduler is a two-part algorithm that balances latency, throughput and power consumption through both course grain and fine grain attributes of the system. The schedulers goal is to optimize for latency based on available hardware and software models. The algorithm inputs are the desired throughput, the neural network model to use, the target Xilinx FPGA, and the data precision. The coarse portion of the scheduling algorithm takes the specified model and examines the layers and provides the configuration with the lowest latency for the FPGA, and, if proper, software layer execution. The configuration output informs the second stage with the optimal number of PEs, data memory offsets for implementation, the size of scratch memory, and the optimal number of active PEs per layer.

3.2 Customizable Design

SCALENet, written in C++ within Xilinx VIVADO HLS, allows for customizing each implemented neural network definition. The design enables block-level building and an iterative data path to accommodate different sized datasets without re-compilation. There are two sets of customization: at compile time and runtime as optimized by the scheduler.

The parameters that are configurable only at compile time are: the maximum number of PEs, the size of a PEs local scratchpad memory, the data precision, and the PE type. The maximum number of PEs is limited by the available FPGA resources, which is a variable of the FPGA family. The design template can be configured to set the scratchpad memory per PE. The memory amount can be increased or decreased depending on the number of PEs and the layer type, CNN or FC.

3.2.1 Flexible Parallelism. In deep neural networks, FC and CNN layers dominate the complexity typically accounting for more than 90% of the computation and memory requirements. Therefore, being capable of supporting and deploying these layers in an efficient methodology is required. SCALENet supports PEs that accelerate both types of layers. For convolution, SCALENet utilizes the *output channel tiling* form of parallelism based on tiling methods [16]. Again, focusing on the convolutional PEs SCALENet supports two different types, direct convolution, and FFT Convolution [1] [2]. To meet latency requirements, the coarse scheduler will choose either a direct or FFT convolution solution. When deploying an all hardware design with direct convolution the scheduler may insert at least one FC PE to accelerate any FC layers as necessary.

3.2.2 Data Precision. The accelerator's design can utilize either fixed-point or floating-point format and varying levels of data precision. The option of a fix-point or floating-point data operation is set at compilation time. The floating-point form has the advantage of supporting dynamic range, underflow/overflow conditions, and a non-uniform scale. This is beneficial for neural networks as layers tend to differ in their dynamic range and filter weights usually follow a normal distribution in which higher precision is needed for smaller values. The downside is that floating-point requires more logic than an equivalent fixed-point implementation. Furthermore, the use of an exponent to support higher dynamic range requires dedicating a subset of bits for the exponent, which leaves fewer bits for the mantissa and hence precision. Figure 3 provides a visual break down of a single PE's resources as a function of the data precision.

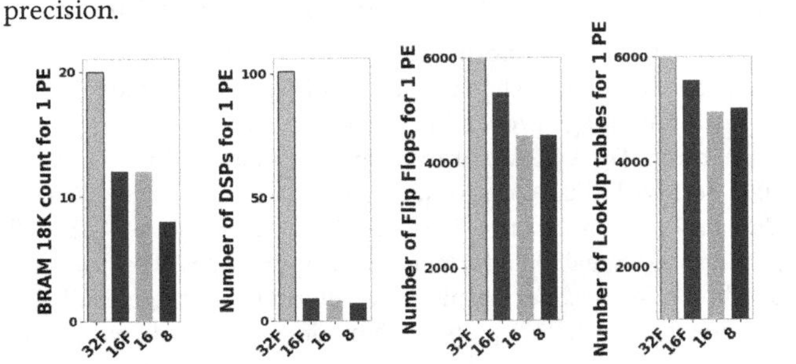

Figure 3: Comparison of floating-point and fixed-point for 32-bit, 16-bit, and 8-bit fixed-point representations regarding required resources for the layer operations associated with direct convolution, max-pooling, and batch normalization. While fixed-point requires fewer resources than the corresponding floating-point, the difference for lower precision, 16-bit Int vs. 16-bit FP becomes minimal.

3.2.3 Clock Gating. Xilinx Vivado HLS does not natively expose user control of the clock enable function for the generated HDL. In SCALENet we explicitly enable the *-clock-enable* option in HLS. This option maps all the clock enables for all clocked resources to be driven by a single top-level enable. SCALENet remaps the generated top level clock enable in HDL to a configurable masking value set by the Acceleration Engine (AE) for each of the PEs. By remapping the control signal, it enables the runtime design to be controlled, by the fine grain scheduler, to turn on and off unused PEs during execution. The clock disablement minimizes power consumption at the expense of latency. With the Xilinx FPGAs, this power savings can range from 1% to 20% [15].

4 CASE STUDIES

4.1 SCALENet Evaluation

A principal aspect of the proposed accelerator to be evaluated is the impact of processing engines on classification throughput, energy, and area utilization. For section 4.2 SCALENet is deployed as a hardware/software co-design with only the convolution, relu, and activation in hardware. In section 4.3 SCALENet is deploy as a hardware only implementation. Figure 4 demonstrates the results of PEs for the four networks trained on the CIFAR dataset. In particular, we see that for a given network increasing the amount of PEs can improve both throughput and energy consumption. Once the throughput begins to saturate, the energy consumption starts negatively impacting the efficiency of the design. Figure 5 highlights the optimal efficiency occurring as a ratio of classification throughput and power consumption (img/sec/watt).

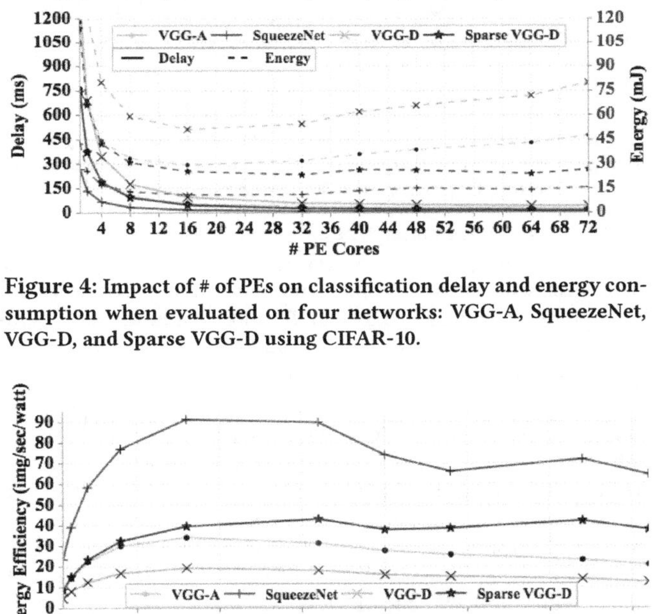

Figure 4: Impact of # of PEs on classification delay and energy consumption when evaluated on four networks: VGG-A, SqueezeNet, VGG-D, and Sparse VGG-D using CIFAR-10.

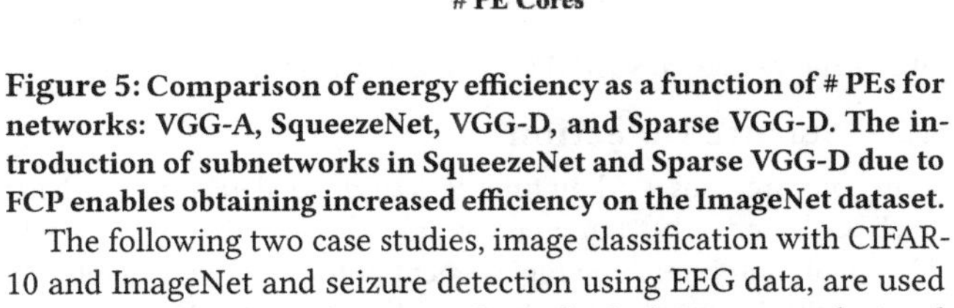

Figure 5: Comparison of energy efficiency as a function of # PEs for networks: VGG-A, SqueezeNet, VGG-D, and Sparse VGG-D. The introduction of subnetworks in SqueezeNet and Sparse VGG-D due to FCP enables obtaining increased efficiency on the ImageNet dataset.

The following two case studies, image classification with CIFAR-10 and ImageNet and seizure detection using EEG data, are used to evaluate SCALENet's use in efficiently deploying convolutional neural networks to resource-bound, real-time embedded systems.

4.2 Image Processing

4.2.1 CIFAR-10 Dataset. The CIFAR dataset consists of 60,000 32x32 color images with ten classes. While the input images are small, achieving good accuracy still requires having reasonably deep neural networks. For this dataset, we target four neural networks including VGG-A, VGG-D, modified SqueezeNet, and Sparse VGG-D [7, 12]. The standard SqueezeNet is designed for the ImageNet dataset with images of size 224x224. We modified the SqueezeNet network for CIFAR-10 by removing a set of convolutional layers and reducing the final pooling layer to cover 4x4 receptive field versus 14x14. Sparse VGG-D is the same network as VGG-D but with three generalized sparsification techniques applied [8]. Figure 6 provides a comparison of the four networks regarding computation, memory, and top-1 test accuracy. Both SqueezeNet and Sparse VGG-D require significantly less computation than VGG-A and VGG-D, relatively, while achieving similar accuracy performance. Sparse VGG-D can reduce computation and memory by 60%, and 93%, respectively. For this dataset, the CPU is a MicroBlaze (μB) on both the Arty A7 FPGA for all networks, but the SqueezeNet is implemented on the Cmod A7.

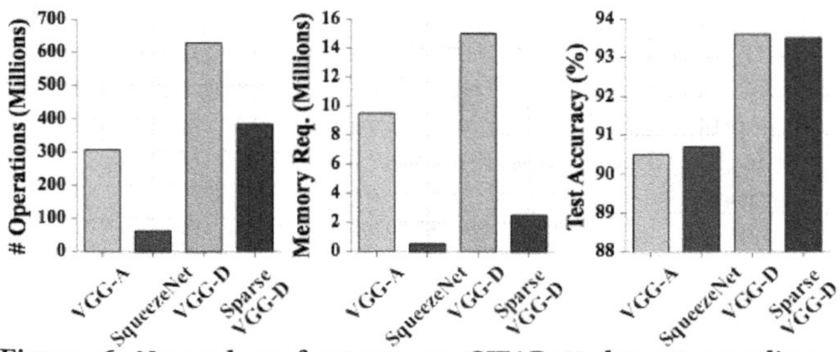

Figure 6: Network performance on CIFAR-10 dataset regarding computation, memory, and top-1 test accuracy. The networks are VGG-A, modified SqueezeNet, VGG-D, and Sparse VGG-D.

4.2.2 ImageNet Dataset. The ImageNet dataset consists of 10 million colored images scaled to 224x224 with 1,000 assigned classes. The specific dataset used comes from the 2012 Large Scale Visual Recognition Challenge (ILSVRC). ILSVRC is a much more difficult dataset and requires a higher complexity network to achieve good accuracy performance. For this dataset, we target four neural networks including AlexNet, Sparse AlexNet, SqueezeNet, and Inception v3. Sparse AlexNet is similar to AlexNet with three sparsification techniques applied in addition to filter factorization and replacing the FC layers with two 3x3 convolutional layers and a spatial pooling layer [8]. Sparse AlexNet, SqueezeNet, and Inception all require substantially less memory than AlexNet by replacing FC layers with convolutional layers. SqueezeNet and Sparse AlexNet, in particular, need 49% and 21% less computation than AlexNet, respectively. Inception requires 635% more computation than AlexNet but can dramatically increase top-5 accuracy by 14%. All datasets utilize the Zedboard's ARM CPU and FPGA fabric.

4.3 Seizure Detection

Using our previous work in time series seizure detection as a basis for EEG detection [9], our architecture is a reduced ResNet-20 with 13 convolution layers and replacement of the last two convolution layers with FC layers. The choice of ResNet is due to our experience in its performance in previous research and its low memory

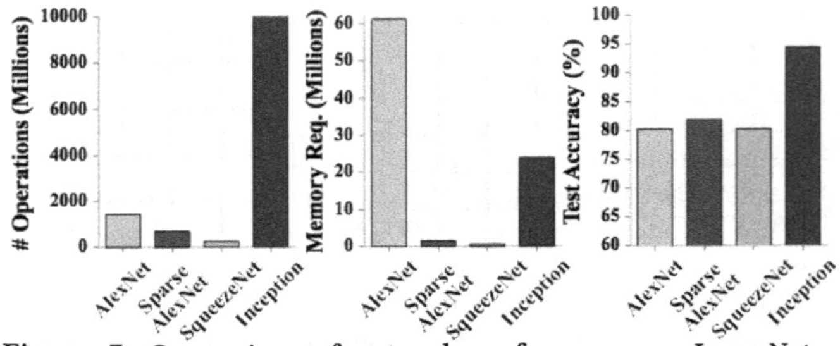

Figure 7: Comparison of network performance on ImageNet dataset in terms of computation, memory, and top-5 test accuracy. The networks include AlexNet, Sparse AlexNet, SqueezeNet, and Inception v3.

requirements for parameters. The input matrix is a fusion of 24 EEG channels from [6] dataset. Here time series samples, 24 consecutive from each channel, are fused to form a 24x24 matrix, and a 3x3 filter is applied.

Each set of fused channels is defined through a sliding window that moves from 1 sample to 24 samples per window, for 24 channels. At the start and end, when there is not enough data to fill the window, samples are set to 0 and shifted in or out. Each matrix of samples passes through the modified network as an image. The constructed model had an accuracy of 86.98%, which is similar in accuracy to [3]. We implemented the ResNet network using both Direct and FFT convolutional PE using SCALENet. The inputs to the SCALENet scheduler where: the modified ResNet model, the latency, the 1 sample every 3-milliseconds (ms) for a 256Hz EEG, a Zynq 7020, and 16-bit FP. The scheduler guided a design for a pure hardware implementation of 32 PEs for the Direct Convolution and 12 FFT Convolution PEs for the FFT based solution and in both cases 2 FC PEs. Due to the latency requirement of 3ms, the scheduler was unable to find a hardware/software co-design that could not meet the deadline of 3ms. Based on these design constraints the resulting solutions produced a decision every 3.05 milliseconds and 2.01 milliseconds, direct and FFT respectively.

5 COMPARISON WITH COTS

5.1 Targeted Platforms and Implementation

To understand the performance of the proposed accelerator, we evaluated SCALENet when running on three FPGA-based SoC platforms for all image processing and seizure detection network architectures. The FPGA platforms are the Zedboard with a Zynq-7000 SoC with dual-core ARM Cortex-A9 and FPGA, the Arty & Cmod A7 containing Artix-7 35T FPGA with Microblaze™ (μB) soft-processors. For each platform, the corresponding CPU is used as a baseline reference. Furthermore, we alternatively target NVIDIAs low-power Jetson TK1 platform containing TK1 SoC with quad-core ARM Cortex-A15 and K1 GPU. Torch, a scientific computing framework with comprehensive support for deep learning algorithms, is used to implement the networks on each platform. While the framework is built on the Lua scripting language, the underlying libraries are developed in C/C++ with support for acceleration on both CPUs and GPUs by utilizing OpenBLAS compiled for the architecture and the necessary CUDA libraries. Using the same framework also enables ensuring consistency across platforms. To use the SCALENet FPGA-based accelerator, a modified version of *SpatialConvolution.lua* is used to call the appropriate accelerator

Database	Network			Host ARM/μB		ARM/μB + SCALENet		Improvement	
	Architecture	Memory (MB)	(GFLOP)	Execution (sec)	Energy (Joules)	Exec (sec)	Energy (Joules)	Exec (%)	Energy (%)
CIFAR	VGG-A	36.22	0.31	0.90	0.85	0.19	0.25	**78.71%**	**70.20%**
	SqueezeNet	2.04	0.06	0.25	0.25	0.05	0.07	**80.14%**	**73.48%**
	VGG-D	57.19	0.63	1.80	1.73	0.30	0.49	**83.48%**	**76.58%**
	Sparse VGG-D	9.56	0.38	0.26	0.26	0.05	0.06	**80.79%**	**75.04%**
ImageNet	AlexNet	233.15	0.80	3.32	5.54	0.39	1.11	**88.28%**	**80.00%**
	Sparse AlexNet	5.76	0.63	0.95	1.61	0.08	0.21	**92.05%**	**86.99%**
	SqueezeNet	4.79	0.40	1.09	1.77	0.07	0.20	**93.42%**	**88.62%**
	Inception	91.05	5.89	16.62	26.76	0.74	2.07	**95.55%**	**92.28%**
Seizure	FFT Conv	0.24	0.4	0.1	0.16	0.00205	0.00328	**99.75%**	**97.9%**
	Direct Conv	0.24	0.4	0.25	0.4	0.00301	0.004816	**99.87%**	**98.8%**

Table 1: Evaluation of SCALENet performance compared to baseline CPU when deploying nine network architectures. All CIFAR processing is based on Arty A7 and MicroBlaze (μB), all ImageNet based on ZedBoard and Cortex-A9. Seizure Detection is all hardware on Zedboard. On average, utilizing the accelerator improves throughput by 10x and energy usage 5.4x

library functions and perform data marshaling. A pre-deployment script is also used to remove all training related details such as gradients in addition to merging sets of convolution, batch normalization, and ReLU layers. We also utilize NVIDIAs CUDA 6.5 framework along with cuDNN v2 library when targeting the K1 GPU of the Jetson TK1.

5.2 Measurement Setup

Each platform is measured in real-time for both the execution time and power consumption required to classify sample data. To accomplish this, we actively record these metrics for a large number of samples and then average to derive the *per classification* performance. For power results, we look to only measure the consumption of both the processor and external DDR memory. While a few platforms include built-in monitoring capabilities, we utilized an external TI INA219 voltage and power IC connected to each system's primary power rails to ensure consistency. For each platform all other peripherals including HDMI, debug circuitry, and additional communication peripherals such as Wi-Fi and Bluetooth were powered off.

5.3 COTS Results

For each of the networks, we performed nine experiments deployed onto the FPGA platforms with and without SCALENet. Networks trained on CIFAR, the Arty platform is using a single SCALENet accelerator. For the ImageNet targeted networks, the Zedboard platform is used and incorporates three PEs of the SCALENet accelerator. For a given layer, the work is split among the three accelerators. Doing so enables avoiding dependencies or starvation conditions among the accelerators. The entire Arty platform containing the μB and SCALENet accelerator has an average measured power consumption of 1.4 Watts when running at 166.67 MHz. The Zedboard containing the dual-core ARM Cortex-A9 and 3 SCALENet PE accelerators have an average measured the power consumption of 2.07 Watts when running at 667.67 MHz. From these results, the proposed SCALENet accelerator can significantly improve classification throughput and energy efficiency when compared to using only the host processor. On average, for all networks evaluated, exploiting the accelerator can dramatically increase classification throughput, up to 10x and decrease total system energy usage by 5.4 for the VGG-A and VGG-D network.

For the modified SqueezeNet trained on CIFAR-10, we targeted the Cmod A7, uses the same FPGA as the Arty, but instead of 256 MB DDR3 memory there is only 512 KB SRAM, and there are no external peripherals. Reduction in memory is possible as SqueezeNet requires a lower number of parameters after compression.

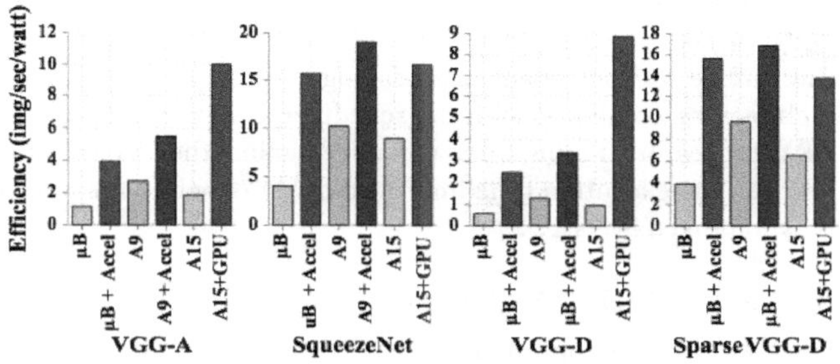

Figure 8: Energy efficiency comparison of platforms with and without accelerator targeted for CIFAR-10 dataset. MicroBlaze™(μB) & μB+Accel are performed using Arty or Cmod A7. While A9 & A9+Accel are performed using Zedboard, and A15 & A15+GPU are using Jetson TK1 platform.

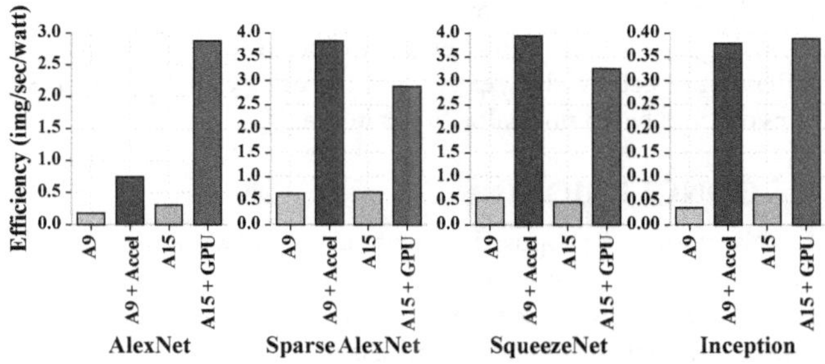

Figure 9: Energy efficiency comparison with and without accelerator targeted for ImageNet dataset. A9 & A9+Accel are using Zedboard, and A15 & A15+GPU are the Jetson TK1 platform.

We also compared SCALENet against NVIDIA's Jetson TK1 mobile GPU platform on all networks. Figure 8 shows the efficiency results of running on the three platforms for the four CIFAR trained networks with and without accelerators. All platforms, there is a

Metrics	[3]	[5]	[16]	**This work**	
Platform	Virtex-5	Zynq	Virtex-7	**Zynq**	Jetson TK1
Precision (bit)	48 Fixed	16 Fixed	322 Float	**16 Fixed**	32 Float
Clock (MHz)	120	150	100	**100**	2320
Network	N/A	N/A	AlexNet	**Inception**	Inception
Network Complexity (GOP)	0.52	0.552	1.33	**15.92**	55.30
Network Performance (GOP/s)	16	25.15	61.62	**1592**	55.30
Total Power (W)	14	8	18.61	**2.07**	12.08
Network Energy Efficiency (GOP/s/W)	1.14	2.90	3.31	**5.70**	4.58

Table 2: Comparison of the proposed accelerator with related works when evaluated on a convolutional network. For this work, measurements are taken when running on Zedboard containing three SCALENet accelerators without sparsification.

large increase in efficiency with the accelerator. The SCALENet accelerator on average can improve efficiency over its host processor by 3x whereas the K1 GPU can increase efficiency by 4.5x over its ARM CPUs. Figure 9 similarly compares the efficiency of the FPGA and GPU platforms when targeting the ImageNet networks. The Zedboard with 3 SCALENet accelerators can achieve an average increase in efficiency of 9x whereas the TK1 accelerated with the GPU can increase efficiency on average by 5x. In Table 2 the last row outlines the power efficiency savings for using the SCALENet architecture, combined with the scheduler, compared to just the ARM processor running torch compiled against the OpenBlast libraries. The execution time improved by 99.7% while the power only improved by 74.10%.

6 COMPARISON WITH EXISTING WORK

Table 2 compares the proposed SCALENet with existing FPGA-based CNN accelerators. Deployed on Zedboard platform with Cortex-A9 running at 667.67 MHz and FPGA running at 100 MHz, the accelerator achieves an energy efficiency of 5.70 GOP/J with total system power of 2.07 W and throughput of 15.92 GOP/s. SCALENet delivers higher energy efficiency for a given network complexity than the previous best accelerators [5] and [16] while targeting a much lower power utilization. Additional gains in efficiency are achieved by exploiting the ability to perform fused convolution, batch normalization, and ReLU.

7 CONCLUSION

In this work, we proposed contributions in two enterprises for deploying convolutional and fully connected neural networks in resource-bound, real-time embedded systems. In the first contribution, we evaluated eight image processing focused networks trained on CIFAR-10 and ImageNet datasets for computation, memory, and accuracy and we assess the use of a modified network for time series EEG seizure detection. In the second contribution, we proposed and evaluated SCALENet: a SCalable Low power Accelerator for real-time deep neural Networks. The accelerator enables deploying a variety of networks through coarse and fine grain configuration as well as acceleration of FC and CNN layers and implementation flexibility for hardware only or hardware and software designs. The proposed accelerator was evaluated in real-time on different FPGA platforms using eight image processing networks and one custom time series network for biomedical seizure detection in EEGs and demonstrated to outperform all other COTS platforms. When accelerating the highest complexity network evaluated, Inception with 11.78 GOP, on the Zedboard platform with a dual-core ARM Cortex-A9 running at 667.67 MHz and FPGA running at 100 MHz, the accelerator achieves an energy efficiency of 5.70 GOP/s/W with a total system power of 2.07 W and throughput of 15.92 GOP/s. SCALENet produces higher energy efficiency than the prior best accelerators as well as Jetson TK1 while targeting a power profile that is more than 4x lower than the Jetson TK1. In the case of time series seizure detection, our SCALENet architecture shows an execution time and power improvement of 99.75% and 97.9% respectively compared to software-only implementations.

REFERENCES

[1] T. Abtahi, A. Kulkarni, and T. Mohsenin. 2017. Accelerating convolutional neural network with FFT on tiny cores. In *2017 IEEE International Symposium on Circuits and Systems (ISCAS)*. 1–4. https://doi.org/10.1109/ISCAS.2017.8050588

[2] T. Abtahi, C. Shea, A. Kulkarni, and T. Mohsenin. 2018. Accelerating Convolutional Neural Network with FFT on Embedded Hardware. *IEEE Transactions on Very Large Scale Integration (VLSI) Systems* (2018).

[3] U. Rajendra Acharya et al. 2017. *Computers in Biology and Medicine* (2017). https://doi.org/10.1016/j.compbiomed.2017.09.017

[4] Y. Chen et al. 2016. 14.5 Eyeriss: An energy-efficient reconfigurable accelerator for deep convolutional neural networks. In *ISSCC*.

[5] Vinayak Gokhale et al. 2014. A 240 G-ops/s mobile coprocessor for deep neural networks. In *CVPRW*.

[6] A. L. Goldberger, L. A. N. Amaral, L. Glass, J. M. Hausdorff, P. Ch. Ivanov, R. G. Mark, J. E. Mietus, G. B. Moody, C.-K. Peng, and H. E. Stanley. 2000 (June 13). PhysioBank, PhysioToolkit, and PhysioNet: Components of a New Research Resource for Complex Physiologic Signals. *Circulation* 101, 23 (2000 (June 13)), e215–e220. Circulation Electronic Pages: http://circ.ahajournals.org/content/101/23/e215.full PMID:1085218; doi: 10.1161/01.CIR.101.23.e215.

[7] Forrest N. Iandola et al. 2016. SqueezeNet: AlexNet-level accuracy with 50x fewer parameters and <1MB model size. *CoRR* (2016).

[8] Adam Page, Ali Jafari, Colin Shea, and Tinoosh Mohsenin. 2017. SPARCNet: A Hardware Accelerator for Efficient Deployment of Sparse Convolutional Networks. *J. Emerg. Technol. Comput. Syst.* 13, 3, Article 31 (May 2017), 32 pages. https://doi.org/10.1145/3005448

[9] A. Page, C. Shea, and T. Mohsenin. 2016. Wearable Seizure Detection using Convolutional Neural Networks with Transfer Learning. In *ISCAS*.

[10] Mohammad Samragh et al. 2017. Customizing Neural Networks for Efficient FPGA Implementation. In *FCCM*. IEEE.

[11] Jaehyeong Sim et al. 2016. 14.6 A 1.42 TOPS/W deep convolutional neural network recognition processor for intelligent IoE systems. In *ISSCC*. IEEE.

[12] Karen Simonyan et al. 2014. Very Deep Convolutional Networks for Large-Scale Image Recognition. *CoRR* (2014).

[13] L. Song et al. 2016. C-Brain: A deep learning accelerator that tames the diversity of CNNs through adaptive data-level parallelization. In *DAC*.

[14] Abdulhamit Subasi et al. [n. d.]. Classification of EEG signals using neural network and logistic regression. *Computer Methods and Programs in Biomedicine* ([n. d.]).

[15] Xilinx. 2011. Power Methodology Guide. (2011).

[16] Chen Zhang et al. 2015. Optimizing FPGA-based Accelerator Design for Deep Convolutional Neural Networks. In *FPGA (FPGA '15)*. ACM.

Improving the Security of Split Manufacturing Using a Novel BEOL Signal Selection Method

Suyuan Chen and Ranga Vemuri
Department of Electrical Engineering and Computing Systems
University of Cincinnati, Cincinnati, Ohio
{chens6,vemurir}@mail.uc.edu

ABSTRACT

Split manufacturing of integrated circuits (IC) was proposed as a possible defense against security issues arising from the use of potentially untrusted foundries. However, split manufactured designs were shown to be vulnerable to a new form of attack known as the proximity attack which attempts to reverse engineer the BEOL (Back End of Line) signals. Hence, care must be exercised in identifying the BEOL signals and their placement and routing. In this paper, we present a secure BEOL signal selection algorithm to defeat proximity attacks. Our method is based on two novel features: First, we introduce a new metric for signal selection based on the effect each signal has on the outputs. Second, we use a multiway partitioning algorithm to find a 'secure' cut-set which is the set of signals assigned to the BEOL layers. Our approach increases the number of BEOL nets while minimizing the impact on performance. We present experimental results which show significant improvement in security (on average by 800%) with only a modest effect on performance (less than 4% on average).

ACM Reference Format:

Suyuan Chen and Ranga Vemuri. 2018. Improving the Security of Split Manufacturing Using a Novel BEOL Signal Selection Method. In *GLSVLSI '18: 2018 Great Lakes Symposium on VLSI, May 23–25, 2018, Chicago, IL, USA.* ACM, New York, NY, USA, 6 pages. https://doi.org/10.1145/3194554.3194564

1 INTRODUCTION

Reverse engineering of an IC design has become a major threat due to the recent advent of fabless design houses and the use of third-party fabrication facilities [15]. *Split manufacturing* has been proposed to alleviate this threat [6]. In split manufacturing, the layout of a design is divided into two sets of layers: Front End of Line (FEOL) layers include the transistor devices and lower levels of metal and Back End of Line (BEOL) layers include the top few metal layers. Thus, the design is split into two parts: FEOL circuit and BEOL signals. FEOL layers are fabricated at a potentially untrusted foundry while the BEOL layers are completed at a trusted foundry or integration facility [6, 10]. When compared with the FEOL layers, the BEOL layers are thicker, have larger pitch and usually have lower routing density. This allows for easier fabrication and integration BEOL layers at a low cost, trusted facility [13]. Split manufacturing method aims to thwart reverse engineering attacks by 'hiding' the signals assigned to BEOL layers from an attacker. Even if FEOL signals are exposed, BEOL signals are unknown to the attacker making it impossible to complete the missing connections to recreate the correct design netlist [16].

In order to make it difficult for an attacker to reverse engineer the entire design, the signals assigned to the BEOL layers must be carefully selected. Too few BEOL nets make reverse engineering feasible while too many nets may significantly increase the cost of BEOL fabrication and may adversely impact the design performance.

In the past decade since split manufacturing was introduced, researchers have proposed several attack algorithms to reconstruct the BEOL signals and their defenses accordingly[8, 21]. Rajendran et al. [13] proposed an attack named *proximity attack*. This pin location based attack algorithm was able to recover more than 90% of the hidden nets correctly by iteratively identifying the missing connections. Furthermore, a network flow based proximity attack showed full recovery of the missing signals is possible [19]. This had significantly shown the vulnerability of split manufacturing under attacks. Meanwhile, the pin swap based defense method proposed in [13] does make the proximity attack take much longer time but doesn't provide sufficient level of defense to thwart the attack.

In this paper, we propose a novel method to identify nets to be assigned to BEOL layers to thwart proximity attacks. Given a gate-level netlist of a logic circuit, a multiway partitioning tool divides the circuit into FEOL partitions and determines a cutset of nets which will be assigned to the BEOL layers as shown in Fig. 1.

We summarize our contributions as follows:

- We present heuristics to attach security-aware weights to the nets in a logic circuit such that min-cut hypergraph partitioning algorithms can generate secure cutsets of nets which when assigned to BEOL layers can thwart proximity based reverse engineering attacks.
- Our net weights are based on three factors critical to defend against proximity attacks: (1) effect of internal signals on primary outputs, (2) number of primary outputs in the output cones of internal signals, and (3) uniqueness of signals in influencing the primary outputs. We define these factors, show how to compute them and combine them into a single weight for each net.
- We evaluate the proposed method using 12 benchmark circuits from the ISCAS-85 [9] and ITC'99 [14] which were widely used in this area [18–20, 22]. We mount the proximity attack on partitioned and placed circuits. Results show significantly reduced attack correctness in terms of the proportion

GLSVLSI '18, May 23–25, 2018, Chicago, IL, USA

ACM ISBN 978-1-4503-5724-1/18/05...$15.00
https://doi.org/10.1145/3194554.3194564

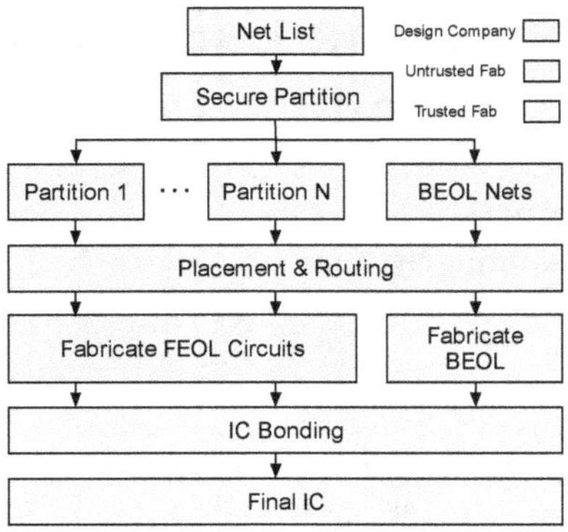

Figure 1: Design Flow for Secure Split Manufacturing

of successfully reconstructed BEOL nets and increased Hamming distance (HD) between the outputs of the original and reconstructed circuits.

2 RELATED WORK

Proximity attack assumes that the attacker has access to the a functionally correct copy of IC from the open market. However, due to the limited observability of packaged ICs, only the correct primary output vectors for given a set of input vectors can be used as a reference. Once the attacker reconstructs a circuit which produces the same outputs as the reference IC on a set of input vectors, it is assumed that IC is correctly recovered. Therefore, HD between the output vectors of the reconstructed circuit and the reference IC, given the same input vectors is an important metric for the attacker to evaluate the attack quality.

Xie [18] proposed a Fiduccia-Mattheyses (FM) algorithm [3] based secure partitioning method. An observability and controllability based weight is utilized to select the nets in BEOL. If a net is recovered incorrectly, this error propagates to the POs thereby increasing the overall HD. However, several nets can propagate their errors to the same primary output pin. Furthermore, placement with perturbation increases the net wire-length in BEOL and thus longer delay and worse performance. This performance overhead is a critical concern as ICs that have a high demand on advanced fabrication processes are also sensitive to signal delay overhead.

3 ATTACK MODEL AND PROBLEM FORMULATION

3.1 Attack Model

In this paper, we use the proximity attack model discussed in [13][18]. This attack attempts to iteratively connect an input pin (of the FEOL circuit but not a primary input) to the nearest output pin (of the FEOL circuit but not a primary output) without causing any combinational loops. For details, we refer the readers to [13].

The correctness of the proximity attack is not only influenced by the physical placement but also on the order of signal selection. In a nominal EDA design flow, at the placement stage, nets with low fanout are unlikely to be placed to obtain minimum net wire-length due to their lower placement priority. Thus, these nets are less likely to be recovered correctly by the proximity attack.

As the attack correctness (percentage of correctly recovered nets) is unknown to the attacker, he can only compare the responses of the reconstructed circuit with those from the working IC given the same inputs. Hence, the HD between the expected and reconstructed circuit responses for an input sequence is a significant metric from the attacker's viewpoint.

3.2 Problem Formulation and Security Metrics

3.2.1 Problem Description. Let $G = (V, E)$ be a hypergraph representation of a combinational logic circuit. Vertices $v_i, 1 \leq i \leq |V|$ represent logic gates and hyperedges $e_j \subseteq V, 1 \leq j \leq |E|$ represent signal nets. Let $H \subseteq E$ be the subset of nets selected to be assigned to the 'hidden' BEOL layers and fabricated at a trusted facility. Remaining circuit $(V, E - H)$ is assigned to the FEOL layers fabricated at a foundry assumed to be untrusted. We assume that the attacker knows $(V, E - H)$. Let H' be the set of nets that the attacker reconstructed in place of H. Hence, the attacker's final circuit is $G' = (V, (E - H) \cup H')$. The problem is to identify a suitable H so that it is computationally hard for the attacker to reconstruct the original circuit. Removing H from G induces a partition $\{V_1, V_2, ..., V_p\}$ on V such that $V = \cup_{i=1,p} V_i$ and $H = \{e \in E | \exists_{v_1, v_2 \in e} : v_1 \in V_i, v_2 \in V_j, i \neq j\}$. Conversely a partition of V into $\{V_1, V_2, ..., V_p\}$ for some p, $2 \leq p \leq |V|$ determines the 'cutset' of nets H to be assigned to the BEOL layers. The problem, therefore, is perform a security-driven multiway partitioning (for a suitable value of p) so as to identify and hide the cutset of nets in the BEOL layers to defeat the proximity attack.

3.2.2 Security Metrics. In order to evaluate the security of split manufacturing, we use two metrics in this paper: (1) attack correctness, and (2) average normalized Hamming distance. To evaluate the efficiency and performance overhead of the defense method, we use execution time and total estimated wire-length [11].

Attack correctness, AC is defined as the proportion of BEOL nets correctly reconstructed by the proximity attack. This is computed as $|H' \cap H|/|H|$. If AC is 100% then the circuit is completely reverse engineered. Even if AC is 90%, the circuit may be secure since the attacker does not know the AC achieved and cannot distinguish the correct connections in H' from incorrect ones.

Hamming Distance (HD) is widely used to quantify the security of circuit obfuscation methods [4, 5, 13, 18, 19]. Let $HD(x, y)$ be the Hamming Distance between two Boolean vectors x and y of the same size. Let $Y = F(X)$ be the Boolean function represented by G. X and Y are vectors of Boolean input and output variables respectively. Let F' be the Boolean function represented by the recovered circuit G'. If x is a specific Boolean input vector then $HD(y, y')$, where $y = F(x)$ and $y' = F'(x)$ is the number of bit positions in which y and y' differ.

For a given input vector x, *Normalized Hamming Distance*, NHD(x) is defined as the ratio $HD(F(x), F'(x))/|F(x)|$ where the denominator denotes the number of output pins. Given a series of input vectors $x_1, x_2, ...x_n$, *Average NHD* (ANHD) is defined as follows:

$$ANHD = \frac{\sum_{i=1}^{n} NHD(x_i)}{n} \quad (1)$$

For a sufficiently large sequence of input vectors, ANHD is either 0% or 100% assumed successful attack as output vectors or its inversion equal to correct output[13, 18]. Two uncorrelated circuits will produce output sequences whose ANHD is in the vicinity of 50% [4, 5]. In this paper, our goal is to hide selected nets in the BEOL layers so as to ensure ANHD in the range 40%-50% over n random input sequences($n \geq 1,000$). This ensures that not only the attack is unable to recover the hidden nets but also that the recovered circuit and the original circuit are functionally uncorrelated [4].

Simulated annealing based algorithms to identify BEOL signals have long execution times and cannot be scaled to large problem sizes [18, 22]. In contrast, our goal is to develop an efficient algorithm scalable to large problems. Overhead of the defense method is usually in terms of decreased performance. We use total half-perimeter wire-length (HPWL) as an estimation of the performance.

4 SECURE PARTITIONING FOR BEOL SIGNAL IDENTIFICATION

Secure bipartition has been used before to identify BEOL layers [18]. We define and assign a novel, security-aware weight to each net in the design and use a generalized weighted cutset minimal multiway partitioning method to identify the BEOL nets. We begin by defining three factors that contribute to the overall weight of a net: Signal Effect on Output, Output Cone Size and Signal Priority.

4.1 Effect of Signals on Primary Outputs

Following reverse engineering by an attacker using proximity attack, a non-zero ANHD shows that the reconstructed circuit is incorrect. However, a small non-zero value (close to zero) indicates a relatively high degree of matching with the correct circuit. In case an incorrect connection influences exactly one primary output, the attacker can easily identify that incorrect connection using his knowledge of the FEOL circuit. We would prefer to embed in the BEOL layers signals which are likely to cause multiple errors in the primary outputs thereby increasing the ANHD value.

To quantify the effect of signals on the primary outputs, we define a parameter named *Signal Effect on Output (SEO)* of a signal. Let s be a signal net. SEO of a signal s in the context of an input vector x is defined as,

$$SEO(s,x) = HD(F(x)|_{s=b}, F(x)|_{s\leftarrow b'}) \tag{2}$$

where, $F(x)$ denotes the output vector when x is applied as input to the circuit, $b(\in \{0,1\})$ denotes the value assumed by s when x is applied, and $F(x)|_{s\leftarrow b'}$ denotes the output vector when the value of s is reversed and forward propagated to the primary outputs while keeping the other values. Thus, SEO(s,x) denotes the sensitivity of the primary outputs to a change in s from b to b' in the 'context' of x. Note that the value of SEO is dependent on x and the direction of change in s. To eliminate the bias of context x, we compute SEO over a large number of input vectors and take the average. Given a series of input vectors $x_1, x_2, ...x_n$, SEO(s) is defined as,

$$SEO(s) = \frac{\sum_{i=1}^{n} SEO(s,x_i)}{n} \tag{3}$$

We use $n \geq 1000$ which is sufficiently large to remove the bias of individual vectors. Average SEO (ASEO) is the average SEO value of all the signals in the design. Finally, we define the *Normalized SEO*, NSEO(s) of a signal s is defined as,

$$NSEO(s) = \frac{SEO(s)}{ASEO} \tag{4}$$

4.2 Primary Output Cone Size

Consider two signals s_1 and s_2 that have the same SEO value over the same vectors. It is possible that $SEO(s_1)$ is attributed to its high influence on one pin or relatively few pins while $SEO(s_2)$ is due to its moderate influence on a large number of pins. To maximize ANHD, we would like to give preference to s_2 for inclusion in the BEOL layers. To capture this weight, we define the *Primary Output Cone*, POC(s), of a signal s as the set of primary output pins in the output cone of of signal s. $|POC(s)|$ is the number of output pins influenced by s. Average Output Cone Size (AOCS) is the average value of $|POC(s)|$ over all the signals in the design. We define *Normalized Output Cone Size*, NOCS(s), of s as,

$$NOCS(s) = \frac{|POC(s)|}{AOCS} \tag{5}$$

4.3 Priority Factor

Consider a signal s which influences only one primary output pin p. Since NSEO(s) and NOCS(s) are both low, it is unlikely that s would be selected for inclusion in the BEOL layers if only these two metrics are considered. However, if s is the only signal which influences p then s should be given a higher priority for inclusion in the BEOL layers in order to ensure that p contributes to the ANHD of an incorrectly reconstructed circuit. To generalize this situation, we introduce a *Priority Factor*, P, of signal s, defined as follows:

$$P(s) = MIN_{p\in POC(s)} \ |\{i : signal \mid p \in POC(i)\}| \tag{6}$$

The lower the priority factor, the higher is the preference to assign the signal to BEOL layers. Detailed procedure to calculate these factors is shown in Algorithm 1. After taking all parameters into consideration, a set of highly efficient signals are selected for BEOL fabrication as we will explain later on.

4.4 Secure Min-Cut Algorithm

We developed a secure min-cut multiway partitioning method based on a hyper-graph partitioning tool called PaToH from OSU [2]. PaToH is a multilevel hypergraph partitioning tool based on the FM algorithm. It generates near-optimal multiway partitioning result for hypergraphs with weighted vertices and edges. We use the three parameters defined in the previous subsection to weigh all the nets. Then, we use the weighted min-cut partitioning of PaToH to generate balanced p-way partitions for various p values.

Since heavily weighted nets are unlikely to be cut, to each signal net s we assign a weight which is directly proportional to P(s) and inversely proportional to NSEO(s) and NOCS(s) as shown below. α is the proportionality constant which is tuned experimentally. For the signals that do not effect primary outputs, the weight is set to the max value allowed by PaToH.

$$W(s) = \begin{cases} \infty & \text{if } |POC(s)| = 0 \\ \alpha * \frac{P(s)}{NSEO(s)*NOCS(s)} & \text{otherwise} \end{cases} \tag{7}$$

Proximity attack aims to recover BEOL nets based on the assumption that nearby FEOL circuit pins are more likely to be connected. By increasing the number of partitions (which together form the FEOL circuit) and assigning the security-aware cut-set nets to BEOL

Algorithm 1: Calculation of Security Weights of Signals

```
Input: SignalNets(S) = s_1, s_2, ..., s_k, InputVectors(X) =
       x_1, x_2, ..., x_n, PrimaryOutputs(O) = O_1, O_2, ..., O_w
Output: SEO[1..k], POC[1..k], P[1..k]
for i in 1 to n do
    y = Primary_Output(PI = x_i);
    Internal_Signal_Value.backup();
    for j in 1 to k do
        Propagate_Signal_Forward(s_j = INV(s_j));
        for m in 1 to w do
            if (y[m] ≠ Current_Output_Value(O_m)) then
                SEO_j[m] += 1;
            end
        end
        Internal_Signal_Value.recover();
    end
end
for j in 1 to k do
    for m in 1 to w do
        if (SEO_j[m] ≠ 0) then
            POC[j] = POC[j] ∪ {O_m};
            POC_Size[j] += 1;
            SEO[j] += SEO_j[m];
            Q[y] += 1;
        end
    end
end
for j in 1 to k do
    for y in POC[j] do
        P[j] = min (P[j], Q[y]);
    end
end
return SEO, POC, P;
```

layers, we are aiming to defeat the proximity attack. In fact, with the number of partitions increases, proximity attack often fails to identify a cycle free connection with a target pin since viable candidate pins have already been incorrectly assigned to other nets.

5 GLOBAL MINIMUM WIRE LENGTH PLACEMENT

Pin placement is critical to defeat location based attack algorithms. If the same weights used in partitioning are used to drive placement, then pins connected by the BEOL nets tend to be placed close to each other thereby allowing the proximity attack to succeed. In order to thwart the attack, pin positions are usually swapped or perturbed thereby increasing wire length and possibly adversely effecting the performance. However, in our approach, such perturbation is not necessary due to the use of different weight functions during partitioning and floor-planning/placement.

We assume that the circuit is placed on a square die and partitions are assigned to a square grid on the die. Also the number of

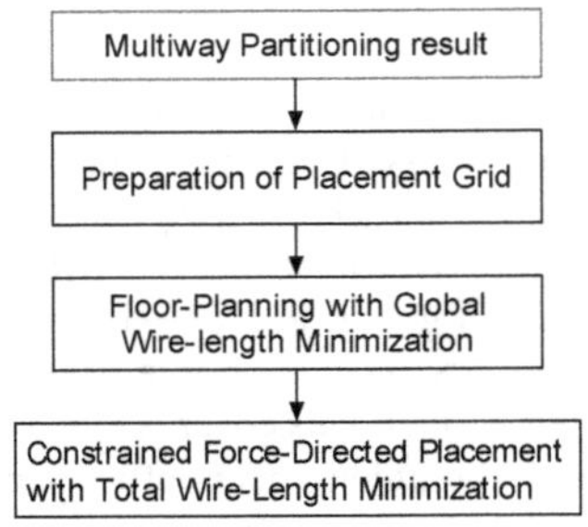

Figure 2: Placement Process

partitions p is 2 (for bipartitioning) or a perfect square of some integer > 1. That is, $p = 2, 4, 9, 16 ....$ The hyper-graph partitioning tool evenly divides the circuit into p balanced partitions. The chances of creating combinational loops during the proximity attack increases significantly in our multiway partitioning approach compared to the bipartition based approach as the former method cuts a fan-out net with p branches up to p-1 times in a p-way partition whereas the latter method cuts the net only once.

For a multiway partitioned circuit, the location of each partition will affect the global wire-length dramatically. Hence, we first perform a floor-planning of the p partitions to minimize total global wire-length. Our placement process is shown in Fig 2. After partitioning, a simulated annealing (SA) based min-weight floor-planning algorithm is implemented to allocate space for each partition. Finally, a global placement of the whole circuit is performed using a constrained force-directed placement algorithm in which the cells in each partition are constrained to stay within the area assigned to that partition.

In the force-directed placement algorithm [12], the ideal target location for any cell can be anywhere in the designated placement area. However, in our case, if the target location for any cell is computed to be outside the region designated for its partition, then we change it to the nearest location within the partition's region.

6 EXPERIMENT SETUP AND RESULTS

6.1 Experimental Setup

We evaluated our algorithms with 7 benchmarks from ISCAS-85 [9] and 5 benchmarks from ITC'99 [14] suits on a Dell M4800 with Intel i7-4800MQ CPU@2.7GHz. These suits were used by previous research [7, 13]. Weight values are calculated using 1,000 randomly generated input vectors for all benchmarks. (We found that using 10,000 vectors, accuracy of SEO computation improves by up to 5% but consumes 10x more time.)

In the secure min-cut algorithm, α is varied from 0.03 to 2 to obtain the best defense against the attack with the lowest performance overhead. In floor-planning and placement, all cells including the I/O buffers are assumed to be of unit size. The chip is divided into p square regions arranged in a $\sqrt{p}$ *$\sqrt{p}$ grid and each partition is assigned to one grid space. For multiway partitioning, we report experimental results with p partitions with $r = \sqrt{p}$ set to 2 to 11 for the large benchmarks, 2 to 7 for middle-sized benchmarks and 2 to 6 for small benchmarks. For bipartitioning, we use a 1x2 grid.

As r increases, the size of each partition can become too small. However, our goal is find enough partitions to yield acceptable security which we define to be 40% ANHD [13]. For larger benchmarks

Table 1: Benchmark Details and Cut-set Comparison

BM	# PI	# PO	# Gate # Nets	# Cut (N)	# Cut (S)	# Cut [18] StateOfTheArt
c499	41	32	202	17	37	45
c880	60	26	383	19	63	NA
c1355	41	32	546	16	38	43
c1908	33	25	880	29	43	37
c3540	50	22	1,669	52	72	74
c6288	32	32	2,416	34	36	NA
c7552	207	108	3,512	25	142	155
b14_1	277	299	6,569	106	471	NA
b15	485	519	8,367	135	707	NA
b21_1	522	512	13,898	86	1163	NA
b20	522	512	19,682	87	867	NA
b17	1,452	1,512	30,777	175	1329	NA

this security goal can be achieved with a relatively small value of r. To evaluate the performance overhead at placement level, we compute Half-Perimeter Wire-Length (HPWL) as it is widely used in several placers [17][1] to estimate performance.

6.2 Normal vs. Secure Bipartitioning

Table 1 shows the comparison between the cut-sizes of normal and secure bipartitioning methods for all the benchmarks as well as the cut-sizes using a state-of-the-art method [18]. The cut-sizes are lower for most benchmarks in our case even though we have included I/O buffers as cells in the netlist thereby increasing the total number of nets. Figure 3 shows the HD values for all benchmarks using normal and secure multiway partitioning. The results show that for 9 of the 12 benchmarks, 40% HD security requirement is achieved using secure bipartitioning with acceptable cut-sizes and performance overhead. For the remaining 3 relatively large benchmarks (b14_1,b15 and b17), multiway partitioning is needed. Table 2 shows the attack correctness (AC) values for normal and secure multiway partitioning. Security improvement afforded by the secure partitioning demonstrated by the reduction in the AC values. Low AC (<5%) values show that perturbation in placement is unnecessary for circuits such as b17 with more than 1,000 cut-sizes.

6.3 Effect of Security-Aware Weights on Nets

In secure partitioning, the partitioning tool does not directly determine if enough number of effective signals are selected. Factor α is utilized to indirectly control the number of signals which are selected by directly controlling the average weight of all the nets. Signal weights have been proved effective for both small and large circuits. For example, while both c499 and b20 attained less than 10% HD using normal insecure min-cut partitioning, we obtain more than 40% HD using secure partitioning although the later benchmark is 100 times larger than the former.

6.4 Multiway Partitioning

For some benchmarks like b14_1, secure bipartitioning is not sufficient to obtain a set of BEOL signals with the desired target HD value of 40%. In Fig. 3, multiway partitioning shows significant improvement in HD. For example, for b17, the HD is 20% for bipartition while it increases to 40% with 16-way partition. This significant

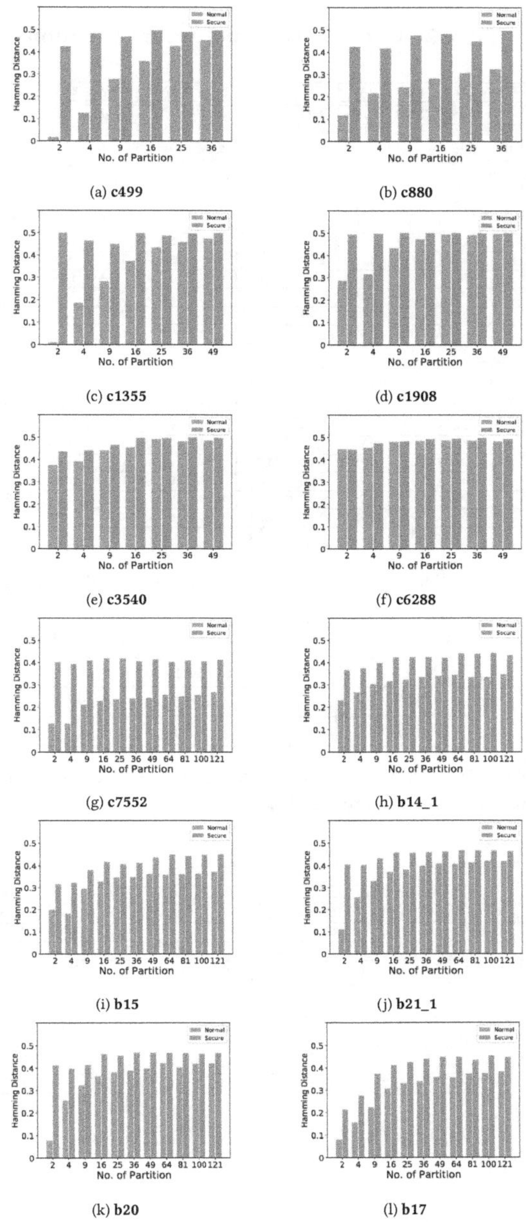

(a) c499 (b) c880 (c) c1355 (d) c1908 (e) c3540 (f) c6288 (g) c7552 (h) b14_1 (i) b15 (j) b21_1 (k) b20 (l) b17

Figure 3: HD for Normal and Secure Partitions

increase comes with only a 3.5% overall wire-length overhead. Table 3 shows the number of partitions and cut-set sizes for benchmarks which needed multiway partitioning. Also, AC keeps decreasing as we increase the number of the partitions. In case of 25-way partition or above, c1355 has AC less than 10% and HD larger than 40% even with insecure partitioning. This result further demonstrates that perturbation in placement is unnecessary as the attacker fails to recover 10% of the missing nets correctly in multiway partitioning with modest wire-length overhead.

6.5 Performance Trade-off

Larger cut-size means higher BEOL cost. From Fig. 4, note that the cut-set size is linearly increasing while we increase the number of

Table 2: AC for Normal and Secure Partitions

BM		2-W	4-W	9-W	16-W	25-W	36-W	49-W	64-W	81-W	100-W	121-W
c499	N	29.4%	23.3%	7.04%	4.9%	2.1%	2.4%	N/A	N/A	N/A	N/A	N/A
	S	2.44%	3.6%	1.83%	1.5%	1.6%	1.9%	N/A	N/A	N/A	N/A	N/A
c880	N	15%	20%	5.9%	8.8%	11.7%	7.4%	N/A	N/A	N/A	N/A	N/A
	S	5.8%	3.85%	2.9%	2.9%	5.4%	3.8%	N/A	N/A	N/A	N/A	N/A
c1355	N	29.4%	14.6%	6.7%	14.8%	3.7%	3.2%	7.5%	N/A	N/A	N/A	N/A
	S	2.5%	0.0%	1.7%	2.4%	1.7%	5.2%	3.4%	N/A	N/A	N/A	N/A
c1908	N	35.5%	19.4%	13.7%	7.5%	10.4%	10%	8.3%	N/A	N/A	N/A	N/A
	S	7.7%	6.3%	2.9%	3.4%	3.8%	2.1%	3.3%	N/A	N/A	N/A	N/A
c3540	N	7.4%	6.7%	3.1%	2.4%	2.5%	3.6%	3.6%	N/A	N/A	N/A	N/A
	S	3%	4.3%	2.0%	1.3%	0.6%	0.5%	1.0%	N/A	N/A	N/A	N/A
c6288	N	26.5%	21.3%	4.7%	5.6%	6.8%	4.5%	7.0%	N/A	N/A	N/A	N/A
	S	9.3%	6.2%	2.6%	4.9%	3.2%	4.5%	4.5%	N/A	N/A	N/A	N/A
c7552	N	9.4%	7.0%	6.3%	5.0%	7.5%	6.2%	7.2%	6.2%	5.7%	4.8%	8.0%
	S	9.1%	5,3%	2.8%	2.7%	2.6%	2.7%	2.7%	2.8%	2.9%	3.4%	3.2%
b14_1	N	9.9%	1.6%	1.6%	1.3%	0.6%	1.0%	1.7%	1.0%	1.3%	1.4%	1.5%
	S	3.1%	0.9%	1.3%	0.6%	0.6%	0.9%	0.8%	0.5%	0.6%	0.4%	0.8%
b15	N	2.2%	1.7%	1.4%	0.7%	0.9%	0.9%	0.9%	1.0%	0.9%	0.9%	1.0%
	S	1.2%	0.4%	0.4%	0.2%	0.2%	0.4%	0.3%	0.4%	0.3%	0.4%	0.3%
b21_1	N	5.3%	2.9%	0.3%	1.4%	1.0%	0.9%	0.8%	1.1%	0.9%	0.8%	1.2%
	S	1.2%	1.2%	0.7%	0.1%	0.2%	0.2%	0.2%	0.3%	0.4%	0.3%	0.3%
b20	N	3.3%	1.8%	1.9%	1.2%	0.6%	1.0%	0.5%	0.5%	0.9%	0.9%	1.0%
	S	0.7%	0.6%	0.2%	0.3%	0.2%	0.2%	0.3%	0.2%	0.4%	0.3%	0.3%
b17	N	2.9%	0.9%	0.9%	0.9%	0.7%	1.1%	0.4%	0.7%	0.7%	0.7%	0.8%
	S	1.1%	0.8%	0.3%	0.2%	0.3%	0.3%	0.2%	0.1%	0.2%	0.1%	0.2%

Table 3: Cut-Sizes for Multiway Partitions with HD > 40%

Benchmark	Part No.	Secure	Normal
b14_1	16	1317	632
b15	16	2418	1092
b17	16	6159	1677

Table 4: Half Perimeter Wire-length (HPWL) overhead between normal and secure deign flow

BM	2-W	4-W	9-W	16-W	25-W	36-W	49-W	64-W	81-W	100-W	121-W
c499	6.33%	13.2%	0.97%	8.34%	6.69%	3.11%	N/A	N/A	N/A	N/A	N/A
c880	5.71%	5.58%	10.2%	4.4%	13.3%	7.4%	N/A	N/A	N/A	N/A	N/A
c1355	-1.9%	2.59%	1.73%	0.16%	2.83%	6.39%	-0.1%	N/A	N/A	N/A	N/A
c1908	2.72%	3.63%	-1.6%	0.16%	6.82%	4.05%	-0.1%	N/A	N/A	N/A	N/A
c3540	1.94%	7.48%	10.9%	6.19%	9.54%	6.36%	12.4%	N/A	N/A	N/A	N/A
c6288	-0.2%	14.6%	15.7%	5.44%	-5.5%	1.94%	-10%	N/A	N/A	N/A	N/A
c7552	-1.5%	-0.7%	-0.6%	3.62%	4%	4.66%	5.11%	4.55%	0.09%	4.85%	1.94%
b14_1	2.26%	-3.5%	1.59%	8%	1.29%	1.48%	-4.5%	6.5%	2.63%	4.17%	5.48%
b15	2.86%	3.33%	5.7%	2.27%	5.25%	5.67%	4.94%	4.08%	7.51%	5.86%	15.5%
b21_1	5.7%	-8.2%	4.85%	-0.5%	11.6%	-0.004%	1.94%	9.17%	3.95%	3.77%	6.49%
b20	1.93%	4.02%	3.68%	5.03%	-1.8%	4.81%	9.75%	9.41%	6.85%	5.07%	-5.4%
b17	-0.9%	2.57%	8.42%	3.23%	3.92%	4.58%	0.47%	2.23%	4.9%	3.38%	3.6%

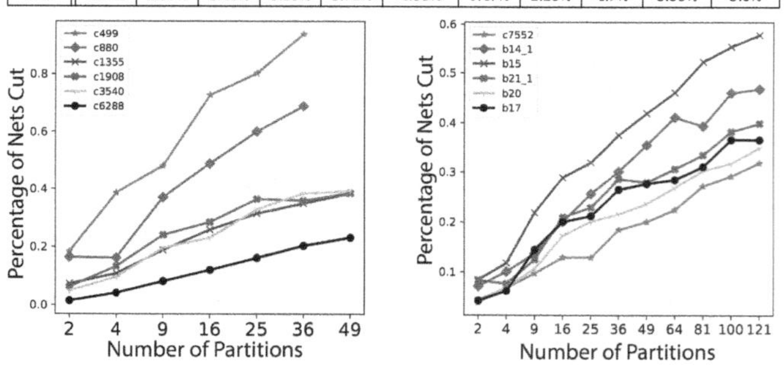

Figure 4: Percentage of Nets Cut vs Number of Partitions

partitions exponentially. Also, our results show less wire-length overhead with multiway partitioning than with bipartitioning with same cut-set size. As Table 4 shows, the increase in HPWL between normal and secure partitions is less than 10%, with some benchmarks such as b21_1 showing a decrease by up to 8.24%. These results show that the performance penalty is minimal.

6.6 Execution Time

Execution times for all the partitioning and placement algorithms are within 1 to 20 seconds for all the benchmarks. Attack algorithm takes from 1 to 200 seconds for various benchmarks and partition sizes.

7 CONCLUSION

Proximity attack is one of the most effective reverse engineering attacks against split manufactured ICs. We propose effective and efficient heuristics and algorithms for the identification of BEOL nets during physical DA to thwart proximity attacks. Our method is based on assigning security-aware weights to nets and performing multiway partitioning followed by floor-planning and placement. We have presented detailed experimental results which demonstrate the effectiveness of our method with minimal performance overhead.

REFERENCES

[1] S. Reda A. B. Kahng and Q. Wang. 2005. Architecture and details of a high quality, large-scale analytical placer. In *2005 ICCAD*. San Jose, California, 891–898.
[2] U. V. Catalyurek. 1999. *Hypergraph Models for Sparse Matrix Partitioning and Reordering*. Ph.D. Dissertation. Computer Engineering and Information Science Bilkent University, Columbus, Ohio. http://bmi.osu.edu/umit/software.html
[3] Charles M. Fiduccia and Robert M. Mattheyses. 1982. A linear-time heuristic for improving network partitions. In *19th DAC*. Las Vegas, Nevada, 175–181.
[4] C. Zhang G. S. Rose Y. Pino O. Sinanoglu J. Rajendran, H. Zhang and R. Karri. 2015. Fault Analysis-Based Logic Encryption. *IEEE Trans. Computers* 64 (2015), 410–424.
[5] O. Sinanoglu J. Rajendran, Y. Pino and R. Karri. 2012. Logic Encryption: A Fault Analysis Perspective. In *2012 DATE*. Munich, Germany, 953–958.
[6] R.W. Jarvis and M.G. McIntyre. 2007. Split manufacturing method for advanced semiconductor circuits. (27 March 2007).
[7] H. Ekin Sumbul Q. Zhu F. Franchetti K. Vaidyanathan, R. Liu and L. T. Pileggi. 2014. Efficient and secure intellectual property (IP) design with split fabrication. In *2014 IEEE International Symposium on HOST*. Arlington, VA, 13–18.
[8] J. Hu W. Mak L. Feng, Y. Wang and J. Rajendran. 2017. Making Split Fabrication Synergistically Secure and Manufacturable. In *2017 ICCAD*. Irvine, California, 313–320.
[9] H. Yalcin M. C. Hansen and J. P. Hayes. 1999. Unveiling the ISCAS-85 Benchmarks: A Case Study in Reverse Engineering. *IEEE Trans. DTC* 16 (1999), 72–80.
[10] M. Sika M. Bajura M. Jagasivamani, P. Gadfort and M. Fritze. 2014. Split-fabrication obfuscation: Metrics and techniques. In *2014 IEEE International Symposium on HOST*. Arlington, VA, 7–12.
[11] J. Rajendran M. Rostami, F. Koushanfar and R. Karri. 2013. Hardware security: threat models and metrics. In *2013 ICCAD*. San Jose, California, 819–823.
[12] U. Schlichtmann P. Spindler and F. M. Johannes. 2008. Kraftwerk2 - A Fast Force-Directed Quadratic Placement Approach Using an Accurate Net Mode. *IEEE Trans. on CAD* 27 (2008), 1398–1411.
[13] J. Rajendran, O. Sinanoglu, and R. Karri. 2013. Is split manufacturing secure?. In *2013 DATE*. Grenoble, France, 1259–1264.
[14] Squillero. 2017. ITC'99 Benchmarks. (2017). https://github.com/squillero/itc99-poli
[15] R. Torrance and D. James. 2011. The state-of-the-art in semiconductor reverse engineering. In *48th DAC*. San Diego, CA, 333–338.
[16] K. Vaidyanathan, B. P. Das, E. Sumbul, R. Liu, and L. Pileggi. 2014. Building trusted ICs using split fabrication. In *2014 IEEE International Symposium on HOST*. Arlington, VA, 1–6.
[17] N. Viswanathan and C. C. N. Chu. 2005. FastPlace: efficient analytical placement using cell shifting, iterative local refinement, and a hybrid net model. *IEEE Trans. on CAD* 24 (2005), 722–733.
[18] Y. Xie, C. Bao, and A. Srivastava. 2015. Security-Aware Design Flow for 2.5D IC Technology. In *TrustED@CCS*. Denver, CO, 31–38.
[19] J. Hu Y. Wang, P. Chen and J. Rajendran. 2016. The Cat and Mouse in Split Manufacturing. In *2016 DAC*. Austin, Texas, 1–6.
[20] J. Hu Y. Wang, P. Chen and J. Rajendran. 2017. Routing Perturbation for Enhanced Security in Split Manufacturing. In *2017 ASP-DAC*. Chiba, Tokyo, 505 – 510.
[21] P. Yang and M. Marek-Sadowskae. 2016. Making Split-Fabrication More Secure. In *2016 ICCAD*. Austin, Texas, 1–8.
[22] T. Ho Z. Chen, P. Zhou and Yier Jin. 2016. How secure is split manufacturing in preventing hardware trojan?. In *2016 IEEE AsianHOST*. Yilan, Taiwan, 1–6.

A Novel Polymorphic Gate Based Circuit Fingerprinting Technique

Tian Wang, Xiaoxin Cui, Dunshan Yu
Institute of Microelectronics, Peking University, Beijing, China
cuixx@pku.edu.cn

Omid Aramoon, Timothy Dunlap, Gang Qu
Department of Electrical and Computer Engineering and Institute for Systems Research, University of Maryland, College Park, USA
gangqu@umd.edu

Xiaole Cui
Key Lab of Integrated Microsystems, Peking University Shenzhen Graduate School, Shenzhen, China
cuixl@pkusz.edu.cn

ABSTRACT

Polymorphic gates are reconfigurable devices that deliver multiple functionalities at different temperature, supply voltage or external inputs. Capable of working in different modes, polymorphic gate is a promising candidate for embedding secret information such as fingerprints. In this paper, we report five polymorphic gates whose functionality varies in response to specific control input and propose a circuit fingerprinting scheme based on these gates. The scheme selectively replaces standard logic cells by polymorphic gates whose functionality differs with the standard cells only on Satisfiability Don't Care conditions. Additional dummy fingerprint bits are also introduced to enhance the fingerprint's robustness against attacks such as fingerprint removal and modification. Experimental results on ISCAS and MCNC benchmark circuits demonstrate that our scheme introduces low overhead. More specifically, the average overhead in area, speed and power are 4.04%, 6.97% and 4.15% respectively when we embed 64-bit fingerprint that consists of 32 real fingerprint bits and 32 dummy bits. This is only half of the overhead of the other known approach when they create 32-bit fingerprints.

KEYWORDS

Polymorphic gate, fingerprinting, satisfiability don't care conditions

ACM Reference format:

Tian Wang, Xiaoxin Cui, Dunshan Yu, Omid Aramoon, Timothy Dunlap, Gang Qu, Xiaole Cui. 2018. A Novel Polymorphic Gate Based Circuit Fingerprinting Technique. In *GLSVLSI '18: 2018 Great Lakes Symposium on VLSI, May 23–25, 2018, Chicago, IL, USA*. ACM, New York, NY, USA, 6 pages. https://doi.org/10.1145/3194554.3194572

ACM ISBN 978-1-4503-5724-1/18/05...$15.00
https://doi.org/10.1145/3194554.3194572

1 INTRODUCTION

Recent achievements in the field of digital circuit design brings a novel reconfigurable scheme based on polymorphic gates (or polymorphic circuits) that was first introduced by A. Stoica in 2001 [1]. With multiple functionalities integrated in one single structure, polymorphic gates/circuits can achieve function transformation in response to control factors such as temperature, supply voltage or external inputs, etc. One typical polymorphic gate that has been fabricated with HP 0.5um technology is a NAND/NOR gate proposed in [2]. It performs as a NAND gate when Vdd is 3.3V and when Vdd drops to 1.8V, this gate works as a NOR gate. Many follow-up works have been reported on designing various types of polymorphic gates based on evolutionary approach [3][4] and on building complex polymorphic circuits using polymorphic gates [5][6].

Polymorphic gates have been applied in many scenarios such as multifunctional adaptive systems [7][8], finite impulse response(FIR) filter [9], self-checking circuits [10,12] and reduction of test vector volume [11], where multiple working modes are supported, and each mode can be enabled with global control signals. Besides these applications, polymorphic gates have great potentials in hardware security, as the flexible built-in multi-functionality enables one or more conceived 'extra' functions in addition to the 'main' one, which makes it feasible to hide function or embed secret information, such as circuit watermark [21]. The embedded information will show up when the 'extra' function gets activated. One straightforward and convenient application is to embed circuit fingerprint, which allows the tracking of every individually sold IP. When a designer suspects IP piracy or counterfeiting, he can detect the embedded fingerprint to locate the source.

In this paper, we propose a circuit fingerprinting scheme with polymorphic gates controlled by external inputs. The scheme targets SDC (Satisfiability Don't Care) conditions that usually appear in non-trivial circuits and replaces the standard library cells holding the SDC conditions by polymorphic gates. The modified circuit delivers correct functionality and the configurations of the polymorphic gates constitute the circuit fingerprint. We also introduce additional replacements to those gate locations without SDC conditions. The control inputs of these polymorphic gates serve as the dummy fingerprints. Any malicious attempt to modify the dummy fingerprints will bring functional changes and make the fingerprinted circuits function incorrectly.

Our works and contributions are specified as follows,

- After a brief review of the existing design approaches of polymorphic gates, we employ the most widely used genetic algorithm. With this modified algorithm, we successfully construct five polymorphic gates whose function transition is controlled by external signals.
- We propose a polymorphic logic based justifiability checking method to determine the SDC conditions and potential locations where standard cells can be replaced by polymorphic gates to embed fingerprints.
- We perform security analysis by considering different attacking scenarios based on the attackers' capabilities, which demonstrates the robustness and reliability of the proposed scheme.
- We evaluate the area, delay and power overhead introduced by our proposed fingerprinting scheme on ISCAS 85 and MCNC benchmark circuits using 0.13um SMIC technology. Results demonstrate that, when we embed 32-bit real fingerprint and 32-bit dummy fingerprint, the benchmark circuits have an average of 4.04%, 6.97% and 4.15% overhead in delay, area and power, respectively. In other words, our scheme can provide sufficiently strong fingerprints (32 bits) with acceptable performance deterioration.

The rest of the paper is organized as follows: Section 2 gives the background and the design of polymorphic gates. Section 3 presents our fingerprinting scheme based on SDC conditions and the security analysis. In Section 4, we validate the proposed technique based on overhead evaluation, and Section 5 concludes.

2 DESIGN OF POLYMORPHIC GATES

2.1 Genetic Algorithm

Polymorphic gates can be implemented with FTPA (field programmable transistor array) [1], CMOS [2], emerging devices such as silicon nanowire and ambipolar devices [13] [14]. For better integration into the mainstream CMOS technology, we only focus on polymorphic gates consisting of CMOS transistors. Table 1 lists some representative polymorphic gates reported in the literature. These gates deliver different outputs for the same input vector depending on the operating environment such as temperature, supply voltage or specific input signals.

While standard logic gates adopt complementary topology, polymorphic gates employ rather unconventional structure at the transistor level. Due to their irregular topology, it is a challenge to find polymorphic gates. Evolutionary approach [3][15] is the most suitable method to search for potential designs that match perfectly with the required functionalities. Genetic algorithm is one of the most popular variants of evolutionary approach. In the general version of genetic algorithm [16], after the genotype (or gene) is mapped to an artificial system and the initial population of candidate individuals are created, a generative process ranks candidate solutions based on a fitness function which incorporates the desired criteria, and selects the fittest candidates for mutation and reproducing the next generation. This process repeats until an acceptable solution is found. In this paper, we tailor the generalized genetic algorithm for designing polymorphic gates, as shown in Algorithm 1. We assign an index to each terminal of transistors, the source, gate and drain. Genes refer to the width and length value of transistors and the index of the terminals that their source, gate or drain are connected to, which are all initialized in Step 1. The genes are mapped to candidate netlists which are later simulated and evaluated in Step 2. The function for fitness evaluation is the hamming distance between the outputs of the candidate solutions and the desired outputs. In step 3, only those with hamming distance less than a threshold are mutated for reproduction of the next generation.

Table 1: Examples of the Existing Polymorphic Gates.

Gate	Control	Control values	#Transistor
AND/OR[1]	T	27/125℃	6
AND/OR[1]	ext. input	3.3V/0V	6
AND/OR[1]	V_{dd}	3.3V/1.2V	8
AND/OR/XOR[1]	ext. input	3.3V/0V/1.5V	10
NAND/NOR[2]	V_{dd}	3.3V/1.8V	6
NAND/NOR[10]	V_{dd}	5V/3.3V	8
NAND/XOR[4]	ext.input	3.3V/0V	9

2.2 Evolved polymorphic gates

We have evolved several polymorphic gates whose function is selected by a specific control input. The functionalities of these gates and their size (in terms of the number of transistors) are summarized in Table 2. For example, the first row shows a polymorphic gate with 6 transistors that behaves as a NOR gate when the control input C=1, and changes to an inverter when C=0.

Table 2: Evolved Polymorphic Gates

Gate functionalities	#Transistor
NOR(C=1) - INV (C=0)	6
NAND(C=1) - INV (C=0)	7
AND(C=1) – BUF (C=0)	9
AND(C=1) – OR (C=0)	9
NAND(C=1) – NOR (C=0)	9

Fig. 1 (a) presents the schematic of the polymorphic AND/OR gate in the second row from the bottom in Table 2. The nine transistors are connected in irregular topology and take unconventional parameters. The function of this gate is shown in Fig. 1 (b). When the input c is logic '1', this gate is an AND gate; when *c* reverses to logic '0', this gate functions as an OR gate.

Algorithm 1-Genetic algorithm for evolving polymorphic gates

Input:
Population_No - number of individuals in each generation
Generation_No- number of generations for evolution
f<c, a, b...> - truth table of the desired gate function, where a,b.... are the input values and c is the external control signal to transform the function
fitness_threshold – threshold of hamming distance between the output of each individual and that of the desired gate function
r - mutation rate of each generation

Output: Gate netlist that performs the desired function.

1.Gene initialization
cnt1 = 0;
for (cnt2 = 0 ; cnt2 < Population_No; cnt2++)
Initialize the genes and generate netlist[cnt2];
end for

2.Simulation and fitness evaluation
for (cnt2 = 0; cnt2 < Population_No; cnt2 ++)
for different c and every input combination of a,b...
f' = Simulate(c,a,b,..netlist[cnt2]);
end for
fitness[cnt2]= matches(f, f');//Hmming distance calculation
end for

3.Selection and reproduction
No_indiv= 0;
for (cnt2 = 0; cnt2 < Population_No; cnt2 ++)
if (fitness[cnt2] > fitness_threshold)
Survival= Survival ∪ netlist(cnt2);No_indiv++;
endif
end for
for every netlist in the set Survival
for(cnt2 = 0; cnt2 <[Population_No/No_indiv];cnt2++)
Change r% of genes in netlist[cnt2];
end for
end for

4.*While*(cnt1 != Generation_No)
Goto step 2~3; cnt1++;
end while

5. Report the netlists in the set Survival.

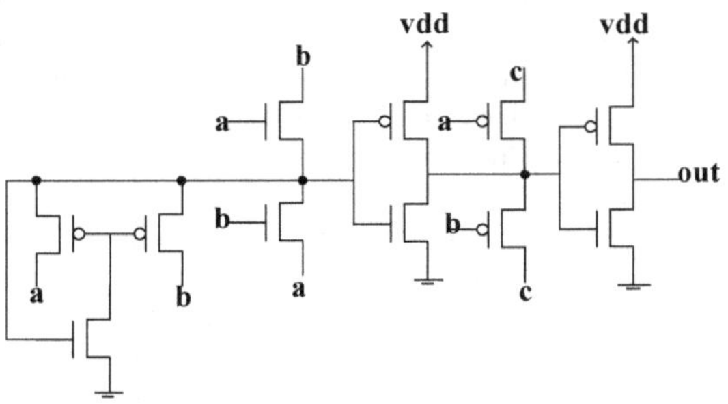

(a)

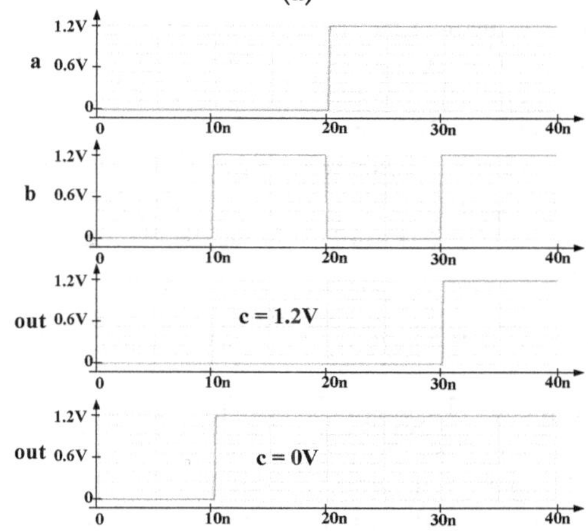

(b)

Figure 1: Polymorphic AND/OR gate. (a) Topology (b) Input and output waveforms (from top to bottom: input a, input b, output with c =1.2V, output with c = 0V).

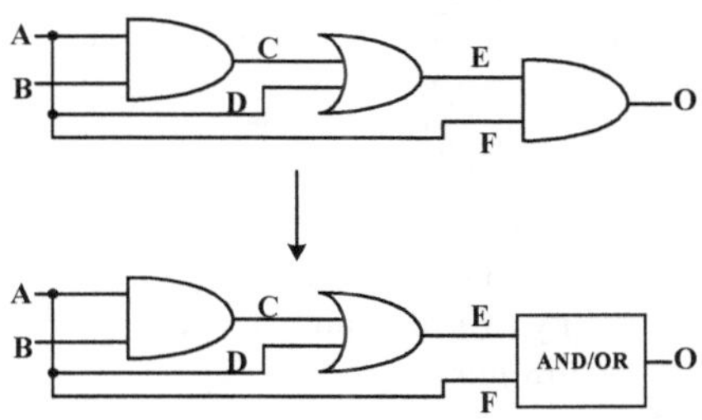

(a)

A	B	C	D	E	F	AND	OR
0	0	0	0	0	0	0	0
0	1	0	0	0	0	0	0
1	0	0	1	1	1	1	1
1	1	1	1	1	1	1	1

(b)

Figure 2: An example of SDC condition based fingerprinting. (a) The original circuit (top) and the one after the AND gate is replaced (bottom) (b) Truth tables of the internal signals and gates AND and OR.

3 POLYMOPHIC GATE BASED FINGERPRINTING WITH SATISFIABILITY DON'T CARE CONDITIONS

3.1 Satisfiability Don't Care(SDC) conditions

Satisfiability Don't Care conditions describe the logic combinations that will not occur in the internal nets given all the combinations that the primary inputs can take. For example, in Fig. 2, the AND gate in (a) cannot have input patterns (1, 0) or (0, 1) as shown in the truth table in (b).

As shown in Algorithm 2, SDC conditions can be determined by using the justification methodology in VLSI testing, which deduces the logic value from an internal net backwards to the primary inputs. If the justification of a logic pattern in a gate fails, there exists a SDC condition for this gate. For example, in Fig. 2(a), for the AND gate to have inputs E=0 and F=1, we have A=F=1, but this makes D=1 and the OR gate will make E=1. Therefore, input pattern (0,1) fails justification and thus it is a SDC condition.

Algorithm 2-Determining gate locations with SDC conditions

```
Function SDC_checking ( gate g, pattern <v1,v2,... ,vn> )
for i = 0; i < n; i ++
    if ( justify ( g's ith input, vi ) = fail )
        return pattern<v1,v2,... ,vn> is a SDC condition; //
The SDC condition exist.
endfor
  return fail;// The SDC condition doesn't exist.
```

```
Function Justify (gate g, justification value v)
if (v != g's existing output value)// conflict occurs
   backtrace();
Endif
Else
  if ( g functions as AND && v == 1)
      for i = 0; i < number of inputs for g; i ++
          if ( justify ( g's ith input, 1) = fail )
              return fail;
      endfor
endif
if ( g functions as AND && v == 0)
      for i= 0; i < number of inputs for g; i ++
          if ( justify ( g's ith input, 0) = success )
              return success;
      endfor
endif
......
```

3.2 Fingerprinting scheme with polymorphic gates

A circuit fingerprinting technique needs to meet the following requirements [17][20]:

1. *Consistency.* The circuit embedded with fingerprints needs to function correctly.
2. *Uniqueness.* Each circuit should have distinct fingerprints so that it is feasible to differentiate different copies.
3. *Robustness.* To enable the trace of source, the fingerprints must remain unchanged in any illegally produced circuits and shouldn't be modified.

In the proposed scheme, we replace standard cells in the netlist with polymorphic gates whose either modes of operation maintain the correct functionality of the circuit. As shown in Fig. 2, by embedding such polymorphic gates, we can generate fingerprinted copies of the original circuits, where the configuration of each polymorphic gate represents one fingerprint bit.

3.2.1 SDC-based fingerprint

We derive the following principles when determining the potential locations for gate replacement.

P1. Only the gates which have the same logic as either modes of polymorphic gates can be potential locations for replacements. For example, if we want to replace standard cells with evolved AND/OR gate, we should only target the 2-input AND gates and 2-input OR gates.

P2. The SDC conditions of potential replacement locations which we aim to find should be the Differentiating Input Value of the polymorphic gates.

Differentiating Input Values (DIV) of a polymorphic gate are the input combinations for which the polymorphic gate produces different output when the control signal changes. For example, input combinations (1,0) and (0,1) are DIVs of the AND/OR gate in Fig. 1. The output of this gate reverses from 0 to 1 as the control signal changes from '1' to '0' when the two inputs are set as '1' and '0', respectively.

After these gates with such SDC conditions are replaced by polymorphic gates, the functionality of the original circuit remains unchanged no matter which configuration the embedded polymorphic gates take. This satisfies the consistency requirement. We assign a binary value to the control input of each polymorphic gates (e.g. the input *c* in Fig. 1) which serves as a one-bit fingerprint. By replacing *p* standard cells with polymorphic gates, we can obtain 2^p distinct fingerprints meeting the uniqueness requirement. In this scheme, we make this type of replacement with the first three polymorphic gates in Table 2. These gates deliver different outputs with only one input combination (1,0). We need to find the standard library gates with one SDC-condition (1,0), which is more likely to appear than the gates with two SDC conditions, (1,0) and (0,1) if we consider introducing NAND/NOR and AND/OR into the original design.

3.2.2 Adding 'dummy' fingerprinting.

Besides the gates with SDC conditions leading in, we also make some additional replacements for those gates without SDC conditions. To ensure the consistency of the circuit function after modification, the additionally inserted polymorphic gates should be configured to the same logic as the original cells. We take the function control input of these gates as the 'dummy' fingerprint bits as their values are constant and cannot be used for identification purposes. Any attempt to modify the dummy fingerprints will cause incorrect function of the circuit. Therefore, the robustness of the fingerprinted circuits against attacks can be enhanced. In this paper we add dummy fingerprint by replacing two-input logic gates with NAND/NOR and AND/OR gate.

The design flow to embed fingerprints is summarized in Fig. 3. After the locations for replacement are determined, we connect the function control inputs of polymorphic gates to the power supply or ground to configure the functions. Thus, the fingerprint values can be embedded in the circuit at the layout design phase. After the fingerprinted copies of the original circuit are fabricated, we can detect the embedded fingerprints by opening up the chip and identifying the configuration type of the polymorphic gates at each location to recover the corresponding bits in the fingerprints.

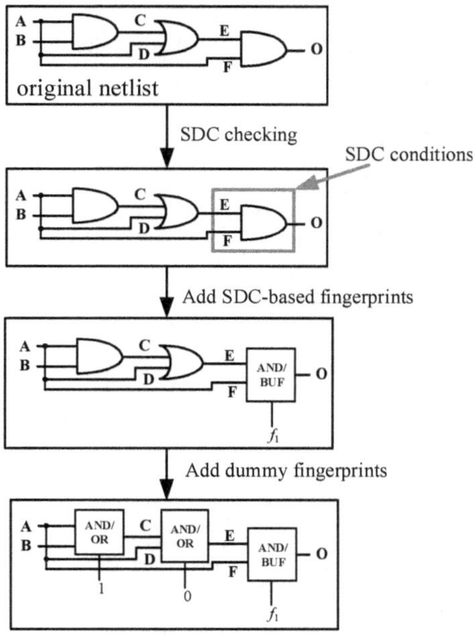

Figure 3: Design flow of the proposed scheme

3.3 Security Analysis

When a suspicious IP or circuit appears, the IP designer needs to recover the fingerprint to trace its source. Attackers who attempt to illegally build the circuit will try to alter the fingerprint to prevent it from being recovered. In this section, we will illustrate that our scheme is resilient against such adversaries and provides robust fingerprints in different attack scenarios.

3.3.1 Fingerprint modification.

Given a single copy of the fingerprinted circuit, the attacker can find the fingerprint locations by targeting the polymorphic gates. The attacker can modify the configuration of these polymorphic gates and change the fingerprint to one that has not been distributed by the vendor. However, this attack requires locating the dummy fingerprint bits as changing these bits would influence the function of the circuits. It is not feasible for the attackers to fully reverse engineer the netlist since the fingerprinted circuit is obfuscated with polymorphic gates. Therefore, the attacker cannot differentiate between the dummy and the real SDC-based fingerprint locations and this attack will become impractical.

3.3.2 Collision attack.

Collision attack is a powerful attack for all fingerprinting schemes where the attacker has access to multiple fingerprinted copies and can compare these copies to determine the fingerprint locations. More specifically, for our proposed scheme, the attacker may extract the fingerprints and compare their values corresponding to different gate locations. If there exists a certain location where the corresponding bit value differs in different copies, this location is a real SDC-based fingerprint location and can be modified. A countermeasure to thwart this attack would be encoding the fingerprint before applying it to the original circuit and checking the parity bits in the extracted fingerprint to help reveal any malicious modifications.

3.3.3 SAT-based attack

SAT-based attacks[18] are powerful adversaries for many logic encryption schemes. As the attacker obtains a gate-level netlist and a functional module of the circuit, he can use the correct input-output pairs to eliminate the wrong configurations of the embedded polymorphic gates for retaining dummy bits, recover the locations of dummy bits, and change them. To gain resilience against these attacks, we can combine schemes like SARLOCK[19], which compares inputs and fingerprint bits to generate a signal that flips the primary outputs. This modification will bring exponential complexity to retrieve the dummy bit locations.

4 SIMULATION VALIDATION AND EVALUATION

We selected several circuits in ISCAS 85 and MCNC benchmarks to perform overhead evaluation. The circuits are described in Verilog HDL and synthesized using 0.13um SMIC technology and the supply voltage is set as 1.2V. For simplicity, the RTL design is mapped to inverters and two-input/three-input/four-input NAND/NOR/OR/AND gates. A program written in C checks all the SDC conditions and replaces the standard cells with the evolved polymorphic gates automatically. The timing and power of the polymorphic gates are measured using Hspice and their layout area are estimated based on the transistor parameters. With these measurements, we incorporate the polymorphic gates into the SMIC 0.13um synthesis library as standard cells. We collect the area, delay and power of the original netlists and the fingerprinted netlists using Synopsys Design Compiler.

The maximum size of fingerprints utilizing SDC conditions and dummy fingerprint locations is listed in Table 3. For most benchmark circuits there are enough number of locations to embed polymorphic gates for our fingerprinting scheme.We set fixed fingerprint width which equals to 16bit and 32bit, respectively and evaluate the overhead. For both cases, we also add dummy fingerprints of equal width. The synthesis results of the fingerprinted netlists are summarized in Table 4 and Table 5. When we add 16-bit real fingerprint and 16-bit dummy fingerprint, the average overhead in delay, area and power is approximately 2%, 3.5% and 4% respectively, which is tolerable; for most benchmarks, performance deterioration is less than 5%. The average overheads rise to 4%, 7% and 5% when we add 16 more bits both in the real fingerprints and dummy fingerprints. Note that in this case, we have 64-bit fingerprints. Compared to the only other similar approach in [17] where their fingerprints are 32 bits, our average overhead is about only half. In addition, the use of dummy fingerprints makes our scheme more robust.

Table 3: Maximum SDC-based and Dummy Fingerprint Size

Circuit	#Gates	#SDC-based fingerprint	#Dummy fingerprint
C880	290	42	114
C1355	424	69	64
C1908	396	52	106
C3540	943	116	124
C5315	1428	47	548
dalu	1228	52	398
des	3483	70	1712
ex5	609	155	64
i8	1174	208	267
i10	1914	134	509

Table 4: Overhead with 16-bit Real Fingerprint and 16-bit Dummy Fingerprint

Circuit	Δdelay(%)	Δarea(%)	Δpower(%)
C880	1.08	8.11	8.16
C1355	5.72	5.9	7.23
C1908	5.1	6.31	4.13
C3540	0.55	3	2.78
C5315	0	1.645	1.93
dalu	2.38	2.56	2.26
des	4.59	0.77	0.50
ex5	0	3.54	13.05
i8	0	1.845	1.79
i10	0.74	1.205	0.77
avg	2.02	3.485	4.26

Table 5: Overhead with 32-bit Real Fingerprint and 32-bit Dummy Fingerprint

Circuit	Δdelay(%)	Δarea(%)	Δpower(%)
C880	1.08	16.31	11.90
C1355	11.74	12.275	8.02
C1908	7.05	13.17	5.09
C3540	1.11	5.835	4.72
C5315	6.8	3.355	2.05
dalu	5.71	4.77	2.49
des	4.59	1.455	0.55
ex5	1.65	6.485	13.26
i8	0	3.635	2.29
i10	0.74	2.4	0.98
avg	4.04	6.97	5.14

5 CONCLUSION

In this paper, we proposed a circuit fingerprinting scheme to resist IP overbuilding and piracy. The proposed scheme utilizes the SDC conditions and make replacements with the polymorphic gates whose functions are controlled by specific inputs into the gate-level netlist. Experiment results demonstrate that our scheme brings low overhead in performance, area and power. One important direction for future work would be investigating the implementation of evolved polymorphic gates and our proposed technique in fabricating real-life circuits.

ACKNOWLEDGMENTS

Omid Aramoon and Gang Qu were supported in part by the National Science Foundation under grant CNS1745466 and by a research agreement between the University of Maryland and the Laboratory for Physical Sciences.

REFERENCES

[1] A. Stoica, R. Zebulum, D. Keymeulen. Polymorphic electronics. *International Conference on Evolvable Systems.* Springer Berlin Heidelberg, 291-302, 2001.

[2] A. Stoica, R. Zebulum, X. Guo, D. Keymeulen, M.I.Ferguson & V.Duong. Taking evolutionary circuit design from experimentation to implementation: Some useful techniques and a silicon demonstration. *IEE Proceedings Computers and Digital Techniques,* 151(4), 295-300, 2004.

[3] L. Sekanina. Evolutionary design of gate-level polymorphic digital circuits. *Workshops on Applications of Evolutionary Computation.* Springer Berlin Heidelberg, 185-194, 2005.

[4] R. Ruzicka. On bifunctional polymorphic gates controlled by a special signal. *WSEAS Transactions on Circuits,* 7(3), 96-101, 2008.

[5] L. Sekanina. Design methods for polymorphic digital circuits. In *Proceedings of the 8th IEEE Design and Diagnostics of Electronic Circuits and Systems* (DDECS), 2005.

[6] W. Luo, Z. Zhang, X. Wang. Designing polymorphic circuits with polymorphic gates: a general design approach. *IET Circuits, Devices & Systems,* 1(6), 470-476, 2007.

[7] L. Sekanina, R. Ruzicka, Z. Vasicek, R. Prokop & L. Fujcik. Repomo32-new reconfigurable polymorphic integrated circuit for adaptive hardware. *IEEE Workshop on Evolvable and Adaptive Hardware,* 2009.

[8] L. Sekanina, L. Starecek, Z. Gajda, Z. Kotasek. Evolution of multifunctional combinational modules controlled by the power supply voltage. In *Proceeding of the 1st NASA/ESA Conference on Adaptive Hardware and Systems,* 86–193, 2006.

[9] L. Sekanina, R. Ruzicka, Z. Gajda. Polymorphic FIR filters with backup mode enabling power savings. *NASA/ESA Conference on Adaptive Hardware and Systems,* 2009.

[10] L. Sekanina, R. Ruzicka, R. Prokop. Physical demonstration of polymorphic self-checking circuits. *14th IEEE International On-Line Testing Symposium,* 2008.

[11] L. Sekanina, L. Starecek, Z. Kotasek, Z. Gajda. Polymorphic gates in design and test of digital circuits. *International Journal of Unconventional Computing,* 4(2), 125, 2008.

[12] L. Sekanina. Evolution of Polymorphic Self-Checking Circuits. In *Proceedings of the 7th Conference on Evolvable Systems: From Biology to Hardware,* 186–197, 2007.

[13] Y. Bi, K Shamsi, J.S. Yuan, P. E. Gaillardon, G.D. Micheli, X. Yin.Emerging technology-based design of primitives for hardware security. *ACM Journal on Emerging Technologies in Computing Systems,* 13(1), 2016

[14] R. Richard and T. Radek. Let's move polymorphism downwards: On the multifunctional logic based on ambipolar behaviour of semiconductor devices. *2016 International Conference on Design and Technology of Integrated Systems in Nanoscale Era* (DTIS), 2016.

[15] J.F. Miller, J. Dominic and K.V. Vesselin. Principles in the evolutionary design of digital circuits—Part I. *Genetic programming and evolvable machines,* 1(1-2), 7-35, 2000.

[16] J.H.Holland. Adaptation in natural and artificial systems: an introductory analysis with applications to biology, control, and artificial intelligence. MIT press, 1992.

[17] C. DunBar, G. Qu. Satisfiability don't care condition based circuit fingerprinting techniques. 2015 *20th Asia and South Pacific Design Automation Conference* (ASP-DAC), IEEE, 815-820, 2015.

[18] P. Subramanyan, S. Ray, and S. Malik. Evaluatingthe Security of Logic Encryption Algorithms. *IEEE International Symposium on Hardware Oriented Security and Trust,* 137–143, 2015.

[19] M. Yasin, B. Mazumdar, J. J. Rajendran, and O. Sinanoglu. SARlock: SAT Attack Resistant Logic Locking. *IEEE International Symposium on Hardware Oriented Security and Trust,* 236–241, 2016.

[20] G. Qu and M. Potkonja, Fingerprinting intellectual property using constraint-addition. *Proceedings of the 37th annual design automation conference,* 587-592, 2000.

[21] T. Wang, X. Cui, D. Yu, O.Aramoon, T.Dunlap, G. Qu, et al. Polymorphic gate based IC watermarking techniques. *Asia and South Pacific Design Automation Conference,* 90-96, 2018.

Cross-Lock: Dense Layout-Level Interconnect Locking using Cross-bar Architectures

Kaveh Shamsi[1], Meng Li[2], David Z. Pan[2], and Yier Jin[1]
[1]ECE Department, University of Florida, Gainesville, FL, USA
[2]ECE Department, University of Texas at Austin, Austin, TX, USA
kshamsi@ufl.edu, {meng_li, dpan}@utexas.edu, yier.jin@ece.ufl.edu

ABSTRACT

Logic locking is an attractive defense against a series of hardware security threats. However, oracle guided attacks based on advanced Boolean reasoning engines such as SAT, ATPG and model-checking have made it difficult to securely lock chips with low overhead. While the majority of existing locking schemes focus on gate-level locking, in this paper we present a layout-inclusive interconnect locking scheme based on cross-bars of metal-to-metal programmable-via devices. We demonstrate how this enables configuring a large obfuscation key with a small number of physical key wires contributing to zero to little substrate area overhead. Dense interconnect locking based on these circuit level primitives shows orders of magnitude better SAT attack resiliency compared to an XOR/XNOR gate-insertion locking with the same key length which has a much higher overhead.

CCS CONCEPTS

• **Security and privacy → Tamper-proof and tamper-resistant designs; Hardware reverse engineering;**

KEYWORDS

Logic Obfuscation; Hardware Security; Logic Locking; SAT Attacks

ACM Reference Format:

Kaveh Shamsi, Meng Li, David Z. Pan, and Yier Jin. 2018. Cross-Lock: Dense Layout-Level Interconnect Locking using Cross-bar Architectures. In *GLSVLSI '18: 2018 Great Lakes Symposium on VLSI, May 16–18, 2018, Chicago, IL, USA.* ACM, New York, NY, USA, 6 pages. https://doi.org/10.1145/3194554.3194580

1 INTRODUCTION

Logic locking and integrated circuit (IC) camouflaging are two closely related techniques for hiding the design of an integrated circuit. These techniques will make it difficult for an attacker to recover the original netlist of the design. This in turn can hinder various attacks such as reverse-engineering, intellectual property (IP) theft, and malicious modification of the design. Recent reports suggest that IP theft is on the rise and concerns about design integrity through the global IC supply chain remain strong [16]. Hence, logic locking and camouflaging if made secure with low overhead can alleviate great concerns in the semiconductor industry.

GLSVLSI '18, May 16–18, 2018, Chicago, IL, USA

ACM ISBN 978-1-4503-5724-1/18/05...$15.00
https://doi.org/10.1145/3194554.3194580

Logic locking is based on inserting additional "key inputs" into the circuit so that the circuit produces incorrect outputs for incorrect keys. The key bits are programmed post-fabrication by a trusted entity hiding the original design from the foundry as well as end-users. IC camouflaging is based on using layout constructs and special fabrication technologies to hinder reverse-engineering. In camouflaging, while the foundry knows the true functionality, it is difficult for an end-user attacker to obtain an accurate netlist of the camouflaged layout through IC delayering and imaging [24].

The security of a locking/camouflaging scheme versus the overhead that it incurs to the design is the primary metric of evaluation. The security of the protection scheme heavily relies on the considered threat model. The "oracle-guided" threat model which is widely used, allows the attacker to make arbitrary input-output queries on a functional/unlocked oracle-circuit. Several attacks are possible under this threat model, the strongest being the notorious SAT [5, 21] attack that uses SAT queries to construct and solve a system of input-output equations to find the correct functionality of the obfuscated netlist.

Several "SAT-resilient" locking/camouflaging schemes [10, 25, 27–29, 31, 32] have been proposed based on inserting large gate-level tree-structures that increase exponentially the minimum number of queries required for the attack. Unfortunately these schemes cannot satisfy entropy criteria due to a fundamental contention between entropy and minimum query count. Hence, they are vulnerable to approximate attacks such as AppSAT [17] and DDIP [19]. In addition they can be vulnerable to removal attacks [30] due to the fixed structure of the inserted trees.

In IC camouflaging it is possible to "flood" the design layout with a prohibitively large number of dummy elements inserted in the abundant empty spaces in the layout [2]. These approaches show a high resiliency against SAT attacks [13] simply by creating very large SAT instances that overwhelm the SAT-solver. These approaches can overcome the fundamental error versus resiliency contention, as they result in complex SAT instances rather than exponentially large minimum query counts. These layout-level approaches however, have not been applied to logic locking. This is primarily due to the key-bit programming circuitry needed for logic locking which not only incurs additional overhead, but also reveals the location of the ambiguous circuit elements, narrowing the search for the attacker. This hinders large-scale layout-level logic locking. As a result, the majority of existing logic locking schemes are forced to insert large gate-level primitives without the ability to exploit special transistor structures.

In this paper however, we start with the design of transistor-level primitives, in particular key bit programming architectures and then build netlist-level routines upon the primitive. We present a layout-inclusive locking scheme based on cross-bar programmable interconnect architectures. We demonstrate how using cross-bar circuit architectures a large number of key elements can be programmed sequentially with a much smaller number of physical key wires. We show that without adding a single gate to the design, just by densely obfuscating interconnects, small circuits can withstand advanced SAT attacks orders of magnitude longer than state-of-art gate-insertion strategies.

The paper makes the following contributions:

- We study various programmable device technologies in terms of attack resiliency and footprint. We focus on metal-to-metal programmable vias and define a general layout-level locking scheme based on these devices with minimal programming structures.
- We analyze the functional level security of the proposed interconnect locking scheme based on these primitives, demonstrating how densely cyclic interconnect locking can result in hard SAT instances for the attack.
- We demonstrate a custom design flow for inserting cross-bar primitives in the layout using a 32/28nm technology library and report design metrics which shows overhead values orders of magnitude better than gate-insertion strategies.

The paper is organized as follows: Section 2 provides a brief background. Section 3 discusses circuit-level locking primitives, and Section 4 discusses netlist-level routines. Section 5 presents experiments and Section 6 concludes the paper.

2 BACKGROUND

Oracle-guided attacks: In studying locking/camouflaging it is a basic assumption that the attacker is able to recover the netlist of the locked/camouflaged IC. Any locked/camouflaged netlist contains a number of ambiguous elements from the attacker's view. These ambiguous parts can be encoded using "key" variables over which a space of possible functions for the netlist is defined. The original circuit is $c_o : I \rightarrow O, I = \mathbb{F}_2^n, O = \mathbb{F}_2^m$ and the locked/camouflaged function is $c_e : I \times K \rightarrow O$ with $K = \mathbb{F}_2^l$. The function space $C = \{c_e(i,k) | k \in K\}$ is defined and $\exists k_* \in K_*$ s.t. $\forall i \in I \ c_e(i,k_*) = c_o(i)$.

Oracle-guided attacks assume input-output access to c_o. The baseline SAT attack [5] starts by finding an input pattern that can distinguish between different keys, namely a discriminating input pattern (DIP), by solving the mitter SAT problem $M \equiv (c_e(i,k_1) \neq c_e(i,k_2))$ with $\hat{i}$, $\hat{k_1}$, and $\hat{k_2}$. It then queries the DIP $\hat{i}$ on the oracle: $\hat{y} = c_o(\hat{i})$, and adds the input-output pair to the SAT problem, $M \leftarrow M \wedge (c_e(\hat{i},k) = \hat{y})$. It terminates once M is not satisfiable, i.e. no more DIPs can be found. At this point any key that satisfies all DIP-output observations is the correct key.

The CycSAT Attacks: While oracle-guided attacks based on solving systems of equations in key variables are generally applicable to any keyed Boolean function (including stateful circuits using model-checking [12]), the baseline SAT attack is only applicable to acyclic combinational circuits. Shamsi et al. [18] proposed using cyclic interconnect obfuscation to thwart the attack. However, Zhou et al. [33] developed an algorithm called CycSAT to add a condition to the mitter M so that the solver avoids cyclic solution breaking cyclic obfuscated circuits. We use the structural CycSAT algorithm as our main attack in this paper.

3 CIRCUIT-LEVEL PRIMITIVES

3.1 Key Storage Element

All locking/camouflaging schemes are built upon a specific physical element that creates ambiguity for the attacker. The security of any netlist/chip-level scheme heavily relies on the security of this physical primitive. For IC camouflaging the main criteria for the element is that it should resist physical IC reverse-engineering procedures while allowing the foundry to resolve and fabricate it. One example for such primitives is vias that have a middle-gap [14] which falsely appear to be connecting two metal layers. Another is Mg-based [1] vias, which when exposed to oxygen during reverse-engineering, all transform into MgO insulating vias hindering the recovery of an accurate netlist.

In logic locking, the physical primitive in addition to being resilient to physical reverse-engineering, should be programmable post-fabrication resulting in fewer options. The size of the device and the programming and read circuitry become important metrics. We study several technologies with respect to these criteria herein.

The first category for logic locking primitives is CMOS based volatile memory elements such as SRAM cells, and D-flip-flops which are all based on the cross-coupled inverter pair. These can store bits as voltage levels on internal wires. In terms of security, since voltage levels are difficult to read on a large scale in advanced technology nodes, these primitives are acceptable[1]. In terms of cell area, the smallest storage unit which is the SRAM cell requires 6 transistors. In terms of programming circuitry while DFFs can be chained together for serial programming of key bits, SRAM cells require memory architectures for programming. The volatility of these elements is problematic as well, since the key must be stored on an external tamper-proof nonvolatile memory and transferred to the device which introduces its own security risks[2].

Embedded Nonvolatile Memory (NVM) technologies such as Flash, EEPROM, Resistive-RAM (RRAM), and Spin-based NVMs that use Magnetic-Tunneling Junctions (MTJs) can be used to store key bits as well. In terms of security, Flash and EEPROMs can be read out with special laborious chip reverse-engineering procedures at small scale [4]. The magnetic polarity of spin-based memory elements such as MTJs can be read with Magnetic Force Microscopy (MFM) with sub-micron resolution on a small scale [7]. RRAM cells are particularly difficult to read under scanning electron microscopy [26]. In terms of area, EEPROM and Flash have 1~2 transistors in their footprint, whereas RRAM cells and MTJs are placed on the metal layers with no substrate area and can be as small as $1F^2$. EEPROM and Flash require CMOS read-out circuits to convert internal charge to digital level voltage. Similarly MTJs require a sense-amplifier to convert the small resistance difference to a logic level voltage. The sense-amplifier can have a minimum of 6 transistors. RRAM cells however, can have very high R_{on}/R_{off}

[1]Non-conventional approaches exist for limited voltage level read-out on integrated circuits [11]. Most are based on pointing a laser beam at the chip and analyzing the variations on the reflected beam that are caused by the electric field between two lines with opposite voltages. A recent study [11] used backside laser imaging which allowed distinguishing between an oscillating signal and a static one on a 60nm FPGA device. Note that if the attacker is able to read voltage levels at a large scale, secure hardware locking/camouflaging is most likely impossible at least with reasonable overhead.

[2]It is possible to overcome the volatility by using CMOS *aging* mechanisms to create bias in the memory element so that it always starts up in the forced state [9]. This comes at the cost of additional aging circuitry.

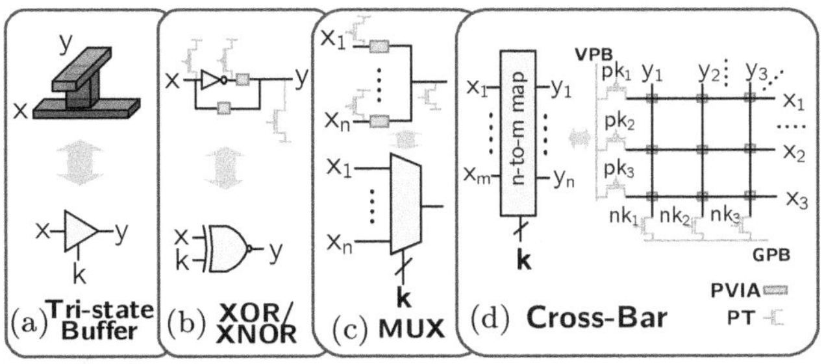

Figure 1: Various PVIA-based locking primtives.

ratios, which allows them to be directly placed on the signal path [23] removing the need for translation circuitry.

The last category is one-time-programmable (OTP) elements such as OTP EPROM, fuse [6] and anti-fuse [3] technologies. These are best suited for logic locking since the locked circuit is typically not configured more than once. Among OTP technologies metal-to-metal anti-fuse devices [3] are particularly suited to interconnect locking. They are a mature technology used in FPGAs and PLAs based on metal-insulator-metal (MIM) structures that connect two adjacent metal layers. They start off in an insulating state and can be made conducting by applying voltage to the two ends. They have a footprint similar to that of conventional vias, and are reasonably secure against invasive attacks [3]. We base our schemes in this paper on this technology, while we do note that any metal-to-metal configurable connector can be used as long as it is secure against invasive attacks, and has a small footprint. We refer to this element as a programmable via (PVIA) in the remainder of the paper.

3.2 PVIA Programming

PVIAs are programmed by applying a programming voltage for a known period of time to the two ends of the device. The specific voltage range for programming is dependent on the particular technology [3]. However, it must remain above the peak AC voltage and current that the element experiences during normal operation to avoid inadvertent programming. It also should be below the gate-oxide breakdown voltage of the logic transistors to avoid damaging them during programming. The power lines of the logic should be separate from the programming circuitry to avoid short circuits. The main approach for PVIA programming is connecting two complementary (NMOS and PMOS) programming transistors (PTs) to the two ends that connect the device terminals to programming supplies [26]. This way by configuring the two transistors and programming supplies, the cell can be programmed and then disconnected from the logic. The PTs can also be replaced with larger multi-level drivers to suppress sneak paths and provide protection.

The key idea that enables area saving is sharing PTs/drivers. If N PVIAs share one terminal they can share a single PT for that terminal. PVIA-based logic locking is any logic locking where the secret values are stored in the PVIAs. It is possible to construct a minimal programming network using this idea for arbitrarily inserted PVIAs in between a set of nets.

3.3 PVIA-based Locking Primitive

While it is possible to randomly insert a series of PVIAs in the netlist and construct a minimal programming structure for them, another strategy is to first use PVIAs to construct several primitives/modules and then perform the locking using these pre-designed primitives. These primitives can be evaluated in terms of their PVIA/PT ratio, sneak-paths and so on.

As seen from Figure 1 PVIAs can be used to implement an array of different locking primitives. Per Figure 1a, the single PVIA implements a tri-state buffer and needs two PTs. The XOR/XNOR gate which is heavily used in traditional logic locking, can be implemented with an inverter, two PVIAs and 3 PTs as seen in Figure 1b. Multiplexers (MUXs) are particularly suited to PVIA implementations. A single-level or multi-level tree can be used to implement an n-to-1 MUX as seen in Figure 1c[3].

The $n \times m$ cross-bar seen in Figure 1d shows the highest PVIA/PT ratio. nm PVIAs can be programmed with only $n + m$ PTs with a sequential write scheme where a horizontal line and a vertical line are connected to opposing voltages while other signals are left floating. If there is only one connected node in each column, the shortest sneak paths will have at least two PVIAs during programming. Otherwise, the non-active lines may need to be configured to a middle-voltage ($\frac{VPG}{2}$) with multi-level drivers. The sequence of configurations is also important in reducing the risk of inadvertent programming. This paper focuses on using cross-bar primitives for interconnect locking which we term *cross-lock*.

Note that the sharing of programming signals can be furthered using the *banking* technique used in memory array designs. Per Figure 1d, the nk_i and pk_i signals of N different cross-bars can be shared while replicating only the VPB and GPB signals N times and using them as arbitrators that select the active cross-bar.

4 NETLIST-LEVEL INTERCONNECT LOCKING

We can perform interconnect locking by inserting individual PVIAs or PVIA-based primitives in the netlist. Security against various attacks per the amount of overhead added to the design is the main criteria for netlist level locking which we discuss herein.

4.1 Security Against SAT Attacks

SAT attacks are the strongest oracle-guided attacks against combinational locking/camouflaging. The SAT attack and its variants are based on constructing and solving systems of input-output equations. The first natural approach towards thwarting these attacks, which includes the majority of the existing literature, is to increase the minimum number of queries (equations) required for the attack to succeed. The second which has seen little progress in literature, is making the SAT instances for querying and system-solving intractable. Due to the fundamental contention between query count and error rate, the only way to achieve a high error rate while maintaining attack resiliency is to ensure that the system of input-output observations cannot be solved efficiently even if it has very few equations (queries) in it.

To better understand SAT attack resiliency it is useful to look at similar problems across other domains. It has been noted in logic obfuscation literature that the SAT attack is related to the problem of active-learning [10] and the "query-by-disagreement probably-approximately-correct (PAC)" learning schemes [17]. While these relations are interesting, they cannot practically help advance SAT attack resiliency checking beyond what simple truth-table based analysis of Boolean functions provides us with.

[3]Note the difference between n tri-state buffers connecting n inputs to one output, and an n-to-1 MUX. In the former multiple inputs can be connected to the output while the latter is a one-hot connection.

A much more useful connection is to the domain of cryptography. A cryptographic function $f(x, k)$ is said to be Chosen-Plaintext-Attack (CPA)-secure, if k cannot be found from arbitrary queries of the form $(x_i, f(x_i, k))$. Researchers have been studying attacks against cryptographic functions for decades. A major category of attacks is *algebraic attacks* in which the main goal is to construct and solve a system of input-output equations to find the key. Algebraic attacks model deobfuscation attacks very closely, with the distinction that in practical algebraic attacks the system is typically pre-compiled and optimized whereas the SAT deobfuscation attack builds the system itself iteratively. Interestingly, in recent years SAT-solvers have become a promising tool for algebraic attacks against various block and stream ciphers [8].

While there are many aspects of this relation that we can exploited, here we focus on the "transition-phase" in the runtime behavior of SAT-based algebraic attacks[8], where SAT instances suddenly becomes intractable when the number of cipher rounds exceeds a certain limit, while fewer rounds are solved in a matter of minutes. In experimenting with interconnect locking we have observed a similar behavior where the SAT queries' search trees begin to explode as the obfuscated circuit graph gets closer to a complete-graph, even though the query count is low and the circuit is relatively small.

Hence we gear our netlist locking routines towards increasing the edge density of parts of the circuit using each cross-bar. These strategies are based on first finding the smallest candidate wire set W where $|W| > max(n, m)$ for each $n \times m$ cross-bar (n MUXs of size m where $m \geq n$). Then n wires are randomly selected from W and opened and routed through the cross-bar which occupies n inputs and n outputs of the cross-bar. Then the remaining $m - n$ cross-bar inputs are also selected from W and connected. The strategies that we implement for picking W include: a) *k-cut*: we search the circuit for a logic cone with k inputs and gradually increase k until a large enough set is found. b) *wire-cut*: we search for a cone with a sufficient number of wires by backward breadth-first-searches on each wire in the circuit. c) *diagonal*: we start exploring the wires in the distance d of each wire in the forward and backward directions while gradually growing d until a sufficiently large candidate set is found. Figure 2 shows an example of inserting a 3×3 cross-bar where $W = \{w_1, w_2, O\}$.

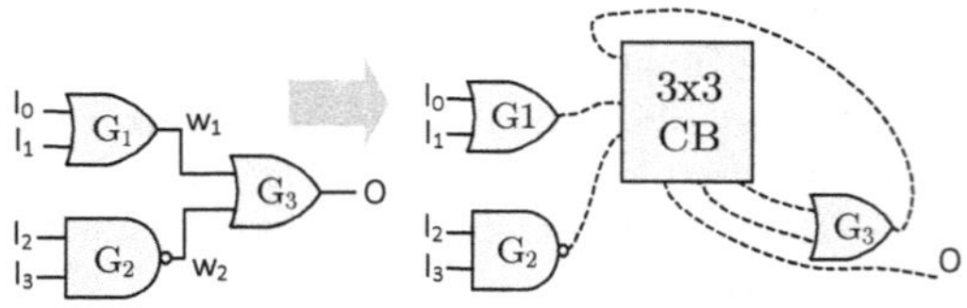

Figure 2: inserting a 3x3 cross-bar in a netlist.

4.2 Security Against Removal Attacks

Removal attacks or oracle-less attacks target special structures in the obfuscated netlist that can allow removing key possibilities without making queries. As for any MUX-based interconnect locking, we discuss two possible removal attacks. First is that if a key-controlled MUX output can reach one of its own inputs without interfering with any other key bit in the circuit, that MUX input can be removed if the assumption is that the original circuit is acyclic (removable backward edge [18]). We check for such edges using a simple readability search on the circuit graph starting from the output wires. We avoid creating such edges in cross-lock. Luckily few such edges arise when density driven selection strategies are used. Another possible removal attack is proximity based attacks that try to connect the given edge to the nearest location. These attacks can be thwarted by avoiding edges between distant nodes in the circuit which is ensured by the density driven selection strategies.

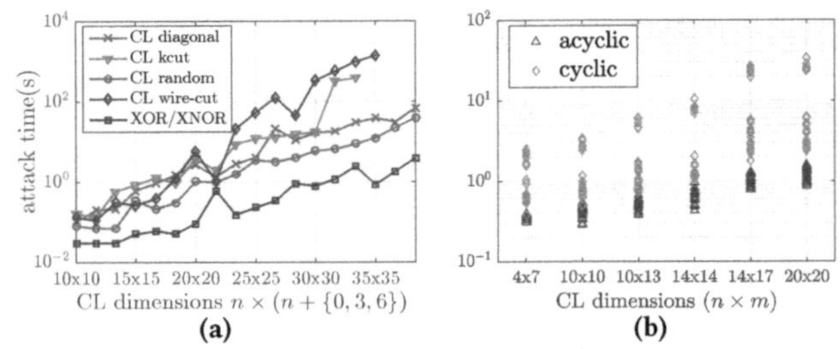

Figure 3: a) Different cross-lock insertion strategies and dimensions on the c432 benchmark circuit versus SAT attack runtime. b) Maximally acyclic versus maximally cyclic insertion attack run-times on random 8-input circuits.

5 EXPERIMENTS

5.1 Resiliency Testing

We first perform netlist-level resiliency tests. Netlist-level attacks and defenses are implemented in a C++ framework. The baseline SAT attack is the structural CycSAT attack with AppSAT intermediate key extraction and error characterization capabilities included, using MiniSat as the back-end SAT-solver. Tests were run on a server machine with 16 Intel Xeon E5 CPUs clocked at 2.6GHz, running linux with 128GB of memory.

CNF-SAT modeling: When deobfuscating an $n \times m$ cross-bar the attacker can model the cross-bar in several ways: a) with n m-input MUXs each of which implemented using a tree of 2-input MUXs and transformed to conjunctive-normal-form (CNF) formula. b) n m-input MUXs each implemented with AND/OR/INV gates. c) nm key-controlled tri-state buffers (TBUF). The CNF formula for a TBUF depicted in Figure 1a is $(\bar{k} + x + \bar{y})(\bar{k} + \bar{x} + y)$. Only the TBUF-based model implements the "subset-MUX" where any subset of m inputs can be connected to the output. When using the TBUF-based model it is important to include a *no-float* condition on the key to ensure that all TBUFs that control a node do not disconnect at the same time. If the TBUF-based model is used there will be a quadratic number of key-bits. Surprisingly, the SAT attack performs better with the much larger TBUF-based model versus MUX-based models. We suspect that this is related to the system of equations becoming "over-defined" [8]. We use TBUF models to favor the attacker in our experiments. We define the equivalent key-length of the cross-bar as its MUX-based model key-length $n\lceil\log_2(m)\rceil$ for comparison with other locking schemes such as random XOR/XNOR insertion [15].

Density versus Resiliency: Figure 3a shows the running time of the attack for one cross-bar inserted in the c432 benchmark which has 160 primitive gates with different insertion strategies. The attack was run 3 times on each netlist. With high error-rate schemes it is important to rerun the attack several times with different SAT-search seeds and report the shortest time. As can be seen from

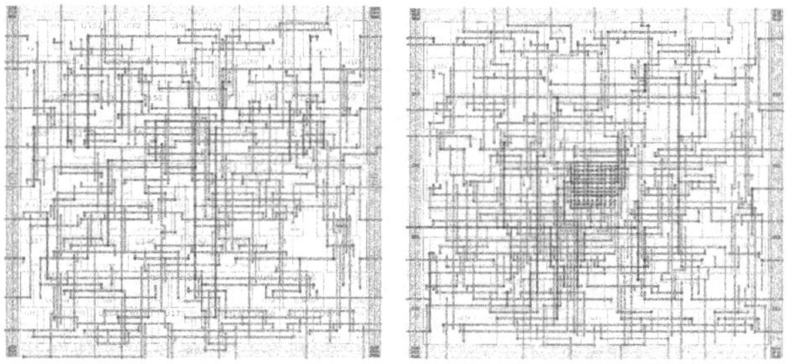

(a) (b)

Figure 4: c432 circuit. a) original layout. b) 10×10 **cross-bar inserted in the middle.**

edge-density		0.05		0.1		0.2		0.3		0.4	
#ins	#gates	#DI	t(s)	#DI	t(s)	#DI	t(s)	#DI	t(s)	#DI	t(s)
4	9.2	3.2	<0.0	5.0	<0.0	8.6	0.01	10.2	0.3	12.2	5.5
5	20.6	13.4	0.04	16.0	0.09	14.2	1895	3.8	44.3	TO	TO
6	39.1	20.6	1106	30.0	2697	TO	TO	TO	TO	TO	TO

Table 1: Runtime and query count average for random circuits versus edge density.

Figure 3a, the high density cone-based selection strategies, k-cut and wire-cut, surpass random cross-lock insertion by an order of magnitude exceeding the 1 hours deadline at smaller dimensions. Diagonal selection performs better than random selection, but is not as formidable as the cone-based strategies. This is while none of the circuits locked with random XOR/XNOR locking of the equivalent key-length resist the attack longer than 5s over various dimensions.

The relationship between density and SAT attack complexity becomes clearer when we try to create a complete-graph in the netlist. That is when every wire can be potentially connected to every other wire from the attacker's point of veiw. This is the case when a fully configurable interconnect similar to an FPGA is used. We generated 10 random circuits for small input widths by synthesizing random truth-tables using ABC [22]. We then began adding dummy edges to each netlist to achieve a certain graph density ($d = \frac{2|E|}{|E|(|E|-1)}$). As can be seen from Table 1 beyond a certain density a small circuit with 5-inputs cannot be resolved within the 3 hour deadline. This is an interesting result, since it takes less than a second for the SAT attack to resolve a 5-input look-up-table that implements all 2^{32} different 5-input Boolean functions! Hence, clearly a transition in the nature of the SAT problems is occurring as density increases. None of the existing logic locking schemes, even SAT-resilient schemes can last hours under the attack on a circuit with such a small number of inputs.

Cyclicness versus Resiliency: Another important question is whether cyclicness of the locked circuit improves resiliency. Figure 3b shows attack runtimes on 50 8-input random circuits with random cross-lock insertion with different dimensions when all added edges are forward edges, versus when most edges are feedback edges. This is done by topologically sorting the wires, and in the acyclic selection connecting wires late in the order to wires earlier in the order, while doing the opposite for the cyclic selection. It can be seen that cyclic insertion results in higher attack runtimes compared to acyclic locked circuits. The non-cyclic condition in the CycSAT attack can also result in a significant number of additional clauses for densely cyclic circuits.

bench	#g	#I/O	CL dim	eq-klen	XOR t(s)	CL t(s)
apex2	610	39/3	$2 \times 30 \times 36$	310	93.2	TO
apex4	5360	10/19	$11 \times 30 \times 36$	1706	1072	TO
c1355	546	41/32	$2 \times 30 \times 36$	310	3715	TO
c1908	880	33/25	$2 \times 30 \times 36$	310	624	TO
c2670	1193	157/64	$3 \times 30 \times 36$	465	TO	TO
c3540	1669	50/22	$4 \times 30 \times 36$	620	109	TO
c432	160	36/7	$1 \times 30 \times 36$	155	1.84	TO
c499	202	41/32	$1 \times 30 \times 36$	155	5.96	TO
c5315	2307	178/123	$5 \times 30 \times 36$	775	1011	TO
c7552	3512	206/107	$8 \times 30 \times 36$	1240	TO	TO
c880	386	60/26	$1 \times 30 \times 36$	155	0.82	TO
dalu	2298	75/16	$5 \times 30 \times 36$	775	308	TO
des	6473	256/245	$13 \times 30 \times 36$	2016	427	TO
i4	338	192/6	$1 \times 30 \times 36$	155	18.1	TO
i7	1315	199/67	$3 \times 30 \times 36$	465	7.08	TO
i8	2464	133/81	$5 \times 30 \times 36$	775	20.2	TO
seq	3519	41/35	$8 \times 30 \times 36$	1240	335	TO

Table 2: ISCAS and MCNC benchmark circuits locked with cross-lock and XOR/XNOR obfuscation under the CycSAT attack.

Benchmark Circuit Tests: We performed cross-lock on a set of ISCAS and MCNC benchmarks from [20] as seen in Table 2. We used one 30×36 cross-bar for every 500 gates in the circuit. Hence, the *des* benchmark ends up with 13 cross-bars inserted. Note that with banking, the final chip needs 30 + 36 + 13 physical wires to configure the 30.36.13 PVIAs sequentially for this benchmark. We used the equivalent key-length times the number of cross-bars for XOR/XNOR obfuscation. As can be seen from Table 2 none of the cross-locked netlist are deobfuscated within the 3 hour deadline, while almost all XOR/XNOR lockings were defeated with the exception of the c2670 benchmark which has an internal AND-tree and the c7552 which overwhelms the attack with 1240 XOR/XNOR key bits. As for AppSAT resiliency, both schemes go through a rapid drop in error value after a certain number of iterations. However, the densely locked circuits that resist the exact attack, do not reach this many iterations within the given deadline.

5.2 Physcial Design

We also performed a proof-of-concept physical design flow. The Synopsys generic 32/28nm library and design kit was used for synthesis and place-and-route. Synopsys Design-Compiler (DC) was used for synthesis and IC-Compiler (ICC) was used for place-and-route. We designed the PVIA cells in Custom-Designer between the M2 and M3 layers and added them to the design as physical-only cells. Existing EDA tools lack a standard flow for automatic best-possible placement and routing of a large number of PVIAs. Hence we manually insert the PVIAs in a grid and try to push standard cells away from under this PVIA grid and perform placement. Then the automatic routing was successful in routing the cross-bar with a grid-like network as seen in Figure 4 without DRC violations. If DRC violations occur the utilization rate can be lowered until they are resolved which was not needed for the single cross-bar layouts reported in Table 3.

For power and delay characterization since the locked circuits are cyclic and can create issues for power/delay calculation routines, we take the acyclic netlist and manually add the additional capacitance due to the PVIAs (chosen as 0.3ff which is half of the minimum inverter capacitance in our technology) and nets to the netlist and calculate power/delay which is reported in Table 3. We compare these results with post-route XOR/XNOR locking with

$n \times n$ CL	original			15					25					35				
circuit	a(μm^2)	p(μW)	d(ns)	aX	pX	pCL	dX	dCL	aX	pX	pCL	dX	dCL	aX	pX	pCL	dX	dCL
c432	176.9	12.9	1.2	172.7	102.2	3.2	91.9	0.0	288.6	209.1	6.7	120.3	5.7	421.1	308.2	34.1	135.0	39.0
c499	526.6	50.9	0.9	40.0	13.5	2.1	58.9	2.2	76.7	47.3	4.8	67.8	4.4	119.7	88.0	11.7	93.3	6.7
c880	390.1	27.1	1.2	62.1	24.4	1.3	47.9	0.0	125.9	75.9	11.3	74.4	3.4	197.9	154.6	7.0	81.2	6.0
c1355	541.6	60.3	0.9	46.6	13.8	0.6	114.8	2.3	97.1	26.1	4.0	137.5	4.5	152.4	56.6	7.7	225.0	6.8
c1908	499.4	47.6	1.3	59.0	8.0	0.3	65.4	0.0	110.8	43.0	10.1	81.1	2.4	165.3	81.0	12.5	103.9	3.1
c2670	664.6	48.7	1.4	49.4	10.7	1.7	37.1	0.0	95.3	43.7	3.2	60.1	0.0	135.0	74.3	22.3	90.9	0.0

Table 3: Place and route results. (a, p, d)X/CL: area, power and delay overhead percentage for XOR/XNOR / cross-lock.

the equivalent key-length. While cross-lock inserts no additional gates to the design it incurs overhead to the entire chip through the programming circuitry that is shared among several cross-bars. An XOR/XNOR locking also requires external key-programming circuitry which is typically a scan-chain of DFFs as long as the key-length not included in Table 3. A detailed comparison of these two key-programming approaches and multi-crossbar layouts is left for future work. However, it is clear that scan-chains will be much larger for such large key-lengths compared to a banked cross-lock implementation.

6 CONCLUSION

In this paper we presented a layout-level dense interconnect locking scheme based on cross-bar architectures that has the potential to create high error rate and SAT resiliency simultaneously while suppressing overhead with layout and circuit level techniques. Chip-level overhead analysis, programming architecture optimization, reliability analysis, and interconnect locking schemes with the highest algebraic complexity are important topics of future research.

ACKNOWLEDGEMENT

This work was partially supported by DARPA (FA8650-18-1-7822).

REFERENCES

[1] Shuai Chen, Junlin Chen, Domenic Forte, Jia Di, Mark Tehranipoor, and Lei Wang. 2015. Chip-level anti-reverse engineering using transformable interconnects. In *Proc. IEEE Int. Symp. on Defect and Fault Tolerance in VLSI and Nanotechnology Systems*. IEEE, 109–114.

[2] Ronald P Cocchi, James P Baukus, Lap Wai Chow, and B Jiangyun Wang. 2014. Circuit Camouflage Integration for Hardware IP Protection. In *Proc. IEEE/ACM Design Automation Conf.*

[3] Actel Corp. 2002. Design Security in Nonvolatile Flash and Antifuse FPGAs. (2002). Actel Corp. Technical Report on QuickLogic FPGAs, http://www.actel.com/documents/DesignSecurity_WP.pdf.

[4] Franck Courbon, Sergei Skorobogatov, and Christopher Woods. 2016. Reverse Engineering Flash EEPROM Memories Using Scanning Electron Microscopy. In *Int. Conf. on Smart Card Research and Advanced Applications*. Springer, 57–72.

[5] Mohamed El Massad, Siddharth Garg, and Mahesh V Tripunitara. 2015. Integrated Circuit (IC) Decamouflaging: Reverse Engineering Camouflaged ICs within Minutes.. In *Network and Distributed System Security Symposium (NDSS)*.

[6] Stephen E Greco. 2011. Integrated circuit fuse. (Nov. 8 2011). US Patent 8,053,862.

[7] Óscar Iglesias-Freire, Miriam Jaafar, Eider Berganza, and Agustina Asenjo. 2016. Customized MFM probes with high lateral resolution. *Beilstein journal of nanotechnology* 7 (2016), 1068.

[8] Philipp Jovanovic and Martin Kreuzer. 2010. Algebraic attacks using SAT-solvers. In *Conference on Symbolic Computation and Cryptography*. 7.

[9] Shahrzad Keshavarz and Daniel Holcomb. 2017. Threshold-based Obfuscated Keys with Quantifiable Security against Invasive Readout. *CoRR* abs/1708.07150 (2017). arXiv:1708.07150 http://arxiv.org/abs/1708.07150

[10] Meng Li, Kaveh Shamsi, Travis Meade, Zheng Zhao, Bei Yu, Yier Jin, and David Z. Pan. 2016. Provably Secure Camouflaging Strategy for IC Protection. In *Proc. Int. Conf. on Computer Aided Design*. 28:1–28:8.

[11] Heiko Lohrke, Shahin Tajik, Christian Boit, and Jean-Pierre Seifert. 2016. No Place to Hide: Contactless Probing of Secret Data on FPGAs. In *International Conference on Cryptographic Hardware and Embedded Systems*. Springer, 147–167.

[12] Mohamed El Massad, Siddharth Garg, and Mahesh Tripunitara. 2017. Reverse Engineering Camouflaged Sequential Integrated Circuits Without Scan Access. *CoRR* abs/1710.10474 (2017). arXiv:1710.10474 http://arxiv.org/abs/1710.10474

[13] Satwik Patnaik, Mohammed Ashraf, Johann Knechtel, and Ozgur Sinanoglu. 2017. Obfuscating the Interconnects: Low-Cost and Resilient Full-Chip Layout Camouflaging. *CoRR* abs/1711.05284 (2017). arXiv:1711.05284 http://arxiv.org/abs/1711.05284

[14] Jeyavijayan Rajendran, Michael Sam, Ozgur Sinanoglu, and Ramesh Karri. 2013. Security Analysis of Integrated Circuit Camouflaging. In *Proc. ACM Conf. on Computer & Communications Security*.

[15] J. A. Roy, F. Koushanfar, and I. L. Markov. 2008. EPIC: Ending Piracy of Integrated Circuits. In *Proc. Design, Automation and Test in Europe (DATE '08)*. 1069–1074.

[16] SEMI. 2012. IP Challenges for the Semiconductor Equipment and Materials Industry. (2012). [Online] http://www.semi.org/sites/semi.org/files/docs/2012_IP_White_Paper.pdf.

[17] Kaveh Shamsi, Meng Li, Travis Meade, Zheng Zhao, David Z. Pan, and Yier Jin. 2017. AppSAT: Approximately Deobfuscating Integrated Circuits. In *Proc. IEEE Int. Symp. on Hardware Oriented Security and Trust*. 46–51.

[18] Kaveh Shamsi, Meng Li, Travis Meade, Zheng Zhao, David Z. Pan, and Yier Jin. 2017. Cyclic Obfuscation for Creating SAT-Unresolvable Circuits. In *Proc. IEEE Great Lakes Symp. on VLSI*. 173–178.

[19] Yuanqi Shen and Hai Zhou. 2017. Double DIP: Re-Evaluating Security of Logic Encryption Algorithms. In *Proc. IEEE Great Lakes Symp. on VLSI*. ACM, 179–184.

[20] Pramod Subramanyan, Sayak Ray, and Sharad Malik. 2015. Evaluating the security of logic encryption algorithms. In *Proc. IEEE Int. Symp. on Hardware Oriented Security and Trust*. IEEE, 137–143.

[21] P. Subramanyan, N. Tsiskaridze, Wenchao Li, A. Gascon, Wei Yang Tan, A. Tiwari, N. Shankar, S.A. Seshia, and S. Malik. 2014. Reverse Engineering Digital Circuits Using Structural and Functional Analyses. 2, 1 (2014), 63–80.

[22] Berkeley Logic Synthesis and Verification Group. 2016. ABC a System for Sequential Synthesis and Verification. (2016). [Online] http://people.eecs.berkeley.edu/~alanmi/abc/.

[23] Xifan Tang, Pierre-Emmanuel Gaillardon, and Giovanni De Micheli. 2014. A high-performance low-power near-Vt RRAM-based FPGA. In *Field-Programmable Technology (FPT), 2014 International Conference on*. IEEE, 207–214.

[24] Randy Torrance and Dick James. 2009. The state-of-the-art in IC reverse engineering. In *Proc. Int. Conf. on Cryptographic Hardw. and Embed. Systems*. Springer, 363–381.

[25] Yang Xie and Ankur Srivastava. 2016. Mitigating sat attack on logic locking. In *Proc. Int. Conf. on Cryptographic Hardw. and Embed. Systems*. Springer, 127–146.

[26] Yufeng Xie, Xiaoyong Xue, Jianguo Yang, Yinyin Lin, Qingtian Zou, Ryan Huang, and Jingang Wu. 2016. A logic resistive memory chip for embedded key storage with physical security. *IEEE Trans. on Circuits and Systems II* 63, 4 (2016), 336–340.

[27] Xiaolin Xu, Bicky Shakya, Mark M Tehranipoor, and Domenic Forte. 2017. Novel Bypass Attack and BDD-based Tradeoff Analysis Against all Known Logic Locking Attacks. In *Proc. Int. Conf. on Cryptographic Hardw. and Embed. Systems*. 189–210.

[28] Muhammad Yasin, Bodhisatwa Mazumdar, Jeyavijayan Rajendran, and Ozgur Sinanoglu. 2016. SARLock: SAT Attack Resistant Logic Locking. In *Proc. IEEE Int. Symp. on Hardware Oriented Security and Trust*. 236–241.

[29] Muhammad Yasin, Bodhisatwa Mazumdar, Ozgur Sinanoglu, and Jeyavijayan Rajendran. 2016. Camoperturb: secure ic camouflaging for minterm protection. In *Proc. Int. Conf. on Computer Aided Design*. IEEE, 1–8.

[30] Muhammad Yasin, Bodhisatwa Mazumdar, Ozugr Sinanoglu, and Jeyavijayan Rajendran. 2017. Removal Attacks on Logic Locking and Camouflaging Techniques. Cryptology ePrint Archive, Report 2017/348. (2017). https://eprint.iacr.org/2017/348.

[31] Muhammad Yasin, Abhrajit Sengupta, M Ashraf, M Nabeel, J Rajendran, and Ozgur Sinanoglu. 2017. Provably-Secure Logic Locking: From Theory To Practice. In *Proc. ACM Conf. on Computer & Communications Security*. 1–1.

[32] Hai Zhou. 2017. A Humble Theory and Application for Logic Encryption. Cryptology ePrint Archive, Report 2017/696. (2017). https://eprint.iacr.org/2017/696.

[33] Hai Zhou, Ruifeng Jiang, and Shuyu Kong. 2017. CycSAT: SAT-Based Attack on Cyclic Logic Encryptions. (2017). Cryptology ePrint archive, Report 2017/626, [Online] https://eprint.iacr.org/2017/626.pdf.

SRCLock: SAT-Resistant Cyclic Logic Locking for Protecting the Hardware

Shervin Roshanisefat
George Mason University
sroshani@gmu.edu

Hadi Mardani Kamali
George Mason University
hmardani@gmu.edu

Avesta Sasan
George Mason University
asasan@gmu.edu

ABSTRACT

In this paper, we claim that cyclic obfuscation, when properly implemented, poses exponential complexity on SAT or CycSAT attack. The CycSAT, in order to generate the necessary cycle avoidance clauses, uses a pre-processing step. We show that this pre-processing step has to compose its cycle avoidance condition on all cycles in a netlist, otherwise, a missing cycle could trap the SAT solver in an infinite loop or force it to return an incorrect key. Then, we propose several techniques by which the number of cycles is exponentially increased with respect to the number of inserted feedbacks. We further illustrate that when the number of feedbacks is increased, the pre-processing step of CycSAT faces an exponential increase in complexity and runtime, preventing the correct composition of loop avoidance clauses in a reasonable time before invoking the SAT solver. On the other hand, if the pre-processing is not completed properly, the SAT solver will get stuck or return incorrect key. Hence, when the cyclic obfuscation in accordance to the conditions proposed in this paper is implemented, it would impose an exponential complexity with respect to the number of inserted feedback, even when the CycSAT solution is used.

ACM Reference Format:
Shervin Roshanisefat, Hadi Mardani Kamali, and Avesta Sasan. 2018. SRCLock: SAT-Resistant Cyclic Logic Locking for Protecting the Hardware. In *GLSVLSI '18: 2018 Great Lakes Symposium on VLSI, May 23–25, 2018, Chicago, IL, USA.* https://doi.org/10.1145/3194554.3194596

1 INTRODUCTION

The cost of building a new semiconductor fab was estimated to be \$5.0 billion in 2015, with large recurring maintenance costs [5][7], and sharply increases as technology migrates to smaller nodes. Due to the high cost of building, operating, managing, and maintaining state-of-the-art silicon manufacturing facilities, many major U.S. high-tech companies have been always fabless or went fabless in recent years (e.g., AMD, Broadcom, Marvell, Nvidia, Qualcomm, and Xilinx, to name a few). Thus, to reduce the fabrication cost, and for economic feasibility, most of the manufacturing and fabrication is pushed offshore [5]. However, many offshore fabrication facilities are considered to be untrusted, which has raised concern over potential attacks in the manufacturing supply chain, with an intimate knowledge of the fabrication process, the ability to modify and expand the design prior to production, and an unavoidable access to the fabricated chips during testing. Hence, fabrication in untrusted fabs has introduced multiple forms of security threats from supply chain including that of overproduction, Trojan insertion, Reverse Engineering, Intellectual Property (IP) theft, and counterfeiting [7].

To prevent the adversaries from such attacks, researchers have proposed various obfuscation methods for hiding and/or locking the functionality of an netlist. However, the validity and strength of logic obfuscation to defend an IP against adversaries in the manufacturing supply chain was seriously challenged as researchers demonstrated that the de-obfuscation attacks leveraging satisfiability (SAT) solvers [13][6] combined with Signal Probability Skew (SPS) attacks [16] could break the existing obfuscation schemes (both locking and camouflaging) in a relatively short time. Cyclic obfuscation [12] was another approach that was considered as a defense mechanism against SAT solvers. However, this technique was later broken by CycSAT attack [18]. The CycSAT added a pre-analysis step to the original SAT attack for detection and avoidance of cycles in the netlist during SAT attack. In this paper, we further investigate the CycSAT attack and illustrate its pre-processing step has to compose the cycle avoidance condition by traversing all cycles in a netlist. We illustrate that by having a small number of methodically constructed feedbacks in a netlist, an exponentially large number of simple and nested cycles could be generated in a netlist, and we propose two different techniques for building such behavior. Since a successful SAT attack on a cyclic circuit requires the avoidance clauses, and time it takes to generate such avoidance clauses has an exponential relation with the number of inserted feedbacks, the CycSAT attack faces exponential runtime at its processing step. Hence, when deploying the CycSAT, the complexity of the problem is not in the SAT solver step of the problem, but in its pre-processing step.

The rest of this paper is organized as follows. In section 2 we cover the background on logic obfuscation. Then in section 3 we elaborate on the limitation of CycSAT and our approach for breaking the CycSAT. In section 4 we introduce our techniques for building an exponential relation between the number of feedbacks and the number of created cycles in a circuit. We also introduce three mechanisms for building a cyclic Boolean function to further increase the complexity of CycSAT pre-processing step. Our experimental results are summarized in section 5. Section 6 concludes the paper.

2 BACKGROUND ON LOGIC OBFUSCATION AND SAT ATTACKS

Logic obfuscation is the process of hiding the functionality of an IP by building ambiguity or by implementing post manufacturing means of control and programmability into a netlist. Gate camouflaging and circuit locking are two of the widely explored obfuscation mechanisms [3][17][4] for this purpose. A camouflaged gate is a gate that after reverse engineering (by means of delayering and lithography) could be mapped to any member of a possible set of gates or may look like one logic gate (e.g., AND), however functionally perform as another (e.g., XOR). In locking solutions, the functionality of a circuit is locked using a number of key inputs such that only when a

GLSVLSI '18, May 23–25, 2018, Chicago, IL, USA

ACM ISBN 978-1-4503-5724-1/18/05...\$15.00
https://doi.org/10.1145/3194554.3194596

correct key is applied, the circuit resumes its expected functionality. Otherwise, the correct function is hidden among many of the 2^K (K being the number of keys) circuit possibilities. The claim raised by such obfuscation scheme was that to break the obfuscation, an adversary needs to try a large number of inputs and key combinations to extract the correct key, and the difficulty of this process increases exponentially as the number of keys and primary inputs increases. Hence, if enough gates are obfuscated, an adversary faces an unacceptably long time (claimed as years to decades) to break the obfuscation scheme. Note that the availability of scan chains (for DFT), allows an adversary to access combinational logic in each stage of a sequential circuit, load the desired input, execute the stage for one cycle, and readout the output.

The validity and strength of logic obfuscation to defend the IP against adversaries in the manufacturing supply chain was seriously challenged as researchers demonstrated that the satisfiability (SAT) solvers, when formulated according to Algorithm 1, could break the obfuscation (both locking and camouflaging) in a matter of minutes as opposed to the promised claim of years and decades [13][6]. As illustrated in algorithm 1, to employ a SAT attack, the obfuscated circuit is transformed into a circuit SAT problem, in which the SAT solver looks for an input value X for which the obfuscated circuit produces two different outputs for two different input keys. Such key is referred to as a *Discriminating Input* X_{DI}. Each time a new X_{DI} is found, the circuit SAT is updated to make sure that the next two keys that will be found in the next iteration of SAT solver invocation, produce the same output for all previously discovered X_{DI}. This is done by building a Discriminating Input Validation Circuit (DIVC) as illustrated in algorithm 1. When the SAT solver can no longer find a X_{DI}, the DIVC circuit contains a complete set of discriminating inputs. At this point, any key that satisfies the DIVC (by calling a SAT solver on this circuit) is the key to the obfuscated circuit [13][6].

Algorithm 1 SAT Attack on Obfuscated Circuits

1: $DIVC = 1;$
2: $SAT_{circut} = C(X, K_1, Y_1) \wedge C(X, K_2, Y_2) \wedge (Y_1 \neq Y_2);$
3: **while** $((X_{DI}, K_1, K_2) \leftarrow SAT_F(SAT_{circut}) = T)$ **do**
4: $\quad Y_f \leftarrow C_{BlackBox}(X_{DI});$
5: $\quad DIVC = DIVC \wedge C(X_{DI}, K_1, Y_f) \wedge C(X_{DI}, K_2, Y_f);$
6: $\quad SAT_{circut} = SAT_{circut} \wedge DIVC;$
7: $KeyGenCircuit = DIVC \wedge (K_1 = K_2)$
8: $Key \leftarrow SAT_F(KeyGenCircuit)$

This reevaluation redirected the attention of the researchers to find harder obfuscation schemes that are more resilient to SAT attacks. SARLock and Anti-SAT [15][14] obfuscation methods were proposed for this purpose, however further research proved that these obfuscation techniques are prone to a simple removal attack after identification of these blocks using Signal Probability Skew (SPS) attack [16], or identification of most key values using approximate SAT attacks [11], leaving the problem of finding a SAT and SPS resilient obfuscation still unresolved.

A different direction for obfuscating a netlist was proposed in [12] where by introducing feedbacks in the netlist, the netlist is no longer a Directed Acyclic Graph (DAG). In their approach each intentionally created cycle had more than one way to be opened, making such cycle irreducible by structural analysis, claiming that the existence of such cycle breaks the original SAT attack in [13][6]. This cyclic obfuscation was later broken with the introduction of CycSAT attack in [18]. In CycSAT attack, before invoking the SAT solver, the netlist is checked for key conditions that may result in the creation of cycles. This conditions are translated to a set of cycle avoidance clauses and are added to the list of clauses that represent the circuit SAT problem. The algorithm 2 illustrates the flow of utilizing the cycle avoidance-clauses in CycSAT attack.

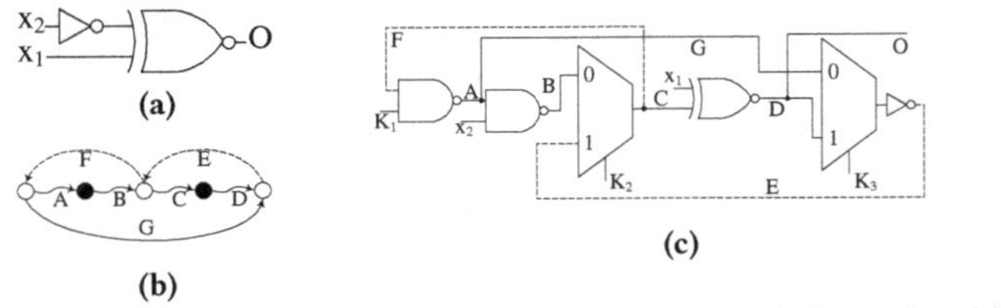

Figure 1: (a) Original circuit (b) Flow diagram of the netlist (c) Obfuscated circuit.

Algorithm 2 CycSAT Attack on Cyclic Obfuscated Circuits

1: Find a set of feedback signals $(w_0, w_1, \dots w_m)$;
2: Compute "no structural path" formulas $F(w_0, w_0'), \dots, F(w_m, w_m')$;
3: $NC(K) = \wedge_{i=0}^{m} F(w_i, w_i')$
4: $C(X, K, Y) = C(X, K, Y) \wedge NC(K)$
5: $SAT_{circut} = C(X, K_1, Y_1) \wedge C(X, K_2, Y_2) \wedge (Y_1 \neq Y_2);$
6: **while** $((X_{DI}, K_1, K_2) \leftarrow SAT_F(SAT_{circut}) = T)$ **do**
7: $\quad Y_f \leftarrow C_{BlackBox}(X_{DI});$
8: $\quad DIVC = DIVC \wedge C(X_{DI}, K_1, Y_f) \wedge C(X_{DI}, K_2, Y_f);$
9: $\quad SAT_{circut} = SAT_{circut} \wedge DIVC;$
10: $KeyGenCircuit = DIVC \wedge (K_1 = K_2)$
11: $Key \leftarrow SAT_F(KeyGenCircuit)$

In this algorithm $(w_0, w_1, \dots w_m)$ is a collection of feedback signals whose break will make the encrypted circuit acyclic and w_i' is a signal that feeds to w_i before the break. The function $F(w_i, j)$ is a function that construct the condition for "*having no structural path*" between signal w_i to signal j. The $F(w_i, j)$ is computed by starting from a feedback signal w_i and constructs a string of clauses that satisfy the following condition while traversing a cycle:

$$F(w_i, j) = \bigwedge_{l \in NK(j)} F(w_i, l) \vee bk(l, j) \tag{1}$$

In this function, the $NK(j)$ are the non-key inputs of signal j, and $bk(l, j)$ is the condition on key assuring key does not affect j. This function is initiated with condition $F(w_i, w_i) = 0$ and finishes after completing the loop. In this case, the condition for no structural path is tested on all discovered feedback signals in line 3 of the algorithm.

3 BREAKING CYCSAT

The computation for $F(w_i, j)$ could be done in two ways: (i) traversing through a cycle starting from w_i until w_i is visited again and ignoring the cycle break conditions imposed by fanins of other nested cycles; or (ii) traversing through one cycle and adding the cycle break conditions imposed by other nested cycle. We demonstrate that the first choice results in missing some NC conditions, leaving cycles in a design that could break the SAT solver, and by choosing the condition (2) we are forced to build the NC condition by visiting all cycles in the netlist.

Considering the obfuscated netlist in Fig. 1 and a topological sort from gate A, the edge E and F are identified as feedbacks. When following rule (i), and building the NC condition we will have:

1: $F(F, A) = F(F, F) \vee bk(k_1) = k_1'$
2: $F(F, F') = F(F, A) \vee bk(k_2) = k_1' \vee k_2$
3: $F(E, C) = F(E, E) \vee bk(k_2) = k_2'$
4: $F(E, E') = F(E, C) \vee bk(k_3) = k_2' \vee k_3'$
5: $NC = F(F, F') \wedge F(E, E') = (k_1' \vee k_2) \wedge (k_2' \vee k_3')$

The problem with this assignment is when $(k_1, k_2, k_3) = (0, 1, 0)$. In this case, the NC condition is satisfied, however, the larger nested cycle *EFGE* is not broken. Hence, the NC condition would not resolve the cycles if nested or multi-path scenarios exist. In this case, if the wrong key $(k_1, k_2, k_3) = (0, 1, 0)$ is chosen by SAT solver, it will enter a loop. Depending on whether the cycle is stateful or oscillating, the SAT solver will either be trapped in an infinite loop or will exit with an incorrect key assignment. Note that this infinite loop happens during the execution of the SAT solver and not during the topological sort used in the original SAT attack proposed in [13][6].

To avoid the problem imposed by rule (i), we need to follow the rule (ii) where the key contribution of all fanins in all stages are considered. When using rule (ii) for building the NC condition for the same circuit we have:

1: $F(F, A) = F(F, F) \vee bk(k_1) = k_1'$
2: $F(F, F') = (F(F, A) \vee bk(k_2)) \wedge (F(F, E) \vee bk(k_2)) = (k_1' \vee k_2) \wedge (k_1' \vee k_3 \vee k_2')$
3: $F(E, C) = F(E, E) \vee bk(k_2) = k_2'$
4: $F(E, E') = (F(E, C) \vee bk(k_3)) \wedge (F(E, G) \vee bk(k_3)) = (k_2' \vee k_3') \wedge (k_2' \vee k_1' \vee k_3)$
5: $NC = F(C, C') \wedge F(E, E') = (k_2' \vee k_3') \wedge (k_1' \vee k_2' \vee k_3) \wedge (k_1' \vee k_2)$.

By following rule (ii), the previous assignment of keys $(k_1, k_2, k_3) = (0, 1, 0)$ will no longer be a valid assignment, preventing the SAT solver from being stuck or suggesting a wrong key. However, in this case, *all cycles in the design have to be traversed and conditioned.* As a matter of fact, given the way the NC is formulated in [18], in order to derive the "no structural path" condition, some of the combinational cycles (such as *EFGE* in Fig. 1) have been visited more than once. Hence, the number of times the key conditions has to be generated is even larger than the number of cycles in a netlist.

The problem of visiting nested cycles more than once in a CycSAT attack could be resolved by a slight modification to the CycSAT pre-processing step. In the modified attack, instead of applying rule (ii) on one-cycle-per feedback, we could apply the rule (i) on all cycles. It is intuitive to see that both approaches produce the same NC clauses. For example, in Fig. 1 when following condition (i), and traversing cycle *EFGE*, the condition $(k_1' \vee k_2' \vee k_3)$ is generated. Hence, by ANDing the generated condition to the two clauses generated by applying the rule (i), the NC condition of rule (ii) is generated. However, in this case, the combinational cycle *EFGE* is only visited once. Even by considering the improvement suggested in CycSAT formulation, it still requires visiting all cycles in a netlist to compose the NC clauses. This necessity is used to break the CycSAT attack in this paper.

A different method of introducing complexity is by eliminating DAG nature of the original netlist and by transforming it into a Boolean cyclic function, which could be represented using a Directed Cyclic Graph (DCG), before subjecting it to cyclic obfuscation. If the original netlist is not a DAG, the CycSAT pre-processing step has to build the NC condition by checking for "*no sensitizable path*" condition [18], instead of "*no structural path*" condition. The no sensitizable path condition from [18] is recited in equation 2:

$$F(w_i, j) = \bigwedge_{l \in fanin(j)} F(w_i, l) \vee ns(l, j) \tag{2}$$

The "no sensitizable path" condition generates a clause for each multi-input gate in a cycle. As the result, NC clauses are much longer and much weaker. Hence, adding even a small number of feedbacks to such circuits (that have valid Boolean cycles) for the purpose of obfuscation, will significantly increase the size of the circuitSAT problem. To illustrate the weaker and longer nature of the NC clauses, the no "sensitizable path condition" for the circuit in Fig. 1 is constructed below:

1: $F(F, A) = F(F, F) \vee ns(F, A) = k_1'$
2: $F(F, B) = F(F, A) \vee ns(A, B) = k_1' \vee x_2'$
3: $F(F, F') = (F(F, B) \vee ns(B, F')) \wedge (F(F, E) \vee ns(E, F')) = (k_1' \vee x_2' \vee k_2) \wedge (k_1' \vee k_3 \vee k_2')$
4: $F(E, C) = F(E, E) \vee ns(E, C) = k_2'$
5: $F(E, D) = F(E, C) \vee ns(C, D) = k_2'$
6: $F(E, E') = (F(E, D) \vee ns(D, E')) \wedge (F(E, G) \vee ns(G, E')) = (k_2' \vee k_3') \wedge (k_2' \vee k_1' \vee x_2' \vee k_3)$
7: $NC = F(F, F') \wedge F(E, E') = (k_1' \vee x_2' \vee k_2) \wedge (k_1' \vee k_3 \vee k_2') \wedge (k_2' \vee k_3') \wedge (k_2' \vee k_1' \vee x_2' \vee k_3)$

The CycSAT pre-processing time, as illustrated in equation 3, is linearly related to the number of discovered cycles N and the time for composing the NC condition per cycle t_{NC}. Our approach for breaking the CycSAT is to exponentially increase the time needed for composing the NC condition in the pre-processing step of CycSAT beyond acceptable. This is achieved by exponentially increasing the number of cycles N in a design with respect to the number of inserted feedbacks m, and increasing the time required for processing each cycle (t_{NC}) by forcing the pre-processing step to consider the "no sensitizable path" condition instead of " no structural path" condition.

$$T_{NC} = \sum_{i=1}^{N} t_{NC} \mid N = Ae^m \tag{3}$$

In the next section we propose two methods for building an exponential relation between the number of cycles in a netlist with the number of inserted feedbacks and subsequently introduce three techniques for transforming a netlist to contain cyclic Boolean functions which forces an attacker to use the "no sensitizable path" condition in CycSAT attack.

4 CYCLIC OBFUSCATION

4.1 Exponentially increasing the number of cycles in a netlist

In order to exponentially increase the number of cycles in a given netlist with respect to the number of inserted feedbacks, we introduce two approaches: (1) building Super Cycles (SC) and, (2) building Logarithmic Feedback Networks (LFN).

4.1.1 *Building Super Cycles (SC).*

The process of building a SC is illustrated in Fig. 2. To define and build a SC, let us first define a Micro Cycle (MC). A MC is a cycle created by following the cycle creation conditions adopted from [12], which are recited below:

MC Condition 1: Any created cycle has to be non-reducible
MC Condition 2: At least $n \geq 2$ edges in each small cycle have to be removable

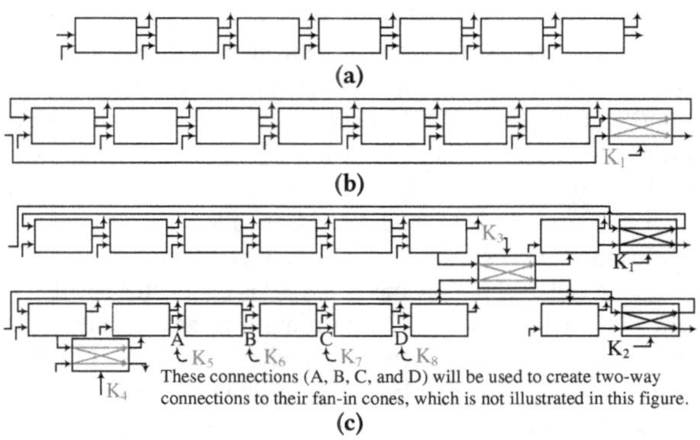

Figure 2: Building a Super Cycle from 7 gate MC. (a) A path segment containing 7 gates, (b) building a Micro Cycle, (c) building a SC by strongly connecting multiple MCs.

A reducible cycle has a single entry point. Hence, the depth-first-search (DFS) traversal of a netlist, that only contain reducible cycles is unique allowing reducible cycles to be opened by removing a unique set of edges which can be found efficiently [12]. By having multiple entries into each MC, the non-reducable condition is satisfied. Combined with having more than one removable edge, this forces an adversary to use the CycSAT pre-processing step to generate the necessary cycle avoidance clauses before invoking the SAT solver. At this point, when each MC is considered as a graph vertice, a SC is the strongly connected graph of these vertices. In graph theory, a strongly connected graph is defined as a graph with at least one path between any two pairs of its vertices. Finally in the last step, the edge density of the SC is increased, creating additional paths between MCs. The process of building a SC is captured in algorithm 3.

Algorithm 3 Steps for building a Super Cycle

1: Construct MCs in the fanin of smallest possible number of primary outputs.
2: Strongly connect all MC cycles (this is illustrated in Fig. 2.b is done by creating a two-way connection between each newly created MC, and the existing SC).
3: Select signals in MCs (A, B, C, D in Fig. 2.c) that are not used for SC connectivity and provide a two way path from them to unused edges in other MCs or random signals in their fanin cone.

By forcing the MC cycles to the fanin of the smallest number of primary outputs, we increase the possibility of shared edges or connecting edges between created MCs. By having all MC cycles strongly connected, we create the possibility of larger combinational cycles. And finally, adding the random connections increase the density of the edges in the strongly connected graph, increasing the number of resulting cycles. In the result section, we illustrate that the number of created cycles, by following the steps in algorithm 3 has an exponential relation with the number of inserted feedbacks.

4.1.2 ***Building Logarithmic Feedback Networks (LFN).*** In this method, as illustrated in Fig. 3.a, several path segments in the fanin cone of the same primary output are selected. By breaking a signal in the midpoint of each path, two path segments are created. The signal entering and the signal exiting each half segment is marked as its start point (SP) and end point (EP) respectively. Then the SP and EP of multiple such path segments are used to build a logarithmic switching network (e.g., Omega, Butterfly, Benes, or Banyan network). When connecting M EPs to M SPs we need $M(1 + log_2(M))$ muxes for a non-blocking logarithmic network. In this case, when the correct key is applied, the switching network is configured correctly, otherwise, an invalid connectivity obfuscates the netlist functionality.

Lemma. *The lower bound on the number of cycles created when using LFN is $\sum_{l=1}^{m}\binom{m}{l}(l-1)!$, when m is the number of inserted feedbacks and l is the log base two of the number of cycles of size l.*

Proof. The proposed LFN is a special case of a complete bipartite graph that contains no odd cycles. Suppose that SE_{ij} indicates a vertex from SP_i to EP_j. Similarly, ES_{ij} indicates a vertex from EP_i to SP_j. For $l = 2$, the cycles are all paths from a SP to its corresponding EP and return path $\{SE_{ii}, ES_{ii}\}$. If we start from SP_i, the second visited node is its EP (EP_i). Since each EP is connected to all SP_s, for intermediate nodes, we have all permutations as possible paths. cycles with $l = 2$, have no intermediate node. So, there are $\binom{m}{1}0!$ cycles when $l = 2$. For $l = 4$, the cycles are paths like $\{SE_{ii}, ES_{ij}, SE_{jj}, ES_{ji}\}$. There is only one intermediate node in cycles when $l = 4$ resulting in $\binom{m}{2}1!$ cycles. Similarly, for $l = 8$, the cycles are paths like $\{SE_{ii}, ES_{ij}, SE_{jj}, ES_{jk}, SE_{kk}, ES_{ki}\}$. Since, we have two intermediate node, j and k, we should consider their permutation as a new cycle, i.e. $\{SE_{ii}, ES_{ik}, SE_{kk}, ES_{kj}, SE_{jj}, ES_{ji}\}$. So, for $l = 8$, we have $\binom{m}{3}2!$. We can extend this relation to all cycles with different length. The summation of these cycles indicates the number of cycles in our logarithmic network, which is $\sum_{l=1}^{m}\binom{m}{l}(l-1)!$. ■

Note that the $\sum_{l=1}^{m}\binom{m}{l}(l-1)!$ is the lower bound of the number of simple and nested cycles created by using the logarithmic network. As a matter of fact, the number of paths from each SP to each EP could be more than 1, and there are possibilities of having a connection between SPs and EPs of the different paths in the original circuit,

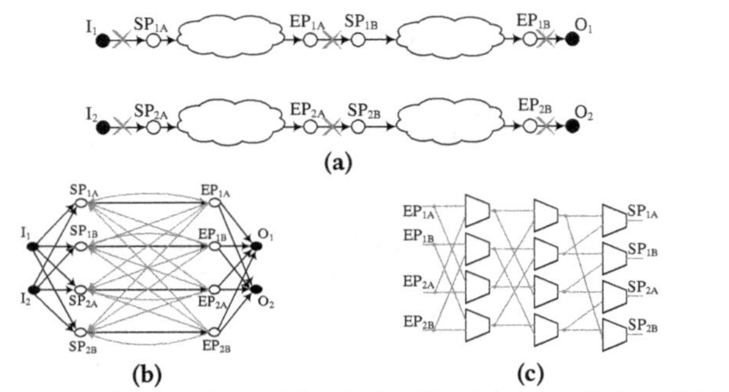

Figure 3: Building a logarithmic feedback network in which the number of cycles exponentially increase with the number of feedbacks.

increasing the number of cycle possibilities to a far larger number. Based on the lower bound formula, the number of created cycles is $O(\sum_{l=1}^{m}\binom{m}{l}(l-1)!) \leq O(m!) = O(m^m)$. Hence, there exists an exponential relation between the number of inserted feedbacks and the number of resulting cycles in the netlist.

4.2 Building Cyclic Boolean Functions

A Boolean function does not need to be acyclic; it is possible to reduce the number of gates in a circuit if a function could be implemented in its acyclic form [2][1][9][10]. For example, the work in [10] presents an n-input 2n-output positive unate Boolean function which can be realized with $2n$ two-input gates when feedback is used but requires $3n - 2$ gates if feedback is not used. Hence, cyclification of a circuit in addition to forcing the CycSAT pre-processing step to consider the "no sensitizable path", could also remedy the area overhead of introducing new gates for cyclic obfuscation. To cyclify a netlist and to increase the t_{NC} in equation 3, we suggest three approaches: (1) Template-based cyclic-function mapping, (2) Input-dependency based cycle generation and, (3) Node-merging based cycle generation.

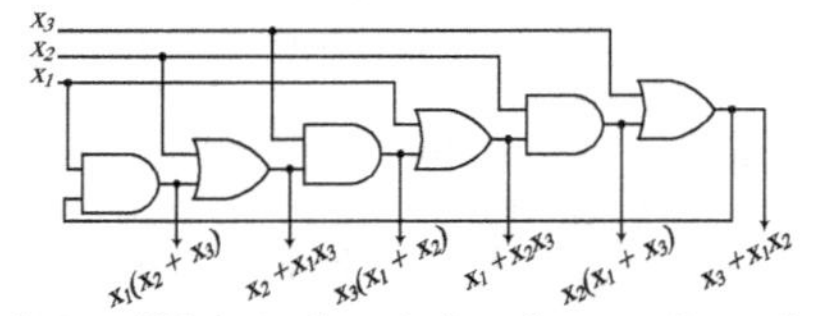

Figure 4: 3-input Rivest circuit implementing six functions.

4.2.1 ***Template-based cyclic-function mapping.*** In this approach, many small cyclic Boolean circuits are collected as templates in our obfuscation library. Then, A netlist is scanned for opportunities (with and without logic manipulation) to replace a cluster of logic gates with such templates. An example of such feedback template is the circuit introduced in [10] where a special case of it (for 3 inputs) is illustrated in Fig. 4. To introduce cycles, the circuit could be modified to introduce at least one of the possible functions in this circuit. The candidate logic cluster is then replaced by the template. To prevent template scanning and removal attacks, in a subsequent camouflaging step (by means of gate and route obfuscation) the template will be hidden. Note that many such templates could be made [10][2][1][9], and by not knowing the template type and the camouflaged technique used to hide the connection, an attacker has no prior information to identify and remove these templates.

4.2.2 ***Input-dependency based cycle generation.*** This method explores the correlations between signals that share common primary inputs in their fanin cone. Considering N such signals in an arbitrary stage of a DAG, some of the 2^N input possibilities may

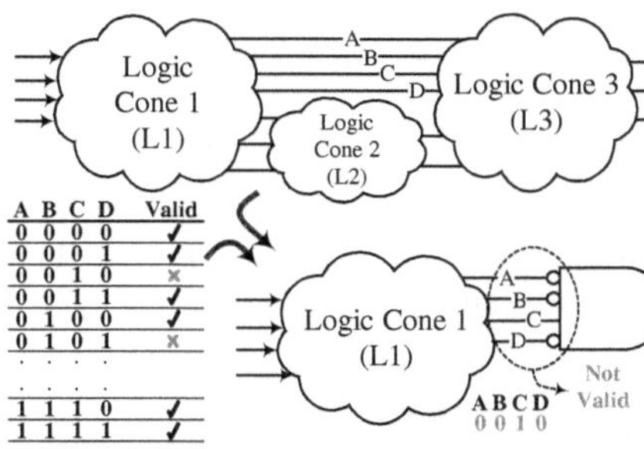

Figure 5: Due to correlation of intermediate signals, certain signal combinations may never occur.

never occur. For example, when tracking 4 signals A, B, C, and D in Fig. 5, we may find that $ABCD = \{0010\}$ could not occur. A SAT solver cold be used for finding the non-occurring input scenarios; This process is illustrated in Fig. 5, where the logic clusters L2 and L3 are removed, and the 4 signals are ANDed together such that for a certain case, for example, $ABCD = 0010$, the output of AND gate is evaluated to 1. Then, this circuit is given to a SAT solver to find a satisfying input assignment. If SAT solver returns UNSAT, this combination of input is chosen since it would never happen, otherwise, a different combination is checked.

In the next step, we use a sequential element and tie the discovered non-occurring input scenario to the state preserving input of the sequential element. For example, by using SR latch in Fig. 6.a, If $SR = 11$ doesn't happen, the Q_{next} is the inverse of input S. Hence, we can build a circuit that ties the discovered non-occurring input scenario to the $SR = 11$. For example, let's assume wires A, B, C and D have a non-occurring combination $ABCD = 0010$ and these signals construct the signal $Y = A + B + CD$. Fig 6.c illustrates the signal Y reconstructed when the non-occurring combination of the inputs is tied to SR input of the latch. In the next step, to hide the correlation between input signals, they are further obfuscated. The SR latch feedback is also obfuscated using a set of muxes that create alternative paths for its feedback signals. This assures that the CycSAT can only generate the correct NC clauses if the "no sensitizable path" condition is processed, otherwise, it breaks the SR latch feedback and invalidates the netlist.

4.2.3 ***Node-merging based cycle generation.*** The third approach for cyclification of a netlist is based on the work in [2] where the logic implication is used to identify cyclifiable structure candidates directly, or to create them aggressively in circuits. At its core, the work in [2] introduces active combinational feedback cycles by merging two nodes in the original DAG. To check the validity of the generated cyclic netlist, they use a SAT-based algorithm and validate whether the formed cycles are combinational or not.

5 RESULTS

In this section, we analyze the effectiveness of our proposed defense against SAT and CycSAT attacks. For finding the list of cycles in a netlist after cyclic obfuscation, the algorithm in [8] was implemented in C++. Our computational platform is a Dell PowerEdge R620 equipped with Intel Xeon E5-2670 2.50GHz and 64GB of RAM. We have used our proposed Super Cycle scheme for exponentially increasing the number of cycles on ISCAS-85 benchmarks, and the input-dependency-based netlist cyclification for forcing the CycSAT pre-processing to use the "no sensitizable path" condition instead of "no structural path" condition. However, similar results are observed when LFN is deployed, or other proposed techniques (template-based cyclification, and node-merging) are used for cyclification of a netlist.

Table 1: SAT-attack and CycSAT execution time after insertion of a SC (N=2) and insertion of a SC and 10 SR latches (N=2 + SR-L=10).

Circuit	N=2			N=2 + SR-L=10			
	SAT	#Cycles	CycSAT-I	SAT	#Cycles	CycSAT-I	CycSAT-II
c432	Inf Loop	23,879	2.561 s	Inf Loop	1.65×10^5	UNSAT	11.691 s
c499	0.56 s	236	0.104 s	Inf Loop	397	UNSAT	0.118 s
c880	Inf Loop	1,601	0.245 s	Inf Loop	7.87×10^6	UNSAT	793.125 s
c1355	Inf Loop	636	0.122 s	Inf Loop	5.00×10^5	UNSAT	53.215 s
c1908	0.28 s	294	0.101 s	Inf Loop	6,467	UNSAT	0.732 s
c2670	Inf Loop	1,570	0.234 s	Inf Loop	7,412	UNSAT	0.927 s
c3540	Inf Loop	5,991	0.756 s	Inf Loop	6,026	UNSAT	0.753 s
c5315	Inf Loop	4,869	0.613 s	Inf Loop	2.59×10^5	UNSAT	26.042 s
c7552	Inf Loop	124	0.189 s	Inf Loop	164	UNSAT	0.195 s

Table 1 captures the behavior of SAT and CycSAT when dealing with obfuscated cyclic and acyclic netlists. For generating the data in this table, we have created a cyclic version of each ISCAS-85 benchmark using input-dependency based obfuscation proposed in section 4.2.2, and then implemented a super cycle with two MCs in each netlist. The pure SAT attack is trapped in an infinite loop in both cases, with an exception of two benchmarks, that SAT solver luckily chooses a sequence of keys that avoid or exit the trap. The CycSAT when uses the "no structural path" condition (CycSAT-I) for the acyclic circuit, breaks the obfuscation easily, however, as illustrated in this table and predicted in equation 3, its runtime (which include the runtime for both pre-processing step and SAT solver's invocation) almost linearly varies with the number of cycles in each netlist. But when the netlist is acyclic, CycSAT-I returns UNSAT as it produces NC clause that breaks the DCG cycles incorrectly. On the other hand, the CycSAT when uses the "no sensitizable path" condition (CycSAT-II), breaks the obfuscation in all cases. However, since the number of created cycles are larger, and the time it takes to compose the NC condition for each cycle based on "no sensitizable path" condition is longer, the runtime of the SAT solver is considerably longer. In short, this table shows the capabilities of SAT, and CycSAT (I and II) for dealing with cyclic and acyclic original netlists, and also express the linear dependence between the CycSAT runtime and the number of created cycles. Hence, if the number of cycles exponentially increase, the runtime of CycSAT (pre-processing step) also exponentially increase.

The number of cycles created in ISCAS-85 benchmarks, when adding N=1, 2, 3, 5, 10, 15 and 20 MCs of size 7 (i.e., 7 gates in a cycle), while building a super cycle is reported in Table 2. As illustrated, the number of cycles created from implementing a super cycle is primarily a function of the number of inserted feedbacks and secondarily a function of the topology of starting netlist. As expected, the number of cycles is aggressively increased by the addition of each MC to the SC. Since the number of created cycles is also a function of topology, no single equation could predict the exact

Table 2: The number of cycles reported during CycSAT attack. The exponential fitting function is in form of $y = Ae^{Bx}$.

Circuit	N=1	N=2	N=3	N=5	N=10	N=15	N=20	Exponential Fit Function
c432	3,384	23,879	2.54×10^6	N/A	N/A	N/A	N/A	–
c499	10	236	397	55,585	N/A	N/A	N/A	–
c880	67	1,601	1,903	8.22×10^6	Timeout	Timeout	Timeout	A=881.953, B=1.75536
c1355	59	636	5.67×10^6	1.96×10^9	Timeout	Timeout	Timeout	A=21.7956, B=3.66316
c1908	13	294	12,594	1.33×10^7	Timeout	Timeout	Timeout	A=0.00174972, B=4.59814
c2670	273	1,570	8,912	2.90×10^5	Timeout	Timeout	Timeout	A=1036.51, B=1.82463
c3540	1,215	5,991	8.69×10^6	4.98×10^8	Timeout	Timeout	Timeout	A=4.0758, B=3.72457
c5315	162	4,869	6,650	1.22×10^9	Timeout	Timeout	Timeout	A=0.0217371, B=4.95008
c7552	11	124	1,558	2.57×10^5	1.15×10^9	Timeout	Timeout	A=9191.65, B=1.10724

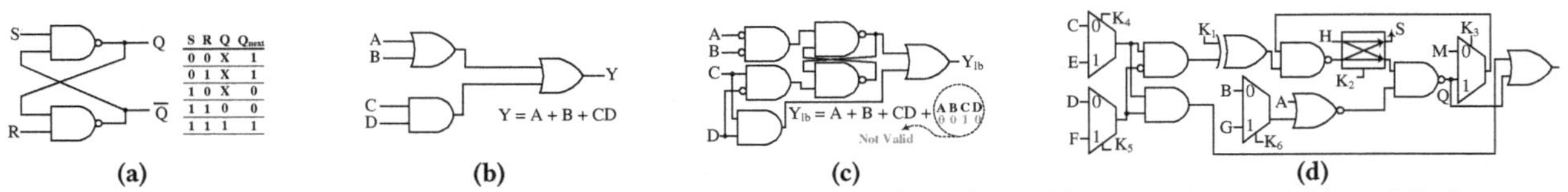

Figure 6: Input-dependency-based cyclification of a Boolean function. (a) SR latch (b) original circuit (c) cyclified circut when $ABCD = 0010$ is non-occuring. (d) obfuscated cyclified circuit using additonal random inputs E, F, G, H and M.

Table 3: Area overhead of SCs versus number of used MCs.

#MCs	N=1	N=2	N=3	N=5	N=10	N=15	N=20
#Gates	6	11	16	26	51	76	101

exponential growth for all benchmarks. Hence, using curve fitting techniques, the number of created cycles in each netlist as a function of the number of feedbacks is also reported in this table. As expected in all cases we see an exponential relation between the number of feedbacks and the number of created cycles. In smaller circuits like c432 and c499, there were not enough gates to create the required MCs for larger super cycles, hence, N/A is reported. For timeout entries, the number of cycles was not determined after 10 hours of execution on our server node. For executions resulted in timeout we also confirmed that initiating the CycSAT with incomplete NC clauses traps the SAT solver in an infinite loop. As illustrated in Table. 2, this is the case for most of the circuits with more than 10 MCs. The area overhead for building the SC in terms of the number of needed switches depends on the number of MCs and the number of gates in each MC. The area overhead for having various number of MCs of size 7 gates when building a SC is reported in Table 3. In short, as the number of inserted feedbacks increases, the pre-processing step of CycSAT faces an exponential increase in its runtime. Hence, by introducing a reasonable number of feedbacks using a methodology that exponentially increases the number of cycles (such as SC or LFN as proposed in this paper), the netlist could be protected against both SAT and CycSAT attacks by means of cyclic obfuscation.

Table 4: Number of cycles in c1908 circuit after inserting different number of cycles and SR latches.

#MCs \ #SR-L	0	1	2	5	10	20
0	0	5	30	245	7,675	7.35×10^6
1	13	189	9,875	4.37×10^6	1.78×10^7	Timeout
2	294	7,574	8.71×10^6	Timeout	Timeout	Timeout
3	12,594	6.82×10^5	1.42×10^7	Timeout	Timeout	Timeout
5	1.33×10^7	2.28×10^7	Timeout	Timeout	Timeout	Timeout
10	Timeout	Timeout	Timeout	Timeout	Timeout	Timeout

Table 4 illustrates the strength of cyclic obfuscation when a netlist (c1908 in ISCAS-85) is first cyclified and then is subjected to cyclic obfuscation. For netlist cyclification, the input-dependency-based technique in section 4.2.2 is used, and for exponentially increasing the number of cycles with respect to number of feedbacks, the SC approach was used. After adding 5 SR-latches and only two MCs, list of cycles could not be generated under 10 hour time limit. This will again prevent the initiation of SAT-attack because cycle avoidance clauses could not be generated. In short, cyclification of a netlist before subjecting it to cyclic obfuscation could increase the runtime of CycSAT pre-processing step exponentially.

6 CONCLUSION

By introducing cycles in a netlist, the straightforward SAT-attack would be trapped in an infinite loop while CycSAT can solve such obfuscation problems. However, the problem with CycSAT is the runtime of its pre-processing step for generating the cycle avoidance clauses, which grow as a linear function of the number of cycles in the netlist. As a mean of defense, we introduced several techniques for exponentially increasing the number of cycles with respect to the number of inserted feedbacks. This, in turn, resulted in an exponential increase in runtime of CycSAT pre-processing step, disabling the SAT attack to be carried in a reasonable amount of time. Based on this study, the cyclic obfuscation when properly implemented poses an exponential runtime on CycSAT attack with respect to the number of inserted feedbacks. Hence, CycSAT or existing SAT-attacks are not an effective mean for breaking cyclic obfuscation.

REFERENCES

[1] V. Agarwal, N. Kankani, R. Rao, S. Bhardwaj, and J. Wang. 2005. An efficient combinationality check technique for the synthesis of cyclic combinational circuits. In *Proc. of the ASP-DAC*. 212–215. https://doi.org/10.1109/ASPDAC.2005.1466160

[2] J. H. Chen, Y. C. Chen, W. C. Weng, C. Y. Huang, and C. Y. Wang. 2015. Synthesis and verification of cyclic combinational circuits. In *IEEE Int'l System-on-Chip Conf. (SOCC)*. 257–262. https://doi.org/10.1109/SOCC.2015.7406959

[3] R. P. Cocchi, J. P. Baukus, L. W. Chow, and B. J. Wang. 2014. Circuit camouflage integration for hardware IP protection. In *2014 51st IEEE Design Automation Conf. (DAC)*. 1–5. https://doi.org/10.1145/2593069.2602554

[4] J. Davis, N. Kulkarni, J. Yang, A. Dengi, and S. Vrudhula. 2016. Digital IP protection using threshold voltage control. In *2016 17th Int. Symposium on Quality Electronic Design (ISQED)*. 344–349. https://doi.org/10.1109/ISQED.2016.7479225

[5] DIGITIMES. 2013. Trends in the global IC design service market. *online http://www.digitimes.com/news/a20120313RS400.html?chid=2* 2013 (2013).

[6] M. El Massad, S. Garg, and M. V. Tripunitara. 2015. Integrated Circuit (IC) Decamouflaging: Reverse Engineering Camouflaged ICs within Minutes. In *NDSS*.

[7] U. Guin, D. Forte, and M. Tehranipoor. 2013. Anti-counterfeit Techniques: From Design to Resign. In *2013 14th International Workshop on Microprocessor Test and Verification*. 89–94. https://doi.org/10.1109/MTV.2013.28

[8] K. A. Hawick and H. A. James. 2008. Enumerating Circuits and Loops in Graphs with Self-Arcs and Multiple-Arcs.. In *FCS*. 14–20.

[9] M. D. Riedel and J. Bruck. 2003. The synthesis of cyclic combinational circuits. In *Proc. 2003. Design Automation Conf. (IEEE Cat. No.03CH37451)*. 163–168. https://doi.org/10.1145/775832.775875

[10] R. L. Rivest. 1977. The Necessity of Feedback in Minimal Monotone Combinational Circuits. *IEEE TC* 26, 6 (1977), 606–607.

[11] K. Shamsi, M. Li, T. Meade, Z. Zhao, D. Z. Pan, and Y. Jin. 2017. AppSAT: Approximately deobfuscating integrated circuits. In *IEEE Int'l Symp. on Hardware Oriented Security and Trust (HOST)*. 95–100.

[12] K. Shamsi, M. Li, T. Meade, Z. Zhao, D. Z. Pan, and Y. Jin. 2017. Cyclic Obfuscation for Creating SAT-Unresolvable Circuits. In *Proc. of the on Great Lakes Symposium on VLSI 2017 (GLSVLSI '17)*. ACM, New York, NY, USA, 173–178.

[13] P. Subramanyan, S. Ray, and S. Malik. 2015. Evaluating the security of logic encryption algorithms. In *2015 IEEE Int. Symp. on Hardware Oriented Security and Trust (HOST)*. 137–143. https://doi.org/10.1109/HST.2015.7140252

[14] Y. Xie and A. Srivastava. 2016. Mitigating sat attack on logic locking. In *International Conference on Cryptographic Hardware and Embedded Systems*. Springer, 127–146.

[15] M. Yasin, B. Mazumdar, J. J. V. Rajendran, and O. Sinanoglu. 2016. SARLock: SAT attack resistant logic locking. In *2016 IEEE Int. Symp. on Hardware Oriented Security and Trust (HOST)*. 236–241. https://doi.org/10.1109/HST.2016.7495588

[16] M. Yasin, B. Mazumdar, O. Sinanoglu, and J. Rajendran. 2017. Security analysis of Anti-SAT. In *2017 22nd Asia and South Pacific Design Automation Conference (ASP-DAC)*. 342–347. https://doi.org/10.1109/ASPDAC.2017.7858346

[17] J. Zhang. 2016. A Practical Logic Obfuscation Technique for Hardware Security. *IEEE Transactions on Very Large Scale Integration (VLSI) Systems* 24, 3 (March 2016), 1193–1197. https://doi.org/10.1109/TVLSI.2015.2437996

[18] H. Zhou, R. Jiang, and S. Kong. 2017. CycSAT: SAT-based attack on cyclic logic encryptions. In *2017 IEEE/ACM Int'l Conf. on Computer-Aided Design (ICCAD)*. 49–56. https://doi.org/10.1109/ICCAD.2017.8203759

Scalable Hardware Accelerator for Mini-Batch Gradient Descent

Sandeep Rasoori
Electrical and Computer Engineering Department
University of California, Davis
srasoori@ucdavis.edu

Venkatesh Akella
Electrical and Computer Engineering Department
University of California, Davis
akella@ucdavis.edu

ABSTRACT

Iterative first-order methods that use gradient information form the core computation kernels of modern statistical data analytic engines, such as MADLib, Impala, Google Brain, GraphLab, MLlib in Spark, among others. Even the most advanced parallel stochastic gradient descent algorithm, such as Hogwild is not very scalable on conventional chip multiprocessors because of the bottlenecks induced by the memory system when sharing large model vectors. We propose a scalable architecture for large scale parallel gradient descent on a Field Programmable Gate Array (FPGA) by taking advantage of the large amount of embedded memory in modern FPGAs. We propose a novel data layout mechanism that eliminates the need for expensive synchronization and locking of shared data, which makes the architecture scalable. A 32-PE system on the Stratix V FPGA shows about 5x improvement in performance compared to state-of-the-art implementation on a 14 core/28 thread Intel Xeon CPU with 64 GB memory and operating at 2.6 GHz.

KEYWORDS

Stochastic Gradient Descent; Mini-Batch Gradient Descent; Machine Learning; FPGA; CPU; Embedded Memories; Caches

ACM Reference Format:
Sandeep Rasoori and Venkatesh Akella. 2018. Scalable Hardware Accelerator for Mini-Batch Gradient Descent. In *GLSVLSI '18: 2018 Great Lakes Symposium on VLSI, May 23–25, 2018, Chicago, IL, USA.* ACM, New York, NY, USA, 6 pages. https://doi.org/10.1145/3194554.3194559

1 INTRODUCTION

Deep neural networks are being widely used in a large number of applications for analyzing and extracting useful information from the hundreds of petabytes of data that is being generated every day. Inference and training are the two modes of operation of a neural network. Training is the most computationally challenging task as it involves solving a large scale optimization problem, typically using the back propagation algorithm (backprop) which is based on gradient descent [2]. In particular Stochastic Gradient Descent (SGD) is a widely used algorithm to overcome the large number of computations. However, for fast convergence large batch sizes are desirable [6], but large batch sizes are extremely inefficient on a CPU or GPU because of poor utilization of caches and synchronization requirements. In the prior work FPGAs have been primarily used in the inference part of the deep neural networks with the network already trained in the back-end CPU or GPU clusters [16–18, 21]. However, the FPGA landscape has changed significantly in the past few years. Intel has announced new platforms that have a tightly coupled FPGA that is cache-coherent with a large scale Broadwell processor [7, 23]. Microsoft has demonstrated the use of FPGAs as accelerators in a data center environment [3, 10] and several works have shown that FPGAs can be more efficient than GPUs in many machine learning applications [8, 22].

In this paper we design and evaluate an accelerator for mini-batch gradient descent on an FPGA. The proposed architecture overcomes the limitations introduced by the memory hierarchy in modern processors to realize a scalable accelerator for SGD computation. Furthermore, FPGAs can take advantage of the limited precision arithmetic (6 bits or even less) [4]. And more importantly we develop an architecture that works well with large mini-batch sizes because instead of using the cache hierarchy for transferring data from the memory to the functional units, we manage the memory explicitly to reduce the number of stalls. We demonstrate a full system implementation on the DE1-SoC board and show the performance on real benchmarks. We identify the bottlenecks that could limit our scalability and project the performance of our implementation on larger FPGAs and compare them with recently published results of comparable implementation on a high end processor [15].

The rest of the paper is organized as follows. We start with a brief background of SGD and then discuss the high level overview of the mini-batch gradient descent implementation on a CPU and show the exact bottlenecks that limit the performance. Next we show the main ideas underlying the proposed implementation with an example. We present the details of the architecture and evaluate its performance. We conclude the paper with discussion of results, related work and directions for future work.

2 BACKGROUND

With the explosion in the available data to train on, machine learning is being widely used in many applications. Typically, machine learning models are trained using a training data set with N examples and f features. This entire data can be thought of as an $N \times f$ matrix A with each row in A representing an example and the columns representing the features. The goal is to find an f-dimensional model vector θ that minimizes an objective function or loss function. In many application domains such as image analysis, natural language processing, the number of examples and features can be in the order of millions or hundreds of millions (Table 1), which results in a very large optimization problem and solving this optimization problem efficiently is the computational bottleneck in large scale machine learning applications.

GLSVLSI '18, May 23–25, 2018, Chicago, IL, USA

ACM ISBN 978-1-4503-5724-1/18/05...$15.00
https://doi.org/10.1145/3194554.3194559

Stochastic Gradient Descent (SGD) is widely used to solve this optimization problem in many applications such as deep learning, matrix factorization etc. because of its superior performance especially with large data sets [2]. However, SGD is inherently a *sequential* algorithm where instead of computing the gradient exactly, each iteration estimates the gradient on the basis of a single randomly picked example x using the equation: $\theta_{t+1} = \theta_t - \alpha.\Delta(x, \theta_t)$ where Δ is the gradient of the loss function and α is the learning rate. Clearly, the update at step $t + 1$ is directly dependent on the previous step t limiting the paralleilization of SGD. Furthermore, the datasets are extremely sparse and the model vector is very large so sharing the model vector across multiple cores on CPU results in significant inter-core communication. Also, the computations performed per memory access is very low, which along with the extreme sparsity of the data makes the memory system the key bottleneck in SGD computation on both CPUs and GPUs. So, there has been a significant interest in the past few years on improving the performance of SGD on conventional CPUs. One approach that has gained lot of attention is the use of *asynchronous* or Hogwild style algorithms [13, 19] that deliberately sacrifice statistical efficiency for hardware efficiency.However, Hogwild style algorithms suffer from excessive cache coherence traffic (almost 60% of the cycles are spent on core-to-core communication [15]) and scale poorly on modern multi socket CPUs because all the threads continuously read and write from the same global model vector that causes excessive cache invalidations as shown in [20]. Another approach for exploiting parallelism in SGD is to use *batching* [6], where instead of a single example, a set of examples called a *batch* are processed together in each iteration. Given that all the examples in a batch use the same model vector, they can be processed in parallel. This approach still requires the large model vector to be shared by multiple CPU cores/threads which results in significant memory/cache traffic but it effectively increases the computation/memory ratio because multiple examples are processed per memory access. However, after processing each batch, the model vector has to be *synchronized* which requires significant inter-core communication. So, the question of interest to us in this work is how to *scale* the performance of large scale SGD to enable next generation machine learning applications with larger and sparser datasets?

FPGAs have increasingly become very attractive as special purpose accelerators/co-processors to CPU/GPU in datacenters [3, 10, 11] to an extent that Amazon now offers FPGA instances for its EC2 cloud computing service. Also, emerging computing platforms from Intel that target datacenters propose to combine a 14 core Broadwell with an ARRIA 10 GX 1150 FPGA on the same package with high bandwidth cache coherent PCI express/QPI links. With CMOS scaling, the amount of embedded memory in a FPGA is growing significantly. For example in Stratix V FPGA there is about 52Mb of embedded memory in the form of 2640 M20K blocks and in Stratix X the amount of embedded memory is 127 Mb with an additional 90Mb in terms of embedded SRAM. In this paper we propose a scheme to take advantage of this embedded memory to overcome the memory system bottleneck that limits the scalability of parallel SGD. We create a custom-memory system that is tailored to the specific dataset and the specific memory access patterns of the various phases of gradient descent algorithm to eliminate the need for inter-processor communication in the mini-batch gradeint descent algorithm to improve the scalability of the implementation.

Table 1: Sample Datasets

Dataset name	Examples	Features	NNZ/Row	Avg/Row
news20.binary	19,996	1,355,191	1-16423	454.987
RCV1-v2	781,265	276,544	4-1585	77.482
RCV1-v1	677,399	47,236	4-1224	73.157
real-sim	72,309	20,958	1-3484	51.295
w8a	64,700	300	1-114	11.652

3 PROBLEM DEFINITION AND OVERVIEW OF THE SOLUTION

Mathematically, for a batch of size B and starting sample x the model vector update is given by: $\theta_{t+B} = \theta_t - \alpha. \sum_{b=x}^{x+B} \Delta(J, b, \theta_t)$ where J is the loss function that depends on the application such as deep learning, matrix factorization, support-vector machine, logistic regression etc and Δ is the gradient and α is the learning rate. For a given input sample x the hypothesis function h helps predicting the output value y. For regression tasks, the hypothesis function is defined as: $h(x) = x\theta^t$ for linear regression and $h(x) = \frac{1}{1+exp(-x\theta^t)}$ for logistic regression where θ is the model vector. The loss function is given by:

$$J(A, \theta) = \frac{1}{2} \sum_{i=1}^{N} (h(x^{(i)}) - y^{(i)})^2 \text{ for linear regression}$$

$$J(A, \theta) = \sum_{i=1}^{N} y^{(i)} log(h(x^{(i)})) + (1 - y^{(i)}) log(1 - h(x^{(i)})) \text{ for}$$

logistic regression where $x^{(i)}$ is an input sample, $y^{(i)}$ is the corresponding label and h is the corresponding hypothesis function. The gradient of the loss function in either cases is given by:

$$\Delta_j(J, x^{(i)}, \theta) = (h(x^{(i)}) - y^{(i)}).x_j^{(i)}$$

Without loss of generality we focus on binary logistic regression that forms the core of many applications. The goal of mini-batch based parallel gradient descent is to compute the combined gradient of a small batch of samples, which can be computed in parallel by different cores/threads (so it exploits inter-example parallelism). This computation can be divided into 3 steps or phases.

- Phase 1: Compute Inner Product and Non Linear Transformation $Z = x.\theta^T$ and $h = \frac{1}{1+exp(-Z)}$
- Phase 2: Compute Gradient $G = x.(h - y)$, where y is the expected output (in supervised learning) of example x
- Phase 3: Update Model $\theta_{t+1} = \theta_t - \alpha.G$

3.1 Illustration of Mini-Batch Implementation

We will use a simple dataset with 8 examples and 8 features, so $N = 8$ and $f = 8$ based on our notation, as shown in Table 2. As shown in the table the dataset has only 16 non-zero entries and to keep things simple we will assume batch size $B = 4$, so we have only 2 batches.

CPU Implementation and Drawbacks: For simplicity let us consider the implementation on CPU with two cores, so each core processes 4 examples. The computations performed by each core during each phase of execution is as follows.

Phase 1:

Table 2: Sample Illustration Dataset

	x_{01}			x_{04}	x_{05}		
		x_{12}					x_{17}
x_{20}							
		x_{32}		x_{34}		x_{36}	
					x_{45}	x_{46}	
	x_{51}	x_{52}					
	x_{61}						x_{67}
			x_{73}				

Table 3: Data Partitioning and Memory Layout

rowRAM0		rowRAM1		colRAM0		colRAM1
r_{01}		r_{32}		c_{02}		c_{40}
r_{04}		r_{34}		c_{10}		c_{43}
r_{05}		r_{36}		c_{15}		c_{50}
r_{12}		r_{51}		c_{16}		c_{54}
r_{17}		r_{52}		c_{21}		c_{63}
r_{20}		r_{61}		c_{23}		c_{64}
r_{45}		r_{67}		c_{25}		c_{71}
r_{46}		r_{73}		c_{37}		c_{76}

Core0:
$h_0 = \delta(z_0) = \delta(x_{01}.\theta_1 + x_{04}.\theta_4 + x_{05}.\theta_5)$
$h_1 = \delta(z_1) = \delta(x_{12}.\theta_2 + x_{17}.\theta_7)$
$h_2 = \delta(z_2) = \delta(x_{20}.\theta_0)$
$h_3 = \delta(z_3) = \delta(x_{32}.\theta_2 + x_{34}.\theta_4 + x_{36}.\theta_6)$
Core1:
$h_4 = \delta(z_4) = \delta(x_{45}.\theta_5 + x_{46}.\theta_6)$
$h_5 = \delta(z_5) = \delta(x_{51}.\theta_1 + x_{52}.\theta_2)$
$h_6 = \delta(z_6) = \delta(x_{61}.\theta_1 + \delta(x_{67}.\theta_7)$
$h_7 = \delta(z_7) = \delta(x_{73}.\theta_3)$

Phase 2:

Core0:
$g_{00} = x_{20}.(h_2 - y_2); g_{10} = x_{01}.(h_0 - y_0)$
$g_{20} = x_{12}.(h_1 - y_1) + x_{32}.(h_3 - y_3)$
$g_{40} = x_{04}.(h_0 - y_0) + x_{34}.(h_3 - y_3); g_{50} = x_{05}.(h_0 - y_0)$
$g_{60} = x_{36}.(h_6 - y_6); g_{70} = x_{17}.(h_1 - y_1)$
Core1:
$g_{11} = x_{51}.(h_5 - y_5) + x_{61}.(h_6 - y_6)$
$g_{21} = x_{52}.(h_5 - y_5)$
$g_{31} = x_{73}.(h_7 - y_7); g_{51} = x_{45}.(h_4 - y_4)$
$g_{61} = x_{46}.(h_4 - y_4); g_{71} = x_{67}.(h_6 - y_6)$
REDUCTION: to compute final gradient from partial gradients thus requiring synchronization amongst the cores.
$g_0 = g_{00}; g_1 = g_{10} + g_{11}$
$g_2 = g_{20} + g_{21}; g_3 = g_{31}$
$g_4 = g_{40}; g_5 = g_{50} + g_{51}$
$g_6 = g_{60} + g_{61}; g_7 = g_{70} + g_{71}$

Phase 3:

$\theta_i^{t+1} = \theta_i^t - \alpha.g_i \;\; \forall\, i = 0, 1, ...7$

There are two major problems that limit scalability on a CPU. **First**, partitioning of the dataset is in terms of the *examples*, which makes sense when the data set is very dense, but introduces significant workload imbalance when the dataset is sparse as indicated by the characteristics of typical datasets used in machine learning literature today (see Table 1, NNZ denotes number of non-zero entries). The load imbalance not only results in stall cycles (the cores are not utilized fully) but also requires barrier synchronization which in particular is inefficient as the number of cores increases. **Second**, if the data is partitioned based on examples (or rows), then the examples for a given feature (the column entries) are spread across different cores. This requires inter-process communication in Phase 2 to compute the gradient for the batch as shown in the *REDUCTION* step in the example. As the number of cores increases, the features are spread across more PEs and this results in significant inter-core communication which drastically reduces the performance of mini-batch algorithm on a conventional processor (CPU or GPU).

3.2 Proposed Implementation Strategy

We show that using the large amount of embedded memory on state-of-the-art FPGAs we can overcome the drawbacks of CPU implementation in the following ways. An offline data partitioning and memory layout tool determines the amount of memory to be allocated to each Processing Element (PE) based on the available embedded memory on the FPGA and also the specific dataset that is under consideration. This includes duplication of memory and customizing the layout of the data in the memory to align with the access patterns in Phase 1 and Phase 2 of the algorithm. The data layout also includes additional meta data of the examples in terms of the row and column address of each non zero entry and it's expected output. Then instead of processing the entire batch B at a time we propose to divide the batch into smaller subsets that can fit in the memory allocated to each PE. Next, the dataset is partitioned and packed into the allocated memory of the PEs based on the number of non-zero elements in the dataset, not the examples. This automatically takes the sparsity of the dataset into account and results in almost perfect load balancing with very little overhead in terms of stall cycles.
FPGA Implementation Illustration: To show how the proposed FPGA implementation works in contrast to the CPU implementation let us consider the example dataset in Table 2 on a system with 2 PEs. The key to the FPGA implementation is the data partitioning and the memory layout which is done by an offline tool. The tool generates the initialization files required to populate the embedded memory and is shown in Table 3. Memory (depth of block RAM) is allocated to each PE after analyzing the dataset that is under consideration. Here, the allocated memory for each PE is 8 entries. Each PE has two memories allocated it to called rowRAM and colRAM and each nonzero entry x_{ij} in i^{th} row and j^{th} column is stored as $< i, j, x_{i,j} >$ in rowRAM and $< y_i, j, i, x_{ij} >$ in colRAM. So, the entry r_{01} in rowRAM0 is $< 0, 1, x_{01} >$ and the entry c_{02} in colRAM0 is $< y_2, 0, 2, x_{20} >$. Also, note that the non-zero entries are not placed sequentially, for example, x_{32}, x_{34}, and x_{36} are allocated to PE1 instead of PE0, to make sure the work is partitioned equally whenever possible. The computation in each PE during each phase of the algorithm is as follows.

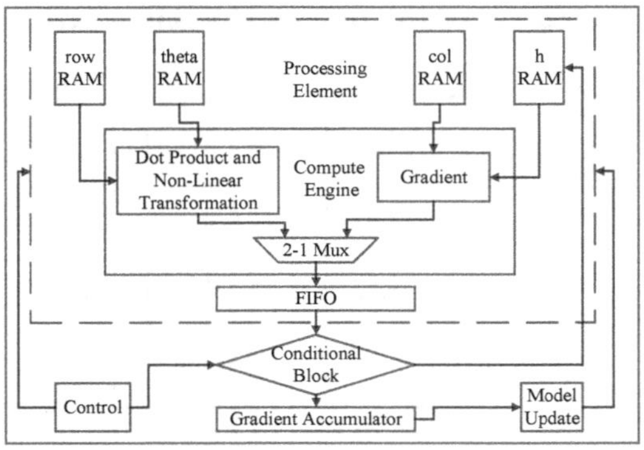

Figure 1: Top level Architecture of a single PE system

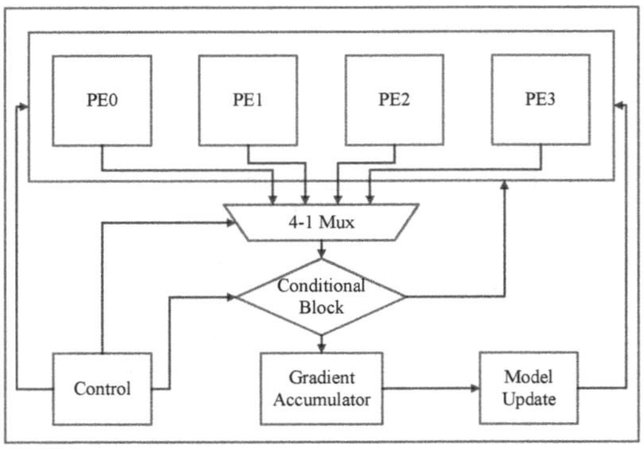

Figure 2: Top Level System with 4 PEs

Phase 1:

PE0:

$h_0 = \delta(z_0) = \delta(x_{01}.\theta_1 + x_{04}.\theta_4 + x_{05}.\theta_5)$
$h_1 = \delta(z_1) = \delta(x_{12}.\theta_2 + x_{17}.\theta_7)$
$h_2 = \delta(z_2) = \delta(x_{20}.\theta_0)$
$h_4 = \delta(z_4) = \delta(x_{45}.\theta_5 + x_{46}.\theta_6)$

PE1:

$h_3 = \delta(z_3) = \delta(x_{32}.\theta_2 + x_{34}.\theta_4 + x_{36}.\theta_6)$
$h_5 = \delta(z_5) = \delta(x_{51}.\theta_1 + x_{52}.\theta_2)$
$h_6 = \delta(z_6) = \delta(x_{61}.\theta_1 + \delta(x_{67}.\theta_7)$
$h_7 = \delta(z_7) = \delta(x_{73}.\theta_3)$

Phase 2:

PE0:

$g_0 = x_{20}.(h_2 - y_2)$
$g_1 = x_{01}.(h_0 - y_0) + x_{51}.(h_5 - y_5) + x_{61}.(h_6 - y_6)$
$g_2 = x_{12}.(h_1 - y_1) + x_{32}.(h_3 - y_3) + x_{52}.(h_5 - y_5)$
$g_3 = x_{73}.(h_7 - y_7)$

PE1:

$g_4 = x_{04}.(h_0 - y_0) + x_{34}.(h_3 - y_3)$
$g_5 = x_{05}.(h_0 - y_0) + x_{45}.(h_4 - y_4)$
$g_6 = x_{36}.(h_6 - y_6) + x_{46}.(h_4 - y_4)$
$g_7 = x_{17}.(h_1 - y_1) + x_{67}.(h_6 - y_6)$

Phase 3:

$\theta_i^{t+1} = \theta_i^t - \alpha.g_i \;\; \forall\, i = 0, 1, \ldots 7$

The key difference between the CPU implementation and the proposed implementation is the fact that the data is partitioned based on the non-zero elements of the dataset, not based on the rows of the dataset, and the duplication of the data so that Phase 1 and Phase 2 can be done by a PE without the need of any inter-processor communication. This makes the proposed implementation extremely scalable and the performance is directly proportional to the number of non-zero elements allocated to each PE and the number of PEs is limited by the available memory on the FPGA.

4 ARCHITECTURE DETAILS

Figure 1 is the high level architecture of each processing element (PE) that implements the three phases of the mini-batch gradient descent algorithm in a pipelined fashion. Each PE consists of 4 memory blocks that are realized using the M20K blocks on a Stratix FPGA - **rowRAM** stores the non-zero elements of the examples in the row major format, the **colRAM** stores the non-zero elements in the column major format. The block **thetaRAM** stores the model vector and the block **hRAM** stores the result of Phase1 (each PE has a copy of the entire model vector and hRAM). The sizing of these memories and the layout of the data in these memories was described in the previous section. In addition to the memory blocks, the core of the PE is the Compute Engine block that has two major blocks. The block (Dot Product and Non-Linear Transformation) computes the inner product and the Sigmoid (logistic function) for Phase 1 and the Gradient block computes the individual gradients in Phase 2 of the algorithm that are placed in a FIFO to be accumulated by the Gradient Accumulator block asynchronously. The Model Update block performs the operation in Phase 3 of the algorithm. As noted earlier we focus on binary logistic regression in this paper but if a different loss function such as a support vector machine or linear regression needs to be implemented then only the block Dot Product and Non Linear Transformation has to be changed.

The proposed architecture can be scaled to a large number of PEs by replicating each PE tile and implementing them as shown in Figure 2. To completely avoid any inter-core communication the block **hRAM** needs to be replicated similar to **thetaRAM**. The PEs need not communicate with each other as the Gradient Accumulator block ensures that the gradient updates are accumulated correctly.

5 IMPLEMENTATION, EVALUATION, AND DISCUSSION

There is significant work that has been done regarding the appropriate bit-width suitable for machine learning algorithms. Based on that prior work we choose a bit-width that is appropriate for fixed-point implementation on FPGAs. The offline tool partitions the dataset and determines the data layout for the embedded memories in each PE based on a given dataset, the number of M20K blocks in the FPGA, and a batch size, and the number of PEs. The entire system has been implemented on the DE1-SoC Development Kit which is a robust hardware design platform built around the Altera System on Chip FPGA, which combines the dual-core Cortex-A9 embedded cores. Altera's SoC integrates the ARM-based hard processor system (HPS) consisting of processor, peripherals and memory interfaces tied seamlessly with the FPGA fabric using a high bandwidth interconnect backbone. We extrapolate the results

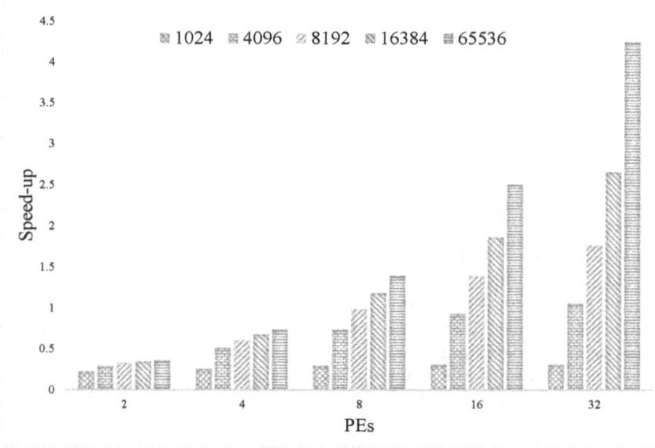

Figure 3: Speedup for varying number of PEs as the batch size is increased for the RCV1 dataset with training size of 512K examples. The speedup is relative to the best implementation in terms of the batch size of MiniBatch from [15]

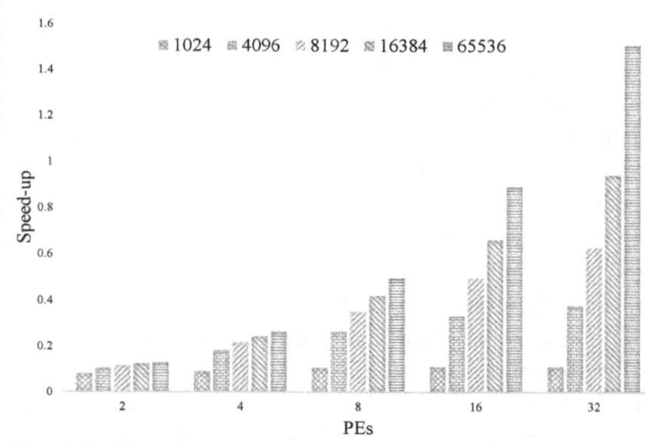

Figure 4: Speedup for varying number of PEs as the batch size is increased for the RCV1 dataset with training size of 512K examples. The speedup is relative to the best state-of-the-art SGD implementation - HogBatch from [15]

from implementation on DE1-SoC to the latest emerging FPGAs like Stratix V and the same are discussed in the rest of this section.

We synthesized, placed, and routed the top level design on a Stratix V device and results are reported for *real-sim* and *RCV1-v1* datasets. We compare our results with the state-of-the-art implementation of large scale stochastic gradient on a CPU described [15] on exactly the same datasets who in turn have outperformed the GPUs. The results in [15] are based on a single socket Intel Xeon E5-2697 v3 Haswell based CPU, with 14 cores (28 threads including Simultaneous Multi-Threading/SMT) running at 2.6 GHz with 64 GB of memory. The TDP of the system is 120W. Note that the proposed design (even with 32 PEs) is well pipelined and runs at fairly high clock frequency and the number of PEs scale with the available memory resources.

5.1 Impact of Batch Size on Performance

Figure 3 and Figure 4 show that the performance improves drastically with larger batch size. This is because in the proposed architecture Phase 3 (updating the model vector) is the bottleneck. For a dataset with a given number of examples, the number of model updates required for smaller batches is higher than that of batches with larger sizes, so the performance is much better with larger batch sizes. HogBatch [15] is a HogWild-style asynchronous algorithm that is different from the mini-batch algorithm for gradient descent computation discussed in this paper. HogBatch trades off statistical accuracy for hardware efficiency so it is faster than mini-batch, but we provided the comparison in Figure 4 so as to compare the proposed FPGA implementation with the state-of-the-art CPU implementation for large scale stochastic gradient descent.

On a CPU smaller batch sizes are chosen to avoid the miss penalties that increases with size of the batch. The computational efficiency decreases due to the limited sizes of the caches and thus the reason for smaller batch sizes on a CPU. However, on the FPGA with embedded memories tailor managed for our purpose the convergence issues can be tackled more efficiently and cache penalties can be avoided. The higher batch sizes are more suitable for this particular architecture to avoid frequent model updates like SGD.

5.2 Scalability and its limitations

As noted before the scalability of the proposed architecture is limited by the available embedded memory on an FPGA. On a given FPGA with fixed number of M20K blocks, the amount of memory available to each PE decreases as the number of PEs increases - this results in each PE processing fewer example during each epoch (same as having a very *small* effective batch size), so majority of the time will be spent on model update (Phase 3) as compared to other two phases and hence the performance will drop.

The state-of-the-art CPU-FPGA heterogeneous system is the Intel Heterogeneous Architecture Research Platform (HARP) where Intel Xeon E5 2600 v2 processor and Altera Stratix V FPGA are integrated. The CPU and FPGA communicate through Intel QuickPath Interconnection (QPI) [23] with 6.4 GT/s full bandwidth. Studies in [23], [7] show that QPI offers much higher bandwidth with low latency, packetized, point-to-point interconnect compared to FSB, which is suitable for continuous, large volume data transfer between heterogeneous devices. The FPGA on chip cache also makes it much more efficient for hardware to access data [17]. The high bandwidth and the faster processor can result in much higher improvement than compared to the results discussed earlier. The scalability is limited only by the amount of embedded memory that is available on the FPGA and the CPU external bandwidth.

6 RELATED WORK

The authors in [9] developed a customizable DNN (deep neural network) accelerator template for FPGAs and demonstrated the advantages of FPGA over GPU. Similar to us they conclude that FPGA implementation can result in higher performance/watt by taking advantage of the embedded memory and hard DSPs to extra fine-grain parallelism. Majority of work in the recent years is on developing better and faster convolutional neural network (CNN) implementation on a FPGA. In [18], the authors propose how to quantitatively analyze throughput and memory bandwidth requirements for a given CNN and in [22] the authors show how a combination of low precision CNNs and high level design methodology may help address the performance and productivity gap between FPGAs and

GPUs. An in-depth investigation of the memory footprint and bandwidth problem in order to accelerate state-of-the-art CNN models is described by authors in [12]. They propose a dynamic-precision data quantization flow to reduce memory footprint and bandwidth requirement while maintaining comparable accuracy. In [16] the authors describe systematic design space exploration methodology to maximize the throughput of an OpenCL-based FPGA accelerator for a given CNN model, considering the FPGA resource constraints such as on-chip memory, registers, computational resources and external memory bandwidth. The authors in [21] propose an analytical performance model and apply it to perform an in-depth analysis on the resource requirement of CNN classifier kernels and available resources on modern FPGAs. They propose a new kernel design to effectively address such bandwidth limitation and to provide an optimal balance between computation, on-chip, and off chip memory access. A novel architecture written in OpenCLTM, which is referred to as a Deep Learning Accelerator (DLA), that maximizes data reuse and minimizes external memory bandwidth is proposed by authors in [1]. The work in [5] proposes an end-to-end FPGA based CNN accelerator with all the layers mapped on one chip so that different layers can work concurrently in a pipelined structure to increase the throughput. In most of these research works it is assumed that the training is done offline. Instead of implementing a specific network such DNN or CNN the work proposed here addresses the most fundamental and time consuming part of large scale machine learning - which is *training* on an FPGA. Back propagation [14] is the widely used algorithm for training in a wide variety of machine learning models and applications and its core computation kernel is large scale stochastic gradient descent. So, the proposed architecture can be used as an accelerator in a wide range of present and future machine learning applications and in large scale optimization which is at the core of data analysis.

7 CONCLUSION AND FUTURE WORK

We propose a scalable architecture for parallel gradient descent on an FPGA by taking advantage of the embedded memory (Block RAMs) that outperforms state-of-the-art CPU based implementation of parallel SGD. The proposed algorithms avoid inter-processor communication and scales with the available memory resources. We show about 5x improvement in performance compared to state-of-the-art implementation on a 14 core/28 thread Intel Xeon CPU with 64 GB memory and operating at 2.6 GHz. Future FPGAs are likely to have even more memory and are more tightly coupled with processors (such as the new CPU+Arria 10 based FPGA from Intel), so our implementation can serve as an accelerator for a wide class of existing and new large scale machine learning applications. We have not explored the use of hard DSP especially one's with floating point capability and embedded SRAM (Stratix 10 has 52 Mb of so-called eSRAM) that is available in next generation FPGAs. That will constitute our future work.

REFERENCES

[1] Utku Aydonat, Shane O'Connell, Davor Capalija, Andrew C Ling, and Gordon R Chiu. 2017. An OpenCL (TM) Deep Learning Accelerator on Arria 10. *arXiv preprint arXiv:1701.03534* (2017).

[2] Léon Bottou. 2010. Large-scale machine learning with stochastic gradient descent. In *Proceedings of COMPSTAT'2010.* Springer, 177–186.

[3] Young-kyu Choi, Jason Cong, Zhenman Fang, Yuchen Hao, Glenn Reinman, and Peng Wei. 2016. A quantitative analysis on microarchitectures of modern CPU-FPGA platforms. In *Design Automation Conference (DAC), 2016 53nd ACM/EDAC/IEEE.* IEEE, 1–6.

[4] Suyog Gupta, Ankur Agrawal, Kailash Gopalakrishnan, and Pritish Narayanan. 2015. Deep Learning with Limited Numerical Precision.. In *ICML.* 1737–1746.

[5] Huimin Li, Xitian Fan, Li Jiao, Wei Cao, Xuegong Zhou, and Lingli Wang. 2016. A high performance FPGA-based accelerator for large-scale convolutional neural networks. In *Field Programmable Logic and Applications (FPL), 2016 26th International Conference on.* IEEE, 1–9.

[6] Mu Li, Tong Zhang, Yuqiang Chen, and Alexander J Smola. 2014. Efficient mini-batch training for stochastic optimization. In *Proceedings of the 20th ACM SIGKDD international conference on Knowledge discovery and data mining.* ACM, 661–670.

[7] Bhyrav Mutnury, Frank Paglia, James Mobley, Girish K Singh, and Ron Bellomio. 2010. QuickPath Interconnect (QPI) design and analysis in high speed servers. In *Electrical Performance of Electronic Packaging and Systems (EPEPS), 2010 IEEE 19th Conference on.* IEEE, 265–268.

[8] Eriko Nurvitadhi, Jaewoong Sim, David Sheffield, Asit Mishra, Srivatsan Krishnan, and Debbie Marr. 2016. Accelerating recurrent neural networks in analytics servers: Comparison of FPGA, CPU, GPU, and ASIC. In *Field Programmable Logic and Applications (FPL), 2016 26th International Conference on.* IEEE, 1–4.

[9] Eriko Nurvitadhi, Ganesh Venkatesh, Jaewoong Sim, Debbie Marr, Randy Huang, Jason Ong Gee Hock, Yeong Tat Liew, Krishnan Srivatsan, Duncan Moss, Suchit Subhaschandra, et al. 2017. Can FPGAs Beat GPUs in Accelerating Next-Generation Deep Neural Networks?. In *Proceedings of the 2017 ACM/SIGDA International Symposium on Field-Programmable Gate Arrays.* ACM, 5–14.

[10] Kalin Ovtcharov, Olatunji Ruwase, Joo-Young Kim, Jeremy Fowers, Karin Strauss, and Eric S Chung. 2015. Accelerating deep convolutional neural networks using specialized hardware. *Microsoft Research Whitepaper* 2, 11 (2015).

[11] Andrew Putnam, Adrian M Caulfield, Eric S Chung, Derek Chiou, Kypros Constantinides, John Demme, Hadi Esmaeilzadeh, Jeremy Fowers, Gopi Prashanth Gopal, Jan Gray, et al. 2014. A reconfigurable fabric for accelerating large-scale datacenter services. In *Computer Architecture (ISCA), 2014 ACM/IEEE 41st International Symposium on.* IEEE, 13–24.

[12] Jiantao Qiu, Jie Wang, Song Yao, Kaiyuan Guo, Boxun Li, Erjin Zhou, Jincheng Yu, Tianqi Tang, Ningyi Xu, Sen Song, et al. 2016. Going deeper with embedded fpga platform for convolutional neural network. In *Proceedings of the 2016 ACM/SIGDA International Symposium on Field-Programmable Gate Arrays.* ACM, 26–35.

[13] Benjamin Recht, Christopher Re, Stephen Wright, and Feng Niu. 2011. Hogwild: A lock-free approach to parallelizing stochastic gradient descent. In *Advances in Neural Information Processing Systems.* 693–701.

[14] David E Rumelhart, Geoffrey E Hinton, and Ronald J Williams. 1985. *Learning internal representations by error propagation.* Technical Report. DTIC Document.

[15] Scott Sallinen, Nadathur Satish, Mikhail Smelyanskiy, Samantika S Sury, and Christopher Ré. 2016. High Performance Parallel Stochastic Gradient Descent in Shared Memory. In *Parallel and Distributed Processing Symposium, 2016 IEEE International.* IEEE, 873–882.

[16] Naveen Suda, Vikas Chandra, Ganesh Dasika, Abinash Mohanty, Yufei Ma, Sarma Vrudhula, Jae-sun Seo, and Yu Cao. 2016. Throughput-optimized OpenCL-based FPGA accelerator for large-scale convolutional neural networks. In *Proceedings of the 2016 ACM/SIGDA International Symposium on Field-Programmable Gate Arrays.* ACM, 16–25.

[17] Chi Zhang, Ren Chen, and Viktor Prasanna. 2016. High throughput large scale sorting on a CPU-FPGA heterogeneous platform. In *Parallel and Distributed Processing Symposium Workshops, 2016 IEEE International.* IEEE, 148–155.

[18] Chen Zhang, Peng Li, Guangyu Sun, Yijin Guan, Bingjun Xiao, and Jason Cong. 2015. Optimizing fpga-based accelerator design for deep convolutional neural networks. In *Proceedings of the 2015 ACM/SIGDA International Symposium on Field-Programmable Gate Arrays.* ACM, 161–170.

[19] Ce Zhang and Christopher Ré. 2014. Dimmwitted: A study of main-memory statistical analytics. *Proceedings of the VLDB Endowment* 7, 12 (2014), 1283–1294.

[20] Huan Zhang, Cho-Jui Hsieh, and Venkatesh Akella. 2016. Hogwild++: A new mechanism for decentralized asynchronous stochastic gradient descent. ICDM.

[21] Jialiang Zhang and Jing Li. 2017. Improving the Performance of OpenCL-based FPGA Accelerator for Convolutional Neural Network. In *Proceedings of the 2017 ACM/SIGDA International Symposium on Field-Programmable Gate Arrays.* ACM, 25–34.

[22] Ritchie Zhao, Weinan Song, Wentao Zhang, Tianwei Xing, Jeng-Hau Lin, Mani Srivastava, Rajesh Gupta, and Zhiru Zhang. 2017. Accelerating Binarized Convolutional Neural Networks with Software-Programmable FPGAs. In *Proceedings of the 2017 ACM/SIGDA International Symposium on Field-Programmable Gate Arrays.* ACM, 15–24.

[23] Dimitrios Ziakas, Allen Baum, Robert A Maddox, and Robert J Safranek. 2010. Intel® quickpath interconnect architectural features supporting scalable system architectures. In *High Performance Interconnects (HOTI), 2010 IEEE 18th Annual Symposium on.* IEEE, 1–6.

MC3A: Markov Chain Monte Carlo ManyCore Accelerator

Lahir Marni
Dept. of Computer Science and Electrical Engineering, University of Maryland, Baltimore County
Baltimore, Maryland
mlahir1@umbc.edu

Morteza Hosseini
Dept. of Computer Science and Electrical Engineering, University of Maryland, Baltimore County
Baltimore, Maryland
hs10@umbc.edu

Tinoosh Mohsenin
Dept. of Computer Science and Electrical Engineering, University of Maryland, Baltimore County
Baltimore, Maryland
tinoosh@umbc.edu

ABSTRACT

The paper presents "MC3A"- Markov Chain Monte Carlo ManyCore Accelerator, a high-throughput, domain-specific, programmable manycore accelerator, which effectively generates samples from a provided target distribution. MCMC samplers are used in machine learning, image and signal processing applications that are computationally intensive. In such scenarios, high-throughput samplers are of paramount importance. To achieve a high-throughput platform, we add two domain-specific instructions with dedicated hardware whose functions are extensively used in MCMC algorithms. These instructions bring down the number of clock cycles needed to implement the respective functions by 10× and 21×. A 64-cluster architecture of the MC3A is fully placed and routed in 65 nm, TSMC CMOS technology, where the VLSI layout of each cluster occupies an area of 0.577 mm^2 while consuming a power of 247 mW running at 1 GHz clock frequency. Our proposed MC3A achieves 6× higher throughput than its equivalent predecessor (PENC) and consumes 4× lower energy per sample. Also, when compared to other off-the-shelf platforms, such as, Jetson TX1 and TX2 SoC, MC3A results in 195× and 191× higher throughput, and consumes 808× and 726× lower energy per sample generation, respectively.

CCS CONCEPTS

• **Hardware** → **Application specific instruction set processors**; • **Computer systems organization** → *Multicore architectures*; • **Mathematics of computing** → Distribution functions;

KEYWORDS

Manycore accelerator, ASIC, VLSI, MCMC, Uniform Random Number Generator, PDF, Metropolis-Hastings (MH)

1 INTRODUCTION

Markov Chain Monte Carlo (MCMC) algorithms are used to obtain samples from any target probability distribution and are widely used in numerical approximations, processing multi-dimensional signals, Bayesian statistics, rare event simulations and most importantly various Machine Learning (ML) applications [7][18][14]. Most of these, find themselves as real-time applications in multi-dimensional sampling, image processing and machine learning algorithms which need results in very limited time and require high throughput [8][15][5][13]. Sampling from complex probability distributions and a large number of multiple channels is often a bottleneck that results in slowing down the speed of the application. In this paper, we propose a programmable MCMC hardware accelerator, MC3A, to achieve a very high-throughput performance by customization of an existing manycore architecture. Domain-specific accelerators consisting of dedicated processing hardware, provide high processing performance and high throughput/watt performance. Programmable domain specific manycore accelerators can outperform general purpose CPUs and GPUs in terms of energy efficiency, as they use low power cores with special instructions and hardware architectures [10][11][1][4][9][2][16]. The proposed MC3A allows programming the manycore to implement various MCMC samplers such as Parallel Tempering (PT), Multiple Parallel Tempering (MPT), Gibbs Sampler depending on the application's requirement. The high throughput sampling is achieved by adding dedicated hardware and instructions to an existing manycore architecture, PENC [17], for functions that are repeatedly used and cause the overhead in most MCMC algorithms. Main contributions of this paper include:

- Proposed MC3A, a low-power, programmable manycore accelerator to efficiently execute MCMC algorithms.
- Design and implement an optimized hardware for MCMC specific instructions without slowing the operating frequency.
- Fully synthesized, placed and routed VLSI layout of the MC3A in 65 nm CMOS technology.
- Evaluation and comparison analysis of MC3A with PENC manycore, embedded NVIDIA Jetson TX1 and TX2 CPU's.

2 BACKGROUND

MCMC sampling consists of two steps: Monte Carlo, that implies that the sampling is a stochastic process, and Markov Chain, that indicates the generation of the next sample is based on the current sample. The sampling is mainly used to convert a complicated integration over a continuous multi-dimensional Probability Distribution Function (PDF) to a discrete summation on the samples, the result of which is used to calculate an expected value. Samples $x^{(t)}$, where t=1 to N, are drawn out from a target distribution. Markov chain is an iterative stochastic process which is initialized to $x^{(1)}$, and determines the next states based on a transition probability, where the transition probability can be described by a first order Markov chain as shown in equation 1:

$$P(x^{(i)}|x^{(i-1)}, x^{(i-2)}, ..., x^{(1)}) = P(x^{(i)}|x^{(i-1)}) \quad (1)$$

GLSVLSI'18, May 23–25, 2018, Chicago, IL, USA

ACM ISBN ISBN 978-1-4503-5724-1/18/05...$15.00
https://doi.org/10.1145/3194554.3194577

Algorithm 1 Metropolis Hastings (MH) Algorithm

Initialize Samples:
x_0 = p(x)
for *i* in 1 to N **do**
  Update Samples:
  x_p = q(x(i) | x(i-1))
  Acceptance Function:
  $\alpha(x_p) = min\{1, \frac{p(x(i-1))}{p(x_p)}\}$ //Use of EXP instruction
  u = Uniform (u; 0, 1) //Use of RAN instruction
  if u < $\alpha(x_p)$ **then**
    Accept the proposed sample: x(i) ← x_p
  else
    Reject the proposed sample: x(i) ← x(i-1)
  end if
end for

MCMC contains iterative interdependent kernels which makes hardware acceleration challenging.

2.1 MH Algorithm

In this paper, we chose the Metropolis-Hastings (MH) algorithm to verify the results and evaluate the performance of our manycore accelerator. MH Algorithm is one of the MCMC samplers that takes random samples from a PDF, p(x), to calculate the value of the required function f(x) that is proportional to PDF. In order to generate samples from p(x), the first sample is always needed to be initialized and then, three steps are performed in each iteration to generate next samples [12]:

2.1.1 Update Samples. Propose a sample, x_p, from a proposal density, q(x), which should be a symmetrical function that suggests a next sample based on the current sample. We use a Gaussian distribution for q(x). In this step, we use the current sample, x, and the target PDF, p(x), to calculate the next suggested value, x_p.

2.1.2 Acceptance function. In this step we calculate the ratio that is used to decide if the sample we had selected in the previous step is accepted or rejected. This ratio is called the acceptance ratio, denoted in equation 2.

$$\alpha = f(x)/f(x_t) \quad (2)$$

Since the PDF, p(x), is proportional to the actual function, f(x), the acceptance ratio can be re-written as equation 3.

$$\alpha = f(x)/f(x_t) = p(x)/p(x_t) \quad (3)$$

2.1.3 Accept or Reject. A uniform random number, u, is generated in the range of [0,1] and the proposed sample is accepted or rejected based on the condition mentioned in equation 4.

$$Accepted : u \leq \alpha, Rejected : u > \alpha \quad (4)$$

The detailed pseudo-code of the MH algorithm is mentioned in the Algorithm 1.

2.2 PENC Manycore

The PENC manycore is composed of 64 processing clusters (192 cores) connected through routers in a two-tier hierarchy: each cluster consists of three processing cores called Nodes, a shared memory that consists of three block memories of size 1024x16 and a low latency bus. At the next tier, all clusters are connected to each other through a hierarchy of routers. A router with five ports connects four clusters and keeps one port open for communication to the next router [17][10]. Each core processor has 128 30-bit words for storing instructions and 128 16-bit words for data storage and a six-stage processor pipeline for all instructions.

IN and OUT instructions are used to pass data between different cores. The bus is used to read the data from output FIFO and to place data into the input FIFO of the destination core. Bus arbiter takes care of granting the bus to different cores for communication. The bus has five ports connecting three cores, one Distributed Cluster Memory (DCM) and the router for communication with cores outside the cluster. The processing core contains a 32-element content-addressable memory (CAM) to store packets from the bus and allows a finite state machine to find a word corresponding to the source core field in the IN instruction. Inside each cluster, the three cores have access to the DCM using load (LD) and store (ST) instructions.

3 MC3A IMPLEMENTATION

Two important instructions, RAN and EXP, are additionally implemented in the PENC manycore in order to boost the performance and increase the throughput, as all the MCMC methods use these functions extensively throughout their algorithms [3]. RAN is a Uniform Random Number Generator, and EXP is an Exponent Function Instruction. Figure 1(A) shows the cluster architecture of the MC3A integrating the three cores, shared memory and a low latency bus. Figure 1(B) is the Post-layout view of bus-based cluster implemented in 65nm, 1V TSMC CMOS technology using Cadence Encounter. Figure 1(C) shows the 6-stage pipeline. In the execution stage of the 6-stage pipeline, ALU instructions and the RAN instruction can be completed in a single clock cycle, whereas EXP instruction is executed in 20 clock cycles and has a dedicated hardware, explained in detail in section 3.2 of this paper. Figure 1(D) shows post-layout implementation results for a single cluster of MC3A.

3.1 Uniform Random Number Generator - RAN Instruction

Uniform Random Number Generator or RAN instruction is a new addition to the MC3A architecture. Uniform Random Number Generation (URNG) is a very pivotal and extensively used operation in MCMC algorithms. In order to implement a URNG hardware, Linear Feedback Shift Registers (LFSR) are of common practice. However, In order to reduce the hardware overhead, we take advantage of a new URNG schematic proposed by [6]. The implemented URNG, whose hardware is shown in Figure 2, eliminates the barrel-shifter by introducing a simpler bit-masking block, that results in a shrunk hardware, thereby reducing the total area of MC3A. The used URNG has a high repeating period of 2^{175}. RAN R1 instruction generates a 16-bit random number and stores it in the R1 register. The implementation of RAN takes advantage of 9 Shift Registers (that are practically wires and registers, unlike in a barrel-shifter that shifts the input dynamically), 3 AND and 9 XOR gates. RAN instruction

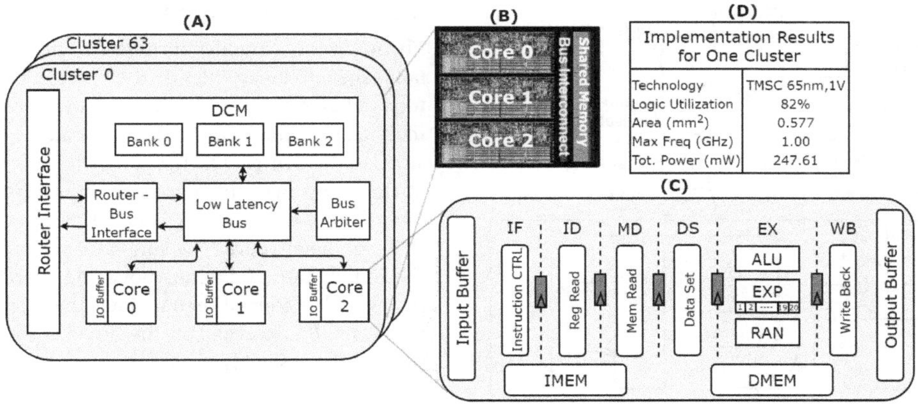

Figure 1: (A) 64 Clusters of MC3A are interconnected with routers. Each cluster consists of a distributed cluster memory (DCM), a low latency bus and three processing cores, bus arbiter and router-bus interface. (B) Post-layout view of MC3A implemented in 65nm, 1V TSMC CMOS technology. (C) Processing core architecture consisting of 6 pipeline stages where, IF, ID, MD, DS, EX and WB are instruction fetch, instruction decode, memory decode, date set, execution, and write-back pipeline stages respectively, Instruction memory(IMEM) and data memory(DMEM) are instruction and local data memory respectively. (D) Post Layout implementation results of MC3A single cluster.

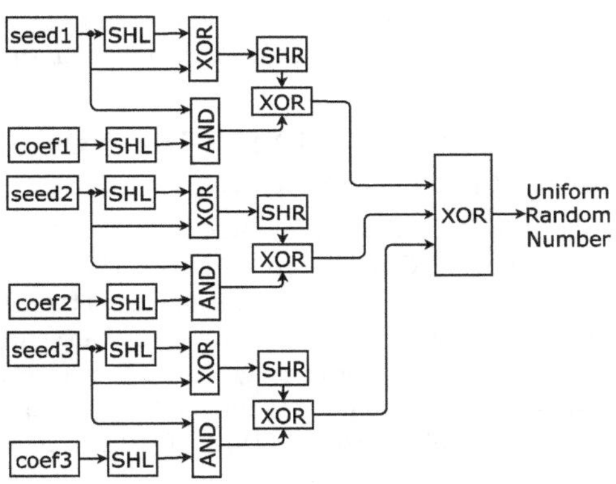

Figure 2: Block Diagram of Uniform Random Number Generator implemented using shift registers, XORs and ANDs

reduces the generation of a uniform random number from 60 clock cycles to 6 clock cycles with only one execution cycle. Figure 3 (A) Shows the alternate assembly instructions to generate the uniform random number with PENC and its equivalent instruction in MC3A. Figure 3 (B) shows the impact in the number of clock cycles with the addition of the RAN instruction.

3.2 Exponent Function - EXP Instruction

In addition, an EXP instruction to calculate the value of exp(-x) has been added to the execution stage of the manycore architecture. The EXP function is optimally implemented using CORDIC algorithm. CORDIC (Coordinate Rotation Digital Computer) is a simple and efficient algorithm to calculate hyperbolic and trigonometric functions such as exponent, logarithm, sine, and cosine, and is mainly used for hardware implementation. CORDIC uses pre-calculated coefficients which are stored in a look-up table, by means of which the function output converges to the actual value typically one bit per iteration. In our exponential function design, the input value is first read, and is assumed to have a temporary exponent value of

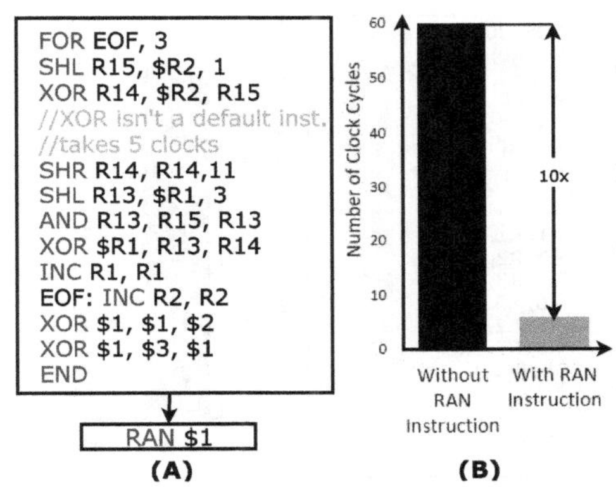

Figure 3: (A) On the above is an assembly program to implement uniform random number generator with PENC (All seeds are pre-loaded in data memory). Below is the equivalent assembly program with MC3A. (B) The graph showing the decrease in number of clock cycles with the addition of RAN instruction.

1. Then, a pre-calculated reference value is read from a ROM and is subtracted from the input value. If the result is negative, then it will replace the input value. Meanwhile, the temporary exponential value will be multiplied by another offset value, read from another ROM. Otherwise, both the input and the temporary exponential values will be passed to the next iteration without any manipulation. After a few iterations, the temporary value converges to the true exponent value. We calculated values for the reference and offset ROMs such that for an exponential function of a negative 16-bit value the process will complete after 20 iterations. If two of the iterations are merged into one clock cycle, then the critical path of the hardware exceeds 1ns, thus slowing down the system frequency below 1GHz. To eliminate this problem, a state machine is developed to implement the 20 iterations in 20 different clock cycles to maintain the minimum clock period of the manycore at 1 ns. "EXP R1, R2" reads the value from R2 in <8,8> binary fixed-point format,

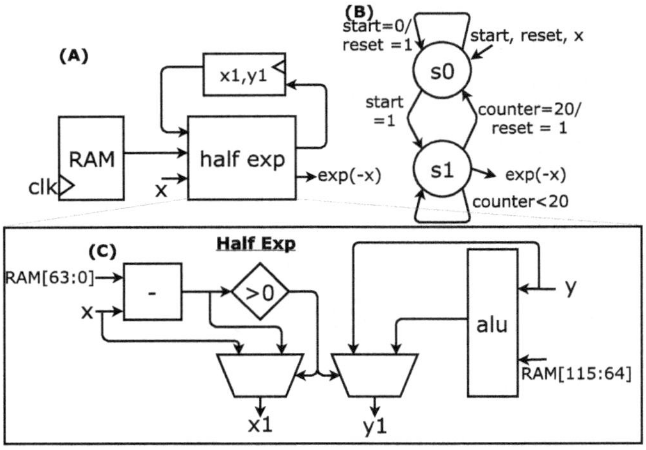

Figure 4: (A) Block diagram of exp(-x) implemented using half exp functions. All the coefficients and offset values are stored in RAM. The functionality of half exp is shown in Figure 4 (B) State Machine that implements exp(-x). (C) Block diagram for the single iteration of the half exp implemented using CORDIC.

```
FOR EOF, 20
SHL R1, R0, $1
SHL R2, R0, $2
SHL R3, R0, $3
SUB R4, R15, $4
MUL R5, R0, $5
//MUL should followed by
//NOP instructions as it takes
//more than one clockcycle.
MUL R1, R1, $6
MUL R2, R2, $7
MUL R3, R3, $8
ADD R6, R5, R1
ADD R6, R2, R6
ADD R6, R3, R6
BL EOF, R4, 0
MOV R15, R4
MOV R2, R6
EOF: NOP
END
```

```
EXP R15, R1
```

(A)

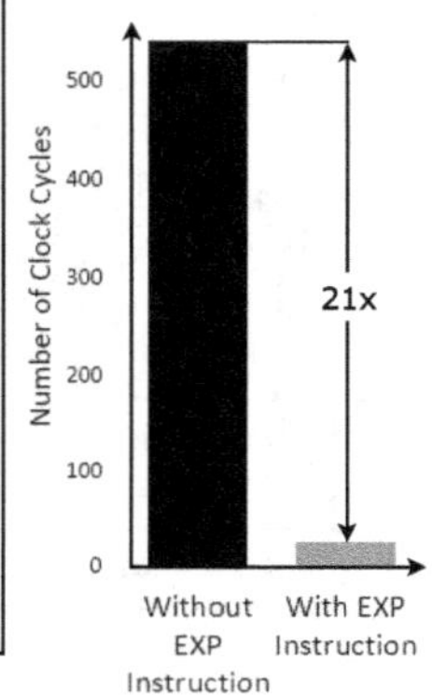

(B)

Figure 5: (A) On the above is an assembly program to implement exp(-x) in PENC (All coefficients are pre-loaded in data memory). Below is the equivalent assembly program with MC3A. (B) The graph showing the decrease in number of clock cycles with the addition of EXP instruction.

computes the value of exp(-x) and stores it in R1 as <0,16> binary fixed-point format. <0,16> binary point format is chosen because the values of exp(-x) always lie between 0 and 1. Figure 4 (A) Shows an iteration of the EXP function using Half Exp functions. Figure 4 (B) shows the state machine that divides the CORDIC exponent algorithm into sequential logic. Figure 4 (C) shows the combination logic of Half Exponent function. Implementing the EXP instruction reduces the calculation of exp(-x) from 542 clock cycles to 25 clock cycles. Figure 5 (A) Shows the alternate assembly instructions to calculate exp(-x) with PENC manycore and how the additional hardware reduces it in the proposed MC3A. Figure 5 (B) Shows the impact in the number of clock cycles with the addition of the EXP instruction.

3.3 Programming the Manycore

The manycore compiler, written in Python, converts the assembly language into binary files. It also reads in the initial values of registers and memories, and converts them into bin files for each core individually, which can be directly loaded on the manycore. A java simulator is written which is completely a software implementation of the manycore which assists with running, debugging, testing and refining the assembly code before loading it as binary files to the actual manycore. The simulator reads the assembly code and the initial state of data memory and registers, then models it as per assembly code. It then updates the final states of registers and memories. It also evaluates the summary of clock cycles it takes to execute the assembly program.

3.4 Hardware Evaluation

We implemented our algorithm on hardware for evaluating the energy consumption, execution time, area and power analysis of our proposed MC3A. The hardware model is simulated using NC-Verilog. The complete MC3A is placed and routed to generate a VLSI Layout in 65 nm 1V CMOS technology using the Cadence Encounter tool. The resulting VLSI layout is used to calculate the accurate area analysis, clock frequency and power consumption.

4 IMPLEMENTATION RESULTS AND PLATFORM COMPARISON

The MH algorithm of MCMC, presented in section 2.1, is implemented on both the PENC and MC3A manycore. The MH algorithm samples from a uni-variate Gaussian distribution as the target PDF. The results are evaluated in terms of throughput, execution time, energy and area metrics. To better gauge the performance of MC3A, the same algorithm is implemented on NVIDIA Jetson TX1 SoC CPU platform and NVIDIA Jetson TX2 SoC CPU. In-order to achieve a low power platform, the rule of thumb is to use the least number of clusters possible.

4.1 Implementation Results on NVIDIA Jetson TX1 and TX2 SoC

The MH algorithm is also implemented on the NVIDIA Jetson TX1 and the NVIDIA Jetson TX2 processors. The results of TX1 and Tx2 are scaled up (from 28nm) to match 65nm technology to be comparable with MC3A and PENC. Before collecting the power and timing analysis for the TX1 and TX2, we made sure that all the other components such as GPU, HDMI are turned off and there is no power consumption from any of these components.

4.2 Area Efficiency Analysis

To evaluate the area efficiency, we use the throughput per unit area (TPA) metric. TPA is the ratio between the throughput of each core to the total area of the core. There is a 4.7× performance increase in the TPA despite the increase in the area, because of the dedicated hardware to MC3A compared to PENC manycore. Figure 6 shows the graphical analysis of layout area of the complete cluster and the TPA metric.

Table 1: Hardware implementation results for MC3A compared with PENC manycore, NVIDIA Jetson TX1 and TX2 (CPU). For a fair comparison with Jetson TX1 and TX2 CPUs, the results are scaled to 65 nm as shown in the table

	MC3A	PENC (Base)	Improvement Over PENC	TX1 CPU	Improvement over TX1 CPU	TX2 CPU	Improvement over TX2 CPU
Technology (nm)	65	65	-	28	-	28	-
Frequency(MHz)	1000	1000	-	1224	-	1267.2	-
Cluster area (mm^2)	0.577	0.528	**0.9x**	-	-	-	-
Scaled Throughput/Area(Msps/mm^2)	166.5	35.02	**5x**	-	-	-	-
Execution Time(nS)	42.9	247.6	**6x**	8400	**195x**	8200	**191x**
Throughput(Msps)	23.31	4.04	**6x**	0.11	**195x**	0.12	**191x**
Total Power (mW)	247.61	226.78	-	2373.33	-	2185.5	-
Scaled Power(mW)	247.61	226.78	**0.9x**	5508.75	**22x**	5072.32	**21x**
Scaled Energy Consumption(uJ)	10.6	41.29	**4x**	8587.8	**808x**	7719.85	**726x**

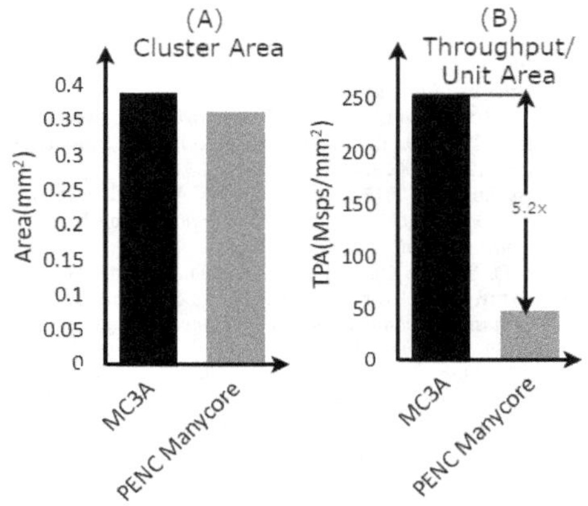

Figure 6: (A) Graph showing the areas for a single cluster of MC3A and the PENC manycore. (B) Graph showing the Throughout per unit area (TPA) of the core and the performance improvement of MC3A. The units of TPA are million samples/second/mm²

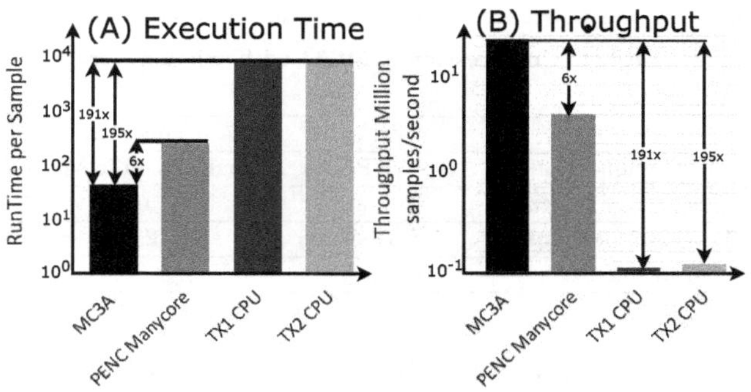

Figure 7: (A) Graph showing the Execution time and the amount of speed-up of MC3A compared to PENC manycore, TX1 CPU and TX2 CPU. (B) Graph showing the throughput (million samples per second) and the amount of increase in throughput of MC3A compared to PENC manycore, TX1 CPU and TX2 CPU. (All the graphs are plotted in logarithmic scale)

4.3 Execution Time and Throughput Analysis

It takes the MC3A 42.9 ns to generate a single sample using MH algorithm achieving a throughput of 23.3 million samples per second. A speed-up of around 6× is achieved compared to the PENC manycore. Figure 7 shows the execution time analysis per sample and throughput per second of the MC3A versus the PENC manycore. The results of this experiment show an improvement of 191× and 195× more throughput over Jetson TX1 and Jetson TX2 CPU platforms respectively.

4.4 Energy Efficiency Analysis

Although there is a considerable amount of hardware overhead to achieve great speed and high throughput, a significant decrease in the energy consumption was achieved. The power consumption per cluster has increased to 247.6 mW, but there is 4× decrease in the amount of energy consumed compared to PENC manycore. Figure 8 shows the power and energy analysis of the MC3A versus the PENC manycore and illustrates the energy efficiency it brings in the MCMC algorithms. The results of this experiment shows an improvement of 808× and 726× over TX1 and TX2 CPU platforms respectively.

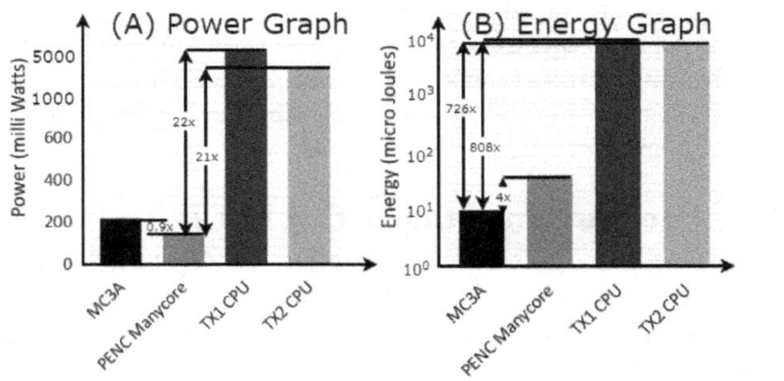

Figure 8: (A) Graph showing the Power in mW for MC3A compared to PENC manycore, TX1 CPU and TX2 CPU. (B) Graph showing the energy (μJ) in logarithmic scale and the amount of decrease in energy of MC3A compared to PENC manycore, TX1 CPU and TX2 CPU.

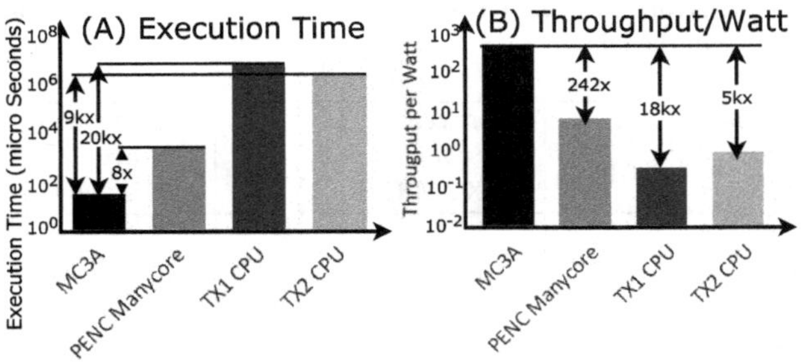

Figure 9: (A) Comparison graph of time taken to generate 10000 sample for 100 channels across MC3A, PENC, TX1 and TX2 CPUs. (B) Graph comparing efficiency metric (million samples per second/watt) to generate 10000 samples for 100 channels across MC3A, PENC, TX1 and TX2 CPUs (For both (A) and (B) quad-core CPU parallel, all channels evenly distributed among all the processes, and processes are distributed evenly among all the cores of the CPU)

Table 2: Compression of MC3A with existing work

	[7]	This Work
Implementation	Artix-7 FPGA	Domain-specific Manycore
Frequency (MHz)	200	1000
Throughput (Msps)	5.04	23.31
Improvement	Base	5x

4.5 Comparison with Parallel Multi-Core CPU

Applications that use MCMC algorithms usually need many samples from multiple channels following the distribution of data in the channel. So, the present MH algorithm is scaled to 10000 samples and 100 channels. The scaled results of the MC3A are compared across various platforms, PENC manycore, TX1 (quad-core) and TX2 (quad-core). Figure 9 (A) shows the performance increase in the execution time. Figure 9 (B) shows an increase in efficiency compared to other platforms. Over TX1 and TX2 each channel is run as a separate thread using pthreads, since there are 4 processor cores in TX1 and TX2 CPUs, 4 different processes are created using MPI (Message Paring Interface) and each process is mapped with 25 threads to ensure maximum parallelism that can be achieved over TX1 and TX2 CPUs.

4.6 Comparison with existing work

We compare our work with a similar existing work [7]. We consider only 1 chain Parallel Tempering (PT) from [7], which is equivalent to MH sampler algorithm. Table 2 summarizes the comparison, where MC3A achieves 4.6× higher throughput when compared with [7].

5 CONCLUSION

In this work, we proposed a programmable, high-throughput and energy-efficient manycore for MCMC algorithms - named "MC3A" that contains customized instructions, and an architecture that is modified to speed-up the MCMC algorithms. The proposed work is then fully placed and routed using 65nm 1V, TSMC CMOS technology. The VLSI post-layout results show that the proposed MC3A has a throughput of 23 Msps which is 6× higher over the PENC manycore, and consumes an energy of 10.6 μJ per sample generation per cluster which is a 4× improvement over PENC. Also, we implemented the MH algorithm on NVIDIA Jetson TX1 and TX2 CPUs where MC3A achieves 195× and 191× speedup respectively, and 808× and 726× better energy efficiency respectively.

REFERENCES

[1] T. Abtahi, A. Kulkarni, and T. Mohsenin. 2017. Accelerating convolutional neural network with FFT on tiny cores. In *2017 IEEE International Symposium on Circuits and Systems (ISCAS)*. 1–4. https://doi.org/10.1109/ISCAS.2017.8050588

[2] T. Abtahi, C. shea, A. Kulkarni, and T. Mohsenin. 2018. Accelerating Convolutional Neural Network with FFT on Embedded Hardware. *IEEE Transactions on Very Large Scale Integration (VLSI) Systems* (2018).

[3] Narges Bani Asadi et al. 2008. Reconfigurable computing for learning Bayesian networks. In *Proceedings of the 16th international ACM/SIGDA symposium on Field programmable gate arrays*. ACM, 203–211.

[4] N. Attaran, A. Puranik, J. Brooks, and T. Mohsenin. 2018. Embedded Low-Power Processor for Personalized Stress Detection. *IEEE Transactions on Circuits and Systems II: Express Briefs* PP, 99 (2018), 1–1. https://doi.org/10.1109/TCSII.2018.2799821

[5] Ter Braak and Cajo JF. 2006. A Markov Chain Monte Carlo version of the genetic algorithm Differential Evolution: easy Bayesian computing for real parameter spaces. *Statistics and Computing* 16, 3 (2006), 239–249.

[6] R. Gutierrez, V. Torres, and J. Valls. 2012. Hardware Architecture of a Gaussian Noise Generator Based on the Inversion Method. *IEEE Transactions on Circuits and Systems-II* 8 (2012), 501–505.

[7] Morteza Hosseini et al. 2017. A Scalable FPGA-based Accelerator for High-Throughput MCMC Algorithms. In *IEEE Symposium on Field- Programmable Custom Computing Machines (FCCM)*.

[8] Z. Ji, Y. Xia, Q. Sun, Q. Chen, D. Xia, and D. D. Feng. 2012. Fuzzy Local Gaussian Mixture Model for Brain MR Image Segmentation. *IEEE Transactions on Information Technology in Biomedicine* 16, 3 (2012), 339–347. https://doi.org/10.1109/TITB.2012.2185852

[9] A. Kulkarni, T. Abtahi, C. Shea, A. Kulkarni, and T. Mohsenin. 2017. PACENet: Energy efficient acceleration for convolutional network on embedded platform. In *2017 IEEE International Symposium on Circuits and Systems (ISCAS)*. 1–4.

[10] A. Kulkarni, T. Abtahi, E. Smith, and T. Mohsenin. 2016. Low Energy Sketching Engines on Many-Core Platform for Big Data Acceleration. In *Proceedings of the 26th Edition on Great Lakes Symposium on VLSI (GLSVLSI '16)*. ACM, New York, NY, USA, 57–62. https://doi.org/10.1145/2902961.2902984

[11] A. Kulkarni, A. Page, N. Attaran, A. Jafari, M. Malik, H. Homayoun, and T. Mohsenin. 2017. An Energy-Efficient Programmable Manycore Accelerator for Personalized Biomedical Applications. *IEEE Transactions on Very Large Scale Integration (VLSI) Systems* PP, 99 (2017), 1–14.

[12] Scott M. Lynch. 2007. Introduction to Applied Bayesian Statistics and Estimation for Social Scientists. (2007), 107–130.

[13] Alireza S. Mahani and Mansour T.A. Sharabiani. 2014. SIMD Parallel MCMC Sampling with Applications for Big-Data Bayesian Analytics. *Computational Statistics and Data Analysis* (2014), 1–41. https://doi.org/10.1016/j.csda.2015.02.010

[14] Lahir Marni, Morteza Hosseini, Hopp Jennifer, Mohseni Pedram, and Tinoosh Mohsenin. 2018. A Real-Time Wearable FPGA-based Seizure Detection Processor Using MCMC. In *IEEE proceedings of International Symposium on Circuits and Systems (ISCAS)*.

[15] G. Mingas and C. S. Bouganis. 2012. A Custom Precision Based Architecture for Accelerating Parallel Tempering MCMC on FPGAs without Introducing Sampling Error. In *2012 IEEE 20th International Symposium on Field-Programmable Custom Computing Machines*. 153–156. https://doi.org/10.1109/FCCM.2012.34

[16] Grigorios Mingas and Christos-Savvas Bouganis. 2012. Parallel tempering MCMC acceleration using reconfigurable hardware. In *International Symposium on Applied Reconfigurable Computing*. Springer, 227–238.

[17] A. Page, N. Attaran, C. Shea, H. Homayoun, and T. Mohsenin. 2016. Low-Power Manycore Accelerator for Personalized Biomedical Applications. In *Proceedings of the 26th Edition on Great Lakes Symposium on VLSI (GLSVLSI '16)*. ACM, New York, NY, USA, 63–68. https://doi.org/10.1145/2902961.2902986

[18] Grigorios Mingas Shuanglong Liu and Christos-Savvas Bouganis. 2016. An Unbiased MCMC FPGA-based Accelerator in the Land of Custom Precision Arithmetic. *IEEE TRANSACTIONS ON COMPUTERS* PP, 99 (2016), 1–1.

AEAS - Towards High Energy-efficiency Design for OpenSSL Encryption Acceleration through HW/SW Co-design

Chunhua Xiao*
Chongqing University
Chongqing, China

Yuhua Xie
Chongqing University
Chongqing, China

Lei Zhang
Chongqing University
Chongqing, China

ABSTRACT

Entering the Big Data Era leads to the rapid development of web applications which provide high performance sensitive access on large data centers. OpenSSL has been widely deployed as a freely available implementation of SSL/TLS protocol that secures transactions over the Internet. In order to accelerate the speed of OpenSSL, many alternative encryption approaches are designed. However, energy consumption has been ignored in the rush for performance. Energy efficiency becomes a challenge with the increasing demands for performance and energy saving in data centers. In this paper, we present the *Adaptive Encryption Acceleration System* (AEAS), an OpenSSL encryption acceleration scheme. It provides high energy-efficiency encryption through HW/SW co-design. The essential idea is exerting the superiorities of energy efficiency for different encryption approaches and making full use of system resource through the *Dynamic Management Mechanism* including *RequestAllocation* algorithm and *DynamicScheduler* algorithm. Specifically, this scheme supports instruction set and hardware to process the computation compatibly by the *Adaptive Control Crypto* (*ac_crypto*) engine. Experimental results show that AEAS can improve energy efficiency by up to 933.5%, 68.8%, and 483.7% comparing with software, AES-NI and QAT, respectively.

ACM Reference Format:
Chunhua Xiao, Yuhua Xie, and Lei Zhang. 2018. AEAS - Towards High Energy-efficiency Design for OpenSSL Encryption Acceleration through HW/SW Co-design. In *GLSVLSI '18: 2018 Great Lakes Symposium on VLSI, May23–25, 2018, Chicago, IL, USA.* ACM, 6 pages. https://doi.org/10.1145/3194554.3194584

1 INTRODUCTION

A strong tide of constructing green data center has engendered with the rapid development of Web Server in Internet industry [12]. Continuously developing of transaction-intensive web applications makes the security become increasingly important [19]. More and more transactions require transfer of sensitive information kept on data center through the Internet. However, Internet is an insecure medium. The Secure Socket Layer (SSL) protocol and its successor Transport Layer Security (TLS) protocol can be used to secure applications that communicate over the Internet [21]. The most widely deployed, freely available implementation of SSL/TLS protocol is the OpenSSL [20]. The core library of OpenSSL implements basic cryptographic functions and various utility functions [22]. The cryptographic functions, such as symmetric key ciphers, are extremely compute-intensive. OpenSSL dose these expensive computations through software implementations. It may not be able to compete with the increasing need for performance of encryption services. In order to accelerate the speed of OpenSSL, there are two typical solutions raised to overcome this problem, one is instruction set, the other is hardware accelerators. However, energy consumption of encryption has been ignored in the rush for performance.

According to the survey in 2011 by Professor Jonathan G. Koome [13], electricity used in global data centers accounted for 1.1-1.5% of total electricity use. Moreover, there is a huge waste of energy. The utilization rate of energy in data center is generally low. Data center is rapidly being throttled by the constraints of power delivery and cooling, generating a *energy wall* for high-density servers that seek to maximize commercial server encryption capacity [10]. As Luiz Andr Barroso said [2], developing computing infrastructure, the focus should be broader than performance alone. Breaking through this *energy wall* requires a focus on Performance per Watt instead of absolute performance [14]. Thus, energy efficiency is an emerging challenge with the increasing demands for performance and energy saving from data centers.

As discussed in Section 2.2, for secure communication with SSL/TLS, software encryption is not so energy efficient as AES-NI or hardware accelerators. However, neither the encryption approach with special instructions nor crypto-accelerators could perform well for various data blocks. Why not take full advantages of these solutions in a same system to select the most suitable encryption mechanism adaptively? Therefore, we propose *Adaptive Encryption Acceleration System* (AEAS), which is an OpenSSL encryption acceleration system through HW/SW co-design. The goal of this system is to provide a high energy-efficiency encryption service. The essential idea is to exert respective superiorities of energy efficiency for instruction set and hardware accelerators, meanwhile make full use of system resource. Specifically, we design *Adaptive Control Crypto* (*ac_crypto*) engine with a *Dynamic Management Mechanism* for OpenSSL. As to *Dynamic Management Mechanism*, we first set up a threshold policy to dynamically choose instruction set encryption or hardware

*Corresponding author:Chunhua Xiao Email: xiaochunhua@cqu.edu.cn

GLSVLSI '18, May23–25, 2018, Chicago, IL, USA

ACM ISBN 978-1-4503-5724-1/18/05...$15.00
https://doi.org/10.1145/3194554.3194584

encryption for requests through *RequestAllocation* algorithm. Besides, in order to maximize the utilization rate of CPUs, we propose *DynamicScheduler* algorithm to dynamically manage requests according to the utilization of hardware accelerators.

The main contributions of this work are listed as follows.

- To the best of our knowledge, the proposed AEAS is the first adaptive encryption solution towards high energy efficiency, which could invoke the most suitable method dynamically according to the size of data and the utilization of hardware to get the best Performance per Watt. The experiment shows that AEAS has great improvement comparing with others.
- We propose a detailed crypto-engine along with a *Dynamic Management Mechanism* for AEAS, which schedules requests adaptively for exerting the superiorities of each encryption approaches and making full use of system resource. Proposed design methodology possesses universal properties. It could be applied to other similar crypto-acceleration systems.
- We explore and analyze the energy efficiency of existing software, instruction set and hardware encryption approaches by quantifying Performance per Watt. We argue that it is essential to further the research on the energy efficiency optimizing for OpenSSL.

The rest of this paper is organized as follows. Section 2 discusses the existing encryption approaches for OpenSSL performance improvement and the challenges of them on energy consumption. Section 3 presents the design of *Adaptive Encryption Acceleration System* (AEAS) including the *Adaptive Control Crypto* (*ac_crypto*) engine and the *Dynamic Management Mechanism*. Section 4 presents the experimental evaluation results. This paper is concluded in Section 5.

2 BACKGROUND AND MOTIVATION

2.1 Background

Nowadays, using OpenSSL to protect data security is economical, efficient and easy to manage [9]. OpenSSL itself implements basic software library for cryptographic functions and provides various utility functions [22]. However, the speed of software implementation is not fast enough for incorporating encryption ubiquitously for all computing needs. There are some solutions raised to overcome this problem.

Most systems support cryptographic instructions set, such as Advanced Encryption Standard New Instructions (AES-NI) [17]. It is an extension to the x86-based architecture. It performs several compute-intensive parts of algorithm thus accelerating the execution of encryption. ARMv8 architecture also has user-level instructions to implement AES rounds [8].

Many manufacturers have developed hardware devices to accelerate encryption. For example, *qat_dh895xcc* [5] accelerator card with Intel QuickAssist Technology (QAT) [6]. It accelerates compute-intensive operations to enhance security and compression performance in cloud, networking and big data. It can free up CPU for offloading compute-intense security protocols. Most studies also proposed hardware solutions [1, 7, 11, 16]. Mohamed Khalil-Hani *et al.* [11] has proposed an FPGA-based embedded system integrating hardware that accelerates the cryptographic algorithms used in the SSL/TLS protocol. Vishnu P. Nambiar *et al.* [16] has implemented hardware based on FPGA to perform AES, which achieved a faster encryption for embedded system.

There is no doubt that these works make effective efforts for the acceleration in encryption services. Nevertheless, the research on energy consumption of encryption is far less than need. These works concentrated more on the technique implementation itself, and hardly taken into account the energy efficiency of cryptographic operations. Therefore, this paper focus on how to design a high energy-efficiency system for OpenSSL encryption acceleration.

2.2 Challenges of existing approaches

AES-NI and QAT are two main alternative methods to achieve encryption function for OpenSSL. These approaches mainly devote to improving the encryption performance. However, one fundamental property needs to be researched if the approaches should be deployed in large data centers: How is the energy efficiency of these approaches?

To explore the energy efficiency of state-of-the-art encryption approaches, we run OpenSSL *speed* benchmark with algorithm AES-256-CBC on an x86-based server connected with a digital power meter. As shown in Figure 1, we use Performance per Watt (PPW) to denote the energy efficiency for encryption methods, which is defined by the maximum performance divided by its energy consumption.

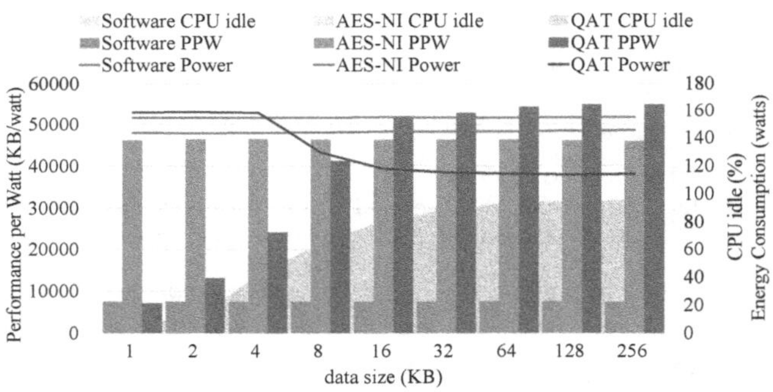

Figure 1: Energy efficiency of OpenSSL encryption methods with algorithm AES-256-CBC.

The experimental results reveal problems of the existing encryption approaches.

- For both encryption performance and energy consumption, OpenSSL software implementation is inferior to other two alternative methods.
- For small data blocks, QAT takes the highest energy consumption, but achieves low performance.
- For large data blocks, AES-NI spends more energy than QAT but gets lower performance.
- Software and AES-NI take up all the CPU resource, while QAT can significantly release CPU resource by offloading computing-intensive operations.

Based on the above analysis, software implementation should not be deployed in large data centers for its poor energy efficiency. In addition, we argue that the high energy-efficiency system for OpenSSL encryption acceleration should consider both advantages and disadvantages of these state-of-the-art encryption approaches. In order to maximize the energy efficiency, we should choose appropriate method to implement the encryption for different situations. Considering the underused CPU resource in hardware case, we should enhance their energy efficiency to increase the performance for whole system.

3 ADAPTIVE ENCRYPTION ACCELERATION SYSTEM

3.1 System architecture of AEAS

As discussed in Section 2.2, we have a knowledge of the characteristic of energy efficiency for instruction set implementation and hardware implementation. In this paper, toward a high energy-efficiency design for OpenSSL encryption acceleration, we propose *Adaptive Encryption Acceleration System* (AEAS) through HW/SW co-design. The design of AEAS is based on two observations.

First, it is obvious that no matter what size the data is, instruction set implementation has a stable and nice energy efficiency. Nevertheless, for large data blocks, hardware implementation has an edge over instruction set implementation. For small data blocks, the overhead of hardware initialization and interrupt processing neutralizes the benefit of hardware acceleration. For higher energy efficiency, encryption requests should be dispatched to appropriate method according to the data size.

Second, each encryption task implemented by instruction set occupies one CPU. Hardware offloads compute-intense operations and frees up CPUs. The idle resource in hardware case should be utilized to boost the system performance even further and reduce the cost of energy consumption.

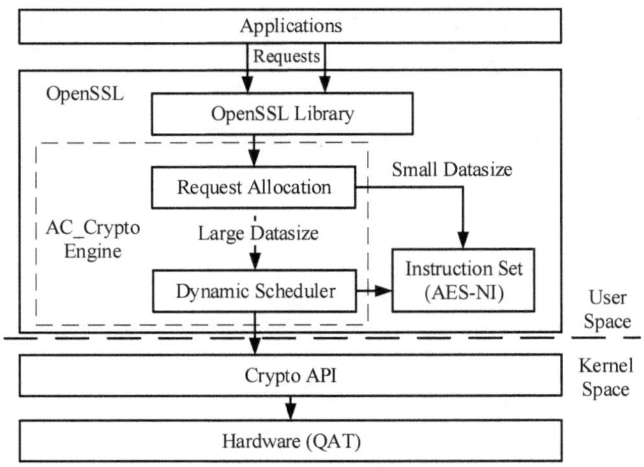

Figure 2: The Architecture of Adaptive Encryption Acceleration System (AEAS).

Figure 2 shows the architecture of AEAS. It consists of three components: OpenSSL, Crypto API and Hardware accelerators. Besides the core library with cryptographic functions and utility functions, we design *Adaptive Control Crypto* (*ac_crypto*) engine with a *Dynamic Management Mechanism* for OpenSSL. When encryption requests issued by upper layer applications reach OpenSSL, the *ac_crypto* engine dynamically dispatches and manages encryption tasks between instruction set and hardware through the *Dynamic Management Mechanism*, which is composed of *RequestAllocation* algorithm and *DynamicScheduler* algorithm. The following section describes the design methodology of AEAS in more detail.

3.2 Adaptive Control Crypto Engine

When compiling OpenSSL, we can choose whether to use the instruction set function via the configuration options *./configure [no-asm]*. On x86-based platform, the system supports AES-NI function by default, so OpenSSL can directly use this function through the interface *aesni_cbc_encrypt*. Besides, OpenSSL supports *ENGINE* mechanism since version 0.9.6 [4]. The *ENGINE* framework extends OpenSSL by providing the ability to add various hardware encryption devices to the system. It makes hardware accelerators more transparent and easy to be used.

However, the conventional *EGNINE* framework can only support either hardware or software/instruction set. To make OpenSSL compatibly work with both hardware algorithms and instruction set algorithms at the same time, we design an *Adaptive Control Crypto* engine named *ac_crypto* based on traditional *ENGINE* mechanism. Figure 3 shows the scheme of the *Adaptive Control Crypto* engine. To implement HW/SW co-design, the *ac_crypto* engine needs to contain the following components.

Register unit. It registers the third-party algorithms to OpenSSL protocol library, such as *ac_crypto_aes_cbc*, *ac_crypto_aes_192_cbc* and *ac_crypto_aes_256_cbc*. After loading *ac_crypto* engine, the newly added algorithms will replace the default encryption algorithm of OpenSSL.

Scheduler unit. Through a function pointer, OpenSSL gets the interface of instruction set and expands it to the process of hardware implementation. Therefore, *ac_crypto* engine supports instruction set encryption and hardware encryption in the meantime. In order to take full energy efficient advantages of different encryption methods and make the most use of system resource, *scheduler unit* dynamically manages encrypted tasks between hardware and instruction set.

Control unit. The parameters of encryption, such as IV, key and source data address, are encapsulated into the data structure which saves the context of the engine. The data object from OpenSSL needs to be processed for supporting hardware algorithm. If the hardware encryption function returns error message, *control unit* will call the instruction set algorithm to encrypt the data. *Control unit* makes the system run in a safe and stable state.

Interaction unit. It receives requests from OpenSSL and transmits them to Crypto API, which is the standard encryption frame for dealing with various encryption operations in Linux kernel.

In order to ensure hardware accelerators for normal use when encryption requests arrive at Crypto API, hardware

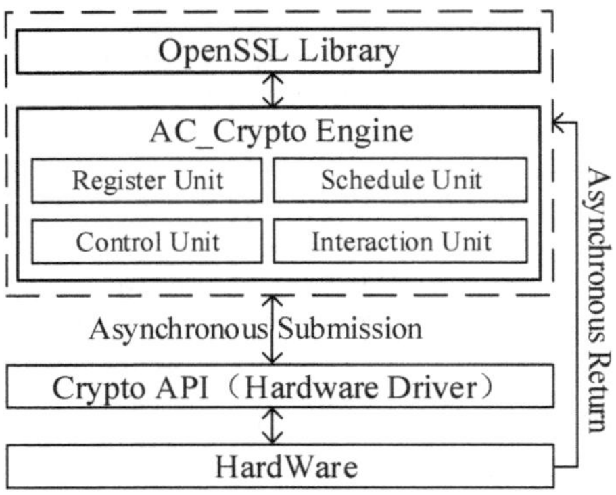

Figure 3: The scheme of Adaptive Control Crypto Engine.

driver must register corresponding encryption algorithm with the highest priority to Crypto API first. Hardware encryption is based on asynchronous mechanism. Processes submit encryption requests to hardware device in an asynchronous manner, and then processes enter the sleeping state. After finishing the operation of encryption, hardware accelerator wakes up the correspondingly sleeping process by interruption and returns the result asynchronously. Therefore, when OpenSSL encrypts large data blocks with hardware, the system has a lot of idle CPU resource.

The essential part of *ac_crypto* engine is the *schedule unit*, which dispatches requests with a *Dynamic Management Mechanism* according to the request size and system resource. In the next section, we discuss in detail how the *Dynamic Management Mechanism* works.

3.3 Dynamic management mechanism

In AEAS, we propose *RequestAllocation* algorithm and *DynamicScheduler* algorithm to implement the *Dynamic Management Mechanism* for *schedule unit* in *ac_crypto* engine.

From the previous analysis in Section 2.2, we can know that, for large data blocks, hardware encryption with accelerating device can get better PPW and has the advantages of energy consumption comparing with software and instruction set encryption. But when the data size is small, even software encryption has advantages over hardware. In AEAS, OpenSSL and Engine run in user space. To guarantee the universality, the system adopts standard Crypto API framework in kernel space for the invocation of hardware, which includes the overhead of mode switch and context switch. The overhead of hardware implementation is inevitable, and neutralizes the benefit of hardware acceleration for small data blocks. Besides, as to instruction set, the encryption function is accelerated directly through instructions without additional operations needed. Thus, for small data blocks, the performance of hardware is inferior to instruction set.

In order to bring respective superiorities of instruction set and hardware accelerators into full play, we set up a threshold policy to dynamically dispatch requests between instruction set and hardware. As shown in Algorithm 1, when the upper application submits a new encryption request to OpenSSL, *RequestAllocation* obtains the size of plaintext first. If the data size is greater than the given threshold T, this request will be pushed into hardware encryption queue *HW_Queue*, otherwise it will be assigned to instruction set queue *IS_Queue*.

ALGORITHM 1: *RequestAllocation*

```
Input: Req: Encrypted requests from applications to OpenSSL.
Output: HW_Queue: request queue encrypted by hardware.
        IS_Queue: request queue encrypted by instruction set.
Get Req from the upper-level applications;
Let Size ← get_request_size(Req);
if size > T then
    Add Req to HW_Queue;
else
    Add Req to IS_Queue;
end
```

Each request in *IS_Queue* needs one CPU to implement encryption. However, requests in *HW_Queue* have low utilization rate of CPUs. In order to enhance the energy efficiency of these free CPUs in hardware case, we propose *DynamicScheduler* algorithm dynamically managing requests between *HW_Queue* and *IS_Queue* according to the utilization of hardware accelerators to maximize the use of system resource.

AEAS adopts a background daemon to continuously monitor the utilization rate of hardware device. Algorithm 2 shows how this scheme works. If hardware resource has been fully used and there are still some requests in *HW_Queue*, *DynamicScheduler* will migrate requests from *HW_Queue* to *IS_Queue*. Otherwise, *DynamicScheduler* will transplant request, whose data size is greater than the given threshold T, from *IS_Queue* to *HW_Queue*. *DynamicScheduler* can make sure that hardware accelerators be fully used first, and then make the rest of CPU resource bring more PPW with instruction set for OpenSSL.

ALGORITHM 2: *DynamicScheduler*

```
Input: HW_Queue: original queue encrypted by hardware.
       IS_Queue: original queue encrypted by instruction set.
Output: HW_Queue: queue after scheduling encrypted by
        hardware. IS_Queue: queue after scheduling encrypted
        by instruction set.
while 1 do
    if hardware utilization is full then
        if HW_Queue not empty then
            Req ← get_hw_queue_req();
            migrate Req from HW_Queue to IS_Queue;
        end
    else
        if IS_Queue not empty then
            Req ← get_is_queue_req();
            Size ← get_request_size(Req);
            if size > T then
                migrate Req from IS_Queue to HW_Queue;
            end
        end
    end
end
```

4 EVALUATION

4.1 Experimental setup

We conduct our experiment on a Dell Precision Tower 7910 (Dell 0215PR) x86 server equipped with 16 Intel Xeon C-PUs E5-2630 v3 at 2.40GHz, 128G RAM, and 256G SSD. The operating system of the server is Ubuntu 17.04 with a kernel version 4.13. OpenSSL-1.0.2j is utilized to perform software encryption and instruction set (AES-NI) encryption through cryptographic library *libcrypto*. All the hardware cryptographic operations are executed through an external QAT accelerator card *qat_dh895xcc*. *RequestAllocation* and *DynamicScheduler* are also integrated into OpenSSL with *ac_crypto* engine for efficient utilization of instruction set and hardware accelerators. In this paper, we set the threshold T to 8KB based on the above experimental results in Section 2.2.

Energy measurement. As one of our goals is to evaluate the energy consumption of OpenSSL encryption operation, we connect the server to a *YOKOGAWA WT310E* digital power meter [3]. In the meanwhile, the instrument connects with a PC to save measured data and change the setting of it via software *WTViewerFreePlus*. It accepts two input parameters: voltage and current; the accuracy is $\pm 0.1\%$ of reading 0.05% of range [15]. Moreover, we get the maximum active power every third of a second. We keep the temperature in the server room constant.

Performance benchmark. Benchmark *speed*, a part of OpenSSL package, runs for the encryption performance tests. It measures the throughput on various ciphers in terms of the number of bytes processed in a time unit. The OpenSSL *speed* command, by default, runs through every single algorithm in every single supported mode and option, with several different sizes of data, for 3 seconds [18]. At the end of testing, *speed* reports the encryption performance results in 1000s of bytes per second processed. Before the experiment, in order to get steady and multiple results of energy consumption and performance, we control the testing time from 3 to 10 seconds by modifying the *SECONDES* in *OpenSSL-1.0.2j/apps/speed.c* and add several different data size cases.

4.2 Experimental Results

For getting the energy efficiency of different methods with algorithm AES-256-CBC, we record the performance, energy consumption and CPU utilization of OpenSSL encryption approaches in the condition of variable data size, including 1KB, 2KB, 4KB, 8KB, 16KB, 32KB, 64KB, 128KB and 256KB, and divide the performance by its energy consumption to get the PPW. Table 1 shows the energy efficiency of four different OpenSSL encryption methods, including software, instruction set, hardware and AEAS.

As shown in Table 1, when data size is smaller than 8KB, the PPW of AEAS gradually increased from 41251.7KB/watt to 43114.4KB/watt. Furthermore, when data size is larger than 8KB, the PPW of AEAS increased from 73084.7KB/watt to 77710.5KB/watt. Regardless of data size, AEAS makes the utmost of CPU and hardware resource.

To better present the energy-efficiency improvement with our proposed AEAS, we show the incremental multiples of PPW for AEAS comparing with software, instruction set and hardware in Figure 4.

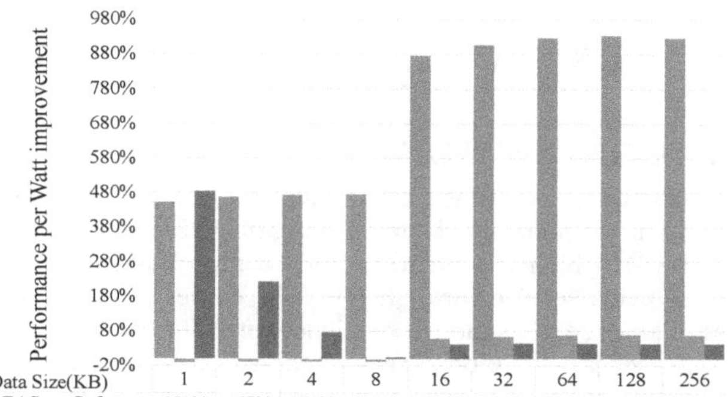

Data Size(KB)	1	2	4	8	16	32	64	128	256
AEAS vs. Software	451%	467%	473%	475%	876%	906%	928%	934%	927%
AEAS vs. AES-NI	-10.5%	-8.7%	-7.6%	-6.9%	58.3%	63.8%	67.4%	68.8%	68.1%
AEAS vs. QAT	483.7%	221.9%	76.4%	4.7%	42.1%	43.9%	43.2%	42.8%	42.4%

Figure 4: Energy-efficiency improvement comparing with Software, Instruction Set and Hardware

AEAS vs. Software implementation. The performance of software encryption is poor, because it has no accelerating measures. As shown in Figure 4, for different data size, the PPW of AEAS remarkably outperforms software method. AEAS gets 451.2% to 933.5% PPW improvement comparing with software implementation.

AEAS vs. Instruction Set implementation. When data size is larger than 8KB, AEAS improves 58.3% to 68.8% PPW over AES-NI. Beyond that, the PPW of AEAS is a little bit lower than AES-NI. The reason is that a fraction of CPU resource is occupied for data size checkout and scheduling decision. Therefore, for the small data size, the maximum performance of AEAS is somewhat lower than instruction set implementation. However, this influence is decreased with the increasing of data size, on account of the reduced frequency for scheduling checkout.

AEAS vs. Hardware implementation. As shown in Table 1, the energy efficiency of hardware encryption is worse for small data blocks, and smaller the data block, worse the energy efficiency. As we can see from the results in Figure 4, for small data blocks that less than 8KB, AEAS could get several times PPW improvement comparing with only hardware encryption with QAT, and smaller the data block, bigger the improvement. The reason behind this is the adaptive scheduler avoiding low performance of accelerators. For large data blocks, which typically performs well for hardware accelerators, the proposed AEAS still could get around 43% PPW over only hardware implementation. This contribution comes from best utilization of system resource through dynamic management mechanism.

Based on the above analysis, cooperating hardware and instruction set in AEAS exerts their respective superiorities and makes full use of system resource, and contributes a better energy efficiency for OpenSSL in the cases of various situations.

Table 1: Energy Efficiency of 4 different OpenSSL encryption methods with algorithm AES-256-CBC

data size(KB)	1K	2K	4K	8K	16K	32K	64K	128K	256K
Software PPW(KB/watt)	7484.0	7470.8	7484.7	7498.0	7490.2	7516.0	7526.4	7519.0	7511.7
AES-NI PPW(KB/watt)	46113.5	46383.7	46446.6	46331.4	46170.5	46182.9	46194.8	46045.3	45864.2
QAT PPW(KB/watt)	7112.4	13166.4	24197.2	41289.1	51628.6	52744.6	54266.3	54904.8	54898.3
AEAS PPW(KB/watt)	**41251.7**	**42332.0**	**42894.5**	**43114.4**	**73084.7**	**75633.4**	**77346.1**	**77710.5**	**77117.4**

5 CONCLUSION

In this paper, we present an OpenSSL encryption acceleration scheme, named *Adaptive Encryption Acceleration System* (AEAS), which is able to provide a high energy-efficiency encryption service through HW/SW co-design. We explore and analyze the energy efficiency of different encryption approaches with OpenSSL first, and find that software encryption has a very poor energy efficiency for all application scenarios. In addition, instruction set and hardware accelerators have their respective advantages and disadvantages of energy efficiency for different cases. We design the *Adaptive Control Crypto* (*ac_crypto*) engine with a *Dynamic Management Mechanism*, including *RequestAllocation* algorithm and *DynamicScheduler* algorithm. It exerts the superiorities of instruction set and hardware and makes full use of system resource. The *RequestAllocation* algorithm divides the encryption requests into different task queues according to the data size of each request, meanwhile the *DynamicScheduler* algorithm dynamically manages these requests between these task queues. Experimental results show that, for typical encryption algorithm AES-256-CBC, the proposed AEAS can provide energy-efficiency improvement by up to 933.5%, 68.8%, and 483.7% comparing with software, AES-NI and QAT, respectively. Proposed design methodology possesses universal properties. It could be applicable to other kinds of encryption algorithm but differ in effect. In addition, the proposed AEAS can be applied to different applications, such as Nginx, Apache and other web services.

ACKNOWLEDGMENTS

This work is supported by National Natural Science Foundation of China: 61502061, Chongqing Application Foundation and Research in Cutting-edge Technologies: cstc2015jcyjA40016, and the Fundamental Research Funds for the Central Universities: 106112017CDJXY180004.

REFERENCES

[1] Josep Balasch, Benedikt Gierlichs, Kimmo Ja, Ingrid Verbauwhede, et al. 2014. Hardware/software co-design flavors of elliptic curve scalar multiplication. In *Electromagnetic Compatibility, 2014 IEEE International Symposium on*. IEEE, 758–763.

[2] Luiz André Barroso. 2005. The price of performance. *Queue* 3, 7 (2005), 48–53.

[3] Christopher B Barth, Intae Moon, Yutian Lei, Shibin Qin, CN Robert, et al. 2015. Experimental evaluation of capacitors for power buffering in single-phase power converters. In *Energy Conversion Congress and Exposition (ECCE), 2015 IEEE*. IEEE, 6269–6276.

[4] Lilian Bossuet, Michael Grand, Lubos Gaspar, Viktor Fischer, and Guy Gogniat. 2013. Architectures of flexible symmetric key crypto enginesa survey: From hardware coprocessor to multi-crypto-processor system on chip. *ACM Computing Surveys (CSUR)* 45, 4 (2013), 41.

[5] Intel Corp. 2013. Intel Xeon Processor E5-2600 v2-Based Platforms for Large-Scale Communications Infrastructure Systems. (2013). https://www.intel.com/content/www/us/en/intelligent-systems/highland-forest/xeon-e5-2600-v2-large-scale-communications-brief.html

[6] Intel Corp. 2015. Programming Intel QuickAssist Technology Hardware Accelerators for Optimal Performance. *White Paper* (2015).

[7] R Cowart, D Coe, J Kulick, and A Milenković. 2017. An Implementation and Experimental Evaluation of Hardware Accelerated Ciphers in All-Programmable SoCs. In *Proceedings of the SouthEast Conference*. ACM, 34–41.

[8] Richard Grisenthwaite. 2011. Armv8 technology preview. In *IEEE Conference*.

[9] Li Gui-hong, Zheng Hua, and Li Gui-zhi. 2010. Building a secure web server based on OpenSSL and apache. In *E-Business and E-Government (ICEE), 2010 International Conference on*. IEEE, 1307–1310.

[10] Alex K Jones. 2017. Green Computing: New Challenges and Opportunities. In *Proceedings of the on Great Lakes Symposium on VLSI 2017*. ACM, 3–3.

[11] Mohamed Khalil-Hani, Vishnu P Nambiar, and MN Marsono. 2010. Hardware Acceleration of OpenSSL cryptographic functions for high-performance Internet Security. In *Intelligent Systems, Modelling and Simulation (ISMS), 2010 International Conference on*. IEEE, 374–379.

[12] Donald Kline, Nikolas Parshook, Xiaoyu Ge, Erik Brunvand, Rami Melhem, Panos K Chrysanthis, and Alex K Jones. 2016. Holistically evaluating the environmental impacts in modern computing systems. In *Green and Sustainable Computing Conference (GSC-C),2016 Seventh International*. IEEE, 1–8.

[13] Jonathan Koomey. 2011. Growth in data center electricity use 2005 to 2010. *A report by Analytical Press, completed at the request of The New York Times* 9 (2011).

[14] James Laudon. 2005. Performance/watt: the new server focus. *ACM SIGARCH Computer Architecture News* 33, 4 (2005), 5–13.

[15] Yokogawa Digital Power Meter. 2013. *WT310/WT310HC/WT330 Digital Power Meter User's Manual*. https://www.yokogawa.com/pdf/provide/E/GW/IM/0000027039/0/IMWT310-17EN.pdf.

[16] Vishnu P Nambiar, Mohamed Khalil-Hani, and Muhammad M Zabidi. 2009. Accelerating the AES encryption function in OpenSSL for embedded systems. *International Journal of Information and Communication Technology* 2, 1-2 (2009), 83–93.

[17] Jeffrey Rott. 2010. Intel advanced encryption standard instructions (aes-ni). *Technical Report, Technical Report, Intel* (2010).

[18] Anthony J Stieber. 2006. OpenSSL hacks. *Linux Journal* 147 (2006), 74–77.

[19] Subashini Subashini and Veeraruna Kavitha. 2011. A survey on security issues in service delivery models of cloud computing. *Journal of network and computer applications* 34, 1 (2011), 1–11.

[20] John Viega, Matt Messier, and Pravir Chandra. 2002. *Network security with openSSL: cryptography for secure communications.* O'Reilly Media, Inc.

[21] Judson Wilson, Riad S Wahby, Henry Corrigan-Gibbs, Dan Boneh, Philip Levis, and Keith Winstein. 2017. Trust but Verify: Auditing the Secure Internet of Things. In *Proceedings of the 15th Annual International Conference on Mobile Systems, Applications, and Services*. ACM, 464–474.

[22] Eric A Young, Tim J Hudson, and R Engelschall. 2011. Openssl: The open source toolkit for ssl/tls. (2011).

A Machine Learning Attack Resistant Dual-mode PUF

Qian Wang, Mingze Gao, Gang Qu
Department of Electrical and Computer Engineering and Institute of Systems Research
University of Maryland, College Park, MD
{qwang126,mgao1,gangqu}@umd.edu

ABSTRACT

Silicon Physical Unclonable Function (PUF) is arguably the most promising hardware security primitive. In particular, PUFs that are capable of generating a large amount of challenge response pairs (CRPs) can be used in many security applications. However, these CRPs can also be exploited by machine learning attacks to model the PUF and predict its response. In this paper, we first show that, based on data in the public domain, two popular PUFs that can generate CRPs (i.e., arbiter PUF and reconfigurable ring oscillator (RO) PUF) can be broken by simple logistic regression (LR) attack with about 99% accuracy. We then propose a feedback structure to XOR the PUF response with the challenge and challenge the PUF again to generate the response. Results show that this successfully reduces LR's learning accuracy to the lower 50%, but artificial neural network (ANN) learning attack still has an 80% success rate. Therefore, we propose a configurable ring oscillator based dual-mode PUF which works with both odd number of inverters (like the reconfigurable RO PUF) and even number of inverters (like a bistable ring (BR) PUF). Since currently there are no known attacks that can model both RO PUF and BR PUF, the dual-mode PUF will be resistant to modeling attacks as long as we can hide its working mode from the attackers, which we achieve with two practical methods. Finally, we implement the proposed dual-mode PUF on Nexys 4 FPGA boards and collect real measurement to show that it reduces the learning accuracy of LR and ANN to the mid-50% and low 60%, respectively. In addition, it meets the PUF requirements of uniqueness, randomness, and robustness.

KEYWORDS

Physical Unclonable Functions; Configurable ring oscillator; Modeling attacks; Artificial Neural Network

ACM Reference Format:
Qian Wang, Mingze Gao, Gang Qu. 2018. A Machine Learning Attack Resistant Dual-mode PUF. In *GLSVLSI '18: 2018 Great Lakes Symposium on VLSI, May 23–25, 2018, Chicago, IL, USA.* ACM, New York, NY, USA, 6 pages. https://doi.org/10.1145/3194554.3194590

1 INTRODUCTION

Physical Unclonable Functions (PUFs) have been widely accepted as a promising hardware security primitive and recently adopted in many security applications such as hardware fingerprinting and authentication, secure key generation, and secure storage for ciphers. One of the most important features of PUF is that it can map challenges (inputs) to responses (outputs) based on the intrinsic physical variation in the hardware devices. The properties of unclonability and unpredictability among others give PUFs certain advantages over conventional cryptography based solutions in many security applications, in particular on systems where computing, power, and storage resources are limited.

There are three representative PUFs that can generate challenge-response pairs (CRPs) exponential to the number of bits in the challenges: the classic arbiter PUFs [1] where the challenge determines the delay paths, the reconfigurable ring oscillator (RO) PUFs [2] where the challenge determines whether the inverter in each stage will be included in the delay path, and the bistable ring PUF [3] which can generate a stable random bit based on the challenge applied to each of its stage. However, due to the fact that the exponential number of CRPs in these PUFs are generated from hardware units (such as MUXes and inverters) that are linear to the number of bits in the challenge, it is not surprising that they are facing severe threats from (machine) learning based attacks. In such modeling attacks, the attackers can utilize a subset of CRPs to build mathematical models for the PUF and then use the model to predict the response of the other challenges thus breaking the PUF. Arbiter PUFs and reconfigurable RO PUFs are vulnerable to linear learning techniques such as logistic regression (LR) [4–6] and the bistable ring PUF can be broken by differential and linear analysis [7].

Our goal is to seek novel PUF structures that are highly resistant to machine learning attacks based on both linear models and non-linear models. This paper makes the following contributions towards achieving this goal:

(1) We apply the machine learning attacks on conventional arbiter PUF and RO PUF. Both the linear model based attack (Logistic regression, LR) and the non-linear model based attack (artificial neural network, ANN) can break the PUFs with about 99% accuracy.
(2) We introduce a feedback structure in the PUF where we perform bitwise XOR of the challenge and its response and use the result as input to challenge the PUF again in order to create the real response. This hides the direct relationship between challenge and real response because the attacker cannot observe the first response. This approach successfully reduces LR's learning ability to the low 50%, but ANN's learning accuracy is still above the 80%.
(3) We propose a novel dual-mode feedback PUF on the reconfigurable RO-PUF platform which can behave as either an RO PUF or a bistable ring PUF to confuse the attacker. We implement the dual-mode PUF on FPGA and the measured

GLSVLSI '18, May 23–25, 2018, Chicago, IL, USA

ACM ISBN 978-1-4503-5724-1/18/05...$15.00
https://doi.org/10.1145/3194554.3194590

data show that we are able to reduce the learning accuracy of LR to the mid-50% and that of the ANN to the low 60%.

(4) We evaluate the quality of the proposed dual-mode PUF in terms of randomness, uniqueness, and reliability (against temperature changes). The results based on real FPGA chip measurement show that the dual-mode PUF meets all these requirements.

The remainder of the paper is organized as follows: Section 2 introduces the related PUF designs and their vulnerability to modeling attacks; Section 3 presents the proposed design of configurable dual-mode PUF. In addition, the challenge obfuscation and masking schemes are introduced in this section; Section 4 provides the experimental results for the modeling attack and demonstrates that the dual-mode PUF could resist the state-of-art modeling attacks. Section 5 presents the quality analysis of the innovated PUF structure, and then Section 6 concludes this paper.

2 PUF DESIGNS AND THEIR VULNERABILITY TO MODELING ATTACKS

For machine learning attacks, it is necessary to collect reasonably amount of training data. Therefore, in this section, we briefly discuss PUFs capable of generating large amount of CRPs and their vulnerability to modeling attacks.

2.1 Arbiter PUF and basics of modeling attack

The classic arbiter PUF [1] consists of two MUX arrays, at each stage of the array there are two MUXes, both connecting to the two MUXes in the next stage. Two signals start from the two MUXes in the first stage simultaneously and choose their path according to the value of the selection bit to the MUX in each stage. These selection bits are known as challenge. Due to manufacture variation, the two signal will not go through the last stage at the same time and this delay discrepancy defines a PUF bit, which is called response.

In a modeling attack, the input of the training data is the challenge of PUF: $C = c_1 \cdots c_k$; and the label will be the 1-bit response $r \in \{0, 1\}$. The arbiter PUF could be modeled as a linear additive model since a response bit is generated based on the summation of delay segment in each stage depending on the challenge C[4, 5]. The delay difference Δ can be expressed as

$$\Delta = \omega^T \Phi \tag{1}$$

where ω is the delay vector for each of the segment in the arbiter PUF structure and Φ is the following function of the k-bit challenge C

$$\Phi(C) = (\Phi^1(C), ..., \Phi^k(C), 1)^T \tag{2}$$

where $\Phi^j(C) = \prod_{i=j}^{k}(1 - 2c_i)$ for j = 1, ..., k (Note: different types of PUF would have different Φ function to map a challenge C to a real value). If $\Delta > 0$, the response bit r will be '1'. Otherwise, r will be '0'.

The goal of a machine learning attacker is to find out an estimate of ω that can represent the actual delay vector of physical PUF structure. With sufficient number of CRPs, the delay information ω of each stage in the arbiter PUF can be learned with high accuracy [4, 8, 9]. Now the general assumption is that such attack requires less than 10% of the total number of CRPs [10].

There are several methods proposed to resist the modeling attacks on PUFs. One solution is to complicate the modeling attack by altering the PUF structure and reducing the correlation between challenges and responses, e.g., the XOR-mixed PUF [5] and the twisted PUF [11]. These attempts provide some modest defenses over the linear learning algorithm; however, simply adding nonlinearity in the PUF structure cannot defend more powerful learning techniques that could solve non-linear classifications.

Another efficient approach to confuse the adversary is to introduce redundancy in the challenges[12]. In this approach, the challenges are obfuscated either by adding another redundant challenge or by padding some unused bits in the original challenge in order to hide the real challenge from the adversary. This will definitely increase hardware cost in both the PUF instance and the authentication server. Also, it will cause longer response time as both the PUF and the server need a pre-processing procedure before the authentication.

2.2 Reconfigurable RO PUF and Bistable PUF

The original RO PUF uses the delay difference between two ring oscillators with an odd number of inverters to create one bit of information. Its main application is to generate a secret key and does not support CRPs. Modification to the RO PUF structure has been proposed to enable CRP, for example, by having two inverters at each stage and use the challenge bit to select one. In the highly flexible reconfigurable RO PUF, a selection bit decides at each stage whether the inverter will be included in the RO. Thus different challenges, which are called configuration vectors, may result in different response [2, 13]. Delay in the reconfigurable RO PUF structure could be mapped as linear additive functions, which demonstrate vulnerabilities to machine learning methods.

The concept of bistable ring PUF (BR PUF) was proposed in [3] where even number of inverters are connected from head to tail to force it into two arbitrary Boolean states, logic 0 or logic 1. The security evaluation of BR PUF has been studied in [11], where the resilience of BR PUF against modeling attacks is evaluated and it is stated that a possible mapping relationship between challenge and response may cause the PUF response to be predictable. Furthermore, it shows that the alternative twisted bistable rings PUF (TBR PUF) is immune to learning algorithms. However, it still leaks some correlations between the challenges and the final stable states, which could be learned by specific learning strategy.

Our proposed dual-mode PUF design is developed based on the architecture of the reconfigurable RO PUF but allow the use of an even number of inverters to provide features of bistable ring PUF. Thus, depending on the challenge (i.e. the configuration vector), the dual-mode PUF may work either as an RO PUF or as a BR PUF. Because these are two different types of PUF and existing machine learning models to attack them are different (to the best of our knowledge, there has not been any efficient model reported working for both the delay ring and bistable ring), it will be very challenging for model-based attacks to break the proposed dual-mode PUF.

3 DESIGN OF DUAL-MODE PUF

In the following, we will first discuss the design of unit cell and propose our dual mode topology. Then we will introduce the technique applied in the dual mode PUF design to thwart the modeling attacks.

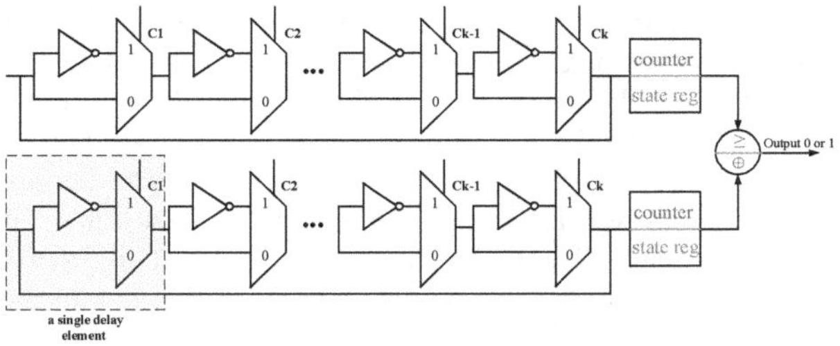

Figure 1: The architecture of K-stage reconfigurable dual-mode PUF, a single delay element is marked in shaded box

3.1 Dual-mode PUF structure

As shown in Fig.1, the basic delay element which consists of an inverter and a multiplexer has been placed in parallel and connected from head to tail. The corresponding challenge bit of stage i is c_i which controls the inverter to be selected or not. If the selection bit is "1", the delay of this stage would be $d_{path1} = d_{mux}+d_{inv}+d_{wire}$; otherwise, the delay of the inverter would not be included and the delay would be $d_{path0} = d_{mux} + d_{wire}$.

By connecting the basic delay element, we build the dual mode configurable PUF. Unlike those delay based RO-PUFs, which require odd number inverters in the chain to guarantee the oscillation, our new design would work on both odd and even number inverters. More precisely, the working mode of our PUF depends on the parity of the challenge as shown in Fig.1. For the odd mode, the circuit drawn in a rectangular box works as a counter which counts the oscillating frequency, and the circular shape module represents a comparator which compares the frequency and generates 1-bit response based on the difference. For the even mode, the functionality of the rectangular box is a state register which stores the stable state is whether 5 (0101) or A (1010). The following module is an exclusive-or function generates 1-bit response from two separated rings to make the even structure compatible to the odd structure. Moreover, the exclusive-or (XOR) logic has the linearly non-separable attribute, which would offering intrinsic resilience to linear machine learning attacks. In addition, the output of XOR logic is of uniform distribution as long as one of the inputs is uniformly distributed. Therefore, XOR logic gate standouts other logics like AND, OR, etc. in our design.

3.2 Overcoming the learning vulnerability of bistable ring

Our basic delay element shown in Fig.1 has some significant changes compared to the bistable ring shown in Fig.2. First, we only deploy one inverter and the compared delay path as $path_0$ is generated by the intrinsic delay of the wire and the MUX. Compared to the bistable ring, we get rid of the duplicated inverter and the demultiplexer for each stage which could definitely save the hardware cost.

Besides, our design overcomes the modeling attack vulnerability of bi-stable ring discussed in [7]. In the traditional bistable ring, the driving behavior of one fixed inverter is compared to the inverter in the adjacent stage. With this assumption, the author defined the difference between the pull-up and pull-down capability of the inverter as strength t_i for the ith stage. And all the even stages will contribute toward the positive response as t_i, the odd stages will contribute toward the strength as $-t_i$. Thus the attacker can model the competition behavior based on the strength of each stage.

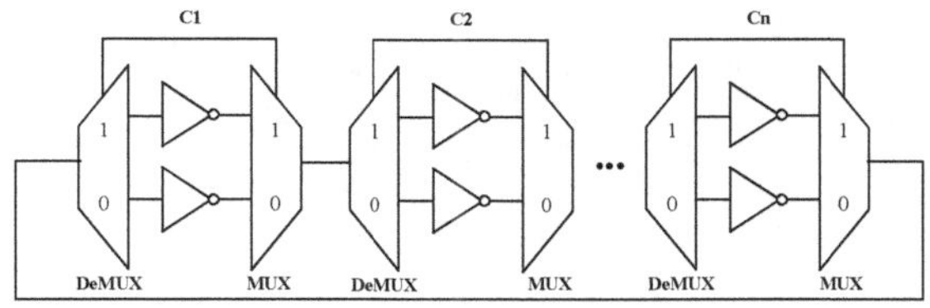

Figure 2: Delay element of bistable ring PUF

However, this model would not work in our dual mode design because we do not fix the odd stages to be pull-up and the even stages to be pull-down. On the contrary, each stage in our design could either be the pull-up or pull-down determined by the input challenges. When the selection bit for this stage is 0, the inverter in this stage would be bypassed and the input signal would directly drive on the next selected inverter. This could avoid the fixed adjacent "strong-weak" pattern in the bistable ring. Moreover, the connecting wires and the MUXs could influence on the output resistance of the inverter which indeed impacts the driving capability of it. All of the aspects make it infeasible to accurately model the behavior of our new design of bistable ring by the pull-up and pull-down strength.

3.3 Hiding the working mode by challenge obfuscation and masking

The work mode of the dual-mode PUF is purely determined by the parity of the input challenge. If the adversary could learn the parity of challenge in advance, he may build two separate models for the dual-mode PUF and the complexity of learning the PUF would be halved. Here, we designed two mechanisms to hide the working mode of our dual mode PUF to mitigate the security concern as the adversary could know the parity of the challenges.

3.3.1 Challenge obfuscation. Fig. 3 shows the flow chart of our challenge obfuscating and masking approaches. The original challenge C would pass the challenge obfuscated circuit first, and several bits of C are modified to make the parity of the new generated challenge C' is unknown to the adversary. As a result of this, the attacker cannot build separate learning models even though he knows how the dual mode PUF works. Note that the challenge obfuscation circuit is built with the PUF instance in hardware; there is no I/O ports for the adversary to acquire the new generated challenge C'.

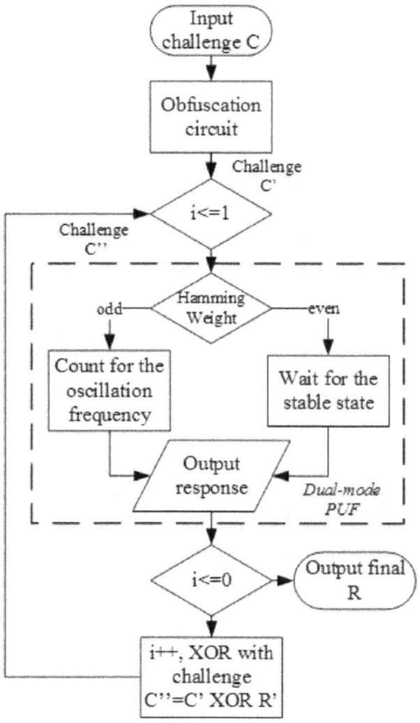

Figure 3: The flow chart of two-round Dual mode PUF illustrating the challenge obfuscation and masking

A 16-bit challenge case is shown in Fig.4. The input challenge is divided into 4 parts (the length of the challenge is the multiple of 4). We determinatively choose one bit from each part (colored in yellow), and generate the boolean value by bitwise AND or OR operation. Next, we assign the new boolean value to the selected positions (e.g. bit 8 and bit 9 in this example). The goal for this challenge obfuscation is to confuse the adversary on the parity of the challenge. Even though some bits are unchanged from the original challenge after the obfuscation, this would not hamper the effect we expect. We conduct statistical analysis on our obfuscation mechanism and results show that for both even and odd inputs, the parity flip rate is 0.5 which is as the same as random flip rate.

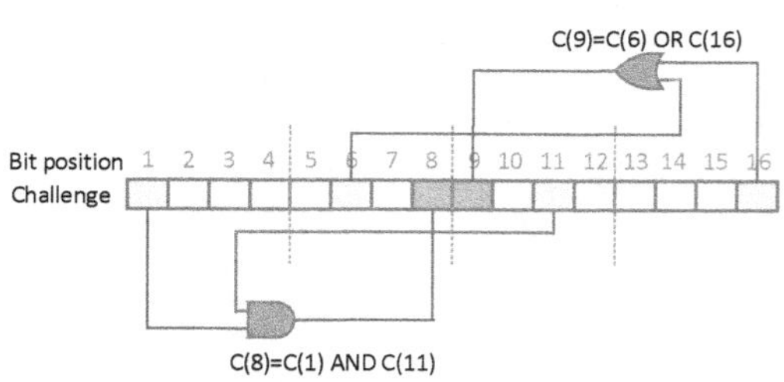

Figure 4: Challenge obfuscation example, when the challenge bit is 16 and each sub-block has 4 bits

3.3.2 Challenge masking. From the first step, the obfuscation circuit successfully hides the parity of the input challenge but some bits of are still exposed to the attacker. It is necessary to find an approach to hide the input pattern from the malicious attackers without hampering the PUF property. Thus, we design a two-round masking scheme to conceal the input challenge to the adversary shown in Fig. 3. In the first round, the challenge after the obfuscation circuit C' would input to the PUF directly and the same length output is generated as $R' = \text{PUF}(C')$, where we place the same number of rings to keep the length of output unchanged. Then, the response R' would be exclusive-or with the input challenge C' in obtaining a new challenge as $C'' = C' \oplus R'$ which is the input to the PUF in the second round. This procedure masks the challenge of the second round which not only conceals the parity but also hides the relationship of challenge and response to the attacker. The intermediate result R' and C' would input to the PUF in the next step immediately, thus leaving no time for the attacker to intercept them. Therefore, the adversary can only use the input challenge with two-round response (C, R) to train a model. The direct additive relationships between challenge and response pairs are confused by the XOR function and the two-round iteration. The intermediate responses are required in order to derive the final response, but the intermediate results are invisible. Hence, those CRPs leak limited information to an adversary in modeling the PUF.

After implementing the challenge obfuscation and masking, the adversary faces a big challenge to find out the appropriate model for the PUF. Since the parity of the input challenges is hidden to the adversary, he can only randomly guess the combination of work mode of the PUF from 4 possible patterns: odd-odd, odd-even, even-odd and even-even. However, the adversary has no knowledge on how to distinguish the CRPs from the four patterns. If he arbitrary choose one mode, there are 3/4 noise CRPs which he could not figure out. We will theoretically prove the upper bound of the prediction of accuracy in the following. It has been demonstrated that a relationship between machine learning complexity and noise of input labels is subject to the noise bit corruption rate η , where a value of $\eta = 0$ means that none of the labels are corrupted, and $\eta = 0.5$ means that values are completely corrupted by random noise.

The adversary can guess, among all the candidate mode, given an incoming CRP, the adversary can have 1/D chance to guess the correct working mode. In our case, for two-round dual mode PUF, as D=2, the successful rate of the guess would be $1/D \times 1/D = 1/4$. We define the mode uncertainty for one step would be as $\varepsilon_u(D) = 1 - 1/D$. Thus, for the dual mode PUF the mode uncertainty would be 1-1/4=3/4. Besides, we assume that the learning noise for a certain mode would be η_e , and the learning noise after apply the working mode uncertainty would be

$$\eta_a(n) = 1 - [\varepsilon_u(D) \cdot \eta_e(n) + (1 - \varepsilon_u(D)) \cdot (1 - \eta_e(n))] \quad (3)$$

We can get the noise of input labels by experiment and plug into the equation to get the bound for the final noise level. By plugging the noise level of 0.046 from experiment [14], the noise after two rounds would be a level of 0.273, and the advantages would grows with D.

4 EXPERIMENTAL RESULTS

We choose the most representative two methods (LR and ANN) to test our dual-mode PUF design. To make a comparison, we also

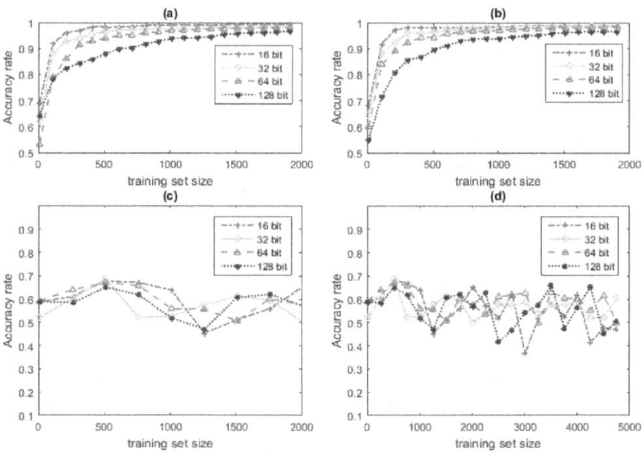

Figure 5: Results of modeling attack (logistic regression) on (a) RO PUF, (b) Arbiter PUF, and (c) Dual mode PUF with 2000 CRPs (d) Dual mode PUF with 5000 CRPs

test the traditional arbiter PUF and RO-PUF by the same learning algorithms. Also, we will verify the potential of anti-modeling on different proposed dual-mode PUF structures.

4.1 Results from logistic regression

4.1.1 Test results on a single pair of ROs. We first test a single pair of RO with different stage size as 16, 32, 64, 128. The CRPs for arbiter and RO-PUF are from the simulated data. Paper [5] demonstrates that modeling attacks would work both on simulated and silicon data, and the only difference is that the results on simulated data are noise free. However, by using more CRPs in training stage, results from the real silicon could achieve the same accuracy rate (e.g., 99%) compare to the simulated data.

The logistic regression attack results for three kinds of PUFs are shown in Fig.5. We sweep the training size from 10 to 2000 for the traditional arbiter and RO-PUFs and enlarge it to 5000 for our dual-mode PUF. The y-axis represents the learning accuracy rate and the maximum value is 1 which means the PUF responses can be completely predicted. For ideal learning resistant case, the accuracy should be around 0.5, meaning that the machine learning prediction is no better than the random guess.

It can be seen in Fig.5 (a) and (b) the learning rates are near 1 (100%) when the training set is around 2000 which indicates that the logistic regression successfully models the arbiter and RO-PUF. The learning accuracy got from the dual mode PUF is dramatically different from the above, shown in the 5 (c). The learning rate is oscillating around 0.55 nearing the randomly guess rate. Moreover, even we enlarge the training set to 5000 shown in the Fig. 5 (d)(nearly double size we used for delay based PUFs), the predication rates has no trend in increasing. From the results summarized above, it is confident to conclude that our dual mode PUF could resist the logistic regression learning attack.

4.1.2 Test results on PUF array. Further, we apply the attack method on PUF array structure in section 3.3. As discussed before, the attacker may group the challenge based on its parity and build different learning models separately. To solve this problem, we propose the array structure to break the linear relationship of the challenge and response as discussed in section 3.3. We place in total 32 ring instances on the FPGA and each ring consists 32 stages. We name this structure as (32,32) PUF array. To keep consistent, the single pair of ROs we studied above is named as (32,1) structure.

The array structure masks the actual challenge of the second round C'' by the first round response R' as $C'' = C' \oplus R'$. We choose XOR function because it could add resilience to the linear learning model. As a result of this, the learning accuracy rate shown in Table 1 goes down to around 0.5 when using logistic regression to model the masked PUF arrays. To make a comparison, we also list the attack result of a single pair of 32-bit ROs shown in the table as (32,1). Results from the Table 1 shows that the logistic regression method fails in modeling the array structure. The reason is because LR is a linear learning algorithm and only works for the linear separable models. The masking method applied on the input challenges introduces the intrinsic non-linearity, thus making the logistic regression ineffective. However, the state-of-art neural network could overcome the limitation of the linear learning algorithms. Therefore, we also test the same array structure design under the neural network based learning method.

4.2 Results from neural network

The ANN method could model non-linearity based on the multilayer network structure and the non-linear activation function. The ANN learning network structure we used in the experiment is a 2-layer MLP with 40 nodes in each layer. The learning results from the ANN method are shown on the right side of Table 1. We observe that the ANN method greatly improves the learning rate for the arbiter PUF and RO PUF, but still fails to learn the dual-mode PUF.

Table 1: Attack results for three type of PUFs

Type	LR		ANN	
	(32,32)	(32,1)	(32,32)	(32,1)
Arbiter PUF	0.5132	0.9851	0.8192	0.9933
RO PUF	0.5009	0.9906	0.8132	0.9982
Dual Mode PUF	0.5404	0.5580	0.6162	0.6105

5 PUF QUALITY ANALYSIS

In this section, we evaluate the quality of the two kind of implementations for the dual-mode PUF: one is the single pair of ROs which has 16 bit, 32 bit, 64 bit and 128 bit challenge width respectively; the other is the array structure, where n pairs of dual-mode rings (n delay elements for each) are placed and the length of the controlled configurable bit is chosen as $n = 16, 32$.

We evaluate the uniformity(randomness of the output) of a single pair RO based on the response collected from FPGA board. The uniformity checks the distribution of "0" and "1" under different configuration inputs. The good PUF should have the ideal value of 0.5 as uniformly distributed. The results of uniformity per bit under 50000 random selected challenges are shown in the table 2. We further examine the same statistical properties of the (16,16) and (32,32) PUF arrays. Results show that conducting XOR on the intermediate response will have extra good effects on the uniformity. This is because the output of XOR gate would have uniform distribution if the input is uniformly distributed. From the results in Table 2, we could observe that the (32,32) array has better properties in uniformity, which makes it as a good candidate in real applications. The slight bias from the ideal value (0.5) might be caused by multiple reasons. First, since we use the data acquired from the FPGA board, factors such as the disturbance from FPGA surrounding logics and the noise could drift the response, this phenomenon has also been observed in the FPGA based PUFs [15]. As lots of effective solutions have been discussed in the literature to solve this [16], this problem is not the key point we should follow in our paper.

Table 2: Statistical evaluation on the dual mode PUF with 50K CRPs

Type	**16**	**32**	**64**	**128**	**(16,16)**	**(32,32)**
Uniformity	0.4108	0.4465	0.4874	0.4923	0.4377	0.4765

To analyze the reliability of our dual-mode PUFs, we also test the 32-bit PUF instance at several different temperatures from 0°C to 65°C. Taking the CRPs measured at 25°C as the reference, we calculated the average bit flip rates under each temperature. Fig 6 shows the results got from different temperatures, which confirms the temperature sensitivity observed in others' implementations [3]. However, the temperature sensitivity of PUFs has already been solved either by error correction [17] or by the extended authentication protocol for environmental-condition-sensitive PUFs[18]. We could take use of those techniques to overcome the reliability drawback of our dual-mode PUF.

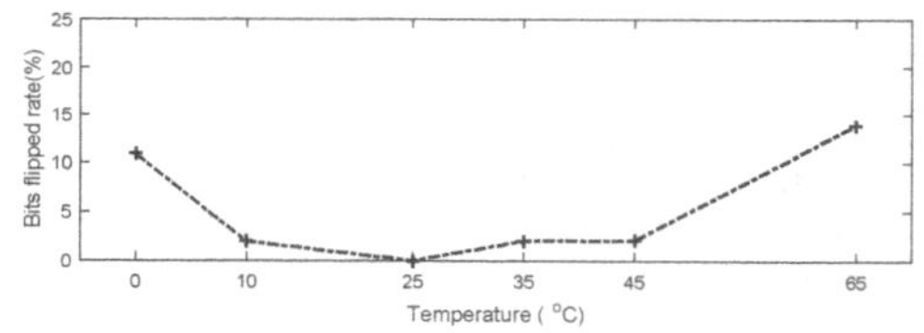

Figure 6: Reliability of dual mode PUF

6 CONCLUSION

Modeling attack is one of the most powerful threats to the PUF based security applications. In this paper, we propose such a PUF design based on both the delay-based PUF and the memory-based PUF which could work effectively in defending the modeling attacks. We implemented the PUF design on the Nexys 4 FPGA board and collected real challenge-response pairs from the board. We tested the learning results using those data and it demonstrated that our design could successfully resist the modeling attacks.

ACKNOWLEDGMENT

This work was supported in part by AFOSR MURI under award number FA9550-14-1-0351.

REFERENCES

[1] Blaise Gassend, Dwaine Clarke, Marten Van Dijk, and Srinivas Devadas. Silicon physical random functions. In *Proceedings of the 9th ACM conference on Computer and communications security*, pages 148–160. ACM, 2002.

[2] Mingze Gao, Khai Lai, and Gang Qu. A highly flexible ring oscillator puf. In *2014 51st ACM/EDAC/IEEE Design Automation Conference (DAC)*, pages 1–6. IEEE, 2014.

[3] Qingqing Chen, György Csaba, Paolo Lugli, Ulf Schlichtmann, and Ulrich Rührmair. The bistable ring puf: A new architecture for strong physical unclonable functions. In *Hardware-Oriented Security and Trust (HOST), 2011 IEEE International Symposium on*, pages 134–141. IEEE, 2011.

[4] Ulrich Rührmair, Frank Sehnke, Jan Sölter, Gideon Dror, Srinivas Devadas, and Jürgen Schmidhuber. Modeling attacks on physical unclonable functions. In *Proceedings of the 17th ACM conference on Computer and communications security*, pages 237–249. ACM, 2010.

[5] Ulrich Rührmair, Jan Sölter, Frank Sehnke, Xiaolin Xu, Ahmed Mahmoud, Vera Stoyanova, Gideon Dror, Jürgen Schmidhuber, Wayne Burleson, and Srinivas Devadas. Puf modeling attacks on simulated and silicon data. *IEEE Transactions on Information Forensics and Security*, 8(11):1876–1891, 2013.

[6] Qian Wang, An Wang, Gang Qu, and Guoshuang Zhang. New methods of template attack based on fault sensitivity analysis. *IEEE Transactions on Multi-Scale Computing Systems*, 3(2):113–123, 2017.

[7] Dai Yamamoto, Masahiko Takenaka, Kazuo Sakiyama, and Naoya Torii. Security evaluation of bistable ring pufs on fpgas using differential and linear analysis. In *Computer Science and Information Systems (FedCSIS), 2014 Federated Conference on*, pages 911–918. IEEE, 2014.

[8] Yuntao Liu, Yang Xie, Chongxi Bao, and Ankur Srivastava. An optimization-theoretic approach for attacking physical unclonable functions. In *Proceedings of the 35th International Conference on Computer-Aided Design*, page 45. ACM, 2016.

[9] Yuntao Liu, Yang Xie, Chongxi Bao, and Ankur Srivastava. A combined optimization-theoretic and side-channel approach for attacking strong physical unclonable functions. *IEEE Transactions on Very Large Scale Integration (VLSI) Systems*, 26(1):73–81, 2018.

[10] Meng-Day Mandel Yu, Matthias Hiller, Jeroen Delvaux, Richard Sowell, Srinivas Devadas, and Ingrid Verbauwhede. A lockdown technique to prevent machine learning on pufs for lightweight authentication. *IEEE Transactions on Multi-Scale Computing Systems*, 2(3):146–159, 2016.

[11] Xiaolin Xu, Ulrich Rührmair, Daniel E Holcomb, and Wayne Burleson. Security evaluation and enhancement of bistable ring pufs. In *International Workshop on Radio Frequency Identification: Security and Privacy Issues*, pages 3–16. Springer, 2015.

[12] Yansong Gao, Damith C Ranasinghe, Said F Al-Sarawi, Omid Kavehei, and Derek Abbott. Emerging physical unclonable functions with nanotechnology. *IEEE access*, 4:61–80, 2016.

[13] Mingze Gao, Khai Lai, Jiliang Zhang, Gang Qu, Aijiao Cui, and Qiang Zhou. Reliable and anti-cloning pufs based on configurable ring oscillators. In *Computer-Aided Design and Computer Graphics (CAD/Graphics), 2015 14th International Conference on*, pages 194–201. IEEE, 2015.

[14] Meng-Day Yu, Ingrid Verbauwhede, Srinivas Devadas, and David M'RaïHi. A noise bifurcation architecture for linear additive physical functions. In *Hardware-Oriented Security and Trust (HOST), 2014 IEEE International Symposium on*, pages 124–129. IEEE, 2014.

[15] Daniel E Holcomb, Wayne P Burleson, and Kevin Fu. Power-up sram state as an identifying fingerprint and source of true random numbers. *IEEE Transactions on Computers*, 58(9):1198–1210, 2009.

[16] Chi-En Yin and Gang Qu. Improving puf security with regression-based distiller. In *Proceedings of the 50th Annual Design Automation Conference*, page 184. ACM, 2013.

[17] Chi-En Yin and Gang Qu. Temperature-aware cooperative ring oscillator puf. In *Hardware-Oriented Security and Trust, 2009. HOST'09. IEEE International Workshop on*, pages 36–42. IEEE, 2009.

[18] Zdenek Paral and Srinivas Devadas. Reliable and efficient puf-based key generation using pattern matching. In *Hardware-Oriented Security and Trust (HOST), 2011 IEEE International Symposium on*, pages 128–133. IEEE, 2011.

A Distributed Power Grid Analysis Framework from Sequential Stream Graph

Chun-Xun Lin
Dept. of ECE, UIUC
IL, USA
clin99@illinois.edu

Tsung-Wei Huang
Dept. of ECE, UIUC
IL, USA
twh760812@gmail.com

Ting Yu
Austin, TX, USA
yuting20031918@gmail.com

Martin D. F. Wong
Dept. of ECE, UIUC
IL, USA
mdfwong@illinois.edu

ABSTRACT

The ever-increasing design complexities have overwhelmed what is offered by existing EDA tools. As a result, the recent EDA industry is driving the need for distributed computing to leverage large-scale compute-intensive problems, in particular, *power grid analysis*. In this paper, we introduce a distributed power grid analysis framework based on the stream graph model. We show that the stream graph model has better programmability over the MPI and enables flexible domain decomposition without limited by hardware resource. In addition, we design an efficient scheduling policy for this particular workload to maximize the cluster utilization to improve the performance. The experimental results demonstrated the promising performance of our framework that scales from single multi-core machines to a distributed computer cluster.

ACM Reference Format:
Chun-Xun Lin, Tsung-Wei Huang, Ting Yu, and Martin D. F. Wong. 2018. A Distributed Power Grid Analysis Framework from Sequential Stream Graph. In *GLSVLSI '18: 2018 Great Lakes Symposium on VLSI, May 23–25, 2018, Chicago, IL, USA.* ACM, New York, NY, USA, 6 pages. https://doi.org/10.1145/3194554.3194560

1 INTRODUCTION

As the technology continues to advance, analyzing a power distributed network that corporates billions of transistors becomes a critical challenge. Traditionally, power analysis engineers partitioned the problem into smaller and manageable pieces, and ran each on a single multi-threading machine. However, according to [1], analyzing a power grid with 136 million nodes on a single multi-core machine can take hundreds of GBs of memory and several hours to finish. Building such a high-end computer is expensive and unscalable to the ever-increasing design complexities. As a result, EDA vendors are driving the need of distributed power grid analysis.

Researchers have proposed parallel computing methods for power grid analysis [2] [3] [4] [5] [6]. Existing works are based on either multi-threading in a shared memory storage or distributed computations across different nodes. The work by [2] [3] developed parallel power grid simulators by taking the advantage of multi-cores with shared memory to speed up the computing. Although the shared memory model is advantageous in data communication, it relies on expensive hardware resources to gain more scalability. The work by [4] [5] designed parallel computing schemes by partitioning data and distributing the computations across multiple machines using the low-level massage passing interface (MPI) library [7]. While MPI provides a layer of abstraction over the network communication, it suffers from many distinct notations to express the parallelism. The bottom-up design principle of MPI is analogous to assembly languages in terms of writing parallel code. For example, users have to manually name the machines for process mapping and hard-code message passing for serialization and deserialization. It also requires a significant amount of coding efforts when the software changes to the next generation. Putting these issues together discourages developers from being productive and innovative. Nevertheless, building a distributed power grid analysis beyond MPI remains an open problem.

While existing big-data tools offer many promises in distributed computing [8], EDA researchers remain skeptical about the applicability for many reasons [9]. First, power grid analysis is compute-intensive whereas the big data computing focuses on I/O processing. Second, MapReduce paradigm assumes data can be split into independent chunks while the power grid data are not easily separable. Third, the mainstream programming languages of the big data are JVM languages that do not appeal to the language need of power grid (C/C++). As a consequence, we need a specialized distributed framework for power grid analysis.

In this paper, we introduce a distributed power grid analysis framework based on the stream graph model. The goal of this paper is, instead of solving the power grid analysis with domain-specific techniques, to investigate into the programmability, extensibility, and scalability of distributed power grid analysis at framework level. We summarize our contributions as follows:

- We show that with the use of the *stream graph* programming paradigm, programming distributed power grid analysis can be greatly simplified. Unlike MPI which is based on low-level message passing API, the stream graph is a higher-level abstraction to express parallelism. Users can focus on developing the framework based on the algorithmic specification, without wrestling with system-specific implementation details.
- We show that with a customized scheduler, we are able to maximize the resource utilization in a cluster. Our scheduler is tailored for the compute-intensive power grid analysis. We demonstrate our scheduler can effectively leverage the CPU usage for this particular workload.

GLSVLSI '18, May 23–25, 2018, Chicago, IL, USA

ACM ISBN 978-1-4503-5724-1/18/05...$15.00
https://doi.org/10.1145/3194554.3194560

- We show that our framework is a more flexible and scalable alternative to MPI-based solutions. We can flexibly partition the power grid to different subdomains regardless of the number of cores, which is instead impossible in MPI due to its architectural limitation.

We implement our framework on DtCraft[1] [10], a distributed execution engine for high-performance applications, for our experiment. The experimental results show that our distributed power grid framework achieves comparable performance to MPI-based solutions. We also demonstrated the effectiveness of our scheduler over the default scheduler of DtCraft in an emulated production environment.

2 DISTRIBUTED POWER GRID ANALYSIS

The goal of power grid analysis is to solve following system of equations extracted from the associated circuit:

$$GV = I,$$

G : A matrix formed by the conductance of components

V : A vector consists the voltage of nodes (unknown)

I : A vector consists the independent current sources

By solving above linear system, the voltage drop at each node can be derived by comparing the node voltage V with the supply voltage. One feasible way to solve the system is the domain decomposition [3] [11] [12] which partitions the problem into subsets and solves them in parallel. The Additive Schwarz Method (ASM), one type of the domain decomposition methods, is especially suitable for large sparse system [4]. In this paper, we adopt the geometric ASM method with 2D partitioning proposed by [4] for distributed direct current (DC) analysis, which is proved to have minimum data communication. The geometric ASM method for DC analysis can be summarized as four steps:

(1) Partition the circuit into subdomains.
(2) Solve each subdomain independently.
(3) Synchronize and exchange the boundary values of subdomains.
(4) Go to (2) if any of the subdomains does not converge.

The geometric ASM method is a natural fit for distributed computing as it can be directly parallelized by assigning the subdomains to different processors.

2.1 Existing Works and Limitations

Based on the geometric ASM method, researchers developed a number of distributed power grid analysis systems using MPI [4] [11] [12]. The MPI programming model is processor-centric. A MPI program consists of several processes with each process attached to a processor, and a typical MPI program can have number of processes less than or equal to the number of available processors. Even though oversubscription is possible in MPI, it's discouraged by the official due to performance degradation. The processes form a communication group and each process has a unique number called rank for identification. Processes can send or receive data through using the rank in a set of APIs. Based on the message passing model, a distributed DC analysis program with MPI is shown in Algorithm 1

Algorithm 1: MPI-based Distributed DC analysis

```
   Input: C: circuit, W: width, H: height
1  MPI_Init();
2  rank ← MPI_Rank();
3  subdomains ← ∅;
4  if rank == 0 then
5  |  PartitionGrid(C, W, H);
6  end
7  MPI_Sync();
8  subdomains[rank] ←ReadGrid(rank);
9  bd_value_num ← CountBD(subdomains[rank]);
10 MPI_Gather( 0, bd_nums, bd_value_num);
11 if rank == 0 then
12 |  bd_array ← CreateBoundaryArray(bd_nums)
13 end
14 converge ← False;
15 while !converge do
16 |  solution ← Solve(subdomains[rank]);
17 |  bd_value ← ExtractBoundary(solution);
18 |  converge ← Check(solution);
19 |  MPI_Gather( 0, bd_array, bd_value);
20 |  MPI_Gather( 0, result, converge);
21 |  if rank == 0 then
22 |  |  converge ← IsConverge(result);
23 |  |  Reorder(bd_array);
24 |  end
25 |  MPI_Scatter(0, bd_array, bd_value);
26 |  UpdateBD(bd_value, solution);
27 |  MPI_broadcast(0, converge);
28 end
```

In Algorithm 1, the power grid is partitioned into $W \times H$ subdomains and the MPI program launches $W \times H$ processes with each process assigned a subdomain. Notice that in line 8, a process handles the subdomain based on the rank automatically assigned by MPI and the rank is limited by the number of available CPU cores. Although users can implement a distributed computing program by directly including the MPI library and utilizing the low-level APIs, there are several disadvantages of the MPI-based implementation:

- The number of subdomains is limited by the available processors. Also, this is a constraint to launching the program (`mpirun -n [number of cores]`). This fundamentally restricts our problem-solving logic to deliver an effective and scalable solution.
- To manage all processes running concurrently in the MPI model, an MPI program needs to explicitly use conditional instructions or branch predicate to separate the execution flows of different processes. This complicates the program structure and also makes the MPI program difficult to be extended to incremental analysis [13], where some processes might change the values in subdomains.

[1] We use DtCraft version 0.0.1 for the implementation.

As a result, it's desirable to have a novel distributed computing framework that does not suffer from the above issues.

3 DISTRIBUTED POWER GRID ANALYSIS BASED ON STREAM GRAPH

3.1 Stream Graph Model

Stream graph [10] is a new programming model that aims for distributed computing, especially for high performance (compute-intensive) applications. A stream graph is a high-level abstraction that describes the program as a directed graph, where vertices and edges encapsulate the data flow and a sequence of computations. The computations are asynchronous, i.e. computations are only executed when the associated data arrive. This makes the stream graph a competitive solution for performance-driven applications.

3.2 DC Analysis in Stream Graph

Based on the stream graph programming paradigm, we formulate the DC analysis as a stream graph with two types of vertices: synchronization vertex and worker vertex. The stream graph of DC analysis consists of one synchronization vertex and N worker vertices where N is the number of subdomains, and there are two directed edges connecting the synchronization vertex and each worker vertex. In general, the synchronization vertex serves as a hub that exchanges data between worker vertices and determines whether the solution converges or not, while the worker vertex is responsible for solving a subdomain and reporting the result to the synchronization vertex. Algorithm 2 presents the stream graph for DC analysis. A synchronization vertex is first inserted into the graph in line 5. Then we insert a worker vertex and two directed edges to the graph (line 7 - 11) and execute the graph in line 12.

Algorithm 2: DC analysis using stream graph

```
   Input: C: circuit, W: width, H: height
1  Graph G;
2  workers ← {} ;
3  to_worker ← {} ;
4  to_sync ← {} ;
5  sync ← InsertV(G, sync_cb(C,W,H,to_worker));
6  N ← W ∗ H ;
7  for i = 1 to N do
8  |   workers[i] ← InsertV(G, worker_cb());
9  |   to_worker[i] ← InsertE(G, sync, workers[i], worker_edge_cb(
   |     )) ;
10 |   to_sync[i] ← InsertE(G, workers[i], sync, sync_edge_cb()) ;
11 end
12 dispatch(G);
```

The program initializes required data from invoking the synchronization vertex's callback once to prepare subdomains. Then the synchronization vertex notifies the worker vertices of the corresponding subdomains by sending a signal through edges. Algorithm 3 presents the callback of the synchronization vertex. In line 1, the power grid is first partitioned into W×H subdomains and then each subdomain index is passed to a worker vertex along the directed edge (line 2 - 7).

Algorithm 3: Callback of a synchronization vertex

```
  Input: C: circuit, W: width, H: height, edges: edges to worker
         vertices
1 PartitionGrid(C, W, H);
2 for i = 1 to W do
3 |   for j = 1 to H do
4 |   |   id ← SubdomainId(i, j);
5 |   |   send( edges[i][j], id );
6 |   end
7 end
```

For the input edge callbacks of both types of vertices, we use finite state machines to establish a communication protocol to react to different types of input data. Algorithm 4 shows the details in the callback of a synchronization vertex at input side. The callback has two states: *CHECK* and *RECV*. In line 3, the CHECK state gathers the results from worker vertices and informs all worker vertices the global status once all results are received (line 4 - 11). The callback is removed when reaching convergence (line 10). From line 13 to 23, in the RECV state the synchronization vertex collects and sends the new boundary values to the worker vertices.

Algorithm 5 presents the callback of a worker vertex at input side. The callback has three states: *INIT*, *COMPUTE* and *WAIT_RESULT*. In the INIT state, each worker vertex first receives a subdomain index from the synchronization vertex (line 2 - 6). Then a worker vertex solves its own subdomain and replies the result and transits to the WAIT_RESULT state (line 22 - 27). In the WAIT_RESULT state, the worker vertex waits for the global result. The callback is removed if the whole solution converges (line 9 - 11); otherwise the worker vertex sends the boundary values to the synchronization vertex and transits to the COMPUTE state (line 12 - 14). In the COMPUTE state (line 17 - 19), when a worker vertex receives the updated boundary values, it proceeds to solve the subdomain with the new values and send the result back.

Our proposed distributed framework has several benefits over the MPI model:

- In contrast to the static (manual) mapping of processes to processors in MPI, the callbacks in the stream graph can be executed on any core in an asynchronous manner, allowing users to create more partitions than the available processors.
- By packaging the callbacks (sequential block) into a parallel program, the stream graph formulation has better code readability and makes debugging easier, whereas the MPI program is more complex as processes with different execution trajectories are put in the same block.
- The stream graph formulation lets users to assign the resource requirements for individual subgraph, which allows the scheduler to make a more effective cluster resource utilization.

Combining above benefits, our framework has better programmability and scalability than the MPI. We believe our framework stands out as a unique solution to distributed power grid analysis, considering the software design and the architectural decision we made.

Algorithm 4: Input edge callback of a synchronization vertex

```
Input: id: edge id, N: number of worker vertices, edges: edges to
       worker vertices
switch state do
    case CHECK do
        recv( results[id] );
        if all workers are recv then
            done ← AllConverge(results) ? True : False;
            for i = 1 to N do
                send( edges[i], done );
            end
            state = RECV;
            return done ? REMOVE_THIS_CB:DEFAULT;
        end
    end
    case RECV do
        recv( bd_vectors[id] );
        if all workers are recv then
            Reorder(bd_vectors);
            for i = 1 to N do
                send( edges[i], bd_vectors[i] );
            end
            state = CHECK;
            return DEFAULT;
        end
    end
end
```

Algorithm 5: Input edge callback of worker vertex

```
Input: id: edge id, edge: edge to synchronization vertex
switch state do
    case INIT do
        recv( subdomain_id );
        my_subdomain ← ReadGrid( subdomain_id );
        go to 22;
    end
    case WAIT_RESULT do
        recv( result );
        if result then
            return REMOVE_THIS_CB;
        end
        state ← COMPUTE;
        send(edge, bd_value);
        return DEFAULT;
    end
    case COMPUTE do
        recv( bd_value );
        UpdateBD(bd_value, solution);
        go to 22;
    end
end
solution ← Solve(my_subdomain) ;
bd_value ← ExtractBoundary(solution) ;
converge ← Check(solution);
state ← WAIT_RESULT;
send( edge, converge );
return DEFAULT;
```

4 APPLICATION-SPECIFIC RESOURCE CONTROL PLUG-IN

Job scheduling is an important issue in distributed computing as the scheduling has a huge impact on overall system performance. In this section, we first outline the default scheduler in DtCraft, then we introduce a scheduler that is tailored for CPU bound applications such as the power grid analysis to enhance the system performance.

4.1 Default Scheduler

The default scheduler in DtCraft adopts a best-fit method to match a job's tasks to machines based on their resource (CPU + memory) requirements. Unlike CPUs that are shared among processes, memory claimed by a process will not be available to others during execution. As a result, memory is regarded as a hard constraint and any process violates the memory constraint will be terminated. The policy of the default scheduler is first-come-first-serve and non-preemptive. Whenever the scheduler receives a job from users, it seeks to find a feasible scheduling for the job if no jobs are waiting ahead. The scheduler first takes a snapshot of the current status of machines, then for each task in the job, the scheduler collects the machines that have enough memory to accommodate the task, and among those candidates the best-fit machine, the one with the least amount of memory, is matched to the task. A job cannot be scheduled if any of its task fails to be matched to a machine. A failed job will be stored in a queue for future processing. Whenever a job finishes execution and releases the memory, the scheduler will examine the queue to process the waiting jobs. The idea of this method is to reduce memory fragmentation which could spare more room to have more jobs scheduled.

4.2 Proposed Scheduler

One deficiency of the default scheduling policy is the underutilization of CPUs since the default scheduler tends to assign jobs to the machines that are partially loaded while there still exists idle machines. To have better utilization of the cluster resource, we propose a scheduler for balancing the workload of cluster machines. In order to evenly distribute the workload we integrate the CPU usage and average CPU load in the past one minute into scheduling to decide the deployment. We record the CPU demands of tasks allocated on each machine and define the ratio of total CPU demands to the number of CPUs on the machine as load index. During the job scheduling, we first collect the machines that satisfy the memory requirement. Then, rather than selecting the machine with the least available memory, a task is matched to the machine with the smallest load index and in case of a tie, the machine with smaller average CPU load in the past one minute is preferred. The goal of using load index to determine the task placement is to proportionally distribute the workload. Algorithm 6 presents the algorithm of the proposed scheduler. In Line 8 - 15, the scheduler finds the machines with enough memory and then deploys the task on the least utilized machine by comparing their load indices and average load over past one minute for tie-breaking.

Algorithm 6: Load-aware scheduling algorithm

```
Input: M: machines, J: a job
Output: P: packings
snapshot ← {};
foreach m ∈ M do
    snapshot ← snapshot ⋃ m;
end
foreach t ∈ J do
    best ← null;
    foreach s ∈ snapshot do
        if s.memory >= t.memory then
            if s.load < best.load or best == null then
                best ← s;
            end
            else if s.load == best.load and
             s.loadavg < best.loadavg then
                best ← s;
            end
        end
    end
    if best == null then
        P ← ∅;
        break;
    end
    else
        P ← P ⋃ (t, best);
        best.memory− = t.memory;
        best.load+ = t.cpu/best.cpu;
    end
end
```

5 EXPERIMENTAL RESULTS

We first compare two implementations of distributed DC analysis: the stream graph and the MPI model on both the single machine and the distributed environment. Next we compare the proposed scheduler with the default scheduler in an emulated production environment.

5.1 Stream Graph versus MPI

We conduct experiments on a set of power grid benchmarks released by IBM [14]. We use the network file system (NFS) to allow file sharing across the machines. In the single machine experiment, the machine is equipped with a 2.4 GHz quad-core CPU and 35 GB memory. Due to the available number of cores, we partition the circuit into four (2×2) subdomains to evaluate the MPI program. Since the stream graph does not have the processor binding issue, we further test the stream graph model with the 3×3 and 4×4 partitions to investigate possible performance improvement.

Table 1 lists the results of the single machine experiment. We record the total execution time (including the generation of partitioned files) and the matrix solving time. For the 2×2 partitions, the runtime of stream graph is only moderately higher than the MPI's and both exhibit a similar performance scale. Considering the 3×3 and 4×4 partitions, the performance is further improved by partitioning the circuit into smaller subdomains to reduce the matrix solving time.

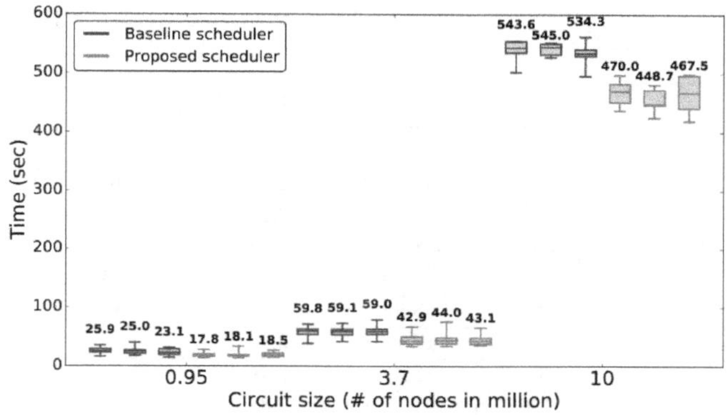

Figure 1: The runtime (sec) distribution for the three sizes of benchmarks in all runs. The number on the top of each box is the median value, and the top and bottom whiskers represent the maximum and minimum values.

Next we evaluate their performance in a cluster consisting of 9 machines with each has a 3.2 GHz quad-core CPU and 24 GB memory. We experiment four partition sizes: 3×3, 4×4, 5×5 and 6×6. For the sake of fairness, in the stream graph model a subdomain is assigned one CPU core. Table 2 shows the matrix solving and total runtime (including the latency of transferring partitioned files on NFS). In all types of partitions, the matrix solving time of stream graph is close to the MPI model's and the difference does not scale with the circuit size, indicating the performance of stream graph is comparable to the MPI model.

5.2 Production-Mode Evaluation

The scheduler experiments are undertaken on Amazon's Elastic Compute Cloud and we use 10 EC2 instances where each instance has 4 CPUs and 16 GB memory. The first experiment is to evaluate the schedulers on handling workload composed of jobs in different scales. We select three types of circuits whose power grids have 0.95, 3.7 and 10 million nodes respectively to represent jobs with small, medium and large scale. The stream graph each has 4 (small), 8 (medium) and 16 (large) worker vertices respectively. There are one hundred jobs in total and the number of jobs for each types are 27, 68 and 5, which is distributed normally to simulate the job composition in realistic situations. The jobs are randomly permuted and we submit a job every 10 seconds.

We run three times for both the default scheduler and the proposed scheduler and record all results. Table 3 shows the total time from submitting the first job to the finish of the last job. Compared with the baseline scheduler, the proposed scheduler effectively reduces the total time by an average of 10%.

To understand the impact of schedulers on the runtime of each job, Figure 1 records the distribution of completion time on jobs with different sizes. With the proposed scheduler, the average runtime of the small, medium and large-sized jobs is reduced by 24%, 22% and 14% respectively.

Lastly, we evaluate the schedulers with jobs arriving in Poisson distribution manner. We set the average arrival rate to 0.1 (i.e. the

Table 1: Runtime (sec) of MPI versus Stream graph on single machine

Testcase	Size	Solve Time (2x2)		Total Time (2x2)		Solve time (stream graph)		Total Time (stream graph)	
		MPI	Stream graph	MPI	Stream graph	3x3	4x4	3x3	4x4
y200	10513442	1,061.45	1,246.63	1,133.46	1,302.94	544.44	749.20	592.30	795.65
y250	6727562	628.15	717.60	676.21	754.30	262.03	266.03	294.22	296.09
y300	4688899	251.82	294.99	284.67	320.52	156.08	154.70	178.36	176.37
y400	2627442	48.72	68.38	66.82	82.49	45.96	49.61	58.14	61.25
y500	1680602	25.77	36.31	37.94	45.43	25.76	25.29	33.69	32.95
y600	1171822	12.50	18.41	20.77	24.74	18.25	15.50	23.96	20.99
y800	655896	6.44	10.71	11.07	14.51	7.82	7.49	10.97	10.68
y1000	419522	2.85	5.27	5.79	7.61	4.21	4.17	6.27	6.18

Table 2: Runtime (sec) of MPI versus Stream graph (ours) on a cluster with 9 machines

Testcase	Decomposition	Solve Time		Total Time	
		MPI	Ours	MPI	Ours
y200	6 x 6	90.60	109.12	149.42	163.40
y250	6 x 6	34.40	45.36	70.583	82.29
y300	5 x 5	22.52	28.06	43.95	52.59
y400	5 x 5	7.52	10.04	19.35	22.75
y500	4 x 4	5.21	6.77	14.79	16.87
y600	4 x 4	3.26	5.03	9.96	12.54
y800	3 x 3	2.25	3.65	7.54	7.97
y1000	3 x 3	1.10	2.58	4.41	5.63

Table 3: The execution time (minutes) for the three runs.

	1st		2nd		3rd	
	Base	Ours	Base	Ours	Base	Ours
Runtime	25.32	23.05	26.0	22.58	25.42	22.77

average arrival time of a job is 10 seconds) and submit 100 medium-sized jobs. Table 4 shows that the proposed scheduler's average completion time of a job is around 20% smaller than the default scheduler's. We observe that the number of vertices deployed on each machine can vary greatly in the default scheduler, resulting in a low resource utilization and slower performance.

6 CONCLUSION

This paper introduces a distributed power grid analysis framework based on the stream graph programming model. The framework enables flexible power grid decomposition regardless of the available CPU cores. Moreover, a load aware scheduler is proposed to balance the machine workloads and effectively promote the overall system resource utilization. The experimental results show that the framework has comparable performance as the MPI-based framework and the effectiveness of the load aware scheduler. We believe we open a new direction for the distributed power grid analysis. Our idea can inspire EDA engineers to rethink the way to parallelize EDA algorithms.

Table 4: The average runtime (sec) of a benchmark for the three runs.

	1st		2nd		3rd	
	Base	Ours	Base	Ours	Base	Ours
Runtime	62.53	48.44	63.51	42.95	62.47	42.89

7 ACKNOWLEDGMENT

This work is partially supported by the National Science Foundation under Grant CCF-1421563 and CCF-171883.

REFERENCES

[1] C. J. Wei, H. Chen, and S. J. Chen. Design and Implementation of Block-Based Partitioning for Parallel Flip-Chip Power-Grid Analysis. *TCAD*, 31(3):370–379, March 2012.

[2] James W. Demmel, John R. Gilbert, and Xiaoye S. Li. An Asynchronous Parallel Supernodal Algorithm for Sparse Gaussian Elimination. *SIAM J. Matrix Anal. Appl.*, 20(4):915–952, July 1999.

[3] V. Y. Voronov and N. N. Popova. Parallel power grid simulation on platforms with multi core processors. In *2009 International Conference on Computing, Engineering and Information*, pages 144–148, April 2009.

[4] T. Yu, Z. Xiao, and M. D. F. Wong. Efficient parallel power grid analysis via Additive Schwarz Method. In *IEEE/ACM ICCAD*, pages 399–406, Nov 2012.

[5] Laura Grigori, James W. Demmel, and Xiaoye S. Li. Parallel Symbolic Factorization for Sparse LU with Static Pivoting. *SIAM Journal on Scientific Computing*, 29(3):1289–1314, 2007.

[6] Q. He, W. Au, A. Korobkov, and S. Venkateswaran. Parallel power grid analysis using distributed direct linear solver. In *2014 IEEE International Symposium on Electromagnetic Compatibility (EMC)*, pages 866–871, Aug 2014.

[7] MPICH. https://www.mpich.org/.

[8] M. Zaharia, M. Chowdhury, A. Dave T. Das, J. Ma, M. McCauley, M. J. Franklin, S. Shenker, and I. Stoica. Resilient distributed datasets: A fault-tolerant abstraction for in-memory cluster computing. In *NSDI*, pages 2–2. USENIX Association, 2012.

[9] T. W. Huang, M. D. F. Wong, D. Sinha, K. Kalafala, and N. Venkateswaran. A distributed timing analysis framework for large designs. In *ACM/IEEE DAC*, pages 1–6, June 2016.

[10] T.-W. Huang, C.-X. Lin, and Martin D. F. Wong. DtCraft: A Distributed Execution Engine for Compute-intensive Applications. In *IEEE/ACM ICCAD*, pages 757–765, Nov 2017.

[11] Kai Sun, Quming Zhou, Kartik Mohanram, and D. C. Sorensen. Parallel domain decomposition for simulation of large-scale power grids. In *IEEE/ACM ICCAD*, pages 54–59, Nov 2007.

[12] PETSC. http://www.mcs.anl.gov/petsc/.

[13] P. Sun, X. Li, and M. Y. Ting. Efficient incremental analysis of on-chip power grid via sparse approximation. In *ACM/IEEE DAC*, pages 676–681, June 2011.

[14] Sani R. Nassif. Power grid analysis benchmarks. In *IEEE/ACM ASP-DAC*, pages 376–381, 2008.

A Distributed Parallel Random Walk Algorithm for Large-Scale Capacitance Extraction and Simulation

Mingye Song, Zhezhao Xu, Wei Xue, Wenjian Yu
Department of Computer Science and Technology, BNRist
Tsinghua University, Beijing, China
songmy16@mails.tsinghua.edu.cn,zhezhaoxu@gmail.com,xuewei@tsinghua.edu.cn,yu-wj@tsinghua.edu.cn

ABSTRACT

Due to the advantages on scalability and reliability, the floating random walk (FRW) algorithm has been widely adopted for calculating the capacitances among three-dimensional (3-D) conductors. This is evidenced by the industrial practice of interconnect capacitance extraction during the design of high-performance very large-scale integrated (VLSI) circuits. In this work, the FRW algorithm is enhanced through the distributed parallel computing. With an efficient and adaptive task allocation scheme, the communication among different computer nodes is largely reduced. A distributed algorithm for accelerating the space management is also proposed. They have been implemented with Message Passing Interface (MPI) and applied to the high-precision capacitance simulation for touch-screen design and the interconnect capacitance extraction of VLSI circuits. Experiments on a computer cluster show that the proposed techniques achieve up to 114X speedup while using 120 cores, and build up the space management structure for a VLSI case including two million conductor blocks in just 22 seconds (37X parallel speedup on 60 cores).

ACM Reference Format:
Mingye Song, Zhezhao Xu, Wei Xue, Wenjian Yu. 2018. A Distributed Parallel Random Walk Algorithm for Large-Scale Capacitance Extraction and Simulation. In *Proceedings of Great Lakes Symposium on VLSI 2018 (GLSVLSI'18)*. ACM, New York, NY, USA, 6 pages. https://doi.org/10.1145/3194554.3194568

1 INTRODUCTION

Capacitance extraction and simulation is a fundamental topic of computer-aided design (CAD) [4, 11]. For accurate validation of the delay, signal integrity, and other performance metrics, the interconnect capacitances should be accurately extracted while designing nanometer integrated circuits. Another relevant scenario is during the design of touchscreen. For validating its functionality, simulating the capacitances of the touch sensor structures becomes an important and frequent task. The geometry complexity in touch-screen design and high-accuracy demand for coupling capacitance pose a challenge to the existing capacitance simulation techniques [9].

GLSVLSI'18, May 23–25, 2018, Chicago, IL, USA

ACM ISBN 978-1-4503-5724-1/18/05...$15.00
https://doi.org/10.1145/3194554.3194568

High-precision capacitance simulation needs three-dimensional (3-D) field-solver methods. They can be classified into the following categories [11]: domain descretization method, including the finite difference methods (FDM) and the finite element methods (FEM), boundary element method, and the floating random work (FRW) method [1, 3, 7, 12]. The FRW method is more stable in accuracy and scalable to very large case, due to its nature of a discretization-free method. And as it is based on the Monte Carlo method, the FRW method has better parallelism, and becomes favorable nowadays due to the population of parallel computing infrastructures. A lot of work has been devoted to the FRW method to improve its efficiency and extend its ability [3, 9, 10, 13–15]. Most of them only consider the single-thread or multi-thread implementation on a single computer.

To tackle very large computing task, the parallel computing using GPU or multiple computers should be considered [1, 8, 9, 13]. In [1, 13], GPU accelerated FRW algorithms were proposed showing several tens times speedup over the FRW algorithm with serial-computing. Although the parallel computing on GPU is generally more energy-efficient, implementing a GPU-friendly FRW algorithm requires much algorithmic change, and thus induces much labor on software development and maintenance. And, due to the workload divergence among different walk paths, parallelizing FRW on GPU is not easy, or can hardly achieve high parallel speedup [13]. In contrast, the distributed parallel FRW algorithm on computer cluster or the *cloud* is more feasible. This has been evidenced by industrial practice for multi-net or full-chip extraction tasks. Its basic idea is to assign subsets of nets to each machine and then collect their results on a host machine [8]. This method with coarse-grained workload distribution can cause large workload unbalance, and is not suitable for the extraction of a single net. In [9], a distributed parallel FRW algorithm was proposed to speed up the single-net computation for obtaining accurate coupling capacitances in the touchscreen design. It distributes the random walk procedure to the computers in a cluster, and achieves 67X speedup at most using 120 CPU cores. This method has two major drawbacks: 1) There is still much inter-machine communication which leads to not high enough parallel speedup. 2) It does not distribute the construction of the space management structure among the machines, which makes it inefficient while handling cases with a large number of conductors.

In this work, we focus on fine-grained workload distribution during the FRW based capacitance simulation, which results in an efficient parallel FRW algorithm on computer cluster. We propose an adaptive task allocation scheme and a distributed construction algorithm for the grid-based spatial structure, to minimize the communication cost. They accelerate the random walk procedure and the space management step respectively, without loss of accuracy. With this distributed parallel FRW algorithm, we have tested structures from touchscreen design and VLSI design. The experiments on a cluster show that the parallel speedup is up to 4.9X larger than that of the algorithm in [9]. And, with 60 cores the space management structure can be built in 22 seconds for a VLSI case including two million conductor blocks. It corresponds to a 37X speedup on the space management construction step.

2 PRELIMINARIES

The FRW method for capacitance extraction is based on the integral formula for electric potential [7, 12]:

$$\phi(\mathbf{r}) = \oint_S P(\mathbf{r}, \mathbf{r}^{(1)})\phi(\mathbf{r}^{(1)})d\mathbf{r}^{(1)}, \tag{1}$$

where $\phi(\mathbf{r})$ is the potential of point $\mathbf{r}$ and $P(\mathbf{r}, \mathbf{r}^{(1)})$ is called surface Green's function. The domain enclosed by S is called transition domain, which includes $\mathbf{r}$. $P(\mathbf{r}, \mathbf{r}^{(1)})$ can be regarded as a probability density function (PDF). With the Monte Carlo method, $\phi(\mathbf{r})$ can be estimated as the statistical mean of $\phi(\mathbf{r}^{(1)})$.

When computing the capacitances related to a master conductor i, one should first construct a Gaussian surface G_i enclosing it (see Fig. 1). According to the Gauss theorem, the charge of conductor i is:

$$Q_i = \oint_{G_i} F(\mathbf{r}) g \oint_{S^{(1)}} \omega(\mathbf{r}, \mathbf{r}^{(1)})\tilde{P}(\mathbf{r}, \mathbf{r}^{(1)})\phi(\mathbf{r}^{(1)})d\mathbf{r}^{(1)}d\mathbf{r}, \tag{2}$$

where $F(\mathbf{r})$ is the dielectric permittivity at point $\mathbf{r}$, $\tilde{P}(\mathbf{r}, \mathbf{r}^{(1)})$ is the PDF for sampling on $S^{(1)}$ which may be different from $P(\mathbf{r}, \mathbf{r}^{(1)})$, and $\omega(\mathbf{r}, \mathbf{r}^{(1)})$ is the weight value [7, 12]. Thus, Q_i can be estimated as the statistical mean of sampled values on G_i, which is further the mean of sampled potentials on $S^{(1)}$ multiplying the weight value. If the potential of a sample point $\mathbf{r}^{(1)}$ is unknown, Eq. (1) is substituted into (2) recursively. The computation can be decribed as a floating random walk (FRW) procedure. The walk starts from the Gaussian surface, and repeatedly jumps from a transition domain's center to its surface, until reaching conductor surface. After performing a number of walks, the statistical mean of the weight values for the walks terminating at conductor j approximates the capacitance C_{ij} between conductors i and j.

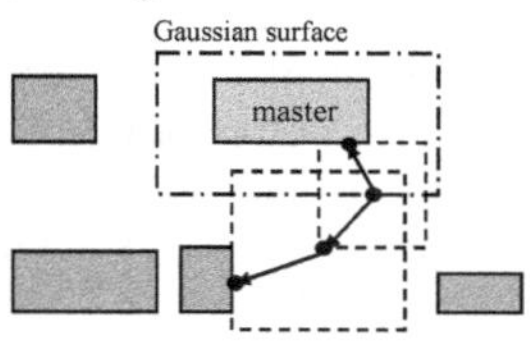

Figure 1: Two examples of random walk in the FRW method for capacitance extraction (a 2-D top view).

The cubic transition domain is widely adopted because it fits well the Manhattan-shaped interconnects in VLSI circuit. This means larger probability for terminating a walk earlier. The sampling probability and weight value for a cube domain can be pre-calculated and tabulated, so as to accelerate the sampling operation.

Another key is the space management techniques [14], which are useful for quickly finding the nearest conductor for constructing the transition cube, especially for simulating a case including thousands of conductor blocks. A grid-Octree hybrid spatial structure was proposed in [14], which enables better efficiency of conductor inquiry than existing grid or Octree based structures. In [15], a multi-thread parallel algorithm was proposed for constructing the Octree structure. On a machine with 8 cores it achieves 4.5X parallel speedup.

The flowchart of the distributed parallel FRW algorithm in [9] is shown in Fig. 2. Its focus is on accelerating the random walk process without paying attention to the construction of the space management structure. However, a block-level or chip-level VLSI structure can involve more than a million conductor blocks. Constructing the spatial structure for such large case can be much more costly than running the FRW procedure to extract a net's capacitances.

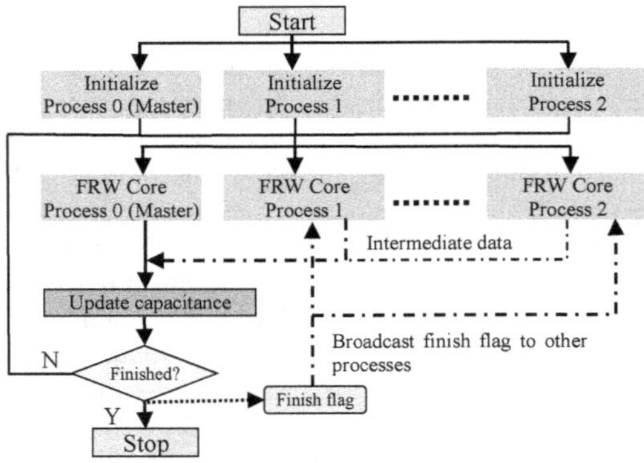

Figure 2: The Flowchart of the distributed parallel FRW algorithm in [9].

3 EFFICIENT DISTRIBUTED PARALLEL FRW ALGORITHM

3.1 Basic Idea

To speed up the FRW algorithm in dealing with both VLSI and touchscreen design problems, many techniques have been adopted, such as space management techniques [11, 15], dielectric pre-characterization method [9], etc. However, for high-accuracy and/or large-scale simulation, the cost of FRW algorithm is still expensive.

Distributed parallel computing is a crucial technique to solve the large and high-accuracy capacitance calculation problems. For large circuit with many conductor blocks, the construction of space management is slow relatively compared with the random walk procedure. Notice that more conductors usually mean faster convergence of the random walk procedure. For touchscreen design, the random walk procedure needs more walks to achieve the demanded high accuracy, so it becomes the bottleneck. In these scenarios, we need a distributed parallel FRW algorithm with fine-grained workload distribution, where efficiently parallelizing both the space management construction and the random walk procedure becomes crucial.

3.2 Distributed Parallel Random Walk Procedure

The random walk procedure of the FRW algorithm is suitable for parallelization naturally, since each random walk is independent to each other. In [12], the parallel FRW algorithm is implemented with pthread APIs. However, the speedup is limited by the condition of a single machine and the number of CPU cores. To achieve higher speedup, in [9], a parallel FRW algorithm was implemented on a Cluster Environment with MPI (see Fig. 2). First, the algorithm initializes each process including parsing input file and loading GFT/WVT tables. After that, each process starts to execute the random walk procedure independently and all processes send intermediate data to the master process every m walks (typically $m = 1000$). Process 0 serves as master process and is responsible for collecting the intermediate data from other processes. Once the termination criteria is satisfied, the master process broadcasts the finish flag to all other processes to terminate the whole computation. Because all processes except master process need to send intermediate result to the master process frequently, the communication overhead is large. If the simulation needs a plenty of random walks, the parallel speedup of this scheme will become disappointing. For tackling the problem, we figure out a new parallel random walk algorithm to reduce the communication overhead.

From [11], we can derive that the estimated error of capacitance err is inversely propositional to the square root of number of walks n_{walk} as follows,

$$err \propto \frac{1}{\sqrt{n_{walk}}}, \tag{3}$$

where n_{walk} means the total number of walks. For a given termination criterion of the FRW algorithm ϵ, the program stops when $err \leq \epsilon$ is satisfied. If we have $m_{process}$ processes, each process should be assigned $\frac{n_{walk}}{m_{process}}$ walks to balance workload. According to Eq. (3), we can derive the error of capacitance achieved with the random walk performed on each process, which corresponds to a FRW procedure set the following termination criterion:

$$\epsilon' = \sqrt{m_{process}} \cdot \epsilon. \tag{4}$$

This means we just set the termination criterion in Eq. (4) to each process at the beginning, and then no more communication among processes is needed during the FRW procedure.

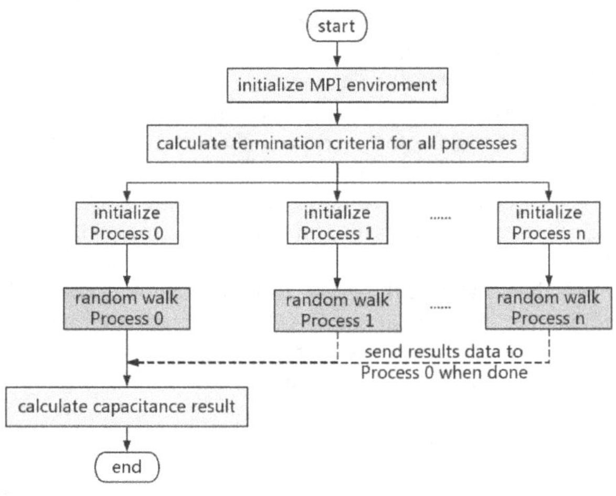

Figure 3: Flowchart of the proposed distributed parallel FRW procedure.

With this idea, we propose a distributed parallel FRW procedure which is shown in Fig. 3. It avoids the communication during the FRW procedure. After every process finishes their work, they send result data to the master process. On the master process the final capacitance result is calculated. Obviously, this method has little communication overhead.

The proposed walk assignment strategy attempts to divide the whole task into independent equal small tasks. However, its basis, Eq. (3) holds approximately. Therefore, if all processes terminates after reaching the condition in (4) sometimes the final capacitance cannot satisfy the error criterion ϵ. To overcome this drawback, a trick is setting the distributed termination criterion a little stricter than the result of Eq. (4). This is empirically proven an effective way to guarantee the accuracy of final result.

The above treatment is based on an assumption that the performance of different machines in the cluster is the same, but it is not always true. When it comes to the fact that the performance of machines are different, an adaptive allocation scheme should be conducted. Before we start our task, we run a quick and standard random walk program to measure actual performance of each machine. Assuming that the runtime for the testing procedure on computing node j is t_j and we have m computing nodes each corresponding to a MPI process, we should allocate

$$n_{walk}^{(j)} = \frac{\frac{1}{t_j}}{\sum_{i=1}^{m} \frac{1}{t_i}} \cdot n_{walk} \tag{5}$$

random walks to process j. Based on Eq. (3), we then should set the termination criterion ϵ_j' for process j:

$$\epsilon_j' = \sqrt{\frac{\sum_{i=1}^{m} \frac{1}{t_i}}{\frac{1}{t_j}}} \cdot \epsilon. \tag{6}$$

This will achieve the best balance of workload, and results in the shortest runtime of the whole distributed parallel computing.

3.3 Distributed Parallel Space Management

In order to improve the procedure of building space management, parallelization is a key technique. There are several spatial data structures, such as uniform grid and Octree. Octree is applied in [12, 15], while for parallel application, sending partial information of Octree between processes and rebuilding the whole data structure are more complex than those of uniform grid. And, as shown in [11], the grid with candidate list has similar performance to the Octree structure, and they both are slightly inferior to the grid-Octree hybrid spatial structure. As the grid structure is more suitable for parallel computing, we choose the grid-based approach to develop the distributed parallel FRW algorithm.

Fig. 4 shows the grid with candidate list structure. Every grid cell contains a list of candidate list that consists of the conductor blocks which can be the nearest to the points in the grid cell. Generating these candidate lists are the major work of construction of this grid spatial structure. During construction, conductor blocks nearby should be inserted into the candidate list according to the judgment of domination relationship. Because the candidate lists of different grid cells are independent to each other, the grid cells can be assigned to different processes or threads without conflict. After all processes finish the candidate list generation for assigned cells, the information sent among processes simply includes conductor IDs and grid cell IDs and they are enough to rebuild the whole spatial structure for the further computation. For the cell with too long candidate list, it can be divided as a second-level grid structure.

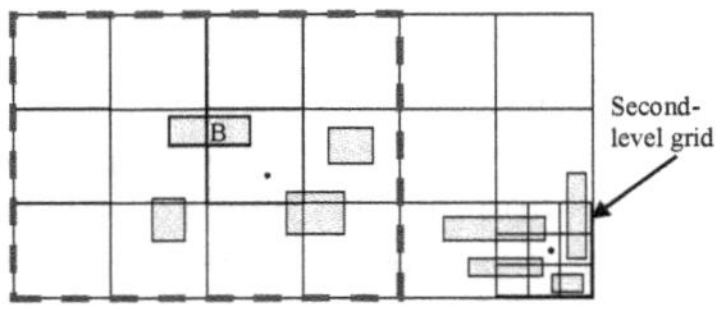

Figure 4: A two-level grid structure. The neighbor cells of conductor B are outlined with the *blue dashed* line [11].

The flowchart of the proposed distributed parallel space management is shown in Fig. 5. Firstly, we split the whole grid cells into cell sets, then assign them to different processes separately and subsequently calculate the candidate list for each cell. Finally, we can gather all information together to build the complete spatial data structure.

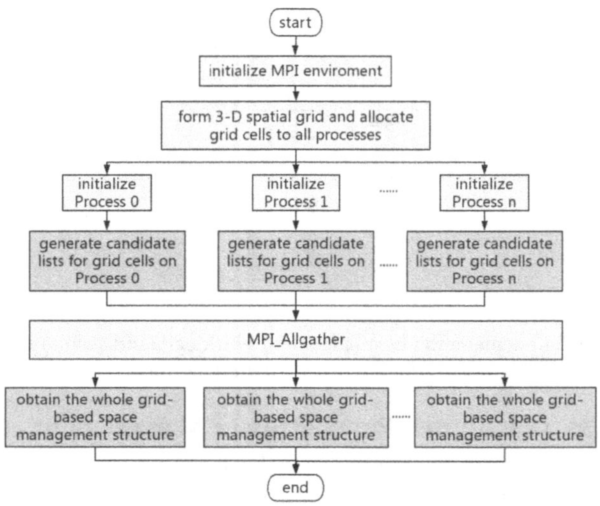

Figure 5: Flowchart of the proposed algorithm on parallel space management construction.

It should be pointed out that the communication cost between processes is not negligible. A well-designed communication scheme benefit the speedup and vice versa. There are two issues. One is how to communicate between processes and the other is what to send.

For the first issue, it is common to use send/receive pairs, which means to use MPI_ISend and MPI_IRecv functions in MPI. MPI_ISend and MPI_IRecv are similar to MPI_Send and MPI_Recv, and the difference between them is that the former functions are non-blocking [6]. If we use MPI_ISend and MPI_IRecv functions, all the $m_{process}$ processes broadcast the message to all the other processes and they send $m_{process}(m_{process} - 1)$ messages totally (see Fig. 6(a)). This makes too many messages occupy the channel. And, synchronization delay becomes prominent when the number of processes is large. So, it is time-consuming and not efficient. We propose to use collective communication in MPI, which is MPI_Allgather function. It gathers data from all tasks and then distributes the combined data to all tasks (see Fig. 6(b)) [2, 5]. Compared with simple send/receive pairs, collective communication performs better. The programmer should allocate sufficient size of receiving buffer to avoid overflowing. The required size of receiving buffer depends on the actual case and how the space management construction task is allocated. Too large and too small receiving buffer both cause problem. For this reason, we cannot allocate a constant-size receiving buffer prior to the computation and the buffer should be dynamically allocated. Actually, for a given case, no matter how many processes are set, the sum of lengths of candidate lists is constant if the grid partition is set. So, the size of receiving buffer does not increase as the number of processes increases. We can calculate its upper bound according to the maximum length of messages. Before each process sends the message of the candidate lists, we let them firstly send the length of messages so that we can find out the maximum length. Therefore, we can set and allocate a sufficiently large receiving buffer. As shown in Fig. 6(b), the receiving buffer can be treated as a two-dimensional array where each row stores all the candidate lists from one single process. Because MPI_Allgather does not return the length of message, we should also set a finish flag to mark the end of each receiving message. This communication scheme is efficient both on storage and latency.

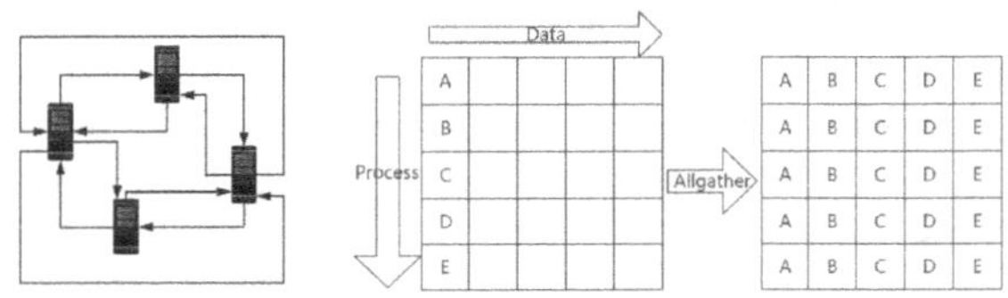

(a) Send/receive (b) Allgather

Figure 6: Two communication mechanisms.

For the second issue, a trivial way is to send a type of structure that contains conductor block ID and grid cell ID, which are both represented as integer. The rebuilding step is inserting the conductor block into the corresponding cell according to the grid cell ID. However, it is obvious that some information is redundant because blocks in the same grid cell share the same grid cell ID. Inspired by sparse matrix storage format, we design a compressed grid cell format that we combine all conductor block IDs in the same cell together along with grid cell ID and use a division flag to distinguish blocks from each other. Each process is responsible to a cell set which includes the grid cells requesting the generation of candidate list. Suppose $size_{max}$ is the maximum total number of candidate conductors in a cell set, and $m_{process}$ is the number of processes. The trivial way needs at most

$$Buffer\_size_1 = 8m_{process} \cdot size_{max} \quad (7)$$

bytes storage for the receiving buffer. In contrast, the compressed one only needs at most

$$Buffer\_size_2 = 4m_{process} \cdot size_{max} + 4n_{cell} \quad (8)$$

bytes for the receiving buffer, where n_{cell} is the number of grid cells. Notice $m_{process} \cdot size_{max}$ is multiplies of the number of all conductor blocks in the problem, and the number of all conductor blocks is much larger than n_{cell} (e.g., $n_{cell} = 2048$ in our experiments). Therefore, the compressed message format can almost reduce the size of sent messages and the buffer size to the half.

4 EXPERIMENTAL RESULTS

The proposed FRW methods are all implemented in C++ with MPI. They are tested with structures from both touchscreen design and VLSI design. If not explicitly stated otherwise, all experiments are carried out on a computer cluster where each node includes 12-core Intel Xeon X5670 CPU at 2.93GHz and nodes are connected with the infiniband QDR network. Half of the computing nodes are equipped with 32GB memory and half 48GB.

Five structures are tested. The first three are from real touchscreen design [9], and the last two are from VLSI design. Their details are listed as follows.

Case 1: This case contains 1423 conductor blocks in two metal layers. The dielectric layers have relative permittivity of 4.0, 3.2, 4.0, 1.0. The metal heights in the two layers are 70nm and 220nm.

Case 2: This case is a small structure with 11 conductor blocks in two metal layers. The dielectric layers have relative permittivity of 4.0, 3.5, 7.0. The heights of the two metal layers are both 100nm.

Case 3: This case contains 808 conductor blocks in four metal layers. The dielectric layers have relative permittivity of 3.9, 6.5, 3.5, 6.5, 4.2, 3.2, 4.0, 1.0. The heights of the four metal layers are 340nm, 220nm, 400nm and 70nm, respectively.

Case 4: This case contains 484,441 conductor blocks forming 12,149 nets. Different from the former cases with non-Manhattan shape generally, the latter two cases are mostly Manhattan shape.

Case 5: This case contains 2,302,995 conductor blocks forming 1,163,751 nets.

4.1 Test Cases from Touchscreeen Design

The first three cases are tested with the distributed parallel FRW algorithm. Because these cases do not include many conductors, the multi-process parallel space management construction is not applied. We have also implemented the algorithm in [9] for comparison. To obtain accurate coupling capacitances, the FRW algorithms are run with 0.1% 1-σ error criterion on the self-capacitance. The parallel runtime of the algorithm in [9] and the proposed algorithm are listed in Table 1, with different number of processes.

Because of the communication and synchronization costs among different processes, the speedup of the algorithm in [9] is far from the ideal situation. The best speedup is only 67.1X with 120 processes and the worst is 23.4X. In contrast, the proposed algorithm with task assignment based on estimated error reduces the communication cost significantly. It achieves up to **114X** speedup for Case 2 with 120 processes, which is about **4.9X** larger that of the algorithm in [9]. For Case 2, the FRW algorithms consumes as many as 5,000,000 random walks, ten times larger than that for Case 3. Because the proposed method minimizes the communication during the random walk procedure, it performs best for Case 2.

Table 1: The parallel runtime of the algorithm in [9] and the proposed FRW algorithm.

$m_{process}$	Case 1		Case 2		Case 3	
	[9](s)	ours(s)	[9](s)	ours(s)	[9](s)	ours(s)
1	3661	3668	12904	12838	7452	5937
12	363	321	1425	1074	644	621
24	217	162	905	554	349	307
36	163	107	747	362	259	205
48	144	81	678	278	200	157
60	124	65	676	221	170	125
72	111	55	647	187	150	106
84	108	47	590	158	138	91
96	102	41	588	141	129	80
108	99	37	516	124	152	72
120	96	33	551	113	111	65

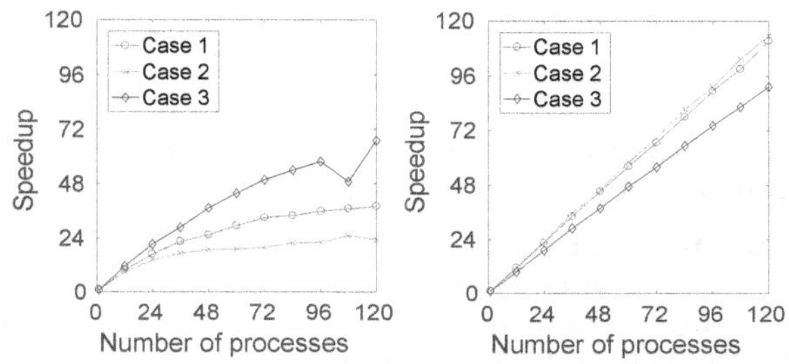

(a) The method in [9] (b) The proposed method

Figure 7: The parallel speedup vs. number of processes for Cases 1-3.

The comparison between two algorithms is also illustrated in Fig. 7. It is apparent that the proposed method achieves better performance. Moreover, the trick guaranteeing that the given termination criterion ϵ is satisfied involves a relatively small runtime cost, but ensures the accuracy.

An experiment is also carried out to evaluate the proposed adaptive workload distribution scheme. We test the parallel FRW algorithms with the uniformly distributed criterion Eq. (4) and the nonuniformly distributed criterion Eq. (6) respectively, on a cluster with two machines. One machine is equipped with Intel Xeon E5-2630 2.3GHz CPU with 24 cores, and the other is with Xeon E5-2630 2.4GHz CPU with 32 cores. The experimental results show that in 32 processes, the parallel FRW algorithm with the nonuniformly distributed criterion further reduces the runtime from 13.32 seconds to 10.32 seconds by **22.5%** compared with the algorithm with uniformly distributed criterion. This validates the effectiveness of the proposed technique.

4.2 Test Cases from VLSI Design

We use Case 4 and 5 to test the distributed parallel grid-based space management construction technique. As we have introduced, the space management construction may dominate the overall runtime in those cases with a large number of conductor blocks and just a

Table 2: The results on space management construction for two large VLSI cases.

$m_{process}$	Case 4		Case 5	
	time(s)	speedup	time(s)	speedup
1	52.12	1.00	824.11	1.00
12	6.55	7.96	76.72	10.74
24	3.90	13.36	42.55	19.37
36	3.15	16.55	29.91	27.55
48	2.58	20.20	23.75	34.70
60	2.27	22.96	22.05	**37.37**

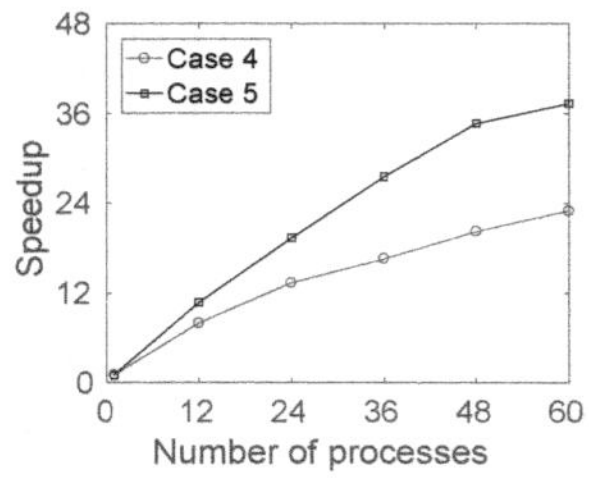

Figure 8: The parallel speedup on space management construction vs. the number of processes.

few of nets for extraction. The experimental results on the VLSI design cases are listed in Table 2.

The parallel speedup of the space management construction is also shown in Fig. 8. For Case 5, with 60 processes the runtime for building the grid with candidate list is reduced from 824.11 seconds in serial computing to 22.05 seconds, which means a **37.4X** speedup. For this larger case with two million conductor blocks the proposed algorithm demonstrates satisfied performance. Notice for Case 4, the construction time has been reduced to just 2 seconds.

The runtime breakdown for exacting a single net with the proposed algorithm is listed in Table 3. It is for Case 5, with 0.5% 1-σ error criterion on self-capacitance. t_{sp} and t_{walk} denotes the runtime for space management construction and the random walk procedure, respectively. Accordingly, $speedup_{sp}$ and $speedup_{walk}$ are the parallel speedup for the both parts. t_{pre} denotes the preparation time in the FRW algorithm that contains all the work done before starting the random walk procedure, including parsing input file, loading GFT/WVT tables and space management construction. With 60 processes, the parallel speedup of space management construction is 37.4X, while that of random walk reaches 38.8X. The total runtime equals to $t_{pre} + t_{walk}$, which is 41.3 seconds. Notice there is about 12 seconds for parsing the input file including two million conductors, which is serially executed.

For Case 5, the maximum number of conductor blocks $size_{max}$ equals to 60,850 in 60 processes. According to Eq. (7) and (8), the trivial message format needs 27.85MB receiving buffer for each process, while the proposed message format only needs 13.94MB. It reveals that the memory overhead is well acceptable.

5 CONCLUSIONS

Parallelization is crucial for capacitance calculation problems when high-accuracy demand and/or a large number of conductors are

Table 3: The runtime breakdown of the proposed algorithm for Case 5.

$m_{process}$	t_{sp}(s)	t_{pre}(s)	t_{walk}(s)	$speedup_{sp}$	$speedup_{walk}$
1	824.11	836.73	189.47	1.00	1.00
12	76.72	90.06	18.59	10.74	10.19
24	42.55	57.11	9.87	19.37	19.20
36	29.91	43.89	6.73	27.55	28.15
48	23.75	38.83	5.13	34.70	36.93
60	22.05	36.41	4.89	37.37	38.75

involved. With an adaptive task allocation scheme and a grid-based distributed space management construction technique, we propose an efficient FRW algorithm suitable for large computer cluster environment. The experiments validate the effectiveness and advantages of the proposed algorithm, with comparison with existing techniques.

ACKNOWLEDGMENTS

This work is supported by NSFC (Grant No. 61422402). W. Xue's work is supported by the National Key R&D Program of China (Grant No. 2016YFA0602100) and NSFC (Grant No. 91530323). W. Yu is the corresponding author.

REFERENCES

[1] Narain D Arora, Steven Worley, and Dilip R Ganpule. 2015. FieldRC, a GPU accelerated interconnect RC parasitic extractor for full-chip designs. In *Proc. EDSSC.* 459–462.

[2] Blaise Barney. 2017. Message Passing Interface (MPI), Online tutorials. (2017). https://computing.llnl.gov/tutorials/mpi/.

[3] S. H. Batterywala and M. P. Desai. 2005. Variance reduction in Monte Carlo capacitance extraction. In *Proc. 18th Int. Conf. VLSI Design.* 85–90.

[4] A. N. Bhoj, R. V. Joshi, and N. K. Jha. 2013. 3-D-TCAD-based parasitic capacitance extraction for emerging multigate devices and circuits. *IEEE Trans. VLSI* 21, 11 (2013), 2094–2105.

[5] Victor Eijkhout. 2012. *Introduction to High Performance Scientific Computing.* Lulu.com.

[6] George M. Karniadakis and Robert M. Kirby. 2003. *Parallel scientific computing in C++ and MPI.* Cambridge University Press.

[7] Y. Le Coz and R. B. Iverson. 1992. A stochastic algorithm for high speed capacitance extraction in integrated circuits. *Solid-State Electronics* 35, 7 (1992), 1005–1012.

[8] N Sawhney, S. Batterywala, N. Shenoy, and R. Rudell. 2004. Parallelizing a statistical capacitance extractor. In *Proc. VLSI Design and Test.* 253–267.

[9] Zhezhao Xu, Wenjian Yu, Chao Zhang, Bolong Zhang, Meijuan Lu, and Michael Mascagni. 2016. A parallel random walk solver for the capacitance calculation problem in touchscreen design. In *Proc. GLSVLSI.* 1661–1666.

[10] Z. Xu, C. Zhang, and W. Yu. 2017. Floating random walk based capacitance extraction for general non-Manhattan conductor structures. *IEEE Trans. Computer-Aided Design* 36, 1 (2017), 120–133.

[11] Wenjian Yu and Xiren Wang. 2014. *Advanced Field-Solver Techniques for RC Extraction of Integrated Circuits.* Springer Science & Business.

[12] Wenjian Yu, Hao Zhuang, Chao Zhang, Gang Hu, and Zhi Liu. 2013. RWCap: A Floating Random Walk Solver for 3-D Capacitance Extraction of Very-Large-Scale Integration Interconnects. *IEEE Trans. Computer-Aided Design* 32, 3 (2013), 353–366.

[13] K. Zhai, W. Yu, and H. Zhuang. 2013. GPU-Friendly floating random walk algorithm for capacitance extraction of VLSI interconnects. In *Proc. DATE.* 1661–1666.

[14] C. Zhang and W. Yu. 2013. Efficient space management techniques for large-scale interconnect capacitance extraction with floating random walks. *IEEE Trans. Computer-Aided Design* 32, 10 (2013), 1633–1637.

[15] Chao Zhang and Wenjian Yu. 2014. Efficient techniques for the capacitance extraction of chip-scale VLSI interconnects using floating random walk algorithm. In *Proc. ASP-DAC.* 756–761.

A Fast and Fuzzy Functional Simulator of Inexact Arithmetic Operators for Approximate Computing Systems

Justine Bonnot
Univ Rennes, INSA Rennes, CNRS, IETR - UMR 6164
jbonnot@insa-rennes.fr

Karol Desnos
Univ Rennes, INSA Rennes, CNRS, IETR - UMR 6164
kdesnos@insa-rennes.fr

Maxime Pelcat
Univ Rennes, INSA Rennes, CNRS, IETR - UMR 6164
Institut Pascal UMR CNRS 6602
mpelcat@insa-rennes.fr

Daniel Menard
Univ Rennes, INSA Rennes, CNRS, IETR - UMR 6164
dmenard@insa-rennes.fr

ABSTRACT

Inexact operators are developed to exploit the tolerance of an application to imprecisions. These operators aim at reducing system energy consumption and memory footprint. In order to integrate the appropriate inexact operators in a complex system, the Quality of Service of the approximate system must be thoroughly studied through simulation. However, when simulating on a PC or workstation, the custom bit-level structures of inexact operators are not implemented in the instruction set of the simulating architecture. Consequently, the simulation requires a costly emulation, leading to expensive bit-level simulations. This paper proposes a new "Fast and Fuzzy" functional simulation method for inexact operators whose probabilistic behavior is correlated with the Most Significant Bits of the input operands. The proposed method processes real signal data and simplifies the error model for inexact operators, accelerating the simulation of the system. The modelization accuracy of the error can be controlled by a parameter called fuzzyness degree F. Using the proposed method, the bit-accurate logic-level simulation of inexact operators is replaced by an exact operator to which a pseudo-random error variable is added. Experiments on 16-bit operators show that the proposed simulation method, when compared to a bit-accurate logic level simulation, is up to 44 times faster.

ACM Reference Format:
Justine Bonnot, Karol Desnos, Maxime Pelcat, and Daniel Menard. 2018. A Fast and Fuzzy Functional Simulator of Inexact Arithmetic Operators for Approximate Computing Systems. In *GLSVLSI '18: 2018 Great Lakes Symposium on VLSI, May 23–25, 2018, Chicago, IL, USA.* ACM, New York, NY, USA, 6 pages. https://doi.org/10.1145/3194554.3194574

1 INTRODUCTION

According to the Semiconductor Industry Association and Semiconductor Research Corporation, the total energy required for computing will exceed the estimated world's energy production in 2040, if no significant improvement is obtained in terms of energy-aware computing systems [2]. In this context, approximate computing is an active field of research that trades-off the output quality of a system for its energy consumption. Approximate computing benefits from the error resilience of algorithms in signal, image or video processing and data mining fields. Among the numerous existing approximate computing techniques, inexact operators have been designed to overcome the performance limitations of exact operators. Inexact operators are obtained by making a functional approximation. The boolean function of inexact operators is slightly modified to reduce the logic complexity and/or length of critical paths [9], [4], [17]. The main interest of inexact operators compared to a technique such as fixed-point coding is to generate an error with an error rate (ER) lesser than 1 [13]. Inexact operators can then have varied error profiles in terms of ER, the frequency of error occurrences, and error distance (ED) representing the error amplitude.

A challenge when including inexact operators in an application is to evaluate the impact of the approximation on the quality of service (QoS) λ at the output of the application. Potential approximations have to be analyzed to choose the best inexact operators with respect to the different constraints on the application implementation. The approximation design space exploration (ADSE) is large and requires a fast simulation to evaluate approximation impact on QoS.

Two families of state-of-the-art approaches exist to evaluate the errors induced by approximations on an application: 1) Analytical techniques [20], [11]mathematically express error statistics but the link between these statistics and the application QoS is not straightforward. 2) Functional simulation techniques run the approximate system on data and checks the obtained λ. Nevertheless, to mimic the inexact operator behavior, bit-accurate simulations at the logic-level (BALL simulations) are required. BALL simulations are two or three orders of magnitude more complex than classical simulations with native data types, as shown in Section 4.

In this paper, we propose a fast functional simulation technique for inexact operators. The proposed "Fast and Fuzzy" (FnF) simulator simplifies the approximation error model to fasten the simulation. The BALL simulation of an inexact operator is replaced by the exact operation to which is added a pseudo-random variable (PRV) modeling the approximation error. To take into account the correlation between input values and approximation errors, the input operand set is decomposed into subspaces and a different PRV is associated to each subspace. Each PRV is defined to mimic the error in terms

GLSVLSI '18, May 23–25, 2018, Chicago, IL, USA

ACM ISBN 978-1-4503-5724-1/18/05...$15.00
https://doi.org/10.1145/3194554.3194574

of ER and ED generated by the approximation. The proposed simulator is designed to be operator agnostic and is intended to be used during the ADSE process. The FnF simulator is designed to quickly evaluate the impact of different approximations at the hardware level on the QoS of an application.

The paper is organized as follows: related works on techniques to model and simulate inexact operators are presented in Section 2. Section 3 details the proposed FnF simulation technique. The efficiency of the FnF simulation in terms of time savings and quality, is exposed in Section 4. Finally, Section 5 concludes the article.

2 RELATED WORKS

Inexact operators are designed by making a functional approximation. The functionality of the operator is modified to reduce e.g. the combinatorial logic complexity and the length of critical paths. The effect on the circuit is a reduction in power consumption and/or area. Inexact operators have been developed to overcome the performance limitations of exact arithmetic operators. Many inexact adders have been proposed ([9], [4], [17]) and their performances are compared in [8]. The comparison between adders is done in terms of normalized mean error distance (NMED), ER, and mean relative error distance (MRED). The error profile of inexact operators is often represented as a Probability Mass Function (PMF).

Different approaches have been proposed to characterize the error of an inexact operator. Probabilistic error models in [11] and [10] derive the link between the inputs and the error occurrence in the operator. These techniques are accurate but custom to particular types of operators. In the case of small input bit-width operators, exhaustive simulations can be launched to give an accurate expression of the PMF. In the more general case, inexact operators are long and complex to simulate since they are working at the logic level. For high word-length operators or to avoid exhaustive simulations, Monte-Carlo simulations can be used to compare the performances of different inexact operators [6]. These simulations strongly depend on the chosen input data distribution and on the number of launched simulations. This technique is also non-deterministic and its execution time depends on the required simulation precision.

Analytical methods provide mathematical expressions of an error metric (ER, NMED or MRED) on inexact operators. The chosen error metric can then be quickly evaluated. For instance, when implementing an approximation based on fixed-point coding, the error metric is the error power. To derive the error power, perturbation theory is used [15]. Perturbation theory is however not applicable to inexact operators because it builds on the hypothesis that errors are small compared to signal, which is not the case in most inexact operators. Several analytical methods have thus been proposed to get the impact of an inexact operator on an application. Interval Arithmetic (IA) can be used [1], but usually overestimates the error bounds. To overcome the pessimistic bounds given by IA, Affine Arithmetic (AA)takes into account the first order dependencies between variables [5]. Nevertheless, these techniques do not give information on the ER of inexact operators. Modified Interval (MIA) and Affine (MAA) Arithmetic have also been proposed in [7]. MIA and MAA require a characterization of the PMF of the inexact operator and derive rules to propagate it through the application. However, the number of terms required to propagate

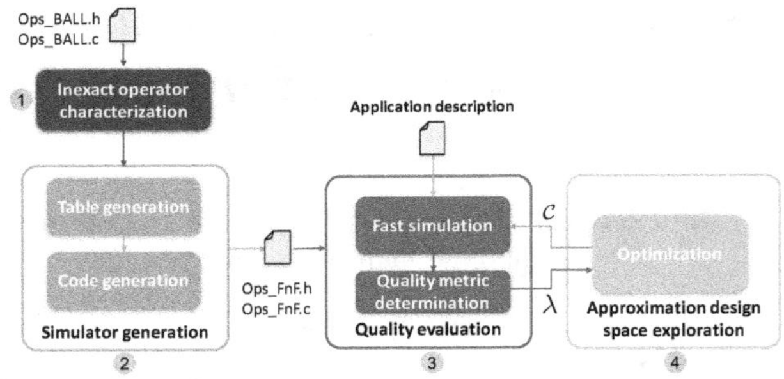

Figure 1: ADSE flow integrating the proposed FnF simulator to evaluate the application QoS with inexact operators

the PMF suffers from range explosion. For instance, to propagate the PMF through 4 Multiply-Accumulate (MAC) operations, 8 million terms are needed [7]. Analytical techniques are completely describing the PMF of an inexact operator but do not give a direct link between the error metric and λ.

The straightforward method to determine the impact of the error on λ is to perform a functional simulation of the application. A functional simulation of an inexact operator simulates the operator at the logic level. Thus, the simulation time is significantly higher than the one obtained with a classical simulation using workstation native data types. The simulation in C code of an Almost Correct Adder (ACA, [17]) on 32-bits takes 197× more time than the floating-point addition natively supported by the processor. When it comes to the Lower-Error Fixed-Width Multiplier (AAM, [16]), a multiplication of two 32-bit operands takes 6250× more simulation time than a floating-point multiplication. Inexact operators are generally more intricate in terms of hardware implementation or memory accesses than their exact implementation.

To the best of our knowledge, no method has been proposed to accelerate the simulation of inexact operators by combining exact computation and statistical methods. The goal of the proposed simulator is to replace the BALL simulation of the inexact operator $\hat{\diamond}$ by the simulation of the exact operator $\diamond$ plus a Pseudo-Random Variable (PRV).

3 PROPOSED FAST AND FUZZY SIMULATOR

Our proposed simulation technique for inexact operators simplifies the modeling of the approximation error to fasten the simulation of inexact operators within the targeted application.

The proposed FnF simulator is set in the design flow presented in Figure 1. The ADSE, corresponding to Block 4 in Figure 1 aims at finding the best inexact operator for each operation in the application as well as the best parameters for their tuning. For each test of a configuration C, λ is evaluated from the results of the fast simulation carried-out with the FnF simulator (Block 3). The technique proposed for the fast simulation is presented in Section 3.1.

The FnF simulator uses pre-computed tables computed in Block 2. The generation of the tables is presented in Section 3.2. The generation of the tables requires the knowledge of the approximation error statistics. These statistics are provided by the characterization process corresponding to Block 1 in Figure 1. Analytical techniques

[11], Monte-Carlo simulations [6] or exhaustive simulations are the different alternatives to obtain these statistics. In the rest of the paper, the statistics on the error have been derived from exhaustive simulations for accuracy and generic purpose.

3.1 Fast and Fuzzy simulation of $x\widehat{\diamond}y$

Let's consider an approximate operator $\widehat{\diamond}$ whose input operands $x \in I_x = [\underline{x};\overline{x}]$ and $y \in I_y = [\underline{y};\overline{y}]$ are encoded on N_x and N_y bits respectively. To avoid a coarse error modeling, the input set $I = I_x \times I_y$ is decomposed in subspaces $S_{ij} = I_{xi} \times I_{yj}$ such that $\bigcup_{i,j} S_{ij} = I$. Since the ER is not equal to 1 in each S_{ij}, our method determines a pseudo-random variable PRV e_{ij} for each S_{ij} with statistical characteristics provided by the inexact operator characterization phase (Block 1). It is important to note that our FnF simulator can take as input the statistics on the error provided by [11], by exhaustive or Monte-Carlo simulations. Our simulator does not output the exact value of the approximate operation but generates the error with the same statistical characteristics as the error at the output of the approximate operator.

Our method reduces the software simulation time of an inexact operator by replacing the BALL simulation of $\widehat{\diamond}$ by the accurate version of the operator $\diamond$ plus a PRV e_{ij} whose statistical characteristics are computed from the error generated by $\widehat{\diamond}$. Figure 2 illustrates this principle.

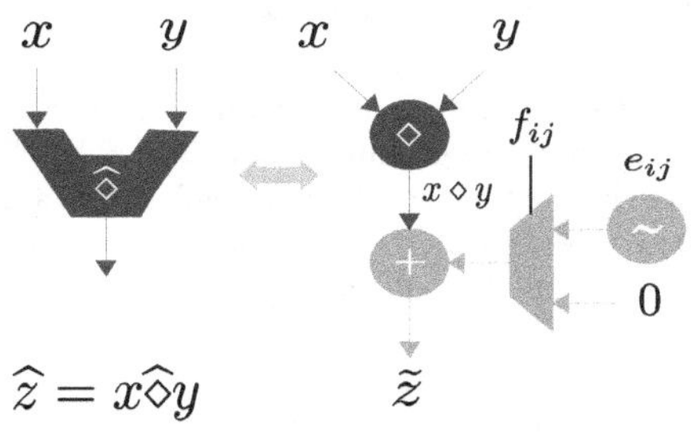

Figure 2: Statistical equivalence between BALL and FnF simulation of $x\widehat{\diamond}y$

According to the ER f_{ij} in S_{ij}, 0 or e_{ij} is added to $x \diamond y$. The input operands sharing the same N-F MSBs (Most Significant Bits) are grouped in the same subspace S_{ij}, and are then associated to the same PRV e_{ij}, hence the error on the result of the simulation. The size of the subspaces S_{ij} controls the modeling grain and is embodied by the user-defined fuzziness degree F. F has an impact on the accuracy of our FnF simulator. Hence, the larger F is, the more different outputs of the simulated operator are summarized with the same PRV e_{ij}, thus increasing the simulation imprecision.

Algorithm 1 details the proposed simulation process for $N_x = N_y = N$ and Figure 3 illustrates the flow of our simulation. The first step of the FnF simulation is to *pre-process* the input operands x and y by extracting their N-F MSBs. This leads to the values x_0 and y_0 respectively. x_0 and y_0 indicate to which subspace S_{ij} x and y belong to. The index $k = \mathcal{T}_{idx}[x_0][y_0]$ indicates if $x\widehat{\diamond}y$ may generate an error. $\mathcal{T}_{idx}$ is a precomputed table that indicates if an error occurs in S_{ij}. Consequently, if k is equal to zero, no error is generated and the accurate version of $x \diamond y$ is directly returned, thus

Algorithm 1 Fast and Fuzzy Simulation of $x\widehat{\diamond}y$

procedure $FnF_{\widehat{\diamond}}(x, y, N, F)$
  $x_0 = x >> F$ ▷ Pre-process operands
  $y_0 = y >> F$
  $k = \mathcal{T}_{idx}[x_0][y_0]$
  if $k == 0$ **then** ▷ Error-free test
    return $x \diamond y$
  else ▷ Pseudo-random number generation
    $M_1 = 2^F - 1$
    p_{ij} = generatePRNumber(M_1, x, y)
    e_{ij} = generateError($p_{ij}, f_{ij}, a_{ij}, b_{ij}$)
    return $x \diamond y + e_{ij}$
  end if
end procedure

avoiding any simulation time overhead. If k is different from zero, a set of statistical characteristics (a_{ij}, b_{ij}, f_{ij}) is used to compute the PRV e_{ij}. The pre-computed table $\mathcal{T}_{err}[k]$ stores the sets of statistical characteristics for each S_{ij} where an error occurs. Section 3.2 presents the generation of the two abovementioned tables. The PRV e_{ij} is computed with the following expression

$$e_{ij} = a_{ij} + b_{ij} * p_{ij}, \tag{1}$$

with p_{ij} a pseudo-random number. In the FnF simulator, p_{ij}, is geerated from the F LSBs of the input operands. Indeed, the LSBs of a signal can be considered as a white random additive noise non-correlated with the input signal as derived in [19]. The F LSBs of x and y are concatenated and finally scrambled by a `xor` operation with a constant K. The purpose of these operations is to map the input operands $(x, y) \in I_x \times I_y$ to $p_{ij} \in [0; 2^{2F}[$ in a bijective way.

Finally, an asset of our simulator is that the execution time depends on the number of errors committed by the original inexact operator. The less errors an operator generates, the faster our FnF simulator.

3.2 Automated simulator construction

The main contribution is to reduce the simulation time to get the value $x\widehat{\diamond}y$ with the method detailed in Section 3.1. The error modeling is simplified using the tables $\mathcal{T}_{idx}$ and $\mathcal{T}_{err}$ to store the characteristics of the PRVs used to compute the output value. The generation of these tables is done only once for each operator and off-line.

Table $\mathcal{T}_{idx}$ indicates if a combination of input operands does or not generate an error. The size of $\mathcal{T}_{idx}$ is $2^{N_x+N_y-2F}$. The N_x-F and $N_y - F$ MSBs of the operands are masked and operands obtaining the same mask value are mapped to the same subspace S_{ij} in $\mathcal{T}_{idx}$. Equation 2 presents the computation of $\mathcal{T}_{idx}$.

$$\mathcal{T}_{idx}[i,j] = \begin{cases} 0 & \text{if } \forall x, y \in S_{ij}, x\widehat{\diamond}y = x \diamond y \\ k & \text{else.} \end{cases} \tag{2}$$

$\mathcal{T}_{err}$ stores the ED characteristics embodied by the affine form (a_{ij}, b_{ij}), and the threshold t_{ij} used to generate an error with the same ER as in S_{ij}. The size of $\mathcal{T}_{err}$ then depends on the number of subspaces where an error occurs.

To generate an error with the same statistical characteristics as the inexact operator, a system with two equations for three unknowns is set. The threshold t_{ij} is then computed to be equal

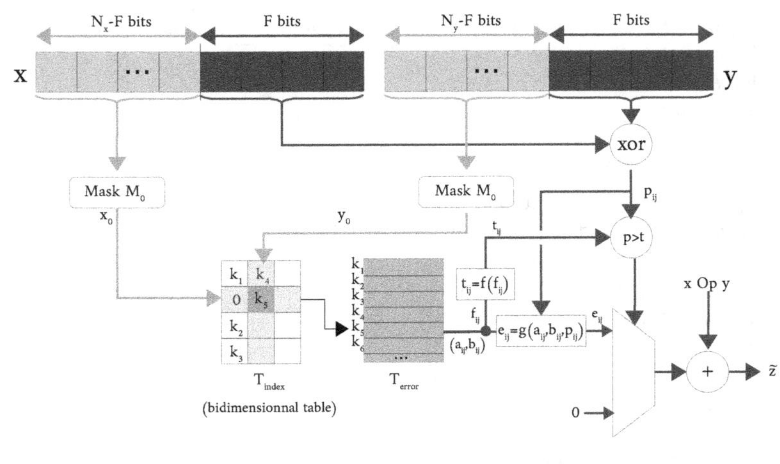

Figure 3: Graph flow of the proposed Fast and Fuzzy simulation

to the number of errors to generate. We then have the system $\mathcal{S}$ in Equation 3 to solve, with f_{ij} representing the ER in S_{ij}, A_{ij}, the maximum ED in S_{ij}, and μ_{ij} the mean ED in S_{ij}.

$$\mathcal{S}:\begin{cases} t_{ij} &= 2^{2*F}(1-f_{ij}) \\ A_{ij} &= a_{ij}+b_{ij}*\max\limits_{i,j}(p_{ij}) \\ \mu_{ij}*f_{ij} &= \frac{\sum_{p=0}^{2^{2*F}-1} a_{ij}+b_{ij}*p}{2^{2*F}} \end{cases} \tag{3}$$

$\mathcal{S}$ is developed to extract a_{ij} and b_{ij} in Equation 4. Indeed, the maximum value of the pseudo-random number p_{ij} is $2^{2F}-1$ and the third equation of the system can be separated to highlight an arithmetic sequence whose first term is t_{ij} and common term 1.

$$\begin{cases} b_{ij} &= \frac{2^{2F+1}\mu_{ij}f_{ij}-2A_{ij}(2^{2F}-1-t_{ij})}{(2^{2F}-1-t_{ij})(2^{2F}-3+t_{ij}-2^{2F+1})} \\ \\ a_{ij} &= A_{ij}-b_{ij}(2^{2F}-1) \end{cases} \tag{4}$$

The error e_{ij} can also be modeled by a constant value if b_{ij} is set to zero, but the accuracy of our simulator decreases. In this case, the threshold t_{ij} is computed for each S_{ij} by equalizing the mean ED of $\widehat{\diamond}$ with the mean ED generated by the FnF simulation of $\widehat{\diamond}$, as presented in Equation 5.

$$\mu_{ij}*f_{ij} = a_{ij}*(1-\frac{t_{ij}}{2^{2*F}}) \tag{5}$$

$$\Leftrightarrow \qquad t_{ij} = 2^{2*F}\cdot(1-\frac{\mu_{ij}\cdot f_{ij}}{a_{ij}}) \tag{6}$$

Besides, an inexact operator can be designed to generate errors always lower or equal to $x\diamond y$. In this case, e_{ij} cannot be greater than the value of the operation $x\diamond y$, since the output of the simulation is $x\diamond y+e_{ij}$. In this case, the generated error e_{ij} is equal to $\max(-\min\limits_{x,y\in S_{ij}}(x\diamond y), A_{ij})$. The maximum ED is not always generated. Consequently, to keep the same mean ED, the threshold t_{ij} has to be lower to generate errors more often. The worst possible case is obtained when e_{ij} is always equal to $x\diamond y$ in S_{ij}: in this case, the value of t_{ij} is presented in Equation 7. Else, e_{ij} is always equal to A_{ij}, the maximum ED in S_{ij}.

$$t_{ij} = 2^{2*F}\cdot(1-\frac{\mu_{ij}\cdot f_{ij}}{-\min\limits_{x,y\in S_{ij}}(x\diamond y)}) \tag{7}$$

4 EXPERIMENTAL RESULTS

The FnF simulator proposes to simulate an inexact operator using a simple error model. To evaluate the impact on the simulation of the proposed method, three points have to be highlighted: the time savings offered by the simulator for the simulation of a single operation presented in Section 4.1, the trade-off simulation time/accuracy of the proposed simulation depending on the fuzzyness degree F, detailed in Section 4.2 and the accuracy of the QoS evaluation compared to the time savings in an ADSE process, extended in Section 4.3. The results have been obtained on a processor Intel i7-6700 with 32GBytes of RAM.

4.1 Simulation time savings for the FnF simulator

To quickly test the impact of an inexact operator in an application, the easiest solution is to simulate the application in software with BALL simulation. The simulation time of our FnF simulator is then compared with the software BALL simulation time obtained with the C code from the App Test framework [3] for a single operation and various input operand bit-width. The time required to generate the tables (Block 4 in the flow presented in Figure 1) is less than 140s for the tested 16-bit inexact operators.

Figure 4a represents the simulation times for the ACA and Figure 4b for the Lower-Error Fixed-Width Multiplier (AAM), an approximate array multiplier presented in [16]. The time for simulating a single operation is represented depending on the operand bit-width. The obtained times have been **averaged** for all the possible configurations of carry-chain length (for the ACA) and all the possible values of F for both operators. A BALL simulation of the ACA on 16-bit takes 300 more time than classical simulation of the exact operator with native data types, and the BALL simulation of the AAM, for the multiplication of two 16-bit operands takes 4200 more time than a simulation with native data types.

The simulation times for the FnF simulator are represented for $b_{ij} \neq 0$ and $b_{ij} = 0$, the affine modeling being slightly longer to simulate than when $b_{ij} = 0$. For the ACA, the FnF simulation is always faster than the BALL one with operand bit-width greater than 5 if $b_{ij} = 0$, else greater than 6. On a single 16-bit addition, the BALL simulation takes 3.5 more time than the FnF simulation. The gain for this operator is reasonable since the design of the ACA is quite simple and can easily be reproduced with C-code. However, when it comes to the AAM, whose design is much more complex than the one of the ACA, the FnF simulation is always faster and the BALL simulation takes 44 more time than the FnF simulation on a single 16-bit operation.

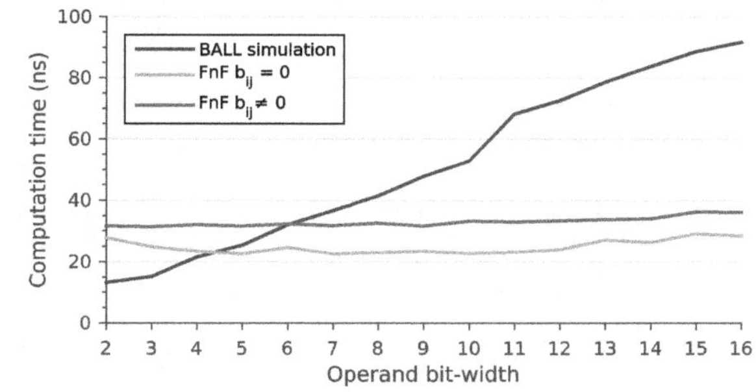

(a) ACA inexact operator

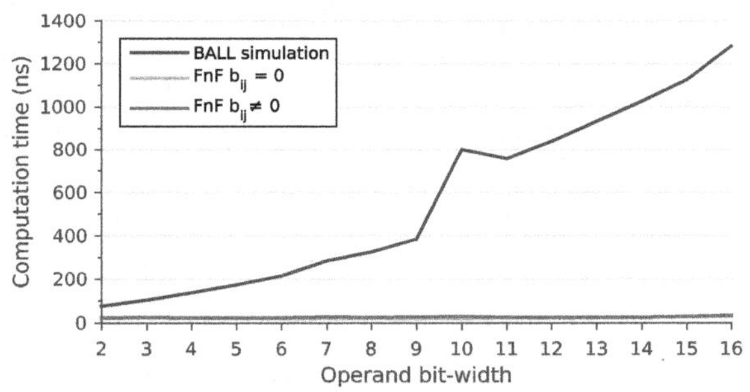

(b) AAM inexact operator

Figure 4: Simulation time for the FnF and the BALL simulation of one operation.

4.2 Trade-off simulation time/quality

The number of Fuzzy bits F embodies a trade-off between the simulation time, the size of the tables to store and the quality of the simulation. Figure 5 represents the Normalized Rooted Mean Squared Error (NRMSE) of the FnF simulation of the ACA compared to the BALL simulation of the inexact operator, $\delta_{FnF/BALL}$, for two input operand bit-widths. The NRMSE of the inexact operator simulated with BALL simulation compared to the exact operator, $\delta_{BALL/ex}$, is equal to 0.35. When $F = N - 1$, a single PRV is used to model the errors, $\delta_{FnF/BALL}$ and $\delta_{BALL/ex}$ are of the same order of magnitude. When $F = 0$, the simulator behaves like a Look-Up Table (LUT) containing the error due to inexact operation. Thus, $\delta_{FnF/BALL}$ is equal to zero. Besides, the relative difference between the FnF simulation and BALL simulation stays lower than 10% for $N - F$ higher than 4.

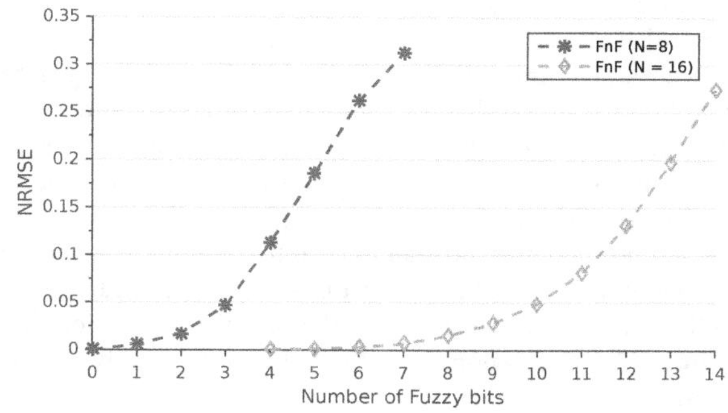

Figure 5: NRMSE between the FnF simulation and the BALL simulation of $\widehat{\diamond}$ (ACA with a carry chain length cut at $N/2$)

The fuzzyness degree F has also an impact on the simulation time as demonstrated in Figure 6 for the AAM. The FnF simulation time is represented for different input bit-widths, depending on the fuzzyness degree. The highest F, the smallest the tables and the least cache misses. For instance, for $N = 13$, F has to be at least equal to 3 to be faster than the BALL simulation (simulation time gain of 2.4) and the maximum simulation time gain if $F = N - 1$ is equal to 49.2.

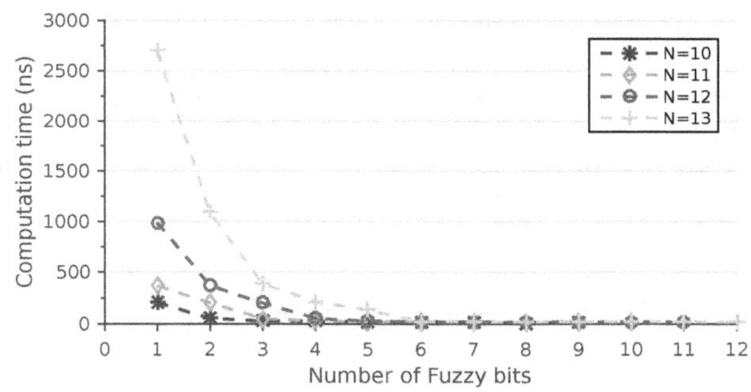

Figure 6: FnF simulation time depending on the fuzzyness degree F for the AAM

4.3 ADSE for a stereo vision application

Designing an application with approximate computing, several parameters have to be tuned during the ADSE. During this phase, the application is run several times to measure the quality of the result at the output of the application with the chosen parameters, to finally select the parameters leading to the best performances with respect to the designer's constraints. To give an idea of the intensiveness of this phase, several tunable parameters are given hereafter (non exhaustive list). The percentage of replaced operators, the replaced operations, the inexact operator that is used (ex: AAM or AWM), if the operator is tunable, the parameter to tune (ex: carry-chain length for the ACA) and finally, the set of inputs on which the algorithm has to be tested, are tunable parameters.

To illustrate the DSE phase, the stereomatching algorithm is considered [12]. This computer vision algorithm outputs a depth map given two rectified input images. Approximate computing is particularly interesting for this algorithm since it is computationally expensive. In this experiment, only the most computation intensive kernel of this algorithm is considered for the ADSE. Only taking into account the percentage of operators as well as the operations to replace, but no tuning of the operators, 158 simulations are needed. If the replacement of multiply operations is solely considered, testing all the possible configurations with the BALL simulation takes **8.82 hours**. The simulation using the FnF simulator only requires **12.71 minutes**.

This test has been done using solely an input image from a test set extracted from the Middlebury database [14]. To validate the approximation on the stereomatching algorithm, the test needs to be done on a complete data set, hence increasing the number of simulations to perform. Several configurations have been tested and are presented in Table 1. The quality metric used to measure the difference between FnF and the BALL simulation is the SSIM presented in [18]. The terms r_{ADD} and r_{MULT} represent the ratio of respectively addition and multiplication which use an inexact operator. The gain $G_t = \frac{t_{BALL}}{t_{FnF}}$ in term of simulation time of the proposed approach compare to a BALL simulation is provided. The accuracy degradation of the application QoS evaluation is provided through Δ_a that measures the relative difference between the SSIM of both output images obtained with FnF and BALL simulations. The multiply operations have been replaced by the AAM and the additions have been replaced by the ACA with a carry-chain length equal to 7. Both operators are on 16-bit. The most important accuracy degradation for QoS evaluation depends on which operation is impacted by the approximation, but the degradation is always lower than 6%. The FnF simulator leads to an accurate QoS evaluation and allows to save a non negligible simulation time by dividing the simulation time between 1.38 to 87.59.

F	r_{ADD} (%)	r_{MPY} (%)	G_t	Δ_{acc}
5	0	14.3	65.59	< 0.1%
5	0	14.3	66.01	< 0.1%
5	0	14.3	65.71	< 0.1%
5	0	28.6	84.44	< 0.1%
5	0	28.6	83.37	< 0.1%
5	0	28.6	87.59	< 0.1%
8	20	0	1.38	5.69%
5(AAM) - 8(ACA)	20	14.3	52.24	0.578 %

Table 1: ADSE for the stereomatching algorithm. Simulation time gain G_t and quality degradation Δ_{acc} of the proposed approach compared to a BALL simulation for different configurations r_{ADD} and r_{MULT}

5 CONCLUSION

This paperhas proposed a simulator of inexact arithmetic operators that simplifies the modeling of the approximation error to fasten the simulation. The "Fast and Fuzzy" simulator explores the functional accuracy of operators in potentially large applications. The simulator is demonstrated to induce an acceptable loss of simulation accuracy in exchange for large simulation speedups. Simulation speedups of 3.5× and 44× are observed respectively for an inexact 16-bit adder and an inexact 16-bit multiplier.

This project has received funding from the French Agence Nationale de la Recherche under grant ANR-15-CE25-0015 (ARTEFaCT project).

REFERENCES

[1] G Alefeld. 1999. Interval arithmetic tools for range approximation and inclusion of zeros. In *Error Control and Adaptivity in Scientific Computing*. Springer, 1–21.

[2] Semiconductor Industries Association and Semiconductor Research Corporation. 2015. Rebooting the IT Revolution, a Call for Action. https://www.src.org/newsroom/rebooting-the-it-revolution.pdf. (2015).

[3] Benjamin Barrois, Olivier Sentieys, and Daniel Menard. 2017. The hidden cost of functional approximation against careful data sizing: a case study. In *Proceedings of DATE*. European Design and Automation Association, 181–186.

[4] Vincent Camus, Jeremy Schlachter, and Christian Enz. 2016. A low-power carry cut-back approximate adder with fixed-point implementation and floating-point precision. In *Proceedings of the 53rd Annual Design Automation Conference*. ACM, 127.

[5] Claire Fang Fang, Rob A Rutenbar, Markus Püschel, and Tsuhan Chen. 2003. Toward efficient static analysis of finite-precision effects in DSP applications via affine arithmetic modeling. In *Proceedings of the 40th annual Design Automation Conference*. ACM, 496–501.

[6] Jiawei Huang and John Lach. 2011. Exploring the fidelity-efficiency design space using imprecise arithmetic. In *Design Automation Conference (ASP-DAC), 2011 16th Asia and South Pacific*. IEEE, 579–584.

[7] Jiawei Huang, John Lach, and Gabriel Robins. 2011. Analytic error modeling for imprecise arithmetic circuits. *Proc. SELSE* (2011).

[8] Honglan Jiang, Jie Han, and Fabrizio Lombardi. 2015. A comparative review and evaluation of approximate adders. In *Proceedings on Great Lakes Symposium on VLSI*. ACM.

[9] Yongtae Kim, Yong Zhang, and Peng Li. 2013. An energy efficient approximate adder with carry skip for error resilient neuromorphic VLSI systems. In *Proceedings of the International Conference on Computer-Aided Design*. IEEE Press.

[10] Sana Mazahir, Osman Hasan, Rehan Hafiz, and Muhammad Shafique. 2017. Probabilistic Error Analysis of Approximate Recursive Multipliers. *IEEE Trans. Comput.* (2017).

[11] Sana Mazahir, Osman Hasan, Rehan Hafiz, Muhammad Shafique, and Jorg Henkel. 2017. Probabilistic error modeling for approximate adders. *IEEE Trans. Comput.* 66, 3 (2017), 515–530.

[12] Judicaël Menant, Muriel Pressigout, Luce Morin, and Jean-Francois Nezan. 2014. Optimized fixed point implementation of a local stereo matching algorithm onto C66x DSP. In *Design and Architectures for Signal and Image Processing (DASIP), 2014 Conference on*. IEEE.

[13] Jongsun Park, Jung Hwan Choi, and Kaushik Roy. 2010. Dynamic bit-width adaptation in DCT: an approach to trade off image quality and computation energy. *IEEE transactions on very large scale integration (VLSI) systems* 18, 5 (2010).

[14] Daniel Scharstein and Richard Szeliski. 2003. High-accuracy stereo depth maps using structured light. In *Computer Vision and Pattern Recognition, 2003. Proceedings. 2003 IEEE Computer Society Conference on*, Vol. 1. IEEE.

[15] Changchun Shi and Robert W Brodersen. 2004. A perturbation theory on statistical quantization effects in fixed-point DSP with non-stationary inputs. In *Circuits and Systems, 2004. ISCAS'04. Proceedings of the 2004 International Symposium on*, Vol. 3. IEEE, III–373.

[16] Lan-Da Van, Shuenn-Shyang Wang, and Wu-Shiung Feng. 2000. Design of the lower error fixed-width multiplier and its application. *IEEE Transactions on Circuits and Systems II: Analog and Digital Signal Processing* 47, 10 (2000).

[17] Ajay K Verma, Philip Brisk, and Paolo Ienne. 2008. Variable latency speculative addition: A new paradigm for arithmetic circuit design. In *Proceedings of the conference on Design, automation and test in Europe*. ACM.

[18] Zhou Wang, Alan C Bovik, Hamid R Sheikh, and Eero P Simoncelli. 2004. Image quality assessment: from error visibility to structural similarity. *IEEE transactions on image processing* 13, 4 (2004).

[19] Bernard Widrow and István Kollár. 2008. Quantization noise. *Cambridge University Press* 2 (2008).

[20] Yi Wu, You Li, Xiangxuan Ge, and Weikang Qian. 2017. An Accurate and Efficient Method to Calculate the Error Statistics of Block-based Approximate Adders. *arXiv preprint arXiv:1703.03522* (2017).

Battery-aware Design Exploration of Scheduling Policies for Multi-sensor Devices

Yukai Chen, Daniele Jahier Pagliari, Enrico Macii and Massimo Poncino
Department of Control and Computer Engineering
Politecnico di Torino, Turin, Italy
yukai.chen@polito.it;daniele.jahier@polito.it;enrico.macii@polito.it;massimo.poncino@polito.it

ABSTRACT

Lifetime maximization is a key challenge in battery-powered multi-sensor devices. Battery-aware power management strategies combine task scheduling with dynamic voltage scaling (DVS), accounting for the fact that the power drawn by the device is different from that provided by the battery due to its many non-idealities. However, state-of-the-art techniques in this field do not take into account several important aspects, such as the impact of sensing tasks on the overall power demand, the (operating point dependent) losses due to multiple DC-DC conversions, and the dynamic modifications in battery efficiency caused by different distributions of the currents in the temporal and in the frequency domains. In this work, we propose a novel approach to identify optimal power management solutions, that addresses all these limitations. Specifically, using advanced battery and DC-DC converter models, we propose methods to explore the scheduling space both statically (at design time) and dynamically (at runtime), accounting not only for computation tasks, but also for communication and sensing. With this method, we show that the battery lifetime can be increased by as much as 23.36% if an optimal power management strategy is adopted.

CCS CONCEPTS

• **Applied computing** → **Computer-aided design**; *Electronics*; • **Computing methodologies** → *Modeling and simulation*; Planning and scheduling; • **Theory of computation** → Scheduling algorithms; • **Networks** → Wireless access networks;

KEYWORDS

IoT devices; Power Management; Battery-aware Scheduling; Sensor-based Systems

ACM Reference format:
Yukai Chen, Daniele Jahier Pagliari, Enrico Macii and Massimo Poncino. 2018. Battery-aware Design Exploration of Scheduling Policies for Multi-sensor Devices. In *Proceedings of 2018 Great Lakes Symposium on VLSI, Chicago, IL, USA, May 23--25, 2018 (GLSVLSI '18)*, 6 pages.
https://doi.org/10.1145/3194554.3194588

GLSVLSI '18, May 23--25, 2018, Chicago, IL, USA

ACM ISBN 978-1-4503-5724-1/18/05...$15.00
https://doi.org/10.1145/3194554.3194588

1 INTRODUCTION

Dynamic power management (DPM) of battery-powered multi-sensor devices (ranging from wearable electronics to wireless sensor nodes) has been intensively studied by researchers, and many strategies have been proposed over the years[1--7]. Many of these solutions are battery-aware, in the sense that they specifically take into account the fact that there is a substantial difference between the power consumed by the hardware and the one actually provided by the battery [3--7]. The reason for this discrepancy is twofold: first, a DC-DC converter is typically placed between the battery and the load. Second, a battery cannot provide any arbitrary amount of power with the same efficiency; this is due to the so-called "rated capacity" effect, which states that a battery is less efficient in providing increasingly larger currents.

The many solutions in the literature that account for these non-idealities are mostly focused on the power management of the hardware in terms of *scheduling of the computational tasks executed on the microprocessor*[3, 4, 6]. While these works provide relevant general guidelines for task scheduling, they show several shortcomings. First, the great majority of these works focuses only on *computational tasks*, despite the fact that *sensing tasks* normally have significantly larger power demands [7, 8], and thus impact on the battery depletion. Moreover, sensing tasks are typically independent from each other, thus they can be freely parallelized or serialized, if this is beneficial for the battery (e.g. in order to minimize peak currents or to maximize idle intervals). Second, most works neglect the fact that each system component may work at a different voltage level. In general, each sensor requires a dedicated DC-DC converter, different from that of the micro controller unit (MCU) or core and from that of the RF transceiver. Each of these converters will be working in a different operating point, with consequently different efficiencies. Third, the battery models used in these works (e.g., the one of [9]) are *steady-state*: they are not able to track the instantaneous changes in voltage and state-of-charge (SOC) of the battery, and rather calculate the overall duration of the battery for a given workload. Therefore, most solutions only propose *static* scheduling algorithms, i.e. in which the schedule is fixed throughout the system operation [3, 4, 6, 7]. Moreover, many of these works overrate the so-called recovery effect in batteries, providing solutions that are biased towards the insertion of idle times among operations. However, recent works have shown that in typical Li-Ion batteries the recovery effect is virtually absent [10].

In this work we proposed a novel design exploration method for battery-aware power management in multi-sensor devices, that targets all the aforementioned limitations. Our approach accounts for the impact of all major system tasks, including sensing and communication, and considers the scheduling freedom offered by the independence of sensing operations as a new optimization dimension for battery lifetime optimization. Moreover, it makes use of a DC-DC converter efficiency model that accounts for dependencies on the operating point of each component [11], and of an advanced circuit-equivalent battery model [12], capable of expressing battery non-idealities related to instantaneous current values distribution and frequency spectrum. Thanks to these models, we are able to show that a *dynamic* scheduling solution, in which the scheduling is recomputed at the beginning of every sampling interval, can provide additional lifetime benefits compared to a static approach. In Section 4, we show that scheduling according to our exploration can provide up to 18.48% lifetime increase if computed statically, and up to 23.36% if updated dynamically.

2 MOTIVATION

The workload of a multi-sensor device is structured as a periodic sequence of the following major tasks: sensing, computation, and transmission. Figure 1-(a) shows an example timing diagram in which the sensing tasks are started **in parallel** at the start of the period, and followed by processing and transmission. After these operations (of a total duration of T_{active}) the system enters an idle state for a time $T_{idle} \gg T_{active}$, resulting in a typically very low duty cycle $D = T_{active}/T_{idle}$.

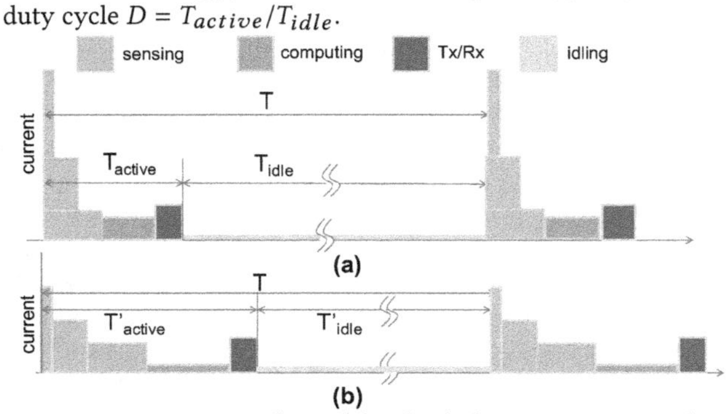

Figure 1: Conceptual workload of the system considered in this work: (a) one in which T_{active} is minimized, and (b) one in which T_{active} is maximized while keeping the current peaks as low as possible.

This schedule is driven by the objective of *maximizing the idle time*. Therefore, multiple sensing operations are run in parallel, and for the same reason the computation task is run at the maximum possible speed in order to shorten T_{active} as much as possible. While this might be reasonable from the perspective of the power consumed by the system, it might lead to sub-optimal results when a battery is involved. As a matter of fact, it is well-known that a battery is particularly sensitive to large current variations [13, 14]. Stacking together multiple sensing tasks, which are incidentally the most power-hungry operations, would unnecessarily deplete battery charge. Similarly, relaxing execution speed of the MCU might help avoid a too strong depletion of the battery. Figure 1-(b) shows an alternative schedule with the sensing tasks serialized and the computing task executed at the lowest possible speed. This yields a duty cycle $D' = T'_{active}/T'_{idle} > D$.

Nevertheless, when the system is in idle state, the power consumption P_{off} is likely to be 2 or 3 orders of magnitude smaller than in the active phase. Therefore, there will be a limit in stretching the activity phase after which an increase of the duty cycle will not be convenient anymore. The objective of this work is to provide an insight of such trade-off by exploring different alternatives using a power model of a battery that can accurately track the battery efficiency as a function of current distribution (and not just instantaneous current values) [12] in order to derive the optimal tasks scheduling policy for prolonging the lifetime of designed system.

3 METHOD AND ALGORITHMS

3.1 System Characterization

3.1.1 System Architecture. The device consists of the following components:

- A wireless transceiver implementing some given protocol. We assume that each received and sent message has a fixed-size payload so that transmission requires always the same time T_{tx} and T_{rx}. Power consumed during transmission and reception are P_{tx} and P_{rx} respectively, with $P_{tx} > P_{rx}$. We assume also that the transceiver has approximately zero power when idle. Notice that in our scenario, without loss of generality, we assume that the devices only transmit the sensed information to a central gateway and do not receive any data.
- A set of N_s sensors, each sensing a different quantity. Each sensor takes a time $T_{s,i}$ to complete sensing and requires a power $P_{s,i}$. Notice that we assume that the sensing task includes analog-to-digital conversion.
- A micro controller unit (MCU) that executes a given algorithm on the sensed data. We assume that the MCU has N_p power states associated to different voltage/frequency points. At a given voltage/frequency point $i = 1, ..., N_p$, the MCU takes $T_{c,i}$ to execute and requires a power $P_{c,i}$. Without loss of generality we assume that lower indices represent lower power levels, $T_{c,i} > T_{c,i+1}$ and $P_{c,i} < P_{c,i+1}$.
Besides these active states, the MCU has an off state in which it consumes a power $P_{off} > 0$ due to static power consumption. In this state the CPU cannot execute instructions.

Table 1 summarizes the key parameters of the components of the system.

Component	Mode	Exec. Time	Power
Transceiver	TX	T_{tx}	P_{tx}
	RX	T_{rx}	P_{rx}
Sensors	Active	$T_{s,i}$	$P_{s,i}$
	Idle	--	$P_{offs,i}$
MCU	Active	T_c	$P_{on}(T_c)$
	Idle	--	P_{offmcu}

Table 1: Power/Performance parameters of the system.

3.1.2 Workload Characterization. As described in Section 2, the workload is structured as a periodic sequence of the following major tasks: sensing, computation, and transmission. We assume that there exist two degrees of freedom in the possible temporal sequence of the workload: (1) the scheduling of the sensing operations, and (2) the power state at which the computational phase is executed. Transmission is assumed to take a fixed time. How these two phases are executed will determine the resulting T_{active}, and since T is considered to be fixed (determined by the application constraints), it will also determine the duty cycle D.

3.1.3 Characterization of the Power Domains. An accurate analysis of the impact on the battery of the different workload distributions in a period implies an accurate characterization of the various power domains involved in the system. Considering only the power consumed by each task as in Table 1 to determine the battery depletion in each cycle would not be accurate at all. Conversely, it is essential to consider the actual voltage and current levels of each component.

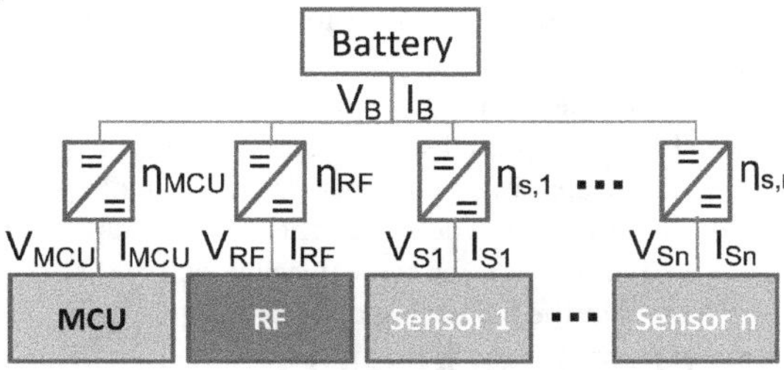

Figure 2: Characterization of the power domains involved.

Figure 2 suggests that each component operates in a different *power domain* with its own voltage level and current consumption [15]. Furthermore, such power level is in general different from the output power of the battery, and therefore each power domain must be "adapted" by an appropriate DC/DC converter. Obviously, if multiple components share the same voltage level, a single DC/DC converter can be shared accordingly. This has important consequences for the assessment of the battery lifetime for two reasons:

(1) the DC-DC converters are not ideal components, and each one does not fully convert 100% of the battery power into usable power. The lost power is dissipated as heat. This is represented by an efficiency factor $\eta < 1$; for instance, $P_{MCU} = \eta_{MCU} \cdot P_{battery}$. This implies that the power consumption by a component actually translates in a larger power demand to the battery P/η.
(2) Due to the implementation of such converters, normally the efficiency decreases for low output currents [15], which, incidentally, is the exactly what we target when we maximize the idle time.

Therefore, besides an accurate battery model that can track current variations and its distribution, a model of DC/DC converters in which efficiency is (at least) sensitive to output current is needed.

3.2 Models

3.2.1 Component Models. From the perspective of the battery energy, all components can be regarded as generic **loads** that consume an instantaneous power given by the product of a current demand and a voltage level. Therefore, components that are assumed to be non power-manageable such as the transceiver and the sensors, are simply characterized by their current and voltage (Figure 2).

Conversely, the MCU has N_p power states, each one corresponding to a given (voltage, frequency) pair and an associated current consumption I_i. The frequency of power state i impacts the computation time $T_{c,i}$, whereas the voltage V_i and I_i determine the power level. Notice that as each power state is associated to a different voltage level, it will result in a different efficiency of the corresponding DC/DC converter.

3.2.2 Battery Model. Analyzing the impact of workload scheduling on battery lifetime requires an advanced battery model, able to accurately account for the effects of load current variations on the usable battery capacity. Specifically, the model must express both the capacity dependency on current *magnitude*, and on current *dynamics* [12]. Indeed, recent works have shown that the available capacity is influenced by the current *value* distribution (e.g. constant and varying load currents with the same average value affect the capacity differently), as well as by its *frequency* spectrum (e.g. periodic load currents with the same amplitude and shape, but different frequencies). To account for all these effects, we employ the circuit equivalent battery model described in [12], shown in Figure 3.

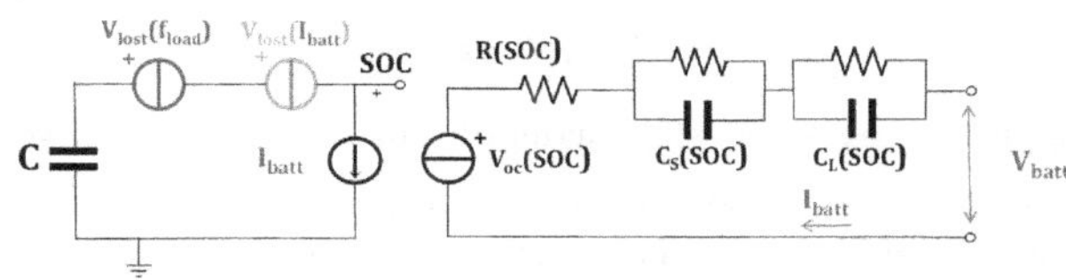

Figure 3: Battery model incorporating current magnitude and frequency dependence.

The circuit consists of two main sections. On the left, the capacitor C represents the nominal battery capacity in Ah; the current generator models the load current (I_{batt}), and the two voltage generators express the dependency of capacity on load current magnitude and frequency respectively. On the right side, the voltage-controlled oscillator models the dependence of the battery open-circuit voltage V_{oc} on the SOC of the battery. Finally, the RC network represents the internal impedance of the battery. All the model parameters can be extracted directly from the battery datasheet [12].

3.2.3 Converter Model. DC-DC converters connecting different power domains to the battery are characterized by an efficiency factor $\eta < 1$, defined as:

$$\eta = \frac{P_{out}}{P_{battery}} = \frac{P_{out}}{P_{battery} + P_{loss}} \tag{1}$$

We use the efficiency model introduced in [11], which expresses η as a quadratic function of the converter input voltage, output voltage, and current.

3.3 Exploration Algorithm

We envision two scenarios of increased accuracy and complexity. A **static** scenario, in which the schedule is determined off-line based on the effect of each possible schedule on the battery charge, with the latter assumed to be 100% charged. Such optimal schedule is then kept fixed throughout the lifetime of the battery. In the **dynamic** scenario, the schedule is re-determined at the beginning of each new sampling interval; this is because, as the battery gets discharged, its capability of handling large current decreases, and therefore it is possible that the best schedule changes according to the battery state-of-charge.

3.3.1 Static Scenario. In this case, the optimal scenario is obtained by evaluating off-line all possible schedules and assessing their impact on the SOC of battery. Since the degrees of freedom in the schedule are the arrangement of the sensing tasks and the power/speed of the computation task, the evaluation simply consists of an exhaustive exploration of all possible schedules. This is feasible since both the number of possible sensors and the power states of the MCU are small (< 10, and typically about 3--5).

In spite of the small number of sensors, the possible combinations of schedules increases rapidly. The number of combinations is 14 for 3 tasks, 81 for 4 tasks, and 821 for 5 tasks. Figure 4 shows the 13 possible schedules of three sensing tasks, shown for simplicity as all requiring the same time and current. The top left configuration does all the sensing in parallel, whereas those on the second row are different combinations of a serialized sensing.

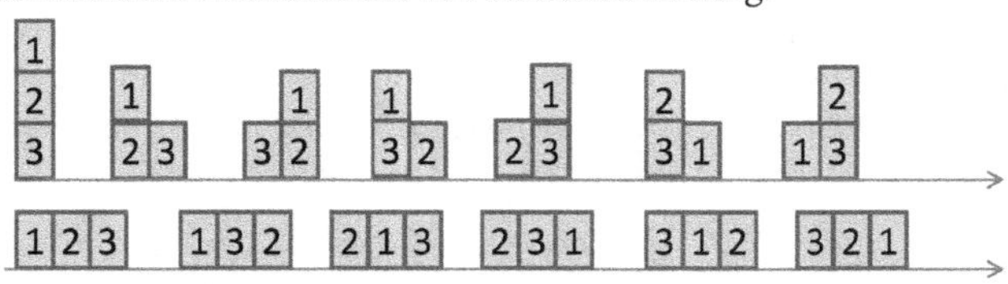

Figure 4: The 13 possible schedules of three sensing tasks.

Notice that in principle we should consider all possible orders of executions, since the battery is sensitive to different current demand over time. However, as shown in [4], it can be proved that among all possible schedules of a set of tasks, those in non-increasing order of power consumption are always the most battery-efficient ones. This well-known result implies that some schedules will be dominated by non-increasing ones and can simply be disregarded. For instance in Figure 4, three of the schedules in the first row (i.e., (3), (1 + 2), (2), (1 + 3), and (1), (2 + 3)) can be neglected in the enumeration. As a result, the actual number of possible schedules to be explored depends on the specific power consumption associated to each task and cannot be enumerated analytically.

The search algorithm is thus a straightforward exhaustive search in the space of the possible schedules:

```
1.  foreach combination of sensing tasks
2.    foreach power mode of the MCU
3.      build schedule S
4.      if (S is not-increasing in current values)
5.        S ➡ current and voltage waveform (I(t), V(t))
6.        transform (I(t), V(t)) into I_batt(t), V_batt(t)
          using the converter efficiencies
7.        apply I_batt(t), V_batt(t) to the battery and
          evaluate the SOC loss ΔSOC
8.        if (ΔSOC < ΔSOC_min)
9.          S_opt ← S
10.       endif
11.     endif
12.   endfor
13. endfor
```

3.3.2 Dynamic Scenario. In this scenario, the only difference with respect to the previous case is that the calculation of the battery SOC loss resulting from the schedule ΔSOC (Line 7 in the algorithm) is done not by calculating it on a fully charged battery but rather accumulating them over each cycle. More precisely if the optimal schedule in cycle i results in a loss ΔSOC_i for a battery with capacity C_i at the beginning of that cycle, in the next cycle the power demand impact of the schedules will be applied to a battery of capacity $C_{i+1} = C_i - \Delta SOC_i$.

Notice that the implementation of this scenario requires that at the beginning of an interval some code calculates or estimates such optimal, SOC-aware scheduling and arranges the tasks accordingly. Notice that in this case the timing profile Figure 1 should be slightly modified to insert a small computation/estimation task at the beginning of the period.

The calculation of the optimal schedule would clearly have a significant overhead and an exhaustive exploration could not be executed in a real-life implementation; we therefore report results for the dynamic scenario mostly as a reference, in order to show how accounting for the battery SOC in the calculation might affect the overall battery lifetime and the resulting schedule.

Given the unfeasibility of an on-line implementation of the search, an interesting challenge becomes the extraction of a rule of thumb for the selection of the scheduling that could help at least approaching the optimal solution. For instance, a qualitative indication about preferring a compact (with minimal T_{active}) vs. a stretched schedule as a function of the battery SOC. In the result section we will try to infer some possible policy that could be quickly estimated at the beginning of each cycle.

4 EXPERIMENTAL RESULTS

4.1 Simulation Setup

4.1.1 System used in the simulation. We used SystemC to specify a multi-sensor device equipped with four sensors, namely, infrared, wind speed and direction, gas and PM2.5 sensors. The multi-sensor device is based on the system proposed in [7]; we added two additional sensors in our experiment to enlarge the space for exploration in order to extend our analysis to a more complex system. We assume that the MCU takes care of the scheduling of the sensors activities by controlling their power state (idle, active).

Table 2 lists all components in such system, and their corresponding electrical characteristics, power supply voltage and current, within different modes.

Component	Mode	Voltage (V)	Current (mA)
CC2420 [16]	TX	1.8	18.8
	RX	1.8	17.4
	Idle	0.0	0.00
Infrared Sensor [7]	Active	5.0	10.0
	Idle	2.5	0.0001
Wind Sensor [17]	Active	12.0	50.0
	Idle	5.0	0.0010
Gas Sensor [7]	Active	5.0	168.9
	Idle	2.0	0.0015
PM2.5 Sensor [18]	Active	5.0	220.0
	Idle	2.0	2.00
Atmega128l [19]	Active	2.0 − 3.0 − 5.0	1.0 − 6.0 − 18.0
	Idle	3.0	0.002

Table 2: Electrical parameters of the designed system.

The different voltage and current values of the 8-bit Atmega1281 microcontroller shown in the last row of table 2 mean that it has three different power modes, they are 2.0V with 1.0mA, 3.0V with 6.1mA and 5.0V with 18.0mA.

Parameters	UR16650ZT	CSC93-3B0024
Rated Capacity	2100mAh	2000mAh
Nominal Voltage	3.7V	3.9V
Weight	41.0g	17.0g
Cut-off voltage	3.0V	2.0V

Table 3: Manufacturer's parameters of the selected batteries.

4.1.2 Battery used in the simulation. We selected two popular rechargeable Lithium batteries for our experiments, namely, the PANASONIC UR16650ZT and the ELECTROCHEM CSC93--3B0024. Table 3 shows the key specifications of both batteries. They have similar nominal capacities, 2100mAh and 2000mA respectively. The weight of battery is a critical point when design such kind of multi-sensor devices, therefore, the main advantage of CSC93-3B0024 is its lightness (less than half of the weight of the Panasonic UR16650ZT), while its weak point is its lower power rating, which makes it more sensitive to the larger currents compared to the UR16650ZT.

We used the methodology described in [14] to extract a circuit-equivalent model of the two batteries that includes also the dependence on current magnitude and load frequency as shown in section 3.2. This model cannot track the capacity recovery-effect during idle intervals, which was widely used in many previous works on scheduling of wireless sensor nodes. However, as shown in recent research [10], the recovery effect is overrated and often misinterpreted; the experimental analyses of [10] do not show any evidence of the recovery effect in Lithium-Ion batteries.

4.1.3 DC-DC converter used in the simulation. Each component has its individual DC-DC converter to connect to the battery in the system. We selected LTC3789 buck-boost switching mode DC-DC converter from Linear Technology [20], whose main applications are distributed DC power systems and high power battery-operated devices. Similar to the battery model, we used the manufacturer's information to extract the parameters for the converter loss model[15]. We adopted the model proposed in [11] and whose conversion efficiency is function of input voltage, output voltage and current as shown in section 3.2.

4.2 Static scheduling

In this experiment, we first simulate the UR16650ZT. As illustrated in [14], the rated capacity effect of such battery becomes very evident when battery current exceeds $\approx 0.9A$. For this reason, only schedules in which all the sensors work in parallel can strongly affect the available capacity of this battery, while the others ones only limitedly stress the battery. Figure 5 shows the distribution of the battery lifetime for all possible scheduling policies. Since the PANASONIC UR16650ZT has good capability to provide higher current without losing much available capacity, the difference between shortest lifetime and longest lifetime is only 4.53%.

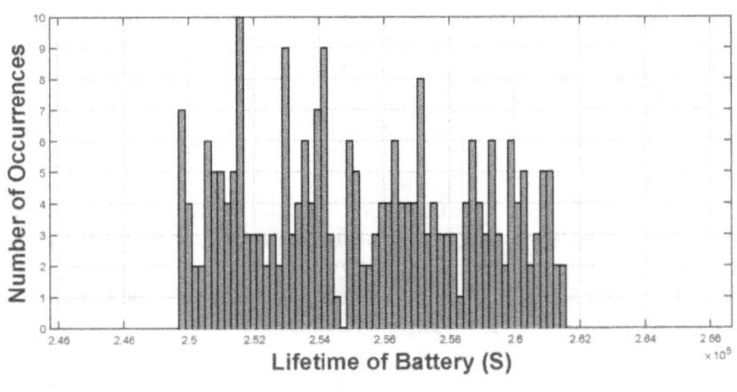

Figure 5: UR16650ZT Lifetime Distribution.

The longest lifetime shown in the Figure 5 is $2.6156 \cdot 10^5$ seconds, whose corresponding optimal scheduling is illustrated in Figure 6. The PM sensor and GAS sensor work in series at first, then WIND sensor and IR sensor work in parallel. Although the MCU has three different power states related to different voltage and current, the optimal scheduling does not select the low power state. The reason is that the current in 5.0V power state is only 18mA which does not significantly deplete the available capacity of the battery.

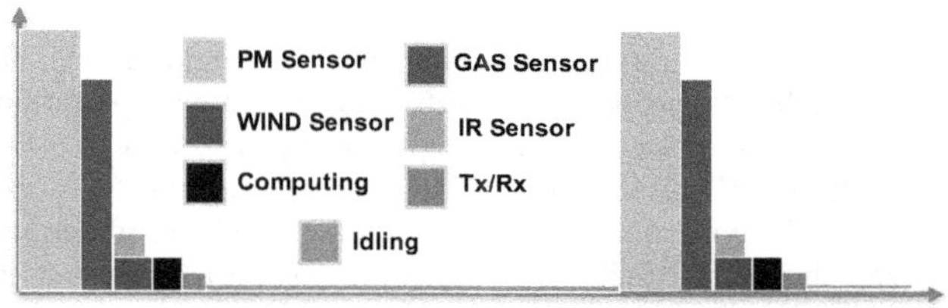

Figure 6: The Optimal Static Scheduling for UR16650ZT .

Our experiments also reveal that, as expected, the worst scheduling policies are the ones with all sensors working in parallel, because the aggregate currents impact the usable capacity. Due to space limits, we do not show the temporal diagram of worst case; Figure 7 shows the battery current profile for both worst- and best-case scheduling over four cycles. Notice that these current profiles do not match the current values listed in Table 2, because the actual battery current is determined by (i) the voltage ratio between battery and each component, and (ii) by the efficiency of DC-DC converter.

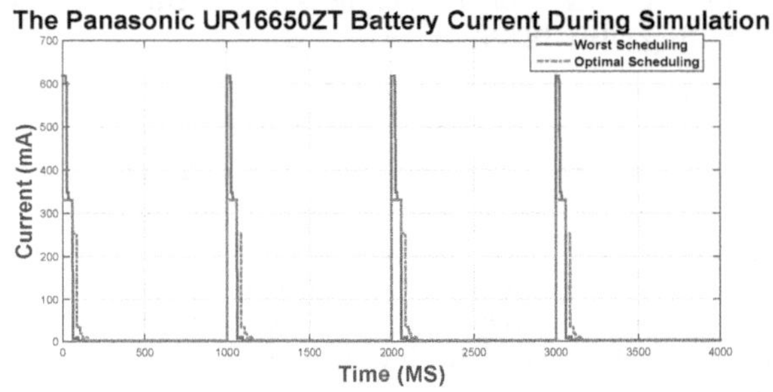

Figure 7: Battery Current Profiles of Worst/Best Schedules.

We then used the CSC93-3B0024 and run all possible schedules. Figure 8 exhibits the battery lifetime distribution for all possible schedules. The difference between the best and worst scheduling is now more pronounced due to the higher sensitivity of the CSC93-3B0024 to larger currents. The best/worst battery lifetimes are $2.5952 \cdot 10^5/2.1155 \cdot 10^5$, respectively, a 18.48% difference. The scheduling that yields the longest battery duration almost identical to the one for the UR16650ZT shown in Figure 6, with the minor difference that the execution by the MCU uses 3.0V power state as opposed to the 5.0V of the UR16650ZT.

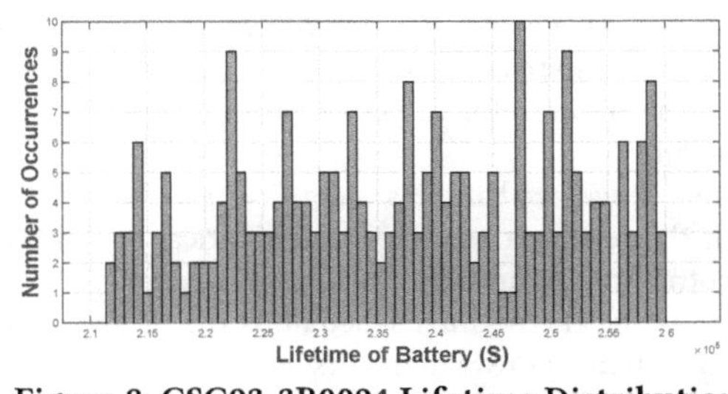

Figure 8: CSC93-3B0024 Lifetime Distribution.

In the above analysis we set the period T at 1 s. While this is a reasonable value, for some applications it might be case that the system does not need to sense data that frequently. For the designer it is important to know for which values of T the impact of different schedules is relevant. Intuitively, as T gets larger, the active section of the period (sensing + computation + transmission) will take an increasingly smaller portion and the power consumption will be dominated by idle power. We therefore ran the same exploration of static schedules for different lengths of the cycle time and for both batteries. We used values of T of 1s, 60s, 600s and 1800s and calculated the normalized range (max-min) of the battery lifetime. Figure 9 shows the results: the lifetime range expectedly decreases with larger cycle times.

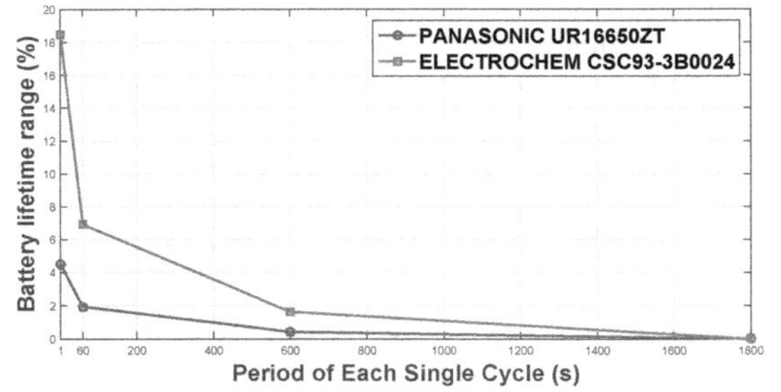

Figure 9: Lifetime difference between optimal and worst scheduling with different period values.

This analysis is essential to assess if and when the scheduling is a relevant dimension of the power optimization of the device. Our analysis show that for cycle times longer than a few minutes the impact of the scheduling in terms of battery duration becomes negligible (below 2% for the weakest battery). Therefore, our exploration of schedules is relevant for multi-sensor devices with activation periods in the order of seconds to minutes. Notice that this consideration applies to **all** methods in the literature discussed in Section 1; however, such analysis was not carried out before.

4.3 Dynamic Scheduling

For the dynamic scheduling scenario, we assume that at the beginning of each cycle, the MCU executes a small task in which it explores the optimal schedule in order to get smallest SOC loss, as described in Section 3.3.2. We assume that the MCU consumes approximately the same power required for the processing of the sensing data in the state that consumes the most power in Table 2.

Since a cycle-specific schedule aims at the smallest SOC loss per cycle, the corresponding lifetime of battery will be longer than the static scheduling scenario. For instance, when $T = 1$s, our results show that the longest battery lifetimes of UR16650ZT and CSC93-3B0024 are $2.6999 \cdot 10^5$ and $2.7604 \cdot 10^5$ seconds, respectively, the lifetimes are prolonged of 3.266% and 6.368% compared to the longest lifetimes for the same batteries under the optimal static schedule.

We tested above two batteries using $T = 1$s and $T = 60$s. Results show that the resulting schedules are identical for both periods and for both batteries and change three times during the battery lifetime. Initially, the optimal schedule is the same as the static schedule shown in Figure 6; in the first change, wind and IR sensor eventually start to operate serially; the second and third changes correspond to the MCU switching to a lower power state. Notice that the time-points at which the changes of scheduling occur are different for the two batteries with two different T, as reported in Table 4. As expected, the CSC93-3B0024 battery always changes schedule before the earlier than UR16650ZT due to its higher sensitivity to higher current values.

$T = 1s$			
Battery	1st Change	2nd Change	3rd Change
UR16650ZT	68133s	204399s	233715s
CSC93-3B0024	54499s	163156s	201244s
$T = 60s$			
Battery	1st Change	2nd Change	3rd Change
UR16650ZT	733320s	2380380s	2777160s
CSC93-3B0024	641040s	2014860s	2289720s

Table 4: Times of schedule change with $T = 1s$ and $T = 60s$.

5 CONCLUSIONS

In this paper, we present a framework to evaluate static and dynamic schedules to optimize the lifetime of multi-sensor devices powered by batteries. We use advanced battery and DC-DC converter models in our experiments to get more accurate results. The two proposed scheduling algorithms have been applied to two different batteries and two different working situations for estimating the increment of lifetime. Our results show that the optimal schedule according to our exploration can achieve a 18.48% lifetime increment when using a static schedule, and as much as 23.36% for the dynamic schedule.

REFERENCES

[1] Simunic, T., Benini, L., Glynn, P. and De Micheli, G., "Dynamic power management for portable systems," Proc. MobiCom 2000, pp. 11-19.
[2] Shin, Y., Choi, K. and Sakurai, T., "Power optimization of real-time embedded systems on variable speed processors," Proc. IEEE/ACM ICCAD 2000, pp. 365-368.
[3] Luo, J. and Jha, N.K., "Battery-aware static scheduling for distributed real-time embedded systems," Proc. IEEE DAC 2001, pp. 444-449.
[4] Chowdhury, P. and Chakrabarti, C., "Static task-scheduling algorithms for battery-powered DVS systems," IEEE Trans. VLSI Syst., vol. 13, no. 2, pp. 226-237, 2005.
[5] Yu, X., Xiaosong, X. and Wenyong, W., "Priority-based low-power task scheduling for wireless sensor network," Proc. IEEE ISADS 2009, pp.1-5.
[6] Wei, K., Zhang, W., Yang, Y., Song, G. and Zhang, Z., "Battery-Aware Task Scheduling for Energy Efficient Mobile Devices," IEICE Trans. Fundamentals, vol. E97-A, no. 9, pp. 1971-1974, 2014.
[7] Hong, S., Kim, D. and Kim, J.E., "Battery aware real time task scheduling in wireless sensor networks," Proc. IEEE RTCSA 2005, pp. 269-272.
[8] Schonle, P., et al, "A multi-sensor and parallel processing SoC for wearable and implantable telemetry systems," Proc. IEEE ESSCIRC 2017, pp. 215-218.
[9] Rakhmatov, D., Vrudhula, S. and Wallach, D.A., "A model for battery lifetime analysis for organizing applications on a pocket computer," IEEE Trans. VLSI Syst., vol. 11, no. 6, pp. 1019âĂŞ1030, 2003.
[10] Narayanaswamy, S., et al, "On battery recovery effect in wireless sensor nodes," ACM TODAES vol. 21, no. 4 (2016): pp. 60:1-60:28.
[11] Park, S., Wang, Y., Kim, Y., Chang, N. and Pedram, M., "Battery management for grid-connected PV systems with a battery," Proc. ACM/IEEE ISLPED 2012, pp. 115-120.
[12] Chen, Y., Macii, E. and Poncino, M., "A circuit-equivalent battery model accounting for the dependency on load frequency," Proc. IEEE DATE 2017, pp. 1177-1182.
[13] Doerffel, D. and Sharkh, S.A., "A critical review of using the Peukert equation for determining the remaining capacity of lead-acid and lithium-ion batteries," J. Power Sources 155, no. 2, (2006): pp. 395-400.
[14] Chen, Y., Macii, E. and Poncino, M., "Frequency domain characterization of batteries for the design of energy storage subsystems," Proc. IFIP/IEEE VLSI-SoC 2016, pp. 1-6.
[15] Lee, W., Wang, Y., Shin, D., Chang, N. and Pedram, M., "Power conversion efficiency characterization and optimization for smartphones," Proc. ISLPED 2012, pp. 103-108.
[16] http://www.ti.com/lit/ds/symlink/cc2420.pdf
[17] http://www.fischer-barometer.de/katalog/dokumente/meteo/E451213_14.pdf
[18] http://breathe.indiaspend.org/wp-content/uploads/2015/11/nova_laser_sensor.pdf
[19] http://www.atmel.com/products/microcontrollers/avr/default.aspx
[20] http://cds.linear.com/docs/en/datasheet/3789fc.pdf

Accelerating Coverage Directed Test Generation for Functional Verification: A Neural Network-based Framework

Fanchao Wang, Hanbin Zhu, Pranjay Popli, Yao Xiao, Paul Bodgan and Shahin Nazarian
University of Southern California
Los Angeles, CA, USA
{fanchaow,hanbinzh,ppopli,xiaoyao,pbogdan,shahin.nazarian}@usc.edu

ABSTRACT

With increasing design complexity, the correlation between test transactions and functional properties becomes non-intuitive, hence impacting the reliability of test generation. This paper presents a modified coverage directed test generation based on an Artificial Neural Network (ANN). The ANN extracts features of test transactions and only those which are learned to be critical, will be sent to the design under verification. Furthermore, the priority of coverage groups is dynamically learned based on the previous test iterations. With ANN-based screening, low-coverage or redundant assertions will be filtered out, which helps accelerate the verification process. This allows our framework to learn from the results of the previous vectors and use that knowledge to select the following test vectors. Our experimental results confirm that our learning-based framework can improve the speed of existing function verification techniques by 24.5x and also also deliver assertion coverage improvement, ranging from 4.3x to 28.9x, compared to traditional coverage directed test generation, implemented in UVM.

CCS CONCEPTS

• **Computing methodologies → Machine learning**; • **Hardware → Simulation and emulation**; *Coverage metrics*; *Assertion checking*;

KEYWORDS

Coverage Directed Test Generation; Neural Networks; UVM

ACM Reference format:
Fanchao Wang, Hanbin Zhu, Pranjay Popli, Yao Xiao, Paul Bodgan and Shahin Nazarian. 2018. Accelerating Coverage Directed Test Generation for Functional Verification: A Neural Network-based Framework. In *Proceedings of 2018 Great Lakes Symposium on VLSI, Chicago, IL, USA, May 23–25, 2018 (GLSVLSI '18)*, 6 pages.
https://doi.org/10.1145/3194554.3194561

1 INTRODUCTION

Gordon Moore's [15] observation that the number of transistors in modern chips doubles approximately every 2 years, has also resulted in exponential escalation of the complexity of modern technologies and systems. Furthermore, with the increasing customer needs for ASIC, design specifications are becoming elusive, which leads to disagreement on implementation of the functional models in HDL. Upon consensus of a system design, RTL designers translate specifications into RTL, which makes it difficult to verify all possible corner cases. In addition to misinterpretation of spec, the design flow, namely synthesis and physical design and optimization steps may introduce more functional bugs.

As the heterogeneity and complexity of state-of-the-art systems, such as those in IoT and cloud systems, grow [5][6][10][17], systematic functional verification plays a more significant role in making chips functionally reliable for users. It is not feasible to exhaustively simulate every possible case and state of the system. For example, a typical 64-bit adder calls for 2^{129} possible test vectors to cover all corner cases. Assuming a 2 GHz processor is used to run it and one stimulus per 16 cycles since the depth of modern pipeline is 15-20, roughly 2^{76} years are needed to verify a simple adder. On the other hand, formal verification techniques, necessitate a detailed understanding of the design well ahead of time and also may suffer from state explosion. Therefore, compared to the design of an actual chip, verification adds more energy, cost, complexity, and especially time [8]. Traditionally, a combination of constrained-random simulation-based and formal verification has been used in literature and industry to mitigate the cost of verification and achieve high coverage. However the increasing complexity of systems with larger number of inputs, states, interfaces and protocols, as well as tighter time-to-market enforced by market, have led the designers to seek beyond traditional verification algorithms towards machine learning algorithms to mitigate the verification challenges.

In the simulation-based verification, test stimuli are randomly generated under spec constraints and applied to DUV (Design Under Verification). CDG (Coverage-directed Test Generation) can be incorporated to increase the coverage rate within the limited time. However the traditional CDG can under-perform in progressively complex environments due to manual bias. For example, in state-of-the-art micro-architectures, features such as out-of-order executions would make it difficult to predict what constraints would produce tests with high coverage [11][12].

In this work, we aim to revisit the problem of verification of ASIC blocks that are typically complex RTL blocks with high chance of error bugs, due to complex functional specifications and parameters associated with them. We understand many of those parameters may turn out to be irrelevant, therefore we aim to design a verification platform that automatically learns the important dependencies and utilizes the knowledge it gains from previous test failures in order to increase the coverage and also the speed of verification. To guide test generation toward high coverage rate, we introduce an

GLSVLSI '18, May 23–25, 2018, Chicago, IL, USA

ACM ISBN 978-1-4503-5724-1/18/05...$15.00
https://doi.org/10.1145/3194554.3194561

ANN (Artificial Neural Network) module into CDG with the goal of increasing the probability of selecting high coverage test cases. We use assertions coverage as the main metric of coverage rate. The assertions are grouped based on their functional and structural dependencies. Next the randomly generated transactions (i.e., test vectors) are classified using the ANN. Only the transactions with high probability of high coverage will be sent to the DUV. To further enhance the verification process, the assertion groups are prioritized and the priorities of the groups are dynamically changed. Also the low-coverage or redundant assertions will be filtered out. Given the limited verification time, our framework achieves significantly higher assertion coverage than that of the traditional CDG-based frameworks.

The rest of the paper is organized as follows. Section 2 presents the related work on verification acceleration. Section 3 describes the proposed methodology including coverage-directed test generation, assertion grouping, and the ANN setup. Section 4 provides the experimental results on performance improvement of our framework against traditional UVM. Section 5 concludes this paper.

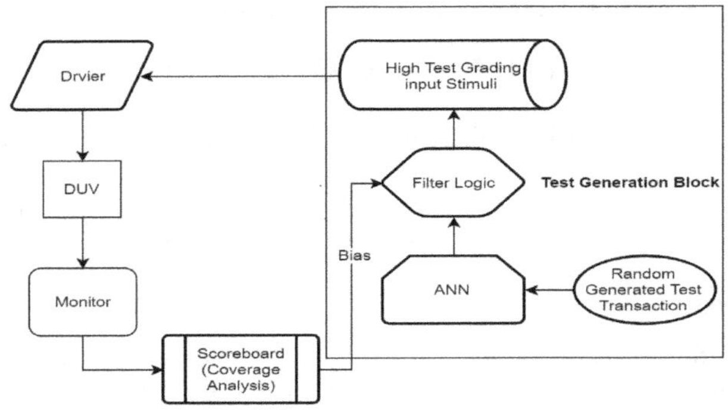

Figure 1: ANN-based CDG process. In the simulation phase, randomly generated transactions will be classified. Next, based on the previous simulation, the ANN eliminates irrelevant transactions and the remaining transactions will be treated as stimuli for the next round. This procedure is repeated several times to meet overall coverage requirement.

2 PRIOR WORK

Several research works have utilized machine learning for formal verification based on BDDs [14] (Binary Decision Diagrams [1][2]) and SAT solvers [3][7]. Simulation-based verification has been used as a complement to formal verification, especially in cases that lack detailed understanding of design specifications.

A great amount of effort has been dedicated to improving simulation performance, using simulator optimizations such as GPGPUs, emulators, and sampling. Event-driven gate level simulation, proposed in [4], was accelerated by general-purpose graphics processing units (GPGPUs). Also a gate level design is leveraged to exploit advantages of low switching activity under large hardware designs. New algorithms for netlist partitioning were developed and optimized for GPGPUs by first doing levelization to make parallelization of the netlist easier and then executing one level in parallel only when at least one of its input values have changed, which is event-driven. Finally, Nvidia's CUDA architecture was performed to offer a programming interface which could enable users to write software applications based on the underlying GPGPUs.

The CDG-based verification, proposed in [9], uses Bayesian networks to model coverage information and testbench directives. A dependency graph based on causal relationships between testbench directives (cause) and coverage parameters (effect) is created, which is then trained and evaluated. It can achieve full coverage faster as compared to manual test directives. However, it is more suitable for automatic creation of test directives as compared to human users.

3 OUR VERIFICATION FRAMEWORK

3.1 Coverage-Directed Test Generation

This section proposes a new test generation process to replace manual generation of transactions. Since the relationship between the test transactions and the assertions are non-intuitive, we propose an ANN-based framework that captures the non-intuitive relations and patterns, which ultimately enhances the quality of verification in terms of speed and coverage both. In addition to the relations between test transactions and assertions, there exist patterns among various design bugs (e.g., because designers tend to make similar mistakes in different parts of the design). Also considering the high complexity of the verification flow, AI can be very effective in capturing dependencies and filtering the parameters that turn out to have no impact on the outcome. We have found ANN as an effective learning methodology for the CDG process. Before elaborating the detail in each step, several terms are needed to be clarified. The transaction represents random generated test vectors under design specs. Based on the previous simulation, bias is generated by scoreboard to control the direction in following simulation. The steps of our ANN-based CDG process are as follows in Figure 1.

Step 1: This step is performed to prepare the training data for the ANN. Randomly generated vectors are sent to DUT. Depending on which assertions they trigger, they will be labeled. Noted that a single test vector is possibly labeled by multiple groups because it tests different aspects of the design. The design properties are written using assertions. As explained in the next section, the assertions are clustered (grouped) using the assertion grouping model.

Step 2: The ANN is trained with labeled transactions generated in the Step 1. Once the ANN is well-trained, it will be embedded as the ANN module into the modified CDG process for the rest of the verification process. Note that to efficiently use the limited verification process, our framework utilizes a conventional CDG, at start while the ANN is being trained, and switches to ANN-based CDG when the training is complete.

Step 3: As shown in the test generation block, the randomly generated test transactions are fed into the trained ANN to predict which assertion group they may target. In case they trigger assertion groups with high priorities (criticality) they will be forwarded to the DUV. Otherwise they will be filtered out. One main key to the efficiency of our approach is that our ANN would be significantly faster than the DUV simulator or emulator.

Step 4: In this step, the stimuli, chosen in step 3, is applied to the DUV (c.f. figure 1). The simulation results are monitored. if there exists any assertion group which hasn't been tested, the scoreboard will give a bias to the filter logic to skew future tests focusing on that assertion group.

Step 5: If overall coverage achieves the test plan expectation, terminate the CDG process, otherwise jump to step 3 with the bias generated in step 4.

Theoretically, in the worst case scenario the number of labels is too large for the ANN to handle, because each assertion can in the worst case be treated as a separate category (i.e., assertion group.) However in practice the number of assertion groups can be very low. This is thanks to the fact that many assertions are related and therefore own common patterns that can be recognized by the ANN. We will show that only 6 assertion groups are sufficient for a dual-core processor with various tricky bugs, to provide significantly higher verification quality.

3.2 Assertion Grouping

Typically, different assertions may overlap with each other in terms of the design specifications they target. We refer to those assertions as related, and we aim to cluster them into the same group. The reason for multiple assertions to be related, is that same design structures are tested, which means some control signals, execution paths, and arithmetic/memory resources are common. Another reason for related assertions is that the designer tends to make similar mistakes, leading to assertions having overlaps, i.e., one failing would imply that the related assertions have a high probability of failing too. Clustering these similar assertions to the same group can significantly increase the efficiency of verification in terms of verification time and coverage. Assertion grouping has the following benefits: (1) It helps reducing the overall simulation time by shrinking the assertion set. During the functional verification, coverage is the main metric to evaluate the completeness of the test. Each assertion should be triggered by test stimuli to ensure the design meets its specification. If assertion set is too large, enormous time will be consumed to find stimuli which can trigger assertions. Therefore, shrinking the overall assertion set helps engineers avoid redundancy and save efforts and time. (2) In case a certain assertion fails in simulation, design bugs may exist in any components related to this assertion, therefore it is reasonable to put extra effort in verifying those components. With assertion grouping, since assertions in the same group are interrelated, each time one assertion fails, testing other assertions in the same group can help verify the related resources (datapath, etc.) with high failure probabilities.

In our grouping method, there are three factors contributing to the calculation of correlation, namely number of common structural signals (denoted by $\{f_0\}$), length of the shared datapath ($\{f_1\}$), and common resources ($\{f_2\}$). All 3 factors or a subset of those could be used for assertion grouping. We must however address this concern: Is the process of assertion grouping based on the $\{f_0, f_1, f_2\}$ limited to designs for which the designer knows exactly which structure would relate to which assertion? In other words, if an assertion is written based on a high level behavioral view of the design without clear understanding of how the structure of the corresponding behavior would turn out post-synthesis, would assertion grouping fail? The answer is No. Even for those assertions based on the design behavior, the common control signals can be used to group the assertions. Each factor generates its own grouping results. Since there are limited number of resources in a design, every resource can have its own assertion group, i.e., size of f2 is small. However the scenario space of f0 and f1 is vast for complex designs, therefore it is infeasible to create one group per scenario. We as part of our assertion group method, propose a clustering technique based on edge-labeled graph modeling to convey the correlation between assertions and efficiently cluster the assertions into groups. Similar ideas are also used in [16] and [13] to reduce the overall assertion size and clustering hardware checker. As shown in Figure 2, the edge-labeled weighted graph is defined as the Assertion Graph $(AG) = \{V, E\}$. The set of vertices, defined as $V = \{v_0, v_1, v_2, \ldots, v_n\}$ represents all assertions required to be inserted for the DUV, with v_n, representing assertion n. The weight of edge $w^i_{a\_b}$ denotes the correlation between two assertions a and b when considering factor i.

To make each edge weight into a dimensionless quantity, $w^i_{a\_b}$ denotes the standard weight between assertions a and b, while considering factor i. We apply the following normalization function to make the weight scale consistent across different factors:

$$w^i_{a\_b} = \frac{w'^i_{a\_b} - \mu_i}{\sigma_i}$$

$$\mu_i = \frac{1}{N_i} \sum_{ab} w'^i_{a\_b}$$

$$\sigma_i = \sqrt{\frac{\sum_{ab}(w'^i_{a\_b} - \mu_i)^2}{N_i - 1}}$$

where N_i is the number of weights given the factor i, $w'^i_{a\_b}$ is the raw weight between two vertices $\{v_a, v_b\}$, μ_i is the mean and σ_i is the standard deviation of all edge raw weights for the factor i. After calculating each edge weight, two adjacent nodes with weight higher than threshold δ_{corr} will be grouped together, edge weight lower than δ_{corr} pair will be considered as belonging to two distinct group. All assertions get grouping by three different factors separately. After group merging, the final grouping result will be a assertion group set $G_{assertion} = \{g_1, g_2, g_3, \cdots, g_n\}$ and each individual group contains all related assertion vertices $g_i = \{v_1, v_2, v_3, \cdots, v_n\}$. Note that factors f0, f1, and f2 impact the relation between assertions, i.e., the edge weight of two adjacent nodes depends on them. The following is an example of assertion grouping for a pipelined processor with 5 assertions groups:

$A_1 : ID_{op} == R_{type} \&\& ALU_{src} == ADD \mapsto \#\#[3:4] WB_{out} == ADD_{ref}$

$A_2 : ID_{op} == R_{type} \&\& ALU_{src} == SUB \mapsto \#\#[3:4] WB_{out} == SUB_{ref}$

$A_3 : ID_{op} == M_{type} \&\& MEM_{sl} == SD \mapsto \#\#[2:3] MEM_{wen}$

$A_4 : ID_{op} == M_{type} \&\& MEM_{sl} == LD \mapsto \#\#[2:3] MEM_{en}$

$A_5 : ID_{op} == BEZ \&\& Reg_0 == 0 \mapsto WB_{out} == branch_{taken}$

The following describes each factor and shows how they should be considered towards calculating the raw weights:

3.2.1 Number of Overlapping Control Signals f_0. It aims to capture the similarity between two assertions when considering their control signals. The ratio of the number of shared signals with average number of two assertion signals is defined by the raw weight. For example, for assertion A_3 and A_4, there are one common control

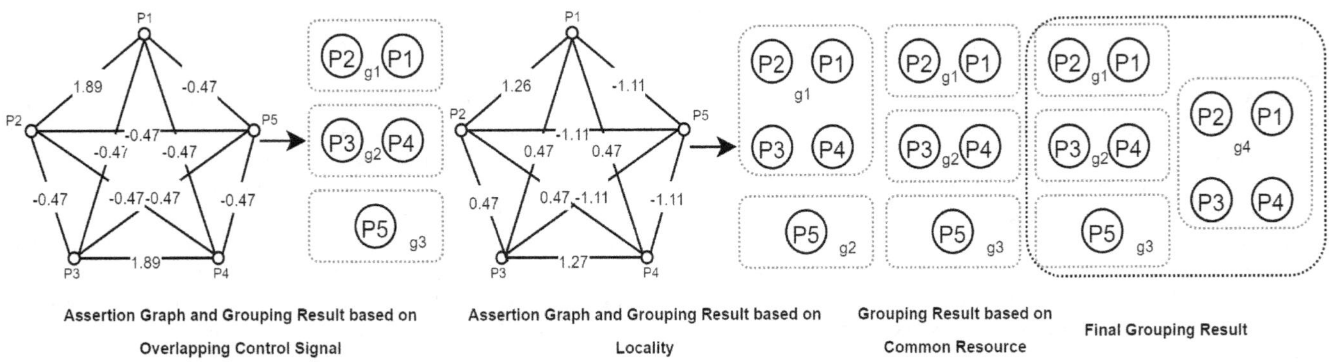

Figure 2: Overview of assertion grouping procedure. First two weighted graphs are constructed based on the structural similarities between assertions. Next, any edge with a weight lower than δ_{corr} is considered as irrelevant, which means the corresponding pair of vertices, i.e., assertions are irrelevant. Finally only the relevant edges remains which means the corresponding pairs of vertices are group. Also the "common resources" would be directly used for grouping. Finally the 3 grouping results are merged into distinct groups.

signal ($ID_{op} == M_{type}$) and two different signals ($MEM_{sl} == SD$ and $MEM_{sl} == LD$). Therefore the raw weight is 1/2.

3.2.2 Locality f_1. This factor is used to merge two assertions into a group if their majority execution data paths are overlapped. The ratio of the shared data path with the average individual total data path is calculated as the raw weight for two adjacent assertion vertices. E.g., A_1 relates to four stages and A_3 relates to three stages. The common data path between A_1 and A_3 is three stages. Therefore, the edge weight between A_1 and A_3 is 3/3.5.

3.2.3 Common Resource f_2. We assume the number of resources for a given design (DUV) is limited, therefore each resource has its own assertion group. Here, A_1 and A_2 are sharing ALU, A_3 and A_4 are sharing memory block and A_5 uses branch predictor exclusively.

As the last step of assertion group algorithm, the groups are checked to see whether any two or more groups perfectly match each other, i.e., they have identical assertions, which means they should merge into one group. Note that groups will have common assertions, therefore groups have overlaps, however merging would occur, if and only if the exact set of assertions appear in two or more groups.

3.3 ANN Setting

Considering the non-trivial relations between the input vectors and the assertion groups, we utilize ANN to identify patterns within transactions. The first layer of ANN focuses more on the local patterns whereas the following layers are set to capture the patterns from the former layers on a higher perspective. The final layer therefore makes decisions from a higher perspective, based on local and more global patterns. This relation between layers and property patterns is advantageous to realize the relationship between input test vectors and the assertion groups. For instance, for the CPU design, the opcode is straightforward and we can anticipate that if certain ALU operations have bugs, then it may relate to certain opcodes. However, the relationship between certain opcodes and whether they will lead to the data dependency problem is not straightforward. Therefore, the ANN can be used to find the correlation in terms of above questions.

We have examined two configurations: In the first configuration, 32-bit vectors are sent directly to the ANN, which means the input layer has 32 neurons and each input is either 0 or 1. In the second configuration, we categorize the vector bits into opcode, rt, rs, and ALUopcode/offset. Our testing results show that configuration number one, i.e., uncategorized vector bits, produces more accurate results. This implies that the patterns could be too complicated to be manually identified for designers. Therefore, we should let the ANN automatically figure out the patterns and choose configuration 1 as the ANN setting for our experiments.

In terms of the layers and hidden neurons within each layer, we performed several experiments to calculate the optimal configuration. We have chosen a 3-layer ANN including 1 input layer, 1 hidden layer, and 1 output layer with 32, 128, and 128 neurons in each layer, respectively. The number of neurons in the input layer is the same as the number of input bits. We use the ReLU activation function and also cross entropy loss function as the training objective. It is also worth noting that since the input data for our verification problem is not as large as the image or voice data, deep convolutional neural network might not be a proper solution for this problem.

The output layers are the assertion groups. We use the softmax function as the output layer, therefore the output numbers will be fractions, rather than 0 or 1. To classify the vectors into assertion groups, we can either use the probability (i.e., choose the group with the highest probability) or use a threshold for the output value and in case the output value is higher than the threshold, the vector would be associated with the corresponding assertion group.

3.4 Test Phase

After the ANN is well-trained, it will be embedded into the test phase of the verification flow. During the test phase (c.f. figure 3), the randomly generated transactions will first be sent into the ANN for classification. The ANN will filter the redundant transactions that have no relationship with the existing assertion groups and

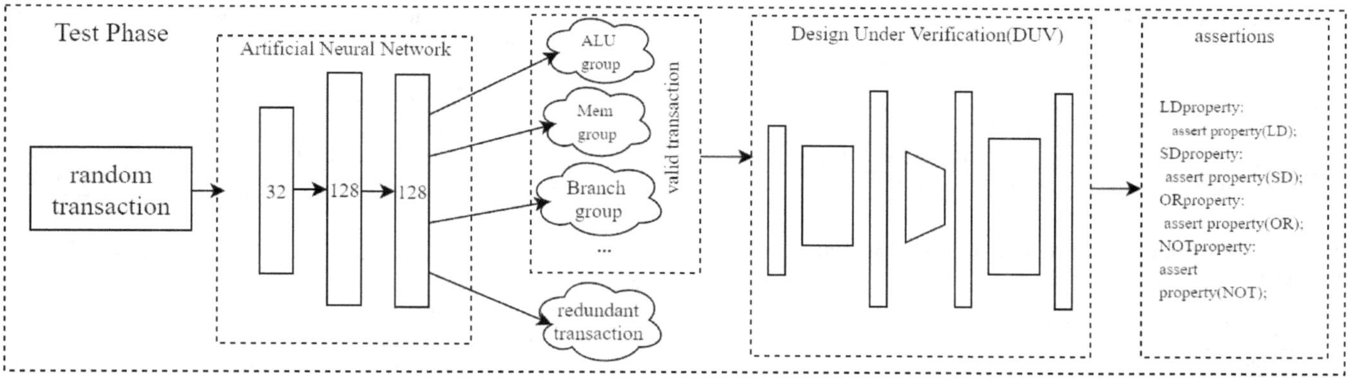

Figure 3: Overview of the test phase. The randomly generated transactions will be first classified by the ANN. The redundant transactions will be filtered whereas the rest of the transactions are valid and will be classified into related assertion groups. After ANN classification, the valid transaction will be sent to the DUV and trigger assertions in order to achieve a higher coverage.

Table 1: Training Time for Different Assertion Groups.

	AG0	AG1	AG2	AG3	AG4	AG5
# Neuron	30	30	30	10	30	20
Time (s)	11.3	9.98	13.4	12.1	10.1	11.6

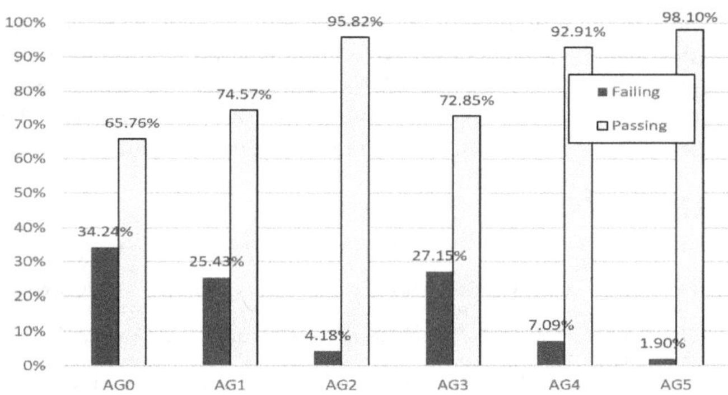

Figure 4: The distribution of passing and failing vectors.

classify the rest of the transactions to the related assertion group. The previous assertion groups proved that the assertions within each assertion group are highly correlated. The ANN extracts the relations between the input transactions and the assertion groups. Therefore, the classified transaction will target more on the assertions within assertion groups and have higher probability to trigger the assertions. Therefore, within the limited time, the ANN-based CDG process can achieve a higher functional coverage.

4 EXPERIMENTAL RESULTS

To test the effectiveness of our ANN-based verification framework we have implemented a dual-core RISC processor, which includes two cores with a static pipeline and DMEM unit, as well as a dispatcher unit and a unified memory. We use the assertion grouping algorithm discussed in Section 3.2 to cluster all processor's assertions into 6 separated groups, i.e., AG0 to AG5. These assertions cover processor specifications such as control hazard handling, arithmetic calculation correctness, memory read/write, etc.

4.1 Configuration and Distribution of Vectors

We chose the Neural Net Pattern Recognition toolbox of MATLAB as our ANN platform. In this experiment, we tested the different number of neurons in the hidden layer to find the best configuration with the least error rate and training time for assertion groups. In our experiments, a total of 83620 vectors were randomly generated. 70% of those vectors were used for training; 15% of those vectors for testing; and the remaining 15% for validation. Note that the randomly generated vectors are the ones which are correctly classified and misclassified due to some structural and behavioral bugs, such as misconnections of control signals or wrong data forwarding. The vectors that result in failure were labeled based on which assertion group they trigger. Six labels are one-bit numbers $d_5, d_4, \ldots, d_0$ where $d_i = 1$ means the vector passes all the assertions of group i and $d_i = 0$ means it triggers at least one assertion in group i. These labels are stored and used for the ANN training. Figure 4 illustrates the distribution of passing and failing vectors for each of the 6 assertion groups. Note that the distribution varies from assertion groups, due to the nature of properties related to each assertion group as discussed in Section 3.2. Table 1 presents the training times for the 6 ANNs corresponding to the 6 assertion groups, given the number of neurons in the hidden layer. Note that the number of neurons is selected such that accuracy over training time is maximized. The training times of the 6 ANNs corresponding to the 6 assertion groups should overlap in time, to maximize the parallelism. As reported in Table 1, the training times of the ANNs are almost identical, which helps with the parallel training of these ANNs.

4.2 Failing Vector Prediction Rate (FVPR)

There are 4 possibilities for the ANN in terms of how it would treat a given test vector:

Case 1: ANN: Fail, DUV: Fail;
Case 2: ANN: Pass, DUV: Fail;
Case 3: ANN: Fail, DUV: Pass;
Case 4: ANN: Pass, DUV: Pass.

Out of the 4 cases, only vectors in cases 1 and 3 are identified by ANN as vectors to be fed into the DUV. Vectors in cases 2 and 4 are eliminated, as the ANN calculates them as passing all assertions. Also note that among the 4 cases, vectors in case 2 are wrongly eliminated. Therefore the Failing Vector Prediction Rate (FVPR) of the ANN is formulated as $\frac{Case1}{Case2+Case1}$.

Table 2 shows the Failing Vector Prediction Rate for each assertion group, calculated during the test phase. The number of test vectors during the test phase is 15% of total 83620, i.e., 12543. Note that FVPR is calculated based on the ratio of row 2 in Table 2 divided by its row 3. Also note that FVPR for

Table 2: Success rate and assertion hit results for the 6 ANNs.

	Testing Data					
	AG0	AG1	AG2	AG3	AG4	AG5
FVPR	34.36	95.55	86.54	43.06	51.11	71.20
Case 1	1660	2986	463	1518	415	136
Case 1 + Case 2	4831	3125	535	3525	812	191

Table 3: FVPR comparison between our ANN-based and the traditional CDG.

	AG0	AG1	AG2	AG3	AG4	AG5
Traditional CDG	380	201	16	271	89	8
ANN-based CDG	1660	2986	463	1518	415	136
Improvement	4.37	14.86	28.94	5.60	4.66	17

each ANN is independent of the FVPRs of the other ANNs. All the 6 ANNs are used in parallel to decide whether a future vector should be applied to DUV or pruned. A vector is pruned only when all the 6 ANNs report it as a passing vector. This implies that the average FVPR among all the 6 ANNs would be a measure of the quality of verification in terms of managing the randomly generated vectors, i.e., dropping them, or applying them to DUV.

4.3 Performance Evaluation

In addition to using FVPR to make comparisons among different ANN-based implementations of our framework, there are two metrics to evaluate the performance of our ANN-based framework when compared to a baseline technique: one is the measure of the quality of verification in terms of vectors triggering assertions in a limited time. This could be regarded as a measure of coverage, because the higher the number of triggered assertions, the higher the number of detected design errors. Another measure of performance is the time it takes to analyze a given set of test vectors. First we compare our ANN-based CDG verification process with the traditional CDG assuming both are given a fixed verification time limit. This comparison helps us measure the impact of ANN training time overhead. As shown in Table 3, given the same time, our ANN-based CDG determines 1660 vectors for AG0, as case 1 vectors (as defined in section 4.2), which means that these vectors are predicted to trigger at least one assertion in AG0, and they indeed trigger at least one assertion, when applied to DUV. However, using the traditional CDG, only 380 vectors are able to trigger an assertion from AG0. This shows a minimum assertion coverage improvement of 4.37x considering a limited verification time. Note that the assertion coverage improvement is as high as 28.94x. Next we consider the same number of randomly generated vectors (in this case about 12000 vectors) and compare our framework with the traditional CDG in terms of the verification time. The traditional CDG takes 1.84 seconds, whereas our ANN-based CDG takes a maximum of 0.075 seconds, which means that our ANN-based CDG is 24.5 times as fast as the traditional CDG. The reason is that our ANN-based framework can label the vectors and prune the passing vectors without driving them into the DUV, which is much faster than the simulation on DUV.

5 CONCLUSIONS

Design complexity of modern processing systems has significantly impacted the reliability of the conventional test generation. Our framework integrates ANN into the CDG (Coverage-Directed test

Table 4: Simulation time comparison between our ANN-based and the traditional CDG.

	AG0	AG1	AG2	AG3	AG4	AG5
Traditional CDG	1.84	1.84	1.84	1.84	1.84	1.84
ANN-based CDG	0.075	0.0747	0.073	0.0534	0.0672	0.0586
Speedup	24.53	24.63	25.20	34.46	27.38	31.40

Generation) process to accelerate the verification process and increase the coverage in a limited verification time. The assertions are clustered using an algorithm for assertion grouping with the goal of efficiently managing properties and the relations among them. The ANN is used to label the randomly generated vectors based on the corresponding assertion group. If test vectors trigger assertion groups with high probability, they will be driven into the DUV whereas the irrelevant transactions are pruned. Our experimental results confirm that our ANN framework can eliminate as high as 40.2% of test vectors with much faster runtime, when compared to a standard testbench implemented in SystemVerilog UVM. The resulting speedup reaches 24.5x and assertion coverage improvement ranges from 4.37x to 28.94x.

6 ACKNOWLEDGEMENT

The authors gratefully acknowledge the support by the the U.S. Army Defense Advanced Research Projects Agency (DARPA) under grant no. W911NF-17-1-0076, DARPA Young Faculty Award under grant no. N66001-17-1-4044, the National Science Foundation under CAREER Award CPS-1453860 and the Okawa Foundation Award.

REFERENCES

[1] R. E. Bryant. "Graph-based algorithms for boolean function manipulation". In: *TC*. 1986.
[2] R. E. Bryant. "Symbolic Boolean manipulation with ordered binary-decision diagrams". In: *CSUR*. 1992.
[3] B. Bünz and M. Lamm. "Graph Neural Networks and Boolean Satisfiability". In: 2017.
[4] D. Chatterjee, A. DeOrio, and V. Bertacco. "Event-driven gate-level simulation with GPGPUs". In: *DAC*. 2009.
[5] M. Cheng, J. Li, and S. Nazarian. "DRL-cloud: Deep reinforcement learning-based resource provisioning and task scheduling for cloud service providers". In: *ASPDAC*. 2018.
[6] S. Crago, K. Dunn, and P. Eads. "Heterogeneous cloud computing". In: *CLUSTER*. 2011.
[7] D. Devlin and B. O'Sullivan. "Satisfiability as a classification problem". In: *AICS*. 2008.
[8] D. Ernst. "Complexity and internationalisation of innovation". In: *IJIM*. 2005.
[9] S. Fine and A. Ziv. "Coverage directed test generation for functional verification using bayesian networks". In: *DAC*. 2003.
[10] M. Guevara, B. Lubin, and B. C Lee. "Navigating heterogeneous processors with market mechanisms". In: *HPCA*. 2013.
[11] O. Guzey and L. Wang. "Coverage-directed test generation through automatic constraint extraction". In: *HLVDT*. 2007.
[12] C. Ioannides and K. I Eder. "Coverage-directed test generation automated by machine learning–a review". In: (2012).
[13] M. H. Neishaburi and Z. Zilic. "Enabling efficient post-silicon debug by clustering of hardware-assertions". In: *DATE*. 2010.
[14] M. L. Rebaiaia, J. M. Jaam, and AM Hasnah. "A neural network algorithm for hardware-software verification". In: *ICECS*. 2003.
[15] R. R. Schaller. "Moore's law: past, present and future". In: *IEEE spectrum*. 1997.
[16] J. G Tong, M. Bottlé, and Z. Zilic. "Assertion clustering for compacted test sequence generation". In: *ISQED*. 2012.
[17] Y. Xue, J. Li, S. Nazarian, and P. Bogdan. "Fundamental Challenges Toward Making the IoT a Reachable Reality: A Model-Centric Investigation". In: *TODAES*. 2017.

Effective In-Situ Chip Health Monitoring with Selective Monitor Insertion Along Timing Paths

Hadi Ahmadi Balef[1], Hamed Fatemi[2], Kees Goossens[1,3], José Pineda de Gyvez[1,2]
[1]Eindhoven University of Technology, Eindhoven, The Netherlands
[2]NXP Semiconductors, Eindhoven, The Netherlands
[3]Topic Embedded Systems, Best, The Netherlands
{h.ahmadi.balef,k.g.w.goossens,j.pineda.de.gyvez}@tue.nl,hamed.fatemi@nxp.com

ABSTRACT

In-situ delay monitoring is an advanced technique to monitor the robustness of digital circuits. Conventionally, in-situ delay monitors are inserted at the end-points of timing paths. To reduce the number of monitors and to increase their observability, intermediate points have been considered. In sharp contrast to these works, we propose a low overhead technique where the insertion points are selected along the timing paths such that timing violations can be predicted without false negative detections. With our approach, the number of required monitors is reduced by up to ~11X compared to end-point insertion techniques. The observability to delay degradation is ~8X better with our approach, compared to techniques with straight monitor placement at intermediate points.

KEYWORDS

Reliability, Digital Circuit, CMOS Variability, In-Situ Delay Monitoring

ACM Reference Format:
Hadi Ahmadi Balef[1], Hamed Fatemi[2], Kees Goossens[1,3], José Pineda de Gyvez[1,2]. 2018. Effective In-Situ Chip Health Monitoring with Selective Monitor Insertion Along Timing Paths. In *GLSVLSI '18: 2018 Great Lakes Symposium on VLSI, May 23–25, 2018, Chicago, IL, USA.* ACM, New York, NY, USA, 6 pages. https://doi.org/10.1145/3194554.3194563

1 INTRODUCTION

CMOS technology scaling has been the driving force of the semiconductor industry for decades. In the Nano-scale era, however, the increased variability effects can nullify the benefits of the technology scaling by jeopardizing the robustness of designs. A variety of physical phenomena, such as aging effects (*e.g.* hot carrier injection and bias temperature instability), voltage droops, process variations, etc., are sources of variability. Variability effects on electrical parameters of a circuit are manifested as delay variation of logical gates. Delay variation may cause erroneous capturing of data at the flip-flops, *i.e.* a timing error happens. If the timing error is not masked properly, a timing failure occurs in the system. Traditionally, integrated circuits (ICs) are over-designed statically to improve their robustness, by designing at worst-case corners. However, the cost of worst-case design can be reduced by chip health monitoring at run-time, and compensating for the variability effects accordingly. Furthermore, chip health monitoring is essential for safety-critical applications in which the robustness of the system must be guaranteed. Chip health monitoring is performed based on physical sensors [1], replica paths [11], or in-situ delay monitors [3, 4, 7, 10]. The physical sensor and the replica path based techniques require calibration and thus have a diagnosis overhead. Besides, those techniques provide less correlation to the variation of the main circuit as they are not truly in the system. On the other hand, in-situ monitoring allows a truly in-system monitoring but the main challenges for this technique are the prohibitive design overheads, limited observability to the variation effect, and design intrusion.

GLSVLSI '18, May 23–25, 2018, Chicago, IL, USA

ACM ISBN 978-1-4503-5724-1/18/05...$15.00
https://doi.org/10.1145/3194554.3194563

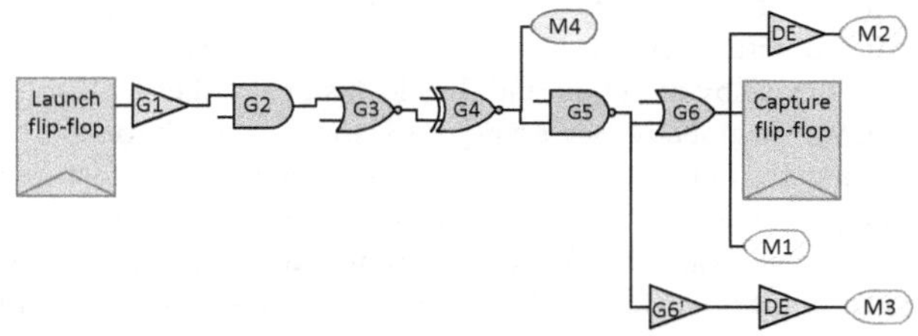

Figure 1: The insertion points of monitors along the timing paths of digital circuits for different in-situ delay monitoring techniques.

In Fig. 1, an example of a timing path and the possible insertion points of in-situ monitors are illustrated. A timing path, starts from the launch flip-flop, goes through combinational logic gates (see G1 to G6) and ends into a capture flip-flop. Conventionally, in-situ delay monitors are inserted at the end-point of timing paths [4] (see M1). A timing error is detected with end-point monitoring by sensing if the data arrival time is delayed to the next clock cycle. To avoid metastability in the main flip-flops and to avoid the complexity and overheads of error correction [5], guard banding is applied between the detection at the monitors and the actual timing error in the main flip-flops. The guard banding is performed by adding delay margin between the insertion point and the input of monitor (see DE before M2). Inserting the monitors at every flip-flop of the design adds a huge design cost due to the large number of added monitors. Moreover, the detection of timing degradation by the in-situ monitors depends on the excitation of the monitored paths, *i.e.* the paths which end into the monitors. The monitored paths are not always excited since path excitation is data dependent. Therefore, in-situ monitoring may have limited *observability* to the variability effect. In [6], the monitors are inserted at intermediate points along timing paths to reduce the number of monitors. Since the first part of any timing path is excited more than the full path, the observability is increased by inserting the monitors within timing paths. In [6], the unmonitored part of the paths are accounted by adding a pessimistic delay margin between the insertion point and the input of the monitor (see G6' in Fig. 1). Note that the guard banding is still applied by adding another delay margin before the monitor (see DE before M3 in Fig. 1). To reduce the design overhead per monitor, the monitors are therefore preferably inserted almost at the end of the timing paths. In some works, the timing error is predicted within one clock cycle to perform correction at the end of clock cycle by manipulating the clock signal either locally (see *e.g.*[8, 9]), or globally (see *e.g.*[7]). However, the excitation of the path up to the monitor insertion point may not propagate to the end of the path due to logic masking, causing performance reduction due to unnecessary clock manipulations. In [8, 9], the temporal middle point of critical timing paths is monitored to check if the increased delay to the insertion point causes a transition after half of the clock signal. The insertion points are identified based on the timing report of all critical paths. To have the list of all critical paths, path-based static timing analysis is required which is not feasible for this purpose due to the complexity of the analysis [2] and the huge list of critical paths to be monitored. Furthermore, in [8, 9] no delay margin is added for guard banding assuming that the delay of monitored and unmonitored parts of the paths degrade in similar fashion.

In this paper, we propose a new in-situ chip health monitoring technique with reduced number of monitors compared to end-point monitoring and improved observability to delay degradation through selective insertion at intermediate points along timing paths. We add implicit guard banding by inserting the monitors at particular points of the critical paths and reduce design cost per monitor by removing additional delay margins (see M4 in Fig. 1). Furthermore, we employ a novel technique which is based on graph-based static timing analysis to make sure that all critical paths are monitored while the drawbacks of path-based static timing analysis are avoided. To reduce design intrusion, we propose a new implementation flow that does not disturb the timing and layout of the main design during monitor insertion.

The remainder of this paper is organized as follows. In section 2, the proposed in-situ chip health monitoring scheme is discussed. The new technique to insert in-situ delay monitors in the design is explained in section 3. The experimental results of using the proposed technique are provided in section 4. Finally, section 5 concludes the paper.

2 IN-SITU DELAY MONITORING WITHIN TIMING PATHS

The design of in-situ delay monitor is shown in Fig. 2. The monitor detects delay degradation by checking if any late data transition occurs during the second half of the clock period. Therefore, the insertion points for this monitor are the points where the maximum delay of the timing paths up to the insertion point is less than half of clock period, during normal circuit operation. The monitor consists of a latch with active high clock and an XOR gate. The data value

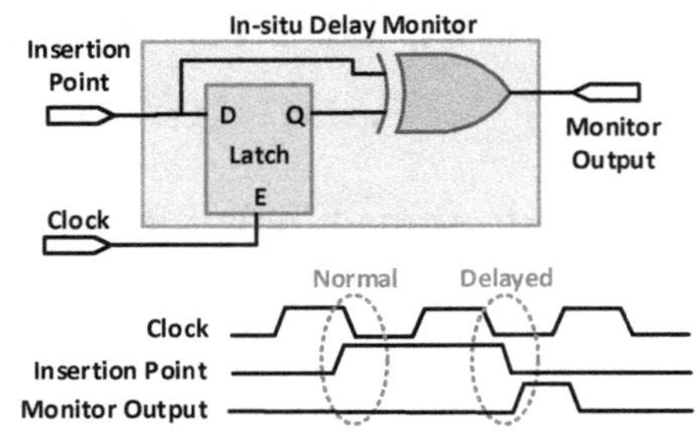

Figure 2: The design of in-situ delay monitor and the corresponding waveforms for the normal and delayed data.

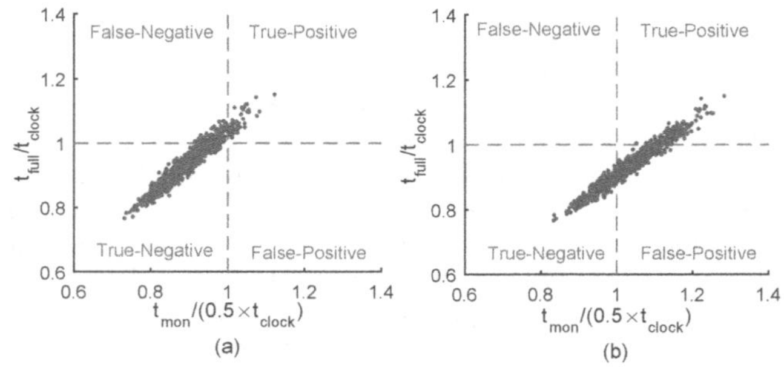

Figure 3: Scatter plot obtained from Monte Carlo simulations of a critical path delay of an industrial design showing t_{full} versus t_{mon} for the cases where (a) t_{mon}= 0.5×t_{clock}, and (b) t_{mon}= 0.55×t_{clock}.

at the insertion point is captured by the latch at the negative clock edge. The XOR gate then flags any transition which occurs during the second half of the clock cycle. Delayed data arrival time to the insertion point implies delay degradation in the circuit and is detected by the monitor.

Notice that when the monitor is inserted at the temporal middle point of the timing paths, it does not capture the effect of timing spread on the remaining logical gates which are located after the insertion point in the timing path. To investigate this effect, we performed Monte Carlo simulations on the spice netlist of a critical path of an industrial design. The Monte Carlo simulation is performed to capture the effect of local and global process variations on the delays of gates in the path. In Fig. 3-(a), the scatter plot of delay samples is shown for full path delay t_{full}, versus the delay of the path up to the insertion point of the monitor t_{mon}. In this figure, t_{full} and t_{mon} are normalized to clock period t_{clock} and 0.5×t_{clock}, respectively. The dashed lines in the figure divide the space into four regions according to the timing checks performed on t_{mon} and t_{full}. These checks are at half of the clock cycle for t_{mon}, and at the end of the clock cycle for t_{full}. Each sample then occurs in one of these regions

- True-Negative region: $t_{full} < t_{clock}$ and $t_{mon} < 0.5 \times t_{clock}$. Therefore the monitor truly detects no timing violation in the design.
- True-Positive region: $t_{full} > t_{clock}$ and $t_{mon} > 0.5 \times t_{clock}$. Therefore the monitor truly detects timing violation in the design.

- False-Negative region: t_{full}> t_{clock} and t_{mon}< $0.5\times t_{clock}$. Therefore the monitor falsely detects no timing violation in the design.
- False-Positive region: t_{full}< t_{clock} and t_{mon}> $0.5\times t_{clock}$. Therefore the monitor falsely detects timing violation in the design.

True-Negative and True-Positive detection is acceptable, while False-Negative and False-Positive detection should be avoided. False-Negative detection must be avoided, since in this case the delays of the gates after the insertion points increase, but the monitors are falsely showing that the system is robust. On the other hand, False-Positive detection can be acceptable for chip health monitoring since it reflects delay degradation of some gates in the circuit while the full path still has enough margin. In fact, during normal circuit operation, only True-Negative detections are acceptable, and as the circuit degrades, it is preferred to have False-Positive detections before True-Positive ones, to have a guard band between the detection of delay degradation with the monitors and the actual timing violation in the design. Note that this guard banding is implemented without additional design cost, by selecting the insertion points properly.

By inserting the monitor at a point closer to the end-point more samples with t_{mon}> $0.5\times t_{clock}$ fall in the False-Positive region. The scatter plots shown in Fig. 3-(a) and (b) are for the cases in which the insertion point is selected so that the average value of t_{mon} is about $0.5\times t_{clock}$ and $0.55\times t_{clock}$, respectively. By inserting the monitors at the points which are after the temporal middle point of the timing path (*i.e.* t_{mon}> $0.5\times t_{clock}$), guard banding is implicitly applied without additional cost of delay margin. Also, note that False-Negative cases are avoided at the cost of more False-Positive ones which are actually acceptable for chip health monitoring. The achieved guard banding is therefore

$$t_{gb} = t_{mon} - 0.5 \times t_{clock}. \tag{1}$$

In the next section, a technique is introduced to identify the set of insertion points based on the selected t_{mon}, such that all critical paths of the circuit are monitored.

3 SELECTIVE POINTS FOR IN-SITU MONITORING

We define critical timing paths as those paths whose delay is longer than a specific value. Therefore, we define the maximum monitored slack , slk_{max}, as the constraint for selecting the critical timing paths to be monitored, *i.e.* the critical paths are all the paths whose delay is more than (t_{clock}-slk_{max}). In one approach, the monitor insertion points are identified using the list of all critical timing paths. However, this approach is based on the path-based static timing analysis, which is extremely compute-intensive. Fast and feasible timing analysis is performed using the graph-based static timing analysis. In the graph-based static timing analysis, the maximum delay to each circuit node is calculated with summation and maximum operations. Hence, we employ the graph-based static timing analysis (see G_STA in Algorithm 1) to determine the maximum delay to each circuit node, from the nodes in a starting set V_{start}. The inputs of G_STA are therefore the circuit graph and V_{start}.

Algorithm 1 The procedure of graph-based timing analysis to identify the maximum delay to circuit points starting from a set of points V_{start}.

procedure G_STA
input: G, V_{start}
  $D \leftarrow \{d_i \in R_{-\infty} | d_i = 0 \text{ if } v_i \in V_{start}; \text{ else: } d_i = -\infty\}$
  $V_f \leftarrow V_{start}$
  while $V_f \neq \emptyset$ **do**
    $V_{fn} \leftarrow \emptyset$
    for $v_i \in V_f$ **do**
      $V_{fn} \leftarrow V_{fn} \cup Adj(G, v_i)$
      for $v_j \in Adj(G, v_i)$ **do**
        $d_j \leftarrow \max\{d_j, d_i + e_{ij}\}$
      end for
    end for
    $V_f \leftarrow V_{fn}$
  end while
  return D
end procedure

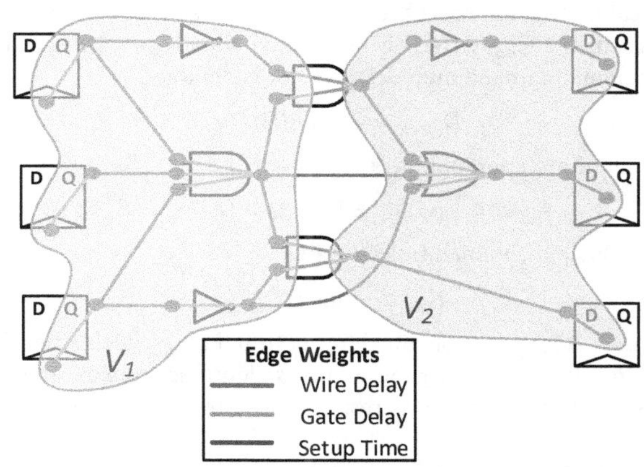

Figure 4: An example circuit graph and a cut $C = (V_1, V_2)$.

The timing graph of a digital circuit is a weighted directed graph G. The set of vertices in G representing the ports and instance pins is $V(G)$, and the set of directed edges in G representing the timing arcs is $E(G)$. The timing arc from vertex $v_i \in V(G)$ to vertex $v_j \in V(G)$ is represented by $e_{ij} \in E(G)$. From an implementation perspective, we employ the Standard Delay Format (SDF) output of the circuit to generate G. The set of adjacent vertices to the vertex $v_i \in V(G)$ is

$$Adj(G, v_i) = \{v_j \in V(G) | e_{ij} \in E(G)\}. \tag{2}$$

G_STA returns the vector $D \in R^{n\times 1}_{-\infty}$, where $R_{-\infty}$=$R \cup \{-\infty\}$. The vector D=G_STA(G,V_{start}) contains the maximum delay from the vertices in V_{start} to each vertex $v_i \in V(G)$. The maximum delay to vertex $v_i \in V(G)$ is represented as $d_i \in D$. In Algorithm 1, the maximum delays are accumulated iteratively within each pipeline stage, up to the capturing flip-flops. If there is no timing path from any vertex in V_{start} to $v_i \in V(G)$, then d_i =-∞.

Without loss of generality, we assume an ideal clock tree in this analysis. Note that during the clock tree synthesis, the design tool attempts to make the delay from the clock ports to the clock pin of all flip-flops the same. Naturally, in a more accurate analysis, clock skew should also be included. To find the set of insertion points, first, the maximum delay vector from the clock pins is calculated as

$$D_{ck,pins} = \text{G\_STA}(G, \{\text{clock pin of all flip-flops}\}). \quad (3)$$

A cut $C = (V_1, V_2)$ is created based on t_{mon} and $D_{ck,pins}$, where

$$V_1 = \{v_i \in V(G) | d_i < t_{mon}\}, \quad (4)$$

and

$$V_2 = \{v_i \in V(G) | d_i \geq t_{mon}\}. \quad (5)$$

In (4) and (5), $d_i \in D_{ck,pins}$ is obtained from (3), and t_{mon} is the maximum delay to the monitor insertion point within timing path, as was discussed in the previous section. In Fig. 4, an example timing graph and the cut are illustrated. The set of boundary vertices, $V_{bnd} \subset V_1$, is defined as

$$V_{bnd} = \{v_i \in V(G) | e_{ij} \in E(G), v_i \in V_1, v_j \in V_2\}. \quad (6)$$

where V_1 and V_2 are obtained from (4) and (5), respectively. The vertices in V_{bnd} are candidates for placement of the monitors. A screening is performed on V_{bnd} to find the vertices which are in the critical paths, and insert the monitors at those vertices. Therefore, for each $v_i \in V_{bnd}$, G_STA is performed with $V_{start} = \{v_i\}$, and the corresponding maximum delay vector is obtained

$$D_{bnd,i} = \text{G\_STA}(G, \{v_i\}). \quad (7)$$

The set of insertion points is

$$V_{inp} = \{v_i \in V(G) | v_i \in V_{bnd}, t_i > (t_{clock} - slk_{max})\}. \quad (8)$$

where V_{bnd} is obtained from (6), and

$$t_i = d_i + \max\{D_{bnd,i}\}, \quad (9)$$

where $d_i \in D_{ck,pins}$ is obtained from (3), and $D_{bnd,i}$ is obtained from (7). Once the set of insertion points is identified from (8), the monitors are inserted at the corresponding gate pins of all vertices in V_{inp}.

The monitors are conventionally added to the design after the place and route step (see *e.g.* [6, 7]). However, such an implementation flow perturbs the layout and the timing of the main design [6]. To minimize the perturbation, we propose the implementation flow illustrated in Fig. 5. In the proposed flow, the monitors are added at the synthesis stage with dangling insertion point inputs. Yet, the clock input of the monitors is connected, such that their loading effect is taken into account during clock tree synthesis. The design with unconnected monitors, then goes through synthesis and back-end design steps. The insertion points of the monitors are identified based on the SDF output, when timing closure is achieved after the place and route step. The monitors are then truly inserted into the design by connecting them to the identified insertion points (*i.e.* V_{inp}). The insertion is done by generating a TCL script which contains Engineering Change Order (ECO) commands. Then, optimization is performed to compensate for the loading effects of the monitors on the timing closure of the main circuit. The target slack of the latch in monitors is set to $-t_{gb}$, to preserve guard banding and avoid over-optimization of the circuit during the final optimization.

Hence, in the proposed implementation flow, the number of monitors n_{mon} is decided at the front end. Since the monitored paths are the critical paths identified by slk_{max}, with a given n_{mon}, we obtain a path coverage in terms of slk_{max}. Intuitively, by increasing n_{mon}, a higher slk_{max} is possible since more paths are monitored. To compare our results against the end-point monitoring approach, we define $n_{ff,crt}$ as the number of critical end-points for a given slk_{max}. Therefore, the number of monitors relative to the number of critical end-points, $n_{mon}/n_{ff,crt}$, represents the effectiveness of the proposed technique compared to end-point monitoring in terms of number of monitors.

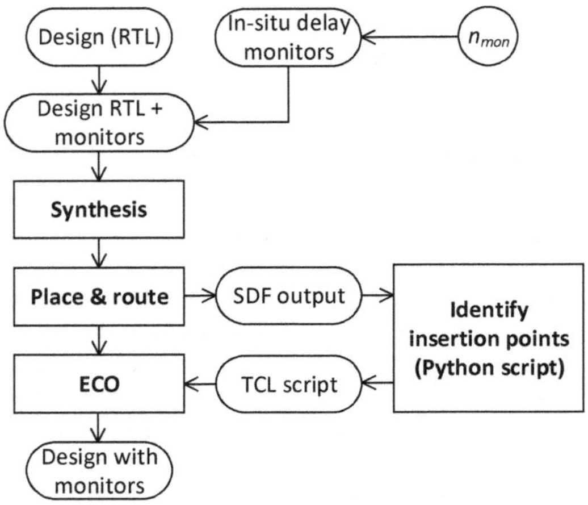

Figure 5: The proposed implementation flow.

Table 1: The implementation details of the benchmark circuit (ARM Cortex M0 processor implemented in 40nm technology).

Target frequency	200MHz
Number of gates	8441
Number of flip-flops	841
Number of IOs	136
Power (mW)	2.24
Area (μm^2)	18877

4 EXPERIMENTAL RESULTS

The proposed technique is employed for in-situ monitoring in an ARM Cortex M0 processor, implemented in an industrial 40nm technology. Cadence Genus and Cadence Innovus are used for synthesis and back-end design, respectively. The design specifications are provided in Table 1. The benchmark application for netlist simulation and power calculation is an infinite impulse response filter.

In Fig. 6, $n_{mon}/n_{ff,crt}$ is plotted versus t_{mon} in the range of 0.5× t_{clock} to t_{clock}, for slk_{max} = 5%, 10%, 15%, and 20% of the clock period. As it can be observed, the maximum effectiveness of the technique (*i.e.* minimum $n_{mon}/n_{ff,crt}$) is achieved when t_{mon}=0.7×t_{clock}, independent of slk_{max}. Furthermore, it can be observed that by increasing slk_{max}, $n_{mon}/n_{ff,crt}$ increases. To illustrate the dependency of the number of insertion points on slk_{max}, we fixed t_{mon} to 0.7× t_{clock} and swept slk_{max} from 5% to 30% of the clock period and show n_{mon} and $n_{ff,crt}$ in Fig. 7. Based on these results we can see that, to monitor all paths whose slack is less than 5% of the clock period,

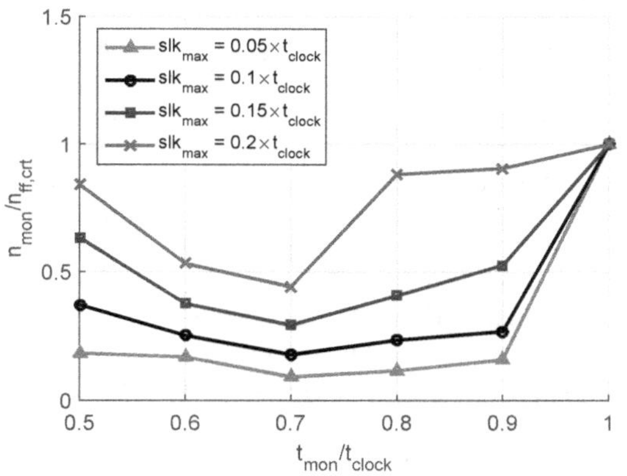

Figure 6: The number of the insertion points of monitors relative to the number of critical flip-flops versus t_{mon} ranging from $0.5{\times}t_{clock}$ to $0.9{\times}t_{clock}$, for slk_{max} from $0.05{\times}t_{clock}$ to $0.2{\times}t_{clock}$. The target speed of the design is 200MHz.

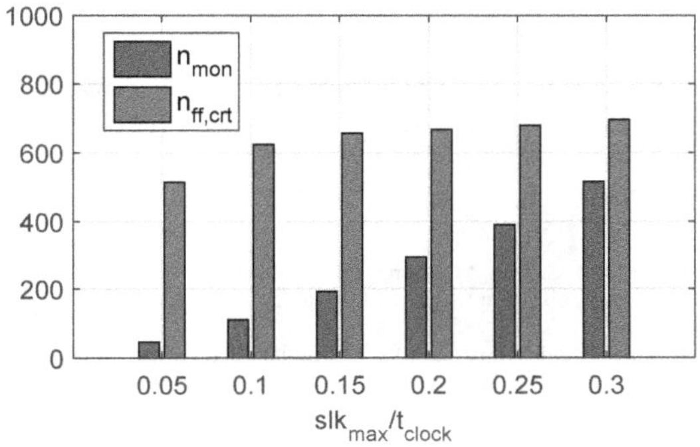

Figure 7: The effect of changing slk_{max} on the number of required monitors $n_{mon}$and the number of critical flip-flops $n_{ff,crt}$for the design with 200MHz target frequency, considering t_{mon}=$0.7{\times}t_{clock}$.

the number of required monitors is ~11X lower compared to the traditional end-point monitoring approach.

The target speed of the design, f_{clock}, affects the topology of the circuit and its timing graph. To investigate the effect of f_{clock} on the effectiveness of the proposed technique, f_{clock} is varied from 50MHz to 250MHz. n_{mon} and $n_{ff,crt}$ are calculated for each new design considering slk_{max}=$0.1{\times}t_{clock}$. Fig. 8 shows n_{mon} and $n_{ff,crt}$ plotted versus f_{clock}. The design with f_{clock}=50MHz is so relaxed that no critical path exists for slk_{max}=$0.1{\times}t_{clock}$. Therefore, both n_{mon} and $n_{ff,crt}$ are zero. The effectiveness of the proposed technique in terms of the number of monitors, is ~8X higher than the traditional end-point monitoring, when the speed target is f_{clock}=100MHz and it reduces at higher frequencies.

Following the implementation flow which was discussed in the previous section, we added the monitors to the design with f_{clock}=200MHz. Table 2 shows the overheads for n_{mon}=64 and 128 considering t_{mon}=$0.7{\times}t_{clock}$. Furthermore, slk_{max} and the corresponding $n_{ff,crt}$ are provided in the Table to indicate the path coverage and the higher overhead of end-point monitoring techniques. Inserting more monitors in the design allows for a higher slk_{max} at

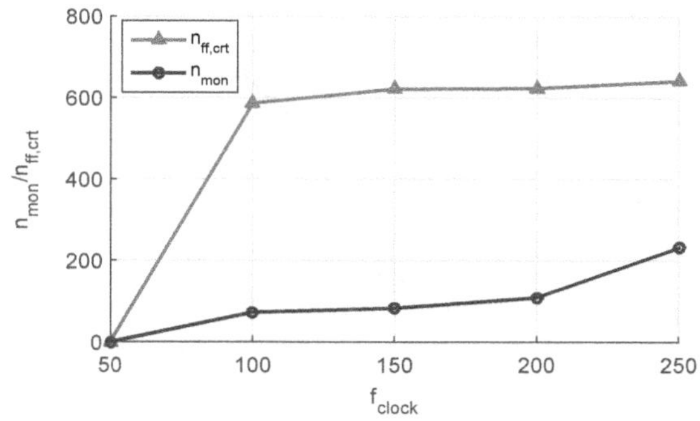

Figure 8: The effect of changing f_{clock}, on $n_{mon}/n_{ff,crt}$, considering t_{mon}=$0.7{\times}t_{clock}$ and slk_{max}=$0.1{\times}t_{clock}$.

Table 2: The power, area, and speed overheads of adding monitors to the design with f_{clock}=200MHz, with the corresponding slk_{max} and $n_{ff,crt}$, considering 64 and 128 monitors, and t_{mon}=$0.7{\times}t_{clock}$.

n_{mon}	64	128
Power Overhead	7.6%	10.5%
Area Overhead	9.7%	11.25%
Speed Overhead	0.5%	1.2%
slk_{max}	$0.07{\times}t_{clock}$	$0.12{\times}t_{clock}$
$n_{ff,crt}$	518	651

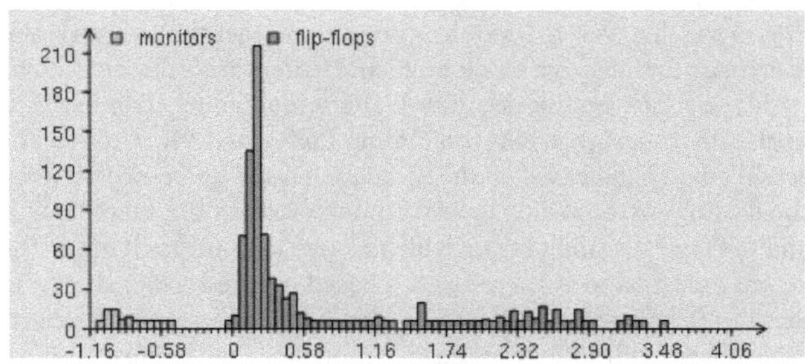

Figure 9: The histogram of the monitor slacks and the slack of the flip-flops with t_{mon}=$0.7{\times}t_{clock}$.

the expense of more power, area, and speed overhead. In Fig. 9, the histogram of worst case monitor slacks, and of the main design, are shown for the slow corner and for t_{mon}=$0.7{\times}t_{clock}$. Based on the histogram shown in Fig. 9, and considering (1), t_{gb} is distributed from ~0.5ns to ~1ns, (*i.e.* in the range of 10% to 20% of clock period). Next, a netlist simulation was performed with the annotated timing at the typical corner. The simulation testbench runs the benchmark application on the processor. Delay degradation is modelled by using a scaling factor during the generation of the SDF output used for timing annotation. The number of monitors which are excited (*i.e.* detection of a late data arrival) is obtained by counting the timing violations happening in the latch of the monitors. In Fig. 10-(a) the number of excited monitors is plotted versus the scaling factor used for SDF generation. No monitor excitation happens up to 1.3X delay degradation. By scaling more the delays, the monitor

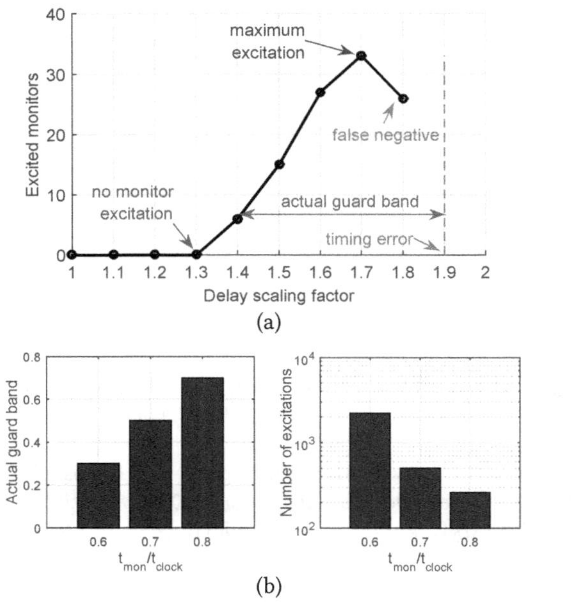

Figure 10: Netlist simulation results with timing annotated at the typical corner. (a) The number of excited monitors versus the delay scaling factor considering t_{mon}=0.7×t_{clock}. (b) The effect of t_{mon} selection on the actual guard band, and the total number of excitations.

excitation starts and reaches its maximum value of 33 when the scaling factor is 1.7X. The monitor excitation decreases afterwards due to the fact that the monitor does not detect the late arrival if it crosses the positive clock edge and enters into the next clock cycle (*i.e.* false negative detection). The actual timing error happens in the main design when the scaling factor of 1.9X is used. The actual guard band based on the simulation is the difference between the scaling factor which causes timing error in the main design, and the lowest scaling factor which causes monitor excitation. The actual guard band is therefore 0.5 based on the results shown in Fig. 10-(a). Furthermore, the excitation rate of the monitors reflects their observability to delay degradation since with more monitor excitation rate, delay degradation is detected faster. Hence, the maximum number of excitations during the simulation indicates the monitor observability and depends on t_{mon}, since shorter part of a path is excited more frequently compared to longer part of the path. Therefore, we considered three t_{mon} values of 0.6×t_{clock}, 0.7×t_{clock}, and 0.8×t_{clock} to investigate more the effect of t_{mon} on the actual guard banding and the observability of monitors. The effect of t_{mon} on the guard band, and the total number of excitations are shown in the bar plots illustrated in Fig. 10-(b). It can be observed that the actual guard band increases when the insertion points of monitors are adjusted with higher t_{mon}. On the other hand, more observability to delay degradation is possible by adjusting the monitor insertion points with lower t_{mon}. When the monitors are inserted with t_{mon}=0.6×t_{clock}, more than ~8X higher observability to delay degradation is obtained compared to the case where $t_{mon} \geq$ 0.8×t_{clock}. Hence, the insertion points can be adjusted to find the optimal set of insertion points in terms of observability to delay degradation, guard banding, and the number of monitors.

5 CONCLUSIONS

A new in-situ chip health monitoring technique is proposed in which the insertion points are selected at intermediate points along the critical timing paths. It is shown that with effective guard banding, the unmonitored part of the paths are protected such that false negative detections are avoided. The guard banding is implemented without additional overhead per monitor by properly selecting the insertion points. The number of required monitors depends on the number of monitored paths which are selected based on their minimum slacks. With the proposed technique, the number of monitors is reduced by up to ~11X compared to the traditional end-point monitoring techniques, to monitor all timing paths which their minimum slacks are less than 5% of clock period. Furthermore, ~8X more observability to delay degradation is obtained compared to other techniques which insert the monitors at intermediate, but close to end, point of the critical paths. Finally the design intrusion is minimized by adding the monitors at the front-end of design, and connecting the insertion points after the design is placed and routed.

ACKNOWLEDGMENT

This research has been partially supported by NL grant STW ZERO (2016/STW/00157176) and EU grant ECSEL SILENSE (2017/ECSEL/00737487).

REFERENCES

[1] M. Agarwal, B. C. Paul, M. Zhang, and S. Mitra. 2007. Circuit Failure Prediction and Its Application to Transistor Aging. In *Proceedings of IEEE VLSI Test Symposium (VTS'07)*. 277–286.

[2] H. Cherupalli and J. Sartori. 2015. Graph-based Dynamic Analysis: Efficient Characterization of Dynamic Timing and Activity Distributions. In *Proceedings of IEEE/ACM International Conference on Computer-Aided Design (ICCAD'15)*. 729–735.

[3] M. Choudhury, V. Chandra, K. Mohanram, and R. Aitken. 2010. TIMBER: Time Borrowing and Error Relaying for Online Timing Error Resilience. In *Proceedings of Design Automation and Test in Europe Conference and Exhibition (DATE'10)*. 1554–1559.

[4] S. Das, C. Tokunaga, S. Pant, W. H. Ma, S. Kalaiselvan, K. Lai, D. M. Bull, and D. T. Blaauw. 2009. RazorII: In Situ Error Detection and Correction for PVT and SER Tolerance. *IEEE Journal of Solid-State Circuits (JSSC)* 44, 1 (January 2009), 32–48.

[5] D. Fick, N. Liu, Z. Foo, M. Fojtik, J. s. Seo, D. Sylvester, and D. Blaauw. 2010. In Situ Delay-Slack Monitor for High-Performance Processors Using An All-Digital Self-Calibrating 5ps Resolution Time-to-Digital Converter. In *Proceedings of IEEE International Solid-State Circuits Conference - (ISSCC)*. 188–189.

[6] L. Lai, V. Chandra, R. C. Aitken, and P. Gupta. 2014. SlackProbe: A Flexible and Efficient In Situ Timing Slack Monitoring Methodology. *IEEE Transactions on Computer-Aided Design of Integrated Circuits and Systems (TCAD)* 33, 8 (August 2014), 1168–1179.

[7] S. M. Londono and J. P. de Gyvez. 2012. A Better-Than-Worst-Case Circuit Design Methodology Using Timing-Error Speculation and Frequency Adaptation. In *Proceedings of IEEE International SOC Conference*. 15–20.

[8] V. Mahalingam, N. Ranganathan, and R. Hayman. 2012. Dynamic Clock Stretching for Variation Compensation in VLSI Circuit Design. *ACM Journal on Emerging Technologies in Computing Systems (JETC)* 8, 3, Article 16 (Aug. 2012), 16:1–16:13 pages.

[9] M. Nejat, B. Alizadeh, and A. Afzali-Kusha. 2014. Dynamic Flip-Flop Conversion: A Time-Borrowing Method for Performance Improvement of Low-Power Digital Circuits Prone to Variations. *IEEE Transactions on Very Large Scale Integration Systems (TVLSI)* 23, 11 (November 2014), 2724 – 2727.

[10] M. Nicolaidis. 1999. Time Redundancy Based Soft-Error Tolerance to Rescue Nanometer Technologies. In *Proceedings of IEEE VLSI Test Symposium (VTS'99)*. 86–94.

[11] J. Tschanz, K. Bowman, S. Walstra, M. Agostinelli, T. Karnik, and V. De. 2009. Tunable Replica Circuits and Adaptive Voltage-Frequency Techniques for Dynamic Voltage, Temperature, and Aging Variation Tolerance. In *Proceedings of IEEE Symposium on VLSI Circuits (VLSIC'09)*. 112–113.

Low Complexity Burst Error Correcting Codes to Correct MBUs in SRAMs

Abhishek Das and Nur A. Touba
Computer Engineering Research Center,
University of Texas at Austin, TX-78712
abhishekdas@utexas.edu, touba@ece.utexas.edu

ABSTRACT

[1]Multiple bit upsets (MBUs) caused by high energy radiation is the most common source of soft errors in static random-access memories (SRAMs) affecting multiple cells. Burst error correcting Hamming codes have most commonly been used to correct MBUs in SRAM cell since they have low redundancy and low decoder latency. But with technology scaling, the number of bits being affected increases, thus requiring a need for increasing the burst size that can be corrected. However, this is a problem because it increases the number of syndromes exponentially thus increasing the decoder complexity exponentially as well. In this paper, a new burst error correcting code based on Hamming codes is proposed which allows much better scaling of decoder complexity as the burst size is increased. For larger burst sizes, it can provide significantly smaller and faster decoders than existing methods thus providing higher reliability at an affordable cost. Moreover, there is frequently no increase in the number of check bits or a very minimal increase in comparison with existing methods. A general construction and decoding methodology for the new codes is proposed. Experimental results are presented comparing the decoder complexity for the proposed codes with conventional burst error correcting Hamming codes demonstrating the significant improvements that can be achieved.

KEYWORDS

Burst error correction; Hamming codes; multiple bit upsets; SRAM; low complexity decoder

ACM Reference Format:

Abhishek Das and Nur A. Touba. 2018. Low Complexity Burst Error Correcting Codes to Correct MBUs in SRAMs. In *GLSVLSI '18: 2018 Great Lakes Symposium on VLSI*, May 23–25, 2018, Chicago, IL, USA. ACM, NY, NY, USA, 6 pages. https://doi.org/10.1145/3194554.3194570

1 INTRODUCTION

Soft errors caused by radiation poses a significant reliability concern for SRAMs [4]. With technology scaling, the susceptibility of SRAMs to soft-errors has significantly increased as well [8]. In current nanoscale technology nodes, device geometries are small, and with technology scaling, devices are getting smaller. Thus, a particle strike might affect more than one cell causing a multiple bit upset [13]. The smaller the device geometries, more the number of cells that are affected by a single particle strike. A b-bit burst error caused by such a particle strike can cause multiple bits to be flipped within the b-bit burst window. Thus, codes aimed to correct MBUs in SRAMs should be able to correct all possible error combinations within a b-bit burst window including all b-bits getting flipped.

Burton Code [5] was one of the early codes that dealt with MBUs by correcting a single phased burst error or a single symbol error. But they can only correct b-bit burst error if it falls within a single symbol which is not always guaranteed. It is also possible to use multi-symbol error correction to correct all b-bit burst errors regardless of their position, but this increases the decoder complexity as well as the decoder latency. Over the years, many different and better codes have been devised to address the problem of correcting burst errors independent of their position. The most common method to address MBUs in SRAMs was to use a simple single error correcting double error detecting (SEC-DED) code in tandem with word-interleaving in such a way that each MBU would affect only a single bit for each word instead of multiple bits of a single word. This scheme made it possible to correct MBUs and reduce the soft error rate (SER) using a SEC-DED error correcting code (ECC) [3]. The degree of interleaving defined the amount of adjacent error protection for a memory system. However, such a scheme is no longer beneficial due to constraints such as memory aspect ratio, performance and power consumption which limits the degree of interleaving.

Error correcting codes (ECCs) with one-step majority logic decoding have been studied and extended to address the problem of MBUs for SRAMs. [7] proposed a general theory on adjacent error correcting orthogonal Latin square (OLS) codes for various burst sizes. [15] proposed a method to correct triple adjacent errors with the same amount of redundancy as a double error correcting OLS code. [14] proposed a method to correct MBUs in SRAMs using majority logic-decodable difference set codes. [16] proposed a new class for double adjacent error correction (DAEC) SEC-DED-DAEC codes from OLS codes. Although these classes of majority-logic decodable (MLD) codes have very low access latencies which is good for the overall performance of the memory system, the MLD codes suffer from very high redundancy. Other low redundancy codes have also been extensively studied for correcting MBUs in SRAMs. [11] proposed a parallel double error correcting Bose-Chaudhuri-Hocquenghem (BCH) code. [10] proposed a single-bit and double

GLSVLSI '18, May 23–25, 2018, Chicago, IL, USA

ACM ISBN 978-1-4503-5724-1/18/05...$15.00
DOI: https://doi.org/10.1145/3194554.3194570

adjacent error correcting parallel decoder for BCH codes. But such codes have very high decoder area and decoder latency. Multidimensional codes have also been proposed in the literature specifically to correct MBUs in SRAMs. [9] proposed a two-dimensional coding method to correct multiple bit errors in caches. [2] proposed a matrix-based code which combined Hamming codes and Parity codes to detect and correct multiple errors. But both these codes have high area and power consumption compared to general burst error correcting Hamming codes. Recently, Hamming codes have also been studied and extended to correct MBUs in SRAMs. These codes provide balanced trade-off between the amount of redundancy required and the decoding complexity and decoding latency. Thus, they are an attractive solution specific to SRAMs. [6] first extended the traditional SEC-DED Hamming code to correct two adjacent errors for tolerating multiple bit upsets in small memories. [17] proposed a general solution for burst (local) error correcting codes working in conjunction with random (global) error correcting codes to correct MBUs in SRAMs. [12] presented a code with the basic SEC-DED coverage as well as both DAEC and scalable adjacent error detection (xAED) while reducing the adjacent/nonadjacent double-bit error mis-correction probability. [1] proposed a SEC-DAEC-TAEC and 3-bit burst error correction codes which reduced the total number of ones in the parity check matrix to optimize the decoder complexity and decoder latency. For all such Hamming extended codes, the decoding procedure still relies on a syndrome based matching method. As the burst size increases, the number of syndromes also increases exponentially, thus increasing the decoder complexity exponentially as well.

In this paper, a general b-bit burst error correcting code is proposed which aims to reduce the decoder complexity for a similar amount of redundancy as general burst error correcting Hamming codes. The proposed codes correct all possible combination of errors within a b-bit burst and achieve much better decoder complexity and decoder latency for higher burst sizes. The rest of the paper is organized as follows. Section 2 briefly describes the concepts for burst error correcting Hamming codes along with an analysis on syndromes. Section 3 describes the proposed codes, its construction and its decoding procedures. Section 4 evaluates the proposed codes and makes a comparison to the general burst error correcting Hamming codes. Finally, sec. 5 presents the conclusion of this work.

2 BURST ERROR CORRECTING HAMMING CODES

Extensive research has been done on burst error correcting Hamming codes as discussed previously. The key concepts related to burst error correcting codes remains the same. For a Hamming code to be b-bit burst error correcting, it needs to satisfy the following conditions [17]:

1. Each column of the parity check matrix is unique.
2. The bitwise XOR of any combination of columns within b-adjacent columns is unique.

Condition-1 ensures that all single errors are recognized and corrected. Condition-2 ensures that not only adjacent errors, but any combination of errors within the burst size b are recognized and corrected. The parity check matrix can be constructed in an algorithmic manner by extending [6] or using a Boolean SAT solver [17]. An example of a parity check matrix for a 3-bit burst error correcting code for information length k = 16 bits and with redundancy r = 8 bits has been shown in Figure 1.

$$\left(\begin{array}{cccccccccccccccc|cccccccc}
0&1&1&1&1&1&0&0&0&0&0&1&0&0&0&0&1&0&0&0&0&0&0&0\\
0&1&1&0&0&0&1&1&0&0&0&0&1&0&0&0&0&1&0&0&0&0&0&0\\
1&0&0&1&0&0&0&0&1&0&0&0&0&1&0&0&0&0&1&0&0&0&0&0\\
0&1&0&0&0&0&1&0&0&1&0&0&0&0&1&0&0&0&0&1&0&0&0&0\\
1&0&0&0&1&0&0&0&1&0&1&0&0&0&0&1&0&0&0&0&1&0&0&0\\
0&0&0&0&1&0&0&1&0&0&1&0&0&1&0&0&0&0&0&0&0&1&0&0\\
1&0&0&1&0&1&1&0&1&1&0&1&0&0&1&0&0&0&0&0&0&0&1&0\\
1&0&1&0&0&1&0&1&0&1&1&0&1&0&0&1&0&0&0&0&0&0&0&1
\end{array}\right)$$

Figure 1: Parity check matrix of a 3-bit burst error correcting code for k = 16.

2.1 Syndrome Analysis

The total number of syndromes for a b-bit burst error correcting code for each b-adjacent column code is given by equation (1). Only syndromes affecting information bits are taken into account as there is no necessary requirement to correct the parity check bits. Since for each information bit a b-bit burst might exist, the total number of useful syndromes for a b-bit burst error correcting code is given by equation (2), where k is the total number of information bits.

$$\#Syndromes/Burst = {}^{b}C_1 + {}^{b}C_2 + \dots + {}^{b}C_b = 2^b - 1 \quad (1)$$

$$\#\ Syndromes = k(2^b - 1) \quad (2)$$

As can be seen from equation (2), the total number of syndromes is a linear function of the length of information bits, and an exponential function of the burst size b. Thus, as the burst size increases the number of syndromes increase exponentially thereby increasing the decoder hardware exponentially. For a b-bit burst error, any combination of errors within b-adjacent bits is possible. Table I shows all the possible errors that can occur involving data bit d_i within a 4-bit burst window. For each type of error within b-adjacent bits, there is a unique syndrome which defines the pattern and location of the error.

Table I: Possible Errors for a Data Bit Within a 4-Bit Burst Window

Number of bits in error	Location of errors
1	*i*
2	*(i,i+1); (i,i+2); (i,i+3);(i-3,i); (i-2,i); (i-1,i)*
3	*(i-3,i-2,i); (i-3,i-1,i); (i-2,i-1,i); (i-2,i,i+1); (i-1,i,i+1); (i,i+1,i+2); (i-1,i,i+2); (i,i+1,i+3); (i,i+2,i+3)*
4	*(i-3,i-2,i-1,i); (i-2,i-1,i,i+1); (i-1,i,i+1,i+2); (i,i+1,i+2,i+3)*

2.2 Decoding Procedure

The decoding procedure for most methods is based on syndrome matching i.e. each syndrome is mapped to particular data bit(s) being in error. Each syndrome is mapped to their corresponding data bits and the relevant syndrome is the OR of all corresponding syndromes. This indicates whether a bit is in error or not, and if it is in error, the data bit is flipped. Thus, as the burst size or the block length increases, the number of syndromes increases and so does the complexity of the decoding circuit.

3 PROPOSED CODES

For a burst size of b, the key idea of the proposed codes is to partition the parity check matrix in a manner such that the upper b-rows of the parity check matrix is used to compute the error pattern within the b-bit burst, and the lower (r-b) rows of the parity check matrix are used to compute the location of the burst. To compute the error pattern, the upper b-rows of the parity check matrix are organized in such a manner that for each consecutive b-columns there is exactly one non-zero entry per row. This is easily done by interleaving the 1s every b-columns. Next, the lower (r-b) rows of the parity check matrix are constructed in such a manner that they satisfy the conditions for a b-bit burst error correcting Hamming Code:

1. All columns of the parity check matrix are unique.
2. The bitwise XOR of any combination of columns within b-adjacent columns are also unique.

Similar to burst error correcting Hamming codes, Condition-1 ensures that all single errors are recognized and corrected. Condition-2 ensures that not only adjacent errors, but any combination of errors within the burst size b are recognized and corrected. This condition is necessary because MBUs do not necessarily flip consecutive bits, and there might be cases were the MBU flips a few non-consecutive bits within a burst size. The general form of the parity check matrix for a b-bit burst error correcting code has been shown in Figure 2. In this case H^* refers to the lower (r-b) rows constructed as described previously. The parity check matrix for a 4-bit burst error correcting code has been shown in Figure 3.

$$H = \begin{pmatrix} I_b & I_b & \cdots & I_b & \multirow{2}{*}{I_r} \\ & & H^* & & \end{pmatrix}$$

Figure 2: General form of the parity check matrix of proposed codes.

$$\left(\begin{array}{cccccccccccccccc:cccccccccc}
1&0&0&0&1&0&0&0&1&0&0&0&1&0&0&0&1&0&0&0&0&0&0&0&0&0\\
0&1&0&0&0&1&0&0&0&1&0&0&0&1&0&0&0&1&0&0&0&0&0&0&0&0\\
0&0&1&0&0&0&1&0&0&0&1&0&0&0&1&0&0&0&1&0&0&0&0&0&0&0\\
0&0&0&1&0&0&0&1&0&0&0&1&0&0&0&1&0&0&0&1&0&0&0&0&0&0\\
0&1&1&1&1&0&0&0&0&0&1&0&0&0&0&0&0&0&0&0&1&0&0&0&0&0\\
0&1&0&0&0&1&1&0&0&0&0&1&0&0&0&0&0&0&0&0&0&1&0&0&0&0\\
1&0&1&1&0&0&0&1&1&0&0&0&1&0&0&0&0&0&0&0&0&0&1&0&0&0\\
1&1&1&0&1&1&0&1&1&1&0&0&0&1&0&0&0&0&0&0&0&0&0&1&0&0\\
1&0&0&0&0&1&1&1&0&1&1&0&0&0&1&0&0&0&0&0&0&0&0&0&1&0\\
1&0&0&1&1&0&1&0&1&1&0&1&0&0&0&1&0&0&0&0&0&0&0&0&0&1
\end{array}\right)$$

Figure 3: Parity check matrix of a 4-bit burst error correcting proposed codes for $k = 16$.

The proposed codes are also systematic by design. Thus, the encoding procedure is the same as general Hamming codes. The parity bits are computed by XORing data-bits based on the parity check matrix and are appended to the data-bits to form the final codeword. As a result, the proposed codes do not add any complexity to the encoding procedure.

3.1 Decoding Procedure

The decoding procedure involves two parts: the error pattern computation and the error location computation. The error pattern is directly computed from the upper b-rows of the parity check matrix. Since the upper b-rows of the parity check matrix are arranged in an interleaved fashion, any error within a b-bit burst produces a syndrome equal to that of the error pattern. The location of the burst error is computed through the lower (r-b) rows. If an error occurs within a b-bit burst starting from location i, the syndrome is given by equation (3).

Thus, the decoding works by considering each group of b-adjacent columns as a single symbol and decoding on a per symbol basis. Any data bit d_i then is part of b symbols of b-bit each. An example has been shown for a 4-bit burst error correcting code in Figure 4, the data but d_i is part of 4-bit symbols B_{i-3}, B_{i-2}, B_{i-1} and B_i. A b-bit burst error simply means an error in one of the b-bit symbols, and thus can be computed through equation (4). If for any of the b-bit symbols that the data bit is a part of equation (4) is satisfied, that means the data bit is in error. The error pattern of the data bit is simply the syndrome value S_α where α is the row amongst the upper b-rows for which the corresponding column is a 1. Thus, the location of error for any data bit is the AND of all b-bit symbols of which it is a part. A data bit will not be in error only if it does not satisfy equation (4) for all b-bit symbols of which it is a part.

$$\begin{bmatrix} S_1 \\ S_2 \\ \vdots \\ S_b \\ S_{b+1} \\ S_{b+2} \\ \vdots \\ S_r \end{bmatrix} = \begin{bmatrix} e_i \\ e_{i+1} \\ \vdots \\ e_{i+b-1} \\ h_{b+1,i}e_i \oplus h_{b+1,i+1}e_{i+1} \cdots \oplus h_{b+1,i+b-1}e_{i+b-1} \\ h_{b+2,i}e_i \oplus h_{b+2,i+1}e_{i+1} \cdots \oplus h_{b+2,i+b-1}e_{i+b-1} \\ \vdots \\ h_{r,i}e_i \oplus h_{r,i+1}e_{i+1} \cdots \oplus h_{r,i+b-1}e_{i+b-1} \end{bmatrix} \quad (3)$$

$$h_{b+\beta,i}S_1 \oplus h_{b+\beta,i+1}S_2 \cdots \oplus h_{b+\beta,i+b-1}S_b \oplus S_{b+\beta} = 0 \quad \forall \beta \in \{1, 2, \ldots r-b\} \quad (4)$$

The above method has a clear advantage over syndrome matching based decoding methods specifically for larger burst sizes. This is because as the burst size increases, the number of syndrome increases exponentially, as shown in equation (2). Thus, the amount of hardware needed to decode also increases exponentially in syndrome matching based decoding. But in the proposed decoding scheme, an increase in burst size results in addition of another term in equation (4). This essentially means a linear increase in the amount of XOR, AND and OR gates in the decoder design. A partial error pattern generator design for a 3-bit burst error correcting code for k=16 is shown in Figure 5. Similarly, the partial error pattern generator design for a 4-bit burst error correcting code for k=16 is shown in Figure 6. From Figure 5 and Figure 6, it can be seen that an increase in the burst size adds only a few XOR gates, an extra input to the AND gate and depending on the lower (r-b) rows, possibly an extra input to the OR gate per symbol $B_\alpha \, \forall \, \alpha \in \{1, \ldots, k\}$.

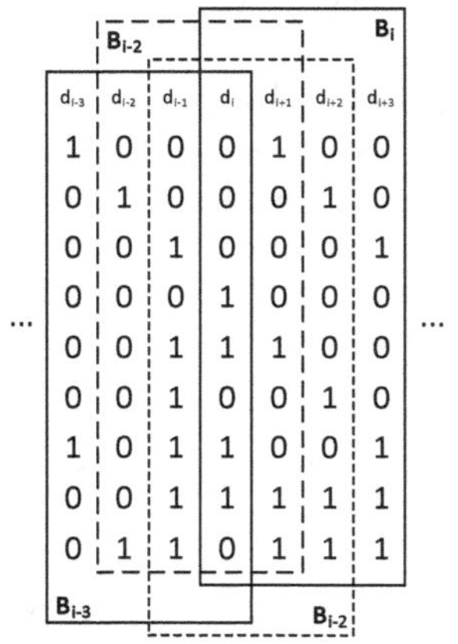

Figure 4: Symbols data bit d_i is part of for a 4-bit burst error correcting proposed code.

3.2 Area and Delay Optimization

In a general Hamming Code, there are two optimization criteria that can be used on its parity check matrix to reduce the decoder complexity and decoder latency:

1. Minimize the total number of 1's in each row of the parity check matrix.

2. Minimize the total number of 1's in the parity check matrix.

The first criterion minimizes the decoder latency while the second criterion reduces the decoder complexity. A similar optimization can be done for the proposed codes as well but with a simple modification. Considering the general parity check matrix of the proposed codes shown in Figure 2, it can be seen that the upper b-rows of the matrix is already sparse and has the minimum number of 1's both on a row basis and in total. Thus, the two optimization criteria of the Hamming code can be applied to the lower (r-b) rows of the matrix to achieve the same optimizations. This is because, minimizing the number of 1's in each row simply reduces the number of bits that need to be XORed together for the syndrome as well as for equation (4). Thus, the optimization results in lesser XOR operations thereby reducing the decoder delay. And minimizing the total number of 1's in the lower (r-b) rows of the parity check matrix reduces the total number of XOR gates thus reducing the complexity. Thus, optimization techniques proposed in [1] are orthogonal to the proposed codes and can be used in place of burst error correcting Hamming codes.

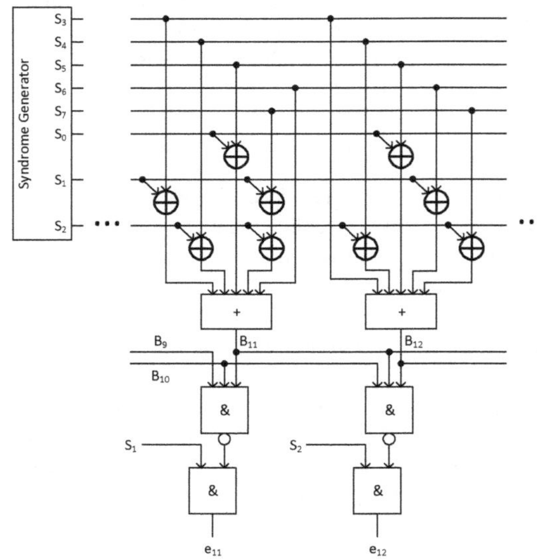

Figure 5: Partial schematics of the error pattern generator for a 3-bit burst error correcting proposed codes for k=16.

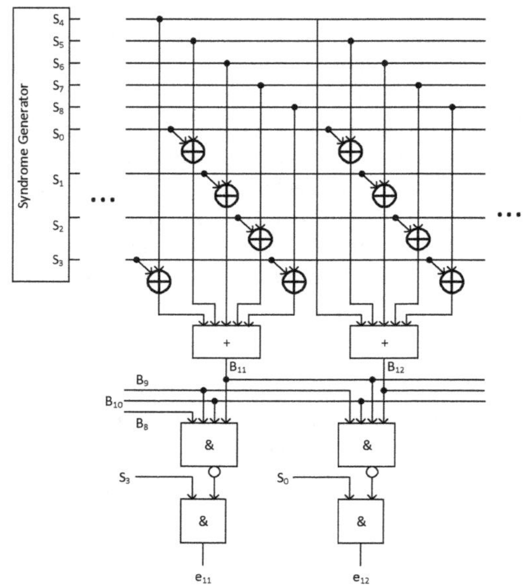

Figure 6: Partial schematics of the error pattern generator for a 4-bit burst error correcting proposed codes for k=16.

4 EVALUATION

The burst error correcting codes for different burst sizes were constructed by extending the codes proposed in [17]. The proposed codes and the general burst error correcting Hamming codes were synthesized on Synopsys Design Compiler using NCSU FreePDK45 45nm library for information length k = 16, 32 and 64 bits, and burst sizes b = 3, 4, 5, 6 and 7 bits. For the general burst error correcting Hamming codes, the codes in [17] were used to construct the parity check matrix for difference burst sizes. But [17] doesn't explicitly define a decoding procedure and simply mentions the decoding procedure to be the same as a Hamming Code. Thus, the syndrome matching based decoding from [6] was extended to the appropriate burst sizes for the constructed parity check matrix derived from [17]. The proposed codes and the general burst error correcting Hamming codes were implemented using Dataflow model in Verilog and errors were injected to ensure that all errors within the burst size was corrected. Exhaustive testing was done for all different error patterns within the burst size and for various locations of the burst errors. Table II shows the comparison of redundancy, decoder

Table II: Comparison of redundancy, decoder latency, decoder area and decoder cell usage between traditional Hamming code and Proposed Codes.

#Data bits (k)	Burst error size (*b*-bits)	Burst error correcting Hamming Codes				Proposed Codes			
		#check bits (r)	*Latency (ns)*	*#cells*	*Area (μm²)*	*#check bits (r)*	*Latency (ns)*	*#cells*	*Area (μm²)*
16	3	8	0.89	302	807	8	0.79	225	892
	4	9	1	531	1327	9	0.93	252	977
	5	11	1.31	1015	2396	12	0.9	269	963
	6	13	1.33	1559	3570	13	1.23	339	1162
	7	15	1.5	2795	6360	15	1.16	276	921
32	3	8	1.11	529	1480	9	1.08	450	1711
	4	10	1.29	1108	2759	10	1.15	506	2020
	5	12	1.59	2115	4983	12	1.29	674	2708
	6	14	1.9	4354	9915	14	1.4	727	2965
	7	15	2.39	7753	17482	16	1.27	650	2493
64	3	9	1.47	1056	2967	10	1.18	858	3150
	4	11	1.89	2032	5171	11	1.22	1016	3657
	5	13	1.8	4102	9696	13	1.4	1270	4774
	6	14	2.51	8952	20296	14	1.58	1724	7022
	7	16	2.52	15958	36124	16	1.77	1748	7495

area, number of cells in decoder and decoder latency, between the proposed codes and the general burst error correcting Hamming codes, for different information lengths and different burst error sizes. The number of information bits in a codeword is given by k. The burst size b refers to the maximum number of bits in a single burst that the code can correct. The redundancy is given by the total number of check-bits (r) required to correct a single burst error for the given number of information bits. The decoder latency is the longest timing path between the codeword and the decoded message bits.

4.1 Redundancy

Table II shows the comparison of redundancy for $k = 16$, 32 and 64 bits for various burst error sizes $b = 3$, 4, 5, 6 and 7 bits. The redundancy column shows the number of check bits required to correct the b-bit burst error for different information lengths k. It can be seen that the redundancy in all the cases is either the same or very close to the redundancy of the general burst error correcting Hamming codes. Thus, the proposed codes add negligible amount of redundancy compared to the general burst error correcting Hamming codes.

4.1 Hardware Complexity

Table II shows the comparison of decoder latency, number of cells as well as decoder area for $k = 16$, 32 and 64 bits for various burst error sizes $b = 3$, 4, 5, 6 and 7 bits. It can be seen that the decoder area for general burst error correcting Hamming codes increases almost exponentially with the increase in burst size. This in turn affects the decoder latency as well since the gate depth also increases with the increase in burst size. The decoder area for the proposed codes increases almost linearly with an increase in burst size as shown in Figure 7, which plots the decoder area for both the general burst error correcting Hamming codes and the proposed codes for different information lengths k and different burst error sizes b. The decoder area is much less for the proposed codes compared to the general burst error correcting Hamming codes for higher burst sizes. This also leads to a slower increase in decoder latency compared to the general burst error correcting Hamming codes. Figure 8 plots the decoder latency for the general burst error correcting Hamming codes and the proposed codes for different information lengths k and different burst error sizes b. Thus, the decoder latency is also lower for higher burst sizes compared to the general burst error correcting Hamming codes. It is also seen that in the cases of $k = 16$ and 32, the decoder complexity and the decoder latency for burst size $b = 7$ is lower compared to burst size $b = 5$, 6. This is because the H-matrix for the proposed codes is constructed using a greedy algorithm, that selects the lowest Hamming weight column that satisfies the conditions described in Sec. 3. This inadvertently creates a very sparse H-matrix, i.e. it has lesser total number of 1s, in some cases compared to other cases. The constructed H-matrix from our algorithm is sparser for burst size $b = 7$ compared to the H-matrix of burst size $b = 5$, 6, which in turn reduces the decoder complexity for burst size $b = 7$.

5 CONCLUSION

This paper proposes a new burst error correcting code by modifying the parity check matrix of a general burst error correcting Hamming code along with its decoding procedure. The proposed codes achieve significant reduction in decoder area as well as a non-negligible reduction in the decoder latency for similar amount of

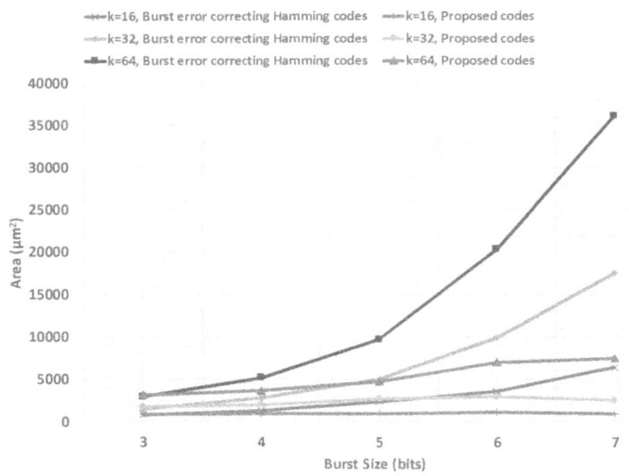

Figure 7: Comparison of decoder area for different information lengths k and different burst sizes b.

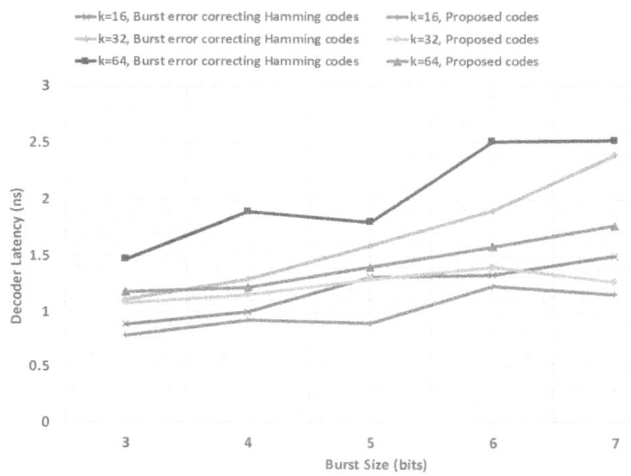

Figure 8: Comparison of decoder latency for different information lengths k and different burst sizes b.

redundancy compared to a general burst error correcting Hamming Code. Also, the proposed codes can be used in tandem with other burst error correction optimization methods to achieve better decoder latency as well as better decoder complexity. Thus, the proposed codes are highly suitable for correcting MBUs in SRAMs specifically for lower technology nodes where the burst size from a single particle strike is expected to increase.

ACKNOWLEDGMENTS

This research was supported in part by the National Science Foundation under Grant No. CCF-1617665.

REFERENCES

[1] L. S. Adalid, P. Reviriego, P. Gil, S. Pontarelli and J. A. Maestro, "MCU Tolerance in SRAMs Through Low-Redundancy Triple Adjacent Error Correction," in *IEEE Transactions on Very Large Scale Integration (VLSI) Systems*, vol. 23, no. 10, pp. 2332-2336, Oct. 2015.

[2] C. Argyrides, D. Pradhan and T. Kocak, "Matrix codes for reliable and cost efficient memory chips," in *IEEE Transactions on Very Large Scale Integration (VLSI) Systems*, vol. 19, no. 3, pp. 420-428, Mar. 2011.

[3] S. Baeg, S. Wen and R. Wong, "SRAM Interleaving Distance Selection with a Soft Error Failure Model," in *IEEE Transactions on Nuclear Science*, vol. 56, no. 4, pp. 2111-2118, Aug. 2009.

[4] R. Baumann, "Soft errors in advanced computer systems," in *IEEE Design & Test of Computers*, vol. 22, no. 3, pp. 258-266, May-Jun. 2005.

[5] H. O. Burton, "Some asymptotically optimal burst-correction codes and their relation to single-error-correcting reed-solom codes," in *IEEE Transactions on Information Theory*, vol. 17, no. 1, pp. 92–95, Jan. 1971.

[6] A. Dutta and N.A. Touba "Multiple Bit Upset Tolerant Memory Using a Selective Cycle Avoidance Based SEC-DED-DAEC Code," in *Proc. of IEEE VLSI Test Symposium*, pp. 349-354, 2007.

[7] R. Datta and N.A. Touba, "Generating Burst-Error Correcting Codes from Orthogonal Latin Square Codes - A Graph Theoretic Approach," in *Proc. of IEEE Symposium on Defect and Fault Tolerance*, pp. 367-373, 2011.

[8] E. Ibe, H. Taniguchi, Y. Yahagi, K. Shimbo and T. Toba, "Impact of scaling on neutron-induced soft error in SRAMs from a 250 mm to a 22 nm design rule," in *IEEE Transactions on Electron Devices*, vol. 57, no. 7, pp. 1527-1538, Jul. 2010

[9] J. Kim, N. Hardavellas, K. Mai, B. Falsafi and J. Hoe, "Multi-bit error tolerant caches using two-dimensional error coding," in *Annual IEEE/ACM International Symposium on Microarchitecture (MICRO)*, pp. 197–209, 2007.

[10] K. Namba, S. Pontarelli, M. Ottavi and F. Lombardi, "A Single-Bit and Double-Adjacent Error Correcting Parallel Decoder for Multiple-Bit Error Correcting BCH Codes," in *IEEE Transactions on Device and Materials Reliability*, vol. 14, no. 2, pp. 664-671, Jun. 2014.

[11] R. Naseer and J. Draper, "Parallel double error correcting code design to mitigate multi-bit upsets in SRAMs," in *Proc. of Eurpoean Solid-State Circuits Conference (ESSCIRC)*, pp. 222-225, 2008.

[12] A. Neale and M. Sachdev, "A new SEC-DED error correction code subclass for adjacent MBU tolerance in embedded memory," in *IEEE Transactions on Device and Materials Reliability*, vol. 13, no. 1, pp. 223–230, Mar. 2013.

[13] D. Radaelli, H. Puchner, S. Wong and S. Daniel, "Investigation of multi-bit upsets in a 150 nm technology SRAM device," in *IEEE Transactions on Nuclear Science*, vol. 52, no. 6, pp. 2433-2437, Dec. 2005.

[14] P. Reviriego, M. Flanagan, S.-F. Liu and J. Maestro, "Multiple cell upset correction in memories using difference set codes," in *IEEE Transactions on Circuits and Systems-I: Regular Papers*, vol. 59, no. 11, pp. 2592–2599, Nov. 2012.

[15] P. Reviriego, S. Liu, J.A. Maestro, S. Lee, N.A. Touba and R. Datta, "Implementing Triple Adjacent Error Correction in Double Error Correction Orthogonal Latin Square Codes," in *Proc. of IEEE Symposium on Defect and Fault Tolerance*, pp. 167-171, 2013.

[16] P. Reviriego, S. Pontarelli, A. Evans and J. A. Maestro, "A Class of SEC-DED-DAEC Codes Derived from Orthogonal Latin Square Codes", in *IEEE Transactions on Very Large Scale Integration (VLSI) Systems*, vol. 23, no. 5, pp. 968-972, May 2015.

[17] S. Shamshiri and K. T. Cheng, "Error-locality-aware linear coding to correct multi-bit upsets in SRAMs," in *Proc. of IEEE International Test Conference (ITC)*, Paper 7.1, 2010.

Loss is Gain: Shortening Data for Lifetime Improvement on Low-Cost ECC Enabled Consumer-Level Flash Memory

Yejia Di*, Liang Shi*, Congming Gao*, Qiao Li‡, Kaijie Wu† and Chun Jason Xue‡*

*College of Computer Science, Chongqing University †Tandon School of Engineering, New York University

‡Department of Computer Science, City University of Hong Kong

ABSTRACT

Reliability has been a challenge in the development of NAND flash memory, due to its technology size scaling and bit density improvement. To ensure the data integrity, error correction codes (ECC) with high error correction capability have been suggested. However, much higher costs will be introduced which cannot be supported for cost-limited consumer-level flash memory. Thus, low-cost ECCs are usually applied. In this work, a reliability improvement scheme is proposed for low-cost ECC enabled consumer-level flash memory. The scheme is motivated by the finding that low-cost ECC is able to protect shortened encoded data with improved reliability. This is because that the less the encoded data are, the less the errors will be occurred. With this motivation, a design is proposed to construct the shortened data case for a low-cost ECC when it cannot be able to provide the reliability requirement. Second, two relaxation approaches are proposed to relax the space reduction as it has bad effects on flash memory. A model guided evaluation is finally presented, and the results show that the lifetime can be significantly improved with little space reduction.

ACM Reference Format:

Yejia Di*, Liang Shi*, Congming Gao*, Qiao Li‡, Kaijie Wu† and Chun Jason Xue‡. 2018. Loss is Gain: Shortening Data for Lifetime Improvement on Low-Cost ECC Enabled Consumer-Level Flash Memory. In *GLSVLSI '18: 2018 Great Lakes Symposium on VLSI, May 23–25, 2018, Chicago, IL, USA.* ACM, 6 pages. https://doi.org/10.1145/3194554.3194571

1 INTRODUCTION

During the last decades, NAND flash memory has been widely deployed as the storage devices, due to many advantages, such as non-volatility, high access performance, power efficiency and so on. For further development, the cost of flash memory is reduced by density improvement and technology scaling, even being staked as 3D flash memory [10]. However, the reliability becomes decreasing, where flash memory is easier to get errors. Thus, ECCs with high error correction capability are recommended for data integrity, such as low density parity codes (LDPC) [23]. However, higher costs will be introduced, including the large implementation areas, high energy consumption and long decoding latencies [19]. Thus, high capability ECCs are not applicable for consumer-level flash memory, which usually has cost limitations. In this paper, we focus on the reliability improvement for flash memory devices equipped with low-cost ECCs.

The reliability issue is due to the physical characteristics of flash memory. Flash memory is possibility to get errors for several reasons, such as program/erase (P/E) cycling [1], retention loss [14][3], program disturb [2], and cell-to-cell interference [1]. A series of methods are proposed to improve the reliability which can be classified into two groups. The first group is to use signal processing schemes, such as finding the optimal reference voltages [1], using a slow programming voltage [22][19], and so on. However, these works need to redesign the chip to support new commands. Another group is to use refresh operations when the storage time of the data is approaching the supported retention time of flash blocks [1]. However, the refresh operations need to be conducted online, which cannot be guaranteed in consumer-level flash memory all the time.

In this paper, a data shortened scheme is proposed to improve the reliability of flash memory equipped with low-cost ECCs. The proposed scheme is motivated by the finding that if ECC only needs to protect part of the ECC unit, the probability of correcting errors successfully is increased, representing reliability is improved. This is because that the number of errors is reduced with shortening protected data. In detail, with 50% of data shortened, the reliability can be improved by 100%. Based on the motivation, the basic idea of the data shortened scheme is to make a tradeoff between storage space and reliability improvement. In this case, the low-cost ECC is enabled with shortened data to continuously protect data integrity. However, there are several challenges for the basic idea: First, the size of shortened part is unknown to the designer. Because the reliability of flash memory is varied during the lifetime, the size of shortened part should be determined correspondingly. Second, the storage space is reduced with the increases of shortened part. If the space is significantly reduced, the lifetime and performance can be impacted. In order to solve above issues, the shortened scheme is designed as follows: First, a mapping unit shorten design is proposed to realize the data shortened case. Basically, the mapping unit of state-of-the-art flash memory is generally much smaller than the flash page size. In this case, once the reliability cannot be supported with the low-cost ECC, one more mapping unit is shortened for a flash page. Second, two space relaxation approaches are proposed. The first one is to exploit the process variation (PV) of flash memory to only shorten the weak blocks. The second one is to exploit

*Corresponding author: Liang Shi. Email: shi.liang.hk@gmail.com.

GLSVLSI '18, May 23–25, 2018, Chicago, IL, USA

ACM ISBN 978-1-4503-5724-1/18/05...$15.00

https://doi.org/10.1145/3194554.3194571

the different reliability characteristics of the multiple bits in multiple level cell (MLC) flash memory. With the significantly increased volume of flash memory devices, we believe that using small space to trade for lifetime improvement is very attractive to the consumer level flash devices. A model guided evaluation is performed, and the results show that the proposed scheme can improve the lifetime significantly with little space reduction. The paper has following contributions:

- Presented the data shortened opportunity of low-cost ECC on reliability improvement;
- Presented a design to enable a low-cost ECC on flash memory by shortening data;
- Proposed two methods to relax the storage space reduction;
- Presented model-guided evaluations. Experimental results show that the proposed approach is able to achieve expected lifetime improvement with tolerable space overhead.

The following of the work is organized as follows: In Section 2, the background and related work are discussed. In Section 3, the data shorten motivation is presented. In Section 4, the mapping unit shortened design is proposed. In Section 5, the evaluations on lifetime, storage space are presented. Finally, the work is concluded in Section 6.

2 BACKGROUND AND RELATED WORK

2.1 Background

There are three operations in flash memory, write, read and erase. The write and read unit of flash memory is a flash page, while the erase unit is a flash block, where a flash block consists of hundred times of flash pages. Due to the asymmetric operation units, out-of-place updates by invalidating the original data and writing updated data to new pages are applied. Besides, a mapping table is used for recording data locations. There are three mapping types: block-level mapping, page-level mapping, and finer-grained mapping, where logical pages are mapped to arbitrary physical pages, any pages, and several finer-grained units. A trend for the future flash memory is the large page size which will be employed to reduce the circuit complexity and improve the I/O bandwidth [10]. For large page size flash memory, finer-grained mapping is recommended, where the mapping unit is smaller than the page size, such as 4KB mapping unit for 32KB page [10].

Flash memory is written by charging electronics to the flash cells, where 2^n voltage states are defined for n bit per cell flash memory, such as 4 states for 2 bits per cell called MLC flash memory as shown in Figure 1. These two bits belongs to different pages, the least significant bit (LSB) page and the most significant bit (MSB) page. During programming, LSB page is first programmed and then is the MSB page for reliability concern. The voltage states are distinct with noise margins for distinguished data read. However, margins have possibilities to be decreased, as there are many adverse effects, including P/E cycling [1], retention loss [1][14][3], program disturb [2], cell-to-cell interference [1], and so on. If voltage is affected from one state to another, data will be read out incorrectly. The possibility of data getting errors is called raw bit error rate (RBER), which is mainly due to the adjacent state changes [12]. As the red arrows shown in Figure 1, we can find that MSB page has higher possibility to get errors than that of LSB page. With the development of multiple bits per cell and wearing of flash memory, RBER will be increased. For data integrity, error correction codes (ECCs) are equipped in flash controller to correct errors, where data are encoded as writing and decoded as reading. Usually, the page size is times of ECC-unit sizes [19]. However, the error correction capability of ECC is limited. In this case, flash memory can only be used reliably with limited lifetime that is with limited P/E cycles.

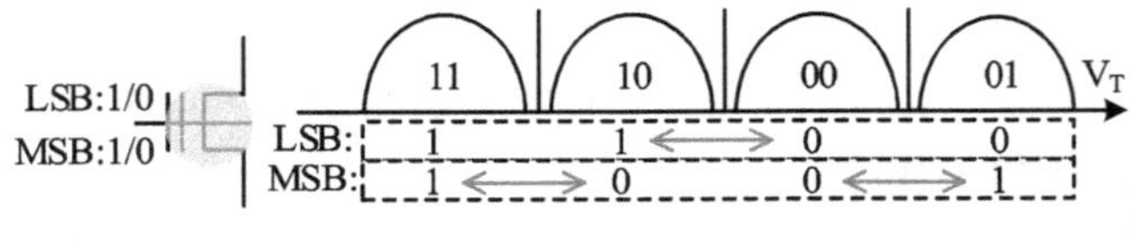

Figure 1: Traditional MLC data states, where the red arrows represent the high-probability error cases with state changes.

2.2 Related Work

Due to the degraded reliability of flash memory, most of recent works proposed to use strong ECC [23] or multiple ECCs [20] to provide higher error correction capability. However, strong ECC always comes with high costs to the storage systems [19]. In order to solve the reliability issue, many works also proposed to reduce the adverse effects with low-cost ECC for flash memory. Cai *et al.* [1] built a precise model to eliminate the cell-to-cell interference effects. Zhang *et al.* [22] proposed to use slow write to form a larger noise margin. Cai *et al.* [1] proposed to relax retention time by refreshing to reduce the charge loss effects. However, these works either need to redesign the flash chips for new commands, or need to keep system online for refreshing, which are not applicable for consumer-level flash memory. In this work, a method is proposed to increase the reliability of flash memory taking advantage of the characteristic of ECC.

On the other hand, flash memory can tolerate some space reduction for lifetime improvement. In tradition, bad block management (BBM) mechanism is applied for flash memory allowing some bad blocks, where occurred errors cannot be corrected by ECC [17]. Usually, the ratio of bad block is 5%. Thus, the BBM mechanism can only prolong lifetime in a little degree. And then, a set of finer-grained space reduction methods are proposed to prolong the lifetime. For example, previous works found that the wearing of flash pages are different [8][17]. Thus, the flash page can be used as the bad unit. Then, the space reduction speed is reduced. Besides, other works also proposed to revive to-be bad pages to further improve lifetime. There is a theory that if only one bit is stored in the multiple bits cell, the reliability can be improvement. Thus, several works proposed to only store one bit per cell when the reliability cannot be supported by ECC [7][21]. Furthermore, Lin *et al.* [11] proposed to reuse two bad pages as one normal page. In this work, a graceful space reduction method is proposed for lifetime improvement. More importantly, a low-cost ECC is used.

As the algebra operation principle of BCH codes, the encoded data length can be shorter than the designed length, called shortened BCH codes [4]. This is because the shortened contents can be regarded as all '0's in the algebra operation. And the shortened BCH codes can provide better reliability [4]. The proposed work is enlightened but different from the shortened BCH codes, as the data alignment of the ECC unit must be obeyed.

3 DATA SHORTENED MOTIVATION

In this section, the motivation on the proposed scheme is presented. The motivation is on the finding that if the encoded data of ECC unit is shortened, the error correction probability will be increased. Considering ECC alignment of flash page, data shortened case is shown in Figure 2. Figure 2(a) shows the traditional ECC structure with ECC-unit-size contents. While Figure 2(b) shows the shortened case, where part of ECC-unit-size contents are encoded by ECC called real encoded data, and the remaining space with all '1's are called padding. With the case of Figure 2(b), the size of contents requiring protection by ECC becomes shorter, so that the number of errors will be reduced.

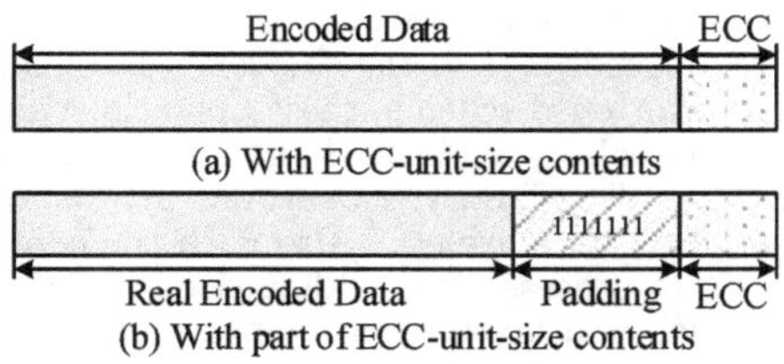

Figure 2: The ECC structures with different-size encoded data.

Here, the reliability benefit is formulated as follows, where available raw bit error rate (RBER) is regarded as the reliability of flash memory, as it represents the maximum tolerated probability to get errors of raw data. The higher the available RBER is, the longer the lifetime will be achieved [1]. For low-cost BCH *(n,k,t)*, where the encoded data length is *k*, the generated codedata length is *n*, and it can correct *t* errors. Then the probability of *m* errors occurred is:

$$pr(m,n,RBER) = \binom{n}{m} \cdot RBER^m \cdot (1 - RBER)^{n-m} \quad (1)$$

If *m* is lower than *t*, errors can be corrected by ECC and the UBER will be 0. Otherwise, *m* is larger than *t*, and there are uncorrectable errors. Thus, the uncorrectable bit error rate (UBER) has the following relationship with RBER.

$$UBER = \frac{\sum_{m=t+1}^{n} m * pr(m,n,RBER)}{n} \quad (2)$$

With the Formula, Figure 3 presents the quantified results of the relationship of BCH(17264, 16400, 57). As shown in the figure, the larger the RBER is, the larger the UBER is. However, in general, the UBER should be guaranteed to be lower than a threshold for reliability, e.g. 10^{-15}.

With part of ECC-unit-size contents, the reliability can be improved with larger available RBER. Assume that the padding length is *l*. If the errors in prior *(k-l)*-length encoded data are corrected, the data integrity can be protected by ECC. Thus, the relationship between RBER and UBER becomes:

$$UBER = \frac{\sum_{m=t+1}^{n-l} m * pr(m,n-l,RBER)}{n} \quad (3)$$

Here, we define shortened percentage as the fraction between padding length and the traditional encoded data length. And the shortened percentages of the encoding data are measured by varying from 0% to 50%. Figure 3 shows the reliability benefits with part of ECC-unit-size contents, where x-axis is the RBER and y-axis is the UBER. As shown in the figure, with the increasing of shortened percentages, the available RBER is increased. When the shortened percentage is 10%, the available RBER is increased by 12%. While with 50%

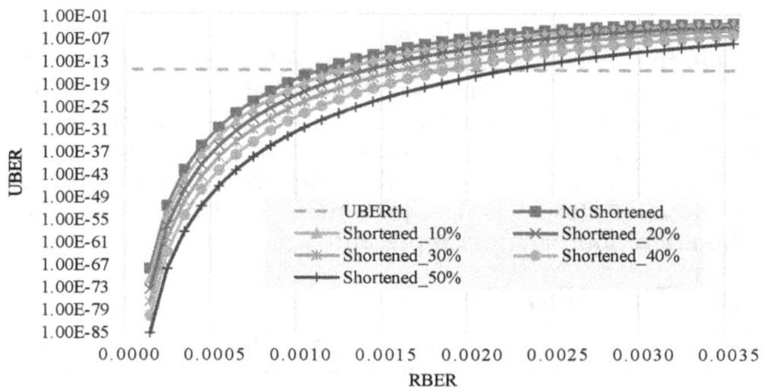

Figure 3: With increased shortened percentage, larger RBER can be tolerated. Where UBERth represents the UBER threshold.

shortened percentage, the available RBER can be improved by 100%. In this work, the opportunity motivates us to improve the reliability by shortening data.

4 MAPPING UNIT SHORTENED DESIGN

With the data shortened motivation, the reliability can be improvement by shortening data for each ECC unit, where a flash page basically contains multiple of ECC units. In the following, we propose to deploy the data shortened scheme to a 4KB-mapping unit flash memory device with a large page size, such as 32KB. This configuration is a popular setting for state-of-the-art flash device in smartphones and tablets, especially for 3D NAND flash. This is because that large page size is employed to reduce the circuit complexity and improve the I/O bandwidth [10] and finer-grained mapping (e.g. 4KB-mapping) is applied as the request size is usually smaller than the page size [10][9]. Note that the data shortened scheme can also be easily extended to page and block mapping devices without mapping issue due to the smaller request sizes [10][9], and we will discuss them in our future work.

4.1 Overview

In the mapping unit shortened design, once the ECC cannot support the reliability, one or more mapping units are shortened with receiving data. And the data shortened scheme is applied by dividing the received data to each ECC unit. Figure 4 shows an example of the overall structure of the proposed design. In the above half of the figure, assume there are four ECC units for one flash page. L_1 unit data are received for storage and L_2 units are shortened. In the bottom half of the figure, the data are evenly distributed to each ECC unit as encoded data. The paddings are filled with '1's as there are no data. Actually, the cells for paddings will be worn less than other cells [9], and the benefits will be exploited in the future work.

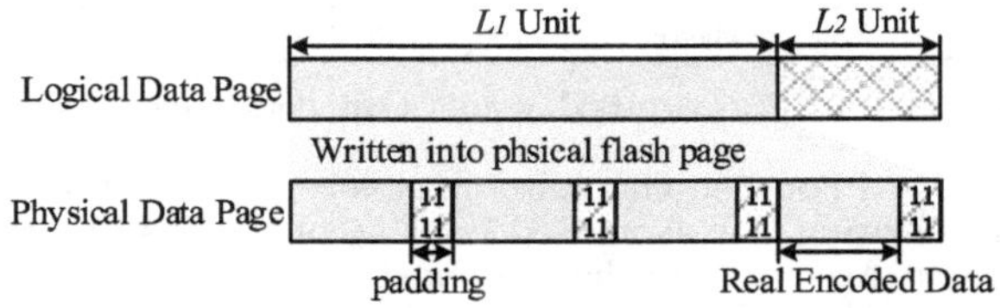

Figure 4: The overview of the mapping unit shortened design.

However, there are challenges on the design. The first one is the shortened data size, where the reliability of flash blocks get worse with the wearing, so that the shortened data size should be determined reliably. The second one is the space reduction, which is increased with the shortened data size, bringing bad effects on flash memory. In the following, the detailed design is first presented. And then, two space relaxation approaches are presented.

4.2 Detailed Design

The basic idea is to gradually shorten data in the granularity of mapping-unit for lifetime improvement. Shortened unit ratio decides the padding ratio, and then introduces related reliability improvement. The larger the shortened unit ratio is, the larger the reliability improvement will be. Here, we call flash page without data shortened is level 0, and with one mapping unit shortened is level 1, and so on. There are totally $\frac{S_{page}}{S_{mapping}}$ levels, and the last level is the flash page with only one mapping-unit received data, where the page size is S_{page}, and the mapping unit size is $S_{mapping}$. For 4KB-mapping with 32KB page size, there are totally 8 levels. In the following, the shortened level is represented as L_2, and the shortened level determination and related write and read processes are presented.

Shortened Level Determination: Initially, flash page is reliable without shortened data. Once the flash page becomes unreliable, the next level is applied to the flash page, and so on. The shortened unit level is determined when reading. During reading, pages in block are read out with acknowledging the error number. If all the error number of the block is less than a threshold, denoted as E_{th}, the current shortened unit level can be used reliability. Otherwise, the shortened unit should be increased to the next level for reliability improvement. If the current shortened level is $\frac{S_{page}}{S_{mapping}} - 1$, the block is regarded as bad. New shortened level will be used for the next round of usage for flash blocks. Each block only needs to maintain one shortened level, which is costless. Note, E_{th} is selected with a smaller number than error correction capability of ECC for conservation.

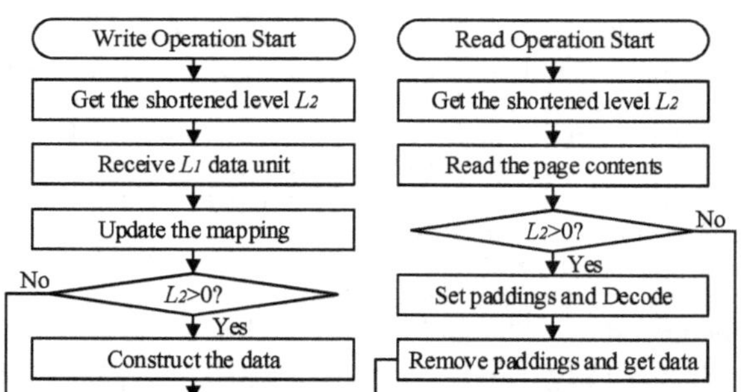

Figure 5: The related write and read processes.

Write Process: The write process is shown in Figure 5. When writing, the shortened level L_2 of the flash block is first got. According to the shortened level, L_1 unit data are received. Then, the mapping table is updated, where one-to-one mapping is used, and the prior L_1 mapping units are mapped with storing these data. Next, data will be encoded and written into flash pages. If the shortened level is 0, that is without data shortened, the data can be directly encoded and then written into flash pages. Otherwise, the data should be constructed first as shown in Figure 4. For constructing, the L_1 unit data are evenly divided to be stored into each ECC unit as real encoded data. For example, when page size is 32KB, mapping unit size is 4KB, ECC unit size is 1KB, and shortened level is 2, the 6 4KB-unit data will be divided, and each 0.75KB to be stored in each ECC unit.

Read Process: For finer-grained mapping flash, the request data is in the finer-grained unit. The read process is shown in Figure 5. When reading, the shortened level L_2 is got first. Second, the whole page data are read out. Then, the decoding and getting data operations are performed according to the shortened level. If the shortened level is 0, that is without data shortened scheme, these operations are directly performed. Otherwise, paddings will be set with all '1's before decoding. After decoding, the paddings are removed, and then the required data are got. Also with the configuration example in write process, the padding size is 0.25KB in each ECC unit which will be set and removed for decoding and getting data.

Expect the write and read operations, there are also operations requiring write or read operations, such as update, garbage collection, wear leveling and so on. For these operations, all data are written and read with related write and read processes.

4.3 Space Relaxation

Data shortened scheme will introduce space reduction for lifetime improvement, introducing user space concern. The user space can be maintained taking advantage of the invisible space, over-provision space (OPS). However, the OPS is usually configured with 15%~25% of SSD capacity, which is also limited. On the other hand, the use frequency of OPS will become larger, including the introduced update number and garbage collection frequency [6]. Larger use frequency of OPS would affect the performance, though the dominate access pattern of the consumer-level devices is sequential access. In this work, besides the gradual shortened method, two physical characteristics of flash memory are exploited to further relax the space reduction: (1) the block endurance variation, (2) the differential reliability characteristics of the multiple bits in a cell.

4.3.1 Block Endurance Variation Awareness. With the technology scaling and density improvement, process variation (PV) has been a prominent characteristic of flash memory, especially for consumer-level devices. PV indicates that flash blocks have different endurance and larger than the industry data [13][18]. In this work, the variation can be exploited for space relaxation, where only weak blocks need to be shortened. To exploit PV, many measurements can be metrics, such as maximum P/E cycles [15][13], bit error rates (BER) [13][18][8], programming speed [16], and so on[18]. In this work, the maximum error criteria like RBER can work to exploit the reliability variations of flash blocks.

4.3.2 Differential Reliability of LSB and MSB. Multiple bits per cell flash memory has been dominant devices. And the differential reliability characteristics of the multiple bits is exploited here to further relax space reduction. Here, MLC flash memory is discussed, the method can be easily extended to more bits per cell flash memory, such as triple level cell (TLC). For MLC, the data shortened scheme is proposed to be only applied on MSB page. The relaxation approach is based on two observations. First, MSB pages are generally weaker than LSB page as shown in Figure 1. MSB page has larger possibilities to get errors than that of LSB page by almost 2 times [1]. Second, if MSB page is shortened, the reliability of the corresponding part of LSB page is also improved. As shown in Figure 6, when padding in MSB page are set to all '1's, the stored states in LSB page become only '11' and '01', two states. In that case, the possibility of getting errors is decreased almost to 0 for the corresponding contents in LSB page.

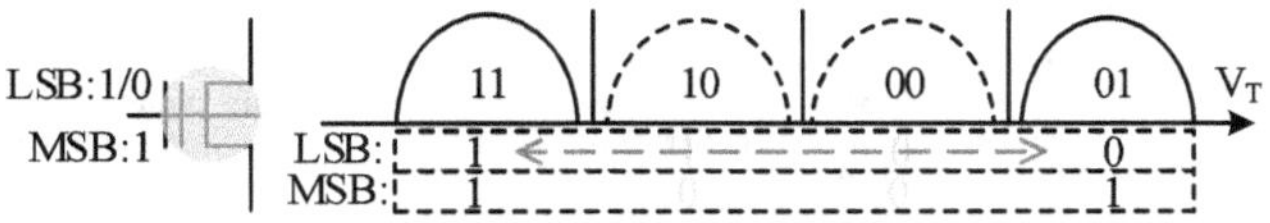

Figure 6: LSB data states with shortening MSB.

5 EXPERIMENT AND RESULTS

5.1 Experiment Setup

A 16GB flash chip is configured as the default storage device. Table 1 presents the parameters. For 32KB page size, 4KB is used as the mapping unit. Thus, there will be 8 shortened levels, and 4KB is the shortened data unit for each level. In flash controller, the low-cost ECC, BCH(17264,16400,57), will be applied.

Parameter	Value
Page/Block Size	32KB/2MB
Plane/Die Size	4GB/8GB
Total Chip Capacity	16GB

Table 1: The parameters for the evaluated consumer-level flash device.

5.1.1 *Reliability Model.*

In the evaluation, RBER is regarded as the reliability metric. The higher the available RBER is, the more reliable the flash memory is. To quantify the RBER, a reliability model is constructed based on error characteristics of flash memory.

There are two dominant factors on RBER, the wearing (w) and retention time (d), both are proportional to RBER. Through analyzing the measured error characteristics of real flash memory, we find that RBER is exponentially increased with w, and almost linearly increased with d. Furthermore, the RBER can be formulated as follows [14].

$$RBER(w,d) = d_r(w) \cdot d \tag{4}$$

Where d is assumed to be 10 years, and $d_r(w)$ was the deterioration rate, which can be represented as follows, where c and k both are constants.

$$d_r(w) = c \cdot w^k \tag{5}$$

For the wearing of blocks, P/E cycles and its endurance under PV are the main effects. Considering PV, the maximum P/E cycles vary among blocks. Assume that blocks are worn linearly, wearing can be represented as follows, where PE represents its P/E cycles and WD represents the wearing degree for each P/E cycle.

$$w = PE * WD \tag{6}$$

Combining the Formulas from 4 to 6, the reliability model is constructed.

In the evaluation, the default PV distribution on flash memory is assumed as normal distribution, N(8524,1318^2), for the maximum P/E cycles, while the factory index is just 3000 [18]. For each flash block, the wearing degree is the fraction between 3000 and the real maximum P/E cycles.

Four platforms are evaluated here, that is DS_Original, DS_PV, DS_MSB, and DS_ALL. DS_Original represents the gradual mapping unit shortened design. DS_PV takes the block endurance variations into consideration. DS_MSB only applies the data shorten scheme for the MSB page. And DS_ALL takes all relaxation approaches into consideration.

5.2 Experiment Results

In this subsection, the lifetime improvement under various shortened percentages is first presented. With the improvement of lifetime, the data amount under each space reduction is presented. At last, the performance effects are discussed.

Table 2 shows the wearing extension with data shortened scheme. As shown in the table, the wearing of flash can be extended with increasing shortened percentages. Compared with the baseline of 0%, when the mapping unit is shortened one by one, with shortened percentages of 12.5%, 25%, 37.5%, 50%, 62.5%, 75%, 87.5%, the tolerated wearing can be improved by 7.8%, 18.2%, 31.5%, 49.6%, 77.2%, 125%, 238%. As wearing is increased with P/E cycles, improved tolerated wearing means improved lifetime.

Shortened Percentages	0%	12.5%	25%	37.5%
Tolerated wearing (w)	3000	3235	3545	3944
Shortened Percentages	50%	62.5%	75%	87.5%
Tolerated wearing (w)	4488	5317	6749	10142

Table 2: The wearing benefits under various shortened percentages.

With PV, the wearing degrees (WD) of flash blocks are different, so the block can achieve different P/E cycles, based on Formula 6. While the larger the space reduction is, the smaller the available space for data will be. To evaluate lifetime improvement, we simulate to erase blocks one-cycle-by-one and compute the corresponding written data amounts and space reductions. The written data amount represents the amount of data can be written to the flash memory, which is a popular metric in representing the lifetime. During the usage of flash memory, traditional wear leveling scheme is assumed to be applied. Here, without considering PV, the wearing ratio is regarded as 1. Otherwise, the real wearing ratio is taken into consideration considering PV. Figure 7 shows the normalized amount of written data under different space reduction ratios. From the results, several observations can be concluded: First, with the increases of space reduction ratios, the amount of data is significantly increased. Second, to achieve an increased written data amount, the proposed space relaxation approaches can relax the space reduction. In detail, to achieve 10% data amount increases, the DS_Original platform requires 23% space reduction, while the DS_PV requires only 4%, DS_MSB requires 11%, and DS_ALL only requires 2%. Besides, with considering PV, the space reduction ratio becomes smoothing. For DS_ALL platform, the amount of written data can be increased by 34% with only 12% space reduction.

Besides, we also make an evaluation on the performance effects. For evaluation, a widely used simulator, SSDsim [5], is used. The SSDsim is configured with traditional operation latencies shown in [17], and 15% OPS. We collected a typical

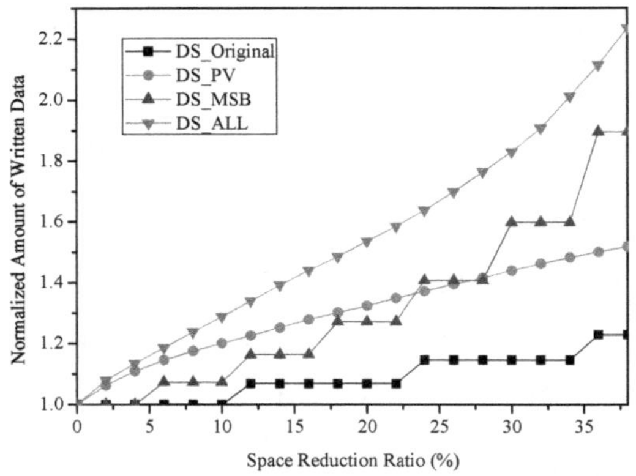

Figure 7: The normalized amount of written data under different space reduction ratios.

workload for consumer-level device. The workload is to copy a movie from the computer to a Sandisk USB, which is collected by Diskmon. Three mapping schemes are evaluated, including 4KB-mapping, page-mapping and block-mapping. For 4KB-mapping, the mapping is first deployed and then the 4KB-mapping unit shortened design is applied in the simulator. For page-mapping, the shortened design is implemented with receiving part of page-size data. Similarly for block-mapping, the mapping is deployed with only receiving part of block-size data. With given shortened percentage, the receiving data size can be got. As shown in Figure 8, with 12.5% shortened percentage, the write performance is slightly affected, by only 6% for page/block-mapping and 9% for 4KB-mapping, which is acceptable for consumer devices. From the results, we find that the performance effects of page/block-mapping are the same. This is because that all the data size is smaller than the block size, and the effects both exist in the additional page writing. In addition, there is almost no read performance differences as there are only a small amount of sequential read requests.

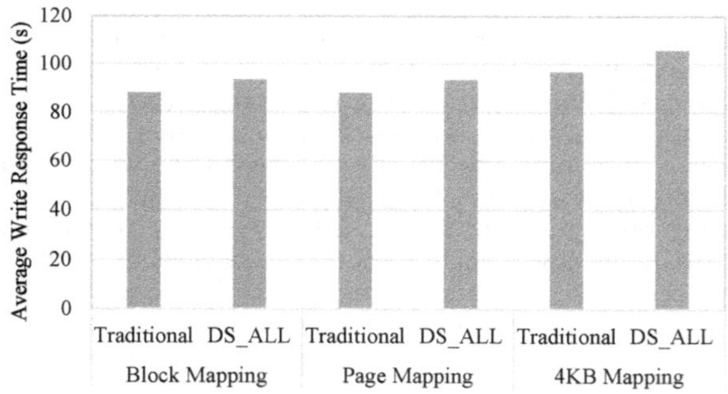

Figure 8: The performance effects.

6 CONCLUSIONS

The reliability of the low-cost enabled flash memory is a challenge. While we find that if encoded data are shortened in each ECC unit, the reliability can be significantly improved. With the motivation, a design deployed on 4KB-mapping flash is proposed to construct the motivation case for lifetime improvement. However, there are two challenges, that is the shortened data determination and space reduction. First, the design is proposed to gradually shortening 4KB-mapping unit with reliable shortened level, and the related write/read process are presented. Second, two space reduction relaxation approaches are proposed for relaxing large space reduction. At last, the experiment results show that the proposed work can improve the lifetime of flash memory significantly with negligible effects.

ACKNOWLEDGMENTS

This work is supported by the NSFC (61772092 and 61572411).

REFERENCES

[1] Yu Cai, Saugata Ghose, Erich F. Haratsch, Yixin Luo, and Onur Mutlu. 2017. Error Characterization, Mitigation, and Recovery in Flash-Memory-Based Solid-State Drives. *Proc. IEEE* 105, 9 (2017), 1666–1704.

[2] Yu-Ming Chang, Yung-Chun Li, Yuan-Hao Chang, Tei-Wei Kuo, Chih-Chang Hsieh, and Hsiang-Pang Li. 2015. On Relaxing Page Program Disturbance over 3D MLC Flash Memory *(ICCAD)*.

[3] Y. Di, L. Shi, K. Wu, and C. J. Xue. 2016. Exploiting process variation for retention induced refresh minimization on flash memory. In *DATE*. 391–396.

[4] H. Helgert and R. Stinaff. 1973. Shortened BCH codes (Corresp.). *IEEE Transactions on Information Theory* (1973).

[5] Yang Hu, Hong Jiang, Dan Feng, Lei Tian, Hao Luo, and Shuping Zhang. [n. d.]. Performance Impact and Interplay of SSD Parallelism Through Advanced Commands, Allocation Strategy and Data Granularity. In *ICS'11*.

[6] Ping Huang, Guanying Wu, Xubin He, and Weijun Xiao. 2014. An Aggressive Worn-out Flash Block Management Scheme to Alleviate SSD Performance Degradation. In *EuroSys*.

[7] Xavier Jimenez, David Novo, and Paolo Ienne. 2012. Software controlled cell bit-density to improve NAND flash lifetime. In *DAC*.

[8] Xavier Jimenez, David Novo, and Paolo Ienne. 2014. Wear unleveling: improving NAND flash lifetime by balancing page endurance.. In *FAST*.

[9] Jung Hoon Kim, Sang Hoon Kim, and Jin Soo Kim. 2015. Subpage programming for extending the lifetime of NAND flash memory. In *DATE*. 555–560.

[10] Myungsuk Kim, Jaehoon Lee, Sungjin Lee, Jisung Park, and Jihong Kim. 2017. Improving Performance and Lifetime of Large-Page NAND Storages Using Erase-Free Subpage Programming. In *DAC*. 1–6.

[11] Han-Yi Lin and Jen-Wei Hsieh. 2015. HLC: Software-based half-level-cell flash memory. In *DATE*.

[12] T. Nakamura, Y. Deguchi, and K. Takeuchi. 2017. AEP-LDPC ECC with Error Dispersion Coding for Burst Error Reduction of 2D and 3D NAND Flash Memories. In *IMW*. 1–4.

[13] Yangyang Pan, Guiqiang Dong, and Tong Zhang. 2013. Error Rate-Based Wear-Leveling for nand Flash Memory at Highly Scaled Technology Nodes. *TVLSI* 21, 7 (2013), 1350–1354.

[14] Heejin Park, Jaeho Kim, Jongmoo Choi, Donghee Lee, and Sam H. Noh. 2015. Incremental redundancy to reduce data retention errors in flash-based SSDs. In *MSST*.

[15] Roman A. Pletka and Saša Tomić. 2016. Health-Binning: Maximizing the Performance and the Endurance of Consumer-Level NAND Flash *(SYSTOR)*.

[16] L. Shi, Y. Di, M. Zhao, C.J. Xue, K. Wu, and E.H.-. Sha. 2015. Exploiting Process Variation for Write Performance Improvement on NAND Flash Memory Storage Systems. *TVLSI* PP, 99 (2015).

[17] D. Wei, L. Deng, L. Qiao, and P. Zhang. 2016. PEVA: A Page Endurance Variance Aware Strategy for the Lifetime Extension of NAND Flash. *TVLSI* (2016).

[18] Yeong-Jae Woo and Jin-Soo Kim. 2013. Diversifying wear index for MLC NAND flash memory to extend the lifetime of SSDs. In *EMSOFT*. 1–10.

[19] Guanying Wu, Xubin He, Ningde Xie, and Tong Zhang. 2013. Exploiting Workload Dynamics to Improve SSD Read Latency via Differentiated Error Correction Codes. *ToDAES* (2013).

[20] Ningde Xie, Guiqiang Dong, and Tong Zhang. 2011. Using lossless data compression in data storage systems: Not for saving space. *TC* (2011).

[21] Ming-Chang Yang, Yuan-Hao Chang, Chei-Wei Tsao, and Chung-Yu Liu. 2016. Utilization-Aware Self-Tuning Design for TLC Flash Storage Devices. *TVLSI* (2016).

[22] L. Zhang, B. Neely, D. Franklin, D. Strukov, Y. Xie, and F. T. Chong. 2016. Mellow Writes: Extending Lifetime in Resistive Memories through Selective Slow Write Backs. In *ISCA*.

[23] Kai Zhao, Wenzhe Zhao, Hongbin Sun, Tong Zhang, Xiaodong Zhang, and Nanning Zheng. 2013. LDPC-in-SSD: making advanced error correction codes work effectively in solid state drives. In *FAST*.

A Novel Fault-Tolerant Last-Level Cache to Improve reliability at Near-Threshold Voltage

Wei Liu
College of Computer Science and Technology, Wuhan University of Technology, China
Hubei Key Laboratory of Transportation Internet of Things, Wuhan, China
wliu@whut.edu.cn

Zhigang Wei
College of Computer Science and Technology, Wuhan University of Technology, China
weizhigang@whut.edu.cn

Wei Du
College of Computer Science and Technology, Wuhan University of Technology, China
Hubei Key Laboratory of Transportation Internet of Things, Wuhan, China
whutduwei@whut.edu.cn

ABSTRACT

Near-threshold voltage computing (NTC) improves power and energy efficiency of cache by scaling transistor voltage. However, in large SRAM structures, such as last-level cache (LLC), a great number of bit-cell errors will occur when supply voltage scales to near-threshold voltage. In this paper, we propose a novel fault-tolerant LLC design (NFTLLC) to deal with a high failure rate which is higher than 1% at near-threshold voltage. NFTLLC corrects the single-error and compresses multi-error in Cache entry to improves the reliability of last-level cache. To validate the efficiency of NFTLLC, we implement NFTLLC and prior works in gem5, and simulate with SPEC CPU2006. The experiment shows that compared with Concertina when bit-cell failure rate is 1.1%, the performance of NFTLLC with 4-byte subblock size improves by 6.8% and the Cache capacity increases by 20.8%. Besides, miss rate decreases more than 53%, and overhead increases by 16.8% in minimum.

Keywords

near-threshold voltage; fault-tolerant last-level cache; ECC; compression mechanism

ACM Reference Format:

Wei Liu, Zhigang Wei and Wei Du. 2018. A Novel Fault-Tolerant Last-Level Cache to Improve reliability at Near-Threshold Voltage. In *GLSVLSI '18: 2018 Great Lakes Symposium on VLSI*, May 23–25, 2018, Chicago, IL, USA. ACM, NY, NY, USA, 6 pages. https://doi.org/10.1145/3194554.3194583

1 INTRODUCTION

Over the past five decades, the number of transistors on a chip has increased exponentially in accordance with Moore's law [1]. However, the number of transistors integrated in a die has been very large, and heat removal limits at the package level have further restricted more advanced integration. So we are facing such a curious design dilemma: more gates can now fit on a die, but a growing fraction cannot actually be used due to strict power limits [2].

The most straightforward way to reduce energy dissipation is to scale supply voltage(Vdd), since the energy consumption in CMOS circuits can be reduced quadratically by lowering Vdd. Near-threshold voltage computing (NTC) [3] is a novel approach that demonstrates greater energy efficiency and provides much more flexible tradeoffs between energy and delay than the conventional sub-threshold computing circuits [4]. Although NTC is a promising energy-efficient solution to circuit design, it brings its own sets of complications. Process variation is one of key barriers faced by NTC, which will cause mismatch in device and result in functional failure in SRAM cell. High cell failure rate relevant to increased process variation in LLC will slow down the application execution, produce incorrect results, and even crash the system [2].

Existing research to improving cache reliability can be classified into two types: circuit-level and architecture-level. Circuit-level techniques improve bit cell reliability by either upsizing transistors [5] or using alternative SRAM cell designs, such as eight-transistor (8T) [6], ten-transistor(10T) [7] or Schmitt trigger-based (ST) SRAM cells [8]. These techniques can have a great improvement on reliability of LLC in NTC, while they incur significant area overhead, higher power consumption and higher access latency.

At architecture-level, the reliability of Cache is improved in many different ways. Zeshan Chishti et al. propose MS-ECC to correct multi-bit error by sacrificing half of cache ways at fine sub-cache line granularities [9]. Alameldeen et al. propose VS-ECC to design an energy-efficient cache [1], which combines SECDED and 4EC5ED to correct bit-cell errors in cache line. Hijaz et al. propose a new cache architecture by correcting the data stored in cache using ECC, and disabling the cache lines which can't be corrected by ECC [10]. Duwe et al. rearrange the logical bit to physical bit mapping to transform the uncorrectable error patterns in logical words into correctable ones [11]. Ferrerón et al. propose Concertina, a compression mechanism that compresses cache blocks in order that they can be allocated

GLSVLSI '18, May 23–25, 2018, Chicago, IL, USA

ACM 978-1-4503-5724-1/18/05...$15.00
https://doi.org/10.1145/3194554.3194583

to cache entries with faulty cells [12]. Palframan et al. present iPatch, which rely on existing microarchitectural structures and mechanisms to "patch" the faulty parts of caches [13]. Jung et al. manage data by cache coherence states and several layers of cache organization [14]. All of these techniques have a good impact on cache reliability when bit-cell failure rate is less than 0.5%. However, it is not suitable for current SRAM cell which has a higher failure rate such as 1% at near-threshold voltage.

In this paper, we present a novel fault-tolerant last-level cache (NFTLLC) based on compression mechanism. NFTLLC uses a detector to detect the null subblocks in the incoming block and compress the block into a smaller block which has no null subblocks. Then, an ECC encoder encodes the compressed block with a simple error correction code. Using a simple ECC technique to correct a cache entry with multi-bit error incurs a significant area for the extra circuits to store ECC check bits. We propose an optimized protection policy to achieve a tradeoff between performance and area overhead.

The rest of this paper is organized as follows. Section 2 presents the motivation of our work. Section 3 explains our proposed architecture in detail. Section 4 and 5 present the evaluation methodology and the results of evaluation. Finally, we conclude in section 6.

2 MOTIVATION

With the development of semiconductor technology, MOS device is becoming smaller and smaller. But when the process scale into nanometers, process variation plays a more important role on reducing device reliability. Random Dopant Fluctuation(RDF) is a main factor that changing the threshold voltage of transistors and leading to some SRAM cells weaker than other cells in the cache. Weak cells become faulty as the supply voltage is reduced, the number of which is reflected by bit-cell failure rate. Since these faulty cells are caused by permanent defects (e.g., dopant variation), they can be located using a number of built-in self test (BIST) routines [1, 4]. Some faults at low voltages are due to soft errors that cannot be detected by BIST routines. However, the fraction of such faults caused by soft errors at low voltage is minuscule [15] (by over 5 orders of magnitude at 650mV [9]).

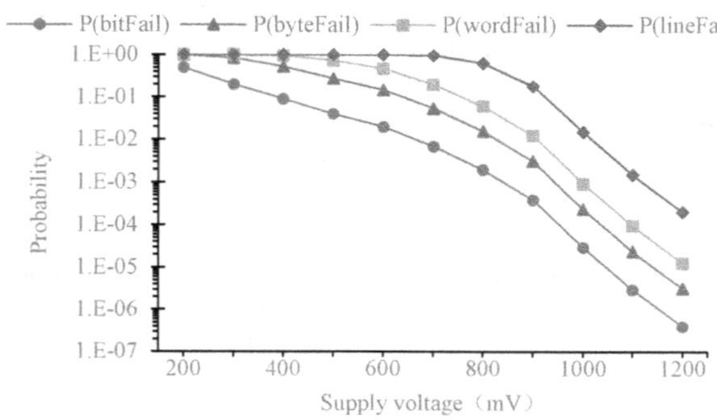

Figure 1: The probability of a single bit failure and the probabilities of a byte, 32-bit word and a line that are faulty in a cache for 65nm SRAM cells.

In Fig. 1, we show the bit failure data from [2], indicating the probability of a single 65nm SRAM bit failure ($P_{bitFail}$) across a range of voltages. We also assume that SRAM failures are random in nature [16]. So we compute the probabilities of having errors in a byte ($P_{byteFail}$), a 32-bit word ($P_{wordFail}$) and a cache line ($P_{lineFail}$) as follows:

$$P_{byteFail} = 1 - (1 - P_{bitFail})^8 \quad (1)$$

$$P_{wordFail} = 1 - \left(1 - P_{byteFail}\right)^4 \quad (2)$$

$$P_{lineFail} = 1 - (1 - P_{wordFail})^{16} \quad (3)$$

The probabilities $P_{byteFail}$, $P_{wordFail}$ and $P_{lineFail}$ are also plotted in Fig. 1. By examining Fig. 1, we observe that the probability of a block having errors increases with the decrease of supply voltage. When the supply voltage scales to 650mV, the probability of a bit failure increases to 1.1%. This failure rate means more than 99% of cache entries are faulty, which leads to functional failure in LLC.

Considering that LLC requires a large capacity and low miss rate to reduce average latency of data requests from L1 Cache, NFTLLC is proposed to improve performance and reliability of LLC at near-threshold voltage with an acceptable area overhead.

3 ARCHITECTURE DESIGN AND IMPLEMENT

We present NFTLLC, a novel fault-tolerant last-level cache that combined with compression mechanism and weak ECC techniques. Compression mechanism compresses data by ignoring the null subblocks in a data block and stores the data into a cache entry which has disabled the faulty subentries, while there are too much faulty subentries in an entry at near-threshold voltage. In order to increase the available capacity of a cache entry, we use a weak ECC to correct the faulty cells in each entry. The combination of compression and error correction mechanisms ensure a minimal degradation on performance and improve the cache reliability.

3.1 Operation and Component Description

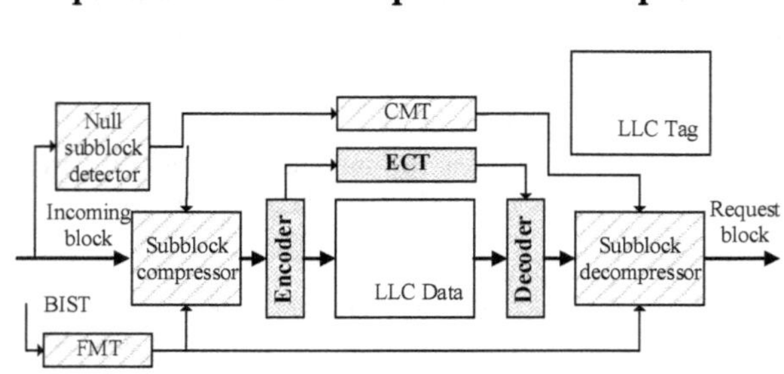

Figure 2. NFTLLC design overview

Our proposed NFTLLC is shown in Fig. 2, it consists of 3 parts: conventional LLC module, compression module and ECC module. Conventional LLC is the area which the background color is white. Compression module is filled with light grey, and ECC module is filled with dark grey. We recognize that the additional logic inserted on the critical path of a cache access may result in an extra latency, and its overhead is presented in Section 4.

When a data block is evicted from L1 Cache and written back to LLC, our proposed NFTLLC performs in three steps. First, NFTLLC detects the location of null subblocks in a block by null subblock detector. The detector transfers the location information to subblock compressor and compression map table (CMT). Then, Subblock compressor combines the location information with the distribution of faulty subentries in selected entry to rearrange the non-null subblocks into non-faulty subentries. Finally, the cache entries containing compressed block are encoded by Encoder, which use SECDED to protect data and generate ECC check bits.

When a read request comes from L1 Cache or a compressed block need to be evicted from LLC, our proposed NFTLLC firstly uses Decoder to check if the data stored in selected cache entry is correct. Decoder corrects the faulty subentries if these subentries are correctable. Then, we use null subblock decompressor to reconstruct the original block by rearranging corrected subblocks according the information from CMT and the distribution of faulty subentries from fault map table (FMT). After decompressing the compressed block, we finally get the original block stored in LLC.

3.2 Compression Mechanism Design

Compression mechanism in our proposed LLC is based on Concertina [12]. During a cache access, FMT and CMT play a key role on compressing/decompressing and rearranging data. For the FMT, we set '1' in each bit to indicates whether the subentry is non-faulty or correctable. If the subentry is faulty and uncorrectable, we set the corresponding bit with '0'. The problem that if a subentry is correctable can be judged from ECT (ECC check table), which will be presented in Section 3.3. For the CMT, bit value '0' means the subblock is filled with zero and bit value '1' shows that the subblock has valid data. A subblock filled with zero can be compressed, it can be removed when written into cache and can be refilled to its original location when read from LLC. The granularity of compression can be, such as 1-byte, 2-byte and 4-byte subblock etc. For example, a 64-byte block can be divided into 16 4-byte subblocks, so each entry requires 16 bits to store corresponding information in CMT and FMT.

CMT is generated by null subblock detector, and it changes with data incoming. We consider that the number and the location of faulty cells do not change during LLC working. So FMT comes from a built-in self-test routine (BIST) that can be executed at boot up time and tests the last-level cache at the target low voltage [4, 11, 17]. The initialization of FMT can be seen in Procedure 1. We first initialize FMT with faulty-free subentries, for faulty-free subentry can hold right data. Then, we Initialize ECT to correct the correctable faulty subentries which can right hold data by using ECC. Finally, we update FMT with these correctable faulty subentries to increase the number of available subentries in an entry.

CMT combines with FMT compresses and rearranges a data block to a cache entry by subblock compressor. We can use an example (Fig. 3) to explain the process of compressing the incoming blocks. CMT indicates the location of corresponding block, and each non-null subblock is rearranged to non-faulty subentries. The detailed process circuit can be seen in Concertina [12], and the subblock decompressor has a similar circuit.

We set N as the number of subentries (subblocks) in a cache entry (block). So we need extra $2N$ bits to compress an entry, which lead to a great increase on area overhead. To guarantee robustness at low voltages, we assume a 10T SRAM based implementation for CM and UFM. The compression logic requires N^2 comparators of $log2(N)$ bits, and N^2 tri-state buffers. When the subentry size decreases (finer granularity), both the number of the comparators and the size of their inputs increase, but overall, the overhead is still low.

Procedure 1 FMT initialization

```
Input: Empty FMT array, LLC array
Output: Configured FMT array
for each Entry in LLC do
  for each subentry in Entry do
    //Initialize FMT with each subentry
    if subentry is faulty-free then
      Index bit of corresponding subentry in FMT ← 1;
    else
      Index bit of corresponding subentry in FMT ← 0;
    end if
  end for
  Correct faulty subentries with ECT array;
  for each subentry in Entry do
    if subentry is faulty and correctable in ECT then
      //This subentry can hold data correctly.
        Update index bit of corresponding subentry in FMT
      with '1';
    end if
  end for
end for
return UFM;
```

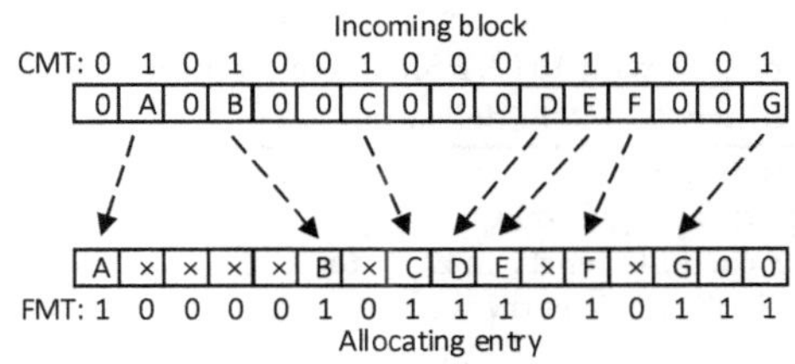

Figure 3. Example of compressed block to be rearranged to a faulty entry

3.3 Implement of Error Correction Code Module

When we insert a block to LLC, ECC encoding is the second phase in our proposed NFTLLC. Typically, most proposed ECC techniques are based on BCH code. SECDED is a weak ECC technique based on BCH code. We use SECDED as our ECC technique for its low latency overhead with only one cycle.

However, SECDED doesn't meet the requirement of cache at high failure rate, which has multi-error in a cache entry. Besides, the employ of other complex ECCs such as 4EC5ED leads to more latency increase. When 4EC5ED is implemented in cache, it adds one extra cycle latency in encoding and at least 7 cycles latency in decoding, and a significant performance degradation occurs [1].

Considering that multi-bit correction requirement and the overhead of access latency. We divide a whole cache entry into multiple subentries with a sort of correction granularity. 1-byte, 2-byte and 4-byte subentry size can be selected as correction granularity, and the correction granularity are required to be the same as compression granularity. Then, we use SECDED to protect data in each subentry. To decrease the area of ECT, we propose an optimized protection policy.

For M subentries in a cache entry, we try to protect k ($k<M$) faulty subentries using SECDED. When the value k increases, the number of subentries that can be protected and corrected increases correspondingly. E.g. a 64-byte cache entry has 16 subentries for a 4-byte subentry, we set $k=4$. Then, the architecture of ECT (ECC Check Table) is shown in Fig. 4.

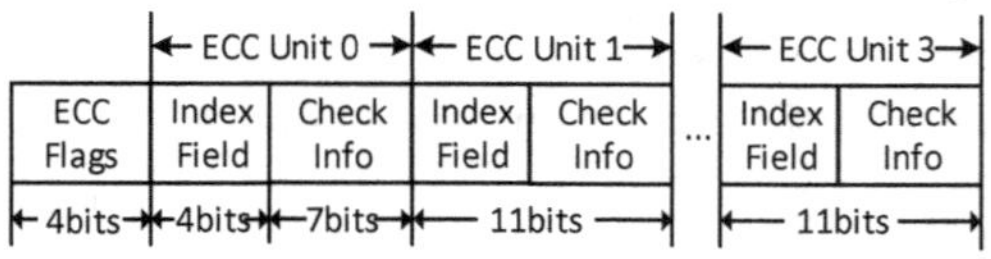

Figure 4. The architecture of ECT

ECT consists of ECC Flags and 4 ECC Units. ECC Flags indicate whether the ECC Units are used, and the size of ECC Flags is equal to the number of ECC Units. Each ECC Unit contains 11 bits, and it consists of Index Field and Check Info. Index Field indicates the index of subentry protected by this ECC Unit, which use 4 bits to represent the identity of each subentry. Check Info containing 7 bits is check code generated by Encoder. Each time LLC gets read request, Check Info is fetched to check whether the subentry from LLC is right and correct the subentry if it is faulty. ECT is defective at near-threshold voltage, so we implement ECT with 10T ST SRAM cell to keep it reliable.

Procedure 2: ECT initialization

```
Input: Empty ECT array, Cache entry
Output: Configured ECT array
for each ECCenrty in ECT do
  Initialize ECCentry with '0';
  for each Unit in ECCentry do
    if cache entry has correctable subentries then
      Get a correctable subentry from the cache entry;
      if Unit is unused then
        IndexField ← Index of subentry;
        Set Unit in use;
      end if
    end if
  end for
end for
return ECT;
```

NFTLLC(k=4) needs 52 bits in total to implement ECT with 4 ECC Units. And 12k bits are needed when we want to protect k subentries in a cache entry. By analyzing the failure rate of 1.1% in LLC, we find the average number of faulty subentries ranges from 4.77 to 5.42 in different subentry sizes, so we set k range from 4 to 7 for it having an impact on performance and area overhead.

Only Check Info in ECT are set and updated during regular cache accesses, while all other bits in the ECT are set at runtime by BIST that can be executed at boot up time. First, BIST initializes all the bits in ECT array with '0'. Then, it tests each subentry of a cache entry, and a subentry will be protected by an unused ECC Unit if the subentry is faulty and correctable. More details of initializing ECT can be seen in Procedure 2.

3.4 Replacement Policy

In this paper, our proposed NFTLLC based on compression mechanism has variable number of faulty subentries in each entry, and variable number of null subblocks with incoming blocks. So, we use Fit-LRU policy, a LRU-based management policy to deal with different between entries and blocks [12]. When a block is to be inserted, we first find a set of entries that can accommodate the compressed block. Then we search the set of entries for a LRU entry. If there is no available entry to store the compressed block, we write back this block to main memory directly. By this policy, we avoid writing a block to a cache entry which can't accommodate the compressed block. Thus, the reliability of LLC is improved and the data is kept right in LLC.

4 EVALUATION METHODOLOGY

To evaluate the impacts of NFTLLC, we use Gem5 simulator to construct the CMP platform [18]. The important architectural parameters used for evaluation are shown in Table 1. We assume a frequency of 1 GHz at 650 mV (our target near-threshold Vdd) and set the bit-cell failure rate to 1.1%. L1 caches are built with robust SRAM cells and, therefore, they can run at lower voltages without suffering the bit-cell functional failure. As in previous studies [4, 12], we assume that LLC tag arrays are built with 10T SRAM [8], for it having significantly smaller latency and area overhead compared to LLC Data arrays.

Table 1. Architectural parameters used for evaluation

Cores	8, in-order, single-threaded, 1 GHz@650mV
L1 DCache	32KB, 4-way associative, private, 2 cycles
L1 ICache	32KB, 4-way associative, private, 2 cycles
L2 Cache (LLC)	1MB, 8-way associative, shared, 8 cycles, 1 extra cycle for decompression/compression, 1 extra cycle for ECC decoding/encoding
Coherence protocol	MOESI, Full-map, directory-based
Memory	2 channels, 2GB per channel, raw access time 50 ns
Network	Mesh, 1 cycle link latency

We use a set of 10 multiprogrammed workloads built from SPEC CPU 2006 as our benchmarks [19]. Each workload is combined with 8 programs random selected from the 29 programs in SPEC CPU 2006, with no special distinction between integer and floating point. We run cycle-accurate simulations including 300 million cycles to warm up the memory hierarchy and 700 million cycles for data collection.

We compare NFTLLC with Concertina and "Correction+ Disabled" at near-threshold voltage. Concertina is a novel technique that use compression mechanism to make full use of cache subentries that are fault-free [12]. "Correction+Disabled" is modified from [10] for its unsuitable on high failure rate. To improve the reliability of this work, we use SECDED to protect fine-grained subblocks such as 1-byte subblocks, 2-byte subblocks and 4-byte subblocks. We implement an ideal cache as baseline, which is assumed that has no extra latency overhead and 100% available capacity at all voltages.

5 EVALUATION RESULTS

In this section, we present the evaluation results for our NFTLLC. We first present available capacity of last-level caches with different techniques in different subblock/sub-entry sizes. Then, we explore performance and access miss rate variety at different situations. Finally, we analyze the area overhead.

5.1 Available cache capacity

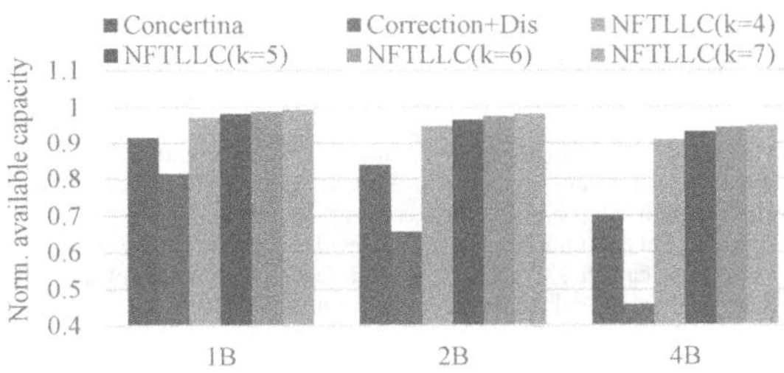

Figure 5. Available capacity of different caches in different subblock/subentry sizes

Reliable Cache design can address the faulty cells and improve available cache capacity, for faulty cells causing a great loss on available capacity. Fig. 5 shows available cache capacity variety at different situations and the results are normalized with ideal cache. The available cache capacity in a LLC architecture increases with the decrease of subblock/subentry sizes. We can get maximal available capacity at 1-byte subblock/subentry size, and minimal ones at 4-byte grain size. For a 4-byte subblock/ subentry, "Correction+Disabled" has only 45.68% available capacity compared with ideal cache, and the available cache capacity of Concertina reaches to 70.17%, while that of NFTLLC is more than 90.95%, which is far larger than others. When k varies from 4 to 7, available capacity improves from 90.95% to 94.94% of ideal cache capacity, and the capacity improves slowly. This means that NFTLLC(k=4) has a good effect on available cache capacity, and the increase of k has less effect on it.

5.2 Miss rate of LLC accesses

As we can see from Fig. 6, miss rate of LLC accesses increases with the increase of subblock/subentry size. For caches using 4-byte subblocks/sub-entries, normalized miss rate of Concertina is about 2.33 times of ideal cache, and "Correction+Disabled" increases 21% than ideal cache on the number of access misses. Normalized miss rate of NFTLLC ranges from 1 to 1.095, and it almost reaches the same miss rate of ideal cache at some situation, such as NFTLLC(k=7) with 1-byte subblocks/sub-entries. Besides, the miss rate of NFTLLC increases with the increase of subblock/subentry size and the decrease of value k. As the value of k increase, the number of corrected subentries and non-faulty subentries is increasing in each entry. So more entries are available to hold compressed data in one cache set, which will lead to a great decrease on miss rate.

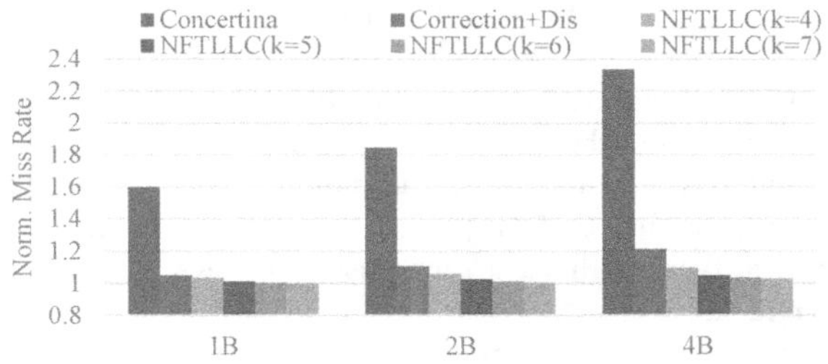

Figure 6. Miss rate of different caches in different sub-block/subentry sizes

5.3 Performance

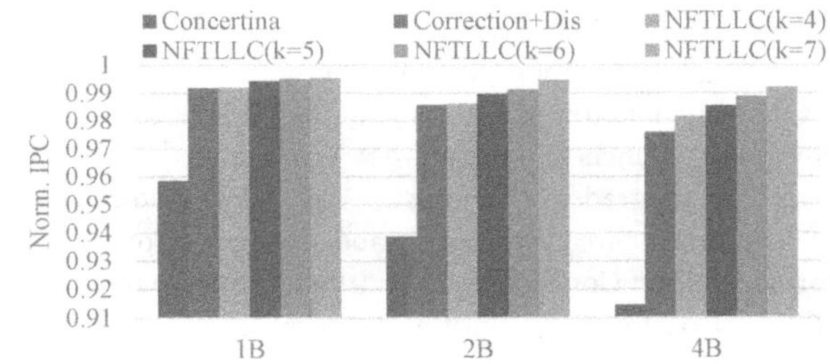

Figure 7 Performance of different caches in different sub-block/subentry sizes

Fig. 7 shows the performance of NFTLLC relative to Concertina and "Correction+Disabled". We use IPC (Instructions Per Cycle) to reflect the performance of CPU. And a reliable cache takes a great impact on performance. As is shown in Fig. 7, the normalized IPC of our NFTLLC with 4-byte subblocks/ subentries ranges from 0.982 to 0.992, while the normalized IPC of Concertina is 0.914 and "Correction+Disabled" is 0.976. Compared with Concertina, the IPC of NFTLLC(k=4) improves by 6.8%. This means that miss rate of LLC access has a greater impact on performance than access latency, and NFTLLC have a significantly lower performance degradation than other cache designs at the same subblock/subentry size. In addition, the performance of LLC increases with the subblock/subentry size decreasing, and it improves with k increasing in NFTLLC.

5.4 Overhead Analysis

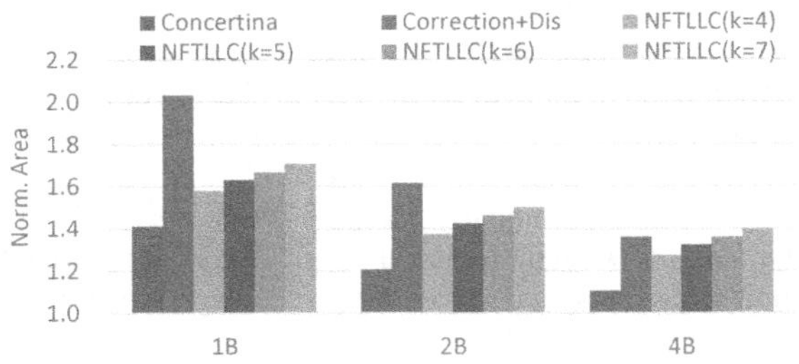

Figure 8. Area overhead compared to ideal LLC in different block/subentry sizes

FMT, CMT and ECT array in our NFTLLC need some storage circuits to store the information, which increases the area overhead. Besides, the area overhead of ECT array changes with value *k*. We use CACTI [20] to quantify these costs, and normalize them with ideal cache using 6T SRAM. Results are shown in Fig. 8.

Concertina takes the least extra area overhead compared with other architecture at different subblock/subentry sizes in Fig. 8, while "Correction+Disabled" has the largest area overhead. Compared with ideal cache, the area overhead of NFTLLC varies from 27.2% to 70.5%, and it takes at least 16.8% extra area overhead relative to Concertina at 4-byte subblock/subentry size. Fig. 7 shows that performance of NFTLLC increases little with the decrease of subblock/subentry size. So we can get the least area overhead and a good performance with NFTLLC(*k*=4) at 4-byte subblock/subentry size among all the NFTLLCs.

Although Concertina has the least area overhead, its performance degrades the most. And "Correction+Disabled" takes the most area overhead above others for its better performance than Concertina. In contrast to prior work, NFTLLC has the best performance with a little area overhead increasing, while it ensures the most of available cache capacity.

6 CONCLUSIONS

Near-threshold voltage technique presents some challenges on cache reliability, functional failure of SRAM cells is one of the largest barriers. A lot of architectures are proposed to deal with low bit-cell failure rate in cache. However, bit-cell failure rate is becoming higher for the scaling of device and supply voltage. NFTLLC are proposed to explore a higher failure rate at near-threshold. We propose an error correction module based on SECDED, and correct faulty subentries in last-level cache. And a compression mechanism is proposed to compress the incoming block and the uncorrectable faulty subentries of each entry. Our NFTLLC incurs at least 6.8% performance improvement at 4-byte subblock/ subentry size compared with Concertina, and takes minimally 16.8% extra area overhead.

ACKNOWLEDGMENTS

This paper is supported by the Ministry of Education Project of Humanities and Social Sciences (Project Name, Research on fuzzy QoE aware and trustworthy cloud services selection in mobile commerce, Project No. 16YJCZH014), the Natural Science Foundation of Hubei Province of China (Project Name, Research on the replica-aware data acquiring mechanism for mobile cloud computing, Project No. 2016CFB466), and the Fundamental Research Funds for the Central Universities (WUT:2016III028).

REFERENCES

[1] A. R. Alameldeen, I. Wagner, Z. Chishti, W. Wu, C. Wilkerson and S. L. Lu. Energy-efficient cache design using variable-strength error-correcting codes. ACM International Symposium on Computer Architecture, 2011, pp. 461-472.

[2] R. G. Dreslinski, M. Wieckowski, D. Blaauw, D. Sylvester and T. Mudge. Near-Threshold Computing: Reclaiming Moore's Law Through Energy Efficient Integrated Circuits. Proceedings of the IEEE, 2010, vol. 98, no. 2, pp. 253-266.

[3] D. Markovic, C. C. Wang, L. P. Alarcon, T. T. Liu and J. M. Rabaey. Ultralow-Power Design in Near-Threshold Region. Proceedings of the IEEE, 2010, vol. 98, no. 2, pp. 237-252.

[4] A. Ansari, S. Feng, S. Gupta and S. Mahlke. Archipelago: A polymorphic cache design for enabling robust near-threshold operation. IEEE International Symposium on High Performance Computer Architecture, 2011, pp. 539–550.

[5] S. T. Zhou, S. Katariya, H. Ghasemi and S. Draper. Minimizing total area of low-voltage SRAM arrays through joint optimization of cell size, redundancy, and ECC. IEEE International Conference on Computer Design, 2010, vol. 41, no. 3, pp. 112-117.

[6] L. Chang, R.K. Montoye, Y. Nakamura, K.A. Batson, R. J. Eickemeyer and R. H. Dennard. An 8T-SRAM for variability tolerance and low-voltage operation in high-performance caches. IEEE Journal of Solid-State Circuits, 2008, vol. 43, no. 4, pp. 956-963.

[7] B. H. Calhoun and A. P. Chandrakasan. A 256-kb 65-nm sub-threshold SRAM design for ultra-low-voltage operation. IEEE Journal of Solid-State Circuits, 2007, vol. 42, no. 3, pp. 680-688.

[8] J. P. Kulkarni, K. Kim and K. Roy. A 160mV robust schmitt trigger based subthreshold SRAM. IEEE Journal of Solid-State Circuits, 2007, vol. 42, no. 10, pp. 2303-2313.

[9] Z. Chishti, A. R. Alameldeen, C. Wilkerson, W. Wu and S. L. Lu. Improving cache lifetime reliability at ultra-low voltages. IEEE/ACM International Symposium on Microarchitecture, 2009, pp. 89-99.

[10] F. Hijaz, Q. Shi and O. Khan. A private level-1 cache architecture to exploit the latency and capacity tradeoffs in multicores operating at near-threshold voltages. International Conference on Computer Design, 2013, pp. 85-92.

[11] H. Duwe, X. Jian, D. Petrisko and R. Kumar. Rescuing uncorrectable fault patterns in on-chip memories through error pattern transformation. International Symposium on Computer Architecture, 2016, pp. 634-644.

[12] A. Ferrerón, D. Suarez-Gracia, J. Alastruey-Benede, T. Monreal-Arnal and P. Ibanez. Concertina: Squeezing in Cache Content to Operate at Near-Threshold Voltage. IEEE Transactions on Computers, 2016, vol. 65, no. 3, pp. 755-769.

[13] D. J. Palframan, N. S. Kim and M. H. Lipasti. iPatch: Intelligent fault patching to improve energy efficiency. IEEE International Symposium on High Performance Computer Architecture, 2015, pp. 428-438.

[14] D. Jung, H. Lee and S. W. Kim. Lowering Minimum Supply Voltage for Power-Efficient Cache Design by Exploiting Data Redundancy. ACM Transactions on Design Automation of Electronic Systems, 2015, vol. 21, no. 1, pp. 1-24.

[15] H. Duwe, X. Jian, and R. Kumar. Correction prediction: Reducing error correction latency for on-chip memories. IEEE, International Symposium on High PERFORMANCE Computer Architecture IEEE, 2015:463-475.

[16] Mukhopadhyay, S., Mahmoodi, H. and Roy, K. Modeling of failure probability and statistical design of sram array for yield enhancement in nanoscaled cmos. IEEE Transactions on Computer-Aided Design of Integrated Circuits and Systems, 2005, 24(12), 1859-1880.

[17] J. Wang, Y. Han, H. Li and X. Li. Exploring Variation-Aware Fault-Tolerant Cache under Near-Threshold Computing. International Conference on Parallel Processing IEEE, 2016:149-158.

[18] N Binkert, B Beckmann and G. Black. The gem5 simulator. ACM Sigarch Computer Architecture News, 2011, vol. 39, no. 2, pp. 1-7.

[19] Standard Performance Evaluation Corporation. Spec cpu2006. Available: www.spec.org/cpu2006.

[20] N Muralimanohar, R Balasubramonian and N P. Jouppi. CACTI 6.0: A Tool to Model Large Caches. Bragantia, 2009.

AB-Aware: Application Behavior Aware Management of Shared Last Level Caches

Suhit Pai, Newton Singh and Virendra Singh
{suhitpai, newton, viren}@ee.iitb.ac.in
Computer Architecture and Dependable Systems Laboratory
Indian Institute of Technology Bombay, India

ABSTRACT

In modern multicore systems, Last-Level Cache (LLC) is usually shared among multiple cores. Though it benefits applications by sharing and utilizing cache resources efficiently; the benefits come at the cost of increased conflict misses due to interference among applications. In shared LLC, conventionally used LRU-based cache replacement policies logically partition the cache on-demand basis. Thus, cache friendly applications sharing LLC with streaming applications, suffer due to high data demands and low reuse of streaming applications. Apart from different data locality behavior, applications also show different memory access behavior while accessing the LLC. Some applications inherently have parallel memory accesses while others have more isolated long-latency accesses. The cost of idle cycles processor spends waiting for off-chip memory accesses is shared by parallel misses. However, misses which occur in isolation hurt the performance most. This adds another dimension to application's behavior. We propose an application behavior aware cache replacement policy to manage shared LLC. The proposed policy simultaneously reduces the negative interference among applications sharing the LLC and the miss-penalty associated with each LLC miss. Evaluation on SPEC CPU2006 benchmarks shows that our replacement policy improves performance on dual-core systems and quad-core system by up to 15.9% and 23.8% respectively over SRRIP for shared LLC. It is worth to note that effectiveness of our policy improves with the increase in the number of cores.

ACM Reference Format:
Suhit Pai, Newton Singh and Virendra Singh. 2018. AB-Aware: Application Behavior Aware Management of Shared Last Level Caches. In *GLSVLSI '18: 2018 Great Lakes Symposium on VLSI, May 23–25, 2018, Chicago, IL, USA.* ACM, New York, NY, USA, 6 pages. https://doi.org/10.1145/3194554.3194573

GLSVLSI '18, May 23–25, 2018, Chicago, IL, USA

ACM ISBN 978-1-4503-5724-1/18/05...$15.00
https://doi.org/10.1145/3194554.3194573

1 INTRODUCTION

In the last couple of decades, microprocessors' performance has improved almost thousand-folds mainly due to core micro-architectural innovations and transistor-speed scaling. However, the DRAM access latency has not improved as significantly as the CPU's speed. This disparity in the speeds of DRAM and CPU has resulted in a memory bottleneck known as *Memory Wall*. Hence, modern processors dedicate a large portion (~40%) of die area to on-chip caches for reducing off-chip memory accesses. Processors use a large on-chip L3 cache as the LLC. It acts like a victim cache for L1 and L2 caches and also helps in maintaining cache-coherency in a multicore system. Each LLC miss stalls the CPU for ~200 cycles and significantly degrades processor's performance [2].

Sharing LLC enables dynamic allocation of cache space between multiple cores. However, multiple cores utilizing the LLC also compete with each other to make the most of the shared resource. At times, these conflicts result in negative interference among the competing cores. One core may evict the useful data of the other core, resulting in unnecessary off-chip memory accesses to the main memory, thus reducing the system performance. *Hence, effective management of LLC is very critical to the performance of a multicore system.*

Conventionally, LRU-based policies are used to manage LLC. Such policies perform sub-optimally for LLC as most of the temporal and spatial regularity present in the data is filtered-out by the higher level caches (L1 and L2). Caches benefit by utilizing the locality present in the data. Hence, a filtered access pattern makes LRU-based policies inefficient in managing the LLC. The problem further aggravates as such policies allocate cache resources on the basis of access rates of the competing applications. The cache is implicitly partitioned in favor of application having high access rate. However, a highly demanding application may not have high data locality, resulting in a poor resource utilization. Thus, considering application's data-reuse behavior can be beneficial while allocating LLC resources among applications with different access rates. Data-reuse pattern of cache blocks brought by an application can be assimilated to better understand application's behavior and limit the negative interference of high access rate applications.

Apart from different data-reuse behavior, applications also show different memory access pattern. Some applications have multiple memory accesses which can be parallelly serviced, while others have more isolated accesses. The ability to process multiple memory operations concurrently is called Memory Level Parallelism (MLP) [10]. The penalty per miss

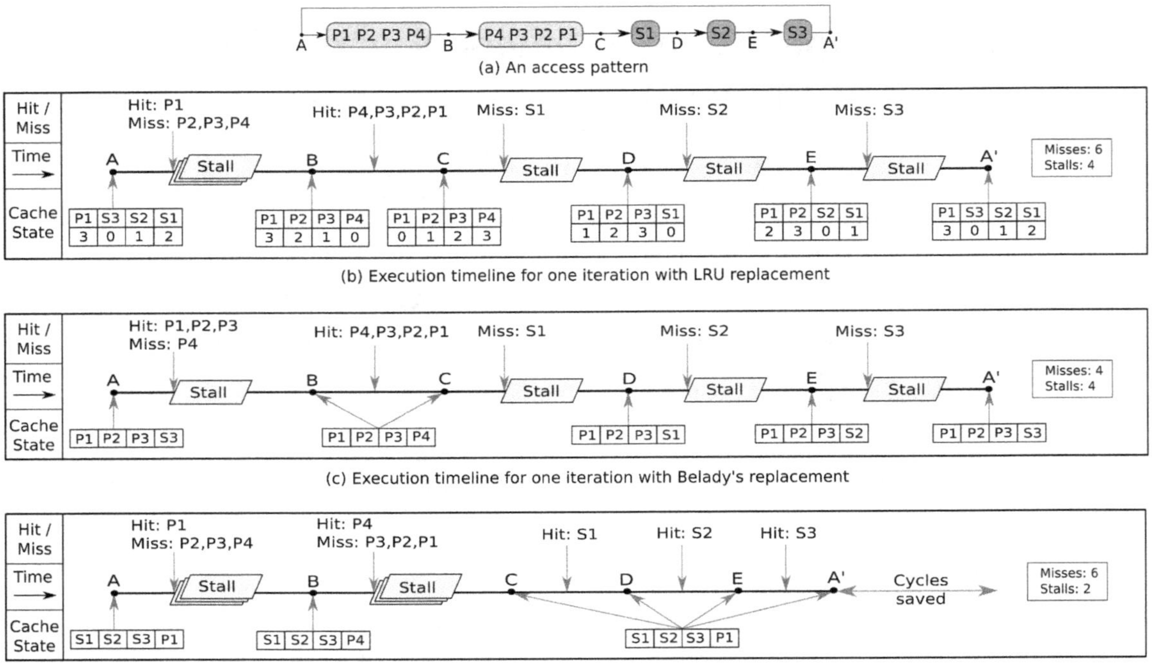

(a) An access pattern

(b) Execution timeline for one iteration with LRU replacement

(c) Execution timeline for one iteration with Belady's replacement

(d) Execution timeline for one iteration with MLP-aware replacement

Figure 1: The drawback of MLP-unaware Cache Replacement

incurred while servicing parallel misses is less than that of isolated misses. Most of the LRU-based cache management policies focus only on reducing the number of LLC misses, assuming same cost for each miss. Hence, such policies are oblivious to the observation that servicing N parallel misses may be less costlier than servicing M ($N > M$) isolated misses. MLP information can be useful while managing caches, however, it can complicate the replacement policy. Such a replacement policy is costly for L1 & L2 caches, considering their relatively lower miss penalties as compared to that of LLC. Hence, using both the data-reuse and MLP-behavior of an application can be effective in managing the LLC.

This paper proposes an application behavior aware cache replacement policy for shared LLC. Our policy manages the LLC by considered data-reuse behavior as well as MLP behavior of the applications sharing the LLC. It simultaneously reduces both the number of misses and the cost of misses. Evaluation of SPEC CPU2006 benchmarks on a multicore system sharing LLC shows that our policy outperforms both *state-of-the-art* SRRIP [6] and ABRIP [7] policies.

2 MOTIVATION

Traditional cache replacement algorithms try to reduce the overall number of cache misses assuming same miss penalty for each miss. However, this assumption may not be always true. Consider an example [10] of a loop having 11 memory accesses to LLC as shown in Figure 1(a). A, B, C, D and E are points representing a program's intervals. Blocks *P1*, *P2*, *P3* and *P4* are accessed between interval A & B and B & C. The four accesses of these blocks are close to each other in instruction space and hence, can be serviced in parallel. While *S1*, *S2* and *S3* are the sequential accesses between interval C & A' which result in *isolated misses*. As an example, we consider a fully-associative cache having four cache blocks.

Figure 1(b) shows the behavior of LRU replacement policy for this loop. While managing the cache, LRU replacement policy only considers the recency of a block and is oblivious to the block's MLP behavior. Recency value of each cache block has been shown as cache state (MRU = 0 and LRU = 3). LRU replacement policy results in total 6 misses and 4 stalls. Cache behavior under Belady's OPT is shown in Figure 1(c). Belady's OPT [1] minimizes the number of misses by evicting those blocks which will be referred farthest in future, based on oracle's information. Blocks *P1*, *P2*, *P3* and *P4* are referred more than once as compared to blocks *S1*, *S2* and *S3*. So, in order to minimize the misses, it will try to retain *P* kind of blocks. Belady's OPT replacement is able to reduce parallel misses, making a total of 4 misses and 4 long-latency stalls for every iteration of the loop.

It is interesting to observe, as shown in Figure 1(d), that we can still reduce the number of long-latency stalls from 4 to 2 if our replacement policy is MLP-aware. MLP-aware policy focuses on minimizing isolated misses by not evicting those cache blocks which result in isolated misses. *Thus, the policy prefers retaining S type cache blocks over P type cache blocks.* However, making the replacement policy only MLP-aware will not be sufficient while managing caches, as caches mainly work on the philosophy of utilizing the recency information of data blocks. Several policies have been proposed earlier [5] [6] which consider the recency information of cache blocks to predict their future re-references. Cache blocks which are less likely to be re-referred again or which are going to be re-referred in far future are placed near LRU position and the ones which are likely to be re-referred in the near future are placed near MRU position. However, LRU replacement policy predicts that each newly inserted block will be re-referenced in the near future and thus, places them at MRU position.

Predicting the future re-references of cache blocks becomes more difficult for a multicore system when its LLC is shared among multiple applications running on different cores. In such a case, the LLC experiences mixed access pattern from applications with diverse behavior. Considering only the recency information of cache blocks and being ignorant of the behavior of the application which brought the cache block can be sub-optimal [7]. LRU-based replacement policies and recently proposed policies [6] [5] manage cache by utilizing the recency behavior of cache block. They do not assimilate the recency information of each block to understand the application's behavior better. Applications' data access behavior was utilized in [7] to classify them as cache-friendly (*CF*) or streaming (*STR*) applications. However, insights about applications' data access behavior and MLP-behavior can be used to classify their temporal-varying phases more specifically as *CF-IM* (cache-friendly isolated misses), *CF-PM* (cache-friendly parallel misses), *STR-IM* (streaming isolated misses), and *STR-PM* (streaming parallel misses). In an application's *IM* phase, it suffers from many isolated misses whereas in *PM* phases misses can be parallelized to reduce effective miss penalty. The priority of retaining cache blocks in the LLC of applications should be *CF-IM* > *CF-PM* > *STR-IM* > *STR-PM*. This more specific classification gives more insight into an application's behavior and can be effectively utilized to manage the LLC.

3 APPLICATION BEHAVIOR AWARE LLC MANAGEMENT

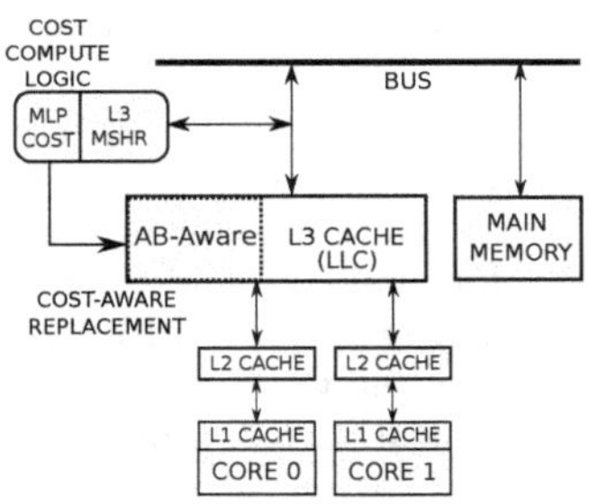

(a)

MLP-based cost value	Quantized value
0-22 cycles	7
23-45 cycles	6
46-68 cycles	5
69-91 cycles	4
92-114 cycles	3
115-137 cycles	2
138-160 cycles	1
160+ cycles	0

(b)

Figure 2: (a) Microarchitecture of AB-Aware policy (b) Quantization of *mlp_cost* to *q_cost*

3.1 Framework for AB-Aware policy

Figure 2(a) shows the microarchitecture of AB-Aware Policy. The LLC consists of a cost-aware replacement engine. It calculates the MLP-based cost for LLC misses according to algorithm 1, as described in section 3.2. The MLP-based cost value is quantized to 3-bits (to limit the storage overhead) and is stored with each cache block. The recency information about a particular block is collected using recency counters at each block. Our proposed policy takes replacement decisions by considering a weighted sum of block's mlp_cost and its recency information.

3.2 Computation of MLP-based cost

The MLP-based cost of each block is computed using the number of LLC accesses to main memory as done in [10]. Whenever a LLC miss occurs, an entry is made in Miss Status Holding Register (MSHR) before sending the request to main memory. The information about the *number of in-flight misses* and *wait-cycles before being serviced* is taken from MSHR. To compute MLP-based cost, a field *mlp_cost* has been added to each entry of MSHR and the entry is set to 0 when a new entry is made in MSHR. The quantized value of the field *mlp_cost* is stored in tag-store entry of each block and is used by replacement algorithm. The *mlp_cost* of a block shows predictability across successive misses to the same block as shown in [10]. Hence, the MLP-behavior of a block captured as its *mlp_cost* shows phasic behavior and can be predicted.

Algorithm 1 Calculation of MLP-based cost for LLC misses

init_mlp_cost(miss): /* when miss enters MSHR */
    $miss.mlp\_cost = 0$
update_mlp_cost(): /* called every cycle */
$N_i \Leftarrow$ Number of outstanding misses from i^{th} core
for each demand miss in MSHR **do**
    $mlp\_cost += (1/N_i)$
end for

We modified the algorithm proposed by Qureshi *et al.* [10] for MLP-based cost calculation to make it suitable for shared LLCs in a multicore system. *mlp_cost* for all the outstanding misses is incremented by (1/Number of outstanding misses from i^{th} core) per cycle, where i is the core-id of the requesting core. The modification accurately calculates *mlp_cost* considering LLC misses *on per core basis instead of total LLC misses from each core.* Consider an example of a 2-core system, where *core-0* is having one outstanding miss and *core-1* is having four outstanding misses at some point in time. Then, considering $N = 5$ as the total number of outstanding memory misses for *mlp_cost* calculation of all misses would be unfair to *core-0*, as it is facing one isolated miss. Without the modification, the isolated miss of *core-0* will be considered as a parallel miss and thus, the MLP-behavior per core will be wrongly understood.

3.3 Quantization of MLP-based cost

In our simulation environment, an isolated LLC miss takes 175 cycles to get serviced. We quantize *mlp_cost* into 3 bits (8 values), according to intervals shown in Figure 2(b). Quantized cost (*q_cost*) is proportional to the degree of parallelism. Note that *mlp_cost* is inversely quantized, as shown in Figure 2(b), to *q_cost* for suitability to AB-Aware policy. High *q_cost* of a block signifies that the block was brought in cache while servicing other parallel misses. A block brought in cache while servicing isolated miss will have low *q_cost*.

3.4 AB-Aware Policy

The proposed replacement algorithm takes into account both MLP-behavior (captured in the *q_cost*) and application's data-reuse behavior assimilated from recency information of each block (captured in the block's ABr value [7]). The victim of the *AB-Aware* policy is selected by a linear function block's recency value and its *q_cost* as

$$ABAr = Br + \alpha * Cr + \lambda * q\_cost \quad (1)$$
$$Victim = max\{Br(i) + \alpha * Cr(i) + \lambda * q\_cost(i)\} \quad (2)$$

In equation 1, Br represents that block's recency value, Cr captures the application's behavior and *q_cost* represents MLP-based cost of the block. A higher value of α gives more weight to core's behavior over block's recency behavior and similarly, a higher value of λ gives more weight to *q_cost*. We tried different combinations of λ and α (2, 4, 8) and experimentally found that the combination ($\lambda = 4$ & $\alpha = 4$) is optimum for the *AB-Aware* policy. The policy selects the victim block as per equation 2. Thus, the policy will protect cache blocks from the core which were isolated misses and showed high data-reuse behavior. The promotion, eviction and insertion policy of the proposed policy is explained below.
Promotion Policy: Hit to any block predicts that next reference of the block will be in the near future. Hence, the recency counter Br of the block is set to 0. The core which brought the block has also shown data-reuse and hence, the Cr counter corresponding to the block is also set to 0.
Eviction Policy On a cache replacement, block to be evicted is selected as per equation 2.
Insertion Policy Each incoming block is inserted at $Br = 2^M - 2$ location, which is closer to LRU.

4 EXPERIMENTAL METHODOLOGY

4.1 Simulator Infrastructure

We use Sniper [3] multicore x86 simulator as the evaluation platform. The baseline processor is 2.67 GHz, 4-wide fetch, 128-entry ROB, x86 Nehalem micro-architecture, with three level memory hierarchy as shown in Table 1. L3 miss penalty is 175 cycles. We evaluate 2-core configuration with 4MB, 8-way LLC and 4-core configuration with 8MB, 8-way LLC. MSHR supports up to 32 outstanding misses.

We use weighted speedup to evaluate our results, as it is a commonly used metric to quantify the performance of multi-core systems [11] [12].

4.2 Benchmarks

We use workloads from SPEC CPU2006 benchmark suite [4] for our evaluation. Using Pin-Points [8], 250M instruction traces of representative regions of these workloads were collected. We use four such traces of each application, i.e., 1 Billion instructions per application, for 2-core and 4-core configurations. Recent works on shared LLC [11] [6] [7] have followed the similar methodology.

L1-D Cache	32KB, 4-Way, Private, 4-cycles, LRU
L1-I Cache	32KB, 4-Way, Private, 4-cycles, LRU
L2 Cache	256KB, 8-Way, Private, 8-cycles, LRU
L3 Cache	2MB per core, 8-Way, Shared, 30-cycles

Table 1: Cache hierarchy of the simulated system

Application	*apki*	*mpki*	Characteristics
bzip	15.44	1.07	cache-friendly (CF)
gcc	28.32	7.24	cache-friendly (CF)
soplex	37.05	14.64	cache-friendly (CF)
sphinx	13.44	4.35	cache-friendly (CF)
lbm	31.92	31.57	Streaming (STR)
libquantum	49.45	35.39	Streaming (STR)
mcf	96.12	56.34	Streaming (STR)

Table 2: Workloads under evaluation

To identify memory characteristics of workloads under evaluation, we run each application with single core configuration under LRU policy. As shown in Table 2, some applications like *bzip*, *sphinx* have low *apki* (accesses per kilo instructions) & low *mpki* (misses per kilo instructions). When these applications are allotted more cache resources, they show commensurate performance improvements; we label them as cache-friendly (CF). However, some applications like *libquantum*, *mcf* have very high *apki*. They have either very large working data set, which does not fit in cache (results into thrashing), or streaming access pattern [5]; we label them as Streaming (STR).

We compare our results with LIN [10] having $\lambda = 4$, SRRIP [6] having 2-bit RRPV and with ABRIP [7] having 2-bit Cr RRPV and $\alpha = 4$. We use the same configuration as baseline ABRIP with 3-bit MLP-cost and $\lambda = 4$.

5 RESULTS AND ANALYSIS

5.1 2-core configuration

We evaluate the proposed replacement policy on 18 combinations of workloads under evaluation. In subsequent performance plots, first 12 workload mixes are of *CF-STR* category, and rest 6 are *CF-CF* mixes. We do not consider *STR-STR* workload mixes, as their performance remains unaffected irrespective of policy used.

Figure 3 shows the comparison of weighted speedup achieved by SRRIP, LIN, ABRIP and AB-Aware. *sphinx-gcc* achieve weighted speedup of 1.988, which is almost equal to the ideal value of weighted speedup (2 for dual-core and 4 for quad-core). LIN, which is MLP aware replacement with LRU as the baseline, performs poorly in all the workload mixes. LIN is MLP-aware, however, it is application behavior un-aware. *lbm* benchmark performs poorly with AB-Aware policy due to the poor predictability of the *mlp_cost* for *lbm's* blocks. AB-Aware policy implicitly assumes that the blocks which had high *mlp_cost* at the time they were brought in the cache will continue to have high *mlp_cost* in their successive access. However, blocks belonging to *lbm* showed large variability in the *mlp_cost* of the blocks across successive accesses. Hence, all workload mixes having *lbm* as one the benchmarks perform poorly with AB-Aware policy. While ABRIP worsens weighted speedup compared to SRRIP, we achieve 1.69% improvement on an average for all mixes.

Figure 4 shows *mpki's* of workload mixes for AB-Aware policy normalized to SRRIP. *Workload mixes having bar less than 2 perform better for AB-Aware policy.* A maximum of 69.22% of reduction is achieved by *bzip* while running with

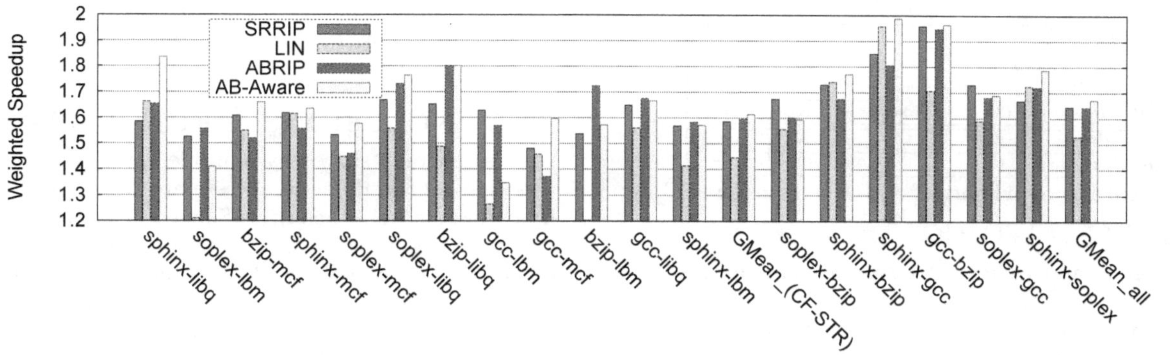

Figure 3: Weighted speedup comparison for 2-core configuration

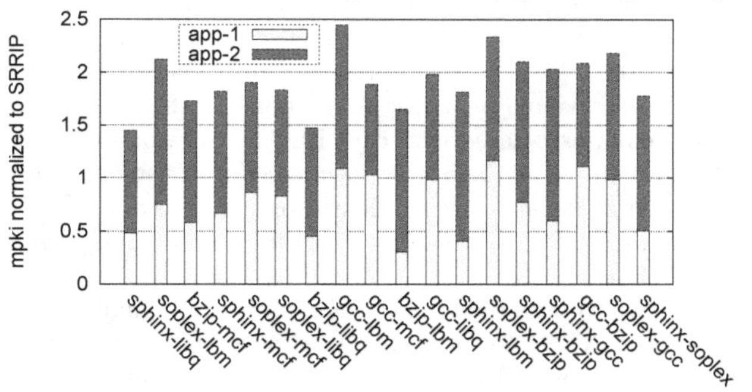

Figure 4: *mpki* reduction of AB-Aware over SRRIP

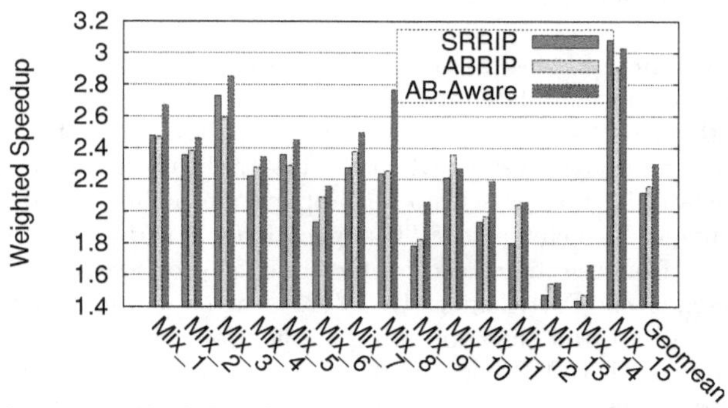

Figure 5: Weighted speedup comparison for 4-core configuration

Workload	Applications	Category
Mix_1	soplex-sphinx-gcc-libq	CF-CF-CF-STR
Mix_2	bzip-gcc-sphinx-lbm	
Mix_3	sphinx-bzip-gcc-mcf	
Mix_4	bzip-soplex-gcc-lbm	
Mix_5	gcc-soplex-sphinx-mcf	
Mix_6	sphinx-soplex-bzip-lbm	
Mix_7	bzip-sphinx-libq-mcf	CF-CF-STR-STR
Mix_8	gcc-sphinx-mcf-libq	
Mix_9	sphinx-bzip-lbm-mcf	
Mix_10	bzip-gcc-libq-lbm	
Mix_11	bzip-gcc-lbm-mcf	
Mix_12	soplex-bzip-libq-lbm	
Mix_13	soplex-libq-mcf-lbm	CF-STR-STR-STR
Mix_14	sphinx-libq-lbm-mcf	
Mix_15	bzip-gcc-sphinx-soplex	CF-CF-CF-CF

Table 3: Workloads under evaluation for quad-core

libq. In CF-STR mixes, *soplex-lbm* and *gcc-lbm* see increased *mpki*, mainly because of misses for *lbm* increase by around 35% due to poor *mlp_cost* predictability as mentioned in the previous paragraph. Even though workload mixes like *sphinx-bzip* and *sphinx-gcc* observe total normalized *mpki* more than 2, they gain in performance over SRRIP as shown in Figure 3 as in the proposed policy *mlp_cost* component sometime increases the total number of misses. However, in such cases, the number of reduced isolated misses overshadow increase in the number of parallel misses.

5.2 4-core configuration

In order to investigate the scalability of our policy, we evaluate our replacement policy on 15 workload mixes (shown in Table 3) with 8 MB LLC shared among four cores. These workload mixes include the following categories: six CF-CF-CF-STR, six CF-CF-STR-STR, two CF-STR-STR-STR and one CF-CF-CF-CF.

Figure 5 shows the comparison of weighted speedup achieved by SRRIP, ABRIP and AB-Aware. AB-Aware outperforms SRRIP in all workload mixes, except Mix_15 (CF-CF-CF-CF). For Mix_15, AB-Aware performs poorly as the policy finds it difficult to allocate cache resources among all CF workloads. AB-Aware outperforms ABRIP in 14 out of total 15 workload mixes and also outperforms SRRIP by 8.71% on an average. As we achieve better performance gains for 4-core system over 2-core system, it shows that AB-Aware policy is scalable and will perform better as the number of cores sharing LLC increases.

5.3 Hardware Overhead

Table 4 details the storage overhead incurred by AB-Aware policy for 2-core and 4-core configurations over SRRIP. 2-core configuration with 4 MB shared LLC has 8192 sets and 4-core configuration with 8 MB shared LLC has 16384 sets. We use 2-bit saturating counter *Cr* as core RRPV, which accounts for 2 bits of storage overhead per core per set. MLP cost (3-bit) is stored in tag-store array, which has a overhead of $(3\ bits * 8\ ways) = 24\ bits$ per set. Also, block RRPV *Br* uses additional 2 bits per set per way, which has a overhead of 16 bits per set. AB-Aware has 0.6% overhead (incurred due to MLP bits) over ABRIP for both 2-core and 4-core configurations.

Overhead	2-core	4-core
Core RRPV (2 bits per core per set)	4 KB	16 KB
Block RRPV bits (16 bits per set)	16 KB	32 KB
MLP Cost storage (24 bits per set)	24 KB	48 KB
Net overhead	44 KB	96 KB
% overhead over LLC	1.1%	1.2%

Table 4: Storage overhead of AB-Aware over SRRIP

6 RELATED WORK

Both academic and industrial research communities have made significant contributions in the development of efficient cache management policies. We summarize prior research work in the area of improving LLC performance through efficient management.

Qureshi *et al.* [10] proposed a low-cost run-time mechanism to compute MLP-cost of in-flight misses and uses the MLP-cost to reduce isolated misses. This replacement scheme uses LRU as its baseline policy. Hence, the policy is not efficient for a multicore system when a STR application high data demand is running with a CF application having low data demand. In such a case, STR application will thrash the data of CF from the shared cache. Qureshi *et al.* proposed a Utility-based Cache Partitioning (UCP) [11] scheme to minimize the miss rate of all the competing applications. It uses Utility Monitor (UMON) counters to find the utility of providing extra *ways* to an application. Based on statistics received from each UMON, replacement policy logically partitions the cache to have the lowest number of misses.

Qureshi *et al.* [9] show that on an average more than 60% of the cache lines are not re-referred before getting evicted as LLC receives filtered data locality. Such *zero reuse* cache lines adversely affect the performance of other applications under LRU policy, as these cache lines spend time traversing from MRU to LRU position before eviction, and therefore consume cache resources without any returns in terms of reuse. *LRU Insertion Policy (LIP)* [9] inserts cache blocks directly at LRU position, so they get evicted without spending much time in cache.

Jaleel *et al.* [6] proposed *Static Re-reference Interval Prediction (SRRIP)*, which predicts re-reference intervals of cache blocks. Instead of maintaining recency counters, SRRIP maintains M-bit saturating counter, which they call *Re-Reference Prediction Value (RRPV)*. $RRPV = 0$ denotes near re-reference interval and $RRPV = 2^M - 1$ denotes distant re-reference interval. SRRIP inserts blocks at $RRPV = 2^M - 2$, which is intermediate re-reference value. Upon hit, the block is promoted to $RRPV = 0$ (promotion policy), which is equivalent to MRU position. SRRIP tries to preserve the data-sets of the application showing good locality, however, some workloads have very high access rates compared to others. Such workloads may still interfere with cache blocks of recency-friendly workloads, especially, if they have low access rates. STR applications may produce misses with high rate, and CF blocks may get evicted before getting the first hit. To address this issue, Lathigara *et al.* [7] propose to add one more RRPV counter at core/application level in *Application Behavior-aware Re-reference Interval Prediction (ABRIP)* policy. However, ABRIP doesn't perform well when workload mixes are CF-CF.

7 CONCLUSIONS & FUTURE WORK

LLC is generally shared by multiple applications having diverse nature and different access pattern. Applications also have different MLP-behavior. Some applications have more parallel misses, whereas other applications have many isolated misses. Conventionally used LRU-based cache replacement policies are unaware of such application behaviors. We proposed an application behavior aware replacement policy AB-Aware. It considered both application's MLP-behavior and data-reuse behavior to manage shared LLC. The proposed policy reduced the negative interference among applications by assimilating each block's recency information to understand application's behavior as a whole. It also reduces the miss-penalty associated with each LLC miss. Experimental results showed up to 15.85% performance improvement (1.69% on an average) for 2-core configuration and up to 23.8% IPC improvement (8.71% on an average) for 4-core configuration over SRRIP.

We plan to investigate the benefits of using Auxiliary Tag Directory (ATD) to dynamically choose the best performing policy among SRRIP and AB-Aware as in few workload mixes SRRIP outperforms AB-Aware policy. AB-Aware policy increases the total number of misses for few workload mixes, we plan to study the energy cost for these increased misses and increased activity in MSHR due to updates in every cycle.

REFERENCES

[1] L. A. Belady. 1966. A Study of Replacement Algorithms for a Virtual-storage Computer. *IBM Syst. J.* 5, 2 (June 1966), 78–101.

[2] Shekhar Borkar and Andrew A. Chien. 2011. The Future of Microprocessors. *Commun. ACM* 54, 5 (May 2011), 67–77.

[3] Trevor E. Carlson, Wim Heirman, Stijn Eyerman, Ibrahim Hur, and Lieven Eeckhout. 2014. An Evaluation of High-Level Mechanistic Core Models. *ACM TACO* (2014).

[4] John L. Henning. 2006. SPEC CPU2006 Benchmark Descriptions. *SIGARCH Comput. Archit. News* 34, 4 (Sept. 2006), 1–17.

[5] Aamer Jaleel, William Hasenplaugh, Moinuddin Qureshi, Julien Sebot, Simon Steely, Jr., and Joel Emer. 2008. Adaptive Insertion Policies for Managing Shared Caches. In *PACT-17*. 208–219.

[6] Aamer Jaleel, Kevin B. Theobald, Simon C. Steely, Jr., and Joel Emer. 2010. High Performance Cache Replacement Using Re-reference Interval Prediction (RRIP). In *ISCA-37*. 60–71.

[7] P. Lathigara, S. Balachandran, and V. Singh. 2015. Application Behavior Aware Re-reference Interval Prediction for Shared LLC. In *ICCD-33*. 172–179.

[8] Harish Patil, Robert Cohn, Mark Charney, Rajiv Kapoor, Andrew Sun, and Anand Karunanidhi. 2004. Pinpointing Representative Portions of Large Intel® Itanium® Programs with Dynamic Instrumentation. In *Micro-37*. 81–92.

[9] Moinuddin K. Qureshi, Aamer Jaleel, Yale N. Patt, Simon C. Steely, and Joel Emer. 2007. Adaptive Insertion Policies for High Performance Caching. In *ISCA-34*. 381–391.

[10] Moinuddin K. Qureshi, Daniel N. Lynch, Onur Mutlu, and Yale N. Patt. 2006. A Case for MLP-Aware Cache Replacement. In *ISCA-33*. 167–178.

[11] Moinuddin K. Qureshi and Yale N. Patt. 2006. Utility-Based Cache Partitioning: A Low-Overhead, High-Performance, Runtime Mechanism to Partition Shared Caches. In *Micro-39*. 423–432.

[12] Carole-Jean Wu, Aamer Jaleel, Margaret Martonosi, Simon C. Steely, Jr., and Joel Emer. 2011. PACMan: Prefetch-aware Cache Management for High Performance Caching. In *Micro-44*.

Towards Near-Data Processing of Compare Operations in 3D-Stacked Memory

Palash Das and Hemangee K. Kapoor
Department of CSE, IIT Guwahati, Guwahati, Assam 781039, India
{palash.das, hemangee}@iitg.ernet.in

ABSTRACT

The gap between the processing speed and memory access speed of the modern multi-core systems has become a bottleneck for the emerging data-intensive workloads. In this scenario, it has become a smarter idea to move some amount of computation closer to the data, thus stimulating the concept of near-data processing (NDP).

Compare or scanning, the core operations of many applications, typically in a database, can leverage the benefits of NDP. We propose *near-data compare unit (NDCU)*, a less-invasive hardware, that can be integrated with the existing ecosystem of the hybrid memory cube (HMC). While integrating NDCU, we have designed two full-system architectures, one is lighter NDP with no parallelism (NNP) and the second is NDP with vault level parallelism (NVLP). While the first architecture is more power and area efficient, the second one is very fast with negligible overheads. With the motive of carrying out scan operation, we have specifically implemented *'compare-n-hit'*, *'compare-n-count'* and *'compare-n-max'* operations on both row-store and column-store databases and found significant improvements over conventional CPU-based system. We get around 2.3x and 37x performance improvement in NNP and NVLP architectures respectively. In both the designs, we reduce the energy consumption by around 8x on an average.

CCS CONCEPTS

• **Hardware** → **Application specific processors**; **Logic synthesis**; *3D integrated circuits*;

KEYWORDS

Near-data processing; Row-store database; Column-store Database; Process in memory; Compare operation; 3D-Stacked Memory; Hybrid Memory Cube

ACM Reference Format:

Palash Das and Hemangee K. Kapoor. 2018. Towards Near-Data Processing of Compare Operations in 3D-Stacked Memory. In *GLSVLSI '18: 2018 Great Lakes Symposium on VLSI, May 23–25, 2018, Chicago, IL, USA.* ACM, New York, NY, USA, 6 pages. https://doi.org/10.1145/3194554.3194578

GLSVLSI '18, May 23–25, 2018, Chicago, IL, USA

ACM ISBN 978-1-4503-5724-1/18/05...$15.00
https://doi.org/10.1145/3194554.3194578

1 INTRODUCTION

The two major metrics for optimizing a system are performance and energy. Along with the processors, the memory hierarchy also plays a crucial role in deciding these metrics. The architectural shift from processors to chip-multiprocessors has given enormous compute capability. However, this aggravated the memory bottleneck as memory bandwidth could not be increased in sync with computational capability due to the limitation of pins. This has lead to the *memory-wall* problem. Besides this, emerging data-intensive workloads are making the system more data-hungry due to its notorious data access pattern, inherent large memory footprints and small amount of computations with a high degree of parallelism. Locality of references being extremely low in these data-intensive workloads, the cache hierarchy often gets immobilized which leads to increased off-chip main memory accesses. Main memory access, being expensive in terms of access latency as well as energy consumption, pulls down the throughput of the entire system. The newly arrived big data workloads have endorsed the movement towards the resurgence of the old unavailing idea of processing in memory (PIM) or near-data processing (NDP). Many researchers have built PIM prototypes since 1990s [6, 10, 16] and have shown promising results. However, that could not be adopted at that time due to several factors. Incorporating costlier logic and memory on the same die was a challenging job. Moreover, newer programming model needed to be grappled by the programmers.

But with the advent of 3D-stacked memory like Micron's Hybrid Memory cube (HMC) [2], JEDEC's High Bandwidth Memory (HBM) [25] etc., there is scope for PIM on account of the tight integration of logic and memory with the help of Through-Silicon-Vias (TSVs). 3D-stacked memories have logic layer (LoB) and high internal bandwidth that can be used by NDP approaches. This reduces the cost of data movement altogether by offloading certain amount of computations to the processing units placed at or near the memory. Many researchers have even placed processors in the memory [9, 15, 20]. However, full-fledged processors have challenges related to thermal issues [24] as memory devices suffer from cooling technology and have challenges of cache coherence, virtual memory etc.

On the contrary, application specific simple hardware [12, 18, 19] has proven to be an eligible candidate for NDP within the limited thermal, power and area budget of the memory. Flexibility being an issue with the application specific hardware, we have targeted widely used operation like *'compare-n-op'* which is primitive to many applications, typically in a database. The *'compare-n-op'* compares two parameters and based on the result of comparison, some additional simple operations like read, write, finding multiple occurrences, counting the number of occurrence or finding the maximum value, etc., can be performed on a huge dataset. Almost similar operations have been targeted in [12]. Our work is also motivated

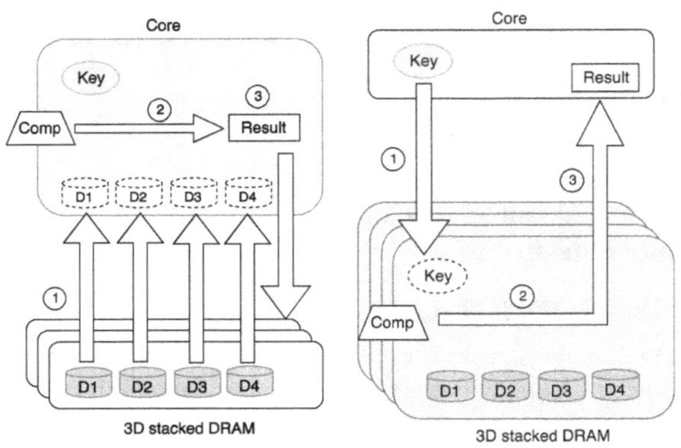

(a) Conventional system (b) NDP based system

Figure 1: Conventional system vs. NDP based system

by the use of hardware for acceleration of the database operations as in [1], however they follow an FPGA based approach which is different from our NDP based approach. In this work, we tried to exploit the high unused internal bandwidth of the HMC for *'compare-n-op'* on huge amount of data with minimal changes to the existing ecosystem of the HMC. Though our proposed model leverages minimum computing capability by keeping complex and unbounded operations on to the host processor, it helps the host processor by behaving like a slave to the master. The applications that comprise of compare operations on huge dataset can be benefited substantially by this model. We have evaluated our system on the database applications because it comprises of maximum number of *'compare-n-op'*.

Fig. 1 depicts two systems (a) Conventional Systems and (b) Systems having NDP capability. Conventional Systems include ① fetching chunk of data one by one from memory ② comparing key with the fetched data ③ storing the results back to the memory. This process uses the external bandwidth heavily, with its heavy off-chip communication, resulting in low system throughput. However, the second approach needs ① sending the key to the memory side processing unit using off-chip connection② comparing the key with target data close to DRAM itself ③ sending the result back to the host processor for further high-level processing using off-chip connection. The second approach is superior to the previous one in terms of system throughput because of its highly reduced off-chip communication: only two in this case. The internal bandwidth being extremely high in a multi-vault HMC, the requirement of using external bandwidth can easily be compensated with its internal bandwidth leading to high-performance computing. This paper makes the following contributions:

- We use NDP to improve the performance of various *'compare-n-op'*s. We present the design of a near-data compare unit (NDCU) which performs *'compare-n-hit'*, *'compare-n-count'* and *'compare-n-max'* operations near the memory.
- We have proposed two full-system NDP architectures. One is having the benefits of NDP with no parallelism (NNP) while the other has vault level parallelism with NDP (NVLP).
- The difference with existing state-of-the-art is the use of 3D-stacked memory environment, dedicated logic units and exploiting vault level data parallelism.

2 BACKGROUND AND MOTIVATION

2.1 Related Work

The approach of NDP has been explored in both 2D and 3D memories. 3D memories are fast due to its high bandwidth and render more scope while integrating logic units with the memories.

2D Process-in-memory: While talking about simple 2D DRAM, building PIM can broadly be classified into two categories. One is integrating logical units on top of the DRAM chip while the second is modifying the DRAM itself to provide computational capabilities. NDA [8], Buffered Compares [12] and JAFAR [18] belong to the first category of integrating logical units with the existing DRAM organizations while Fast Bulk bitwise AND and OR [17] belongs to the later. In NDA, Coarse-Grained Reconfigurable Architecture (CGRA) units are stacked on top of DRAM modules to perform near-memory computation. In [17], they connected 3 cells directly to a bit-line in such a way, so as to provide AND and OR operations depending on the value of one of these cells. In [12], a BCU (Buffered Compare Unit) has been made for compare operation. In [18], select operation in databases are accelerated. JAFAR sends only qualifying data to the processor, whenever select request is sent by the host processor, reducing the traffic between processor and DRAM. Both these works have portrayed a similar approach, but their idea of NDP has been implemented with the traditional 2D DRAM. However, our approach of NDP has been implemented in a completely different setup of 3D memory, specifically HMC [22] and it exploits data parallelism. Experimental results show the evidence of the fact that 3D memories are more desirable candidates for NDP.

NDP on 3D-stacked Memory: Reduced energy consumption with increased performance has been achieved by 3D stacking of layers through TSVs. In 3D-stacked memory, DRAM layers are stacked on each other and a logic layer remains at the bottom of the DRAM layers. The interaction between these layers takes place through high speed, low powered TSV connects. These 3D memories are being used for highly parallel map-reduce operations [15]. It has also been used for data re-organization [4]. In HRL [21], Heterogeneous Reconfigurable Logic has been used as processing unit while incorporating the concept of NDP. The overall throughput of the HRL based system is shown to be substantially better than both fine-grained (FPGA) and coarse-grained (CGRA) reconfigurable logic, while executing MapReduce, graph processing, and deep neural networks. In Logic-in-Memory accelerator [19], a 3D die-stacked DRAM device, which is quite similar to HMC, has been integrated with accelerator. Reasonable performance gain and power efficiency has been obtained with respect to CPU based baseline system while implementing target application like SpGEMM, 2D FFT. Special hardware has also been employed for NDP operations in PIM-Enabled Instructions [5]. Similar to these contributions, we have used specialized hardware for our proposed approach.

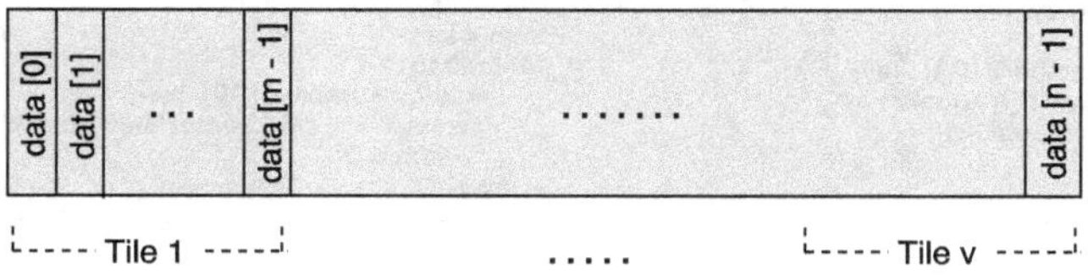

Figure 2: Tiled Data layout for parallel processing

2.2 Hybrid Memory Cube

Generally, HMC [22] consists of 4 to 8 dies of DRAM cell arrays. A 3D memory die is formed by stacking those DRAM layers. Each DRAM layer is made up of DRAM banks. A single logic layer which lies at the bottom of the DRAM layers consists of all the interconnects and controllers to fetch and store data in the memory die. Each of the memory layers is divided into 16 to 32 parts. Every individual stack of these partitions is called a vault. There is a vault controller (VC0, VC1, etc.), in the logic layer (LoB), associated with individual vaults. Each vault controller has the capability of controlling its operation independently in the respective vault. HMC also has a host memory controller and SerDes links for off-stack communication in the logic layer. HMC is generally faster than the normal DRAM device in terms of throughput.

2.3 Table-Scan

Table-scan is predominantly used in database operations. It is a critical operation where the processors have to waste a lot of unnecessary efforts while fetching the data for comparison. It can be performed on column-store databases (TSC) as well as on row-store databases (TSR). Table-scan is specifically efficient for column-store databases [3] as it restricts the fetching of unnecessary data. As a result, the cache hierarchy performs effectively in case of TSC. In NDP, both TSC as well as TSR databases can be effectively used. Our proposed NDCU performs basic operations close to the data and sends results to the host processor making any type of data storage easy to use.

3 SYSTEM ARCHITECTURE AND OPERATIONAL STEPS

The philosophy behind the design has got twofold advantages: (1) leveraging the novelty of NDP by placing the logical unit as close to the data as possible (2) harnessing the hidden parallelism in the scan operation on huge datasets. To exploit (1) we place our NDCU on the logic layer, close to the data. Here, all memory references are managed by the host memory controller instead of individual vault controllers. This architecture is named as NNP, i.e. NDP with no-parallelism. In order to exploit (2), i.e. data parallelism, we propose to place NDCUs with every vault. In particular, each NDCU will parallely operate on data (tile) from its corresponding vault. In our experimental setup, we have 16 vaults and therefore 16 NDCUs. Memory references, in this case, are handled by the individual vault controllers. Our proposed idea is based on the observation of having inherent parallelism in the scan operation. While scanning huge datasets, the entire data can be partitioned into tiles (relatively small pieces of datasets) as shown in Fig. 2. The entire

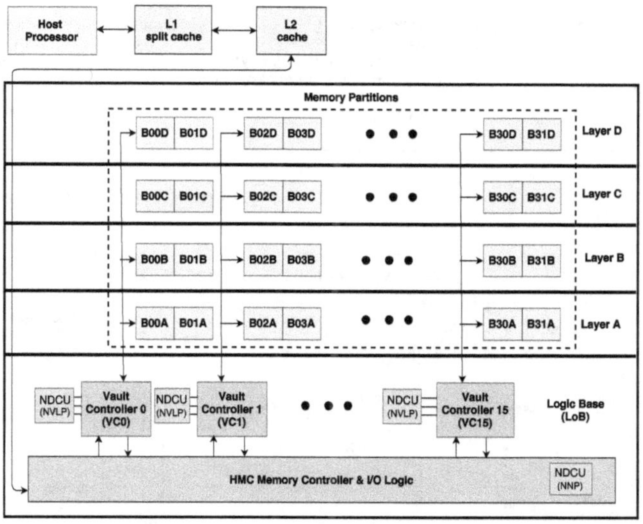

Figure 3: A conceptual view of proposed full system architectures (NNP and NVLP)

dataset of size n has been divided into v number of tiles where each tile has approximately same amount of data (size of m). Here, v is the number of vaults in the HMC. These tiles are distributed by the host processor over different vaults of HMC module (1 tile / vault) for parallel scanning to obtain maximum speedup, leading to our proposed second architecture (NVLP). However, this maximum speedup cannot be obtained in cases when the tiles are mapped unevenly by the host across the vaults. In such cases, some NDCUs may take longer time compared to others which will have an impact on achievable speedup. Fig. 3 shows both the architectures: NNP and NVLP. In NNP architecture, the system has only 1 NDCU component (marked in green) whereas in NVLP, the system has 16 NDCUs (marked in blue). This logic unit (NDCU) has the capability of scanning both row-store and column-store databases. Additionally, it can perform basic arithmetic operations while performing the following three variants of *'compare-n-op'*. The pseudocodes for all the three operations, shown in Fig. 4, are explained below.

- The *'compare-n-hit'* operation is used to search a key, sent by the host processor, on an attribute of the schema. If that key is found in the target data (D[i]), the NDCU informs the host processor about the presence of the corresponding key by setting the hit register.
- In *'compare-n-count'* operation, the number of occurrences of a particular key (sent by the host processor) in the target data (D[i]), is to be counted. The result is sent to the host processor for high-level processing.
- In *'compare-n-max'*, the maximum value (can be found in *'item'* register) of any attribute of the schema is sent to the host processor.

All these operations can be executed on both row-store and column-store databases. The generalized *'compare-n-op'* function becomes a specialized one by the respective opcodes sent by the host processor. The 2-bit opcodes for hit, count and max operations are shown in Fig. 4. NDCU remains in inactive mode when opcode is set to '11'.

```
opcode 00: Compare_n_Hit (key, D[n]) {
    for i = 0 to n−1 {
        result = compare (D[ i ], key)
        if (result == "D[i] equals key") {
            hit reg = 1
            return } } }
```

```
opcode 01 : Compare_n_Count (key, D[ n ]) {
    for i = 0 to n−1 {
        result = compare (D[i], key)
        if (result == "D[i] equals key")
            count = count + 1
    } return }
```

```
opcode 10 : Compare_n_Max (key, D[n]) {
    item = key
    for i = 0 to n−1 {
        result = compare (D[i], item)
        if (result == "D[i] greater than item")
            item = D[i]
    } return }
```

Figure 4: Specialized pseudocode of *'compare-n-op'*

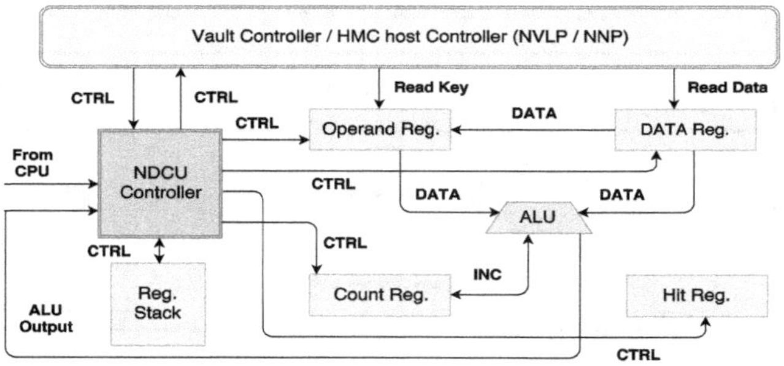

Figure 5: Abstract design of NDCU

Initially, the host processor sets the opcode based on its requirement and sends the key to be processed, along with some additional information, like, initial address and range of data to be processed, to the NDCU. Upon offloading the workload to the slave NDCUs, the host processor becomes free to start some other work. This, indeed, increases the parallelism and thereby the throughput of the proposed system becomes high.

3.1 Operational Steps

The abstract data-path of the NDCU is shown in Fig. 5. NDCU controller is the centroid of the entire data-path. For simplicity, all the communication channels between any two units in the data-path are shown with a single connector. After the processor's intervention, the NDCU controller receives all the relevant information like opcode, initial data address, range of data to be processed etc., from the host processor and stores it in the register stack for further processing. In the next step, the operand register is assigned with the key sent by the host processor. With the help of the vault controller in case of NVLP or the HMC host memory controller in case of NNP, the data items are brought by the NDCU controller one by one to the data register for *'compare-n-op'*. The ALU acts as a processing element which compares the values. Based on the ALU output and the opcode given by the processor, the NDCU controller invokes the corresponding function. Depending on the function to be performed and the ALU output, the NDCU controller sets the hit register for hit operation, whereas it updates the count register in case of count operation. For max operation, NDCU controller transfers the content of the data register to the operand register if the item (content of the operand register) is less than the value of the data register. NDCU controller has separate connections for sending reset and write signals to all the registers of the entire data-path which are not shown in Fig. 5 for simplicity.

4 EXPERIMENTAL EVALUATION

We have chosen database application because it comprises of significant amount of *'compare-n-op'* which justifies the efficacy of the proposed system as well as demonstrates its usefulness.

4.1 Target Applications

4.1.1 Table scan - column store (TSC):. Table-scan is having benefits over index-based database operations in terms of storage, as storing indexes needs extra space on the disk. Specifically, in the context of column-store databases where the data is stored in column-wise format, scan is often used because it fetches only the necessary information while saving the costly memory bandwidth. We have implemented all the variants of *'compare-n-op'* and tested on the *star schema benchmark* [14]. This benchmark is very efficient in measuring the performance of database products. The *'PARTKEY'* attribute of the 'lineorder' fact table is used for *'compare-n-hit'*, *'SUPPLYCOST'* is used for *'compare-n-max'* and *'QUANTITY'* is used for *'compare-n-count'* operation.

4.1.2 Table scan - row store (TSR):. The operations same as those in TSC are performed on the same attributes in this case as well, however the data is stored in row-wise format here. Row-store databases are less efficient as CPU based processing units fetch unnecessary data leading to wastage of memory bandwidth. From

Table 1: Workload Details

Workloads	Details	Workloads	Details
Hit_TSC_best	Best case hit operation	Hit_TSR_worst	Worst case hit operation
Hit_TSC_avg	Average case hit operation	Count_TSC	Count on column-store database
Hit_TSC_worst	Worst case hit operation	Count_TSR	Count on row-store database
Hit_TSR_best	Best case hit operation	Max_TSC	Finding maximum value
Hit_TSR_avg	Average case hit operation	Max_TSR	Finding maximum value

Table 2: Specification of the simulation setup.

Host Processor [GEM5]	
Core	Single core, x86-64, 2 GHz
L1 i-cache	32 KB, private, 4 way associative
L1 d-cache	32 KB, private, 8 way associative
L2 cache	256 KB, shared, 8 way associative
Main Memory	2 GB, DDR3_1600_x64
Proposed logic unit for NDP (NDCU)	
NDCU	1 for NNP, 16 for NVLP. Each has 1 ALU.
Frequency	950MHz on UMC 90nm technology
3D Memory Stack (HMC)	
Timing Parameters	t_{RP} = 7.7ns, tt_{CCD} = 3.3ns, t_{RCD} = 10.2ns, t_{CL} = 9.9ns, t_{WR} = 15ns, t_{RAS} = 21.6ns, t_{CK} = 0.8ns
Energy [22]	3.7 pj/bit for DRAM read, 6.78 pj/bit for SerDes hop
Power[23]	11.08W
Size	2 GB
Logic Die	90nm, dimension 27 X 27 mm^2

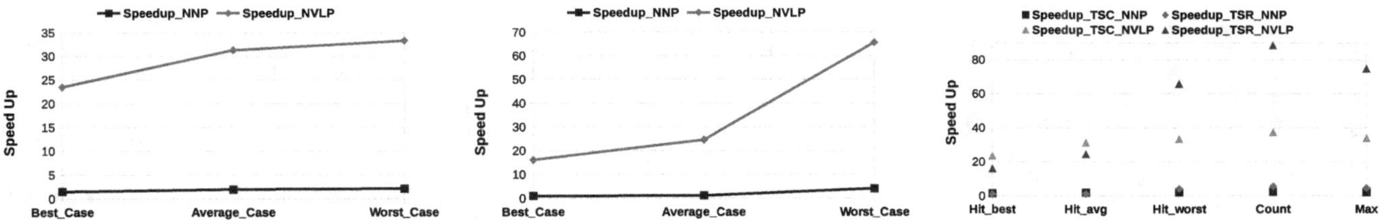

(a) Speed up comparison for TSC (b) Speed up comparison for TSR (c) Performance comparison of TSC vs TSR

Figure 6: Analysis of the proposed system performance on typical cases

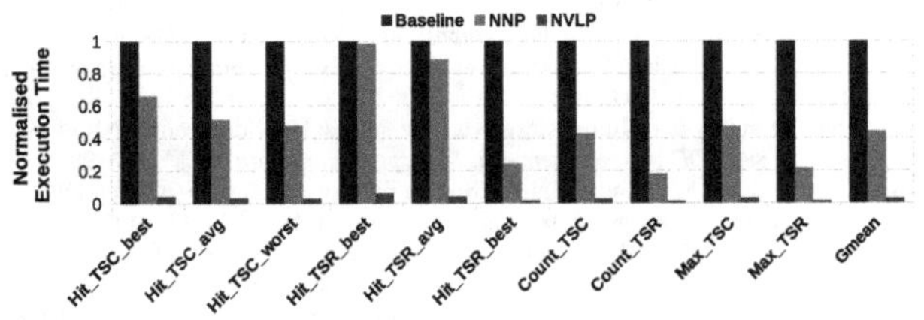

Figure 7: Performance comparison of proposed NDP architecture; normalized w.r.t baseline CPU based model

the result section, it can be verified that our architectures (NNP and NVLP) perform much better in case of TSRs. The reason of this improvement is that in row-store databases, data (target attribute of a schema) does not remain in consecutive memory locations. As a result, cache hierarchy in the conventional CPU based system cannot deliver performance due to lack of spatial locality.

All three operations mentioned above have been performed in the typical column-store (TSC) and row-store (TSR) database, leading to the workloads as shown in Table 1. During the search operation on a given key-value pair, item (to be searched) may be found anywhere. To quantify the performance improvement, we categorize these searches. In particular, we model three cases: (i) Hit_TSx_best- when the item is found in the first 25% of the search space. (ii) Hit_TSx_avg- when the item is found within 25%-50% of the search space and (iii) Hit_TSx_worst- when the item is found after 75% of the search space (when TSx represents both column and row store database).

4.2 Baseline CPU based System

We have used Gem5 [7] to model our baseline system. Gem5 is a cycle accurate simulator which is being extensively used for the full system simulation purpose. We have configured our simulation setup with x86-64bit processing core having working frequency of 2 GHz. Two level cache hierarchy (private L1 and Shared L2) has been implemented with DRAM based main memory system for full system simulation. The energy modeling of the core has been done using McPAT 1.3 [11], and CACTI 6.5 [13] has been used to obtain the energy of the main memory system.

4.3 NDCU hardware

NDCU is a dedicated hardware, designed using Verilog hardware description language. After the initial design, it has been synthesized by Genus Synthesis solution from Cadence. We have used UMC 90nm technology library and the obtained operating frequency of NDCU is around 950 MHz. This NDCU will be placed in the logic layer of HMC. Specification parameters for both baseline and proposed systems are given in Table 2.

4.4 Results

We have obtained motivating results in terms of performance and energy which instigate the concept of near-data processing. Area being a critical aspect for integrating logic on the same memory chip, we have analyzed the area overhead for practical implementation of the proposed architectures.

Performance: For both the architectures (NNP and NVLP), we get improvement in the execution time and speedup over the conventional system, for all the workloads. While the NVLP is extremely fast due to its massively parallel architecture, NNP proves its significance in terms of reduced power consumption with negligible area overhead and improved performance compared to baseline. From Fig. 7, we can see substantial improvement in the performance of all the workloads for both NNP and NVLP architectures. We have evaluated the hit operation for best, average and worst case scenario. Here, the execution time of NNP and NVLP architecture includes both the computation time as well as the data fetching time from the DRAM die to the logic layer. Similarly, in the case of baseline, the execution time comprises of the computation time of the CPU and the data fetching time through the conventional memory hierarchy.

The novelty of our approach is that the speed up (in TSC as shown in Fig. 6a and TSR as shown in Fig. 6b) is monotonically increasing from the best case to the worst case for both NNP and NVLP architectures. The reason behind this is that, with the increasing number of *'compare-n-op'*, the off-chip communication also increases which pulls down the system performance of the conventional CPU based system. However, our NDP based approach is working near the memory. As a result, the effect of costly off-chip communication is avoided and high internal bandwidth utilization is obtained.

Another important observation is that our proposed approach is doing well under typical data layouts. If we observe Fig. 6c, we can see that the performance of TSR has dominated the performance of TSC both for NNP and NVLP architectures with the increasing number of *'compare-n-op'*. Initially, TSC has not been dominated by TSR because the number of *'compare-n-op'* was less. However, with the increasing dataset, the scenario has changed. Conventional CPU

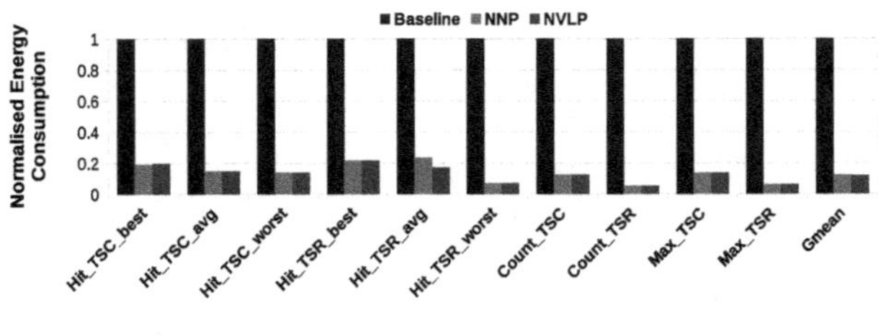

Figure 8: Reduction in energy consumption w.r.t baseline CPU based model

based system suffers from row-store databases. The reason for this is that unnecessary data has to be fetched by the CPU in row-store databases which not only wastes the memory bandwidth but also increases the off-chip communication. Even in this typical scenario, both the NNP and NVLP architectures leverage the benefits of NDP and minimize the costly off-chip communication. On an average, we obtained around 2.3x speed up in NNP and around 37x speed up in NVLP, over the baseline.

Energy Savings: Power analysis of baseline has been done using McPAT and CACTI. We analyzed the power consumption of the proposed NDCU units in Genus Synthesis solution from Cadence. Using this value, we analyzed the total power consumption of the two proposed system (NNP and NVLP). Energy consumption depends on the execution time as well as power consumption. Though NNP architecture is more power efficient, the energy consumption is almost same as NVLP because the execution time of NNP architecture is longer than NVLP architecture. In both the proposed models, we obtained substantially better results in terms of energy consumption over the baseline. The comparison of energy consumption between the baseline and proposed models is shown in Fig. 8. On an average, we obtained around 8x saving in energy in both NNP and NVLP architecture with respect to the baseline.

Area analysis: Since memory industries are extremely area sensitive, area overhead of the logical units should be analyzed thoroughly. We performed a detailed area analysis on the NDCU net-list, generated after the post synthesis simulation done by the Genus. We used Innovus (from Cadence tool-set) and our net-list got placed on 0.18mm X 0.18mm square box at 90nm technology. In NNP architecture, this incorporated the area overhead of 0.032mm^2 which is only 0.004% of the logic die area, which is negligible. In case of NVLP architecture, the total area overhead due to multiple NDCUs is 0.52mm^2 which is 0.07% of the entire logic die. Even this area overhead is quite reasonable considering its overall throughput.

5 CONCLUSIONS

Scan or compare operations being primitive in nature, can be used in a wide variety of applications. The inherent parallelism in scan operation over the tiled data layout has made it a lucrative candidate for near-data processing. In this paper, we have implemented our proposed design of NDCU hardware unit, dedicatedly built for memory scan operation, while performing some additional tasks like hit, count and max. We have designed two full system architectures (NNP and data parallel NVLP) to harness the benefits of NDP. Both have substantial improvements over CPU based baseline in terms of performance and power with negligible area overhead. While the system can achieve 2.3x and 37x speedup in NNP and NVLP architectures respectively, it reduces the energy consumption by 8x, on an average, for both the architectures.

This work can be carried forward in several directions: optimizing the design, reducing the overhead of result accumulation from the host processor, technology scaling, increasing the clock frequency, thermal issues, etc. The results of this research encourage the use of NDP for data parallel applications, like table-scan, by the use of dedicated hardware rather than fully functional processors.

REFERENCES

[1] Jared Casper and Kunle Olukotun. 2014. Hardware acceleration of database operations. In *ACM/SIGDA Int. symposium on FPGA*. ACM, 151–160.

[2] Hybrid Memory Cube Consortium et al. 2013. Hybrid memory cube specification 1.0. *Last Revision Jan* (2013).

[3] Abadi et al. 2008. Column-stores vs. row-stores: How different are they really?. In *ACM SIGMOD Int. conference on Management of data*. ACM, 967–980.

[4] Akin et al. 2015. Data reorganization in memory using 3D-stacked DRAM. In *ACM SIGARCH Computer Architecture News*, Vol. 43. ACM, 131–143.

[5] Ahn et al. 2015. PIM-enabled instructions: A low-overhead, locality-aware processing-in-memory architecture. In *ISCA*. IEEE, 336–348.

[6] Ahn et al. 2015. A scalable processing-in-memory accelerator for parallel graph processing. In *ISCA*. IEEE, 105–117.

[7] Binkert et al. 2011. The gem5 simulator. *ACM SIGARCH Computer Architecture News* 39, 2 (2011), 1–7.

[8] Farmahini-Farahani et al. 2015. NDA: Near-DRAM acceleration architecture leveraging commodity DRAM devices and standard memory modules. In *HPCA*. IEEE, 283–295.

[9] Gao et al. 2015. Practical near-data processing for in-memory analytics frameworks. In *PACT*. IEEE, 113–124.

[10] Kang et al. 2012. FlexRAM: Toward an advanced intelligent memory system. In *ICCD*. IEEE, 5–14.

[11] Li et al. 2009. McPAT: an integrated power, area, and timing modeling framework for multicore and manycore architectures. In *MICRO*. IEEE, 469–480.

[12] Lee et al. 2017. Excavating the Hidden Parallelism Inside DRAM Architectures With Buffered Compares. *IEEE Trans. on VLSI Syst.* (2017).

[13] Muralimanohar et al. 2009. CACTI 6.0: A tool to model large caches. *HP laboratories* (2009), 22–31.

[14] O'Neil et al. 2009. The star schema benchmark and augmented fact table indexing. In *Technology Conference on Performance Evaluation and Benchmarking*. Springer, 237–252.

[15] Pugsley et al. 2014. NDC: Analyzing the impact of 3D-stacked memory + logic devices on MapReduce workloads. In *ISPASS*. IEEE, 190–200.

[16] Schaffner et al. 2015. DRAM or no-DRAM? Exploring linear solver architectures for image domain warping in 28 nm CMOS. In *DATE*. IEEE, 707–712.

[17] Seshadri et al. 2015. Fast bulk bitwise AND and OR in DRAM. *IEEE Computer Architecture Letters* 14, 2 (2015), 127–131.

[18] Xi et al. 2015. Beyond the wall: Near-data processing for databases. In *Proceedings of the 11th Int. Workshop on Data Management on New Hardware*. ACM, 2.

[19] Zhu et al. 2013. A 3D-stacked logic-in-memory accelerator for application-specific data intensive computing. In *3D Systems Integration Conference (3DIC), IEEE Int.* IEEE, 1–7.

[20] Zhang et al. 2014. TOP-PIM: throughput-oriented programmable processing in memory. In *23rd Int. symp. on High-performance parallel and distributed computing*. ACM, 85–98.

[21] Mingyu Gao and Christos Kozyrakis. 2016. HRL: efficient and flexible reconfigurable logic for near-data processing. In *HPCA*. Ieee, 126–137.

[22] Joe Jeddeloh and Brent Keeth. 2012. Hybrid memory cube new DRAM architecture increases density and performance. In *VLSI Technology (VLSIT), 2012 Symposium on*. IEEE, 87–88.

[23] J Thomas Pawlowski. 2011. Hybrid memory cube (HMC). In *Hot Chips 23 Symposium (HCS), 2011 IEEE*. IEEE, 1–24.

[24] Kiran Puttaswamy and Gabriel H Loh. 2006. Thermal analysis of a 3D die-stacked high-performance microprocessor. In *GLSVLSI*. ACM, 19–24.

[25] JEDEC Standard. 2013. High bandwidth memory (hbm) dram. *JESD235* (2013).

Utility Aware Snoozy Caches for Energy Efficient Chip Multi-Processors

Ashwini A. Kulkarni[1], Shounak Chakraborty[2], Shrinivas P. Mahajan[1], and Hemangee K. Kapoor[2]
[1]College of Engineering Pune, Pune, Maharashtra 411005, India
[2]Department of CSE, IIT Guwahati, Guwahati, Assam 781039, India
{aak15.extc, spm.extc}[1]@coep.ac.in, {c.shounak, hemangee}[2]@iitg.ernet.in

ABSTRACT

Heavy leakage power consumption of on-chip last level caches (LLCs) has become the primary obstacle for architecting chip multi-processors (CMPs) in recent times. As leakage power has a direct relationship with the supply voltage, hence, periodic access profile based dynamic voltage scaling (DVS) in the LLC banks can be a promising option towards reducing this heavy cache leakage. A plethora of prior attempts have reduced this by anticipating working set size (WSS) of the applications and eventually putting some portions of the cache banks in low power mode. This proposed work aims to reduce leakage by putting a whole LLC bank into a low power (snoozy) mode through exploiting DVS at cache banks having minimal usages. Additionally, the resulting performance impacts of the low power snoozy mode are alleviated further by putting some snoozy banks in active mode on-demand. Experimental evaluations using full system simulation on a multi-banked 2MB 8-way set associative L2 cache show 10% more leakage savings on an average over a prior drowsy technique.

CCS CONCEPTS

• **Hardware** → **Power estimation and optimization**; • **Computer systems organization** → *Multicore architectures*;

KEYWORDS

Leakage Energy; EDP (Energy Delay Product); Multi-banked Caches; LLCs; Usage Statistics; Dynamic Energy; Snoozy Cache; IPC (Instructions Per Cycle);

ACM Reference Format:

Ashwini A. Kulkarni[1], Shounak Chakraborty[2], Shrinivas P. Mahajan[1], and Hemangee K. Kapoor[2]. 2018. Utility Aware Snoozy Caches for Energy Efficient Chip Multi-Processors. In *GLSVLSI '18: 2018 Great Lakes Symposium on VLSI, May 23–25, 2018, Chicago, IL, USA.* ACM, New York, NY, USA, 6 pages. https://doi.org/10.1145/3194554.3194581

1 INTRODUCTION

Ultra-scale logic integration of a large number of cores along with multi-level on-chip caches drastically improves performance of the modern chip multi-processors (CMPs) by ameliorating the ever increasing processor-memory gap, undoubtedly. In addition with this hiked performance, these heavy integration also escalates the on-chip power density which in turn may prohibitively have adverse effects on the chip circuitry, battery life etc. According to the available literature [18, 20], majority of these power consumption is coming from the LLC leakage, due to the largest area occupancy of LLCs on the wafer real-estate. Table 1 listed the amount of power consumption shared by the LLCs in some contemporary CMPs which can motivate the architects and designers towards lowering these numbers.

Microprocessor	Power Consumed by on-chip Caches with respect to total power
ARM 920T	44%
Strong ARM SA-110	27%
21164 DEC Alpha	25 – 30%
Niagra	12%
Niagra2	21%
Alpha 21364	13%
Xeon (Tulsa)	13%

Table 1: Power consumed by on-chip caches [18, 20]

Shrinking in LLC size can be a promising option to significantly reduce the leakage consumption, but, random reduction in LLC size can aggravate the system performance by incorporating more capacity and conflict misses. Moreover, dynamic resizing of caches needs some extra stall cycles for data management and conventional delays in gating circuitry [10]. Practically, complete shutdown of cache portions needs eviction of its blocks with proper management measures which incur complex procedures from the actual design perspective. As a contrast to this, Flautner et al. in 2002 have proposed Drowsy cache, where supply voltage of the cache is controlled by exploiting MTCMOS circuitry [7] where extra overhead of cache resizing has been minimised by preserving the blocks' status in a low power mode. As leakage power has a direct dependency on supply voltage (and running chip temperature), hence, reduction in supply voltage (i.e. DVS) reduces leakage power significantly, with a negligible impact on performance. This DVS can be exclusively applied either at the data array or at the tag array or can also be applied at both. But, reducing power supply at both the arrays simultaneously may slowdown the request processing at the caches. As data array consumes the majority of the cache leakage, hence, controlling its power supply alone is also able to save a significant portion of total power consumption. In this work, we apply DVS only at the data array, and keep tag array unchanged for the early detection of cache miss/hit. We choose the least accessed banks as the candidates for DVS, towards reducing performance degradation, as cache exploits locality of reference.

Recently, Tiled CMP (TCMP), as shown in Figure 1, has been evolved as a scalable design for the small scale upcoming CMPs, which is baseline architecture of our work. A TCMP is formed

GLSVLSI '18, May 23–25, 2018, Chicago, IL, USA

ACM ISBN 978-1-4503-5724-1/18/05...$15.00
https://doi.org/10.1145/3194554.3194581

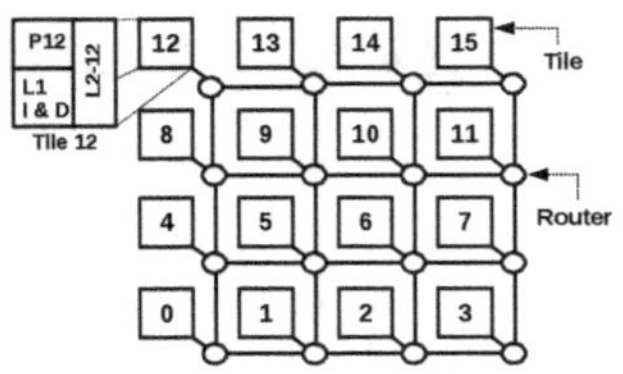

Figure 1: Tiled CMP architecture

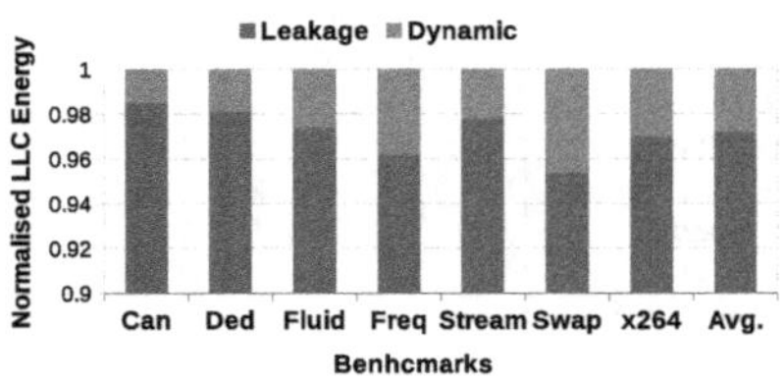

Figure 2: Total Energy Consumption break-up (Dynamic + Leakage) for an LLC of size 2MB.

by exploiting a 2D mesh interconnection of a set of replicated tiles, where each tile contains a processor core, a local split L1-cache (Instruction and Data) and a slice/bank of (shared) L2-cache (considering L2-cache as LLC). Multi-level inclusion of the cache blocks is maintained among the cache hierarchies. However, LLC banks of a TCMP are accessed in a non-uniform fashion throughout the execution of the application(s) [15]. Hence, scaling down supply voltage of the least utilised banks will save leakage with minimal degradation in performance. However, scaling down of voltages at several banks may aggravate the performance by incurring extra clock cycles at the bank level for accessing of the data blocks.

The major contributions of this work are: (i) Applying DVS at the least used cache banks to reduce the leakage. (ii) Scale up the supply voltage if the number of accesses to a snoozy bank increases. Our experimental results show that, the policy saves static energy by 50% and EDP by 45% than our baseline architecture for a 2MB 8 way set associative L2 cache. For a larger 4MB cache with 8 way associativity we also able to save static energy by 47% and EDP by 46%. This proposed policy also shows better results compared to a prior state preserving policy: Drowsy cache [3], which puts some of the cache ways in a low-power mode to save leakage.

Rest of this article is organised as follows. Section 2 discusses about the background and motivations of our proposed policy. The proposed work is illustrated in Section 3 and our used energy model is given in Section 4. We discuss our experimental analyses in Section 5. The prior works are discussed in Section 6 before concluding the paper in Section 7.

2 MOTIVATION

Concomitant to the available literature and our own simulation analyses, it has been noticed that, majority of the LLC energy is coming from its leakage, which has a direct dependency on the supply voltage. However, Figure 2 shows the break-up of dynamic and leakage consumption for a set of PARSEC applications, generated by executing them on our simulation framework (ref. Section 5). As

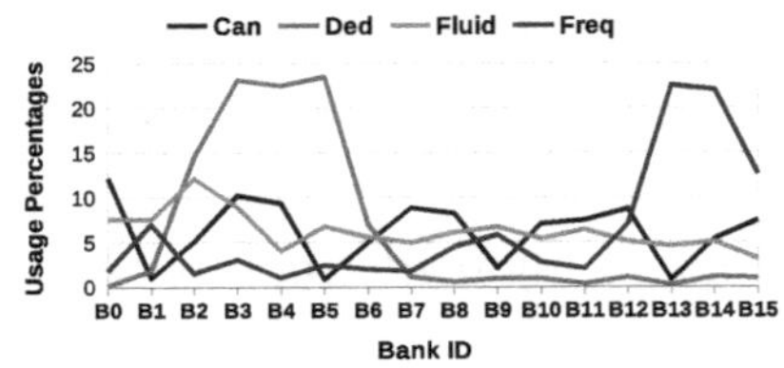

Figure 3: Non-uniform accesses to the LLC banks for a set of memory intensive PARSEC applications. The Y-axis represents usage percentage of the banks w.r.t. the total LLC accesses. X-axis represents the bank ID (Bi).

leakage consumption has a direct dependency on supply voltage, it can be stated that, controlling the same in LLC can be the most promising optimisation knob towards leakage minimisation. This power supply control can be done in a couple of ways [18, 20]: (a) Scaling down the supply voltage (State Preserving policy), or (b) Gating the power supply (State Destroying policy). Gating of power supply is although the best option as leakage will become zero in turned-off cache area, but, has adverse effect on performance due to critical data management during and after cache resizing.

State destroying policy evicts blocks from the victim locations forcibly and either migrates them to some other on-chip cache area [15] or writes them back to the lower level memory. The on-chip block transfer during resizing and post-resizing request redirection increase both NoC latency and power consumption while handling these extra traffic. However, authors in [15] (sub-)optimally handled these overheads by making their dynamic cache resizing policies sensitive to the locality of reference. But, still for the smaller caches this technique may be costlier due to lack of adequate cache space while running applications with larger working set sizes (WSSs). Hence, for the smaller caches, state destroying methods may not be an efficient strategy towards leakage minimisation especially in performance critical systems. On the other end of the spectrum, state preserving snoozy caches never include any extra load of request or block remapping but still save significant amount of leakage by applying DVS on the caches. However, awakening up from snoozy to normal incurs negligible latency [7].

The runtime cache accesses across the banks are distributed unevenly, for a multibanked SNUCA based cache architecture. For four memory intensive PARSEC [4] applications, we derived the bank accesses (through our simulators) shown in Figure 3 for a TCMP architecture having 16 L2 banks with a size of 2MB and 8 way set-associativity. This figure shows enough diversities in cache accesses across the applications at a certain time-stamp during execution. Usually, in case of cache memory, the accesses follow locality of reference, which anticipates that, a heavily (lightly) used cache portion will also be used heavily (lightly) in future. For a certain set of applications, this property works fine especially in uniprocessor systems, but, in case of modern multi-tasking CMP based environments, this property is prominently violated for the long running applications. Figure 4 shows the violation in locality of reference for three memory intensive PARSEC applications. For each application, 4 banks out of 16 have been randomly selected to

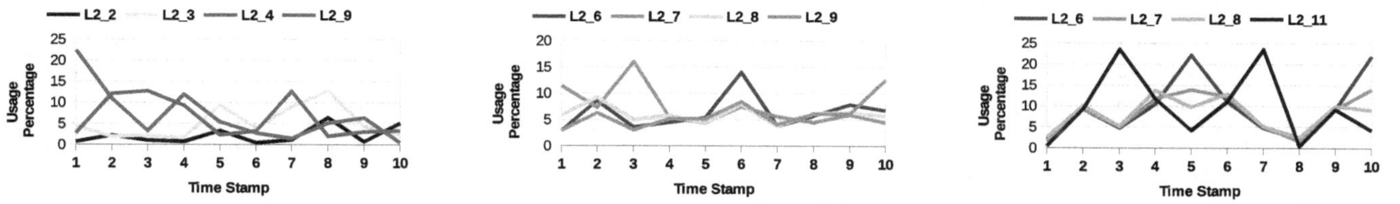

(a) canneal (b) dedup (c) fluid

Figure 4: Violation in Locality of Reference.

Algorithm 1 Usage based Snoozy Cache Banks.

```
1: T : Reconfiguration interval
2: δ : Permissible percentage increment in accesses.
3: m : Maximum limit on snoozy banks.
4: j = 0 : Number of snoozy banks. Initially zero.
5: Run system for T_Normal clock cycles (cc).
6: while (j ≤ m) and application is running do
7:     Run application for T number of cc. ;
8:     Sort banks in non-decreasing order according to their usages over last T cc.
9:     if current bank is in first 75% least used banks then
10:        if current bank is not snoozy & access increment over last T cc < δ then
11:            Make this bank snoozy.
12:            j++
13:        end if
14:    else
15:        if current bank is snoozy & access increment over last T cc ≥ δ then
16:            Awake this bank.
17:            j--
18:        end if
19:    end if
20: end while
```

maintain clarity in the figures. Here, X-axis represents uniform time-intervals, where each interval has a uniform length of 0.8 micro seconds (which has been taken based upon the average across the benchmarks). However, this violation in locality motivates us to use both snoozy as well as awaken states repeatedly on demand.

3 PROPOSED WORKS

Our experimental analyses discussed in the previous section show that, cache banks are unevenly accessed during process execution, with exploitation of locality of reference for a short time-span. This phenomena motivates us to apply snoozy technique for the least used banks (unlike ways [3]) for better leakage minimisation and further dynamically keep track of the bank usages during process execution to awake the cache bank(s) on demand towards performance compensation.

The L2 banks, those are rarely accessed over a period of execution will be chosen as the candidates for snoozy. Hypothetically, according to the temporal locality the banks having lesser accesses in the current time stamp, will have fewer accesses in future. Thus making these banks snoozy will not at all hamper the system performance and at the same time it will save leakage significantly. However, we need to keep track of change in bank access patterns. While transitioning to the snoozy mode, if access-count over the last stipulated predefined interval crosses a given threshold, we do not put this bank in snoozy mode. Rather, this bank will become active if it is snoozy currently. Bank usage statistics are analysed periodically and an active bank will become snoozy when its access count is below the limit. In case the changes in accesses of an awaken bank is within limit but the number of snoozy banks reaches its maximum permissible value, no more further banks will be put into snoozy mode. This limit can be fixed through experimental analysis. The complete method is given in Algorithm 1: Initially, in line number 1-4, all the basic variables are initialised. In the practical implementation, all of these variables are to be put into reset mode before kicking off the execution. Once, execution starts, the system will run for an amount of initial clock cycles called as warm-up cycles (T_{Normal}) and during this period no changes will be made (line number 5). On completion of warming up the application will run for another T cycles and during which no changes in voltage level is also permitted (line number 7). At the end of T, the cache banks will be sorted based upon their usages over the last T cycles (line 8). The banks, which belong to the first 75% least used set, has a chance of switching over to the snoozy mode (line 9). And out of this set, if any non-snoozy bank's accesses are not increased beyond the preset threshold value (δ), the bank will become snoozy after incrementing j, the snoozy counter, by 1 (line 10 to 12). On the other hand, on violation of the above constraint, system will awake a cache bank and updates all necessary parameters (line 15 to 17). This whole voltage scaling process will continue till the end of the process execution. The process will be conducted by invoking a (per bank) small counter based logic for profiling and controlling voltage regulator in LLC controller, and other levels of cache hierarchies are kept transparent completely about this procedures. Additionally, this process does not need any extra hardware for book keeping of the remapping information as it is done in prior state destroying policies mentioned in [18, 20]. The full process is implemented in our simulation framework (ref. Section 5).

4 ENERGY MODEL

We use the energy model of [1] in this work, that computes total energy consumption of the cache as:

$$E_{total} = E_{dynamic} + E_{static} + E_{off-cache} \quad (1)$$

where $E_{dynamic}$ represents dynamic component of energy required for each cache access, E_{static} represents static or leakage component and $E_{off-cache}$ is the energy needed for off-cache access.

The dynamic energy consumption can be broken as:

$$E_{dynamic} = (\#bank\ accesses \times E_{bank\ access} + \#flit\_transmissions \times E_{flit\_transmission} + \#flit\_traversals \times E_{flit\_traversal}) \quad (2)$$

$E_{bank\ access}$ represents dynamic energy consumed per bank access and the energy consumption for flit traversals ($E_{flit\_traversal}$) and transmissions ($E_{flit\_transmission}$) are related to the energy consumed by the interconnection network.

Static power can be summed up in the following way:

$$E_{static} = (\#banks \times P_{bank\ static} + \#switches \times P_{switch\ static}) \times execution\ time \quad (3)$$

The leakage power, $P_{bank\ static}$, consumed by each cache bank has been generated using the CACTI tool [17] and the static power of the interconnection network, $P_{switch\ static}$, is obtained from the Orion tool [6]. The product of power values and total execution time derives the energy values.

Off-cache energy is consumed during accesses to the next level from L2-cache. DDR2 memory system is assumed as next level, which needs $E_{off-cache-access}$ energy for each access with a value of 12200 pJ [15]. So the overall value is:

$$E_{off-cache} = \#off\_cache\_accesses \times E_{off-cache-access} \quad (4)$$

The bank usage percentages need to be calculated dynamically which can be obtained by using the following formula:

$$L2BankUsage(i, j) = \frac{totalAccesses(i, j)}{totalL1Misses(j)} \times 100\% \quad (5)$$

Here in equation 5, i is L2 bank-id and j is remap-period. So, the term $L2BankUsage(i, j)$ represents the bank usage percentage for bank-id i in jth interval. Note that, power consumption of the snoozy banks are simulated in CACTI.

5 EXPERIMENTAL ANALYSIS

5.1 Simulation Setup

A multi-core timed-based full system simulator Gem5 [11] (includes Ruby memory module) is used to simulate our CMP, and CACTI 6.5 [17] is used for cache power simulation. Table 2 contains configuration details of the processor, memory and NoC configuration used in our experiments. Following applications from multithreaded PARSEC benchmark suite having emerging applications [4] are used to validate the proposed architecture-canneal (can), dedup (ded), fluidanimate (fluid), freqmine (freq), streamcluster (stream), swaptions (swap) and x264 (x264). We executed all of them with 16 threads, with fixing T at 3 million and T_{Normal} at 5 million ruby cycles [2] for all of our simulations. For a 128KB cache bank, leakage power consumption is 44.86mW with per access dynamic energy is around 0.148nJ while the supply voltage is 0.9v. In snoozy mode, supply voltage is reduced to 0.6v and corresponding leakage power per bank is 29.92mW with dynamic energy 0.068nJ per access.

5.2 Results and Analysis

Our proposed policy scales down the supply voltage for a number of least used cache banks. Initially, we fixed this limit at 50%, i.e. 8 banks will become snoozy for a 2MB cache. According to our simulation results, this configuration does not show any noticeable degradation in system performance, hence, we decided to set this drowsy limit at 12 banks i.e. 75% of the total. All of our experiments are performed with 8-way set associative cache.

Table 2: System Configurations

CACTI Parameters	Values	Syst. Components	Values
Cache Level	L2	#Tiles	16
L2 Bank-size	256KB/128KB	Processor	x86
Block Size	64 Bytes	L1 I/D Cache	64KB, 4-way
Technology	32nm	L2 Cache bank	256KB/128KB
Associativity	8	Memory bank	1GB, 4KB/page
Cache Model	NUCA	Flit Size, Buffer Size	16 bytes, 4
Temperature	360K	#Pipeline Stages	5-stages
Cache Size	4 MB/2 MB	#Virtual Networks	5

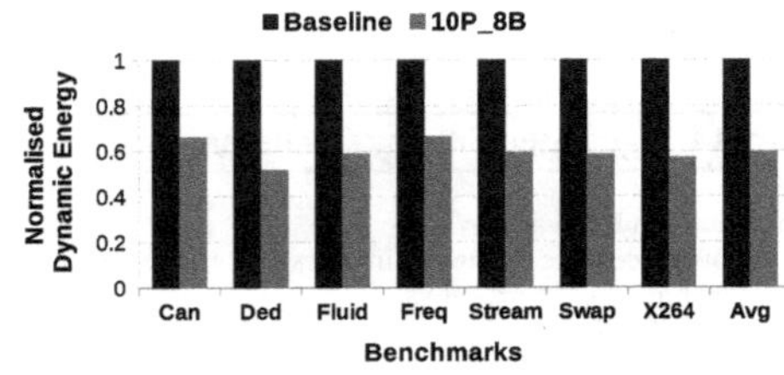

Figure 5: Reduction in Dynamic Energy for a 2MB L2 cache.

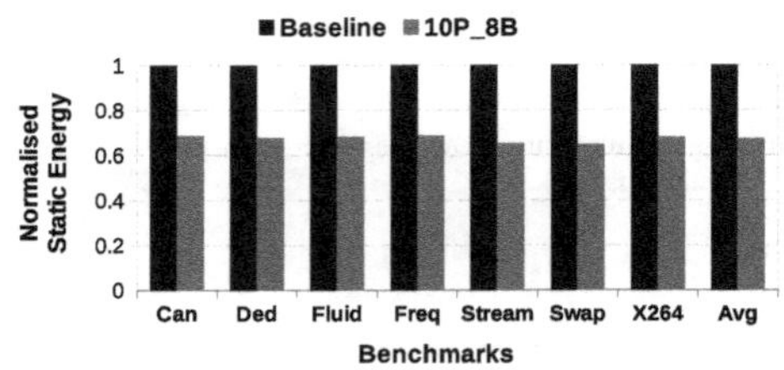

Figure 6: Reduction in Static Energy for a 2MB L2 cache.

We compare our proposed snoozy cache bank policy with another prior Drowsy technique [3] (*DR_H*) that puts half number of cache ways from each bank in low-power mode. The normally evicted data from active ways are placed in the drowsy area and eventually written back to the main memory. Note that, **xP_yB** represents our policy with $\delta = x$ and $m = y$, respectively.

Dynamic & Static Energy Savings. For a set of PARSEC benchmarks, the proposed technique (denoted as 10P_8B in Figures 5 and 6) has a dynamic energy saving of 40% while static saving is around 33% on an average, with respect to baseline architecture. We have limited our number of snoozy banks (m in Algorithm 1) to 8 and set δ as 10% for making snoozy or wake up decision.

Change in Performance & EDP Gains. Figure 7 and 8 show the normalised IPC and EDP values for a 2MB 8-way L2 cache, respectively. The average reduction in IPC is around 2%, which is very less as compared to prior state destroying techniques [18]. However, smaller change in IPC achieves a significant average EDP gains of 29% due to noticeable reduction in static energy. All obtained benefits are shown with respect to the baseline architecture.

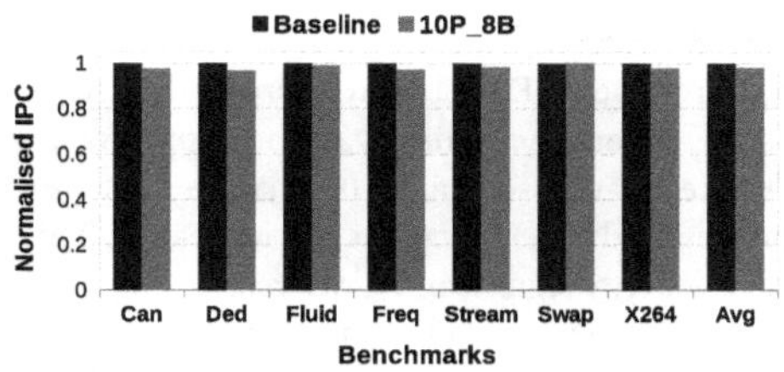

Figure 7: IPC change with Snoozy banks for a 2MB cache.

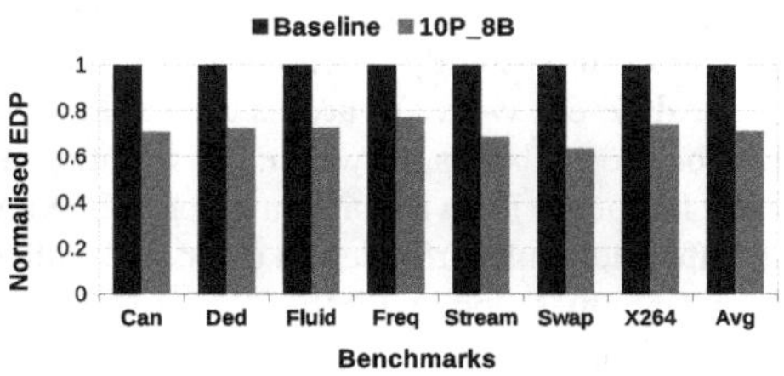

Figure 8: EDP gains for a 2MB L2 cache with Snoozy banks.

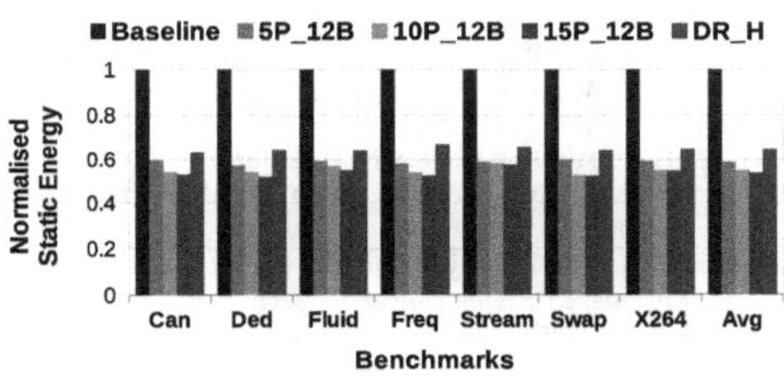

Figure 9: Static energy with Snoozy banks for a 2MB L2: $m = 12$ and δ is 5%, 10% and 15%.

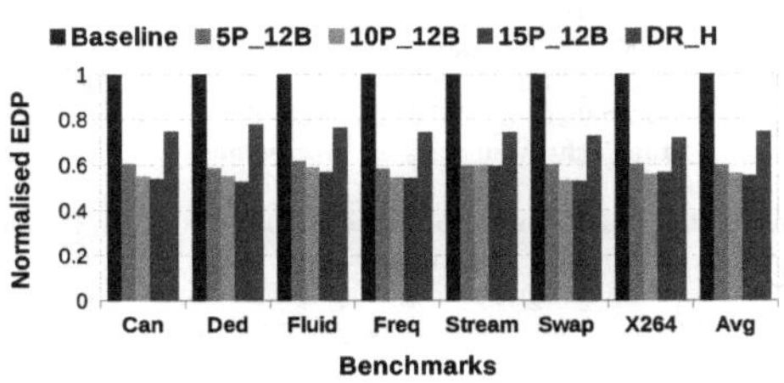

Figure 10: EDP Gains with Snoozy banks for a 2MB L2: $m = 12$ and δ is 5%, 10% and 15%.

5.2.1 Variations in m and δ in Algorithm 1. Smaller IPC degradation in our above experiment motivates us to save more leakage by setting m at 12. For various design space explorations, we further vary the value of δ from 5% to 15% and compared results with *DR_H* after implementing it in our same simulation framework.

For all of our policies, we saved more than 40% of dynamic energy on an average, whereas *DR_H* saves 20% of dynamic energy. Actually, cache lines in our snoozy banks are always accessed in low power mode unlike *DR_H*, where drowsy lines are accessed during replacement and eviction of LRU blocks. Hence, *DR_H* consumes more dynamic energy than our proposed ones. However, reduction in dynamic energy excogitates no remarkable effects in total power consumption of the caches built up with lesser technology nodes, as static component dominates the total power consumption.

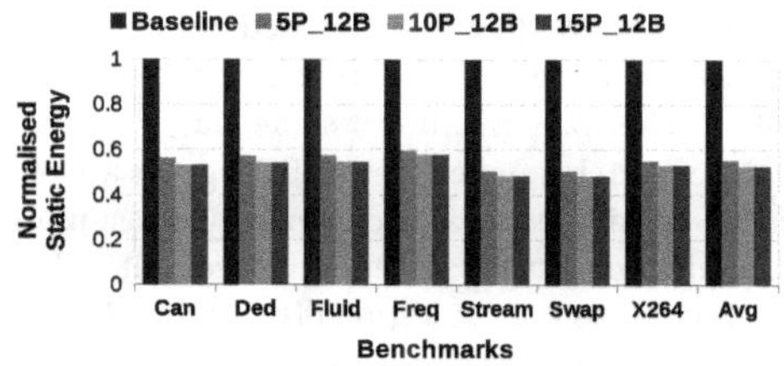

Figure 11: Static energy with Snoozy banks for a 4MB L2: $m = 12$ and δ is 5%, 10% and 15%.

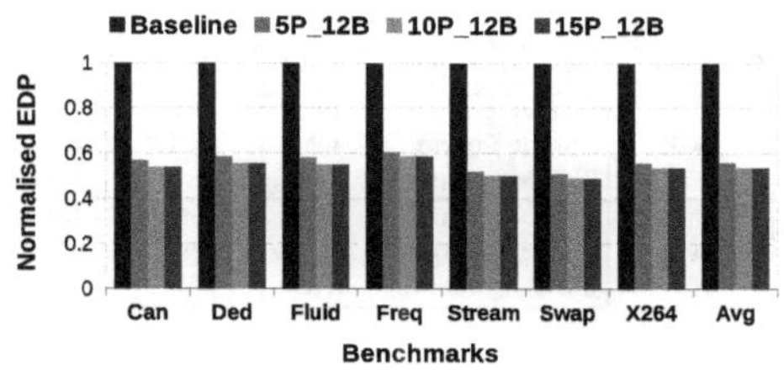

Figure 12: EDP gains with Snoozy banks for a 4MB L2: $m = 12$ and δ is 5%, 10% and 15%.

Savings in static energy for our applications are shown in Figure 9. With $\delta = 5\%$, comparatively lesser reduction is noticed, as for a few benchmarks (like can, ded, swap etc.) the accesses to the banks are changed often more than 5% across the intervals (T), but mostly this (application dependent) change is lesser than 10%. Hence, while $\delta = 5\%$, the banks are more frequently switches between active and snoozy modes, which slightly raised up the power consumption unlike other values. However, in case of *DR_H*, the amount of drowsy ways are fixed for all the banks and saves 36% of static energy, whereas our snoozy bank saves 46% leakage and thus outperforms *DR_H*. This significant reduction in leakage gives an average EDP gains of 46% for $\delta = 15\%$, whereas *DR_H* has an average saving of 25%, which is remarkably lower than our policies. The EDP values for all of our test cases along with *DR_H* is shown in Figure 10. The performance degradation in our case is almost similar to *DR_H* which varies in between 2 – 3%, on an average.

5.2.2 Experiment with larger caches. Towards showing the scalability, we further simulate our policy with 4MB L2 cache, and significantly save leakage energy by 48%, on an average, with an average EDP gain of around 46%. The results for leakage savings and EDP gains for a 4MB cache are shown in Figures 11 and 12, respectively. We have also varied δ like earlier, but for the larger cache, savings are almost similar for all the cases. We fixed m at 12 for all of our experiments with 4MB cache.

5.2.3 Summary. We have summarised our obtained results for all of our cases in Table 3. The static energy savings we obtained for both the cache sizes are almost same, but IPC hardly changes in case of larger cache, hence, better EDP gains are achieved. As static energy dominates total cache energy consumption, hence, significant reduction in in static energy excogitates the amount of EDP gains very close to it. Additionally, for the 2MB caches, with almost same changes in performance, we obtained better energy savings than *DR_H*.

Table 3: Summary of improvement over baseline.

Cache Size	Parameters	5P_12B	10P_12B	15P_12B
2MB	EDP gains	40%	44%	45%
	Static Energy	42%	45%	47%
	IPC Degradation	1.5%	1.8%	2.6%
4MB	EDP gains	44%	46%	46%
	Static Energy	45%	47%	47%
	IPC Degradation	1.4%	1.6%	1.7%

6 RELATED WORKS

In recent years a plethora of attempts have been taken to reduce leakage of the LLCs [18, 20]. Gated-VDD [10], a circuit level policy, has minimal impact on performance can also efficiently work as a heart of different cache resizing techniques, which comes under the category of state destroying cache resizing policy. By keeping Gated-VDD as their backbone, a prediction based [2] and LLC usage based [15] dynamic cache resizing policies have been proposed to reduce cache leakage. On the other end of the spectrum, Flautner et al. in 2002, have coined DVS technique for caches [7] by using MTCMOS as their backbone circuitry. This policy is further exploited by plenty of state preserving leakage reduction techniques [3, 3, 5, 8, 9, 12–14, 16, 19]. This DVS technique is applied at different granularities of cache memory from different implementation perspectives, while considering performance constraint. In their way level drowsy cache, Fitzgerald et al. saves more than 40% leakage with negligible drops in performance [3]. In another exploration [19], around 26% of energy is saved by L1 data cache tuning in a heterogeneous dual-core system. Loghi et al. [9] move a large chunk of tag bits from the cache into an external register which works as an identifier of the current locality of the cache references, which achieves both dynamic and static energy efficiency. In [12], an access behaviour cognizant adaptive cache reconfiguration achieved a total energy saving of 30% on an average with a performance degradation of 2.1%, in a single core system, implemented with large technology nodes, hence, the solution for leakage was not remarkable.

Most of the policies mentioned above applied DVS at multiple granularities of the caches. As DVS has minimal impact on performance [7], hence, in this work, we adopt it at the bank level granularity for a multi-banked shared LLC to keep our control logic simpler than implementing it at some deeper level granularities. Moreover, a low power snoozy bank can significantly reduce the leakage consumption with negligible impact on performance.

7 CONCLUSIONS

This paper proposes a DVS based energy efficient cache design, snoozy cache, where dynamically cache supply voltage is scaled down at the least accessed cache banks. The voltage is scaled up further on-demand when accesses are increased. This voltage reduction saves energy significantly, whereas scaling up voltage compensates performance degradation, however, overall EDP gain is significant although. The proposed policy shows 45% gains in EDP while saving leakage around 50% for a 2MB and 8-way associative L2 cache. Our policy also outperforms an earlier drowsy cache technique [3] that makes a bank partially drowsy by putting some of its ways in low power mode. All of these gains are obtained without much degradation in system performance. We have also shown our policy for different values of access threshold with different limit values for snoozy banks. However, the variation in cache reconfiguration frequency (T in Algorithm 1) for different workloads can further offer more insightful design choices for different cache sizes and associativities along with the respective changes in data distributions & their accesses, that we intend to take as our future work.

REFERENCES

[1] A. Bardine et al. 2007. Analysis of Static and Dynamic Energy Consumption in NUCA Caches: Initial Results. *ACM MEDEA* (Septemeber 2007), 105–112.

[2] A. Mandke Dani et al. 2011. Adaptive Power Optimization of On-chip SNUCA Cache on Tiled Chip Multicore Architecture using Remap Policy. *Second Workshop on Architecture and Multi-Core Applications* (2011), 12–17.

[3] B. Fitzgerald et al. 2013. Drowsy Cache Partitioning for Reduced Static and Dynamic Energy in the Cache Hierarchy. *International Green Computing Conference (IGCC)* (June 2013), 1–6.

[4] C Bienia et al. 2008. The PARSEC Benchmark Suite: Characterization and Architectural Implications. *Princeton University Tech. Rep. TR-811-08* (2008).

[5] G. Keramidas et al. 2007. Applying decay to reduce dynamic power in set-associative caches. *HiPEAC* (2007), 38–53.

[6] Hang-Sheng Wang et al. 2002. Orion: a power-performance simulator for interconnection networks. In *MICRO-35.* 294 – 305.

[7] K. Flautner et al. 2002. Drowsy caches: simple techniques for reducing leakage power. In *Proceedings of 29th Annual Int. Symp. on Comp. Arch.* 148–157.

[8] K. Inoue et al. 1999. Way-predicting set-associative cache for high performance and low energy consumption. In *Proceedings of Int. Symp. on Low power electronics and design.* ACM, 273–275.

[9] M. Loghi et al. 2009. Tag overflow buffering: Reducing total memory energy by reduced-tag matching. *IEEE Trans. on VLSI systems* 17, 5 (2009), 728–732.

[10] M. Powell et al. 2000. Gated-Vdd: A Circuit Technique to Reduce Leakage in Deep-submicron Cache Memories. In *Proceedings of Int. Symp. on Low Power Electronics and Design.*

[11] N. Binkert et al. 2011. The Gem5 Simulator. *ACM SIGARCH Computer Architure News* 39, 2 (Aug. 2011), 1–7.

[12] S. Dropsho et al. 2002. Integrating adaptive on-chip storage structures for reduced dynamic power. In *Proceedings of Parallel Architectures and Compilation Techniques.* IEEE, 141–152.

[13] Y. Guo et al. 2011. Energy-efficient hardware data prefetching. *IEEE Trans. on VLSI Systems* 19, 2 (2011), 250–263.

[14] Z. Huiyang et al. 2003. Adaptive Mode Control: A Static Power Efficient Cache Design. *ACM Trans. on Embedded Comp. Syst.* 2, 3 (August 2003), 347–372.

[15] H. K. Kapoor et al. 2015. Static energy reduction by performance linked cache capacity management in Tiled CMPs. In *ACM SAC.*

[16] G. H. Loh. 2008. 3D-stacked memory architectures for multi-core processors. In *35th Int. Symp. on Comp. Arch.* IEEE, 453–464.

[17] Naveen M. et al. 2008. CACTI 6.0: A Tool to Understand Large Caches. (2008).

[18] S. Mittal. 2014. A survey of architectural techniques for improving cache power efficiency. *Sust. Comp.: Informatics and Systems* 4, 1 (2014), 33 – 43.

[19] M. Rawlins and A. Gordon-Ross. 2011. On the interplay of loop caching, code compression, and cache configuration. In *Proceedings of the 16th Asia and South Pacific Design Automation Conference.* IEEE Press, 243–248.

[20] W Zang and A Gordon-Ross. 2013. A Survey on Cache Tuning from a Power/Energy Perspective. *ACM Comput. Surv.* 45, 3 (July 2013), 32:1–32:49.

SARO: A State-Aware Reliability Optimization Technique for High Density NAND Flash Memory

Myungsuk Kim
Department of Computer Science and Engineering
Seoul National University
morssola75@davinci.snu.ac.kr

Youngsun Song
Department of Computer Science and Engineering
Seoul National University
ysunsong@davinci.snu.ac.kr

Myoungsoo Jung
School of Integrated Technology
Yonsei University
mj@camelab.org

Jihong Kim
Department of Computer Science and Engineering
Seoul National University
jihong@davinci.snu.ac.kr

ABSTRACT

Recent advances in flash technologies, such as scaling and multi-leveling schemes, have been successful to make flash denser and secure more storage spaces per die. Unfortunately, these technology advances significantly degrade flash's reliability due to a smaller cell geometry and a finer-grained cell state control. In this paper, we propose a state-aware reliability optimization technique (SARO), new flash optimization that improves the flash reliability under diverse scaling and multi-leveling schemes. To this end, we first reveal that reliability-related flash errors are highly *skewed* among flash cell states, which was not captured by prior studies. The proposed SARO exploits then the different per-state error behavior in flash cell states by selecting the most error-prone flash states (for each error type) and by forming narrow threshold voltage distributions (for the selected states only). Furthermore, SARO is applied only when the program time gets shorter because of flash cell aging, thereby keeping the program latency unchanged. Our experimental results with real MLC and TLC flash devices show that SARO can reduce a significant number of flash bit errors, which can in turn reduce the read latency by 40%, on average.

ACM Reference Format:
Myungsuk Kim, Youngsun Song, Myoungsoo Jung, and Jihong Kim. 2018. SARO: A State-Aware Reliability Optimization Technique for High Density NAND Flash Memory. In *GLSVLSI'18: 2018 Great Lakes Symposium on VLSI, May 23–25, 2018, Chicago, IL, USA.* ACM, New York, NY, USA, 6 pages. https://doi.org/10.1145/3194554.3194591

1 INTRODUCTION

Many recent advances and innovations in flash technologies (such as 3D flash, 10-nm node process, and TLC cells) enabled dramatic increases in the flash memory capacity. However, the fundamental relationship between the capacity and reliability of flash memory remains unchanged: *the higher the flash chip capacity, the lower the flash reliability* [1]. As the feature size of technologies shrinks, neighboring flash cells are getting closer and located in a smaller space geometry. Unfortunately, a narrow spacing between adjacent cells tend to be more vulnerable to noise effects such as cell-to-cell interference, thus lowering the flash reliability [1]. In addition, the m-bit multi-leveling technique (e.g., 3-bit triple-level cell (TLC)) significantly lowers the flash reliability because it increases the storage capacity by distinguishing the same threshold voltage (V_{th}) distribution of a cell transistor with 2^m different states. Since a higher m allows a smaller noise margin (between the adjacent cells), the m-bit multi-leveling technique degrades the flash reliability, compared to the single-level cell (SLC) flash device.

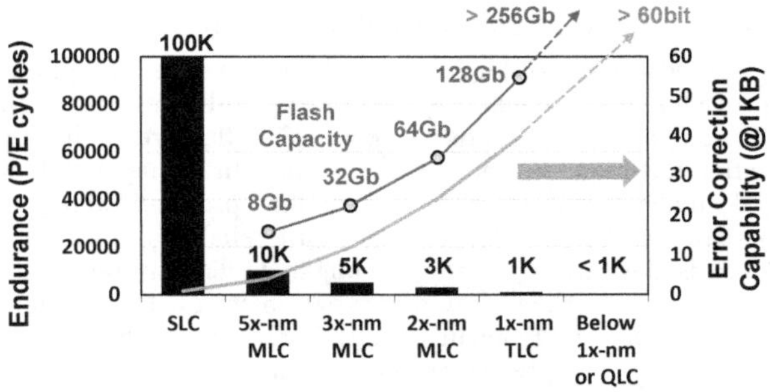

Figure 1: Trends in the flash capacity and flash reliability over advances in flash technologies.

Figure 1 shows how the flash reliability has deteriorated by process scaling and m-bit multi-leveling techniques, which have been the driving force behind the recent growth in the storage capacity in flash. For example, while flash's storage capacity was increased from 8G bits to 128G bits, the flash endurance has been worsened by 10 times. To handle the poor reliability introduced by such advanced techniques, a flash controller should employ 40-bit error correction codes (ECC) rather than 4-bit ECC at the system-level.

To secure a better reliability in flash, a straightforward approach is to keep V_{th} distributions of adjacent program states as distant as possible so that the interference between neighboring cells can be minimized. One simple technique is to reduce the V_{th} width of each program state. Although narrowing V_{th} distributions for program states makes program states *error-resistant*, it slows down the program speed because a program step voltage (V_{ispp}) should be reduced for forming a narrow V_{th} distribution. Since V_{ispp} is inversely proportional to the program latency, it is inevitable to sacrifice the program latency if the reliability is improved in a way that reduces V_{ispp}. Furthermore, many emerging applications (such as real-time big-data analytics, autonomous cars and virtual-reality applications) require both high capacity and high performance from

[1] Over 2D flash, 3D flash is more reliable with a higher capacity. However, within 3D flash, this relationship still holds.

GLSVLSI'18, May 23–25, 2018, Chicago, IL, USA

ACM ISBN 978-1-4503-5724-1/18/05...$15.00
https://doi.org/10.1145/3194554.3194591

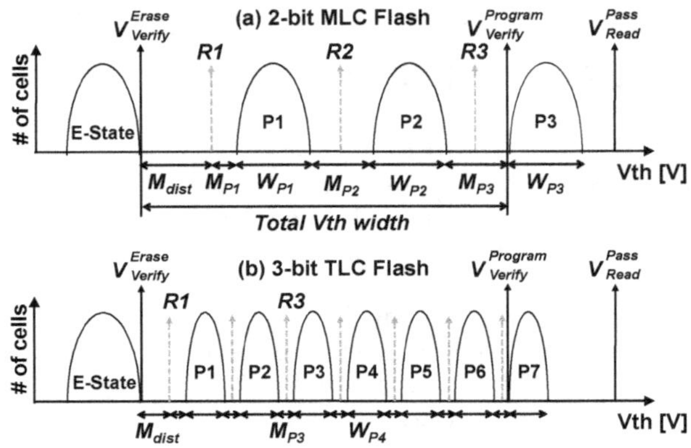

Figure 2: V_{th} distributions of 2^m-state flash memory.

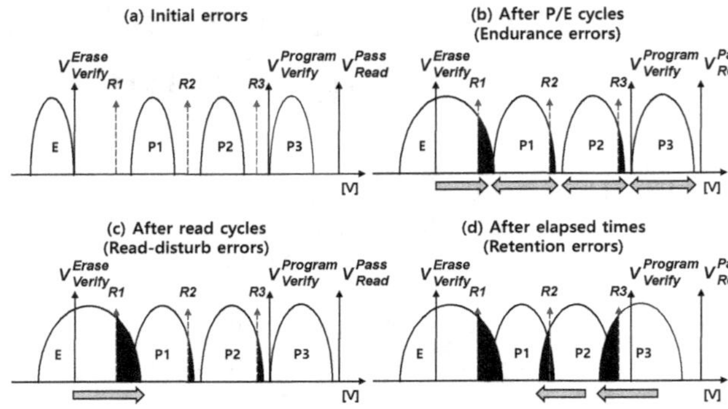

Figure 3: Change patterns in V_{th} distributions depending on different error types.

flash-based storage systems, thus making it even less desirable to improve the flash reliability by slowing down the program latency.

In this paper, we propose a new NAND flash reliability optimization technique that addresses the reliability issue of high density flash memories without sacrificing their program latency. Our proposed technique, called as state-aware reliability optimization (SARO), is motivated by our key finding that reliability-related flash errors are highly skewed among program states. That is, not all flash reliability errors occur equally likely among different program states. To be precise on the per-state error characteristics, we performed comprehensive evaluations using 2x-nm TLC flash chips and validated that a few program states are responsible for most reliability errors. SARO narrows V_{th} distributions of these error-prone states only, thus significantly reducing the overheads imposed by applying a fine-grained V_{ispp}. Our SARO also exploits a well-known flash phenomenon that the program latency is decreased as flash cells get older because of traps in the damaged tunnel oxide [2]. Specifically, we employ a fine-grained V_{ispp} only when the program latency gets shorter, which can in turn make SARO achieve high flash reliability while keeping the program latency unchanged.

For the validation of SARO, we built per-state error models using 2x-nm TLC flash chips. Based on the per-state error models, we devise a simple but effective method of selectively modifying V_{ispp} values under given flash cell status (such as P/E cycles). Our experimental results show that SARO can improve the reliability of MLC and TLC flash devices by 100% and 50%, respectively. As a direct result of the improved reliability, SARO shortens the read latency by 40%, on average, by reducing the number of read retry operations.

The rest of this paper is organized as follows. Before SARO is presented, we explain the key trade-off relationship between the reliability and program latency in flash devices using real MLC and TLC flash chips. The key schemes of SARO are presented in Section 3. Section 4 describes the SARO implementation details. Experimental results follow in Section 5, and related work is summarized in Section 6. Section 7 concludes with a summary and future work.

2 BACKGROUND

2.1 Reliability vs. V_{th} Design Parameters

For writes, flash changes target cell's V_{th} states based on the content information (per bit). In the case of reads, flash reconstructs the content by sensing the V_{th} state of target cells. Figure 2 illustrates V_{th} distributions for 2^m-state flash devices, which stores m bits within a cell by using 2^m distinct V_{th} states (i.e., m is 2 and 3 for MLC and TLC, respectively). Since the primary V_{th} design parameters shown in Figure 2 (i.e., W_{Pi}'s, M_{Pi}'s, M_{dist}, V^{Erase}_{Verify}, and $V^{Program}_{Verify}$) directly affect both the flash reliability and flash performance, how to set these parameters is a critical decision for NAND flash manufacturers. Once the V_{th} design parameters are fixed during the flash design time, the flash reliability largely depends on how V_{th} distributions are disturbed by various causes. Bit errors in flash memory occur when the V_{th} distribution of one state is shifted to neighboring state's V_{th} regions so that two overlapping V_{th} distributions cannot be distinguished as two different states.

In general, we can categorize bit errors in flash into four groups as shown in Figure 3. When a page is written, a small number of bit errors are inevitable as shown in Figure 3(a). These initial errors are caused by process variations and inherent noise effects (such as cell-to-cell interference, back pattern dependency, and random telegraph noise) [3]. More serious bit errors, which mandate to employ a strong error-correction scheme (such as LDPC codes) in a flash controller, are related to defects in the tunnel oxide layer of flash cells [4]. As a flash device experiences P/E cycles, the width of V_{th} distributions tend to get wider because of traps in tunnel oxide layer which are caused by applying a high program/erase voltage frequently. The traps in the tunnel oxide layer generated by P/E cycles also exacerbate the program disturbance. When flash cells are programmed, neighboring cells belonging to the E-state are softly programmed, so that their V_{th} move to the right. As shown in Figure 3(b), these errors are called endurance errors. The repeated read operations also shift V_{th} of E-state cells to the right. When flash cells are read, V^{Pass}_{Read} (6~7V) is applied to all the wordlines (WLs) in the same block except for the target wordline [2]. When pages in the same block are frequently read, E-state cells in the block are softly programmed, thus shifting their V_{th}s to the right. These errors, as shown in Figure 3(c), are called read-disturb errors. If flash cells are left for a long time after a program operation, a charge loss occurs by the stress-induced leakage current (SILC) through traps in the tunnel oxide layer. These errors, as shown in Figure 3(d), are called retention errors. The charge loss shifts the V_{th} of program states to the left. Furthermore, higher program states experience a greater amount of the charge loss, and hence show a larger V_{th} shift compared to lower program states [5].

When V_{th} distributions are sufficiently moved, V_{th} distributions may overlap with read reference voltages (i.e., R1, R2 and R3 in Figure 3), thus producing flash bit errors. For example, the shaded regions in Figure 3 indicate such overlapped V_{th} distributions. If

[2]The memory cells are packed to form a matrix structure. As shown in Figure 9, cells share a wordline (WL) horizontally and a bitline (BL) vertically.

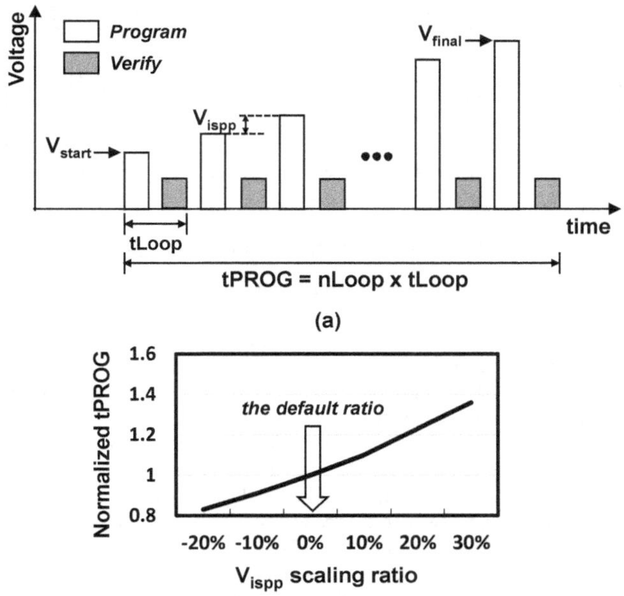

Figure 4: An overview of the ISPP scheme: (a) Key parameters for *tPROG* and (b) Normalized *tPROG* over varying V_{ispp} scaling ratios

there is an insufficient V_{th} margin between the states, flash bit errors sharply increase as V_{th} distributions are disturbed. When the number of flash bit errors reaches over a pre-defined upper limit, which is generally determined by the error correction capability of an ECC engine in a flash controller, the flash page cannot be correctly read, resulting in a read-failure status. Thus, to guarantee the reliability of a flash device, sufficient M_{dist} and M_{Pi} should be secured considering the maximum V_{th} changes after the maximum number of P/E cycles, read cycles, and retention times.

2.2 Reliability vs. Program Latency

Typically, a flash device employs an *incremental step pulse programming* (ISPP) scheme [6] to control the width W_{Pi} of program states. As shown in Figure 4(a), the ISPP scheme gradually increases the program voltage by V_{ispp} at a time until all their cells in a page are completely programmed. For each program loop that takes *tLOOP*, once cells are verified to have been sufficiently programmed by a verify operation, those cells are excluded from the next program loop. Since the width W_{Pi} of the *i*-th program state is proportional to V_{ispp}, a simple solution to ensure sufficient M_{dist} and M_{Pi} is to narrow W_{Pi} by reducing V_{ispp} during a program operation. Even though the V_{ispp} reduction can improve the flash reliability, it increases the total number of *nLoop* of program loops because a smaller V_{ispp} value needs to repeat the program loop more to reach V_{final} for the maximum program state. Therefore, the program latency is inversely proportional to V_{ispp}. Figure 4(b) shows that the program latency directly increases as V_{ispp} is scaled down.

Figure 5 shows the results of reliability test over various V_{ispp} scaling ratios using real 2x-nm node MLC and TLC chips [3]. (For a detailed description on the evaluation settings, refer to Section

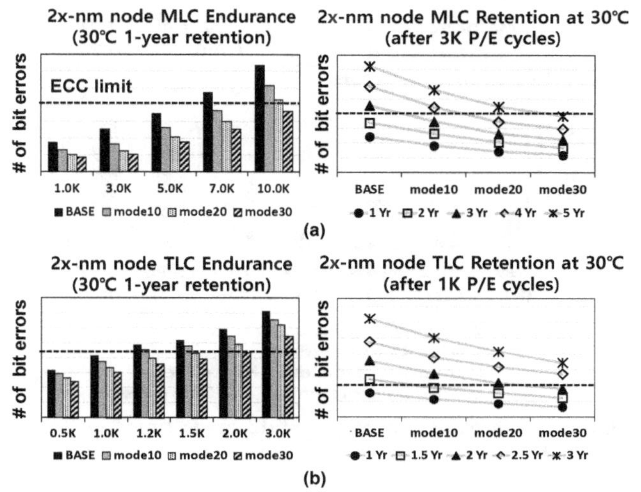

Figure 5: Reliability of flash devices over various V_{ispp} scaling ratios: (a) 2x-nm MLC flash and (b) 2x-nm TLC flash

5.) As expected, both the endurance and retention capability were significantly improved with a smaller V_{ispp} value. In 2x-nm MLC flash chips, the maximum number of P/E cycles is increased from less than 7,000 to more than 10,000 when V_{ispp} is reduced by 30% (i.e., mode*30*). The data retention capability is also increased under mode*30* from about 2 years to 5 years [4].

As shown in Figure 4 and 5, there is a trade-off relationship between the flash reliability and the flash program latency when V_{ispp} varies. Our main goal of the proposed SARO technique is to investigate if we can achieve the same flash reliability improvement from a smaller V_{ispp} value without sacrificing the program latency.

3 SARO: BASIC IDEA

3.1 State-Aware Reliability Characterization

Since the program latency is proportional to *nLoop* and *nLoop* is, in turn, inversely proportional to V_{ispp}, reducing V_{ispp} directly increases the program latency and vice versa. In order to mitigate the impact of a smaller V_{ispp} on the program latency, we investigated whether flash errors occur in a *state-oblivious fashion* or in a *state-aware fashion* using 2x-nm TLC flash chips. Our intention was that if flash bit errors occurred differently over different program states, we can apply a smaller V_{ispp} value only to those states with higher probability of bit errors while not reducing V_{ispp} for the other states. By combining a small V_{ispp} value with a larger one, we can effectively lessen the impact of V_{ispp} on the program latency while, hopefully, achieving the same reliability improvement.

Figure 6 shows a breakdown of per-state flash bit errors on our characterization study with 2x-nm TLC flash. Our results strongly indicate that flash bit errors occur in a *state-aware fashion.* That is, different error types occur in different program states. Most of endurance and read-disturb errors occur between the E and P1 state by the overlapped V_{th} distribution of the E-state cell and R1 read reference voltage level. In Figure 6, about 43% of the total endurance and read-disturb errors occur between E and P1 states. On the other hand, most of retention errors occur in higher states. In Figure 6,

[3]When the V_{ispp} scaling ratio is set to *X*%, V_{ispp} is reduced by *X*% of the nominal V_{ispp}. We call this V_{ispp} setting by mode*X*. BASE represents the baseline technique where V_{ispp} scaling ratio is 0%.

[4]The data retention capability is measured under the retention temperature of 30°C after the maximum P/E cycles (3,000 for MLC flash and 1,000 for TLC flash) and 1,000 read cycles for each block. This evaluation setting is a de facto standard for NAND manufactures.

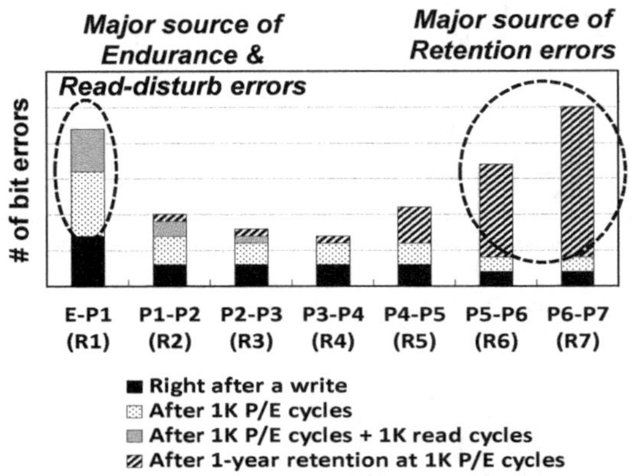

Figure 6: A breakdown of per-state error types on 2x-nm TLC flash.

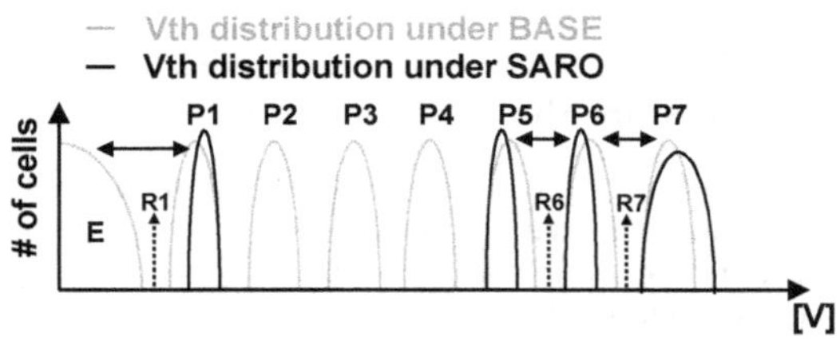

Figure 7: An overview of the state-aware selective programming scheme on a TLC flash device.

retention errors between the P5 and P6 states account for about 31% of the total retention errors while retention errors between the P6 and P7 states are responsible for 50% of the total retention errors.

Based on our characterization results, SARO employs a state-aware program scheme, optimizing each program state based on its own reliability requirement. As shown in Figure 7, we apply the reduced V_{ispp} value to most error-prone states (e.g., P1, P5, and P6 in Figure 7) only so that most bit errors can be avoided with a small increase in the program latency. In addition to the reliability optimization from a finer V_{ispp} control, SARO improves the read latency as well. For example, in Figure 7, as M_{P1}, M_{P6}, and M_{P7} get wider, we adjust R1, R6, and R7 accordingly. This adjustment contributes to reducing the number of read retry operations required. Furthermore, since P7 has no right-side neighbor, we *increase* its V_{ispp} so that P7 program latency can be further reduced.

Our SARO technique can be easily generalized to 2^m-state flash as follows:

- Reduce V_{ispp} and increase the verify and read reference voltage (Rx) of the lowest program state (i.e., P1) to improve the endurance and read disturb error.
- Reduce V_{ispp} of program states from (2^m-2) state to $2^m-(2^{m-2}+1)$ state to improve the retention error.
- Increase V_{ispp} of (2^m-1) (i.e., the highest) program state to reduce the performance degradation.
- Decrease Rx of program states from (2^m-1) state to (2^m-2^{m-2}) state to make the read latency shorter.

3.2 Slack-Aware Adaptive NAND Programming

In order to minimize the performance degradation from reducing V_{ispp}, we devised a slack-aware scheme which accurately estimates the *tPROG* acceleration ratio as flash cells get aged. For an accurate

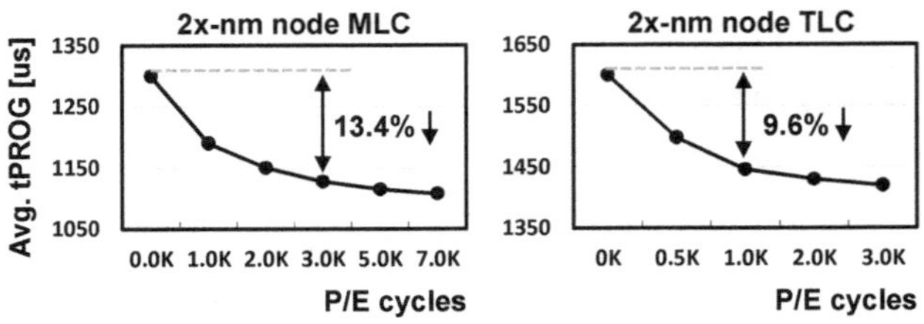

Figure 8: *tPROG* speed changes over varying P/E cycles.

estimate of *tPROG*, we performed a flash characterization study while varying the number of P/E cycles. As shown in Figure 8, the average latency for a page programming constantly decreases as the number of P/E cycles increases. In MLC flash devices, after applying 3,000 P/E cycles, the average program latency decreases by 13.4%, compared to an initial value (1,300 μs). The average program latency of TLC flash devices also decreases by 9.6% after 1,000 P/E cycles. The effect of *tPROG* acceleration over P/E cycles can be explained using traps in the tunnel oxide layer. As the number of P/E cycles increase, traps also increase because a high program/erase voltage damages the tunnel oxide layer. As the tunnel oxide layer gets damaged, its insulation capability gets worse, thus allowing electrons to move easily into flash floating gate. As a consequence, programming the aged pages (e.g., experienced a lot of P/E cycles) requires lesser number of program loops to complete the program operation.

Based on the *tPROG* acceleration model, SARO applies a finer V_{ispp} value only when *tPROG* gets faster. In order not to introduce any latency overhead, SARO tries to match an increase from a finer V_{ispp} value with a decrease in *tPROG*. Although this solution is helpful to improve the flash reliability and easy to implement without any hardware modification, if we apply the proposed slack-aware V_{ispp} adjustment technique only without exploiting per-state error behavior of Section 3.1, its effect on the flash reliability is rather limited. Since the decrease of the program latency (even) at the end of the flash lifetime is about 10% of the default program latency, V_{ispp} can be reduced up to 10% only. For TLC flash, the reliability improvement is marginal, i.e., about 10% only, as shown in Figure 5(b).

4 SARO: IMPLEMENTATION DETAILS

4.1 State-Aware Selective NAND Programming

To support state-aware programming, a flash device should apply different V_{ispp} values to cells in the same WL. Fortunately, since NAND flash memory supports a bit-by-bit selective operation with the self boosting program inhibit (SBPI) scheme [6], state-aware selective programming can be easily implemented by modifying the *BL* operating conditions without an additional hardware modification.

Figure 9 illustrates how the SBPI scheme supports bit-by-bit selective program operations. When a page WL_k is programmed, its i-th cell within the page is selectively programmed depending on the value of BL_i. If BL_i is set to 1 (i.e., Vcc), the i-th cell is not programmed (i.e., inhibited) because there is an insufficient voltage difference by channel boosting effect (P1 in Figure 9(a)). If BL_i is set to 0 (i.e., 0V), the i-th cell is programmed because there is an enough voltage difference to move the electron into the floating-gate (P6 in Figure 9(b)). Based on a conventional SBPI, when the i-th cell is programmed, the *effective* V_{ispp} for the i-th cell during a program operation can be reduced by forcing a specific voltage into the channel connected to *BL*. For example, when a program

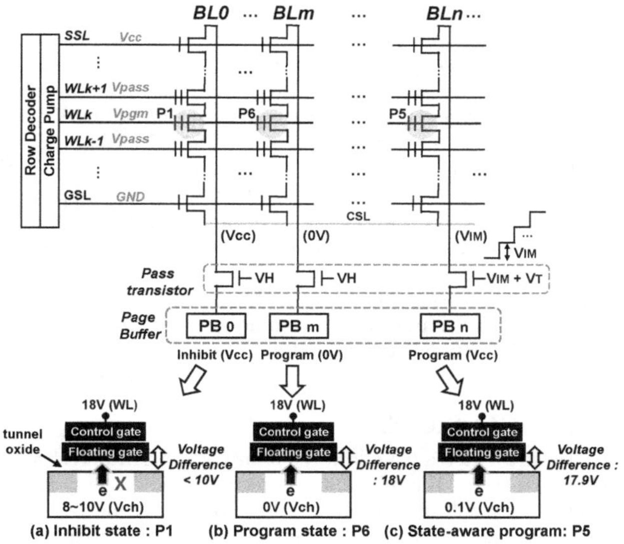

Figure 9: Design Schematics to implement state-aware selective programming using conventional SBPI scheme and page buffer operation.

voltage is increased from 18V to 18.4V by V_{ispp} (= 0.4V), the *effective* V_{ispp} can be reduced to 0.3V by applying 0.1V to the channel. In our example, P1 state is inhibited (Figure 9(a)), P6 state is normally programmed by 0.4V V_{ispp} (Figure 9(b)), and P5 state in BL_n is programmed in a state-aware fashion (Figure 9(c)). At the start of P5 state programming (assuming that the start program voltage of P5 state is 18V), the WL gate is set to 18V by the target row decoder, and the PB_n forces Vcc to the BL_n. Since the gate of the pass transistor connected with BL_n is set to $V_{IM}+V_T$ (i.e., V_T is a threshold voltage of the pass transistor), the voltage which can be transfered to the BL_n becomes V_{IM}. Therefore, the voltage difference between the channel and floating-gate of P5 state is reduced by V_{IM}, which indicates that the effective V_{ispp} is 0.4V$-V_{IM}$. As the program loops of the target program state proceed, the gate voltage of the pass transistors is increased by V_{IM} to maintain the reduced effective V_{ispp}.

4.2 SaFTL: SARO-aware FTL

In order to take advantage of the SARO technique in flash-based storage systems, we modified an existing page-level FTL to support SARO. (We call this modified FTL `SaFTL`, SARO-aware FTL.) The main goal of `SaFTL` is to manage various operating parameters based on the program latency measured from NAND flash memories. Figure 10 shows an overall organization of `SaFTL`. `SaFTL` monitors the program latency from a flash device. The measured program latency is compared to its initial (non-accelerated) *tPROG*. Depending on the difference between the measured *tPROG* and the initial *tPROG*, the *Mode Selector* module decides a proper *Mode* for a program request. For example, if the measured *tRPOG* is faster than the initial *tPROG* by 3%, the next program request is programmed using *Mode* 3 entry of the *Parameter Table*. The *Parameter Table* contains all the necessary values for V_{th} design parameters for a given *Mode* type.

In order for `SaFTL` to properly work, the initial program latency and *Mode* should be maintained for every programmed page. However, in order to reduce the memory overhead for implementing

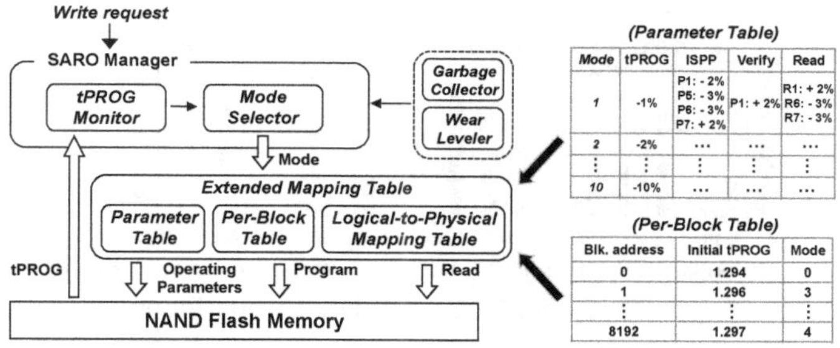

Figure 10: An Organizational overview of `SaFTL`

SARO, a mode selection is applied in a per-block basis. (That is, all the pages in the same block is programmed using the same *Mode*.) Since variations in *tPROG* within the same block is negligible (e.g., less than 3 μs in our evaluations), per-block mode selection is an effective solution to minimize both the memory overhead and the *tPROG* monitoring overhead.

In order to maintain up-to-date status per each block, `SaFTL` uses the *Per-Block Table* which can be implemented with a small memory overhead. For example, a flash device with 8,192 blocks needs extra 22-KB memory for *Per-Block Table*. The initial program latency is measured when the flash device is first programmed, and stored in a pre-defined area. The current program latency is determined by monitoring only one last WL per block.

5 EXPERIMENTAL RESULTS

We conducted experiments using 20 real 2x-nm TLC and MLC flash chips, respectively, to evaluate the effectiveness of the proposed optimization technique. In order to minimize the potential distortion of the evaluation results from process variations, we evenly selected 30 test blocks from each chip at different physical block locations, and tested all the pages in each selected test block. As a result, a total of 115,200 pages (on TLC flash chips) and 76,800 pages (on MLC flash chips) were used to obtain statistically significant experimental results. Using an in-house custom test board (equipped with a NAND controller and a thermal controller), we conducted comprehensive reliability and performance evaluations varying key variables such as P/E cycles, read cycles, and retention times. For example, in MLC flash chips, the endurance test was performed with increasing the P/E cycles from 0 (an initial condition) to 10,000. Similarly, the retention capability was evaluated by changing the elapsed time (since the program operation) from 1 year to 5 years.

Figure 11 (a) and (b) show how the flash endurance and retention capability change under four different operation modes, BASE, mode*10*, mode*30*, and SARO. SARO improves endurance and retention capability by 100% in MLC flash chips and 50% in TLC flash chips over BASE, respectively. To better understand why SARO outperforms BASE, we measured flash bit errors in each pages. The number of flash bit errors in SARO is reduced by 56.1% in MLC flash chips and 25.2% in TLC flash chips over BASE because SARO increases the V_{th} margin between an error-prone adjacent states, thus improving the error tolerance of a flash device. As expected, mode*30* shows the best reliability improvement, but it also degrades the program latency by about 20% as shown in Figure 11(c). SARO, on the other hand, barely affects the program latency. For TLC flash chips, SARO increases the program latency by 1.8% which is negligible overhead.

In order to understand the impact of the improved reliability on the read latency, we evaluated how the number of read retry operations changes under SARO. The read retry operation is initiated

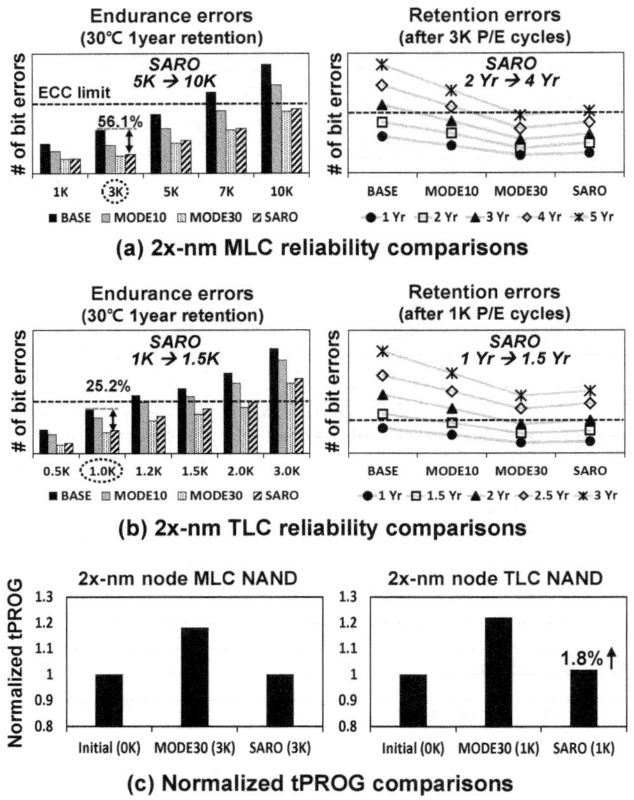

Figure 11: Comparisons of reliability and performance metrics of four different operation modes.

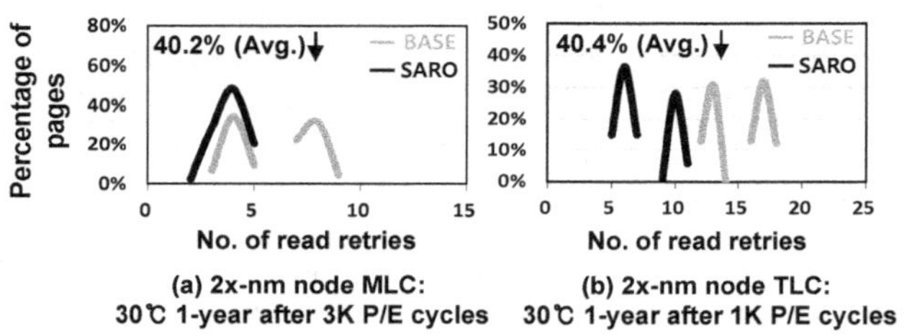

Figure 12: Changes in the number of read retry operations under SARO **over the baseline technique.**

when uncorrectable errors are detected, and repeated until errors can be corrected by the ECC scheme. Since the read latency of a flash device is directly proportional to the number of repeated read retry operations, the read latency is significantly improved when the number of read retry operations is reduced. Figure 12 shows the number of read retry operations under BASE and SARO in MLC and TLC flash chips. SARO reduces the average number of read retry operations by 40% on average over BASE.

6 RELATED WORK

There have been several studies that attempt to improve the reliability of flash devices. Pan *et al.* [7] proposed a technique which can reduce V_{ispp} with P/E cycles to optimize the reliability and performance of NAND flash memory. However, this technique changes V_{ispp} of all program states without considering different error patterns among different program states. Therefore, this technique is rather limited to apply for high-density flash devices, such as TLC flash devices. Park *et al.* [8] also proposed a technique which can change program operating parameters according to P/E cycles. However, their technique is different from SARO in that they did not explore per-state error characteristics. In addition, their technique targets SLC flash devices only so that it cannot be applied for high-density flash devices. The *DPES* technique proposed by Jeong *et al.* [9] is similar to our SARO in that it dynamically changes erase and program parameters of a flash device. However, unlike SARO, it improves the flash endurance only by reducing a stress to flash cells. SARO is different from this technique in that SARO improves the flash reliability in a comprehensive fashion by considering all the different error types including the endurance errors.

7 CONCLUSIONS

We have presented a new flash reliability optimization technique, SARO, that solves the reliability problem of high-density NAND flash memory without sacrificing the program latency. Our proposed technique is based on the state-aware selective programming scheme, which enables each program state to be programmed by a different V_{ispp} value. Since SARO improves the error tolerance of a flash device by selectively reducing V_{ispp} for the most error-prone NAND states only, it is an effective solution to maximize the reliability improvement while minimizing the performance degradation. In order to keep the performance unchanged, SARO parameters are fine-tunned exploiting the flash characteristics that the program latency decreases with cell aging. Our evaluation results with real flash chips show that SARO is effective in improving the flash reliability thanks to the significant decrease in NAND bit errors. It also improves the read latency by 40% on average due to the reduction of read retry operations.

The current version of SARO can be extended in several directions. For example, since a finer V_{ispp} value is more effective for higher flash reliability, we plan to better exploit various system hints (e.g., latency-insensitive program operations) to more aggressively reduce V_{ispp} without affecting the program latency.

ACKNOWLEDGMENT

This work was supported by Samsung Research Funding & Incubation Center of Samsung Electronics under Project Number SRFC-IT1701-11.

REFERENCES

[1] Y. Park et al. 2014. Scaling and Reliability of NAND Flash Devices. In *Proc. IEEE Int. Reliability Physics Symposium.*

[2] Y. Woo et al. 2013. Diversifying Wear Index for MLC NAND Flash Memory to Extend the Lifetime of SSDs. In *Proc. Int. Conf. on Embedded Software.*

[3] R. Micheloni et al. 2010. Inside NAND Flash Memories. Springer.

[4] N. Mielke et al. 2017. Reliability of Solid-State Drives Based on NAND Flash Memory. In *Proc. IEEE*, Vol. 105(9). 1725–1750.

[5] Y. Cai et al. 2015. Data retention in MLC NAND flash memory: Characterization, optimization, and recovery. In *IEEE Int. Symposium on High Performance Computer Architecture.*

[6] K. Suh et al. 1995. A 3.3V 32 Mb NAND Flash Memory with Incremental Step Pulse Programming Scheme. In *IEEE Tran. on Consumer Electronics*, Vol. 30(11). 1149–1156.

[7] Y. Pan et al. 2011. Exploiting Memory Device Wear-Out Dynamics to Improve NAND Flash Memory System Performance. In *Proc. USENIX Conf. on File and Storage Technologies.*

[8] S. Park et al. 2012. Adaptive Program Verify Scheme for Improving NAND Flash Memory Performance and Lifespan. In *IEEE Asian Solid-State Circuits Conf.*

[9] J. Jeong et al. 2014. Lifetime Improvement of NAND Flash-based Storage Systems Using Dynamic Program and Erase Scaling. In *Proc. USENIX Conf. on File and Storage Technologies.*

Simultaneous Timing Driven Tree Surgery in Routing with Machine Learning-based Acceleration

Peishan Tu, Chak-Wa Pui, Evangeline F. Y. Young
Department of Computer Science and Engineering
The Chinese University of Hong Kong, NT, Hong Kong
pstu,cwpui,fyyoung@cse.cuhk.edu.hk

ABSTRACT

In global routing, both timing and routability are critical criterions to measure the performance of a design. However, these two objectives naturally conflict with each other during routing. In this paper, a tree surgery technique is presented to adjust routing tree topologies in global routing to fix timing. We formulate the problem as a quadratic program (QP), which adjusts routing topologies of all the nets from a global perspective and takes congestion into consideration to trade off timing and routability objectives. We also apply machine learning-based techniques to accelerate our algorithm, which offers a fast and effective way to solve the problem. Experimental results on ICCAD 2015 benchmarks show that our algorithms can achieve 10.12% timing improvement with no significant degradation in routability and wirelength. With machine learning-based acceleration (MLA), our results can be obtained in almost negligible runtime.

CCS CONCEPTS

• **Hardware** → **Wire routing**;

ACM Reference Format:
Peishan Tu, Chak-Wa Pui, Evangeline F. Y. Young. 2018. Simultaneous Timing Driven Tree Surgery in Routing with Machine Learning-based Acceleration. In *GLSVLSI '18: 2018 Great Lakes Symposium on VLSI, May 23–25, 2018, Chicago, IL, USA.* ACM, New York, NY, USA, 6 pages. https://doi.org/10.1145/3194554.3194556

1 INTRODUCTION

As design complexity increases, achieving timing closure becomes even more challenging. Modern designs demand improved routing strategies to meet timing requirements [12].

Since global routing plays an important role in both the placement and routing phases, there are numerous previous works on global routing. NCTUgr [15] began with rectilinear minimum spanning tree (RMST) topologies and utilized the rectilinear steiner minimum tree (RSMT) topologies to guide the following monotonic routing and negotiation-based rip-up and reroute. NTHURoute [2] also decomposed nets to two-pin nets based on routing tree topologies. Next, it utilized a rip-up and reroute approach, based on the congested region identification, to further improve routability. FastRoute [18] first built routing trees for all the nets and then adjusted the routing edges to reduce congestion. It then performed multi-source multi-pin maze routing and 3-bend routing with an adaptive cost function. MaizeRouter [17] initialized tree construction by FLUTE [6], which is an approach to build RSMT. It then shifted and retracted the edge to optimize congestion. Followed by layer assignment, the maze routing was performed. Overall, these global routers achieved good performance in terms of wirelength and routing congestion. However, timing is not considered in these routers.

Besides congestion driven routers mentioned above, some works optimized timing and congestion together. The work [7] proposed a global routing approach to incorporate both congestion and timing optimization. However, it took tens of seconds to handle at most 400 nets, which may not be fast enough for current designs. In addition, it targeted at small number of module nets instead of large number of standard cell nets. The unified timing and congestion optimizing (UTACO) [11] algorithm adopted a shadow price mechanism which considered timing and congestion as the sum of the price. It first built the minimum wire length steiner tree and performed rip-up and reroute by optimizing the price of congestion and timing. However, it modeled the delay of each net individually which may neglect interaction among adjacent nets because actual gate delay is affected by values from upstream and downstream nets. The work [5] targeted at optimizing Chemical-Mechanical Polishing(CMP) and timing in global routing besides congestion. It modeled timing by a guide of wire density. However, the gate model it considered is the lumped resistance model. The work [19] proposed a routing algorithm that considered timing optimization, buffer insertion and power reduction. It first constructed minimum steiner trees and additional detoured trees and buffered trees are then built to reduce congestion and timing. Next, it formulated an ILP to decrease power consumption. However, the buffer tree construction was time consuming and only wire delay was optimized without gate delay considered.

In most global routers, a tree topology will be assigned to each net, better timing can be achieved by considering timing in construction of the routing tree topologies. Several algorithms [1] [3] are proposed to build timing aware routing trees to achieve good performance on balancing net and gate delay. However, most of them adopt simple lumped resistance model as their gate delay model, which is inaccurate and inadequate for modern designs. Moreover, modern gate delay model requires that tree topologies should not be optimized individually. Hence, in timing aware global

The work described in this paper was partially supported by a grant from the Research Grants Council of the Hong Kong Special Administrative Region, China (Project No. CUHK14206015).
GLSVLSI '18, May 23–25, 2018, Chicago, IL, USA

ACM ISBN 978-1-4503-5724-1/18/05...$15.00
https://doi.org/10.1145/3194554.3194556

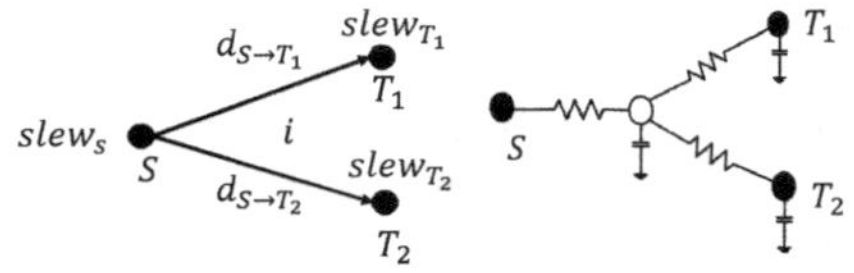

(c) **interconnection** (d) **RC model**

Figure 1: Delay in the circuit.

routers, methods are needed to capture delay more accurately and to consider the topologies of all the nets simultaneously.

In this work, we propose an algorithm to adjust the tree topologies of all the nets to fit timing from a global perspective and consider routing congestion simultaneously. Our contributions are summarized as follows:

- To optimize the tree topologies globally, a QP is formulated to determine how to adjust the most critical sink connection to optimize timing and congestion.
- We study various circuit properties and identified those that contribute to timing. Later, these features will be used to accelerate the QP-based tree surgery technique by a machine learning-based technique.
- Experimental results show that we can improve timing of the design significantly with small increase in routing congestion.

The remaining of this paper is organized as follows. Section 2 introduces basic knowledge in timing analysis. Section 3 defines our tree surgery technique (TST) in global route and its formulation. Section 4 contains details of our algorithms, including quadratic programming based TST and machine learning-based acceleration technique. Section 5 shows the experimental results and we finally conclude the work in Section 6.

2 PRELIMINARY

A simple circuit structure is shown in Figure 1(a). It consists of circuit elements, IO pins and interconnections. The circuit elements can be combinational logic elements or sequential elements. When signals travel from the primary inputs to the primary outputs of the circuit, the circuit elements and their interconnections will have delays which affect the performance of the circuit.

2.1 Delay and Slew Calculation

A circuit element shown in Figure 1(b) is extracted from Figure 1(a) which is marked red. It consists of input A, input B and output Y, which is the source gate of net k. Based on a nonlinear delay model (NLDM), gate delay $gd_{A\to Y}$ is estimated based on a 2-dimensional table with inputs slew $slew_A$ and capacitance cap_k. Generally, given specific index values x and y, gate delay can be estimated by Equation (1). Assuming $x_1 < x < x_2$ and $y_1 < y < y_2$, solutions of the bilinear interpolation can be computed as in Equation (1) and the coefficients can be obtained by Equation (2) using z_{11}, z_{12}, z_{21} and z_{22}. Details of the calculation are shown in [8].

$$L(x, y) = a_0 + a_1 \cdot x + a_2 \cdot y + a_3 \cdot x \cdot y \tag{1}$$

$$\begin{bmatrix} 1 & x_1 & y_1 & x_1y_1 \\ 1 & x_1 & y_2 & x_1y_2 \\ 1 & x_2 & y_1 & x_2y_1 \\ 1 & x_2 & y_2 & x_2y_2 \end{bmatrix} \begin{bmatrix} a_0 \\ a_1 \\ a_2 \\ a_3 \end{bmatrix} = \begin{bmatrix} z_{11} \\ z_{12} \\ z_{21} \\ z_{22} \end{bmatrix}. \tag{2}$$

Interconnect delay is calculated according to Elmore delay. We make use of the slew calculation as proposed by [8].

2.2 Timing Analysis

Generally, timing analysis is propagated from the primary input to the output to obtain the actual arrival time (aat) and from the output to the input to obtain the required arrival time (rat). We quantify the timing of a circuit at each node by the term slack which is computed by $slack = rat - aat$. Statistic Timing Analysis (STA) [8] is always performed to check the timing of the design.

3 PROBLEM FORMULATION

Given the placement of a design, nets are routed and timing information are obtained by STA. Our objective is to maximize the total negative slack (TNS) by adjusting routing topologies, which is called TST. In our work, TST tries to reconnect critical sinks to maximize TNS by reducing wire delay and gate delay on the critical path, which is formulated as Equation (3).

$$\begin{aligned} \max \quad & \text{TNS}, \\ s.t. \quad & x_i \in \{0, 1\} \quad \forall i \in N_c, \end{aligned} \tag{3}$$

where x_i denotes whether the most critical sink of each net $i \in N_c$ is reconnected and N_c is a set of net such that any net $i \in N_c$ with P_i sinks should satisfy the following constraints:

$$j_x^i = \underset{l \in P_i, \text{slack}_l < 0}{\arg\min} \quad slack_l, \tag{4}$$

$$\text{parent}[j_x^i] \neq s_i, \tag{5}$$

where j_x^i is the sink in net i whose slack is the most negative and the parent of j_x^i is not the source s_i. If the slack of every sink in net i is positive, the routing topology of net i will remain unchanged. Equation (5) requires that the sink j_x^i with the worst negative slack is not connected to the root. It may then be possible to connect it to the root to improve the timing.

The explicit formulation of our objective is explained in the following section.

4 TREE SURGERY TECHNIQUE (TST)

TST is an approach to modify the tree structure, such as reconnection. TST is first formulated as a QP to maximize the total negative slack while congestion is also considered in the formulation. We then extract circuit properties which can influence timing and a machine learning based acceleration method is further proposed to speed up the QP-based TST. The notations of variables in this section are listed in Table 1.

4.1 QP-based TST (QPTST)

4.1.1 Timing Optimization. In order to achieve timing closure, STA is used to detect the timing problem of a design. It measures

Table 1: Variable notations in Section 4.1.

s_i	the source of net i
j_x^i	the sink of net i whose slack is negative and the worst
l	the input pin of the gate of s_i which affects actual arrival time of s_i
j	the net of input pin l
$L(cap_i, slew_l)$	gate delay $gd_{l \to S}$ from input l to source node S of net i
$d^o_{s_i \to j_x^i}$	delay from s_i to j_x^i before reconnection on net i
$d_{s_i \to j_x^i}$	delay from s_i to j_x^i after reconnection on net i
$\Delta d_{s_i \to j_x^i}$	delay difference before and after reconnection on net i, $d^o_{s_i \to j_x^i} - d_{s_i \to j_x^i}$
cap_i^o	lumped capacitance of node i before deciding whether performing reconnection on net i
cap_i	lumped capacitance of node i after deciding whether performing reconnection on net i, $cap_i^o - \Delta cap_i x_i$
Δcap_i	capacitance changed when reconnection is performed on net i
$slew_l^o$	slew of pin l before deciding whether performing reconnection on net j
$slew_l$	slew of pin l after deciding whether performing reconnection on net j, $slew_l^o - \Delta slew_l x_j$
$\Delta slew_l$	slew changed when reconnection is performed on net j
ΔL_i	gate delay difference of source s in net i considering reconnection of net i and net j

slack ($slack_{po} = rat_{po} - at_{po}$) at each timing end point $po \in PO$, where PO is a set of primary outputs and register data ports. In STA, timing failure can be detected if the slack of a timing end point is negative ($slack_{po} < 0$). In order to reduce timing failure, our objective is to maximize TNS at critical timing endpoints, which is formulated in Equation (6). PO_n denotes the set of timing end points with negative slack.

$$\max \sum_{po \in PO_n} rat_{po} - aat_{po}. \tag{6}$$

The negative slacks of PO_n is mainly related to the nets with negative slack sinks, which are called critical nets N_c. Hence, in this work, we will improve the slack of critical nets instead of directly optimizing the slack on the primary outputs, which is shown in Equation (7).

$$\max \sum_{i \in N_c} \sum_{l \in P_i^c} rat_l - aat_l, \tag{7}$$

where P_i^c is the set of critical sinks of net i. Since simultaneously optimizing all the critical sinks of a net is hard to achieve and may cause congestion, we further simplify the problem such that only the most critical sink of each critical net will be considered and formulate it as Equation (8).

$$\max \sum_{i \in N_c} rat_{j_x^i} - aat_{j_x^i}. \tag{8}$$

Since the slack value on one critical timing path is the same, for each net, optimizing the slack of the source is equivalent to optimize the slack of the most critical sink. Hence, Equation (8) can be transformed into Equation (9).

$$\begin{aligned} &\max \sum_{i \in N_c} rat_{s_i} - aat_{s_i} \\ &= \max \sum_{i \in N_c} rat_{j_x^i} - d_{s_i \to j_x^i} - aat_l - gd_{l \to s_i} \end{aligned}, \tag{9}$$

where $d_{s_i \to j_x^i}$ is the net delay from s_i to j_x^i, $gd_{l \to} s_i$ is the gate delay and the input pin l of the gate containing node s_i determines the actual arrival time of source s_i. By assuming $rat_{j_x^i}$ and aat_l are constant, we can further simplify the problem as Equation (10).

$$\begin{aligned} &\min \sum_{i \in N_c} d_{s_i \to j_x^i} + gd_{l \to s_i} \\ &= \min \sum_{i \in N_c} d_{s_i \to j_x^i} + L(cap_i, slew_l) \end{aligned}, \tag{10}$$

where gate delay can be represented as $L(cap_i, slew_l)$.

In this work, we minimize delay $d_{s_i \to j_x^i}$ in Equation (10) by reconnecting the critical sink j_x^i directly to its source s_i. However, reconnecting all the nets N_c will increase total capacitance cap_i of each net i due to longer wirelength, which will increase the gate delay $L(cap_i, slew_l)$. In order to maximize the delay reduction $d_{s_i \to j_x^i} + L(cap_i, Slew_l)$, the set of net that will be reconnected is found by Equation (11).

$$\begin{aligned} &\max \sum_{i=1}^{n} (\beta \cdot \Delta L_i + \Delta d_{s_i \to j_x^i} \cdot x_i), \\ &s.t. \quad x_i = \{0, 1\} \quad \forall i \in N_c, \end{aligned} \tag{11}$$

where x_i is a binary variable indicating whether net i is reconstructed. β is a user defined parameter. $\Delta d_{s_i \to j_x^i}$ is the difference of interconnect delay on the path from the critical sink j_x^i to its source s_i before and after reconnecting it to the root, which is computed by Equation (12).

$$\Delta d_{s_i \to j_x^i} = d^o_{s_i \to j_x^i} - d_{s_i \to j_x^i}. \tag{12}$$

ΔL_i implies how much gate delay at node s_i can be reduced, which is computed by Equation (13).

$$\begin{aligned} \Delta L_i &= L(cap_i^o, slew_l^o) - L(cap_i, slew_l) \\ &= a_1 \cdot (cap_i^o - cap_i) + a_2 \cdot (slew_l^o - slew_l), \\ &+ a_3 \cdot (cap_i^o \cdot slew_l^o - cap_i \cdot slew_l) \end{aligned} \tag{13}$$

where $L(cap_i^o, slew_l^o)$ and $L(cap_i, slew_l)$ are the gate delay before and after reconnection respectively. The value of ΔL_i is determined by reconnection of net i and net j, where net j influences the input slew at node l. It is easy to see that ΔL_i can be rewritten in the form of summation of terms with x_i and x_j as in Equation (14), where a_0, a_1, a_2 and a_3 can be obtained as shown in Section 2.1.

$$\begin{aligned} \Delta L_i &= (a_1 + a_3 \cdot slew_l^o) \cdot \Delta cap_i \cdot x_i \\ &+ (a_2 + a_3 \cdot cap_i^o) \cdot \Delta slew_l \cdot x_j \\ &- a_3 \cdot \Delta cap_i \cdot \Delta slew_l \cdot x_i \cdot x_j \end{aligned} \tag{14}$$

With Equation (11) and Equation (14), we can formulate a QP to determine which net to be reconnected such that the total negative slacks is optimized.

4.1.2 Congestion Optimization. When we improve the timing by reconnecting sinks to their sources, routing congestion may be increased. Hence, routability needs to be considered when we optimize timing by reconnection. The general idea is to avoid reconnecting the critical sink which may go through congested routing regions.

More specifically, a penalty factor of each critical sink is obtained and such penalty will be added to the objective function in order to consider routability. The penalty factor of each critical sink is calculated from the overflow values of its source, which can be obtained after global routing. To honor our original tree topologies, both the steiner points and pins of each tree are treated as pins in the global router. How we calculate the overflow penalty po_i of critical sink i is illustrated by an example given in Figure 2, where a, b, c are the possible locations of the critical sink and s is the source. For each critical sink i, po_i can be obtained from the overflow values of its source, which are o_{e_u}, o_{e_r}, o_{e_d} and o_{e_l} in this example. There are two kinds of situations as follows:

(1) The routing grid of the critical sink is either horizontal or vertical to the one of its source, such as critical sinks a, c.
(2) Otherwise, such as critical sinks b.

For the first situation, po_i is equal to the overflow of the edge cut through by the connection between the sink and source. For the other situation, po_i is equal to the maximum overflow of the edges cut through by the bounding box of the sink and source. In Figure 2, the overflow penalties of a, b and c are o_{e_u}, $\max(o_{e_u}, o_{e_r})$ and o_{e_r} respectively.

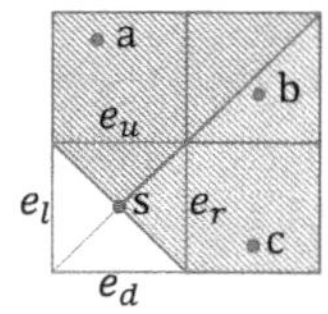

Figure 2: An example of how to calculate potential routing overflow.

By adding overflow penalty po_i into the objective function as shown in Equation (15), we can optimize timing and congestion simultaneously.

$$\max \sum_{i=1}^{n} (\beta \cdot \Delta L_i + (\Delta d_{s \to j_x^i} + \alpha \cdot po_i) \cdot x_i) \qquad (15)$$
$$s.t. \quad x_i = \{0, 1\} \quad \forall i \in N_c$$

4.2 Machine Learning-based Acceleration (MLA)

In this section, we first study how the circuit properties will affect the reconnection decisions. For example, the critical sink may have a large detour to the source in the original tree topology and the slew of the critical sink will be improved a lot after reconnection. We will select some of these properties as features and use a classification

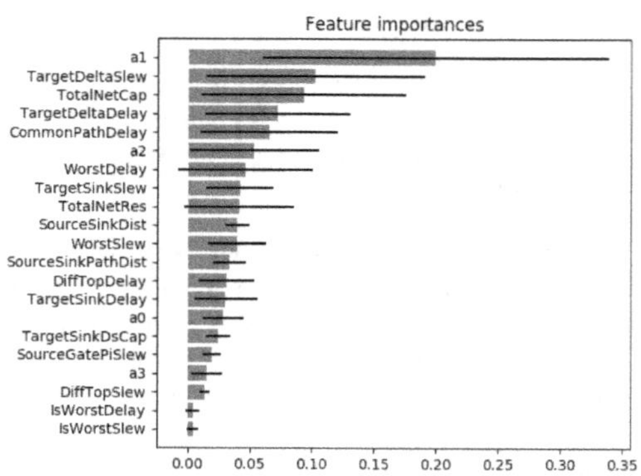

Figure 3: Feature Importances.

approach to speed up QPTST. In the following parts, we assume each net i has n sinks and a source s_i and sink j_x^i is the most critical one.

The circuit properties we study can be categorized into three types: (1) slew and delay related features as shown in Table 2, (2) distance and length related features as shown in Table 3, and (3) physics related features as shown in Table 4.

Since the ranges of the values of the extracted features f vary a lot, Equation (16) is used for normalization.

$$f' = \frac{f - min(f)}{max(f) - min(f)}, \qquad (16)$$

where $max(f)$ and $min(f)$ are obtained in the training set.

Large number of features may cause inefficiency and overfitting. Hence, we need to reduce the number of features and features are selected according to their importance. The importances of features are obtained by a machine learning model. As shown in Figure 3, features are ranked according to their importance produced by Random Forest (RF) [14].

After feature selection and preprocessing, we formulate our MLA problem as a classification problem. To be specific, a binary classifier is applied to each critical net to decide whether it should be reconnected and the results of QPTST are used to label the data. Accuracy of the classifier is based on the results of QPTST. We use the RF as our classification model and the top 15 important circuit properties shown in Figure 3 are selected as final features. If congestion is also considered, factor po_i of each net i is added to our features during classification.

Table 2: Delay And Slew Related Features.

DiffTopSlew (*DiffTopDelay*)	The difference of sink j_x^i slew (delay) and the largest slew (delay) of net i except slew (delay) of sink j_x^i.
IsWorstSlew (*IsWorstDelay*)	Whether slew (delay) of sink j_x^i is worst in net i.
WorstSlew (*WorstDelay*)	Value of the worst slew (delay) of net i.
TargetSinkSlew (*TargetSinkDelay*)	The slew (delay) of sink j_x^i.
TargetDeltaSlew (*TargetDeltaDelay*)	The difference slew (delay) of sink j_x^i before and after connecting to root.
CommonPathDelay	The delay accumulated on branches which connects s to j_x^i path.

Table 3: Distance And Length Related Features.

SourceSinkPathDist	The path length from source to the sink j_x^i on the routing tree.
SourceSinkDist	The Manhattan distance between the position of source s and sink j.

Table 4: Physics Related Features.

TotalNetCap	The total capacitance of net i.
TotalNetRes	The total net resistance.
a_0,a_1,a_2 and a_3	The coefficients of lookup table function of source s.

5 EXPERIMENTAL RESULTS

In the experiments, the benchmarks of the contest in ICCAD 2015[13] are used and these benchmarks provide timing information. OpenTimer [9] is used for STA. Our work is implemented in C++ and tested on a 2.1 GHz Intel Linux machine with a 64 GB memory. IBM ILOG CPLEX V12.7.0 [10] is used to solve the QP.

5.1 QPTST Results

5.1.1 Timing Results. The results of QPTST is shown in Table 6. Evaluation is performed by Opentimer [9] and our results provide

Table 5: ICCAD 2015 Benchmarks Information

Designs	#nodes	#nets	clock periods (ns)
superblue10	1876103	1898119	10
superblue1	1209716	1215710	9
superblue16	981559	999902	5.5
superblue18	768068	771542	7
superblue3	1213253	1224979	10
superblue4	795645	802513	6
superblue5	1086888	1100825	9
superblue7	1931639	1933945	5.5

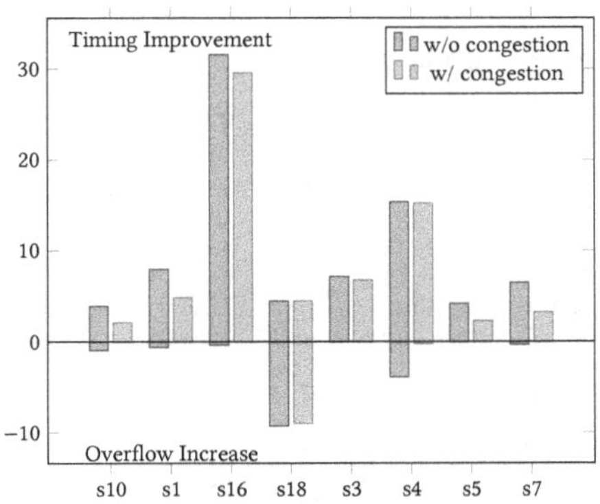

Figure 4: Performance analysis on timing and routing congestion.

interconnection information to it. FLUTE Baseline shows timing results when all the nets are constructed by FLUTE, which does not optimize timing. Direct Connection is the experiment that the most critical sink of every net is reconnected to its source. It can shorten path length of all the nets but will increase wirelength a lot. QPTST is our result and congestion-aware QPTST is the algorithm described in Section 4.1.2. β is set to 2500. QPTST takes 27.6*s* while congestion-aware QPTST takes 30.71*s* on average. r_wns and r_tns denote WNS and TNS improvement over the FLUTE baseline. r_stwl and r_d denote tree length improvement over the FLUTE baseline and direct connection. Direct Connection improves timing by 1.10% on worst negative slack (WNS) and 6.81% on total negative slack (TNS). However, it increases 18.74% wirelength as expected. QPTST obtains 2.05% and 10.12% improvement on WNS and TNS. The wirelength is only worse by −0.55%. If we also consider congestion in the objective function, timing is not as good as QPTST but can still get 1.74% and 8.55% improvement on WNS and TNS. The wirelength is improved compared with QPTST. All the results of our algorithms achieve better wirelength and timing compared with the FLUTE baseline and direct connection.

Besides using FLUTE as baseline, we also performed QPTST experiments on timing driven routing tree constructed by the PD method mentioned in [1]. Shown in Table 7, our algorithm achieves 1.7% and 7.11% improvement on WNS and TNS with loss of 0.39% wirelength. It shows that our algorithm is efficient on both non-timing aware trees and timing driven routing.

5.1.2 Congestion Results. Nets are decomposed to two-pin nets by FLUTE first and NCTUgr [16] is performed to measure congestion. As shown in Table 8, r denotes the improvement compared with FLUTE based net decomposition. The overflow of QPTST and congestion aware QPTST increases 1.91% and 1.15% respectively. Wirelength increases 1.29% and 0.79% respectively. In congestion aware TST, α is set to 1000. Our algorithm QPTST can improve timing around 10% but congestion is increased by 1.91%.

5.1.3 Analysis. Figure 4 shows the analysis of performance of our algorithms on timing and congestion. The part above 0 of the chart is timing improvement and the other part is plotted as increase of overflow. It is obvious that our algorithms can achieve significantly timing improvement with small increase in congestion.

5.2 Machine Learning-based Acceleration Results

As mentioned in Section 4.2, top 15 features are selected in our experiments. Data from 4 benchmarks (superblue4, superblue16, superblue18 and superblue7) with scaled features are fed into cross validation and our machine learning model is trained by random forest method. In addition to designs listed in Table 5, we also adopt placement results generated by top 3 contestants in [13]. Therefore, test benchmark sets (superblue1, superblue3, superblue5 and superblue10) with each of 7 placement results are tested. Benchmarks (superblue4, superblue16, superblue18 and superblue7) with untrained placement results from contestants are also tested.

The average evaluation of each benchmark is shown in the Table 9. We can see from the table that runtime is reduced a lot. Moreover, we achieves a relative high accuracy classification rate. The final timing and wirelength improvement are also listed in Table 9. Classification Over Base shows timing results compared with baseline and Classification Over QP shows the comparison with the results of QPTST. The timing and wirelength quality are very compatible compared with our QPTST results.

6 CONCLUSION

Timing is a critical issue for the design optimization and it is hard to improve timing without increasing routing congestion. In this work, we formulate the tree surgery problem as a QP, which optimizes gate delay and net delay with adjacent nets considered. In order to enhance routability, congestion is also optimized in our algorithm. To speed up the process, a machine learning-based algorithm is proposed and features related to timing optimization are extracted from the design. In the experimental results, our algorithms can achieve high quality of timing improvement.

REFERENCES

[1] Charles J Alpert, Andrew B Kahng, CN Sze, and Qinke Wang. 2006. Timing-driven steiner trees are (practically) free. In *Proceedings of the 43rd annual Design Automation Conference*. ACM, 389–392.

[2] Yen-Jung Chang, Yu-Ting Lee, Jhih-Rong Gao, Pei-Ci Wu, and Ting-Chi Wang. 2010. NTHU-route 2.0: a robust global router for modern designs. *IEEE Transactions on Computer-Aided Design of Integrated Circuits and Systems* 29, 12 (2010), 1931–1944.

[3] Genjie Chen, Peishan Tu, and Evangeline FY Young. 2017. SALT: Provably Good Routing Topology by a Novel Steiner Shallow-Light Tree Algorithm. In *Proceedings of the 2017 IEEE/ACM international conference on Computer-aided design*. ACM.

[4] Minsik Cho and David Z Pan. 2007. BoxRouter: a new global router based on box expansion and progressive ILP. *IEEE Transactions on Computer-Aided Design of Integrated Circuits and Systems* 26, 12 (2007), 2130–2143.

[5] Minsik Cho, David Z Pan, Hua Xiang, and Ruchir Puri. 2006. Wire density driven global routing for CMP variation and timing. In *Proceedings of the 2006 IEEE/ACM international conference on Computer-aided design*. ACM, 487–492.

[6] Chris Chu and Yiu-Chung Wong. 2008. FLUTE: Fast lookup table based rectilinear steiner minimal tree algorithm for VLSI design. *IEEE Transactions on Computer-Aided Design of Integrated Circuits and Systems* 27, 1 (2008), 70–83.

Table 6: Experimental Results of Tree Surgery Technique.

Benchmarks	FLUTE Baseline**						Direct Connection*			QPTST					Congestion Aware QPTST				
	WNS	r_wns	TNS	r_tns	stWL	r_stwl	r_wns	r_tns	r_stwl	r_wns	r_tns	r_stwl	r_d	CPU(s)	r_wns	r_tns	r_stwl	r_d	CPU(s)
superblue10	-1.65	1.00	-33.10	1.00	2.05	1.00	0.47%	2.47%	-13.92%	0.92%	3.88%	-0.79%	11.52%	69.73	0.00%	2.11%	-0.48%	11.80%	77.03
superblue1	-0.50	1.00	-0.46	1.00	0.96	1.00	-0.26%	3.20%	-19.76%	1.76%	7.92%	-0.38%	16.18%	15.60	1.78%	4.81%	-0.37%	16.19%	25.05
superblue16	-0.46	1.00	-0.76	1.00	0.93	1.00	3.58%	25.18%	-14.74%	3.94%	31.58%	-0.38%	12.52%	6.42	3.94%	29.57%	-0.36%	12.54%	15.21
superblue18	-0.46	1.00	-1.03	1.00	0.58	1.00	-0.75%	2.10%	-23.30%	2.27%	4.45%	-0.18%	18.75%	17.93	2.27%	4.45%	-0.18%	18.75%	13.01
superblue3	-1.01	1.00	-1.50	1.00	1.14	1.00	4.82%	5.79%	-18.87%	5.61%	7.16%	-0.11%	15.78%	6.12	5.37%	6.76%	-0.09%	15.80%	15.10
superblue4	-0.62	1.00	-3.47	1.00	0.71	1.00	0.90%	10.81%	-18.51%	1.60%	15.33%	-1.79%	14.10%	48.95	0.47%	15.19%	-1.58%	14.29%	57.36
superblue5	-2.57	1.00	-6.95	1.00	1.08	1.00	0.07%	1.42%	-17.24%	0.32%	4.17%	-0.62%	14.18%	11.93	0.12%	2.29%	-0.27%	14.48%	22.02
superblue7	-1.51	1.00	-1.84	1.00	1.40	1.00	0.00%	3.54%	-23.56%	0.00%	6.46%	-0.13%	18.96%	44.13	0.00%	3.21%	-0.08%	19.00%	20.91
Average	-1.10	1.00	-6.14	1.00	1.11	1.00	1.10%	6.81%	-18.74%	2.05%	10.12%	-0.55%	15.25%	27.60	1.74%	8.55%	-0.43%	15.35%	30.71

*Direct Connection: directly connect the critical sinks to the source for all nets.

**WNS is in $10^4 ps$. TNS is in $10^6 ps$. stWL is in $10^8 um$.

Table 7: Comparisons Between PD Based Tree Construction and QPTST.

Benchmarks	PD Baseline						Direct Connection			QPTST				
	WNS	r_wns	TNS	r_tns	stWL	r_stwl	r_wns	r_tns	r_stwl	r_wns	r_tns	r_stwl	r_d	CPU(s)
superblue10	-1.66	1.00	-33.14	1.00	2.12	1.00	4.65%	2.78%	-10.97%	5.12%	4.12%	-0.60%	9.34%	57.87
superblue1	-0.50	1.00	-0.47	1.00	1.01	1.00	-0.86%	1.53%	-14.78%	0.90%	5.46%	-0.24%	12.67%	14.14
superblue16	-0.46	1.00	-0.69	1.00	0.96	1.00	2.41%	11.21%	-12.12%	3.10%	19.44%	-0.28%	10.56%	6.01
superblue18	-0.45	1.00	-1.04	1.00	0.63	1.00	-0.74%	-0.29%	-18.12%	1.10%	2.41%	-0.14%	15.23%	4.43
superblue3	-1.01	1.00	-1.51	1.00	1.22	1.00	2.02%	2.90%	-14.80%	2.71%	4.15%	-0.07%	12.84%	5.91
superblue4	-0.63	1.00	-3.54	1.00	0.75	1.00	-0.63%	9.66%	-14.50%	-0.02%	13.20%	-1.29%	11.53%	39.80
superblue5	-2.57	1.00	-6.95	1.00	1.11	1.00	-0.18%	0.12%	-13.43%	0.10%	2.91%	-0.45%	11.44%	12.08
superblue7	-1.52	1.00	-1.81	1.00	1.51	1.00	0.00%	1.06%	-18.69%	0.56%	5.24%	-0.09%	15.67%	11.46
Average	-1.10	1.00	-6.14	1.00	1.16	1.00	0.83%	3.62%	-14.68%	1.70%	7.11%	-0.39%	12.41%	18.96

Table 8: Comparisons Before and After Considering Congestion in QPTST.

	FLUTE Based Net Decomposition				QPTST				Congestion Aware QPTST			
Benchmarks	WL	r	Overflow	r	WL	r	Overflow	r	WL	r	Overflow	r
superblue10	1.71	1.00	7696.32	1.00	1.72	-1.69%	7768.53	-0.94%	1.71	-1.03%	7697.78	-0.02%
superblue16	0.98	1.00	684.93	1.00	0.98	-0.15%	688.89	-0.58%	0.98	0.17%	685.04	-0.02%
superblue18	.63	1.00	74.81	1.00	0.63	0.37%	75.08	-0.36%	0.63	0.55%	74.81	0.00%
superblue1	0.78	1.00	3297.61	1.00	0.82	-3.16%	3603.07	-9.26%	0.82	-2.46%	3593.22	-8.96%
superblue3	1.07	1.00	2538.63	1.00	1.07	-0.83%	2538.63	0.00%	1.07	-0.83%	2538.63	0.00%
superblue4	0.77	1.00	749.92	1.00	0.78	-2.24%	778.55	-3.82%	0.77	-0.18%	751.39	-0.20%
superblue5	0.73	1.00	3060.91	1.00	0.73	-1.72%	3060.80	0.00%	0.73	-1.72%	3060.80	0.00%
superblue7	.37	1.00	3972.55	1.00	1.38	-0.93%	3984.21	-0.29%	1.37	-0.81%	3972.87	-0.01%
Average	1.01	1.00	2759.46	1.00	1.01	-1.29%	2812.22	-1.91%	1.01	-0.79%	2796.82	-1.15%

Table 9: Experimental Results of Machine Learning Acceleration (MLA).

Benchmarks	Classification Accuracy						Classification Over Base			Classification Over QP		
	TP	FP	FN	TN	ACC	CPU(s)	r_wns	r_tns	r_wl	r_wns	r_tns	r_wl
superblue18	2047.17	63.00	41.33	1483.67	97.13%	1.21	0.09%	3.89%	-0.18%	-0.01%	0.01%	0.00%
superblue16	3037.67	122.50	96.33	1833.33	95.53%	1.54	5.24%	29.54%	-0.32%	0.10%	0.14%	0.00%
superblue7	3392.20	119.80	157.00	1769.00	94.91%	1.59	0.00%	5.49%	-0.13%	0.00%	0.41%	0.00%
superblue4	15374.83	92.83	151.33	12844.83	99.14%	6.39	1.55%	13.87%	-1.78%	-0.02%	0.11%	0.00%
superblue1	4651.14	798.71	1201.43	4932.86	82.74%	2.98	1.71%	6.10%	-0.38%	0.42%	1.28%	-0.06%
superblue3	1587.14	310.00	288.57	1211.43	82.38%	1.13	3.67%	5.32%	-0.10%	0.37%	1.26%	-0.05%
superblue5	5552.86	707.14	1182.57	3803.57	83.19%	2.97	0.25%	3.40%	-0.57%	0.05%	0.06%	-0.01%
superblue10	20330.29	2107.29	1974.43	9563.00	87.99%	7.73	0.73%	3.71%	-0.76%	0.07%	0.55%	-0.08%

[7] Jiang Hu and Sachin S Sapatnekar. 2000. A timing-constrained algorithm for simultaneous global routing of multiple nets. In *Proceedings of the 2000 IEEE/ACM international conference on Computer-aided design*. IEEE Press, 99–103.

[8] Jin Hu, Greg Schaeffer, and Vibhor Garg. 2015. TAU 2015 contest on incremental timing analysis. In *Computer-Aided Design (ICCAD), 2015 IEEE/ACM International Conference on*. IEEE, 882–889.

[9] Tsung-Wei Huang and Martin DF Wong. 2015. OpenTimer: A high-performance timing analysis tool. In *Proceedings of the IEEE/ACM International Conference on Computer-Aided Design*. IEEE Press, 895–902.

[10] IBM. 2017. CPLEX. (2017). https://www-01.ibm.com/software/commerce/optimization/cplex-optimizer/

[11] Tong Jing, Xianlong Hong, Haiyun Bao, Yici Cai, Jingyu Xu, Chungkuan Cheng, and Jun Gu. 2003. UTACO: a unified timing and congestion optimizing algorithm for standard cell global routing. In *Proceedings of the 2003 Asia and South Pacific Design Automation Conference*. ACM, 834–839.

[12] Andrew B Kahng. 2015. New game, new goal posts: A recent history of timing closure. In *Proceedings of the 52nd Annual Design Automation Conference*. ACM, 4.

[13] Myung-Chul Kim, Jin Hu, Jiajia Li, and Natarajan Viswanathan. 2015. Iccad-2015 cad contest in incremental timing-driven placement and benchmark suite. In *Proceedings of the IEEE/ACM International Conference on Computer-Aided Design*. IEEE Press, 921–926.

[14] Andy Liaw, Matthew Wiener, et al. 2002. Classification and regression by randomForest. *R news* 2, 3 (2002), 18–22.

[15] Wen-Hao Liu, Wei-Chun Kao, Yih-Lang Li, and Kai-Yuan Chao. 2013. NCTU-GR 2.0: multithreaded collision-aware global routing with bounded-length maze routing. *IEEE Transactions on computer-aided design of integrated circuits and systems* 32, 5 (2013), 709–722.

[16] Wen-Hao Liu, Cheng-Kok Koh, and Yih-Lang Li. 2013. Optimization of placement solutions for routability. In *Design Automation Conference (DAC), 2013 50th ACM/EDAC/IEEE*. IEEE, 1–9.

[17] Michael D Moffitt. 2008. MaizeRouter: Engineering an effective global router. *IEEE Transactions on Computer-Aided Design of Integrated Circuits and Systems* 27, 11 (2008), 2017–2026.

[18] Min Pan, Yue Xu, Yanheng Zhang, and Chris Chu. 2012. FastRoute: An efficient and high-quality global router. *VLSI Design* 2012 (2012), 14.

[19] Ahmed Youssef, Zhen Yang, Mohab Anis, Shawki Areibi, Anthony Vannelli, and Mohamed Elmasry. 2010. A power-efficient multipin ILP-based routing technique. *IEEE Transactions on Circuits and Systems I: Regular Papers* 57, 1 (2010), 225–235.

Electromigration Design Rule aware Global and Detailed Routing Algorithm*

Xiaotao Jia, Jing Wang, Yici Cai, Qiang Zhou
Tsinghua National Laboratory for Information Science and Technology
Department of Computer Science and Technology, Tsinghua University, Beijing, China
jiaxiaotao@outlook.com,j-w16@mails.tsinghua.edu.cn,{caiyc,zhouqiang}@tsinghua.edu.cn

ABSTRACT

Electromigration (EM) in interconnects is becoming a major concern as the scaling of technology nodes. Electromigration affects chip performance and signal integrity seriously by generating shorts or opens, and then shortens the life-time of integrated circuits. In this paper, we propose an EM-aware routing algorithm in both global and detailed routing stages. Based on physics-based EM modeling and analysis, EM issue is modeled as physical design rule. In global routing stage, an efficient EM-aware Mazerouting algorithm is implemented. An concurrent EM-aware detailed router is then proposed based on multi-commodity flow method. Experimental results show that comparing with general routing algorithm, the proposed EM-aware algorithm could effectively reduce EM risk of signal wires by 92% with slight increasing of wire length and via count.

KEYWORDS

Electromigration, Global Routing, Detailed Routing, Design Rule

ACM Reference Format:
Xiaotao Jia, Jing Wang, Yici Cai, Qiang Zhou. 2018. Electromigration Design Rule aware Global and Detailed Routing Algorithm. In *Proceedings of Great Lakes Symposium on VLSI 2018 (GLSVLSI'18).* ACM, New York, NY, USA, 6 pages. https://doi.org/10.1145/3194554.3194567

1 INTRODUCTION

Electromigration (EM) is becoming a major concern for current VLSI designs as the technology nodes advance into the nanometer regime. It occurs when the current density flowing through the conductor is high enough to cause the drift of metal ions. EM decreases the reliability of integrated circuits (ICs). An EM failure may cause either a void (open) or a hillock (short) as shown in Fig. 1, which eventually leads to circuit functional error. The 2012 edition of the ITRS roadmap has predicted that all minimum-sized interconnects would be EM-affected by 2018, potentially restricting any further downscaling of wire sizes (Fig. 2 [12]). In the latest edition of the ITRS roadmap, EM is reported as one difficult challenge for 16 *nm* technology.

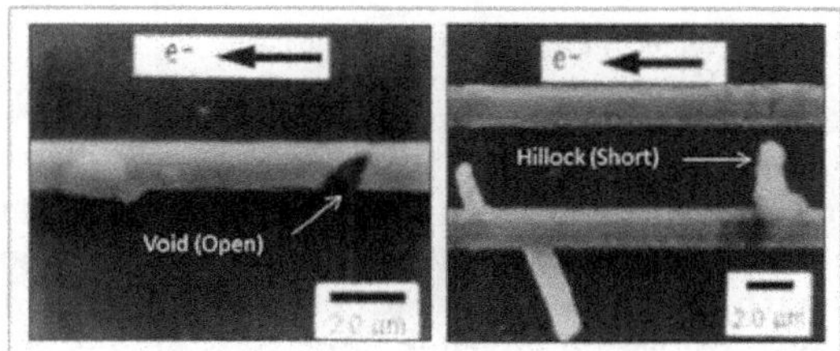

Figure 1: EM-failures: Void (open circuit) and hillock (short circuit) [5].

Analog designers have become aware of EM issue for a long time, and digital designers are now being affected as well. At 90 *nm* and before, EM impact on digital ICs, particularly signal nets, has been minimal, making signal EM analysis and fixing an optional design step. At 45 *nm* and beyond, this is no longer the case. Metal widths are shrinking because of pitch scaling. Interconnects become thinner and thinner. Wire length continuously increases to meet the complex device integration demands. These thin and long interconnects switch at gigahertz speed in order to the push for higher performance. Once combined, these factors result in higher current densities, which amplify the effects of signal EM at advanced technology nodes [5]. With the shrinking of technology nodes, EM becomes even more critical in digital circuits on signal nets [11]. As declared by Synopsys, there are more EM violations on signal interconnects at 28 *nm* compared to those at 65 *nm* and 40 *nm*.

Analysis, prevention and fixing are three main components of an optimal EM solution [6]. EM analysis provides theoretical guidance for EM violation prevention and fixing. Analysis accuracy could significantly affect the final EM results. EM violations fixing is usually processed in post-layout stage. It is not acceptable to fix those violations manually by experienced engineers nowadays. Nano-technology requires fixing method to be automatic, accurate, timing and design rule checking aware. However, only performing fixing in post-stage is not an ideal strategy as it would be iterative and may break down existing results. Furthermore, post-layout fixing could not make obvious improvement because the increasing design complexity leaves very limited space for post-layout

*This work was supported by the National Natural Science Foundation of China (Grand No. 61774091).

ACM ISBN 978-1-4503-5724-1/18/05...$15.00
https://doi.org/10.1145/3194554.3194567

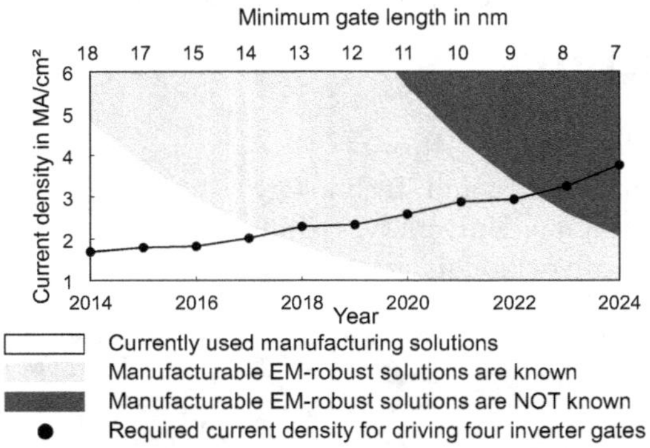

Figure 2: Expected evolution of required and maximum IC wires. While the required current density scales with frequency and reducing cross-section, the maximum tolerable current density is shrinking due to smaller structure sizes [12].

optimization. As described in [8], current density, temperature, segment width and segment length are several main factors that cause EM violations. For a given design, the layout is mainly determined in routing stage during which the segment length and width could be controlled to lower the probability of EM violation generation. For modern complex and challenging ICs, the best way to effectively prevent signal EM violations is to address it as early as possible during physical design stage.

Related Works: The EM issue was originally discovered by Gerardin over 100 years ago [5]. It started to become of practical interest in 1966 with the introduction of the first ICs. EM has become a significant concern in analog circuits. There are many research works that address EM issue in routing and post-routing stage. In digital circuits, the EM issue has been a significant concern in power delivery networks for many years. But as the shrinking of technology nodes, the EM problem on interconnects *i.e.* metal wires and vias is addressed by both academics and industries. Generally, existing works related to EM could be classified as two terms: current-driven and design-rule driven.

As described in [6], an integrated clock signal EM solution is provided during routing stage by IC Compiler. A prevention flow is implemented for clock nets during clock tree synthesis stage. It also includes a signal EM analysis and fixing flow after routing stage on a timing / route DRC clean database. The work in [3] presents a design strategy using special signal non-default rules to re-route the wire segments of critical nets which present a high density and are EM-unsafe. The work in [14] proposes an EM-aware redundant via insertion algorithm that considers current distribution with different via layouts. However, post-layout optimization space is limited. In routing stage, EM issue on 3D ICs has been considered especially around TSVs in [13]. However the work does not consider other design rules such as spacing. Magma Inc. introduced Blast Fusion and Blast Noise in order to achieve a current-density-correct routing of signal nets. Public Ltd. offered an integrated routing solution Lyric AMS for analog and mixed-signal IC designs with the consideration of pin current for current-density-correct routing.

There are likewise some works that model design rules for EM issue such as [3]. In industrial area, complexity of metal and via EM rules are also proposed depending on segment width and segment length [4]. The major challenge facing any current-driven signal routing is the inherent feature that exact segment currents are only known after the entire topology of the net has been laid out. Combining current density and net's layout requirement together as physical design rules could effectively reduce the EM risk in nanometer ICs.

Our Contributions As described above, EM generation in ICs is mainly affected by current density, temperature, segment width and segment length. The best way to reduce the EM risk is combining these factors together in design stage. In this paper, an EM design rule aware routing algorithm in both global and detailed routing stages is proposed. The main contributions of this work are listed as follows.

- EM design rule is proposed based on EM modeling and analysis. With the EM design rule, it is much easy and reasonable to consider EM issue in routing stage.
- A sequential EM design rule aware global routing algorithm is proposed. The proposed algorithm could effectively reduce the EM-unsafe global segments.
- An EM design rule aware detailed routing algorithm based on multi-commodity flow theory is proposed, for the first time to our best knowledge. With the guidance of global routing results, the proposed concurrent detailed routing algorithm could significantly reduce the EM risk.

The remainder of this paper is organized as follows. Section 2 reviews the EM modeling of signal nets. Section 3 demonstrates the overall flow of the proposed routing algorithms. Section 4 proposes EM design rule and discusses the EM-aware global routing and detailed routing algorithm. Experimental results are demonstrated in Section 5, followed by the conclusion in Section 6.

2 EM MODELING

Mostly EM reliability assessments are mainly based on the semi-empirical Black's equation [1] to estimate the mean time-to-failure (MTTF). Thus, many EM works during physical design stage also utilize this model such as the work in [3]. However, Black's equation suffers some major problems in today's chip design. It is an over-simplified model of the actual physics for EM failure mechanisms and only works for constant temperature and current density. Recently, a more physics-based EM model have been proposed to mitigate the shortcomings of Black's equation [8]. In the work of [8], a dynamic EM model under time-dependent current and temperature stressing is proposed and a fast stress calculation method (Eqn. (1)) is also proposed to demonstrate what happened before the MTTF.

$$\sigma = \sigma_T + \frac{eZ\rho jl}{\Omega}\left(\frac{1}{2} - \frac{x}{l} - 4\sum_{n=0}^{\infty}\frac{cos\left(\frac{(2n+1)\pi x}{l}\right)}{(2n+1)^2\pi^2}e^{-\kappa\frac{(2n+1)^2\pi^2}{l^2}t}\right) \quad (1)$$

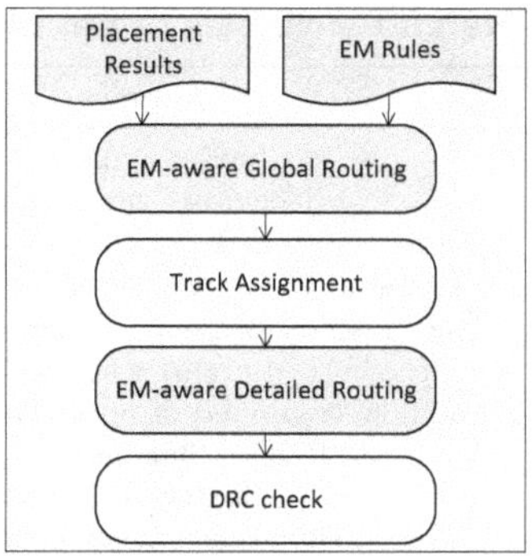

Figure 3: Overall flow of the proposed EM-aware routing algorithm.

Here, l is segment length, j is the current density, σ_T is the thermal stress. e, Z and ρ are electronic constants. The details of these symbols are described in [8].

From Eqn.(1) we can find that the stress is only associated with current density j, temperature T, segment width w and segment length l. Lower current density (lower current or wider wire), lower temperature and shorter segment length could reduce the increasing speed of stress, and then increase the lifetime of chip. This conclusion agrees with the well-known "Blech Length" [2] which indicates that any wire whose length is shorter than this threshold will have a stretched limit for electromigration.

3 OVERALL FLOW

Fig. 3 shows the overall flow of the proposed EM design rule aware routing algorithm. The inputs are placement results and EM design rules. Placement results are stored in OpenAccess (OA) format. And EM design rules vary for different parameters (current density, wire width, wire length, etc.). Then the proposed EM design rule aware global routing algorithm is performed on the basis of traditional Mazerouting algorithm in a 3D global routing graph. It will penalize the routing results which violate the EM design rules. Traditional track assignment algorithm is executed taking the global routing results as inputs. As the track assignment is performed layer by layer, EM issue can not be avoided by a large margin. So it is not considered in this stage. The last routing stage is EM design rule aware detailed routing based on multi-commodity flow method. EM design rules are translated into constraints of an integer linear program (ILP) problem. These constraints are used to restrict the generation of EM-unsafe wires. The ILP problem is solved by a commercial solver. The final step is the design rule checking (DRC) including open, short, spacing, minarea, EM etc. and the DRC violations will also be reported.

4 EM DESIGN RULE AWARE ROUTING ALGORITHM

In this section, we firstly propose EM design rule based on the EM modeling and analysis described in section 2. Then an EM-aware routing algorithm restricted by the proposed EM design rule is presented. In our routing algorithm, divide-and-conquer mechanism is utilized to to reduce the complexity of the routing problem. The full routing flow is constructed with global routing, track assignment and detailed routing. EM design rules are incorporated into global routing stage and detailed routing stage.

4.1 EM design rule

The theoretical analysis and modeling of EM prove that the final layout of chip has significant effects on EM results. It is therefore necessary to consider EM-related design parameters as early as possible in the physical design flow, especially in routing stage.

In the IC design flow, exact wire currents are only known after the entire topology of the net has been laid out. Current calculation based on Kirchhoff's current law requires the sequence of all terminals. Since it is very hard to calculate the real time currents in routing stage, the current is usually treated as a constant value. maximum current and mean current are commonly used. The constant value could be estimated by some technology files such as process design kit (PDK). In other words, the current could be a given and constant value in routing stage and different nets have different values. Thus, only wire width and wire length are variable factors in routing stage. Fortunately, it is also the basic task of routing algorithm that generates physical layout with the requirement of wire shape. In order to reduce the EM occurrence risk, EM design rules based on this observation are proposed in this work. For a given net, the proposed EM design rule requires that the value of $s(j, l, w)$ should be less than a threshold. The threshold is associated with signal net parameters such as temperature, working frequency, expected MTTF. In modern ICs, the wire width on each layer is suggested being uniform. Thus, the EM design rule could be further simplified as a wire length and current density dependent design rule in each layer.

4.2 EM-aware Global Routing Algorithm

The implemented global routing algorithm is built on graph-search technique. The algorithm is guided by the congestion information associated with routing regions and net topologies. Before the graph-search technique is implemented in routing, a global routing graph (GRG) should be constructed firstly. A global router is used to obtain the coarse solution of GRC to GRC paths for all nets on a GRG. There are many graph-search techniques for global routing including Steiner tree based technique, A^* algorithm and Mazerouting algorithm. Each of them has its own advantages and disadvantages. In this paper, a multi-level Mazerouting algorithm is implemented to perform global routing in a $3D$ routing graph.

At each level, an EM-aware Mazerouting algorithm is applied as shown in Algorithm 1. The routing process is executed window by window at all routing levels. For each given window, the inputs are net terminal positions and EM constraints of all nets locating at this window. At the beginning, the actual length *ActLen* of graph edge in current routing level is calculated using window size and routing grid count (line 1). Then the algorithm will route all the nets one by

Algorithm 1 EM-aware global routing algorithm

```
Input: Routing window information, routing nets information,
       EM constraints
 1: CalActualLength(window, track_count) → ActLen;
 2: for each net i do
 3:     GetWireWidth() → width
 4:     EMConstr[i] × width/ActLen → σ
 5:     Mazerouting :
 6:       ...
 7:       getPathLength() → L
 8:       ⌊L/σ⌋ → α
 9:       StdCost · 2^α → EMCost
10:       AddEMCost2RoutingCost()
11:       ...
```

one. Based on the specified EM constraints, current density, wire width (may vary for different metal layers) of the net, we can calculate the maximum step that the router can run (lines 3–4). Then is the EM-aware $3D$ Mazerouting. Different from the traditional one, EM design aware routing algorithm penalizes the paths that exceed the maximum step by Eqn. (2) (lines 7–10). It is obvious that the penalty value is exponential with the quotient of path length and maximum step. The longer the path, the higher the routing cost. The *StdCost* in Algorithm 1 and Eqn. (2) represents the routing cost of an edge used in general purpose routing algorithm. Finally, the algorithm will select a path with the lowest routing cost.

$$EMCost = \begin{cases} StdCost & if\ \sigma \leq L \\ StdCost \cdot 2 & if\ \sigma < L \leq 2 \cdot \sigma \\ \vdots & \\ StdCost \cdot 2^{n-1} & if\ (n-1) \cdot \sigma < L \leq n \cdot \sigma \end{cases} \tag{2}$$

After the global routing, track assignment is implemented to assign global routing segments to each routing track. Then the detailed routing algorithm described in the following section will take its results as inputs.

4.3 EM-aware Concurrent Detailed Routing Algorithm

It has been found during our experiments that after the track assignment, there are many segments that have a high probability of generating EM violations because of long distance, even though EM-aware global routing algorithm is implemented. Thus, it is necessary to propose an EM-aware detailed routing algorithm to shorten the long wires by some techniques such as net detour or layer shifting. In this section, an EM-aware concurrent detailed routing algorithm is proposed based on multi-commodity flow method.

4.3.1 Concurrent Detailed Routing Model. Normally, the detailed routing problem of a chip is divided into many subproblems based on global routing cells. Each subproblem is simplified as a path-finding problem. To finish the routing task, a routing graph based on given routing resources (routing layers, routing grids, blockages etc.) is built firstly. Because there are always several available routing layers, the routing graph $G = (N, A)$ is three dimensional. The concurrent detailed routing model is based on multi-commodity flow method. In order to indicate the commodity flow direction, the routing graph is formulated as directed. Some set symbols and variables are listed in TABLE 1 to describe the routing model based on the routing graph. The meaning of each set or variable is described in the second column. Based on those sets and variables, multi-commodity flow based ILP formulation of detailed routing problem is built as Eqn. (3). The objective function (3a) is to minimize the total routing cost. Constraints (3b) are used to connect all the terminals of a net together *i.e.* ensure that there are no open nets after routing. Arc and node capacity constraints (3e)(3f) could guarantee no short violations are generated. In order to build a practical detailed router, spacing design constraints learning from [9, 10] are also formulated in this work. Our ILP formulation is very similar to that in [9, 10]. However, EM related constraints are seamlessly integrated in our model which will be described in the following sections.

Table 1: Sets and variables of detailed routing

set/notion	meaning
A / N / S	arc/node/signal net set
A_{n_j}	adjacent arc set of node n_j
$A_{n_j,o}/A_{n_j,in}$	arc set that starts from / end at the node n_j
$A_{n_j,w}/A_{n_j,v}$	metal wire / via arc set of node n_j
$c(a_i)$	the capacity of arc a_i with value of 0 or 1
$p(a_i)$	the cost of arc a_i with positive value
$r(s_k, n_j)$	the flow command of node n_j with value of -1, 0, or 1 that net s_k requires
$f(s_k, a_i)$	binary variable, flow of signal net s_k goes through arc a_i

$$\textbf{min.} \quad \sum_{k=1}^{|S|} \sum_{i=1}^{|A|} (f(s_k, a_i) \cdot p(a_i)) \tag{3a}$$

$$\textbf{s.t.} \quad \eta(s_k, n_j) - \gamma(s_k, n_j) = r(s_k, n_j), \qquad \forall s_k \in S, \forall n_j \in N, \tag{3b}$$

$$\eta(s_k, n_j) = \sum_{a \in A_{n_j,o}} f(s_k, a) \tag{3c}$$

$$\gamma(s_k, n_j) = \sum_{a \in A_{n_j,in}} f(s_k, a) \tag{3d}$$

$$\sum_{k=1}^{|S|} f(s_k, a_i) \leq c(a_i), \qquad \forall a_i \in A, \tag{3e}$$

$$\sum_{k=1}^{|S|} \sum_{a \in A_{n_j}} f(s_k, a) \leq 2, \qquad \forall n_j \in N, \tag{3f}$$

$$f(s_k, a_i) \in \{0, 1\}, \qquad \forall s_k \in S, \forall a_i \in A. \tag{3g}$$

4.3.2 Algorithm of Finding Net Detour Window. As discussed above, EM design rule aware detailed router is desirable to reduce the EM occurrence risk. However, it is not necessary that all the routing windows execute EM-aware detailed routing. For a given segment, if it is too long that may generate EM violation, only part of windows that it goes through need integrate the EM constraints. The integration of EM constraints makes the ILP problem much hard to solve and may increase the wirelength and via count. Therefor, by this way, we can not only achieve the goal of reducing EM occurrence risk but also maintain the routing quality and reduce runtime. In this section, an algorithm of finding net detour window is proposed as Algorithm 2 before detailed routing. For a given global segment on layer i, assuming that the segment length is l and the maximum length for EM-safe calculated by EM rules, current density and layer width is σ (line 2–3). If $l \leq \sigma$, no EM ILP constraints are needed for this segment. Otherwise only $n = \lfloor l/\sigma \rfloor$ window(s) needs to

Algorithm 2 Algorithm of finding net detour window

Input: Track assignment results, EM constraints
for each segment s **do**
  getLength(s) $\rightarrow l$; getWidth(s) $\rightarrow width$
  getMaxLength($width, EMConst$) $\rightarrow \sigma$
  if $l > \sigma$ **then**
    $n = \lfloor l/\sigma \rfloor$
    for $k = \{1, 2, ..., n\}$ **do**
      getWindow(s, k) $\rightarrow w$
      $w.unsafe\_segs$.push_back(s)
for each routing window w **do**
  model ILP formulation as Eqn.(3)
  if $w.unsafe\_segs$.size()> 0 **then**
    add EM constraints to Eqn.(3)
  solve ILP problem

build EM ILP constraints for this segment. If $l > \sigma$, the segment is termed as **EM-unsafe segment** in this paper. Then the segments will be partitioned evenly by n points. Those windows where the partition points locating at need to build EM ILP constraints for this segment. In routing stage, detailed router will be executed window by window. For each window, if there are one or more segments that have to be detoured in it, EM design rule based constraints described in 4.3.3 will be formulated and added into Eqn. (3).

4.3.3 EM design rule based ILP constraints. Algorithm 2 collects all the windows in which EM-aware detailed routing algorithm is performed. At the same time, it determines the segment set that need to formulate EM ILP constraints for each window. Now EM-aware detailed routing model is proposed. On the basis of concurrent detailed routing model in section 4.3.1, EM ILP constraints are formulated in order to detour the corresponding wires by Algorithm 3. For a given routing window, firstly we need to estimate whether or not it is an EM-unsafe window. If yes, EM ILP constraints will be formulated. Concurrent detailed routing model could route two-terminal and three-terminal nets simultaneously, but this work will only formulate EM ILP constraints for two-terminal nets. Because EM modeling of multi-branch and $3D$ wires is still inadequate. Based on the results of Algorithm 2, we could get access of the necessary segment information such as terminal position. It is restricted that two terminals ($T1$ and $T2$) of an EM-unsafe segment are located at the same row or column, otherwise, EM constraints will be not formulated. Based on the segment information, EM ILP constraint(s) are formulated as Equation (4). The equation is under construction to make sure that the wire has a detour in other layer rather than goes through the window by a line. It is to be noted that not all the variables in this routing region need to be collected into EM ILP constraints. Assuming that the segment is horizontal and the row index that the segment locating at is r. k is the net index that the segment is owned to. The constraint only collects the edge variables associated with net k and row r, but associated via edges are not collected as Eqn.(4) shows.

$$\sum_{j=1,j=j+2}^{col\_cnt} \sum_{a\in A_{n_j,w}} f(s_k, a) \le col\_cnt - 2 \quad (4)$$

Here, n_j is the node in the rth row. *col_cnt* is the routing track count, so there are *col_count* $- 1$ edges (ignore edge

Algorithm 3 Algorithm of formulating EM ILP constraints

Input: Routing window w
Input: routing nets information
if $w.unsafe\_segs$.size() ≤ 0 **then**
  continue;
for each s in $unsafe\_segs$ **do**
  if $s.T1.row = s.T2.row$ and $s.T1.col = s.T2.col$ **then**
    modelEMConstraints(s)//based on Eqn. (4)

direction). If routing path is forbidden to go through the window by a line, *col_count* $- 2$ edges could be used at most. Thus the right hand value of Eqn. (4) is *col_cnt* $- 2$.

In order to make the work easier to comprehend, global and detailed routing algorithm with the consideration of EM issue are simplified as **EMGR** and **EMDR**, respectively, otherwise are **QGR** and **QDR** (routing-quality-driven global/detailed routing algorithm [10]).

5 EXPERIMENTAL RESULTS

The proposed EM-aware routing algorithm is implemented with C++ language on Linux server with 2.6 GHz Intel Xeon CPU and 16 GB memory. In detailed routing stage, GUROBI [7] is applied as our ILP solver. Our experiments are executed on five industry benchmarks with 45 *nm* library on OA format which are cited from [10] and have been placed by Encounter. However, we could only get access to the physical layout information of these benchmarks and no current information could obtain. In our experiments, the maximum length of each net is assigned randomly with the range of 6 to 10 times of GRC width. These random length values could be replaced by real current information if it is available.

In order to demonstrate the effectiveness of the proposed algorithm, some comparisons are made between routing algorithms with and without the consideration of EM issue. The metrics for comparison in the experiments are total wire length (WL) measured by millimeter, total via count (#Via), DRC violation count (#DRC) and runtime (Time) measured by second. Furthermore, we propose another comparison parameter, EM-unsafe wire length (EMWL). It is calculated by the length sum of global segments or metal wires whose length exceeds the corresponding EM threshold. The larger the EM-unsafe wire length, the greater the probability of EM violation generation.

5.1 Effectiveness of EM-aware global routing algorithm

In this section, some experimental results are demonstrated to prove the effectiveness of the proposed EM-aware global routing algorithm. In TABLE 2, the first column indicates two global routing algorithm QGR and EMGR. The second column shows four comparison metrics. Columns 3-7 are experimental results of five different benchmarks. The last column is the comparison results in average. The third row in TABLE 2 shows the net count of each benchmark. It could be seen from the comparison that comparing with QGR, EMGR could averagely reduce the EM-unsafe wire length by 26% at the cost of slight increasing of wire length, via count and runtime by 1%, 3% and 12%, respectively.

Table 2: Effectiveness of EM-aware GR algorithm

Routing Flow	Metrics	Benchmarks					Comp.
		chip1	chip2	chip3	chip4	chip5	
#Net	-	36k	52k	10k	91k	100k	-
QGR	WL	645	820	1657	1519	1691	1
	#VIA	351	380	738	665	739	1
	EMWL	219	429	953	902	1019	1
	Time	27.65	23.55	54.18	50.27	52.07	1
EMGR	WL	645	823	1667	1528	1701	1.01
	#VIA	354	391	766	693	769	1.03
	EMWL	165	324	718	662	752	0.74
	Time	28.91	26.01	61.04	58.72	58.47	1.12

Table 3: Comparison of different routing flow

Routing Flow	Metrics	Benchmarks					Comp.
		chip1	chip2	chip3	chip4	chip5	
Flow1: QGR + QDR	WL	647	827	1674	1536	1709	1
	#VIA	370	401	780	704	780	1
	EMWL	117	218	471	444	504	1
	#DRC	61	94	166	156	164	1
	Time	1033	1165	2154	1925	2302	1
Flow2: EMGR + QDR	WL	649	831	1682	1543	1717	1.00
	#VIA	371	406	793	717	796	1.02
	EMWL	92	168	355	332	371	0.75
	#DRC	56	81	168	160	177	1.04
	Time	1038	1115	2228	2001	2268	1.01
Flow3: QGR + EMDR	WL	651	836	1693	1553	1729	1.01
	#VIA	373	409	798	722	802	1.02
	EMWL	11	16	42	38	42	0.09
	#DRC	62	79	171	159	181	1.02
	Time	2061	2566	4926	4447	5087	2.22
Flow4: EMGR + EMDR	WL	652	835	1692	1552	1728	1.01
	#VIA	373	405	788	712	789	1.01
	EMWL	11	15	39	37	40	0.08
	#DRC	58	83	152	170	152	0.93
	Time	1900	2269	4349	3906	4414	1.96

5.2 Effectiveness of EM-aware detailed routing algorithm

Even though the EM-aware global routing algorithm could reduce the EM-unsafe wire length a lot, there is still much optimization space for that. In this section, we compare the routing results of routing quality driven routing flow and the proposed EM-aware routing flow. Four routing flows are implemented based on different combinations of global routing and detailed routing algorithms as shown in the first column of TABLE 3. Firstly, we continue to evaluate the effect of the `EMGR` algorithm by the comparison between `Flow1` and `Flow2`. As the results show, even though the same detailed routing algorithm is used, `EMGR` could provide better guidance for detailed routing than `QGR`. Experimental results show that in the final layout EM-unsafe wire length is reduced by 25% and DRC count has an increasement of 4%. While the total wire length, via count and runtime are almost the same. Secondly, we study the effectiveness of EM-aware detailed routing algorithm from the comparison between `Flow1` and `Flow3`. The length of EM-unsafe wire decreases with the proposed detailed routing algorithm by 91% on average while the routing quality in terms of total wire length, via count and DRC number remains basically the same. However, the runtime of EM-aware detailed routing is 2.22× of `Flow1`. It is because that ILP formulation of detailed routing problem become hard to solve after the consideration of EM issue. Thirdly, we study the effectiveness of overall EM-aware routing flow i.e. `Flow4`. Comparing with `Flow3`, `Flow4` could further reduce the EM-unsafe wire length by 5%. Meanwhile, DRC count is also decreased by 9%. Compared with `QGR`, `EMGR` reduces the subproblem count that should take EM into consideration in detailed routing stage. So detailed routing in `Flow4` spends less time that in `Flow3`. Finally, the entire runtime of `Flow4` is reduced by 12% comparing with `Flow3`. While the routing quality is almost the same. Comparing with `Flow1`, `Flow4` finally reduces the EM-unsafe wire length by 92% at the cost of 1.96× runtime. The results prove the effectiveness of `EMGR` once again. These comparisons indicate that the proposed EM-aware routing algorithm could effectively reduce the EM-unsafe wire length, thus, reduce the probability of EM violation generation. At the same time, there are only a minor loss of the routing quality.

6 CONCLUSION

In this paper, electromigration issue is considered as a design rule based on physics-based EM modeling and analysis. EM-aware global routing and detailed routing algorithms are proposed to reduce the EM violation generating probability. Experiments demonstrate that the proposed algorithms reduce the EM-unsafe wire length by 92% which is helpful to increase the chip reliability. In the future work, we will take via EM model into consideration to make the algorithm much complete and test the proposed algorithm using benchmarks with advanced technology nodes.

REFERENCES

[1] James R Black. 1969. ElectromigrationA brief survey and some recent results. *IEEE TES* 16, 4 (1969), 338–347.
[2] Illan A Blech. 1976. Electromigration in thin aluminum films on titanium nitride. *Journal of Applied Physics* 47, 4 (1976), 1203–1208.
[3] Lucas de Paris, Gracieli Posser, and Ricardo Reis. 2016. Electromigration aware circuits by using special signal non-default routing rules. In *Proc. ISCAS*. IEEE, 2795–2798.
[4] Chan Gary and TSMC. 2011. Hybrid IR/EM Analysis Flow with EM Rule Extension. In *SNUG Conference*.
[5] Bradley Geden. 2011. Understand and Avoid Electromigration (EM) IR-drop in Custom IP Blocks. In *Synopsys White Paper*.
[6] Rangarajan Geetha and Deng James. 2013. Addressing signal electromigration (EM) in todays complex digital designs.
[7] Gurobi Optimization Inc. 2017. Gurobi Optimizer Reference Manual. http://www.gurobi.com. (2017).
[8] Xin Huang, Tan Yu, Valeriy Sukharev, and Sheldon X-D Tan. 2014. Physics-based electromigration assessment for power grid networks. In *Proc. DAC*. ACM, 1–6.
[9] Xiaotao Jia, Yici Cai, Qiang Zhou, Gang Chen, Zhuoyuan Li, and Zuowei Li. 2014. MCFRoute: a detailed router based on multi-commodity flow method. In *Proc. ICCAD*. IEEE, 397–404.
[10] Xiaotao Jia, Yici Cai, Qiang Zhou, and Bei Yu. 2018. A Multi-commodity Flow-Based Detailed Router With Efficient Acceleration Techniques. *IEEE TCAD* 37, 1 (Jan 2018), 217–230.
[11] Andrew B Kahng, Siddhartha Nath, and Tajana S Rosing. 2013. On potential design impacts of electromigration awareness. In *Proc. ASPDAC*. IEEE, 527–532.
[12] Jens Lienig. 2013. Electromigration and its impact on physical design in future technologies. In *Proc. ISPD*. ACM, 33–40.
[13] Jiwoo Pak, Sung Kyu Lim, and David Z Pan. 2012. Electromigration-aware routing for 3D ICs with stress-aware EM modeling. In *Proc. ICCAD*. ACM, 325–332.
[14] Jiwoo Pak, Bei Yu, and David Z Pan. 2015. Electromigration-aware redundant via insertion. In *Proc. ASPDAC*. IEEE, 544–549.

A Comparative Study of Local Net Modeling Using Machine Learning

Jackson Melchert, Boyu Zhang, and Azadeh Davoodi
University of Wisconsin - Madison
{jmelchert,bzhang93,adavoodi}@wisc.edu

ABSTRACT

Local nets are by default ignored during global routing but can contribute to a high percentage (up to 30%) of total number of nets in the design. Prior work proposed simple models for how local nets are routed and showed benefits such as better congestion analysis post-placement, integration with global routing, and better track assignment. In this work we study local net modeling using machine learning. Our model predicts utilization by local routes inside each global cell. We model this as a regression problem and as reference use local route utilization data from the detailed routing stage using a commercial tool. To solve the problem we identify suitable machine learning algorithms. Within our modeling, we study and rank different features which utilize various layout attributes. We identify the most beneficial features and show our model performs superior to prior work which were based on pin density and Steiner tree models. Our model also performs better for the subset of local nets which are routed in more than one global cell.

CCS CONCEPTS

• **Computing methodologies → Machine learning**; • **Hardware → Very Large Scale Integration Design; Modeling and parameter extraction; Physical design (EDA)**;

KEYWORDS

Machine Learning, Local Nets, Global Routing

ACM Reference Format:

Jackson Melchert, Boyu Zhang, and Azadeh Davoodi. 2018. A Comparative Study of Local Net Modeling Using Machine Learning . In *GLSVLSI '18: 2018 Great Lakes Symposium on VLSI, May 23–25, 2018, Chicago, IL, USA*. ACM, New York, NY, USA, 6 pages. https://doi.org/10.1145/3194554.3194579

1 INTRODUCTION

Obtaining a routable layout and removing violations have turned into key physical design challenges in modern designs. Addressing these challenges has recently inspired new routability-driven placement algorithms, and better algorithms and metrics for global routing and violation-free track assignment [2, 3, 6, 9, 11–14].

GLSVLSI '18, May 23–25, 2018, Chicago, IL, USA

ACM ISBN 978-1-4503-5724-1/18/05...$15.00
https://doi.org/10.1145/3194554.3194579

Local nets are one of the factors which challenge obtaining a routable and violation-free layout. They are by default ignored during global routing and track assignment. However, they contribute up to about 30% of the total number of nets in a design. Some recent works have considered modeling local nets using simple models and shown improvement in global routing, post-placement congestion analysis, and track assignment. However, the local net model itself has not been verified against how these nets actually get routed at the detailed routing stage.

In this work, we study modeling the local nets using machine learning. Our contributions are outlined below.

- Using local route utilization from the detailed routing stage as reference data, we use machine learning algorithms to create a model at the post-placement stage.
- We evaluate and rank various post-placement and post-global-routing features to identify the ones which are most beneficial for modeling.
- We show that the use of post-placement features which utilize information about the neighboring global cells help improve the modeling accuracy.
- We show *consistent* improvement across all designs compared to prior work which used Steiner tree or pin density to predict the local nets. Our work is also the first to use local net data from the detailed routing stage for comparison.

In the remainder of the paper we first review preliminaries and prior work in Section 2. We discuss our modeling process in Section 3. This is followed by simulation results and conclusions.

2 PRELIMINARIES AND PRIOR WORK

2.1 Preliminaries

At the post-placement stage, we are given a 3-dimensional *placement grid*, $P = \{0, \dots, X_P\} \times \{0, \dots, Y_P\} \times \{0, \dots, L\}$. The design consists of a set of nets $N = \{T_1, T_2, \dots, T_{|N|}\}$, where each net $T_n \in N$ consists of a set of pin locations on P. Before performing global routing, this detailed placement grid is replaced with a less-refined *global routing grid*, $G = \{0, \dots, X_G\} \times \{0, \dots, Y_G\} \times \{0, \dots, L\}$.

The global routing grid is made of rectangular regions called global cells (gcells) where the coordinates of the placement grid fall inside or on the boundaries of the gcells. Each gcell contains a number of routing tracks which are uniformly spaced and the width of each track is known. Before performing global routing a grid-graph is created from the global routing where each gcell is represented by a vertex and the boundary of two adjacent gcells is represented by an edge known as *global edge*. Each global edge e has a capacity c_e representing the number of routing tracks that can pass the corresponding boundary of its two adjacent gcells. At this point the nets are divided into either local or global nets. A net T_ℓ is a local net if all its pins are located inside the same gcell.

Otherwise if a net has its pins in two or more gcells then it is called a global net. Once global routing is performed, all global nets are routed and local nets are by default ignored. After global routing, each global edge will have a utilization u_e representing the number of routing tracks used to route global nets in the corresponding boundary of its two adjacent gcells. The overflow of a global edge is defined as $o_e = \max(u_e - c_e, 0)$. An overflow higher than 0 indicates that the global edge is utilized beyond its capacity.

2.2 Applications of Local Net Modeling

Some recent works try to predict how local nets will be routed prior to performing global routing in order to have a more realistic estimate of the available capacity of each global edge. The work [12] models local routes and uses reduced global edge capacities (as some routing tracks are predicted to be utilized by local routes). This allows performing a more accurate global routing congestion analysis. Local-route-aware congestion analysis can also be performed prior to routing of global nets, during or after a routability-driven placement stage. This is assuming the global routing grid is known. The work [11] also models local routes and integrates their impact during global routing by introducing a vertex capacity in the global routing grid-graph. The capacity of a vertex is the area of its gcell after subtracting the utilization of its (expected) local routes.

In this work, we also aim to model local nets. Our goal is to model *local route utilization* for each gcell. Our model computes how much the routing tracks will be utilized after local nets are routed for each gcell. While local nets by definition have all their pins inside the same gcell, it is not necessary for a local net to be routed completely inside the same gcell and a small number of local nets may additionally be routed in the neighboring gcells. Our model accounts for this issue and generates a utilization number per gcell by local routes which are expected to fall inside it.

2.3 Prior Work on Local Net Modeling

Here we review two models of local route utilization which have been studied in prior work. First the authors in [12] model local route utilization inside each gcell to be proportional to the number of pins in the gcell. The proportionality factor is decided as a technology-dependent parameter. This model was developed based on the observation that each pin may be connected to a set of local wires, and the number of pins in a gcell is a good indicator of the number of local routes and a first-order estimate of the number of blocked routing tracks. The main benefit of this model is that it can be evaluated very quickly and at the post-placement stage because it only requires knowledge of pin locations and the global routing grid. This model is therefore useful for integration with a congestion analysis tool which may be evoked many times during routability-driven placement. In this work we made comparison with pin-density model in [12]. *Since the technology parameter used in [12] did not match the 65nm node used by our designs, in our implementation of [12] we obtained the highest accuracy when we used linear regression to fit the pin density of each gcell to the local route utilization in the subset of designs which were used for training. This fitting was done using the same tool (Weka [5]) which implemented our machine learning algorithm. This approach produced the best results to implement [12] in our experimental setup.* The proportionality factor was then used to validate during testing.

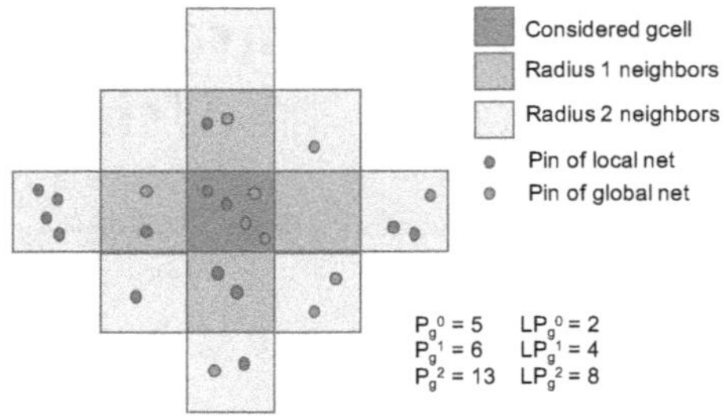

Figure 1: Example showing some post-placement features

The second model used for local net modeling is based on Steiner tree wirelength which has been used in [12]. In this model first a Steiner tree is generated based on the subset of the pins of a net which falls inside the same gcell. Therefore the net maybe a local net, or a global net in which some pins are located in the same gcell. Depending on where the edges of the Steiner tree fall, the corresponding routing tracks are computed and get blocked in the nearest global edge. These are done for the gcells in M2 and M3 based on the observation that the vast majority of local nets are routed on these two metal layers. After processing all the local nets, the number of blocked tracks at the boundary of each gcell is then computed and used to update the available capacity of each global edge. Similar to the pin density model, the work [12] used empirically-tuned parameters to scale the horizontal and vertical Steiner wirelength to the number of blocked tracks.

Compared to the pin density model, the Steiner wirelength model takes significantly longer to generate. Other variations of the Steiner wirelength model are also used in works such as [9, 10, 13] and typically applied as a first step in congestion analysis and in track assignment. In this work, since we model local route utilization inside the gcell (and not number of blocked tracks), we directly use the Steiner wirelength of each local net which we generate using FLUTE [4]. The work [11] also models local nets by first routing them on metals M2 and M3 using a rip-up and reroute technique. The corresponding tracks are then blocked and used to update the available tracks inside each gcell.

3 MACHINE LEARNING FRAMEWORK

We first introduce the features collected for our modeling and rank them to identify the top ones. Next we discuss our modeling process.

3.1 Feature Selection and Ranking

For a considered gcell g we define the following features.

- P_g^i (numPins): cumulative pin density inside gcells at radius i from g; a special case is P_g^0 which indicates pin density solely inside g. Also, P_g^1 corresponds to the immediate neighbors of g, P_g^2 corresponds to the neighbors of neighbors of g.
- LP_g^i (numLocalNetPins): cumulative pin density of local nets inside gcells at radius i from g; a special case is LP_g^0 which shows pin density of local nets inside g.
- EW_g (estimatedWirelength): wirelength of local nets inside gcell g; to compute this feature, first the local pins inside g are traversed, and a minimum bounding box is constructed between each pair of consecutive pins of the same local net. The sum of half-perimeter bounding box values across all local nets is computed as the estimated local wirelength of g.

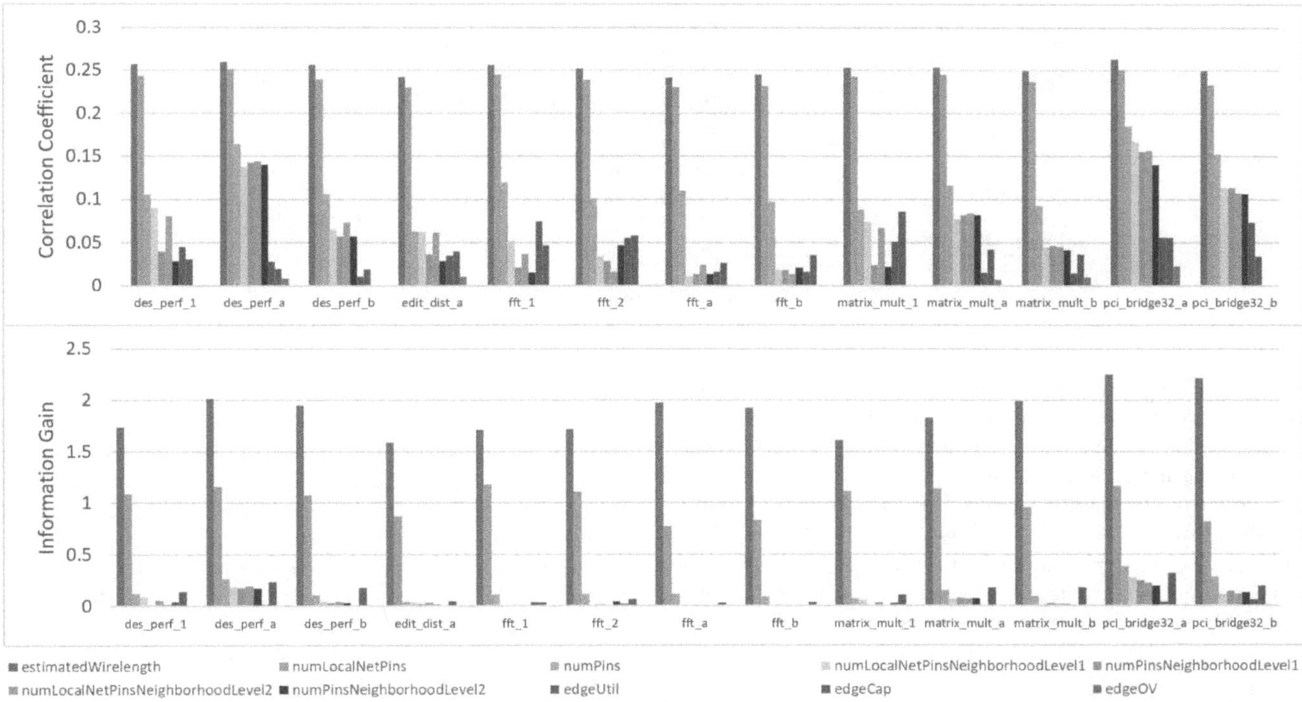

Figure 2: Comparison of layout features in predicting local route utilization using the IG and CC metrics in each benchmark

- U_g (edgeUtil): sum of global routing edge utilizations corresponding to the four boundaries of g.
- C_g (edgeCap): sum of global routing edge capacities corresponding to the four boundaries of g.
- O_g (edgeOV): overflow of g is computed based on its utilization and capacity: $\max(0, U_g - C_g)$.

In the above list, the features P^i_g, LP^i_g, EW_g can be extracted at the post-placement stage, using information about the global routing grid (so the locations of the gcells are known). In our modeling framework, we collect the values of these features for $i = \{0, 1, 2\}$ so that a total of 7 post-placement features per g-cell. Figure 1 shows these features for a simple example and how various post-placement features (except EW_g) are computed. The 3 additional features O_g, U_g and C_g are collected at the post-global routing stage so they require to first perform global routing.

For the post-placement features, we did not include radius-3 features because we observed that almost all local nets were routed within a radius of at most 1, i.e., they are routed either completely within the gcell or its immediate neighbors. So we just included radius 2 features in case of a potential domino effect when multiple gcells of high pin density are adjacent to each other.

Next, we used two metrics, information gain (IG) and correlation coefficient (CC), to measure the importance of each feature in predicting local route utilization. Information gain is the measure of reduction in the entropy of a variable achieved by learning the state of another random variable [8]. Correlation coefficient is a number that quantifies correlation between two variables. These metrics were measured with the Weka tool [5] using the data collected for each benchmark individually together with the reference data (of actual local route utilization) at the detailed routing stage.

In this work we used the 2015 ISPD contest benchmark suite [2]. Specifically, we used the subset of benchmarks implemented in 65nm technology node all of which had 5 routing layers. We provide details about our experimental setup later.

Before measuring the IG and CC metrics we applied some preprocessing on the collected data. This was in order to highlight the difference in predictive ability of each feature. First, we discarded every gcell with 0 local route utilization to get a more meaningful representation of the predictive power of the features, especially in relation to the CC measurement.

The reason that removing these instances helped to differentiate features is that when a gcell has 0 local route utilization, it must have 0 local net pins, 0 estimated wirelength, and in most cases, values of 0 for every feature. This leads to very high correlation scores for every feature in benchmarks where there is little local route congestion, making it difficult to differentiate the features based on actual predictive power. Also, in these gcells, the prediction is trivial, and we observed that whenever the machine learning algorithm sees a gcell with 0 local net pins and 0 estimated wirelength, it will almost always predict 0 local route utilization.

Another preprocessing step that we took was to discretize the attributes into 10 equal frequency bins based on local route utilization. This again allowed to better compare the features in cases where local route utilization in all gcells was heavily skewed.

Figure 2 shows the ranking of each feature for each benchmark. For both IG and CC, the most important feature is estimatedWirelength (EW), followed by numLocalNetPins (LP^0). Both of these features are directly related to local route utilization, so it is not surprising that they contribute the most information in order to predict local route utilization.

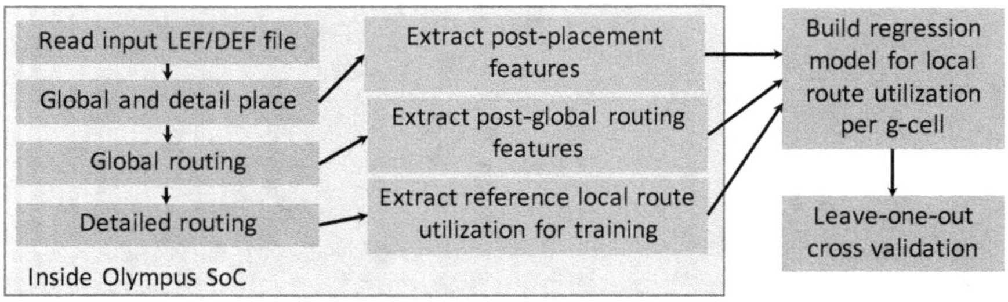

Figure 3: Flow chart of our modeling process

Post-global routing features clearly do not add much predictive ability to the model, and the fact that they need to be collected after completing global routing makes them even less useful. The level 1 and level 2 neighborhood features seem to be useful in some benchmarks but not in others, leading us to believe that in most cases, neighboring gcells do not impact local routes significantly.

We selected 5 features as input to our final machine learning algorithm: EW_g, LP_g^0, P_g^0, LP_g^1, P_g^1. While it is clear that EW_g, LP_g^0, and P_g^0 are the three most useful features overall, we wanted to include the radius 1 neighborhood features to help predict local route utilization in cases where local nets are routed outside of their own gcells, *something that prior works did not consider.*

3.2 Our Modeling Process

Figure 3 shows overview of our modeling process. We used Olympus SoC [1] to collect the values of these features in the 65nm ISPD 2015 designs. First, the Olympus placement tool was used to do placement on each benchmark. The values of post-placement features were extracted at this point. Next, Olympus global router was called to generate a solution. The values of global routing features were extracted at this point. Finally, the Olympus track router was called to generate a detailed routing solution and the local route utilization as reference data. These features were all extracted using TCL scripting inside Olympus.

To extract the values of post-placement and post-global routing features, we first built a 2D-projection of the solution corresponding to that stage and computed the values of those features for the g-cells of that 2D-projected grid-graph. This allowed storing significantly smaller set of data.

To test each design, the values of the features were extracted from the remaining designs and used to train the model. This technique is known as **leave-one-out cross validation**. It not only enables us to have relatively more training instances to train our models, which is always good, but also gives us an unbiased evaluation about how well the algorithm works on current dataset. *We note we used the same leave-one-out evaluation technique for implementing and comparing with other prior work in our experiments.*

Our goal was to model local route utilization inside each gcell in the 2D projected global routing grid-graph. During our modeling, we experimented with different machine learning algorithms.

We note the reason we do feature extraction and modeling for the 2D-projected global routing graph is because we observed the vast majority of local routes were located on metal layers M2 and M3. Breakdown of the local route utilization between M2 and M3 followed a constant ratio across the benchmarks (about 48% on M2 and 40% on M3).

4 EXPERIMENTAL RESULTS

We used the modeling process explained in Figure 3 in Section 3. We experimented with the 65nm ISPD 2015 designs all of which had 5 routing layers. (Extension to evaluate designs from other technology nodes will be considered in our future work.) We used the tool Weka [5] which allowed data mining with various machine learning algorithms as well as simple linear regression (to implement prior work). We compared various machine learning algorithms and prior work. These were calculated in Olympus by comparing the predicted local route utilization versus the true local route utilization (at the detailed routing stage) per gcell.

For evaluation of accuracy we first define a Relative Absolute Error metric which is defined below.

$$RAE_{gcells} = \frac{\sum_{\forall g \in gcell} |LU^g_{approach} - LU^g_{ref}|}{\sum_{\forall g \in gcell} |E[LU_{ref}] - LU^g_{ref}|}$$

where $LU^g_{approach}$ is the local route utilization predicted by a specific approach for a gcell, LU^g_{ref} is the reference local utilization of the gcell and $E[LU_{ref}]$ is the average of reference local utilizations across all the gcells. This error metric first computes an error in local utilization per gcell compared to its true value obtained from detailed routing. These errors are then added up across all gcells, and then the sum is normalized with respect to a reference value given in the denominator. The above formula for RAE allows handling cases when the true local route utilization of a gcell is 0.

We first give a comparison of accuracy among various machine learning algorithms, then present comparison with prior works in terms of accuracy, runtime and outlier cases.

4.1 Comparing Machine Learning Algorithms

We trained and tested five machine learning models using the feature set we selected in Section 3.1 and the leave-one-out cross validation technique explained in Section 3.2. The machine learning algorithms are summarized below:

(1) `RandomTree` constructs a tree that considers K randomly chosen features at each node.

(2) `MultilayerPerceptron` creates a shallow neural network model.

(3) `DecisionTable` constructs a simple decision tree with default majority mapping rule [7].

(4) `RandomForest` is an ensemble learning method for classification, regression and other tasks. During training, RandomForest constructs a multitude of decision trees where each decision tree is built based on a random sampling of the training instances and a random subset of the feature vector.

Table 1: Relative Absolute Error over all gcells of different machine learning models trained with the top ranked features identified in Section 3.1. All results are obtained via leave-one-out cross validation.

	RandomTree	MultilayerPerceptron	DecisionTable	RandomForest	REPTree
mgc_des_perf_1	37.14%	23.29%	32.26%	24.97%	25.83%
mgc_des_perf_a	10.48%	40.82%	16.16%	7.39%	7.40%
mgc_des_perf_b	21.38%	14.31%	27.88%	14.62%	14.24%
mgc_edit_dist_a	16.15%	25.99%	27.04%	12.90%	12.89%
mgc_fft_1	35.91%	27.76%	32.46%	27.10%	27.58%
mgc_fft_2	31.85%	26.59%	33.91%	23.90%	24.47%
mgc_fft_a	9.64%	28.08%	28.86%	7.39%	7.63%
mgc_fft_b	9.88%	25.86%	24.20%	7.73%	7.68%
mgc_matrix_mult_1	37.19%	26.46%	33.97%	27.23%	27.45%
mgc_matrix_mult_a	9.56%	7.31%	11.95%	6.85%	7.03%
mgc_matrix_mult_b	9.60%	8.14%	19.25%	7.08%	7.15%
mgc_pci_bridge32_a	13.11%	24.10%	20.51%	9.35%	9.57%
mgc_pci_bridge32_b	8.55%	6.69%	21.39%	6.03%	6.23%
Total Average	19.26%	21.95%	25.37%	14.04%	14.24%

Table 2: Error metrics in all gcells and outlier gcells of different approaches. The table also shows percentage of local nets out of all the nets, and percentage of outlier local nets out of all the local nets.

		Error in all gcells				Error in outlier nets		
	LN	PD	ST	ML	Outlier-LN	PD	ST	ML
mgc_des_perf_1	31.77%	97.48%	80.19%	25.83%	0.85%	84.38%	33.84%	15.77%
mgc_des_perf_a	20.82%	50.59%	18.01%	7.40%	0.91%	78.22%	36.21%	26.41%
mgc_des_perf_b	22.64%	85.65%	37.14%	14.24%	0.32%	87.43%	33.64%	25.66%
mgc_edit_dist_a	14.62%	101.65%	21.87%	12.89%	2.71%	132.25%	45.58%	42.29%
mgc_fft_1	32.26%	95.12%	75.93%	27.58%	0.88%	44.89%	33.02%	16.10%
mgc_fft_2	29.06%	92.25%	50.17%	24.47%	1.50%	46.69%	30.47%	19.45%
mgc_fft_a	15.68%	79.40%	12.83%	7.63%	0.56%	73.90%	61.31%	61.21%
mgc_fft_b	18.25%	69.68%	13.51%	7.68%	0.99%	83.22%	49.64%	48.16%
mgc_matrix_mult_1	31.92%	105.72%	83.89%	27.45%	1.04%	41.50%	34.26%	15.48%
mgc_matrix_mult_a	26.48%	44.51%	16.15%	7.03%	0.71%	64.49%	36.19%	25.22%
mgc_matrix_mult_b	19.76%	60.88%	14.45%	7.15%	0.54%	88.38%	41.16%	38.01%
mgc_pci_bridge32_a	29.65%	54.98%	25.27%	9.57%	1.06%	56.83%	41.68%	31.21%
mgc_pci_bridge32_b	25.12%	59.78%	12.93%	6.23%	0.37%	57.39%	39.36%	40.18%
Average	24.46%	76.74%	35.56%	14.24%	0.96%	72.27%	39.72%	31.17%

During testing, it outputs the mean prediction of each individual tree. Compared to decision tree, Random Forest is less likely to overfit its training data, and it is more robust to outliers and noise. (5) REPTree first builds a decision tree based on all the training instances and the feature vector, then it uses a reduced error pruning method to reduce the size of the tree by removing sections of the tree that provide little power to make prediction. Thus, the pruned tree generalizes better and gives higher accuracy because the complexity of the tree is reduced so it is less likely to overfit the training data.

We used the default settings in Weka in our experiments. In Table 1 we report the RAE over all gcells of these five different models. As can be seen from the table, RandomForest and REPTree have significantly lower error than the other three models.

RandomTree has the disadvantage that only a randomly picked subset of features are considered at each node, thus the model may not correctly utilize the most correlated feature(s). Even though each tree in RandomForest is very similar to a random tree, the ensemble mechanism ensures that the final prediction made by RandomForest is much better than an individual random tree. MultilayerPerceptron and DecisionTable perform worse than REPTree, possibly due to the fact that these two algorithms may overfit the training data. In contrast, REPTree reduces the chance of overfitting by pruning decision trees, thus increases the prediction accuracy.

While REPTree and RandomForest have similar error results, REPTree is faster to train. On average, RandomForest took 48 seconds to train the model for a benchmark, while REPTree took 1.3 seconds. We identify REPTree as the suitable model for our problem and use it as our default algorithm hereafter.

4.2 Comparison with Other Prior Work

To put our machine learning approach into perspective, in Table 2 we compare the best Machine Learning (ML) algorithm identified above (REPTree) with the approaches proposed by other prior works.

Specifically, we compare with the Pin Density (PD) and Steiner Tree (ST) models explained in Section 2.3.
For linear regression in PD we used Weka [5] and as explained before, this generated the highest accuracy to implement this approach in our experimental setup. Furthermore, we used the same leave-one-out cross validation technique for all PD, and ML models during our training and testing. Leave-one-out cross validation has not been used for the ST model since the ST model does not require training.

In Table 2 Column 2 we report the percentage of Local Nets (LN) of all nets in a benchmark which is on average close to 25% of all the nets. First, we consider the RAE metric reported in Columns 3 to 5. As can be seen, the ML model is significantly and *consistently* better than PD and ST across all the benchmarks. Even though the ST model is significantly better than the PD model, it is still worse than the ML model. The superiority of the ML may be caused by the fact that it can learn more knowledge about local route utilization from new features such as local pin density and radius-1 neighbors, as well as the interaction between all the features. Also, our estimated wirelength (*EW*) feature works well as an estimate to Steiner wirelength because we observed that often times a local net inside a g-cell has a very small number of pins.

Table 3: Runtime Comparison

	Runtime (minutes)		
	PD	ST	ML
mgc_des_perf_1	0.92	36.50	1.04
mgc_des_perf_a	0.85	22.87	1.18
mgc_des_perf_b	0.87	25.76	1.03
mgc_edit_dist_a	0.98	19.55	1.23
mgc_fft_1	0.29	10.82	0.34
mgc_fft_2	0.29	9.77	0.35
mgc_fft_a	0.27	4.99	0.51
mgc_fft_b	0.28	5.93	0.51
mgc_matrix_mult_1	1.32	50.72	1.48
mgc_matrix_mult_a	1.29	40.93	2.12
mgc_matrix_mult_b	1.22	30.29	2.01
mgc_pci_bridge32_a	0.26	8.86	0.34
mgc_pci_bridge32_b	0.27	7.48	0.50
Average	0.70	21.11	0.97

4.3 Runtime Comparison

We observed that predicting local route utilization using the ML and PD models were much faster than prediction using the ST model. (Note, our final error measurements followed the same procedure for all methods and took approximately 2 minutes to complete for each benchmark regardless of the used model.) Therefore for runtime comparison, we only compare the time it takes to collect the data for each method and train and evaluate the models. On average, the data collection took 0.69, 0.52, and 0.95 minutes for the PD, ST, and ML models respectively. Therefore, the main difference in runtime resulted from evaluating the Steiner tree wirelength using FLUTE (in ST) versus training and testing the ML and PD models using Weka. Training and testing the PD and ML models were very fast, at most taking a few seconds to complete while Steiner tree computation using FLUTE was comparatively slow, taking at maximum 49 minutes to complete. As can be seen in Table 3, the ST model took on average 21.11 minutes to complete, while both the PD and ML models took an average of less than 1 minute to complete. Our ML model achieved better results than the ST model in a fraction of the time.

4.4 Comparison Among Outlier Local Nets

In the final part of this experiment we compute a relative absolute error for a small subset of local nets which we define as "outlier" nets. We define a local net to be outlier if it is routed in more than one gcell. A gcell is then defined as outlier if it includes at least one outlier local net. Outlier local nets and gcells are first identified per design from the detailed routing data and then used to perform this experiment. In Table 2 we report the percentage of outlier local nets compared to all local nets in Column 6 which is a very small value (hence the name outlier). Here, we first compute a relative absolute error for each outlier local net (denoted by *outnet*) by computing and averaging the errors across its corresponding outlier gcells (denoted by *outgcell*). After computing an error per outlier local net, we then report the average of these errors across all outlier local nets. This is described in the formula below.

$$RAE_{outnet} = \frac{\sum_{\forall n \in outnet} \frac{\sum_{\forall g \in outgcell(n)} \frac{|LU^g_{approach} - LU^g_{ref}|}{LU^g_{ref}}}{\#outgcells(n)}}{\#outnets}$$

We note, this error is ultimately a net-based metric (to capture error across outlier local nets) while the previous error was a gcell-based metric (computed for each gcell).

The results for the error of outlier nets is reported in Columns 7 to 9 in Table 2. Here ML has consistently lower error than ST and PD. In one case for the *mgc_edit_dist_a* benchmark and the PD approach, the error is higher than 100%. This is because the predicted LU by the PD approach was significantly higher than the reference one per gcell.

Overall, we conclude that our ML model consistently generates the most accurate prediction compared with the other methods proposed by prior works.

5 CONCLUSIONS

We modeled the route utilization by local nets inside individual gcells using various machine learning algorithms. Compared to prior work, first the machine learning model was validated using detailed routing data of local nets and a commercial tool. Also it included new features such as steiner tree wirelength estimation, local pin density, neighborhood information, as well as interaction among the features. When ranking different features, we concluded that post-global routing features and radius-2 neighborhood features did not cause much difference and consistent improvement in modeling. We compared different machine learning algorithms and identified the most suitable one, and showed significantly lower modeling error compared to prior work.

ACKNOWLEDGMENTS

This research is supported by National Science Foundation under award 1608040.

REFERENCES

[1] Olympus-SoC: Place and route for advanced node designs.
[2] I. S. Bustany, D. G. Chinnery, J. R. Shinnerl, and V. Yutsis. ISPD 2015 benchmarks with fence regions and routing blockages for detailed-routing-driven placement. In *International Symposium on Physical Design*, pages 157–164, 2015.
[3] W. J. Chan, P. Ho, A. B. Kahng, and P. Saxena. Routability optimization for industrial designs at sub-14nm process nodes using machine learning. In *ACM International Symposium on Physical Design*, pages 15–21, 2017.
[4] C. Chu and Y. C. Wong. FLUTE: Fast lookup table based rectilinear steiner minimal tree algorithm for VLSI design. *IEEE Transactions on Computer-Aided Design of Integrated Circuits and Systems*, 27(1):70–83, 2008.
[5] E. Frank, M. A. Hall, and I. H. Witten. The WEKA Workbench. Online Appendix for "Data Mining: Practical Machine Learning Tools and Techniques". *Morgan Kaufmann, Fourth Edition*, 2016.
[6] C. Huang, C. Chiou, K. Tseng, and Y. Chang. Detailed-routing-driven analytical standard-cell placement. In *Asia and South Pacific Design Automation Conference*, pages 378–383, 2015.
[7] R. Kohavi. The power of decision tables. *Machine learning: ECML-95*, pages 174–189, 1995.
[8] T. M. Mitchell. *Machine Learning*. The Mc-Graw-Hill Companies, Inc, 1997.
[9] D. Shi and A. Davoodi. Improving detailed routability and pin access with 3D monolithic standard cells. In *ACM International Symposium on Physical Design*, pages 107–112, 2017.
[10] D. Shi, E. Tashjian, and A. Davoodi. Dynamic planning of local congestion from varying-size vias for global routing layer assignment. *IEEE Transactions on Computer-Aided Design of Integrated Circuits and Systems*, 36(8):1301–1312, 2017.
[11] H. Shojaei, A. Davoodi, and J. T. Linderoth. Planning for local net congestion in global routing. In *ACM International Symposium on Physical Design*, pages 85–92, 2013.
[12] Y. Wei, C. C. N. Sze, N. Viswanathan, Z. Li, C. J. Alpert, L. N. Reddy, A. D. Huber, G. E. Téllez, D. Keller, and S. S. Sapatnekar. GLARE: global and local wiring aware routability evaluation. In *IEEE/ACM Design Automation Conference*, pages 768–773, 2012.
[13] M. Wong, W. Liu, and T. Wang. Negotiation-based track assignment considering local nets. In *IEEE Asia South Pacific Design Automation Conference*, pages 378–383, 2016.
[14] V. Yutsis, I. Bustany, D. G. Chinnery, J. R. Shinnerl, and W. Liu. ISPD 2014 benchmarks with sub-45nm technology rules for detailed-routing-driven placement. In *ACM International Symposium on Physical Design*, pages 161–168, 2014.

Fast Timing Analysis of Non-Tree Clock Network with Shorted Wires

Kiwon Yoon, Daijoon Hyun, and Youngsoo Shin
School of Electrical Engineering, KAIST
Daejeon 34141, Korea

ABSTRACT

A non-tree clock network, such as crosslink and mesh, includes some shorted wires to reduce clock skew. A short-circuit current that flows through the shorted wires makes conventional static timing analysis (STA) inapplicable. Transistor-level simulation may be applied but takes long time. We address a fast timing analysis of non-tree clock network. A partial circuit made of drivers, shorted wires, and receivers is extracted and represented as voltage-dependent current sources with π-model of RC load. Given voltage waveforms at driver inputs, we calculate the waveform at each shorted node by repeating nodal analysis for each time step; the waveform is represented as piecewise linear function. As the waveform propagates to receiver input via RC tree, the responses for all linear segments are obtained and merged into a full waveform. The waveform at receiver input then passes through receiver to produce a linear waveform at receiver output. Finally, timing parameters from the waveform at receiver output are transferred to STA, such that it utilizes the parameters to analyze the remaining circuit from receiver outputs to clock sinks. Experiments with a few test circuits demonstrate that analysis time is reduced by 10× with only 1% error on average (both in delay and transition time) compared to SPICE.

ACM Reference Format:
Kiwon Yoon, Daijoon Hyun, and Youngsoo Shin. 2018. Fast Timing Analysis of Non-Tree Clock Network with Shorted Wires. In *Proceedings of Great Lakes Symposium on VLSI 2018 (GLSVLSI'18)*. ACM, New York, NY, USA, 6 pages. https://doi.org/10.1145/3194554.3194598

1 INTRODUCTION

A non-tree clock network, such as crosslink and mesh, contains some shorted connections to reduce clock skew. Figure 1 illustrates a simplified mesh structure, which consists of drivers, shorted wires in the form of mesh, and receivers. Non-tree clock network has been adopted in high-performance microprocessors [1, 2] and some ASICs [3, 4].

Shorted wire causes short-circuit current from one driver to the other, meaning that the current from one driver is not entirely used to charge load capacitance. This is against the basic assumption made in static timing analysis (STA); the voltage waveform at shorted node is not simple increasing or decreasing (see the second waveform in Figure 1), which is also against STA paradigm. This is one of reasons why non-tree clock network is still limitedly used because timing should be checked through lengthy transistor-level simulation such as SPICE; this can be compared to more popular clock tree in which its synthesis can be performed while timing is checked by using convenient STA.

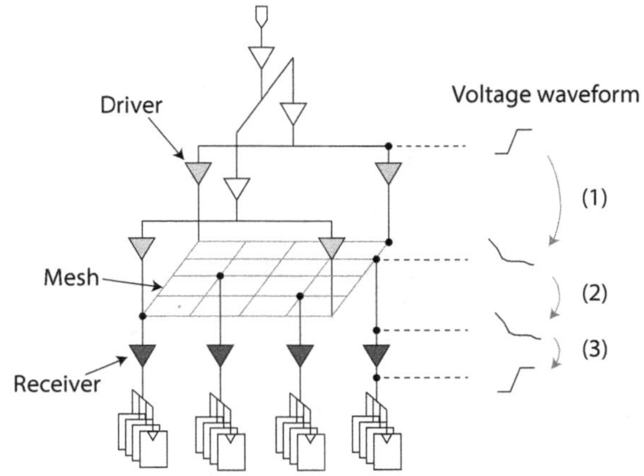

Figure 1: Mesh clock network with proposed timing analysis steps.

A few prior works have addressed the timing analysis of non-tree clock network. One approach is to perform SPICE repeatedly on each partition of mesh and its associated clock tree, where RC network outside the partition is simplified [5]; as a result, simulation is completed for large circuits that SPICE cannot finish, but it still takes a long time. Also, an efficient driver model is applied to reduce simulation time of non-tree clock network, which uses voltage-dependent current source and dynamic capacitance [6]; however, timing analysis with this model is not considered, and it still depends on SPICE. In industry, on the other hand, a method that employs both STA and SPICE is proposed for practical application, in which a portion of clock network including shorted wires is simulated by SPICE, and the remaining circuit is analyzed by STA. This method reduces the size of circuit on which SPICE is performed, but it still consumes heavy runtime for the clock network of large circuits.

In this paper, we address the overall methodology for timing analysis of non-tree clock network. We define a partial clock network as the circuit from driver inputs to receiver outputs because the linear waveforms at receiver outputs are compatible with STA. The circuit is effectively simplified with voltage-dependent current sources and π-model of RC load to minimize the runtime with small

GLSVLSI'18, May 23–25, 2018, Chicago, IL, USA

ACM ISBN ISBN 978-1-4503-5724-1/18/05...$15.00
https://doi.org/10.1145/3194554.3194598

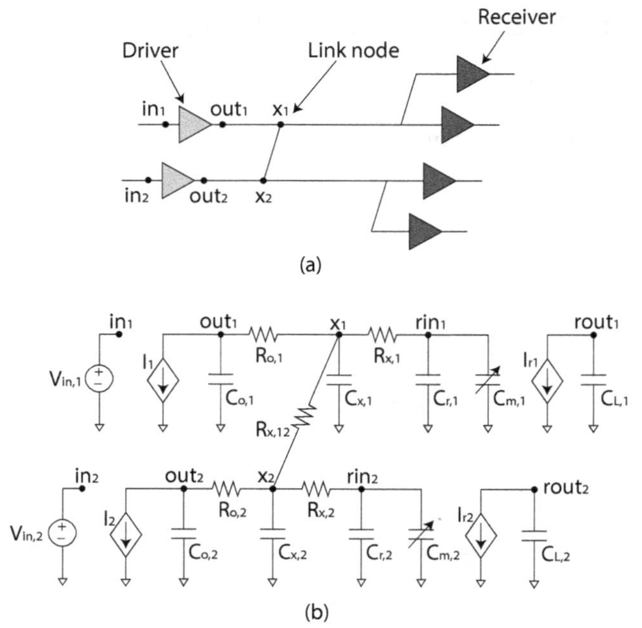

Figure 2: (a) A clock network with shorted wires and (b) equivalent circuit model.

accuracy loss. We perform the waveform calculation in three nodes sequentially; the waveform at link node, connected to shorted wire, is calculated by repeating nodal analysis for each time step; the resulting waveform is represented as piecewise linear function, and corresponding responses of RC tree are obtained and merged to form a full waveform at receiver input; the waveform then passes through receiver to produce a linear waveform at receiver output.

The remainder of this paper is organized as follows. Overall flow of proposed timing analysis and circuit modeling are addressed in Section 2, and Section 3 presents the proposed method of calculating waveform. Experimental results are demonstrated in Section 4, in which we show the effectiveness of proposed method in terms of runtime and accuracy. Conclusion is drawn in Section 5.

2 OVERVIEW

2.1 Analysis Flow

The goal of timing analysis for non-tree clock network is to obtain timing parameters, such as arrival time and transition time, at clock sinks. Initial STA is performed on the clock network, and voltage waveforms at driver inputs are obtained. We extract the circuit from driver inputs to receiver outputs including shorted wires, such as crosslink and mesh, and the circuit is modeled with voltage-dependent current source and simplified RC network. Our approach consists of three steps as described in Figure 1: (1) voltage waveform at link node is obtained by iterative nodal analysis, (2) the resulting waveform is represented as piecewise linear function, and the corresponding responses of RC tree are obtained for all time intervals; they are then merged to make a full waveform at receiver input, (3) linear waveform is produced through receiver buffer. Finally, the timing parameters from the waveform at receiver output are transferred to STA, such that it deploys the parameters to analyze the timing of remaining clock network from receiver outputs to clock sinks.

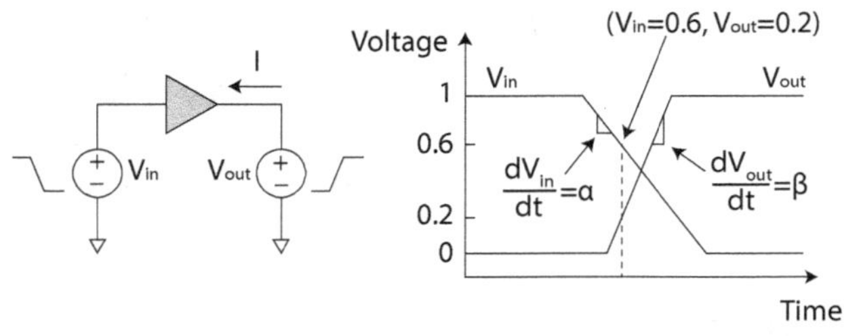

Figure 3: Current source characterization with ramp input and ramp output voltages.

2.2 Circuit Modeling

For a fast nodal analysis, we perform circuit modeling that can accurately represent circuit characteristics with fewer nodes. To calculate waveform at link node, the circuit from driver inputs to receiver outputs is modeled with voltage-dependent current sources and simplified RC network.

Consider a clock network with a shorted wire in Figure 2(a), where each driver drives two receivers, and the shorted wire connects two link nodes, x_1 and x_2. Each driver is modeled as a current source I that varies with input voltage V_{in}, output voltage V_{out}, and their derivatives which reflect the current from Miller effect; it is defined as

$$I = f(V_{in}, V_{out}, \frac{dV_{in}}{dt}, \frac{dV_{out}}{dt}). \quad (1)$$

The current source is pre-characterized by using ramp input and ramp output as shown in Figure 3, where we measure current I at dotted time, and it corresponds to $f(0.6, 0.2, \alpha, \beta)$. In this way, we store the current values of clock buffer under various input and output conditions in look-up table.

The shorted wire and the wires between driver output and link node are represented as π-model, in which two capacitance values are set to the same; this is because current flows through the wires in both directions. In addition, RC trees from link node to receiver inputs are approximated to driving-point admittance in the form of π-model [7]. Multiple receivers are modeled as one clock buffer, which size is determined as the closest one to the average size of receivers; this is represented as current source I_r in the same manner as Equation (1). Miller effect in the receiver is considered using variable capacitance C_m, which depends on the input and output voltages of receiver. The circuit model for clock network with a shorted wire is finally shown in Figure 2(b).

Figure 4 shows the effect of Miller capacitance in non-tree clock network with crosslink, where blue line represents the voltage waveform without Miller capacitance while Miller effect is considered in red line. We observe that the waveform at link node is affected by steep rising transition at receiver output; this causes a

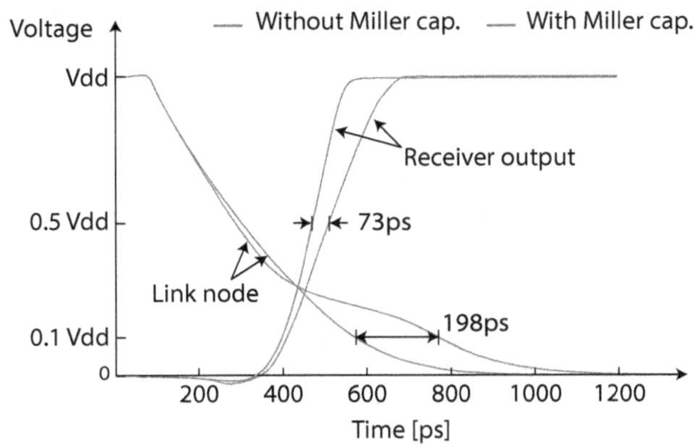

Figure 4: Waveforms at link node and receiver output without Miller capacitance (blue) and with Miller capacitance (red).

large difference, 198ps, in falling transition time at link node, which results in 73ps difference in arrival time at receiver output.

3 WAVEFORM CALCULATION

This section describes how to propagate voltage waveform at driver input to receiver output over three stages: (1) obtain waveform at link node by repeating nodal analysis for each time step, (2) represent resulting waveform as piecewise linear function, and obtain ramp input response of RC tree for each linear segment; those responses are merged to form a waveform at receiver input, and (3) pass the waveform to receiver to create a linear waveform at receiver output.

3.1 Link Node

Given a circuit model and waveforms at driver inputs, the waveform at link node is obtained by iterative nodal analysis for each time step.

The initial voltage of each node is set to the value before its transition; for an instance, if the driver input is rising and its output is falling, the voltage at driver input and output are set to zero and Vdd, respectively; all voltage derivatives are set to zero. At each time step, the voltages at driver inputs and their derivatives are updated following the waveforms at driver inputs; while the voltages at the other nodes are changed using Euler method in Equation (2) for the next time step.

$$V_n(t + \Delta t) = V_n(t) + \frac{dV_n(t)}{dt}\Delta t,\ n \in \mathbb{N} \tag{2}$$

where Δt is a time step, and $\mathbb{N}$ denotes a set of all nodes in the model except driver inputs.

We now calculate voltage derivatives using voltages at current time step. Kirchhoff's current law (KCL) equations for the nodes of i-th driver are expressed as:

$$I_i(t) + C_{o,i}\frac{dV_{out,i}(t)}{dt} + \frac{V_{out,i}(t) - V_{x,i}(t)}{R_{o,i}} = 0, \tag{3}$$

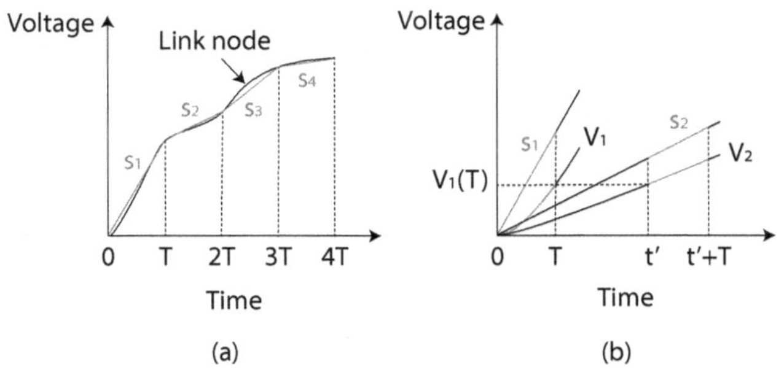

Figure 5: (a) Waveform at link node and its piecewise linear approximation (blue) and (b) ramp inputs with different slopes and their RC tree responses (red).

$$C_{x,i}\frac{dV_{x,i}(t)}{dt} + \frac{V_{x,i}(t) - V_{out,i}(t)}{R_{o,i}} + \frac{V_{x,i}(t) - V_{rin,i}(t)}{R_{x,i}} + \sum_j \frac{V_{x,i}(t) - V_{x,j}(t)}{R_{x,ij}} = 0, \tag{4}$$

$$(C_{r,i} + C_{m,i}(t))\frac{dV_{rin,i}(t)}{dt} + \frac{V_{rin,i}(t) - V_{x,i}(t)}{R_{x,i}} = 0, \tag{5}$$

$$I_{r,i}(t) + C_{L,i}\frac{dV_{rout,i}(t)}{dt} = 0, \tag{6}$$

where j represents the index of driver that is connected to i-th driver by a shorted wire. Miller capacitance $C_{m,i}$ is also calculated for each time step, where the gain of input voltage change over output voltage change is used by considering the direction in current source; it is shown in Equation (7).

$$C_{m,i}(t) = -C_{r,i}\frac{V_{rin,i}(t) - V_{rin,i}(0)}{V_{rout,i}(t) - V_{rout,i}(0)}. \tag{7}$$

Voltage derivatives at x_i and rin_i are obtained by solving Equation (4) and (5); however, voltage derivatives at out_i cannot be computed in Equation (3) because it is also one of the inputs of I_i. To solve this problem, we list the candidates of $dV_{out,i}/dt$, which ranges from 0.9 times to 1.1 times the value of the previous time step; for those candidates, we calculate two values of I_i using Equation (1) and (3), where the candidate with the minimum difference between two current values is determined as $dV_{out,i}/dt$. Same method is applied to find the voltage derivative at $rout_i$ in Equation (6).

If the voltages and their derivatives at all nodes are obtained, t is increased by Δt and the voltages for next time step are updated again. This process is repeated until the voltages at link nodes are saturated. If the time step is large, the error from the approximation in Equation (2) increases, and the waveform can be oscillated. In this case, we reduce the time step and calculate the waveform again. In our experiment, this oscillation problem is not observed when the time step is reduced to 0.1ps in worst case.

3.2 Receiver Input

Once the waveform at link node is obtained, the waveform is propagated to the receiver inputs via RC tree. However, the waveform has several bends as shown in Figure 5(a), and it cannot be represented with a single ramp input. So we divide the waveform by the same

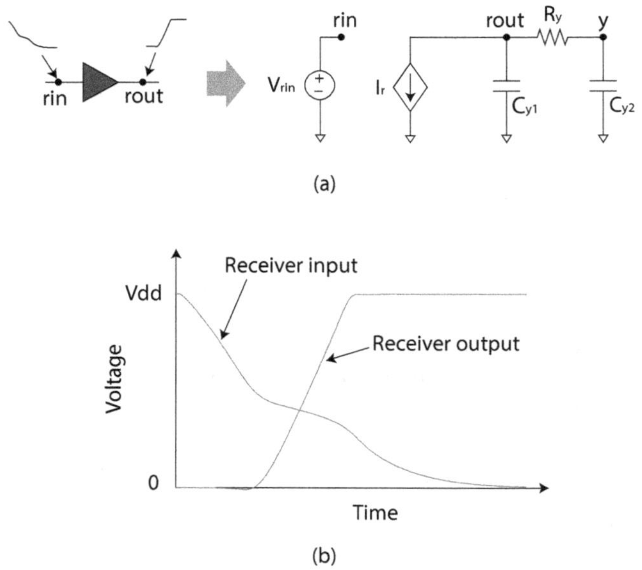

Figure 6: (a) Equivalent circuit model to calculate the receiver output waveform and (b) nonlinear receiver input waveform versus linear receiver output waveform.

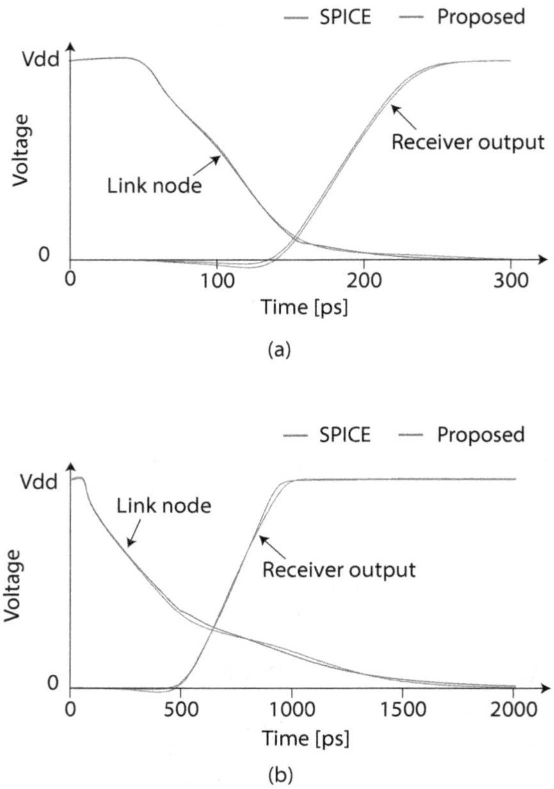

Figure 7: Voltage waveforms obtained by SPICE (blue) and proposed method (red) at (a) crosslink clock network and (b) mesh clock network.

time interval T (in our case, T is set to 10ps), and the waveform is linearly modeled in each interval as shown in blue line. For each linear function, ramp input response of RC tree is formulated as [8]:

$$V_s(t) = s[t - \tau(1 - e^{-t/\tau})], \quad (8)$$

where s represents the slope of ramp input, and τ indicates Elmore delay from link node to receiver input.

We merge the ramp input responses to form the full waveform at receiver input. Figure 5(b) shows the responses, V_1 and V_2, from two ramp inputs, s_1 and s_2. V_1 from zero to T is the waveform for the first interval (see red line of V_1), and the last value in the first interval, $V_1(T)$, is the initial value of second interval. To find the time that corresponds to $V_1(T)$ in V_2, inverse function of Equation (8) is derived as:

$$t_s(V) = \frac{V}{s} + \tau[1 + ln(1 - e^{-(\frac{V}{s\tau}+1)})]. \quad (9)$$

By using Equation (9), we can find the start time of each response analytically, and combine the waveforms for T. Finally, the entire waveform at receiver input is completed by merging all responses.

3.3 Receiver Output

The waveform at receiver input is still incompatible with STA; however, when the waveform passes through the receiver, it becomes a linear curve at receiver output. As illustrated in Figure 6(a), receiver is modeled with a voltage-dependent current source, and RC tree at receiver output is represented as π-model [7]. We apply iterative nodal analysis in Section 3.1 again, where Euler method and nodal analysis are repeatedly applied for each time step until the waveform at receiver output is saturated; Equation (10) and (11) are used for the nodal analysis.

$$I_r(t) + C_{y1}\frac{dV_{rout}(t)}{dt} + \frac{V_{rout}(t) - V_y(t)}{R_y} = 0, \quad (10)$$

$$C_{y2}\frac{dV_y(t)}{dt} + \frac{V_y(t) - V_{rout}(t)}{R_y} = 0. \quad (11)$$

Figure 6(b) shows the waveforms at receiver input and at receiver output, where nonlinear waveform at receiver input (in blue) is linearly transformed at receiver output (in red); it proves that the waveform at receiver output is compatible with STA. We extract arrival time and transition time of the waveform, and transfer them to STA for timing analysis in the remaining clock network from receiver output to clock sinks.

4 EXPERIMENTAL RESULTS

Experiments are carried out on a set of sequential circuits from ISCAS, ITC, and OpenCores [9–11], which are listed in the second column of Table 1. Each circuit is synthesized using 28-nm industrial library. In physical synthesis, clock network is constructed with mesh and crosslink, where inverter is used as driver and receiver; the clock structure of each circuit is shown in the first column. First eight circuits are implemented with mesh, in which clock mesh

Table 1: Comparison of timing analysis runtime: SPICE, fast SPICE, and proposed method

Clock structure	Circuit	#Drivers	#Receivers	Runtime SPICE [sec]	Runtime Fast SPICE [×]	Runtime Proposed [×]
Mesh	s38584	4	89	11	1.00	0.09
	b17	9	125	13	0.77	0.07
	b19	9	129	14	0.71	0.08
	usb	9	144	14	0.77	0.07
	reed	25	519	35	0.59	0.11
	des3	25	684	45	0.50	0.13
	ethernet	25	823	53	0.53	0.15
	vga	49	1362	104	0.43	0.11
Crosslink	fft	206	657	80	0.52	0.07
	tate	304	987	131	0.48	0.07
Average					0.63	0.09

drives local clock buffer (LCB); in other words, LCB is the receiver of clock mesh. The size of mesh grid is empirically determined by the number of clock sinks. Each grid is driven by a driver, and the number of drivers is shown in column 3. Another two circuits have the clock network with crosslink, where crosslink also drives LCB. We randomly select the pair of drivers, such that the driver outputs are connected each other. Each crosslink connects only two drivers; thus, the number of crosslinks in a circuit is the half of the number of drivers.

For the clock network of each circuit, we extract a partial circuit from driver inputs to receiver outputs, and SPICE is applied to the partial one, which is served as reference. Fast SPICE as well as proposed method are used to obtain the waveforms at receiver outputs, and they are assessed in terms of runtime and accuracy. Figure 7(a) and (b) show the results of waveform propagation in our proposed method for crosslink and mesh, respectively, where the waveform at link node is falling in non-linear form and the signal at receiver output is linearly rising. The waveforms of proposed method (in red) follow those of SPICE (in blue) similarly. In Figure 7(b), the transition time at link node is very large due to large load capacitance; nevertheless, the waveform in the proposed method is very accurate.

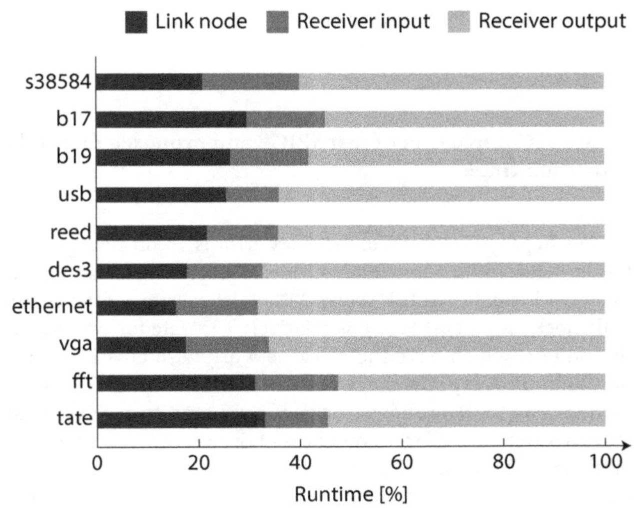

Figure 8: Runtime breakdown of calculating waveforms at link node, receiver input, and receiver output.

4.1 Runtime

The analysis runtimes of fast SPICE and proposed method are shown in columns 6-7, respectively, which are normalized by the reference in column 5. Fast SPICE has the average runtime of 37% less than SPICE; on the other hand, the proposed method reduces the runtime by more than 90%. In fast SPICE, the number of nodes is reduced by 82% on average of test circuits, while the proposed method achieves a larger runtime gain by circuit modeling with less than 1% of nodes.

The runtimes of all three methods depend on the number of receivers in column 4, and that of proposed method is also affected by output transition times of driver and receiver, because nodal analysis is repeated until the signal is saturated. There are 89 receivers in s38584, much smaller than 144 in usb; however, the runtime of s38584 is a little larger than that of usb. It comes from the difference of the repeated number of nodal analysis; s38584 has larger transition time (593ps) at link node compared to usb (387ps), on average.

Figure 8 shows the runtime ratio at each step of the waveform calculation. On average, the waveform calculation at receiver output takes up the largest runtime portion, because it requires many iterations of nodal analysis due to a large number of receivers. The runtime ratio of link node has large variation from 15% (ethernet) to 32% (tate), which is proportional to the ratio of the number of drivers to the number of receivers.

4.2 Accuracy

The accuracy of proposed method is assessed in terms of the delay from driver input to receiver output and the transition time at receiver output. Figure 9(a) and (b) show the error distributions in delay and transition time, respectively, where red boxplot represents that of proposed method, and the results of fast SPICE are shown

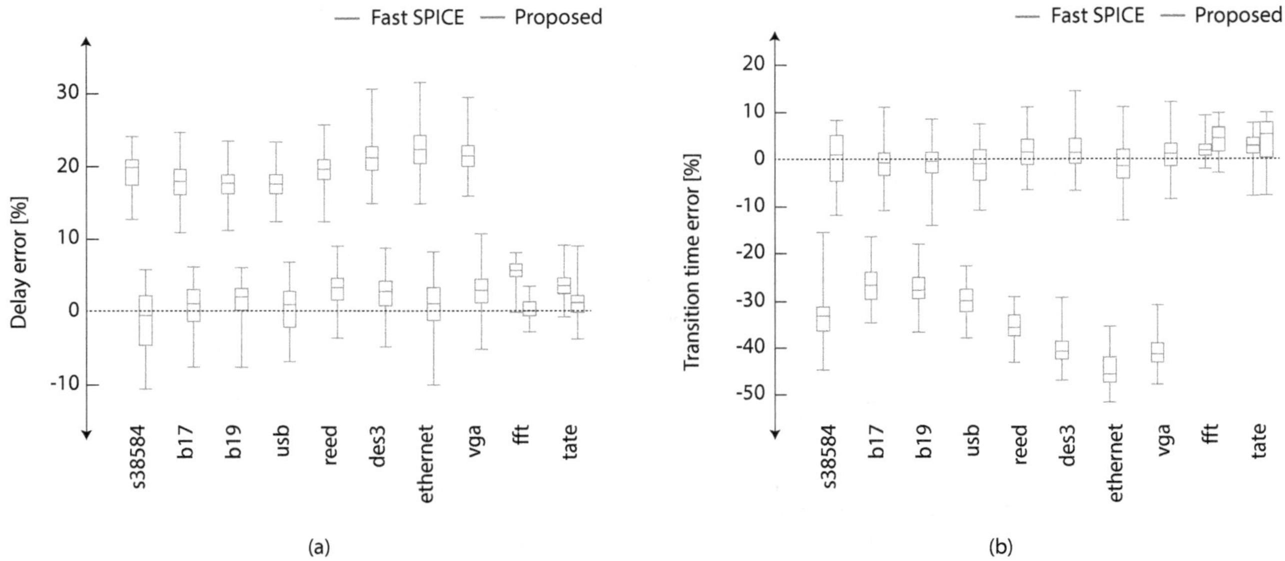

Figure 9: Comparison of fast SPICE and proposed method in (a) clock delay (from driver input to receiver output) and (b) clock transition time.

in blue. In proposed method, the delay error is 1% on average of the test circuits, and the maximum absolute error is less than 11%; on the other hand, fast SPICE shows 20% of delay error for the circuits with clock mesh. Fast SPICE is relatively accurate for two circuits, fft and tate, which have the clock network with crosslink. From our additional experiment, we observe that error in fast SPICE increases as there are fewer drivers compared to receivers; and crosslink cases have larger numbers of drivers per a receiver than mesh cases. In addition, the proposed method shows the average error of 1% even at the transition time in mesh cases, which is very accurate compared to 27% average error of fast SPICE.

To check the impact of timing errors in proposed method on circuit timing, STA analyzes the timing of whole circuit with the timing parameters at receiver outputs, and the results are compared to those obtained by SPICE. In vga, the maximum error of arrival time at clock sinks is 4%, which is smaller than 10% in the delay error; average error is less than 1%. With respect to setup constraint, the proposed method shows 15ps of optimism in worst negative slack compared to SPICE, and it corresponds to less than 1% of clock period.

5 CONCLUSION

We have addressed fast timing analysis method for non-tree clock network. A partial circuit from driver inputs to receiver outputs is extracted and modeled with voltage-dependent current source and simplified RC network. Our method consists of three steps. In the first step, we perform iterative nodal analysis to obtain the voltage waveform at link node. In the second step, the resulting waveform is represented as piecewise linear function, and corresponding responses of RC tree are obtained for each time interval; they are then merged to make a full waveform at receiver input. Finally, linear waveform is produced at receiver output. The timing parameters at receiver output are transferred to STA for timing analysis on the remaining clock network. Experiments have demonstrated that our method achieves 90% runtime reduction with 1% of accuracy loss in the timing parameters, on average of a few test circuits in 28-nm technology.

ACKNOWLEDGMENT

This work was supported by Samsung Electronics.

REFERENCES

[1] T. Singh, J. Bell, and S. Southard, "Jaguar: A next-generation low-power x86-64 core," in *Proc. Int. Solid-State Circuits Conf.*, Feb. 2013, pp. 52–53.
[2] D. Shan *et al.*, "Resonant clock mega-mesh for the IBM z13^{TM}," in *Proc. Symp. Very Large Scale Integr. VLSI Circuits*, Jun. 2015, pp. C322–C323.
[3] S. Lu, Z. Zhang, and M. Papaefthymiou, "A 5.5GHz 0.84TOPS/mm^2 neural network engine with stream architecture and resonant clock mesh," in *Proc. Asia Solid-State Circuits Conf.*, Nov. 2016, pp. 133–136.
[4] L.-T. Pang *et al.*, "A shorted global clock design for multi-GHz 3D stacked chips," in *Proc. Symp. Very Large Scale Integr. VLSI Circuits*, Jun. 2012, pp. 170–171.
[5] H. Chen *et al.*, "A sliding window scheme for accurate clock mesh analysis," in *Proc. Int. Conf. Computer-Aided Design*, Nov. 2005, pp. 939–946.
[6] G. Venkataraman *et al.*, "Combinatorial algorithms for fast clock mesh optimization," in *Proc. Int. Conf. Computer-Aided Design*, Nov. 2006, pp. 563–567.
[7] P. O'brien and T. Savarino, "Modeling the driving-point characteristic of resistive interconnect for accurate delay estimation," in *Proc. Int. Conf. Computer-Aided Design*, Nov. 1989, pp. 512–515.
[8] E. Friedman and J. Mulligan, "Ramp input response of RC tree networks," in *Proc. Int. ASIC Conf. Exh.*, Sep. 1996, pp. 63–66.
[9] ISCAS'85 benchmark circuits. [Online]. Available: http://www.cbl.ncsu.edu/benchmarks/ISCAS85
[10] ITC99. [Online]. Available: http://www.cerc.utexas.edu/itc99-benchmarks/bench.html
[11] OpenCores. [Online]. Available: http://www.opencores.org/

Reliable On-Chip Voltage Regulation for Sustainable and Compact IoT and Heterogeneous Computing Systems

Longfei Wang
University of South Florida
Tampa, Florida
longfei@mail.usf.edu

Selçuk Köse
University of South Florida
Tampa, Florida
kose@usf.edu

ABSTRACT

As an essential part of modern power delivery networks, on-chip voltage regulation consisting of multiple distributed voltage regulators provides the required power and voltage levels for localized load circuits. The harsh application environment of internet of things (IoT) and heterogeneous computing systems including, but not limited to, high temperature and large load current variations, can lead to significant and uneven performance degradations of on-chip voltage regulators due to aging. Investigating sustainable on-chip voltage regulation schemes considering the lifetime of different distributed voltage regulators becomes imperative. Furthermore, techniques to mitigate the aging induced voltage regulator degradations can consume the scarce on-chip area resource. In this work, a new reliable on-chip voltage regulation technique is explored to simultaneously mitigate the performance degradation and reduce the area cost of distributed on-chip voltage regulators to achieve sustainable and compact design and satisfy the needs of different IoT and heterogeneous computing systems considering the interactions among different regulators. A brief survey of reliable design challenges and potential solutions is also provided.

KEYWORDS

On-chip voltage regulation; reliability; internet of things; heterogeneous computing

ACM Reference Format:
Longfei Wang and Selçuk Köse. 2018. Reliable On-Chip Voltage Regulation for Sustainable and Compact IoT and Heterogeneous Computing Systems. In *GLSVLSI '18: 2018 Great Lakes Symposium on VLSI, May 23–25, 2018, Chicago, IL, USA.* ACM, New York, NY, USA, 6 pages. https://doi.org/10.1145/3194554.3194602

1 INTRODUCTION

The increasing number of internet connected devices enables more advanced applications such as smart homes and smart cities beyond conventional stand-alone smart devices [34]. Efficient social systems can be constructed with the support of vast deployment of internet of things (IoT) devices and the integration of heterogeneous computing systems [28]. Besides the popularity of IoT devices, challenging design requirements such as power efficiency, cost, security, and reliability are also emerging. Similarly, there are open research problems such as workload partitioning, task mapping, and thermal and power management [5, 8, 26] for performance and energy efficiency improvement of heterogeneous computing systems.

On-chip voltage regulation, as an essential part of both IoT and heterogeneous computing systems, can greatly affect most of these design concerns. Considerable amount of research has been performed to improve the power efficiency of on-chip voltage regulators [9, 15, 29, 38] and further the energy efficiency of the underlying microprocessors [6]. Meanwhile, voltage regulators have been leveraged as a low overhead solution to enhance the security of the load circuits [16, 21, 37, 48–54]. On the other hand, reliability issue of on-chip voltage regulator has recently drawn attention [3, 32, 41–43]. However, as the application environment and load current demand of different IoT devices and different portion of heterogeneous computing systems can vary a lot, a homogeneous methodology by designing voltage regulators for the worst case scenario may lead to an over-design problem, which potentially increases the area and cost of devices.

While intensive technology scaling has enabled increasingly outstanding circuit performance, transistor aging induced circuit performance degradation has also become more dramatic [2]. A large circuit delay can be introduced and even circuit failure can occur [46]. Transistor aging induced circuit performance degradation is a strong function of temperature, electrical stress, and the amount of time the transistor is under stress. It is thus important to consider the variations of these parameters within IoT and heterogeneous computing systems to achieve the targeted design specifications. Furthermore, the reliability design constraints can be relaxed within a certain portion of a chip that has less degree of aging to reduce the total area cost or to spare additional area for heavily aged regions.

Techniques to mitigate aging induced voltage regulator performance degradations are investigated. As on-chip voltage regulation with distributed voltage regulators becomes prominent in recent design paradigms [18, 22, 36, 39, 40, 42], reliable on-chip voltage regulation within the context of distributed voltage regulators is also explored. Furthermore, reliable on-chip voltage regulation considering the varying application environment and lifetime requirement of IoT devices and heterogeneous computing systems is discussed.

The rest of the paper is organized as follows. Background information regarding on-chip voltage regulation, IoT devices, and heterogeneous computing systems is introduced in Section 2. Major transistor aging mechanisms and aging-aware on-chip voltage regulators are discussed in Section 3. Reliable on-chip voltage regulation

GLSVLSI '18, May 23–25, 2018, Chicago, IL, USA

ACM ISBN 978-1-4503-5724-1/18/05...$15.00
https://doi.org/10.1145/3194554.3194602

for sustainable and compact designs is investigated in Section 4. Conclusion is offered in Section 5.

2 BACKGROUND

On-chip voltage regulation provides certain advantages as compared to off-chip implementations such as reduced voltage noise, fast dynamic voltage and frequency scaling (DVFS) capability, reduced number of power/ground pins, more compact design, and reduced power loss due to parasitic impedance, which serves as an ideal power supply solution for IoT and heterogeneous computing systems.

2.1 Internet of things

IoT covers a wide range of application domains such as smart home, smart city, wearable device, automotive industry, agriculture, and health care [33]. Different applications may impose different lifetime requirements. Furthermore, even with the same lifetime requirement, the aging speed of functional circuits within IoT devices can be quite different. For example, it would be acceptable to have a lifetime requirement of only five years for smart home devices such as Amazon Echo and Google Home, since functions of these devices may quickly run out of date as technology advances and replacement of them can be effortless. It would be, however, more desirable to set a lifetime target of more than ten years for implantable medical devices to reduce potentially costly and painful operations.

On the other hand, temperature sensors for IoT applications may experience quite challenging environmental changes. A digital temperature sensor with a wide industrial temperature range of -40°C $\sim$ 150°C [12], may operate around room temperature or near the low/high temperature boundaries. Individual transistors age much faster in high temperature operations as discussed in Section 3. The desired circuit level performance such as accuracy of the temperature sensor may degrade faster as well within a high temperature environment. For two identical temperature sensors with quite different operating temperatures, performance degradations between them can also significantly vary after a five-year period. In order to have similar performance degradation and operate with acceptable accuracy, temperature sensors operating mostly in higher temperature may need to be designed with a higher level of reliability standard at design time. Similarly, for low temperature operations, reliability constraint can be relaxed to reduce cost or design complexity.

2.2 Heterogeneous computing systems

Increasing number of IoT devices generates huge amount of data that needs to be processed by microprocessors. These data can be transmitted to specialists or servers for analysis. However, the transmission bandwidth and latency can limit the applications [1]. Edge computing has become a promising way to directly equip IoT devices with sufficient computation capability to overcome data transmission induced bandwidth, latency, and energy consumption limitations [1]. The emerging edge computing necessitates heterogeneous computing systems at either chip-level or network-level [1]. As IoT devices can have different functions and data characteristics, design requirements for IoT microprocessors also vary a lot. Such varying demands can be fulfilled with chip-level solution with heterogeneous cores on a single chip or network-level approach with different cores for different devices [1]. Regardless of chip-level or network-level strategy, the existence of heterogeneity demands heterogeneous on-chip power delivery among different cores or different part of the chip.

2.3 On-chip voltage regulation

On-chip voltage regulation is widely adopted in processors [9, 14, 36], energy harvesting devices [7, 24, 27, 29], and wearable devices [30, 44, 45], enabling various IoT applications. Three commonly used voltage regulator topologies including buck or boost converter, switched-capacitor (SC) converter, and low dropout regulator (LDO) cover most IoT application scenarios due to their respect advantages. A buck converter can achieve high power conversion efficiency over a wide load current range and voltage conversion ratios [29, 30] while a boost converter is needed for certain energy harvesting applications [17, 47] due to low input voltage levels. SC converters gain popularity due to the easiness of integration and higher power density over inductive approach. LDOs can achieve sub-ns response time and are adopted in the most recent IBM POWER8 and POWER9 processors [14, 36].

Although a single voltage regulator is typically implemented for most applications, distributed on-chip voltage regulation [14, 18, 22, 36–40, 42], where multiple parallel voltage regulators are distributed across the chip, has recently drawn significant attention. Better voltage noise performance and fast localized load response can be achieved. By adaptively turning on/off some of the distributed voltage regulators, a high power conversion efficiency can be obtained over a wide dynamic load range [37, 38]. It also provides a degree of freedom to mitigate hot spots on a certain chip and simultaneously optimize power efficiency, on-chip temperature, and voltage noise profile [19, 20].

3 RELIABLE ON-CHIP VOLTAGE REGULATION

Despite the advantages of on-chip voltage regulation, less attention has been paid to the reliability issues and aging induced on-chip voltage regulator performance degradations especially within IoT and heterogeneous computing system applications. To realize reliable on-chip voltage regulation, it is essential to first understand major transistor aging mechanisms and mitigate their side effects on individual voltage regulators.

3.1 Transistor aging mechanisms

Major transistor aging mechanisms include bias temperature instability (BTI), hot carrier injection (HCI), time dependent dielectric breakdown (TDDB), and electromigration (EM) [46]. BTI, which includes positive BTI (PBTI) for NMOS transistors and negative BTI (NBTI) for PMOS transistors, is the dominant reliability concern among others [11, 25, 35]. NBTI (PBTI) is caused by negatively (positively) applied transistor gate to source voltage V_{gs} and it can introduce significant threshold voltage V_{th} degradations. BTI induced V_{th} degradation is related to the generated Si/SiO_2 interface traps when electrical stress is applied [4]. $|V_{th}|$ increases when electrical stress is applied and partially recovers when electrical stress

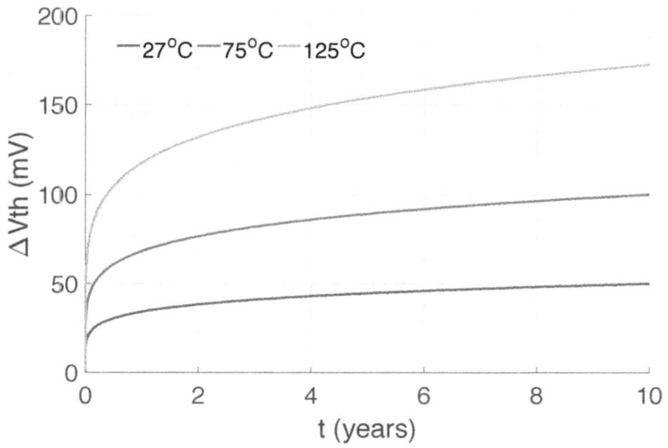

Figure 1: NBTI induced threshold voltage degradation with different temperature.

is removed. BTI induced $|V_{th}|$ degradation with time t and activity factor α can be expressed as [35]

$$\Delta V_{th} = \chi K_{lt} \sqrt{C_{ox}(|V_{gs}| - |V_{th}|) e^{\frac{-E_a}{kT}}} (\alpha t)^{\frac{1}{6}} \quad (1)$$

where α is the percentage of time the transistor is under stress and k, T, and C_{ox} are Boltzmann constant, temperature, and the oxide capacitance, respectively. K_{lt} and E_a are fitting parameters to match the model with experimental data [35]. As α is included in the model, the BTI recovery effect is already considered.

Utilizing the PMOS transistor parameters in 32 nm metal gate, high-k strained-Si CMOS technology from PTM model library [10], which is typically used in the literature for reliability study [2, 13, 25, 35], NBTI induced V_{th} degradation under different temperature is demonstrated in Fig. 1. As shown in Fig. 1, more than 150 mV V_{th} degradation can be introduced within a ten-year time frame with a temperature of 125°C. Even with a room temperature of 27°C, 50 mV V_{th} degradation can be introduced. NBTI induced ΔV_{th} can be significant as compared to the initial value of 491.55 mV.

Transistor V_{th} degradation can further lead to circuit level performance degradations. As demonstrated in [3], aging can induce degradation of current sensing accuracy of multiphase buck converter, mismatches between each phase, and degradation of power efficiency. Important performance metrics of a digital LDO (DLDO), including maximum current supply capability, load response time, and magnitude of the transient voltage droop, are shown to experience significant degradation as the power transistor array ages [41]. Experimental results in [43] also demonstrate side effects of aging on LDO DC performance and electromagnetic interference (EMI) immunity level. Local hotspots near voltage regulators can occur and further lead to transistor breakdown, top metal rupture, and even system level malfunction [32]. Furthermore, within an on-chip power delivery network consisting of many distributed individual voltage regulators, unbalanced current sharing among different voltage regulators can occur due to parasitic on-chip power grid resistance mismatches. This unbalanced current distribution causes different aging speed of metal wires connected to each voltage regulator due to electromigration (EM) induced wear-out [42]. The mean time to failure (MTTF) of metal wires which provide larger current can be much less than those providing less current. This phenomenon may lead to the earlier failure of the whole on-chip power delivery network [42]. Thus, a reliability-aware design approach should be adopted and reliability enhancement techniques need to be investigated for on-chip voltage regulators.

3.2 Aging-aware on-chip voltage regulators

A rotational phase shedding scheme for multiphase buck converters is proposed in [3] to mitigate the aging induced efficiency degradation especially under light load. For conventional multiphase buck converters, only one phase can be active under light load. For medium and heavy load conditions, additional phases are activated. The conventional phase activation scheme imposes too much electrical stress on a certain phase P_1 among all the N phases (P_1 to P_N) as P_1 is always activated at light load condition. The phase shedding scheme [3] rotationally turns on one of the N phases to make sure that electrical stress can be evenly distributed among all the phases at light load condition. The scheme may not work well under all the load current conditions as it is only activated at light load. A decoding methodology to decide which portion of the power transistor array to be turned on is proposed in [32] to mitigate or eliminate the hotspots generated by DLDOs. The power transistor array is divided into n rows and m columns. One power transistor in a certain row and middle column is turned on first and the one in the adjacent column and next row is activated as load current increases. A code rotation scheme is formed to spread the current distribution under all load conditions. The implementation cost of the proposed scheme is not clear and it may also introduce side effects on DLDO performance such as increased output voltage ripple. A lightweight aging mitigation scheme for DLDO is proposed in [41]. Instead of utilizing the conventional bidirectional shift register, a unidirectional shift register is proposed by simple modifications of the control circuit. The proposed NBTI-aware DLDO works well under arbitrary load conditions with little side effects on the performance of DLDO as the number of power transistors activated/deactivated per clock cycle remains the same. The power and area overhead incurred by the proposed technique are also negligible. Within the context of distributed on-chip voltage regulation, an effective current balancing scheme is proposed in [42] that can be applied to most regulator types which need a reference voltage to operate. Through balancing the current distribution among all the regulators, EM induced metal wear-out effects can be minimized.

4 RELIABLE VOLTAGE REGULATION FOR SUSTAINABLE AND COMPACT DESIGN

Besides aging mitigation techniques for individual on-chip voltage regulators, the application environment of on-chip voltage regulator needs to be considered to fully exploit the benefits of reliable on-chip voltage regulation. Seen from (1), temperature effects on ΔV_{th} can be more significant than α and $|V_{gs}|$. Thus, thermal management techniques can be essential for reliable on-chip voltage regulation. Thermally aware on-chip voltage regulation is investigated in [19] by turning on/off distributed voltage regulators in a thermally aware fashion. A nearly optimal chip-wide temperature profile can be achieved and up to 20°C maximum temperature

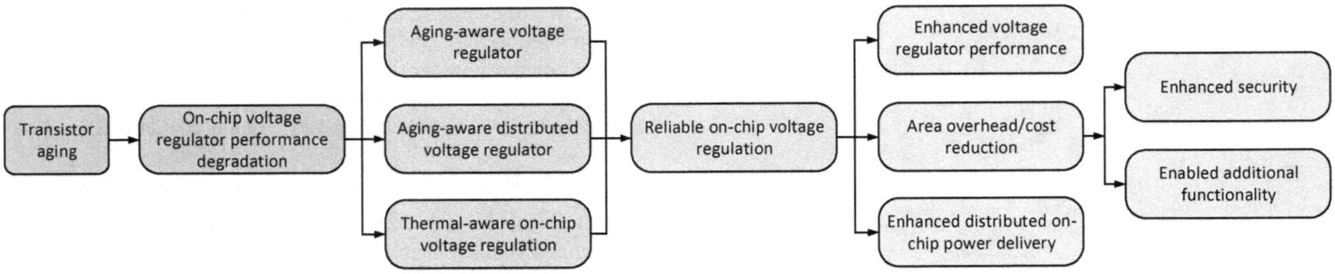

Figure 2: Road map to reliable on-chip voltage regulation for sustainable and compact design.

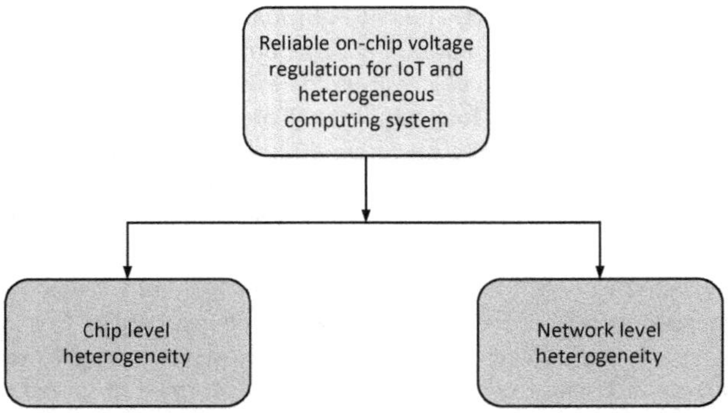

Figure 3: Reliable on-chip voltage regulation for IoT and heterogeneous computing systems.

reduction can be obtained as compared to a voltage noise optimal approach. The benefits of temperature reduction regarding reliability can be prominent as shown in Fig. 1. Furthermore, it is also important to consider different load current profile of each voltage regulator. It is demonstrated in [3, 31] that light and medium load current are consumed most of the time for mobile and microprocessor applications. However, voltage regulators need to be designed for the maximum load current supply capability, which may lead to varying aging speed of different voltage regulator portions [41] or individual voltage regulators. Balancing load current distribution among each power transistor, distributed voltage regulator, and different functional blocks through, respectively, reliability enhancement techniques [3, 32, 41], balanced current sharing schemes[36, 42], and reconfigurable voltage regulation [23, 31] can be beneficial. The road map to achieve reliable on-chip voltage regulation is summarized in Fig. 2.

Furthermore, different portions (functional block) of a chip can have quite different load current and temperature profiles. As investigated in [19, 41], the representative temperature profile among a load store unit, an execution unit, an instruction fetch unit, an instruction scheduling unit, and a cache can vary from 62^oC to 90^oC. The maximum load current varies from 1.356A to 12.092A. On the other hand, for IoT applications where various devices are connected to the Internet, temperature and load current profile vary at the network level. It is thus necessary to consider the heterogeneity characteristics at both the chip level and network level, as shown in Fig. 3 to implement reliable on-chip voltage regulation for IoT and heterogeneous computing systems. On-chip voltage regulator design simultaneously considering temperature, load current, and lifetime requirement, needs to be adopted for reliable on-chip voltage regulation.

Benefits of reliable on-chip voltage regulation can be manifold as summarized in Fig. 2. Reliability enhancement techniques for individual voltage regulators directly translate into improved voltage regulator performance such as reduced steady state output voltage ripple, faster load response, and lower voltage noise characteristics. Enhanced individual voltage regulator performance further strengthens distributed on-chip power delivery benefits and helps achieve faster and more accurate DVFS capability. Also, aging-aware on-chip voltage regulator can essentially reduce the area/power overhead needed for mitigation of aging induced voltage regulator performance degradation. For example, the NBTI-aware DLDO proposed in [41] only induces ~ 2.6% area overhead and achieves up to 43.2% DLDO performance degradation mitigation. A conventional DLDO designed in an aging-unaware fashion may need extra decoupling capacitors to achieve the equivalent performance after aging. The area overhead of deploying an additional decoupling capacitor can be much larger than that induced by implementation of NBTI-aware DLDO. Reliable on-chip voltage regulation by adopting a heterogeneous on-chip power delivery network design at both the chip level and network level further reduces the area cost of on-chip voltage regulators. Not only sustainable and compact IoT and heterogeneous computing systems can be realized through reliable on-chip voltage regulation, but also significant area savings can be reaped. As area can be a stringent resource for IoT applications, area savings can be leveraged for enhanced security performance and even added functionality. Increased battery capacity, more number of voltage regulators, and reduced fabrication cost can also be enabled.

5 CONCLUSION

Reliable on-chip voltage regulation is investigated to realize sustainable and compact IoT and heterogeneous computing systems. The characteristics of IoT devices necessitate the embedded application of heterogeneous computing features and on-chip voltage regulation provides an optimal power supply solution for such systems with enhanced security. Transistor aging induced threshold voltage increase can lead to on-chip voltage regulator performance degradations. Aging mitigation techniques for individual voltage regulators as well as thermal-aware on-chip voltage regulation are critical nodes on the road map to reliable on-chip voltage regulation. Heterogeneous voltage regulators tailored for the special needs of different functional blocks of a certain chip and even different portions of the IoT network enable significant area overhead savings, which further translate into enhanced security, improved power delivery performance, and additional functionality.

ACKNOWLEDGMENTS

This work is supported in part by the National Science Foundation CAREER award under Grant CCF-1350451 and by a Cisco Research Award.

REFERENCES

[1] Tosiron Adegbija, Anita Rogacs, Chandrakant Patel, and Ann Gordon-Ross. 2018. Microprocessor optimizations for the Internet of Things: a survey. *IEEE Transactions on Computer-Aided Design of Integrated Circuits and Systems* 37, 1 (Jan. 2018), 7–20. https://doi.org/10.1109/TCAD.2017.2717782

[2] Innocent Agbo, Mottaqiallah Taouil, Daniel Kraak, Said Hamdioui, Halil Kukner, Pieter Weckx, Praveen Raghavan, and Francky Catthoor. 2017. Integral impact of BTI, PVT variation, and workload on SRAM sense amplifier. *IEEE Transactions Very Large Scale Integration (VLSI) Systems* 25, 4 (April 2017), 1444–1454. https://doi.org/10.1109/TVLSI.2016.2643618

[3] Youngkook Ahn, Inho Jeon, and Jeongjin Roh. 2014. A multiphase buck converter with a rotating phase-shedding scheme for efficient light-load control. *IEEE Journal of Solid-State Circuits* 49, 11 (Nov. 2014), 2673–2683. https://doi.org/10.1109/JSSC.2014.2360400

[4] M.A. Alam and S. Mahapatra. 2005. A comprehensive model of PMOS NBTI degradation. *Microelectronics Reliability* 45, 1 (2005), 71 – 81. https://doi.org/10.1016/j.microrel.2004.03.019

[5] Shoukat Ali, Tracy D. Braun, Howard Jay Siegel, and Anthony A. Maciejewski. 2001. Heterogeneous computing. *Encyclopedia of Distributed Computing* Kluwer Academic (2001).

[6] Toke M. Andersen, Florian Krismer, Johann W. Kolar, Thomas Toifl, Christian Menolfi, Lukas Kull, Thomas Morf, Marcel Kossel, Matthias Brandli, and Pier Andrea Francese. 2017. A 10 W on-chip switched capacitor voltage regulator with feedforward regulation capability for granular microprocessor power delivery. *IEEE Transactions Power Electronics* 32, 1 (Jan. 2017), 378–393. https://doi.org/10.1109/TPEL.2016.2530745

[7] Hansraj Bhamra, Jui-Wei Tsai, Yu-Wen Huang, Quan Yuan, Jay V. Shah, and Pedro Irazoqui. 2017. A sub-mm^3 wireless implantable intraocular pressure monitor microsystem. In *International Solid-State Circuits Conference.*

[8] Ganapati Bhat, Yier Jin, Ali K. Unver, and Umit Y. Ogras. 2018. Algorithmic optimization of thermal and power management for heterogeneous mobile platforms. *IEEE Transactions on Very Large Scale Integration (VLSI) Systems* 26, 3 (March 2018), 544–557. https://doi.org/10.1109/TVLSI.2017.2770163

[9] Edward A. Burton, Gerhard Schrom, Fabrice Paillet, Jonathan Douglas, William J. Lambert, Kaladhar Radhakrishnan, and Michael J. Hill. 2014. FIVR-fully integrated voltage regulators on 4th generation Intel core SoCs. In *Proceedings of the IEEE International Applied Power Electronics Conference and Exposition.*

[10] Yu Cao. 2011. *Predictive technology model for robust nanoelectronic design.* Springer.

[11] Tuck-Boon Chan, John Sartori, Puneet Gupta, and Rakesh Kumar. 2011. On the efficacy of NBTI mitigation techniques. In *Proceedings of the Design, Automation and Test in Europe Conference & Exhibition.*

[12] European Editors. 2013. How to interface sensors to the internet of things. (Oct. 2013). Retrieved Feb, 2018 from https://www.digikey.com/en/\articles/techzone/2013/oct/how-to-interface-sensors-to-the-internet-of-things

[13] Jianxin Fang and Sachin S. Sapatnekar. 2013. The impact of BTI variations on timing in digital logic circuits. *IEEE Transactions on Device and Materials Reliability* 13, 1 (Jan. 2013), 277–286. https://doi.org/10.1109/TDMR.2013.2237910

[14] Christopher Gonzalez, Michael Floyd, Eric Fluhr, Phillip Restle, Daniel Dreps, Michael Sperling, Rahul Rao, David Hogenmiller, Christos Vezyrtis, Pierce Chuang, Daniel Lewis, Ricardo Escobar, Vinod Ramadurai, Ryan Kruse, Juergen Pille, Ryan Nett, Pawel Owczarczyk, Joshua Friedrich, Jose Paredes, Timothy Diemoz, Saiful Islam, Donald Plass, and Paul Muench. 2018. The 24-Core POWER9 processor with adaptive clocking, 25-Gb/s accelerator links, and 16-Gb/s PCIe Gen4. *IEEE Journal of Solid-State Circuits* 53, 1 (Jan. 2018), 91–101. https://doi.org/10.1109/JSSC.2017.2748623

[15] Yong-Min Ju, Se-Un Shin, Yeunhee Huh, Sang-Hui Park, Jun-Suk Bang, Ki-Duk Kim, Sung-Won Choi, Ji-Hun Lee, and Gyu-Hyeong Cho. 2017. A hybrid inductor-based flying-capacitor-assisted step-up/step-down DC-DC converter with 96.56% efficiency. In *International Solid-State Circuits Conference.*

[16] Monodeep Kar, Arvind Singh, Sanu Mathew, Anand Rajan, Vivek De, and Saibal Mukhopadhyay. 2017. Improved power-side-channel-attack resistance of an AES-128 core via a security-aware integrated buck voltage regulator. In *International Solid-State Circuits Conference.*

[17] Janko Katic, Saul Rodriguez, and Ana Rusu. 2018. A high-efficiency energy harvesting interface for implanted biofuel cell and thermal harvesters. *IEEE Transactions on Power Electronics* 33, 5 (May 2018), 4125–4134. https://doi.org/10.1109/TPEL.2017.2712668

[18] Ahmed Waheed Khan, Tanya Wanchoo, Gokhan Mumcu, and Selçuk Köse. 2017. Implications of distributed on-chip power delivery on EM side-channel attacks. In *Proceedings of the IEEE International Conference on Computer Design.*

[19] S. Karen Khatamifard, Longfei Wang, Weize Yu, Selçuk Köse, and Ulya R. Karpuzcu. 2017. Thermogater: thermally-aware on-chip voltage regulation. In *Proceedings of the IEEE International Symposium on Computer Architecture (ISCA).*

[20] Selçuk Köse. 2014. Thermal implications of on-chip voltage regulation: upcoming challenges and possible solutions. In *Proceedings of the IEEE/ACM Design Automation Conference (DAC).*

[21] Selçuk Köse. 2017. Efficient and secure on-chip reconfigurable voltage regulation for IoT devices. In *Proceedings of the ACM/IEEE Great Lakes Symposium on VLSI.*

[22] Selçuk Köse and Eby G. Friedman. 2012. Distributed on-chip power delivery. *IEEE Journal on Emerging and Selected Topics in Circuits and Systems* 2, 4 (Dec. 2012), 704–713. https://doi.org/10.1109/JETCAS.2012.2226378

[23] Woojoo Lee, Yanzhi Wang, and Massoud Pedram. 2015. Optimizing a reconfigurable power distribution network in a multicore platform. *IEEE Transactions on Computer-Aided Design of Integrated Circuits and Systems* 34, 7 (July 2015), 1110–1123. https://doi.org/10.1109/TCAD.2015.2396998

[24] Chao-Chieh Li, Min-Shueh Yuan, Chih-Hsien Chang, Yu-Tso Lin, Chia-Chun Liao, Kenny Hsieh, Mark Chen, and Robert Bogdan Staszewski. 2017. A 0.2V trifilar-coil DCO with DC-DC converter in 16nm FinFET CMOS with 188dB FOM, 1.3kHz resolution, and frequency pushing of 38MHz/V for energy harvesting applications. In *International Solid-State Circuits Conference.*

[25] Mohamed Mounir Mahmoud, Norhayati Soin, and Hossam A. H. Fahmy. 2014. Design framework to overcome aging degradation of the 16 nm VLSI technology circuits. *IEEE Transactions on Computer-Aided Design of Integrated Circuits and Systems* 33, 5 (May 2014), 691–703. https://doi.org/10.1109/TCAD.2014.2299713

[26] Sparsh Mittal and Jeffrey S. Vetter. 2015. A survey of CPU-GPI heterogeneous computing techniques. *Journal ACM Computing Surveys (CSUR)* 47, 4 (2015), 1–35. https://doi.org/10.1145/2788396

[27] Phillip Nadeau, Mark Mimee, Sean Carim, Timothy K. Lu, and Anantha P. Chandrakasan. 2017. Nanowatt circuit interface to whole-cell bacterial sensors. In *International Solid-State Circuits Conference.*

[28] Yuichi Nakamura, Hideyuki Shimonishi, Yuki Kobayashi, Kozo Satoda, Yashuhiro Matsunaga, and Dai Kanetomo. 2017. Novel heterogeneous computing platforms and 5G communications for IoT applications. In *Proceedings of the IEEE/ACM International Conference on Computer-Aided Design.*

[29] Arun Paidimarri and Anantha P. Chandrakasan. 2017. A buck converter with 240pW quiescent power, 92% peak efficiency and a 2x10^6 dynamic range. In *International Solid-State Circuits Conference.*

[30] Young-Jun Park, Ju-Hyun Park, Hong-Jin Kim, Hocheol Ryu, SangYun Kim, YoungGun Pu, Keum Cheol Hwang, Youngoo Yang, Minjae Lee, and Kang-Yoon Lee. 2017. A design of a 92.4% efficiency triple mode control DC-DC buck converter with low power retention mode and adaptive zero current detector for IoT/wearable applications. *IEEE Transactions on Power Electronics* 32, 9 (Sept. 2017), 6946–6960. https://doi.org/10.1109/TPEL.2016.2623812

[31] Divya Pathak, Houman Homayoun, and Ioannis Savidis. 2017. Smart grid on chip: work load-balanced on-chip power delivery. *IEEE Transactions Very Large Scale Integration (VLSI) Systems* 25, 9 (Sept. 2017), 2538–2551. https://doi.org/10.1109/TVLSI.2017.2699644

[32] Pradipta Patra, Ramnarayanan Muthukaruppan, and Sumedha Mangal. 2015. A reliable digitally synthesizable linear drop-out regulator design for 14nm SOC. In *Proc. IEEE Symposium on Nanoelectronic and Information Systems (iNIS).*

[33] Rahul. 2016. IoT applications spanning across industries. (Jan. 2016). Retrieved Feb, 2018 from https://www.ibm.com/blogs/internet-of-things/iot-applications-industries/

[34] Sandip Ray, Yier Jin, and Arijit Raychowdhury. 2016. The changing computing paradigm with internet of things: A tutorial introduction. *IEEE Design and Test of Computers* 33, 2 (Feb. 2016), 76–96. https://doi.org/10.1109/MDAT.2016.2526612

[35] Daniele Rossi, Vasileios Tenentes, Sheng Yang, Saqib Khursheed, and Bashir M. Al-Hashimi. 2016. Reliable power gating with NBTI aging benefits. *IEEE Transactions Very Large Scale Integration (VLSI) Systems* 24, 8 (Aug. 2016), 2735–2744. https://doi.org/10.1109/TVLSI.2016.2519385

[36] Zeynep Toprak-Deniz, Michael Sperling, John Bulzacchelli, Gregory Still, Ryan Kruse, Seongwon Kim, David Boerstler, Tilman Gloekler, Raphael Robertazzi, Kevin Stawiasz, Timothy Diemoz, George English, David Hui, Paul Muench, and Joshua Friedrich. 2014. Distributed system of digitally controlled microregulators enabling per-core DVFS for the POWER8^{TM} microprocessor. In *International Solid-State Circuits Conference.*

[37] Orhun Aras Uzun and Selçuk Köse. 2014. Converter-gating: a power efficient and secure on-chip power delivery system. *IEEE Journal on Emerging and Selected Topics in Circuits and Systems* 4, 2 (June 2014), 169–179. https://doi.org/10.1109/JETCAS.2014.2315880

[38] Orhun Aras Uzun and Selçuk Köse. 2014. Regulator-gating methodology with distributed switched capacitor voltage converters. In *IEEE Computer Society Annual Symposium on VLSI.*

[39] Inna P. Vaisband and Eby G. Friedman. 2016. Stability of distributed power delivery systems with multiple parallel on-chip LDO regulators. *IEEE Transactions on Power Electronics* 31, 8 (Aug. 2016), 5625–5634. https://doi.org/10.1109/TPEL.2015.2493512

[40] Inna P. Vaisband, Renatas Jakushokas, Mikhail Popovich, Andrey V. Mezhiba, Selçuk Köse, and Eby G. Friedman. 2016. *On-chip power delivery and management, Fourth Edition.* Springer.

[41] Longfei Wang, S. Karen Khatamifard, Ulya R. Karpuzcu, and Selçuk Köse. 2018. Mitigation of NBTI induced performance degradation in on-chip digital LDOs. In *Proceedings of the Design, Automation and Test in Europe Conference & Exhibition.*

[42] Longfei Wang, S. Karen Khatamifard, Orhun Aras Uzun, Ulya R. Karpuzcu, and Selçuk Köse. 2017. Efficiency, stability, and reliability implications of unbalanced current sharing among distributed on-chip voltage regulators. *IEEE Transactions Very Large Scale Integration (VLSI) Systems* 25, 11 (Nov. 2017), 3019–3022. https://doi.org/10.1109/TVLSI.2017.2742944

[43] Jianfei Wu, Alexandre Boyer, Jiancheng Li, Sonia Ben Dhia, and Rongjun Shen. 2013. Characterization of changes in LDO susceptibility after electrical stress. *IEEE Transactions on Electromagnetic Compatibility* 55, 5 (Oct. 2013), 883–890. https://doi.org/10.1109/TEMC.2013.2242471

[44] Taiyang Wu, Fan Wu, Jean-Michel Redoute, and Mehmet Rasit Yuce. 2017. An autonomous wireless body area network implementation towards IoT connected healthcare applications. *IEEE Access* 5 (June 2017), 11413–11422.

[45] Long Yan, Jerald Yoo, Binhee Kim, and Hoi-Jun Yoo. 2010. A 0.5-uV$_{rms}$ 12-uW wirelessly powered patch-type healthcare sensor for wearable body sensor network. *IEEE Journal of Solid-State Circuits* 45, 11 (Nov. 2010), 2356–2365. https://doi.org/10.1109/JSSC.2010.2065831

[46] Hyunbean Yi, Tomokazu Yoneda, Michiko Inoue, Yasuo Sato, Seiji Kajihara, and Hideo Fujiwara. 2011. A failure prediction strategy for transistor aging. *IEEE Transactions Very Large Scale Integration (VLSI) Systems* 20, 11 (Nov. 2011), 1951–1959. https://doi.org/10.1109/TVLSI.2011.2165304

[47] Kye-Seok Yoon, Sung-Wan Hong, Jun-Suk Bang, Sang-Han Lee, Sung-Won Choi, and Gyu-Hyeong Cho. 2017. A 1452-% power extraction improvement energy harvesting circuit with simultaneous energy extraction from a piezoelectric transducer and a thermoelectric generator. In *2017 Symposium on VLSI Circuits.*

[48] W. Yu and S. Kose. [n. d.]. Exploiting Voltage Regulators to Enhance Various Power Attack Countermeasures. *IEEE Transactions on Emerging Topics in Computing* ([n. d.]), 1. https://doi.org/10.1109/TETC.2016.2620382

[49] Weize Yu and Selçuk Köse. 2015. Time-delayed converter-reshuffling: an efficient and secure power delivery architecture. *IEEE Embedded Systems Letters* 7, 3 (Sept. 2015), 73–76. https://doi.org/10.1109/LES.2015.2433175

[50] Weize Yu and Selçuk Köse. 2016. Charge-withheld converter-reshuffling (CoRe): a countermeasure against power analysis attacks. *IEEE Transactions on Circuits and Systems II: Express Briefs* 63, 5 (May 2016), 438–442. https://doi.org/10.1109/TCSII.2015.2505261

[51] Weize Yu and Selçuk Köse. 2016. A voltage regulator-assisted lightweight AES implementation against DPA attacks. *IEEE Transactions on Circuits and Systems I: Regular Papers* 63, 8 (Aug. 2016), 1152–1163. https://doi.org/10.1109/TCSI.2016.2555810

[52] Weize Yu and Selçuk Köse. 2017. False key-controlled aggressive voltage scaling: a countermeasure against LPA attacks. *IEEE Transactions on Computer-Aided Design of Integrated Circuits and Systems* 36, 12 (Dec. 2017), 2149–2153. https://doi.org/10.1109/TCAD.2017.2682113

[53] Weize Yu and Selçuk Köse. 2017. Security-adaptive voltage conversion as a lightweight countermeasure against LPA attacks. *IEEE Transactions on Very Large Scale Integration (VLSI) Systems* 25, 7 (July 2017), 2183–2187. https://doi.org/10.1109/TVLSI.2017.2670537

[54] Weize Yu, Orhun Aras Uzun, and Selçuk Köse. 2015. Leveraging on-chip voltage regulators as a countermeasure against side-channel attacks. In *Proceedings of the IEEE/ACM Design Automation Conference.*

Low-Energy Architectures of Linear Classifiers for IoT Applications using Incremental Precision and Multi-Level Classification

Sandhya Koteshwara
University of Minnesota, Twin Cities
Minneapolis, MN
kotes001@umn.edu

Keshab K. Parhi
University of Minnesota, Twin Cities
Minneapolis, MN
parhi@umn.edu

ABSTRACT

This paper presents a novel *incremental-precision classification* approach that leads to a reduction in energy consumption of linear classifiers for IoT applications. Features are first input to a low-precision classifier. If the classifier successfully classifies the sample, then the process terminates. Otherwise, the classification performance is incrementally improved by using a classifier of higher precision. This process is repeated until the classification is complete. The argument is that many samples can be classified using the low-precision classifier, leading to a reduction in energy. To achieve incremental-precision, a novel data-path decomposition is proposed to design of *fixed-width* adders and multipliers. These components improve the precision *without* recalculating the outputs, thus reducing energy. Using a linear classification example, it is shown that the proposed incremental-precision based multi-level classifier approach can reduce energy by about 41% while achieving comparable accuracies as that of a full-precision system. [1]

ACM Reference Format:
Sandhya Koteshwara and Keshab K. Parhi. 2018. Low-Energy Architectures of Linear Classifiers for IoT Applications using Incremental Precision and Multi-Level Classification. In *GLSVLSI '18: 2018 Great Lakes Symposium on VLSI, May 23–25, 2018, Chicago, IL, USA.* ACM, New York, NY, USA, 6 pages. https://doi.org/10.1145/3194554.3194603

1 INTRODUCTION

There is a growing trend towards connecting millions of devices to form what is termed as the Internet-of-Things (IoT). Reducing the energy consumption of these IoT devices connected to the network has become critical. Also, there is an increasing need to incorporate machine learning algorithms onto resource-constrained hardware to perform several tasks. Hence, low-energy solutions for IoT machine learning applications have become important. In this paper, we approach classification using bit-width reduction and a multi-level approach. This means that we compute features and perform classification using the lowest possible precision and then improve classification accuracy in a step by step manner based on certain criteria. The argument is that significant amount of data can be classified using the lowest precision components and only the remaining data need to be processed using higher precision components. Thus, overall energy consumption can be reduced.

The paper presents an incremental-precision algorithm for classification termed as *multi-level* classification. To process the data in each stage of the algorithm, we need hardware components which start processing in low precision and then increase precision as needed. This necessitates the design of basic components such as adders and multipliers which can perform the required *incremental-precision* operation. The required adders and multipliers are designed using *fixed width* components based on novel data-path decomposition techniques. Using multi-level classification implemented with incremental-precision components, we demonstrate energy reduction in a linear classification system.

The rest of the paper is divided as follows: Section 2 describes the incremental-precision addition and subtraction units. In Section 3, the incremental-precision multiplier based on approximation is introduced. The multi-level classification algorithm is presented in Section 4. Finally, using a linear classification example, results with respect to both accuracy and energy consumption are presented in Section 5.

2 INCREMENTAL-PRECISION ADDITION AND SUBTRACTION

Consider the sum of two N bit numbers A and B given by $S = A+B$. If we split A and B into their MSB and LSB parts, we obtain the sum in the following format:

$$S = A_{MSB} + 2^{-p}A_{LSB} + B_{MSB} + 2^{-p}B_{LSB}$$

In this equation, p represents the number of bits of the MSB. The sum can now be rewritten as the following:

$$\begin{aligned} S &= (A_{MSB} + B_{MSB}) + 2^{-p}(A_{LSB} + B_{LSB}) \\ &= S_M + 2^{-p}S_L \end{aligned} \quad (1)$$

This is termed as *data-path decomposition* and has been proposed in the context of error-tolerant applications [1].

The hardware architecture of a signed 8-bit incremental-precision adder/subtractor unit decomposed into two 4-bit adders/subtractors is illustrated in Figure 1. The top adder operates on 4 MSB bits of the data and stores it in memory. If a 4-bit output is desired, this output can be read. Instead, if an 8-bit output is desired, the sum of the MSB terms can be read from memory and combined with the output

[1]This research was supported in part by the National Science Foundation under grant number CCF-1749494.

GLSVLSI '18, May 23–25, 2018, Chicago, IL, USA

ACM ISBN 978-1-4503-5724-1/18/05...$15.00
https://doi.org/10.1145/3194554.3194603

from the lower 4-bit adder/subtractor. The combination equations for both addition and subtraction are also presented in Figure 1. Note that the carry information from the lower adder needs to be included in the combination equation. Also since sign bits are considered, appropriate sign extensions are required for subtraction operation. The decomposition can be extended further on the upper or lower adder to create various combinations of incremental precision adders with precision 2-bit/4-bit/6-bit/8-bit. The decomposition of adder/subtraction units and combining the outputs of different precisions leads to an error-free result. However, this is not the case for computing multiplication using incremental-precision, as discussed in next section.

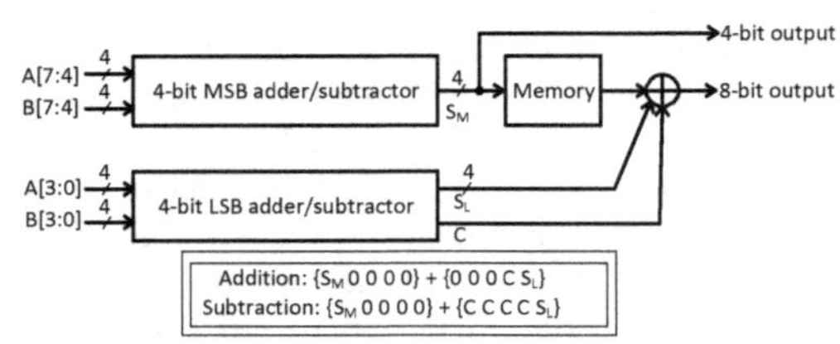

Figure 1: Decomposition and subsequent combination operations on 8-bit inputs to create incremental-precision adder/subtraction unit. The 8-bit inputs are decomposed into two 4-bit inputs in this example.

3 INCREMENTAL-PRECISION FIXED-WIDTH MULTIPLIERS

Consider the multiplication of two inputs x and y. Data-path decomposition can be applied on the multiplication operation of these two inputs as given by Equation (2).

$$P = x \times y = x_{MSB}\ y + 2^{-p}\ x_{LSB}\ y \tag{2}$$

x_{LSB} can be further decomposed to produce multiplication in the form of Equation (3), where p' is the number of bits in x_{LSB1}.

$$P = x_{MSB}\ y + 2^{-p}\ x_{LSB1}\ y + 2^{-(p+p')}\ x_{LSB2}\ y \tag{3}$$

This process can be continued on the LSB bits to produce a decomposed multiplier whose precision improves with every stage. The data flow of the decomposed multiplier is presented in Figure 2. To implement the products in this decomposition, fixed-width multipliers are required. Several approaches to implementation of fixed-width multipliers have been presented in the literature. Among them, the approach proposed in [2] is a technique which results in low-error implementations of fixed-width multipliers. This technique is described in detail in the next subsection. The following subsections discuss the modifications required to convert these fixed-width multipliers to *incremental-precision* fixed-width multipliers using certain approximations.

3.1 Fixed-width multipliers

Consider multiplication of two inputs x and y of length W bits. The resultant output after multiplication is a value P which is of width $2W - 1$ bits. To perform multiplication, the coefficient y is first recoded into y' bits using Booth recoding techniques. This results

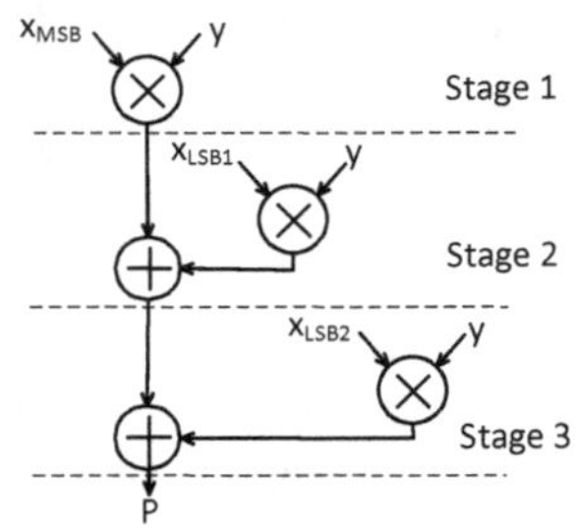

Figure 2: Data-path decomposition of multiplier into multiple stages by incrementally increasing the precision of x and maintaining y at a constant precision.

in less number of partial products that need to be finally summed to generate the terms of the product. The fixed-width multiplier based on Booth recoding is illustrated in Figure 3.

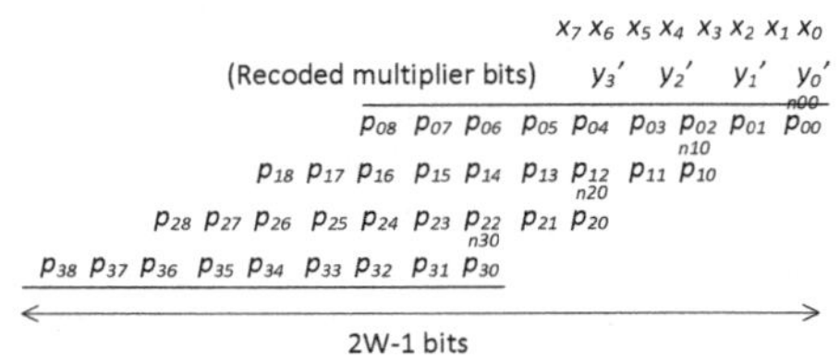

Figure 3: Multiplication of two 8-bit inputs by applying Booth recoding on the input y. The resultant output is of length $2W - 1$ bits.

For a fixed-width multiplier, we constrain the number of terms in the final output to be of length W bits. If direct truncation is used, the resultant outputs produced will have high error. Hence, appropriate rounding needs to be performed and this idea is illustrated in Figure 4. In this figure, the final output is presented as three terms: MP, LP_major and LP_minor which represent the most significant part, the major part of the least significant part, and the minor part of the least significant part, respectively. The MP part needs to be computed precisely. This means that all the partial products required for this part need to be generated. The rest of the output can be approximated using an actual carry and approximate carry value whose details are discussed next. The final carry is termed as *error compensation bias*.

3.2 Approximate carry generation

The partial products of LP_major need to be computed precisely. For the terms of the LP_minor, statistical analysis can be used to derive an approximate carry value. Consider Table 1 which lists partial products for all possible combinations of recoding (represented by three adjacent bits of y) and combinations of adjacent x inputs. It can be seen that when the recoded value is greater than or equal to 1 (represented by $y'' = 1$), the expected value of partial products is $E[p_{i,j}] = 1/2$. Considering Figure 4, we see that the contribution of each y'' bit on the expected value of LP_minor is 2^{-1}. Thus, the

Table 1: Table of partial products and the expected values of partial products for every combination of recoded bits y' and input $x_j x_{j-1}$

					Partial products with $x_j x_{j-1}$ $(p_{i,j})$				Expected value $(E[p_{i,j}])$
y_{2i+1}	y_{2i}	y_{2i-1}	y'	y''	00	01	10	11	
0	0	0	0	0	0	0	0	0	0
0	0	1	1	1	0	0	1	1	1/2
0	1	0	1	1	0	0	1	1	1/2
0	1	1	2	1	0	1	0	1	1/2
1	0	0	-2	1	1	0	1	0	1/2
1	0	1	-1	1	1	1	0	0	1/2
1	1	0	-1	1	1	1	0	0	1/2
1	1	1	0	0	0	0	0	0	0

total expected value of LP_minor is given by :

$$E[LP\_minor] = 2^{-1}[y_0'' + y_1'' + y_2''] \tag{4}$$

The carry signals are generated depending on the values of y_0''

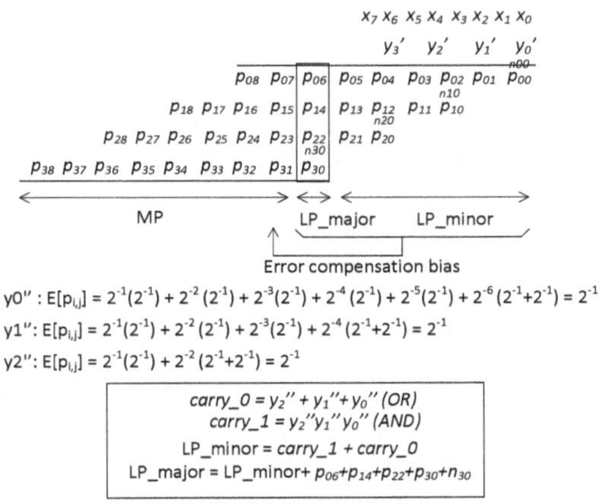

Figure 4: Calculation of the error compensation bias terms *LP_major* and *LP_minor* based on carry signals.

to y_2''. The maximum value of carry in this case occurs when all values of y_0'', y_1'' an y_2'' are equal to 1. This is equal to a value of $E[LP\_minor] = 1.5$ which can be rounded to a value of 2. Note that y_3'' does not contribute to the approximate carry value. For an expected value of 2, the number of carry signals required is 2. Solving for all values of y_0'' to y_2'' using Karnaugh maps, we obtain the required equations for the carry signals as shown in Figure 4.

3.3 Two-stage incremental-precision multipliers

From Equation (2), we require the computation of two products: $x_{MSB} \times y$ and $x_{LSB} \times y$. Observe that the coefficient y is of the same width while x is split into MSB and LSB parts. Hence, the previous example of 8×8 bit multiplication requires the decomposition of 8-bit operand x into two parts and the multiplication result is approximated. This can be achieved by separating the partial products and redesigning the carry generation circuit as illustrated in Figure 5. The top part of the figure presents the approximate multiplier

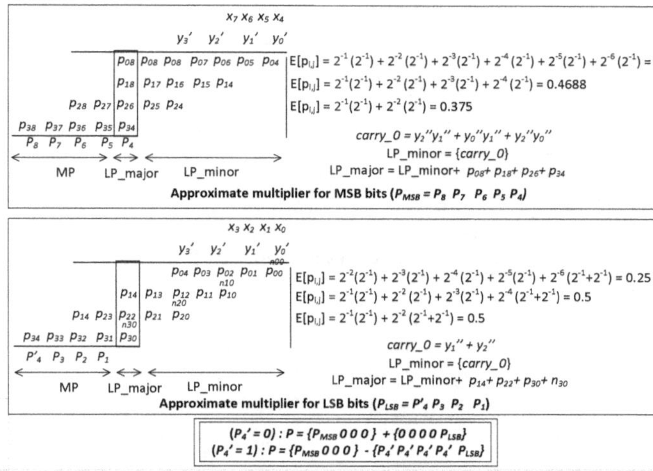

Figure 5: Splitting the 8-bit multiplier into two approximate multipliers of 4 bits each.

required for computation of the MSB bits. Note that the sign bit n_{t0}, where t denotes the row of the partial product, is not present in any of the partial product arrays. However, partial products p_{t8} is required in the calculations. The carry signal is also modified and reduced to just one compared to the 8-bit fixed-width multiplier presented in Figure 4.

The bottom part of the figure presents the approximate multiplier required for computation of LSB bits. In this case, the additional partial products (p_{t8}) are not present. However, the sign bit n_{t0} is processed by the bottom part. This requires the calculation of different carry signals. Note again that only one carry signal is required for this multiplier compared to two in the full precision fixed-width multiplier. The two data-paths can now operate *independently* of each other and produce approximate multiplication outputs. The combination of the two products is illustrated in Figure 5. The precision of the 4-bit multiplier operating on the MSB bits is improved by combining the product generated by operating on the LSB bits. The final output obtained through this combination will be an approximation of the full 8-bit precision fixed width output. This is because of the loss of precision during approximation of the products. Approximation is inherently introduced by the fixed-width multipliers as well as the incremental-precision architectures. It may be noted that approximations have been used in other contexts [3–5].

3.4 Multi-stage incremental-precision multipliers

The approximate multiplier required to compute the LSB bits can be further split into two as given by Equation (3). This idea is illustrated in Figure 6. The difference between the two multipliers is that the top multiplier does not account for the sign bit n_{t0} (similar to the multiplier operating on MSB bits). The final output is a combination of the product from MSB bits overlapped with the product from the middle multiplier operating on the first two LSB bits and the last multiplier operating on the last two LSB bits. With each step, precision is improved.

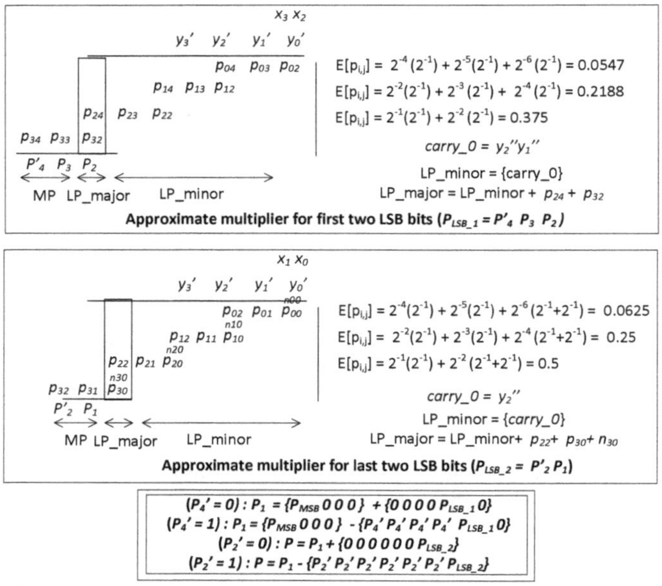

Figure 6: Splitting the LSB 4-bit multiplier into two approximate multipliers of 2 bits each.

We combine the three multipliers to produce a multi-stage incremental precision multiplier. Note that in the case of splitting an 8-bit multiplier into three stages of 4-bit, 2-bits and 2-bits, stage 2 and stage 3 of 2-bit multiplication can be performed using the same multiplier in a time-multiplexed or folded manner [6]. This idea is illustrated in Figure 7. The incremental-precision multiplier structure also requires a memory unit. The computation of intermediate stages are stored in memory.

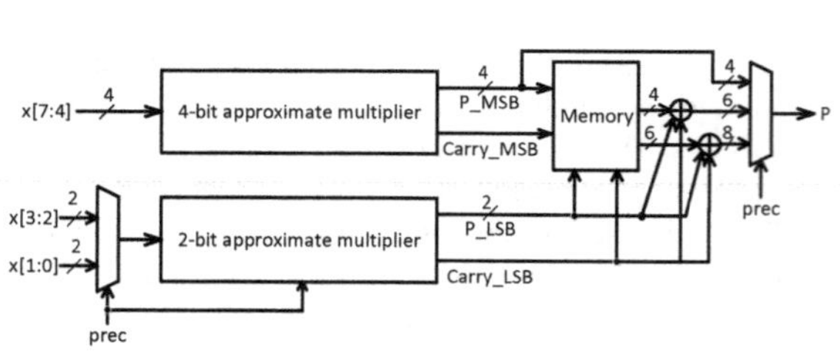

Figure 7: Incremental-precision 8-bit multiplier using one 4-bit multiplier and one time-multiplexed 2-bit multiplier. Intermediate outputs are stored in memory.

For example, if only a 4-bit precision output is demanded by the application, the MSB multiplier functions to generate a 4-bit output. The output along with a carry bit are stored in memory. If the application now demands a 6-bit output, the LSB multiplier is functional (with sign bit set to 0) and the memory unit is accessed to retrieve the MSB outputs. The combination of the two outputs is generated as the 6-bit output and also stored in memory along with the carry generated from the second stage. This process continues to provide incrementally higher precision outputs.

4 MULTI-LEVEL CLASSIFICATION ALGORITHM

The incremental-precision components described in this paper can be utilized in a multi-level classification setup where each stage of the classification is based on different precision levels for feature computation as well as classification. In this section, we describe a general multi-level algorithm with a specific example presented in later sections. The basic steps of the algorithm are illustrated in Figure 8.

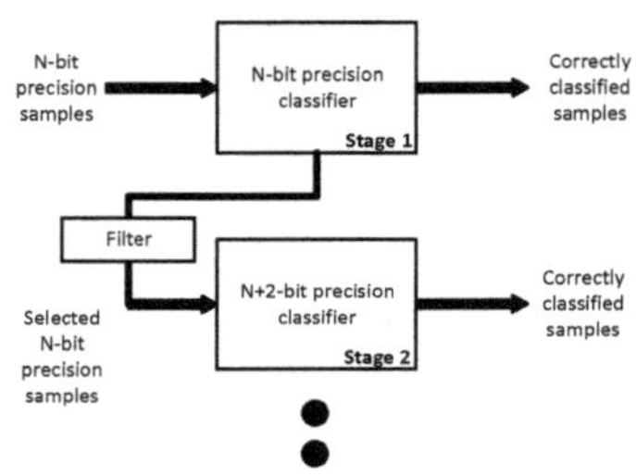

Figure 8: Steps of the multi-level classification algorithm with increasing precision classifier at each stage.

Training algorithm:

- Start with a low-precision classifier which operates at a precision of N-bits. Samples which are far away from the classification boundary can be easily classified with this classifier.
- Determine a *threshold* to filter out samples which need to be retrained in higher precision. This threshold could be selected based a distance metric which indicates the distance from the classification boundary.
- Using the determined threshold, select samples to be reclassified in the next higher precision of $N + l$-bits. Here l is the increment in precision between stages.
- This process can be continued till no further improvement in classification accuracy is obtained or for a predetermined number of steps.

Testing algorithm:

- For each test sample, use the first classifier of N-bit precision and obtain a distance metric or probability measure.
- Use the threshold determined in training process to select the samples which need to be reclassified.
- For the test samples which are reselected apply the next $N + l$-bit precision classifier.
- Continue till all stages of classifiers are applied or till no test sample is reselected.

We assume that training occurs offline and the testing/inference algorithm is implemented on hardware. For the first step of testing, a low-precision (N-bit) classifier is used. This implies that all computation can be carried out using the top-level of the decomposed hardware (Figure 1 and Figure 7). If a sample is reselected to be classified at the next level, the bottom level of the decomposed hardware is used to increment the precision of the classification output. Note that it is not necessary to recompute the first N bits of the classification output. Since most of the samples can be classified using low-precision (N-bit) classifiers, the increment operation is utilized as needed. This leads to significant savings in energy consumption.

5 EXPERIMENTAL RESULTS

In this section we discuss a binary classification problem based on linear classifiers. Note that even though this is a simple example, the operations involved (namely multiplication with weights and addition of bias) are also fundamental to most machine learning algorithms such as logistic regression, linear Support Vector Machines (SVM), perceptron *etc.* Hence, the techniques in this paper can be applied to these algorithms as well after necessary extensions.

5.1 Multi-level linear classification

This example considers classification between samples of the Fisher's Iris data set [7]. Two classes of data belonging to two species are picked from this set. There are 50 samples in each category which are randomly divided into training and test data. 60% of the samples form the training set while 40% of the samples are considered for testing. For simplicity, only two features out of the four available features are considered. A linear classifier attempts to train weights to fit a straight line that separates the data. The classification problem can then be defined as the following:

$$sign(w_1x_1 + w_2x_2 + w_0) > 0 \implies Class = 1 \quad (5)$$

In this equation, the features are represented as x_1 and x_2 while the weights are represented as w_0, w_1 and w_2. We observe that while the training process involves calculation of weights, the testing process involves multiplication and addition operations. Hence, we incorporate the incremental-precision components in this classification system.

Consider the multi-level classification algorithm described in the previous section with a starting precision $N = 2$ bits and an increment $I = 2$ bits. The plots of the data with the separating line in different precisions are presented in Figure 9. Note that this figure also presents a margin above and below the separating line which represents the *threshold* calculated in the training process. All samples lying beyond this threshold need not be retrained. The calculation of the threshold value is obtained after computing the value $w_1x_1 + w_2x_2 + w_0$ for each sample and setting the threshold equal to the average of the magnitudes of the computed value for all training samples. Note that other techniques for threshold calculations can be used with associated trade-offs.

5.2 Accuracy of classification

The results of training using a full-precision (8-bit) classifier and the multi-level classification algorithm are presented in Table 2. The table also provides the number of samples reselected at each stage. For the multi-level classification algorithm, the class labels for the samples selected at each stage are replaced with new class labels and the classification accuracy for the entire training set is calculated. We observe that the classification accuracy improves with each stage and the number of samples reselected at each step also reduces.

Using the generated classifier models and the calculated thresholds from the training process, we generate the test accuracy at each stage of the algorithm. The test accuracy measures along with the number of reselected samples are also presented in Table 2. Stage-4 does not provide any improvement in accuracy and hence the algorithm can be stopped after 3 stages. These results are obtained using an assumption that the components used to implement the testing algorithm provide accurate precision values. In the next section we provide practical implementation results along with the reduction in energy consumption after employing incremental-precision components in hardware.

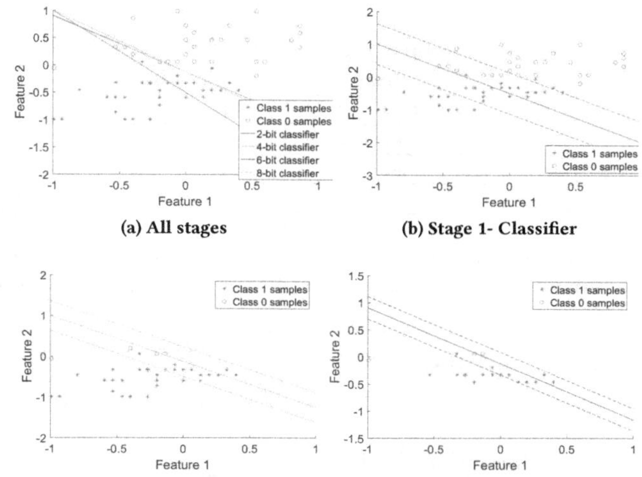

(a) All stages (b) Stage 1- Classifier (c) Stage-2 Classifier (d) Stage-3 Classifier

Figure 9: Classification of samples using multi-level classification algorithm.

Table 2: Accuracy of classification for the training and testing process using full-precision single stage and incremental-precision multi-level classifier

Classifier	Training accuracy	Samples trained	Testing accuracy	Samples tested
Full-prec (8-bit)	93.33%	100%	95%	100%
Stage 1 (2-bit)	50 %	100%	50%	100%
Stage 2 (4-bit)	93.33%	56.67%	90%	77.50%
Stage 3 (6-bit)	95%	31.67%	95%	20%
Stage 4 (8-bit)	95%	21.67%	95%	12.5%

5.3 Test accuracy and reduction in energy using incremental-precision components

The classifier using both single stage and multi-level algorithm is implemented in Verilog Hardware Description Language and synthesized using Design Compiler with a 65 nm technology library.

Table 3: Accuracy of the classifier based on implementations of the full-precision and multi-level algorithms

Classifier implemented in hardware	With original thresholds		After recalculation of thresholds	
	Testing accuracy	Samples tested	Testing accuracy	Samples tested
Full-precision (8-bit)	92.5%	100%	92.5%	100%
Stage-1 (2-bit)	37.5%	100%	37.5%	100%
Stage-2 (4-bit)	72.5%	72.5%	85%	100%
Stage-3 (6-bit)	77.50%	17.5%	92.5%	35%

Table 4: Area, Power, Timing and Energy consumption per test sample for the single stage full-precision and multi-level incremental precision algorithms (Numbers in paranthesis indicate values after recalculation of threshold)

Classifier	Without time-multiplexing				With time-multiplexing			
	Area (um^2)	Total Power (mW)	Total time (ns)	Energy per test sample (pJ)	Area (um^2)	Total Power (uW)	Total Time (ns)	Energy per test sample (pJ)
Full-precision (8-bit)	1123	1.480	167	0.155	1123	1.48	167	0.155
Stage-1 (2-bit)	-	0.284 (0.284)	181 (181)	-	-	0.284 (0.284)	181 (181)	-
Stage-2 (4-bit)	-	0.234 (0.323)	150 (207)	-	-	0.249 (0.344)	151 (209)	-
Stage-3 (6-bit)	-	0.071 (0.143)	25 (50)	-	-	0.073 (0.145)	26 (53)	-
Incremental-precision	987	0.589 (0.75)	356 (438)	0.068 (0.086)	867	0.606 (0.773)	358 (443)	0.072 (0.091)

All implementations are clocked at a frequency of 100 MHz and performance is measured in terms of area, power and time required for testing all samples as well as the energy required per sample.

The testing accuracy obtained is reported in Table 3. Note that with a full-precision system, an accuracy of 92.5% can be obtained. This is lower than the value obtained through simulation and can be attributed to errors in the multiplication hardware. For the incremental-precision system, we observe that using the original thresholds calculated through simulation, high test accuracies cannot be obtained. This is due to lack of accounting for the additional approximation of the incremental-precision components. After recalculation of the thresholds, the incremental-precision system is able to achieve the same accuracy as that of the fixed-width full-precision classification system.

Performance measures as well as resource consumption after synthesis are presented in Table 4. While the area consumption is not dependent on the number of samples processed at each step, the power consumption and timing requirements are presented based on the number of samples processed. We present the energy consumption per sample after summing the energy requirements for each stage (obtained as a product of the power and timing requirement) and then dividing by the total number of test samples. Implementations both with time-multiplexing of the lower stage and without time-multiplexing are discussed. For each implementation, the values before and after recalculation of thresholds are also presented.

We observe that the energy consumption for the incremental-precision system with the original thresholds is reduced by about 56% compared to the full-precision system. After recalculation of thresholds, the energy reduction is about 45%. With the multiplexed hardware, these values correspond to 53% and 41%, respectively. While the implementation without multiplexing reduces the area of the incremental-precision system by 12%, multiplexing further reduces the area consumption by 22%. The improvements in energy and area consumption are achieved at an expense of increase in the time to process. This is because of the overheads associated with comparison and combination. This timing overhead can be reduced by use of pipelining techniques such that multiple samples can be processed in parallel [6].

6 CONCLUSIONS

This paper presents a novel multi-level classification algorithm and corresponding incremental-precision adders and multipliers that can be used to implement it. Note that the incremental-precision idea is not limited to the classifiers and can be applied to the features as well. Also, the proposed algorithms and architectures are not limited to linear classification and can be used in several machine algorithms with more sophisticated classifiers. The corresponding error-energy trade-off needs to be carefully considered.

REFERENCES

[1] Sai Zhang and Naresh R Shanbhag. 2016. Embedded Algorithmic Noise-Tolerance for Signal Processing and Machine Learning Systems via Data Path Decomposition. *IEEE Transactions on Signal Processing* 64, 13 (2016), 3338–3350.

[2] Kyung-Ju Cho, Kwang-Chul Lee, Jin-Gyun Chung, and Keshab K Parhi. 2004. Design of low-error fixed-width modified booth multiplier. *IEEE Transactions on Very Large Scale Integration (VLSI) Systems* 12, 5 (2004), 522–531.

[3] S Hamid Nawab, Alan V Oppenheim, Anantha P Chandrakasan, Joseph M Winograd, and Jeffrey T Ludwig. 1997. Approximate signal processing. *Journal of VLSI signal processing systems for signal, image and video technology* 15, 1-2 (1997), 177–200.

[4] Jongsun Park, Jung Hwan Choi, and Kaushik Roy. 2010. Dynamic bit-width adaptation in DCT: an approach to trade off image quality and computation energy. *IEEE transactions on very large scale integration (VLSI) systems* 18, 5 (2010), 787–793.

[5] Charbel Sakr, Ameya Patil, Sai Zhang, Yongjune Kim, and Naresh Shanbhag. 2016. Understanding the Energy and Precision Requirements for Online Learning. *arXiv preprint arXiv:1607.00669* (2016).

[6] Keshab K Parhi. 1999. *VLSI digital signal processing systems: design and implementation.* Wiley, New York.

[7] Ronald A Fisher. 1936. The use of multiple measurements in taxonomic problems. *Annals of human genetics* 7, 2 (1936), 179–188.

Towards A Universal Power Manager for Multi-Source Energy Scavenging and Storage

Sudip K. Mazumder, *Fellow*, IEEE
University of Illinois, Chicago
851 S. Morgan St, Chicago, IL: 60607
Phone: (312) 355-1315, Fax: (312) 996-6465
E-mail: mazumder@uic.edu

ABSTRACT

Power efficiency of multi-source integrated energy harvesting (EH), storage, and delivery is a fundamental requirement of emerging energy autonomous internet-of-thing (IoT) and internet-of-everything (IoE) devices. To make these energy autonomous devices practical, an enhanced, *universal* power management integrated circuit (PMIC) needs to be developed for efficiently controlling power on-chip. Currently, there exists no universal power manager (UPM) that seamlessly interfaces to DC and/or AC EH sources. The state of the art viable PMICs delivered by industry rely primarily on the following approach: for an unregulated DC source a DC/DC power manager is adopted whereas for an AC source, a front-end rectifier is inserted. This reduces efficiency and enhances distortion, requiring additional filtering.

KEYWORDS

Differential mode, power management, universal power manager, multi-source energy harvesting, energy storage

ACM Reference Format:

Sudip K. Mazumder. 2018. Towards A Universal Power Manager for Multi-Source Energy Scavenging and Storage. In *GLSVLSI '18: 2018 Great Lakes Symposium on VLSI*, May 23–25, 2018, Chicago, IL, USA. ACM, NY, NY, USA, 2 pages. https://doi.org/10.1145/3194554.3194604

1 INTRODUCTION

We outline what follows author's 2016-patented [1] topological differential-mode power manager that circumvents that need by seamlessly interfacing to DC and AC sources (see Figure 1). One experimental preliminary embodiment is show in Figure 2 [2]. Note that Q_{a1} (Q'_{a1}) and Q_{a2} (Q'_{a2}) operate complementarily. If input power drops then the energy storage cap is connected right to the load using a simple bypass switch (not shown).

GLSVLSI '18, May 23–25, 2018, Chicago, IL, USA

ACM ISBN 978-1-4503-5724-1/18/05...$15.00
https://doi.org/10.1145/3194554.3194604

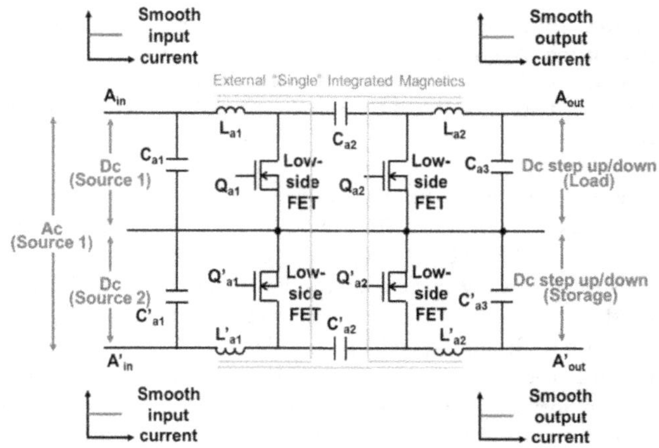

Figure 1: Schematic of the UPM using single integrated magnetics (that can be placed externally to a PMIC). If AC source is not available, then the number of FETs is reduced by 50% by replacing FETs Q_{a2} and Q'_{a2} with diodes. If additional DC sources are needed UPM DC stage can be duplicated without increasing the magnetics count. Similarly, a single additional module (comprising 3 caps and 2 FETs) is needed for each additional AC source phase. Note that Q_{a1} (Q'_{a1}) and Q_{a2} (Q'_{a2}) operate complementarily. If input power fails or drops then the energy storage cap is connected right to the load using a simple bypass switch (not shown).

Equally important, the new power manager yields continuous current at both the source and load ends, significantly reducing electromagnetic-interference (EMI) filtering requirements as needed in boost or buck converters. Yet another feature of the UPM, which only comprises low-side devices thereby simplifying driver complexity and reducing cost, is its ability to integrate single or plurality of sources without using additional switches in series with each source. As a result, the UPM exhibits reduced conduction loss and electronic complexity, and increased reliability.

Figure 2: A high power *discrete* UPM-type experimental prototype. A goal in near future is to synthesize a PMIC realization following the UPM concept at a very low power and voltage at higher power density, with/without magnetics.

Efficient control of the energy budget in UPM PMIC will be maintained in real-time with a radically-new switching-sequence based controller (SBC) [3][4] (see Figure 3). The PMIC will be capable of sensing current at the loads and dynamically scale UPM output voltages within an integrated control loop and based on application specific power objectives. For fast, safe, and power efficient control, the UPM PMIC will employ adaptive bias and compensation mechanisms, hysteresis techniques, and an asynchronous arbitration of harvested power from hybrid (AC and DC) sources. Unlike the state-of-the art PMICs that require a start-up circuitry, start-up sequence will be designed as part of the SBC switching sequences, precluding the need for any soft start.

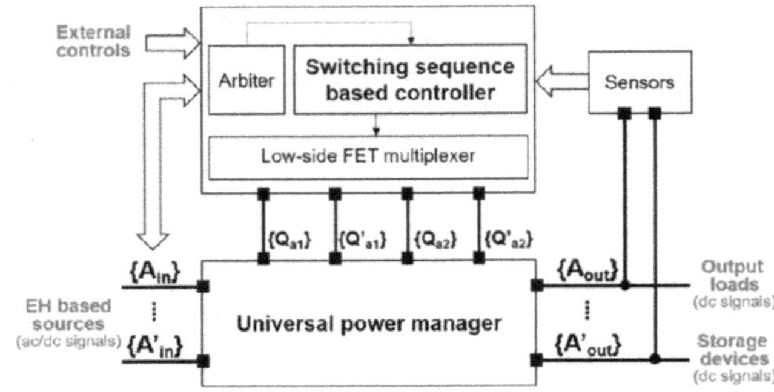

Figure 3. Block diagram of the proposed UPM PMIC. Power from multiple harvesting AC and DC sources is regulated with an SBC-managed UPM and delivered to multiple output loads and storage devices.

The SBC controlled UPM provides a scalable platform for co-designing power control techniques for distributed voltage regulation, grid control, and switching loss mitigation. To address the challenges of hybrid multi-source energy harvesting, existing power optimization techniques (*e.g.*, maximum power point tracking and synchronous electric charge extraction) will be co-designed on an application specific basis. Thus, in the proposed UPM PMIC, power harvesting, system-wide power efficiency, and quality of power will be jointly optimized in real-time.

REFERENCES

[1] S.K. Mazumder, "Scalable single-stage differential power converter," USPTO Patent# 9379640, awarded on June 28, 2016.

[2] S. Mehrnami and S.K. Mazumder, "Discontinuous modulation scheme for a differential-mode Cuk inverter," *IEEE Transactions on Power Electronics*, vol. 30, no. 3, pp. 1242-1254, 2014.

[3] S.K. Mazumder and T. Geyer, "Next generation time-domain control of power electronics systems using predictive switching sequences," Invited Tutorial, *IEEE Energy Conversion Congress and Exposition*, 2015.

[4] A. Tajfar and S.K. Mazumder, "Sequence-based control of an isolated dc/ac matrix inverter," *IEEE Transactions on Power Electronics*, vol. 31, no. 2, pp. 1757-1773, 2016.

Efficient Wireless Power Transfer for Heterogeneous Adaptive IoT Systems

Inna Partin-Vaisband, *Member, IEEE*
University of Illinois at Chicago
vaisband@uic.edu

ABSTRACT

To support the demand for energy autonomy, many of the future IoT edge devices will be powered from non-conventional, energy harvesting and wireless power sources. While convenient, sustainable, and robust, wireless power transfer (WPT) exhibits limited efficiency compared with the traditional wired power approaches, presenting a primary design challenge for practical IoT systems. Non-radiative mid-range WPT from a single power source to several power loads and from several power sources to a single power load has recently been experimentally demonstrated. Alternatively, WPT among multiple, simultaneously transmitting and receiving devices is a primary concern in future IoT systems with numerous interconnected heterogeneous objects. Furthermore, the dynamic nature of certain distributed IoT systems has a significant effect on WPT interactions among the numerous, mobile in space power devices. WPT that exploits the lossless characteristics of strong-coupled resonant regime is explored in this work as a method for efficiently transferring power among multiple, dynamically connected and disconnected IoT end devices. The efficiency of the power transfer is investigated in dense and sparse IoT systems in terms of the number of IoT devices located within limited space. Based on the results of this work, interactions among wirelessly powered devices have significant effect on the power transfer. Efficiency of power transfer increases with increasing transmitter-receiver coupling. Alternatively, densely clustered power transmitters or receivers may degrade the system-wide power transfer and efficiency. Intuition behind systematically optimized utilization of the WPT-based energy budget in future IoT systems is also provided.

KEYWORDS

Wireless power transfer, MIMO WPT, resonant coupling, IoT, adaptive power management, power efficiency, load power

ACM Reference Format:
Inna Partin-Vaisband, *Member, IEEE*. 2018. Efficient Wireless Power Transfer for Heterogeneous Adaptive IoT Systems. In *GLSVLSI '18: 2018 Great Lakes Symposium on VLSI, May 23–25, 2018, Chicago, IL, USA.* ACM, New York, NY, USA, 6 pages. https://doi.org/10.1145/3194554.3194605

GLSVLSI'18, May 23–25, 2018, Chicago, IL, USA
© 2018 Association for Computing Machinery.
ACM ISBN 978-1-4503-5724-1/18/05...$15.00
https://doi.org/10.1145/3194554.3194605

1 INTRODUCTION

Efficiently and securely managing high quality power is a primary challenge in Internet of Things (IoT) systems. Based on current projections, future IoT will provide vast interconnectedness with up to trillions of embedded devices and sensors, many of which will be powered up wirelessly from spatially distributed power supplies or locally from energy harvesting (EH) sources [2]. The energy budget, constrained by inherently lower efficiency of these non-traditional power sources, will become a critical system resource and a primary limiting factor for scalability of future IoT systems.

Recently, strong-coupled resonant circuits have been fabricated for efficient mid-range wireless power transfer (WPT) of up to several meters and a few times the characteristic sizes of the resonators [6]. Based on these WPT systems, energy can be efficiently transmitted from a single power source (input) to a single load device (output) placed at mid-range or longer distances from the source [4, 5, 7, 9]. WPT from a single power source to multiple power loads and from multiple power loads to a single power source has also been demonstrated [1, 3, 8]. The power efficiency of these single-input-multiple-output (SIMO) and multiple-input-single-output (MISO) systems has been shown to increase with number of WPT devices.

While practically novel, the WPT is very well timed with the advances in integration technology and scaling of power design constraints in high performance ICs. With the introduction of three-dimensional (3-D) integrated circuits (ICs) and advances in 3-D enabling technologies, a natural platform for efficient integration of heterogeneous IoT devices has emerged [10, 11]. These modern integration capabilities and continuous advances in wireless power technology are expected to enable efficient WPT in next generation IoT systems. Alternatively, the dynamic nature of distributed IoT systems has a significant effect on WPT interactions among the numerous, mobile in space power devices. To systematically optimize the utilization of the WPT based energy budget in future IoT systems, enhanced understanding of distributed WPT in multiple-input-multiple-output (MIMO) systems as a function of number, density, and physical characteristics (e.g., resonant frequency and spatial mobility) of IoT devices is required.

Distributed MIMO WPT is explored in this paper. A heterogeneous MIMO WPT-based IoT system is illustrated in Figure 1. The efficiency of the power transfer is investigated in dense and sparse IoT systems in terms of the number of IoT devices located within limited space. Based on the results of this work, interactions among wirelessly powered densely clustered devices have significant effect on the power transfer, degrading the overall power efficiency in dense IoT systems with increasing number of devices. To compensate for the adverse interactions among the individual transmitters

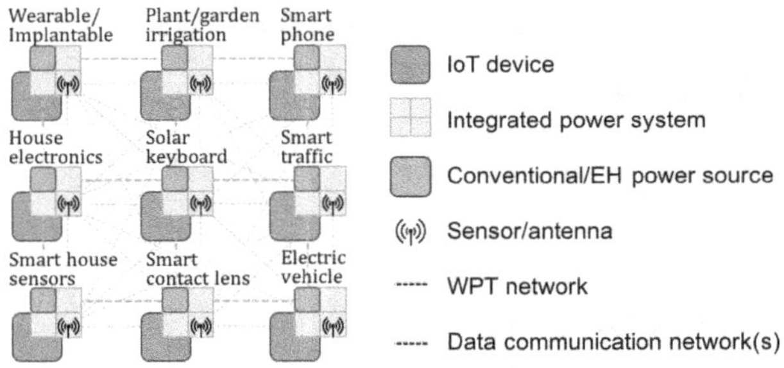

Figure 1: IoT system with distributed wireless power transfer.

and among the individual receivers, resonant frequency of system components should be adjusted at the expense of additional power consumption. The tradeoff among the system-wide efficiency, power load, adjustment power losses, and system size are described in this paper and a FOM is proposed for determining the preferred number of wirelessly connected devices.

The rest of the paper is organized as follows. Background on mid-range wireless power transfer is presented in Section 2. A multi-source multi-load WPT model and analytic expressions for the wireless power efficiency are described in Section 3. Concluding remarks are provided in the final section of the paper.

2 BACKGROUND

Transmission of radiative energy over large distances is possible by the means of electromagnetic (EM) wave propagation [w. 4,9,14]. To optimally utilize the transmitted energy, complex pointing, tracking, and reflection mechanisms are required that enhance the efficiency of the power transfer for long distances. Alternatively, non-radiative WPT has recently been proposed that exploits the lossless characteristics of strong-coupled resonant regime to efficiently transmit energy over a range of several meters [6]. A typical coupled resonator system is presented in Figure 2, comprising a sinusoidal power source with amplitude V_s and input resistance R_S, energy transmitter with R_{TX}, L_{TX}, C_{TX}, energy receiver with R_{RX}, L_{RX}, C_{RX}, and AC current load R_L . The WPT efficiency is a function of the system coupling (increases with L_{TX}, L_{RX}) and losses (increases with R_{TX}, R_{RX}) and is evaluated here based on strong-coupling parameter, U — the ratio between the rate of transferred and dissipated energy,

$$U = \omega k \sqrt{\frac{L_{TX} L_{RX}}{R_{TX} R_{RX}}} = \omega \frac{M}{\sqrt{R_{TX} R_{RX}}}, \tag{1}$$

where M is the mutual inductance and k is the magnetic coupling coefficient [Mur-Miranda],

$$k \approx \frac{1}{2} \left(\frac{r_{TX} r_{RX}}{d^2} \right)^{3/2}, \tag{2}$$

where r_{TX} and r_{RX} are the effective radii of, respectively, the source and load resonating coals, and d is the physical distance between the devices.

To enhance the efficiency of the power transfer in the SISO scheme, depicted in Figure 2, the power supply and the load are designed with the same resonant frequency, $\omega_0 = \omega_{TX} = \omega_{RX}$,

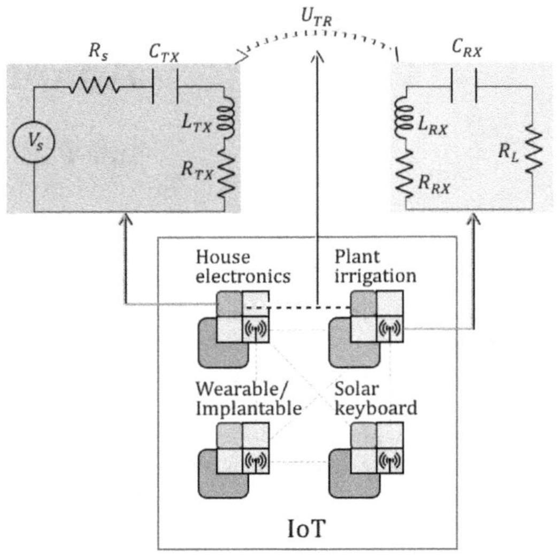

Figure 2: Power supply and load coupled within a resonator system.

and system parameters R_{TX}, L_{TX}, R_{RX}, and L_{RX}, are designed to meet the following design constraint [cite witricity],

$$\omega_0 = 1/\sqrt{L_{TX} C_{TX}} = 1/\sqrt{L_{RX} C_{RX}}, \tag{3}$$

$$\left(\frac{R_S}{R_{TX}} \right)^2 = \left(\frac{R_L}{R_{RX}} \right)^2 = 1 + U^2. \tag{4}$$

Efficiency of power transfer under the design constraint (4) is maximized, yielding

$$\rho_{WPT}^{opt} = \left(\frac{P_L}{P_s} \right)_{\max} = \frac{U^2}{\left(1 + \sqrt{1 + U^2}\right)^2} \xrightarrow[U>>1]{} 1. \tag{5}$$

Note that the maximum efficiency of a SISO WPT system increases with the strong-coupling parameter, U ($\partial \rho_{WPT}^{opt} / \partial U > 0$) and increases with higher frequency, larger inductive resonators, lower radiative losses (see equation (1)), and shorter distance (see equation (2)), approaching 100% WPT efficiency when system loss $\sqrt{R_{TX} R_{RX}}$ are significantly smaller than the system coupling, $\omega_0 \sqrt{L_{TX} L_{RX}}$. Alternatively, in MIMO WPT system, where multiple distributed sources wirelessly power up multiple IoT loads, the system-wide WPT efficiency is also a strong function of interaction among all the devices.

3 DISTRIBUTED WIRELESS POWER TRANSFER

Wireless power transfer among multiple distributed energy sources and power loads in an IoT system is explored in this section. A MIMO system with N power transmitters and M power receivers is shown in Figure 3. Power transfer in this general case is determined based on the set of linear equations, as described in equation (6). In this equation $I_{TX}^{(i)}$ and $I_{RX}^{(j)}$ are the currents at, respectively, the transmitter i and receiver j, $V_S^{(i)}$ is the source voltage at transmitter i, and $Z_T^{(i)}$ and $Z_R^{(j)}$ is self impedance of respectively the transmitter

$$\left[\begin{array}{cccc|cccc} Z_T^{(1)} & j\omega_0 M_{TX}^{(1,2)} & \dots & j\omega_0 M_{TX}^{(1,N)} & M_{TR}^{(1,1)} & M_{TR}^{(1,2)} & \dots & M_{TR}^{(1,M)} \\ j\omega_0 M_{TX}^{(2,1)} & Z_T^{(2)} & \dots & j\omega_0 M_{TX}^{(2,N)} & M_{TR}^{(2,1)} & M_{TR}^{(2,2)} & \dots & M_{TR}^{(2,M)} \\ \vdots & \vdots & \ddots & \vdots & \vdots & \vdots & \ddots & \vdots \\ j\omega_0 M_{TX}^{(N,1)} & j\omega_0 M_{TX}^{(N,2)} & \dots & Z_T^{(N)} & M_{TR}^{(N,1)} & M_{TR}^{(N,2)} & \dots & M_{TR}^{(N,M)} \\ \hline j\omega_0 M_{TR}^{(1,1)} & j\omega_0 M_{TR}^{(2,1)} & \dots & j\omega_0 M_{TR}^{(N,1)} & Z_R^{(1)} & j\omega_0 M_{RX}^{(1,2)} & \dots & j\omega_0 M_{RX}^{(1,M)} \\ j\omega_0 M_{TR}^{(1,2)} & j\omega_0 M_{TR}^{(2,2)} & \dots & j\omega_0 M_{TR}^{(N,2)} & j\omega_0 M_{RX}^{(2,1)} & Z_R^{(2)} & \dots & j\omega_0 M_{RX}^{(2,M)} \\ \vdots & \vdots & \ddots & \vdots & \vdots & \vdots & \ddots & \vdots \\ j\omega_0 M_{TR}^{(1,M)} & j\omega_0 M_{TR}^{(2,M)} & \dots & j\omega_0 M_{TR}^{(N,M)} & j\omega_0 M_{RX}^{(M,1)} & j\omega_0 M_{RX}^{(M,2)} & \dots & Z_R^{(M)} \end{array}\right] \left[\begin{array}{c} I_{TX}^{(1)} \\ I_{TX}^{(2)} \\ \vdots \\ I_{TX}^{(N)} \\ \hline I_{RX}^{(1)} \\ I_{RX}^{(2)} \\ \vdots \\ I_{RX}^{(M)} \end{array}\right] = \left[\begin{array}{c} V_S^{(1)} \\ V_S^{(2)} \\ \vdots \\ V_S^{(N)} \\ \hline 0 \\ 0 \\ \vdots \\ 0 \end{array}\right], \quad (6)$$

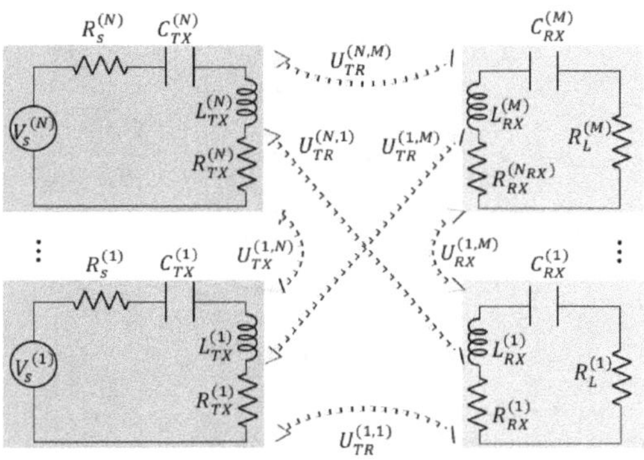

Figure 3: A MIMO WPT system with N power sources and M power loads .

$$Z_T^{(i)} = (R_S^{(i)} + R_{TX}^{(i)}) + j\omega_0 L_{TX}^{(i)} + \frac{1}{j\omega_0 C_{TX}^{(i)}}, \quad (7)$$

$$Z_R^{(j)} = (R_{RX}^{(j)} + R_L^{(j)}) + j\omega_0 L_{RX}^{(j)} + \frac{1}{j\omega_0 C_{RX}^{(j)}}, \quad (8)$$

$i = 1, \dots, N$ (see equation (7)) and the receiver $j = 1, \dots, M$ (see equation (8)). To accurately characterize any given MIMO WPT system, the solution of equation (6) can be obtained numerically. Alternatively, to gain the intuition behind the complex interactions in *dynamically* reconfigurable WPT systems with numerous power devices and loads, simple models and analytic closed-form expressions are required. Closed-form expression for WPT power efficiency and load are derived in this section under the following assumptions:

(1) In a system with $M_{TR}^{(i_0,j)} << M_{TR}^{(i,j)}$, $\forall\ i \neq i_0, j$, most of the current to the loads is supplied from these stronger coupled transmitters, $i \neq i_0$, and receivers j. The overall efficiency of the system with the transmitter i_0 is therefore degraded due to the source current dissipated within this transmitter as compared with the system without the transmitter i_0. To maintain high efficiency of dynamically reconfigurable WPT system, mutual inductance $M_{TR}^{(i,j)} \equiv M_{TR}$ is assumed to be similar for all i and j in this paper.

(2) The amount of wirelessly transferred power in a MISO system with a driving and resonant frequency ω_0 degrades with the increasing number of strong-coupled power supplies. To counteract the degradation in the transferred power load, the driving and/or resonant frequency can be dynamically adjusted [1], ultimately exhibiting similar WPT as compared with the system with weakly coupled power supplies. A WPT system with weakly coupled power supplies, $M_{TX}^{(i_1,i_2)} << M_{TR}^{(i,j)}$, is considered in this paper.

(3) The efficiency and amount of wirelessly transferred power in a SIMO system with a driving and resonant frequency ω_0 degrade with the increasing number of strong-coupled power loads. To counteract the degradation in system efficiency and power load, the driving and/or resonant frequency can be dynamically adjusted [1], ultimately exhibiting similar WPT performance as compared with the system with weakly coupled power loads. A WPT system with weakly coupled power loads, $M_{RX}^{(j_1,j_2)} << M_{TR}^{(i,j)}$, is considered in this paper.

(4) Self impedance of transmitter i and receiver j becomes a real number at the resonant frequency ω_0, yielding respectively $Z_T^{(i)} = R_S^{(i)} + R_{TX}^{(i)}$ and $Z_R^{(j)} = R_{RX}^{(j)} + R_L^{(j)}$. These resistive source and load components as well as supply voltages are controlled by the system designer and assumed to be similar among all the individual transmitters $Z_T^{(i)} \equiv R_T$ and $V_S^{(i)} \equiv V_S, \forall i$ and all the individual receivers $Z_R^{(j)} \equiv R_R, \forall j$.

Under these assumptions, the power transfer interactions as defined by equation (6) can be simplified, yielding

$$\left[\begin{array}{c|c} Z_T \cdot I_N & j\omega M_{TR} \cdot J_{N,M} \\ \hline j\omega M_{TR} \cdot J_{M,N} & Z_R \cdot I_M \end{array}\right] \left[\begin{array}{c} \mathbf{I_{TX}} \\ \hline \mathbf{I_{RX}} \end{array}\right] = \left[\begin{array}{c} \mathbf{V_S} \\ \hline \mathbf{0} \end{array}\right], \quad (9)$$

where I_N is the $N \times N$ identity matrix, $J_{N,M}$ is the $N \times M$ all-ones matrix, $\boldsymbol{I_{TX}}$ and $\boldsymbol{I_{RX}}$ are respectively the transmitter and receiver current vectors, $\boldsymbol{V_S}$ is the supply voltage vector, and $\boldsymbol{0}$ is the zero voltage load vector. The simplified WPT relation yields a set of linear current equations,

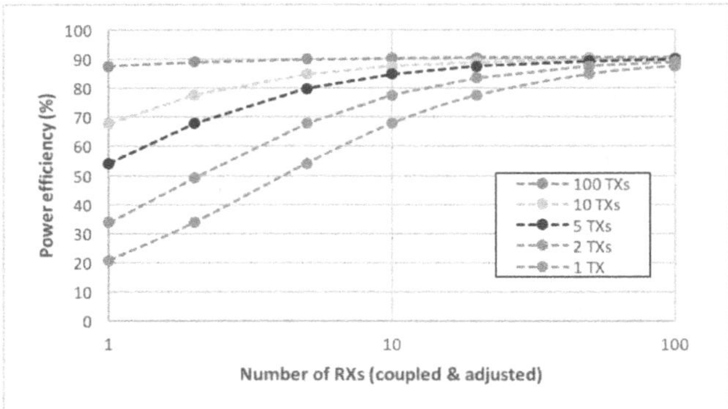

(a)

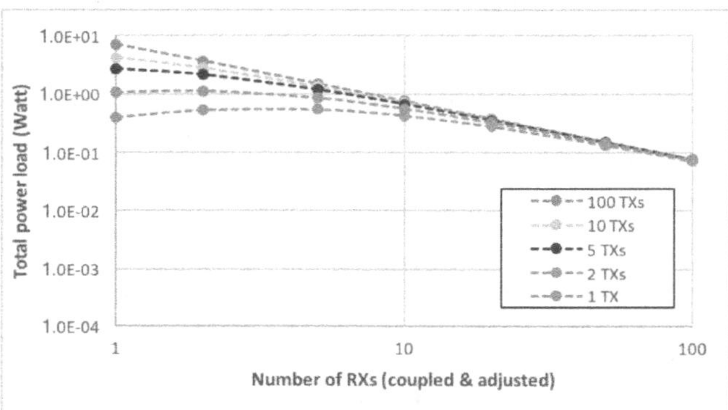

(b)

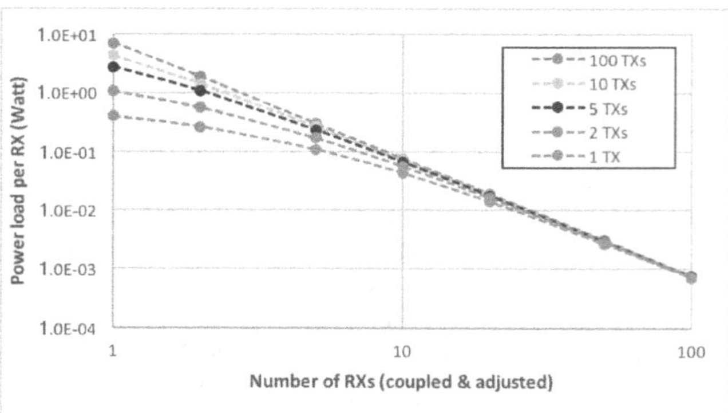

(c)

Figure 4: Performance of a MIMO WPT system with individually decoupled transmitters and receivers, (a) power efficiency, and (b) overall power load, and (c) power load at the individual receivers.

$$\begin{cases} R_T \cdot \boldsymbol{I_{TX}} \approx I_N^{-1}\left[I + \frac{\omega^2}{R_T R_R} \cdot M_{TR} J_{N,M} M_{TR} J_{M,N}\right]^{-1} I_N \boldsymbol{V_S} \\ R_R \cdot \boldsymbol{I_{RX}} \approx -j\omega \cdot I_N M_{TR} J_{M,N} \boldsymbol{I_{TX}} \end{cases} \tag{10}$$

Using the identity, $(I_N + kJ_N)^{-1} = I_N - \frac{k}{1+Nk} J_N$ and solving equation (10) for $\boldsymbol{I_{TX}}$ and $\boldsymbol{I_{RX}}$, the transmitter and receiver currents in a MIMO WPT systems are

$$\begin{cases} \boldsymbol{I_{TX}} \approx \dfrac{R_R}{R_T R_R + \omega^2 NMM_{TR}} \cdot \boldsymbol{V_S}, \\ \boldsymbol{I_{RX}} \approx \dfrac{-j\omega NM_{TR}}{R_T R_R + \omega^2 NMM_{TR}} \cdot \boldsymbol{V_S}. \end{cases} \tag{11}$$

The power efficiency and power load of the WPT MIMO are therefore, respectively,

$$\eta = \frac{\dfrac{R_{RL}}{R_R}}{1 + \left(\dfrac{\sum_{i=1}^{N} \left| I_{TX}^{(i)} \right|^2 \cdot R_T}{\sum_{j=1}^{M} \left| I_{RX}^{(j)} \right|^2 \cdot R_R} \right)} = \frac{U_{eff}^2}{1 + U_{eff}^2} \cdot \frac{R_{RL}}{R_R}, \tag{12}$$

and

$$P_{Load} = \sum_{j=1}^{M} \left| I_{RX}^{(j)} \right|^2 R_R = \left(\frac{U_{eff}}{1 + U_{eff}^2} \right)^2 \cdot \frac{R_{RL}}{R_R} \cdot \frac{V_S^2}{\frac{R_T}{N}}, \tag{13}$$

where U_{eff} is the effective strong-coupling parameter,

$$U_{eff} = \omega_0 \frac{M_{TR}}{\sqrt{\dfrac{R_T}{N} \dfrac{R_R}{M}}}. \tag{14}$$

The energy dissipated within the WPT MIMO system therefore linearly decreases with the increasing number of decoupled transmitters and/or decoupled receivers, increasing the overall system efficiency η, as shown in equations (12) and (14). Alternatively, the total power load decreases with the increasing number of power loads, as shown in equations (13) and (14).

In these strong-coupled MIMO WPT systems with $U_{eff} >> 1$ and large number of transmitters and receivers, the power efficiency and overall power load quickly converges to, respectively,

$$\lim_{N \to \infty} \eta = \lim_{M \to \infty} \eta = \frac{R_{RX}}{R_{RX} + R_L}, \tag{15}$$

and

$$\lim_{N \to \infty} P_{Load} = \frac{R_{Load}}{MU} \cdot V_S^2 \xrightarrow[M \to \infty]{} 0. \tag{16}$$

These tradeoffs among the number of transmitters, number of receivers, WPT efficiency, overall power load, and power load within the individual receivers, as described by equations (12)-(16), are illustrated in Figure 4. The reduced power load is therefore traded off for high power efficiency with the increasing number of power loads. Alternatively, both the power efficiency and load increase with the increasing number of transmitters.

While derived for the systems where coupling among the individual transmitters and individual receiver is significantly weaker than the coupling between the transmitter and receivers, the tradeoffs described here based on equations (9)-(16) are also valid for the

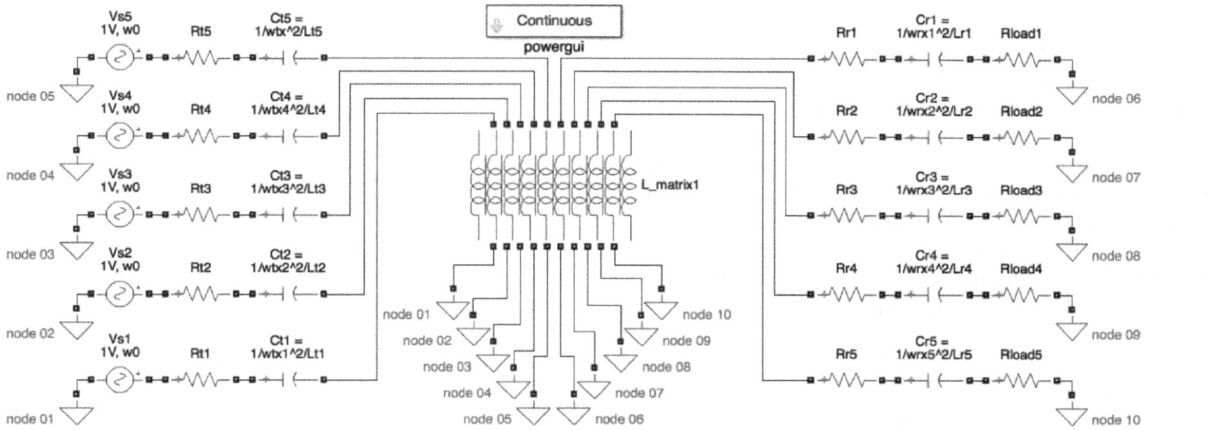

Figure 5: Schematic of a MIMO WPT system with five transmitters and two receivers.

systems with strong-coupled transmitters and/or strong-coupled receivers. The validity of the described tradeoffs among the number of transmitters, number of receivers, WPT efficiency, and overall power load is however conditional on dynamically adjusting the resonant and/or driving frequency as the number of wirelessly connected components within a MIMO WPT changes. To maximize the power efficiency in a SIMO system with M coupled receivers, the resonant frequency should be adjusted, such that [1]

$$\omega_0 \approx \omega_{TX} = \frac{\omega_{RX}}{\sqrt{1+(M-1)k_{RX}}}. \tag{17}$$

Similarly, to maximize the power transfer in a MISO system with N coupled transmitters, the resonant frequency should be adjusted, such that

$$\omega_0 \approx \omega_{RX} = \frac{\omega_{TX}}{\sqrt{1+(N-1)k_{TX}}}. \tag{18}$$

To maximize the overall efficiency and power load in a MIMO WPT system with a driving frequency ω_0, simultaneously adjusting the transmitting and receiving resonant frequency is proposed in this paper, yielding

$$\begin{cases} \omega_{TX} \approx \dfrac{\omega_0}{\sqrt{1+(N-1)k_{TX}}}, \\ \omega_{RX} \approx \dfrac{\omega_0}{\sqrt{1+(M-1)k_{RX}}}. \end{cases} \tag{19}$$

To demonstrate these tradeoffs and proposed frequency adjusting, a MIMO WPT system with five transmitters and five receivers is designed in Simulink. The proposed system is illustrated in Figure 5. The performance of the system is illustrated in Figure 6, demonstrating a) the decreasing efficiency and power load with the increasing number of coupled transmitters and/or receivers, b) the increasing efficiency and power load with the increasing number of decoupled or adjusted transmitters, and (c) the increasing efficiency with the increasing number of decoupled or adjusted receivers. The performance of a MIMO WPT system as described by equations (12), (13), (14), and (19) is compared with the Simulink results, yielding less than 10% error. A comparison of the simulated performance of a decoupled MIMO WPT system with the adjusted system also exhibits less than 10% variations.

To support at runtime the adjustment of resonant frequency in a MIMO WPT system with dynamically (dis)connected transmitters

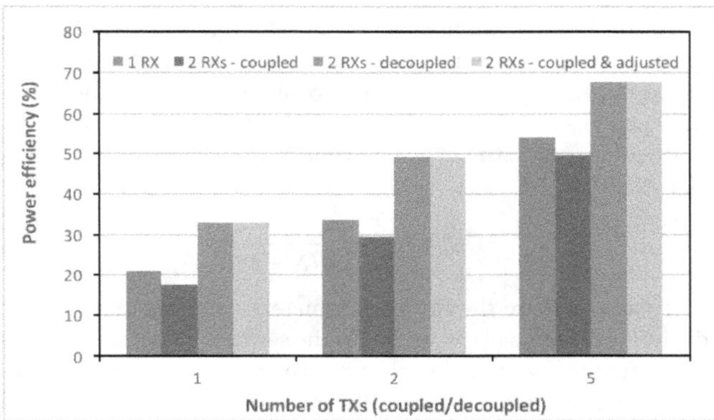

(a)

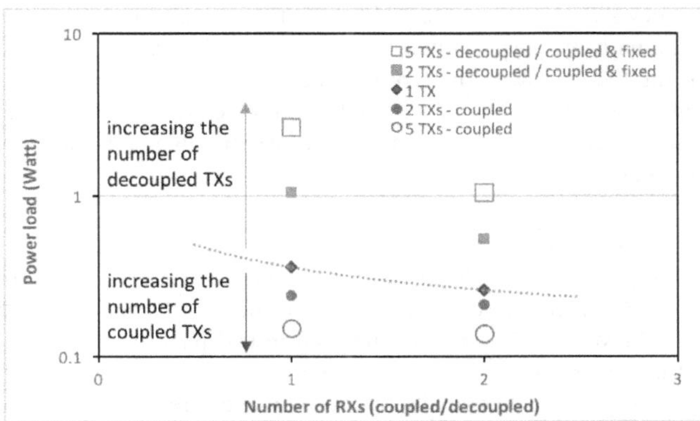

(b)

Figure 6: Performance of a MIMO WPT system with and without adjusting the resonant transmitting and receiving frequency, (a) power efficiency, and (b) power load at the individual receivers.

and receivers, variable dynamically controlled capacitors are integrated within the individual transmitters and receivers, dissipating additional power. Assuming a constant power consumption of P_{adj} watts for each adjustment of an LC tank capacitive component, a bound on the minimum time of a system operation in its updated configuration can be determined which makes the (dis)connection of transmitters and receivers useful. For example, consider adding a transmitter to a MIMO WPT system $S(N, M)$ with N transmitters and M receivers. In the reconfigured system, $S'(N+1, M)$, the transmitting resonant frequency ω_{TX} is adjusted based on equation 19 within each of the N transmitters, dissipating NP_{adj} watts. Alternatively, the efficiency of the system S' with $N+1$ transmitters is increased by $\Delta\eta = \eta'(N+1, M) - \eta(N, M)$. To practically enhance the overall power efficiency $\eta(N, M)$ (see equation (12)) over a period of time T'_{N+1}, the dissipated power NP_{adj} is added to the overall system power consumption, yielding,

$$\eta' = \frac{R_{RL}/R_R}{1 + \left(\dfrac{\sum_{i=1}^{N} \left| I_{TX}^{\prime(i)} \right|^2 \cdot R_T + \dfrac{N \cdot P_{adj}}{T'}}{\sum_{j=1}^{M} \left| I_{RX}^{\prime(j)} \right|^2 \cdot R_R} \right)} \geq \eta. \tag{20}$$

To consider the multiple effects of reconfiguring a MIMO WPT system on the system performance, figure of merit (FOM) is proposed in this paper that simultaneously accounts for the steady state power efficiency, overall power load, and power losses due to frequency adjustment as determined by the size of the system $N + M$.

$$\text{FOM} = \frac{\eta}{P_{Load}^{\alpha}} \cdot \frac{1}{(N+M)^{\beta}}, \tag{21}$$

where α and β are the fitting parameters determined by, respectively, the power load constraints of the system and power efficiency of the frequency adjusting circuits. The proposed FOM is shown in Figure 7 as a function of system size for $\alpha = \beta = 0.1$. Based on the proposed FOM, the performance of those MIMO WPT systems with less transmitters and receivers is dominated by the power efficiency and increases with additional strong-coupled components. Alternatively, the performance in those larger MIMO WPT systems is limited by power losses due to the system reconfiguration and degrades with additional transmitters and receivers. The preferred number of components can therefore be determined for any set of system parameters.

4 SUMMARY

To address the emerging need for dynamically reconfigurable wirelessly powered IoT systems, system-wide power efficiency and load of a MIMO WPT system is analyzed in this paper as a function of the system size. Closed-form expression for power efficiency, power load, and preferred resonant frequency are provided. Based on the analytic expressions, the tradeoffs among the various system performance parameters and size of the system are discussed and demonstrated in Simulink. A FOM is proposed that simultaneously accounts for power efficiency, load, and reconfiguration losses is proposed, yielding the preferred number of wirelessly connected devices in a MIMO WPT system.

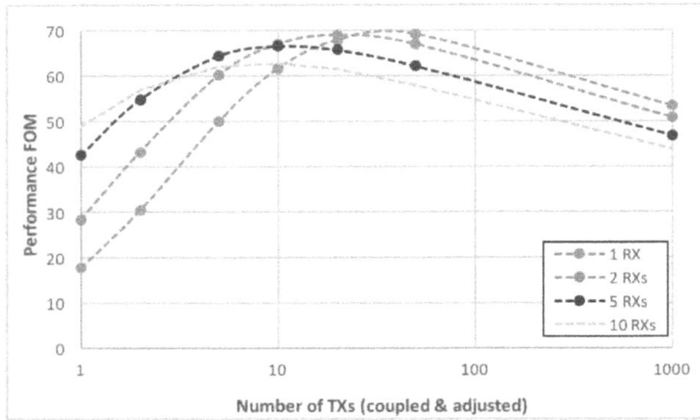

(a)

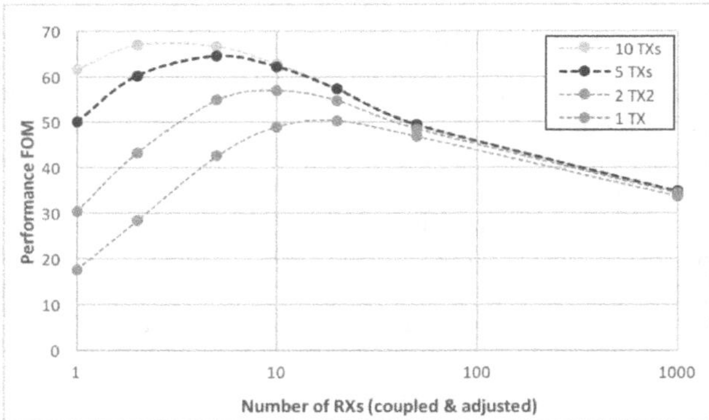

(b)

Figure 7: FOM of performance of a MIMO WPT system as a function of a system size for $\alpha = \beta = 0.1$.

REFERENCES

[1] D. Ahn and S. Hong. 2013. Effect of Coupling Between Multiple Transmitters or Multiple Receivers on Wireless Power Transfer. *IEEE Transactions on Industrial Electronics* 60, 7 (2013), 2602–2613.

[2] Semiconductor Industry Association. 2015. International Technology Roadmap for Semiconductors, 2015 Edition. (2015). Available online: https://www.semiconductors.org.

[3] B. L. Cannon, J. F. Hoburg, D. D. Stancil, and S. C. Goldstein. 2009. Magnetic Resonant Coupling as a Potential Means for Wireless Power Transfer to Multiple Small Receivers. *IEEE Transactions on Power Electronics* 24, 7 (2009), 1819–1825.

[4] S.Y. R. Hui, W. Zhong, and C. K. Lee. 2014. A Critical Review of Recent Progress in Mid-Range Wireless Power Transfer. *IEEE Transactions on Power Electronics* 29, 9 (2014), 4500–4511.

[5] M. Kesler. 2013. Highly Resonant Wireless Power Transfer: Safe, Efficient, and Over Distance. *Witricity corporation* (2013), 1–32.

[6] A. Kurs, A. Karalis, R. Moffatt, J. D. Joannopoulos, P. Fisher, and M. Soljačić. 2007. Wireless Power Transfer via Strongly Coupled Magnetic Resonances. *Science* 317, 5834 (2007), 83–86.

[7] A. Kurs, R. Moffatt, and M. Soljačić. 2010. Simultaneous Mid-Range Power Transfer to Multiple Devices. *Applied Physics Letters* 96, 4 (2010), 044102.

[8] H.-D. Lang, A. Ludwig, and C. D. Sarris. 2014. Convex Optimization of Wireless Power Transfer Systems with Multiple Transmitters. *IEEE Transactions on Antennas and Propagation* 62, 9 (2014), 4623–4636.

[9] S.-H. Lee and R. D. Lorenz. 2011. Development and Validation of Model for 95%-Efficiency 220-W Wireless Power Transfer over a 30-cm Air Gap. *IEEE Transactions on Industry Applications* 47, 6 (2011), 2495–2504.

[10] I. Savidis, B. Vaisband, and E. G. Friedman. 2015. Experimental Analysis of Thermal Coupling in 3-D Integrated Circuits. *IEEE Transactions on Very Large Scale Integration (VLSI) Circuits* 23, 10 (October 2015), 2077–2089.

[11] B. Vaisband, I. Savidis, and E. G. Friedman. 2014. Thermal Conduction Path Analysis in 3-D ICs. In *Proceedings of the IEEE International Symposium on Circuit and Systems*. 594–597.

Low-Power Optical Interconnects based on Resonant Silicon Photonic Devices: Recent Advances and Challenges

Meisam Bahadori
EE Department, Columbia University
New York, NY, USA
mb3875@columbia.edu

Keren Bergman
EE Department, Columbia University
New York, NY, USA
kb2028@columbia.edu

ABSTRACT

The progressive blooming of silicon photonics technology (SiP) over the last decade has indicated that optical interconnects may substitute the electrical wires for data movement over short distances in the future. A key enabler is the resonant structures that can participate in both modulation and demultiplexing of a high throughput wavelength division multiplexed (WDM) photonic link. The optical and electro-optical properties of such devices are subject to various design considerations, operation conditions, and optimization procedures. We present recent technological advances in photonic links based on resonant structures and highlight the key challenges that must be overcome at a large scale. Furthermore, we discuss how the design space of these resonant devices, down to the geometrical parameters and fabrication errors, can affect the performance and reliability of a photonic link.

CCS CONCEPTS

• **Applied computing → Physical sciences and engineering; Computer-aided design;** • **Computing methodologies → Modeling and simulation; Model development and analysis;**

KEYWORDS

Silicon photonics; microring resonators; optical amplitude modulation; optical interconnect; optical power penalty; wavelength division multiplexing

ACM Reference Format:

Meisam Bahadori and Keren Bergman. 2018. Low-Power Optical Interconnects based on Resonant Silicon Photonic Devices: Recent Advances and Challenges. In *GLSVLSI '18: 2018 Great Lakes Symposium on VLSI, May 23–25, 2018, Chicago, IL, USA*. ACM, New York, NY, USA, 6 pages. https://doi.org/10.1145/3194554.3194606

1 INTRODUCTION

Silicon Photonics (SiP) platform has been the subject of intensive research for more than a decade now and its prospects continue to emerge as it enjoys the maturity of CMOS manufacturing industry [2]. SiP foundries all over the world [27] and particularly in the US (AIM Photonics) have been developing reliable photonic design kits (PDKs) that include fundamental SiP building blocks such as wavelength selective modulators and tunable filters. Microring resonators (MRR) are hailed as the most compact devices that can perform both modulation and demodulation in a wavelength division multiplexed (WDM) transceiver design [9]. Although the use of WDM can reduce the number of fibers carrying data, it also makes the design of transceivers challenging [24]. It is probably acceptable to achieve compactness at the expense of somewhat higher transceiver cost and power consumptions. Nevertheless, these two metrics should remain close to their actual values [61] for Datacom applications. An increase of an order of magnitude is clearly not acceptable. For example costs relative to bandwidth for an optical link in a data center interconnect will have to decrease from the current ~\$5/Gbps down to <\$1/Gbps [1, 3]. Additionally, the transceiver itself must remain compact.

Silicon does not exhibit optical absorption at wavelengths in the vicinity of 1550 nm (a transparent material) and has an indirect bandgap. Therefore, silicon-based MRR modulators are designed based on the "electro-refraction" principle [47]. In this type of modulators, the refractive index of the material (silicon) is alternatively changed by applying an electrical signal, resulting in a different optical path length for "0" bits and "1" bits. In 1987, Soref *et al.* [51] characterized how the optical properties (index and absorption) of Silicon change by injecting charge carriers into an undoped sample or by extracting carriers from a doped sample. Although this phenomenon, called the plasma dispersion effect, is fast enough to enable Gb/s modulation speed [58], it still provides a weak perturbation of the refractive index. In addition, unlike the thermo-optic effects [5], the optical absorption of Silicon is also affected through the plasma dispersion effect. In return, electro-refractive modulators are relatively easy to fabricate, robust, and broadband. In contrast to electro-absorptive modulators (EAM) [16], they do not require the presence of Germanium or another absorbing material in the silicon-on-insulator (SOI) fabrication process.

2 SILICON PHOTONIC LINKS

A photonic link is by definition equipped with a transmit unit (Tx) and a receive unit (Rx). The link architecture based on an integrated photonic platform such as Silicon Photonics can be envisaged as the ones presented in Fig. 1 [7, 10]. The Tx requires input optical power in the form of serialized/combined optical wavelengths. Each wavelength provides one channel of optical data. One convenient solution is to use a multi-wavelength laser source such as a comb laser source [11]. The optical power is then injected into the Tx using vertical grating couplers or edge couplers. This process inflicts optical loss and is unavoidable. Grating couplers with

GLSVLSI '18, May 23–25, 2018, Chicago, IL, USA

ACM ISBN 978-1-4503-5724-1/18/05...\$15.00
https://doi.org/10.1145/3194554.3194606

more than 75% coupling efficiency [54] and less than 4 dB loss [26] have already been demonstrated.

The architecture in Fig. 1(b) consists of cascaded microring modulators. Each modulator is designated to a specific wavelength through thermo-optic tuning of its resonance, while modulating light through fast charge carrier based electro-optic effects in silicon. The output data streams of all modulators are combined and multiplexed inside the bus waveguide and extracted from the Tx unit into a carrier fiber through another optical coupler. As can be seen in Fig. 1(b), multiplexing of optical channels in a transmitter architecture based on MRR modulators is achieved at no additional cost because of the wavelength-selective property of MRRs.

The Rx unit is equipped with a wavelength demultiplexer since WDM scheme is used [6]. Light from each channel, accompanied by optical crosstalk [8], is incident on a photodiode, which is then converted to electrical current. The electrical current is converted to electrical voltage signal and amplified and finally deserialized to recover each individual electrical data stream. Although inclusion of a clock-and-data recovery (CDR) module is a common choice for the Rx units, forwarded clock schemes have also been proposed for MRR-based links [18].

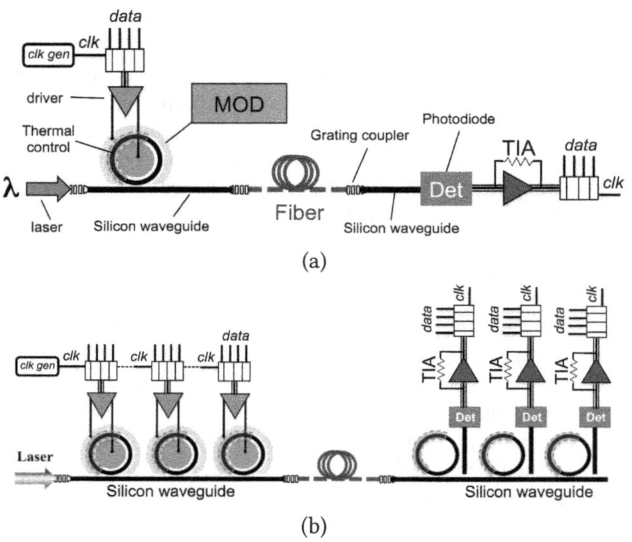

Figure 1: (a) Structure of a single-λ photonic link with a microring modulator at the transmitter and no spectral filtering at the receiver. (b) Anatomy of a WDM link based on microring resonators. Multiplexing of wavelengths is easily achieved due to the wavelength-selective nature of MRRs. Spectral filtering is required at the receiver to select individual channels.

Figure 2(a) depicts the inter-relations of optical and electrical parts of a link to target a specific throughput and energy/bit metric. A link design problem can be formulated in several ways: 1) Maximizing the total throughput (aggregated bandwidth) of the link by finding the best combination of number of channels and data rate per channel for a given optical power budget; 2) minimizing the energy/bit metric for a given throughput; 3) maximizing the throughput for a given energy/bit metric. In [9], we showed that a silicon photonic link under ideal electronics circuitry can provide up to 2 Tb/s of aggregation. However, later on we included more realistic models for the modulator drivers and TIAs based on 65nm CMOS node and concluded a maximum supported throughput of 1.6 Tb/s for the best energy/bit metric (~1.5 pJ/bit) [7]. In a more recent work, we added an optimization of the microring resonators based on realistic fabrication limitations (e.g. the coupling gaps are in the range of 100nm–400nm) and found out that the maximum supported bandwidth is limited to less than 1 Tb/s [10]. Figure 2(b) shows the result of optimization of the link for various throughput targets and Fig. 2(c) shows the breakdown of the calculated energy/bit metrics. This shows that both electronic and photonic components play a significant role in determining the capacity of a silicon photonic link.

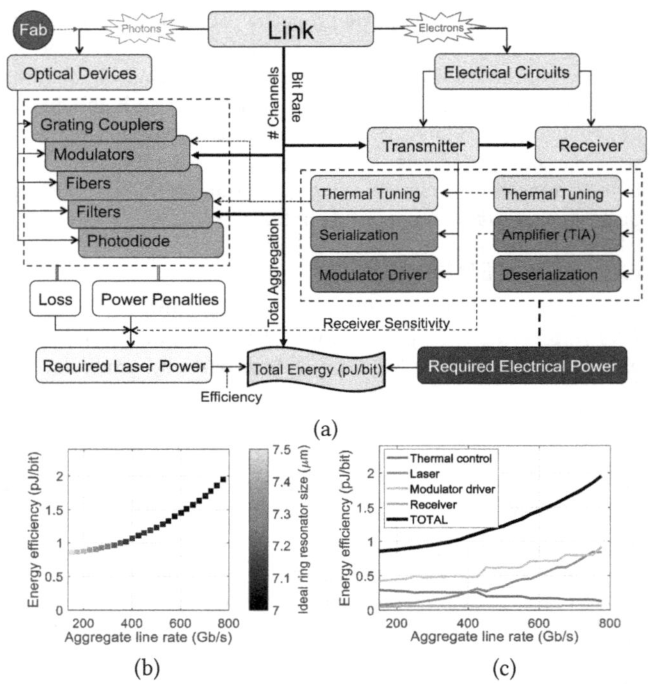

Figure 2: (a) Diagram of electrical and optical interplays for designing and analyzing a photonic link. Both electronics and photonics play important parts in the energy consumption of the link (in units of pJ/bit). (b) A recent example of optimizing an MRR-based silicon photonic link for various throughputs. (c) Breakdown of energy consumption of a link for various aggregations.

3 MICRORING MODULATORS

In 2005, it was first demonstrated that silicon MRRs can provide adequate phase shift by taking advantage of the plasma dispersion effect (PN or PIN diode). The device had a compact footprint (12 μm diameter) while achieved more than 10 dB of extinction ratio with a low insertion loss [59]. Since then, many researchers have proposed various modulator designs based on MRRs for low-power and high-speed modulations. MRRs with free spectral range as large as 22 nm (diameter <10 μm) have been demonstrated for dense WDM systems, capable of operating at 15 Gb/s [50]. Dynamic energy consumptions as low as 7 fJ/bit have been demonstrated for an MRR operating at 25 Gb/s with 1 V peak-to-peak drive voltage [23]. In 2013, the first 50 Gb/s modulation at 1.96 V peak-to-peak drive voltage for a silicon racetrack MRR was demonstrated [4]. In order to enhance the modulation efficiency and reduce the effective junction capacitance, MRRs with ZigZag [56] and interdigitated [43] junctions have been proposed. MRRs have also been used for higher-order amplitude modulation formats such as four-level pulse amplitude modulation (PAM4) [48] at 80 Gb/s and PAM8 at 45 Gb/s [15], with a power consumption of 7 fJ/bit and 1 fJ/bit, respectively. Due to the nonlinear spectral response of MRR, a single PN phase shifter requires unequal voltage steps to realize a high-order PAM. To resolve this, designs with two separate phase shifters embedded in one MRR have been proposed [42]. Phase modulation such as binary phase shift keying (BPSK) at 10 Gb/s has also been realized with MRRs [25]. Table 1 provides a summary of recent notable demonstrations of microring modulators.

Table 1: Notable demonstrations of SiP microring modulators.

Structure	Bit rate (Gb/s)	Modulation Format	Extinction Ratio (dB)	Year	Ref.
MRR-PIN	12.5	NRZ	>9	2007	[58]
MRR-PIN	15	NRZ	NA	2016	[50]
MRR-PN	25	NRZ	>5	2011	[23]
MRR-PN	40	PAM4	NA	2017	[42]
MRR-PN	25	NRZ	4.5	2012	[57]
MRR-PN	44	NRZ	3.01	2012	[56]
MRR-PIN	50	NRZ	4.58	2013	[4]

4 MICRORING FILTERS

The use of cascaded MRR modulators at the transmitter to achieve WDM signaling mandates the presence of a wavelength demultiplexer at the receiver end. As shown in Fig. 1(b), MRRs in the form of add-drop structures are capable of performing wavelength demultiplexing due to their wavelength selective spectral response. Based on the desired passband and the rejection ratio of the filter, first-order [8, 12–14] or higher-order [19, 32, 46, 55] add-drop filters are used. Higher order filters provide a better rejection ratio but suffer from a higher loss in their passband.

Recently we showed that it is possible to perform an optimization on the add-drop filters to minimize the optical power penalty of the demultiplexing array [6]. Such optimization of microrings requires a deeper understanding of how these structures operate. MRRs in a demux array are subject to multiple physical and optical constraints. For example, the radius must be large enough to prevent undesired high bending losses [19], but not too large in order to avoid interference of other resonances in the optical bandwidth of interest. Moreover, the 3dB optical bandwidth of a ring used in a WDM add-drop configuration should be large enough to accommodate the bandwidth of the optical signal to be dropped. A too narrow bandwidth will result in heavy, and undesired, truncation of the signal spectrum, thus distortions [9] (truncation power penalty). However, a too large bandwidth can cause a severe optical crosstalk problem (crosstalk power penalty) if the channel density is high [8, 19, 39].

Under these multiple constraints, the selection of an MRR with right parameters is not a straightforward and easy task. For example, a larger radius results in a strong coupling of the ring to the waveguides while at the same time it results in a smaller optical loss of the ring. Furthermore, in some cases no realistic MRR matching all the requirements exists. In order to characterize the design space of MRR filters, recently we developed accurate compact models [49] that incorporate the effect of physical dimensions (width, height, gap size, radius) on the optical response of first order and higher order structures. Such compact models allow us to characterize the design space of a first-order MRR as shown in Fig. 3. In Fig. 3(a), we calculate the contours of optical loss in the passband of the filter and gray out losses worse than 1 dB. In Fig. 3(b), the maximum extinction of the filter outside of its passband is calculated and the values greater than -30 dB are ruled out. In Fig. 3(c), the optical bandwidth of the passband is plotted and the region from 10 Ghz to 50 Ghz is selected. Finally, the design space shown in Fig. 3(d) is obtained by overlaying the contours of all the parameters. The center point of the design space corresponds to a radius of 9 μm and coupling gaps of 180 nm. The center point still

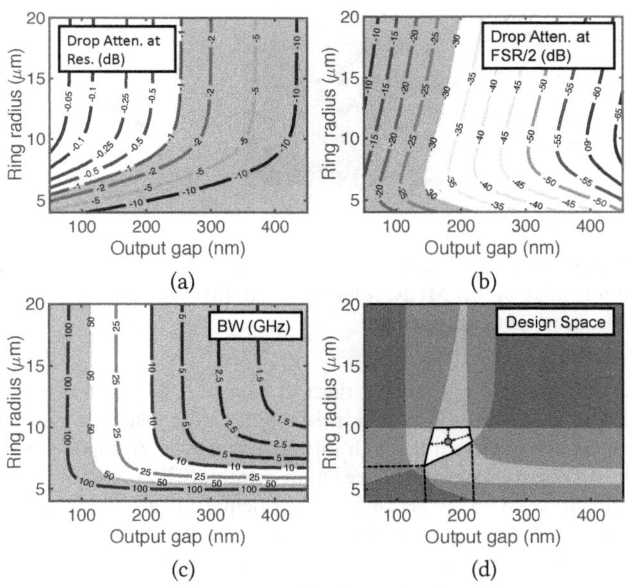

Figure 3: Design space exploration of silicon-based first-order MRR. (a) Contours of optical loss in the passband. (b) Contours of rejection ratio outside of the passband. (c) Optical bandwidth. (d) Design space. Output gap refers to the distance between the ring and the drop waveguide.

remains in the white zone even with the presence of small variations on the gap or radius.

5 CHALLENGES AT SCALE

Although the physical principles behind the operation of MRRs are well-known, a significant amount of engineering effort must be put together to make a MRR-based transceiver fully functional. Here, we briefly review four obstacles that negatively affect the optical performance of MRRs.

5.1 Thermal Sensitivity of MRRs

Thermal effects significantly change the optical behavior of silicon-based devices due to the strong thermo-optic coefficient of silicon material (dn_{Si}/dT = 1.8×10^{-4} K^{-1}) [20]. For very narrow-band optical devices such as MRRs, thermal susceptibility can be significantly detrimental, and requires accurate monitoring and control of the temperature to maintain desired behavior and performance over a long period of operation [17, 31, 60]. The resonance of a typical silicon MRR is shifted by ~10 Ghz (~0.07 nm) for each degree Kelvin change in the temperature of the MRR [34, 44]. A single degree of temperature variation is therefore sufficient to create significant spectral distortion of on-off keying (OOK) signals for dense wavelength-division multiplexing (DWDM) systems that employ the link architecture of Fig. 1(b). In order to experimentally verify the sensitivity of a silicon MRR as shown in Fig. 4(a), we put it inside a temperature chamber (oven) shown in Fig. 4(b) and tracked the resonance wavelength by increasing the tempearture (Fig. 4(c)). As expected, a linear relation between shift of resonance and temperature was observed indicating a thermal sensitivity of 0.067 nm/K of the resonance.

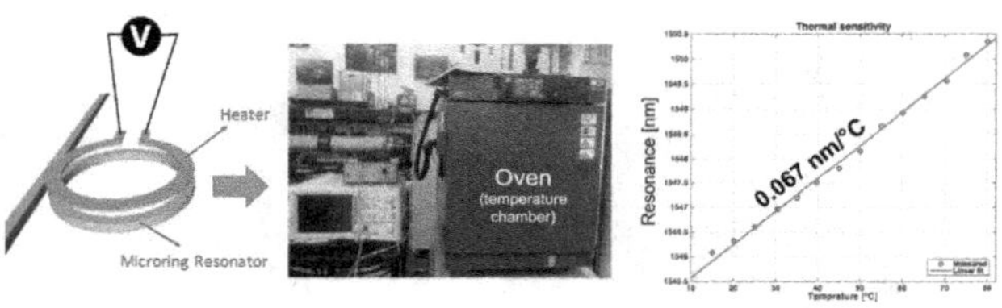

(a) (b) (c)

Figure 4: (a) Structure of an MRR with a microheater. (b) An oven hosting an MRR. (c) Measured shift of resonance as a function of temperature.

The popular solution for thermal control of MRRs is based on active thermal feedback control [40, 41] and consists of sending an electrical current through integrated metallic or doped-silicon based micro-heaters to induce Ohmic heating. This method of operation is based on the heat diffusion principle which is a rather slow process. The thermo-optic bandwidth of the heater-MRR structure is typically limited to 50–100 kHz. Recently, we investigated the main tradeoffs between the thermo-optic bandwidth (i.e., heating speed) and the thermo-optic efficiency (i.e., shift of resonance as a function of heater power, in units of nm/mW) for MRRs [5] and concluded that reaching a higher efficiency leads to a lower speed. The rise time and fall time of thermo-optic response typically falls on the order of micro-seconds. Such low speed response imposes challenges in real-time monitoring and wavelength locking of MRRs. On the plus side, the small thermo-optic bandwidth of the MRR can be utilized to actuate the heater with electrical digital signals such as pulse width modulation (PWM), hence eliminating the need for digital to analog converters [35].

5.2 Self-heating and bistability of MRRs

Due to the resonant nature of MRRs, there is a strong build-up of optical power inside the resonator. The enhancement of optical power is proportional to the finesse (Q-factor) of the resonator for a critically coupled MRR [33]. At the presence of such high optical power inside the ring, even a slight inherent absorption can lead to a noticeable change in the temperature of the ring which causes a thermal drift of resonance, hence deteriorating the optical OOK data. Although for the short period of a "1" bit (e.g., 100 pico-second for 10 Gb/s OOK) this effect is not tangible, for a long stream of consecutive "1" bits it poses a severe threat to the operation of both MRR modulators and filters. A recent transceiver design has clearly pointed out this problem [52] and proposed a thermal tuning algorithm based on the statistics of the data stream. It is worth noting that addition of more electronic circuitry for such algorithms will add-up to the overall energy consumption of the photonic link.

5.3 Fabrication variations and nonuniformity

The spectral parameters of an MRR such as resonance wavelength, free spectral range (FSR), and the optical bandwidth mainly depend on the geometrical properties of the MRR. It is quite known that current silicon photonic fabrication imposes variations on the dimensions of the waveguides (typically in the range of ~5 nm) [21] and the radius of the ring. This results in deviations of the resonance wavelength from the original design [36, 38] and requires thermal tuning, hence degrading the energy efficiency of the link. Furthermore, identical devices experience different variations based on their location on the silicon wafer (fabrication nonuniformity) [37]. Therefore, in order to predict the yield of the fabrication and include that in the optical budget of the link, a wafer-scale statistical model of the variations for the photonic devices should be developed [21, 29, 45]. Most likely, such statistical models vary from one silicon photonic foundry to another which may impose challenges on predicting the yield for a particular transceiver design. Unconventional designs such as multi-mode waveguides have been proven to mitigate the impact of fabrication variations on the resonance of MRRs [30].

5.4 Sidewall roughness and backscattering inside MRRs

Narrow-band spectral response of MRRs in conjunction with high-speed data streams puts stringent requirements on the design of MRRs for high-performance links. It has been shown that in applications where very narrow linewidths (i.e. Q > 10000) are required, even a slight roughness on the sidewalls of the ring will cause backscattering (BS) inside the ring [22, 28]. The effect of backscattering in MRRs is typically observed in the form of a splitting of the resonance in the spectral response of the ring [28]. Such spectral distortion adds extra complexity that further narrows down the design space of MRRs for minimizing power penalties. An increase of optical bandwidth (thus a decrease of the Q-factor) limits the attenuation of the high-frequency components of the dropped signals, but may lead to a truncated filtering shape that inflicts higher losses and spectral distortions on the central frequency components of the dropped signals. Figure 5(a) shows the spectral response of one of our fabricated add-drop MRRs exhibiting a significant resonance splitting. Figure 5(b) compares the simulated response of an MRR with and without the observed backscattering. A loss of 5dB in the passband is inflicted onto the optical data which can significantly impact the bit-error-rate of the optical link.

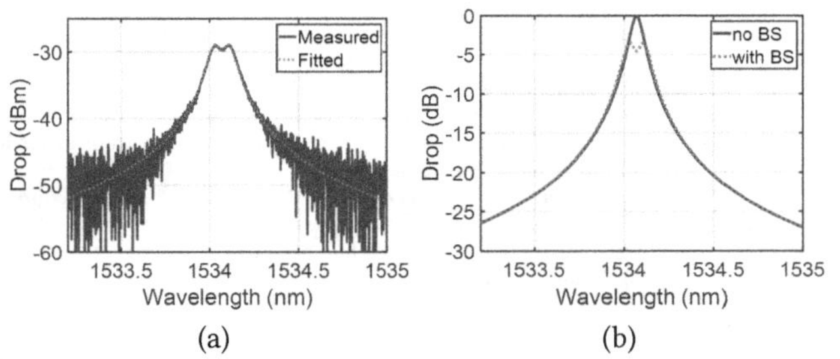

Figure 5: (a) Measured spectral response of a first-order add-drop with strong backscattering (BS). (b) Simulated MRR with and without backscattering (BS).

6 CONCLUSIONS

Our recent studies indicate that silicon photonic links based on microring resonators can provide data aggregations in the range of 0.5–1 Tb/s at energy efficiencies in the range of 1.5–3 pJ/bit. While the design space of MRRs is not hard to explore for the optimum designs, significant amount of engineering effort still needs to accompany that to overcome challenges such as thermal sensitivity of MRRs, optical absorption and self heating, fabrication variations, and backscattering effects. The potential of silicon photonics for monolithic integration with CMOS electronics [53] is driving engineers to find the best solutions for all the problems that MRRs are facing.

ACKNOWLEDGMENTS

This work is supported in part by Air Force Research Laboratory (FA8650-15-2-5220), ARPA-E ENLITENED project (DE-AR00000843), and by Department of Energy under LLNS subcontract (B621301).

REFERENCES

[1] Erik Agrell, Magnus Karlsson, AR Chraplyvy, David J Richardson, Peter M Krummrich, Peter Winzer, Kim Roberts, Johannes Karl Fischer, Seb J Savory, Benjamin J Eggleton, and others. 2016. Roadmap of optical communications. *Journal of Optics* 18, 6 (2016), 063002.

[2] Luca Alloatti, Mark Wade, Vladimir Stojanovic, Milos Popovic, and Rajeev Jagga Ram. 2015. Photonics design tool for advanced CMOS nodes. *IET optoelectronics* 9, 4 (2015), 163–167.

[3] Mehdi Asghari. 2008. Silicon photonics: a low cost integration platform for datacom and telecom applications. In *National Fiber Optic Engineers Conference*. Optical Society of America, NThA4.

[4] Takeshi Baba, Suguru Akiyama, Masahiko Imai, Naoki Hirayama, Hiroyuki Takahashi, Yoshiji Noguchi, Tsuyoshi Horikawa, and Tatsuya Usuki. 2013. 50-Gb/s ring-resonator-based silicon modulator. *Optics express* 21, 10 (2013), 11869–11876.

[5] Meisam Bahadori, Alexander Gazman, Natalie Janosik, Sébastien Rumley, Ziyi Zhu, Robert Polster, Qixiang Cheng, and Keren Bergman. 2018. Thermal Rectification of Integrated Microheaters for Microring Resonators in Silicon Photonics Platform. *Journal of Lightwave Technology* 36, 3 (2018), 773–788.

[6] Meisam Bahadori, Dessislava Nikolova, Sébastien Rumley, Christine P Chen, and Keren Bergman. 2015. Optimization of microring-based filters for dense WDM silicon photonic interconnects. In *Optical Interconnects Conference (OI), 2015 IEEE*. IEEE, 84–85.

[7] Meisam Bahadori, Robert Polster, Sébastien Rumley, Yvain Thonnart, José-Luis Gonzalez-Jimenez, and Keren Bergman. 2016. Energy-bandwidth design exploration of silicon photonic interconnects in 65nm CMOS. In *IEEE Optical Interconnects Conference (OI), 2016*. IEEE, 2–3.

[8] Meisam Bahadori, Sébastien Rumley, Hasitha Jayatilleka, Kyle Murray, Nicolas AF Jaeger, Lukas Chrostowski, Sudip Shekhar, and Keren Bergman. 2016. Crosstalk penalty in microring-based silicon photonic interconnect systems. *Journal of Lightwave Technology* 34, 17 (2016), 4043–4052.

[9] Meisam Bahadori, Sébastien Rumley, Dessislava Nikolova, and Keren Bergman. 2016. Comprehensive design space exploration of silicon photonic interconnects. *Journal of Lightwave Technology* 34, 12 (2016), 2975–2987.

[10] Meisam Bahadori, Sébastien Rumley, Robert Polster, Alexander Gazman, Matt Traverso, Mark Webster, Kaushik Patel, and Keren Bergman. 2017. Energy-performance optimized design of silicon photonic interconnection networks for high-performance computing. In *Proceedings of the Conference on Design, Automation & Test in Europe*. European Design and Automation Association, 326–331.

[11] Chin-Hui Chen, M Ashkan Seyedi, Marco Fiorentino, Daniil Livshits, Alexey Gubenko, Sergey Mikhrin, Vladimir Mikhrin, and Raymond G Beausoleil. 2015. A comb laser-driven DWDM silicon photonic transmitter based on microring modulators. *Optics express* 23, 16 (2015), 21541–21548.

[12] Long Chen, Nicolás Sherwood-Droz, and Michal Lipson. 2007. Compact bandwidth-tunable microring resonators. *Optics letters* 32, 22 (2007), 3361–3363.

[13] John E Cunningham, Ivan Shubin, Xuezhe Zheng, Thierry Pinguet, Attila Mekis, Ying Luo, Hiren Thacker, Guoliang Li, Jin Yao, Kannan Raj, and others. 2010. Highly-efficient thermally-tuned resonant optical filters. *Optics Express* 18, 18 (2010), 19055–19063.

[14] Po Dong, Wei Qian, Hong Liang, Roshanak Shafiiha, Ning-Ning Feng, Dazeng Feng, Xuezhe Zheng, Ashok V Krishnamoorthy, and Mehdi Asghari. 2010. Low power and compact reconfigurable multiplexing devices based on silicon microring resonators. *Optics express* 18, 10 (2010), 9852–9858.

[15] Raphaël Dubé-Demers, Sophie LaRochelle, and Wei Shi. 2016. Ultrafast pulse-amplitude modulation with a femtojoule silicon photonic modulator. *Optica* 3, 6 (2016), 622–627.

[16] Dazeng Feng, Wei Qian, Hong Liang, Cheng-Chih Kung, Zhou Zhou, Zhi Li, Jacob S Levy, Roshanak Shafiiha, Joan Fong, B Jonathan Luff, and others. 2013. High-speed GeSi electroabsorption modulator on the SOI waveguide platform. *IEEE Journal of Selected Topics in Quantum Electronics* 19, 6 (2013), 64–73.

[17] Alexander Gazman, Colm Browning, Ziyi Zhu, Liam P Barry, and Keren Bergman. 2017. Automated Thermal Stabilization of Cascaded Silicon Photonic Ring Resonators for Reconfigurable WDM Applications. *ECOC, September* (2017).

[18] Michael Georgas, Jonathan Leu, Benjamin Moss, Chen Sun, and Vladimir Stojanović. 2011. Addressing link-level design tradeoffs for integrated photonic interconnects. In *Custom Integrated Circuits Conference (CICC), 2011 IEEE*. IEEE, 1–8.

[19] Hasitha Jayatilleka, Michael Caverley, Nicolas AF Jaeger, Sudip Shekhar, and Lukas Chrostowski. 2015. Crosstalk limitations of microring-resonator based WDM demultiplexers on SOI. In *Optical Interconnects Conference (OI), 2015 IEEE*. IEEE, 48–49.

[20] J Komma, C Schwarz, G Hofmann, D Heinert, and R Nawrodt. 2012. Thermo-optic coefficient of silicon at 1550 nm and cryogenic temperatures. *Applied Physics Letters* 101, 4 (2012), 041905.

[21] Patrick Le Maître, Jean-Francois Carpentier, Charles Baudot, Nathalie Vulliet, Aurélie Souhaité, Jean-Baptiste Quélène, Thomas Ferrotti, and Frederic Bœuf. 2015. Impact of process variability of active ring resonators in a 300mm silicon photonic platform. In *Optical Communication (ECOC), 2015 European Conference on*. IEEE, 1–3.

[22] Ang Li, Thomas Vaerenbergh, Peter Heyn, Peter Bienstman, and Wim Bogaerts. 2016. Backscattering in silicon microring resonators: a quantitative analysis. *Laser & Photonics Reviews* 10, 3 (2016), 420–431.

[23] Guoliang Li, Xuezhe Zheng, Jin Yao, Hiren Thacker, Ivan Shubin, Ying Luo, Kannan Raj, John E Cunningham, and Ashok V Krishnamoorthy. 2011. 25Gb/s 1V-driving CMOS ring modulator with integrated thermal tuning. *Optics Express* 19, 21 (2011), 20435–20443.

[24] Jun Li, Xuezhe Zheng, Ashok V Krishnamoorthy, and James F Buckwalter. 2016. Scaling trends for picojoule-per-bit WDM photonic interconnects in CMOS SOI and FinFET processes. *Journal of Lightwave Technology* 34, 11 (2016), 2730–2742.

[25] Qi Li, Yang Liu, Kishore Padmaraju, Ran Ding, Dylan F Logan, Jason J Ackert, Andrew P Knights, Tom Baehr-Jones, Michael Hochberg, and Keren Bergman. 2014. A 10-Gb/s silicon microring resonator-based BPSK link. *IEEE Photonics Technology Letters* 26, 18 (2014), 1805–1808.

[26] Peicheng Liao, Meer Sakib, Fei Lou, Jongchul Park, Mitchell Wlodawski, Victor I Kopp, Dan Neugroschl, and Odile Liboiron-Ladouceur. 2015. Ultradense silicon photonic interface for optical interconnection. *IEEE Photonics Technology Letters* 27, 7 (2015), 725–728.

[27] Andy Eu-Jin Lim, Junfeng Song, Qing Fang, Chao Li, Xiaoguang Tu, Ning Duan, Kok Kiong Chen, Roger Poh-Cher Tern, and Tsung-Yang Liow. 2014. Review of silicon photonics foundry efforts. *IEEE Journal of Selected Topics in Quantum Electronics* 20, 4 (2014), 405–416.

[28] Brent E Little, Juha-Pekka Laine, and Sai T Chu. 1997. Surface-roughness-induced contradirectional coupling in ring and disk resonators. *Optics letters* 22, 1 (1997), 4–6.

[29] Zeqin Lu, Jaspreet Jhoja, Jackson Klein, Xu Wang, Amy Liu, Jonas Flueckiger, James Pond, and Lukas Chrostowski. 2017. Performance prediction for silicon photonics integrated circuits with layout-dependent correlated manufacturing variability. *Optics express* 25, 9 (2017), 9712–9733.

[30] Ying Luo, Xuezhe Zheng, Shiyun Lin, Jin Yao, Hiren Thacker, Ivan Shubin, John E Cunningham, Jin-Hyoung Lee, Stevan S Djordjevic, Jock Bovington, and others. 2016. A Process-Tolerant Ring Modulator Based on Multi-Mode Waveguides. *IEEE Photonics Technology Letters* 28, 13 (2016), 1391–1394.

[31] Andri Mahendra, Chunle Xiong, Xiang Zhang, Benjamin J Eggleton, and Philip HW Leong. 2017. Multiwavelength stabilization control of a thermo-optic system with adaptive reconfiguration. *Applied optics* 56, 4 (2017), 1113–1118.

[32] CL Manganelli, P Pintus, F Gambini, D Fowler, M Fournier, S Faralli, C Kopp, and CJ Oton. 2017. Large-FSR thermally tunable double-ring filters for WDM applications in silicon photonics. *IEEE Photonics Journal* 9, 1 (2017), 1–10.

[33] Christina Manolatou and Michal Lipson. 2006. All-optical silicon modulators based on carrier injection by two-photon absorption. *Journal of lightwave technology* 24, 3 (2006), 1433.

[34] Adil Masood, Marianna Pantouvaki, Guy Lepage, Peter Verheyen, Joris Van Campenhout, Philippe Absil, Dries Van Thourhout, and Wim Bogaerts. 2013. Comparison of heater architectures for thermal control of silicon photonic circuits. In *Group IV Photonics (GFP), 2013 IEEE 10th International Conference on*. IEEE, 83–84.

[35] Hiroyuki Matsuura, Satoshi Suda, Ken Tanizawa, Keijiro Suzuki, Kazuhiro Ikeda, Hitoshi Kawashima, and Shu Namiki. 2017. Accelerating switching speed of thermo-optic MZI silicon-photonic switches with" turbo pulse" in PWM control. In *Optical Fiber Communications Conference and Exhibition (OFC), 2017*. IEEE, 1–3.

[36] Mahdi Nikdast, Gabriela Nicolescu, Jelena Trajkovic, and Odile Liboiron-Ladouceur. 2015. Silicon Photonic Integrated Circuits under Process Variations. In *Asia Communications and Photonics Conference*. Optical Society of America, ASu2A–12.

[37] Mahdi Nikdast, Gabriela Nicolescu, Jelena Trajkovic, and Odile Liboiron-Ladouceur. 2016. Chip-scale silicon photonic interconnects: A formal study on fabrication non-uniformity. *Journal of Lightwave Technology* 34, 16 (2016), 3682–3695.

[38] Mahdi Nikdast, Gabriela Nicolescu, Jelena Trajkovic, and Odile Liboiron-Ladouceur. 2016. Photonic integrated circuits: A study on process variations. In *Optical Fiber Communication Conference*. Optical Society of America, W2A–22.

[39] Mahdi Nikdast, Jiang Xu, Luan Huu Kinh Duong, Xiaowen Wu, Xuan Wang, Zhehui Wang, Zhe Wang, Peng Yang, Yaoyao Ye, and Qinfen Hao. 2015. Crosstalk noise in WDM-based optical networks-on-chip: A formal study and comparison. *IEEE Transactions on Very Large Scale Integration (VLSI) Systems* 23, 11 (2015), 2552–2565.

[40] Kishore Padmaraju, Dylan F Logan, Xiaoliang Zhu, Jason J Ackert, Andrew P Knights, and Keren Bergman. 2013. Integrated thermal stabilization of a microring modulator. *Optics express* 21, 12 (2013), 14342–14350.

[41] Kishore Padmaraju, Lian-Wee Luo, Xiaoliang Zhu, Madeleine Glick, Raj Dutt, Michal Lipson, and Keren Bergman. 2014. Wavelength locking of a WDM silicon microring demultiplexer using dithering signals. In *Optical Fiber Communication Conference*. Optical Society of America, Tu2E–4.

[42] Samuel Palermo, Kunzhi Yu, Ashkan Roshan-Zamir, Binhao Wang, Cheng Li, M Ashkan Seyedi, Marco Fiorentino, and Raymond Beausoleil. 2017. PAM4 silicon photonic microring resonator-based transceiver circuits. In *Optical Interconnects XVII*, Vol. 10109. International Society for Optics and Photonics, 101090F.

[43] Marianna Pantouvaki, Hui Yu, Michal Rakowski, Phillip Christie, Peter Verheyen, Guy Lepage, Nele Van Hoovels, Philippe Absil, and Joris Van Campenhout. 2013. Comparison of silicon ring modulators with interdigitated and lateral PN junctions. *IEEE Journal of Selected Topics in Quantum Electronics* 19, 2 (2013), 7900308–7900308.

[44] Paolo Pintus, Costanza Manganelli, Fabrizio Gambini, Fabrizio Di Pasquale, Maryse Fournier, Olivier Lemonnier, Christophe Kopp, and Claudio J Oton. 2016. Optimization of integrated silicon doped heaters for optical microring resonators. In *ECOC 2016; 42nd European Conference on Optical Communication; Proceedings of*. VDE, 1–3.

[45] James Pond, Jackson Klein, Jonas Flückiger, Xu Wang, Zeqin Lu, Jaspreet Jhoja, and Lukas Chrostowski. 2017. Predicting the yield of photonic integrated circuits using statistical compact modeling. In *Integrated Optics: Physics and Simulations III*, Vol. 10242. International Society for Optics and Photonics, 102420S.

[46] Miloš A Popovic, Tymon Barwicz, Michael R Watts, Peter T Rakich, Luciano Socci, Erich P Ippen, Franz X Kärtner, and Henry I Smith. 2006. Multistage high-order microring-resonator add-drop filters. *Optics letters* 31, 17 (2006), 2571–2573.

[47] Graham T Reed, G Mashanovich, FY Gardes, and DJ Thomson. 2010. Silicon optical modulators. *Nature photonics* 4, 8 (2010), 518.

[48] Ashkan Roshan-Zamir, Binhao Wang, Shashank Telaprolu, Kunzhi Yu, Cheng Li, M Ashkan Seyedi, Marco Fiorentino, Raymond Beausoleil, and Samuel Palermo. 2016. A 40 Gb/s PAM4 silicon microring resonator modulator transmitter in 65nm CMOS. In *IEEE Optical Interconnects Conference (OI), 2016*. IEEE, 8–9.

[49] Sébastien Rumley, Meisam Bahadori, Dessislava Nikolova, and Keren Bergman. 2016. Physical layer compact models for ring resonators based dense WDM optical interconnects. In *ECOC 2016; 42nd European Conference on Optical Communication; Proceedings of*. VDE, 1–3.

[50] M Ashkan Seyedi, Rui Wu, Chin-Hui Chen, Marco Fiorentino, and Ray Beausoleil. 2016. 15 Gb/s transmission with wide-FSR carrier injection ring modulator for Tb/s optical links. In *CLEO: Science and Innovations*. Optical Society of America, SF2F–7.

[51] RICHARDA Soref and BRIANR Bennett. 1987. Electrooptical effects in silicon. *IEEE journal of quantum electronics* 23, 1 (1987), 123–129.

[52] Chen Sun, Mark Wade, Michael Georgas, Sen Lin, Luca Alloatti, Benjamin Moss, Rajesh Kumar, Amir H Atabaki, Fabio Pavanello, Jeffrey M Shainline, and others. 2016. A 45 nm CMOS-SOI monolithic photonics platform with bit-statistics-based resonant microring thermal tuning. *IEEE Journal of Solid-State Circuits* 51, 4 (2016), 893–907.

[53] Chen Sun, Mark T Wade, Yunsup Lee, Jason S Orcutt, Luca Alloatti, Michael S Georgas, Andrew S Waterman, Jeffrey M Shainline, Rimas R Avizienis, Sen Lin, and others. 2015. Single-chip microprocessor that communicates directly using light. *Nature* 528, 7583 (2015), 534.

[54] Mark T Wade, Fabio Pavanello, Rajesh Kumar, Cale M Gentry, Amir Atabaki, Rajeev Ram, Vladimir Stojanović, and Miloš A Popović. 2015. 75% efficient wide bandwidth grating couplers in a 45 nm microelectronics CMOS process. In *Optical Interconnects Conference (OI), 2015 IEEE*. IEEE, 46–47.

[55] Shijun Xiao, Maroof H Khan, Hao Shen, and Minghao Qi. 2007. A highly compact third-order silicon microring add-drop filter with a very large free spectral range, a flat passband and a low delay dispersion. *Optics express* 15, 22 (2007), 14765–14771.

[56] Xi Xiao, Xianyao Li, Hao Xu, Yingtao Hu, Kang Xiong, Zhiyong Li, Tao Chu, Jinzhong Yu, and Yude Yu. 2012. 44-Gb/s silicon microring modulators based on zigzag PN junctions. *IEEE Photonics Technology Letters* 24, 19 (2012), 1712–1714.

[57] Xi Xiao, Hao Xu, Xianyao Li, Yingtao Hu, Kang Xiong, Zhiyong Li, Tao Chu, Yude Yu, and Jinzhong Yu. 2012. 25 Gbit/s silicon microring modulator based on misalignment-tolerant interleaved PN junctions. *Optics express* 20, 3 (2012), 2507–2515.

[58] Qianfan Xu, Sasikanth Manipatruni, Brad Schmidt, Jagat Shakya, and Michal Lipson. 2007. 12.5 Gbit/s carrier-injection-based silicon micro-ring silicon modulators. *Optics express* 15, 2 (2007), 430–436.

[59] Qianfan Xu, Bradley Schmidt, Sameer Pradhan, and Michal Lipson. 2005. Micrometre-scale silicon electro-optic modulator. *nature* 435, 7040 (2005), 325.

[60] William A Zortman, Anthony L Lentine, Douglas C Trotter, and Michael R Watts. 2013. Bit-error-rate monitoring for active wavelength control of resonant modulators. *IEEE Micro* 33, 1 (2013), 42–52.

[61] Maurizio Zuffada. 2012. The industrialization of the silicon photonics: technology road map and applications. In *Solid-State Device Research Conference (ESSDERC), 2012 Proceedings of the European*. IEEE, 7–13.

Wavelength-Routed Optical Networks-on-Chip: Design Methods and Tools to Bridge the Gap Between Logic Topologies and Physical Ones in 3D Architectures

Davide Bertozzi
Dipartimento di Ingegneria,
University of Ferrara
Via Saragat, 1
44122 Ferrara, Italy
davide.bertozzi@unife.it

Marco Gavanelli
Dipartimento di Ingegneria,
University of Ferrara
Via Saragat, 1
44122 Ferrara, Italy
marco.gavanelli@unife.it

Maddalena Nonato
Dipartimento di Ingegneria,
University of Ferrara
Via Saragat, 1
44122 Ferrara, Italy
maddalena.nonato@unife.it

ABSTRACT

Silicon photonics is gaining momentum as a candidate technology platform for future intra- and inter-chip communications. However, its industrial uptake depends not only on technology maturity, but also on the capability to bridge the abstraction gap between technology developers and system designers. This paper presents an early-stage cross-layer refinement methodology of wavelength-routed optical network-on-chip topologies, linking logic topology synthesis to the physical implementation steps.

CCS CONCEPTS

• **Hardware → Emerging optical and photonic technologies;**

KEYWORDS

Optical network-on-chip, Wavelength routing, Design technology, Synthesis methodology

ACM Reference Format:
Davide Bertozzi, Marco Gavanelli, and Maddalena Nonato. 2018. Wavelength-Routed Optical Networks-on-Chip: Design Methods and Tools to Bridge the Gap Between Logic Topologies and Physical Ones in 3D Architectures. In *GLSVLSI '18: 2018 Great Lakes Symposium on VLSI, May 23–25, 2018, Chicago, IL, USA.* ACM, New York, NY, USA, 6 pages. https://doi.org/10.1145/3194554.3194607

1 INTRODUCTION

Photonic integration of multi- and many-core architectures via optical networks-on-chip (ONoCs) has been extensively studied in literature [5, 8, 12, 13, 19, 23]. Proposals use different topologies, routing and flow control mechanisms, and optical wavelength organizations. However, the analyzed design solutions still represent a small subset of the whole design space, which is still largely unknown. This is a typical trend in the early stage of an emerging technology, which is characterized by two interrelated concerns: (i) overcoming technology barriers; (ii) developing proof-of-concept architectures.

However, as silicon photonics gains acceptance as a viable technology platform for on-chip and off-chip communications, another concern comes to the forefront: bridging the gap between technology developers and system designers. This implies the possibility to specify abstract descriptions of interconnection and switching fabrics, matching the requirements of the system at hand, and to refine them into actual implementations. This requires a greater research emphasis on design space exploration, on design flexibility and on vertically-integrated methods to bridge the abstraction gap.

ONoC literature is lagging far behind in this respect, although there are indications of a turning point. In fact, contributions at several abstraction layers are laying the groundwork for future synthesis toolflows of ONoC topologies, such as exploration of communication protocols [10], early-stage analysis of physical properties [16], populating methods of the design space [24], device parameter selection strategies [7], or placement and routing frameworks [2].

The timely evolution and growth of this emerging research field requires a more systematic and coherent effort though [1], aiming at understanding all design points in the context of a unified design framework, and at linking logic solutions with their physical implementations through a consistent refinement flow. This paper takes on this challenge in the field of wavelength-routed ONoC (WRONoC) topologies, that deliver contention-free optical communications and have showed promising results for 2.5D/3D integration [11]. We provide a *unified and vertically-integrated view* to the problem of refining an abstract connectivity specification into a placed and routed netlist of ONoC components on the optical layer of a 3D-stacked system. We define the intermediate steps of the refinement flow, and provide early-stage design space exploration and/or synthesis methodologies at each step. Experimental results show off the capability of the presented framework to gain visibility of a largely unknown design space, with awareness of physical design constraints.

GLSVLSI '18, May 23–25, 2018, Chicago, IL, USA

ACM ISBN 978-1-4503-5724-1/18/05...$15.00
https://doi.org/10.1145/3194554.3194607

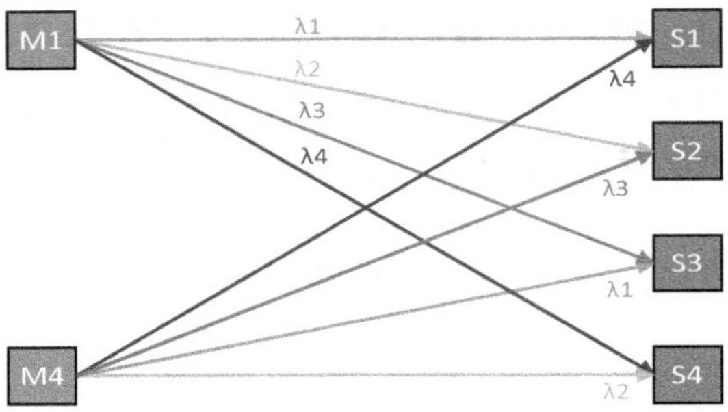

Figure 1: Wavelength-selective routing: concept.

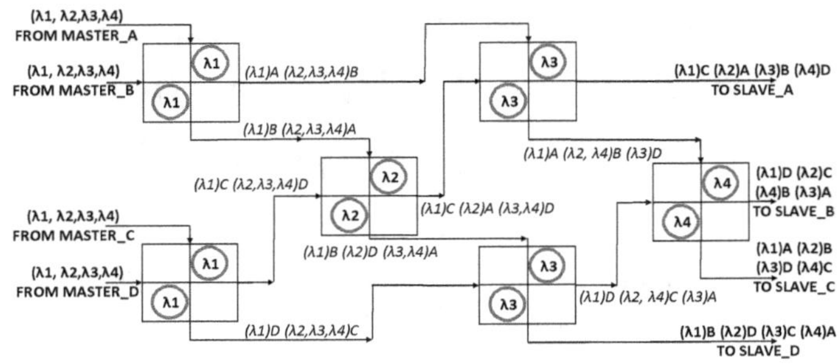

Figure 2: The tightly-intertwined add and drop functions at work in a 4×4 λ-router WRONoC topology.

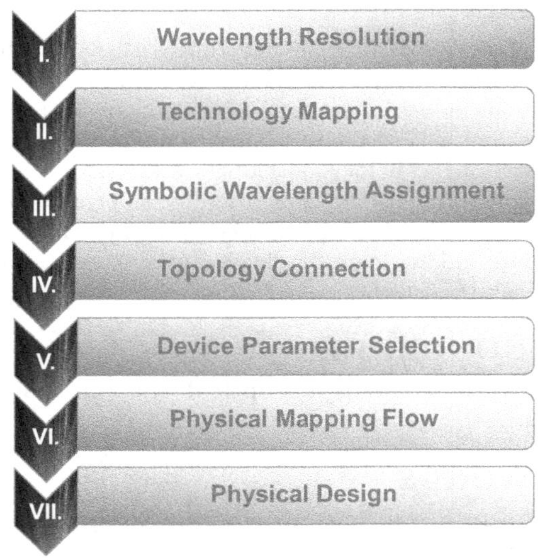

Figure 3: Intervening steps in the synthesis methodology of a WRONoC topology.

2 WAVELENGTH-ROUTED ONOCS

Wavelength-routed optical NoCs (WRONoCs) rely on the principle of wavelength-selective routing (Fig.1), which statically associates an optical channel modulated onto a specific wavelength (*wavelength channel* from now on) to each source-destination pair. In particular, master $M1$ uses n wavelengths λ_1 to λ_n to reach slaves $S1$ to Sn, respectively. At the same time, each slave receives packets from masters $M1$ to Mn on different wavelengths. The intermediate topology (not shown in figure) should be synthesized in such a way that same-wavelength optical channels never overlap on the topology waveguides to avoid interference (hence loss of information). The distinctive property of wavelength-selective routing is that it delivers contention-free concurrent all-to-all connectivity without any form of resource arbitration.

A well-known 4×4 WRONoC topology is illustrated in Fig.2, named λ-router [4]. Boxes represent add-drop filters, which progressively resolve wavelength-division multiplexed (WDM) signals from source nodes into their individual components (*drop function*), and recombine them into the output WDM signals for each receiver (*add function*).

3 REFINEMENT METHODOLOGY

Fig.3 defines the key steps of the proposed refinement methodology for WRONoC topologies, which improves state-of-the-art in terms of cross-layer visibility and vertical integration. This was achieved by identifying suitable abstractions for optical switching, and by consistently refining them with implementation details in the context of a comprehensive floorplanning strategy for 3D integration.

At first, all the *wavelength resolution* steps implied in the connectivity specification are made explicit. At this stage, the drop function of a WRONoC topology is captured by means of an abstract resolution primitive of optical channels.

Next, *technology mapping* takes place: the basic drop operators are aggregated together for the sake of mapping onto real optical switching devices. The add function is implicit in the connectivity of such devices.

The third step consists of assigning *symbolic resonant wavelengths* to the photonic switching elements. Symbolic wavelength channels should then be refined into optical carriers at exact wavelength values to be selected. At the same time, specifying such wavelengths implies the definition of micro-ring resonator (MRR) radius lengths inside photonic switches, since optical channels should be on-resonance with specific MRRs, and off-resonance with all others. The key constraint at this *device parameter selection* stage is to avoid routing faults, i.e., unintended misroutings of optical packets.

The synthesis methodology is completed by the *physical mapping flow*, which consists of the floorplanning, placement and routing of WRONoC topologies on the optical layer of a 3D-stacked parallel computing system.

Last but not least, the *back-end physical design* steps take place, which end up in the mask set generation for the actual photonic integrated circuit. This will not be illustrated in this paper, since photonic integrated circuit design is a well-established field, which relies on mainstream commercial tools [6], although coping with such large-scale designs as ONoCs remains an open challenge.

3.1 Front-End Methodology

State-of-the-art is still far from automatically synthesizing an ONoC topology for a set of input design requirements (e.g., connectivity, bandwidth requirements). Our current

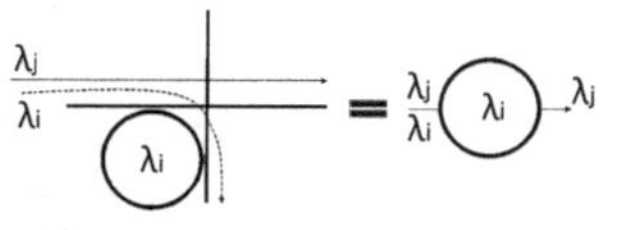

(a) A 1×2 drop filter, and its symbolic representation.

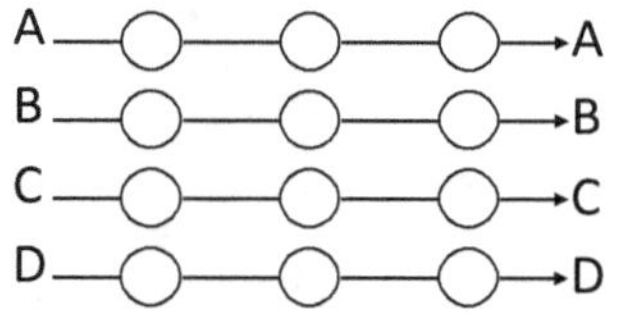

(b) Generic wavelength resolution graph.

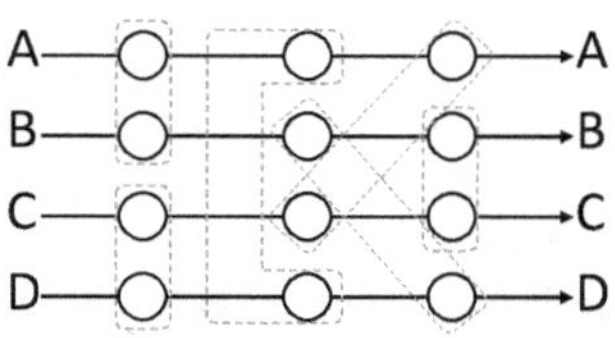

(c) Technology mapping example.

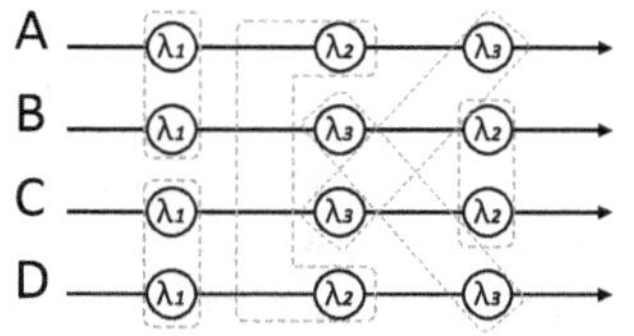

(d) Wavelength assigment example.

Figure 4: Front-end synthesis methodology of WRONoC logic topologies.

contribution at this stage is to provide a methodology to populate the design space of $n \times n$ WRONoC topologies much beyond the few design points available in literature. The latter have been directly inspired by designers' intuition, while we build on communication abstractions and exploit the power of design automation.

More specifically, this paper identifies the 1×2 drop filter (DF) as the universal primitive to synthesize any WRONoC topology (see Fig.4a). With this approach, the WDM input signal from any master node undergoes the drop function by crossing $n - 1$ DFs, each filter resolving the wavelength channel for a specific destination. This process can be pictorially illustrated as a *wavelength resolution graph (WRG)*, reported in Fig.4b for a 4×4 generic WRONoC topology. Fixing the parameters of the WRG indirectly prunes the design space and biases the methodology toward a specific topology design point.

The next step consists of technology mapping, since the 1×2 DFs should be mapped to the photonic swiching elements (PSEs) of a technology library. In most cases, this implies a clustering of the original primitives for the sake of compact implementations. However, not any combination of DFs is legal. In fact, we should avoid coupling rows of the WRG twice, since this would result in a lack of connectivity and in the risk of same-wavelength channel interference.

As an example, let us assume the 1×2 DFs are mapped into compact 2×2 PSEs. In this case, pairs of DFs should be identified on the WRG, and replaced by a PSE. The legal mappings are the combinations without repetitions $C(n, 2)$ for picking 2 unordered outcomes from n possibilities. When assuming 4 masters (A,B,C,D) connected with 4 slaves, the number of mappings is C(4,2)=6, namely AB, AC, AD, BC, BD, CD. One legal mapping example is illustrated in Fig.4c.

When assigning symbolic resonant wavelengths to the MRRs of the PSEs, we should prevent some destinations

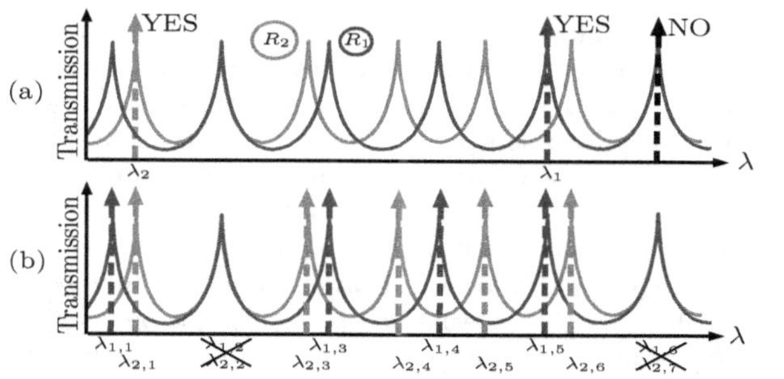

Figure 5: The routing fault concern: (a) constraining wavelength selection; (b) limiting parallelism.

from becoming unreachable and other ones from being overprovisioned. For this, one constraint should be enforced on the WRG: the resonant wavelengths of the DFs along a single row should be different from each other. That is, λ_1, λ_2, λ_3, λ_4 is a valid drop order for the WDM signal from a given master, while λ_1, λ_1, λ_2, λ_3 is not. We have proposed a greedy algorithm in [24] to perform legal wavelength assignment. When applying the algorithm to the technology mapping of Fig.4c, the legal assignment in Fig.4d is derived.

Finally, it is possible to draw the connectivity pattern of the topology. In particular, the reader can easily prove himself that the topology in Fig.4d is exactly the λ-router topology presented in Fig.2. There is a key difference though: the exact connectivity pattern of the λ-router has been materialized while making use of 3 resonator types only instead of 4. In section 4, it will be shown that this potentially leads to a higher communication parallelism. For further details on the complete front-end refinement methodology, the interested reader is referred to [24].

3.2 Device Parameter Selection

At this stage, two tighly intertwined device parameters have to be selected:

a) The exact radius length of the MRRs inside PSEs;

b) The exact values of the n wavelengths used by each initiator in an $n \times n$ fully-connected WRONoC.

These parameters should be selected in such a way that routing faults (an issue not visible at higher abstraction layers) are prevented, which are key limiters (together with static power) of topology scalability and throughput. A routing fault takes place when a wavelength channel ends up on-resonance with a non-intended MRR as an effect of the periodic transmittance of the latter. In this case, the signal mistakenly drops into the wrong MRR and is misrouted.

As an example, Fig.5(a) shows the transmittance of two MRRs used in a generic topology. The free spectral range FSR of the two MRRs (i.e., the wavelength range between any two resonant peaks) depends on radius length. Since it is not the same, resonant peaks from the two MRRs might overlap. As a consequence, if an optical carrier coinciding with overlapped peaks were chosen for transmission, a **routing fault** would occur in the network. The problem can turn into a feasibility limitation when increasing the network size, since the proliferation of PSEs and of wavelength channels may limit the availability of non-overlapped transmission peaks.

Even for a feasible network size, the routing fault concern turns out to be a fundamental limiter for communication parallelism as well. For instance, the former λ_1 channel for a specific 1-bit connection might be augmented to $\lambda_{1,j}$ channels, with $j = 1..M$, for an M-bit extended communication. Fig.5(b) shows that overlapped peaks cannot be chosen for transmission, hence limiting the maximum parallelism that can be sustained on both optical channels to 4. We propose a formal methodology to correctly and efficiently select WRONoC physical parameters.

3.2.1 Maximizing Communication Parallelism. The problem of finding the maximum bit-level parallelism on all I/O connections of a WRONoC topology connecting n senders with n receivers has been addressed in our previous work in [7]. The need to avoid routing faults while selecting device parameters leads to a Constrained Optimization Problem, which is formulated by means of a well-known declarative technology in Artificial Intelligence called Answer Set Programming (ASP). More specifically, the idea is to look for a feasible solution to increase the level of parallelism until the problem turns infeasible. A feasible solution is an s-tuple providing the radius lengths for each of the s MRR types a topology consists of. At the same time, for each radius, the wavelengths for bit-parallel communication are returned, chosen among the overlap-free resonant wavelengths of that MRR type. To account for fabrication tolerances, adjacent resonant peaks of different MRRs are conservatively discarded if they fall within the variability range of the FSRs of the two MRRs (i.e., if they may turn out to be overlapped after fabrication). The objective function consists of maximizing the common communication parallelism n_λ to all I/O connections.

3.2.2 Quality of solutions. It turns out that the solution provided by the ASP model consists of resonant wavelengths suboptimally spaced over the band. This may lead to transmission bandwidth limitations, post-fabrication tuning range inefficiencies, or interchannel crosstalk concerns.

We therefore search for other feasible solutions with the same level of parallelism as the maximum one, whose resonances are distributed differently. Formally, suppose to be given a candidate set of nR radii (the fabrication space), and a given degree of parallelism n_λ (maximized by the ASP framework). We have to select s radii (among the available nR) and n_λ *resonating* wavelengths for each selected radius, so that routing faults are prevented. We consider two variants of this problem, which have the same set of feasible solutions but have different targets, corresponding to different interpretations of the concept of *optimal spacing* of optical channels.

In the first problem (*spacing selected wavelengths*), the target is to *equitably space* the $n_\lambda \times s$ selected wavelengths in the bandwidth $\bar{\Lambda} = [\lambda_{min}, \lambda_{max}]$, in order to facilitate tuning, maximize bitrate, or align with existing off-chip standards. We solve the problem in [17] by means of Mixed Integer Linear Programming (MILP). The problem is formalized as a cardinality-constrained shortest path on an acyclic graph, and solved by an iterative procedure that exploits the objective function properties.

In the second problem (*spacing all wavelengths*), our target is to maximize the minimum difference between any selected resonant wavelength and any other resonant peak of the chosen radii. This way, interchannel crosstalk is indirectly minimized. The problem is addressed in our work in [9], where it is modeled and solved by Constraint Logic Programming on Finite Domain (CLP(FD)).

Note that each approach is currently the most effective tool to solve the problem with respect to its own specific objective function. In theory, the MILP approach could be modified to optimize the same criterion as CLP(FD), but it could not take advantage of the iterative approach in [17] any longer for better scalability. On the contrary, at present CLP(FD) is not very efficient when using the MILP objective function.

3.3 Physical Mapping Flow

In this paper, the target environment for the physical mapping of WRONoC topologies is a clustered 3D many-core architecture, composed of an electronic layer and an optical layer vertically stacked on top of it. For the time being, we assume the off-chip generation of unmodulated optical power.

There are vertical alignment dependencies that determine the location of the optical network interfaces (or hubs) on the optical plane [3, 18]. This gives rise to floorplanning constraints for the placement and routing problem of an ONoC on the optical layer. As a result, sender and receiver placement in the topology logic scheme cannot be typically preserved in the final layout, thus causing a deviation between the logic and the physical topologies. The latter then results in an increase of insertion loss (e.g., additional number of waveguide crossings), hence of laser power requirements in order to meet photodetector sensitivity. Such design predictability gap should be minimized.

Our PROTON+ tool for the place-and-route (P&R) of WRONoC topologies targets the minimization of the worst-case insertion loss across all the optical paths (hereafter named the *critical path*), whatever the optical carrier they modulate [2] [1]. For the best results, this objective function should be matched with the laser power generation system (see [2] for details).

Insertion loss is mainly dominated by propagation losses and crossing losses, which might be contradictory objectives, as shown in Fig.6. Thus, PROTON+ minimizes a weighted sum of propagation loss and crossing loss during P&R, so that users can potentially search for the best combination that yields superior physical mapping properties for the topology and technology at hand. Since the position of the waveguides is not available during placement, waveguide length and

[1] PROTON+ has been jointly developed by the MPSoC group at University of Ferrara (Davide Bertozzi) and the EDA group at TU München (Ulf Schlichtmann).

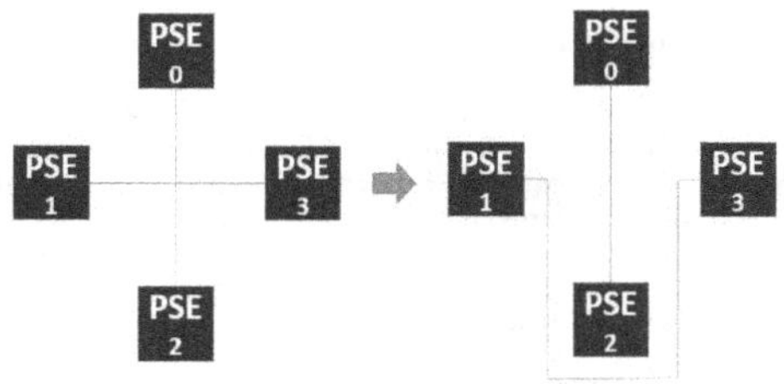

Figure 6: Minimizing propagation loss or crossing loss can be contradictory objective functions.

number of crossings have to be approximated for each path. The placement problem is finally solved with the help of nonlinear optimization.

For routing, PROTON+ uses a modified version of a maze router [14]. Maze routers, as well as all routing algorithms for the design of electronic systems, do not allow crossings of wires. PROTON+ thus adapts the maze router by enabling waveguide crossings, while at the same time penalizing them to reduce the number of their occurrences.

Recently, a follow-up framework of PROTON+, named PLATON, has been proposed by TU München [25], targeting scalability improvements. While featuring several similarities with PROTON+ (e.g., same objective function, maze router), PLATON relies on a force-directed placement algorithm based on Kraftwerk [22]. Because of this, PLATON achieves 86% shorter runtimes on 8×8 WRONoC topologies, and handles P&R of 16×16 topologies in tens of seconds (99.7% lower than PROTON+). Interestingly, PROTON+ still yields more power-efficient topologies for 8×8 networks (from 7 to 31%), while on 16×16 networks PLATON reduces laser power requirements by 99.3%. Again, designers can choose based on the requirements of the system at hand.

4 EXPERIMENTAL RESULTS

Despite the early stage of development, we hereafter document the unique capability of the proposed refinement flow to shed light on the design space of WRONoC topologies with layout awareness.

4.1 Topology Design Space

By running the front-end synthesis methodology in Section 3.1, the complete design space for 4×4 WRONoC topologies is exhaustively generated, built out of 2×2 PSEs. The total population amounts to 1296 topologies. Among them, we found well-known topologies reported in literature, such as λ-router and *snake* [21]. For each topology, we measured the critical path with respect to the insertion loss, which we approximate as the optical path with the highest number of waveguide crossings. With this approximation, the critical path may not be unique. Overall, logic topologies fall into two broad categories. 85% of them fall into the first category, featuring few critical paths (from 1 to 4), with 4 crossings each. The second category, which includes remaining topologies, exhibits a larger number of critical paths (from 4 to 9), but with only 3 crossings each.

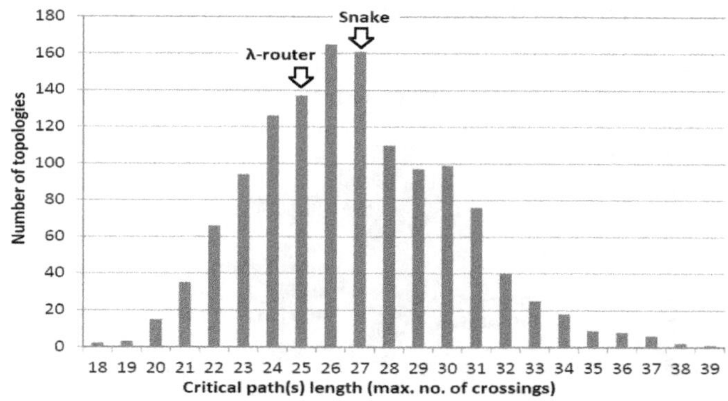

Figure 7: Distribution of the critical path after physical mapping.

The physical mapping of these logic topologies ends up in a broader differentiation of their characteristics though. To prove this, the PROTON+ tool was used to lay out the population of 4×4 topologies. In order to avoid trivial layouts associated with the small radix of the considered networks, they were used in the context of partitioned ONoCs. In practice, 3 replicated 4×4 ONoCs with different floorplanning and connectivity constraints were instantiated to serve different message classes, thus resulting in an 8×8 aggregated topology (details given in [20]). Post-place&route results are reported in Fig.7, where the critical path distribution is reported. Interestingly, now the critical path length ranges from 18 to 39 crossings, thus featuring a much larger variability than in logic schemes. This raises the issue of placement-aware logic synthesis, which is mainstream for electronic design, but is completely new for optical NoCs. An interesting result is that some state-of-the-art solutions (indicated in the figure) are not the optimal ones, since they are part of a richer design space that the proposed methodology brings to light.

4.2 Connectivity and Parallelism

We use the ASP framework recalled in Section 3.2, and verify how the maximum achievable bit-level parallelism $P(s)$ by a WRONoC topology scales with respect to:

i) the network size. In general, larger networks require a higher number of PSE types s, each one defined by a specific MRR radius length.

ii) the fabrication options $R_{opt} = \{R_{min}, R_{step}, R_{max}\}$, including minimum and maximum radius length (R_{min} and R_{max}, respectively), and the intermediate incremental step R_{step}.

iii) the manufacturing non-idealities (ring radius variability R_{tol} and laser center wavelength uncertainty $\Delta\lambda$). We assume worst-case uncertainties $R_{tol} = 0.01\mu$m and $\Delta\lambda = 0.5$nm, while these parameters are set to zero in the ideal case.

Results are in Figure 8. For the first test, we set $R_{opt} = \{5, 1, 25\}\mu$m [15]. Even with ideal fabrication, at most 14×14 topologies can be instantiated without routing faults, which increases only slightly when enabling larger MRR radii ($R'_{\text{opt}} = \{5, 1, 30\}\mu$m). By improving the radius resolution ($R''_{\text{opt}} = \{5, 0.25, 30\}\mu$m), we can extend this upper bound to

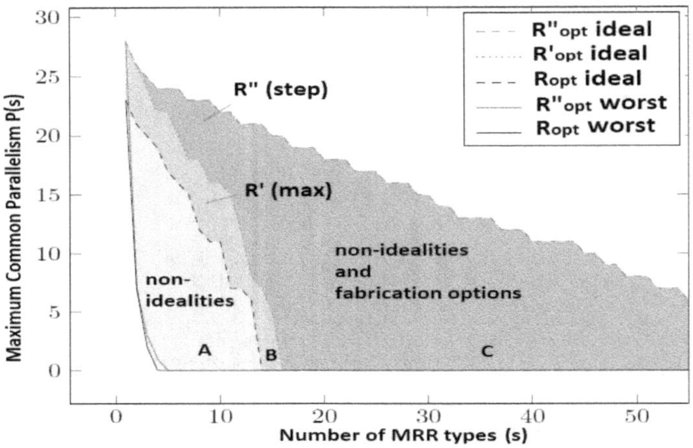

Figure 8: Maximum communication parallelism (common to all I/O paths) as a function of the no. of MRR resonator types in the topology, roughly corresponding to network size.

60×60 topologies. However, the larger the network size the lower the achievable bit-level parallelism.

Finally, when considering R_{opt}, Figure 8 shows that there is a huge inaccessible "performance" gap (see grey area A) that improvements in fabrication and laser generation technology can reduce. With R''_{opt}, this gap is even larger, and is roughly given by the sum of areas A, B and C. For instance, a 32×32 $\lambda-$router may theoretically yield 14-bit parallelism in the ideal case. Instead, with current worst-case assumptions on parameter uncertainty, this network size is infeasible[2].

5 CONCLUSIONS

In this paper, a complete refinement flow has been presented for WRONoC topologies, which brings the philosophy of electronic design automation to the emerging field of silicon nanophotonic networks. It relies on a unified conceptualization framework of topology design points, and on vertically-integrated steps to add implementation details. In future work, we will target the automatic synthesis of WRONoC topologies matching the requirements of the system at hand.

REFERENCES

[1] C. Batten, A. Joshi, V. Stojanovic, and K. Asanovic. 2012. Designing Chip-Level Nanophotonic Interconnection Networks. *IEEE Journal on Emerging and Selected Topics in Circuits and Systems* 2, 2 (2012), 137–153.

[2] Anja Von Beuningen, Luca Ramini, Davide Bertozzi, and Ulf Schlichtmann. 2015. PROTON+: A Placement and Routing Tool for 3D Optical Networks-on-Chip with a Single Optical Layer. *J. Emerg. Technol. Comput. Syst.* 12, 4 (Dec. 2015), 44:1–44:28.

[3] Sébastien Le Beux, Jelena Trajkovic, Ian O'Connor, and Gabriela Nicolescu. 2011. Layout guidelines for 3D architectures including Optical Ring Network-on-Chip (ORNoC). *2011 IEEE/IFIP 19th International Conference on VLSI and System-on-Chip* (2011), 242–247.

[4] M. Briere, B. Girodias, Y. Bouchebaba, G. Nicolescu, F. Mieyeville, F. Gaffiot, and I. O'Connor. 2007. System Level Assessment of an Optical NoC in an MPSoC Platform. In *2007 Design, Automation Test in Europe Conference Exhibition*. 1–6.

[2]Considering worst-case uncertainties is overly pessimistic. In future work, we will explore a statistical notion of manufacturing yield.

[5] Mark J. Cianchetti, Joseph C. Kerekes, and David H. Albonesi. 2009. Phastlane: A Rapid Transit Optical Routing Network. *SIGARCH Comput. Archit. News* 37, 3 (June 2009), 441–450.

[6] European Photonics Industry Consortium. 2015. List of companies in Photonic Integrated Circuits: Company per Value Chain - Company Description. In *http://www.epic-assoc.com/technology/photonic-integrated-circuits/*.

[7] A. Peano et al. 2016. Design technology for fault-free and maximally-parallel wavelength-routed optical networks-on-chip. In *2016 ICCAD*. 1–8.

[8] D. Vantrease et al. 2008. Corona: System Implications of Emerging Nanophotonic Technology. In *2008 ISCA*. 153–164.

[9] Marco Gavanelli, Maddalena Nonato, Andrea Peano, and Davide Bertozzi. 2017. Logic programming approaches for routing fault-free and maximally parallel wavelength-routed optical networks-on-chip. *Theory and Practice of Logic Programming* 17, 5-6 (2017), 800–818.

[10] Paolo Grani and Sandro Bartolini. 2014. Design Options for Optical Ring Interconnect in Future Client Devices. *J. Emerg. Technol. Comput. Syst.* 10, 4 (June 2014), 30:1–30:25.

[11] Paolo Grani, Roberto Proietti, Venkatesh Akella, and S. J. Ben Yoo. 2016. Photonic Interconnects for Interposer-based 2.5D/3D Integrated Systems on a Chip. In *Proceedings of MEMSYS '16*. 377–386.

[12] N. Kirman, M. Kirman, R. K. Dokania, J. F. Martinez, A. B. Apsel, M. A. Watkins, and D. H. Albonesi. 2006. Leveraging Optical Technology in Future Bus-based Chip Multiprocessors. In *2006 IEEE/ACM MICRO'06*. 492–503.

[13] G. Kurian, J. E. Miller, J. Psota, J. Eastep, J. Liu, J. Michel, L. C. Kimerling, and A. Agarwal. 2010. ATAC: A 1000-core cache-coherent processor with on-chip optical network. In *2010 PACT*. 477–488.

[14] C. Y. Lee. 1961. An Algorithm for Path Connections and Its Applications. *IRE Transactions on Electronic Computers* EC-10, 3 (1961), 346–365.

[15] Di Liang and John Bowers. 2010. Recent progress in lasers on silicon. 4 (07 2010), 511–517.

[16] M. Nikdast, J. Xu, L. H. K. Duong, X. Wu, X. Wang, Z. Wang, Z. Wang, P. Yang, Y. Ye, and Q. Hao. 2015. Crosstalk Noise in WDM-Based Optical Networks-on-Chip: A Formal Study and Comparison. *IEEE TVLSI* 23, 11 (2015), 2552–2565.

[17] Maddalena Nonato, Davide Bertozzi, Marco Gavanelli, and Andrea Peano. 2018. A network model for routing-fault-free wavelength selection in WRONoCs design. *Electronic Notes in Discrete Mathematics* 64 (2018), 285 – 294. INOC 2017.

[18] M. Ortin-Obon, M. Tala, L. Ramini, V. Vials-Yufera, and D. Bertozzi. 2017. Contrasting Laser Power Requirements of Wavelength-Routed Optical NoC Topologies Subject to the Floorplanning, Placement, and Routing Constraints of a 3-D-Stacked System. *IEEE TVLSI* 25, 7 (2017), 2081–2094.

[19] Yan Pan, Prabhat Kumar, John Kim, Gokhan Memik, Yu Zhang, and Alok Choudhary. 2009. Firefly: Illuminating Future Network-on-chip with Nanophotonics. In *2009 ISCA*. 429–440.

[20] L. Ramini, D. Bertozzi, and L. P. Carloni. 2012. Engineering a Bandwidth-Scalable Optical Layer for a 3D Multi-core Processor with Awareness of Layout Constraints. In *2012 IEEE/ACM NOCS*. 185–192.

[21] L. Ramini, P. Grani, S. Bartolini, and D. Bertozzi. 2013. Contrasting wavelength-routed optical NoC topologies for power-efficient 3d-stacked multicore processors using physical-layer analysis. In *2013 DATE*. 1589–1594.

[22] P. Spindler, U. Schlichtmann, and F. M. Johannes. 2008. Kraftwerk2 - A Fast Force-Directed Quadratic Placement Approach Using an Accurate Net Model. *IEEE Transactions on Computer-Aided Design of Integrated Circuits and Systems* 27, 8 (2008), 1398–1411.

[23] V. Stojanovic, A. Joshi, C. Batten, Y. j. Kwon, and K. Asanovic. 2009. Manycore processor networks with monolithic integrated CMOS photonics. In *2009 Conference on Lasers and Electro-Optics and 2009 Conference on Quantum electronics and Laser Science Conference*. 1–2.

[24] M. Tala, M. Castellari, M. Balboni, and D. Bertozzi. 2016. Populating and exploring the design space of wavelength-routed optical network-on-chip topologies by leveraging the add-drop filtering primitive. In *2016 IEEE/ACM NOCS*. 1–8.

[25] Anja von Beuningen and Ulf Schlichtmann. 2016. PLATON: A Force-Directed Placement Algorithm for 3D Optical Networks-on-Chip, in ISPD 2016. (04 2016), 27-34 pages.

Cross-Layer Thermal Reliability Management in Silicon Photonic Networks-on-Chip

Sudeep Pasricha, Sai Vineel Reddy Chittamuru, Ishan G. Thakkar
Department of Electrical and Computer Engineering
Colorado State University, Fort Collins, CO, U.S.A.
{sudeep, sai.chittamuru, ishan.thakkar}@colostate.edu

ABSTRACT

Silicon photonics technology is being considered for future networks-on-chip (NoCs) as it can enable high bandwidth density and lower latency with traversal of data at the speed of light. But the operation of photonic NoCs (PNoCs) is very sensitive to on-chip temperature variations. These variations can create significant reliability issues for PNoCs. This paper presents a run-time cross-layer framework to overcome temperature variation-induced reliability issues in PNoCs. The framework consists of a device-level reactive mechanism and a system-level proactive technique to avoid on-chip thermal threshold violations and mitigate thermal reliability issues. Our analysis indicates that this framework can reliably satisfy on-chip thermal thresholds and maintain high network bandwidth while reducing power dissipation over state-of-the-art solutions.

KEYWORDS

Photonic network on chip; thermal management; cross-layer design

ACM Reference Format:
Sudeep Pasricha, Sai Vineel Reddy Chittamuru, Ishan G. Thakkar. 2018. Cross-Layer Thermal Reliability Management in Silicon Photonic Networks-on-Chip. In GLSVLSI '18: 2018 Great Lakes Symposium on VLSI, May 23–25, 2018, Chicago, IL, USA. ACM, NY, NY, USA, 6 pages. *https://doi.org/10.1145/3194554.3194608*

1. INTRODUCTION

Recent advances in the area of silicon photonics have enabled their integration with CMOS circuits [1]. On-chip photonic links provide several significant advantages over their traditional metallic counterparts, including near light speed transfers, high bandwidth density, and low power dissipation [2]. Photonic links also have several times lower data-dependent energy consumption for global on-chip transfers than electrical wires, enabling the design of high-radix networks that are easier to program [3], [4]. Silicon photonics is thus becoming an exciting new option for on-chip communication, and has catalyzed the design of high performance photonic NoCs (PNoCs) for multicore systems [3]-[6].

Typical PNoC architectures employ several photonic devices such as photonic waveguides, couplers, splitters, and multi-wavelength laser sources, along with microring resonators (MRs) as modulators, detectors, and switches. In a typical high bandwidth PNoC, an off-chip laser source generates multi-wavelength light, which is coupled by an optical coupler to an on-chip photonic waveguide. This waveguide guides the input optical power of multiple dense-wavelength-division-multiplexed (DWDM) wavelengths, via a series of optical power splitters, to the individual nodes (e.g., processing cores) on the chip. Each node in the PNoC can connect and communicate to multiple other nodes through such photonic waveguides that can guide the utilized DWDM wavelengths. A wavelength serves as a carrier to a data signal. Typically, multiple data signals are generated at a source node in the electrical domain as sequences of logical 1 and 0 voltage levels. These input electrical data signals are modulated onto the DWDM wavelengths using a bank of modulator MRs. These data-modulated carrier wavelengths traverse a waveguide to a destination node, where an array of detector MR filters remove them and drop them on adjacent photodetectors to regenerate electrical data signals. In general, each node in a PNoC should be able to send and receive data in the optical domain on all of the utilized carrier wavelengths. Therefore, each node has a bank of modulator MRs and a bank of detector MRs. Each MR in a bank is structurally itself a looped waveguide with a small and unique circumference, which makes the MR resonate with and operate on a specific carrier wavelength referred to as the MR's assigned carrier wavelength. Thus, the excellent wavelength selectivity of MRs and DWDM capability of waveguides enable high bandwidth data transfers in PNoCs, under ideal conditions.

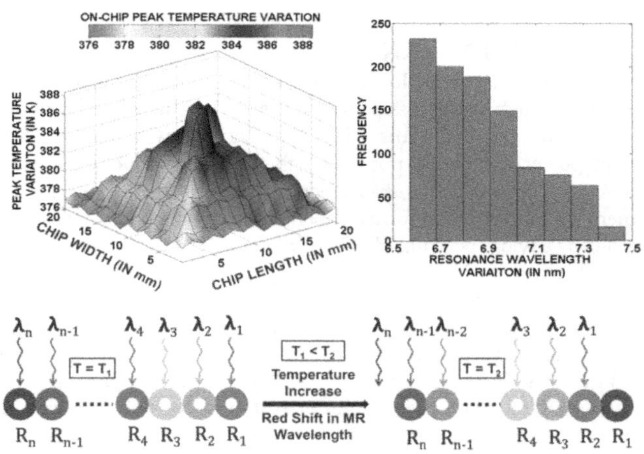

Fig. 1: Impact of temperature increase in DWDM based PNoCs

Unfortunately, MR devices are highly sensitive to temperature fluctuations. As an example, consider the top left of Fig. 1 which shows a plot of the maximum peak temperature of each part of the photonic die (stacked on top of the logic die) for various PARSEC and SPLASH-2 applications executed on a 64-core chip. The main reason for the higher temperature at the center of the chip is the inefficiency of the heat sink to remove heat from the center of the chip. With increase in temperature on the die, the refractive index of an MR device changes, causing a change in its resonance wavelength that has been statically assigned at design-time [7]. The

ACM ISBN 978-1-4503-5724-1/18/05...$15.00.
DOI: *https://doi.org/10.1145/3194554.3194608*

resonance wavelength shifts because of the peak temperature-rises can be as high as 7.4nm, as shown in the histogram at the top right of Fig. 1. This has important implications for communication reliability. The bottom of Fig. 1 depicts MRs R_1-R_n that have been manufactured to resonate on wavelengths λ_1-λ_n respectively at temperature T_1. As the temperature increases, due to the resulting variations in refractive index, each MR now resonates with a different wavelength towards the red end of the visible spectrum (i.e., *red-shift*). This red-shift is shown in the figure where, at temperature T_2, MR R_i will now be in resonance with λ_{i-1}. This phenomenon reduces transmission reliability and wastes bandwidth, e.g., MRs in Fig. 1 are unable to read or write to wavelength λ_n at temperature T_2.

In a typical multicore processor chip, it is quite common to observe on-chip maximum temperature as large as 90^{0}C [10], which can easily result in a mismatch of the resonant wavelengths of MRs and lead to inefficient data transmission. Recent work has proposed localized trimming [9] and thermal tuning [7] mechanisms to re-align the resonant wavelengths of MRs. Trimming alters the free-carrier concentration in an MR core, whereas thermal tuning uses integrated micro-heaters to alter local temperatures at MRs. However, these mechanisms come with considerable power and performance overhead. *Hence, it is essential to intelligently manage temperatures in PNoC-based multicore systems, to achieve reliable communication with minimal local trimming and tuning costs.*

In this work, we aim to minimize the need for (and overheads of) localized thermal tuning and trimming in PNoCs while coping with thermal variations, thereby easing the adoption of PNoCs in future multicore systems. We propose a cross-layer thermal reliability- management framework (SPECTRA) that integrates adaptive MR assignment at the device-level and dynamic thread migration at the system-level for emerging PNoC-based multicore systems. We compare our framework with other thermal management solutions and show significant reduction in maximum temperature and trimming/tuning power consumption compared to the state-of-the-art.

2. RELATED WORK

Traditional electrical NoC communication fabrics are projected to suffer from high power dissipation and severely reduced performance in future multicore systems [1]. The higher bandwidth density and lower power dissipation possible with silicon-photonic links, compared to electrical wires, has made them an attractive option for emerging multicore platforms. Recent research has thus focused on exploring a wide spectrum of network topologies and protocols to enable efficient PNoC architectures [3]-[6], [26]-[32].

One of the key challenges for the widespread adoption of PNoC architectures is thermal management of the silicon-photonic links. Several techniques exist to reduce thermal hotspots and gradients using DVFS [11], workload migration [17] and liquid cooling [12], but these techniques do not consider the unique challenges (e.g., MR resonance wavelength shifts) and constraints (e.g., wavelength match between sender and receiver MR pairs) that exist in PNoCs.

A few prior works have explored thermal management in PNoCs at either the device-level or the system level. The device-level efforts have mainly proposed various athermal photonic devices to reduce the localized tuning/trimming power in MRs. These design time solutions include using various materials such as cladding to reduce thermal sensitivity [13] and using heaters as well as temperature sensors for thermal control [14]. *These device-level techniques either possess high power overhead or require costly changes in the manufacturing process (e.g., larger device areas) that decrease network bandwidth density and area efficiency.*

At the system-level, the overhead associated with localized tuning of MRs is reduced in [7] using the group drift property of co-located MRs as part of a method to trim a group of rings at the same time. A reliability-aware design flow to address variation induced reliability issues is proposed in [15], which uses athermal coating at fabrication-level, voltage tuning at device-level, as well as channel hopping at the system architecture level. In [10] a ring aware thread scheduling policy is proposed to reduce on-chip thermal gradients in a PNoC. To enhance transmission reliability, two encoding techniques PCTM5B and PCTM6B are presented in [8] and a wavelength spacing (WSP) technique is presented in [16] which aim to improve SNR in DWDM-based crossbar PNoC architectures. *None of these system-level solutions for PNoCs consider the impact of run-time workload variations or the relationship between thermal hotspots and transmission reliability.*

To overcome the shortcomings of prior work at the device-level and system-level, we devise a cross-layer thermal management framework for PNoCs that exploits the synergy between new enhancements at both levels to outperform state-of-the-art solutions.

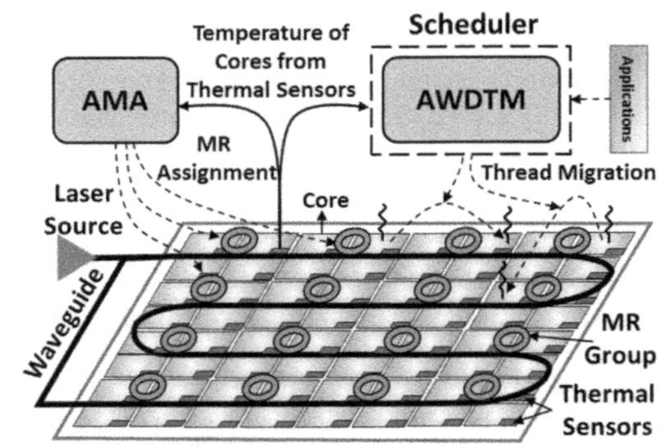

Fig. 2: Overview of SPECTRA, that integrates a device-level adaptive microring assignment mechanism (AMA) and a system-level anti wavelength-drift dynamic thermal management (AWDTM) technique.

3. SPECTRA FRAMEWORK OVERVIEW

Our cross-layer SPECTRA framework enables thermal reliability-aware run-time PNoC management by integrating device-level and system-level enhancements. Fig. 2 gives a high-level overview of our framework. The adaptive microring assignment (AMA) mechanism dynamically assigns a set of MRs for reliable modulation and reception of data from a photonic waveguide in a specific temperature range. This device-level technique aims to adapt to the changing on-chip thermal profile and maintain maximum bandwidth while minimizing trimming and tuning power in the PNoC. However, AMA cannot control maximum on-chip temperature, whose control is critical to further minimize MR trimming and tuning power. Thus, to control maximum on-chip temperature we devise an anti-wavelength-drift dynamic thermal management (AWDTM) scheme that uses support vector regression (SVR) based temperature prediction and dynamic thread migration, to avoid on-chip thermal threshold violations, minimize on-chip thermal hotspots, and reduce thermal tuning power for MRs. The next two sections present details of the two schemes.

4. DEVICE-LEVEL OPTIMIZATION

As discussed earlier, with increase in chip temperature, MR resonance wavelengths change and result in MRs being unable to read or write data to their design-time resonance wavelengths in the waveguide. Fortunately there is a linear dependency between temperature increase and resonance wavelength shift [15], which we exploit to propose a device-level adaptive microring assignment (AMA) mechanism that dynamically assigns a set of MRs to modulate and detect data in a particular temperature range.

Fig. 3 shows how at temperatures T_i and T_{i+1} ($T_{i+1} > T_i$), an MR resonance is in exact alignment with the available wavelengths λ_k and λ_{k+1}, respectively. These temperatures are called ideal resonant temperatures (IRTs). When the MR temperature is in between IRTs T_i and T_{i+1}, as shown in Fig.3, the MR needs to be either *trimmed* to resonate to λ_k (which is the resonance wavelength of an MR at temperature T_i) or thermally *tuned* to resonate to λ_{k+1} (which is the resonance wavelength of an MR at temperature T_{i+1}). To adaptively choose the least power consuming method from trimming and thermal tuning, we divide the temperature range between IRTs T_i and T_{i+1} into two parts: trimming temperature range (Δ_{tr}) and tuning temperature range (Δ_{tu}). For an MR at temperature T, if $(T_i + \Delta_{tr}) > T > T_i$ we perform trimming as it takes the least power, else if $(T_i + \Delta_{tr}) < T < T_{i+1}$ we perform tuning as it takes the least power. At the boundary of the trimming and tuning temperature ranges, where $T_{i+1}\text{-}\Delta_{tu} = T_i\text{+}\Delta_{tr}$, both trimming and tuning consume equal power, and hence, an MR can be either trimmed or tuned. This temperature is called the boundary temperature (BT_i). It has been shown that for a small resonance wavelength shift (<1nm), thermal tuning power is higher compared to trimming power to mitigate the same amount of TV-induced shift [7]. Thus, our *AMA* approach considers a higher trimming temperature range compared to tuning temperature range ($\Delta_{tr} > \Delta_{tu}$), to minimize total trimming and tuning power.

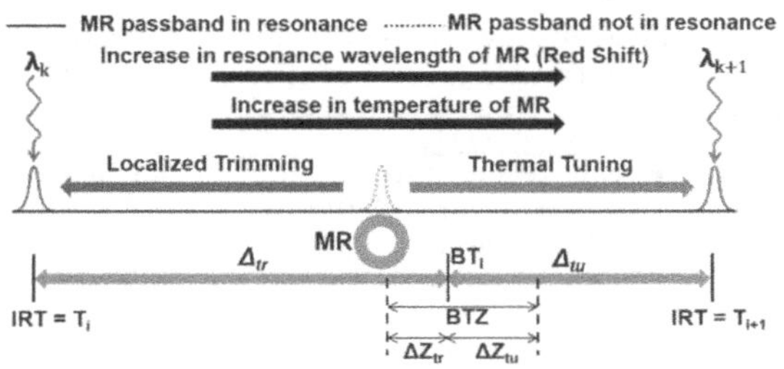

Fig. 3: Red shift of MR with increase in temp. from IRTs T_i to T_{i+1} with trimming and tuning range of temperatures between these IRTs.

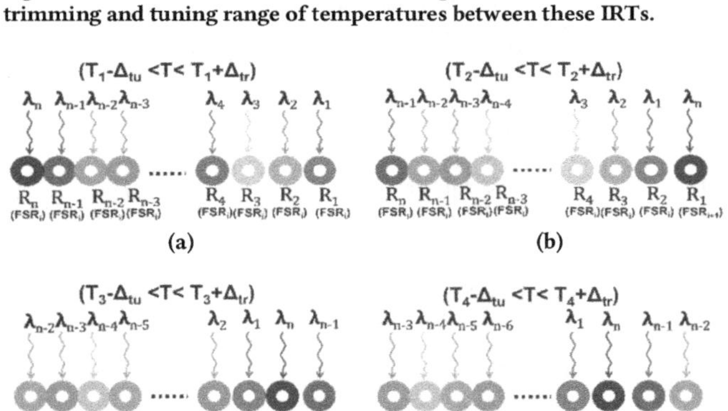

Fig. 4: Thermal aware assignment of microrings ($R_{1\text{-}n}$) to wavelengths ($\lambda_{1\text{-}n}$) at four successive IRTs T_1, T_2, T_3, and T_4 in *AMA* mechanism.

In *AMA*, MRs are dynamically shifted (trimmed or tuned) to an appropriate IRT for correct operation based on their current temperature. Fig. 4(a)-4(d) show four different MR wavelength assignment configurations at successive IRTs T_1, T_2, T_3, and T_4, where $T_4 > T_3 > T_2 > T_1$. If the MR group temperature T is such that $(T_1 - \Delta_{tu}) < T < (T_1 + \Delta_{tr})$ then the assignment in Fig. 4(a) is chosen, otherwise if $(T_2 - \Delta_{tu}) < T < (T_2 + \Delta_{tr})$, $(T_3 - \Delta_{tu}) < T < (T_3 + \Delta_{tr})$, or $(T_4 - \Delta_{tu}) < T < (T_4 + \Delta_{tr})$ then the assignment in Fig. 4(b), 4(c), or 4(d) is chosen, respectively. One critical observation in the assignment shown in Fig. 4(a) is that MRs R_1-R_n are in resonance with λ_1- λ_n within the same Free Spectral Range (FSR_i), whereas, in Fig. 4(b) at IRT T_2, MRs R_2-R_n are in resonance with λ_1-λ_{n-1}, respectively in FSR_i and MR R_1 is in resonance with λ_n of the next FSR (i.e., FSR_{i+1}). In this assignment and the ones shown in Fig. 4(c) and 4(d), there is a need to reposition bits in the electrical domain using backend barrel-shifters or pipelined shift registers. The assignments shown in Fig. 4(b), 4(c), and 4(d) require one, two, and three bit shifts, respectively, to retrieve the original data.

AMA represents a powerful reactive technique to adapt to on-die thermal variations with low overhead while ensuring reliable and high-bandwidth communication in MR based PNoCs. But there is scope for two further enhancements. First, there is a need to proactively control the peak on-chip temperature to reduce the range of on-chip temperature swings, which ultimately limits the number of required bit shifts (this work caps the number bit shifts to three as shown Fig. 4(d)) and reduces the latency to retrieve the original data. Second, at the BT temperature (Fig. 3), maximum trimming or tuning power is required to realign the MR resonances to their nearest carrier wavelengths. Thus, avoiding BT temperatures at MRs can reduce trimming and tuning power overhead. As shown in Fig. 3, we define a boundary temperature zone (BTZ) around each BT_i. This zone includes temperatures T such that $BT_i\text{-}\Delta Z_{tr} < T < BT_i\text{+}\Delta Z_{tu}$ where ΔZ_{tr} and ΔZ_{tu} are designer specified parameters. Cores with corresponding MR bank temperatures that are within BTZs are called boundary temperature cores (BTCs). As BTCs possess the highest trimming and tuning power overhead for their corresponding MR bank, a mechanism that reduces the number of BTCs can save trimming and tuning power. Section 5 describes such a mechanism, which also controls the range of on-chip temperature swings within allowable limits.

5. SYSTEM-LEVEL OPTIMIZATION

To proactively reduce thermal hotspots (which will reduce instances of 'irrecoverable drift') and control on-die temperature (to reduce the number of BTCs), we propose a system-level anti wavelength-drift dynamic thermal management (AWDTM) technique. The primary goals with AWDTM is to maintain the temperature of all the cores on a die below a specified thermal threshold, i.e., for all cores $1 \le i \le N$, $T_i < T_t$ where T_i is the temperature of core i and T_t is threshold temperature. We utilize support vector based regression (SVR) to predict the future temperature of a core. The predicted temperature is compared with a thermal threshold to determine the potential for a thermal emergency. If such a potential exists, threads are migrated to available BTCs. This step has a twofold benefit. First by moving the thread away from a core that could suffer a thermal emergency, we avoid instances of irrecoverable drift in the MR groups of that core. Second, by moving the thread to a BTC, the temperature of the BTC will increase resulting in that core no longer being a BTC (consequently the temperature of the core's MR groups will also increase, taking them outside of their BTZ and closer to IRTs, which will reduce trimming/tuning power).

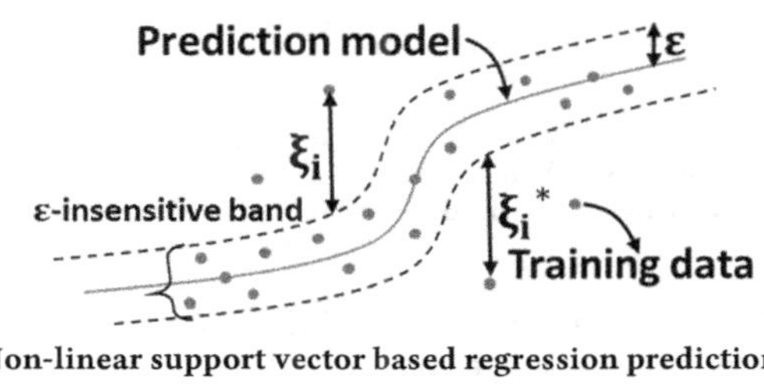

Fig. 5: Non-linear support vector based regression prediction model

5.1 Thermal Prediction

A typical SVR relies on a prediction model that ignores errors that are situated within ε distance of the true value. This type of a prediction model is called an ε-insensitive prediction model. Fig. 5 shows an example of a one-dimensional non-linear SVR based prediction model with an ε-insensitive band. The variables *(ξ and ε)* measure the cost of the errors on the training points. These are zero for all points that are inside the ε-insensitive band. SVR is primarily designed to perform linear regression. To handle non-linearity in data, SVR first maps the input x_i onto an m-dimensional space using some fixed (non-linear) mapping notated as Φ, and then a linear model is constructed in this high-dimensional space. Thus, it overcomes drawbacks of linear and logistic regression towards handling non-linearity in data. This class of SVRs is called *kernel based SVRs.* As on-chip temperature variation data is non-linear in the original space, our SVR model employs a kernel based regression which uses a Radial Basis Function (RBF) Gaussian kernel. The RBF kernel improves the accuracy of SVR when data has non-linearity in the original space.

Our SVR predictor accepts input parameters reflecting the workload for the core under consideration, in terms of instructions per cycle (*IPC_i*), as well as the current core temperature (*CT_i*) and temperatures of surrounding cores (*TN_i*). Once these parameter values are obtained at run-time, the future temperature for the core can be predicted. We trained our SVR model using a set of multi-threaded applications from the SPLASH-2 [22] and PARSEC [18] benchmark suites, specifically: *blackscholes (BS), bodytrack (BT), vips (VI), facesim (FS), fluidanimate (FA), swaptions (SW), barnes (BA), fft (FFT), radix (RX), radiosity (RD)* and *raytrace (RT)* with different thread counts: 2, 4 and 8. We considered different combinations of thread mappings on a 9-core (3×3) floorplan, to train our predictor to determine the temperature of the center (target) core. As the future temperature of a target core is dependent on the average temperature of its immediate neighboring cores, we trained our SVR model with temperature inputs from the target core running a single thread, as well as its surrounding cores running a variable number of threads. Simulations for each of these floorplans allowed us to obtain data to train our SVR model. This data included temperature for the target core and its neighboring core temperatures, as well as instructions per cycle *(IPC)* for the target core. IPC is very useful to determine if there is a phase change in an application and plays a crucial role in maintaining future temperature prediction accuracy, especially when temperatures of a target core and its neighbors are similar at a given time. Our training algorithm involved an iterative process that adjusts the weights and bias values in the SVR predictor to fit the training set.

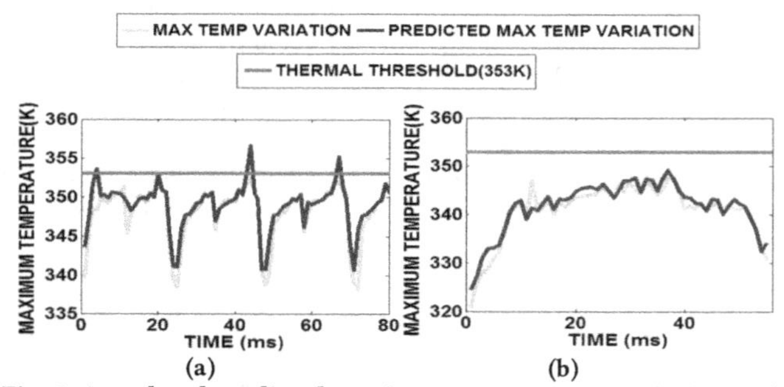

Fig. 6: Actual and predicted maximum temperature variation with execution time for (a) fluidanimate *(FA)* (b) radiosity *(RD)* benchmark applications executed on 64-core platform executing 32 threads.

We verified the accuracy of our SVR model for multi-threaded benchmark workloads (we considered 6000 floorplans, with 70% of input data for training and 30% for testing) and found that it has an accuracy of over 95%. Fig. 6(a) and 6(b) show actual and predicted on-chip temperature variations for a 64-core platform executing 32 threads of the FA and RD benchmarks, respectively. From these figures it can be seen that our temperature predictor tracks temperature quite accurately. When predicted temperature exceeds the thermal threshold our thread migration mechanism (which is discussed next) migrates threads from hotter cores to cooler cores to keep overall maximum temperature below the threshold.

5.2 Thermal-Aware Thread Migration

Algorithm 1 shows the pseudo-code for the AWDTM thread migration procedure. For each core, we periodically monitor the IPC value from performance counters and temperature from on-chip thermal sensors. If a thermal emergency is predicted for a core by the SVR predictor, then AWDTM initiates a thread migration procedure, otherwise no action is taken. Firstly, future temperature *(PT_i)* of the ith core is predicted using the SVR based predictor with inputs: core temperature *(T_i)*, core IPC *(IPC_i)*, and temperature of neighboring cores *(TN_i)* in steps **1-3**. The list of available BTCs (i.e., those that are not currently executing any thread) and available NBTCs is obtained in steps **4-10**. In steps **11-12**, a loop iterates over all cores and checks for possible thread migration conditions (i.e., thermal emergency cases where current core predicted temperature *(PT_i)* is greater than thermal threshold *(T_t)*). If a thread migration is required, then in steps **13-21**, we check for free BTCs, and if they are available then we migrate the thread from current core to the BTC with lowest temperature, else we migrate the thread to a free NBTC with lowest temperature. This AWDTM thread migration is invoked at every epoch (1ms).

Algorithm 1: AWDTM thread migration algorithm

Inputs: Current core temperature (T_i), average neighboring core temperature (TN_i), current core IPC (IPC_i)

```
1:  for each core i do // Loop that predicts future temperature
2:      PTi = SVR_predict_future_temperature (Ti, TNi, IPCi)
3:  end for
4:  for each core i do // Loop that checks for free BTCs and NBTCs
5:      if Ti in BTZ and IPCi == 0 then
6:          List_BTC = Push i //add core to BTC list
7:      else if IPCi == 0 then
8:          List_NBTC = Push i //add core to NBTC list
9:      end if
10: end for
11: for each core i do // Loop that performs thread migration
12:     if PTi ≥ Tt then
13:         if List_BTC ≠ {} then
14:             Migrated_core = Find_min_temperature_core(List_BTC)
15:             Do_thread_migration( core_i ⟶ Migrated_core)
16:             List_BTC = Pop i
17:         else if List_NBTC ≠ {} then
18:             Migrated_core = Find_min_temperature_core(List_NBTC)
19:             Do_thread_migration( core_i ⟶ Migrated_core)
20:             List_NBTC = Pop i
21:         end if
22:     end if
23: end for
```

Output: Thread migration to BTC or NBTC cores

6. EXPERIMENTS

6.1 Experimental Setup

We target a 64-core multicore system for evaluation of our SPECTRA (AMA+AWDTM) framework. Each core has a Nehalem x86 [19] micro-architecture with 32KB L1 instruction and data caches and a 256 KB L2 cache, at 32nm and running at 5GHz. We evaluate our framework on two well-known PNoC architectures: Corona [3] and Flexishare [4]. Corona uses a 64×64 multiple write single read (MWSR) crossbar with token slot arbitration. Flexishare uses 32 multiple write multiple read (MWMR) waveguide groups with a 2-pass token stream arbitration. Each MWSR waveguide in Corona and each MWMR waveguide in Flexishare is capable of transferring 512 bits of data from a source to a destination node.

We modeled and simulated these architectures with the SPECTRA framework for multi-threaded applications from the PARSEC [22] and SPLASH-2 [18] benchmark suites (Section 6.2). Simulations were performed with a "warm-up" period of 100-million instructions and execution period of one billion cycles. Power and instruction traces for the benchmark applications were generated using the Sniper 6.0 [19] simulator and McPAT [20]. We used the 3D-ICE tool [21] for thermal analysis. The ambient temperature was set to 303K and the thermal threshold (T_t) was set to 353K. We considered a three layered 3D-stacked multicore system as advocated in existing PNoC architectures [3]-[4] with a die area footprint of 400mm^2, where the top layer is the core-cache layer, the middle layer is the analog to digital (A/D) and digital to analog (D/A) conversion layer, and the bottom layer is the photonic layer with MRs, waveguides, ring heaters, and ring trimmers for carrier injection. Some of the materials used in the construction of the 3D-stack in the 3D-ICE tool and their properties are shown in Table 1.

The MR thermal sensitivity was assumed to be 0.11nm/°C [15]. For PNoCs, we considered 64 DWDM waveguides sharing the working band 1530–1625 nm with a wavelength channel width of 1.48 nm. The MR trimming power is set to 130μW/nm [9] for current injection (blue shift) and tuning power is set to 240μW/nm [7] for heating (red shift). To compute laser power, we considered detector responsivity as 0.8 A/W [25], MR through loss as 0.02 dB, waveguide propagation loss as 1 dB/cm, waveguide bending loss as 0.005 dB/90^0, and waveguide coupler/splitter loss as 0.5 dB [25]. We calculated photonic loss in components using these values, which sets the photonic laser power budget and the electrical laser power. For energy consumption of photonic devices, we adapt parameters from [25], with 0.42pJ/bit for every modulation and detection event, and 0.18pJ/bit for the driver circuits of MRs.

As presented in section 4, to minimize trimming and tuning power consumption, trimming temperature range (Δ_{tr}) and tuning temperature range (Δ_{tu}) for AMA are calculated as 8.73K and 4.72K respectively. We also set ΔZ_{tr} and ΔZ_{tu} as 2K and 3.5K respectively. Based on our sensitive analysis we get the best accuracy for our SVR-based temperature predictor when parameters C and γ are set to 1000 and 0.1 respectively.

Table 1: Properties of materials used by 3D-ICE tool [21], [23]

Material	Thermal Conductivity	Volumetric Heat Capacity
Silicon	1.30e-4 W/μm K	1.628e-12 J/μm^3 K
Silicon dioxide	1.46e-6 W/μm K	1.628e-12 J/μm^3 K
BEOL	2.25e-6 W/μm K	2.175e-12 J/μm^3 K
Copper	5.85e-4 W/μm K	3.45e-12 J/μm^3 K

6.2 Experiment Results

We compared the performance of our SPECTRA framework with two prior works on multicore thermal management: a ring aware policy (RATM) [10] and a predictive dynamic thermal management (PDTM) framework [17]. RATM distributes threads uniformly across cores that are closer to PNoC nodes first and then distributes the remaining threads in a regular pattern from outer cores to inner cores. PDTM uses a recursive least square based temperature predictor to determine if the predicted temperature of a core exceeds a thermal threshold, and if so then thread migration is done from that core to the coolest core not executing any threads.

Fig. 7 (a)-(b) shows the maximum temperature obtained with the three frameworks across eleven applications from the PARSEC and SPLASH-2 benchmarks suites with 48 and 32 thread counts executed on a 64-core system with the Corona PNoC [3] architecture. From Fig. 7(a) it can be observed that some applications (e.g., FA, SW) with 48 threads exceed the threshold (353K) as there are insufficient number of free cores on the chip whose temperature is below the thermal threshold to migrate threads. However in Fig. 7(b), our SPECTRA framework avoids violating thermal thresholds for all the benchmark applications with 32 threads. On average, SPECTRA has 13.2K and 14.5K lower maximum temperature compared to the RATM policy for 48 and 32 threads, respectively. SPECTRA migrates threads from hotter cores to cooler cores to control maximum temperature, whereas RATM does a simple thread allocation that is unable to appropriately control maximum temperature. For most of the cases, maximum temperatures with PDTM and SPECTRA are below the thermal threshold. As SPECTRA prefers to migrate threads to BTCs instead of to the coolest cores as done in PDTM, maximum temperatures with SPECTRA are sometimes higher compared to maximum temperatures with PDTM, as BTCs have higher initial temperature compared to the coolest cores on the chip. However, despite the higher maximum temperatures, SPECTRA still saves more power than PDTM (and also RATM) as discussed next.

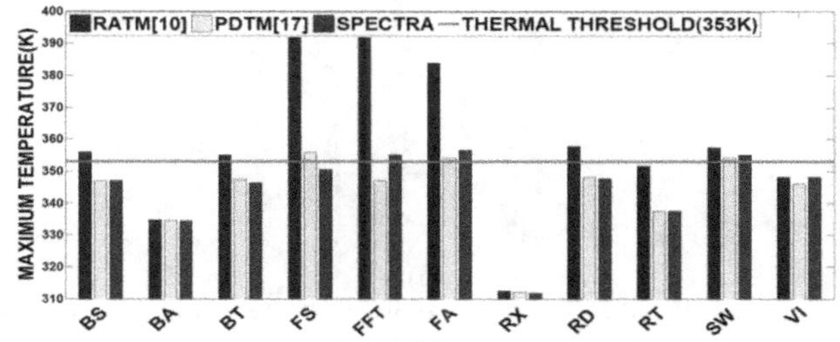

(a)

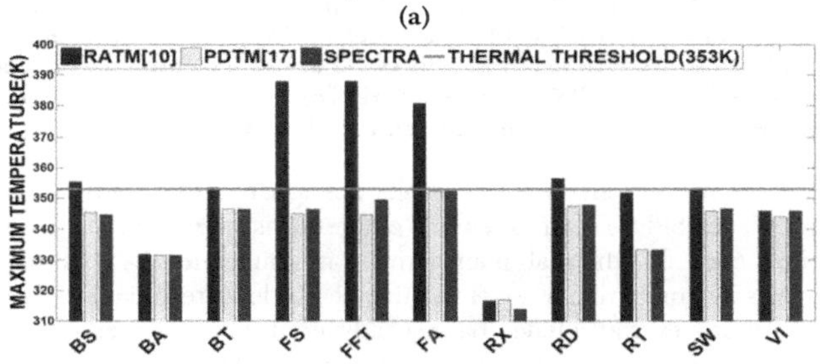

(b)

Fig. 7: Maximum temp. comparison of SPECTRA with RATM [10] and PDTM [17] for (a) 48 (b) 32 threaded PARSEC and SPLASH-2 benchmarks executed on 64-core system with Corona PNoC.

Fig. 8 shows the power dissipation comparison for the three frameworks across multiple 48-threaded applications for the Corona [3] and Flexishare [4] PNoC architectures, respectively. One of the main reasons why SPECTRA has lower power dissipation than RATM and PDTM is that it more aggressively reduces trimming and tuning power in both Corona and Flexishare PNoCs. As can be seen in Fig. 8(a), SPECTRA has 73.3% and 72.5% lower trimming and tuning power on an average compared to RATM and PDTM for the Corona PNoC architecture, respectively. Furthermore, as seen in Fig. 8(b), SPECTRA has 72.3% and 71.5% lower trimming and tuning power on average compared to RATM and PDTM for the Flexishare PNoC architecture, respectively. The AMA technique in SPECTRA intelligently conserves trimming and tuning power compared to RATM and PDTM by performing MR reassignment with increase in temperature, while our AWDTM further improves trimming and tuning power savings with its intelligent thread migration to BTCs. In addition, SPECTRA saves considerable trimming/tuning power to ultimately achieve overall power reduction. From the power analysis in Fig.

8(a), it can be observed that SPECTRA with Corona has 45.4% and 44.5% lower total power consumption compared to Corona with RATM and PDTM respectively. Further from Fig. 8(b), it can be seen that Flexishare with SPECTRA has 63.4% and 62.6% lower power dissipation compared to RATM and PDTM.

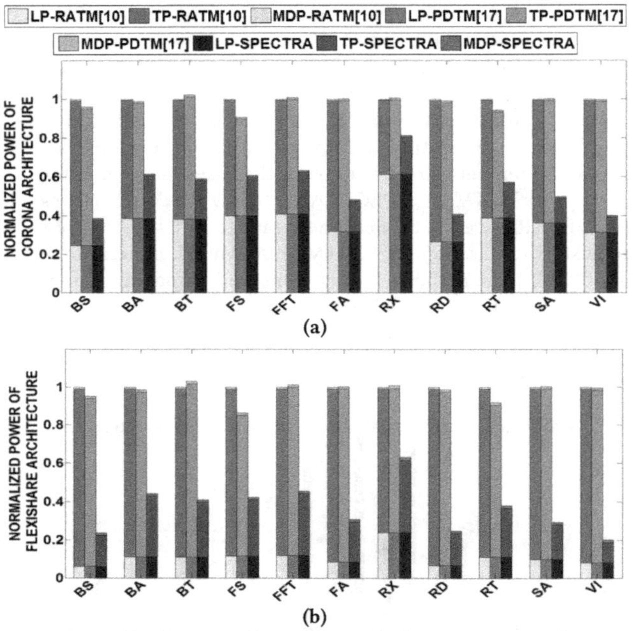

Fig. 8: Normalized power (Laser Power (LP), Trimming and tuning power (TP) and modulating and detecting Power (MDP)) comparison of SPECTRA with RATM [10] and PDTM [17] for 48 threaded applications of PARSEC and SPLASH-2 suites executed on (a) Corona (b) Flexishare PNoC architectures for a 64-core multicore system. Results shown are normalized w.r.t RATM.

In summary, from the above results, it is apparent that our proposed cross-layer SPECTRA framework outperforms previously proposed approaches for thermal management in multicore systems with PNoCs by combining a novel reactive device-level technique (AMA) that improves waveguide channel utilization with a novel system-level proactive thread migration technique (AWDTM). The excellent power savings compared to previous approaches strongly motivate the use of cross-layer techniques in general, and more specifically our proposed cross-layer thermal management framework in future PNoC based multicore architectures.

7. CONCLUSION

We have presented the cross-layer SPECTRA framework that combines two dynamic thermal management mechanisms for the reduction of maximum on-chip temperature and to conserve trimming and tuning power of MRs in DWDM-based PNoC architectures. These techniques (AMA at the device-level, AWDTM at the system-level) constitute a hybrid, cross-layer, reactive-proactive management framework that demonstrated interesting trade-offs between performance and power across two different state-of-the-art crossbar-based PNoC architectures. Our experimental analysis on the well-known Corona and Flexishare PNoC architectures has shown that SPECTRA can notably conserve total power by up to 63.4% and trimming and tuning power by up to 73.3%.

REFERENCES

[1] Y. Xu, S. Pasricha, "Silicon Nanophotonics for Future Multicore Architectures: Opportunities and Challenges", IEEE D&T, 2014.
[2] J. D. Owens, et al., "Research challenges for on-chip interconnection networks," in IEEE Micro, Sep-Oct 2007.
[3] D. Vantrease et al., "Light speed arbitration and flow control for nanophotonic interconnects," in *IEEE/ACM MICRO*, Dec. 2009.
[4] Y. Pan, J. Kim, G. Memik, "Flexishare: Channel sharing for an energy efficient nanophotonic crossbar," in Proc. HPCA, 2010.
[5] S. V. R. Chittamuru, S. Desai, S. Pasricha "A reconfigurable silicon-photonic network with improved channel sharing for multicore architectures," in ACM GLSVLSI, May 2015.
[6] S. Pasricha, S. Bahirat, "OPAL: A Multi-Layer Hybrid Photonic NoC for 3D ICs," in ASPDAC, Yokohama, Japan, Jan 2011.
[7] C. Nitta, M. Farrens, and V. Akella, "Addressing system-level trimming issues in on-chip nanophotonic networks," in Proc. HPCA, 2011.
[8] S. V. R. Chittamuru, S. Pasricha "Crosstalk Mitigation for High-Radix and Low-Diameter Photonic NoC Architectures", IEEE D&T, 2015.
[9] J. Ahn et al., "Devices and architectures for photonic chip-scale integration", Applied Physics A: MSP, 95:989–997, June 2009.
[10] T. Zhang et al., "Thermal management of manycore systems with silicon-photonic networks," in Proc. DATE, 2014.
[11] A. K. Coskun, T. S. Rosing, K. A. Whisnant, and K. C. Gross, "Static and dynamic temperature-aware scheduling for multiprocessor SoCs," Proc. IEEE Trans. on VLSI, vol. 16, no. 9, pp. 1127–1140, 2008.
[12] A. K. Coskun, J. L. Ayala, D. Atienza, and T. S. Rosing, "Modeling and dynamic management of 3D multicore systems with liquid cooling," in IFIP/IEEE Int'l Conference on VLSI-SoC, 2009, pp. 35–40.
[13] Z. Li et al., "Reliability modeling and management of nanophotonic on-chip networks," IEEE TVLSI, vol. 20, no. 1, pp. 98–111, 2012.
[14] C. T. DeRose et al., "Silicon microring modulator with integrated heater and temperature sensor for thermal control," in CLEO, 2010.
[15] M. Mohamed et al., "Reliability-Aware Design Flow for Silicon Photonics On-Chip Interconnect," IEEE Transactions on Very Large Scale Integration (VLSI) Systems, 22(8), pp. 1763–1776, 2014.
[16] S. V. R. Chittamuru, S. Pasricha, "Improving Crosstalk Resilience with Wavelength Spacing in Photonic Crossbar-based Network-on-Chip Architectures", in IEEE MWSCAS, 2015.
[17] I. Yeo, C. Liu, and E. Kim, "Predictive dynamic thermal management for multicore systems," in Proc. DAC, 2008, pp. 734–739.
[18] S. C. Woo et al., "The SPLASH-2 programs: characterization and methodological considerations," in ISCA, 1995, pp. 24–36.
[19] T. E. Carlson et al., "Sniper: Exploring the level of abstraction for scalable and accurate parallel multi-core simulations," in SC, 2011.
[20] S. Li et al., "McPAT: An integrated power, area, and timing modeling framework for multicore and manycore architectures," MICRO, 2009.
[21] A. Sridhar et al., "3D-ICE: Fast compact transient thermal modeling for 3d ICs with inter-tier liquid cooling," in Proc. ICCAD, Nov. 2010.
[22] C. Bienia et al., "The PARSEC benchmark suite: Characterization and Architectural Implications," in Proc. PACT, 2008, pp. 72–81.
[23] http://www.mt-berlin.com/frames_cryst/descriptions/quartz.htm
[24] D. Harris et al., "Support Vector Regression Machines", in Advances in Neural Information Processing Systems NIPS, 1996, MIT Press.
[25] P. Grani, S. Bartolini, "Design Options for Optical Ring Interconnect in Future Client Devices," JETC, 2014.
[26] S. Bahirat, S. Pasricha, "METEOR: Hybrid Photonic Ring-Mesh Network-on-Chip for Multicore Architectures", ACM Trans. on Embedded Computing Systems (TECS), 13(3):116:1-116:33, Mar 2014.
[27] S. Bahirat, S. Pasricha, "A Particle Swarm Optimization Approach for Synthesizing Application-specific Hybrid Photonic Networks-on-Chip", IEEE ISQED, Mar. 2012.
[28] S. Bahirat, S. Pasricha, "UC-PHOTON: A Novel Hybrid Photonic Network-on-Chip for Multiple Use-Case Applications", ISQED 2010.
[29] S. V. R. Chittamuru, S. Desai, S. Pasricha, "SWIFTNoC: A Reconfigurable Silicon-Photonic Network with Multicast Enabled Channel Sharing for Multicore Architectures", ACM Journal on Emerging Technologies in Computing Systems (JETC), Jun 2017.
[30] I. Thakkar, S. V. R. Chittamuru, S. Pasricha, "Improving the Reliability and Energy-Efficiency of High-Bandwidth Photonic NoC Architectures with Multilevel Signaling," IEEE/ACM NOCS, Oct 2017.
[31] I. Thakkar, S. V. R. Chittamuru, S. Pasricha, "A Comparative Analysis of Front-End and Back-End Compatible Silicon Photonic On-Chip Interconnects," ACM/IEEE SLIP, Jun 2016.
[32] I. Thakkar, S. V. R. Chittamuru, S. Pasricha, "Run-Time Laser Power Management in Photonic NoCs with On-Chip Semiconductor Optical Amplifiers," IEEE/ACM International Symposium on Networks-on-Chip (NOCS), Aug 2016.

Silicon Photonic Interconnects: Minimizing the Controller Latency

Felipe Gohring de Magalhães
PPGCC/PUCRS
Ecole Polytechnique Montréal
felipe.magalhaes@acad.pucrs.br

Mahdi Nikdast
Colorado State University
mahdi.nikdast@colostate.edu

Yule Xiong
Ciena Corp.
yule.xiong.ele@gmail.com

Fabiano Hessel
PPGCC/PUCRS
fabiano.hessel@pucrs.br

Odile Liboiron-Ladouceur
McGill University
odile.liboiron-ladouceur@mcgill.ca

Gabriela Nicolescu
Ecole Polytechnique Montréal
gabriela.nicolescu@polymtl.ca

ABSTRACT

Silicon photonic interconnects (SPIs) have emerged as a promising solution to outperform the communication infrastructure in multiprocessor systems-on-chip (MPSoCs). Routing a message from one node to another in an MPSoC integrating SPIs, several photonic components (e.g., switching elements) need to be configured to realize an optical path between sending and receiving nodes. Such configurations are performed in an electronic controller, which, if not fast, imposes high latency in SPIs, constraining the application of SPIs in MPSoCs. Realizing a full exploitation of SPIs, this paper presents a lookup-table-based centralized controller (LUCC). We indicate that LUCC has the lowest latency among the state-of-the-art controllers for SPIs while it can be applied to different SPI architectures. Employing acceleration techniques based on off-line routings, we report (simulation and prototyping) a worst-case control latency smaller than 5 ns. Moreover, LUCC is experimentally integrated with a photonic switch in the lab, where we show contention resolution in one clock cycle.

CCS CONCEPTS

• **Hardware** → **Photonic and optical interconnect**; **Emerging optical and photonic technologies**; *Metallic interconnect*; • **Networks** → **Network control algorithms**;

KEYWORDS

Silicon Photonic Interconnects; Low-Latency Controller

ACM Reference Format:

Felipe Gohring de Magalhães, Mahdi Nikdast, Yule Xiong, Fabiano Hessel, Odile Liboiron-Ladouceur, and Gabriela Nicolescu. 2018. Silicon Photonic Interconnects: Minimizing the Controller Latency. In *GLSVLSI '18: 2018 Great Lakes Symposium on VLSI, May 23–25, 2018, Chicago, IL, USA*. ACM, New York, NY, USA, 4 pages. https://doi.org/10.1145/3194554.3194609

GLSVLSI '18, May 23–25, 2018, Chicago, IL, USA

ACM ISBN 978-1-4503-5724-1/18/05...$15.00
https://doi.org/10.1145/3194554.3194609

1 INTRODUCTION

Silicon photonic interconnects (SPIs) can boost the communication in multiprocessor systems-on-chip (MPSoCs) and data centers, but their full capabilities are curbed by high latency electronic controllers [1]. Such controllers are essential to configure different photonic elements (e.g., switching elements), realizing an optical path between sending and receiving nodes in an MPSoC integrating SPIs. Different techniques have been proposed for controlling and multiplexing SPIs, namely path, time and wavelength division. Path division (PD) techniques have great scalability [8], while time division (TD) ones, deployed as centralized cores, present high system controllability [4]. Still, such techniques impose high control latency in SPIs, hence further improvement in controllers response time is required for practical deployment of SPIs in MPSoCs.

In this paper, we present the design and integration of a lookup-table-based centralized controller (LUCC) for SPIs. Comparing LUCC with the state-of-the-art controllers [5, 6, 11], it has a low latency when computing requests and performing the network configuration in SPIs, while being flexible and applicable to different network topologies. LUCC enables all connections to be configured within a single clock cycle even when the switch configuration dynamically changes due to various node requests. In particular, LUCC is designed based on using a lookup table with a fast algorithm for conflict resolution. It takes advantage of an optimization algorithm to reduce the size of the lookup table, and hence reducing the memory utilization. We indicate LUCC simulation and FPGA prototyping results with a latency smaller than 5 ns in the worst case. Furthermore, we integrate LUCC with a fabricated Mach-Zehnder Interferometer (MZI)-based photonic switch for experimental validation and demonstration, where we report a low latency in the switch performance when using LUCC.

2 LUCC: A LOW-LATENCY CONTROLLER FOR SPIS

Considering silicon photonic interconnects, the data path is through optical communication (i.e., light propagation), decreasing the network latency, where the network routing and configuration are addressed using an electronic controller. For example, in emerging 3D stacked hybrid optical-electronic networks, the electronic layer is responsible to configure the photonic elements on the photonic layer [2]. The controller receives requests from input nodes (i.e., processing cores) and solves conflicts to guarantee message transmissions. Also, the controller is responsible for configuring different photonic switching elements, setting up optical paths between sending and receiving nodes. Control latency is the key parameter to ensure the benefits of SPIs in terms of high throughput and low latency, hence its design must focus on reducing the execution time.

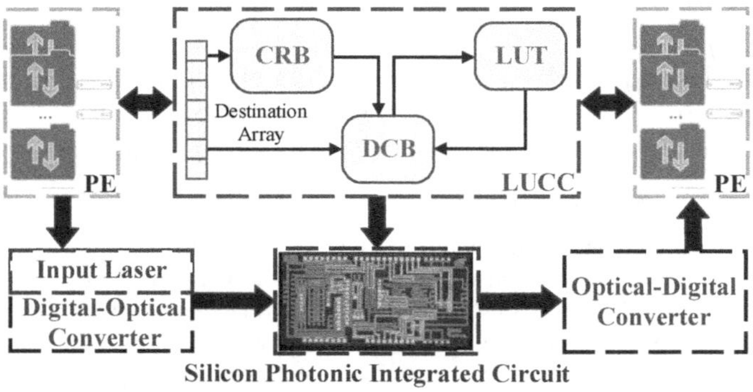

Figure 1: An abstract overview of the proposed LUCC controller architecture.

LUCC is designed to improve the control latency in SPIs. Fig. 1 illustrates an overview of LUCC architecture and how it can interact with different processing elements (PEs) and SPIs [3]. As can be seen, the main building blocks are:

- **Conflicts Resolution Block (CRB)**: this block is responsible for detecting and solving destination conflicts using a given algorithm;
- **Lookup Table (LUT) - Memory**: this block is used to store static data in a form of a lookup table, available to the controller during the runtime. Using a lookup table in the memory, we can reduce the path configuration time, thus reducing control latency, and;
- **Dynamic Setup Block (DSB)**: this block is responsible for on-line calculations (e.g., path attribution and reading memory addresses) employing a real-time calculation (RTC) unit.

LUCC design methodology can be divided into off-line routing analysis and on-line requests computations. Off-line routing analysis seeks to find the best routes in the network, using Shortest Path First (SPF) algorithms, such as Dijkstra algorithm [7]. The routes information is stored in fast access memories (i.e., a lookup table). During the execution, LUCC relies on three main blocks (see Fig. 1): the CRB, the memory arrays created off-line in the LUT, as well as the DSB.

CRB is a hardware block responsible for detecting conflicts in targeted PEs. A conflict is defined as any situation in which two or more source PEs are targeting the same destination PE at the same time. CRB works as follows: firstly, it analyzes all the input requests, looking for a conflict. Secondly, if a conflict is found, a Round-Robin (RR) algorithm is applied to determine which PE should have its access granted. Detecting a conflict, a matrix method is used, in which for every new request, all the source-destination pairs are mapped to a matrix $\mathcal{R}$ of requests. Then, each column j is checked

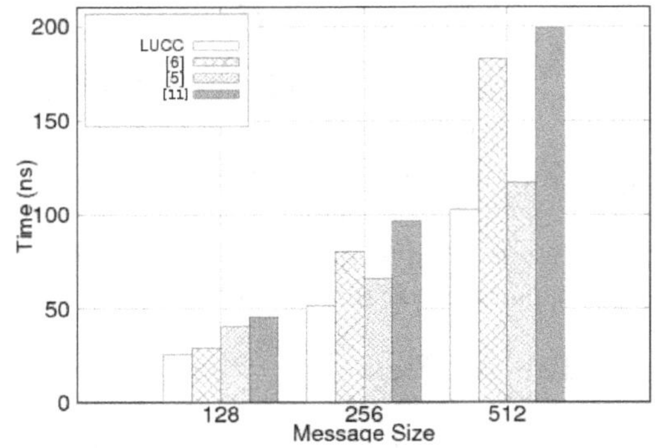

Figure 2: Comparing LUCC latency with that of the state-of-the-art controllers under different message sizes.

for any possible conflicts. The matrices are created based on the indices of the requesting input port(s) and the requested output port(s). For example, $\mathcal{R}(i, j) = 1$ denotes the input port I_i requests to access the output port O_j in the switch, such that:

$$\forall_{ij},\ I_i \text{ request } O_j \leftrightarrow \mathcal{R}(i, j) = 1.$$

As a result, the $\mathcal{R}$ matrix for a 3×3 photonic switch, for example, where all the inputs are requesting to communicate with the output two (i.e., $\langle 0 \longrightarrow 2, 1 \longrightarrow 2, 2 \longrightarrow 2\rangle$) can be defined as:

$$\mathcal{R} = \begin{bmatrix} 0 & 0 & 1 \\ 0 & 0 & 1 \\ 0 & 0 & 1 \end{bmatrix}.$$

Considering the matrix $\mathcal{R}$, a conflict can be detected as:

$$\forall ii'j, i \neq i', \neg XOR[R(i, j)] \wedge OR[R(i', j)] \implies \text{conflict}(O_j) = 1.$$

As the matrix can be accessed directly (i.e., the hardware implementation is a register), no extra processing is needed, thus accelerating the conflict detection.

The DSB is the central core of LUCC that evaluates the status signals (i.e., conflict or no conflict) from the CRB block as well as the routes accessed in the LUT. The DSB simplifies the physical design implementation, without which the CRB and the LUT would imply a prohibitive resource usage. In other words, if only the CRB and LUT blocks were considered, a large (physically unbearable) chip area would be needed, as the memory array scales with an increase in the number of paths combinations. Employing the DSB, the original LUT is compressed, and the DSB executes on-line calculations to access the correct LUT positions. We apply a reduction method to the LUT, which is generated off-line, reducing its size, enabling using the LUT when the network size scales. The reduction method is based on finding repeated (i.e., redundant) entries in the LUT, which reduces its final memory print.

3 RESULTS AND DISCUSSION

Complement and all-to-all traffic patterns are considered to assess LUCC performance under various request conditions. The complement traffic pattern is used to verify the largest paths in the network, while the all-to-all one comprises all possible communication combinations in the network (i.e., all the PEs request access

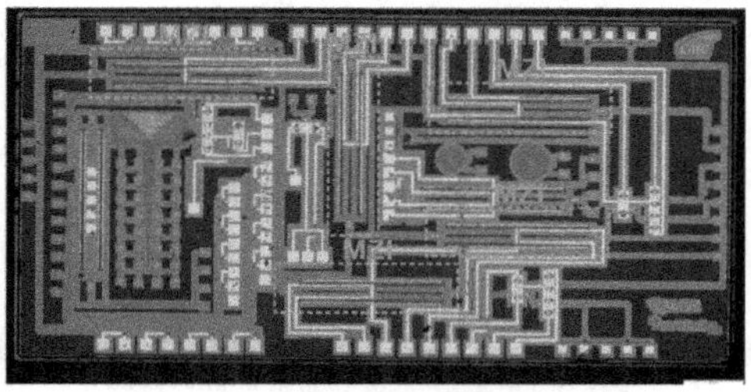

(a) Prototyped MZI-based photonic switch

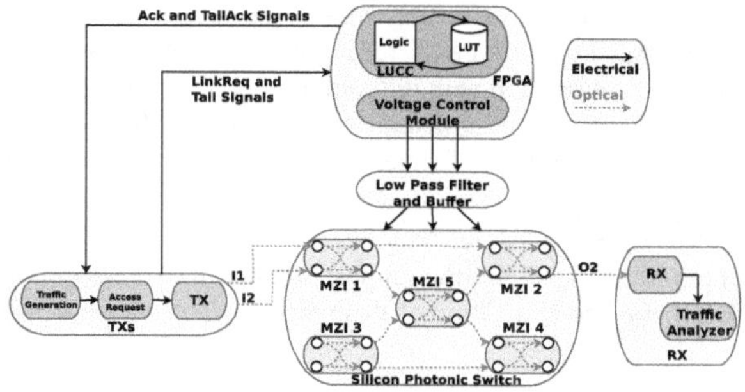

(b) Schematic overview of LUCC and the photonic switch integration

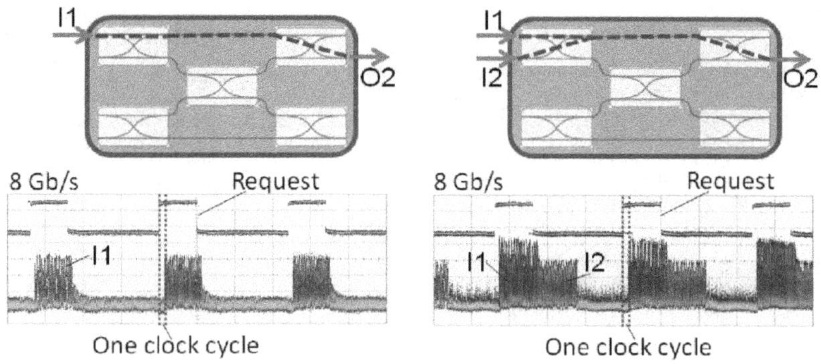

(c) Photonic switch readings

Figure 3: (a) MZI-based prototyped photonic switch; (b) overview of the FPGA-based LUCC co-designed with the MZI-based multistage photonic switch; and, (c) 4×4 MZI-based photonic switch readings.

to each other one by one). In our validations, the traffic load is not considered due to the fact the that a validation based on a traffic load usually aims at evaluating topologies, while we focus on the controller evaluation. Simulations are performed in commercial simulation tools and LUCC is prototyped on Altera's and Xilinx's FPGAs. The obtained results for the Altera Stratix IV FPGA showed a top operation frequency of 270 MHz (≈3.7 ns period). As for Xilinx's Virtex V FPGA, the top operation frequency is 295 MHz (≈3.4 ns period). Also, the design was synthesized using the proposed flow for the STMicroelectronics 65 nm technology process. The minimum period for this technology is ≈ 1.1 ns.

Fig. 2 compares LUCC latency with the state-of-the-art controllers in an 8×8 Beneš network, in which we indicate LUCC has the lowest latency under different message sizes. Considering a predefined photonic switch latency, the latency for each optical bit to pass through the network is rounded to 200 ps. The comparison is performed by analyzing the total time it takes for a message to be arbitrated and passes through the network: TotalTime = CL + Nob× TD. Here, CL is the control latency, Nob is the number of transmitted bits, and TD is the transmission delay. Three different message sizes (128 B, 256 B, 512 B) are considered. According to Fig. 2, the solution in [6] deploys a centralized control core without any acceleration techniques, which compromises its latency and scalability. Also, the approach proposed in [11] relies on PD techniques, which can lead to a high latency as the network scales (i.e., >8×8). Finally, the solution presented in [5] is based on an operation frequency of 5 GHz, and hence the validations are under behavioral simulations only, not considering a realistic physical implementation.

Fig. 3(a) illustrates the prototyped MZI-based photonic switch, integrated with LUCC for a realistic demonstration [9, 10]. The photonic switch is a 4×4 integrated Silicon Photonic (SiP) switch based on a Spanke-Beneš topology with five integrated 2×2 MZIs directly controlled by LUCC (see the middle block in Fig. 3(b)). Fig. 3(b) indicates the setup schematic of the FPGA-based LUCC co-designed with the MZI-based photonic switch. LUCC is prototyped in commercial FPGA from Altera. Fig. 3(c) presents the readings for the photonic switch being controlled by LUCC, in which we indicate the measured dynamic switching of a payload signal. It is generated at the FPGA running at 50 MHz for gate signal (bar and cross). Both LUCC and payload traffic are executed in the FPGA. At the receiver, we employ a photodetector connected to a digital communication analyzer (DCA) for the readings. Considering the observed waveform, it is possible to see the contention resolution in one clock cycle, as the payload is read in the switch output.

4 CONCLUSION

This work presents LUCC, a centralized controller for silicon photonic interconnects. Results, obtained through simulation, FPGA prototyping, as well as experimental integration with a fabricated photonic switch, show a fast response time when employing LUCC in SPIs. Indeed, it takes only one clock cycle delay to compute each request in the network. Our future work comprises extending LUCC's scalability, employing LUCC for larger-radix networks. Also, for a realistic demonstration with different photonic switches, the integration of LUCC with prototyped microring resonator (MR)-based photonic switches will be performed.

ACKNOWLEDGMENT

The authors gratefully acknowledge the support provided by ReSMiQ, CAPES and NSERC for the realization of this work.

REFERENCES

[1] A. Biberman, B. G. Lee, N. Sherwood-Droz, M. Lipson and K. Bergman. 2010. Broadband Operation of Nanophotonic Router for Silicon Photonic Networks-on-Chip. *IEEE Photonics Technology Letters* 22, 12 (2010), 926–928. DOI: http://dx.doi.org/10.1109/LPT.2010.2047850

[2] E. Fusella and A. Cilardo. 2017. H^2ONoC: A Hybrid Optical-Electronic NoC Based on Hybrid Topology. *IEEE Transactions on Very Large Scale Integration (VLSI) Systems* 25, 1 (January 2017), 330–343. DOI: http://dx.doi.org/10.1109/TVLSI.2016.2581486

[3] F. G. de Magalhães, R. Priti, M. Nikdast, F. Hessel, O. Liboiron-Ladouceur and G. Nicolescu. 2016. Design and Modelling of a Low-Latency Centralized Controller for Optical Integrated Networks. *IEEE Communications Letters* 20, 3 (2016), 462–465.

[4] H. Yan, D. A. Maltz, H. Gogineni and Z. Cai. 2007. Tesseract: A 4D Network Control Plane. In *NSDI*. USENIX Association, Cambridge, MA. https://www.usenix.org/conference/nsdi-07/tesseract-4d-network-control-plane

[5] J. Chan and K. Bergman. 2012. Photonic Interconnection Network Architectures Using Wavelength-selective Spatial Routing For Chip-scale Communications. *IEEE/OSA Journal of Optical Communications and Networking* 4, 3 (2012), 189–201.

[6] J. Jian, M. Lai and L. Xiao. 2016. A Fast Hierarchical Arbitration in Optical Network-on-Chip Based on Multi-Level Priority QoS. *IEICE Transactions on Communications* E99.B, 4 (2016), 875–884. DOI: http://dx.doi.org/10.1587/transcom.2015EBP3382

[7] N. Jasika, N. Alispahic, A. Elma, K. Ilvana, L. Elma and N. Nosovic. 2012. Dijkstra's Shortest Path Algorithm Serial and Parallel Execution Performance Analysis. In *International Convention MIPRO.*

[8] P. Lotfi-Kamran, M. Modarressi and H. Sarbazi-Azad. 2016. An Efficient Hybrid-Switched Network-on-Chip for Chip Multiprocessors. *IEEE Transactions on Computers* 65, 5 (2016), 1656–1662. DOI: http://dx.doi.org/10.1109/TC.2015.2449846

[9] Y. Xiong, F. G. de Magalhães, B. Radi, G. Nicolescu, F. Hessel and O. Liboiron-Ladouceur. 2016. Towards a Fast Centralized Controller for Integrated Silicon Photonic Multistage MZI-based Switches, In Optical Fiber Communication Conference - paper W1J.2. *Optical Fiber Communication Conference - paper W1J.2* (2016).

[10] Y. Xiong, F. G. de Magalhães, G. Nicolescu, F. Hessel and O. Liboiron-Ladouceur. 2017. Co-design of a Low-latency Centralized Controller for Silicon Photonic Multistage MZI-based Switches, In Optical Fiber Communication Conference - paper Th2A.37. *Optical Fiber Communication Conference - paper Th2A.37* (2017).

[11] Z. Li and T. Li. 2013. ESPN: A Case For Energy-star Photonic-on-Chip Network. In *IEEE International Symposium on Low Power Electronics and Design*. 377–382.

Leveraging RF Power for Intelligent Tag Networks

Emre Salman
Stony Brook University
Stony Brook, NY 11794, USA
emre.salman@stonybrook.edu

Milutin Stanaćević
Stony Brook University
Stony Brook, NY 11794, USA
milutin.stanacevic@stonybrook.edu

Samir Das
Stony Brook University
Stony Brook, NY 11794, USA
samir.das@stonybrook.edu

Petar M. Djurić
Stony Brook University
Stony Brook, NY 11794, USA
petar.djuric@stonybrook.edu

ABSTRACT

A novel framework and related methodologies are described to leverage RF power for building intelligent and battery-free devices with communication and computation capabilities. These passive devices are envisioned to make significant impact for the popular vision of *smart dust* due to extreme low power operation. The communication framework relies on tag-to-tag backscattering with very limited energy resources. The computing framework relies on a novel AC computing methodology that facilitates local data processing with an order of magnitude less power consumption. These enabling technologies, as described in this paper, revitalize the concept of *smart dust* with significant impact on various application domains such as smart spaces, implantable devices, and environmental/structural monitoring.

KEYWORDS

backscatter-based communication; RFID; RF tags; power harvesting; RF power; wireless energy; adaptive power management; wireless sensing; AC computing; decision making

ACM Reference Format:
Emre Salman, Milutin Stanaćević, Samir Das, and Petar M. Djurić. 2018. Leveraging RF Power for Intelligent Tag Networks. In *GLSVLSI '18: 2018 Great Lakes Symposium on VLSI, May 23–25, 2018, Chicago, IL, USA.* ACM, New York, NY, USA, 6 pages. https://doi.org/10.1145/3194554.3194621

1 INTRODUCTION

The powerful vision of smart dust, proposed in the late 1990s, consists of tiny mote-like devices that are distributed throughout an environment and possess critical capabilities such as sensing, computation, and wireless communication [13]. Despite the significant impact this vision had in the field of wireless sensor networks, the original anticipated framework has not yet come true since delivering power to each of these devices has been a primary barrier. Existing battery technologies are not only highly costly, but also impractical since it would require hundreds of millions of battery changes a day. Furthermore, limited power densities of conventional electrochemical charge storage techniques place stringent constraints on form factor.

ACM ISBN 978-1-4503-5724-1/18/05.
https://doi.org/10.1145/3194554.3194621

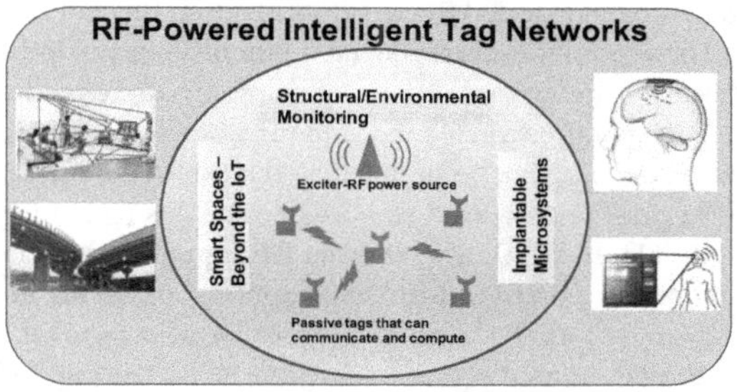

Figure 1: RF-powered intelligent tags that can communicate with each other through backscattering and achieve local computation through efficient AC computing methodology.

In this paper, tiny tags that are powered by harvesting available RF energy are introduced, as conceptually illustrated in Fig. 1. RF power can be provided both from ambient sources such as cellular, TV or WiFi signals as well as from dedicated wireless power sources such as RF exciters. Dedicated RF power sources have been successful in providing the required energy for radio frequency identification (RFID) and wireless charging applications.

Contrary to traditional approaches that are based on active radios, the communication among the tags is achieved by backscattering principle where the data are transmitted by reflecting an incident RF signal while modulating the input impedance of the tag antenna. The receiving tag decodes the transmitted signal through passive and low power envelope detection. Furthermore, the backscattering principle is exploited to monitor the wireless channel and therefore carry out *wireless sensing*, where the tags can detect new object in proximity. This requires energy-efficient local processing and decision making, which is achieved by the proposed AC computing methodology. Contrary to conventional methods that rely on rectifying the harvested AC signal and conventional DC-based computing, in the proposed method, the local processing core directly uses the harvested AC signal by leveraging adiabatic circuit theory. Thus, the significant losses related to rectification are eliminated and the computing is performed significantly more efficiently due to adiabatic charging and charge-recycling. The proposed passive tags have enormous implications both for (a) near-field (range limited) applications such as brain implantable devices for neural recording and stimulation and (b) for far-field applications such as smart spaces.

The rest of the paper is organized as follows. Related background material is provided in Section 2. Contributions of this work are highlighted in Section 3. The proposed tag architecture and critical components are detailed in Section 4. Several related applications where the proposed tags can be utilized are discussed in Section 5. Finally, conclusions are offered in Section 6.

2 BACKGROUND

Conventional RF-powered tags utilize RF power harvesting and backscatter communication to deliver sufficient functionality to communicate small amounts of information. Backscattering is based on modulating an external RF signal incident on the antenna of the device. The modulation is achieved by modifying the impedance levels seen by the antenna, thereby changing its reflection coefficient. This requires very small amount of power which, with appropriate circuits, can be supplied by the external RF signal itself. Today, the most widely used embodiment of this technology is in RFIDs [10, 11]. In RFID, the external RF signal is provided via a relatively higher power embedded computer, possessing an active radio, referred to as the 'reader.' The reader also receives and interprets the modulated signal backscattered by the tag. RFID has long been standardized and is now widely deployed in logistics and inventory applications to perform identification and tracking [1]. Variations of RFID exist as research platforms such as tags with sensors [9, 47] and tags with programming/computational ability (Computational RFID) [32, 47].

Two recent innovations have improved the possibility of ubiquitous deployment of such tags. These include 1) use of ambient RF signals (e.g., TV or WiFi) to provide the external RF signal and/or to power the tag [17, 21] and 2) tag-to-tag backscatter communications [3, 21, 26]. Use of ambient RF signals enables the tags to be deployed anywhere with no other infrastructure support necessary. Tag-to-tag backscatter implies that there is no need to have high-powered reader devices in the neighborhood to read the tag signals; the tags themselves can read and in turn relay the information using multihop routing. This enables highly scalable deployment.

3 CONTRIBUTIONS

This work benefits from existing tag-to-tag backscattering principle, but significantly enhances the basic technique for improved robustness and range. Furthermore, conventional tags suffer from lack of sufficient compute ability due to limited available power. Transmitting large amounts of raw data is not practical due to significant power cost and additional latency for the decision making process. Thus, an AC computing methodology is proposed to enhance the energy efficiency by more than an order of magnitude. Conventional digital logic in these applications typically relies on ultra-low voltage design with subthreshold operation [19]. Even though power levels in the range of nanowatts are achieved, an important limitation of these approaches is significant reduction in performance (clock frequency in range of several kHz) which is critical for applications where real-time inference and decision making are required.

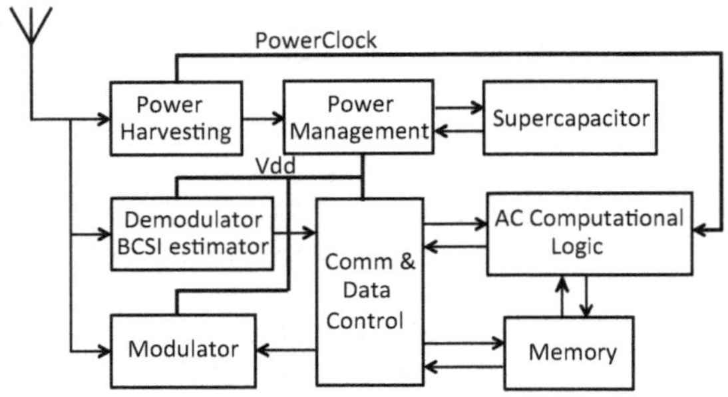

Figure 2: Proposed tag architecture depicting different modules.

4 PROPOSED TAG ARCHITECTURE

A high level block diagram of the proposed tag architecture, the principle building block of an intelligent tag network, is shown in Fig. 2. The architecture is similar to the traditional RFID tag with additional functionality and revised communication module optimized for tag-to-tag communication. The tag comprises antenna, RF energy harvesting and power management modules, modulator and demodulator for tag-to-tag communication, DC control and AC computational logic, along with memory and energy storage element, a supercapacitor, within a small form-factor.

A single frequency RF energy harvesting at 915 MHz or at 2.4 GHz is possible, as well as multi-band RF energy harvesting with more complex antenna design [5, 18, 38]. The incident RF signal is divided between sinusoidal power-clock signal required for the operation of AC logic, a DC supply voltage generated through AC-DC conversion for operation of DC logic and communication module, with extra energy being stored. The tags are designed to operate on a *harvest-use-store* principle with a supercapacitor as an energy storage element. Based on the incident RF power, stored energy and possible actions that can be taken, the logic implemented in the power management module directs the operation of the tag. The tag can integrate different ultra-low power stand-alone sensors. Additionally, the backscatter links themselves provide a form of sensing ability (sensing of backscatter channel state information(BCSI) integrated in demodulator) that can be exploited to perform network-wide inference. The computational logic, based on the collected data, is used for extracting information about the tag's environment.

4.1 RF Energy Harvester

The RF energy harvesting circuit comprises voltage multiplier that converts the incident AC signal to DC voltage as well as several signal conditioning blocks to obtain the required AC signals (power-clock) for AC computational logic. Different number of stages of the voltage multiplication can be used to boost the DC voltage. The energy efficiency, which is the amount of energy transfered by the voltage multiplier, in the conventional voltage multiplier is optimized for a certain small range of input powers. While the tag is listening for or receiving the message from another tag, the incident power at the antenna input is split between the energy harvester and the demodulator. In conventional RFID tags, due to a high modulation index of the received signal, the power ratio is determined solely by the optimization of the energy harvesting.

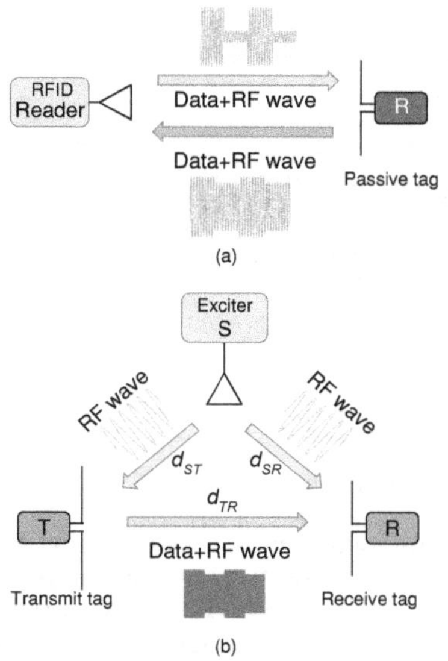

Figure 3: (a) General RFID communication setup, (b) Backscatter tag-to-tag communication network setup.

However, in the tag-to-tag link, the low modulation index not only adds complexity to the design of the demodulator itself, but also calls for the co-design of the energy harvester and demodulator. As an example of this optimization strategy, we examined the performance of the demodulator for different ratios of power division between the demodulator and power harvester. We demonstrated that there exists optimal power ratio that optimizes the energy transfer and voltage sensitivity of the demodulator circuit [2].

Design of the energy harvester with high energy efficiency over a wide input power range presents significant challenge. Structures like dual-path rectifier have been proposed in the literature [23, 24], however the range of the input powers over which the efficiency was optimized is narrow compared to the range of the incident powers at which the tag should operate. An energy-aware architecture of the energy harvester that will optimize the energy efficiency over a wide range of the incident power is a potential research direction.

4.2 Tag-to-Tag Link Design

The focus in the design of the communication module of the proposed tag is to achieve robust and reliable tag-to-tag communication link across a wide range of incident power. In conventional RFID reader-tag links, a tag demodulates a signal with a very high modulation index which greatly increases the robustness of the link, as illustrated in Fig. 3(a). The backscatter tag-to-tag link is illustrated in Fig. 3(b). The amplitude of the baseband signal depends on the input power at both the transmitting and receiving tags, along with the phase at which the transmitting tag backscatters due to the relative phase difference between the superimposing excitation and backscatter signals. The detailed analysis is presented in [14]. The tag-to-tag link is asymmetric as the tag closer to the RF source, when it backscatters, produces signal with high modulation index, while when it is receiving, the modulation index of the received signal is low due to high input power.

4.2.1 Modulator Design. The traditional backscatter modulator transmits data by switching between two different terminating impedances connected to the antenna. In tag-to-tag link, the amplitude of the baseband signal depends on the relationship between the relative phase difference between the superimposing RF source excitation signal and the signal backscattered from transmitting tag, and the phase of the terminating impedance at the transmitter tag. At specific distances between the tags, there exists a null in the response at the receiving tag, that is no distinction between the received signals for both states of the modulator of transmitting tag. We have analyzed this problem in detail and proposed a transmission scheme in which modulator transmits messages at two orthogonal transmitter phases [36]. If signal is canceled in one transmitter phase, the amplitude will be maximum in the other phase. We implemented the modulator that reflects the incident signal at a different phase using variable terminating impedance. This increases the robustness of the link by preventing nulls in the response at the receiving tag at specific distances between tags [36].

4.2.2 Demodulator Design. The signal reception using passive envelope detection [7, 16, 30] has been widely explored in the context of backscatter systems. However, application to tag-to-tag communication system gives rise to unique challenges. While in the forward (reader to tag) link of traditional RFID systems, the incoming signal at the tag has a very large modulation index, in tag-to-tag link, the Rx tag receives a much weaker backscatter signal from a Tx tag in the presence of a much stronger external excitation signal. This means that the modulation index of the incoming signal is at least an order of magnitude lower.

We use the envelope detector as the input circuit at the interface with antenna followed by the passive filter to improve signal-to-noise ratio (SNR), as in the conventional RFID tags [6, 7, 15, 40]. If there would be preceding RF gain stage, the power consumption of the tag would exceed 50 μW [4], which is much higher than the power available to RF energy harvesting tags. The envelope detector is implemented as voltage doubler. Since we want to resolve small modulation index, the envelope detector is followed by architecture comprising an amplifier with integrated band-pass filter followed by comparator. The integrated high-pass filtering removes the baseline from the modulated signal. The high-gain amplifier is implemented as low-noise, low-power folded cascoded amplifier.

The proposed demodulator architecture with voltage doubler followed by an amplifier with integrated high-pass filtering was simulated in 45 nm CMOS technology with supply voltage of 1.1 V. Averaged gain of amplifier is 64 which is enough to detect very weak signal. To demonstrate how the incoming signal with low modulation index can be distinguished, the input power to the tag was held at -28 dBm with ASK modulation and data rate of 10 kbps. At this incident power, we are able to resolve the received backscatter signal with the modulation index as low as 0.6% [14]. The power consumption of the demodulator is 1.2 μW.

4.2.3 Prototype platform for tag-to-tag communication. We have fabricated a discrete prototype of RF backscattering tag, shown in Fig. 4. In the initial prototype, RF power harvesting is not implemented and the tag is powered by a CR 1620 coin cell battery. The prototype tag includes a single dipole antenna and uses a discrete component conventional architecture of the modulator and the

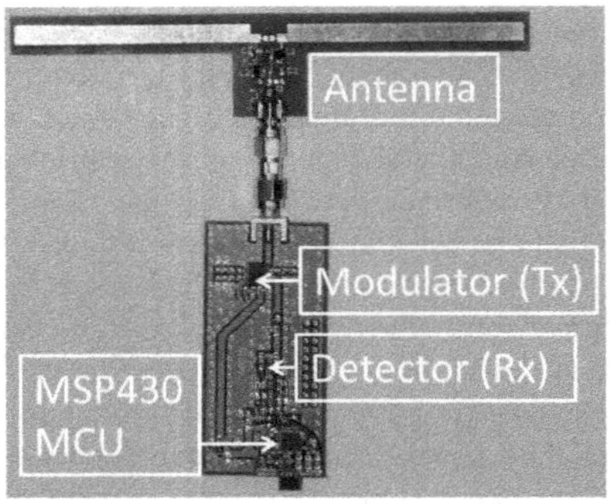

Figure 4: Prototype RF tag with dipole antenna and conventional modulator and demodulator implementation.

demodulator. In the demodulator, a two stage voltage multiplier, implemented using zero bias Schottky diode HSMS-285x series from Avago Technologies, is used for envelope extraction. To demonstrate the tag-to-tag link, we have performed experiments with dedicated RF source providing CW signal at 915 MHz in lab environment. We have demonstrated that the maximum communication distance between tags at the incident power of −20 dBm at both tags is 3 m and that at the incident power of −15 dBm the range extends to 7 m.

4.3 Adaptive Power Management

For the operation of a tag in a network of tags, in addition to the outlined challenges in the circuit design, the management of the operation of the tag on RF harvested energy and with a low capacity energy storage element introduces some unique challenges compared to the energy management of a traditional sensor node. Sensory nodes incorporate active radios that dominate the power budget, although significant steps have been made in reducing their power consumption [4, 8, 12, 27, 31]. The sensor nodes with energy harvesting have optimized energy-neutral operation that maximizes their performance with respect to the available energy, either on node level or application level [22, 25, 29, 33, 37, 39]. The balance between energy and performance is achieved through a wide range of adaptive techniques that control parameters like duty-cycle of the operation, transmit power of active radio and sensor reliability [20, 35, 41]. Backscatter-based communication in the proposed tag reduces the energy cost of the communication by a few orders of magnitude compared to the sensor node with active radio. This results in a different energy budget distribution for different modes of operation compared to the conventional sensor node and calls for different management techniques to be used in the tag's implementation.

In a network of tags, the power needed for backscattering at the Tx tags is small relative to the power needed to demodulate a signal. The power needed for demodulation again depends on the modulation index (lower power for higher modulation index) and is thus variable. The available RF power could be harvested in the supercapacitor on-tag (Fig. 2) that could be used if instantaneous power availability is limited for the function at hand (either transmit, receive or processing). However, due to the small size of the tag, the supercapacitor capacity is limited. Overall, the above issues lead to

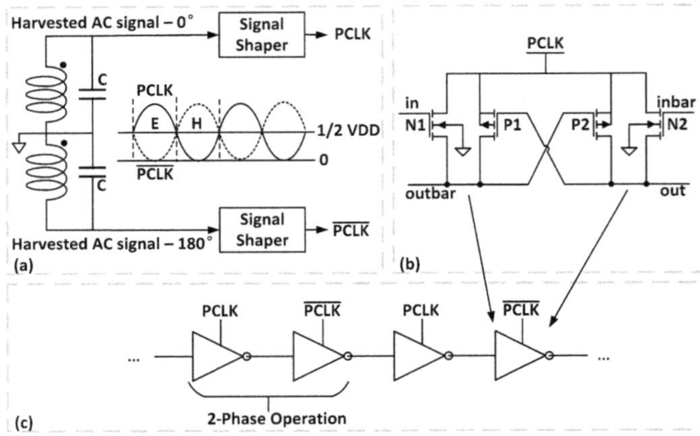

Figure 5: Adiabatic logic based AC computing approach: (a) 2-phase power-clock generation and signal shapers to eliminate negative voltage components, (b) schematic of a PAL based inverter, (c) chain of PAL logic gates powered with AC power-clock signals with 180° phase difference.

an interesting power management plus network formation problem. Depending on the available RF power on a tag (this may depend on the exciter and tag locations and is different for different tags), the tag must decide on whether to demodulate a relatively weak backscatter signal from a neighbor. Due to the inherent redundancy in the network, the value of this action may not be significant relative to the needed energy. Thus, the network "links" that are to be used for communication are not well-defined even in a static network setting. The weaker links may only be occasionally used depending on the available RF power on the Rx tag and the value of using that link, By contrast, stronger links could be used more frequently as they may be less power constrained. A challenge here is the development of algorithms and protocols so that the links are used 'optimally' in the sense that the value of using a specific link for data routing is balanced with the energy budget of its Rx tag.

4.4 On-Site AC Computing

The proposed AC computing methodology enables energy-efficient data processing unit that can potentially be integrated within the passive tag [43]. AC computing leverages adiabatic circuit theory developed in the early 1990s [34, 46]. Extreme low power operation is achieved by eliminating rectification for logical operation and recycling charge during computation.

Existing adiabatic logic families should be reinvented for interoperability with the RF energy harvester described in Section 4.1. In this work, pass transistor adiabatic logic (PAL) [28] is used as an example, as as illustrated in Fig. 5 A PAL gate consists of two NMOS transistors N1, N2, and a pair of cross-coupled charging/recovering PMOS transistors P1, P2. The primary advantage of PAL is the ability to fully recycle charge since the NMOS transistors are connected to AC power supply. In addition, note that PAL is a two-phase logic where the AC supply of each consecutive gate is 180° out-of-phase, as depicted in Fig. 5(c). Thus, when one of the gates is at the "evaluation" phase, the preceding gate is at the "hold" phase, maintaining the input signals stable for the evaluating gate. Note that the two inductors within the energy harvester are configured such that the

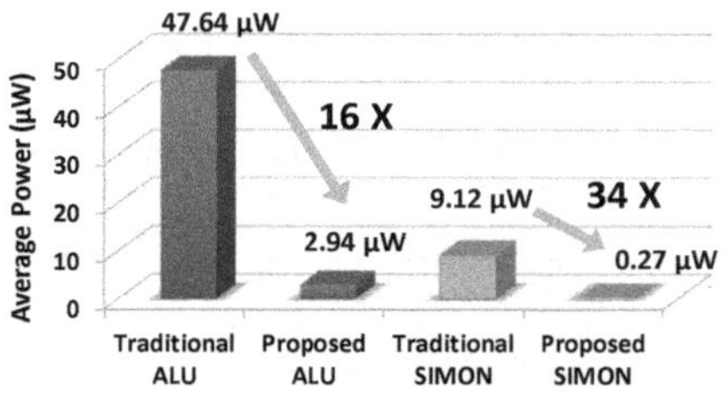

Figure 6: Comparison of power consumed by the 8-bit ALU and SIMON32/64 core, implemented using the proposed AC computing method and conventional method that relies on rectification and DC computing.

two harvested AC signals have 180° phase difference. PAL, however, cannot correctly operate with the harvested AC signal that has both positive and negative voltage components. To mitigate this limitation, a low complexity and efficient signal shaper was developed, as described in [42]. Another approach is to rely on efficient charge recovery logic based AC computing, as described in [45].

The feasibility of the proposed approach has been demonstrated by recent results where the power consumed by a processing block (that relies on RF power and AC computing) has been reduced by more than an order of magnitude. Two examples that are implemented with AC computing include an 8-bit arithmetic logic unit to implement general purpose digital functions and a bit serialized SIMON32/64 (32-bit plaintext with a 64-bit key) core for lightweight encryption [44]. Both blocks operate with the harvested 13.56 MHz carrier signal, which serves as both the power and clock signal. Both ALU and SIMON are also implemented with a conventional approach that relies on rectification and DC computing. The overall power consumption is compared in Fig. 6 for both blocks. For the 8-bit ALU, the proposed approach achieves up to 16.2X reduction in power whereas for the SIMON core, power is reduced by up to 34X and the energy efficiency (kb/sec/μW) is enhanced by 27X. The larger reduction for the SIMON core is primarily due to the existence of a large number of registers (required for bit serialized architecture) where AC computing is highly beneficial due to much smaller and efficient register implementation.

An important future work for AC computing is the development of a system-level energy management methodology. Since the modulation/demodulation and memory blocks as well as the supercapacitor require a DC voltage, the energy management module should determine how to split the harvested energy into DC and AC paths, depending upon the incoming data, required data processing, and power consumption of each block. Another interesting direction would be to investigate on-chip AC energy storage methods such as a flywheel manufactured on-chip by utilizing MEMS technology. AC energy storage would eliminate rectification loss when storing energy that would be later used by the data processing block.

5 APPLICATIONS

5.1 Smart Spaces - Beyond the IoT

The proposed technology will make possible that all objects in our living-, working-, and traveling-spaces will be tagged with miniature passive RF-addressable tags, which can autonomously communicate and interact among themselves without the need for a centralized control. These interactions will enable 'smart spaces' wherein objects can collaboratively understand the 'space' around them and recognize dynamic activities and events therein. Such context-aware intelligent physical spaces will enable new levels of automated human-object interaction and control through efficient exchange of information and knowledge. The tags in this vision will be designed for seamless and ubiquitous deployment, with low cost, and with size and form factor which will allow them to blend with all objects in our everyday spaces; from furniture to smaller objects such as clothes, wallets or keys. This vision goes beyond today's IoT (Internet of Things), where IoT concept is limited to only powerful devices - typically possessing an embedded processor and traditional network communication, such as thermostats, cameras or light bulbs.

5.2 Floating Implantable Microsystems

The proposed research can be highly beneficial for brain implantable microsystems. The number of applications for implantable systems has been growing in the recent years with significant impact on disease treatment and general healthcare. In the design of implantable devices, providing wireless power to the device and data communication link are critical parts of the system design. Power harvesting and telemetry through inductive coupling present a commonly used solution. As the bandwidth of the communication link is limited, raw sensor data need to be processed and compressed before transmission. Since the power is highly limited, performing these computational tasks requires extremely efficient computational techniques. Furthermore, the ability of the multiple implanted devices to communicate via backscattering exhibits significant opportunities in terms of real-time and closed-loop distributed sensing and decision making.

5.3 Environmental and Structural Health Monitoring

Wide deployment of wireless sensor nodes has been limited by the maintenance cost incurred by the battery replacement. Alternatively, proposed tags require only ambient RF signals to operate autonomously in these environments. In most of these applications, the detection of specific events (rather than continuous logging of sensor data) is critical. Unfortunately, detecting these critical events by processing raw sensor data increases the computational burden and therefore the overall energy cost. Proposed tags are able to carry out most of the processing locally and make decisions cooperatively with neighboring tags. We anticipate that the reduction in the energy cost for both computing and tag-to-tag communication achieved in this work will enable many of the potential applications that have been traditionally impeded.

6 CONCLUSIONS

Key enabling technologies have been described to develop RF-powered passive tags with wireless communication and computation capabilities. These tags represent the foundation for building intelligent tag networks, revitalizing the popular vision of smart dust. Critical enabling technologies include adaptive power management for backscatter based tag-to-tag communication and AC computing for energy-efficient and local decision making. The proposed framework is highly applicable to smart spaces and environmental/structural health monitoring where frequent battery changes are impractical, and brain implantable devices where a closed-loop system is essential for fast and efficient stimulation.

REFERENCES

[1] 2005. *Class 1 Generation 2 UHF Air Interface Protocol Standard Version 1.0.9.* EPCGlobal Inc.

[2] A. Athalye, J. Jian, Y. Karimi, S.R. Das, and Petar M. Djurić. 2016. Analog Front End Design for Tags in Backscatter-Based Tag-to-Tag Communication Networks. In *IEEE Int. Symposium on Circuits and Systems (ISCAS).*

[3] Akshay Athalye, Vladimir Savic, Miodrag Bolic, and Petar M Djuric. 2013. Novel semi-passive RFID system for indoor localization. *Sensors Journal, IEEE* 13, 2 (2013), 528–537.

[4] J. Blanckenstein, J. Klaue, and H. Karl. 2015. A Survey of Low-Power Transceivers and Their Applications. *IEEE Circuits and Systems Magazine* 15, 3 (2015), 6–17.

[5] Aniello Buonanno, Michele D'Urso, and Domenico Pavone. 2011. An ultra wide-band system for RF Energy harvesting. In *Antennas and Propagation (EUCAP), Proceedings of the 5th European Conference on.* IEEE, 388–389.

[6] W. Che, Y. Yang, C. Xu, N. Yan, X. Tan, Q. Li, H. Min, and J. Tan. 2009. Analysis, design and implementation of semi-passive Gen2 tag. In *IEEE International Conference on RFID.* 15–19.

[7] H. Dagan, A. Shapira, A. Teman, A. Mordakhay, S. Jameson, E. Pikhay, V. Dayan, Y. Roizin, Eran E. Socher, and A. Fish. 2014. A Low-Power Low-Cost 24 GHz RFID Tag With a C-Flash Based Embedded Memory. *IEEE Journal of Solid-State Circuits* 49, 9 (2014), 1942–1957.

[8] D. Daly and A. Chandrakasan. 2007. An energy-efficient OOK transceiver for wireless sensor networks. *IEEE Journal of Solid-State Circuits* 42, 5 (2007), 1003–1011.

[9] Alanson P. Sample Daniel J. Yeager and Joshua R. Smith. 2008. *RFID Handbook: Applications, Technology, Security, and Privacy.* CRC Press, Chapter WISP: A Passively Powered UHF RFID Tag with Sensing and Computation.

[10] D. M. Dobkin. 2007. *The RF in RFID: Passive UHF RFID in Practice.* Elsevier - Newnes.

[11] Klaus Finkenzeller. 2003. *RFID Handbook: Fundamentals and Applications in Contactless Smart Cards and Identification.* John Wiley & Sons, Inc., New York, NY, USA.

[12] Xiongchuan Huang, Pieter Harpe, Guido Dolmans, Harmke de Groot, and John R Long. 2014. A 780–950 MHz, 64–146 μW power-scalable synchronized-switching ook receiver for wireless event-driven applications. *IEEE Journal of Solid-State Circuits* 49, 5 (2014), 1135–1147.

[13] J. M. Kahn, R. H. Katz, and K. S. J. Pister. 1999. Next Century Challenges: Mobile Networking for Smart Dust. In *Proc. of the ACM/IEEE Int. Conf. on Mobile Computing and Networking.* 271–278.

[14] Y. Karimi, A. Athalye, S. Das, P. Djurić, and M. Stanaćević. 2017. Design of Backscatter-Based Tag-to-Tag System. In *IEEE Int. Conference on RFID (RFID).*

[15] U. Karthaus and M. Fischer. 2003. Fully integrated passive UHF RFID transponder IC with 16.7-μW minimum RF input power. *IEEE Journal of Solid-State Circuits* 38, 10 (2003), 1602–1608.

[16] U. Karthaus and M. Fischer. 2003. Fully integrated passive UHF RFID transponder IC with 16.7uW minimum RF input power. *IEEE Journal of Solid-State Circuits* 38, 10 (2003), 1602 – 1608.

[17] Bryce Kellogg, Aaron Parks, Shyamnath Gollakota, Joshua R. Smith, and David Wetherall. 2014. Wi-fi Backscatter: Internet Connectivity for RF-powered Devices. In *Proceedings of the 2014 ACM Conference on SIGCOMM (SIGCOMM '14).* ACM, New York, NY, USA, 607–618. https://doi.org/10.1145/2619239.2626319

[18] V. Kuhn, C. Lahuec, F. Seguin, and C. Person. 2015. A Multi-Band Stacked RF Energy Harvester With RF-to-DC Efficiency Up to 84%. *IEEE Transactions on Microwave Theory and Techniques* 63, 5 (May 2015), 1768–1778.

[19] Y. Lee, D. Blaauw, and D. Sylvester. 2016. Ultralow Power Circuit Design for Wireless Sensor Nodes for Structural Health Monitoring. *Proc. IEEE* 104, 8 (Aug 2016), 1529–1546.

[20] S. Lin, J. Zhang, G. Zhou, L. Gu, J. Stankovic, and T. He. 2006. ATPC: adaptive transmission power control for wireless sensor networks. In *Proc. of the Int. Conf. on Embedded Networked Sensor Systems.* 223–236.

[21] Vincent Liu, Aaron Parks, Vamsi Talla, Shyamnath Gollakota, David Wetherall, and Joshua R. Smith. 2013. Ambient Backscatter: Wireless Communication Out of Thin Air. In *Proc. ACM SIGCOMM.*

[22] Xiao Lu, Ping Wang, Dusit Niyato, Dong In Kim, and Zhu Han. 2015. Wireless networks with RF energy harvesting: A contemporary survey. *IEEE Communications Surveys & Tutorials* 17, 2 (2015), 757–789.

[23] Y. Lu, H. Dai, M. Huang, M. K. Law, S. W. Sin, S. P. U, and R. P. Martins. 2017. A Wide Input Range Dual-Path CMOS Rectifier for RF Energy Harvesting. *IEEE Transactions on Circuits and Systems II: Express Briefs* 64, 2 (Feb 2017), 166–170.

[24] Y. S. Luo and S. I. Liu. 2017. A Voltage Multiplier With Adaptive Threshold Voltage Compensation. *IEEE Journal of Solid-State Circuits* 52, 8 (Aug 2017), 2208–2214.

[25] Clemens Moser, Lothar Thiele, Davide Brunelli, and Luca Benini. 2007. Adaptive power management in energy harvesting systems. In *Proceedings of the conference on Design, automation and test in Europe.* EDA Consortium, 773–778.

[26] P.V. Nikitin, S. Ramamurthy, R. Martinez, and K.V.S. Rao. 2012. Passive tag-to-tag communication. In *RFID (RFID), 2012 IEEE International Conference on.* 177 –184.

[27] Emil Nilsson and Christer Svensson. 2014. Power consumption of integrated low-power receivers. *IEEE Journal on Emerging and Selected Topics in Circuits and Systems* 4, 3 (2014), 273–283.

[28] V.G. Oklobdzija, D. Maksimovic, and Fengcheng Lin. 1997. Pass-transistor adiabatic logic using single power-clock supply. *IEEE Transactions on Circuits and Systems II: Analog and Digital Signal Processing* 44, 10 (1997), 842–846.

[29] Chulsung Park and Pai H Chou. 2006. Ambimax: Autonomous energy harvesting platform for multi-supply wireless sensor nodes. In *Sensor and Ad Hoc Communications and Networks, 2006. SECON'06. 2006 3rd Annual IEEE Communications Society on,* Vol. 1. IEEE, 168–177.

[30] V. Pillai, H. Heinrich, D. Dieska, P.V. Nikitin, R. Martinez, and K.V.S. Rao. 2007. An ultra-low-power long range battery/passive RFID tag for UHF and microwave bands with a current consumption of 700 nA at 1.5 V. *IEEE Transactions on Circuits and Systems I: Regular Papers* 54, 7 (2007), 1500–1512.

[31] Nathan M Pletcher, Simone Gambini, and Jan Rabaey. 2009. A 52 muW Wake-Up Receiver With −72 dBm Sensitivity Using an Uncertain-IF Architecture. *IEEE Journal of solid-state circuits* 44, 1 (2009), 269–280.

[32] B. Ransford, S. Clark, M. Salajegheh, and K. Fu. 2008. Getting things done on computational RFIDs with energy-aware checkpointing and voltage-aware scheduling. In *Proceedings of USENIX Workshop on Power Aware Computing and Systems (HotPower).*

[33] Srinivas S. Reddy and C.R. Murthy. 2012. Dual-stage power management algorithms for energy harvesting sensors. *IEEE Transactions on Wireless Communications* 11, 4 (2012), 1434–1445.

[34] S. Younis and T. Knight. 1994. Asymptotically zero energy computing using split-level charge recovery logic. Technical Report AITR-1500, MIT AI Laboratory. (June 1994).

[35] Z. Safarian and H. Hashemi. 2014. Wirelessly Powered Passive Systems With Dynamic Energy Storage Mechanism. *IEEE Transactions on Microwave Theory and Techniques* 62, 4 (2014), 1012–1021.

[36] Z. Shen, A. Athalye, and P. M. DjuriÄĞ. 2016. Phase Cancellation in Backscatter-Based Tag-to-Tag Communication Systems. *IEEE Internet of Things Journal* 3, 6 (Dec 2016), 959–970. https://doi.org/10.1109/JIOT.2016.2533398

[37] Farhan Simjee and Pai H Chou. 2006. Everlast: long-life, supercapacitor-operated wireless sensor node. In *Low Power Electronics and Design, 2006. ISLPED'06. Proceedings of the 2006 International Symposium on.* IEEE, 197–202.

[38] C. Song, Y. Huang, P. Carter, J. Zhou, S. Yuan, Q. Xu, and M. Kod. 2016. A Novel Six-Band Dual CP Rectenna Using Improved Impedance Matching Technique for Ambient RF Energy Harvesting. *IEEE Transactions on Antennas and Propagation* 64, 7 (July 2016), 3160–3171.

[39] S. Sudevalayam and P. Kulkarni. 2011. Energy harvesting sensor nodes: Survey and implications. *IEEE Communications Surveys & Tutorials* 13, 3 (2011), 443–461.

[40] N. Tran, B. Lee, and J-W. Lee. 2007. Development of long-range UHF-band RFID tag chip using Schottky diodes in standard CMOS technology. In *IEEE Radio Frequency Integrated Circuits (RFIC) Symposium.* 281–284.

[41] Christopher M Vigorito, Deepak Ganesan, and Andrew G Barto. 2007. Adaptive control of duty cycling in energy-harvesting wireless sensor networks. In *Sensor, Mesh and Ad Hoc Communications and Networks, 2007. SECON'07. 4th Annual IEEE Communications Society Conference on.* IEEE, 21–30.

[42] T. Wan, Y. Karimi, M. Stanaćević, and E. Salman. 2017. Energy efficient AC computing methodology for wirelessly powered IoT devices. In *Circuits and Systems (ISCAS), 2017 IEEE International Symposium on.* 1–4.

[43] T. Wan, Y. Karimi, M. Stanaćević, and E. Salman. 2017. Perspective Paper: Can AC Computing Be an Alternative for Wirelessly Powered IoT Devices? *IEEE Embedded Systems Letters* 9, 1 (2017), 13–16.

[44] T. Wan and E. Salman. 2018. Ultra Low Power SIMON Core for Lightweight Encryption. In *Circuits and Systems (ISCAS), 2018 IEEE Int. Symp. on.*

[45] T. Wan, M. Stanaćević, and E. Salman. 2016. A new circuit design framework for IoT devices: Charge-recycling with wireless power harvesting. In *Circuits and Systems (ISCAS), 2016 IEEE International Symposium on.* 2046–2049.

[46] S. G. Younis and T. F. Knight. 1995. Non-dissipative rail drivers for adiabatic circuits. In *Proceedings of the Conference on Advanced Research in VLSI.* 404–414.

[47] H. Zhang, J. Gummeson, B. Ransford, and K. Fu. 2011. *Moo: A Batteryless Computational RFID and Sensing Platform.* Technical Report UM-CS-2011-020. Department of Computer Science, University of Massachusetts Amherst, Amherst, MA. http://www.cs.umass.edu/publication/details.php?id=2114

Quasi-self-powered Infrastructural Internet of Things: The Mackinac Bridge Case Study

Kenji Aono*
Computer Science and Engineering
Washington University in St. Louis
St. Louis, Missouri
kaono@acm.org

Hassene Hasni
Civil & Environmental Engineering
Michigan State University
East Lansing, Michigan
hasniha1@msu.edu

Owen Pochettino
Electrical and Systems Engineering
Washington University in St. Louis
St. Louis, Missouri
owen.pochettino@wustl.edu

Nizar Lajnef
Civil & Environmental Engineering
Michigan State University
East Lansing, Michigan
lajnefni@egr.msu.edu

Shantanu Chakrabartty†
Electrical and Systems Engineering
Washington University in St. Louis
St. Louis, Missouri
shantanu@wustl.edu

ABSTRACT

Autonomous, continuous and long-term monitoring systems are required to prognosticate failures in civil infrastructures due to material fatigue or extreme events like earthquakes. While current battery-powered wireless sensors can evaluate the condition of the structure at a given instant of time, they require frequent replacement of batteries due to the need for continuous or frequent sampling. On the other hand, self-powered sensors can continuously monitor the structural condition without the need for any maintenance; however, the scarcity of harvested power limits the range at which the sensors could be wirelessly interrogated. In this paper, we propose a quasi-self-powered sensor that combines the benefits of self-powered sensing and with the benefits of battery-powered wireless transmission. By optimizing both of the functionalities, a complete sensor system can be designed that can continuously operate between the structure's maintenance life-cycles and can be wirelessly interrogated at distances that obviates the need for taking the structure out-of-service. As a case study, in this paper we present the design considerations involved in prototyping quasi-self-powered sensors for deployment on the Mackinac Bridge in northern Michigan, with a target operational life span greater than 20 years.

CCS CONCEPTS

• **Hardware** → **Application-specific VLSI designs**; **Full-custom circuits**; **Hardware test**; • **Computer systems organization** → *Embedded and cyber-physical systems*; • **Applied computing** → Physical sciences and engineering;

*Also with, Computer Science and Engineering, Michigan State University.
†Corresponding Author

GLSVLSI '18, May 23–25, 2018, Chicago, IL, USA

ACM ISBN 978-1-4503-5724-1/18/05...$15.00
https://doi.org/10.1145/3194554.3194622

KEYWORDS

Piezo-Floating-Gate Sensor; Quasi-self-powered; Infrastructural Internet of Things; Structural Health Monitoring

ACM Reference Format:
Kenji Aono, Hassene Hasni, Owen Pochettino, Nizar Lajnef, and Shantanu Chakrabartty. 2018. Quasi-self-powered Infrastructural Internet of Things: The Mackinac Bridge Case Study. In *GLSVLSI '18: 2018 Great Lakes Symposium on VLSI, May 23–25, 2018, Chicago, IL, USA.* ACM, New York, NY, USA, 6 pages. https://doi.org/10.1145/3194554.3194622

1 INTRODUCTION

With growth of the world economy and its population, there is an ever increasing dependency on larger and more complex networks of civil infrastructure as evident in the billions of dollars spent by federal, state and local governments to upgrade or repair transportation systems and utilities. Despite these large expenditures, the nation continues to suffer staggering consequences from infrastructural decay. According to the American Society of Civil Engineers 2017 Infrastructure Report Card, the overall health of America's infrastructure is at a D+ grade, with bridges and roads at C+ and D, respectively [30]. As part of the solution, they recognize the cost and difficulty of using, maintaining, and improving the nation's infrastructure; further, they note the importance of supporting research into innovative new technologies, such as structural health monitoring (SHM) to expedite repairs or replacement, and to promote cost savings. Due to the forces of nature that act on infrastructure, it is impossible to have a complete understanding of how these structures will act in deployment conditions; therefore, a method for sensing the state of these structures periodically is necessary. Currently, the primary method of determining the health of infrastructure is visual inspection, resulting in a mostly qualitative assessment of damage [1–3]. In contrast to this qualitative methodology, several quantitative methods are also employed, such as the measurement of structural damage through the use of electrical impedance [19] and ground penetrating radar [4].

However, in order to provide a more expansive method of sensing, several groups have proposed a method of structural monitoring through the use of wireless sensor networks (WSNs). Advantages of this approach are many, as they are relatively low cost and

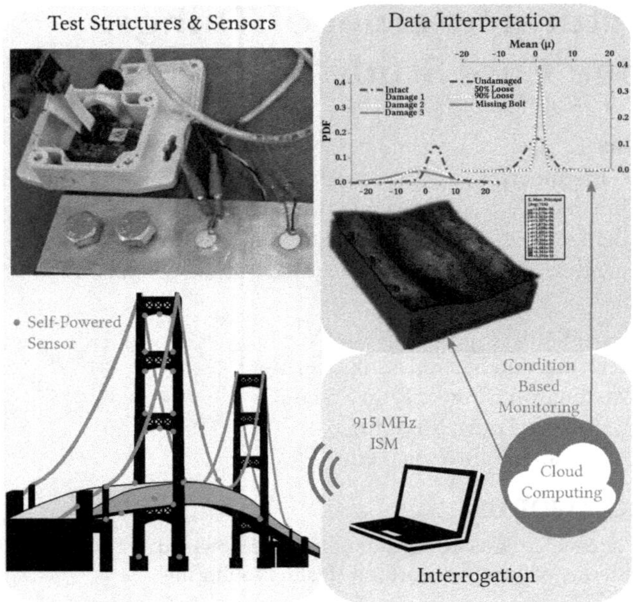

Figure 1: Vision of infrastructural Internet of Things (*i*-IoT).

provide a wide swath of coverage over a majority of the structure. In addition, these sensor nodes have a relatively low cost of installation and require a relatively low amount of maintenance [29]. These sensor networks collect several types of relevant structural data such as acceleration, stress, load, and vibration [29]. Yet even these methodologies are limited, as they frequently use battery powered instruments for sensing as well as the transmission of data; the method of obtaining power and the life of external power supply continues to be the bottleneck in the design of these WSN for the purpose of SHM [29]. On the other end of the spectrum are self-powered SHM systems [13, 31] that require zero-maintenance (no replacement of batteries) and can continuously operate over the useful life-span of the structure without experiencing any down-time. The self-powered sensors have been the basis of our ongoing work in the area of infrastructural Internet of Things (*i*-IoT), which uses a widespread network of self-powered sensing devices with the ability to monitor the impact and strain that are applied to structures.

The goal of the *i*-IoT framework, as shown in Fig. 1, is to provide a robust methodology that can easily deploy on a variety of different structures without compromising or interfering with the integrity of that structure. However, a key aspect of the *i*-IoT framework is ability to collect data from an array of self-powered sensors embedded inside a structure, without taking the structure out-of-service. Self-powered operation is limited in its ability to wirelessly transmit the stored data over long distances due to high energy requirements. Therefore, in this paper we are proposing a quasi-self-powered sensing system that combines the benefits of self-powered sensors that are continuously active and battery-powered transmitters that are sporadically active. The combination of the two techniques results in ultra-low average power consumption of the entire system implying that they can be deployed on real-world structures for a long periods of time with relatively low amounts of maintenance. In this paper we present a case study of a quasi-self-powered SHM sensor that has been designed for deployment on the Mackinac Bridge in northern Michigan, which is one of the largest suspension bridges in North America.

2 PFG SENSING PRINCIPLE

Over the last decade our research group has investigated an alternate approach for designing SHM sensors, which are powered directly by the sensing signal itself [18], which for an SHM application are mechanical strain and the mechanical acceleration. If a sensor could self-power itself from the energy latent in the strain-variations and in the mechanical acceleration, then the device can continuously monitor for events of interest without experiencing any down-time. The challenge is that less than a microwatt of power is available when the sensor is embedded inside a structure like concrete [14, 16]. At this power-level it is practically impossible to implement a continuous monitoring system comprising of energy converters, energy regulators, analog-to-digital converters, signal processors and wireless transceivers. Also, given that SHM sensors have to be operational for more than 20 years, raw strain-measurements cannot be stored due to the limitations on the silicon area and the instantaneous measurements cannot be transmitted wirelessly due to limitations on In [11, 12, 15, 25, 28] we reported a piezo-floating-gate (PFG) sensing technique that self-powers by harvesting energy from micro-strain variations.

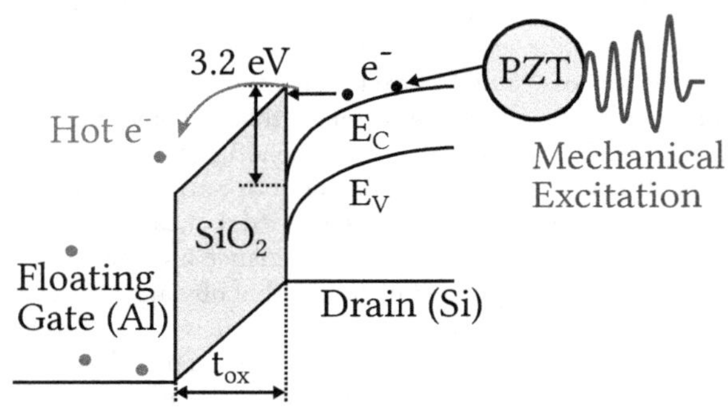

Figure 2: Simplified principle of PFG operation.

The principle of the PFG sensor is illustrated in Fig. 2 where a piezoelectric transducer (in this case a lead zirconate titanate, or PZT) harvests energy from mechanical strain variations to generate high-energy electrons (or hot-electrons) in the channel of a MOSFET transistor. When the energy of some of these electrons (with the right momentum vector) exceeds the energy barrier (3.2 eV) of the silicon, silicon-di-oxide interface (as shown in Fig. 2), these electrons surmount the barrier and get trapped onto a floating-gate. Because the floating-gate is electrically isolated by a high quality insulating oxide, the injected electrons remain trapped for a long period of time. As the piezoelectric transducer is periodically excited, more electrons are injected onto the floating-gate and the cumulative charge stored on the floating gate is a function of the duration and the magnitude of the mechanical excitation. This approach directly couples the physics of piezoelectric energy harvesting with the physics of hot-electron injection to sense, compute and store mechanical usage statistics and hence can be used to push the fundamental limits of self-powered sensing of mechanical strain. The floating-gate also serves as a non-volatile storage memory from which the mechanical usage data could be retrieved at a later stage for offline analysis. This leads to a "sense-now, analyze-later" paradigm which has been the basis of several PFG based sensors [17, 23, 24, 27, 32, 33]. The difference between the respective PFG sensor designs is the interface circuit that connects the piezoelectric transducer with the floating-gate memory. By modifying the topology of the injector interface circuit, the sensor can also be designed to record different statistics of the strain signal, like strain-levels [24, 32], strain-rates [23], or time of occurence [34].

3 EXPERIMENTAL VERIFICATION

We demonstrated the efficacy of our proposed monitoring methods with an experimental that consists of a steel plate under an in-plane tension load. The steel plate under consideration is notched in the middle to introduce damage, as shown in Fig. 3, with the notch in the vertical direction to give better control over the crack size under uniaxial tensile loading; a deviation in the notch location or direction would not significantly alter the results using the methodology proposed by [22]. The damaged segment is surrounded by PZT transducers affixed to the surface of the steel plate, in turn, the transducers are connected to our self-powered PFG sensors that will log the cumulative strain experienced by the transducer. As the damage grows in the steel plate, the strain experienced by each transducer increases near the crack tip of the notch — since the sensors are continuously logging the statistics of this strain, it becomes possible to periodically collect data from the sensors and still deduce the damage progression [5, 9, 10, 20–22].

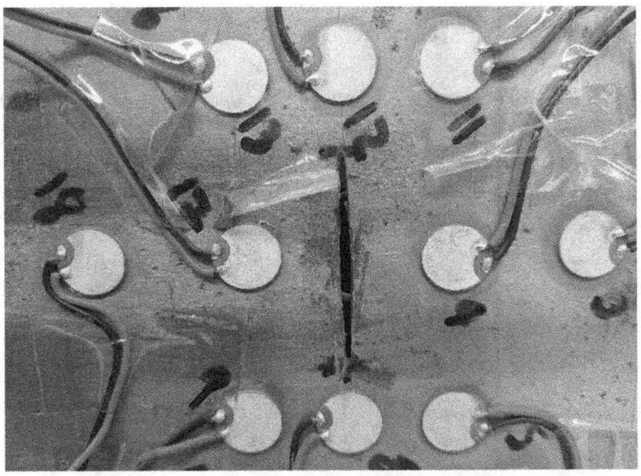

Figure 3: In-lab testing of a steel plate with controlled damage, surrounded by several piezoelectric transducers [22].

For verification purposes, the number of sensors is more than required, in practice, one could use a finite element simulation to predetermine segments of the structure that are more susceptible to damage and prioritize the placement of sensors accordingly. Even with modeling, it is exceedingly difficult to select an optimal sensor placement a priori since the type of damage is unknown. Therefor, a sensor fusion strategy was developed to improve the detection performance using spatial measurements, this "group effect" strategy has been reported in [5, 21]. Even if the location of damage is not known in advance, the group effect can be utilized for condition-based monitoring.

The performance of the self-powered PFG sensor has been experimentally validated on other laboratory test-beds, with a sampling of results given in the Data Interpretation block of Fig. 1. The top left portion of the figure shows results from detection of a bottom up crack in asphalt concrete pavement [20], the top right shows the detection of localized failures such as the loosening of a bolt [6], and the bottom illustrates a simulation verifying the data interpretation [5].

4 MACKINAC BRIDGE SENSOR DESIGN

The PFG sensor was fabricated through MOSIS as a system-on-chip that includes all necessary components (the piezoelectric transducer notwithstanding) for self-powered sensing and data logging. The PFG core and pad ring requires $1.5 \times 1.5\,\text{mm}^2$ as shown in Fig. 4, and relevant characteristics are listed in Table 1.

Table 1: Fabricated PFG Characteristics

CMOS Process	OnSemi 0.5 µm
Chip Size	$1.5 \times 1.5\,\text{mm}^2$
Minimum Energy (Self-powered)	100 nJ
Supply Voltage (Readout)	1.8 V
Power Dissipation (Readout)	75 µW
Programming Resolution	> 12 bits

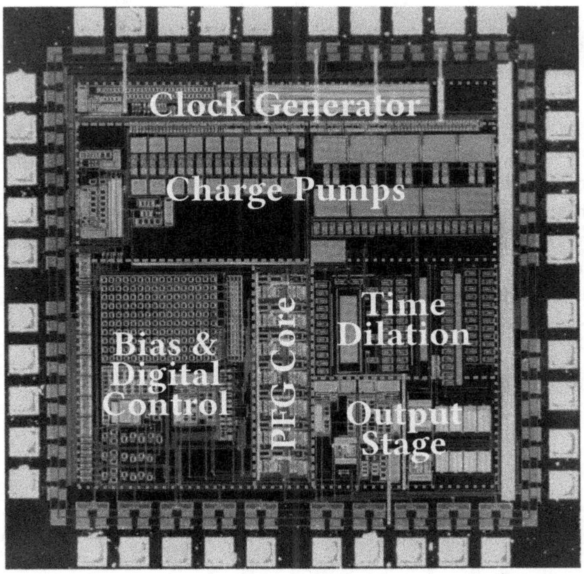

Figure 4: Die micrograph of the $1.5 \times 1.5\,\text{mm}^2$ chip.

4.1 Design Considerations

4.1.1 Analog to Digital Conversion. As evident in the chip micrograph of Fig. 4, die space is at a premium when designing the SoC to fit on a MOSIS tiny core (note that some areas of the die that appear empty are filled with passive resistors). In the pursuit of maintaining a reduced design complexity, some design choices were made that will require consideration when taking the chip outside of a controlled lab environment. The first such consideration is the use of a pulse encoder ADC in lieu of a more robust conversion method to interface the PFG's stored charge to external digital devices. The pulse encoder output frequency as a function of the input voltage (i.e. Floating-Gate Voltage), is presented as Fig. 5, which highlights the non-monotonic behavior of the ADC. In the initial state, the floating-gate voltage would be high, and as the sensor experiences mechanical excitation the injected electrons will reduce the voltage output, thus increasing the output frequency. At an inflection point near 470 mV, this trend reverses as the discharge branch of the ADC becomes too weak to respond in a timely fashion. By observing the duty cycle of the output pulse train, as presented in the bottom trace of Fig. 5, we can decode the floating-gate voltage even though the output frequency is not monotonic.

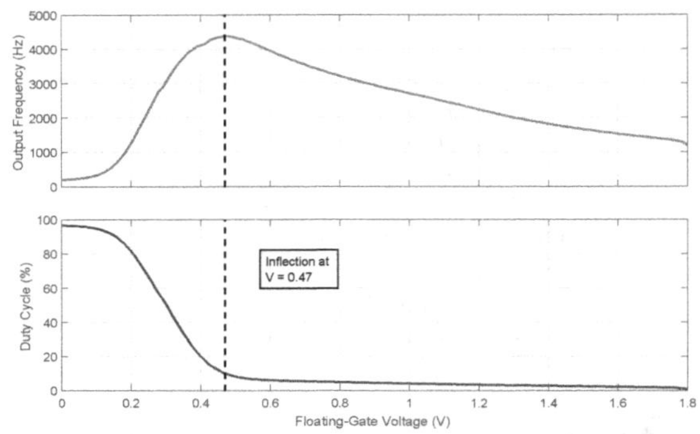

Figure 5: Simulation showing (top) frequency as a function of input voltage, and (bottom) duty cycle of same.

4.1.2 Voltage Reference. Another aspect to consider is the temperature dependence of the self-biased current source used for generating on-chip voltage biases. In simulation, one will observe a large deviation in the output frequency of the pulse encoder as a function of temperatures we'd expect at the Mackinac Bridge installation site, as shown in Fig. 6.

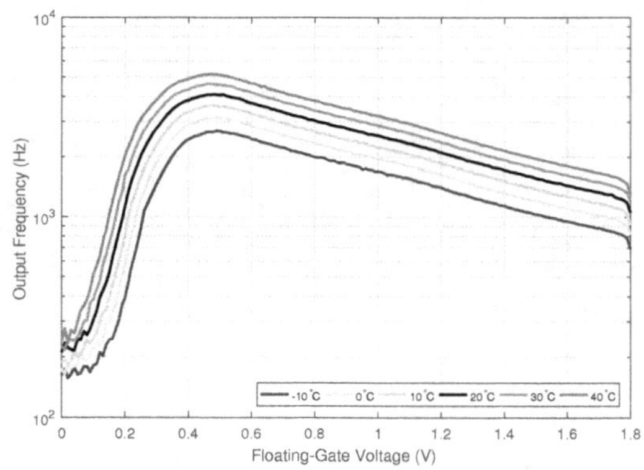

Figure 6: Simulation of pulse encoder output frequency when sweeping the input voltage and ambient temperature.

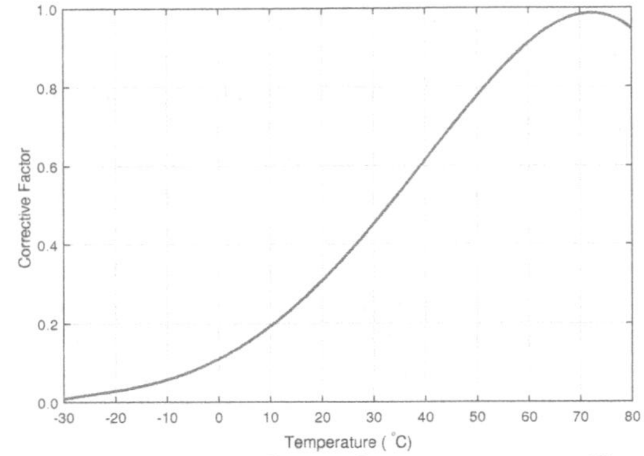

Figure 7: Corrective factor for temperature effects.

To account for the temperature effect, we developed a corrective factor as illustrated in Fig. 7. This factor was derived from averaging the response of three fabricated chips that were initialized to an output frequency of 1.15 kHz at lab room temperature of 21.5 °C and subjected to temperatures from −30 °C to 80 °C in a climate chamber. The data in subsequent discussions are processed using the appropriate corrective factor considering the observed ambient air temperature during data collection and are thus presented as unitless.

5 FIELD TEST

5.1 System Enclosure

We previously demonstrated a backscatter RF interface for data retrieval [13, 24], yet in the case of communication in the dense steel structure of the Mackinac Bridge, for long ranges, they are not feasible. Thus, we opted to swap out the backscatter interrogation unit with an active Radio Frequency (RF) link – leading to a quasi-self-powered platform since the continuous sensing is self-powered, but the interrogation is not [9]. A preliminary feasibility test using a short-term deployment on the Mackinac Bridge [8] was successfully completed and we miniaturized the design to make a more robust platform for an active RF interface, as shown in Fig. 8. Note that modules b & f are self-powered for continuous monitoring, the remaining modules only power up for sporadic RF communications.

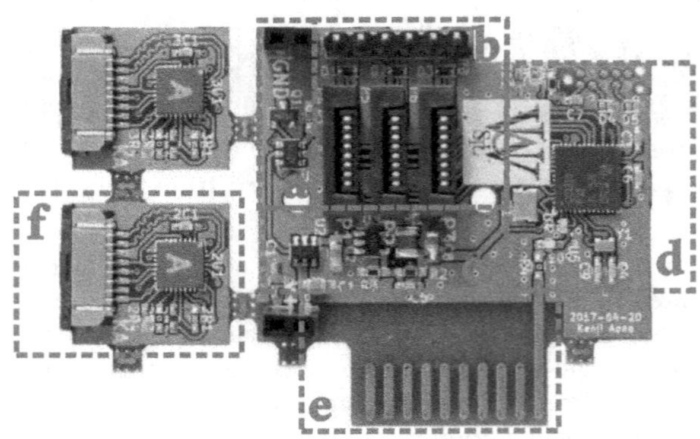

Figure 8: PCB for: (a) timer; (b) piezo input; (c) battery management; (d) micro-controller; (e) antenna; (f) PFG module.

An assembled board with sensors and battery mounted in a weatherproof enclosure is shown in the top left of Fig. 1, operational details of the system are listed in Table 2. To take advantage of the quasi-self-powered architecture, an ultra-deep sleep mode that draw less than 50 nA from the battery (≈35 nA for the TPL5111 from Texas Instruments and another ≈15 nA leakage through bypass capacitors) is enabled by Fig. 8(a), this module places the active portion of the system into a non-responsive deep sleep mode for 300 s at a time, before waking up the micro-controller (MCU). Upon wakeup, the MCU will idle while waiting for a command, if a read command is detected it will pull the data from the PFG sensors, else it goes back to sleep. The PFG sensor modules (Fig. 8(f)) are connected using a Flag Flexible Cable(Fig. 8(b)), which allows for easy swapping in and out of the sensors depending on application. Similarly, (Fig. 8(b)) allows for the piezo transducers to be swapped. In the case of the Mackinac Bridge, the sensors are configured for measuring upwards of two million loading cycles of mechanical strain [10]. (Fig. 8(c)) takes the ≈3 V supplied by ½AA Lithium Thionyl Chloride Cells from Tadiran to 1.8 V to power the MCU (Fig. 8(d)) and RF communication through the integrated antenna (Fig. 8(e)). RF communication is enabled by a Texas Instruments CC1310 using a proprietary protocol on the 915 MHz band.

Table 2: System Enclosure Specification

Parameter	Value
Enclosure Size	$59 \times 94 \times 35\,\text{mm}^3$
Sensors per Enclosure	3
Radio Band	915 MHz ISM
Transmit Power	up to 10 dBm
Transmit Distance	>100 m
Transmit Current	2.5 mA
Transmit Time (Max)	13.5 s
Receive Sensitivity	−112 dBm
Receive Current	225 µA
Receive Time (Max)	6 s
Sleep Current	50 nA
Sleep Duration	300 s

From the specifications in Table 2, we can estimate average current consumption when there is no request for data (no energy spend on RF transmission) and for when there is a request as:

$$\text{Request} = \frac{I_{\text{on}}t_{\text{on}} + I_{\text{search}}t_{\text{search}} + I_{\text{off}}t_{\text{off}}}{t_{\text{on}} + t_{\text{search}} + t_{\text{off}}} = \frac{2.5\,\text{m} \cdot 13.5 + 225\,\mu \cdot 6 + 50\,\text{n} \cdot 300}{13.5 + 6 + 300} < 110\,\mu\text{A}$$

$$\text{No request} = \frac{I_{\text{search}}t_{\text{search}} + I_{\text{off}}t_{\text{off}}}{t_{\text{search}} + t_{\text{off}}} = \frac{225\,\mu \cdot 6 + 50\,\text{n} \cdot 300}{6 + 300} < 5\,\mu\text{A}$$

Working under the assumption that commands are sent only 1% of the time (that is, approximately two or three readings a day), and incorporating an 85% derating factor on the battery, a single ½ AA battery with 1.2 Ah capacity would last:

$$1.2\,\text{Ah} \div (0.99 \cdot 5\,\mu + 0.01 \cdot 110\,\mu)\,\text{A} \cdot 0.85 \cdot \left(\frac{1\,\text{yr}}{8766\,\text{h}}\right) \approx 20\,\text{years}.$$

Once the battery lasts 20 years, other components (weatherproof seals, capacitors, PZT, etc.) may begin to fail before the system enclosure requires a battery change. In this way, the quasi-self-powered system presents a viable method for developing an *i*-IoT framework by leveraging self-powered sensors to move the system bottleneck away from battery technology.

5.2 Mackinac Measurements

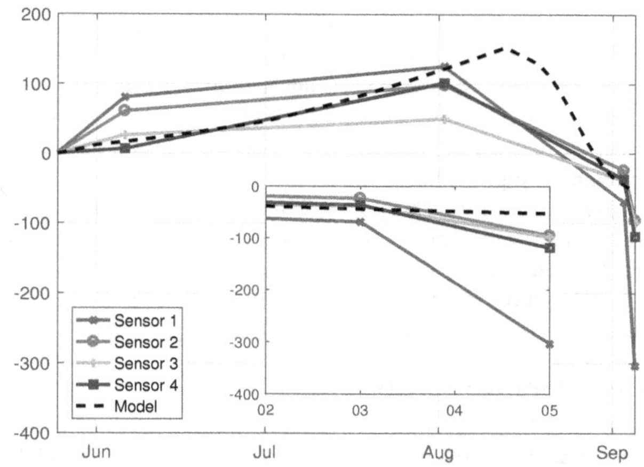

Figure 9: Data from four sensors, dashed black line shows expected results from model. Inset showing before and after Labor Day (Sep 04).

The data collected between May 25th and September 5th of 2017 are presented in Fig. 9 after having the corrective factors applied. Sensors 1 through 3 are at the same installation site and show the same trend in data logging, with some difference in peak frequency as well as injection rate due to fabrication mismatch. Sensor 4 was on a different installation site, but had a similar configuration in terms of PZT size (see Fig. 10 for the types of locations under consideration) and PFG tuning parameters. The sparse data collection appears to follow the trend that we expected based on the PFG characterizations from in-lab testing [7, 10, 17, 26, 34] and the traffic statistics of the Mackinac Bridge. The trend line is shown as the dashed black. The inset of Fig 9 shows the data collected before and after the Mackinac Bridge Labor Day Walk (on Sep. 4th), which drew a crowd of over 25,000 people, much greater than usual traffic on the bridge. It shows that during the event the sensors logged

Figure 10: Mackinac Bridge used for deployment study.

a much larger amount of data than it had in the days before. The deviation from the model trace, which is based on monthly traffic statistics, highlights the extra strain that the Labor Day Walk placed on the sensors. Note that we are only showing a unit-less, corrective-factor-applied frequency output of a single channel from each PFG sensor, from which a layperson may have trouble extracting any meaningful information.

6 CONCLUSIONS

In this paper we presented a system level design of a quasi-self-powered sensor that combined the benefits of continuously active self-powered sensors with sporadically active wireless transmission. The paper also presented a design case study where the sensor was prototyped for field deployment on the Mackinac Bridge in northern Michigan. The prototype was designed to continuously operate over a duration of 20 years and with a transmission range greater than 100 m. Our preliminary deployment results and measured data show the sensors to be functional over a period of a few months. An introspection into the information gleaned from the data will appear in forthcoming publications.

ACKNOWLEDGMENTS

This material is based upon work supported by the National Science Foundation under Grant Nos. DGE-0802267, DGE-1143954 and CNS-1646380. Any opinions, findings, and conclusions or recommendations expressed in this material are those of the author(s) and do not necessarily reflect the views of the National Science Foundation. The presented work was supported in part by a USDoT contract (DTFH6113H00009). Authors thank the Mackinac Bridge Authority for their continued assistance in carrying out this work.

REFERENCES

[1] AASHTO. 2016. Manual for Bridge Evaluation (2nd Edition) with 2011, 2013, 2014, 2015 and 2016 Interim Revisions. (2016).

[2] Federal Highway Administration. 2001. Reliability of Visual Inspection for Highway Bridges Volume I: Final Report. (2001).

[3] Federal Highway Administration. 2011. Bridge Inspector's Reference Manual. (2011).

[4] Amir M. Alani, Aboutalebi Morteza, and Kilic Gokhan. 2013. Applications of ground penetrating radar (GPR) in bridge deck monitoring and assessment. *Journal of Applied Geophysics* 97 (2013), 45–54.

[5] Amir H. Alavi, Hassene Hasni, Nizar Lajnef, Karim Chatti, and Fred Faridazar. 2016. Damage detection using self-powered wireless sensor data: An evolutionary approach. *Measurement* 82 (2016), 254–283.

[6] Amir H. Alavi, Hassene Hasni, Nizar Lajnef, Karim Chatti, and Fred Faridazar. 2016. An Intelligent Structural Damage Detection Approach Based on Self-powered Wireless Sensor Data. *Automation in Construction* 62 (2016), 24–44.

[7] Kenji Aono, Tracey Covassin, and Shantanu Chakrabartty. 2014. Monitoring of repeated head impacts using time-dilation based self-powered sensing. In *IEEE International Symposium on Circuits and Systems, ISCAS 2014, Melbourne, Victoria, Australia, June 1-5, 2014.* 1620–1623. https://doi.org/10.1109/ISCAS.2014.6865461

[8] Kenji Aono, Sri Harsha Kondapalli, Nizar Lajnef, Gokhan Pekcan, Fred Faridazar, and Shantanu Chakrabartty. 2017. Self-powered Sensors to Facilitate Infrastructural Internet-of-Things for Smart Structures. In *ANCRiSST 13th International Workshop on Advanced Smart Materials and Smart Structures Technology, Tokyo, Japan, July 22-23, 2017.* https://www.researchgate.net/publication/323456921

[9] Kenji Aono, Nizar Lajnef, Fred Faridazar, and Shantanu Chakrabartty. 2016. Infrastructural health monitoring using self-powered Internet-of-Things. In *IEEE International Symposium on Circuits and Systems, ISCAS 2016, Montréal, QC, Canada, May 22-25, 2016.* 2058–2061. https://doi.org/10.1109/ISCAS.2016.7538983

[10] Wassim Borchani, Kenji Aono, Nizar Lajnef, and Shantanu Chakrabartty. 2016. Monitoring of Postoperative Bone Healing Using Smart Trauma-Fixation Device With Integrated Self-Powered Piezo-Floating-Gate Sensors. *IEEE Trans. Biomed. Engineering* 63, 7 (2016), 1463–1472. https://doi.org/10.1109/TBME.2015.2496237

[11] Shantanu Chakrabartty. 2010. Self-powered Strain-rate Sensor. (2010). Patent No. 7757565, Issued 2010.

[12] Shantanu Chakrabartty. 2016. Self-powered Strain-gauge. (2016). Patent No. 9331265, Issued 2016.

[13] Shantanu Chakrabartty, Tao Feng, and Kenji Aono. 2012. Gen-2 RFID Compatible, Zero Down-time, Programmable Mechanical Strain-monitors and Mechanical Impact Detectors. In *Proceedings Volume 8692, Sensors and Smart Structures Technologies for Civil, Mechanical, and Aerospace Systems, San Diego, CA, USA, Apr 19, 2013.* 86921A. https://doi.org/10.1117/12.2011956

[14] Shantanu Chakrabartty and Nizar Lajnef. 2009. Infrasonic Power-Harvesting and Nanowatt Self-Powered Sensors. In *2009 IEEE International Symposium on Circuits and Systems.* 157–160.

[15] Shantanu Chakrabartty, Nizar Lajnef, Niell Elvin, and Amit Gore. 2011. Self-powered Sensor. (2011). Patent No. 8056420, Issued 2011.

[16] Niell G. Elvin, Nizar Lajnef, and Alex A. Elvin. 2006. Feasibility of structural monitoring with vibration powered sensors. *Smart Materials and Structures* 15, 4 (2006), 1422–1429.

[17] Tao Feng, Kenji Aono, Tracey Covassin, and Shantanu Chakrabartty. 2015. Self-Powered Monitoring of Repeated Head Impacts Using Time-Dilation Energy Measurement Circuit. *IEEE Trans. Biomed. Circuits and Systems* 9, 2 (2015), 217–226. https://doi.org/10.1109/TBCAS.2015.2403864

[18] National Science Foundation. 2015. Warding off failure. (2015). https://nsf.gov/discoveries/disc_summ.jsp?cntn_id=134022&org=NSF Discovery Briefing.

[19] Park Gyuhae, Hoon Sohn, Charles R. Farrar, and Daniel J. Inman. 2003. Overview of piezoelectric impedance-based health monitoring and path forward. *Shock and Vibration Digest* 35, 6 (2003), 451–464.

[20] Hassene Hasni, Amir Alavi, Pengcheng Jiao, Nizar Lajnef, Karim Chatti, Kenji Aono, and Shantanu Chakrabartty. 2017. A New Approach for Damage Detection in Asphalt Concrete Pavements Using Battery-Free Wireless Sensors with Non-Constant Injection Rates. *Measurement* 110 (2017), 217–229. https://doi.org/10.1016/j.measurement.2017.06.035

[21] Hassene Hasni, Amir H. Alavi, Pengcheng Jiao, and Nizar Lajnef. 2017. Detection of fatigue cracking in steel bridge girders: A support vector machine approach. *Archives of Civil and Mechanical Engineering* 17, 3 (2017), 609–622.

[22] Hassene Hasni, Amir H. Alavi, Nizar Lajnef, Mohamed Abdelbarr, Sami F. Masri, and Shantanu Chakrabartty. 2017. Self-powered piezo-floating-gate sensors for health monitoring of steel plates. *Engineering Structures* 148 (2017), 584–601.

[23] Chenling Huang and Shantanu Chakrabartty. 2011. Compact self-powered CMOS strain-rate monitoring circuit for piezoelectric energy scavengers. *Electronics Letters* 47, 4 (2011), 277–278(1).

[24] Chenling Huang and Shantanu Chakrabartty. 2012. An Asynchronous Analog Self-Powered CMOS Sensor-Data-Logger With a 13.56 MHz RF Programming Interface. *IEEE Journal of Solid-State Circuits* 47, 2 (2012), 476–489. https://doi.org/10.1109/JSSC.2011.2172159

[25] Chenling Huang, Nizar Lajnef, and Shantanu Chakrabartty. 2011. Rail-to-Rail, Linear Hot-Electron Injection Programming of Floating-Gate Voltage Bias Generators at 13-Bit Resolution. *IEEE Transactions on Circuits and Systems I: Regular Papers* 57, 3 (2011), 556–567. https://doi.org/10.1109/TCSI.2009.2024976

[26] Chenling Huang, Pikul Sarkar, and Shantanu Chakrabartty. 2011. Rail-to-Rail, Linear Hot-Electron Injection Programming of Floating-Gate Voltage Bias Generators at 13-Bit Resolution. *IEEE Journal of Solid-State Circuits* 46, 11 (2011), 2685–2692. https://doi.org/10.1109/JSSC.2011.2167390

[27] Nizar Lajnef, Wassim Borchani, Rigoberto Burgueño, and Shantanu Chakrabartty. 2015. Self-powered Piezo-floating-gate Smart-gauges based on Quasi-static Mechanical Energy Concentrators and Triggers. *IEEE Sensors Journal* 15, 2 (2015), 676–683.

[28] Nizar Lajnef, Niell G. Elvin, and Shantanu Chakrabartty. 2008. A Piezo-Powered Floating-Gate Sensor Array for Long-Term Fatigue Monitoring in Biomechanical Implants. *IEEE Transactions on Biomedical Circuits and Systems* 2, 3 (2008), 164–172.

[29] Adam B. Noel, Abderrazak Abdaoui, Tarek Elfouly, Mohamed Hossam Ahmed, Ahmed Badawy, and Mohamed S. Shehata. 2017. Structural Health Monitoring Using Wireless Sensor Networks: A Comprehensive Survey. *IEEE Communications Surveys & Tutorials* 19, 3 (2017).

[30] American Society of Civil Engineers. 2017. 2017 Infrastructure Report Card: A Comprehensive Assessment of America's Infrastructure. (2017). https://www.infrastructurereportcard.org

[31] Praveen Pasupath, Mingxiang Zhu Zhou, Dean P. Neikirk, and Sharon L. Wood. 2008. Unpowered Resonant Wireless Sensor Nets for Structural Health Monitoring. In *2008 IEEE Sensors.* 697–700.

[32] Pikul Sarkar and Shantanu Chakrabartty. 2013. Compressive Self-powering of Piezo-Floating-Gate Mechanical Impact Detectors. *IEEE Transactions of Circuits and Systems* 60, 9 (2013), 2311–2320.

[33] Pikul Sarkar, Chenling Huang, and Shantanu Chakrabartty. 2013. An Ultra-Linear Piezo-Floating-Gate Strain-Gauge for Self-Powered Measurement of Quasi-Static-Strain. *IEEE Transactions on Biomedical Circuits and Systems* 7, 4 (2013), 437–450.

[34] Liang Zhou, Kenji Aono, and Shantanu Chakrabartty. 2018. A CMOS Timer-Injector Integrated Circuit for Self-Powered Sensing of Time-of-Occurrence. *IEEE J. Solid-State Circuits* PP (2018), 1–11. https://doi.org/10.1109/JSSC.2018.2793531

New GPR System Integration with Augmented Reality Based Positioning

Mauricio Pereira
School of Engineering, University of Vermont
Burlington, Vermont
mauricio.pereira@uvm.edu

Dylan Burns
School of Engineering, University of Vermont
Burlington, Vermont
dylanburns802@gmail.com

Daniel Orfeo
School of Engineering, University of Vermont
Burlington, Vermont
dan.orfeo@gmail.com

Robert Farrel
School of Engineering, University of Vermont
Burlington, Vermont
bobby.farrel@uvm.edu

Dryver Huston
School of Engineering, University of Vermont
Burlington, Vermont
dhuston@uvm.edu

Tian Xia
School of Engineering, University of Vermont
Burlington, Vermont
txia@uvm.edu

ABSTRACT

The development of modern cities heavily relies on the availability and quality of underground utilities that provide drinking water, sewage, electric power, and telecommunication services to sustain its growing population. However, the information of localization and condition of subterranean infrastructures is generally not readily available, especially in areas with congested pipes, which impacts urban development, as poorly documented pipes may be hit during construction, affecting services and causing costly delays. Furthermore, aging components are prone to failure and may lead to resources waste or the interruption of services. Ground penetrating radar (GPR) is a promising remote sensing technique that has been recently used for mapping and assessment of underground infrastructure. However, current commercial GPR survey systems are designed with wheel-encoders or GPS for positioning. Wheel-encoder based GPR surveys are restrained to linear-route only, preventing the use of GPR for accurate localization of city wide underground infrastructure inspection. While GPS signal is degraded in urban canyons and unavailable in city tunnels. In this work, we present a new GPR system integration with augmented reality (AR) based positioning that can overcome the limitations of current GPR systems to enable arbitrary-route scanning with a high fidelity. It has the potential for automation of GPR survey and integration with AR smartphone applications that could be used for better planning in urban development.

CCS CONCEPTS

• **Hardware** → **Sensor applications and deployments**; **Sensor devices and platforms**;

KEYWORDS

ground penetrating radar; smart cities; augmented reality; visual-inertial odometry; underground infrastructure

ACM Reference Format:

Mauricio Pereira, Dylan Burns, Daniel Orfeo, Robert Farrel, Dryver Huston, and Tian Xia. 2018. New GPR System Integration with Augmented Reality Based Positioning. In *GLSVLSI'18:2018 Great Lakes Symposium on VLSI, May 23–25, 2018 Chicago, IL, USA.* ACM, New York, NY, USA, 6 pages. https://doi.org/10.1145/3194554.3194623

1 INTRODUCTION

The development of modern cities relies heavily on underground utilities that provide drinking water, electric power, sewage, telecommunications, among other services. However the information of the localization and condition of underground infrastructures is generally not readily available, impacting urban development and maintenance. For aging infrastructures, the degraded conditions and defects may result in resources waste and potential service outage. Recently, smart city approaches have been explored to address the issue of city wide mapping and assessing of underground infrastructure [1]. GPR is a remote non-destructive sensing technique [16, 17] that has been used to both image underground infrastructure and assess buried pipe condition [5, 7, 8, 15]. However, for city wide mapping and assessment of underground infrastructure, an accurate positioning system is required. Current commercial GPR are based on wheel-encoders for local positioning and GPS for global positioning. Wheel-encoders provide linear accuracy only, implying that surveys have to be performed in straight-line routes for correct localization of underground features. While GPS provides flexibility, its resolution is rough for precisely positioning subsurface objects. Moreover GPS signals may be degraded in urban canyons, or unavailable in certain areas, i.e. in tunnels. These factors result in significant limitations for employing existing commercial GPRs for city wide survey applications, especially in dense urban areas where underground infrastructure is critical. Hence, a versatile, accurate, low-cost positioning solution is required to fully explore GPR potentials for underground infrastructure mapping and assessment.

GLSVLSI'18, May 23–25, 2018, Chicago, IL, USA

ACM ISBN 978-1-4503-5724-1/18/05...$15.00
https://doi.org/10.1145/3194554.3194623

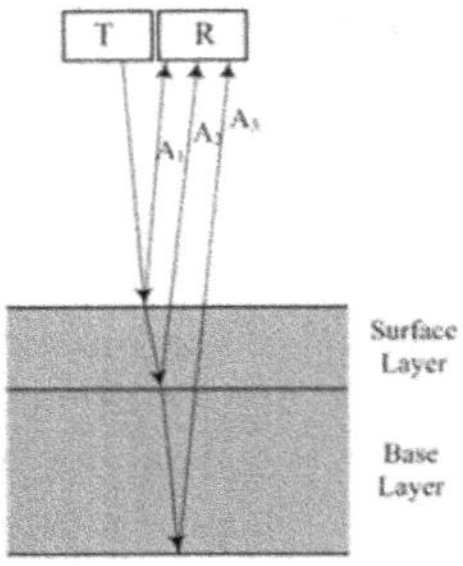

Figure 1: Scheme of a typical GPR system [14].

Recently, there has been great technology advancement in augmented reality (AR) applications for smartphones. For instance, Google created a framework named Tango for the development of AR applications [2]. This framework leverages on photogrammetry techniques that, combined with smartphone's IMU data, enable accurate local positioning.

In this work, a Tango enabled Lenovo Phab 2 Pro smartphone, here denominated the Tango device, was integrated with a GSSI SIR 30 GPR system using an Arduino microcontroller equipped with an XBee bluetooth (BT) shield and a relay for GPR scan triggering. A smartphone application using the Tango framework was developed with Unity, a game development platform that supports mobile AR applications [4]. The application controls communication with the BT shield, sends GPR scan triggering messages to the Arduino and logs device position. This integrated system enables GPR scanning in an arbitrary route with good positioning accuracy, expanding GPR survey capabilities.

This paper is organized as follows, section 2 describes the fundamentals of GPR sensing, section 3 introduces the Tango framework features, section 4 explains the system integration and operation, section 5 shows results demonstrating that this new GPR system is capable of performing arbitrary-route GPR survey, and section 6 presents the concluding remarks.

2 GROUND PENETRATING RADAR

GPR is a non-destructive evaluation technique that has been traditionally used to image the subsurface structure or detect the burying objects. Recently it has been applied to the mapping and assessment of underground infrastructure [8, 9]. A typical GPR consists of a transmitting antenna that sends an electromagnetic wave into the subsurface and a receiving antenna that collects scattered signals as illustrated in Fig. 1. Signals are scattered at every change in the dielectric property of the media, such that GPR can detect both metallic and non-metallic objects [10].

The corresponding received signal, denominated an A-scan, is shown in figure 2. The A_0 peak is the direct coupling between transmitter and receiver, A_1 is the ground reflection, A_2 and A_3 are signals due to the difference in layers dielectric properties. In a GPR survey, signal A_2 would be produced by the presence of buried pipes or other subterranean infrastructure.

Current GPR surveys are conducted over a straight-line route, collecting several A-scans to compose a B-scan. B-scans are represented as a grayscale image whose intensity is proportional to

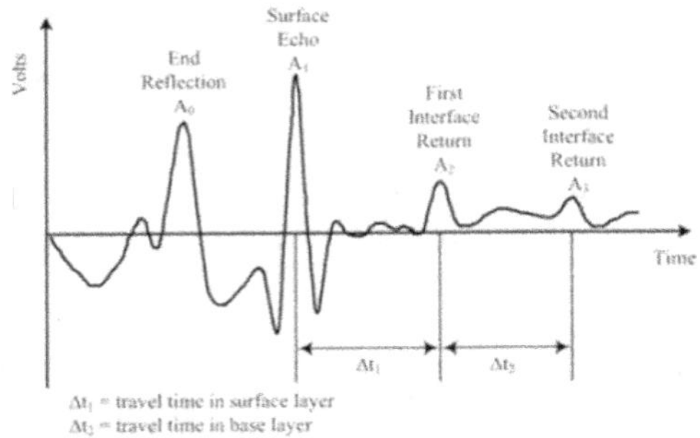

Figure 2: Example of a GPR A-scan signal [14].

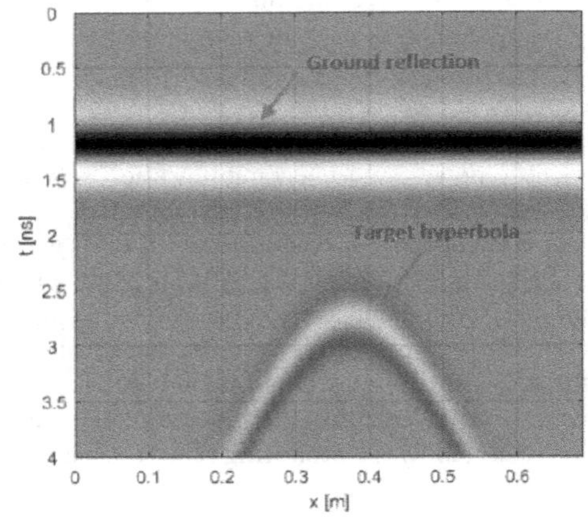

Figure 3: Example of a GPR B-scan. Each pixel column corresponds to an A-scan.

the received signal. For a target buried in the ground, as the GPR system scans, the time index of the scattering corresponding to the target varies, and achieves the lowest value when the GPR is right over the target which is reflected in B-scans as hyperbolas, illustrated in Fig. 3.

By evaluating a B-scan image, it is possible to localize an underground feature and infer subsurface structure conditions [6, 7]. However, for mapping purposes, the A-scans must be associated to a position in the survey area.

In wheel-encoder based GPR systems, each A-scan collection is triggered off of the wheel-encoder signal and each A-scan can be correlated to a linear position. However, the wheel-encoder does not take into consideration variations in height or deviations of the straight-line route. As a result, the subsurface features can be incorrectly positioned. In challenging terrains, wheel-encoder based GPR survey may become unfeasible. Furthermore, for a complete mapping of the area, multiple B-scans have to be collected and composed to form a C-scan, which is a tedious and slow process both for collection and post processing as the operator must carefully keep track of the relative position among B-scans.

Figure 4: Tango feature points (yellow dots) detected using its fish-eye and RGB cameras.

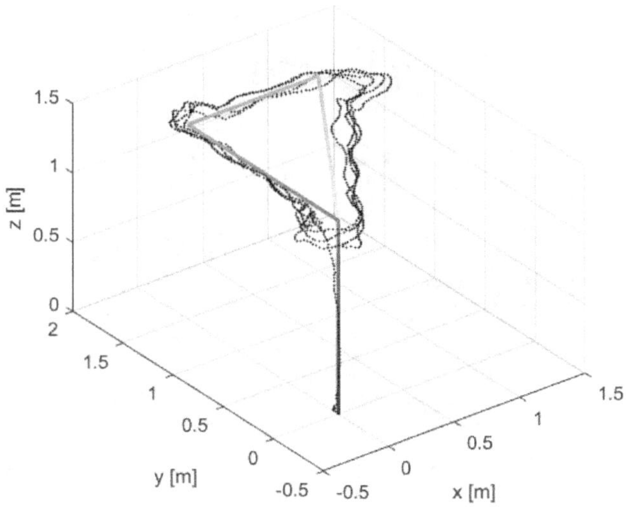

Figure 5: Position tracked by Tango (dots) and ground truth (gradient line). Tango accurately captures height and horizontal displacement in all directions.

3 TANGO

Recent advances in smartphone technology have endowed these devices with an array of sensors beyond the traditional RGB camera, such as a wide-angle fish-eye camera and time-of-flight camera that enabled the use of advanced visual-inertial odometry (VIO) algorithms for AR applications. Google Tango project provides a VIO framework for smartphones and features mapping capability to mitigate IMU drifts through loop closures. A Tango device provides long-term position accuracy and has been used to map and reconstruct large-scale areas [13]. Furthermore, the framework is suited for integration with AR technology of interest for smart city applications [11, 12].

3.1 Tango Framework

Tango is a framework for the development of AR applications that explores VIO for localization and mapping [2]. Localization and mapping in Tango are based on three core features: motion tracking, where IMU and camera data are fused to provide accurate position estimate; local area mapping, where key visual features of the environment are stored and later used for device relocalization; depth sensing, where a 3D understanding of the environment is achieved based on time-of-flight camera. For our GPR integration, the main features of interest are motion tracking, and local area mapping and device relocalization. The latter is described in more detail in the next section.

3.2 Local Area Mapping and Relocalization

Tango creates local area maps based on features in the images captured by its fish-eye camera and RGB camera. During mapping, Tango applications track distinguished visual features of the environment such as edges, corners and other visual cues [2]. Figure 4 shows an example of visual features tracked by the RTAB-Map Tango application [3]. Maps hold key features of the environment in a compact indexed form such that map querying is performed in real time and the device can be quickly relocalized. Relocalization, or loop closure, is achieved by matching features in the current view of the device camera to those stored in the map. Through loop closure, IMU drifting can be mitigated.

3.3 Tango Device Evaluation

To illustrate Tango positioning capability, tracking of a small scale indoor loop route was performed. The setup is as follows, the device is started at ground level, and height is also tracked by Tango. The device is brought at a height of 1.4m, moved 1.5m ahead, turned right and moved 1m in that direction. Finally, the device is brought back to the starting position. This route was looped through 4 times to evaluate Tango accuracy. Fig. 5 shows the assumed ground truth, depicted by the gradient colored line, and the position as tracked by Tango. Notice that all loops are close to each other and in good agreement with the ground truth, as well as the indicated height. This demonstrates that Tango has good accuracy, on sub-meter range, in all directions for an indoor, static environment case.

However, Tango accuracy is affected by several factors, for instance, change in lighting conditions, or an excessively dynamic environment, as well as potential drifts when area learning was not performed. To illustrate Tango performance in an outdoor, dynamic environment, an experiment tracking a long-distance walk (>50m) on the University of Vermont campus was performed. In this experiment, a measured ground truth was not available. Instead we evaluate how well would the local positions match the traveled path when transformed to a geographic coordinate, by overlay on satellite imagery. In the experiment, only the motion tracking feature was used, hence drift mitigation by loop closure was not present. The smartphone Tango application program was set to log position by every 1 inch displacement. The local position is given in relation to the device starting pose. By keeping track of the initial position and orientation in relation to a geographic coordinate system, it is possible to obtain global coordinates by adding the local map recorded. In this experiment, we used the Esri ArcGIS software suite to add the recorded local map to a global map. In this experiment, a footpath at the University of Vermont campus is followed, and involves the following challenges: long distance

Figure 6: Position tracked by Tango overlaid on satellite imagery corresponding to its global position. Notice that the recorded position stays within the footpath. Arrows indicate both a subtle change in the linear-route (left) and a curve (right) that are not detectable with current wheel-encoder based GPR.

Figure 7: A GPR cart with the GSSI SIR-30 control unit, a 400MHz antenna, the Tango device and the Arduino board with the BT shield and relays.

measurement, dynamic environment, and curves. The tracked path is shown in Fig. 6. The walk started on the left side of the indicated route. Notice that Tango accurately kept track of the distance covered, closely matching the footpath in spite of not using the loop closure feature, indicating meter-range accuracy or better. Furthermore, changes in relation to a perfect linear-route are indicated, in particular a subtle change at a crosswalk and a 90 degrees turn at the end of the walk. Such nonlinear route change can not be tracked by wheel-encoders in GPR systems. Nevertheless our GPR system is capable of pinpoint the position for each A-scan wave collected.

4 SYSTEM INTEGRATION AND OPERATION

The integrated system is composed of the Tango device, the Arduino microcontroller with both the BT shield and relay, and the GSSI SIR-30 radar system (see Fig. 7).

The GSSI GPR includes a 400MHz antenna and a SIR-30 control unit. The Tango device is mounted in front of the cart and communicates with the Arduino microcontroller via BT. The Arduino and relays are connected to the SIR-30 and control scan triggering.

Before GPR sensing, a visual mapping of the area is performed using the Google Tango Explorer application program. In the GPR sensing phase, the previously recorded map is loaded by our smartphone application. Once relocalization occurs, the Tango framework can be used to retrieve the device position and attitude. Position is described in terms of cartesian coordinates in relation to the survey area map reference frame, while attitude is given by a quaternion describing the rotation in relation to that reference frame.

A high-level diagram of the integrated system is presented in Fig. 8. The Tango device sends a trigger signal to the Arduino microcontroller should its spatial position changes by a predefined threshold. While the threshold of the Tango device spatial offset can

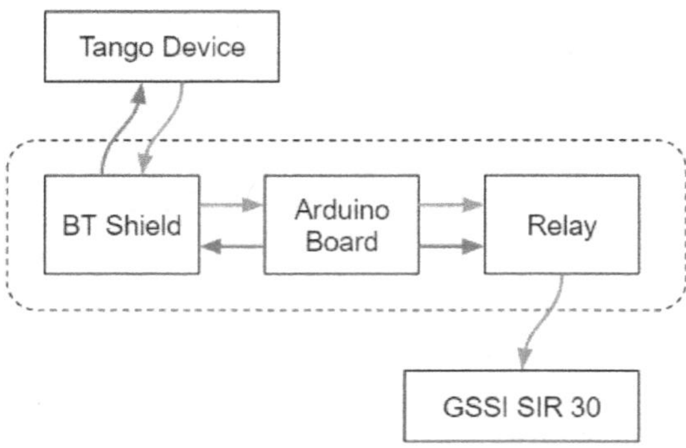

Figure 8: Diagram of the system integration.

be set to an arbitrary value, our operation experience suggests that for mid to long range scans, setting 1 inch threshold allows Tango framework to reach optimum ranging performance. Therefore in our GPR system integration, 1 inch threshold value is adopted.

Correspondingly the Arduino controls the relay to trigger GPR scan operation. As Arduion microcontroller receives the Tango message, it turns on the relay to trigger GPR to perform A-scans. Relay contact time is set to an interval of 25ms compromising between acquisition frequency and preventing relay excessive stress. With the relay adopted, its minimum callback time can be set to 5ms. An alternative option is to use transistors with nano second triggering time to replace the relay. After the relay is turned off, the Arduino microcontroller sends a callback signal to the smartphone informing that it is ready to receive another triggering signal. Radar triggering and location registration are performed simultaneously, such that each A-scan can be matched to a position in the reference map such tha the detected features can be correctly positioned.

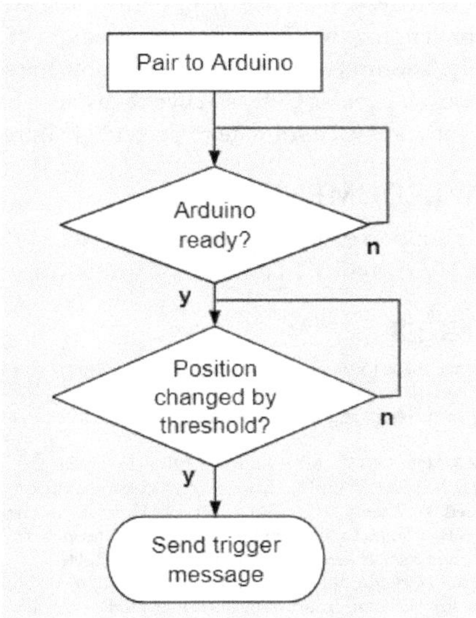

Figure 9: Application logic on the Tango device side.

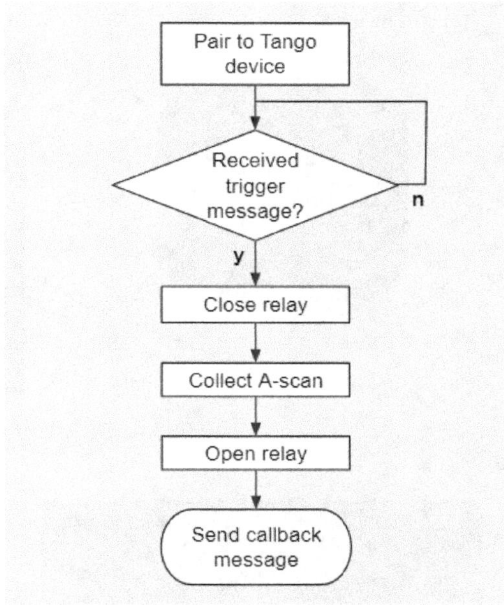

Figure 10: Application logic on the Arduino side.

4.1 Bluetooth Controller

To establish the BT communication, the TechTweaking Bluetooth adapter library for Unity was used. The library offers BT pairing capability, and sending and receiving streaming functions.

4.1.1 Tango device side. The diagram shown in Fig. 9 depicts the logic flow on the Tango application. First the Tango device and the Arduino BT shield must be paired to exchange messages. Once paired, an internal variable on the Tango device keeps track of whether the Arduino is ready to receive another trigger signal. If the Arduino is ready, a change in position check is performed. If the distance threshold is achieved, a trigger message is sent to the Arduino and the current device position is logged. These checks are performed at every application frame rendering. When the Arduino relay is opened, the Arduino will respond with a message informing that it is ready to receive another trigger message. Arduino readiness is determined on the Arduino side as a function of the relay status.

4.1.2 Arduino side. The diagram in Fig. 10 shows Arduino logic flow. As Tango device and the XBee BT shield are paired, a communication channel is established, and a stream reader can be used to receive messages sent by the Tango device. If a trigger message is received, the relay will be closed for 25ms, activating the A-scan collection by the GSSI SIR-30. Upon release, the Arduino uses the stream channel to send a callback message to the smartphone, signaling the release of the relay.

5 RESULTS

A circular long-range GPR scan was performed at the University of Tennessee, Chattanooga, using the new GPR system integrated with the Tango device. The 3D imaging of the subsurface is depicted in Fig. 11a in local coordinates. This local area map can be anchored to a world coordinate of choice, and have the detected features positioned in a geographic coordinate system. To perform this last step, the starting position and orientation of the survey in relation to a geographic coordinate system must be known, in particular its orientation in relation to the north and its starting latitude and longitude. In this survey, we used Esri ArcGIS to add our local recorded positions to a geographic coordinate system. The overlay of the tracked path and satellite imagery is shown in Fig. 12 as a yellow curve. The recorded position successfully matches the surveyed area.

As an example of positioning of detected targets, consider the detail of the 3D image highlighting a detected underground feature, possibly a pipe connected to an adjacent sink, in Fig. 11b. The position of this target is assumed to be at the top of the hyperbola, and both the local position and the corresponding latitude and longitude are shown. In Fig. 12 we indicate the corresponding global position of this feature as a red dot. It corresponds to the expected position, adjacent to one of the sinks present in the area, thus successfully correlating a feature detected in a nonlinear GPR scan to a geographic coordinate.

This survey demonstrates that our new GPR system is capable of performing nonlinear GPR scans with good position accuracy and that recorded positions can be readily associated to geographic coordinates. This opens venue for the automation of GPR survey since scans can be collected continuously as well as potential integration with AR technology applications.

6 CONCLUSIONS

In this paper a new GPR system integration with AR based positioning available on smartphones was introduced. The fundamentals of GPR sensing and the Google Tango AR technology were presented.

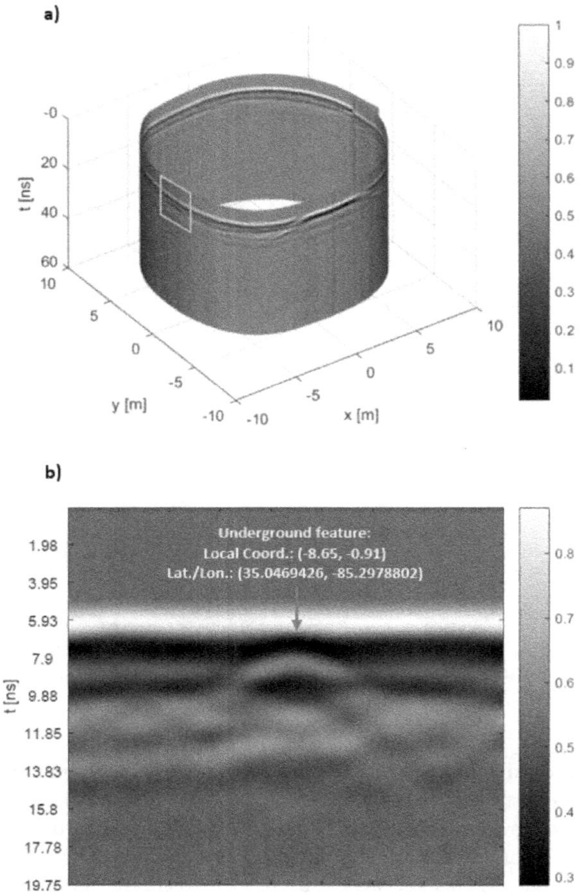

Figure 11: (a) 3D subsurface imaging of the surveyed area in local coordinates and (b) Detail of an underground detected feature showing both its local and global coordinates.

Figure 12: Top view of the survey area with circular path tracked by Tango. Highlighted red point indicates the position of the feature detailed above.

This new GPR system is capable of performing arbitrary route scanning, challenging the GPR industry paradigm of linear-route scanning only. The system capability was demonstrated by successfully performing a circular GPR scan over a distance of 50m and by assigning a geographic coordinate to detected features.

ACKNOWLEDGMENTS

This work is supported by the NSF Grants No. 1647095 and No. 1640687, the UVM SparkVT Fund, and VT EPSCoR.

REFERENCES

[1] 2017. Chicago maps its underground maze. (2017). https://www.cnet.com/news/chicago-maps-its-underground-maze-rahm-emanuel/

[2] 2018. https://developers.google.com/tango/. (2018). https://developers.google.com/tango/

[3] 2018. RTAB-Map. (2018). http://introlab.github.io/rtabmap/

[4] 2018. Unity Mobile AR. (2018). https://unity3d.com/solutions/mobile-ar

[5] Amr Ahmed, Yu Zhang, Dylan Burns, Dryver Huston, and Tian Xia. 2016. Design of UWB antenna for air-coupled impulse ground-penetrating radar. *IEEE Geoscience and Remote Sensing Letters* 13, 1 (2016), 92–96.

[6] L. Capineri, P. Grande, and J. A.G. Temple. 1998. Advanced image-processing technique for real-time interpretation of ground-penetrating radar images. *International Journal of Imaging Systems and Technology* 9, 1 (1998), 51–59. https://doi.org/10.1002/(SICI)1098-1098(1998)9:1<51::AID-IMA7>3.0.CO;2-Q

[7] Sevket Demirci, Enes Yigit, Ismail H. Eskidemir, and Caner Ozdemir. 2012. Ground penetrating radar imaging of water leaks from buried pipes based on back-projection method. *NDT and E International* 47 (2012), 35–42. https://doi.org/10.1016/j.ndteint.2011.12.008

[8] Dryver Huston, Tian Xia, Yu Zhang, Taian Fan, Dan Orfeo, and Jonathan Razinger. 2017. Urban underground infrastructure mapping and assessment. April (2017), 101680M. https://doi.org/10.1117/12.2263530

[9] Dryver Huston, Tian Xia, Yu Zhang, Taian Fan, Dan Orfeo, and Jonathan Razinger. 2017. Urban underground infrastructure mapping and assessment. In *Sensors and Smart Structures Technologies for Civil, Mechanical, and Aerospace Systems 2017*, Vol. 10168. International Society for Optics and Photonics, 101680M.

[10] Harry M. Jol. 2009. *Ground penetrating radar: theory and applications* (1 ed.). Elsevier Science, Amsterdam, Netherlands.

[11] Boris Pokric, Srdan Krco, and Maja Pokric. 2014. Augmented Reality Based Smart City Services Using Secure IoT Infrastructure. *2014 28th International Conference on Advanced Information Networking and Applications Workshops* (2014), 803–808. https://doi.org/10.1109/WAINA.2014.127

[12] Gerhard Schall, Erick Mendez, Ernst Kruijff, Eduardo Veas, Sebastian Junghanns, Bernhard Reitinger, and Dieter Schmalstieg. 2009. Handheld Augmented Reality for underground infrastructure visualization. *Personal and Ubiquitous Computing* 13, 4 (2009), 281–291. https://doi.org/10.1007/s00779-008-0204-5

[13] Thomas Schneider, Marcin Dymczyk, Marius Fehr, Kevin Egger, Simon Lynen, Igor Gilitschenski, and Roland Siegwart. 2017. maplab: An Open Framework for Research in Visual-inertial Mapping and Localization. (2017). https://doi.org/10.1109/LRA.2018.2800113 arXiv:1711.10250

[14] Anbu Selvam Venkatachalam. 2013. *RF Circuit Development for Ultra-wideband Ground Penetrating Radar Evaluating Highway Pavement and Bridge Deck Surface.* Master's thesis. University of Vermont, Burlington, VT.

[15] Tian Xia, Xianlei Xu, Anbu Vekatachalam, and Dryver Huston. 2012. Development of a High Speed UWB GPR for Rebar Detection. In *14th International Conference on Ground Penetrating Radar (GPR)*.

[16] Yu Zhang, Anbu Selvam Venkatachalam, Dryver Huston, and Tian Xia. 2014. Advanced signal processing method for ground penetrating radar feature detection and enhancement. In *Nondestructive Characterization for Composite Materials, Aerospace Engineering, Civil Infrastructure, and Homeland Security 2014*, Vol. 9063. International Society for Optics and Photonics, 906318.

[17] Yu Zhang, Anbu S Venkatachalam, and Tian Xia. 2015. Ground-penetrating radar railroad ballast inspection with an unsupervised algorithm to boost the region of interest detection efficiency. *Journal of Applied Remote Sensing* 9, 1 (2015), 095058.

MTJ Magnetization Switching Mechanisms for IoT Applications

Abdelrahman G. Qoutb and Eby G. Friedman
Department of Electrical and Computer Engineering, University of Rochester
Rochester, New York 14627
a.qoutb@rochester.edu, friedman@ece.rochester.edu

ABSTRACT

Different magnetization mechanisms, structures, and electrical properties of MTJ-based MRAM are described in the context of IoT applications. MTJ-based MRAM provides non-volatility (high retention time), low power, and high speed. This memory has a broad variety of applications. One important example is IoT. A comparative study of the magnetization mechanisms provides insight into which MTJ structures and magnetization mechanisms best support different IoT applications.

ACM Reference format:

A. G. Qoutb and E. G. Friedman. 2018. MTJ Magnetization Switching Mechanisms for IoT Applications. In *Proceedings of ACM Great Lakes Symposium on VLSI, Chicago, Illinois, USA, May 23-25, 2018 (GLSVLSI'18)*, 6 pages.
DOI: http://dx.doi.org/10.1145/3194554.3194624

1 INTRODUCTION

The internet of things (IoT) or the internet of everything has become a primary vehicle for connecting multiple nodes throughout a large network. Each of these nodes may include a small processing unit to collect information, communicate with other nodes, and respond to stimuli. Integrated memory will be needed in all of these IoT applications. Form factor, initialization time, power dissipation, read/write speed, and cost are primary design criteria. Magnetic tunnel junction (MTJ)-based magnetic random access memory (MRAM) is a potentially important solution for IoT applications. MTJ-based MRAM provides a nonvolatile memory able to operate at low latency, low leakage current, and high density. These capabilities support MRAM becoming the universal memory as compared to other nonvolatile memories such as e-Flash, phase change RAM, or resistive RAM [1].

This discussion is outlined as follows. In section 2, the physical behavior and parameters affecting MTJ device performance are described. Different forms of magnetization operation are also discussed in section 2. In section 3, the primary magnetization mechanisms for different structures are characterized. A comparative study of the different magnetization mechanisms described in section 3 is provided in section 4, emphasizing scaling, power dissipation, and circuit speed. A discussion of the effects of thermal variations on the different magnetization mechanisms for IoT applications is provided in section 5. Appropriate magnetization mechanisms applicable for different IoT applications are also described in sections 4 and 5. A summary is provided in the conclusions section.

2 MTJ STRUCTURES FOR MRAM

Tunneling magnetoresistance (TMR) was discovered in 1975 by Julliere [2] within a structure called a magnetic tunnel junction. It was not until the mid-1990s when fabrication of reliable MTJs became possible with the development of certain growth techniques and lithographic processes [3,4] did MTJ become a commercially interesting technology. The basic MTJ structure is composed of two ferromagnetic (FM) materials separated by a nonmagnetic insulator, where the conductivity of the structure is determined by the angle between the magnetization direction of the two ferromagnetic layers. Maximum conductivity is achieved when both magnetization directions are in parallel, and minimum conductivity when anti-parallel (AP). Slonczewski describes the conductance of the structure as a function of θ, the angle between the magnetization direction in the two FM materials, as [5]

$$G(\theta) = G_o(1 + P^2 cos\, \theta), \quad (1)$$

where P is the spin polarization of the ferromagnetic/barrier couple, and G_o is the conductance of the AP configuration. A primary parameter characterizing the quality of an MTJ is the *TMR*,

$$TMR = \frac{G_P - G_{AP}}{G_{AP}}, \quad (2)$$

where G_P and G_{AP} are, respectively, the conductivity of the parallel ($\theta = 0^o$) and anti-parallel ($\theta = 180^o$) configurations.

This research is supported in part by the National Science Foundation under Grant No. CCF-1329374, CCF-1526466, and CCF-1716091, IARPA under Grant No. W911NF-14-C-0089, AIM Photonics under Award No. 059447-007, the Intel Collaborative Research Institute for Computational Intelligence (ICRI-CI), Singapore Ministry of Education Tier 2 under Grant No. MOE2014-T2-2-105, and by grants from Cisco Systems, Qualcomm, and 0eC.

GLSVLSI'18, May 23-25, 2018, Chicago, IL, USA.

ACM ISBN 978-1-4503-5724-1/18/05...$15.00.
DOI: http://dx.doi.org/10.1145/3194554.3194624

The ability to control the MTJ conductivity by the difference in magnetization angle θ is the key concept in using an MTJ as a building block for magnetic memory (such as MRAM). The FM layer is pinned while controlling the direction of magnetization of the other FM free layer (the storage layer). The FM layers are fabricated as uniaxial anisotropy layers (with a preferable single magnetization axis). The magnetization dynamics in the free layer are derived from the Landau–Lifshitz–Gilbert (LLG) equation [6,7], as

$$\frac{\partial M}{\partial t} = -\gamma\, M \times H_{eff} + \alpha\, M \times \frac{\partial M}{\partial t} - \gamma\, \Sigma \tau_i\,, \quad (3)$$

where $\vec{M}$ is the free layer magnetization, t is the time variable, $\vec{H}_{eff}$ is the effective magnetic field applied to the free layer, γ is the gyromagnetic ratio, α is the Gilbert damping factor, and $\vec{\tau}_i$ is the applied torque due to other switching mechanisms such as spin transfer torque (STT) or spin orbital torque (SOT). The effective magnetic field applied to the free layer $\vec{H}_{eff}$ is [8]

$$H_{eff} = H_{UA} - H_{dem} + H_c + H_{APP} - H_{VCMA} + H_{th}\,, \quad (4)$$

where $\vec{H}_{UA}$ is the uniaxial anisotropy field, $\vec{H}_{dem}$ is the demagnetization field, $\vec{H}_c$ is the coupling field due to the other FM layer, $\vec{H}_{APP}$ is the applied magnetic field, $\vec{H}_{VCMA}$ is due to the voltage controlled magnetic anisotropy (VCMA), and $\vec{H}_{th}$ is the stochastic magnetic field due to thermal variations.

MTJ structures are based on uniaxial anisotropy which means the magnetization direction prefers stability over a single axis (easy axis), ensuring the free layer is either in the parallel state or antiparallel state with respect to the pinned reference layer. Switching is controlled by applying a perturbing field by injecting current, applying an external magnetic field, or some other means. Uniaxial magnetic anisotropy (MA) is achieved by different MTJ structures to obtain either an in-plane MTJ (IMTJ) or perpendicular MTJ (PMTJ). Shape magnetic anisotropy is the main source for in-plane magnetic anisotropy where an elliptical MTJ is preferred as the magnetization tends to be directed along the long axis. A circular shape is preferred in the case of a perpendicular MTJ (PMTJ). Perpendicular magnetic anisotropy (PMA) in a PMTJ is due to two reasons, magneto-crystalline anisotropy of the crystalline lattice of the FM layer or by an interfacial magnetic anisotropy due to coupling at the interface between the FM layer and a neighboring layer (such as Co/Pt and Co/Pd [9]).

The pinned reference FM layer is achieved through the exchange bias effect by attaching an FM layer to an antiferromagnetic material. A synthetic antiferromagnetic structure (SAF) is preferred to achieve the pinned FM layer by using two antiparallel FM layers separated by a nonmagnetic (NM) metallic layer, reducing any stray fields affecting the free layer, as shown in Figure 1.

Numerous developments in MTJ structures have been achieved to enhance the TMR and other performance metrics. Different configurations used to switch the MTJ magnetization are discussed in section 3. Switching by applying a magnetic field or injecting a current through the MTJ structure is described. Other forms of assistive switching, such as thermally assisted switching, are also discussed.

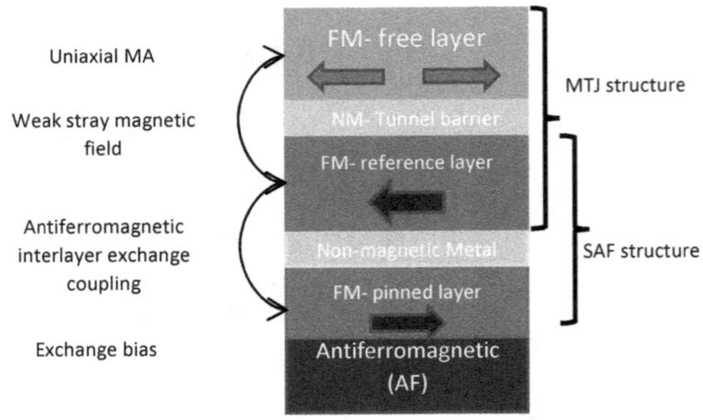

Figure 1. Stacking structure of IMTJ with SAF

3 MTJ-BASED MRAM MAGNETIZATION MECHANISMS

Several magnetization mechanisms of MTJ-based MRAM have been developed. Controlling the magnetization direction of the free layer can be achieved by applying an external magnetic field (induced by current passing through a nearby wire) [10], injecting current through an MTJ structure to cause thermal perturbations to affect device magnetization properties (thermally assisted) [11], injecting greater current to induce spin transfer torque to the magnetization layer [12], or by adding an additional perpendicular magnetization layer within an IMTJ to enhance STT performance to reduce the write current [13]. Recently developed magnetization mechanisms in MRAM are also discussed in this section.

3.1 Field-Induced Magnetic Switching MRAM (FIMS-MRAM)

The magnetic field required to switch an MTJ is governed by the relationship, $\mu_o H_{write} = 2K/M_s$, where K is a constant characterizing the magnetic anisotropy of the MTJ. The Stoner-Wohlfarth MRAM (ST-MRAM) was the first demonstrated MTJ-based MRAM, based on Stoner-Wohlfarth (SW) switching, as shown in Figure 2 [14]. Two orthogonal magnetic fields - one along the easy axis - are applied to an MTJ structure. The total field applied over the x and y axis, respectively, H_x and H_y, based on (5), sets the lower limit of the write field,

$$H_x^{23} + H_y^{23} = \left(\frac{2K_u}{M_s}\right)^{23}, \quad (5)$$

where K_u is the magnetic anisotropy constant and M_s is the saturated magnetization. The upper limit of the switching operation is bounded by the MTJ shape, where the easy axis field is lower than the anisotropy field, $H_K = 2K_u/M_s$.

An improved field written mechanism has been achieved by Savtchenko [15], where two orthogonal fields are oriented at an angle of 45° to the MTJ easy axis. The write operation is performed in a toggle form to maintain full magnetization operation, hence called "Toggle MRAM." The spin flip flop field H_{spin_flop} is

$$\mu_o M_s H_{spin\_flop} = 2\sqrt{K_{eff}\left(\frac{A}{t} + K_{eff}\right)}\,, \quad (6)$$

assuming the two FM layers are identical with a thickness t (a symmetric MTJ). K_{eff} is the effective anisotropy, and A is the interfacial coupling through the spacer (the tunnel barrier).

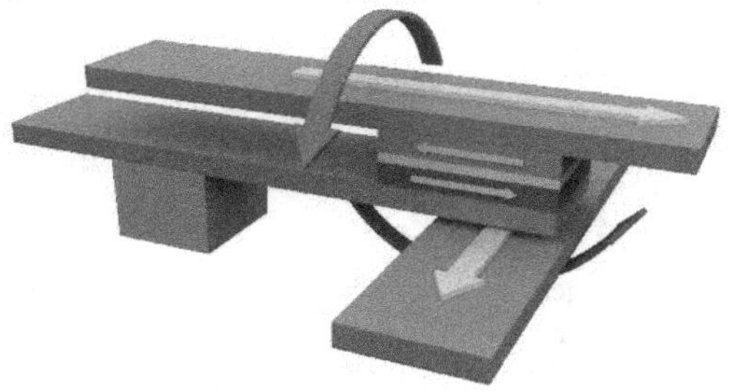

Figure 2. IMTJ writing using FIMS

3.2 Spin Transfer Torque MRAM (STT-MRAM)

In STT-MRAM, switching the magnetization of the free layer is achieved by passing a polarized electric current through an MTJ structure, where the polarized moving electrons exert a torque on the magnetic storage layer. When a normal unpolarized current passes through an FM layer, the current becomes polarized by the FM layer with a spin polarization factor [5]. Based on whether the current direction is into or out of the MTJ structure (the pinned layer), respectively, an antiparallel or parallel configuration is achieved, as shown in Figure 3.

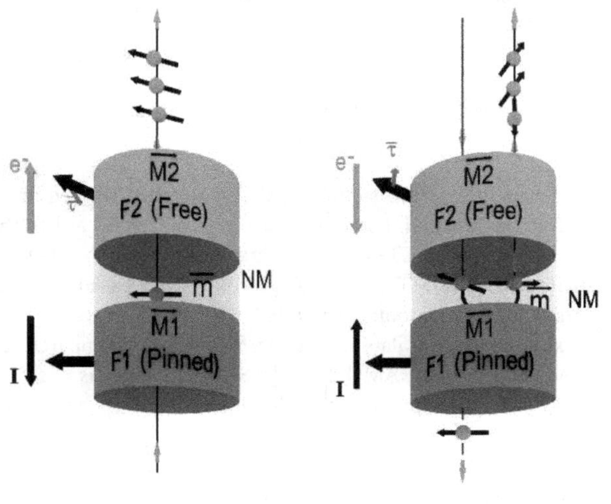

Figure 3. IMTJ writing using STT

The switching current should be greater than a critical magnitude, where the level depends upon the device dimensions and materials. For an IMTJ, the critical current density J_{co} to switch the FM layer is described by (8). The critical current is affected by thermal variations and depends upon the width of the current pulse. The critical current $J_c(t)$ is described by (7),

$$J_c(t) = J_{co}\,[1 - \frac{K_B T}{K_u V_{FL}} ln\left(\frac{t}{\tau_o}\right)] \,, \quad (7)$$

$$J_{co} = \frac{2e\alpha\mu_o M_s t_{FL}(H_{K\parallel}+(\frac{M_s}{2}))}{\hbar\eta} \,, \quad (8)$$

where e is the electron charge, μ_o is the permeability of free space, t_{FL} is the thickness of the FM, $H_{K\parallel}$ is the in-plane magnetic anisotropy field, $\hbar$ is the reduced plank constant, η is the spin transfer efficiency, t is the pulse width, K_B is the Boltzmann constant, T is the temperature, K_u is the uniaxial magnetic anisotropy constant, V_{FL} is the volume of the FM layer, and $\tau_o \sim 1$ is the inverse of the frequency factor or the attempt frequency of the thermal reaction.

For an IMTJ, the magnetization configuration does not efficiently support both thermal stability and writability [8]. Other configurations to reduce the critical current in an IMTJ are

- Dual MTJ: where the storage FM layer is sandwiched between two pinned FM layers, hence the current passing through the structure exerts a larger torque (2x), reducing the critical current to switch the layer [16].
- Perpendicular polarizer: where a perpendicular polarizer is stacked within an MTJ [17], enhancing the precessional switching. The storage layer acquires an out-of-plane component due to the added magnetic precessional movement.
- Reduced demagnetized field: where either volume or interfacial perpendicular magnetic anisotropy is added – by changing the barrier and FM materials – decreasing the demagnetizing field effect, thereby reducing the critical current [18].

MTJ structures that exhibit magnetic anisotropy normal to the surface are faster, dissipate less power, and are higher density than an IMTJ due to a lower critical current and the circular shape of the magnetic cell. A PMTJ-based MRAM is therefore more appropriate for IoT applications than an IMTJ. The critical current density J_{co} for a PMTJ is described by (9) where $H_{K\perp}$ is the perpendicular-to-plane magnetic anisotropy,

$$J_{co} = \frac{2e\alpha\mu_o M_s t_{FL}(H_{K\perp} - M_s)}{\hbar\eta} \,. \quad (9)$$

A PMTJ suffers from a higher Gilbert damping factor α than an IMTJ. In addition, it is difficult to fabricate the crystalline PMTJ structure to produce perpendicular magnetic anisotropy. The critical procedures of annealing and oxidation are required to grow a PMTJ. That leads to a preferential choice between IMTJ and PMTJ based on the manufacturing difficulty. A comparative study between IMTJ and PMTJ in terms of IoT applications is provided in section 4.

3.3 Thermally assisted MRAM (TA-MRAM)

In TA-MRAM, thermal variations are induced by passing current through an MTJ and/or using a high thermal conductivity material. The magnetic anisotropy constant is lower at higher temperatures which affects the magnetic field writing to the storage layer. Accordingly, a thermal assist mechanism is integrated within the FIMS-MRAM structure, achieving higher performance [19].

The same concept can be applied to an STT-MRAM, where the same current line is used for heating and switching the cell. The write operation is composed of multiple stages. The first stage heats the cell by passing a current for a specific duration. A lower level of current is applied for a different duration to switch the state. The cell is left to cool, storing the written state [20].

4 COMPARATIVE STUDY

A PMA-based STT-MRAM structure exhibits better performance, as listed in Table 1, due to a higher density and reduced power [21]. Research is on-going for determining the optimum device characteristics to provide acceptable performance as a replacement memory technology. Research on different structures, materials, and mechanisms suggests that a PMTJ-based MRAM is more applicable for those IoT applications that require higher operating speed.

Table 1. Advantages and disadvantages of different MTJ structures

Technique	Advantages	Disadvantages
IMA	• Controlled retention time	• Density, power consumption
Interfacial PMA	• Higher density • Optimizing I_c and α	• Low retention time
Crystalline PMA	• Higher density	• Larger α • Low retention time
SAF pinned layer	• Symmetric MTJ switching	• Increases height of MTJ stack
Dual MgO/Free layer interface	• Enhance interfacial PMA • Reduces α	• Increases MTJ resistance ($R|_{MTJ}$)
Dual tunnel barrier with dual PL	• Reduces I_c, α	• Increases $R|_{MTJ}$ • Increases height of MTJ stack
Tilted magnetic anisotropy(MA)	• Reduces I_c	• Reduces TMR ratio • Difficult to fabricate
Orthogonal pinned layer	• Reduces I_c without affecting TMR ratio	• Increases height of MTJ stack • Difficult to fabricate

A comparison of magnetization mechanisms for MTJ-based MRAM is summarized in Table 2 [22,1]. A FIMS-MRAM is based on an IMTJ, requiring large cells (which suffers from scaling and bit selectivity due to stray field disturbance from the writing magnetic field from neighboring cells). FIMS consumes large power (due to the large write current to induce the write magnetic field) but exhibits long retention times and thermal stability.

Toggle based MRAM solves the selectivity problem but can place the memory bit in an undefined state – requiring the read operation to be performed before the write operation. A toggle MRAM is predicted to not be highly scalable below 90 nm [1]. FIMS is a robust technology, exhibiting high reliability, endurance, and resistance to radiation, making it a good candidate for automotive, sensor-based weather forecasting, and IoT applications [8,25].

Table 2. Performance of different magnetization mechanisms

	Scalability	Endurance	Write time	Write current
FIMS	Poor	10^{16}	>10 ns	~ 10 mA
Toggle	Good	10^{15}	>30 ns	>30 mA
TAS	Good	10^{12}	>20 ns	~ 1 mA
STT	Very good	10^{16}	<5 ns	~100 µA
TAS+STT	Best	10^{12}	<8 ns	~100µA

The advantages and disadvantages of STT-MRAM are illustrated in Figure 4 [24], where the reliability is improved by optimizing the read/write currents, utilizing novel FM and barrier materials, or applying different magnetization mechanisms such as VCMA or SOT. Spin orbit torque MRAM (SOT-MRAM) shows promising potential due to the separate read and write paths, supporting symmetric switching.

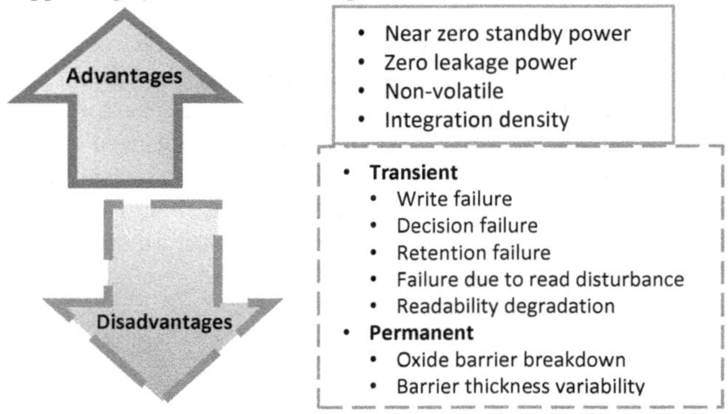

Figure 4. Advantages and reliability challenges of STT-MRAM

The thermally assisted switching (TAS) mechanism requires less writing power and is higher speed than FIMS, although difficult to scale. STT-based mechanisms exhibit better performance for both IMTJ and PMTJ [1,21-24]. TAS-based MRAM suffers from the same problems as FIMS. Merging TAS with STT-MRAM exhibits better scalability and performance as compared to FIMS, TAS, and STT-MRAM [22,1]. TAS+STT-MRAM is a good candidate for IoT applications which require high speed while dissipating low power.

5 MTJ-BASED MRAM FOR DIFFERENT TEMPERATURES

The operation of an MTJ-based MRAM as a nonvolatile memory is composed of three states. The write state with one magnetization mechanism, the retention state, describing how long the memory can maintain the written information, and the read state. The key objective in MTJ-based MRAM is to maintain low read/write/idle power consumption, high retention time, a wide operating temperature range, and low read and write delays. Each of these objectives are affected by the thermal stability factor Δ, as expressed in (10),

$$\Delta = \frac{\Delta E}{K_B T} = \frac{\mu_o M_s^2 t_{FL}^2 (A_R - 1) w}{K_B T}\Big|_{IMTJ} = \frac{[(K_v - (1/4)\mu_o (3N_z - 1) M_s^2) t_{FL} + K_s]\frac{\pi}{4} w^2}{K_B T}\Big|_{PMTJ}, \quad (10)$$

where $\Delta E = K_{eff} V_{FL}$ is the barrier height of the magnetic material. For an elliptically shaped FM IMTJ layer, A_R is the aspect ratio of the ellipse with width w. A circular FM PMTJ layer has a diameter w, K_v is the PMA constant, K_s is the surface energy, and N_z is the perpendicular-to-plane demagnetization coefficient.

The thermal stability factor decreases with scalability, as shown in (10), directly affecting the retention time and power consumption. The integration density, error rate, and thermal stability of MTJs are presented in [26], as shown in Figure 5, describing the critical integration level while maintaining an acceptable error rate.

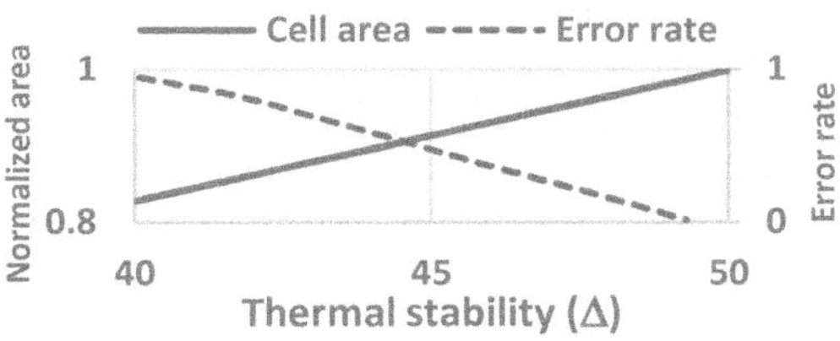

Figure 5. Impact of thermal stability on cell area and error rate

Thermal variations affect the electrical device characteristics (K_{eff}, J_{co}, TMR) in a stochastic manner. TMR was discovered in a Fe-GeO-Co structure at 4.2 K [2]. By the mid-1990s, a *TMR* ratio of 10 to 70% at room temperature was achieved [3], [4]. Later, after 2004, giant TMR exhibited a ratio of 250% - reaching up to 600% - at room temperature by using a monocrystalline magnesium oxide (MgO) barrier [27–29]. These developments achieve a PMTJ with perpendicular anisotropy with low switching current and high thermal stability [22,30] which is appropriate for ultra-low power sensor nodes used in IoT applications. Toggle MRAM exhibits a wide range of operating temperatures, from 0 to 70°C for commercial applications [19,28] and −40 to 125°C for automotive and military applications. These different operating temperatures are particularly relevant for IoT-based sensor nodes and processing units located in extreme environmental conditions.

6 MTJ-BASED MRAM FOR DIFFERENT IoT APPLICATIONS

Wireless sensor networks are a form of IoT, where the sensors are located at far distances and operate autonomously and for a long time. The nodes are expected to survive extreme environmental conditions while conserving energy. The sensor node behaves as an embedded system where an operating system is located within local memory. More than ten year retention time is a useful capability for those memories supporting IoT systems. Retention time, power consumption, and thermal stability are directly proportional to the current levels (which is proportional to the size of the MTJ), as described in Table 3 for STT-MRAM [31].

Table 3. Retention time versus write latency for STT-MRAM

Retention Time	10 ms	1 sec	10 years
Write Latency (ns)	3	6	11
I_c (μA)	61	82	114

MRAM with different magnetization mechanisms has been integrated into commercial applications, as shown in Figure 6 [30]. Everspin Technologies recently released a 1 Gb DDR4 Spin Torque MRAM. GlobalFoundries and eVaderis announced the development of an ultra-low power microcontroller based on an embedded magnetoresistive non-volatile memory.

MRAM provides a fast write-read and low power consumption with no static power which positions this technology for many IoT applications. For those IoT applications which require intermittent access with fast working memory, TAS with STT-MRAM is a good candidate, while greater development is needed to enhance read access and read failure rates.

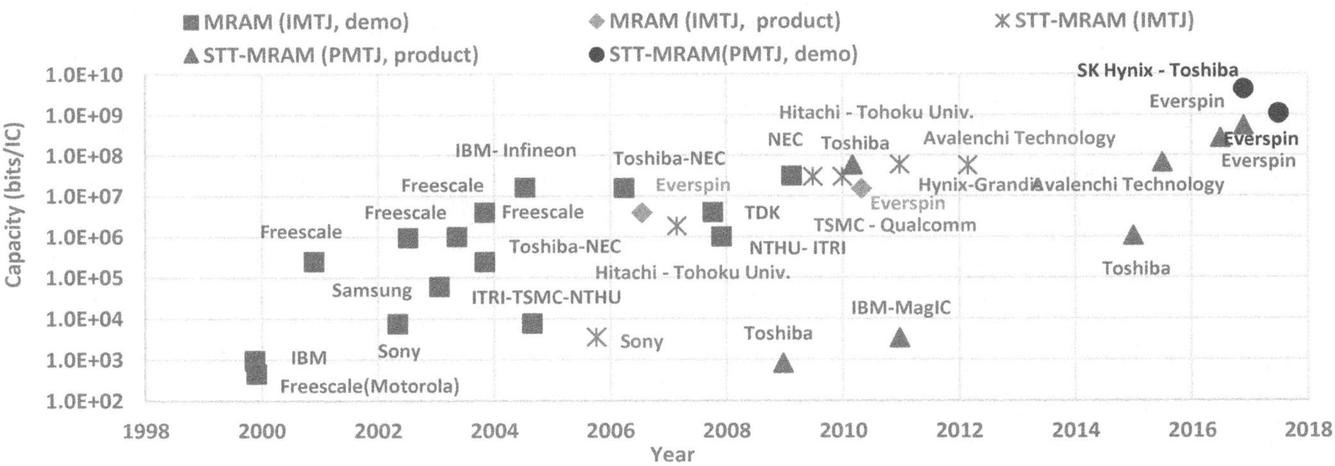

Figure 6. MRAM development trend

Toggle MRAM is a good candidate for those IoT applications requiring long periods of standby current as this technology is non-volatile with fast write times. TAS with STT-MRAM within a PMTJ structure is a better choice for ultra-low power, battery operated IoT nodes, as this application requires zero standby energy with a fast power-up time.

6 CONCLUSIONS

MTJ-based MRAM is an effective candidate technology for the specialized memory needed in IoT applications. PMTJ structures exhibit higher density and lower power than IMTJ due to the circular shape and perpendicular interfacial or magnetocrystalline anisotropy. STT-MRAM assisted with TAS provides enhanced speed and power as compared to FIMS, toggle, TAS, and STT-MRAM. The ability to maintain a ten year retention time operating at extremely low energy makes MRAM highly appropriate for IoT applications, particularly for sensor nodes located in harsh environmental conditions.

REFERENCES

[1] S. Senni, *et al.*, "Exploring MRAM Technologies for Energy Efficient Systems-On-Chip," *IEEE Journal on Emerging and Selected Topics in Circuits and Systems*, Volume 6, No. 3, pp. 279–292, September 2016.

[2] M. Julliere, "Tunneling Between Ferromagnetic Films," *Physics Letters A*, Volume 54, No. 3, pp. 225–226, September 1975.

[3] T. Miyazaki and N. Tezuka, "Giant Magnetic Tunneling Effect in Fe/Al2O3/Fe Junction," *Journal of Magnetism and Magnetic Materials*, Volume 139, No. 3, pp. L231–L234, January 1995.

[4] J. S. Moodera, L. R. Kinder, T. M. Wong, and R. Meservey, "Large Magnetoresistance at Room Temperature in Ferromagnetic Thin Film Tunnel Junctions," *Physical Review Letters*, Volume 74, No. 16, pp. 3273–3276, April 1995.

[5] J. C. Slonczewski, "Current-Driven Excitation of Magnetic Multilayers," *Journal of Magnetism and Magnetic Materials*, Volume 159, No. 1–2, pp. L1–L7, June 1996.

[6] T. L. Gilbert and H. Ekstein, "Basis of the Domain Structure Variational Principle," *The Bulletin of the American Physical Society*, Volume 1, p. 25, 1956.

[7] T. L. Gilbert, "Classics in Magnetics a Phenomenological Theory of Damping in Ferromagnetic Materials," *IEEE Transactions on Magnetics*, Volume 40, No. 6, pp. 3443–3449, November 2004.

[8] B. Dieny, R. B. Goldfarb, and K.-J. Lee, *Introduction to Magnetic Random-Access Memory*. Wiley-IEEE Press, 2016.

[9] K. Yakushiji, *et al.*, "Ultrathin Co/Pt and Co/Pd Superlattice Films for MgO-Based Perpendicular Magnetic Tunnel Junctions," *Applied Physics Letters*, Volume 97, No. 23, p. 232508, December 2010.

[10] R. Patel, *et al.*, "Reducing Switching Latency and Energy in STT-MRAM Caches With Field-Assisted Writing," *IEEE Transactions on Very Large Scale Integration (VLSI) Systems*, Volume 24, No. 1, pp. 129–138, January 2016.

[11] I. L. Prejbeanu, *et al.*, "Thermally Assisted MRAM," *Journal of Physics: Condensed Matter*, Volume 19, No. 16, p. 165218, April 2007.

[12] A. V Khvalkovskiy, *et al.*, "Basic Principles of STT-MRAM Cell Operation in Memory Arrays," *Journal of Physics D: Applied Physics*, Volume 46, No. 7, p. 74001, February 2013.

[13] H. Liu, *et al.*, "Ultrafast Switching in Magnetic Tunnel Junction Based Orthogonal Spin Transfer Devices," *Applied Physics Letters*, Volume 97, No. 24, p. 242510, December 2010.

[14] E. C. Stoner and E. P. Wohlfarth, "A Mechanism of Magnetic Hysteresis in Heterogeneous Alloys," *Philosophical Transactions of the Royal Society A: Mathematical, Physical and Engineering Sciences*, Volume 240, No. 826, pp. 599–642, May 1948.

[15] S. Leonid, *et al.*, "Method of Writing to Scalable Magnetoresistance Random Access Memory Element," U.S. Patent No. 6,545,906B1, October 2001.

[16] Z. Diao, *et al.*, "Spin Transfer Switching in Dual MgO Magnetic Tunnel Junctions," *Applied Physics Letters*, Volume 90, No. 13, p. 132508, March 2007.

[17] D. Houssameddine, *et al.*, "Spin-Torque Oscillator Using a Perpendicular Polarizer and a Planar Free Layer," *Nature Materials*, Volume 6, No. 6, pp. 447–453, June 2007.

[18] S. Mangin, *et al.*, "Current-Induced Magnetization Reversal in Nanopillars with Perpendicular Anisotropy," *Nature Materials*, Volume 5, No. 3, pp. 210–215, March 2006.

[19] J. Wang and P. P. Freitas, "Low-Current Blocking Temperature Writing of Double Barrier Magnetic Random Access Memory Cells," *Applied Physics Letters*, Volume 84, No. 6, pp. 945–947, February 2004.

[20] E. Gapihan, *et al.*, "FeMn Exchange Biased Storage Layer for Thermally Assisted MRAM," *IEEE Transactions on Magnetics*, Volume 46, No. 6, pp. 2486–2488, June 2010.

[21] X. Fong, *et al.*, "Spin-Transfer Torque Memories: Devices, Circuits, and Systems," *Proceedings of the IEEE*, Volume 104, No. 7, pp. 1449–1488, July 2016.

[22] H. Cai, *et al.*, "Exploring Hybrid STT-MTJ/CMOS Energy Solution in Near-/Sub-Threshold Regime for IoT Applications," *IEEE Transactions on Magnetics*, Volume 54, No. 2, pp. 1–9, February 2018.

[23] R. De Rose, *et al.*, "Impact of Voltage Scaling on STT-MRAMs through a Variability-Aware Simulation Framework," *Proceedings of the International Conference on Synthesis, Modeling, Analysis and Simulation Methods and Applications to Circuit Design*, pp. 4–7, June 2017.

[24] S. Salehi, D. Fan, and R. F. Demara, "Survey of STT-MRAM Cell Design Strategies: Taxonomy and Sense Amplifier Tradeoffs for Resiliency," *ACM Journal on Emerging Technologies in Computing Systems*, Volume 13, No. 3, pp. 1–16, April 2017.

[25] J. Heidecker, "MRAM Technology Status: NASA Electronic Parts and Packaging (NEPP) Program Office of Safety and Mission Assurance," Pasadena, California, February 2013.

[26] B. Del Bel, *et al.*, "Improving STT-MRAM Density through Multibit Error Correction," *Proceedings of the IEEE Design, Automation & Test in Europe Conference*, pp. 1–6, March 2014.

[27] S. S. P. Parkin, *et al.*, "Giant Tunnelling Magnetoresistance at Room Temperature with MgO (100) Tunnel Barriers," *Nature Materials*, Volume 3, No. 12, pp. 862–867, December 2004.

[28] S. Yuasa, *et al.*, "Giant Room-Temperature Magnetoresistance in Single-Crystal Fe/MgO/Fe Magnetic Tunnel Junctions," *Nature Materials*, Volume 3, No. 12, pp. 868–871, December 2004.

[29] S. Ikeda, *et al.*, "Tunnel Magnetoresistance of 604% at 300K by Suppression of Ta Diffusion in CoFeB/MgO/CoFeB Pseudo-Spin-Valves Annealed at High Temperature," *Applied Physics Letters*, Volume 93, No. 8, p. 82508, August 2008.

[30] S. Ikeda, *et al.*, "Recent Progress Of Perpendicular Anisotropy Magnetic Tunnel Junctions for Nonvolatile VLSI," *SPIN*, Volume 2, No. 3, p. 1240003, September 2012.

[31] A. Jog, *et al.*, "Cache Revive: Architecting Volatile STT-RAM Caches for Enhanced Performance in CMPs," *Proceedings of the IEEE/ACM Design Automation Conference*, pp. 243-252, June 2012.

Structured Weight Matrices-Based Hardware Accelerators in Deep Neural Networks: FPGAs and ASICs

Caiwen Ding*[1], Ao Ren*[1], Geng Yuan[1], Xiaolong Ma[1], Jiayu Li[1], Ning Liu[1], Bo Yuan[2], Yanzhi Wang[1]

[1]Syracuse University, [2]City University of New York, City College.
{cading,aren,geyuan,xma27,jli221,nliu03,ywang393}@syr.edu,byuan@ccny.cuny.edu

ABSTRACT

Both industry and academia have extensively investigated hardware accelerations. In this work, to address the increasing demands in computational capability and memory requirement, we propose structured weight matrices (SWM)-based compression techniques for both *field programmable gate array* (FPGA) and *application-specific integrated circuit* (ASIC) implementations. In algorithm part, SWM-based framework adopts block-circulant matrices to achieve a fine-grained tradeoff between accuracy and compression ratio. The SWM-based technique can reduce computational complexity from $O(n^2)$ to $O(n \log n)$ and storage complexity from $O(n^2)$ to $O(n)$ for each layer and both training and inference phases. For FPGA implementations on deep convolutional neural networks (DCNNs), we achieve at least 152X and 72X improvement in performance and energy efficiency, respectively using the SWM-based framework, compared with the baseline of IBM TrueNorth processor under same accuracy constraints using the data set of MNIST, SVHN, and CIFAR-10. For FPGA implementations on long short term memory (LSTM) networks, the proposed SWM-based LSTM can achieve up to 21X enhancement in performance and 33.5X gains in energy efficiency compared with the baseline accelerator. For ASIC implementations, the SWM-based ASIC design exhibits impressive advantages in terms of power, throughput, and energy efficiency. Experimental results indicate that this method is greatly suitable for applying DNNs onto both FPGAs and mobile/IoT devices.

CCS CONCEPTS

• **Computer systems organization → Embedded systems**;

KEYWORDS

Deep learning, FPGA, ASIC, Accelerator, Structured weight matrices

ACM Reference Format:
Caiwen Ding[1][1], Ao Ren[1][1], Geng Yuan[1], Xiaolong Ma[1], Jiayu Li[1], Ning Liu[1], Bo Yuan[2], Yanzhi Wang[1]. 2018. Structured Weight Matrices-Based Hardware Accelerators in Deep Neural Networks: FPGAs and ASICs. In *GLSVLSI '18: 2018 Great Lakes Symposium on VLSI, May 23–25, 2018, Chicago, IL, USA.* ACM, New York, NY, USA, 6 pages. https://doi.org/10.1145/3194554.3194625

*Caiwen Ding and Ao Ren contributed equally to this work.

GLSVLSI '18, May 23–25, 2018, Chicago, IL, USA
© 2018 Association for Computing Machinery.
ACM ISBN 978-1-4503-5724-1/18/05...$15.00
https://doi.org/10.1145/3194554.3194625

1 INTRODUCTION

Deep learning has increasingly drawn attentions in many research fields, such as speech recognition [13], computer vision [12, 18], self-driving cars [14, 32], and unmanned aircraft systems [25]. Large-scale deep neural networks (DNNs) typically consist of multiple layers, and at least millions of weight parameters for the entire model [18]. One major advantage of the larger-scale DNNs is that they extract more complex high-level features from the inputs (e.g., images/videos, speeches), and as a result, achieving a significant improvement in model accuracy [32].

On the other hand, as the size of DNNs grows continuously, there exist tremendous demands in increasing computational capability and memory requirement. Therefore, improving the performance and energy efficiency while maintaining the accuracy of DNNs becomes extremely critical. Two trends have characterized the research advance in order to achieve higher performance and energy efficiency. The first trend is *hardware acceleration*. FPGA-based accelerators have the advantage of friendly programmability and high-degree parallelism. Stochastic Computing (SC), in which all the inputs and weight values are represented as streams of random bits, has been investigated and successfully applied to hardware acceleration of DNNs [22–24, 29, 30, 37]. Data-path optimization technique [8] have also been studied to map a limited number of Processing elements (PEs) on FPGA and reuse the mapped PEs by iterating data through them. On the other hand, ASIC-based implementations have been explored to further accelerate DNNs. A substantial number of high-tech companies have declared their ASIC chip designs in DNNs such as Google [15] and IBM TrueNorth [6]. In the field of academia, Eyeriss [2], EIE [10], and DaDianNao [1] mainly focus on the convolutional layers, the fully-connected layers, and the memory design/organization at the architectural level, respectively.

The second trend is *model compression* motivated by energy efficiency limitation of large DNN models. Weight pruning [11] and lower rank approximation [33] have aimed to the reduce the number of operations involved in DNNs. They achieve a parameter reduction to some extent with inconsequential accuracy degradation. However, they have brought the new challenges into DNNs such as irregular network structure caused by sparsity regularization [36], and increased training complexity caused by the additional pruning process [11] or low rank approximation step [33].

In this work, to address the limitations of existing works in model size compression and acceleration and to achieve ultra-high energy efficiency and performance for FPGA and ASIC-based hardware implementations, we propose the structured weight matrices (SWM)-based compression technique on both FPGA and ASIC implementations. The SWM-based framework adopts the general block-circulant matrices to achieve a fine-grained tradeoff between accuracy and compression ratio. For FPGA implementations on DCNNs, we achieve at least 152X and 72X improvement in performance and energy efficiency, respectively using SWM-based framework, compared with the baseline of IBM TrueNorth processor under same accuracy constraints using the data set of MNIST, SVHN, and CIFAR-10. For FPGA implementations on LSTM networks, the proposed SWM-based method can achieve up to 21X enhancement in performance and 33.5X gains in energy efficiency compared with ESE, respectively. For ASIC implementations, the proposed SWM-based design exhibits impressive advantages in terms of power, throughput, and energy efficiency. It indicates that this method is greatly suitable for applying DNNs onto both FPGAs and mobile/IoT devices.

2 BACKGROUND OF DNNS

2.1 Deep Convolutional Neural Networks

DNN systems consist of many different architectures such as DCNNs, recurrent neural network (RNNs), and deep belief networks (DBNs). Although different network structures target at specific applications, they have the similarity in construction principle, i.e., multiple layers connected in series for feature extraction [16, 21]. DNNs are commonly made up of three-layer types: Fully-connected (FC) and convolutional layers (CONV), and pooling layers (POOL).

FC layer is the most storage-intensive layer in DNNs [10, 28] since its neurons are fully connected with neurons in previous layer. The computation of an FC layer consists of matrix-vector arithmetics followed by the activation function, described as: $\mathbf{y} = \psi(\mathbf{W}\mathbf{x} + \theta)$, where $\mathbf{W} \in \mathbb{R}^{m \times n}$ is the weight matrix of the synapses between this FC layer (with m neurons) and its previous layer (with n neurons); $\theta \in \mathbb{R}^m$ is the bias vector; and $\psi(\cdot)$ is the activation function. The calculation of $\mathbf{Wx}$ dominates computational complexity because the rest has lower complexity of $O(n)$.

CONV layer performs a multi-dimensional convolution to extract features from its inputs that will be fed into subsequent layers for extracting higher-level features. A CONV layer is associated with a set of learnable filters (or kernels) [19]. A filter-sized moving window is applied to the input feature maps, calculating the convolution of the filter and input feature maps in the moving window. In practical DNN models, the CONV layers are often associated with multiple input and multiple output feature maps. As a result, the CONV layer can be expressed in *tensor computations*: $\mathcal{Y}(x, y, p) = \sum_{i=1}^{r} \sum_{j=1}^{r} \sum_{c=1}^{C} \mathcal{F}(i, j, c, p)\mathcal{X}(x + i - 1, y + j - 1, c)$, where $\mathcal{X} \in \mathbb{R}^{W \times H \times C}$, $\mathcal{Y} \in \mathbb{R}^{(W-r+1)\times(H-r+1)\times P}$, $\mathcal{F} \in \mathbb{R}^{r \times r \times C \times P}$ represent the input, output, and weight "tensors" of the CONV layer, respectively. Here, W and H are the spatial dimensions of the input maps, C is the number of input maps, r is the size of the convolutional kernel, and P is the number of output maps.

POOL layer performs a subsampling operation on the extracted features to reduce the data dimensions and mitigate overfitting issues. Max pooling is the dominant type of pooling strategy in state-of-the-art DCNNs due to its higher overall accuracy and convergence speed [1, 2].

The majority of computations occur in CONV and FC layers, while the POOL layer has a lower computational complexity of $O(n)$. The storage requirement of DNNs is due to the weight matrices $\mathbf{W}$'s in the FC layers and the convolutional kernels $\mathbf{F}$'s in CONV layers. As a result, the FC and CONV layers become the major research focuses for energy-efficient implementation of DNNs.

2.2 Recurrent Neural Networks

RNNs have been investigated and have many applications in natural language processing, speech recognition, and machine translation [31]. As one popular type of RNNs, long short term memory (LSTM) has been broadly studied as shown in Fig. 1 [31]. An LSTM-based RNN accepts an input sequence $\mathbb{X} = (\mathbf{x}_1; \mathbf{x}_2; \mathbf{x}_3; \ldots; \mathbf{x}_T)$ (each of $\mathbf{x}_t$ is a vector corresponding to time t) with the output sequence from last step $\mathbb{Y}^{T-1} = (\mathbf{y}_0; \mathbf{y}_1; \mathbf{y}_2; \ldots; \mathbf{y}_{T-1})$ (each of $\mathbf{y}_t$ is a vector). It computes an output sequence $\mathbb{Y} = (\mathbf{y}_1; \mathbf{y}_2; \mathbf{y}_3; \ldots; \mathbf{y}_T)$ by using the following equations iteratively from $t = 1$ to T:

$$\mathbf{i}_t = \sigma(\mathbf{W}_{ix}\mathbf{x}_t + \mathbf{W}_{ir}\mathbf{y}_{t-1} + \mathbf{W}_{ic}\mathbf{c}_{t-1} + \mathbf{b}_i), \quad (1a)$$

$$\mathbf{f}_t = \sigma(\mathbf{W}_{fx}\mathbf{x}_t + \mathbf{W}_{fr}\mathbf{y}_{t-1} + \mathbf{W}_{fc}\mathbf{c}_{t-1} + \mathbf{b}_f), \quad (1b)$$

$$\mathbf{g}_t = \sigma(\mathbf{W}_{cx}\mathbf{x}_t + \mathbf{W}_{cr}\mathbf{y}_{t-1} + \mathbf{b}_c), \quad (1c)$$

$$\mathbf{c}_t = \mathbf{f}_t \odot \mathbf{c}_{t-1} + \mathbf{g}_t \odot \mathbf{i}_t, \quad (1d)$$

$$\mathbf{o}_t = \sigma(\mathbf{W}_{ox}\mathbf{x}_t + \mathbf{W}_{or}\mathbf{y}_{t-1} + \mathbf{W}_{oc}\mathbf{c}_t + \mathbf{b}_o), \quad (1e)$$

$$\mathbf{m}_t = \mathbf{o}_t \odot \mathbf{h}(\mathbf{c}_t), \quad (1f)$$

$$\mathbf{y}_t = \mathbf{W}_{ym}\mathbf{m}_t, \quad (1g)$$

where symbols $\mathbf{i}$, $\mathbf{f}$, $\mathbf{o}$, $\mathbf{c}$, $\mathbf{m}$, and $\mathbf{y}$ represent the input gate, forget gate, output gate, cell state, cell output, and projected output, respectively. The $\odot$ operation represents element-wise multiplication, and the + operation is matrix addition. The $\mathbf{W}$ terms represent weight matrices (for instance, $\mathbf{W}_{ix}$ is the weight matrix from the input vector $\mathbf{x}_t$ to the input gate), and the $\mathbf{b}$ terms are the bias vectors. Additionally, weight matrices $\mathbf{W}_{ic}$, $\mathbf{W}_{fc}$, and $\mathbf{W}_{oc}$ are diagonal matrices for peephole connections, which can be considered as vectors during matrix-vector multiplication. Therefore, $\mathbf{W}_{ic}\mathbf{c}_{t-1}$ can be calculated using $\odot$ operation. σ is the logistic activation function and h is a self-defined activation function. In this model we use hyperpolic tangent (tanh) activation function as h.

3 STRUCTURED WEIGHT MATRIX

This section discusses the inference and training algorithms of SWM-based DNNs (e.g., [5, 35]). The advantage is two-fold: *1)* it is possible to derive a fine-grained tradeoff between accuracy and compression/acceleration by changing the block size; and *2)* the method applies to both FC and CONV layers. The theoretical foundation is also derived from [38], which shows that the "effectiveness" of SWM-based DNNs is the same compared with DNNs without compression. Experimental results in [5, 35] have demonstrated a good ratio of model compression (i.e., from 41× to 256×) with small (less than 2%) overall accuracy degradation. In the following, we discuss the inference and training algorithms for FC layer, details of the CONV layer algorithms are provided in [5].

The key idea of SWM-based FC layers is to partition the original weight matrix $\mathbf{W} \in \mathbb{R}^{m \times n}$ into blocks of square sub-matrices, and each sub-matrix is a circulant matrix. The illustrations are shown in Fig. 2. Let k denote the *block size* (size of each sub-matrix) and assume there are $p \times q$ blocks after partitioning $\mathbf{W}$, where $p = m \div k$ and $q = n \div k$. Then $\mathbf{W} = [\mathbf{W}_{ij}]$, $i \in \{1 \ldots p\}$, $j \in \{1 \ldots q\}$. The input $\mathbf{x}$ is also partitioned as $\mathbf{x} = [\mathbf{x}_1^T, \mathbf{x}_2^T, \ldots, \mathbf{x}_q^T]^T$. Then, the *forward propagation* of FC layer in the inference is given by (with

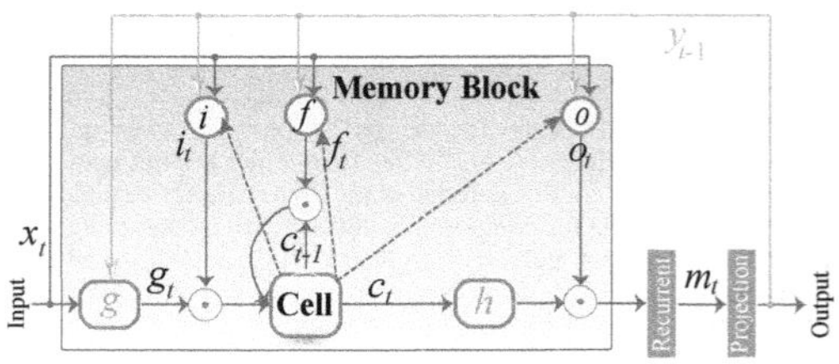

Figure 1: An example of LSTM based RNN architecture.

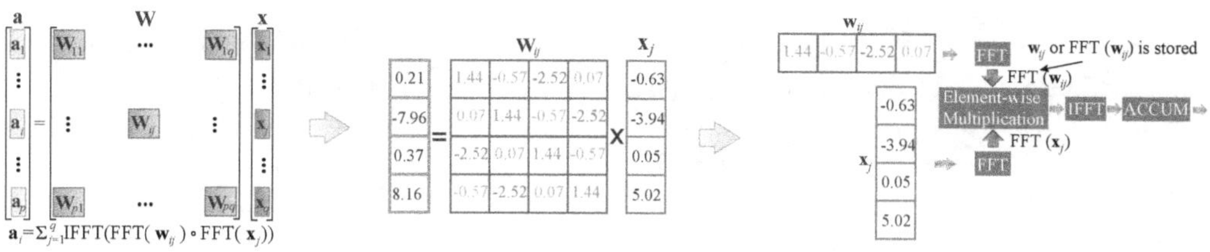

Figure 2: FFT-Based Calculation in SWM-based FC Layer.

bias and ReLU omitted for simplicity):

$$\mathbf{a} = \mathbf{W}\mathbf{x} = \begin{bmatrix} \sum_{j=1}^{q} \mathbf{W}_{1j}\mathbf{x}_j \\ \sum_{j=1}^{q} \mathbf{W}_{2j}\mathbf{x}_j \\ \dots \\ \sum_{j=1}^{q} \mathbf{W}_{pj}\mathbf{x}_j \end{bmatrix} = \begin{bmatrix} \mathbf{a}_1 \\ \mathbf{a}_2 \\ \dots \\ \mathbf{a}_p \end{bmatrix}, \quad (2)$$

where $\mathbf{a}_i \in \mathbb{R}^k$ is a column vector. Assume each circulant matrix $\mathbf{W}_{ij}$ is defined by a vector $\mathbf{w}_{ij}$, i.e., $\mathbf{w}_{ij}$ is the first row vector of $\mathbf{W}_{ij}$. According to the *circulant convolution theorem* [27], the calculation of $\mathbf{W}_{ij}\mathbf{x}_j$ can be performed as $\text{IFFT}(\text{FFT}(\mathbf{w}_{ij}) \circ \text{FFT}(\mathbf{x}_j))$, where $\circ$ denotes element-wise multiplications. The operation procedure is shown on the right of Fig. 2. For the inference phase, the computational complexity of this FC layer is $O(pqk \log k)$, which is equivalent to $O(n \log n)$ for small p, q values. Similarly, the storage complexity is $O(pqk)$ because only $\mathbf{w}_{ij}$ or $\text{FFT}(\mathbf{w}_{ij})$ for each submatrix needs to be stored, which is equivalent to $O(n)$ for small p, q values. Therefore, the simultaneous acceleration and model compression are achieved.

4 MODEL COMPRESSION AND ACCURACY

To reduce the computation complexity and storage complexity, many researchers have investigated to reduce the number of weight parameters or the number of bits for weight representation. However, the compression techniques will cause the model accuracy degradation. In this section, we will discuss the trade-off between model compression and model accuracy loss of the SWM-based technique.

4.1 Quantization and Weight Reduction

Data quantization on weights and neurons is a commonly used method for model compression. We attempt to use low-bit fixed-point data to represent the neurons and weights instead of using floating point data. We design a bit-wise simulator using C++ to verify the total number of bits for both integer and fractional part. Structure weight matrix, as a low-rank representation, uses one or several block circulant matrices to replace the original weight matrix as discussed in Section. 3. Shown in Fig. 2, by partitioning the original weight matrix $\mathbf{W} \in \mathbb{R}^{m \times n}$ into $p \times q$ blocks of square sub-matrices, the total number of weights are reduced from $m \times n$ to $\frac{m}{k} \times \frac{n}{k} \times k = (m \times n)/k$, where each block is a $k \times k$ matrix. We further investigate the SWM-based DNN models including DCNNs and LSTMs regarding the compression ratio (block size) and model accuracy.

4.2 Accuracy Evaluation

4.2.1 Accuracy Evaluation on DCNNs. The weight storage (model size) reduction, and the test accuracy on various image recognition datasets and DCNN models: MNIST (LeNet-5), CIFAR-10, SVHN, STL-10, and ImageNet (using AlexNet structure) [3, 4, 17, 18, 26]) are discussed in [5]. 16-bit data quantization is adopted and the

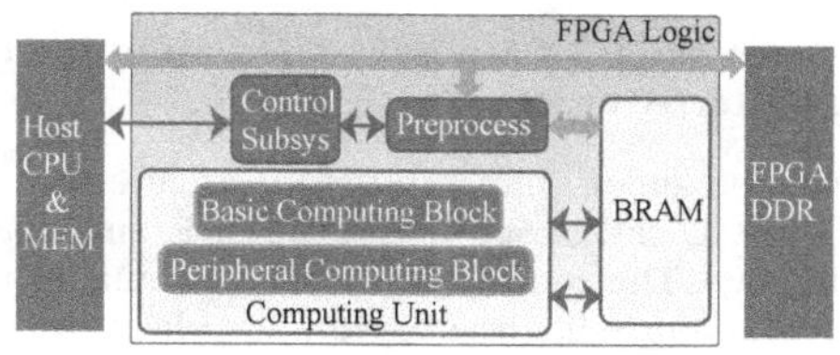

Figure 3: Overall system architecture of the proposed SWM-based FPGA compression framework.

baselines are the original DCNN models with unstructured weight matrices and 32-bit floating point representations. The SWM-based compression technique enables 400×-4000+× reduction in model size in the corresponding FC layers. On the other hand, the accuracy is close to original DCNN models and the accuracy degradation is negligible. Moreover, another advantage of the SWM-based technique is that the storage process of weight parameter after compression is regular, while reference works [11] bring in irregularity in storing the weight parameter. The introduced irregularity requires extra index per weight parameter and therefore affects the available parallelism degree.

4.2.2 Accuracy Evaluation on LSTM. We evaluate the structure matrices based compression technique using TIMIT benchmark, the most commonly used dataset for automatic speech recognition (ASR) application. The LSTM network is built by stacking multiple LSTM layers. The Google LSTM model [31] with unstructured weight matrix is selected as the baseline model. We preprocess the TIMIT audio data using FFT-based filterbank as discussed in [34]. The input speech data have the same number of features and same architecture as ESE [9]. Phone Error Rate (PER) is adopted to evaluate the model prediction accuracy.

The block-circulant matrix based LSTM model enables a comprehensive tuning of model compression ratio by varying the block size k. The PER is close to baseline LSTM when the block size is 2 using SWM-based compression technique. For the SWM-based LSTM models with a block size of 8 and 16, 7.6X and 14.6X model size reduction can be achieved compared with baseline LSTM, respectively. On the other hand, the computational complexity is reduced by 2.6X and 3.7X while the PERs are only 0.32% and 1.23% higher than the baseline.

5 SWM-BASED HARDWARE DESIGN

5.1 FPGA

5.1.1 Overall Architecture. The overall SWM-based architecture is shown in Fig. 3. The Host CPU is responsible for issuing workload or instructions to the FPGA logic block and monitoring the working stats. The FPGA logic part includes computing unit (containing the basic computing block and the peripheral computing block), the control subsystem, BRAM block, and the preprocess block for certain designs when the data loaded from external memory requires

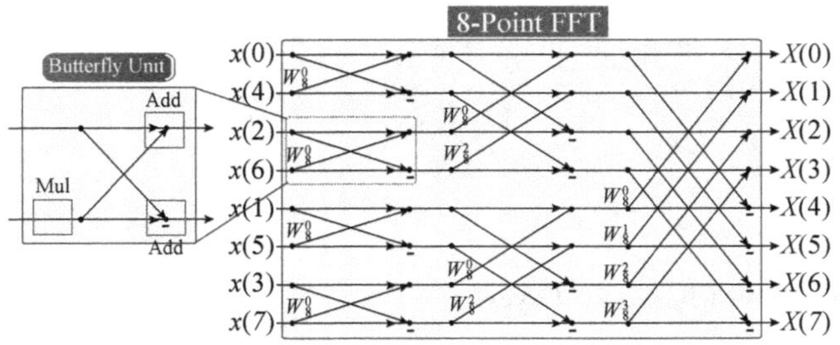

Figure 4: An example of 8-point basic computing block for FFT using butterfly units.

preprocess. The memory hierarchy of the architecture primarily consists of three blocks: Host MEM, FPGA DDR, and on-chip block memory (BRAM). The control subsystem coordinates the actual FFT/IFFT operations in the basic computing block and peripheral computing block. The control subsystem also determines the input size of FFT/IFFT operations. The twiddle factors in FFT/IFFT operations are stored in BRAM (i.e., the W_n^i values including both real and imaginary parts); the weights, e.g., the FFT results $\text{FFT}(\mathbf{w}_{ij})$ are also stored in BRAM.

5.1.2 Computing Unit Designs. In the computing unit, the peripheral computing block mainly focuses on component-wise multiplication, activation (ReLU, Tanh, and Sigmoid), pooling etc., which need lower computational cost and hardware footprint. The basic computing unit consists of an FFT operation with a parallelization degree of N and depth of $\log N$. Fig. 4 shows an example of 8-point FFT operation in the basic computing block using butterfly units. The IFFT operation can also be implemented using the N inputs basic computing unit in addition to a division operation (i.e., $\div N$) and two conjugations.

5.2 ASIC

In order to apply DNNs onto mobile/IoT devices, the DNN applications should be implemented in ASICs, due to the benefit of small hardware volume. The great reduction in both parameter size and computational time complexity makes our SWM-based method suitable for ASIC implementations. Figure 5 shows the architecture of our end-to-end ASIC implementation of the SWM-based DNNs. The architecture consists of four main blocks: input/output interface, storage system, processing system, and global controller.

The input/output interface is in charge of communicating with the external environment of the chip and the on-chip storage system. The input interface is composed of an input IO buffer and an input distributor. Similarly, the output interface is composed of an output IO buffer and an output distributor. In the view of data flow, the input IO buffer first receives and buffers data, including input images, weights, and biases from the external environment. For the reason that the number of IO pads are usually limited to a small number, whereas the bandwidth of the processing system is rather large for achieving high parallelism of computation. This mismatch in bandwidth requires an input distributor to temporally hold the external data until the size of the data reaches the bandwidth requirement of the storage system. Besides, there are three storage modules inside the storage system for respectively storing inputs/intermediate activations, weights, and biases, the global controller will decide where the buffered data should flow. With the similar idea, the output distributor will receive final activations from the storage system and be controlled to distribute a portion of activations into the output IO buffer, which will further send them back to the external system.

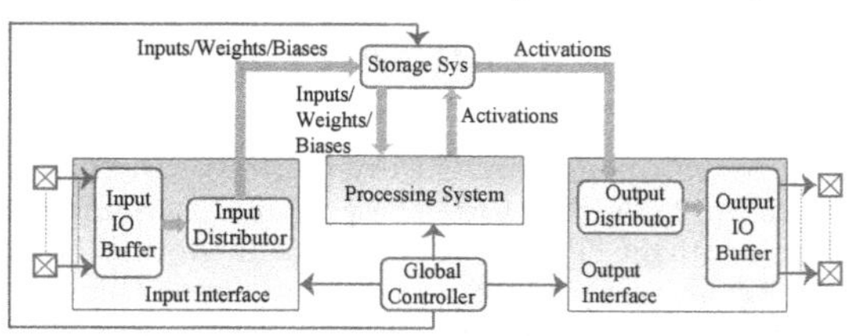

Figure 5: The architecture of the SWM-based chip.

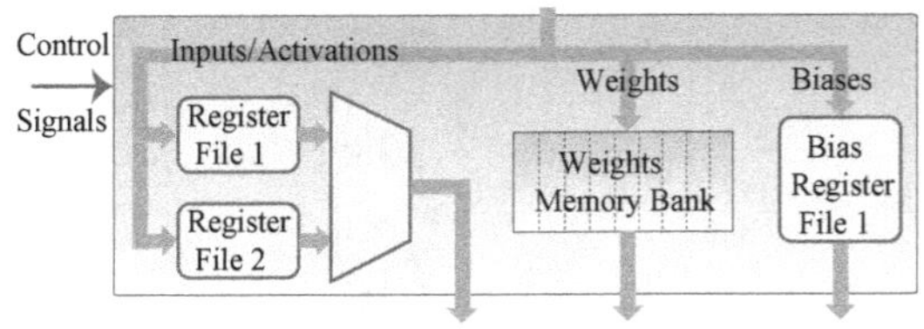

Figure 6: The architecture of the storage system.

As depicted in Figure 6, the storage system composes three subsystems, including a memory bank for storing weights, a register file for storing biases, and a ping-pong buffer (i.e., two alternating register files) for storing image inputs and intermediate activations.

The processing system achieves following equation for each layer: $\mathbf{y}_j = h(\Sigma\text{IFFT}(\text{FFT}(\mathbf{w}_{ij}) \circ \text{FFT}(\mathbf{x}_j)) + \mathbf{b}_j)$, where $\mathbf{w}_{ij}$ is the vector of weights at the ith row and jth column of the weight matrix, $\mathbf{x}_j$ and $\mathbf{b}_j$ are respectively the jth vector of inputs/activations and biases, and $h(\cdot)$ is an activation function. According to above equation, the processing system should contain the modules that are illustrated in Fig. 7. As the first step in the core computation, the image inputs are loaded from the storage system to the FFT module. Since the weights are repeatedly used without changes, what the weight memory bank stores are the weights in frequency domain. Thus the inputs of the multiply module are $\text{FFT}(\mathbf{x}_j)$ and $\text{FFT}(\mathbf{w}_{ij})$. Next, the IFFT module performs the inverse FFT operation over the element-wise production vector, converting the vector from frequency domain to time domain. Then the summation is performed by the Accumulator module that generates the dot-product of inputs and weights. Finally, the Biase module adds up the biases to the dot-products, and the Activation module produces a vector of activations.

Another crucial module in the architecture is the global controller, which takes the responsibility to generate control signals to guarantee the whole system to function correctly.

6 EVALUTATION

6.1 FPGA

We implement the proposed framework on small to medium scale DNNs using the benchmarks of MNIST, SVHN, and CIFAR-10 on

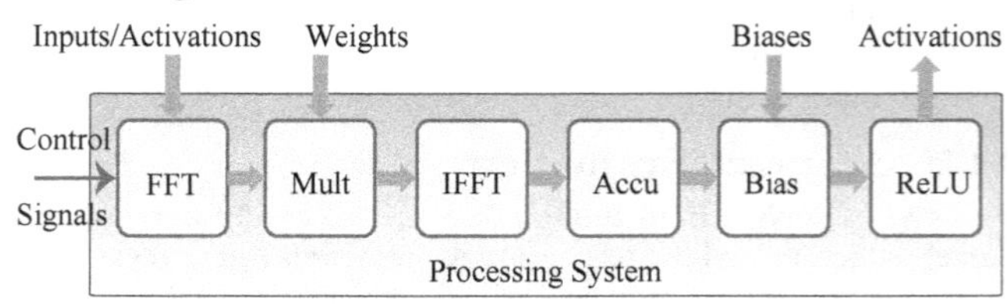

Figure 7: The architecture of the processing system.

Table 1: Comparison results on accuracy, performance, and energy efficiency of the proposed SWM-based FPGA designs and baselines.

DNN Name	Dataset	Platform	Data Quantization	Accuracy	Performance (kFPS)	Energy efficiency (kFPS/W)
Proposed MNIST 1	MNIST	CyClone V	12 bits	92.9%	8.6×10^4	1.57×10^5
Proposed MNIST 2	MNIST	CyClone V	12 bits	95.6%	2.9×10^4	5.2×10^4
Proposed MNIST 3	MNIST	CyClone V	12 bits	99.0%	363	659.5
Proposed SVHN	SVHN	CyClone V	12 bits	96.2%	384.9	699.7
Proposed CIFAR-10 1	CIFAR-10	CyClone V	12 bits	80.3%	1383	2514
Proposed CIFAR-10 2	CIFAR-10	CyClone V	12 bits	94.75%	13.95	25.4
TrueNorth ([6])	MNIST	TrueNorth	2 bits	99%+	1.0	9.26
TrueNorth ([6])	MNIST	TrueNorth	2 bits	95%	1.0	250
TrueNorth ([7])	SVHN	TrueNorth	2 bits	96.7%	2.53	9.85
TrueNorth ([7])	CIFAR-10	TrueNorth	2 bits	83.4%	1.25	6.11
LSTM Name	**Dataset**	**Platform**	**Data Quantization**	**PER Degradation**	**Performance**	**Energy efficiency**
Proposed LSTM1	TIMIT	ADM-7V3	16 bits	1.23%	330.275	14.359
Proposed LSTM1	TIMIT	KU060	16 bits	1.23%	371.095	-
Proposed LSTM2	TIMIT	ADM-7V3	16 bits	0.32%	179.687	8.168
Proposed LSTM2	TIMIT	KU060	16 bits	0.32%	195.312	-
ESE [9]	TIMIT	KU060	12 bits	0.30%	17.544	0.428

the low-power FPGA Intel (Altera) CyClone V 5CEA9. And we implement the proposed method LSTM on the platforms of Xilinx KU060 and Alpha Data's ADM-7V3. The ADM-7V3 board contains a Xilinx Virtex-7 (690t) FPGA and a 16GB DDR3 memory and the Xilinx KU060 platform contains a Xilinx XCKU060 FPGA and two 4GB DDR3 memory. We connect the ADM-7V3 to the host through PCI-e 3.0 X8 interface and the host machine used in the experiment is a sever configured with an Intel Core i7-4790 CPU. The proposed FPGA implementations of LSTMs are operating at 200MHz on both platforms.

We compare the accuracy, performance (kFPS), and energy efficiency (kFPS/W) of the proposed SWM-based FPGA implementation with the state-of-the-art IBM TrueNorth neurosynaptic processor ([6]) for DCNNs, and the state-of-the-art ESE accelerator on the platform of Xilinx KU060 [9] for LSTMs. We first demonstrate the results of three MNIST datasets targeting at different accuracies, one SVHN dataset, and two CIFAR-10 datasets targeting at different accuracies. The first two DNNs of MNIST datasets are multi-layer perceptron (MLP) models which can achieve the accuracy of 92.9% and 95.6%, respectively. The third DNN of MNIST dataset has a CNN structure similar to LeNet-5 [20], which achieves 99.0% accuracy. The first DNN of CIFAR-10 has a simple structure while the second DNN of CIFAR-10 adopts a wide ResNet model [12] which can achieve 94.75% accuracy. The baseline system (IBM TrueNorth) has two different DNNs of MNIST datasets at two accuracy levels. Experimental results show that under the similar accuracy constraint, the gains of the SWM-based framework in performance and energy efficiency are at least 152X and 72X, respectively. For the LSTM implementation, we propose two structures: (i) the proposed LSTM1 adopts a block size of 16 (FFT16), which the relative PER degradation of the model is 1.23%; (ii) the proposed LSTM2 uses a block size of 8 (FFT8), which the relative PER degradation of the model is 0.32%. On the platform of KU060, we achieve 21X and 11X performance speedup for the proposed LSTM1 and LSTM2 based compression techniques compared with ESE. On the platform of AMD-7v3, compared with ESE, we achieve 18.8X and 10.2X and performance enhancement and 33.5X and 19.1X energy efficiency gains using the proposed LSTM1 and LSTM2, respectively. Since the power consumption of SWM-based LSTM is only half of the ESE, the energy efficiency gain is higher than performance. Please note that the manufacturing process of XCKU060 FPGA is 20nm while the process of Virtex-7 is 28nm, which means the actual energy efficiency gain should be more than the report here.

Table 2: Hardware Performance of SWM-Based Neural Network Implemented in ASIC

Metrics	Performance
Clock Frequency (MHz)	200
Area (mm^2)	1.3
Power (W)	0.14
Throughput ($Images/s$)	1.14×10^6
Energy Efficiency ($Images/J$)	8.08×10^6

6.2 ASIC

In this work, we implement an ASIC design of the SWM-based neural network for the image recognition task, and it is tested with the MNIST dataset. The implemented neural network has the original structure of $512 \times 512 - 512 \times 512 - 512 \times 64 - 64 \times 10$, and this network is transferred into an SWM-based structure. The FFT module implemented in this work is a 64-point FFT, that is, it takes a vector of 64 real value numbers as inputs and generates their frequency domain representations. Consequently, the weight matrices has the structure of $8 \times 8 \times 64 - 8 \times 8 \times 64 - 1 \times 8 \times 64 - 64 \times 10$, where $(m \times n \times s)$ represents the weight matrix has m rows and n columns, and each element is a vector containing s weights (s is 64 in this case). Our weight matrix transformation is not applied to the output layer, so the weights in this layer still keep the original structure of 64×10.

Our ASIC design is implemented with SMIC 40nm technology (including memories) and synthesized with Synopsys Design Compiler 2016. Table 2 shows the hardware performance of our design. It can be observed from the table, the SWM-based neural network exhibits impressive advantages in terms of power ($0.14W$), throughput ($1.14 \times 10^6 Images/s$), and energy efficiency ($8.08 \times 10^6 Images/J$), suggesting that this method is greatly suitable for applying DNNs onto mobile/IoT devices.

7 CONCLUSION

In this work, we propose and evaluate the SWM-based compression technique on both FPGA and ASIC implementations. The SWM-based framework adopts the general block-circulant matrices to achieve a fine-grained tradeoff of accuracy and compression ratio and it works for both FC and CONV layers and contains a mathematically rigorous proof. For FPGA implementations, we achieve at least 152X and 72X improvement in performance and energy efficiency, respectively using SWM-based framework, compared with the baseline of IBM TrueNorth processor under same accuracy constraints using the data set of MNIST, SVHN, and CIFAR-10. For the LSTM network, the proposed SWM-based LSTM can achieve up to 21X enhancement in performance and 33.5X gains in energy efficiency compared with ESE, respectively. For ASIC implementations, the proposed SWM-based design exhibits impressive advantages in terms of power, throughput, and energy efficiency. Experimental results indicate that this method is greatly suitable for applying DNNs onto both FPGAs and mobile/IoT devices.

8 ACKNOWLEDGEMENT

This work is funded by the National Science Foundation Awards CNS-1650469, CCF-1733701, CNS-1704662, CCF-1657333, CNS-1739748, and CCF-1733834.

REFERENCES

- [1] Yunji Chen, Tao Luo, Shaoli Liu, Shijin Zhang, Liqiang He, Jia Wang, Ling Li, Tianshi Chen, Zhiwei Xu, Ninghui Sun, et al. 2014. Dadiannao: A machine-learning supercomputer. In *Proceedings of the 47th Annual IEEE/ACM International Symposium on Microarchitecture*. IEEE Computer Society, 609–622.
- [2] Yu-Hsin Chen, Tushar Krishna, Joel S Emer, and Vivienne Sze. 2017. Eyeriss: An energy-efficient reconfigurable accelerator for deep convolutional neural networks. *IEEE Journal of Solid-State Circuits* 52, 1 (2017), 127–138.
- [3] Adam Coates, Honglak Lee, and Andrew Y Ng. 2010. An analysis of single-layer networks in unsupervised feature learning. *Ann Arbor* 1001, 48109 (2010), 2.
- [4] Li Deng. 2012. The MNIST database of handwritten digit images for machine learning research [best of the web]. *IEEE Signal Processing Magazine* 29, 6 (2012), 141–142.
- [5] Caiwen Ding, Siyu Liao, Yanzhi Wang, Zhe Li, Ning Liu, Youwei Zhuo, Chao Wang, Xuehai Qian, Yu Bai, Geng Yuan, Xiaolong Ma, et al. 2017. CirCNN: accelerating and compressing deep neural networks using block-circulant weight matrices. In *Proceedings of the 50th Annual IEEE/ACM International Symposium on Microarchitecture*. ACM, 395–408.
- [6] Steve K Esser, Rathinakumar Appuswamy, Paul Merolla, John V Arthur, and Dharmendra S Modha. 2015. Backpropagation for energy-efficient neuromorphic computing. In *Advances in Neural Information Processing Systems*. 1117–1125.
- [7] Steven K Esser, Paul A Merolla, John V Arthur, Andrew S Cassidy, Rathinakumar Appuswamy, Alexander Andreopoulos, David J Berg, Jeffrey L McKinstry, Timothy Melano, Davis R Barch, et al. 2016. Convolutional networks for fast, energy-efficient neuromorphic computing. *Proceedings of the National Academy of Sciences (PNAS)* (2016), 201604850.
- [8] Vinayak Gokhale, Jonghoon Jin, Aysegul Dundar, Berin Martini, and Eugenio Culurciello. 2014. A 240 g-ops/s mobile coprocessor for deep neural networks. In *Proceedings of the IEEE Conference on Computer Vision and Pattern Recognition Workshops*. 682–687.
- [9] Song Han, Junlong Kang, Huizi Mao, Yiming Hu, Xin Li, Yubin Li, Dongliang Xie, Hong Luo, Song Yao, Yu Wang, et al. 2017. ESE: Efficient Speech Recognition Engine with Sparse LSTM on FPGA.. In *FPGA*. 75–84.
- [10] Song Han, Xingyu Liu, Huizi Mao, Jing Pu, Ardavan Pedram, Mark A Horowitz, and William J Dally. 2016. EIE: efficient inference engine on compressed deep neural network. In *Proceedings of the 43rd International Symposium on Computer Architecture*. IEEE Press, 243–254.
- [11] Song Han, Huizi Mao, and William J Dally. 2015. Deep compression: Compressing deep neural networks with pruning, trained quantization and huffman coding. *arXiv preprint arXiv:1510.00149* (2015).
- [12] Kaiming He, Xiangyu Zhang, Shaoqing Ren, and Jian Sun. 2016. Deep residual learning for image recognition. In *Proceedings of the IEEE Conference on Computer Vision and Pattern Recognition*. 770–778.
- [13] Geoffrey Hinton, Li Deng, Dong Yu, George E Dahl, Abdel-rahman Mohamed, Navdeep Jaitly, Andrew Senior, Vincent Vanhoucke, Patrick Nguyen, Tara N Sainath, et al. 2012. Deep neural networks for acoustic modeling in speech recognition: The shared views of four research groups. *IEEE Signal Processing Magazine* 29, 6 (2012), 82–97.
- [14] Brody Huval, Tao Wang, Sameep Tandon, Jeff Kiske, Will Song, Joel Pazhayampallil, Mykhaylo Andriluka, Pranav Rajpurkar, Toki Migimatsu, Royce Cheng-Yue, et al. 2015. An empirical evaluation of deep learning on highway driving. *arXiv preprint arXiv:1504.01716* (2015).
- [15] Norman P Jouppi, Cliff Young, Nishant Patil, David Patterson, Gaurav Agrawal, Raminder Bajwa, Sarah Bates, Suresh Bhatia, Nan Boden, Al Borchers, et al. 2017. In-datacenter performance analysis of a tensor processing unit. *arXiv preprint arXiv:1704.04760 (published in ACM ISCA 2017)* (2017).
- [16] Andrej Karpathy, George Toderici, Sanketh Shetty, Thomas Leung, Rahul Sukthankar, and Li Fei-Fei. 2014. Large-scale video classification with convolutional neural networks. In *Proceedings of the IEEE conference on Computer Vision and Pattern Recognition*. 1725–1732.
- [17] Alex Krizhevsky and Geoffrey Hinton. 2009. Learning multiple layers of features from tiny images. (2009).
- [18] Alex Krizhevsky, Ilya Sutskever, and Geoffrey E Hinton. 2012. Imagenet classification with deep convolutional neural networks. In *Advances in neural information processing systems*. 1097–1105.
- [19] Yann LeCun, Léon Bottou, Yoshua Bengio, and Patrick Haffner. 1998. Gradient-based learning applied to document recognition. *Proc. IEEE* 86, 11 (1998), 2278–2324.
- [20] Yann LeCun, LD Jackel, Leon Bottou, A Brunot, Corinna Cortes, JS Denker, Harris Drucker, I Guyon, UA Muller, Eduard Sackinger, et al. 1995. Comparison of learning algorithms for handwritten digit recognition. In *ICANN*, Vol. 60. Perth, Australia, 53–60.
- [21] Honglak Lee, Roger Grosse, Rajesh Ranganath, and Andrew Y Ng. 2009. Convolutional deep belief networks for scalable unsupervised learning of hierarchical representations. In *Proceedings of the 26th annual international conference on machine learning*. ACM, 609–616.
- [22] Ji Li, Ao Ren, Zhe Li, Caiwen Ding, Bo Yuan, Qinru Qiu, and Yanzhi Wang. 2017. Towards acceleration of deep convolutional neural networks using stochastic computing. In *The 22nd Asia and South Pacific Design Automation Conference (ASP-DAC). IEEE.*
- [23] Ji Li, Zihao Yuan, Zhe Li, Caiwen Ding, Ao Ren, Qinru Qiu, Jeffrey Draper, and Yanzhi Wang. 2017. Hardware-driven nonlinear activation for stochastic computing based deep convolutional neural networks. *arXiv preprint arXiv:1703.04135* (2017).
- [24] Ji Li, Zihao Yuan, Zhe Li, Ao Ren, Caiwen Ding, Jeffrey Draper, Shahin Nazarian, Qinru Qiu, Bo Yuan, and Yanzhi Wang. 2017. Normalization and dropout for stochastic computing-based deep convolutional neural networks. *Integration, the VLSI Journal* (2017).
- [25] Konstantinos Makantasis, Konstantinos Karantzalos, Anastasios Doulamis, and Nikolaos Doulamis. 2015. Deep supervised learning for hyperspectral data classification through convolutional neural networks. In *Geoscience and Remote Sensing Symposium (IGARSS), 2015 IEEE International*. IEEE, 4959–4962.
- [26] Yuval Netzer, Tao Wang, Adam Coates, Alessandro Bissacco, Bo Wu, and Andrew Y Ng. 2011. Reading digits in natural images with unsupervised feature learning. In *NIPS workshop on deep learning and unsupervised feature learning*, Vol. 2011. 5.
- [27] Victor Pan. 2012. *Structured matrices and polynomials: unified superfast algorithms*. Springer Science & Business Media.
- [28] Jiantao Qiu, Jie Wang, Song Yao, Kaiyuan Guo, Boxun Li, Erjin Zhou, Jincheng Yu, Tianqi Tang, Ningyi Xu, Sen Song, et al. 2016. Going deeper with embedded fpga platform for convolutional neural network. In *Proceedings of the 2016 ACM/SIGDA International Symposium on Field-Programmable Gate Arrays*. ACM, 26–35.
- [29] Ao Ren, Zhe Li, Caiwen Ding, Qinru Qiu, Yanzhi Wang, Ji Li, Xuehai Qian, and Bo Yuan. 2017. Sc-dcnn: Highly-scalable deep convolutional neural network using stochastic computing. In *Proceedings of the Twenty-Second International Conference on Architectural Support for Programming Languages and Operating Systems*. ACM, 405–418.
- [30] A. Ren, Z. Li, Y. Wang, Q. Qiu, and B. Yuan. 2016. Designing Reconfigurable Large-Scale Deep Learning Systems Using Stochastic Computing. *Proc. of ICRC* (2016).
- [31] Haşim Sak, Andrew Senior, and Françoise Beaufays. 2014. Long short-term memory recurrent neural network architectures for large scale acoustic modeling. In *Fifteenth annual conference of the international speech communication association*.
- [32] Jürgen Schmidhuber. 2015. Deep learning in neural networks: An overview. *Neural networks* 61 (2015), 85–117.
- [33] Cheng Tai, Tong Xiao, Yi Zhang, Xiaogang Wang, et al. 2015. Convolutional neural networks with low-rank regularization. *arXiv preprint arXiv:1511.06067* (2015).
- [34] Shuo Wang, Zhe Li, Caiwen Ding, Bo Yuan, Qinru Qiu, Yanzhi Wang, and Yun Liang. 2018. C-LSTM: Enabling Efficient LSTM using Structured Compression-Techniques on FPGAs. In *Proceedings of the 2018 ACM/SIGDA International Symposium on Field-Programmable Gate Arrays (FPGA)*. ACM.
- [35] Yanzhi Wang, Caiwen Ding, Geng Yuan, Siyu Liao, Zhe Li, Xiaolong Ma, Bo Yuan, Xuehai Qian, Jian Tang, Qinru Qiu, and Xue Lin. 2018. Towards ultra-high performance and energy efficiency of deep learning systems: an algorithm-hardware co-optimization framework. In *AAAI Conference on Artificial Intelligence, (AAAI-18)*. AAAI.
- [36] Jiecao Yu, Andrew Lukefahr, David Palframan, Ganesh Dasika, Reetuparna Das, and Scott Mahlke. 2017. Scalpel: Customizing DNN Pruning to the Underlying Hardware Parallelism. In *Proceedings of the 44th Annual International Symposium on Computer Architecture*. ACM, 548–560.
- [37] Zihao Yuan, Ji Li, Zhe Li, Caiwen Ding, Ao Ren, Bo Yuan, Qinru Qiu, Jeffrey Draper, and Yanzhi Wang. 2017. Softmax Regression Design for Stochastic Computing Based Deep Convolutional Neural Networks. In *Proceedings of the Great Lakes Symposium on VLSI*. ACM, 467–470.
- [38] Liang Zhao, Siyu Liao, Yanzhi Wang, Jian Tang, and Bo Yuan. [n. d.]. Theoretical properties for neural networks with weight matrices of low displacement rank. In *2017 International Conference on Machine Learning (ICML) (available on ArXiv)*. ACM/IEEE.

Challenges and Rewards of Implementing and Benchmarking Post-Quantum Cryptography in Hardware

Kris Gaj
George Mason University
Fairfax, Virginia
kgaj@gmu.edu

ABSTRACT

Practical quantum computers have been recently selected as one of 10 breakthrough technologies of 2017 by the MIT Technology Review. Although various fields of human activity, such as chemistry, medicine, and materials science, are likely to be dramatically affected by practical quantum computers, the most likely immediate impact will take place in the area of cryptography and cyber security. As a result of this potential threat, a new field of science has emerged, called Post-Quantum Cryptography (PQC). PQC is devoted to the design and analysis of cryptographic algorithms that are resistant against any known attacks using quantum computers, but by themselves can be implemented using classical computing platforms, based on traditional modern semiconductor technologies. In this paper, we provide an overview and motivation for the PQC, NIST Standardization Effort, cryptographic competitions, and hardware benchmarking of candidates in cryptographic contests. Five major families of PQC schemes, code-, hash-, isogeny-, lattice-, and multivariate-based, are shortly introduced. The challenges of fair and comprehensive hardware benchmarking of PQC submissions are highlighted, together with the possible ways of overcoming these difficulties, such as the use of a common API, development packages, specialized libraries, and high-level synthesis.

CCS CONCEPTS

• **Security and privacy → Public key (asymmetric) techniques; Security in hardware;**

KEYWORDS

post-quantum cryptography; hardware benchmarking; cryptographic standards; security primitives

ACM Reference Format:

Kris Gaj. 2018. Challenges and Rewards of Implementing and Benchmarking Post-Quantum Cryptography in Hardware. In *GLSVLSI '18: 2018 Great Lakes Symposium on VLSI, May 23–25, 2018, Chicago, IL, USA.* ACM, New York, NY, USA, 6 pages. https://doi.org/10.1145/3194554.3194615

GLSVLSI '18, May 23–25, 2018, Chicago, IL, USA

ACM ISBN 978-1-4503-5724-1/18/05...$15.00
https://doi.org/10.1145/3194554.3194615

1 INTRODUCTION

Practical quantum computers have been recently selected as one of ten breakthrough technologies of 2017 [2]. Major investment by companies, such as Google, IBM, Intel, Microsoft, and NTT led to the first general-purpose quantum processors, with up 72 physical qubits [22], and specialized processors reaching 2048 qubits [5]. In parallel, significant progress has been made in the area of languages for describing quantum computing algorithms (such as Q# by Microsoft [8] and OpenQASM from IBM), software development kits (such as QISKit from IBM), open-source quantum computing simulators (such as QuTiP and OpenFermion), and cloud-based quantum computing services, such as IBM Q Experience [4], which enable programmers to remotely run educational and scientific experiments on a publicly-available quantum processor. An era of so-called quantum supremacy, when quantum computers can solve problems beyond the reach of practical computers, seems to be on the horizon, with remaining difficulties mostly in the realm of engineering and technology [43].

Although various fields of human activity, such as chemistry, medicine, and materials science, are likely to be dramatically affected by practical quantum computers, the most likely immediate impact will take place in the area of cryptography and cyber security. In particular, practical quantum computers would easily break all current American federal and banking standards in the area of public-key cryptography, including algorithms protecting the majority of the Internet traffic, such as RSA, Elliptic Curve Cryptography (ECC), Digital Signature Algorithm (DSA), and Diffie-Hellman. All traditional methods of dealing with growing computational capabilities of potential attackers, such as increasing key sizes, would be futile [7].

As a result of this potential threat, a new field of science has emerged, called Post-Quantum Cryptography (PQC) [7]. PQC is devoted to the design and analysis of cryptographic algorithms that are resistant against any known attacks using quantum computers, but by themselves can be implemented using classical computing platforms, such as smartphones, tablets, PCs, servers, specialized hardware, etc. Of particular interest to the attendees of this conference are emerging implementations of post-quantum cryptography in FPGAs and standard-cell ASICs, using traditional modern semiconductor technologies.

The scientists pursuing PQC have established a series of conferences, called PQCrypto, held regularly since 2006. In Feb. 2016, American National Institute of Standards and Technology (NIST) published a draft report and announced its plans of starting the standardization effort in the area of PQC. This effort was predicted to last several years and result in an entire portfolio of algorithms capable of replacing current public-key cryptography schemes. The initial announcement was followed by the official "Call for Proposals and Request for Nominations for Public-Key Post-Quantum Cryptographic Algorithms," issued in Dec. 2016 [36]. Nov. 30, 2017 was set as the candidate submission deadline. After the initial review by the NIST staff, it appeared that 69 distinct algorithms (each with multiple parameter sets corresponding to up to 5 different security strengths) were recognized as valid submissions, and their corresponding specifications and software implementations posted on the NIST website [37]. None of the 69 submissions for the future NIST PQC standard included a corresponding hardware implementation.

After publishing the submission packages on the NIST website on Dec. 22, 2017, the evaluation process started almost immediately, with first analyses and comments focused on security and efficiency in software posted on the same day. The evaluation is likely to last between three and five years and be similar to that conducted in the case of earlier NIST cryptographic standards, such as Advanced Encryption Standard (AES) and Secure Hash Algorithm 3 (SHA-3). In each of these cases, the number of candidates was gradually narrowed down, in consecutive rounds, to those with adequate security (typically less than 1/3rd of the initial pool), and the final selection was based on software and hardware efficiency. In both of the aforementioned competitions, the candidate most efficient in hardware (and in ASICs in particular) was announced the winner.

The challenges of implementing and benchmarking PQC candidates in hardware include the large number of algorithms, their complex mathematical descriptions, non-standard fundamental operations, large public and private key sizes, multiple parameter sets, a multitude of possible optimization targets, etc. Only a few Register-Transfer Level (RTL) implementations of the earlier versions of the PQC candidates, most of them with much different parameter sets, have been reported at the past PQCrypto and CHES conferences, and in related journals. In this paper, we discuss lessons learned from the previous cryptographic competitions, as well as from the pilot studies conducted before the start of the NIST standardization process, aimed at overcoming these difficulties. We also highlight the potential benefits of moving toward new cryptographic algorithms, resistant against quantum computers, and incorporating them in the existing secure protocols and communication systems.

2 CRYPTOGRAPHIC CONTESTS

Starting in late 1990s, cryptographic contests have emerged as a commonly accepted way of developing new cryptographic standards. This trend started from the NIST Advanced Encryption Standard (AES) competition for a secret-key block cipher, conducted in the period 1997-2000 [15]. It was followed by the NESSIE (2000-2002) and eSTREAM (2004-2008) [1] contests in Europe, and CRYPTREC (2000-2002) in Japan. Then, between 2007 and 2012, NIST conducted the second major competition, for a new federal cryptographic hash function standard, SHA-3 [30]. The most recent standardization effort, called CAESAR, Competition for Authenticated Encryption: Security, Applicability, and Robustness, organized by an independent group of world-renowned cryptographers, started in 2013 and at the time of this paper's writing, in March 2018, is still in progress [9]. CAESAR focused on a class of algorithms called authenticated ciphers and sought an improvement over an existing NIST standard AES-GCM.

The benefits of the contests include transparency and involvement of the entire cryptographic community, which helps to avoid any back-door theories and significantly speeds up the development and acceptance of a new standard. The challenges of contests include a large number of candidates, limited time for evaluation, need to select a single winner (or at least small portfolio) based on limited information, the fact that the results are final and the winner(s) will remain in use for tens of years, in applications and scenarios hard to predict at the time of the standard development.

The primary evaluation criteria are security, software efficiency (in general-purpose and embedded processors), hardware efficiency (in FPGAs and ASICs), flexibility, simplicity, and the lack of any licensing encumbrances. Although, by general consensus, the security is by far the most important selection criterion, it rarely by itself can determine a winner. This is because at the later stages of the competitions, all remaining candidates are found to have adequate security, and developing any new attacks is too time consuming. At this stage, traditionally, hardware and software efficiency have been used to break a tie. In particular, during the AES contest, the future winner, Rijndael, was found to be the fastest in ASICs and second fastest in FPGAs (only slightly below a much slower in software Serpent) [15]. In the SHA-3 contest, the future winner, Keccak, distinguished itself, already in Round 2 (with 14 candidates remaining) as the best in terms of throughput and close to the best in terms of throughput/area ratio, when implemented in FPGAs and ASICs [17, 18, 28, 30]. Finally, in the most recent CAESAR competition, among the three finalists in the Use Case 2, concerning high-performance applications, two algorithms, AEGIS and MORUS, were found to be the fastest (14-16 times faster than the current standard AES-GCM) when implemented in FPGAs [12, 26].

3 PQC STANDARDIZATION EFFORT

The NIST PQC Standardization process has been defined to be similar to the previous NIST cryptographic competitions, such as AES and SHA-3, but with a few important differences [36]. First, although similar to the previous competitions, the evaluation is going to be performed in rounds (each lasting between 12 and 18 months), with the goal of narrowing a pool of candidates after each of them, the majority of candidates that do not qualify to a narrowed pool may be still considered for the standardization at a later date, unless they are explicitly withdrawn by their submitters or declared unsuitable for the standardization by NIST. Secondly, there may not be a single winner, understood as a candidate "better" than the remaining ones, but rather a group of algorithms may emerge at the end of the process as potential candidates for the standardization by NIST in the future years.

On the technical side, the primary difference amounts to taking into account quantum attacks, possible only on computing platforms that do not exist at the time of the standard development. The other major differences include a variety of mathematical foundations (some of them not fully understood), making the direct comparison in terms of security strength much more challenging, as well as much more complex requirements for public-key

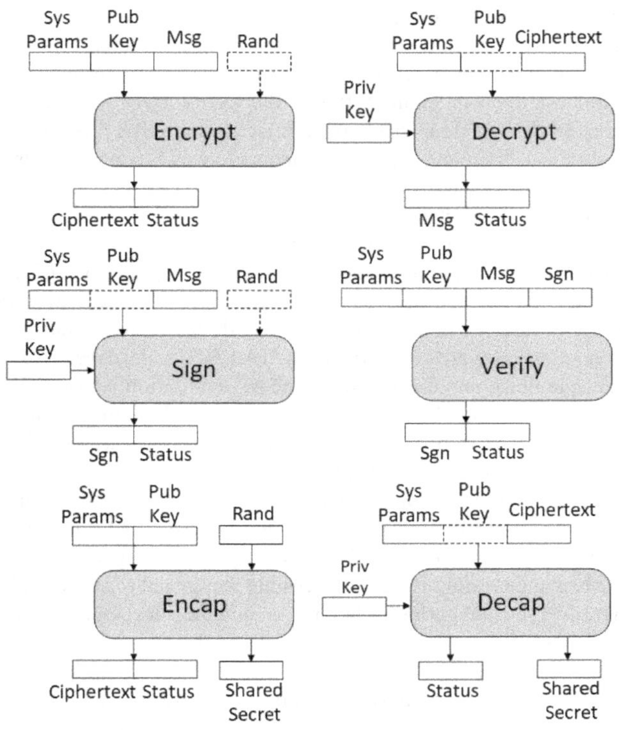

Figure 1: Inputs and outputs of the encryption, signature, and KEM schemes. Optional inputs marked with dashed boxes.

Table 1: NIST PQC Security Strength Categories

Category	Minimum complexity of the best attack
1	AES128 key search
2	SHA256/SHA3-256 collision search
3	AES192 key search
4	SHA384/SHA3-384 collision search
5	AES256 key search

Table 2: Number of PQC Round 1 submissions with division into signature schemes and encryption/encapsulation schemes

Family	Signature	Encryption/ KEM	Total
Lattice-based	5	23	28
Code-based	3	17	20
Multivariate	8	2	10
Hash-based	3	0	3
Isogeny-based	0	1	1
Other	2	5	7
Total	21	48	69

Table 3: Major families of classical and post-quantum public-key cryptosystems and the underlying mathematical problems

Classical	
RSA	Factoring large integers
Discrete logarithm-based	Discrete logarithm problem
Elliptic Curve Cryptography	Elliptic Curve discrete logarithm problem
Post-quantum	
Lattice-based	Shortest Vector Problem, Closest Vector Problem
Code-based	Hardness of decoding in a random linear code
Multivariate	Solving a set of multivariate quadratic equations
Hash-based	Collision resistance of a hash function
Isogeny-based	Finding the isogeny mapping between two elliptic curves with the same number of points

algorithms, compared to secret-key ciphers, hash functions, and authenticated ciphers evaluated in the major previous cryptographic competitions.

Each submission to the NIST Process was expected to support one or more of the following three functionalities: public-key encryption, digital signature, and Key Encapsulation Mechanism (KEM). The primary inputs and outputs of the respective schemes are schematically shown in Fig. 1.

In Table 1, we summarize the five major security strength categories, as defined in the NIST Call for Proposals. For each category, the best known classical or quantum attack against the existing NIST standard (AES, SHA-2, or SHA-3) is used as a lower bound for the complexity of all known attacks against a given PQC candidate variant.

The majority of known PQC algorithms can be classified, based on the underlying mathematical problem, as belonging to one of the following five major families: code-based, hash-based, isogeny-based, lattice-based, and multivariate [3]. In Table 2, the number of PQC Round 1 submissions belonging to each of these major families (as well as to the group of Others) is summarized [40]. As the encryption and KEM functionalities can generally be interconverted, they are treated as a single class for the purpose of this summary. The underlying mathematical problems for the major families of classical and post-quantum public-key cryptosystems are summarized in Table 3. All classical cryptosystems listed in this table are breakable in polynomial time using Shor's algorithm assuming the availability of a sufficiently powerful and scalable quantum computer [7].

4 HARDWARE BENCHMARKING IN PREVIOUS CONTESTS

During the first cryptographic contest, AES, hardware benchmarking was focused primarily on the maximum throughput. Only a single hardware architecture, optimized for maximum throughput for a single long message, was considered for the majority of candidates. The first modern Xilinx FPGA, Virtex, was used for the implementations of five AES finalists. ASIC benchmarking of the same candidates was limited to post-synthesis results [15].

During the later SHA-3 contest (2007-2012), substantial improvements have been made. Both high-speed and lightweight implementations were considered. Multiple hardware architectures (e.g., folded, unrolled, and pipelined) were used in both cases [18]. Benchmarking was performed using multiple FPGA families and ASIC standard-cell libraries [17, 24, 28, 30, 31]. Specialized tools, such as ATHENa [19], were used to select optimum options of FPGA tools. Post-layout and experimental results were generated for ASIC implementations [15]. For the first time, it became common practice to make all implementations open source for the full transparency of the evaluation and to facilitate further optimizations by other groups [10]. The evaluation using FPGAs included the use of embedded resources, such as block memories and DSP units [18].

In the CAESAR contest (2013-2018), a new trend emerged. The submitters of candidates qualified to Round 2 were requested to provide Register-Transfer Level (RTL) hardware implementations in VHDL or Verilog [9]. As a result, the number of candidates implemented in hardware reached about 50% of all initial Round 1 submissions, and hardware efficiency played a major role at much earlier stages of the competition, saving countless hours of complex cryptanalysis [12]. Three use cases, corresponding to different application domains and optimization targets were considered (lightweight, high-performance, and defense in depth).

For the first time, a common hardware Application Programming Interface (API) was developed and approved by the organizers of the contest [25]. The specification of this API included minimum compliance criteria, interface, communication protocol, and timing characteristics to be supported by all implementations. Additionally, the comprehensive Implementer's Guide and Development Package for hardware implementations compliant with CAESAR Hardware API were developed [11, 13]. The latter included: a) VHDL code of generic pre-processing and post-processing units, common for all authenticated ciphers, b) a universal testbench to verify the functionality of any CAESAR candidate implemented using the standard hardware API, c) a Python application used to automatically generate test vectors for this testbench, d) several reference implementations of simple dummy authenticated ciphers, implemented using the proposed API [11, 13].

In parallel, High-Level Synthesis (HLS) was adopted for the first time to rank candidates, giving results comparable to those achieved using much more mundane and time-consuming RTL approach [27]. In this new methodology, a designer started from a reference software implementation, provided by the algorithm's designers in C. This implementation was then manually transformed into HLS-ready C code, by the 1) addition of HLS tool directives (specified using pragmas), 2) hardware-driven code refactoring, and 3) extension of the functionality to accommodate differences between the software and hardware API. All of these transformations made the C code more suitable for the hardware modeling, function parallelization, and resource reuse. Once these modifications were completed, the code was verified in software for the correct functionality. Afterward, the HLS-ready C code was processed by Vivado HLS to generate the corresponding RTL HDL code, and the first performance estimates (e.g., the latency in clock cycles and resource utilization) were generated. The obtained code was then simulated for functional correctness, using a traditional HDL simulator, e.g., ModelSim. If the results were correct and the code inferred an expected hardware architecture, the HLS phase of the design was completed. The obtained code was further processed using the tools and optimization strategies identical to those used in the RTL design flow [27].

In order to verify a potential validity of this approach, the described above HLS-based methodology was applied to the comparison of 16 authenticated ciphers, including AES-GCM and the primary variants of 13 Round 3 CAESAR candidates. These implementations were compared to the best RTL code, developed by multiple designers during the CAESAR evaluation process. The study demonstrated high correlation between the rankings of the evaluated algorithms, obtained using both investigated methodologies. In particular, after applying HLS, the algorithm rankings in terms of three major performance metrics - throughput, area, and throughput to area ratio - have either remained unchanged or have been affected only for algorithms with very similar RTL performance. Additionally, HLS results were used to successfully identify a few suboptimal RTL implementations developed by various groups [27].

For the Use Case 1 CAESAR candidates, targeting lightweight applications, such as Internet of Things, and thus particularly vulnerable to side-channel attacks, a new design and benchmarking methodology was developed. This methodology included the development of threshold implementations, protected against first-order differential power analysis. The resistance of the obtained implementations to secret data leakage was verified experimentally using the t-test methodology applied using the modified open-source side channel analysis suite, FOBOS (Flexible Open-source workBench fOr Side-channel analysis). This methodology was successfully applied to the analysis of two Use Case 1 finalists, ACORN and Ascon, and demonstrated the significant advantages of these two algorithms over the existing standard, AES-GCM, in terms of the minimum achievable area, power, and energy per bit for the equivalent security-strength side-channel protected FPGA implementations [14].

5 PQC HARDWARE BENCHMARKING

Benchmarking PQC algorithms in hardware involves its own unique set of challenges. The biggest of them is the complexity of the algorithms and their often highly mathematical specifications, incomprehensible for hardware designers with limited exposure to number theory and abstract algebra. As a result, the workload for even a single algorithm, implemented using the traditional RTL approach, can easily reach several man-months. Close collaboration with the algorithm designers is highly recommended and often indispensable.

The HLS approach, attempted during the CAESAR contest, appears to be very appealing (especially in light of a very large number of Round 1 PQC candidates and the availability of reference and optimized implementations in C). However, to our knowledge, this approach has not been yet reported for any PQC algorithm, not to mention contrasted, with the RTL approach in terms of performance and/or resource utilization. If attempted, it may lead to potentially unfair comparisons, due to the lack of any clear indication when the optimization of the HLS-ready C code should end and the limited experience of both hardware designers and software programmers with this new methodology.

The second challenge is the storage of large public keys, private keys, and internal state, inside of a hardware module, which may prohibit truly lightweight implementations and effect the key agility of all hardware implementations.

The other difficulty is the requirement for random numbers, used as inputs for encryption, signature generation, and key encapsulation (as shown in Fig. 1) with the specific (e.g., the uniform or Gaussian) distribution. The circuits used to generate such numbers are rarely used in other digital system applications, and may need to be developed from scratch. These circuits are also difficult to validate, and may become the source of considerable side-channel leakage.

The majority of PQC algorithms do not use the same basic operations as classical public-key cryptosystems, not to mention secret-key cryptosystems. As a result, the corresponding building blocks may need to be developed from scratch and thoroughly optimized. If these development efforts are undertaken independently by multiple designers, that may easily lead to unfair and biased comparisons.

Unlike it was the case for secret-key algorithms, the majority of countermeasures against side-channel attacks are algorithm-specific, and yet unexplored for the majority of Round 1 PQC candidates. Their development and experimental validation is likely to require a very considerable and prolonged effort, including substantial modifications and extensions of experimental frameworks. Even constant-time implementations, necessary to protect both high-speed and lightweight implementations against powerful timing attacks, are non-trivial to develop for many PQC algorithms.

In order to simplify the deployment of the newly developed algorithms in real-life applications, such as hardware accelerators for TLS or IPSec, the implemented modules, will need to be plug-and-play replacements for existing public-key cryptography modules, based on classical algorithms. To make matters even more challenging, in the transition period (likely to last several years) hybrid systems, based on both types of public-key algorithms (classical and post-quantum) are likely to be used simultaneously (in the parallel or cascade fashion). This is because the PQC standards may not be fully trusted in terms of resistance to traditional cryptanalytical attacks, while the classical algorithm will face the danger of more and more advanced quantum computers.

Other challenges, common with previous cryptographic competitions, include no clear performance target (caused by a large variety of future applications and possible implementations platforms), the fact that the existing FPGA and ASIC tools are not designed to operate under such assumptions (and instead attempt to always reach a predefined target, rather than the absolute maximum) [16], the difficulty of describing resource utilization in FPGAs using a single metric (due to the use of diverse resources, such as configurable logic blocks, DSP units, memory blocks, hardwired embedded microprocessors, etc.), and differences among the skills and time commitment of hardware designers responsible for implementing particular algorithms.

The first step in addressing the majority of the aforementioned challenges was the development of the PQC Hardware API [6]. This API includes the minimum compliance criteria aimed at the fair evaluation of all developed implementations. For example, the key generation is required to be implemented outside of a PQC module (either in software or in a separate hardware module) as the operations required for this functionality are often substantially different from those used for encryption/decryption, signature generation/verification, and key encapsulation/ decapsulation. On the other hand, the two basic functionalities (e.g., encryption and decryption) are required to be always implemented together to demonstrate the algorithm's potential for resource sharing. A PQC module must also be as complete as possible, and thus include support for various input sizes (including empty messages), processing of incomplete blocks, padding, etc. [6]

The next step will be the creation of the Development Package, containing HDL code that can be shared among multiple PQC candidates (including any pre-processing and post-processing units, libraries of basic operations, and universal testbenches). The experiments with contrasting the results of the corresponding RTL and HLS implementations will most likely follow, in parallel with an effort to develop and validate both universal and algorithm-specific countermeasures against side-channel attacks and fault attacks.

The undertaken effort will greatly benefit from the pilot studies, concerning the implementations of earlier versions of the PQC algorithms, conducted well before the NIST candidate submission deadline of Nov. 30, 2017 [20, 21, 23, 29, 32–35, 38, 39, 41, 42, 44]. However, the results of these earlier studies will need to be used with considerable caution, due to the recent changes in the functionality and parameter values of even well-established candidates, such as NTRUEncrypt, Rainbow, Unbalanced Oil-and-Vinegar, McEliece, etc. Additionally, the old implementations were using very divergent assumptions, optimization targets, APIs, and sources of randomness.

As a result, NIST and other standardization organizations, as well as cryptographers from all over the world involved in developing and/or evaluating PQC submissions, will urgently need the help of the GLSVLSI community. They count on this community's contribution to come up with the most efficient and secure hardware architectures for a multitude of PQC candidates, as well as less time-consuming, but accurate and fair, implementation and benchmarking approaches.

The next 5–10 years are very likely to bring the biggest revolution in cryptography, since the invention of public-key cryptography in mid-1970s. Combined with the emergence of new application areas, such Internet of Things (IoT), Vehicle-to-Vehicle (V2V) Communications, Cloud Computing, and Big Data, the opportunities for new cryptographic systems involving hardware accelerators for speed, enhanced security, reduced power, and energy savings are enormous. By getting involved in the hardware benchmarking of post-quantum cryptography algorithms, hardware designers have a unique opportunity to influence the choice of future cryptographic standards, that are likely to be developed within the next decade and remain in use for the significant portion (if not the rest) of the 21st century. An early involvement may pay of with unique multidisciplinary experiences, knowledge, and skills required to do research and start new businesses in the emerging post-quantum world.

ACKNOWLEDGMENTS

This work was partially supported by the Department of Commerce (NIST) through the grant no. 60NANB15D058.

REFERENCES

[1] 2012. eSTREAM: the ECRYPT Stream Cipher Project. (March 2012). Retrieved March 20, 2018 from http://www.ecrypt.eu.org/stream/

[2] 2017. 10 Breakthrough Technologies 2017. MIT Technology Review. (Dec. 2017). https://www.technologyreview.com/lists/technologies/2017

[3] 2017. Summer School on Post-Quantum Cryptography 2017. (June 2017). Retrieved March 20, 2018 from https://2017.pqcrypto.org/school/schedule.html

[4] 2018. IBM-Q. (March 2018). Retrieved March 20, 2018 from https://www.research.ibm.com/ibm-q/learn/what-is-ibm-q/

[5] 2018. Timeline of quantum computing. (March 2018). Retrieved March 20, 2018 from https://en.wikipedia.org/wiki/Timeline_of_quantum_computing

[6] Ahmed Ferozpuri and Farnoud Farahmand and Viet Dang and Malik Umar Sharif and Jens-Peter Kaps and and Kris Gaj. 2018. Hardware API for Post-Quantum Public Key Cryptosystems. (March 2018). Retrieved March 20, 2018 from https://cryptography.gmu.edu/athena/index.php?id=PQC

[7] Daniel J. Bernstein, Johannes Buchmann, and Erik Dahmen (Eds.). 2009. *Post-quantum cryptography*. Springer, Berlin.

[8] Peter Bright. 2017. Microsoft makes play for next wave of computing with quantum computing toolkit. Ars Technica. (Sept. 2017). https://arstechnica.com/gadgets/2017/09/microsoft-quantum-toolkit/

[9] CAESAR: Competition for Authenticated Encryption: Security, Applicability, and Robustness. 2018. Cryptographic competitions. (March 2018). Retrieved March 20, 2018 from http://competitions.cr.yp.to

[10] CERG. 2015. GMU Source Code of SHA-3 Candidates. (April 2015). Retrieved March 20, 2018 from https://cryptography.gmu.edu/athena/index.php?id=CAESAR_source_codes

[11] CERG. 2017. Development Package for Hardware Implementations Compliant with the CAESAR Hardware API, v2.0. (Dec. 2017). Retrieved March 20, 2018 from https://cryptography.gmu.edu/athena/index.php?id=CAESAR

[12] CERG. 2017. Hardware Benchmarking of CAESAR Candidates. (Dec. 2017). Retrieved March 20, 2018 from https://cryptography.gmu.edu/athena/index.php?id=CAESAR

[13] CERG. 2017. Implementer's Guide to Hardware Implementations Compliant with the CAESAR Hardware API, v2.0. (Dec. 2017). Retrieved March 20, 2018 from https://cryptography.gmu.edu/athena/index.php?id=CAESAR

[14] William Diehl. 2018. *Comparing Costs of Protecting Secret-Key Ciphers Against Differential Power Analysis*. Ph.D. Dissertation. George Mason University.

[15] James Nechvatal et al. 2001. Report on the Development of the Advanced Encryption Standard (AES). *J. Res. Natl. Inst. Stand. Technol.* 106, 3 (May-June 2001), 511–577. https://nvlpubs.nist.gov/nistpubs/jres/106/3/j63nec.pdf

[16] Farnoud Farahmand, Ahmed Ferozpuri, William Diehl, and Kris Gaj. 2017. Minerva: Automated Hardware Optimization Tool. In *2017 International Conference on Reconfigurable Computing and FPGAs - ReConFig 2017, Cancun, Mexico, Dec. 4-6, 2017.* 414–421.

[17] Kris Gaj, Ekawat Homsirikamol, and Marcin Rogawski. 2010. Fair and Comprehensive Methodology for Comparing Hardware Performance of Fourteen Round Two SHA-3 Candidates Using FPGAs. In *Cryptographic Hardware and Embedded Systems, CHES 2010.* Springer, 264–278.

[18] Kris Gaj, Ekawat Homsirikamol, Marcin Rogawski, Rabia Shahid, and Malik Umar Sharif. 2012. Comprehensive Evaluation of High-Speed and Medium-Speed Implementations of Five SHA-3 Finalists Using Xilinx and Altera FPGAs. Cryptology ePrint Archive, Report 2012/368. (2012).

[19] Kris Gaj, Jens-Peter Kaps, Venkata Amirineni, Marcin Rogawski, Ekawat Homsirikamol, and Benjamin Y. Brewster. 2010. ATHENa - Automated Tool for Hardware EvaluatioN: Toward Fair and Comprehensive Benchmarking of Cryptographic Hardware Using FPGAs. In *Field Programmable Logic and Applications (FPL), 2010 International Conference on.* 414–421.

[20] Santosh Ghosh. 2014. On the implementation of McEliece with CCA2 indeterminacy by SHA-3. In *International Symposium on Circuits and Systems, ISCAS, Melbourne, Australia, June 01–05, 2014.* IEEE, 2804–2807.

[21] Santosh Ghosh, Jeroen Delvaux, Leif Uhsadel, and Ingrid Verbauwhede. 2012. A speed area optimized embedded co-processor for McEliece cryptosystem. In *International Conference on Application-Specific Systems, Architectures and Processors, ASAP, Delft, Netherlands, July 9–11, 2012.* IEEE, 102–108.

[22] Martin Giles and Will Knight. 2018. Google thinks it's close to "quantum supremacy." Here's what that really means. MIT Technology Review. (March 2018). https://www.technologyreview.com/s/610274/google-thinks-its-close-to-quantum-supremacy-heres-what-that-really-means/

[23] Tim Guneysu. 2017. Post-Quantum Cryptography for Embedded Systems. Tutorial at CHES 2017, Taipei, Taiwan. (Sept. 2017). https://ches.iacr.org/2017/program.shtml

[24] Xu Guo, Sinan Huang, Leyla Nazhandali, and Patrick Schaumont. 2010. Fair and Comprehensive Performance Evaluation of 14 Second Round SHA-3 ASIC Implementations. In *The Second SHA-3 Candidate Conference.*

[25] Ekawat Homsirikamol, William Diehl, Ahmed Ferozpuri, Farnoud Farahmand, Panasayya Yalla, Jens-Peter Kaps, and Kris Gaj. 2016. CAESAR Hardware API. Cryptology ePrint Archive, Report 2016/626. (June 2016).

[26] Ekawat Homsirikamol, Farnoud Farahmand, William Diehl, and Kris Gaj. 2017. Benchmarking of Round 3 CAESAR Candidates in Hardware: Methodology, Designs and Results. (2017). Retrieved March 20, 2018 from https://cryptography.gmu.edu/athena/presentations/CAESAR_R3_HW_Benchmarking.pdf

[27] Ekawat Homsirikamol and Kris Gaj. 2017. Toward a New HLS-Based Methodology for FPGA Benchmarking of Candidates in Cryptographic Competitions: The CAESAR Contest Case Study. In *2017 International Conference on Field Programmable Technology, FPT 2017.* 120–127.

[28] Ekawat Homsirikamol, Marcin Rogawski, and Kris Gaj. 2010. Comparing Hardware Performance of Fourteen Round Two SHA-3 Candidates Using FPGAs. Cryptology ePrint Archive, Report 2010/445. (2010).

[29] J. Howe, C. Moore, M. O'Neill, F. Regazzoni, T. Guneysu, and K. Beeden. 2016. Lattice-based Encryption Over Standard Lattices In Hardware. In *Proceedings of the 53rd Annual Design Automation Conference, DAC '16, Austin, Texas.* ACM, 162:1–162:6.

[30] Shu jen Chang et al. 2012. *Third-Round Report of the SHA-3 Cryptographic Hash Algorithm Competition.* MIT Research Lab Technical Report NISTIR 7896. NIST.

[31] Miroslav Knezevic, Kazuyuki Kobayashi, Jun Ikegami, Shin'ichiro Matsuo, Akashi Satoh, Unal Kocabas, Junfeng Fan, Toshihiro Katashita, Takeshi Sugawara, Kazuo Sakiyama, Ingrid Verbauwhede, Kazuo Ohta, Naofumi Homma, and Takafumi Aoki. 2012. Fair and Consistent Hardware Evaluation of Fourteen Round Two SHA-3 Candidates. *IEEE Transactions on Very Large Scale Integration Systems* 20, 5 (May 2012), 827–840.

[32] Brian Koziel, Reza Azarderakhsh, Mehran Mozaffari Kermani, and David Jao. 2017. Post-quantum cryptography on FPGA based on isogenies on elliptic curves. *IEEE Transactions on Circuits and Systems I: Regular Papers* 64, 1 (2017), 86–99.

[33] Brian Koziel, Reza Azarderakhsh, and Mehran Mozaffari-Kermani. 2016. Fast hardware architectures for supersingular isogeny Diffie-Hellman key exchange on FPGA. In *Progress in Cryptology–INDOCRYPT 2016: 17th International Conference on Cryptology in India, Kolkata, India, December 11-14, 2016, Proceedings 17.* Springer, 191–206.

[34] Bingxin Liu and Huapeng Wu. 2016. Efficient multiplication architecture over truncated polynomial ring for NTRUEncrypt system. In *IEEE International Symposium on Circuits and Systems, ISCAS 2016, Montreal, QC, Canada, May 22-25, 2016.* IEEE, 1174–1177.

[35] Claudia Patricia Renteria Mejia and Jaime Velasco Medina. 2017. High-Throughput Ring-LWE Cryptoprocessors. *IEEE Trans. VLSI Syst.* 25, 8 (2017), 2332–2345.

[36] National Institute of Standards and Technology. 2017. Post-Quantum Cryptography. (Dec. 2017). Retrieved March 20, 2018 from https://csrc.nist.gov/Projects/Post-Quantum-Cryptography

[37] National Institute of Standards and Technology. 2017. Post-Quantum Cryptography: Round 1 Submissions. (Dec. 2017). Retrieved March 20, 2018 from https://csrc.nist.gov/projects/post-quantum-cryptography/round-1-submissions

[38] Tobias Oder and Tim Guneysu. 2017. Implementing the NewHope-Simple Key Exchange on Low-Cost FPGAs. In *Fifth International Conference on Cryptology and Information Security, Latin America, La Habana, Cuba, September 20-22, 2017.*

[39] Ruhr Universitat Bochum. 2017. Lattice-Based Cryptography and Code-Based Cryptography. (Sept. 2017). Retrieved March 20, 2018 from https://www.sha.rub.de/research/projects/

[40] SAFEcrypto. 2018. Post-Quantum Cryptography Lounge. (March 2018). Retrieved March 20, 2018 from https://www.safecrypto.eu/pqclounge

[41] Malik Umar Sharif, Ahmed Ferozpuri, and Kris Gaj. 2017. Lessons Learned from High-Speed Implementation and Benchmarking of Two Post-Quantum Public-Key Cryptosystems. In *15th Workshop on Cryptographic architectures embedded in logic devices, CryptArchi 2017, Smolenice, Slovakia.*

[42] Shaohua Tang, Haibo Yi, Jintai Ding, Huan Chen, and Guomin Chen. 2011. High-speed hardware implementation of Rainbow signature on FPGA. In *International Workshop on Post-Quantum Cryptography.* Springer, 228–243.

[43] Lieven Vandersypen. 2017. A "spins-inside" quantum computer. Invited talk at PQCrypto 2017. (Dec. 2017). https://2017.pqcrypto.org/conference/schedule.html

[44] Yale CAS Lab. 2018. Post-Quantum Cryptography. (March 2018). Retrieved March 20, 2018 from http://caslab.csl.yale.edu/research.html

Physical Protection of Lattice-Based Cryptography - Challenges and Solutions -

Ayesha Khalid
The Queen's University Belfast,
United Kingdom
a.khalid@qub.ac.uk

Tobias Oder
Ruhr-Universität Bochum, Germany
tobias.oder@rub.de

Felipe Valencia
ALaRI - Università Della Svizzera
Italiana, Switzerland
valena@usi.ch

Maire O' Neill
The Queen's University Belfast,
United Kingdom
m.oneill@qub.ac.uk

Tim Güneysu
Ruhr-Universität Bochum & DFKI,
Germany
tim.gueneysu@rub.de

Francesco Regazzoni
ALaRI - Università Della Svizzera
Italiana, Switzerland
regazzoni@alari.ch

ABSTRACT

The impending realization of scalable quantum computers will have a significant impact on today's security infrastructure. With the advent of powerful quantum computers public key cryptographic schemes will become vulnerable to Shor's quantum algorithm, undermining the security current communications systems. Post-quantum (or quantum-resistant) cryptography is an active research area, endeavoring to develop novel and quantum resistant public key cryptography. Amongst the various classes of quantum-resistant cryptography schemes, lattice-based cryptography is emerging as one of the most viable options. Its efficient implementation on software and on commodity hardware has already been shown to compete and even excel the performance of current classical security public-key schemes. This work discusses the next step in terms of their practical deployment, i.e., addressing the physical security of lattice-based cryptographic implementations. We survey the state-of-the-art in terms of side channel attacks (SCA), both invasive and passive attacks, and proposed countermeasures. Although the weaknesses exposed have led to countermeasures for these schemes, the cost, practicality and effectiveness of these on multiple implementation platforms, however, remains *under-studied.*

ACM Reference Format:
Ayesha Khalid, Tobias Oder, Felipe Valencia, Maire O' Neill, Tim Güneysu, and Francesco Regazzoni. 2018. Physical Protection of Lattice-Based Cryptography - Challenges and Solutions -. In *GLSVLSI '18: 2018 Great Lakes Symposium on VLSI, May 23–25, 2018, Chicago, IL, USA.* ACM, New York, NY, USA, 6 pages. https://doi.org/10.1145/3194554.3194616

1 INTRODUCTION

With the societal shift towards the *Internet of Things*, ensuring security and privacy for an increasing number of heterogeneous connected devices is fast becoming a crucial concern. Moreover, our current public-key security infrastructure needs a complete overhaul since its security could be compromised by a scalable quantum computer in the near future. Quantum computers will be capable of executing Shor's algorithm which can, in polynomial time, break the two hard mathematical problems, i.e., integer factorization and discrete logarithm problem [39], on which RSA and ECC are based. These public-key schemes are used in today's security infrastructure to provide public-key encryption and (authenticated) key exchange. Reacting to this urgency, much research is now being conducted into *quantum-resilient* or *post quantum* cryptography. The concern is also reflected by the stance of government agencies, including NSA and CESG [8, 9, 25, 35]. NSA's Information Assurance Directorate (IAD) announced a transition to quantum resistant public-key cryptography in the near future for their Suite B of recommended algorithms [25]. Also, NIST announced a call requesting new quantum-resilient algorithm candidates to be considered for analysis, standardization and eventually, industry adoption [24].

Of the various flavors of quantum-resilient cryptography proposed to date, lattice-based cryptography (LBC) stands out for various reasons. *Firstly*, these schemes offer security proofs based on NP-hard problems with average-case to worst-case hardness. *Secondly*, in addition to being quantum-age secure, the LBC implementations are notable for their efficiency, primarily due to their inherent linear algebra based matrix/ vector operations on integers. *Thirdly*, LBC constructions offer extended functionality for advanced security services such as identity-based encryption (IBE) [13] attribute-based encryption (ABE) and fully-homomorphic encryption (FHE) [29], in addition to the basic classical cryptographic primitives (encryption, signatures, key exchange solutions) needed in a quantum age [16].

While LBC constructions provide security guarantees in theory, to date, the investigation of LBC implementations resilient to physical attacks remains understudied. Their realization on contemporary computing platforms requires a thorough study of their resilience, especially in the face of advanced side-channel attack techniques, both active attacks and fault attacks. This paper surveys the state of the art in physical attacks and countermeasures undertaken for LBC to date on software and hardware platforms. A significant number of attacks undertaken for non-post-quantum cryptography can be directly applicable in the LBC context, and

GLSVLSI '18, May 23–25, 2018, Chicago, IL, USA

ACM ISBN 978-1-4503-5724-1/18/05...$15.00
https://doi.org/10.1145/3194554.3194616

further vulnerabilities exposed by the inherent structures of LBC schemes need to also be investigated.

The paper is outlined as follows: Section 2 gives a background of LBC proposals and their key components. Section 3 summarizes the state of the art in physical attacks reported against LBC constructions. Section 4 discusses countermeasure proposals to date against these attacks while Section 5 concludes the paper.

2 BACKGROUND

2.1 Lattice-Based Primitives

Lattices are objects in n-dimensional Euclidean space characterized by a regular arrangement of points. More precisely, a lattice in $\mathbb{R}^n$ generated by the basis $\mathrm{B} = \{\mathrm{b}_1, \mathrm{b}_2, \ldots, \mathrm{b}_n\}$, is defined as $\mathrm{L(B)} = \{\mathrm{Bx}, \mathrm{x} \in \mathbb{Z}^n\}$.

A number of hard mathematical problems are used to construct lattice-based schemes. The most commonly used problem is the Learning with Errors problem (LWE) which involves finding a vector $\mathbf{s}$ when given a matrix $\mathbf{A}$ and a vector $\mathbf{b} = \mathbf{As} + \mathbf{e}$ where $\mathbf{e}$ is a small (unknown) error vector. Other popular mathematical problems used to construct lattice-based schemes include the Short Integer Solution (SIS) or NTRU lattices.

There are three classes of lattices that are relevant for cryptography. Schemes that are based on LWE are **standard or random lattice-based schemes**. These schemes have in common that they require computations with large matrices that either need a lot of memory or require costly on-the-fly computations. A further issue with standard lattice-based schemes is that they require matrix-vector multiplication with quadratic complexity. **Ideal or ring lattice-based schemes** are an alternative to standard lattices. The major difference between these classes of lattices is that the matrix that is used in standard lattices is represented by a single row in ring lattices. The remaining rows are generated by cyclic shifts of the first row. Therefore ideal lattice-based schemes are more efficient as they require less memory and the main arithmetic operation is polynomial multiplication instead of matrix-vector multiplication. With the help of the number-theoretic transform (NTT) polynomial multiplication can be accelerated to have a complexity of $O(n \log n)$. In the case of ring lattices the security of the constructed schemes is based on ring variants of the original problems, hence, the Ring-Learning with Errors (R-LWE) or Ring-Short Integer Solution (R-SIS) are the underlying problems used in these schemes.

While ideal lattice-based schemes are more efficient, the additional structure in the lattice might also be exploitable by attacks. So far no strong attack is known that exploits the ring structure or that is better than other attacks that work on standard lattices as well. To have a trade-off between the efficiency of ideal lattices and the trust in the security of standard lattices, **module lattices** were introduced. The difference between module lattices and standard lattices is that in module lattices the matrix has small dimensions and the coefficients of the matrix are no longer simple integers but entire polynomials. Therefore the number-theoretic transform can still be used for efficient polynomial multiplication. The security of module lattice-based schemes is once again based on variants of the original mathematical problems, e.g. Module-LWE or Module-SIS.

As one of the first lattice-based cryptosystems Hoffstein, Pipher, and Silverman introduced the encryption scheme NTRU [14] in 1998 which is based on ring lattices. To date the encryption scheme NTRUEncrypt has withstood cryptanalytic scrutiny provided parameters are chosen correctly, but the NTRU-based digital signature scheme is considered broken. However, a modified version version of the signature scheme has been submitted to the NIST post-quantum call, along with many other proposals.

Table 1 presents a summary of the lattice-based schemes submitted to the NIST standardization process [24] and their related classes of lattices. Out of a total of 69 submissions to the NIST call for post quantum cryptographic proposals for digital signatures and KEM/encryption schemes, 26 are lattice-based proposals. Note that some schemes base their security on multiple assumptions. There are also two submissions based on **polynomial lattices**. This class is very similar to ring lattices and for power-of-two dimensions even equivalent. The table also shows for which key exchange (KEM)/ public key encryption (PKE) schemes the authors claim CCA or CCA2 security in addition to CPA security (which was a requirement for the NIST call). CPA security means that the scheme is mathematically secure against an attacker who has access to a limited amount of plaintext/ciphertext pairs. CCA security on the other hand implies that an attacker has access to a decryption oracle as well. This security can be extended by assuming an adaptive attacker (CCA2).

For most submitted signature schemes the authors claim EUF-CMA security, which means that a signature is existentially unforgeable under chosen-message attacks. This means that an attacker with access to a signing oracle is unable to forge a valid signature of a new message. Strong existential unforgeability under Chosen Message Attacks (SEUF-CMA) is an even stronger security notion that also assumes that an attacker is unable to forge a different signature of a message that he has already seen.

2.2 Basic Blocks for Lattice-Based Cryptography

From an architectural point of view, the key components in lattice based cryptography typically include the calculation of a series of linear algebraic operations and the sampling of values from a discrete Gaussian-distributed random source. For signatures it is beneficial to apply compression techniques (e.g., Huffman encoding) if transmission size reduction is more critical than processing cost. For ideal lattices, polynomial multiplication is typically realized using the number-theoretic transform (NTT). It is a fast Fourier transform (FFT) over a finite field where the n coefficients pass through $\log n$ *butterfly operations*. Many lattice-based cryptosystems require discrete Gaussian distribution for noise generation. In addition to the traditional *rejection sampling*, several other optimized techniques have been proposed including Bernoulli, Cumulative Distribution Table (CDT) sampling (inversion sampling), Knuth-Yao sampling, discrete Ziggurat sampling. All of these schemes have advantages depending on the target application, and hence tackling their vulnerability to side-channel attacks is critical. Random oracles needed by LBC constructions are generally instantiated by cryptographic hash functions, such as ChaCha20, SHA256, or the expandable output function (XOF) SHAKE-128.

Lattice Type	Schemes	
	KEM/PKE	Signatures
Standard	Ramstake[1] Odd Manhattan[1] LOTUS[2] Compact LWE[2] Giophantus FrodoKEM [1]	DRS
Ring, Standard	Lizard[1] Round 2[1] KCL[1] EMBELM/R. EMBELM	
Ring	NTRU Prime[2] NTRU Encrypt[2] Ding Key KINDI [1] LIMA[1] New Hope[1] HILA5 NTRU-RSS-KEM Mersenne-756839	qTESLA FALCON
Ring, Module		pqNTRUsign
Module	CRYSTALS KYBER[2] SABER [1] Three Bears [1]	CRYSTALS DILITHIUM [3]
Polynomial	Titanium [1] LAC[1]	

Table 1: Lattice based proposals submitted to NIST post quantum crytpography call

[1] IND-CCA Security
[2] IND-CCA2 Security
[3] sEUF-CMA security

3 PHYSICAL ATTACKS ON LATTICE-BASED CRYPTOGRAPHY

Physical attacks against lattice based constructions is a research direction largely unexplored. This is mainly due to the fact that lattice based constructions themselves are relatively new and several parameters of the algorithms are still under scrutiny. However, a comprehensive analysis of their resistance against physical attacks is of utmost importance for their widespread deployment. A deep understanding of the physical attack resistance of these construction is also a fundamental parameter for the NIST standardization process. In the reminder of the section, we will introduce the most common physical attacks (timing attacks, power analysis attacks, and fault attacks) and we summarize how they have been applied to lattice based constructions.

3.1 Timing Attacks

Timing attacks were first introduced by Kocher [22], they exploit the differences in time required by a device to perform specific operations, such as the non-constant time to execute two different instructions, different data fetch times due to cache memory hit/miss, programs behavior due to branching, optimizations leading to skipping of unnecessary operations, etc.

The first work discussing timing attacks on lattice-based cryptography is the one of Silverman and Whyte [40]. They mounted a timing attack an implementation of NTRUEncrypt. The attack exploits the difference in the decryption time taken by different (possibly bogus) ciphertexts since they all may require different number of calls to the hash function. To mount the attack, the adversary performs a variable number of pre-computations, and then submits a relatively small number of specially constructed ciphertexts for decryption, measuring the decryption times. Comparison of the decryption times with the precomputed data enables the attacker to recover the key in a much reduced time compared to standard attacks on NTRUEncrypt. Reported results show that for specific parameter sets, an attacker can recover a single key with approximately half of the key bits of effort. The work highlights possible ways to prevent the attack by ensuring a constant number of SHA calls. In [45], Vizev exploited the differing number of hash calls to mount timing side-channel attacks. The proposed countermeasure consists of a padding scheme, which helps ensure a constant timing of operations. A constant time sampler was also used in [6] for key-exchange in the transport layer security (TLS) protocol, based on a R-LWE implementation.

The discrete Gaussian samplers have been shown to be especially vulnerable against the timing attacks. Timing channel was exploited, where the information leaked via cache memory by a CDT based Gaussian sampler was successfully extracted [7]. To disentangle the link between timing information and the samples, Roy *et. al* proposed the use of a Fisher-Yates [11] shuffling algorithm [36, 37]. Saarinen [38] later suggested the shuffling be carried out twice on the set of independently generated samples, before summation. Recent research shows that relying solely on two-stage shuffling may not be sufficient to protect against SCA attacks [27]. Consequently, *multiple sampling and shuffling stages* together with the use of *different convolution parameters* are recommended to ensure adequate protection [27, 28].

3.2 Power Analysis Attacks

These attacks extract secret information by analyzing correlations between the un-intentional power leakage of a target device and the secret values processed during the algorithm execution. In simple power analysis (SPA), the adversary uses a limited set of power traces (possibly as few as one). One example is the single trace attack by Primas *et al.* [30] in which the authors exploit that the `DIV` instruction of an ARM Cortex-M4 microcontroller takes a varying number of cycles to finish depending on the data that is processed. The attacked implementation uses the `DIV` instruction in the modular reduction in the decryption of the R-LWE encryption scheme. The attack is able to fully recover the secret key.

The Differential power analysis (DPA) attacks are much more powerful since they collect many power traces instead to successfully suppress noise and statistically compare a single hypothetical values (*First-order DPA*) or multiple hypothetical values simultaneously (*Higher-order DPA*) with the measured power traces. In contrast to SPA, DPA targets the processed data of the implementation. Atici *et al.* presented the first power analysis attacks on NTRU in [3], targeting implementations on RFIDs. This was followed by Lee *et al.* [23], who considered first and second-order DPA attacks on NTRU. The attacks were based on the leakage of Hamming distance information, generated during the computation of the convolution product. To prevent these attacks the authors proposed to randomize the operation order an add a random value before the computation of the convolution product (a main operation in NTRU) and subtract this value later. This countermeasure is called blinding.

In [46], Wang *et al.* considered the countermeasure proposals of [23] and suggested that blinding during the computation of the convolution products was not sufficient. A DPA was described to exploit the calculation of intermediate values. They exploit that an attacker can trigger decryptions of invalid ciphertexts. Even though illegal intermediate values would be generated, and these values would be prohibited from being output, their calculation during convolution processing stages would still be recordable in the power consumption measurements. The authors then proposed alternative countermeasures, based on random delay insertions, an alternative masking scheme and the use of dummy operations. The authors did not give any indication relating to the performance loss due to the in corporation of these countermeasures.

DPA and SPA are well understood by the community and therefore every implementation of a cryptographic scheme that does not utilize dedicated countermeasures against DPA and SPA is expected to leak secret information. The majority of the research therefore focuses on countermeasures for LBC instead of attacks against implementation of LBC.

3.3 Fault Attacks

For a fault attack the adversary purposely induces a fault and exploits the erroneous behavior of the circuit to gain information about the secret values in the cryptosystem. These errors are typically transient in nature, hence the faults *propagate through the circuit* leaving the device operating normally. The attacks are termed as *first order faults attacks* if the adversary can induce no more than a single fault in the system. The fault injection is shown to be initiated by varying the supply voltage, system clock speed or ambient temperatures, etc. [1, 2]. A further class of invasive attacks were introduced by Skorobogatov in [41, 42], with the use of destructive ion beams and semi-permanent optical fault injection techniques; the faults being shown to induce effects such as changing the values of internal registers, incorrect branching of the program or the skipping of program instructions.

A fault analysis attack against NTRUEncrypt was presented in [17] by Kamal and Youssef, where the fault model assumed the attacker is able to inject faults into the coefficients of the second step of the decryption process. Where NTRU Encrypt is implemented with parameters (N,p,q), the attack is shown to be successful with probability $\approx 1 - 1/p$. In [20], Kamal and Youssef proposed methods for strengthening hardware implementations of NTRUEncrypt against fault analysis attacks using error detection codes and duplication of the decryption operation, using a rotated version of the ciphertext in a redundant computation.

A scan based side-channel attack on NTRU Encrypt was demonstrated in [19], where the scan chain structure of the polynomial multiplication circuits was extracted, thus enabling the secret key to be retrieved. Kamal and Youssef also presented a fault analysis of the NTRU Sign digital signature scheme in [18], where it is assumed that the attacker is able to inject a transient fault into the coefficients of the polynomials in the signing algorithm. When the attacker is also able to skip the norm-bound signature check, the attack requires only one fault for success.

In [4], Bindel *et al.* investigated the vulnerability and resistance of multiple lattice-based signature schemes including BLISS, ring-TESLA and GLP signatures. They considered the first order randomizing, zeroing, and skipping faults and found effective attacks against all the signature schemes. All three schemes were found vulnerable against zeroing faults during the signing and verification, against skipping faults during the key generation, against two kinds of skipping faults during the verification. The work also suggested optimised code modifications as countermeasures against these attacks.

In [44], Valencia *et al.* discuss the vulnerability of R-LWE encryption against fault attacks. The work explored several possible fault injection effects, including single bit flip, single bit zeroing, and skip instructions and examines the consequences and the possibility of recover secret data.

In [10], Espitau *et al.* investigated the implication of early *Loop abort Faults* for various stages of lattice based signature schemes including BLISS, GLP, TESLA and the GPV scheme. For BLISS (and the rest of the Fiat-Shamir family signatures), an early termination of the generation loop for the random commitment element ($y1$) enables a full recovery of the secret key value $s1$. For GPV signature schemes too, reconstruction of the entire secret key is possible by an early loop abort fault considered for the Gaussian sample generation during signature calculation [10].

4 COUNTERMEASURES AGAINST PHYSICAL ATTACKS

This section surveys the countermeasures suggested to protect against the major physical attack vulnerabilities reported to date in LBC constructions. These countermeasures are generally device and attack specific, i.e., some custom hardware vulnerabilities and countermeasures might not be directly applicable to software implementations and vice versa. Moreover, the countermeasures may exhibit side-effects exploitable by an adversary, as shown by Regazzoni *et al.* in [31, 32] where an error detection/correction circuit may aid an adversary by increasing the available exploitable information. The automated application of power/timing attack countermeasures in gate level netlists [12, 43], that has been developed for current cryptographic schemes, is in general also applicable to lattice based circuits.

4.1 Countermeasures against Timing Attacks

The simplest countermeasure against timing attacks is to ensure that the execution time of an implementation is independent of the secret data that is processed. However, especially in the context of a Gaussian sampler, it is often expensive to have a constant-time implementation. There are several possible algorithms that utilise uniform numbers to return Gaussian distributed numbers and they differ from each other in terms of implementation speed, memory, and precision. Constant-time hardware architectures for a wide range of samplers have been proposed [15, 21]. However, to date such proposals have been designed on a case-by-case basis and as yet there has been no proposal of a generic hardware design. The binomial sampler is inherently protected against timing attacks. However, as it only samples from a binomial distribution instead of an exact Gaussian distribution it can only be used in encryption and key exchange schemes as the security proof in signature schemes requires the sampler to have a high precision. To avoid an expensive constant-time Gaussian sampler, shuffling has also been proposed as a countermeasure [36].

4.2 Countermeasures against Power Analysis

Hiding and masking are two commonly used countermeasures against power analysis attacks. While masking tries to avoid the fact that at any point in time a secret value is stored in a register (and thus could be detected by collecting a large amount of traces), hiding uses randomization to increase the noise. While masking schemes can be provably secure as countermeasures against DPA, hiding usually makes DPA more difficult, but does not entirely prevent it. Hiding is better suited as countermeasure against SPA.

The essential goal of hiding is remove the correlation from the data computed by the device and the power consumed by the device during that computation. The most straightforward way of achieving this is to impose that an implementation must consume constant power, however, this, in practice, is extremely hard to be achieved. Another possible approach to realize hiding is to shuffle the order of the executed operations as shown in [27] and [36]. Especially for hardware implementations, it is also possible to instantiate noise generators on the FPGA or ASIC to make it more difficult for an attacker to extract the secret information from the power trace.

The idea of masking is to split the secret value into uniformly random shares and perform computations on each share individually so that an attacker needs to know every share to reconstruct the secret value. First order masking splits the secret value into two shares (i.e. with a single probe, the attacker cannot gain knowledge about the secret value).

Lee *et al.* [23] proposed three countermeasures to protect NTRU, with the aim of thwarting both first and second order attacks. The first countermeasure proposed a random initialization of every register used in the convolution operation, with the random value then subtracted after processing the final result. The second proposal was to blind the intermediate convolution steps, each with a separate random integer value. The final countermeasure was to randomize the order of the array holding the non-zero polynomials.

Masking has also been applied to R-LWE-based schemes in several works [26, 33, 34]. One obstacle when applying masking to R-LWE-based schemes is that R-LWE itself only provides security against chosen-plaintext attackers. For DPA it is essential that an attacker can trigger decryption runs on his own as DPA attacks require millions of power traces. That means that an attacker with access to a decryption oracle does not have to bother with DPA as he can simply break the cryptosystem mathematically. There are indeed use-cases where an attacker can trigger decryption runs but does not get to know the result of the decryption (i.e. DPA can be performed but not chosen-ciphertext attacks), but they are rare. Therefore it is more appropriate to apply masking to a R-LWE-based scheme that is also secure against chosen-ciphertext attackers.

Higher-order security (i.e. security against an attacker with multiple probes) can be achieved using a higher-order masking scheme. However, higher-order masking is usually expensive and therefore in practice it makes sense to combine masking with hiding as higher-order DPA attacks are very susceptible to noise in the power traces.

4.3 Countermeasures Against Fault Attacks

Errors can be intentionally introduced to a system via fault attacks, but they may also arise as a natural consequence of the mathematical constructs of the implementation, for example, calculations that have permissible error rates. When such events occur, an error recovery mechanism will detect the error and instantiate a new calculation. Hence traditional error correction codes can be used for fault error detection (and correction).

The use of the *concurrent error detection (CED)* technique has been proposed so that the normal execution of the algorithm is *suppressed* to avoid any un-intentional leakage of secret values when a fault occurs. One way of doing that is to have duplication of hardware so that in case of a mismatch of results from the two an error detection is reported. Another possibility is re-computation on the same hardware. The first approach is *resource expensive* while the second one has high *execution overhead.* In [5], various countermeasures against fault attacks for software implementations of popular lattice-based signatures are considered. Their effectiveness and overhead is evaluated for schemes including GLP, BLISS, ring-TESLA and GPV-NTRU.

5 CONCLUSIONS AND OUTLOOK

Although lattice based primitives have so far demonstrated resilience against quantum attacks, their implementation on existing commodity hardware and custom hardware will be susceptible to physical attacks. These vulnerabilities need to be addressed before LBC can be considered as a replacement for the public key cryptography suites used today. This work surveys known attacks on LBC constructions including power analysis, timing attacks and fault attacks, all of which could be a potential threat to lattice based implementations. In terms of side channel leakages, power is an important consideration. For software implementations on commodity hardware timing attack vulnerabilities are critical to address since ensuring constant timing for some algorithms, if at all possible, might result in a significant performance penalty.

Most of the countermeasures proposed to date for LBC schemes address a specific threat as they emerge (with no consideration for other threats/ countermeasures simultaneously). Typical hiding/blinding countermeasures include masking, constant time execution, randomization and fault detection. Efforts to benchmark the overhead of one or more of these countermeasures remain limited and are critical to rationalize the practicality of their adoption. There is a wealth of useful techniques to learn from traditional physical attack-resistant cryptographic designs used today but as new lattice-based designs emerge and the volume of their deployment increases, further new attacks will most likely surface and this will continue to be an important area of research going forward.

REFERENCES

[1] Ross Anderson and Markus Kuhn. 1996. Tamper resistance-a cautionary note. In *Proceedings of the second Usenix workshop on electronic commerce*, Vol. 2. 1–11.

[2] Ross Anderson and Markus Kuhn. 1997. Low cost attacks on tamper resistant devices. In *International Workshop on Security Protocols*. Springer, 125–136.

[3] AC Atici, Lejla Batina, Benedikt Gierlichs, and Ingrid Verbauwhede. 2008. Power analysis on NTRU implementations for RFIDs: First results. In *Workshop on RFID Security*. Sl: sn.

[4] Nina Bindel, Johannes Buchmann, and Juliane Krämer. 2016. Lattice-based signature schemes and their sensitivity to fault attacks. In *Fault Diagnosis and Tolerance in Cryptography (FDTC), 2016 Workshop on*. IEEE, 63–77.

[5] Nina Bindel, Juliane Krämer, and Johannes Schreiber. 2017. Hampering fault attacks against lattice-based signature schemes: countermeasures and their efficiency (special session). In *Proceedings of the Twelfth IEEE International Conference on Hardware/Software Codesign and System Synthesis Companion*. ACM, 8.

[6] Joppe W Bos, Craig Costello, Michael Naehrig, and Douglas Stebila. 2015. Post-quantum key exchange for the TLS protocol from the ring learning with errors problem. In *Security and Privacy (SP), 2015 IEEE Symposium on*. IEEE, 553–570.

[7] Leon Groot Bruinderink, Andreas Hülsing, Tanja Lange, and Yuval Yarom. 2016. Flush, Gauss, and Reload–a cache attack on the BLISS lattice-based signature scheme. In *International Conference on Cryptographic Hardware and Embedded Systems*. Springer, 323–345.

[8] CESG. 2016. Quantum Key Distribution: A CESG White Paper. (February 2016). https://www.cesg.gov.uk/white-papers/quantum-key-distribution

[9] CNSS. 2015. Use of Public Standards for the Secure Sharing of Information Among National Security Systems. Committee on National Security Systems: CNSS Advisory Memorandum, Information Assurance 02-15. (July 2015).

[10] Thomas Espitau, Pierre-Alain Fouque, Benoît Gérard, and Mehdi Tibouchi. 2016. Loop-abort faults on lattice-based Fiat-Shamir and hash-and-sign signatures. In *International Conference on Selected Areas in Cryptography*. Springer, 140–158.

[11] Ronald Aylmer Fisher, Frank Yates, et al. 1938. *Statistical tables for biological, agricultural and medical research*. Edinburgh.

[12] Sylvain Guilley, Philippe Hoogvorst, Yves Mathieu, and Renaud Pacalet. 2005. The backend duplication method. In *International Workshop on Cryptographic Hardware and Embedded Systems*. Springer, 383–397.

[13] Tim Güneysu and Tobias Oder. 2017. Towards lightweight Identity-Based Encryption for the post-quantum-secure Internet of Things. In *18th International Symposium on Quality Electronic Design, ISQED 2017, Santa Clara, CA, USA, March 14-15, 2017*. IEEE, 319–324. https://doi.org/10.1109/ISQED.2017.7918335

[14] Jeffrey Hoffstein, Jill Pipher, and Joseph H. Silverman. 1998. NTRU: A Ring-Based Public Key Cryptosystem. In *Algorithmic Number Theory, 1998 (Lecture Notes in Computer Science)*, Joe Buhler (Ed.), Vol. 1423. Springer, 267–288. https://doi.org/10.1007/BFb0054868

[15] James Howe, Ayesha Khalid, Ciara Rafferty, Francesco Regazzoni, and Máire O'Neill. 2016. On Practical Discrete Gaussian Samplers For Lattice-Based Cryptography. *IEEE Trans. Comput.* (2016).

[16] James Howe, Thomas Pöppelmann, Máire O'Neill, Elizabeth O'Sullivan, and Tim Güneysu. 2015. Practical lattice-based digital signature schemes. *ACM Transactions on Embedded Computing Systems (TECS)* 14, 3 (2015), 41.

[17] Abdel Alim Kamal and Amr Youssef. 2011. Fault analysis of the NTRUEncrypt cryptosystem. *IEICE transactions on fundamentals of electronics, communications and computer sciences* 94, 4 (2011), 1156–1158.

[18] Abdel Alim Kamal and Amr M Youssef. 2012. Fault analysis of the NTRUSign digital signature scheme. *Cryptography and Communications* 4, 2 (2012), 131–144.

[19] Abdel Alim Kamal and Amr M Youssef. 2012. A scan-based side channel attack on the NTRUEncrypt cryptosystem. In *Availability, Reliability and Security (ARES), 2012 Seventh International Conference on*. IEEE, 402–409.

[20] Abdel Alim Kamal and Amr M Youssef. 2013. Strengthening hardware implementations of NTRUEncrypt against fault analysis attacks. *Journal of Cryptographic Engineering* 3, 4 (2013), 227–240.

[21] A Khalid, J Howe, C Rafferty, and M O'Neill. 2016. Time-independent discrete Gaussian sampling for post-quantum cryptography. In *Field-Programmable Technology (FPT), 2016 International Conference on*. IEEE, 241–244.

[22] Paul C Kocher. 1996. Timing attacks on implementations of Diffie-Hellman, RSA, DSS, and other systems. In *Annual International Cryptology Conference*. Springer, 104–113.

[23] Mun-Kyu Lee, Jeong Eun Song, Dooho Choi, and Dong-Guk Han. 2010. Countermeasures against power analysis attacks for the NTRU public key cryptosystem. *IEICE Transactions on Fundamentals of Electronics, Communications and Computer Sciences* 93, 1 (2010), 153–163.

[24] Dustin Moody. 2016. Post-Quantum Cryptography: NIST's Plan for the Future. Talk given at PQCrypto '16 Conference, 23-26 February 2016, Fukuoka, Japan. (February 2016). https://pqcrypto2016.jp/data/pqc2016_nist_announcement.pdf

[25] National Security Agency. 2015. Commercial national security algorithm suite. (August 2015). https://www.iad.gov/iad/programs/iad-initiatives/cnsa-suite.cfm

[26] Tobias Oder, Tobias Schneider, Thomas Pöppelmann, and Tim Güneysu. 2018. Practical CCA2-Secure and Masked Ring-LWE Implementation. *IACR Trans. Cryptogr. Hardw. Embed. Syst.* 2018, 1 (2018), 142–174. https://doi.org/10.13154/tches.v2018.i1.142-174

[27] Peter Pessl. 2016. Analyzing the shuffling side-channel countermeasure for lattice-based signatures. In *Progress in Cryptology–INDOCRYPT 2016: 17th International Conference on Cryptology in India, Kolkata, India, December 11-14, 2016, Proceedings 17*. Springer, 153–170.

[28] Peter Pessl, Leon Groot Bruinderink, and Yuval Yarom. 2017. To BLISS-B or not to be: Attacking strongSwan's Implementation of Post-Quantum Signatures. In *Proceedings of the 2017 ACM SIGSAC Conference on Computer and Communications Security*. ACM, 1843–1855.

[29] Thomas Pöppelmann, Michael Naehrig, Andrew Putnam, and Adrián Macías. 2015. Accelerating Homomorphic Evaluation on Reconfigurable Hardware. In *Cryptographic Hardware and Embedded Systems - CHES 2015 - 17th International Workshop, Saint-Malo, France, September 13-16, 2015, Proceedings (Lecture Notes in Computer Science)*, Tim Güneysu and Helena Handschuh (Eds.), Vol. 9293. Springer, 143–163. https://doi.org/10.1007/978-3-662-48324-4_8

[30] Robert Primas, Peter Pessl, and Stefan Mangard. 2017. Single-Trace Side-Channel Attacks on Masked Lattice-Based Encryption. In *Cryptographic Hardware and Embedded Systems - CHES 2017 - 19th International Conference, Taipei, Taiwan, September 25-28, 2017, Proceedings (Lecture Notes in Computer Science)*, Wieland Fischer and Naofumi Homma (Eds.), Vol. 10529. Springer, 513–533. https://doi.org/10.1007/978-3-319-66787-4_25

[31] Francesco Regazzoni, Thomas Eisenbarth, Luca Breveglieri, Paolo Ienne, and Israel Koren. 2008. Can knowledge regarding the presence of countermeasures against fault attacks simplify power attacks on cryptographic devices?. In *Defect and Fault Tolerance of VLSI Systems, 2008. DFTVS'08. IEEE International Symposium on*. IEEE, 202–210.

[32] Francesco Regazzoni, Thomas Eisenbarth, Johann Grossschadl, and Luca Breveglieri. 2007. Power attacks resistance of cryptographic s-boxes with added error detection circuits. In *Defect and Fault-Tolerance in VLSI Systems, 2007. DFT'07. 22nd IEEE International Symposium on*. IEEE, 508–516.

[33] Oscar Reparaz, Ruan de Clercq, Sujoy Sinha Roy, Frederik Vercauteren, and Ingrid Verbauwhede. 2016. *Additively Homomorphic Ring-LWE Masking*. Springer International Publishing, Cham, 233–244.

[34] Oscar Reparaz, Sujoy Sinha Roy, Frederik Vercauteren, and Ingrid Verbauwhede. 2015. *A Masked Ring-LWE Implementation*. Springer Berlin Heidelberg, Berlin, Heidelberg, 683–702.

[35] Steven Rich and Barton Gellman. January 2014. NSA seeks to build quantum computer that could crack most types of encryption. *The Washington Post* (January 2014). https://www.washingtonpost.com/world/national-security/nsa-seeks-to-build-quantum-computer-that-could-crack-most-types-of-encryption/2014/01/02/8fff297e-7195-11e3-8def-a33011492df2_story.html

[36] Sujoy Sinha Roy, Oscar Reparaz, Frederik Vercauteren, and Ingrid Verbauwhede. 2014. Compact and Side Channel Secure Discrete Gaussian Sampling. Cryptology ePrint Archive, Report 2014/591. *ePrint Report 2014/591* (2014). https://eprint.iacr.org/2014/591.

[37] Sujoy Sinha Roy, Frederik Vercauteren, and Ingrid Verbauwhede. 2013. High Precision Discrete Gaussian Sampling on FPGAs. In *SAC*. 1–39. https://www.cosic.esat.kuleuven.be/publications/article-2372.pdf

[38] Markku-Juhani O. Saarinen. 2016. Arithmetic Coding and Blinding Countermeasures for Ring-LWE. *IACR Cryptology ePrint Archive* 2016 (2016), 276. http://eprint.iacr.org/2016/276

[39] P.W. Shor. 1994. Algorithms for quantum computation: discrete logarithms and factoring. *Proceedings 35th Annual Symposium on Foundations of Computer Science* (1994), .

[40] Joseph H Silverman and William Whyte. 2007. Timing attacks on NTRUEncrypt via variation in the number of hash calls. In *Cryptographers' Track at the RSA Conference*. Springer, 208–224.

[41] Sergei Petrovich Skorobogatov. 2005. *Semi-invasive attacks: a new approach to hardware security analysis*. Ph.D. Dissertation. Citeseer.

[42] Sergei P Skorobogatov and Ross J Anderson. 2002. Optical fault induction attacks. In *International Workshop on Cryptographic Hardware and Embedded Systems*. Springer, 2–12.

[43] Mohit Tiwari, Xun Li, Hassan MG Wassel, Bita Mazloom, Shashidhar Mysore, Frederic T Chong, and Timothy Sherwood. 2010. Gate-level information-flow tracking for secure architectures. *IEEE Micro* 30, 1 (2010).

[44] Felipe Valencia, Tobias Oder, Tim Güneysu, and Francesco Regazzoni. 2018. Exploring the Vulnerability of R-LWE Encryption to Fault Attacks. *5th Workshop on Cryptography and Security in Computing Systems - Workshop - HiPEAC* (2018).

[45] Nikolay Vasilev Vizev. 2007. *Side Channel Attacks on NTRUEncrypt*. Ph.D. Dissertation. Bachelor's thesis, Technical University of Darmstadt, Germany, 2007. Available on http://www. cdc. informatik. tu-darmstadt. de/reports/reports/Nikolay_Vizev. bachelor. pdf.

[46] An Wang, Xuexin Zheng, and Zongyue Wang. 2013. Power analysis attacks and countermeasures on NTRU-based wireless body area networks. *KSII Transactions on Internet and Information Systems (TIIS)* 7, 5 (2013), 1094–1107.

Post-Quantum Cryptography on FPGAs: The Niederreiter Cryptosystem

Extended Abstract

Wen Wang
Yale University
New Haven, CT, USA
wen.wang.ww349@yale.edu

Jakub Szefer
Yale University
New Haven, CT, USA
jakub.szefer@yale.edu

Ruben Niederhagen
Fraunhofer SIT
Darmstadt, Germany
ruben@polycephaly.org

ABSTRACT

Our invited presentation will give an introduction to major hardware building blocks needed to implement code-based cryptographic systems. We will present details of a modern, FPGA-based, constant-time implementation of the Niederreiter cryptosystem using binary Goppa codes, including modules for encryption, decryption, and key generation. The presentation will also include a brief summary of other existing implementations of code-based cryptographic systems and it will present research challenges for implementing such systems efficiently.

Currently, there are five promising classes of post-quantum cryptographic algorithms: hash-based, code-based, lattice-based, multivariate, and isogeny-based cryptography. Our work focuses on code-base cryptography, specifically the Niederreiter cryptosystem using binary Goppa codes. The main design challenge within code-based cryptosystems is the tension between cryptographic parameters (i.e., security level) and practical aspects, e.g., the size of keys and computation speed, resulting from the chosen parameters.

The core of the presentation will focus on the FPGA implementation of our binary Goppa code-based Niederreiter cryptosystem, including modules for encryption, decryption, and key generation [2, 3]. We will show how to make the design constant-time in order to protect against timing side-channel analysis and how to make the design fully parameterized in order to support a wide range of parameter choices for security, including binary field size, the degree of the Goppa polynomial, and the code length. The parameterized design also allows users to choose design parameters for time-area trade-offs in order to support a large variety of applications ranging from smart cards to server accelerators. For parameters that are considered to provide "128-bit post-quantum security" (i.e., the cost of an attack on a quantum computer is assumed to be at least 2^{128} quantum operations), our time-optimized implementation requires 966,400 cycles for the generation of both public and private portions of a key and 14,291 cycles to decrypt a ciphertext. The time-optimized design uses only 121,806 ALMs (52% of the available logic) and 961 RAM blocks (38% of the available memory), and results in a design that runs at about 250 MHz on a medium-size Stratix V FPGA (5SGXEA7N).

To achieve this efficient design, a number of building blocks were needed: Gaussian systemizers for matrix systemizations [1], Gao-Mateer additive FFT for polynomial evaluations, a merge-sort module for generating uniformly distributed permutations, and a constant-time Berlekamp-Massey module for decoding [2, 3]. Reasons for making these design choices will be covered in the presentation as well.

Given the increasing interest in code-based cryptography, a number of projects have been focusing on the hardware implementation of the Niederreiter cryptosystem. We will present the performance of our entire Niederreiter cryptosystem with "128-bit post-quantum security" and compare our design with other existing FPGA-based implementations. Prior works have not reached the security level of our design, and this presentation will highlight design choices which allow for achieving a high-security design, while maintaining efficiency. Our current work is the fastest design to date, beating prior FPGA work and optimized CPU-based implementations on recent processors. Based on insights from our work, the presentation will show how to design flexible hardware cores that can be easily configured for different security levels and performance targets.

GLSVLSI '18, May 23–25, 2018, Chicago, IL, USA

ACM ISBN 978-1-4503-5724-1/18/05...$15.00
https://doi.org/10.1145/3194554.3194617

KEYWORDS

Post-Quantum Cryptography, Code-Based Cryptography, Niederreiter Cryptosystem, FPGA, Hardware Implementation.

ACM Reference Format:
Wen Wang, Jakub Szefer, and Ruben Niederhagen. 2018. Post-Quantum Cryptography on FPGAs: The Niederreiter Cryptosystem: Extended Abstract. In *GLSVLSI '18: 2018 Great Lakes Symposium on VLSI, May 23–25, 2018, Chicago, IL, USA.* ACM, New York, NY, USA, 1 page. https://doi.org/10.1145/3194554.3194617

ACKNOWLEDGMENTS

This work was supported in part by United States' National Science Foundation grant 1716541.

REFERENCES

[1] Wen Wang, Jakub Szefer, and Ruben Niederhagen. 2016. Solving Large Systems of Linear Equations over GF(2) on FPGAs. In *Reconfigurable Computing and FPGAs – ReConFig 2016.* IEEE, 1–7.

[2] Wen Wang, Jakub Szefer, and Ruben Niederhagen. 2017. FPGA-based Key Generator for the Niederreiter Cryptosystem Using Binary Goppa Codes. In *CHES 2017 (LNCS),* Wieland Fischer and Naofumi Homma (Eds.), Vol. 10529. Springer, Heidelberg, 253–274.

[3] Wen Wang, Jakub Szefer, and Ruben Niederhagen. 2018. FPGA-based Niederreiter Cryptosystem using Binary Goppa Codes. In *International Workshop on Post-Quantum Cryptography – PQCrypto 2018.*

Going Small: Using the Insect Brain as a Model System for Edge Processing Applications

Angel Yanguas-Gil
Energy Systems Division, Argonne National Laboratory
Lemont, Illinois
ayg@anl.gov

ABSTRACT

In this work I explore bio-inspired architectures for adaptive and smart sensing incorporating two key aspects present on the insect brain that are not found in more traditional neural network approaches: modulated, hierarchical processing and modulated learning. Our architecture incorporates two central ideas: 1) a state-dependent processing of inputs that can be triggered internally or externally, and 2) state-dependent online learning capabilities, in this specific case allowing the system to change the valence associated to different types of input. These ideas are explored through a hybrid design in which information is processed through a spiking neural network, while a recurrent non-spiking component provides the modulatory feedback to the system. The proposed approach exemplifies how neuromorphic computing approaches naturally integrate sensing and processing within a single functional unit. The proposed architecture can be implemented using conventional VLSI processing, though the integration of novel materials can help simplify its implementation.

CCS CONCEPTS

• **Theory of computation** → **Reinforcement learning**; • **Computer systems organization** → **Neural networks**; • **Computing methodologies** → *Logical and relational learning*; • **Hardware** → *Sensor devices and platforms*; *Analog and mixed-signal circuits*; *VLSI design manufacturing considerations*;

KEYWORDS

neuromorphic computing; spiking neural networks; online learning; smart sensors; neuromodulation;insect brain

ACM Reference Format:
Angel Yanguas-Gil. 2018. Going Small: Using the Insect Brain as a Model System for Edge Processing Applications. In *Proceedings of ACM Great Lakes Symposium on VLSI (GLVLSI)*. ACM, New York, NY, USA, 6 pages. https://doi.org/10.1145/3194554.3194610

ACM 978-1-4503-5724-1/18/05...$15.00
https://doi.org/10.1145/3194554.3194610

1 INTRODUCTION

Insects can be viewed as complex, smart sensors able to carry out multiparallel input processing and integration. For instance, the honeybee has 60,000 receptors just in its olfactory system. With an increasingly large body of research consistent with the presence of a complex internal state, [5, 9] they also exhibit remarkable learning capabilities and consume a small amount of power, with a small number of neurons. These properties makes them a fantastic example of how to achieve complex functionality through limited resources. Understanding the design principles of the insect brain and how they can be translated into hardware can therefore be valuable for edge processing and the design of smart sensors that are broadly trained to operate on a changing environment.

An increasing body of research is supporting the idea that the connectome is just one aspect of what provides the functionality to central neural systems: other types of interactions, both through local modulatory interactions, and through volume release of neurotransmitters and neuropeptides, play a central role in modifying the behavior and activity of neurons.[3, 9, 12] A second important role of modulatory signals is regulating online and reinforcement learning, where synaptic weights are reinforced only in presence of a trigger signal.[2]

These ideas can have important implications in how we can design edge processing architectures inspired on neuromorphic systems: from a mathematical point of view, the implication is that rather than a functional transformation between input and output, neural systems could behave as time-dependent *programmable networks*, where an internal state of the system, in the form of local and volume modulatory interactions, controls the the transformation between input and output. This provides an interesting avenue to explore the extension of the concept of programming to neuromorphic architectures, where a sequence of inputs allow us to dynamically control the way information is processed. These principles can also lead to simplified, smaller designs, for instance through the combination of modulation and binary synaptic weights, or by providing a simple way of reusing substructures to perform different tasks. As an example, the network shown in Figure 1 establishes a connectivity pattern for carrying out AND, XOR, and OR operations on the same network based on the modulation of its different neurons.

The olfactive systems of invertebrates is an interesting example of an architecture that takes advantage of modulatory interactions to process information. In Figure 2 we show a scheme of the architecture of the olfactive system of an invertebrate. The antennal lobe acts as the entry level structure of information processing. It is composed of a set of discrete units called glomeruli formed by the synapses between olfactive receptive neurons (ORN) and relay

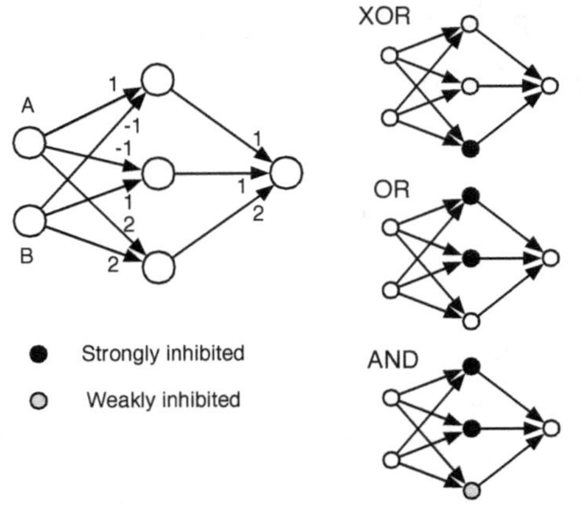

Figure 1: How modulation can drive functionality: a single neural network (left) shows three distinct functionalities when neurons are externally modulated

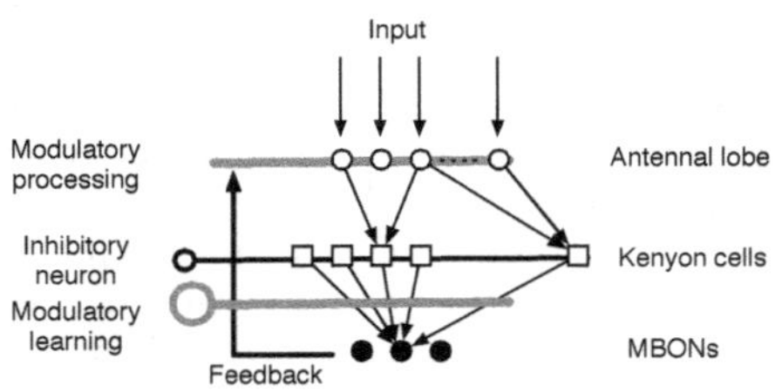

Figure 2: Summary of the early stages of the olfactive system of a higher vertebrate. The parallel processing path to the lateral horn has been removed for simplicity

neurons called projection neurons that take the information into two higher level systems, the mushroom body and the lateral horn (not shown in Figure 2). The antennal lobe is the site of *stateful inhibition*: a set of lateral neurons, which are inhibitory in character, modulate and control the way this information is relayed.[4] The activity of these neurons are themselves modulated through a series of modulatory inputs. The lateral horn has been linked to innate responses, whereas the mushroom body is the site of olfactive learning.[1]

In this work I focus on architectures that incorporate this type of modulation to control information processing. We have implemented heterogeneous architectures involving a fast, spiking component and a slower, modulatory component responsible for two types of modulatory interactions: neuron-level modulation, and neuron-synaptic weight interactions. Our ultimate goal is to understand how to build systems that show adaptive behavior and are broadly trained to perform on a changing environment, and the impact that design choices made at a design stage have on the performance and limitation of such devices.

2 MODEL

The focus of our work are heterogeneous architectures formed by two coupled systems, one responding at a fast scale, in this case implemented as spiking neurons, and a second one reacting at a slower timescale, modulating the performance of the network at the neuron and/or synaptic weight levels, implemented as a non-spiking recurrent system.

2.1 State-based implementation of spiking neurons

Since our goal is to explore architectures that mimic those of biological systems, it is important for us to keep the fundamental aspects of biological systems. However, one of the challenges is how to transform an asynchronous network of analog devices into a physically equivalent model that functions in a synchronous way, respects the analog aspects of the internal state of the neuron, and yet it may be compatible with existing VLSI capabilities. Our approach was to explore a synchronous, recurrent, yet accurate representation of a leaky integrate and fire model.

One of the standard models of spiking neurons is the leaky integrate and fire model, where the neuron dynamics is captured by the following differential equation:[6]

$$\tau \frac{dv_i}{dt} = -v_i + \sum_j w_{ji}\delta(t - t_j) + v_{\text{ext}}^{(i)} \tag{1}$$

Here v_i is the neuron potential, w_{ji} are the different synaptic weights, t_j the firing times of presynaptic neurons, τ controls the leakage of the potential, and $v_{\text{ext}}^{(i)}$ represents other external inputs to the neuron. When the membrane potential reaches the threshold voltage v_0, the neuron spikes, the voltage resets, and the neuron is non-responsive to inputs during an absolute refractory period τ_r.

$$v_i(t) = 1 \Rightarrow v_i(t + t') = 0 \quad \forall \quad t' < \tau_r \tag{2}$$

Our approach takes advantage of the fact that during any time interval $\Delta t \leq \tau_r$ a neuron can spike only once. We can therefore discretize Eq. 1 by integrating over Δt. This allows us to express the output of each neuron during each interval as a binary variable $s_i = 0, 1$

In order to transform the firing times t_j of the neurons projecting into our neuron into time steps n_i, so that $n_j\Delta t \geq t_j < (n_j + 1)\Delta t$, we assume that t_j is homogeneously distributed within that interval: $P(t_j) = \frac{1}{\Delta t}$. Through his approximation we lose any information on the firing times at time scales smaller than Δt. However, as we'll show in the next section the penalty for this is small. This allows us to formulate Eq. 1 as:

$$\begin{aligned} v_i(n) &= (1 - s_i(n-1))\left[\xi_i(n)\left(1 - e^{-1/\tau_m}\right)\right. \\ &\quad \left. + v_i(n-1)e^{-1/\tau_m}\right] \\ &\quad + s_i(n-1)\xi_i(n)\left(1 - \tau_m(1 - e^{-1/\tau_m})\right) \\ s_i(n) &= H(v_i(n) - v_{0i}) \\ \xi_i(n) &= v_{\text{ext}}^{(i)} + \sum_j \frac{w_{ji}}{\tau_r} s_j(n - n_{ji}) \end{aligned} \tag{3}$$

where $H(\cdot)$ is the Heaviside or step function.

The state of a neuron is therefore characterized by a set of two parameters, s_i and v_i: $s_i = 0, 1$ depending on whether the neuron is spiking at that time step, and v_i is the (analog) value of membrane potential. In addition there are several parameters controlling the behavior of the neuron: τ_m is the neuron time constant normalized to the absolute refractory period, and v_{0i} is the firing threshold voltage.

The two terms, one proportional to $(1 - s_i)$ and another to s_i, in Eq. 3 are due to the presence of the absolute refractory period on the evolution of the membrane potential v_i: if the neuron spiked in the prior interval, it will be receptive to input only during a fraction of the next time interval.

If we neglect the impact of the refractory period that we just mentioned from Eq. 3, the recurrence relation for v_i simplifies to:

$$\begin{aligned} v_i(n) &= \left(1 - e^{-1/\tau_m}\right) \xi_i(n) \\ &\quad + ((1 - s_i(n-1))\, v_i(n-1) e^{-1/\tau_m} \\ s_i(n) &= H(v_i(n) - v_{0i}) \\ \xi_i(n) &= v_{\text{ext}}^{(i)} + \sum_j \frac{w_{ji}}{\tau_r} s_j(n - n_{ji}) \end{aligned} \tag{4}$$

Eq. 4 represents a recurrent version of the classic McCulloch-Pitts model. [11] If we can neglect the memory effect on the neuron the classic model is recovered.

2.2 Modulatory interactions

2.2.1 Modulatory processing. The focus of modulated processing is the ability to tune the way input data is processed depending on a state, as shown in the trivial example from Figure 1. A central assumption in our model is that the temporal scale of modulatory interactions is slower than that of spiking neurons. We can then model these slower, modulatory interactions as recurrent systems, so that

$$x(n+1) = \frac{a_i(n)\tau_m + x(n)}{1 + \tau_m} \tag{5}$$

where a_i can be both external or through direct integration of spikes.

This modulatory component can interact with the spiking component in our model in four possible ways: 1) through changes on the threshold voltage v_0 2) through and additional input to the neuron 3) through changes in the characteristic response time of the neuron τ, and 4) through the modulation of all postsynaptic weights.

A key advantage of modulatory processing is that it scales linearly with the number of neurons and not with the number of synapses. They also allow us to build systems that may be flexible yet have fixed or binary connectivity, which can greatly simplify their implementation.

2.2.2 Modulated learning. Spike timing dependent plasticity has been by far the most explored learning approach for spiking neural networks. However, this is not the unique mechanism available. In the case of insects, it has been demonstrated that modulated learning is one of the underlying mechanisms for the acquisition of new knowledge: in the insect brain, the activity of clusters of modulatory neurons correlates with the strengthening of synaptic weights.[1, 2] If in spike timing dependent plasticity the synaptic strength W_{AB} between two neurons A and B is a function of their activity: $W_{\text{AB}} = f(\text{A}, \text{B})$, in the case of modulated learning, the synaptic strength is a function of the pre-synaptic neuron and a *third* neuron C: $W_{\text{AB}} = f(\text{A}, \text{C})$, and optionally the post-synaptic neuron as well in the case of modulated STDP. This provides a substrate to integrate logic and memory through dynamic plasticity: we can actuate learning or strengthen certain pathways by the action of a third input.

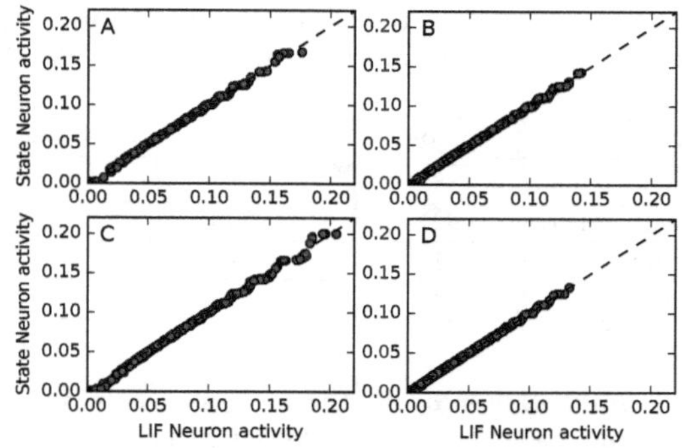

Figure 3: Correlation between the standard LIF model and the state model of a spiking neuron used in this work

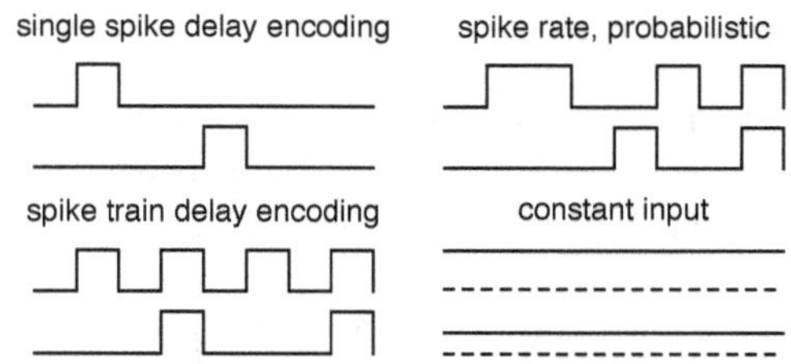

Figure 4: Different encodings implemented in this work

3 RESULTS

3.1 The state based network is functionally equivalent to the asynchronous LIF

In order to understand the impact of our synchronous approximation to a leaky integrate and fire model, we have compared the activity pattern of our model and asynchronous model for a series of randomly connected networks subject to a random set of inputs. In Figure 3 we show the correlation between the activity of a leaky integrate and fire modeled following equation 1 and its corresponding state representation given by Eq. 3.

The correlation between the two models is excellent, indicating that the loss of information of the exact firing times does not negatively impact its functionality for a broad set of conditions. In particular, this allows us to extract the lessons from prior exhaustive studies on the leaky integrate and fire neurons to a recurrent, synchronous model.[6]

3.2 The learning ability of spiking networks is equivalent to non-spiking analog

In order to explore the ability of different encodings to learn and discriminate between different inputs we have used the state model introduced above to benchmark the performance of a shallow network against the MNIST dataset. We have considered the following four types of encoding (Figure 4):

(1) *Single spike delay encoding.* In this case the input is codified as a single spike whose delay with respect to a common epoch decreases with the input intensity.

Table 1: MNIST test accuracy: results for a shallow spiking architecture for different types of encodings and outputs. The state of the art for similar shallow systems is 93%[10]

Encoding	Sigmoidal	Binary non-excl.	Binary excl.
Single spike delay	88%	83%	65%
Spike train delay	90%	90%	87%
Spike rate, prob	91%	91%	87%
Constant	88%	83%	65%

(2) *Spike train delay encoding.* The single spikes from the time encoding are subsequently followed by a periodic train of spikes spaced by an interval equal to the time delay.
(3) *spike rate, probabilistic.* The spiking neurons are fed a constant input proportional to the intensity of each pixel in the input data.
(4) *Constant analog input.* The input is codified as constant input signal.

For each of the proposed encodings, we applied a stochastic gradient descent method to optimize our networks using a cost function that optimized the total number of spikes:

$$C = \frac{1}{N}\sum_i \left(\sum_m a_i(m) - n_i\right)^2 \quad (6)$$

regardless of when those spikes took place.

The results show testing accuracies as high as 90%. This compares well with state of the art results for shallow (no hidden layers) neural networks.[10] In particular, if we optimize a shallow network of non-spiking sigmoidal neurons using the same cost function and stochastic gradient descent method, the resulting accuracy is 91%, as shown in Table 1. If we switch back to a binary output, the differences between the different encodings become more pronounced. The non-exclusive accuracy column includes all cases where the correct digit achieves the maximum number of spikes, regardless of whether other digits also achieves the same number of spikes. In contrast, the exclusive accuracy column considers only those cases where no other digits achieve the maximum number of spikes. The need to distinguish between these to cases comes from the fact that the output is measured in terms of the number of spikes, so two neurons can have identical outputs. According to the results obtained, the single spike encoding's testing (exclusive) accuracy drops below 70%. In contrast, both the spike train time delay and the probabilistic spike rate encodings maintain a high testing accuracy with binary outputs.

3.3 Modulated processing and learning: some simple examples

At a neuron level, the main effect of postsynaptic modulation is to change the transfer function of the neuron from a linear device to a rectified type of transfer function as we reduce postsynaptic modulation. This is shown in Figure 5.

More interesting, we can use modulation to control perception based on expectations. In Figure 6 we show the averaged spike rate of a convolutional layer of a spiking network tracking an array of pixels for 8 consecutive sequences in which an object is moving

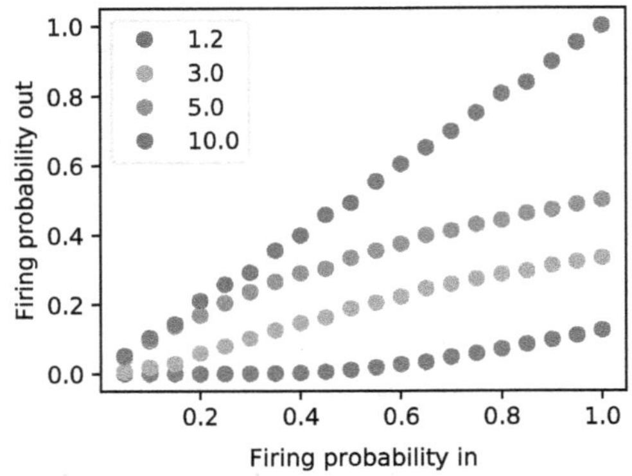

Figure 5: Impact of post-synaptic modulation on the transfer function of a neuron

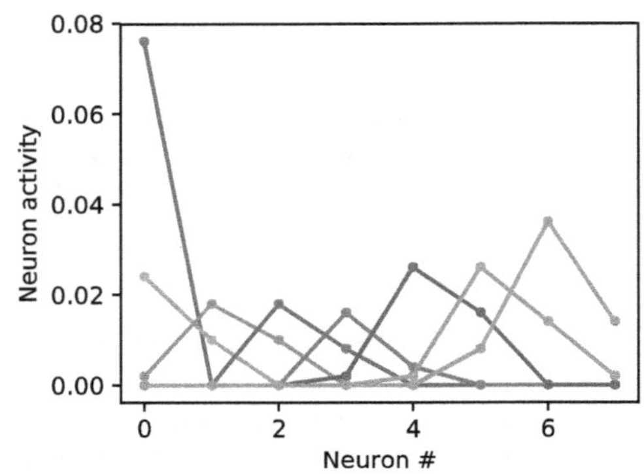

Figure 6: Averaged activity of spiking neurons pooling input from a series of aligned receptive fields.: a reduction on input quality causes a reduction of the activity

from left to right. If we degrade the quality of the input by removing 50% of the spikes after an initial step, the response of the system is, as expected, affected. In contrast, if the activity of this layer is modulated by the expectation that an object is present and moving rightwards, under the same degraded conditions the network is able to successfully track the object, as shown in Fig. 7.

For modulatory learning, we have first explored the case of an agent moving over a 2D space receiving a series of spatially correlated input data. For this particular example we consider a series of point sources randomly distributed over a 2D map (Figure 8). These can be interpreted as either specific set of pulses or frequencies, in the case of radio or visual navigation, or it can be series of molecular signals, for instance different odors. We consider that the intensity of these pulses decay with distance following a gaussian profile.

Our network is a three layer network that mimics the architecture described in Figure 1, with a fan out - fan in architecture that maps input signals to a larger dimensional space through a highly sparse connectivity, which then fans-in to a set of drivers that the system uses to decide when and how to respond. The agent carries out a random walk over the map with a dwell time that is modulated

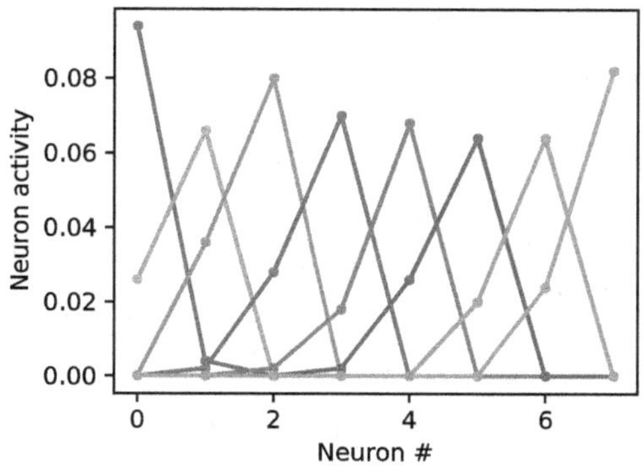

Figure 7: Averaged activity of spiking neurons pooling input from a series of aligned receptive fields: predictive modulation at a neuron level enhances the system's ability to track an object even when the input quality has been severely degraded

by the valence associated to the input. A positive valence leads to longer dwell times during the random walk.

As shown in Figure 8, in absence of modulatory input the dwell time is homogeneously distributed on the map. In order to train the system to spend more time at a preferred location, we introduced a modulatory signal that strengthen the positive response with a certain probability p_0 whenever the agent is within a certain region. A feedback path ensures that, once the system has learned the desired response, the modulatory neuron becomes inactive and the synaptic weights are no longer updated. The system remembers the valence associated to the input, and this alters its behavior. This is shown in Figure 8, where through the use of modulatory signals we can make the system spend more time on desired locations in the map.

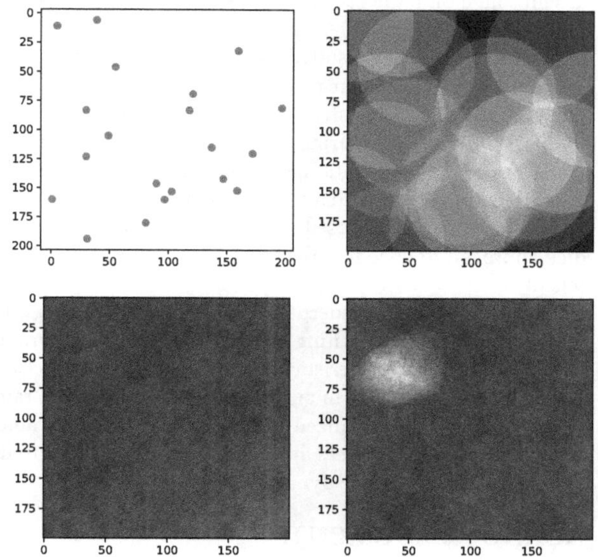

Figure 8: Aggregated dwell times of an agent carrying out a random walk over a 2D map. Top left: spatial distribution of source points providing the input of the system. Top right: fraction of action Kenyon cells as a function of the position. Bottom left: Dwell time distribution in absence of reinforcement. Bottom right: Dwell time distribution after on-line reinforcement of the central position of the map, showing an increase of dwell time close of the excitation area in the top left quadrant.

4 DISCUSSION AND CONCLUSIONS

In the previous section we have introduced two simple examples of systems incorporating modulatory interactions. In the case of neuron-level modulation, it provides a way of controlling functionality without having to introduce drastic changes on the system's connectivity. In principle, the use of neuron-level modulation provides a pathway toward adaptability and programmability that scales linearly with the number of neurons rather than the number of connections. One of the tantalizing possibilities of such type of neuron-level interactions is that it enhances the flexibility of neural network with binary synaptic weights, which would allow to store the network's connectivity as a single bit, reducing the complexity of cross-bar architectures or the size of lookup tables. One of our current areas of research is the design of optimization algorithms for such hybrid architectures, with digital/binary connectivity and continuously varying parameters modulating system performance at a neuron level.

Modulated learning provides a simple yet powerful physical implementation of reinforcement learning. A key advantage of this approach is that it can be readily implemented using existing floating-gate type of technology, as it was already advanced by Mead and collaborators.[7] The use of neurons with binary outputs also simplifies the design of such elements, since they would always operate at a similar DC point, and it is based on local information. Reinforcement learning presents significant advantages for implementations based on memristive type of devices. In the case of our random walker mentioned in the previous section, reinforcement is shut off once a desired level of response is achieved. This means that variabilities at a device performance can be eliminated by the incorporation of such internal feedback loops. In this context we have also explored how to implement real online learning using memristors in a way that it does not interfere with the constant processing of input data: we have found that the combination of voltage-controlled devices with a clear threshold and the use of selector devices preventing current inversion is critical to minimize the cross-talk between sensing and modulated learning.

Our results show that spiking neurons can be as efficient as non-spiking approaches in terms of learning. In particular, in as few as 8 cycles it is possible to achieve accuracies that are as good as the equivalent non-spiking architectures, at least for the case of shallow systems. Consequently, while there is always going to be a trade-off between binary spiking and analog non-spiking systems from a design standpoint, the use of binary spikes do not necessarily lead to a loss in performance. An additional aspect of spiking systems is that they are ideally suited for the processing of pulsed and sparse input streams. Our results also show that performance in fairly insensitive to the structure of the spike trains. This opens the possibility of considering both periodic spike generators, for instance through conventional numerically controlled oscillators, or stochastic generators that take advantage of novel devices, such as spin-torque stochastic oscillators, using concepts such as the spin dice approach to encode inputs as stochastic streams of random bits.[8]

Finally, a key design aspect that makes edge processing different from conventional computing is that the relevant temporal range, and therefore the characteristic time of our *neuromorphic clock* Δt is driven by the input data. In our model, all the relevant parameters of the neuron are normalized to Δt. Consequently, the ability to modulate these parameters at a neuron level enable us to design systems with an adaptive dynamic range.

ACKNOWLEDGMENTS

This material is based upon work supported by Laboratory Directed Research and Development (LDRD) funding from Argonne National Laboratory, provided by the Director, Office of Science, of the U.S. Department of Energy under Contract No. DE-AC02-06CH11357

REFERENCES

[1] Yoshinori Aso, Daisuke Hattori, Yang Yu, Rebecca M. Johnston, Nirmala A. Iyer, Teri-TB Ngo, Heather Dionne, L. F. Abbott, Richard Axel, Hiromu Tanimoto, and Gerald M. Rubin. 2014. The neuronal architecture of the mushroom body provides a logic for associative learning. *eLife* 3 (Dec. 2014), e04577. https://doi.org/10.7554/eLife.04577

[2] Yoshinori Aso, Divya Sitaraman, Toshiharu Ichinose, Karla R. Kaun, Katrin Vogt, Ghislain Belliart-Guérin, Pierre-Yves Plaçais, Alice A. Robie, Nobuhiro Yamagata, Christopher Schnaitmann, William J. Rowell, Rebecca M. Johnston, Teri-T. B. Ngo, Nan Chen, Wyatt Korff, Michael N. Nitabach, Ulrike Heberlein, Thomas Preat, Kristin M. Branson, Hiromu Tanimoto, and Gerald M. Rubin. 2014. Mushroom body output neurons encode valence and guide memory-based action selection in Drosophila. *eLife* 3 (Dec. 2014), e04580. https://doi.org/10.7554/eLife.04580

[3] Cornelia I. Bargmann. 2012. Beyond the connectome: How neuromodulators shape neural circuits. *Bioessays* 34, 6 (June 2012), 458–465. https://doi.org/10.1002/bies.201100185

[4] Matthew E. Berck, Avinash Khandelwal, Lindsey Claus, Luis Hernandez-Nunez, Guangwei Si, Christopher J. Tabone, Feng Li, James W. Truman, Rick D. Fetter, Matthieu Louis, Aravinthan DT Samuel, and Albert Cardona. 2016. The wiring diagram of a glomerular olfactory system. *eLife* 5 (May 2016), e14859. https://doi.org/10.7554/eLife.14859

[5] Gordon J. Berman, William Bialek, and Joshua W. Shaevitz. 2016. Predictability and hierarchy in Drosophila behavior. *PNAS* 113, 42 (Oct. 2016), 11943–11948. https://doi.org/10.1073/pnas.1607601113

[6] Nicolas Brunel. 2000. Dynamics of Sparsely Connected Networks of Excitatory and Inhibitory Spiking Neurons. *Journal of Computational Neuroscience* 8, 3 (01 May 2000), 183–208. https://doi.org/10.1023/A:1008925309027

[7] C. Diorio, P. Hasler, A. Minch, and C. A. Mead. 1996. A single-transistor silicon synapse. *IEEE Transactions on Electron Devices* 43, 11 (Nov 1996), 1972–1980. https://doi.org/10.1109/16.543035

[8] Akio Fukushima, Takayuki Seki, Kay Yakushiji, Hitoshi Kubota, Hiroshi Imamura, Shinji Yuasa, and Koji Ando. 2014. Spin dice: A scalable truly random number generator based on spintronics. *Applied Physics Express* 7, 8 (2014), 083001. http://stacks.iop.org/1882-0786/7/i=8/a=083001

[9] Kang I Ko, Cory M Root, Scott A Lindsay, Orel A Zaninovich, Andrew K Shepherd, Steven A Wasserman, Susy M Kim, and Jing W Wang. 2015. Starvation promotes concerted modulation of appetitive olfactory behavior via parallel neuromodulatory circuits. *eLife* 4 (jul 2015), e08298. https://doi.org/10.7554/eLife.08298

[10] Y. Lecun, L. Bottou, Y. Bengio, and P. Haffner. 1998. Gradient-based learning applied to document recognition. *Proc. IEEE* 86, 11 (Nov 1998), 2278–2324. https://doi.org/10.1109/5.726791

[11] Warren S. McCulloch and Walter Pitts. 1943. A logical calculus of the ideas immanent in nervous activity. *The bulletin of mathematical biophysics* 5, 4 (01 Dec 1943), 115–133. https://doi.org/10.1007/BF02478259

[12] Dick R. Nässel and Åsa M. E. Winther. 2010. Drosophila neuropeptides in regulation of physiology and behavior. *Progress in Neurobiology* 92, 1 (Sept. 2010), 42–104. https://doi.org/10.1016/j.pneurobio.2010.04.010

Energy and Area Efficiency in Neuromorphic Computing for Resource Constrained Devices

Gangotree Chakma, Nicholas D. Skuda
University of Tennessee
Knoxville, TN
[gchakma,nskuda]@utk.edu

Catherine D. Schuman
Oak Ridge National Laboratory
Oak Ridge, TN
schumancd@ornl.gov

James S. Plank, Mark E. Dean, and Garrett S. Rose
University of Tennessee
Knoxville, TN
[jplank,markdean,garose]@utk.edu

ABSTRACT

Resource constrained devices are the building blocks of the internet of things (IoT) era. Since the idea behind IoT is to develop an interconnected environment where the devices are tiny enough to operate with limited resources, several control systems have been built to maintain low energy and area consumption while operating as IoT edge devices. Several researchers have begun work on implementing control systems built from resource constrained devices using machine learning. However, there are many ways such devices can achieve lower power consumption and area utilization while maximizing application efficiency. Spiky neuromorphic computing (SNC) is an emerging paradigm that can be leveraged in resource constrained devices for several emerging applications. While delivering the benefits of machine learning, SNC also helps minimize power consumption. For example, low energy memory devices (memristors) are often used to achieve low power operation and also help in reducing system area. In total, we anticipate SNC will provide computational efficiency approaching that of deep learning while using low power, resource constrained devices.

CCS CONCEPTS

• **Computer systems organization → Neural networks**; **Embedded hardware**;

KEYWORDS

Neuromorphic; memristor; internet of things; machine learning

ACM Reference Format:
Gangotree Chakma, Nicholas D. Skuda, Catherine D. Schuman, and James S. Plank, Mark E. Dean, and Garrett S. Rose. 2018. Energy and Area Efficiency in Neuromorphic Computing for Resource Constrained Devices. In *GLSVLSI '18: 2018 Great Lakes Symposium on VLSI, May 23–25, 2018, Chicago, IL, USA.* ACM, New York, NY, USA, Article 4, 5 pages. https://doi.org/10.1145/3194554.3194611

ACM ISBN 978-1-4503-5724-1/18/05...$15.00
https://doi.org/10.1145/3194554.3194611

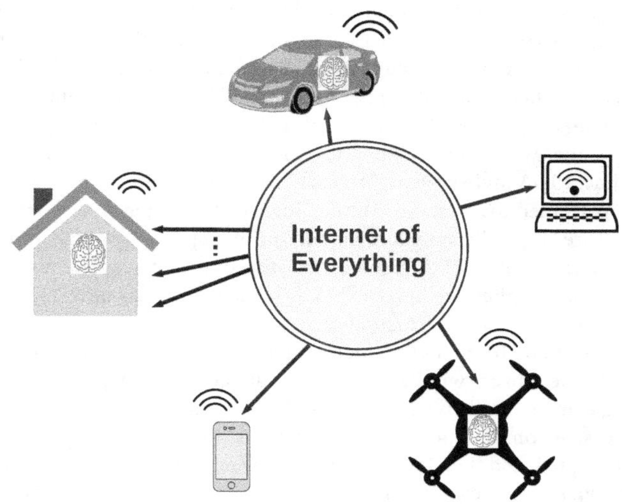

Figure 1: Neuromorphic computing in IoT edge devices.

1 INTRODUCTION

Internet of things applications (IoT) (Fig. 1) are emerging in which many resource constrained devices that compose such systems can benefit from machine learning capabilities. For example, autonomous drone applications can include simple neural networks which actively learn and adapt to subtle variations that will occur as they navigate their environment. Such capability can be particularly advantageous for applications where the drones are used to search for survivors in a disaster zone (e.g., a collapsed building), to provide one example. While such capability would certainly be advantageous, a real challenge exists in providing such on-the-fly learning in systems with limited area and power supply.

Several recent works have explored how deep learning neural networks can be leveraged for resource constrained systems. For example, Leroux *et al.* specifically demonstrated how cascaded neural network layers can achieve small error rates when classifying MNIST characters [9] using IoT devices [11]. Similarly, Motamedi *et al.* demonstrate a system-on-chip (SoC) implementation for convolutional neural networks (CNN) that is particularly useful at reducing the number of threads, and thus power, required for deep learning applications [15]. The prior work in this area has made some important steps toward constructing more efficient deep learning systems for IoT. However, it is the premise of this work that the extreme resource constrained nature IoT demands a more careful study of neuromorphic approaches that are inherently more area and energy efficient than any deep learning approach. Thus, we focus our attention on sparse recurrent neural networks (RNN) that exhibit significant area and energy savings relative to their CNN counterparts.

In [18], Schuman and Birdwell present a genetic algorithm based technique, evolutionary optimization (EO), tailored for implementing area-efficient spiky neuromorphic networks. Typically, EO produces sparse RNN neural networks (small, energy-efficient) that run on the corresponding neuro-inspired dynamic architecture (NIDA) [17]. Further, simplicity in the number and type of parameters is a key feature of the NIDA architecture, making is particularly area and energy efficient relative to other neuromorphic approaches. Thus, NIDA-style systems are particularly well suited for resource constrained IoT systems. While NIDA is itself a high-level architecture (typically only simulated), our group has also begun development on a NIDA-based memristive dynamic adaptive neural network architecture (mrDANNA) [4] that can one day be leveraged in IoT hardware implementations.

Normally for analysis of large or streaming datasets like those from the sensors within IoT devices, data analysis is performed using deep neural networks (DNN's). Traditionally, to avoid needing massive compute power at edge devices, the data is compressed, encrypted, and then broadcast to a data center to handle the calculation, and the response is then sent back to the device. Performing the connection remotely uses much less power than doing the calculation at the endpoint, but this can be slow, insecure, and unreliable in areas without a strong network infrastructure [19]. To avoid these problems, some devices include more powerful processors and more efficient deep learning algorithms to either do all of the deep learning work on-device or process some layers of the DNN on device before sending a smaller message to the remote compute facility [12, 19]. Adding more traditional computing power to a given IoT device may not be desirable or even possible, so work on small, low-power devices is needed.

2 BACKGROUND

2.1 Nano-scale Memristors

Leon O. Chua first introduced the theory behind "memristors" (or "memory resistors") [6] in 1971. A memristor in more recent terms typically refers to a two terminal nanoscale non-volatile device whose resistance can be modulated by the magnitude of voltage across the device and the time for which the voltage is applied. A memristor can attain multiple resistance levels between the two bounds known as the low resistance state (LRS) and the high resistance state (HRS). The LRS and HRS of any memristor is dependent on the switching material, process conditions, noise and environmental conditions. Since memristors are very small in size, they are particularly attractive for designing area efficient systems. Moreover, the energy consumption of a memristor tends to be very low as well, especially for devices whose LRS is relatively large. Hence, memristors have been attractive to the energy efficient neuromorphic chip designer. The used-based switching characteristics of memristors also make them useful for implementing synaptic circuits. Several neuromorphic architectures have been proposed in recent years which leverage a variety of memristive switching materials [10, 13, 20].

The memristor model we have used in this paper is based on [1]. This model was developed from on experimental results for nanoscale hafnium-oxide (HfO_x) memristors fabricated within a 65 nm CMOS process [2, 3]. Fig. 2 shows the current-voltage relationship for an example HfO_x memristor, specifically illustrating the characteristics of the device when switching between the LRS and HRS resistance states. When a voltage greater than a threshold of $1V$ is applied across the memristor, the device will switch from HRS to LRS. Likewise, an applied voltage less than the negative threshold of about $-0.7V$ will cause the device to switch from LRS to HRS. In both cases, the voltage applied should also be held for at least a minimum "switching time" (typically $10 - 100ns$) in order to switch fully between the two extreme resistance states, HRS and LRS. Resistance states between LRS and HRS are also achievable by applying short, nanosecond pulses that essentially "nudge" the resistance. This variety and range of resistance is particularly useful for representing synaptic weights in the spiky neuromorphic model considered. The ability to change these resistance values with controlled pulses is also leveraged to implement online learning mechanisms such as spike time-dependent plasticity (STDP) [4].

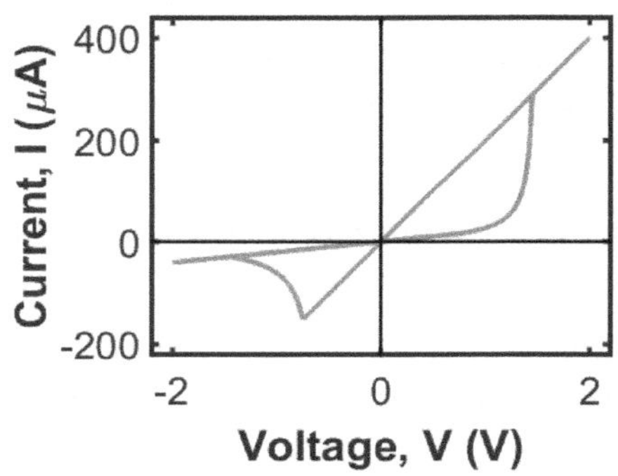

Figure 2: I-V characteristics of memristor model.

2.2 Neuromorphic ASIC Design

Resource constrained IoT devices are always in need of devices and techniques that consume less power and energy, as these are the major constraints for compact systems with limited battery supply. Hence, memristor-based spiky neuromorphic computing architectures are particularly attractive as viable solutions for IoT based machine learning. Moreover, several emergent nano-scale devices (memristors included) are being leveraged in such systems that promise lower area and power consumption [7, 8, 16]. For our part, non-volatile memristors have been used to design synapses that help to ensure low energy consumption while storing synaptic weights. Different materials and their corresponding devices will exhibit differences in energy consumption. For instance, if we consider HfO_x, the energy while the synapse is active, idle and learning is detailed on Table 1. Here, the active phase of the synapse refers to the mode of operation; the idle phase defines the inactive condition and the learning phase includes both the potentiation and the depression of the synaptic weights based on the neuron fires. Each of these synapse states consumes energy depending on the type of memristive device used and the peripheral control circuitry.

Table 1: Energy values for HfO_x synapses [4]

Synapse state	Energy per spike (pJ)
Active	0.48
Idle	0.002
Learning (IncreaseWeight)	0.26
Learning (DecreaseWeight)	0.13

Mixed-signal CMOS neurons can also be designed for energy and area efficiency, specifically when using CMOS integrate-and-fire neurons consisting of very few transistors [5]. The primary concern in terms of area is the size of the capacitors. Capacitor area can also be mitigated via the use of different memristors that will in turn ensure proper incoming current flow into the neuron. The mixed-signal neuron operates in three different phases: *accumulation*, *idle* and the *firing* phases. Energy consumed by the neuron during these phases are listed on Table 2. Here the accumulation energy refers to the energy consumed while accumulating incoming charge/spikes from the synaptic weights. The idle energy is comparatively low since the neuron's functionality is mostly inactive with the exception of peripheral circuitry. Unlike the synapse phases, the neuron does not consume energy specifically relating to the learning process. Instead, the neuron consumes energy while it produces firing spikes. This energy involves the generation of a post-neuron fire when the accumulated charge crosses over the threshold of that particular neuron. Moreover, the shaping of the firing spike is also an important factor for energy consumption since the generated firing pulses would be fed into the next stage of neuromorphic cores.

Table 2: Energy values for CMOS neurons [4]

Neuron phase	Energy per spike (pJ)
Accumulation	9.81
Idle	7.2
Firing	12.5

The neuromorphic architecture (mrDANNA) we consider is mixed-signal in nature. Hence the architecture is significant for low power and area efficiency and includes both the synapse and neuron model described. Several synapses and neurons are gathered to turn into some memristive neuromorphic core which we call mrDANNA cores. Each core contains energy efficient memristive synapses and an analog IAF neuron. The total layout of the design (shown in Figure 3) consists of 36 placements of mrDANNA cores on the right side of the design with the left side containing a digital implementation of the architecture. The advantage of a mixed-signal design is that the connections with the outside signal are fully digital whereas the integration within the core itself is analog. Hence, the mixed-signal memristive neuromorphic system discussed here is digital between cores and analog within the core. Moreover, the mixed-signal approach is also more energy efficient relative to other digital implementations. Since mixed-signal models provide the opportunity to implement synapse and neuron models with better area and power efficiency, we are inclined towards improving the design of our neuromorphic cores for use in multiple different applications including classification, control and anomaly detection.

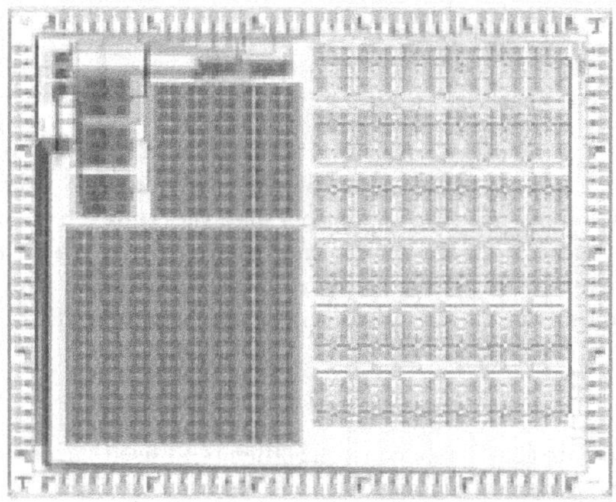

Figure 3: Final layout of first generation mrDANNA test chip submitted for fabrication [3, 4].

3 EXAMPLE: SMALL ROBOT NAVIGATION

One example of a resource constrained environment for computation is the navigation system on an autonomous robot. A robot usually has fixed energy storage and has limits on size and weight to allow it to travel. In this paper we consider the NeoN robot design [14] using a mrDANNA hardware chip. As described by Mitchell et. al, the output spikes from this network are used to signal the motor controller, while input spikes are mostly generated by the robot's sensors (in this case, LIDAR sensors on a servo, which take five measurements in an arc, and limit switches). The goal of the autonomous robot is to explore as much of an area as possible while avoiding any obstacles. In particular, the robot must be able to navigate unfamiliar environments, where the layout of the environment and the obstacles within the environment is unknown.

Networks are developed and trained using evolutionary optimization (EO); in particular, a set of fixed room configurations are used to evaluate how well the network is able to control the robot to perform the objective of covering as much ground as possible while also avoiding obstacles. During the EO, we simulate the neuromorphic system, the robot, and the environments in which the robot navigates (see Figure 4 for a visualization of the simulation), rather than using the actual robot in real environments in training. Though the simulator is relatively primitive, we have deployed network trained in simulation using EO onto another neuromorphic

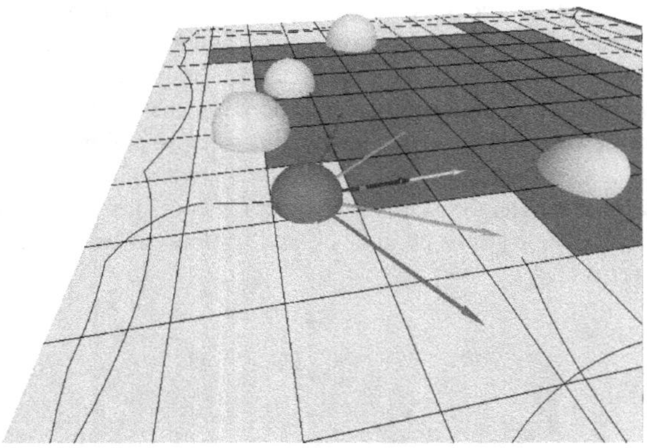

Figure 4: This is the simulator visualization for robot navigation, the floor is divided into a grid – red boxes are unvisited, yellow boxes have been visited. The red sphere is a simple representation of the robot, and the five blue rays represent its sensors. The teal spheres represent obstacles that must be avoided. The black path on the floor is the path that the robot has taken.

architecture (DANNA), which has then been used to successfully control the real robot in unfamiliar environments [14]. As such, we are confident that the resulting mrDANNA network will also perform well on the robot itself in navigating new environments.

The example network generated using the EO to operate the robot uses 31 neurons (9 input neurons, 4 output neurons, and 18 hidden neurons) and utilizes 119 of the synapses for communication (see Figure 5), roughly twice as many as the DANNA implementation described by Parker et. al [14]. The nine input neurons are where the LIDAR sensor information is fed in (five inputs), along with the robot's limit switches information (two inputs), and a bias and random value to help drive activity. The four outputs correspond to forward and backward for both the left and right motors. The network shown in Figure 5 represents a single, sparse neuron layer to handle processing the input and decision-making, and includes many recurrent connections. This different style of handling network layers (as opposed to traditional feed-forward neural networks) makes this network type much smaller than the networks used in traditional deep learning methods.

4 RESULTS

In order to understand how this network would perform on physical mrDANNA hardware, we analyzed the network's performance and measured various types of activity in the network. We use the measurements shown in Tables 1 and 2 to then estimate the power consumption of the network on a physical chip. Analyzing the network's performance showed an average of 4425 spikes in the network per second. When considered with the 20MHz clock frequency, this results in the network being idle the vast majority of the time during this real-time task, as the robot only polls to make a decision five times per second. The average power used by the network is approximately 142.7 μW (see Table 3). It is worth noting

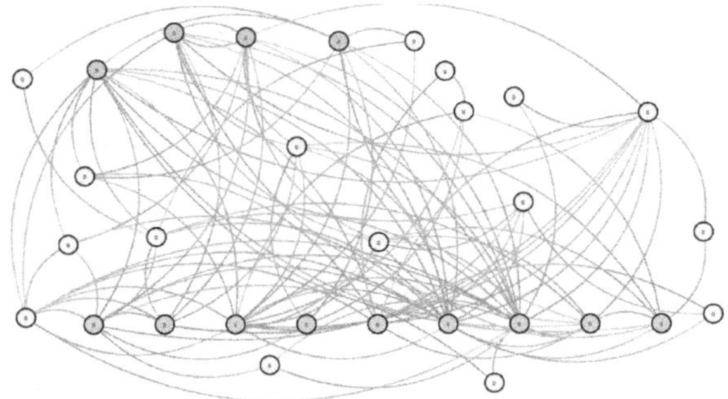

Figure 5: A visualization of the example network. Neurons are represented by colored circles: Blue are input neurons, red are output neurons, and white are hidden neurons. The arcs represent the synapses of the network with the blue end being the pre-neuron and the pink end being the post-neuron.

Table 3: A description of a NeoN mrDANNA network

Number of Neurons	31
Number of Synapses	119
Average Spikes per Second	4425
Power Usage (Core Logic)	142.7 μW

that this value is only measuring the core logic of the neuromorphic system; neither the costs of generating spikes from the input sensors nor converting output spikes to signals to the motor controller are factored into this value, both of which may be non-trivial.

The generated network is generally very sparse but there are some heavily connected nodes, with individual neurons having out-degrees up to 13 and in-degrees up to 11. The connectivity is primarily directly between input and outputs neurons (including many input-to-input connections), with the hidden neurons usually having relatively few synapses.

5 FUTURE WORK AND CONCLUSIONS

The era of IoT devices has compelled us to consider such technologies with opportunities that introduce resource constrained devices having area and power efficiency. Since we are looking at neuromorphic computing with emergent devices, our primary goal is to ensure energy and area efficiency with proper architecture. In this work, we have shown that a network for a neuromorphic architecture using emerging devices (mrDANNA) can be generated using evolutionary optimization to perform an autonomous robot navigation task. The resulting network is relatively small and sparse when compared with most deep learning networks, resulting in area efficiency, while also maintaining power efficiency (142.7 μW).

There is much future work to be done with respect to neuromorphic computing and IoT devices. One potential future direction is the aggregation of data communication among devices connected to each other. Because of the potential power of spiky neuromorphic systems in analyzing streaming data, we also anticipate that neuromorphic systems will play a large role in data analysis at the "edge." Our utilization of EO for training has tended to produce smaller, sparser networks than what is typically seen in deep learning networks, making them well-suited for deployment onto physical, resource-constrained devices. Moreover, we also intend to explore utilizing on-chip plasticity mechanisms to continue learning or training on the device itself. These types of mechanisms will potentially allow for adapting and self-healing systems in the future, which will be especially important for IoT devices that are in remote areas and not easily accessible. We envision to continue our research in the area of big data analysis while ensuring low energy and area consumption for largely connected IoT devices.

6 ACKNOWLEDGEMENTS

The authors would like to thank Grant Bruer, Sagarvarma Sayyaparaju and Sherif Amer from the University of Tennessee, Knoxville for interesting and useful discussions on this topic.

This material is based on research sponsored by Air Force Research Laboratory under agreement number FA8750-16-1-0065 and the U.S. Department of Energy, Office of Science, Office of Advanced Scientific Computing Research, under contract number DE-AC05-00OR22725. The U.S. Government is authorized to reproduce and distribute reprints for Governmental purposes notwithstanding any copyright notation thereon.

REFERENCES

[1] Sherif Amer, Sagarvarma Sayyaparaju, Garrett S. Rose, Karsten Beckmann, and Nathaniel C. Cady. [n. d.]. A Practical Hafnium-Oxide Memristor Model Suitable for Circuit Design and Simulation. In *Proceedings of IEEE International Symposium on Circuits and Systems (ISCAS).*

[2] Karsten Beckmann, Josh Holt, Harika Manem, Joseph Van Nostrand, and Nathaniel C Cady. 2016. Nanoscale Hafnium Oxide RRAM Devices Exhibit Pulse Dependent Behavior and Multi-level Resistance Capability. *MRS Advances* (2016), 1–6.

[3] Nathaniel Cady, Karsten Beckmann, Wilkie Olin-Ammentorp, Gangotree Chakma, Sherif Amer, Ryan Weiss, Sagarvarma Sayyaparaju, Md. Musabbir Adnan, John Murray, Mark Dean, James Plank, Garrett S. Rose, and Joseph E. Van Nostrand. 2018. Full CMOS-Memristor Implementation of a Dynamic Neuromorphic Architecture. In *Proceedings of the Government Microcircuit Applications and Critical Technology Conference (GOMACTech).*

[4] Gangotree Chakma, Md. Musabbir Adnan, Austin R. Wyer, Ryan Weiss, Catherine D. Schuman, and Garrett S. Rose. 2017. Memristive Mixed-Signal Neuromorphic Systems: Energy-Efficient Learning at the Circuit-Level. *IEEE Journal on Emerging and Selected Topics in Circuits and Systems (JETCAS)* PP, 99 (2017). https://doi.org/10.1109/JETCAS.2017.2777181

[5] G. Chakma, S. Sayyaparaju, R. Weiss, and G. S. Rose. 2017. A Mixed-Signal Approach to Memristive Neuromorphic System Design. In *60th IEEE International Midwest Symposium on Circuits and Systems (MWSCAS).* Boston, MA.

[6] L. O. Chua. 1971. Memristor-The missing circuit element. *IEEE Transactions on Circuit Theory* 18, 5 (September 1971), 507–519.

[7] Miao Hu, Hai Li, Yiran Chen, Qing Wu, Garrett S. Rose, and Richard W. Linderman. 2014. Memristor Crossbar-Based Neuromorphic Computing System: A Case Study. *IEEE Trans. Neural Netw. Learning Syst.* 25, 10 (October 2014), 1864–1878. https://doi.org/10.1109/TNNLS.2013.2296777

[8] Giacomo Indiveri, Bernabé Linares-Barranco, Robert Legenstein, George Deligeorgis, and Themistoklis Prodromakis. 2013. Integration of nanoscale memristor synapses in neuromorphic computing architectures. *Nanotechnology* 24, 38 (2013), 384010.

[9] Y. Lecun, L. Bottou, Y. Bengio, and P. Haffner. 1998. Gradient-based learning applied to document recognition. *Proc. IEEE* 86, 11 (November 1998), 2278–2324.

[10] HY Lee, YS Chen, PS Chen, TY Wu, F Chen, CC Wang, PJ Tzeng, M-J Tsai, and C Lien. 2010. Low-power and nanosecond switching in robust hafnium oxide resistive memory with a thin Ti cap. *IEEE Electron Device Letters* 31, 1 (2010), 44–46.

[11] Sam Leroux, Steven Bohez, Tim Verbelen, Bert Vankeirsbilck, Pieter Simoens, and Bart Dhoedt. 2015. Resource-constrained classification using a cascade of neural network layers. In *Neural Networks (IJCNN), 2015 International Joint Conference on.* IEEE, 1–7.

[12] H. Li, K. Ota, and M. Dong. 2018. Learning IoT in Edge: Deep Learning for the Internet of Things with Edge Computing. *IEEE Network* 32, 1 (Jan 2018), 96–101. https://doi.org/10.1109/MNET.2018.1700202

[13] Gilberto Medeiros-Ribeiro, Frederick Perner, Richard Carter, Hisham Abdalla, Matthew D Pickett, and R Stanley Williams. 2011. Lognormal switching times for titanium dioxide bipolar memristors: origin and resolution. *Nanotechnology* 22, 9 (2011), 095702.

[14] J. P. Mitchell, G. Bruer, M. E. Dean, J. S. Plank, G. S. Rose, and C. D. Schuman. 2017. NeoN: Neuromorphic control for autonomous robotic navigation. In *2017 IEEE International Symposium on Robotics and Intelligent Sensors (IRIS).* 136–142. https://doi.org/10.1109/IRIS.2017.8250111

[15] Mohammad Motamedi, Daniel Fong, and Soheil Ghiasi. 2017. Machine Intelligence on Resource-Constrained IoT Devices: The Case of Thread Granularity Optimization for CNN Inference. *ACM Transactions on Embedded Computing Systems (TECS)* 16, 5s (2017), 151.

[16] Mirko Prezioso, Farnood Merrikh-Bayat, BD Hoskins, GC Adam, Konstantin K Likharev, and Dmitri B Strukov. 2015. Training and operation of an integrated neuromorphic network based on metal-oxide memristors. *Nature* 521, 7550 (2015), 61.

[17] C.D. Schuman, J.D. Birdwell, and M. Dean. 2014. Neuroscience-inspired dynamic architectures. In *Biomedical Science and Engineering Center Conference (BSEC), 2014 Annual Oak Ridge National Laboratory.* 1–4. https://doi.org/10.1109/BSEC.2014.6867735

[18] Catherine D. Schuman and J. Douglas Birdwell. 2013. Dynamic Artificial Neural Networks with Affective Systems. *PLoS ONE* 8, 11 (November 2013), e80455. https://doi.org/10.1371/journal.pone.0080455

[19] J. Tang, D. Sun, S. Liu, and J. L. Gaudiot. 2017. Enabling Deep Learning on IoT Devices. *Computer* 50, 10 (2017), 92–96. https://doi.org/10.1109/MC.2017.3641648

[20] J Joshua Yang, MX Zhang, John Paul Strachan, Feng Miao, Matthew D Pickett, Ronald D Kelley, G Medeiros-Ribeiro, and R Stanley Williams. 2010. High switching endurance in TaOx memristive devices. *Applied Physics Letters* 97, 23 (2010), 232102.

Gate-Controlled Memristors and their Applications in Neuromorphic Architectures

Eric Herrmann
EECS, University of Cincinnati
Cincinnati, Ohio
herrmaej@mail.uc.edu

Rashmi Jha
EECS, University of Cincinnati
Cincinnati, Ohio
jhari@ucmail.uc.edu

ABSTRACT

We discuss the theory of gated memristive devices, which exhibit continuous states over three orders of magnitude and can be programmed independently of reading. A model is generated by using knowledge of the device physics and fitting the parameters to measured data. The gate-controlled memristor simplifies the implementation of analog artificial neural network architectures significantly. Using this, a very simple architecture is presented, along with a simulation and its performance metrics. The simulated analog neural neural network is able to achieve 88.9 percent accuracy on the MNIST test set. The objective is to demonstrate the advantages that gated memristors can give to analog neural networks.

CCS CONCEPTS

• **Hardware** → **Non-volatile memory**; *Programmable logic elements*; • **Information systems** → *Storage class memory*; • **Computer systems organization** → *Neural networks*;

KEYWORDS

Neuromorphic Architecture; Memristor; Circuit Design

ACM Reference Format:
Eric Herrmann and Rashmi Jha. 2018. Gate-Controlled Memristors and their Applications in Neuromorphic Architectures. In *GLSVLSI '18: 2018 Great Lakes Symposium on VLSI, May 23–25, 2018, Chicago, IL, USA.* ACM, New York, NY, USA, 6 pages. https://doi.org/10.1145/3194554.3194613

1 INTRODUCTION

Optimizing the training and evaluation of artificial neural networks (ANNs) using traditional CMOS architectures has been a topic of research for many years, with varying levels of success[1, 3]. The obvious reason for this is the increased interest in applying neural networks to machine learning and artificial intelligence problems, yet the problem is very suited to optimization due to the often parallel nature of the problem. What is not new is the implementation of neural networks as arrays of resistive devices, which had been first proposed in the 1960s[4]. This solution to the problem has long been one of the more interesting research topics into analog computing. The advantages are clear, analog multiplication can be done by simple resistive devices, and sums can be done by combining resistive outputs. It is truly parallel in a dense array. For traditional computing methods, computing the output and weight update of a single layer of a network are both $O(N^2)$ operations, but with a resistive crossbar based network, these are constant time operations ($O(1)$).

Recently, progress has continued to be made on this front. A well-performing architecture using phase change memory (PCM) devices and stochastic bit streams to evaluate and train a deep neural network (DNN) using backpropagation has been proposed [1]. However, this architecture lacks the simplicity many may expect from an analog neural network implementation. What we will discuss in this paper is the implications of a three-terminal (3T) non-volatile memory (NVM) cell on ANNs, and propose a simple architecture for $O(1)$ evaluation and learning.

The 3T NVM cell behaves as a resistor with a gate to control its resistance. This allows for greatly simplified architectures compared to two-terminal NVM cells, since with 3T devices the read and write lines are seperated. This means CMOS logic can be used at each cell to program it, and all sneak path problems are eliminated when configuring. The device described has continuous programmable states, making it optimal for this problem. [2]

2 GATED MEMRISTOR

The gated memristor described and simulated below has been fabricated by our group previously [2]. Here we will discuss the theory and testing results of the device, with a focus on how this information can be applied to device modeling.

2.1 Theory

A cross-section of the fabricated device can be seen in Fig. 1. The switching metal oxide used is $SrTiO_3$ (STO), which has been studied for its mobile oxygen ions (O^{2-}) and varying electrical properties at different oxidation states. As O^{2-} migrates, it forms oxygen vacancies (V_O^{2+}) in the material, in this study we are assuming regions depleted of oxygen exhibit higher conductivity. The accepted transport mechanisms through the material generally support this, with oxygen vacancies promoting n-type ohmic conduction [5] and trap-assisted tunneling as well as contact effects. The conduction region of the device is the region between the top electrode (TE) and bottom electrode (BE), a positive voltage on the gate will accumulate V_O^{2+} in this region, and increase conductivity. A negative voltage will deplete this region of V_O^{2+}, and increase resistivity.

The fabricated device exhibits continuous states over 3 orders of magnitude. The set and reset powers are measured in pW for this device[2]. The states are related to the integrated electric field through the STO over time, as will be discussed below.

GLSVLSI '18, May 23–25, 2018, Chicago, IL, USA

ACM ISBN 978-1-4503-5724-1/18/05...$15.00
https://doi.org/10.1145/3194554.3194613

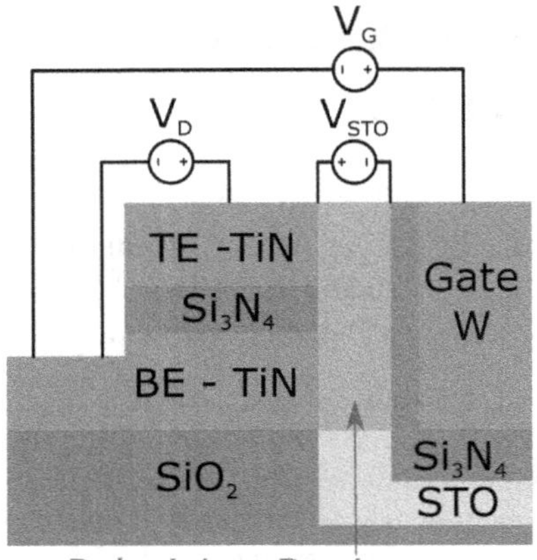

Figure 1: The designed device cross-section. The switching oxide is STO, and the polarizing STO region is between the two electrodes and the gate electrode, where all conduction occurs between the top and bottom electrodes. V_{STO} is defined as the polarization state of the dielectic (potential drop across it when $V_G = 0V$ due to the gradient of V_O^{2+}). V_G is the gate voltage and V_D is the read voltage with the BE as the reference ground.

2.2 Modeling

For the purpose of modeling this device, the STO layer is treated as a slowly-polarizing ionic dielectric. That is:

$$\frac{\partial V_{STO}}{\partial t} = \frac{V_{app} - V_{STO}}{\tau} \tag{1}$$

where V_{STO} is the internal voltage across the STO as shown in Fig. 1, and V_{app} is the applied voltage. This is saying that the material will exhibit ionic polarization linearly with the applied field (as per the charged particle drift equation). As it polarizes, an internal field opposing the applied field will form (as in all dielectrics). However, due to the low ion mobility in STO[5], this will take a significant amount of time. At steady-state, the STO will be fully polarized to the applied voltage, and so the entire voltage drop applied across the device will be seen across the gate insulating layer (Si_3N_4). The parameter τ is an indication of the ionic mobility and device dimensions, and will be a function of temperature. In our study, it is a fitted parameter and assumed constant. V_{app} is defined based on the device structure. In the device shown in Fig. 1, the applied voltage is a function of the gate voltage and the voltage on the TE and BE:

$$V_{app} = V_G - \frac{V_{TE} + V_{BE}}{2} \tag{2}$$

It is important to discuss the assumptions in this relationship. Firstly, if there is a bias across the TE and BE, there will be more complex fields through the STO than can be described by a single potential drop. Second, the non-ionic polarization in STO would also need to be accounted for, since this reduces the effective field through the STO. In (1), the dielectric constant is assumed to be 0 when it is not polarized (all voltage drop is across the STO, none across the gate insulator), and infinity when it is. Third, the only

	$\tau(s)$	$V_T(V)$	$\alpha(V)$	β	$g_{min}(log(S))$
Mean	16.6	.1739	.314	3.12	-11.84
STD	.765	.0571	.0233	.2283	.1949

Table 1: The means and standard deviations of the model parameters were extracted from 5 $100\mu m$ devices

particle effect is assumed to be drift, while diffusion likely also plays a part. These assumptions could be accounted for in future work, but as will be seen below, these assumptions do not significantly compromise the model's effectiveness.

Relating this polarization state to the device conductivity is less intuitive than the polarization model. Fitting (1) to the measured data, the τ can be extracted using voltage sweep data. Since the conductivity of the device should be the same under a given polarization condition, the time constant (τ)can be determined by increasing and then decreasing the polarization state, and aligning each path. This method is visually explained in Fig. 2(a). The device at DC shows a n-channel MOSFET-like characteristic, with an exponential relationship to polarization state in the subthreshold region, and linear transconductance after the threshold. However, in this voltage region, it was found that the $10^{sigmoid}$ relationship was more appropriate due to the high leakage current. The current model is shown here:

$$I_D = 10^{\beta sig(\frac{V_{STO}-V_T}{\alpha})+log_{10}(g_{min})} \tag{3}$$

Where sig is the sigmoid function ($sig(x) = \frac{1}{1+e^{-x}}$), and the fitted parameters are the minimum conductivity (g_{min}), the threshold voltage (V_T), and scaling factors α and β.

These models were fitted to five measured device V_G-I_D sweeps[2]. The voltage between the top electrode (TE) and bottom electrode (BE), V_D, was held at 1V. The gate voltage (V_G) was swept from -5V to 5V and back over the course of 60 seconds, and the current was measured between the TE and BE. Fitting via parameter optimization was done using least squares optimization. The fitted parameters are shown in Table ??, with means and standard deviations on this small set of devices. The results of this model can be seen in Fig. 2.

One major assumption is made in the application of this device. That is that the gate will have high enough capacitance and low enough leakage to retain the device state. This is not an unreasonable assumption, since STO is a high-K dielectric. Realistically, opening the gate terminal would slow the decay rate of the device significantly. However in this study we assume there is no decay due to the trapped charge on the gate.

3 MEMRISTOR NETWORK

The non-volatility of such a device makes it useful for applications traditionally handled by memristors. Specifically, here we explore the applications of such a device to evaluation and training of an ANN applied to a classification problem. The third terminal allows for a feedback training signal. This greatly simplifies the control logic required to train this network.

The basic computations in a network involve computing the dot product of the input and the weight matrix, evaluating the activation function, and finally doing training via gradient descent.

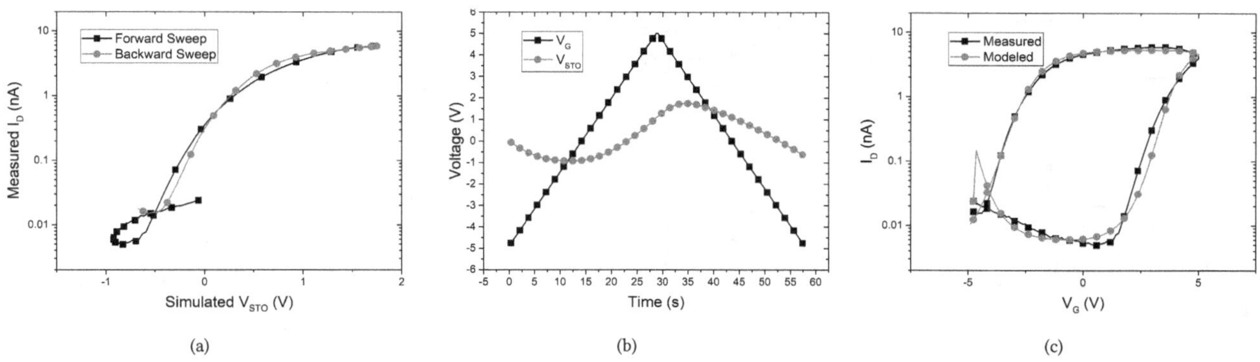

Figure 2: The model fitness. (a) Measured read current (I_D) at $V_D = 1V$ against V_{STO} (simulated polarization state). The curve follows itself in both directions, meaning the time constant is correct, since I_D is a function of only V_{STO} (and V_D, which is constant). (b) V_G against V_{STO}. The simulated dielectic potential (V_{STO}) lags behind the applied voltage due to low ionic mobility, modeled by (1). (c) The measured and modeled read currents (I_D) in a V_G sweep from -5V to 5V and back, showing the accuracy of the model and the low drift from the measured value over time (60 seconds).

The dot product can be expanded into a sum of the form:

$$s_i = \sum_{j=0}^{len(\bar{x})} x_j w_{ij} \tag{4}$$

Where w is the weight matrix, $\bar{x}$ is the input vector, and $\bar{s}$ is the dot product of the two. This can fairly easily be translated to a resistive crossbar array, with the weights equal to the conductivities of the resistors, and s and x being output and input voltages respectively. Using the current law:

$$0 = \sum_{j=0}^{len(\bar{x})} (x_j - s_i) w_{ij} \tag{5}$$

For all i. This can be simplified to:

$$s_i = \frac{\sum_{j=0}^{len(\bar{x})} x_j w_{ij}}{\sum_{j=0}^{len(\bar{x})} w_{ij}} \tag{6}$$

Which is the simple normalized weighted sum of the inputs, and has the same effect as (4).

For activation, the easiest activation function in this context would be the heaviside function, which can be approximated with a voltage comparator. However, activation functions are often forgone in output layers, which we will do in this case. Instead, a winner-take-all (WTA) method is used using a multiple input/output dynamic comparator, which returns a 1 for the highest input, and 0 for the rest. This is similar but not equivalent to the softmax function in software based networks, that are commonly used There are many ways to implement such a circuit.

For training, the gradient descent rule is approximated using boolean logic. The traditional gradient descent rule for a single layer is:

$$\Delta w_{ij} = \eta f_i'(s_i)(y_i - \hat{y}_i)x_j \tag{7}$$

Where f' is the derivative of the activation function with respect to s, y is the desired output of the activation function, $\hat{y}$ is the evaluated output of the activation function ($\hat{y} = f(s)$) , and η is the learning rate.

For our approximation, the derivative of the activation function is removed. Instead, the weights are updated whenever the wrong classification wins, and the derivative is assumed constant. Since all training rules and outputs of the network are binary, the subtraction can be done with boolean logic. There are three possible states for feedback to each dendrite: increase output, decrease output, and do nothing. These are expressed as a 2-bit signal for each output of the network. The first bit of this signal is an output enable (OE), if it is 1 then the weight is updated. Otherwise, the memristor's gate terminal is left open, and no update is applied, so the feedback signal is ignored. The second is the feedback signal, which will be a 1 if the network output should be increased, a 0 otherwise. This is equivalent to subtracting $\hat{y}_i$ and y, expressed at 3 different logic levels (-1,0,1). The boolean logic for this is simple:

$$OE_i = y_i \oplus \hat{y}_i \tag{8}$$

$$feedback_i = y_i \tag{9}$$

The OE signal can also be set to 0 to disable all training, which is done in Fig. 3(d).

The second part of updating needs to be done at each device due to the input dependence as shown in (7). Intuitively, if $feedback$ is 0, then all devices with low input will be potentiated, and all devices with a high input will be depressed, and vice versa if $feedback$ is 1. The output of this is then gated by the OE signal. This is equivalent to multiplying $y_i - \hat{y}_i$ and x_j, if possible values are (-1,0,1). Then the boolean logic for each device is:

$$V_{update,ij} = \begin{cases} \overline{feedback_i \oplus x_j}, & \text{if } OE = 1 \\ \text{open}, & \text{if } OE = 0 \end{cases} \tag{10}$$

The actual weight update is simulated using the device model described in (1), (2), and (3). If the update is 'open', the gate is disconnected and so the applied voltage is equivalent to the potential

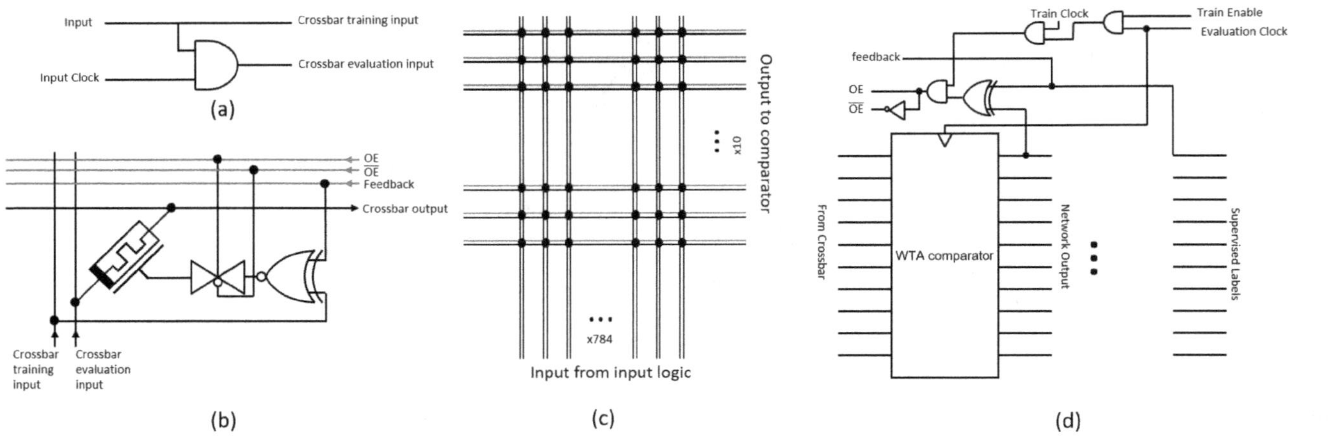

Figure 3: The network architecture. (a) The input logic. This will enable the input while evaluating the network, but once the comparator evaluates, the inputs will disable. This is repeated for each of the 784 inputs. (b) The crossbar intersection circuitry. There is a single gated memristor, a transmission gate, and an xnor at each intersection. (c) The crossbar array, there is a 784-bit binary input, and 10 analog outputs. Each intersection contains a memristive device, and inputs come from the input circuitry. Feedback signals (OE and $feedback$) from the output are marked with red. (d) The output contains a 10-input winner-take-all comparator, which compares the outputs of the crossbar. A one-hot label vector is provided to this block when training. There is some simple control logic that operates on each output/label pair. Training can be disabled with a one bit signal.

stored in the dielectric. (2) can be rewritten with the updated terminology:

$$V_{app,ij} = \begin{cases} V_{update,ij} - \frac{V_{x_i}+V_{s_j}}{2}, & \text{if } OE = 1 \\ V_{STO,ij}, & \text{if } OE = 0 \end{cases} \tag{11}$$

The final term in (4) is the learning rate, η. This is proportional to the time the signal is applied to the gate, and is the same for all devices.

This is the entire network definition, the implementation can be seen in Fig. 3. Realistically, this network would be fabricated with all digital circuitry in silicon, and then the memristive devices would be added in the metal layers (back end of line, BEOL).

The major approximation made with this implementation is that all signals are binary except for the network output, which is then binarized with a WTA comparator. The inputs also need to be binary to allow for them to be used in the weight update. Additionally, the error function is binary, which could cause problems with reaching a good error minimum. However, when not training, analog inputs can be used to evaluate the network.

For usage, the input vector is displayed, and the evaluation/training is controlled with the evaluation clock. It was found that the performance could be improved by grounding the TE/BE terminals of the memristive device when training, this allows the training to be more uniform across devices, this is not strictly necessary however. So, it is assumed that the input vector is grounded after evaluation. This could be accomplished using the inverted evaluation clock through a short delay to gate the input vector, as shown in Fig. 3(a). The training period is then allowed for a set amount of time, while the evaluation clock is high. The learning rate can be modulated by increasing or decreasing this clock frequency/duty cycle. The network described above was constructed and simulated using Python. Discrete time steps were used with a dt of $100\mu s$. The traditional MNIST handwritten number dataset was used for testing, with 784 inputs and 10 outputs. For training, as discussed

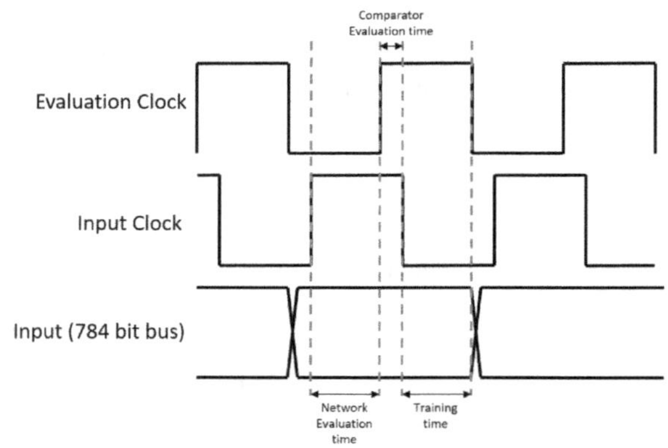

Figure 4: The timing diagram during training, including the evaluation clock which controls the comparator evaluation, the input clock which controls the crossbar evaluation, and the input change times. The network evaluation period is the time the network is allowed to settle, the required time will be a function of the network parasitics. The comparator evaluation time is the time allowed for the comparator to evaluate the crossbar output before removing the input. After the input is removed, the weights are updated for a set amount of time, $100\mu s$ in this experiment.

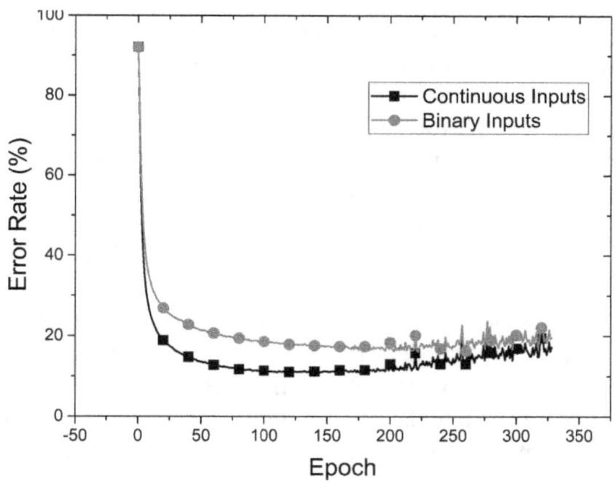

Figure 5: Network error rate on the 10,000 image MNIST test set over 330 epochs. The binary input vector representation rounds the MNIST pixel values to high or low, and is represented by the two logic levels. The continuous input vector scales the input voltage between the two logic levels based on the grayscale pixel value. The The minimum error rate is 10.84 percent with continuous coding, and 16.09 percent with binary.

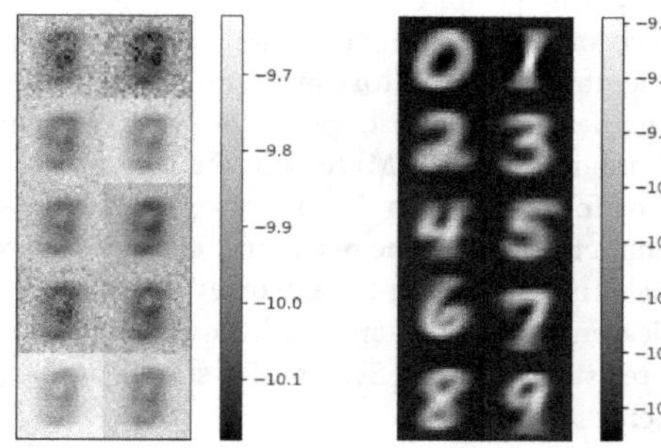

(a) (b)

Figure 6: Conductance matrices after training. The images are arranged into a 2X5 array corresponding to the 10 network outputs. For each, there is a 28X28 array which corresponds to the 784 gated memristor devices. The color scale is in terms of $log_{10}(w)$, where w is the conductance of the gated memristor. (a) The conductance matrix using the WTA comparator described in this paper. (b) The conductance matrix trained using 10 normal output comparators instead, with a threshold voltage of $\frac{V_D}{2}$.

above, the grayscale inputs were rounded to 0 or 255 to create a binary representation (and represented as 0V or V_D internally). At each timestep, a training vector was presented. For the simulation, the network was assumed to evaluate instantaneously. The memristive weights are then trained for a full $100\mu s$ on each sample, with the input vector grounded as discussed. Since the weights are trained for the full dt, this can be thought of as the learning rate, the longer the training signal is applied, the more the device will depress/potentiate. This timing of input and update cycles can be seen in Fig. 4. Realistically, the evaluation clock duty cycle, input clock phase shift, and frequency would be tuned to optimize training speed, learning rate, and performance.

After each set of 60,000 training samples, the network is evaluated by disabling training and testing it using the 10,000 sample test set. This would physically be done by disabling the 'Train enable' signal, and then directly observing the WTA comparator's one-hot output.

The memristive device model used is described above, with the model parameters initialized to the means of parameters shown in Table ??. Logic levels of 0V and 2V were used for the simulation, which is significant because it affects the operating region of the gated memristors. Initial device states were assumed to be normally distributed around their ground states ($V_{STO} = 0$) with a standard deviation of .1V.

4 RESULTS

The network was evaluated over 330 training epochs. The network was trained using the binary vector as discussed above, but can be evaluated using continuous values (analog input is the grayscale pixel values scaled between the two logic levels), which increases performance. This could be accomplished by digital to analog converters (DACs) on the inputs. The network performance on the 10,000 item test set over the 330 epochs is shown in Fig. 5.

Using a binary input vector, as in training, results in a penalty of about 5.5 percent accuracy compared to evaluating the network using continuous values. The error rate converges to over 89 percent accuracy with a continuously coded input, but then begins to degrade as the devices begin to become saturated. However, the network converges to a good minimum before running out of conductance range. Avoiding the saturation of devices would need to be addressed for physical realization.

Fig. 6(a) shows the conductances of the gated memristors in the trained array. There is little visual indication that the network has been trained, which is a result of the WTA comparator, which only enforces separation between outputs, but has no control over the global output level. Fig. 6(b) shows the conductances trained with a similar network to the one described in this paper, except with two-input comparators at the output (heaviside activation) instead of the WTA comparators for training. This hurts accuracy, since multiple outputs can win. Even with a WTA comparator to evaluate the network after training, the performance is worse. The purpose of showing this image is to demonstrate the effect of training on the network conductances. Further work can explore this architecture, these networks may be more noise resistant and could prevent weight saturation.

5 DISCUSSION

The merits of this network are not necessarily due to its performance, indeed many others have shown better performance with single layer neural networks. However, this network is very simple and has very little peripheral circuitry, made possible by the use of 3T memristors. This is a binary voltage level system, which makes implementation straightforward with CMOS technology. Many similar implementations use spiking networks or some kind of pulse width modulation (PWM) to describe continuous values, with a capacitor for integration. In this case, the analog signals are evaluated directly without the need for integration, which can potentially speed up evaluation time. However, the price is that the gradient descent algorithm can only be approximated and the system is less resistant to noise. Even so, for simple problems this may be sufficient.

There are many variations to this. Adding noise will cripple system performance, due to the the similarity of network outputs. This is because once the network obtains the correct output, it will not differentiate the outputs more, due to the binarization of the outputs. This effect could be mitigated by adding some capacitance to the comparator input and leave some integration time. The differentiation could be improved by adding small gated static resistors to ground on the WTA comparator inputs. By only connecting the resistor corresponding to the true value, the output will be lowered during training. This will increase differentiation, and help with noise resilience. Or, a stochastic approach could be taken, by intentionally adding additional noise during training to help differentiate the signals more. As discussed above, a different activation method could also be used, where the outputs are not directly competing during training. These experiments will be left for future work.

There are some obvious improvements that could be made, and will be examined in future work. The physical training time would be very long due to the the low ionic mobility in STO, this could be improved in several ways as has been previously discussed[2]. Adding layers could improve the accuracy. Backpropogation could be implemented in a similar fashion, since all outputs are binary they could be stored in registers and the network could be evaluated in reverse.

6 CONCLUSION

The implications of a gated memristor in neurmorphic applications could potentially be disruptive. It allows for very simple architectures such as the one described here. This is because there doesn't need to be complex logic to control evaluation and training cycles, instead both evaluation of the network and training can be done with no need to share read/write terminals. This also means potential sneak path problems with configuring devices is eliminated. Additionally, the power consumption of such a device is far less than a similar 2-terminal device [2].

More complicated architectures could be developed as well. For instance, more accurate analog operations could be done, as far as analog subtraction and signal mixing, to more adequately approximate the gradient descent algorithm. Or, digital logic could be added, as demonstrated[1], to do stochastic multiplication using an AND gate at the crossbar intersection. Activation and their gradient calculations could be done in digital logic, and then utilize the parallel nature of the crossbar array to do weight updates.

Future work will include varying the device fabrication process to improve characteristics, as well as additional measurements to get a more accurate parameter distribution. The learning architecture can be modeled with distributed device parameters and with added noise. Noise resilience measures could also be tested for effectiveness. The architecture could be extended to multiple layers; Since all signals are binary, the feedback signals can easily be stored in registers to enable backpropagation or even recurrence.

ACKNOWLEDGMENTS

The work was supported by the National Science Foundation under Award ECCS 1556294.

REFERENCES

[1] Tayfun Gokmen and Yurii Vlasov. 2016. Acceleration of Deep Neural Network Training with Resistive Cross-Point Devices: Design Considerations. *Frontiers in Neuroscience* 10 (2016), 333. https://doi.org/10.3389/fnins.2016.00333

[2] Eric Herrmann, Andrew Rush, Tony Bailey, and Rashmi Jha. 2018. Gate Controlled 3-Terminal Metal Oxide Memristor. *IEEE Electron Device Letters* (Feb. 2018). https://doi.org/10.1109/LED.2018.2806188

[3] Cory E. Merkel, Nakul Nagpal, Sindhura Mandalapu, and Dhireesha Kudithipudi. 2011. Reconfigurable N-level memristor memory design. In *The 2011 International Joint Conference on Neural Networks*. IEEE. https://doi.org/10.1109/ijcnn.2011.6033622

[4] Karl Steinbuch. 1961. Die Lernmatrix. *Kybernetic* 1 (1961), 36–45.

[5] J.J. Wang, H Huang, Thorsten Bayer, Ali Moballegh, Ye Cao, Andreas Klein, Elizabeth Dickey, Douglas L. Irving, Clive Randall, and Long-Qing Chen. 2016. Defect chemistry and resistance degradation in Fe-doped SrTiO3 single crystal. *Acta Materialia* 108 (04 2016), 229–240.

Design Exploration of IoT centric Neural Inference Accelerators

Vivek Parmar
Indian Institute of Technology Delhi
New Delhi, Delhi
vivek.p.1990@ieee.org

Manan Suri
Indian Institute of Technology Delhi
New Delhi, Delhi
manansuri@ee.iitd.ac.in

ABSTRACT

Neural networks have been successfully deployed in a variety of fields like computer vision, natural language processing, pattern recognition, etc. However most of their current deployments are suitable for cloud-based high-performance computing systems. As the computation of neural networks is not suited to traditional Von-Neumann CPU architectures, many novel hardware accelerator designs have been proposed in literature. In this paper we present the design of a novel, simplified and extensible neural inference engine for IoT systems. We present a detailed analysis on the impact of various design choices like technology node, computation block size, etc on overall performance of the neural inference engine. The paper demonstrates the first design instance of a power-optimized ELM neural network using ReLU activation. Comparison between learning performance of simulated hardware against the software model of the neural network shows a variation of $\sim 1\%$ in testing accuracy due to quantization. The accelerator compute blocks manage to achieve a performance per Watt of $\sim$ 290 MSPS/W (Million samples per second per Watt) with a network structure of size: 8 x 32 x 2. Minimum energy of 40 pJ is acheived per sample processed for a block size of 16. Further, we show through simulations that an added power-saving of $\sim$ 30 % can be acheived if SRAM based main memory is replaced with emerging STT-MRAM technology.

CCS CONCEPTS

• **Computing methodologies → Artificial intelligence**; • **Computer systems organization → Embedded hardware**; • **Hardware → Application specific integrated circuits**; **Emerging architectures**; **Spintronics and magnetic technologies**;

KEYWORDS

Neural networks, Accelerator, Neuromorphic computing, IoT, Inference engine, STT-MRAM

ACM Reference Format:
Vivek Parmar and Manan Suri. 2018. Design Exploration of IoT centric Neural Inference Accelerators . In *GLSVLSI '18: 2018 Great Lakes Symposium on VLSI, May 23–25, 2018, Chicago, IL, USA.* ACM, New York, NY, USA, 6 pages. https://doi.org/10.1145/3194554.3194614

ACM ISBN 978-1-4503-5724-1/18/05...$15.00
https://doi.org/10.1145/3194554.3194614

1 INTRODUCTION

Recently dedicated neural network hardware has generated tremendous interest due to its widespread applications [5] and performance benefits over software implementation [26]. Both academic and industrial research groups have proposed several new type of neural network accelerators or custom neural network hardware exploiting GPUs, TPUs, FPGAs or ASICs. Hardware neural network implementations exist either as Spiking (SNNs) or non-Spiking Artificial neural network (ANNs) types. Prominent pure CMOS SNN hardware implementations include the SpiNNaker [17], Neurogrid [4], IBM's Truenorth [27] and Intel's Loihi [7]. GPU based implementations have been shown to significantly accelerate computation for intensive deep-learning applications[19], the high power penalty of GPUs limit their scope for IoT type mobile and low-power budget applications [12]. FPGAs have also shown promise on high performance computing tasks [41]. Due to the continuous evolving nature of machine learning/neural network algorithms reconfigurability offered by FPGA based solutions is desirable [10, 30, 32]. In some cases, FPGA based approach has also opened doors for architectures based on low precision data such as Ternary nets [24] and XNOR nets [35]. Among ASIC implementations Google's TPU [16], Intel Movidius's VPU [28], NVIDIA's Xavier DLA [31] are some of the well known architectures from industry. From academia, the most prominent ones are EIE [12], Eyeriss [6], SCNN [33], etc. All industry designs focus on optimizing the matrix computation engine and it's memory interface. However the research designs try to use a compressed version of the network weights to minimize the memory requirements and avoid unnecessary memory traffic. More advance variants that exploit hybrid architectures using emerging non-volatile memory (NVM) technology along with traditional CMOS circuits[18, 25, 38–40, 42] have also been proposed recently.

In this paper, we present a novel neural network inference engine that is based on minimalistic design requirements. The goal of the design was to make a generic extensible/reconfigurable accelerator which can be used primarily for inference tasks in small scale IoT system applications. Section 3 presents the proposed design of the architecture. Section 4 demonstrates the implications on power and performance, using basic neural network workloads for an IoT system to evaluate the design performance . Section 5 presents analysis on potential enhancements for the architecture using emerging STT-MRAM technology.

2 NEURAL INFERENCE ENGINE

Typical artificial neural network designs consist of layers of computational blocks performing weighted summation followed by a non-linear operation. A variety of architectures have been proposed over the years such as MLP[14], RNN[9], ELM[15], CNN[22],etc.

However the computational dataflow for all the aforementioned algorithms/architectures is similar in pure digital CMOS realization. Neural network workloads can be broadly classified into two categories: (1) Training (2) Inference. For IoT centric applications, the neural network is trained less often and mainly used for repeated inference. Re-training is mainly required to optimize network parameters or to adapt to a newer dataset. The standard digital implementation of a neural inference pipeline has following three main components:

(1) Synaptic weight memory
(2) Matrix computation engine
(3) Activation module

Data flow for a typical neural inference engine is shown in Fig 1. This computational pipeline is repeated in a chain for each layer of the neural network. Similarly each neuron is an independent computational unit and hence computation of neuron outputs of the same layer can be pipelined. The weight memory is a buffer to store the weight values for the current layer of the network being processed. This allows multiple samples to be processed in a pipelined fashion. It is typically implemented as a FIFO buffer. The matrix multiplication engine performs the synaptic weighting operation of the neural network. It is implemented as a vector or a matrix level computation where chunks of data are fed in a scheduled order to the co-processor to ensure that maximum throughput can be attained. The third component is a dedicated hardware to improve the latency associated with element-wise processing of activation functions. For defining the hardware realization of a neural inference pipeline the major parameters that a designer can control are:

(1) Precision of data processing
(2) Block size and architecture of the matrix computation co-processor
(3) Activation functions

Owing to the fact that inference tasks require lower precision than training [13], direct mapping of floating-point computation from software-to-hardware typically results in sub-optimal designs [11]. Also augmenting the matrix computation pipeline (vector processing replaced by systolic arrays) gives a possibility to realize a lower latency pipeline implementation [20]. Choice of complex activation functions such as sigmoid or tanh results in a large lookup table to be implemented in hardware [21, 43]. A simpler activation function like ReLU presents an opportunity to reduce hardware complexity and latency significantly [36].

3 PROPOSED ARCHITECTURE

Block level representation of the proposed architecture is represented in Fig. 2. The five primary components of the proposed accelerator are :

- MMA unit (Matrix-Multiply Add)
- ReLU unit (Activation)
- Memory buffers
- Scratch pad memory
- Central controller

Two important parameters of the proposed design are *data precision* and *block size of the computational unit*. The design uses 16-bit

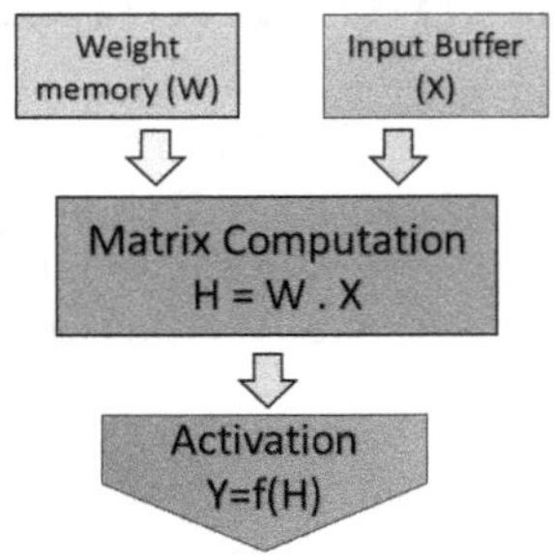

Figure 1: Generic neural inference engine pipeline

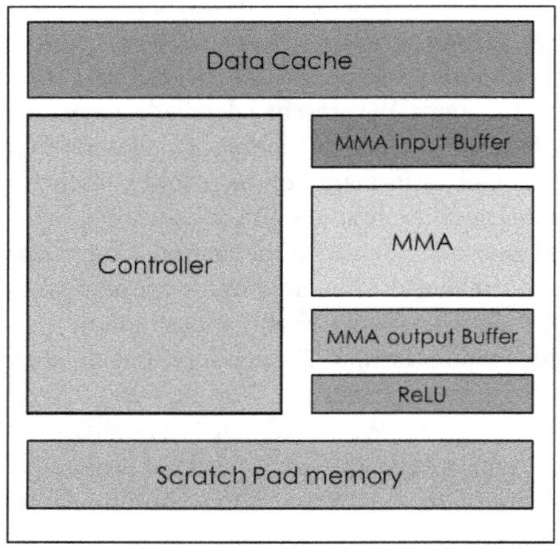

Figure 2: Blocks of the proposed neural network accelerator

fixed point precision (1 sign bit, 3 integer bits, 12 fractional bits) format for the data. The choice of the aforementioned data format was to provide an optimal trade-off between precision and throughput [11]. The second design parameter (block size of the matrix computation) determines the maximum achievable speedup as well as the memory requirements of the accelerator. From literature it is evident that the matrix-multiply operation is the primary bottleneck for compute heavy workloads [16]. For memory heavy workloads, the accelerators need a low latency memory buffer. Conventional memory technologies fail to address these issues. Individual sub-blocks of the proposed design are detailed as follows:

3.1 MMA

Mathematical operation performed by the MMA unit is represented by Eqn 1. A typical workload of a neural inference engine would involve providing decisions on a sizable number of data samples in a pipelined fashion. In order to facilitate this the MMA unit is based on a systolic architecture [20]. This allows us to minimize the initialization interval for the next task on the pipeline. The data flow for the unit is shown in Fig. 3. The basic block of the MMA unit is MLA (multiply add) unit. The MMA unit can process block matrices of given block size as per the design. The implications of varying block size will be further discussed in Section 4.1. We have

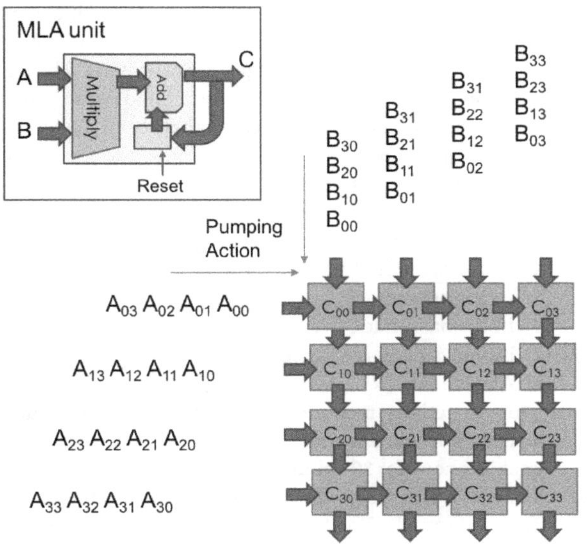

Figure 3: Data flow of MMA unit

also enhanced the MMA unit with a zero-detect capability at the level of a MLA unit. When two inputs to a MLA unit are zero then it skips performing multiplication operation and directly performs an add operation resulting in energy savings. This ensures that in case of sparse weights we can achieve maximum energy savings.

$$Y = A \times B + C \tag{1}$$

3.2 ReLU

Mathematical operation performed by the ReLU unit is represented by Eqn 2. Based on recent research trends, ReLU [29] has become the more preferred choice in comparison to traditional activation functions like sigmoid and tanh [2]. For a hardware-oriented design, ReLU is the most optimal choice due to simpler computations involved. Other traditional activation functions such as sigmoid and tanh would require a lookup table based implementation for fixed point precision based hardware. This would increase the area and latency of the design. In comparison, ReLU performs a max operation that can be realized using a comparator.

$$f(n) = \begin{cases} n & \text{if } n > 0 \\ 0 & \text{if } n <= 0 \end{cases} \tag{2}$$

3.3 Memory and Processor Interface

To remove memory bottlenecks for the MMA and ReLU units, the inference engine would require partitioned memories with different access capabilities managed by a central controller. The controller can ensure that pipeline bubbles [34] are avoided to the maximum possible extent. The major blocks used to realize such an interface are:

(1) **Memory buffers** : For each stage of input and output, a large FIFO buffer is used to store the weights of the network and inputs required for computation.

(2) **Scratch pad memory** : A scratch pad memory is a small memory block that acts as main memory for the controller. It is mapped to a subset of the address space to allow memory access with lower latency. It also stores intermediate computations after each MMA / ReLU operation [16]. Since layer-wise computations would require these intermediate results the central controller must fetch this data from memory. Using a scratch-pad memory allows the controller to schedule operations faster as it is relatively a less expensive operation in terms of both time and energy than a data fetch from DRAM.

(3) **Central controller** : The central control unit manages the data flow and schedules operations on the MMA and ReLU units. In case the data shape is not consistent with the requirement of the accelerator (block size of MMA and ReLU), the control unit performs zero-padding to ensure accurate computation is performed. The controller also manages the data storage on the scratch-pad memory as well as initiating data transfer requests with main memory.

4 PERFORMANCE ANALYSIS SIMULATIONS

We synthesized multiple implementations with different block sizes and at different technology nodes. For performance and power estimation of the design, we created an approximate model based on synthesis stage power and timing estimates. The performance parameters extracted from these implementations can be used to provide a guideline for selecting the best implementation that satisfies any given set of constraints on area, power and latency. Further we have also created a simulation model to derive workload specific energy based on network structure. This simulation also provides an estimate for the learning performance of the network on the simulated hardware.

4.1 Impact of architectural parameters

The key performance parameters of the synthesized modules with varying block sizes are shown in Table 1. The dynamic energy estimates are based on a random test vector input with 50 % switching activity. Other parameters are independent of the workload. From the results it is evident that the speed is marginally affected by increasing block size. Moreover the impact can be minimized (~ 1%) if the block size of the design is a power of 4. The power budget and area is drastically affected. Area and power scales linearly with block size for the ReLU unit while the scaling is exponential for MMA due to the total computation units being n^2 where n is the block size. However increasing block size may also result in more energy savings depending on the workload (network architecture) for the system. If the data being fed into the network is high-dimensional or more hidden units are required in the network, a larger block size will reduce memory transfers and total computation cycles. This lowers down the power dissipation.

Another approach to optimize on energy and speed trade-off would be the choice of technology node. In the second analysis, we have synthesized the basic version of the modules with block size of 4 using three different PDKs (Process Design Kits). The results are summarized in Table 2. We can observe that implementing the design on a lower node increases performance per watt uniformly.

However, the major trade-off would be based on factors like frequency targets, power budget and monetary budget for production.

Table 1: Estimated power and performance with UMC 28 nm technology node synthesis library for MMA architecture variants based on block size

Design name	Frequency (MHz)	Area (mm^2)	Leakage power (uW)	Dynamic energy (pJ)
MLA	156.23	4.75E-04	2.39	0.96
MMA4	135.12	6.20E-03	30.51	11.85
MMA8	131.86	2.88E-02	143.90	38.84
MMA16	133.16	1.29E-01	645.21	157.94
MMA32	114.39	5.53E-01	2,755.35	874.58
ReLU4	699.79	1.97E-04	0.98	0.08
ReLU8	537.92	4.21E-04	2.13	0.11
ReLU16	400.64	8.38E-04	4.22	0.30
ReLU32	352.36	1.66E-03	8.36	0.65

Table 2: Pre-Si estimates derived using Cadence Genus for different technology nodes (Synthesis stage)

Technology lib	Design name	Frequency (MHz)	Area (um^2)	Leakage power (uW)	Dynamic energy (fJ)
UMC 28 nm	ReLU	699.79	197	0.98	76.09
	MLA	156.23	475	2.39	956.49
	MMA	135.12	6.19	30.51	11851.19
TSMC 65 nm	ReLU	1194.74	881	2.97	79.81
	MLA	267.31	2465	12.63	839.98
	MMA	268.24	31568	158.46	9502.51
UMC 90 nm	ReLU	398.09	2146	4.24	151.09
	MLA	103.31	7604	16.09	4055.10
	MMA	85.01	95284	196.70	33805.47

4.2 IoT workload performance modeling

In order to understand and model the operation of an accelerator on different neural networks, we have created a functional model to estimate the total number of operations performed by each unit. These estimates are used in Section 4.3 for power estimation. The preliminary results obtained from this study can open up opportunities to locate bottlenecks in the data flow of the accelerator and thus help in further architectural improvements. For modeling learning performance with the proposed architecture, we have used a simulation test-bench that quantizes the original neural network weights and input data in accordance with the hardware constraints specified in 3. As a case study, we have used networks trained for two datasets as representative of the IoT-centric workloads from the UCI repository [1]:

- Pima Indians Diabetes [37]: This dataset contains medical data of patients to check if the patient shows signs of diabetes according to World Health Organization criteria. The dataset gives eight features for each patient and labels them with two classes based on presence or absence of diabetes. The features used are:
  (1) Number of times pregnant
  (2) Plasma glucose concentration
  (3) Diastolic blood pressure (mm Hg)
  (4) Triceps skin fold thickness (mm)
  (5) 2-Hour serum insulin (mu U/ml)
  (6) Body mass index (weight in kg / (height in m)^2)
  (7) Diabetes pedigree function
  (8) Age (years)
- Human activity recognition [3]: This dataset contain data collected from sensors (gyroscope and accelerometer) of a mobile phone for 30 volunteers. Different time and frequency features were extracted which constitute a 561 feature vector for each sample. The types of activity distinguished are :
  (1) Walking
  (2) Walking Upstairs
  (3) Walking Downstairs
  (4) Sitting
  (5) Standing
  (6) Laying

We have used the ELM (Extreme Learning Machines) [15] network for learning performance analysis primarily for it's simplicity and potential for adaptive learning with low computation cost. This makes it a very good candidate for IoT applications. Our simulated ELM network uses ReLU as the activation function in place of sigmoid. We compared the training and test accuracy for both datasets. The results of the study are summarized in Table 3. Only marginal drop in accuracy was observed for inference tasks.

Table 3: Algorithmic learning performance results

Dataset	Implementation	Train_set accuracy	Test_set accuracy
Pima Indians Diabetes [37]	ELM SW	80.38%	75.00%
	Accelerator model	80.38%	75.52%
Human Activity Recognition [3]	ELM SW	78.28%	78.55%
	Accelerator model	78.31%	78.52%

4.3 Power Analysis

IoT systems typically use a battery or a renewable energy source as the primary source for power. For modeling power, leakage and dynamic power estimates are independently obtained from the implementation (shown in Table 1). Total power budget for given inference workload is modeled by first estimating the number of operations performed. The two components of power i.e. Leakage and Dynamic are modeled independently. The leakage power is directly obtained from the synthesis estimate. Whereas for modeling dynamic power we first estimate dynamic energy per operation. The dynamic power for the accelerator is calculated using Eqn 3. Here OPS means operations per sample. Using the aforementioned power model we show preliminary power estimates for a given value of processed SPS (samples per second) with varying block size. We also present the performance per Watt (PPW) estimates using Eqn 4. Here R_{perf} can be expressed in terms of *SPS* or *OPS*. From the results summarized in Table 4, it is observed that a block size of 16 has reduced overall power budget as it is closely aligned with the network dimensions. The smaller block sizes result in more operations, thereby increasing the dynamic power. Furthermore, for block size of 32, the leakage component increases resulting in higher power dissipation.

$$DynPower_{module} = DynEnergy_{OP} \times OPS \tag{3}$$

$$PPW = \frac{R_{perf}\ (Required\ Performance)}{P_{est}\ (Estimated\ Power)} \tag{4}$$

Table 4: Power Modeling estimates with varying block size for simulation of ELM 8x32x2 at 100 MHz

Block_size	MMA ops	ReLU ops	Estimated energy (pJ/S)	Estimated PPW (MSPS/W)
4	8	8	95.42	1.31
8	1.5	4	58.72	11.35
16	0.25	2	40.08	99.79
32	0.0625	1	55.34	289.11

5 FUTURE SCOPE

In Section 3.1 we have tried to resolve the issue of compute bottleneck by modifying the MMA pipeline to be based upon systolic arrays. As discussed in [16] there are certain inference workloads which may be memory bottlenecked as well. For instance, smart IoT devices which need to perform NLP (Natural Language Processing) tasks the memory bottleneck is a major limiter. There are two primary ways to address this issue:

- Increase the memory allocated to the accelerator so as to hide the latency introduced by the DRAM interface.
- Increase throughput from DRAM memory through a data cache

Emerging memory technologies such as STT-MRAM (Spin transfer torque magneto-resistive RAM) can offer some significant benefits in a hybrid design owing to it's advantages such as high density, non-volatility, etc [23]. To provide a fair comparison between SRAM and STT-MRAM, we simulated performance parameters for a 256 kB RAM with 64-bit data bus-width in Table 5. These parameters are obtained from simulation results generated using NVSim [8]. From the results presented in Table 5, it is evident that STT-MRAM based memory will have comparatively higher write energy (~ 1.5x) and write latency (~ 20x). As leakage power savings for STT-MRAM is high (~ 0.1x) and most operations performed during neural inference tasks are read, these limitations can be mitigated to a large extent. Also since we are targeting IoT architectures, the frequency of operation is not a critical requirement. As a result, the write latency of 5.3 ns is also tolerable as it only limits the frequency of operation to ~ 187 MHz. It is notable that this frequency is much higher than the maximum achieved frequency of the accelerator modules presented in Table 2. This minimizes chances of memory bottleneck. We estimated the power benefits that can be achieved for the neural inference of block-size 4 while using the diabetes dataset [37] with an ELM network of 8x32x2. The approximate ratio of read and write operations to the scratchpad memory would be 3:1. Assuming an operating frequency of 100 MHz, the estimated overall power saving amounts to ~ 30%.

Table 5: Power and performance comparison for RAM Memory using SRAM and STT-MRAM (derived using NVSIM [8])

Memory Technology	Read		Write		Leakage power (mW)	Area (mm2)
	Dynamic energy (pJ)	Latency (ps)	Dynamic energy (pJ)	Latency (ps)		
SRAM	18.93	323	18.85	274	433.44	0.48
STT-MRAM	11.50	459	27.09	5342	33.35	0.17

6 CONCLUSION

This paper presents a novel and reconfigurable design for a neural network inference engine designed specifically for IoT systems. We present a detailed analysis summarizing the impact of variation in design parameters on the performance of the neural inference engine. This analysis was geared towards optimizing the design for power, speed and area based on parameters like block size and technology node. We also proposed performance and power estimation model for the proposed accelerator. This empowers the designer to have an early estimate of the performance per watt for the design for any given application and network structure. Further we present the first instance of an ELM architecture implemented using the ReLU activation function. It was observed that the modification of the ELM network based on ReLU doesn't reduce the learning performance. Best configuration determined was based on a block size of 32 with a performance per watt of ~ 290 MSPS/W at an operating frequency of 100 MHz. We also present an analysis for improvement in memory power-efficiency by replacing the main memory of the proposed accelerator with an emerging memory technology like STT-MRAM. The change in technology can save overall operating power by ~ 30%.

ACKNOWLEDGMENTS

This research activity under the PI Prof. M. Suri is partially supported by the Department of Science & Technology (DST), SERB-EMR Government of India and IIT-D FIRP grants.

REFERENCES

[1] D.J. Newman A. Asuncion. 2007. UCI Machine Learning Repository. (2007). http://www.ics.uci.edu/$\sim$mlearn/{MLR}epository.html

[2] Forest Agostinelli, Matthew Hoffman, Peter Sadowski, and Pierre Baldi. 2014. Learning activation functions to improve deep neural networks. *arXiv preprint arXiv:1412.6830* (2014).

[3] Davide Anguita, Alessandro Ghio, Luca Oneto, Xavier Parra, and Jorge Luis Reyes-Ortiz. 2013. A Public Domain Dataset for Human Activity Recognition using Smartphones.. In *ESANN*.

[4] Ben Varkey Benjamin, Peiran Gao, Emmett McQuinn, Swadesh Choudhary, Anand R Chandrasekaran, Jean-Marie Bussat, Rodrigo Alvarez-Icaza, John V

Arthur, Paul A Merolla, and Kwabena Boahen. 2014. Neurogrid: A mixed-analog-digital multichip system for large-scale neural simulations. *Proc. IEEE* 102, 5 (2014), 699–716.

[5] Tianshi Chen, Yunji Chen, Marc Duranton, Qi Guo, Atif Hashmi, Mikko Lipasti, Andrew Nere, Shi Qiu, Michele Sebag, and Olivier Temam. 2012. BenchNN: On the broad potential application scope of hardware neural network accelerators. In *Workload Characterization (IISWC), 2012 IEEE International Symposium on*. IEEE, 36–45.

[6] Yu-Hsin Chen, Tushar Krishna, Joel S Emer, and Vivienne Sze. 2017. Eyeriss: An energy-efficient reconfigurable accelerator for deep convolutional neural networks. *IEEE Journal of Solid-State Circuits* 52, 1 (2017), 127–138.

[7] Mike Davies, Narayan Srinivasa, Tsung-Han Lin, Gautham Chinya, Prasad Joshi, Andrew Lines, Andreas Wild, and Hong Wang. 2018. Loihi: A Neuromorphic Manycore Processor with On-Chip Learning. *IEEE Micro* (2018).

[8] Xiangyu Dong, Cong Xu, Norm Jouppi, and Yuan Xie. 2014. NVSim: A circuit-level performance, energy, and area model for emerging non-volatile memory. In *Emerging Memory Technologies*. Springer, 15–50.

[9] Jeffrey L. Elman. 1990. Finding structure in time. *COGNITIVE SCIENCE* 14, 2 (1990), 179–211.

[10] Kaiyuan Guo, Lingzhi Sui, Jiantao Qiu, Song Yao, Song Han, Yu Wang, and Huazhong Yang. 2016. From model to FPGA: Software-hardware co-design for efficient neural network acceleration. In *Hot Chips 28 Symposium (HCS), 2016 IEEE*. IEEE, 1–27.

[11] Suyog Gupta, Ankur Agrawal, Kailash Gopalakrishnan, and Pritish Narayanan. 2015. Deep learning with limited numerical precision. In *International Conference on Machine Learning*. 1737–1746.

[12] Song Han, Xingyu Liu, Huizi Mao, Jing Pu, Ardavan Pedram, Mark A Horowitz, and William J Dally. 2016. EIE: efficient inference engine on compressed deep neural network. In *Proceedings of the 43rd International Symposium on Computer Architecture*. IEEE Press, 243–254.

[13] Song Han, Huizi Mao, and William J Dally. 2015. Deep compression: Compressing deep neural networks with pruning, trained quantization and huffman coding. *arXiv preprint arXiv:1510.00149* (2015).

[14] Kurt Hornik, Maxwell Stinchcombe, and Halbert White. 1989. Multilayer feedforward networks are universal approximators. *Neural networks* 2, 5 (1989), 359–366.

[15] Guang-Bin Huang, Qin-Yu Zhu, and Chee-Kheong Siew. 2006. Extreme learning machine: theory and applications. *Neurocomputing* 70, 1-3 (2006), 489–501.

[16] Norman P Jouppi, Cliff Young, Nishant Patil, David Patterson, Gaurav Agrawal, Raminder Bajwa, Sarah Bates, Suresh Bhatia, Nan Boden, Al Borchers, et al. 2017. In-datacenter performance analysis of a tensor processing unit. *arXiv preprint arXiv:1704.04760* (2017).

[17] Muhammad Mukaram Khan, David R Lester, Luis A Plana, A Rast, Xin Jin, Eustace Painkras, and Stephen B Furber. 2008. SpiNNaker: mapping neural networks onto a massively-parallel chip multiprocessor. In *Neural Networks, 2008. IJCNN 2008.(IEEE World Congress on Computational Intelligence). IEEE International Joint Conference on*. Ieee, 2849–2856.

[18] S Kim, M Ishii, S Lewis, T Perri, M BrightSky, W Kim, R Jordan, GW Burr, N Sosa, A Ray, et al. 2015. NVM neuromorphic core with 64k-cell (256-by-256) phase change memory synaptic array with on-chip neuron circuits for continuous in-situ learning. In *Electron Devices Meeting (IEDM), 2015 IEEE International*. IEEE, 17–1.

[19] Alex Krizhevsky, Ilya Sutskever, and Geoffrey E Hinton. 2012. Imagenet classification with deep convolutional neural networks. In *Advances in neural information processing systems*. 1097–1105.

[20] Sun Yuan Kung. 1988. VLSI array processors. *Englewood Cliffs, NJ, Prentice Hall, 1988, 685 p. Research supported by the Semiconductor Research Corp., SDIO, NSF, and US Navy.* (1988).

[21] Hon Keung Kwan. 1992. Simple sigmoid-like activation function suitable for digital hardware implementation. *Electronics letters* 28, 15 (1992), 1379–1380.

[22] Yann LeCun, Yoshua Bengio, et al. 1995. Convolutional networks for images, speech, and time series. *The handbook of brain theory and neural networks* 3361, 10 (1995), 1995.

[23] Kangho Lee and Seung H Kang. 2011. Development of embedded STT-MRAM for mobile system-on-chips. *IEEE Transactions on Magnetics* 47, 1 (2011), 131–136.

[24] Fengfu Li, Bo Zhang, and Bin Liu. 2016. Ternary weight networks. *arXiv preprint arXiv:1605.04711* (2016).

[25] Cory Merkel and Dhireesha Kudithipudi. 2014. Neuromemristive extreme learning machines for pattern classification. In *VLSI (ISVLSI), 2014 IEEE Computer Society Annual Symposium on*. IEEE, 77–82.

[26] Janardan Misra and Indranil Saha. 2010. Artificial neural networks in hardware: A survey of two decades of progress. *Neurocomputing* 74, 1-3 (2010), 239–255.

[27] Dharmendra S Modha. 2014. Introducing a Brain-inspired Computer. *IBM Research, accessed at www. research. ibm. com/articles/brain-chip. shtml* (2014).

[28] David Moloney, Brendan Barry, Richard Richmond, Fergal Connor, Cormac Brick, and David Donohoe. 2014. Myriad 2: Eye of the computational vision storm. In *Hot Chips 26 Symposium (HCS), 2014 IEEE*. IEEE, 1–18.

[29] Vinod Nair and Geoffrey E Hinton. 2010. Rectified linear units improve restricted boltzmann machines. In *Proceedings of the 27th international conference on machine learning (ICML-10)*. 807–814.

[30] Eriko Nurvitadhi, Ganesh Venkatesh, Jaewoong Sim, Debbie Marr, Randy Huang, Jason Ong Gee Hock, Yeong Tat Liew, Krishnan Srivatsan, Duncan Moss, Suchit Subhaschandra, et al. 2017. Can FPGAs Beat GPUs in Accelerating Next-Generation Deep Neural Networks?. In *FPGA*. 5–14.

[31] NVIDIA. 2017. NVIDIA Deep Learning Accelerator. (2017). http://nvdla.org/

[32] Kalin Ovtcharov, Olatunji Ruwase, Joo-Young Kim, Jeremy Fowers, Karin Strauss, and Eric S Chung. 2015. Accelerating deep convolutional neural networks using specialized hardware. *Microsoft Research Whitepaper* 2, 11 (2015).

[33] Angshuman Parashar, Minsoo Rhu, Anurag Mukkara, Antonio Puglielli, Rangharajan Venkatesan, Brucek Khailany, Joel Emer, Stephen W Keckler, and William J Dally. 2017. SCNN: An Accelerator for Compressed-sparse Convolutional Neural Networks. In *Proceedings of the 44th Annual International Symposium on Computer Architecture*. ACM, 27–40.

[34] David A Patterson. 1985. Reduced instruction set computers. *Commun. ACM* 28, 1 (1985), 8–21.

[35] Mohammad Rastegari, Vicente Ordonez, Joseph Redmon, and Ali Farhadi. 2016. Xnor-net: Imagenet classification using binary convolutional neural networks. In *European Conference on Computer Vision*. Springer, 525–542.

[36] Brandon Reagen, Paul Whatmough, Robert Adolf, Saketh Rama, Hyunkwang Lee, Sae Kyu Lee, José Miguel Hernández-Lobato, Gu-Yeon Wei, and David Brooks. 2016. Minerva: Enabling low-power, highly-accurate deep neural network accelerators. In *ACM SIGARCH Computer Architecture News*, Vol. 44. IEEE Press, 267–278.

[37] UCI Machine Learning Repository. 2011. Pima Indians Diabetes Data Set. (2011). https://archive.ics.uci.edu/ml/datasets/pima+indians+diabetes

[38] Lucas L Sanches, Alessandro Fumarola, Severin Sidler, Pritish Narayanan, Irem Boybat, Junwoo Jang, Kibong Moon, Robert M Shelby, Yusuf Leblebici, Hyunsang Hwang, et al. 2017. Multilayer Perceptron Algorithm: Impact of Nonideal Conductance and Area-Efficient Peripheral Circuits. In *Neuro-inspired Computing Using Resistive Synaptic Devices*. Springer, 209–231.

[39] Manan Suri and Vivek Parmar. 2015. Exploiting intrinsic variability of filamentary resistive memory for extreme learning machine architectures. *IEEE Transactions on Nanotechnology* 14, 6 (2015), 963–968.

[40] Manan Suri, Vivek Parmar, Ashwani Kumar, Damien Querlioz, and Fabien Alibart. 2015. Neuromorphic hybrid rram-cmos rbm architecture. In *Non-Volatile Memory Technology Symposium (NVMTS), 2015 15th*. IEEE, 1–6.

[41] Wim Vanderbauwhede and Khaled Benkrid. 2013. *High-performance computing using FPGAs*. Springer.

[42] Shimeng Yu, Zhiwei Li, Pai-Yu Chen, Huaqiang Wu, Bin Gao, Deli Wang, Wei Wu, and He Qian. 2016. Binary neural network with 16 Mb RRAM macro chip for classification and online training. In *Electron Devices Meeting (IEDM), 2016 IEEE International*. IEEE, 16–2.

[43] Babak Zamanlooy and Mitra Mirhassani. 2014. Efficient VLSI implementation of neural networks with hyperbolic tangent activation function. *IEEE Transactions on Very Large Scale Integration (VLSI) Systems* 22, 1 (2014), 39–48.

Leveraging Spintronic Devices for Efficient Approximate Logic and Stochastic Neural Networks

Shaahin Angizi[†], Zhezhi He[†], Yu Bai[‡], Jie Han[*], Mingjie Lin[†], Ronald F. DeMara[†] and Deliang Fan[†]
[†] Department of Electrical and Computer Engineering, University of Central Florida, Orlando, FL 32816
[‡] Department of Engineering and Computer Science, California State University, Fullerton CA, 92831
[*] Department of Electrical and Computer Engineering, University of Alberta, Edmonton, AB T6G 1H9, Canada
dfan@ucf.edu

ABSTRACT

ITRS has identified nano-magnet based spintronic devices as promising post-CMOS technologies for information processing and data storage due to their ultra-low switching energy, non-volatility, superior endurance, excellent retention time, high integration density and compatibility with CMOS technology. As for data storage, spintronic memory has been widely accepted as a universal high performance next-generation non-volatile memory candidate. As for information processing, spintronic computing remains complementary in its features to CMOS technology. In this paper, we present two innovative spintronic computing primitives, i.e. spintronic approximate logic and spintronic stochastic neural network, which both leverage the intrinsic spintronic device physics to achieve much more compact and efficient designs than CMOS counterparts. In spintronic approximate logic, we employ the intrinsic current-mode thresholding operation to implement an accuracy-configurable adder and further demonstrate its application in approximate DSP applications. In spintronic stochastic neural networks, we leverage the stochastic properties of domain wall devices and magnetic tunnel junction to implement a low-power and robust artificial neural network design.

ACM Reference Format:
Shaahin Angizi, Zhezhi He, Yu Bai, Jie Han, Mingjie Lin, Ronald F. DeMara and Deliang Fan. 2018. Leveraging Spintronic Devices for Efficient Approximate Logic and Stochastic Neural Networks. In *Proceedings of 2018 Great Lakes Symposium on VLSI (GLSVLSI '18)*. ACM, New York, NY, USA, 6 pages. https://doi.org/10.1145/3194554.3194618

1 INTRODUCTION

Nowadays, the insufficient ability of modern computing platforms to deliver simultaneously energy efficient and high performance computing solutions leads to a gap between meets and needs. Specially, owing to the boom in machine learning, artificial intelligence and internet of things areas, data analytics can not only rely on conventional computing methods. That's why recently approximate computing [3, 13] and brain-inspired computing [5] have drawn a lot of attentions.Within current Boolean logic and Complementary Metal Oxide Semiconductor (CMOS) based computing platforms, such gap will keep widening mainly due to limitations in devices and computing model. Of all nanoelectronic paradigms, spintronic devices have attracted significant attention over the past decade due to non-volatility, zero leakage current, high integration density, low standby power, and back end of line fabrication with CMOS technology [10]. However, these emerging devices often exhibit strong stochastic switching behaviors and suffer from large variations in both electrical characteristics and device reliability. Therefore, how to efficiently leverage the unique device properties of emerging spintronic devices to facilitate new computing tasks becomes a both intriguing and important research challenge. In this paper, we first present a majority gate design employing intrinsic current-mode thresholding operation of spintronic device to implement an accuracy configurable adder for approximate DSP applications. Moreover, we also show that a stochastic-based soft-limiting artificial neural network (S-ANN) can be efficiently designed for brain-inspired computing employing spintonic devices.

GLSVLSI '18, May 23–25, 2018, Chicago, IL, USA

ACM ISBN 978-1-4503-5724-1/18/05...$15.00
https://doi.org/10.1145/3194554.3194618

2 APPROXIMATE COMPUTING

2.1 Spin-TD

In this section, we present spintronic Threshold Device (Spin-TD) based on a composite device structure consisting of a Domain Wall Motion magnetic stripe (DWS) and Magnetic Tunnel Junction (MTJ). The device structure is shown in Fig. 1a [3, 10]. It consists of a thin and short ($2nm \times 20nm \times 50nm$) magnetic DWS connecting two fixed anti-parallel magnetic domains. When the electrons are injected into the lateral terminals (T1 or T2), they become spin-polarized and exert a Spin-Transfer Torque (STT) on the Domain Wall (DW) (i.e., the transition area between two domains). This spin-polarized current can move DW within DWS. A fixed small magnet and DWS beneath it form a MTJ to read the state of DWS. It is noteworthy that an MTJ consists of two ferromagnetic layers (a free layer and a fixed one as shown in Fig. 1a) with a tunneling oxide (commonly MgO) barrier sandwiched between them [10].

The fixed layer of sense MTJ in Spin-TD is very small ($20nm \times 20nm$). The magnetization of DWS can be identified anti-parallel (AP) or parallel (P) to the fixed layer by injecting a current (larger than critical current) along it from its terminals (T1 to T2) or vice-versa [10]. Hence, the Spin-TD can detect the polarity of current flow at its input node, acting as an ultra-low voltage and compact current comparator. The resistance states are binary, i.e. either high (corresponding to AP configuration) or low (corresponding to P configuration) and can be read employing the Spin-TD sense circuit.

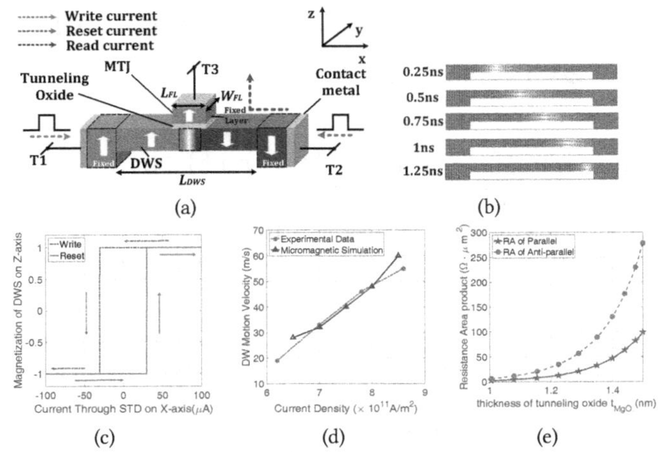

Figure 1: (a) Spin-TD structure, (b) Micro-magnetic simulation for the DW position, (c) Spin-TD transfer function and reset, (d) Simulated DW motion velocity vs. lateral current density, (e) Resistance-area product vs. the thickness of tunneling oxide in AP and P states.

Table 1: Device parameters used in simulation.

Symbol	Quantity	Values
α	Damping coefficient	0.02
K_u	Uniaxial anisotropy constant	$3.5 \times 10^5 J/m^3$
M_s	Saturation magnetization	$6.8 \times 10^5 A/m$
A_{ex}	Exchange stiffness	$1.1 \times 10^{-11} J/m$
P	Polarization	0.6
t_{MgO}	MgO thickness of MTJ	1.5 nm
$(L.W.t)_{DWS}$	DWS dimension	$50 \times 20 \times 2nm^3$

The threshold of Spin-TD, i.e. the minimum current magnitude required to switch the DWS magnetization (move DW from one end to the other end), is determined by the critical current density and DW velocity.

The transient micro-magnetic simulation of DW position (achieved from OOMMF [15]) is illustrated in Fig. 1b, using device dimension shown in Table 1, from 0.25 ns to 1.25 ns. Since the magnetization of DWS beneath the MTJ is fully switched at 1 ns, the Spin-TD intrinsic threshold (I_{th}) of this device can be considered 30μA within 1 ns corresponding to DW velocity of $\sim$ 50m/s. Fig. 1c describes DWS magnetization switch corresponding to the applied current pulse (1 ns). A hysteresis effect can be observed due to DWM critical current density. We benchmarked the micro-magnetic simulation with the experimental data in [11] (the same nano-stripe width of 20nm is fabricated) and it shows a good match as shown in Fig. 1d. The MTJ is modeled using NEGF-LLG solution (non-equilibrium Green's function and Landau-Lifshitz-Gilbert equations) for spin to charge interface and calibrated with experimental data in [8, 11]. Resistance-area product vs. the thickness of tunneling oxide in AP and P states in this work considering a constant voltage of 50mV is plotted in Fig. 1e. For a 1 ns clock cycle, the oxide thickness in this work is chosen to be 1.5 nm that results in a total power dissipation of $\sim$ 1μW for the sensing circuit (including the clocking power). It is worth noting that in the sense circuit, the transient current with short duration (1 ns) and low magnitude ($\sim$ 2μA) flows from T2 to T3, which will not disturb the state of DWS (domain wall position).

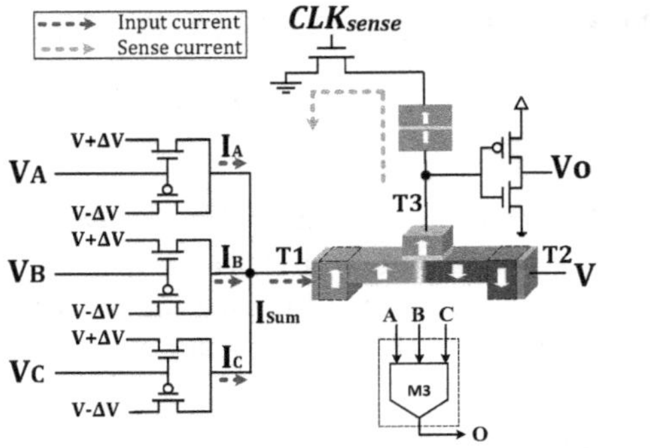

Figure 2: Hybrid Spin-CMOS 3-input majority gate.

2.2 Spin-CMOS majority gate

In this section, we present a highly-scalable spin-CMOS majority gate circuit design based on Spin-TD. The output of an n-input Majority Gate (MG) (*n is odd*) is determined by the majority of its inputs. For instance, the output is asserted to be logic value "1" only when more than ($\frac{n-1}{2}$) of the inputs are "1".

The proposed three-input MG circuit employing Spin-TD is shown in Fig. 2. The input terminal (T1) is connected to a network consisting of 3 pairs of NMOS-PMOS input transistors, in which all of the input transistors work as Deep Triode region Current Sources (DTCS) by applying $V + \Delta V$=550mV and $V - \Delta V$=450mV to the source and drain, respectively. The proposed circuit is controlled by two clock signals ($CLK_{compute}$ and CLK_{sense}) and each clock period is set to be 1 ns to synchronize with next stage circuits. Note that, T2 of Spin-TD is connected to a constant voltage of V=500mV and the voltage difference is ΔV=50mv, leading to an ultra-small voltage drop and correspondingly-low power consumption.

During the computation clock interval, the binary input voltages (VDD,GND) are applied at the gate of the input transistors, leading to input current flowing into (positive) or out of (negative) the connected Spin-TD. According to the principle of conservation of electric charge, the direction and magnitude of total current at intersection node depend on the algebraic sum of the input currents (I_A, I_B and I_C herein). This summation current (I_{Sum}) determines the position of DW as described in Section 2. By properly sizing the input transistors, the current flowing to T1 from each input branch is either +30μA or $-$30μA corresponding to input gate voltages as high ("1") or low ("0"), respectively. For instance, the input combination of (A,B,C)=(0,1,1) leads to (I_A,I_B,I_C)=($-$30μA, +30μA, +30μA) and the total current flowing into T1 is +30μA. Such current is equal to the threshold current of the Spin-TD and relocates the domain wall towards the T1 side, further resulting in the sense MTJ in an anti-parallel high resistance state. During the sense phase, when the CLK_{sense} is high, a voltage divider between Spin-TD's MTJ and a fixed reference MTJ is formed to sense the resistance state of spin-CMOS 3-input MG to produce reliable output voltage right after the inverter. In this case, the sensing circuit will generate a high output representing logic "1".

2.3 Spin-CMOS accuracy-configurable Adder

2.3.1 Functionality Analysis. A full adder (FA) is one of the most frequently-used components in arithmetic circuitry. In addition to its regular use for addition, it is employed in other arithmetic operations such as subtraction, multiplication, and division [3]. For instance, multiplication has been implemented using successive additions. Moreover, FA is the key component and optimization target of many DSP algorithms. Hence, in order to obtain a high performance DSP system, we need to design energy efficient and low complexity adders [14]. While extensive work has been done in designing approximate adders [13, 17], the research efforts on accuracy-configurable approximate adders are limited. Let A, B, and C_{in} be inputs of an accurate full adder, the principle Boolean expression of Carry out (C_{out}) and accurate Sum (Sum_{acc}) of FA cell are as follows:

$$C_{out} = AB + AC_{in} + BC_{in} = M3(A, B, C_{in}) \quad (1)$$

$$Sum_{acc} = ABC_{in} + \bar{A}\bar{B}C_{in} + \bar{A}B\bar{C_{in}} + A\bar{B}\bar{C_{in}} \quad (2)$$

Some Boolean expressions for Sum_{acc} and C_{out} of FA based on inverters and MGs have been reported in [4]. As can be seen in (1), C_{out} can be readily derived with a 3-input MG. Alternatively, Sum_{acc} can be obtained by using 3- and 5-input MG functions as:

$$\begin{aligned} Sum_{acc} &= ABC_{in} + (\overline{AB}.\overline{AC_{in}}.\overline{BC_{in}})(A + B + C_{in}) \\ &= M5(A, B, C_{in}, \overline{C_{out}}, \overline{C_{out}}) \end{aligned} \quad (3)$$

Table 2 shows the truth table of an FA. A close observation clarifies that six of eight outputs are correct if we make $Sum = \overline{C_{out}}$. Based on this observation, we propose a streamlined and cost-effective approximate FA circuit comprising one 3-input MG and one cascaded inverter. The approximate Sum output (Sum_{App}) of this adder is given by:

$$Sum_{App} = \overline{C_{out}} = \overline{M3(A, B, C_{in})} \quad (4)$$

2.3.2 Spin-CMOS Implementation. The proposed spin-CMOS implementation of the accuracy-configurable FA cell is shown in Fig. 3 consisting of two stages: Stage 1 to generate C_{out} and Sum_{app} and Stage 2 to generate Sum_{acc}. The first stage consists of a spin-CMOS MG realizing an approximate FA (App. FA) according to (1) and (4). As shown in Fig. 3, this circuit is designed with an appropriate fan-out for producing Sum_{App} output after one add-on inverter, while C_{out} is already achieved according to the Boolean expression in (1). Meanwhile, the $\overline{C_{out}}$ ($/Sum_{app}$) produced in Stage 1 is then connected to a similarly scaled input transistor network but with a $\frac{2w}{l}$ ratio to provide a double weighted current as expressed in (3). The double weighted current in conjunction with the sum of three primary inputs flow towards the T1 of the Stage 2's MG (realizing a 5-input MG as depicted in the logical schematic in Fig. 3). Consequently, the output voltage of this stage is Sum_{acc} realizing an accurate FA (Acc. FA). To provide the circuit with a proper and streamlined configurability, the wire connection between these two stages is regulated using a CMOS transmission

Table 2: Truth table for accurate and approximate FAs.

A	B	C_{in}	C_{out} (Acc.)	Sum (Acc.)	C_{out} (App.)	Sum (App.)
0	0	0	0	0	0 ✓	1 ✗
0	0	1	0	1	0 ✓	1 ✓
0	1	0	0	1	0 ✓	1 ✓
0	1	1	1	0	1 ✓	0 ✓
1	0	0	0	1	0 ✓	1 ✓
1	0	1	1	0	1 ✓	0 ✓
1	1	0	1	0	1 ✓	0 ✓
1	1	1	1	1	1 ✓	0 ✗

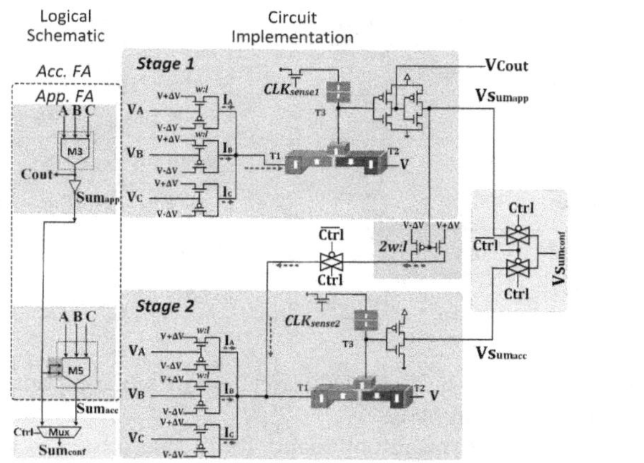

Figure 3: Logical schematic and circuit implementation of Spin-CMOS accuracy-configurable FA.

gate (TG). Furthermore, the sum outputs of both stages are laterally connected to a 2:1 CMOS multiplexer implemented utilizing two TGs to produce configurable sum (Sum_{conf}). Accordingly, the proposed spin-CMOS accuracy-configurable circuit operates in two different modes i.e. precision and approximation. In the precision mode, the control knob (*Ctrl*) is high, so the intermediate TG is ON and the double weighted current is routed to the second stage MG. Consequently, the circuit functions as an accurate adder since the second input of the multiplexer will be transmitted to the output ($Sum_{conf} = Sum_{acc}$). In the approximation mode, the *Ctrl* is low and the double weighted branch is disconnected avoiding any switching activity in second stage. Therefore, the Stage 1's circuit works as a low power approximate adder when $Sum_{conf} = Sum_{app}$.

2.4 Performance

Comparison results between the proposed adder and previously published CMOS-, MTJ-, Spin Hall Effect (SHE)- and Domain Wall Motion (DWM)-based FAs are summarized in Table 3. Various metrics including the device count, total power consumption, and delay are considered for the comparison. Note that the accuracy-configurable circuit in this work is the only adder with the approximation configurability. For fair comparison, we have done fixed-voltage scaling to 180nm process node by using the appropriate scaling factor, which is ($1/S^2$) for area and ($1/S$) for energy [1]. The results clearly show that the proposed accuracy-configurable adder consumes less power than the other designs. For instance, 34.58% and 66% improvement in power consumption can be reported for the precision and approximation modes, respectively, over the best DWM-based FA design in [23]. In addition, compared to the recently-published work by Roohi et al. in [24], the proposed FA in precision mode can show ~ 12.7× and 2.3× smaller power and delay, respectively.

We expect that leveraging the proposed accuracy-configurable adder could provide limited accuracy loss for improvements in other circuit metrics such as power and speed while implementing image processing applications. To examine this, we take widely-used Discrete Cosine Transform (DCT)/ Inverse DCT (IDCT) as an image compression algorithm as an example. We use the approximation mode of the proposed accuracy-configurable FA only in the LSBs

Table 3: Comparison of FA designs.

Designs	Device count	Power	Delay	Config.
CMOS [21]	42 MOSs	$71.1\mu W$ + 0.9nW	2200ps	No
MTJ-based [21]	34 MOSs + 4 MTJs	2100 μW + 0nW	10200ps	No
SHE-based [24]	23 MOSs + 3 SHEs	$710\mu W$ + 0nW	7000ps	No
LPM DWM [23]	20 MOSs + 4 MTJs + 2 DWSs	$85\mu W$+ 0nW	877ps	No
Prop. FA in prec. mode	28 MOSs+ 4MTJs+ 2DWSs	$55.6\mu W$+ 0nW	3000ps	Yes
Prop. FA in approx. mode	28 MOSs+ 4MTJs+ 2DWS	$28.9\mu W$+ 0nW	2000ps	Yes

of adders in a 20-bit DCT-IDCT architecture while exploiting the precision mode in MSBs.

Fig. 4a shows the output quality for the base case and five different degrees of approximations in PSNR. It can be seen that by increasing the approximation degree from the base case to 8 LSBs, the PSNR only drops by 2.93 dB. The power consumption of the DCT-IDCT circuit is evaluated using Synopsys Design Compiler for both pure-CMOS and spin-CMOS circuits as depicted in Fig. 4b. For pure-CMOS and spin-CMOS circuits, a Verilog code describing the truth table in Table 2 is considered for implementing the approximate adder based on existing and developed cell libraries, receptively, which is then used in 8-12 LSBs of a 20-bit DCT-IDCT architecture. Simulation results show that for all cases the power dissipation of the proposed spin-CMOS architecture is less than the CMOS counterpart. Evidently, by changing the degree of approximation, the power consumption of the entire system is changed. For instance, 31.33% power saving is obtained for the spin-CMOS architecture with 12 approximate LSBs in comparison with the base case, although the output quality is degraded to a PSNR of 23.75 dB. In a similar scenario, 8 approximate LSBs provide power saving of 20.4%, although the output quality is slightly degraded to 30.82 dB.

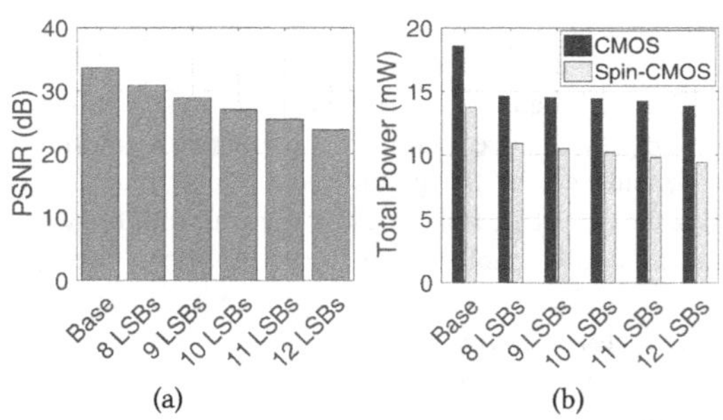

Figure 4: (a) Output quality comparison of different approximations, (b) Power consumption comparison of CMOS and spin-CMOS DCT-IDCT.

3 STOCHASTIC ARTIFICIAL NEURAL NETWORK (S-ANN)

3.1 Architecture of S-ANN

In this section, a stochastic-based ANN using Magnetic Tunnel Junction (MTJ) and domain wall device is presented [5], which has three main motivations. First, current emerging devices can not simply be considered as an alternative to replace CMOS due to large device variations. Thus, a new computation paradigm which embraces and exploits physical characteristics of spintronic devices instead of diminishing or circumventing them is essential. Second, stochastic computing offers much simpler logic operation such as multiplications and additions compared to expensive logic in deterministic method. For example, deterministic multiplications can be replaced with a simple AND operations of two random bit streams. Third, experimental results show that computation in the stochastic domain is much more robust than the deterministic method. The stochastic-based Artificial Neural Network (S-ANN) employs multiple controlled random bit streams instead of weighted sum operation in a deterministic ANN. Mathematically, we model the neuron and synapse function as the following equation:

$$Y = f(\sum X_i \oplus W_i - P_{T_i}) \quad (5)$$

where Y is the neuron output bit stream, X_i and W_i denote the ith input bit stream and its corresponding synapse weighting random bit stream, respectively. In addition, P_{T_i} denotes a threshold in stochastic bit stream and f is the stochastic neuron transfer function. The stochastic soft-limiting function is modeled as:

$$f(v) = \begin{cases} 1 & \text{if} \quad v \geq T_i \\ P_{i-1} & \text{if} \quad T_{i-1} < v < T_i \\ \cdots & \quad \cdots \quad \cdots \\ P_1 & \text{if} \quad T_1 < v < T_2 \\ 0 & \text{if} \quad v < T_1 \end{cases} \quad (6)$$

where v is the weighted sum of inputs in a stochastic bit stream, $T_{(1,\cdots,i)}$ is stochastic threshold range, $P_{(1,\cdots i)}$ is output probability. The training of S-ANN utilizes a conventional training algorithm, i.e. the backpropagation training algorithm. Such training process begins with initial weights, which are chosen randomly. The network processes training data and inputs to the weights and functions in the hidden layers. The resulting outputs are compared with the desired outputs. If there is an error, it then propagates back through the system, causing the system to adjust the weights for application and for the next data that needs to be processed. In training process, the deterministic sigmoid function is selected. Thus, the training process of S-ANN will not add any additional concerns. The training process of S-ANN does not involve in any stochastic and non-linear behavior within the S-ANN system. Once the training process is done, the probable stochastic approximations are applied to trained ANN, such as stochastic computing synthesis [2] and stochastic finite state machine [16]. Currently, most of stochastic ANNs employ finite state machine to approximate learned transfer function [26]. The transfer function is approximated by stochastic state machine using Markov chain theory. In Markov chain theory, each state is connected serially, and the transition of different states is decided by the input, which converts to the stochastic pulse stream. If the incoming pulse is '1' then the state will move forward; otherwise, it will keep at the current state. It is the probability of '1' appearing in the stochastic pulse streams. However, in the S-ANN design, we employ the DW device to approximate state and to integrate the input bitstream. It is feasible to use deterministic learning approach for this non-deterministic system because in S-ANN learning and processing are distinct and approximated by the stochastic algorithm. Fig. 5 shows an architecture of S-ANN. Instead of digital deterministic value, the S-ANN propagates random bit stream.

3.2 Stochastic Switching of MTJ Devices

Numerous experimental results have shown that spintronic devices exhibit complex switching behaviors due to the shifting of their

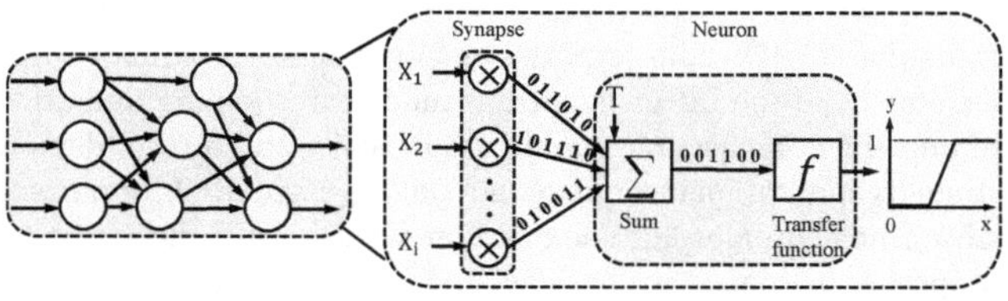

Figure 5: Architecture of stochastic neuron in S-ANN.

intrinsic magnetic moment (spin) of electrons. For example, the spin-torque switching characteristic of MTJ device is highly stochastic and exhibits a well-defined probability as shown in Fig. 6b. Several recent works have realized that the MTJ's switching probability (P_{sw}), depends on its intrinsic switching current and a thermal stability parameter (Δ). The thermal stability parameter Δ is modeled as $\Delta = E_u/k_B T$, E_u, k_B, and T are uni-axial magnetic anisotropy energy, Boltzmann's constant, and temperature, respectively. For example, if an initial state of MTJ is given as parallel state, a write current I_w applied on MTJ device with a pulse duration t can lead to a state switching under certain probability P_{sw}. This switching probability is defined as $P_{sw} = 1 - \exp(-t/\tau_p)$, where τ_p is the switching time constant. Some recent works show how to control the switching probability P_{sw} by changing the applied pulse duration and amplitude [12]. Therefore, using the applied pulse duration and amplitude, the switching probability can be concisely formulated as $P_{sw}(I) = 1 - \exp(-\frac{t}{\tau_p}\exp(-\Delta(1 - I/I_{c0})))$, where I_{c0} is the critical switching current at 0 K. In conclusion, the certain switching probability of a given MTJ device can be modeled by controlling the critical current I_c and the duration of applied pulse current τ_p. In Fig. 6a, experimental and analytical results of switching probability are plotted [22, 25].

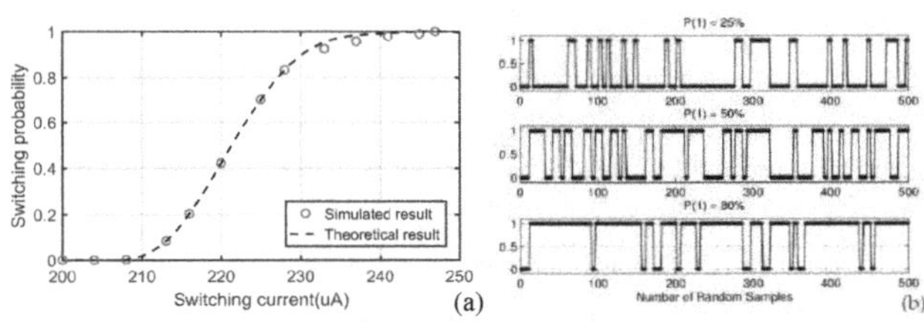

Figure 6: (a) Experimental and analytical results of switching probability [9, 22, 25], (b) SPICE simulation results of random signal generation.

3.3 Stochastic Synapse and Neuron

Fig. 7 shows the stochastic synapse design based on the reconfigurable random sample generator with one MTJ device and one DW device. The key idea of the stochastic synapse is to designing random sample generator by exploiting the stochastic switching behavior of an MTJ device at different input currents under a fixed pulse duration. The S-ANN architecture can be operated by two modes. In configuration mode (Fig. 7a), the proper DW position is programmed according to pre-computed stochastic weights. The required writing current to MTJ is generated upon DW resistance. During the operational mode shown in (Fig. 7b), depending on the applied input either a logic "0" or "1" value, the applied voltage V_c is written into the MTJ on the right hand. However, in order to sense the DW position, a vertical current density must be smaller than its critical value to avoid the shifting of DW position. Thus, a PMOS transistor to amplify a small input current into a larger output current is essential. In Fig. 7 c, d, e, the simulation results have shown that an input small sensing current ($< 30\mu A$) to PMOS transistor terminal can be effectively boosted into a larger current at the output with a supply voltage($V_{cc} = 450mV$). In this paper, we employ the conditional perturbation scheme [7] to generate random sample and achieve a bit rate 2.7 times faster and consume switch energy 6 times lower than conventional MTJ-based random number generator method.

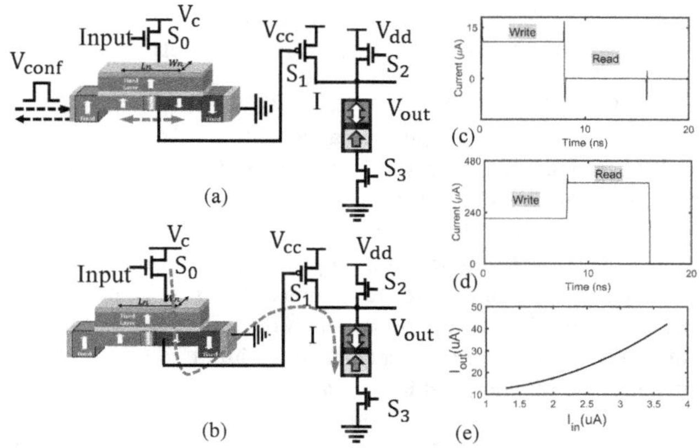

Figure 7: Circuit design of random bit stream generation. (a) Configuration mode, (b) Operational mode. Red curves depict signal directions. (c) Simulation of the current passed through DWS in write and read operation (d) Simulation of the current passed through MTJ, in write procedure, the input current is generated from a DW device and amplified by a PMOS transistor, (e) Output current.

To implement the stochastic neuron, multiple-phase pumping circuit is presented and depicted in Fig. 8b. Differ from deterministic DW device, the spin memristor DW device is employed [27]. In stochastic neuron, three key parameters: $th1$, $th2$, and H are defined. $th1$ and $th2$ denote the starting point and ending point of neural signal transformation, while $\Delta = \frac{H}{th1-th2}$ denotes the slope of a signal change. While a changing magnitude of current input to the stochastic neuron, the DW of DW1 becomes to move. When the I_{in} exceeds the critical of DW1, DW at DW1 starts to move. Finally, the last DWn will start to move, when it receives a signal from its previous stages. Therefore, one signal V_{in} is delivered to the last DW device (DWn) and can be amplified depending on the ($DW_2, ..., DW_n$). Firstly, we model the function of input current and DW movement x as $x_i = f(I_i)$. Using experimental results from DW devices, the function f is approximated as a linear function. Thus, the current passed to the next stage is equal to $\frac{V_{c1}(B\cdot x_1)+C}{A}$, where x_1 and v_{c1} are defined as DW movement and supply voltage in DW1, respectively. Consequently, the second stage output current is equal to $\frac{V_{c2}(B\cdot x_2)+C}{A}$, where x_2 is defined as DW movement in DW2 and equal to $x_2 = f(\frac{V_{c1}(B\cdot x_1)+C}{A})$. The output current at the last DW device can be calculated according to the equation on above. Thus, representing a tri-layered DW structure, the output current at the third DW device is amplified by factor $V_{c3} \cdot V_{c2} \cdot V_{c1}$, approximately.

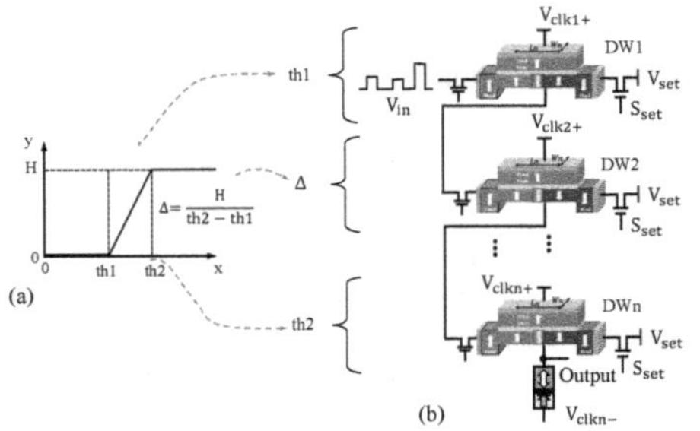

Figure 8: (a) Transfer function of ANN neuron, (b) Architecture of stochastic soft-limiting transfer function neuron.

3.4 Performance

In order to analyze the performance of the S-ANN, we select a well-known neural network task for handwritten digits recognition (MNIST). The MNIST dataset has 60K training samples and 10K testing samples. The simulation process contains two steps: training and pattern matching. In training process, the topology, synapse weights, and neural transfer functions of the S-ANN are obtained using the standard software and open resource code. Afterwards, the S-ANN is built up and predetermined input voltages. We summarize trade-off energy efficiency and recognition performance. In Fig. 9a and b, we present trade-off energy and inaccuracy between S-ANN and conventional CMOS-based stochastic ANN [6, 16, 18, 26]. Each experimental result is repeated ten times in order to minimize random errors. The inaccuracy calculation is based upon comparing the stochastic output with the corresponding probability. Compare to the other stochastic neural networks in CMOS, the S-ANN has high recognition rate. There are three reasons that consider as accuracy degradation: 1) the scaled addition of bit-stream 2) the Inter-stream correlation 3) transfer function FMS-approximation. To improve the accuracy of stochastic ANN, we use KCL summation to overcome scaled addition issue, MTJ-based random number generator to avoid inter-stream correlations, and emerging device soft-limit approximation to reduce the approximation error. In energy comparison, the S-ANN using MTJ-based true random number generator saves 8-10X energy compared with synthesized CMOS-based LFSR [16, 19, 20, 26]. In Fig. 9a and b, we compare the energy and inaccuracy with different bitstream sizes.

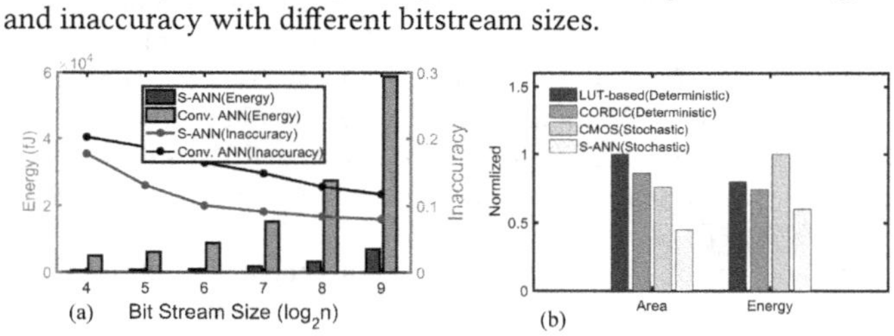

Figure 9: (a) Energy and inaccuracy comparison with different bitstream sizes. (b) Area and Energy comparison at same accuracy level.

4 CONCLUSION

In this paper, we presented two innovative spintronic computing primitives, i.e. spintronic approximate logic and spintronic stochastic neural network, which both leverage the intrinsic spintronic device physics to achieve much more compact and efficient designs than CMOS counterparts. In spintronic approximate logic, we employed the intrinsic current-mode thresholding operation to implement an accuracy configurable adder and further demonstrate its application in approximate DSP applications. In spintronic stochastic neuromorphic computation, we leveraged the stochastic properties of domain wall devices and magnetic tunnel junction to implement a low-power and robust artificial neural network design.

REFERENCES

[1] Zia Abbas and Mauro Olivieri. 2014. Impact of technology scaling on leakage power in nano-scale bulk CMOS digital standard cells. *Microelectronics Journal* 45, 2 (2014), 179–195.

[2] Armin Alaghi and John P Hayes. 2012. A spectral transform approach to stochastic circuits. In *ICCD*. IEEE.

[3] Shaahin Angizi et al. 2017. Composite spintronic accuracy-configurable adder for low power Digital Signal Processing. In *ISQED), 2017*. IEEE, 391–396.

[4] Mostafa Rahimi Azghadi, O Kavehie, and Keivan Navi. 2012. A novel design for quantum-dot cellular automata cells and full adders. *arXiv preprint arXiv:1204.2048* (2012).

[5] Yu Bai et al. 2017. Stochastic-Based Synapse and Soft-Limiting Neuron with Spintronic Devices for Low Power and Robust Artificial Neural Networks. *IEEE TMSCS* (2017).

[6] Bradley D Brown and Howard C Card. 2001. Stochastic neural computation. II. Soft competitive learning. *IEEE TC* 50 (2001), 906–920.

[7] Won Ho Choi et al. 2014. A Magnetic Tunnel Junction based True Random Number Generator with conditional perturb and real-time output probability tracking. In *IEDM*. https://doi.org/10.1109/IEDM.2014.7047039

[8] Xuanyao Fong et al. 2011. KNACK: A hybrid spin-charge mixed-mode simulator for evaluating different genres of spin-transfer torque MRAM bit-cells. In *SISPAD*. IEEE, 51–54.

[9] Xuanyao Fong et al. 2014. Generating true random numbers using on-chip complementary polarizer spin-transfer torque magnetic tunnel junctions. In *72nd DRC*. https://doi.org/10.1109/DRC.2014.6872318

[10] Xuanyao Fong et al. 2016. Spin-transfer torque devices for logic and memory: Prospects and perspectives. *IEEE TCAD* 35, 1 (2016), 1–22.

[11] S Fukami et al. 2013. 20-nm magnetic domain wall motion memory with ultralow-power operation. In *IEDM*. IEEE, 3–5.

[12] Akio Fukushima et al. 2014. Spin dice: A scalable truly random number generator based on spintronics. *Applied Physics Express* 7 (2014), 083001.

[13] Vaibhav Gupta et al. 2011. IMPACT: imprecise adders for low-power approximate computing. In *17th IEEE/ACM ISLPED*. IEEE Press, 409–414.

[14] Jie Han and Michael Orshansky. 2013. Approximate computing: An emerging paradigm for energy-efficient design. In *ETS*. IEEE, 1–6.

[15] http://math.nist.gov/oommf/. [n. d.]. ([n. d.]).

[16] Yuan Ji et al. 2015. A hardware implementation of a radial basis function neural network using stochastic logic. In *DATE, 2015*. 880–883.

[17] Honglan Jiang et al. 2017. A review, classification, and comparative evaluation of approximate arithmetic circuits. *ACM JETC* 13 (2017).

[18] H. Li et al. 2006. A Stochastic Digital Implementation of a Neural Network Controller for Small Wind Turbine Systems. *IEEE TPE* (Sept 2006). https://doi.org/10.1109/TPEL.2006.882420

[19] Peng Li et al. 2012. The synthesis of complex arithmetic computation on stochastic bit streams using sequential logic. In *ICCAD*. ACM.

[20] Z. Li et al. 2016. DSCNN: Hardware-oriented optimization for Stochastic Computing based Deep Convolutional Neural Networks. In *ICCD*. https://doi.org/10.1109/ICCD.2016.7753357

[21] Shoun Matsunaga et al. 2008. Fabrication of a nonvolatile full adder based on logic-in-memory architecture using magnetic tunnel junctions. *Applied Physics Express* 1, 9 (2008), 091301.

[22] N. Onizawa et al. 2014. Analog-to-stochastic converter using magnetic-tunnel junction devices. In *NANOARCH*. 59–64. https://doi.org/10.1109/NANOARCH.2014.6880490

[23] Arman Roohi et al. 2016. A tunable majority gate-based full adder using current-induced domain wall nanomagnets. *IEEE TMAG* 52, 8 (2016), 1–7.

[24] Arman Roohi, Ramtin Zand, et al. 2017. Voltage-based concatenatable full adder using spin Hall effect switching. *IEEE TCAD* 36 (2017).

[25] A.F. Vincent et al. 2015. Spin-Transfer Torque Magnetic Memory as a Stochastic Memristive Synapse for Neuromorphic Systems. *Biomedical Circuits and Systems, IEEE Transactions on* (2015), 166–174.

[26] Shaodi Wang et al. 2017. Hybrid VC-MTJ/CMOS non-volatile stochastic logic for efficient computing. In *Proceedings of the Conference on Design, Automation & Test in Europe*. European Design and Automation Association, 1442–1447.

[27] X. Wang and Y. Chen. 2010. Spintronic memristor devices and application. In *DATE 2010*. 667–672. https://doi.org/10.1109/DATE.2010.5457118

Design Space Exploration of Magnetic Tunnel Junction based Stochastic Computing in Deep Learning

You Wang
Fert Beijing Institute, BDBC and School of Electronic and Information Engineering, Beihang University, Beijing, 100191, China
youwang@buaa.edu.cn

Yue Zhang
Fert Beijing Institute, BDBC and School of Electronic and Information Engineering, Beihang University, Beijing, 100191, China
yz@buaa.edu.cn

Youguang Zhang
Fert Beijing Institute, BDBC and School of Electronic and Information Engineering, Beihang University, Beijing, 100191, China
zyg@buaa.edu.cn

Weisheng Zhao
Fert Beijing Institute, BDBC and School of Electronic and Information Engineering, Beihang University, Beijing, 100191, China
weisheng.zhao@buaa.edu.cn

Hao Cai
Département Communications et Electronique, Télécom-ParisTech, Université Paris-Saclay 75013, France
cai@telecom-paristech.fr

Lirida Naviner
Département Communications et Electronique, Télécom-ParisTech, Université Paris-Saclay 75013, France
lirida.naviner@telecom-paristech.fr

ABSTRACT

Magnetic tunnel junction (MTJ) is considered as a promising memory candidate in the more than Moore era because of high power efficiency, fast access speed, nearly infinite endurance and easy 3D integration. The nondeterministic switching behavior has been profited to exploit new directions for computing methods, such as stochastic computing. In this paper, the application of stochastic switching behavior in stochastic computing is explored for deep neural network (DNN). Stochastic computing method features low logic complexity, low energy consumption and fine-grained parallelism, boosting the performance of DNN system by combining MTJ. As a key block of stochastic computing, MTJ based true random number generator design is presented in details. The functionality has been validated by combining the hardware design and post-processing in software. Simulation results are demonstrated visibly by handwritten digits recognition test to show the accuracy. Furthermore, the performance is investigated in terms of accuracy, energy consumption and memory occupation to find more efficient techniques.

CCS CONCEPTS

• **Computing methodologies → Neural networks**;

KEYWORDS

Magnetic tunnel junction; stochastic computing; deep neural network; true random number generator

GLSVLSI '18, May 23–25, 2018, Chicago, IL, USA

ACM ISBN 978-1-4503-5724-1/18/05...$15.00
https://doi.org/10.1145/3194554.3194619

ACM Reference Format:
You Wang, Yue Zhang, Youguang Zhang, Weisheng Zhao, Hao Cai, and Lirida Naviner. 2018. Design Space Exploration of Magnetic Tunnel Junction based Stochastic Computing in Deep Learning. In *GLSVLSI '18: 2018 Great Lakes Symposium on VLSI, May 23–25, 2018, Chicago, IL, USA.* ACM, New York, NY, USA, 6 pages. https://doi.org/10.1145/3194554.3194619

1 INTRODUCTION

Among the tremendous machine learning (ML) algorithms, deep neural network (DNN) is considered as the most promising one because of high classification accuracy on various computer vision and recognition tasks [1]. However, as large amount of arithmetic operations are usually required in DNN, efficient hardware implementation is critical for DNN relevant systems [2]. Most of the arithmetic operations can be realized by addition and multiplication, which cause area and energy overhead, especially the latter one [3].

Recently, stochastic computing (SC) is regarded as a promising method to reduce energy consumption and save area of DNN hardware implementation. Compared with the conventional fixed-point computation, SC has smaller hardware footprint and higher energy efficiency [3] because the basic multiplication and accumulation operations (MAC) can be executed by AND gate and multiplexer. As a result, very large scale integration of neurons on one chip is much easier to realize using SC than conventional fixed-point hardware. The emergence of non-volatile devices accelerates the hardware implementation of SC and DNN. For example, magnetic tunnel junctions (MTJ) are used to realize stochastic computing methods and deep neural networks in [4–7]. However, there exists barely system integrating SC into DNN. With the rapid development of DNN in artificial intelligence area, the requirement for energy efficient hardware is urgently required to support the software designs [8].

Magnetic Tunnel Junction (MTJ) switched by spin transfer torque (STT) has attracted much attention in research community because of its great potentials in the next generation of non-volatile memories. Compared with conventional memories, STT-MTJ based magnetic random-access memory (MRAM) features high power efficiency, fast speed operation, infinite endurance, high density and compatibility with standard CMOS process [9]. Moreover, MTJ with perpendicular magnetic anisotropy (PMA) behaves better performance in terms of thermal stability, critical current and access speed compared to that with in-plane magnetic anisotropy [10].

The MTJ stochastic switching provides a high-quality entropy source for true random number generator (TRNG), which is an essential element for stochastic computing [11]. Based on unpredictable physical phenomenon, it can supply real random bitstreams by special circuit design. Compared with the conventional CMOS based TRNGs, the MTJ based design can effectively achieve simplified structure, more compact area, higher speed and better energy-efficiency.

This work explores the possibility of using MTJ in stochastic computing for deep neural network. Firstly, the basic structure and principles of stochastic computing is presented. Then, the MTJ based TRNG is described in details. Finally, the performance of SC based DNN is evaluated by performing handwritten digits recognition test using MNIST database [12].

2 MTJ BASED STOCHASTIC COMPUTING

Figure 1 demonstrates the basic structure of stochastic computing system, which mainly consists of three parts:

a) Binary-to-stochastic converter: This part converts the binary numbers into stochastic numbers using MTJ based true random number generators (TRNG). In stochastic computing, the number of '1' existing in the bitstream signifies the binary value. As a result, internal errors can be intrinsically masked by SC. For instance, '10001001' equals to '10010001' and '11000001', they all represent '3/8' in binary numbers. Thus, some errors existing during the stochastic computing process will finally disappear while being converted back to binary numbers.

b) Computation: The multiplication in SC is performed by an AND gate which can significantly reduce the design complexity part [13]. As the sum of 2 stochastic numbers might very well lie beyond the range, it is not possible to carry out precise addition. The scaled addition is performed by a multiplexer which is controlled by another stochastic bitstream. As demonstrated in Figure 1, the result of scaled addition of A_s and B_s is $Y_s = B_s * M_s + A_s * (1 - M_s)$. Because the operation of multiplication is very frequent in deep learning, the computation part is very suit for DNN.

c) Stochastic-to-binary converter: The results of stochastic computing can be simply converted back to binary values by counters.

The advantages of stochastic computing can be demonstrated by a case study of synthesizing polynomial function at Register Transfer Level (RTL) [14]. For instance, we consider the synthesis of the function y described in (1).

$$y = 0.06x^2 + 0.19x + 0.25 \tag{1}$$

With a 10-bit length input signal, we compare the RTL synthesis results of traditional synthesis flow (binary signal) to those from a stochastic synthesis flow. Circuit area is evaluated with 28nm FD-SOI design-kit.

Figure 2 illustrates the realized schematic based on binary signal. The total circuit area is 1122.98 μm^2. It is composed of Carry Select Adder (CSA) trees and multiplexers.

Figure 3 shows the circuit using STT-MTJ based stochastic number generator (SNG) for polynomial function. The cell area of computing part is less than 100 μm^2 according to 28nm design kit. Considering low power family transistors, the estimated propagation delay for stochastic method is 52 ps, which is far below 360.8 ps achieved by traditional deterministic computing synthesis. Detailed description of Bernstein polynomial synthesis can be found in [15]. It is noted that de-randomizer unit is required to reconstruct stochastic results to binary values.

3 MTJ BASED TRUE RANDOM NUMBER GENERATOR

In the aforementioned principles of stochastic computing, the reliability of MTJ based true random number generator (TRNG) is critical for the binary to stochastic conversion which determines the reliability and performance of SC. The conversion circuits induce significant overheads which consume 80-90% of the energy in our CMOS implementations of stochastic circuits and severely limit the overall energy efficiency of SC [5]. This section presents the operation mechanisms of TRNG design using MTJ.

It has been well confirmed, both theoretically and experimentally that a spin-polarized current will deposit its spin-angular momentum into the magnetic system when passing through a small magnetic conductor [16]. Consequently, it causes the magnetic moment to precess or even switch when the spin-current is sufficient [17]. Due to the thermal fluctuation of magnetization, the initial state of free layer magnetic moment is different at each measurement. This leads to the stochastic reversal of free layer magnetization, which is revealed by the random delay for the resistance reversal. As shown in Figure 4, continuous switching probability can be obtained by tuning either the applied current or the stress time. A tunable switching current I_{sw} is applied in this work to investigate the switching probability. The simulation result presented in Figure 4 indicates that $I_{sw} = 84.5\mu A$ is required for a switching probability of 50%.

With continuous scaling down of semiconductor devices, performance degradation induced by process variation becomes a critical issue in CMOS circuits and systems design [18]. Meanwhile, the limited fabrication precision of MTJ induces variable device parameters like the oxide barrier thickness t_{ox}, free layer thickness t_{sl} and TMR ratio [19]. In order to guarantee an accurate probability and high level of randomness, it is necessary to take into consideration the process variations. In the considered 28nm CMOS design kit, process variability is modeled by four worst-case corners [20]. TT is the typical compact model extracted from the "golden die" of the "golden wafer" representing the center-line process technology. On the one hand, the corner models are generated from slow nMOS and slow pMOS (SS) to model the worst-case speed, and from fast nMOS and fast pMOS (FF) to model the worst-case power. On the other hand, the corner models are generated from fast nMOS and slow pMOS (FS) to model the worst-case '1', and from slow nMOS and fast pMOS (SF) to model the worst-case '0' [21]. The worst-case corner models offer for designers capability to simulate the pass/fail results of a typical design and are usually pessimistic. The process variations of MTJ are also integrated in the compact model [19]. Using these models, two current values of worst cases (maximum(FF)

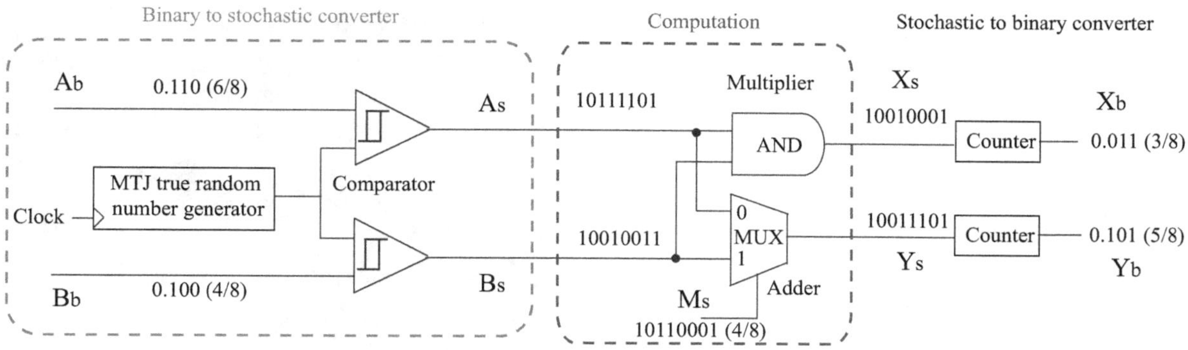

Figure 1: Basic structure of stochastic computing system: Binary numbers are firstly converted to stochastic numbers, then computation is executed and finally the stochastic numbers are converted to binary numbers using counters.

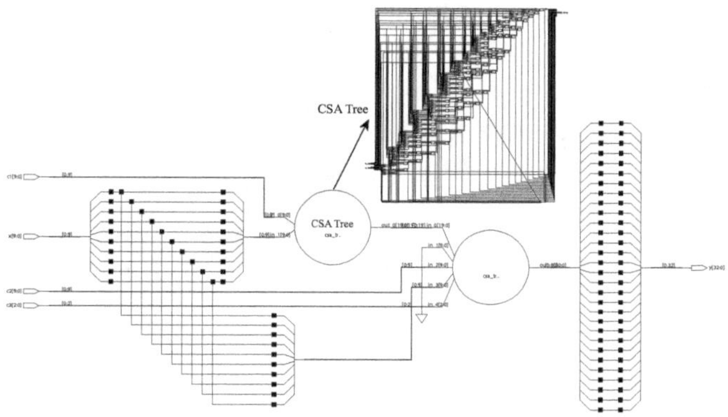

Figure 2: Polynomial function synthesis with traditional binary signal.

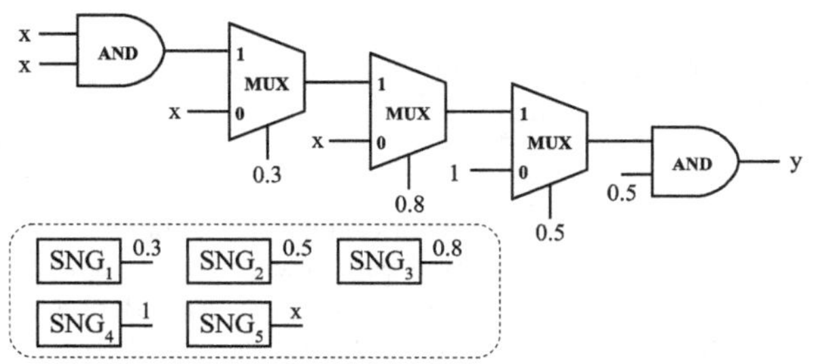

Figure 3: An example of polynomial function synthesis.

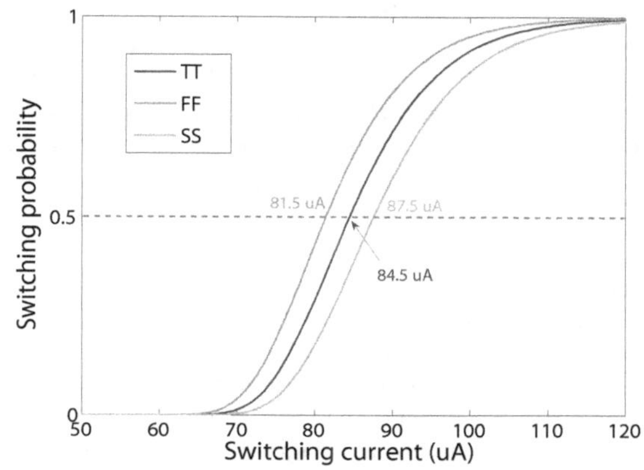

Figure 4: Switching probability of MTJs on function of switching current with 10ns pulse. The current with 50% switching success is indicated above. This figure is obtained by 1000 runs of Monte-Carlo simulation with the same MTJ under voltage pulses.

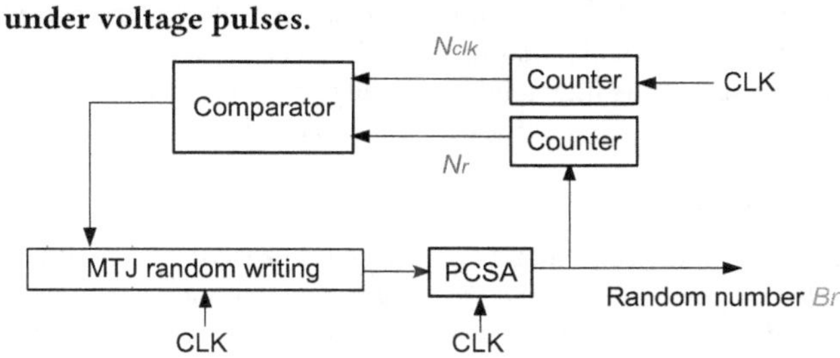

Figure 5: Architecture of proposed MTJ-based true random number generator: The random writing circuit generates a switching current to write the MTJs with 50% success and it is controlled by the correction block; The MTJ writing part enables MTJ switching (generating random number or resetting to initial state); The correction block composed of counter and comparator is used to execute real-time output probability tracking and send feedback to writing block.

and minimum (SS)) are obtained for the switching probability of 50% (shown in Figure 4).

The general architecture of MTJ based true random number generator circuit design is illustrated in Figure 5. It is composed of MTJ random writing part, pre-charge sense amplifier (PCSA) and correction block. By an appropriate choice of transistors dimensions, a particular switching probability can be obtained to get a real random bitstream. In order to improve the reliability, a correction logic block composed of counters and comparator is implemented.

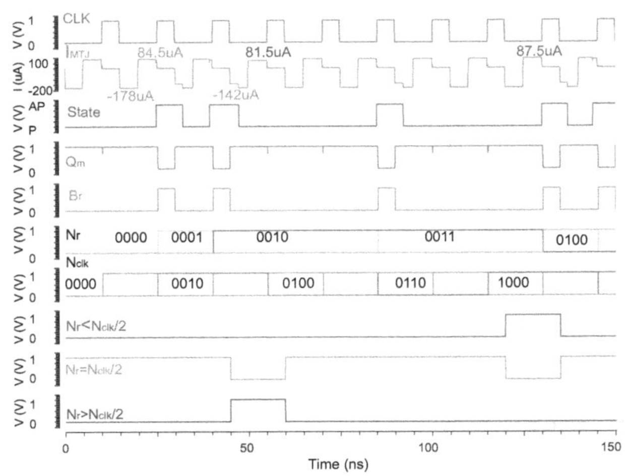

Figure 6: Time-domain diagram of proposed true random number generator. During each cycle, the MTJs are firstly reset to the initial state (with I_r=178μA for P state and I_r=142μA for AP state), then randomly switched, and finally sensed at the output. The initial current is set for 50% of switching success.

This block generates a control signal to modulate the switching current, which guarantees the exact given probability of obtained random number bitstream (ideally with 50% of '1' and 50% of '0').

By using the CMOS 28nm design kit and MTJ compact model, we carried out transient simulation of the proposed TRNG circuit. The corresponding time-domain diagram is presented in Figure 6. Firstly, the switching circuit starts to write with a relatively low current (84.5μA) with the condition of N_r=$N_{clk}/2$ (switching probability P_{sw}=50%). With $N_r > N_{clk}/2$, the switching probability is decreased while the control transistor N_{c0} is opened by the correction block. When N_r is smaller than $N_{clk}/2$, the switching current is increased with the control transistor N_{c2} activated by the correction block. This simulation result matches well the aforementioned design goal and the functionality is well confirmed. The simulation result has passed most of the randomness test [22].

4 PERFORMANCE EVALUATION

In this work, the computation part uses MTJ based logic gates presented in [23]. Thus, the MTJ stochastic switching behavior has a significant impact on the DNN performance. This section investigates the impact of MTJ stochastic switching behavior on the accuracy of stochastic computing based deep neural network. The study is performed on handwritten digits recognition test using the standard MNIST database. Figure 7 displays 10 handwritten digits pattern which usually varies from one to another. Figure 8 displays the standard hierarchy of deep neural network, in which the different layers are composed of MTJ based elements and the connections consist of stochastic computing using MTJ. Then, some switching failures are injected into the CNN to explore the design space. Figure 9 displays the impact of erroneous pixels on the accuracy of CNN for the digit with 1 bit per pixel. It can be observed

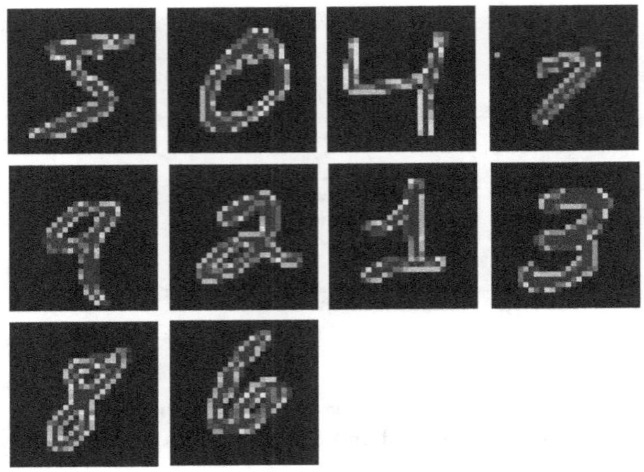

Figure 7: The trained handwritten digits from MNIST database.

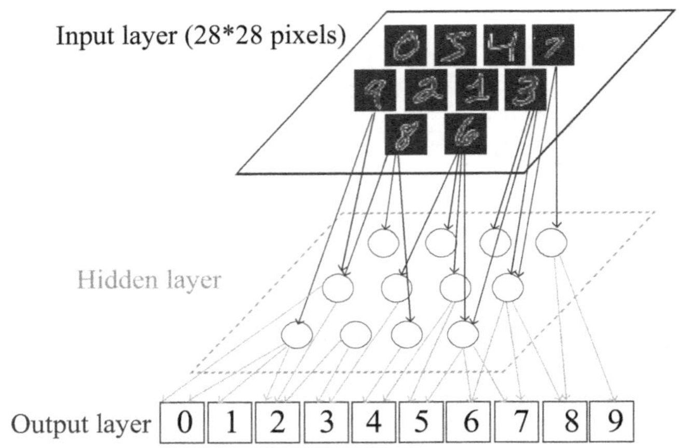

Figure 8: Stochastic computing based deep neural network used for digit recognition.

that the successful switching is critical for the recognition accuracy. As a digit is coded by many pixels with different forms, some of the digits are tolerant to fluctuations, for instance, 0 and 1, others are very sensitive to any degradation of hardware conception, such as 4 and 8.

Figure 10 demonstrates the impact of number of pixels on accuracy. The different colors represent three cases: 1 bit per pixel with errors, 1 bit and 8 bits per pixel with no error. When the number of bits in one pixel is sufficiently large, the accuracy is nearly immune to the number of pixels. Inversely, the accuracy is highly dependent on the number of pixels. Comparing the three groups, it can be assumed that the number of bits per pixel is more critical for the overall accuracy than the number of pixels. Starting from this point, a detailed study between number of bits, MTJ switching success and recognition accuracy is carried out. As illustrated in Figure 11, if the switching probability of MTJ is too small (<10%) or too large (>80%), the number of bits hardly has impact on recognition rate.

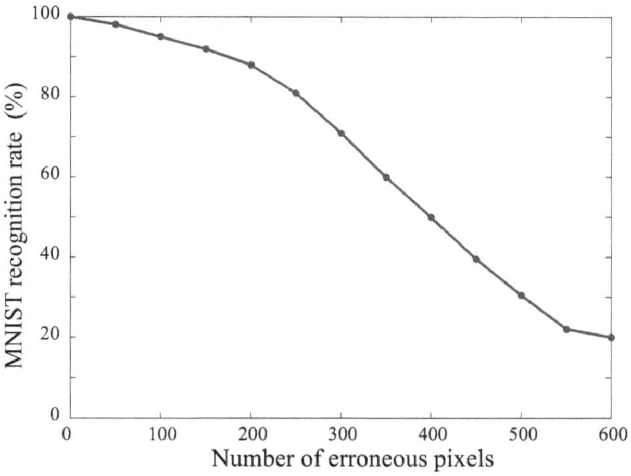

Figure 9: Success probability on function of number of erroneous pixels for image of 1 bit per pixel.

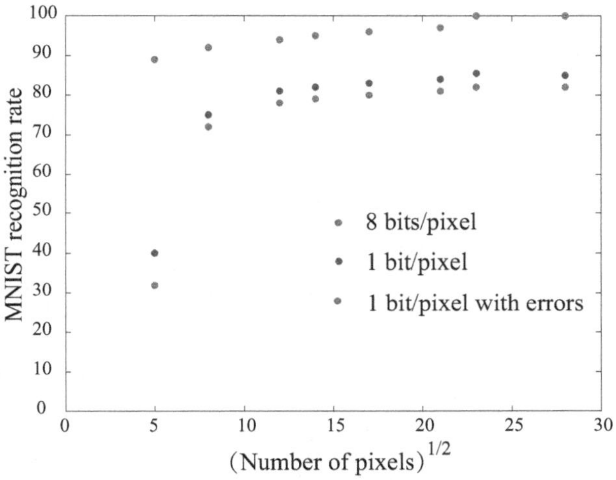

Figure 10: Success probability VS number of pixels.

However, the number of bits have significant impact on recognition rate beyond the two ranges. Figure 12 displays the recognized handwritten digits with 4 bits per pixel and 30% switching success probability. It can be observed that many digits can not be well classified by the DNN system.

As shown in Figure 13, another study is carried out using different machine learning algorithms to verify this assumption, i.e., convolutional neural network (CNN), k-Nearest Neighbor (KNN) and Support Vector Machine (SVM). The three different cases are investigated with stochastic switching behavior of MTJ. In all the cases of different imperfect switching, 1 b/p is much less accurate than other two while 8 b/p with 14*14 pixels nearly has the same accuracy with that of 28*28 pixels. Meanwhile, higher switching error rate of MTJ signifies lower energy consumption and smaller area. It can be deduced that the degradation of tolerable accuracy is efficient to reduce drastically the power consumption. Moreover, CNN is the most accurate algorithm among the three.

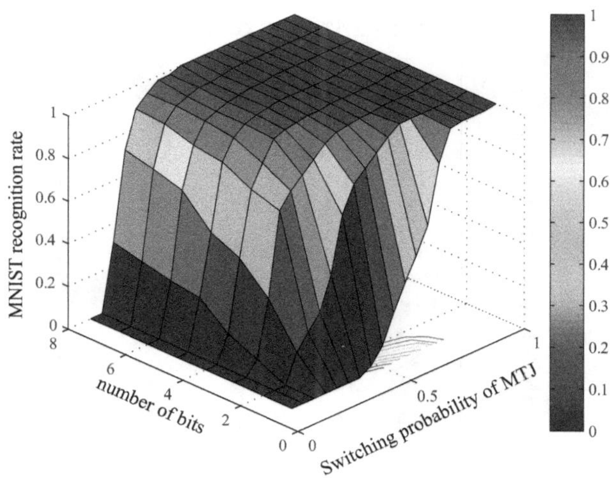

Figure 11: Digit recognition rate VS number of bits per pixel and switching success of MTJ.

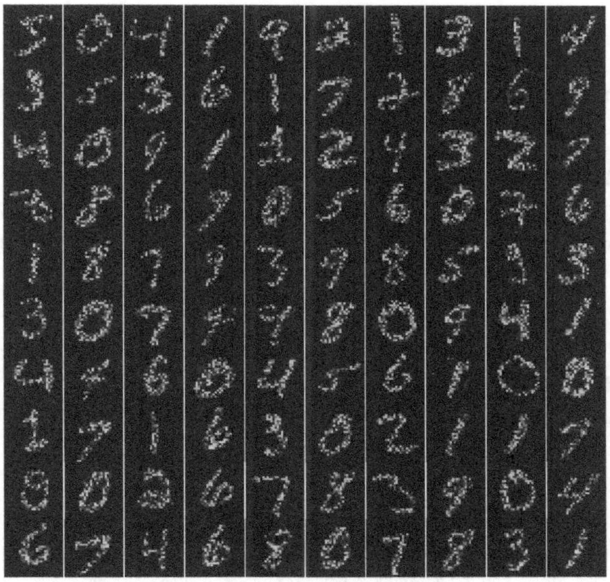

Figure 12: Recognized handwritten digits with MTJ switching errors (4 bits and 30% switching probability).

5 CONCLUSION

This paper explored the application of stochastic switching behavior in stochastic computing for deep neural network (DNN). The functionality has been validated by combining the hardware design and handwritten digits recognition test provided by MNIST database. Simulations results are demonstrated visibly by image processing to show the accuracy. Cases study have been performed to investigate the key parameters impacting the recognition accuracy and learning efficiency. This method can be used to find the most efficient design method of stochastic computing for deep neural network.

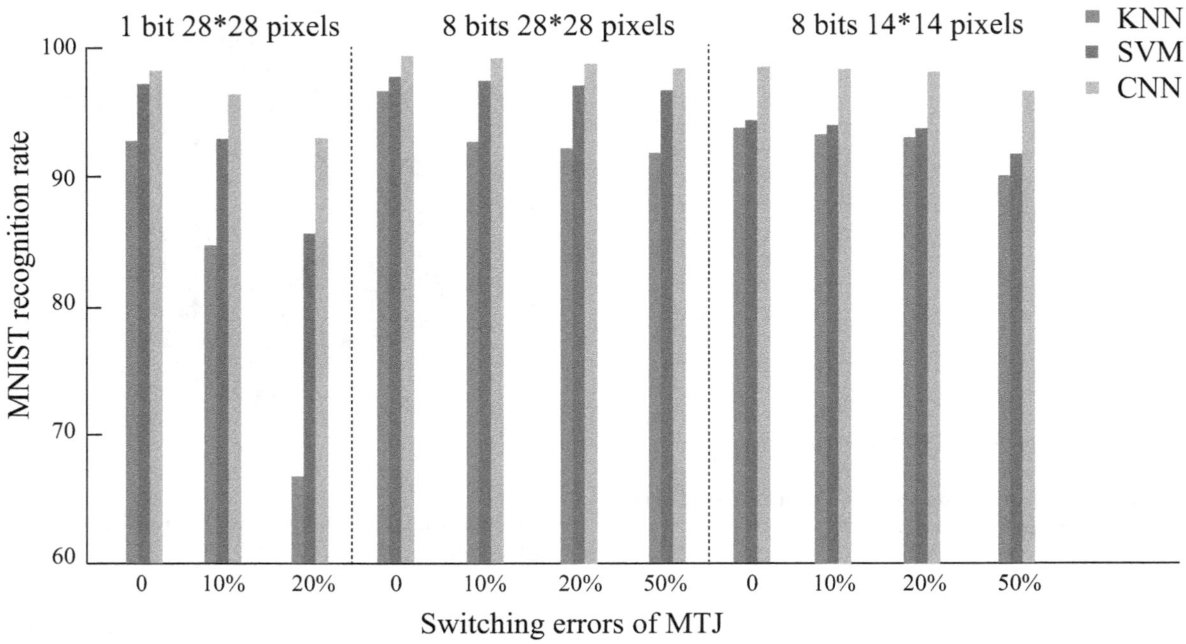

Figure 13: Success probability on function of number of erroneous pixels for image of 1 bit 28*28 pixels, 8 bit 28*28 pixels and 8 bit 14*14 pixels.

ACKNOWLEDGMENT

The authors gratefully acknowledge the National Natural Science Foundation of China (Grant No. 61571023, 61627813), the International Collaboration Project B16001, and the National Key Technology Program of China 2017ZX01032101 for their financial support of this work.

REFERENCES

[1] A. Ardakani, F. Leduc-Primeau, N. Onizawa, T. Hanyu, and W. J. Gross. Vlsi implementation of deep neural network using integral stochastic computing. *IEEE Transactions on Very Large Scale Integration (VLSI) Systems*, 25(10):2688–2699, Oct 2017.

[2] V. Canals, A. Morro, A. Oliver, M. L. Alomar, and J. L. RossellÃş. A new stochastic computing methodology for efficient neural network implementation. *IEEE Transactions on Neural Networks and Learning Systems*, 27(3):551–564, March 2016.

[3] J. Yu, K. Kim, J. Lee, and K. Choi. Accurate and efficient stochastic computing hardware for convolutional neural networks. In *2017 IEEE International Conference on Computer Design (ICCD)*, pages 105–112, Nov 2017.

[4] N. Onizawa, D. Katagiri, W. J. Gross, and T. Hanyu. Analog-to-stochastic converter using magnetic tunnel junction devices for vision chips. *IEEE Transactions on Nanotechnology*, 15(5):705–714, Sept 2016.

[5] R. Venkatesan, S. Venkataramani, X. Fong, K. Roy, and A. Raghunathan. Spintastic: Spin-based stochastic logic for energy-efficient computing. In *2015 Design, Automation Test in Europe Conference Exhibition (DATE)*, pages 1575–1578, March 2015.

[6] G. Srinivasan, A. Sengupta, and K. Roy. Magnetic tunnel junction enabled all-spin stochastic spiking neural network. In *Design, Automation Test in Europe Conference Exhibition (DATE), 2017*, pages 530–535, March 2017.

[7] D. Zhang, L. Zeng, K. Cao, M. Wang, S. Peng, Y. Zhang, Y. Zhang, J. O. Klein, Y. Wang, and W. Zhao. All spin artificial neural networks based on compound spintronic synapse and neuron. *IEEE Transactions on Biomedical Circuits and Systems*, 10(4):828–836, Aug 2016.

[8] D. Querlioz, O. Bichler, A. F. Vincent, and C. Gamrat. Bioinspired programming of memory devices for implementing an inference engine. *Proceedings of the IEEE*, 103(8):1398–1416, Aug 2015.

[9] Weisheng Zhao and Guillaume Prenat. *Spintronics-Based Computing*. Springer, Berlin, Germany, 2015.

[10] S Ikeda, K Miura, H Yamamoto, K Mizunuma, H D Gan, M Endo, S Kanai, J Hayakawa, F Matsukura, and H Ohno. A perpendicular-anisotropy CoFeB-MgO magnetic tunnel junction. *Nature Materials*, 9:721–724, 2010.

[11] Y. Wang, H. Cai, L. A. B. Naviner, J. O. Klein, Jianlei Yang, and W. Zhao. A novel circuit design of true random number generator using magnetic tunnel junction. In *2016 IEEE/ACM International Symposium on Nanoscale Architectures (NANOARCH)*, pages 123–128, July 2016.

[12] Yann LeCun. *The MNIST database of handwritten digits*, 1998.

[13] A. Alaghi, Cheng Li, and J.P. Hayes. Stochastic circuits for real-time image-processing applications. In *Design Automation Conference (DAC), 2013 50th ACM / EDAC / IEEE*, pages 1–6, May 2013.

[14] L. A. de Barros Naviner, H. Cai, Y. Wang, W. Zhao, and A. Ben Dhia. Stochastic computation with spin torque transfer magnetic tunnel junction. In *New Circuits and Systems Conference (NEWCAS), 2015 IEEE 13th International*, pages 1–4, June 2015.

[15] W. Qian, X. Li, M. D. Riedel, K. Bazargan, and D. J. Lilja. An architecture for fault-tolerant computation with stochastic logic. *IEEE Transactions on Computers*, 60(1):93–105, Jan 2011.

[16] T. Devolder, J. Hayakawa, K. Ito, H. Takahashi, S. Ikeda, P. Crozat, N. Zerounian, Joo-Von Kim, C. Chappert, and H. Ohno. Single-shot time-resolved measurements of nanosecond-scale spin-transfer induced switching: Stochastic versus deterministic aspects. *Phys. Rev. Lett.*, 100:057206, Feb 2008.

[17] J. Z. Sun. Spin-current interaction with a monodomain magnetic body: A model study. *Phys. Rev. B*, 62:570–578, Jul 2000.

[18] J. Mazurier, O. Weber, F. Andrieu, A. Toffoli, O. Rozeau, T. Poiroux, F. Allain, P. Perreau, C. Fenouillet-Beranger, O. Thomas, M. Belleville, and O. Faynot. On the variability in planar FDSOI technology: From MOSFETs to SRAM cells. *IEEE Transactions on Electron Devices*, 58(8):2326–2336, Aug 2011.

[19] Y. Wang, H. Cai, L. A. d. B. Naviner, Y. Zhang, X. Zhao, E. Deng, J. O. Klein, and W. Zhao. Compact model of dielectric breakdown in spin-transfer torque magnetic tunnel junction. *IEEE Transactions on Electron Devices*, 63(4):1762–1767, April 2016.

[20] Giorgio Cesana. *The FD-SOI technology for very high-speed and energy efficient SoCs*. STMicroelectronics, july 2014.

[21] S. K. Saha. Compact mosfet modeling for process variability-aware VLSI circuit design. *IEEE Access*, 2:104–115, 2014.

[22] Juan Soto. *The NIST Statistical Test Suite*. National Institute Of Standards and Technology, april 2010.

[23] H. Cai, Y. Wang, L. A. De Barros Naviner, and W. Zhao. Robust ultra-low power non-volatile logic-in-memory circuits in fd-soi technology. *IEEE Transactions on Circuits and Systems I: Regular Papers*, 64(4):847–857, April 2017.

Bit-Wise Iterative Decoding of Polar Codes using Stochastic Computing

Kaining Han
Department of Electrical and Computer Engineering
McGill University
Montreal, Canada
kaining.han@mail.mcgill.ca

Junchao Wang
Department of Electrical and Computer Engineering
McGill University
Montreal, Canada
junchao.wang@mail.mcgill.ca

Warren J. Gross
Department of Electrical and Computer Engineering
McGill University
Montreal, Canada
warren.gross@mcgill.ca

ABSTRACT

Polar codes have received recent attention due to their potential to be applied in advanced wireless communication protocols such as the fifth generation mobile communication system (5G). Among the existing decoding algorithms, Belief Propagation (BP) exhibits high-throughput, low-latency and soft output with a high hardware cost. A form of approximate computing called stochastic computing provides a low-cost implementation solution for the BP algorithm. However, existing stochastic BP decoders suffer from a relatively long decoding latency resulting in low hardware efficiency. In this paper, a novel bit-wise iterative stochastic decoding architecture for the BP algorithm is proposed to improve the throughput and hardware efficiency. Multiple methods at the algorithm and architecture levels are presented to further speed up convergence and hardware efficiency.

CCS CONCEPTS

• **Theory of computation → Stochastic approximation; Error-correcting codes;**

KEYWORDS

Polar code; Belief Propagation; Stochastic Computing

ACM Reference Format:

Kaining Han, Junchao Wang, and Warren J. Gross. 2018. Bit-Wise Iterative Decoding of Polar Codes using Stochastic Computing. In *GLSVLSI '18: 2018 Great Lakes Symposium on VLSI, May 23–25, 2018, Chicago, IL, USA.* ACM, New York, NY, USA, 6 pages. https://doi.org/10.1145/3194554.3194620

1 INTRODUCTION

Polar codes are the first codes with an explicity construction to provably achieve the channel capacity with a low-complexity decoding algorithm [3]. Polar codes have received recent attention due to their potential to be applied in advanced wireless communication protocols such as the fifth generation mobile communication system (5G). In terms of decoding methods of polar codes, Successive Cancellation (SC) decoding and belief propagation (BP) decoding are two common algorithms. Initially, SC decoding was proposed and afterwards Successive Cancellation List decoding was introduced to improve the error-correction performance of SC decoding [18]. However, there are several significant drawbacks for SC and SCL decoding as follows. First, both SC and SCL decoding work in a serial manner, which means the throughput is potentially lower than parallel schemes such as belief propagation. Second, SC and SCL are hard-output decoding algorithms and soft-output is essential for the modern iterative communication systems receivers that incorporate techniques such as Hybrid Automatic Repeat Request(HARQ) [22] [17] [10] [24]. BP decoding was proposed in [3] and [5] and works in a parallel manner resulting in increased throughput. Even though the decoding performance of BP method is not as good as SCL in certain circumstances, BP decoding method can achieve comparable performance with SC decoder when the length of code (N) is relatively short, especially when N is smaller than 512.

In order to achieve the requirements of advanced communication protocols such as 5G wireless communications, the decoding algorithms of polar codes have to achieve relatively low bit error rate. Therefore, the decoders must either increase the list size L for SCL decoding or iteration number I for BP decoding [21]. However, the complexity of the decoders raise with the increase of L and I since the complexities of SCL and BP decoder are $O(LNlogN)$ [11] and $O(INlogN)$ [4]. In other words, there is a trade-off in enhancing the bit-error-rate performance and reducing the complexity of the decoder.

Stochastic computing has received renewed interest in recent years due to its low implementing complexity and high fault tolerance. Stochastic computing is an alternative method of number representation that can carry out complex computations with simple logic. Numbers are represented by random bit steams in stochastic computing. For instance, x = 0.25 can be represented as $X(t)$ = "0,0,1,0,0,0,1,0", where $\Pr\{X_{(t)} = 1\} = x$. Furthermore, multiple complex computations can be mapped to relatively simple logic operations such as multiplication which can be mapped to a single *AND* logic operation [6]. Several stochastic decoders have been proposed for Low-Density Parity Check codes (LDPC) [7] [16] [12], turbo decoders [14], as well as polar decoders [23] [21]. Compared to the original decoder designs, decoders designed by stochastic computing have low hardware cost, short critical path, and high throughput.

In this paper, a hardware efficient bit-wise iterative decoder for polar codes using stochastic computing is proposed. The main

ACM ISBN 978-1-4503-5724-1/18/05...$15.00
https://doi.org/10.1145/3194554.3194620

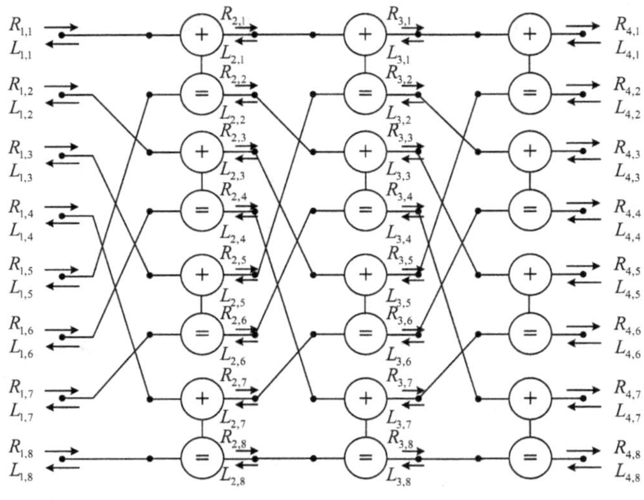

Figure 1: Factor graph for belief propagation decoding of a polar code of length N=8.

contributions of this paper are described next. First, a bit-wise re-randomization based processing unit (PU) to update the messages passed on the factor graph bit by bit, resulting a much faster convergence speed, lower latency and higher throughput. Second, a comb-type re-randomization method is applied to reduce the number of re-randomization modules and reduce hardware cost. Third, the noise dependent scaling method is introduced in the proposed design to lower the error floor of the stochastic BP decoder and further speed up convergence. Finally, a low complexity bit stream generation module is designed to further reduce the hardware cost of the proposed design.

2 PRELIMINARIES

2.1 Polar Codes

A length $N = 2^n$ polar codeword $x_1^N = (x_1, x_2, \ldots, x_{N-1}, x_N)$ is encoded based on a source vector $u_1^N = (u_1, u_2, \ldots, u_{N-1}, u_N)$ as:

$$x_1^N = u_1^N \cdot F^{\otimes N}, \tag{1}$$

where u_1^N is the source vector, $F^{\otimes N}$ is the Kronecker power of base matrix $F = \begin{bmatrix} 1 & 0 \\ 1 & 1 \end{bmatrix}$, and x_1^N is the encoded bit vector. The source vector U is comprised of K information bits and $N - K$ frozen bits, whos values are set to zero. The set of information bit positions is denoted A and the frozen position set is denoted A^c.

2.2 Belief Propagation Decoding

The BP decoding method for polar codes can be represented on a factor graph which is divided into $n = log_2 N$ stages [15], while each stage has $N/2$ basic computation blocks consisting of two left ports and two right ports. For instance, Fig. 1 illustrates the factor graph for $N = 8$. Each node is specified with coordinate (i, j), where i indicates the stage number and j illustrates the node number in the column. The decoding method is the process of passing messages iteratively through the factor graph.

In the decoding process, there are two types of messages passed on the factor graph: the right-to-left message $L_{i,j}$ and the left-to-right message $R_{i,j}$, where i=1,2,..., $log_2 N$ and j=1,2, ..., N. The leftmost and rightmost messages are initialized as (2) and (3):

$$L_{n+1,j} = \frac{P(y_j \mid x_j = 0)}{P(y_j \mid x_j = 1)}, \tag{2}$$

$$R_{1,j} = \begin{cases} 1, & j \in A; \\ 0, & j \in A^c. \end{cases} \tag{3}$$

The messages are updated iteratively from right to left side and left to right side as:

$$L_{i,j}^{(t+1)} = f\left(L_{i+1,2j-1}^{(t)}, g\left(L_{i+1,2j}^{(t)}, R_{i,j+N/2}^{(t)}\right)\right), \tag{4}$$

$$L_{i,j+N/2}^{(t+1)} = g\left(f\left(R_{i,j}^{(t)}, L_{i+1,2j-1}^{(t)}\right), L_{i+1,2j}^{(t)}\right), \tag{5}$$

$$R_{i+1,2j-1}^{(t+1)} = f\left(R_{i,j}^{(t)}, g\left(L_{i+1,2j}^{(t)}, R_{i,j+N/2}^{(t)}\right)\right), \tag{6}$$

$$R_{i+1,2j}^{(t+1)} = g\left(f\left(R_{i,j}^{(t)}, L_{i+1,2j-1}^{(t)}\right), R_{i,j+N/2}^{(t)}\right), \tag{7}$$

where,

$$f(x, y) = \frac{1 + x \cdot y}{x + y}, \tag{8}$$

$$g(x, y) = x \cdot y. \tag{9}$$

After $Iter$ iterations, the decoding result is:

$$\hat{u}_j = \begin{cases} 0, & R_{1,j}^{(Iter)} \geq 1; \\ 1, & Otherwise. \end{cases} \tag{10}$$

2.3 Stochastic BP Decoding

In stochastic computing, a number is represented with a bit stream by comparing it with a uniformly distributed random number as shown in Figure 2 (a). Then the complex arithmetic calculation can be mapped to simple bit wise logic operation. For example, multiplication, which has high hardware cost in the conventional binary system, is mapped to a single *AND* gate in stochastic computing as illustrated in Figure 2 (b).

There have been stochastic polar BP decoders introduced in [23] and [21], in which the messages are represented with bit streams and the message update function is reformulated into stochastic form as:

$$L_{n+1,j}^{(t)} = \begin{cases} 1, & P\left(y_j \mid x_j = 1\right) \geq R(t); \\ 0, & Otherwise, \end{cases} \tag{11}$$

$$R_{1,j}^{(t)} = \begin{cases} 1, & j \in A, 0.5 \geq R(t); \\ 0, & j \in A, 0.5 < R(t); \\ 0, & j \in A^c, \end{cases} \tag{12}$$

where function $F(x, y)$ and $G(x, y)$ are defined as (13) and (14):

$$F(x, y) = x \cdot (1 - y) + (1 - x) \cdot y, \tag{13}$$

$$G(x, y) = \frac{x \cdot y}{x \cdot y + (1 - x) \cdot (1 - y)}. \tag{14}$$

The corresponding stochastic logic architectures are illustrated as Figure 2 (c) and Figure 2 (d).

Benefiting from the simple logic architecture of stochastic computing, the existing stochastic BP decoder shows ultra-low hardware cost compared with the conventional binary based BP decoder.

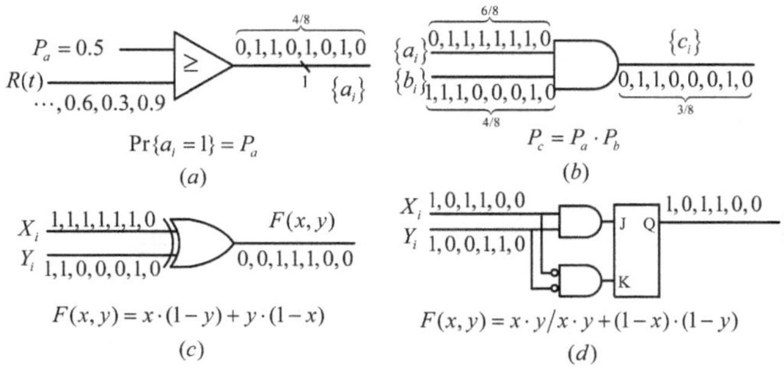

Figure 2: Basic stochastic logic: (a) binary-to-stochastic bit stream conversion, (b) stochastic logic for multiplication, (c) stochastic logic for $F(x, y)$, (d) stochastic logic for $G(x, y)$.

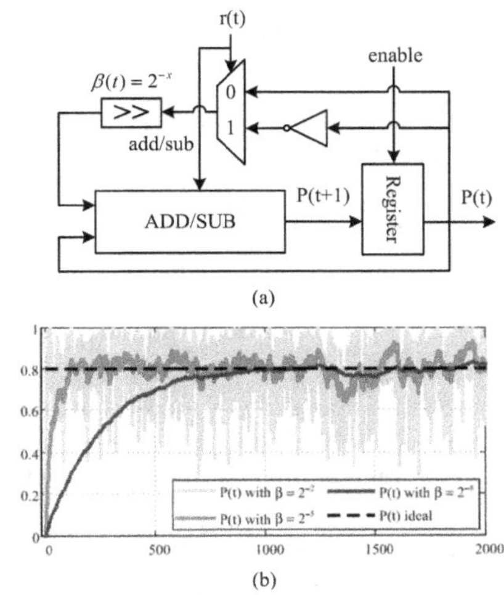

Figure 3: Tracking Forecast Memory (TFM): (a) hardware architecture, (b) simulation results of TFM with $\beta = 2^{-2}, 2^{-5}, 2^{-8}$.

However, the existing stochastic BP decoder is based on a stream-wise iterative scheme: in each iteration, the message is represented with a complete bit stream and after one iteration, the bit stream of each message is re-randomized. The total latency of the stochastic decoder is $m \cdot Iter$, where m is the length of the bit stream and $Iter$ is the number of total iterations. The existing stochastic BP decoders require tens of iterations and hundreds of bits in a bit stream to achieve satisfactory decoding performance.

3 BIT-WISE ITERATIVE STOCHASTIC DECODING

In order to speed up convergence, we propose a bit-wise iterative decoding scheme, where only one bit of the message bit streams is processed in each iteration.

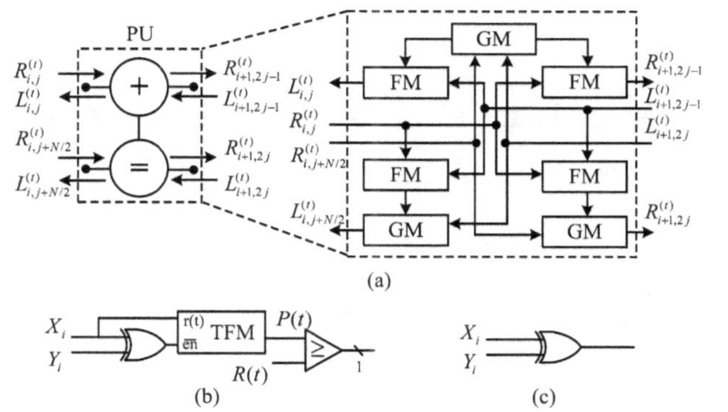

Figure 4: Hardware architecture of the proposed bit-wise PU module. (a) top level architecture of the PU module, (b) bit-wise G function calculation module (GM), (c) F function calculation module (FM).

3.1 Bit-Wise Iterative Message Update

The basic processing unit (PU) updates the bit-wise message $L_{i,j}^{(t)}$ and $R_{i,j}^{(t)}$ based on equations (4)-(7), where the F function is calculated with a single XOR gate using stochastic computing. However, when calculating the G function, the J-K Flip-Flop (FF) based architecture would introduce correlation because of the "hold-state" of J-K FF. For example, when the input of J-K FF, J = 0 and K = 0, the output would hold the same output as in the last clock cycle. For the BP decoding of Polar codes, $\log 2N$ layers of PUs in the message updates degrades the required randomness layer-by-layer, necessitating a re-randomization step after each iteration.

In the proposed design, we introduce a new architecture for the calculation of the G function, which tracks the bit-wise message bit-by-bit and re-randomizes the bit stream in each clock cycle. The proposed new architecture for the calculation of the G function is based on the tracking forecast memory (TFM) [20], which extracts the moving average of a stochastic bit stream based on successive relaxation [13] as:

$$P(t+1) = P(t) + \beta \cdot [r(t) - P(t)] \tag{15}$$

where β is the relaxation coefficient [13] [20] in the form of 2^{-x} to transform the multiplication involved in (15) into a shift operation. The hardware architecture of the TFM is illustrated in Fig. 3 (a). Also the simulation of TFM with $\beta = 2^{-2}, 2^{-5}, 2^{-8}$ as shown in Fig. 3 (b).

Based on the TFM, we designed a bit-wise G updating module to calculate the G function. The proposed bit-wise G updating module tracks the bit stream based on (16). Bit-wise re-randomization is processed based on (17), where $R(t)$ is a uniform distributed random number selected from a random engine. The random engine will be introduced in Section 3.2. The hardware architecture of the proposed bit-wise PU is illustrated in Fig. 4.

$$P(t) = \begin{cases} P(t-1) + \beta \cdot [r(t) - P(t-1)], & x = y; \\ P(t-1), & x \neq y; \end{cases} \tag{16}$$

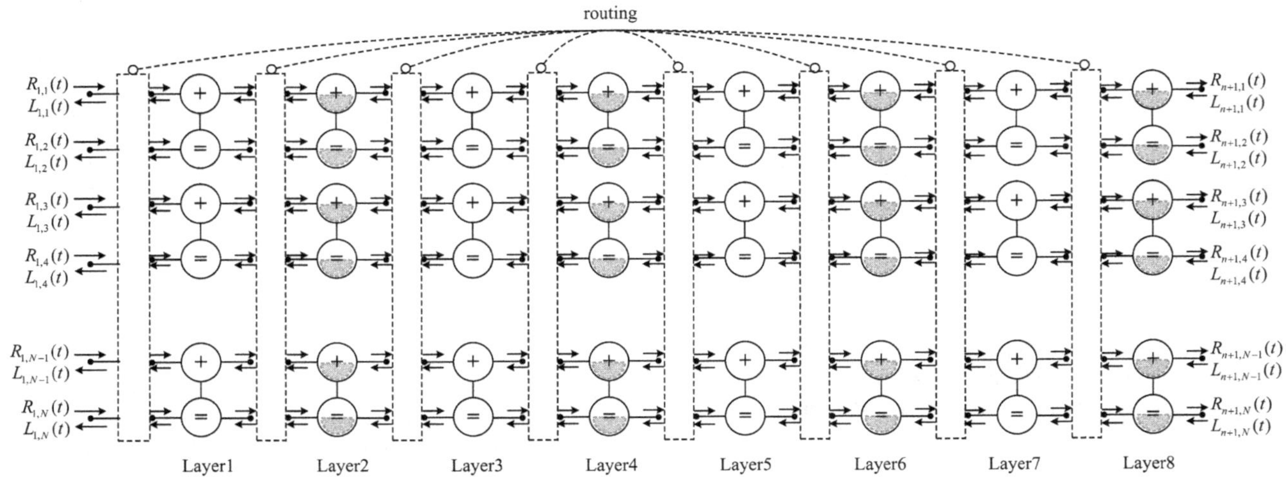

Figure 5: Hardware architecture of the proposed comb-type re-randomization scheme.

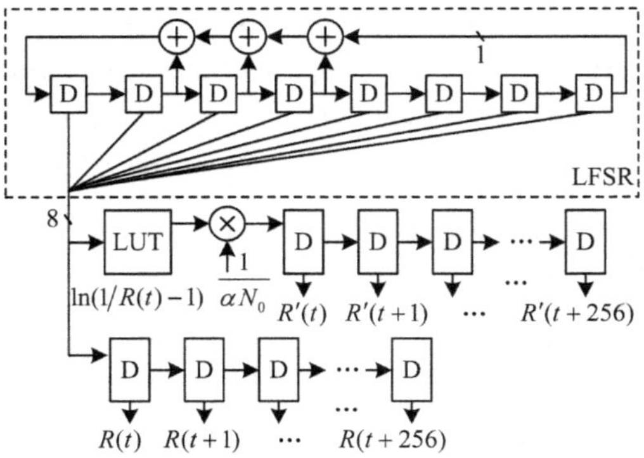

Figure 6: Hardware architecture of the proposed RNE module.

$$G^{(t)}(x,y) = \begin{cases} 1, & P(t) \geq R(t); \\ 0, & P(t) < R(t); \end{cases} \tag{17}$$

The proposed bit-wise G updating module speeds up convergence of the decoder, jowever, as shown in Fig. 4, the hardware cost is higher compared with the J-K FF-based architecture. In order to achieve a good trade-off between hardware cost and convergence, we propose a comb-type re-randomization scheme: the proposed bit wise G updating module is inserted to the stochastic BP decoder in every other layer. The hardware architecture of the comb-type re-randomization for the polar code with N=256 is illustrated in Fig. 5.

3.2 Low Complexity Bit Stream Generation

In stochastic computing-based digital signal processing systems, the first step is to represent the input with bit streams. Bit stream generation adds hardware overhead compared with the conventional binary systems, especially for the proposed parallel BP polar decoder.

First, practical polar decoders typicallt receive input data as log-likelihood ratios (LLRs), i.e.:

$$LLR_j = log\left(\frac{P\left(y_j \mid x_j = 0\right)}{P\left(y_j \mid x_j = 1\right)}\right), \tag{18}$$

$$P\left(y_j \mid x_j = 1\right) = \frac{1}{1 + exp\left(LLR_j\right)}. \tag{19}$$

When we generate the bit stream based on (11) and (19), a large number of exponential operations would be involved, resulting in large hardware cost. In this paper, we propose a direct LLR-to-Stochastic bit stream generation method to remove the exponential operations:

$$L_{n+1,j}^{(t)} = \begin{cases} 1, & LLR_j \leq R'(t); \\ 0, & Otherwise; \end{cases} \tag{20}$$

where $R'(t) \triangleq ln\left[\frac{1}{R(t)} - 1\right]$ can be calculated with the uniformly distributed random number $R(t)$. The proposed LLR-to-Stochastic (LtoS) method is an equivalent form of the original bit stream generation shown in (11). Even though it seems an extra ln operation is involved in (20) to calculate the random number $R'(t)$, we only need one ln calculation for the whole proposed stochastic Polar decoder because of the random number sharing scheme.

In conventional bit stream generation, each bit stream generation module would be equipped with a random number generator to ensure the independence between these random numbers, resulting large extra hardware cost. In this paper, we propose a random number sharing based random number engine (RNE) module to reduce the number of random number generators. The hardware architecture of the proposed RNE module is illustrated in Fig. 6. The multiplication involved in the Fig. 6 is used for the noise dependent scaling and will be introduced in Section 3.3

$$R_j((t)) = R(t + 4j) \tag{21}$$

$$R'_j((t)) = R'(t + 4j) \tag{22}$$

Note that in order to ensure low correlation between each random number, the outputs are selected with a 4 cycle delay [9].

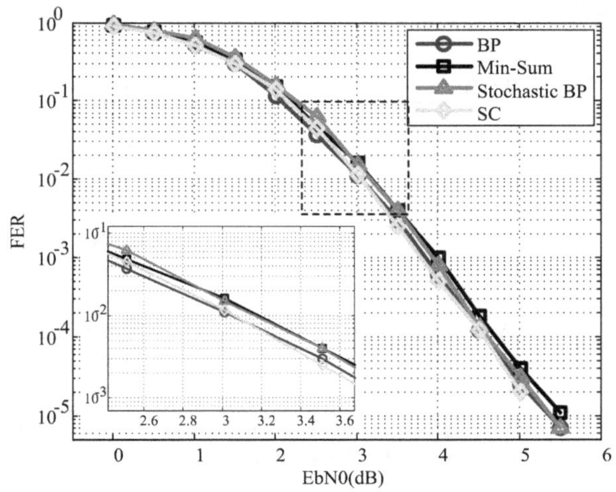

Figure 7: FER simulation results for a (N=256, K=128) polar code.

3.3 Noise Dependent Scaling

As described in Section 3.1, convergence of the decoder will be slowed when the re-randomization modules are in the hold state. In order to reduce the number of hold states, noise dependent scaling (NDS) [19] is used to reduce the error floor and speed up convergence in the proposed decoder:

$$LLR_j^{'} = \alpha \cdot N_0 \cdot LLR_j, \tag{23}$$

where α is the scaling factor obtained through simulation and N_0 is the noise power. For BPSK modulation and a (256,128) Polar code, the scaling factor is selected as $\alpha = 0.6$.

4 EVALUATION AND IMPLEMENTATION

4.1 Evaluation of Performance

We simulated the proposed bit-wise stochastic BP decoder based on a BPSK modulated communication system with a (256,128) polar code. The floating point BP [2], Min-Sum [1] and SC decoder are also simulated and plotted in Fig. 7 as comparison.

The length of the bit streams in the proposed stochastic BP decoder is set to 1500. The number of iterations of BP and Min-Sum decoder is set to 40. It can be observed that the performance of the proposed stochastic BP decoder is similar to the floating point BP decoder, with only 0.2 dB loss. As a result of the NDS, the proposed stochastic BP decoder shows no error floor down to FER = 10^{-5}.

4.2 Analysis of Complexity

As introduced in Section 3.1, a single bit of the bit stream is processed in one iteration with the cost of only one clock cycle. Thus, the total decoding latency of the proposed stochastic BP decoder is 1500 clock cycles, which equals to the length of the bit streams. For the existing stochastic BP decoders in the literature, the total decoding latency is the product of the number of iterations and the length of bit streams, resulting in a latency of 15.3K clock cycles [23].

The proposed design is synthesized for a (256,128) Polar code using 65 nm CMOS technology (SMIC library) and Synopsys Design Complier. We also synthesized the quarter-way message update scheme based Min-Sum decoder in [1] with the same code and CMOS technology as comparison. The synthesis results are shown in Tab. 1.

Form Table 1, we can observe that the maximum decoding latency of the proposed design is 10 times lower compared with the existing stochastic decoder [23], as a result of the efficient bit wise re-randomization and fast convergence. The design in [23] uses a multiple datapath architecture with longer routing delay, resulting a slightly lower clock frequency than this work. The proposed design takes only about 2x more logic with respect to [23].

Compared with the conventional binary system based min-sum decoder, the proposed design shows advantages on logic gate count, area consumption and clock frequency. Despite the longer decoding latency and throughput, the proposed design has a higher hardware efficiency than the min-sum decoder, defined as the ratio of throughput to area consumption.

4.3 Discussion

As a type of hard-decision and non-iterative decoding scheme, the deep-pipelined fast-SSC decoder in [8] shows extremely high throughput and hardware efficiency compared with the BP based decoders even at high SNR region. While, the reason why this paper focuses on the BP based decoder is that for the modern communication system, the soft output of the polar decoder, as the extrinsic information, could be quite helpful to the multiple input multiple output (MIMO) detection, channel estimation and HARQ scheme. For scenarios that require soft-output, the proposed architecture could be a competitive implementation scheme for polar decoders.

5 CONCLUSION

This paper presents a new stochastic BP decoder for polar codes based on an efficient bit-wise re-randomization scheme. A comb-type re-randomization scheme and noise dependent scaling are applied in the proposed design to further reduce the hardware cost and speed up convergence, which contributes to a high hardware efficiency. The proposed decoder significantly reduces the decoding latency with respect to the existing art in stochastic polar decoders and achieves higher area efficiency compared with the conventional min-sum based implementation scheme. The proposed bit-wise iterative decoding scheme could be a good implementation candidate for soft-output polar decoding.

ACKNOWLEDGMENTS

Kaining Han and Junchao Wang would like to thank the China Scholarship Council for supporting their research.

REFERENCES

[1] S. M. Abbas, Y. Fan, J. Chen, and C. Y. Tsui. 2017. High-Throughput and Energy-Efficient Belief Propagation Polar Code Decoder. *IEEE Transactions on Very Large Scale Integration (VLSI) Systems* 25, 3 (March 2017), 1098–1111. https://doi.org/10.1109/TVLSI.2016.2620998

[2] E. Arikan. 2008. A performance comparison of polar codes and Reed-Muller codes. *IEEE Communications Letters* 12, 6 (June 2008), 447–449. https://doi.org/10.1109/LCOMM.2008.080017

Table 1: Comparison of (256,128) polar code hardware implementations.

Design	Bit wise stochastic BP [This work]	Stochastic BP[23]	Min-Sum[1]	Deep-Pipelined Fast-SSC[8]
Technology (nm)	65	65	65	65
Code (N, K)	(256,128)	(256,128)	(256,128)	(256,128)
Frequency (MHz)	700	670	334	500
Logic Gates	250K	121K	574K	778K[a]
Area (mm^2)	0.365	N/A	0.818	1.121
Maximum Latency (cycles)	1500	15300	640	134
Average Latency[b] (cycles@SNR)	230@3.5dB	N/A	61@3.5dB	1
Info Bit T/P [c] (Mbps@SNR)	389@3.5dB	N/A	700@3.5dB	64000
Soft-Output	Yes	Yes	Yes	No
Hardware Efficiency (Mbps/mm^2)	1092	N/A	855	57091

[a]Logic gates consumption is calculated based on 1 gate = 1.44μm^2 in SMIC 65 nm library. [b]The average decoding latency is measured using the CRC-based early stopping criteria. [c]Information bits only are accounted for in the throughput computation.

[3] Erdal Arikan. 2009. Channel polarization: A method for constructing capacity-achieving codes for symmetric binary-input memoryless channels. *IEEE Transactions on Information Theory* 55, 7 (2009), 3051–3073. https://doi.org/10.1109/tit.2009.2021379

[4] Erdal Arıkan, Haesik Kim, Garik Markarian, U Ozgur, and Efecan Poyraz. 2009. Performance of short polar codes under ML decoding. *Proc. ICT MobileSummit,(Santander, Spain)* (2009), 10–12.

[5] U. U. Fayyaz and J. R. Barry. 2013. Polar codes for partial response channels. In *Proc. IEEE Int. Conf. Communications (ICC)*. 4337–4341. https://doi.org/10.1109/ICC.2013.6655247

[6] Brian R Gaines. 1969. Stochastic computing systems. In *Advances in information systems science*. Springer, 37–172. https://doi.org/10.1007/978-1-4899-5841-9_2

[7] Vincent A Gaudet and Anthony C Rapley. 2003. Iterative decoding using stochastic computation. *Electronics Letters* 39, 3 (2003), 299–301. https://doi.org/10.1049/el:20030217

[8] P. Giard, G. Sarkis, C. Thibeault, and W. J. Gross. 2016. Multi-Mode Unrolled Architectures for Polar Decoders. *IEEE Transactions on Circuits and Systems I: Regular Papers* 63, 9 (Sept. 2016), 1443–1453. https://doi.org/10.1109/TCSI.2016.2586218

[9] K. Han, J. Hu, J. Chen, and H. Lu. 2018. A Low Complexity Sparse Code Multiple Access Detector Based on Stochastic Computing. *IEEE Transactions on Circuits and Systems I: Regular Papers* 65, 2 (Feb. 2018), 769–782. https://doi.org/10.1109/TCSI.2017.2722692

[10] K. Han, Z. Zhang, J. Hu, and J. Chen. 2016. A High Performance Joint Detection and Decoding Scheme for LDPC Coded SCMA System. In *Proc. IEEE Globecom Workshops (GC Wkshps)*. 1–6. https://doi.org/10.1109/GLOCOMW.2016.7848813

[11] X. Liang, C. Zhang, M. Xu, S. Zhang, and X. You. 2015. Efficient stochastic list successive cancellation decoder for polar codes. In *Proc. 28th IEEE Int. System-on-Chip Conf. (SOCC)*. 421–426. https://doi.org/10.1109/SOCC.2015.7406997

[12] Ali Naderi, Shie Mannor, Mohamad Sawan, and Warren J Gross. 2011. Delayed stochastic decoding of LDPC codes. *IEEE Transactions on Signal Processing* 59, 11 (2011), 5617–5626. https://doi.org/10.1109/tsp.2011.2163630

[13] James M Ortega and Werner C Rheinboldt. 1970. *Iterative solution of nonlinear equations in several variables*. Vol. 30. Siam. https://doi.org/10.1137/1.9780898719468

[14] Isaac Perez-Andrade, Shida Zhong, Robert G Maunder, Bashir M Al-Hashimi, and Lajos Hanzo. 2016. Stochastic Computing Improves the Timing-Error Tolerance and Latency of Turbo Decoders: Design Guidelines and Tradeoffs. *IEEE Access* 4 (2016), 1008–1038. https://doi.org/10.1109/access.2016.2523063

[15] Jin Sha, Xing Liu, Zhongfeng Wang, and Xiaoyang Zeng. 2015. A memory efficient belief propagation decoder for polar codes. *China Communications* 12, 5 (2015), 34–41. https://doi.org/10.1109/cc.2015.7112042

[16] Saeed Sharifi Tehrani, Warren J Gross, and Shie Mannor. 2006. Stochastic Decoding of LDPC Codes. *IEEE Communications Letters* 10, 10 (2006), 716–718. https://doi.org/10.1109/LCOMM.2006.060570

[17] W. C. Sun, W. H. Wu, C. H. Yang, and Y. L. Ueng. 2015. An Iterative Detection and Decoding Receiver for LDPC-Coded MIMO Systems. *IEEE Transactions on Circuits and Systems I: Regular Papers* 62, 10 (Oct. 2015), 2512–2522. https://doi.org/10.1109/TCSI.2015.2468998

[18] Ido Tal and Alexander Vardy. 2011. List decoding of polar codes. In *Information Theory Proceedings (ISIT), 2011 IEEE International Symposium on*. IEEE, 1–5. https://doi.org/10.1109/isit.2011.6033904

[19] S. Sharifi Tehrani, S. Mannor, and W. J. Gross. 2008. Fully Parallel Stochastic LDPC Decoders. *IEEE Transactions on Signal Processing* 56, 11 (Nov. 2008), 5692–5703. https://doi.org/10.1109/TSP.2008.929671

[20] S. Sharifi Tehrani, A. Naderi, G. A. Kamendje, S. Hemati, S. Mannor, and W. J. Gross. 2010. Majority-Based Tracking Forecast Memories for Stochastic LDPC Decoding. *IEEE Transactions on Signal Processing* 58, 9 (Sept. 2010), 4883–4896. https://doi.org/10.1109/TSP.2010.2051434

[21] M. Xu, X. Liang, C. Zhang, Z. Wu, and X. You. 2016. Stochastic BP Polar Decoding and Architecture with Efficient Re-Randomization and Directive Register. In *Proc. IEEE Int. Workshop Signal Processing Systems (SiPS)*. 315–320. https://doi.org/10.1109/SiPS.2016.62

[22] J. Yeo, S. Park, J. Oh, Y. Kim, and J. Lee. 2017. Partial Retransmission Scheme for HARQ Enhancement in 5G Wireless Communications. In *Proc. IEEE Globecom Workshops (GC Wkshps)*. 1–5. https://doi.org/10.1109/GLOCOMW.2017.8269132

[23] Bo Yuan and Keshab K Parhi. 2016. Belief propagation decoding of polar codes using stochastic computing. In *Circuits and Systems (ISCAS), 2016 IEEE International Symposium on*. IEEE, 157–160. https://doi.org/10.1109/iscas.2016.7527194

[24] Z. Zhang, K. Han, J. Hu, and J. Chen. 2016. Joint Detection and Decoding Schemes for Turbo Coded SCMA Systems. In *Proc. IEEE Globecom Workshops (GC Wkshps)*. 1–6. https://doi.org/10.1109/GLOCOMW.2016.7848941

Comparative Study of Approximate Multipliers

Mahmoud Masadeh , Osman Hasan and Sofiène Tahar
Dept. of Electrical and Computer Engineering, Concordia University, Montréal, Québec, Canada
{m_masa,o_hasan,tahar}@ece.concordia.ca

ABSTRACT

Approximate multipliers are widely being advocated for energy-efficient computing in applications that exhibit an inherent tolerance to inaccuracy. In this paper, we identify three decisions for design and evaluation of approximate multiplier circuits: (1) the type of approximate full adder (FA) used to construct the multiplier, (2) the architecture, i.e., array or tree, of the multiplier and (3) the placement of sub-modules of approximate and exact multipliers in the target multiplier module. Based on FA cells implemented at the transistor level (TSMC65nm), we developed several approximate building blocks of 8x8 multipliers, as well as various implementations of higher order multipliers. These designs are evaluated based on their power, area, delay and error and the best designs are identified. We validate these designs on an image blending application using MATLAB, and compare them to related work.

CCS CONCEPTS

• **Hardware** → *Arithmetic and datapath circuits*; *Circuits power issues*;

KEYWORDS

Approximate Computing; Approximate Multiplier; Power-efficiency

ACM Reference Format:
Mahmoud Masadeh , Osman Hasan and Sofiène Tahar. 2018. Comparative Study of Approximate Multipliers. In *GLSVLSI '18: 2018 Great Lakes Symposium on VLSI, May 23–25, 2018, Chicago, IL, USA*. ACM, New York, NY, USA, 4 pages. https://doi.org/10.1145/3194554.3194626

1 INTRODUCTION

The pervasive, portable, embedded and mobile nature of present age computing systems has led to an increasing demand for ultra low power consumption, small footprint, and high performance. Approximate computing (AC) [1] is a nascent computing paradigm that allows us to achieve these objectives by compromising the arithmetic accuracy. Many systems used in domains, like multimedia and big data analysis, exhibit inherent tolerances to a certain level of inaccuracies in computation, and thus can benefit from AC.

Functional approximation [2], in hardware, mostly deals with the design of approximate arithmetic units, such as adders and multipliers, at different abstraction levels, i.e., transistor, gate, register tansfer level and application. Some notable approximate adders include *speculative adders, segmented adders, carry select adders* and *approximate full adders* [3]. The transistor level approximation provides the highest flexibility due to the ability to tweak most of the design parameters at this level. Various approximate full adder (FA) at the transistor level have been proposed including the mirror adders [4], the XOR/XNOR based FA [5] and the inexact FA [6].

Approximate multipliers have been mainly designed using three techniques, i) *Approximation in partial products generation*, ii) *Approximation in partial product tree*, and iii) *Approximation in partial products summation*. Jiang et al.[7] compared the characteristics of different approximate multipliers, implemented in VHDL based on these different techniques. *We target approximate multipliers based on approximation in partial products summation.*

In this paper, we evaluate and compare the accuracy and circuit characteristics of different approximate multipliers. These multipliers are designed based on three identified decisions: (1) the type of approximate FA used to construct the multiplier, (2) the architecture of the multiplier, and (3) the placement of sub-modules of approximate and exact multipliers in the target multiplier module.

2 PROPOSED METHODOLOGY

The design space for approximate multipliers based on different approximate FAs and compressors is quite huge. However, it is difficult to select the most suitable design for a specific application. Figure 1 presents an overview of our proposed methodology to build different approximate multipliers and compare their design metrics to select the most suitable design. It consists of the following steps:

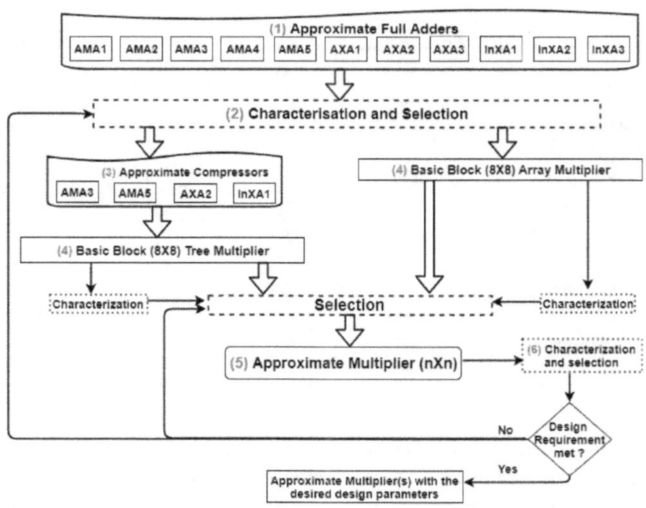

Figure 1: Methodology Overview

GLSVLSI '18, May 23–25, 2018, Chicago, IL, USA

ACM ISBN 978-1-4503-5724-1/18/05...$15.00
https://doi.org/10.1145/3194554.3194626

(1) *Building a library of elementary approximate FAs using the TSMC65nm technology in Cadence Spectre*: We use the default transistors of this technology to build 11 approximate FA designs comprising of 5 mirror FAs, 3 XOR/XNOR FAs and 3 inexact FAs.

(2) *Characterization and early space reduction*: We perform area, power, latency and quality characterizations of different approximate FAs to filter out non-Pareto designs.

(3) *Building a library of approximate compressors*: We build a Cadence library of approximate compressors using the optimal approximate FAs, as recommended by [4].

(4) *Building approximate multipliers basic blocks*: Based on approximate FAs and compressors, we design various approximate 8x8 array and tree multipliers, respectively.

(5) *Designing target approximate multipliers*: Based on different configurations of 8x8 approximate multipliers, the target multiplier modules are designed and characterized.

(6) *Selection of design points*: Considering the required quality constrains of a specific application, a subset of power-efficient design points are selected.

In order to evaluate the efficiency of the proposed approximate designs, *power consumption* and *area*, represented by the number of transistors used, are measured. Circuit performance is measured by the maximum *delay* between changing the inputs and observing the output(s). Besides these basic design metrics, we also measure *accuracy* using, among others, Error Rate (ER) and Normalized Mean Error Distance (NMED) [8].

3 APPROXIMATE FAS AND COMPRESSORS

Low power approximate binary adders are generally constructed by replacing the accurate FAs with approximate FAs. We consider five approximate mirror adders (AMA1, AMA2, AMA3, AMA4 and AMA5) [4], three approximate XOR/XNOR based full adders (AXA1, AXA2 and AXA3) [5] and three inexact adder cells (InXA1, InXA2 and InXA3) [6].

Table 1: Characteristics of Different Approximate FAs

FA Type	Size (A)	Power(nw) (P)	Delay(ps) (D)	# of Error Cases (E)	PDP(fJ)
Exact FA	28	763.3	244	0	186.25
AMA1 (M1)	20	612	195	2	119.34
AMA2 (M2)	14	561.1	366	2	205.36
AMA3 (M3)	11	558.1	360	3	200.92
AMA4 (M4)	15	587.1	196	3	115.07
AMA5 (m5)	8	412.1	150	4	61.82
AXA1 (X1)	8	676.2	1155	4	781
AXA2 (X2)	6	358.7	838	4	300.59
AXA3 (X3)	8	396.5	1467	2	582
InXA1 (In1)	6	410	740	2	303.4
InXA2 (In2)	8	355.1	832	2	295.44
InXA3 (In3)	6	648	767	2	753.5

Table 1 shows the characteristics of the 11 considered approximate FAs including Size (A), Power consumption (P), Delay (D), number of Erroneous outputs (E), which indicates the likelihood of at least one output (Cout or Sum) being wrong, and Power-Delay-Product (PDP). *All approximate FAs are Pareto-points*, i.e., they provide less area and power consumption compared to the exact design at the cost of compromising accuracy [9]. In [10], AMA5 is considered as a *wire* with zero area and zero power consumption. However, this is unrealistic as the output of AMA5 has to drive other signals. Thus, we used two buffers instead of two wires to design it. Assuming that the characteristics of approximate FAs are linearly applied to approximate arithmetic circuits, there is no single approximate FA, which is superior in all aspects. Therefore, we propose to use a *fitness function* to evaluate FA designs, or any approximate circuit, based on its design metrics.

$$Fitness = C1 * A + C2 * P + C3 * D + C4 * E \quad (1)$$

where *C1*, *C2*, *C3* and *C4* are application-dependent design coefficients within the range [0,1] which provide weights to specific design metrics for a specific application, e.g., E equals zero for the exact design, and P is small for low power designs. *A minimal fitness value is preferred since the goal is to minimize A, P, D and E.* For the remainder of this work, we use all 11 Pareto-design approximate FAs as elementary cells to construct approximate array multipliers.

Higher-order compressors, e.g., 5-to-3 and 8-to-4 [11], allow us to construct high speed tree multipliers. Therefore, we also developed approximate FA based compressors, for evaluation purposes. Considering all options, the total combination of compressor settings grows exponentially, e.g., for an 8-to-4 compressor, we have O((# of FA designs)$^{\text{\# of FAs in compressor}}$) = O $(11)^4$ = 14641 combinations. Therefore, in order to show the effectiveness of designing approximate compressors based on approximate FAs, we chose four FAs only, i.e., *AMA5*, *AXA2*, *InXA1* and *AMA3* as explained in detail in [8]. These selected FAs are used to build approximate high-order compressors, which in turn can be used for designing approximate tree multipliers. A detailed overview of the characteristics for the chosen approximate compressors can be found in [8]. However, these selected compressors are not guaranteed to be optimal. But, they exhibit some improvements compared to the exact designs.

4 MULTIPLIER BASIC BLOCKS

In this section, we use the approximate FAs and compressors, described earlier, to design 8x8 array and tree based multipliers, respectively. Which will act as our basic blocks for designing higher-order multipliers, e.g., 32x32 , as it will be discussed in Section 5.

4.1 8x8 Array Multiplier

An n-bit array multiplier [12] is composed of n^2 AND gates for partial products generation, and *n-1* n-bit adders for partial products accumulation. The design space of an *nxn* approximate array multiplier is quite huge, since it depends on the type of FA used in the array, and the *number* of approximate FAs (from 0 to *n*) used in the n-bit adder. Considering all options, the total combination of multiplier settings grows exponentially O((# of FAs)$^{\text{MultiplierSize}^2}$) = O $((11)^{n^2})$ = $(11)^{64}$ in our case.

We have used all 11 Pareto approximate FAs, described in Section 3, to construct 8x8 approximate array multipliers, based on only one FA type per design to avoid the exponential growth of the design space. Regarding the degree of approximation, we have used two options: i) all FAs are approximate, and ii) FAs that contribute to the least significant 50% of the resultant bits are approximated in order

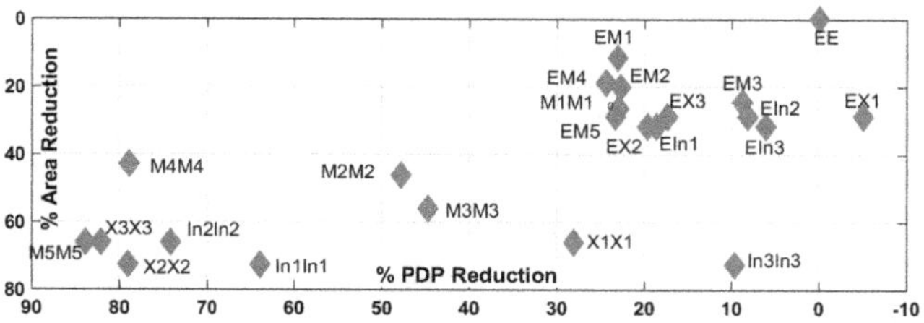

Figure 2: Area and PDP Reduction of 8x8 Array Multiplier

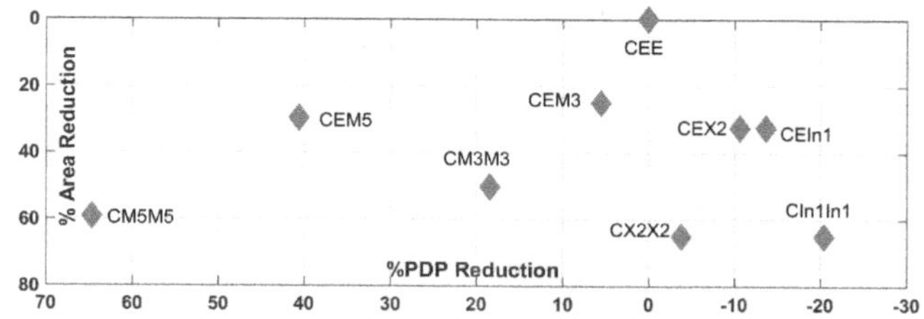

Figure 3: Area and PDP Reduction of 8x8 Tree Multiplier

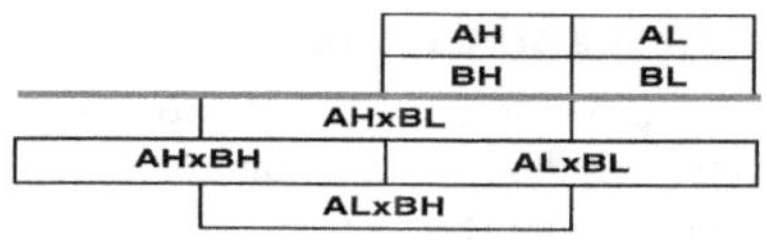

Figure 4: 16x16 Multiplier

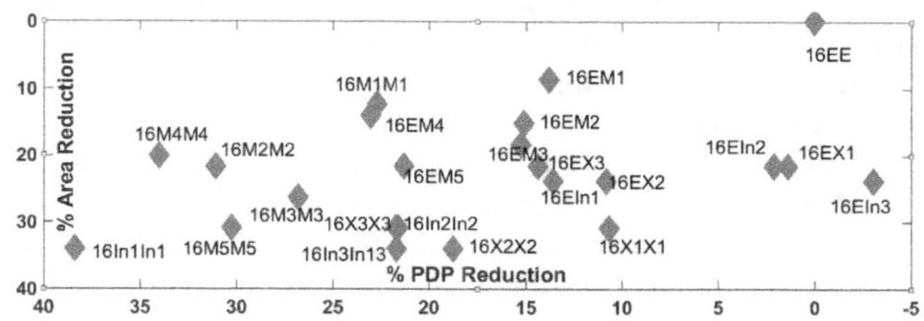

Figure 5: Area and PDP Reduction of 16x16 Array Multiplier

to maintain acceptable accuracy as recommended by [4]. Thus, we have designed, evaluated and compared 22 different options for building 8x8 approximate array multipliers, using the TSMC65nm technology. Various tables showing the design characteristics for the considered approximate multipliers can be accessed from [8]. The name of the 8x8 array multiplier consists of two parts. For example, for the EM1 multiplier, the most significant part is based on an exact (E) adder and the least significant part is based on the mirror adder 1 (M1). Fully approximate multipliers have high NMED. The approximate multiplier size exhibits a linear relationship with the degree of approximation. There is no single design that is superior in all design metrics. Therefore, a Pareto-analysis for the improvements in area and PDP is shown for different proposed designs throughout this work.

Figure 2 shows the area and PDP reduction of 8x8 array multipliers. The best designs are located on the bottom left corner. *M5M5* is a Pareto-design with PDP reduction of 84% and area reduction of 65%. The design *X3X3* is non-Pareto because it has the same area reduction as the *M5M5* but with a smaller PDP reduction. However, we have to consider other *error metrics*. Some designs such as *EX1* have increased PDP due to excessive switching activity compared to the original design.

4.2 8x8 Tree Multiplier

The design space for approximate 8x8 tree multipliers is also quite large, depending on the *compressor type* and *approximation degree*. To avoid the exponential growth of the design space, we choose to use compressors of the same type. Also, we use two options for approximation degree: i) all compressors are approximate, and ii) compressors that contribute to the lowest significant 50% of the resultant bits are approximated to maintain an acceptable accuracy. Thus, based on the four shortlisted compressors, explained in Section 3, we compared 8 options for approximate 8x8 tree multipliers and the full results are given in [8]. The name of the multiplier consists of three parts. For example, CEM1 represents a compressor based multiplier (C), where the most significant part is based on an exact (E) compressor and the least significant part is composed of the mirror adder 1 (M1) based compressor. There is no single design superior is all metrics, but some designs are the best in some metrics. As depicted in Figure 3, the best designs are on the left bottom corner, i.e., *CM5M5* and *CX2X2* are Pareto designs while *CEM5* is a non-Pareto design.

5 HIGHER-ORDER MULTIPLIERS

The 8x8 multiplier basic modules can be used to construct higher-order target multiplier modules. In this paper, we use the example of designing a 16x16 multiplier to illustrate this process. The partial product tree of the 16x16 multiplication can be broken down into four products of 8x8 modules, which can be executed concurrently, as shown in Figure 4. We choose to design 16x16 multipliers with an exact AHxBH multiplier, and with exact MSBs and approximate LSBs for both AHxBL and ALxBH, and a fully approximate or approximate LSBs for ALxBL. Any other approximation degree can be found based on the required accuracy metric.

5.1 16x16 Array Multiplier

The simulation results for 16x16 approximate array multipliers, shows high similarities with the 8x8 version. The multiplier name is based on the type of ALxBL module. Fully approximate designs exhibit the minimal delay due to reduced circuit complexity. Generally, designs based on approximate mirror adders have the lowest power consumption, due to the elimination of static power dissipation. Since, the design size grows linearly with the FA size, fully approximate designs based on 6 transistors cells have the smallest area. As depicted in Figure 5 for area and PDP reduction, the best designs are on the lower left corner, i.e., *16In1In1* and *16In3In3* are Pareto designs while *16M4M4* is a non-Pareto design.

5.2 16x16 Tree Multiplier

The characterization of 16x16 and 8x8 approximate tree multipliers shows high similarities. As depicted in Figure 6, regarding area and PDP reduction, *16CEM5*, *16CEIn1* and *16CM5M5* are Pareto designs while *16CEM3* is a non-Pareto design.

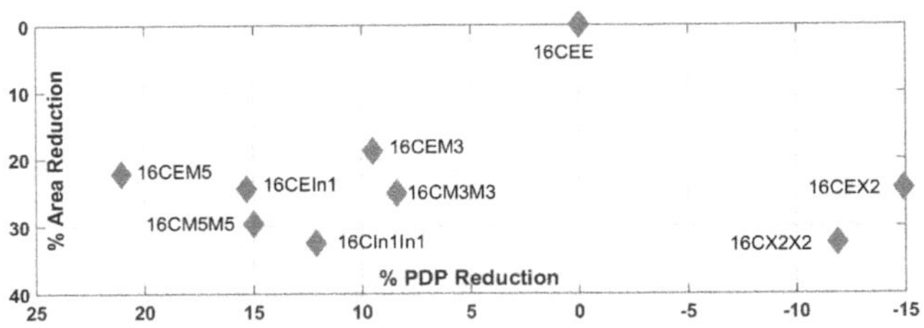

Figure 6: Area and PDP Reduction of 16x16 Tree Multiplier

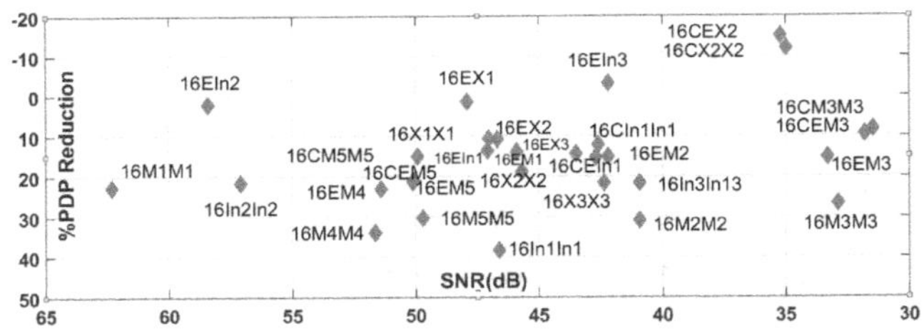

Figure 7: %PDP Reduction and SNR of Multipliers

5.3 Discussion and Comparison

The considered approximate multipliers are implemented using Cadence's Spectre based on TSMC65nm process, with V_{dd} = 1.0V at T=27C^{o}. The circuit inputs are provided by independent voltage sources, and a load of 10fF is utilized. We evaluated and compared the design characteristics (Area, Power and Delay). We found out that the 8x8 exact tree multiplier exhibits lower delay, power and size compared to the 8x8 exact array multiplier.

Several multiplier designs, based on *AMA5*, have the lowest delay and power consumption, due to the basic structure of the FA cell, which is composed of two buffers only. Also, they have the lowest NMED and a small size. Regarding accuracy, the designs based on *InXA1* have low ER and NMED. Similarly, the designs based on the 6 transistors FA, have the minimal size. Thus, it can be observed that the characteristics of approximate FA are generally propagated in the corresponding approximate multipliers as well.

In terms of architecture, we found out that the tree multiplier designs tend to have a lower power consumption than the array multipliers, especially the designs based on low power consumption FAs, such as *AMA3* and *AMA5*. In terms of the 8x8 sub-module placement to form higher-order multipliers, with a fixed configuration for AHxBH, AHxBL and ALxBH, we have noticed that the quality-loss increases, while the size, power consumption and delay decrease for designs with fully approximate ALxBL.

Compared to the 24 different designs reported in [7], where 92% of the designs have ER close to 100%, only 80% of our proposed designs have high ER. Regarding NMED, almost all our designs have a value less than 10^{-5}, which is the minimum value reported by the 24 approximate designs in [7]. Comparing the PDP reduction, most of the designs in [7] have a high PDP reduction because they are based on truncation and a high degree of approximation. However, our designs are superior in PDP reduction for designs with a high degree of approximation.

6 APPLICATION

We evaluate and compare the accuracy of the built approximate multipliers based on an image blending application, where two images are multiplied pixel-by-pixel. While in previous sections, we used Cadence Spectre to build the circuits and evaluate their area, performance and power consumption, for experimentation purposes, here we use MATLAB to evaluate error metrics for an image processing application. The library of implemented cells and multiplier circuits, and the results of the image blending application can be found at *https://sourceforge.net/projects/approximatemultiplier*. The signal to noise ratio (SNR) is used to measure the image quality for different designs. Figure 7 shows a comparison of the SNR and the percentage of PDP reduction for different approximate multipliers. Clearly, designs on the bottom left corner, have the highest PDP reduction and the best quality (high SNR) [8]. Generally, all multiplier designs have an acceptable SNR (acceptable quality).

7 CONCLUSIONS

In this paper, we designed, evaluated and compared approximate multipliers, based on approximation in partial product summation. The design space of approximate multipliers is found to be primarily dependent on the type of the approximate FA used, the architecture, and the placement of 8x8 sub-modules in the higher-order nxn multipliers. The proposed designs are compared based on PDP, area, delay, power, ER and NMED. Various optimal designs have been identified in terms of the considered design metrics. An image blending application is used to compare the proposed multiplier designs in terms of SNR and PDP. Our designs show comparative results compared to 24 different approximate designs reported in [7]. In the future, we plan to investigate the design space of higher-order multiplier modules (e.g., 64x64) using the already considered metrics and configurations. Moreover, we also plan to evaluate the possibility of having mixed FAs in the 8x8 multiplier block.

REFERENCES

[1] J. Han and M. Orshansky, "Approximate computing: An emerging paradigm for energy-efficient design," in *IEEE ETS*, 2013, pp. 1–6.

[2] P. Kulkarni, P. Gupta, and M. Ercegovac, "Trading accuracy for power with an underdesigned multiplier architecture," in *IEEE VLSI Design*, 2011, pp. 346–351.

[3] H. Jiang, J. Han, and F. Lombardi, "A comparative review and evaluation of approximate adders," in *ACM GLSVLSI*, 2015, pp. 343–348.

[4] V. Gupta, D. Mohapatra, A. Raghunathan, and K. Roy, "Low-power digital signal processing using approximate adders," *IEEE Transactions on Computer-Aided Design of Integrated Circuits and Systems*, vol. 32, no. 1, pp. 124–137, 2013.

[5] Z. Yang, A. Jain, J. Liang, J. Han, and F. Lombardi, "Approximate xor/xnor-based adders for inexact computing," in *IEEE Nanotechnology*, 2013, pp. 690–693.

[6] H. A. F. Almurib, T. N. Kumar, and F. Lombardi, "Inexact designs for approximate low power addition by cell replacement," in *IEEE DATE*, 2016, pp. 660–665.

[7] H. Jiang, C. Liu, N. Maheshwari, F. Lombardi, and J. Han, "A comparative evaluation of approximate multipliers," in *IEEE Nanoscale Architectures*, 2016, pp. 191–196.

[8] M. Masadeh, O. Hasan, and S. Tahar, *Comparative Study of Approximate Multipliers*, Technical Report, ECE Department, Concordia University, Montreal, QC, Canada. http://arxiv.org/abs/1803.06587, 2018.

[9] Z. Yang, J. Yang, K. Xing, and G. Yang, "Approximate compressor based multiplier design methodology for error-resilient digital signal processing," in *IEEE ICSIP*, 2016, pp. 740–744.

[10] S. Rehman, W. El-Harouni, M. Shafique, A. Kumar, and J. Henkel, "Architectural-space exploration of approximate multipliers," in *ACM DAC*, 2016, pp. 1–8.

[11] A. Momeni, J. Han, P. Montuschi, and F. Lombardi, "Design and analysis of approximate compressors for multiplication," *IEEE Transactions on Computers*, vol. 64, no. 4, pp. 984–994, 2015.

[12] J. M. Rabaey, A. Chandrakasan, and B. Nikolic, *Digital Integrated Circuits*. Prentice-Hall, 2002.

Dataflow-Based Mapping of Spiking Neural Networks on Neuromorphic Hardware

Anup Das
Computer Engineering, Drexel University, Philadelphia
19104, PA, USA
anup.das@drexel.edu

Akash Kumar
Computer Science, TU Dresden
01062 Dresden, Germany
akash.kumar@tu-dresden.de

ABSTRACT

Spiking Neural Networks (SNNs) are powerful computation engines for pattern recognition and image classification applications. Apart from *application performance* such as recognition and classification accuracy, *system performance* such as throughput becomes important when executing these applications on a hardware. We propose a systematic design-flow to map SNN-based applications on a crossbar-based neuromorphic hardware, guaranteeing application as well as system performance. Synchronous Dataflow Graphs (SDFGs) are used to model these applications with extended semantics to represent neural network topologies. Self-timed scheduling is then used to analyze throughput, incorporating hardware constraints such as synaptic memory, communication and I/O bandwidth of crossbars. Our design-flow integrates `CARLsim`, a GPU-accelerated application-level SNN simulator with $\texttt{SDF}^3$, a tool for mapping SDFG on hardware. We conducted experiments with realistic and synthetic SNNs on representative neuromorphic hardware, demonstrating throughput-resource trade-offs for a given application performance. For throughput-constrained applications, we show average 20% reduction of hardware usage with 19% reduction in energy consumption. For throughput-scalable applications, we show an average 53% higher throughput compared to a state-of-the-art approach.

ACM Reference Format:

Anup Das and Akash Kumar. 2018. Dataflow-Based Mapping of Spiking Neural Networks on Neuromorphic Hardware. In *GLSVLSI '18: 2018 Great Lakes Symposium on VLSI, May 23–25, 2018, Chicago, IL, USA*. ACM, New York, NY, USA, 4 pages. https://doi.org/10.1145/3194554.3194627

1 INTRODUCTION

Spiking Neural Networks (SNNs) [12] are computational models inspired by the dynamics of human brain. In recent years, SNNs have matured significantly in terms of applications, algorithms and hardware implementation. Despite these advances, research in these domains are still conducted in isolation. As an example, algorithm developers do not consider application performance (e.g., accuracy loss) due to hardware constraints such as limited synaptic memory and I/O bandwidth, or scheduling aspects associated with spike communication on a time-multiplexed interconnect. On the other hand, hardware developers demonstrate energy efficiency using toy applications only. Recently, mapping of large applications on neuromorphic hardware are targeted. These efforts are usually ad-hoc [9] or specific to a hardware [14], with no consideration of system performance [4].

Dataflow-based mappings of neural networks on neuromorphic hardware are recently proposed. In [7], the authors propose to model iterative applications using SDFGs, extended to explicitly model loop structures hierarchically to be automatically parallelized on many-core systems. A dataflow architecture called the row-stationary is proposed in [3] to reduce data movement across the processing elements of a deep neural network accelerator. Other approaches in this category are [1, 11, 18]. These approaches suffer from the limitations outlined before.

We propose a systematic design-flow for mapping and scheduling SNN-based applications on neuromorphic hardware. Synchronous Data Flow Graphs (SDFGs) are used to model applications, with extended semantics to represent neural network topologies. Self-timed scheduling is then used to analyze throughput, incorporating hardware constraints such as synaptic memory, communication and I/O bandwidth of crossbars. Our design-flow is demonstrated using Monte-Carlo-based mapping strategy. Experiments are conducted with realistic and synthetic application SNNs on representative neuromorphic hardware, generating throughput-resource trade-offs for a given application performance.

Rest of this paper is organized as follows. Introduction to SDFGs is provided are Section 2 highlighting SNN-specific semantics and throughput computation. Our end-to-end design-flow is introduced in Section 3. Results of our analysis are presented in Section 4. Finally, the paper is concluded in Section 5 with future works.

2 OPERATIONAL SEMANTICS

2.1 Introduction to SDFG

Synchronous Data Flow Graphs (SDFGs, see [10]) are often used to model modern DSP applications and to design concurrent multimedia applications implemented on multi-processor systems. Both pipelined streaming and cyclic dependencies between tasks can be easily modeled in SDFGs. Tasks are modeled by the vertices of an SDFG called *actors*; they represent functions that are computed by reading *tokens* (data items) from their input ports and writing the results of the computation as tokens on the output ports. The number of tokens produced or consumed in one execution of an actor is called port *rate*, and remains constant. The rates are visualized as port annotations. Actor execution is also called *firing*. The edges in the graph, called *channels*, represent dependencies among different actors. Figure 1(a) shows an example of a SDFG.

GLSVLSI '18, May 23–25, 2018, Chicago, IL, USA

ACM ISBN 978-1-4503-5724-1/18/05...$15.00
https://doi.org/10.1145/3194554.3194627

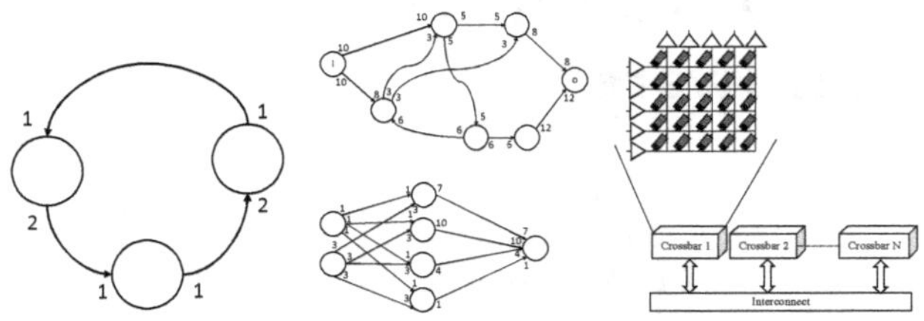

(a) Example SDFG. (b) Example SNN. (c) Example hardware.

Figure 1: Examples of SDFG, SNN and hardware.

2.2 Introduction to SNN

Neural networks are collection of neurons interconnected with synapses. Figure 1(b) shows two example SNN topologies. It is important to observe the similarity between neural networks (Figure 1(b)) and SDFGs (Figure 1(a)). This motivates us to use SDFG to represent SNN, with actors representing neurons, edges representing synaptic connections and tokens representing spikes. Three restrictions apply – (1) tokens produced by an actor (neuron) are all consumed at once during one firing of the connected actors, (2) when an actor fires, it produces the same number of tokens on all output ports, and (3) the synaptic weights ω_i are modeled inside the neuron. Figure 1(c) shows the general architecture of a modern neuromorphic hardware. The architecture consists of multiple crossbars of fully connected neurons. Crossbars communicate with each other using an interconnect. Traffic on the interconnect is time-multiplexed. Key differences between crossbar-based neuromorphic architectures and conventional many-core architectures are that in neuromorphic architectures, (1) neuron computations are carried out in-parallel inside a cossbar; (2) synaptic weights for neuron computation are stored locally inside a crossbar; and (3) memory bandwidth limitations are eliminated.

2.3 Mapping and Throughput Analysis

For the purpose of neuron mapping and throughput analyis, we introduce the following notations.

$\mathcal{G}(\mathcal{A}, \mathcal{S})$	= SNN SDFG with set of actors (neurons) $\mathcal{A}$ and set of connections (synapses) $\mathcal{S}$
$\boldsymbol{a}_i \in \mathcal{A}$	= $\langle \tau_i, \Omega_i \rangle$, where τ_i is the execution time of $\boldsymbol{a}_i$ and Ω_i are the synaptic weights to compute output of $\boldsymbol{a}_i$
$s_{i,j} \in \mathcal{S}$	= synaptic connections between $\boldsymbol{a}_i$ and $\boldsymbol{a}_j$. $\mathbb{R}(s_{i,j})$ is the number of spikes communicated on the synapse.
$\mathcal{H}(C, \mathcal{E})$	= neuromorphic architecture with set of crossbars C and the set of edges between the crossbar $\mathcal{E}$
$c_k \in C$	= $\langle N_k, I_k, O_k \rangle$, where N_k is the size of crossbar c_k in terms of number of neurons and $I_k(O_k)$ is its input (output) spike bandwidth
$e_{k,l} \in \mathcal{E}$	= connection between crossbar c_k and c_l. $\mathbb{L}(e_{k,l})$ is the communication latency of the link e_{k_l}
$\mathcal{G} \xrightarrow[M]{} \mathcal{H}$	= Mapping of SNN SDFG $\mathcal{G}(\mathcal{A}, \mathcal{S})$ on neuromorphic architecture $\mathcal{H}(C, \mathcal{E})$
$x_{i,k}$	= a binary variable representing the assignment of actor $\boldsymbol{a}_i$ on crossbar c_k.

Mapping: Mapping neurons on a neuromorphic hardware involves determining $x_{i,k}$ with the following constraints.

- a neuron is allocated to one crossbar only i.e.,
$$\sum_k x_{i,k} = 1 \; \forall \; i \tag{1}$$
- memory constraint of a crossbar must be satisfied i.e.,
$$\sum_{i,j} x_{i,k} \cdot x_{j,k} \leq N_k^2 \; \forall \; k \tag{2}$$
In the above equation, we note that a crossbar is a fully connected architecture of neurons and therefore the maximum number of synapses in a crossbar is N_k^2. Furthermore, $x_{i,k} \cdot x_{j,k}$ evaluates to 1 iff $\boldsymbol{a}_i$ and $\boldsymbol{a}_j$ are both mapped to the same crossbar.
- spike bandwidth of a crossbar must be satisfied i.e.,
$$\sum_i x_{i,k} \sum_{j,i} (1 - x_{j,k}) \cdot \mathbb{R}(s_{j,i}) \leq I_k \; \forall \; k \tag{3}$$
$$\sum_i x_{i,k} \sum_{i,j} (1 - x_{j,k}) \cdot \mathbb{R}(s_{i,j}) \leq O_k \; \forall \; k \tag{4}$$
In the above equation, $x_{i,k} \sum_{j,i}(1-x_{j,k}) \cdot \mathbb{R}(s_{j,i})$ equates to 1 for all incoming synapses to actor $\boldsymbol{a}_i$ that are not mapped to the crossbar c_k. Similarly, $x_{i,k} \sum_{i,j}(1-x_{j,k}) \cdot \mathbb{R}(s_{i,j})$ equates to 1 for all outgoing synapses of actor $\boldsymbol{a}_i$ that are not mapped to the crossbar c_k.

Scheduling: Self-timed execution [13] is widely used for scheduling SDFGs on multiprocessor systems. Self-timed scheduling is extended for a multi-crossbar neuromorphic hardware as follows. First, we consider a mapping M (refer to Section 3 to generate the mapping). We introduce virtual nodes in the SNN SDFG for every synapse mapped on the interconnect. Execution time of the virtual node is the latency $\mathbb{L}$ of the interconnect link to which the synapse is mapped. Next, we a use list-scheduler to compute the periodic schedule for every crossbar in the neuromorphic architecture using the mapping M (i.e., the variables $x_{i,k}$). Essentially, a list is maintained to store the actors that are ready to fire at any given instance of time. To enable parallel computation in a crossbar, at most N_k actors from the ready list are fired at once. Finally, time slices are allocated for the actors on a crossbar using a binary search algorithm, which guarantees that a time slice allocation satisfies the throughput constraint. The original mapping and schedule generation tool SDF^3 [15, 16] is extended to compute throughput for a given mapping with the neuromorphic hardware specific modifications.

Note: In our formulation, firing of an actor is delayed until the desired number of tokens (i.e., spikes) are received. As a result the spike rate at the input of a neuron is unaltered (similar to the spike rate analyzed using an application simulator). The classification/prediction accuracy, which is interpreted in terms of spike rate, remains the same. Thus, implicitly our approach enforces the same accuracy while using a real hardware. One exception to this is when inter-spike interval is used as information coding instead of spike rate. In this scenario, the accuracy using the hardware is usually lower than what is predicted using an application simulator. However, our approach reduces spike latency, improving accuracy over state-of-the-art approaches (refer to Section 4.3).

3 END-TO-END DESIGN-FLOW

Figure 2 shows our proposed end-to-end design-flow. A reference neuromorphic hardware, CxQuad [8] is shown in the figure. CxQuad consists of four crossbars, each with 128 pre- and 128 post-synaptic

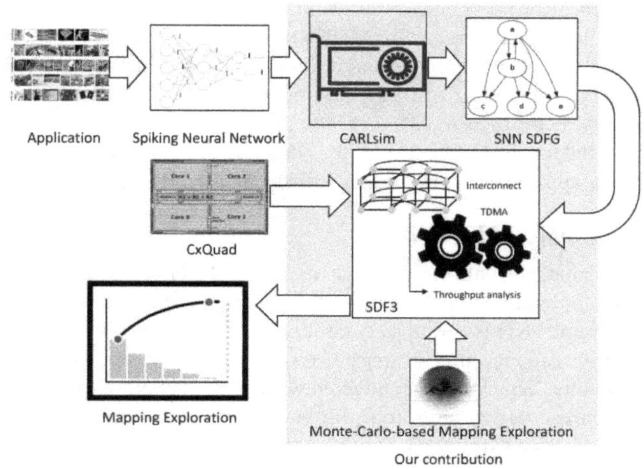

Figure 2: End-to-end design flow.

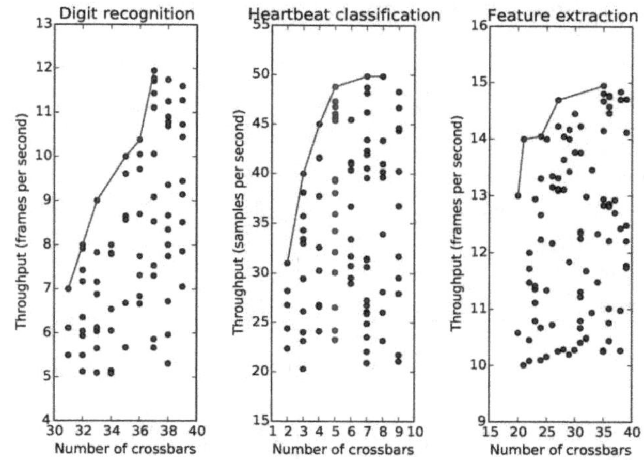

Figure 3: Monte-Carlo-based mapping exploration.

neurons, implementing a full 16K (128x128) local synapses per crossbar. The crossbars are interconnected using a NoC-tree, which time-multiplexes global synaptic connections. In our evaluation, we use neuromorphic hardware models similar to CxQuad. A SNN-based application such as digit recognition is simulated using the `CARLsim` simulator [2], which generates a trained SNN with adjusted synaptic weights and spike counts on every synapse in the SNN. This is encoded as SDFG in XML representation. The neuromorphic hardware is also represented in XML. Next we propose Monte-Carlo-based mapping strategy to generate neuron mapping on the hardware. For every valid mapping, the SDF^3 tool [16] is used to evaluate the throughput and resource utilization using the SDFG and the neuromorphic hardware XMLs. The mapping, throughput and resource results are stored during the exploration.

4 RESULTS

We conducted experiments using three realistic applications – digit recognition [6], heartbeat classification [5] and feature extraction [17]. These applications implement respectively, recurrent, recurrent and feedforward SNN topologies. A range of synthetic feedforward SNNs are also considered.

4.1 Throughput-Resource Trade-offs

To demonstrate throughput-resource trade-offs using our design-flow, Figure 3 plots the Monte-Carlo mapping exploration results for the three applications – digit recognition with 1984 neurons, heart-rate estimation with 80 neurons and feature extraction with 1280 neurons. These applications are executed on a neuromorphic hardware with 64 neurons per crossbar and a time-multiplexed NoC interconnecting the crossbars. For every valid mapping generated using the Monte-Carlo technique, the throughput (frames per second for the first and third applications and samples per second for the second application) and resource usage (in terms of number of crossbars used in the mapping) are computed. These mappings are represented as points on the scatter plot. As can be clearly seen from the figure, for a given resource usage, several mapping choices exist, with wide variations of throughput. This is because

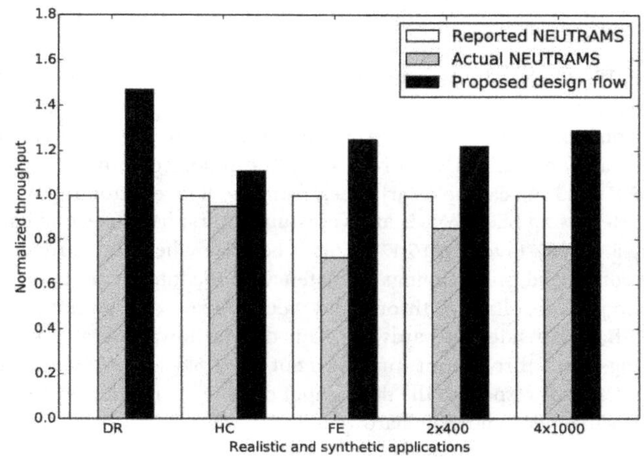

Figure 4: Maximum throughput wrt NEUTRAMS [9].

different mappings result in different delays on the interconnect due to different allocation of interconnected neurons on crossbars. This impacts throughput. Our design-flow can be extended with minimal efforts to output highest throughput mapping or minimum resource mapping for a given throughput constraint.

4.2 Maximum Throughput Comparison

Figure 4 plots the maximum throughput obtained using our design-flow for the three realistic applications – digit recognition (DR), heartbeat classification (HC) and feature extraction (FE) and two synthetic applications – `2x400`, with two hidden layers of 400 neurons each and `4x1000`, with 4 hidden layers of 1000 neurons each. These applications are executed on a hardware platform with 32 crossbars with 64 neurons per crossbar. These crossbars are interconnected using NoC-tree, replicating the CxQuad hardware. The figure plots three bars for each application. The first bar is the reported throughput obtained by applying the default approach of

Table 1: Resource usage for a given throughput.

Metric	DR		HC	
	NEUTRAMS [9]	Proposed	NEUTRAMS [9]	Proposed
Crossbars	40	35	4	2
Memory (kB)	118.8	110.5	4.2	4.1
I/O Bandwidth (bits/sec)	0.5	0.2	0.4	0.3
Latency (cycles)	108	70	99	69
Accuracy (%)	95	95	93	96
Energy Reduction (%)	–	23.3	–	17.8
Metric	FE		2x400	
	NEUTRAMS [9]	Proposed	NEUTRAMS [9]	Proposed
Crossbars	23	22	15	13
Memory (kB)	76.0	70.3	48.5	45.0
I/O Bandwidth (bits/sec)	0.8	0.5	1.1	0.89
Latency (cycles)	394	386	216	171
Accuracy (%)	87	87	–	–
Energy Reduction (%)	–	18.1	–	16.5

NEUTRAMS [9]. The second bar is the actual throughput obtained using NEUTRAMS on a neuromorphic hardware. The third bar is throughput result obtained using our design-flow. Throughput values are normalized with respect to the reported throughput of NEUTRAMS. As can be clearly seen from the figure, throughput reported using NEUTRAMS is an overestimate (first bar vs second bar) by 5% – 28% (average 16.4%). This is because when real hardware is considered, spike timings and latency on the interconnect comes into play, resulting in throughput value lower than that obtained without considering hardware. Our design-flow generates mappings with throughput improvement of 16.8% – 73.6% (average 53.3%) with respect to the throughput obtained using NEUTRAMS on the same neuromorphic hardware.

4.3 Throughput-Constrained Performance

Table 1 reports the resource usage of our design-flow for a given throughput constraint for 3 real and 1 synthetic application. The throughput constraints are set as follows: digit recognition @ 8 frames/second, heartbeat classification @ 33 samples/second, feature extraction @ 14 frames/second and synthetic SNN 2x400 @ 100 frames/second. Results using our approach are compared with respect to NEUTRAMS [9]. As can be seen from the table, our design-flow results in 4.3% – 50% (average 20%) reduction in the number of crossbars compared to NEUTRAMS. This improvement is because, the modeling technique allows better and faster exploration, generating mappings that are optimal with respect to available resources for a given throughput constraint. Reduction of resources directly impacts the energy consumption. Our design-flow also results in a reduction of 2.3% – 7.5% (average 6%) in synaptic memory usage. This saving further reduces the energy consumption. In terms of I/O bandwidth, improvement using our design-flow is between 19% and 60% (average 35%). Finally, in terms of latency, our design-flow reduces latency by 2% – 35% (average 22%). It is to be noted that reducing the latency has impact on the classification accuracy when the information is encoded as inter-spike intervals (e.g., hearbeat classification). For this application we noted a 3% improvement in accuracy with respect to NEUTRAMS. Accuracy for the synthetic application is not reported as it does not represent any real task. Finally, the energy consumption of our approach is lower than NEUTRAMS by 16.5% – 23% (average 19%). The energy numbers are reported for the CxQuad chip [8]. These results prove the relevance of our approach for throughput constrained applications.

5 CONCLUSION

We propose a data-flow based mapping of SNNs on neuromorphic hardware. Synchronous Dataflow Graphs (SDFGs) is used to represent SNN based applications. Our design-flow uses Monte-Carlo-based mapping strategy and performs throughput-resource trade-offs. Experiments conducted with evolving SNN applications on representative neuromorphic hardware demonstrate 53% improvement of throughput for throughput-scalable applications. For throughput-constrained applications, we show 20% reduction of hardware and 19% reduction in energy consumption over a state-of-the-art approach. In future, we will consider accuracy impact for inter-spike interval coding.

REFERENCES

[1] Marco Bacis et al. 2017. A pipelined and scalable dataflow implementation of convolutional neural networks on FPGA. In *International Parallel and Distributed Processing Symposium Workshops (IPDPSW)*.

[2] Michael Beyeler et al. 2015. CARLsim 3: A user-friendly and highly optimized library for the creation of neurobiologically detailed spiking neural networks. In *International Joint Conference on Neural Networks (IJCNN)*.

[3] Yu-Hsin Chen, Joel Emer, and Vivienne Sze. 2017. Using Dataflow to Optimize Energy Efficiency of Deep Neural Network Accelerators. *IEEE Micro* 37, 3 (2017), 12–21.

[4] Anup Das et al. 2018. Mapping Of Local and Global Synapses On Spiking Neuromorphic Hardware. In *Proceedings of the Conference on Design, Automation and Test (DATE)*.

[5] Anup Das et al. 2018. Unsupervised heart-rate estimation in wearables with Liquid states and a probabilistic readout. *Neural Networks* (2018).

[6] Peter U Diehl and Matthew Cook. 2015. Unsupervised learning of digit recognition using spike-timing-dependent plasticity. *Frontiers in computational neuroscience* 9 (2015).

[7] Hyesun Hong, Hyunok Oh, and Soonhoi Ha. 2017. Hierarchical Dataflow Modeling of Iterative Applications. In *Proceedings of the Annual Design Automation Conference (DAC)*.

[8] Giacomo Indiveri, Federico Corradi, and Ning Qiao. 2015. Neuromorphic architectures for spiking deep neural networks. In *IEDM*.

[9] Yu Ji et al. 2016. NEUTRAMS: Neural network transformation and co-design under neuromorphic hardware constraints. In *International Symposium on Microarchitecture (MICRO)*.

[10] Edward A Lee and David G Messerschmitt. 1987. Synchronous data flow. *Proc. IEEE* 75, 9 (1987), 1235–1245.

[11] Wenyan Lu et al. 2017. FlexFlow: A Flexible Dataflow Accelerator Architecture for Convolutional Neural Networks. In *HPCA*.

[12] Wolfgang Maass. 1997. Networks of spiking neurons: the third generation of neural network models. *Neural networks* 10, 9 (1997), 1659–1671.

[13] Sundararajan Sriram and Shuvra Bhattacharyya. 2009. *Embedded multiprocessors: Scheduling and synchronization*. CRC press.

[14] Evangelos Stromatias et al. 2015. Scalable energy-efficient, low-latency implementations of trained spiking deep belief networks on SpiNNaker. In *International Joint Conference on Neural Networks (IJCNN)*.

[15] Sander Stuijk, Twan Basten, MCW Geilen, and Henk Corporaal. 2007. Multiprocessor resource allocation for throughput-constrained synchronous dataflow graphs. In *Proceedings of the Annual Design Automation Conference (DAC)*.

[16] Sander Stuijk, Marc Geilen, and Twan Basten. 2006. SDF^3: SDF for free. In *ACSD*.

[17] Amirhossein Tavanaei, Timothée Masquelier, and Anthony S Maida. 2016. Acquisition of visual features through probabilistic spike-timing-dependent plasticity. In *International Joint Conference on Neural Networks (IJCNN)*.

[18] Shouyi Yin et al. 2017. Learning Convolutional Neural Networks for Data-Flow Graph Mapping on Spatial Programmable Architectures. In *FPGA*.

Design of Dynamic Range Approximate Logarithmic Multipliers

Peipei Yin, Chenghua Wang, Weiqiang Liu*
College of Electronic and Information Engineering
Nanjing University of Aeronautics and Astronautics
Nanjing, China
{ppyin, chwang, liuweiqiang}@nuaa.edu.cn

Fabrizio Lombardi
Department of Electrical and Computer Engineering
Northeastern University
Boston, USA
lombardi@neu.edu

ABSTRACT

Approximate computing is an emerging approach for designing high performance and low power arithmetic circuits. The logarithmic multiplier (LM) converts multiplication into addition and has inherent approximate characteristics. A method combining the Mitchell's approximation and a dynamic range operand truncation scheme is proposed in this paper to design non-iterative and iterative approximate LMs. The accuracy and the circuit requirements of these designs are assessed to select the best approximate scheme according to different metrics. Compared with conventional non-iterative and iterative 16-bit LMs with exact operands, the normalized mean error distance (NMED) of the best proposed approximate non-iterative and iterative LMs is decreased up to 24.1% and 18.5%, respectively, while the power-delay product (PDP) is decreased up to 51.7% and 45.3%, respectively. Case studies for two error-tolerant applications show the validity of the proposed approximate LMs.

KEYWORDS

Approximate computing; logarithmic multiplier; operand truncation; low power

ACM Reference Format:
Peipei Yin, Chenghua Wang, Weiqiang Liu, and Fabrizio Lombardi. 2018. Design of Dynamic Range Approximate Logarithmic Multipliers. In Proceedings of ACM Great Lakes Symposium on VLSI (GLSVLSI'18). ACM, New York, NY, USA, 4 pages. https://doi.org/10.1145/3194554.3194628

1 INTRODUCTION

Approximate circuit design [1] provides an emerging approach to address the high power consumption of integrated circuits. For many applications, computational results using approximate circuits are still of a reasonable good quality; for example, multimedia (such as audio, image, and video) can tolerate errors due to the limited human perception. Therefore, full accuracy is not always necessary, thus enabling approximate computing to be employed for this type of applications.

As a basic operation for an arithmetic processor, multiplication is particularly attractive to approximation due to the high cost incurred in terms of power, area, and delay. Generally, a multiplier consists of three stages: partial product generation, accumulation, and a final addition. So methodologies based on these stages are also used for the approximate design of a multiplier. Another approximation methodology focuses on the operands. In [2], the input operands are split into two parts: a multiplication part that includes a number of higher order bits and a non-multiplication part made of the remaining lower order bits. In [3-4], a leading-1 detector (LOD) is used to provide accuracy higher than by simply truncating the operands, although it incurs in considerable area and power consumption.

Multipliers using the logarithmic transformation (which has inherent approximate characteristics) convert multiplication into addition. The logarithmic multiplier (LM) was first proposed by Mitchell [5]; broadly, LMs can be classified into two categories, non-iterative [6-10] and iterative [11-12]. In the LM architecture, circuits such as LODs are included to detect the most significant operand bit. Thus, if the operands are truncated from the first significant one, no more LOD is needed.

This paper proposes a method combining Mitchell's approximation and the approximation in operands, so-called dynamic range approximate LMs are presented. Both non-iterative and iterative approximate LM designs are studied.

This paper is organized as follows. Section 2 provides a brief review of LM arithmetic. Section 3 presents the designs of the approximate LMs. Section 4 assesses the accuracy and circuit-level metrics of different approximate designs. Section 5 shows the applications of the proposed LMs. Finally, Section 6 provides the conclusion.

2 REVIEW

LMs can be broadly classified into two categories: non-iterative and iterative LMs. This section briefly reviews these two types of LM.

2.1 Non-iterative logarithmic multiplier

Mitchell [2] introduced the first LM. The binary representations of two n-bit input numbers A and B are expressed as:

$$A = 2^{k_1}(1 + x_1) \tag{1}$$

$$B = 2^{k_2}(1 + x_2) \tag{2}$$

where k_1 and k_2 denote the most significant operand bit with value of '1' of A and B, respectively. x_1 and x_2 in the range [0,1], denote the fractional parts [12]. The base-2 logarithm of the product of operands A and B is given by:

$$log_2 P = (k_1+k_2) + log_2(1 + x_1) + log_2(1 + x_2) \tag{3}$$

GLSVLSI '18, May 23–25, 2018, Chicago, IL, USA

ACM ISBN 978-1-4503-5724-1/18/05 $15.00
https://doi.org/10.1145/3194554.3194628

In Mitchell's algorithm, if $0 \leq x < 1$, $log_2(1+x)$ is approximately equal to x; so the logarithm of the product and the product are expressed as per Eq. (4) and Eq. (5):

$$log_2 P \approx (k_1+k_2) + x_1 + x_2 \tag{4}$$

$$P \approx \begin{cases} 2^{k_1+k_2}(1+x_1+x_2), & x_1+x_2<1 \\ 2^{k_1+k_2+1}(x_1+x_2), & x_1+x_2 \geq 1 \end{cases} \tag{5}$$

The sum of the characteristic numbers determines the most significant bit of the product; the sum is then shifted left by k_1+k_2 or by k_1+k_2+1 positions, depending on $x_1 + x_2$.

2.2 Iterative logarithmic multiplier

The iterative LM has been proposed to reduce the multiplication error. The exact product is given by:

$$P = 2^{k_1+k_2}(1+x_1+x_2+x_1x_2)$$
$$= \begin{cases} 2^{k_1+k_2}(1+x_1+x_2) + 2^{k_1+k_2}x_1x_2, \\ \qquad x_1+x_2<1 \\ 2^{k_1+k_2+1}(x_1+x_2) + 2^{k_1+k_2}(1-x_1)(1-x_2), \\ \qquad x_1+x_2 \geq 1 \end{cases} \tag{6}$$

Compared with Eq. (5), the correction terms $2^{k1+k2}x_1x_2$ or $2^{k1+k2}(1-x_1)(1-x_2)$ are added to the approximate product. The computation of the correction terms requires multiplication (this is computed as per Eq. (5)).

3 PROPOSED DYNAMIC RANGE APPROXIMATE LMS

In the following subsections, the proposed dynamic range non-iterative and iterative ALM designs are discussed in detail.

3.1 Non-iterative approximate LM

The proposed architecture of a non-iterative approximate logarithmic multiplier is shown in Fig. 1. In a conventional LM, the most significant '1's are first located in the input operands. Thus, from the most significant '1', the operands can be dynamically truncated with different length according to the accuracy requirement. As the product of a LM is always smaller than its exact counterpart, the last bit of the truncated operands is set to logic one to compensate negative errors [4]. In Fig. 1, LOD and dynamic truncation complete this process. For the truncated fractional operands x_t and their exponents k, a smaller adder is used after the logarithmic converter. An OR operation on the last bit of the addition product and a logic one are added to compensate the result. After the antilogarithmic converter, the result is then shifted according to the location of the two leading ones to generate the final approximate result.

The product terms in Eq. (5) after dynamic truncation and compensation of the fractional portions are as follows:

$$P \approx \begin{cases} 2^{k_1+k_2}\left(1+x_{1t}+x_{2t}+2^{-(t-1)}\right), \\ \qquad x_{1t}+x_{2t}+2^{-(t-1)}<1 \\ 2^{k_1+k_2+1}\left(x_{1t}+x_{2t}+2^{-(t-1)}\right), \\ \qquad x_{1t}+x_{2t}+2^{-(t-1)} \geq 1 \end{cases} \tag{7}$$

where t denotes the truncation width. To assess the most appropriate t, an error analysis of the logarithmic multiplier is carried out in section 4.

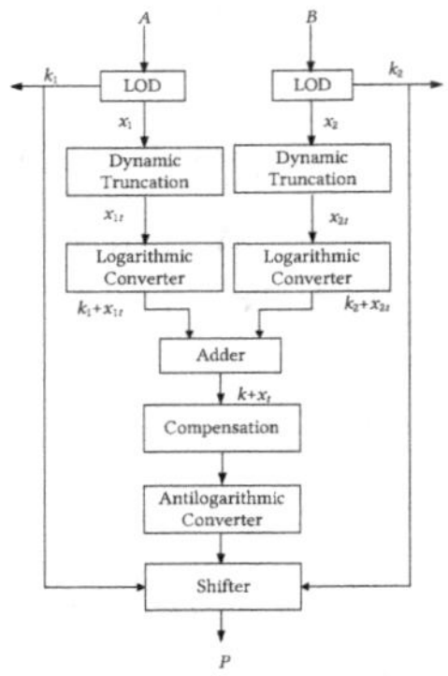

Fig. 1: Non-iterative Approximate LM Architecture.

3.2 Iterative approximate LM

The previously proposed approximate LM is used as the basic iterative unit; the product terms in Eq. (6) after dynamic truncation and compensation of the fractional portions are as follows:

$$P \approx \begin{cases} 2^{k_1+k_2}\left(1+x_{1t}+x_{2t}+2^{-(t-1)}\right) \\ \quad + 2^{k_1+k_2}x_{1t'}x_{2t'}, \\ \qquad x_{1t}+x_{2t}+2^{-(t-1)}<1 \\ 2^{k_1+k_2+1}\left(x_{1t}+x_{2t}+2^{-(t-1)}\right) \\ \quad + 2^{k_1+k_2}(1-x_1)_{t'}(1-x_2)_{t'}, \\ \qquad x_{1t}+x_{2t}+2^{-(t-1)} \geq 1 \end{cases} \tag{8}$$

where t and t' denotes the truncation width for the first and the second iterations, respectively.

4 SIMULATION RESULTS

In this section, the accuracy and hardware requirements are assessed for the proposed non-iterative approximate LMs with L_i-bit input operand (ALM-L_i) and iterative approximate LMs with L_i-bit input operand in iteration 1 and L_j-bit input operand in iteration 2 (IALM-L_i-L_j) along with their exact non-iterative LM design (LM) and iterative LM design (ILM).

4.1 Accuracy

To quantify the accuracy, the errors of the ALM and IALM are assessed for different truncation length of the input operands. Recent approximate LMs namely, ALM-SOA [13] and IALM-SL [13] are also simulated and assessed. The NMED is defined as the normalization of the mean error distance (MED) by the maximum output of the accurate design [14].

Assume that the input data is uniformly distributed in the full range of the 16-bit fixed-point format. The NMEDs are reported in Table 1. In the proposed ALM, the error due to truncation is evident; with an increase in truncation length (L), the NMED rapidly decreases and from L = 6 it slightly increases. For L = 5, the NMED is almost the same as with no truncation, so precision is best at L = 6. When L = 6 or 7, the NMED of the proposed LM is smaller than for ALM-SOA [13].

The IALMs are also simulated. To evaluate the NMED of an IALM, the same truncation is initially used for iteration 2. The NMEDs of an IALM with different length of input operands in iteration 1 (L_1) are reported in Table 2. When L_1>12, the NMED is close to ILM. Next, the NMED of an IALM (Table 3) is analyzed for L_1=12, 14 and by changing the length of the input operand in iteration 2 (L_2). By decreasing the truncation length in iteration 2, the NMED steadily decreases and starting at L_2 = 6, it increases rapidly for either L_1=12 or 14. Both the NMEDs of IALM-12-6 and IALM-14-6 are smaller than ILM and IALM-SL [13]; by using the iterative technique, the NMED is significantly improved.

4.2 Circuit-level assessment

All designs are implemented and simulated by the Synopsys Design Compiler using the Nangate 45nm Open Cell Library. Table 4 and 5 present the delay, area and power consumption of the proposed and previous non-iterative and iterative approximate LMs, respectively. From Table 4, a decrease in L for an approximate LM leads to a reduction in PDP; when the L for the proposed ALM decreases to 6, the PDP is lower than for ALM-SOA. The assessment from Table 5 shows that a decrease in L either in iteration 1 or 2 for an IALM leads to a reduction in PDP. When L for the proposed IALM decreases to 14, the PDP is lower than for IALM-SL. As per the accuracy of a IALM presented in Section 4.1, the IALM with L_1 = 12 or 14 shows very good error features. Then further truncation in iteration 2 with L_1 = 12 or 14 is implemented.

The NMEDs and PDPs of the above non-iterative and iterative LMs whose NMEDs are close to their conventional counterparts, are shown in Fig. 2. Fig. 2(a) shows the NMEDs and PDPs comparison of non-iterative LMs. The proposed ALMs and the previous design ALM-SOA [13] (Fig. 2(a)) have better performance than a conventional LM. ALM-6 is the best proposed non-iterative design, achieving up to 51.7% improvement in PDP and 24.1% improvement in NMED compared with a conventional LM (exact). Fig. 2(b) shows the NMED and PDP comparison for iterative LMs. The proposed IALMs and the previous design IALM-SL [13] (Fig. 2(b)) both have better performance than a conventional ILM. IALM-12-6 is the best proposed iterative design achieving up to 45.3% improvement in PDP and 18.6% improvement in NMED compared with a conventional ILM (exact). IALM-14-6 has a slightly lower NMED, but higher PDP than IALM-12-6. Fig. 2(c) shows the overall comparison of non-iterative and iterative LMs. In general, non-iterative ALMs have a significantly lower PDP, but a higher NMED than iterative ALMs.

5 APPLICATIONS

In this section, the best proposed non-iterative design (ALM-6) and iterative design (IALM-12-6) are applied to digital signal processing and image processing applications.

Table 1: NMED of 16-bit Non-iterative Approximate LMs with Different Length of Input Operand

Non-iterative LMs	L	NMED(10^{-2})
LM	16	0.926
ALM-12	12	0.925
ALM-10	10	0.866
ALM-8	8	0.823
ALM-7	7	0.762
ALM-6	**6**	**0.703**
ALM-5	5	0.923
ALM-4	4	1.821
ALM-3	3	4.133
ALM-SOA[13]	-	0.806

Table 2: NMED of 16-bit Iterative Approximate LMs (IALM) with Different Length of Input Operand (L_1) in Iteration 1

Iterative LMs	L_1	NMED(10^{-4})
ILM	16	3.476
IALM-14-14	**14**	**3.411**
IALM-12-12	**12**	**3.498**
IALM-10-10	10	4.261
IALM-8-8	8	9.716
IALM-6-6	6	35.371

Table 3: NMED of 16-bit Iterative Approximate LMs (IALM) with Different Length of Input Operand (L_1) in Iteration 1 and Different Length of Input Operand (L_2) in Iteration 2

Iterative LMs	L_1	L_2	NMED(10^{-4})
IALM-12-10	12	10	3.372
IALM-12-8		8	3.157
IALM-12-6		**6**	**2.829**
IALM-12-4		4	7.470
IALM-14-10	14	10	3.307
IALM-14-8		8	3.052
IALM-14-6		**6**	**2.724**
IALM-14-4		4	7.415
IALM-SL[13]	-	-	2.870

Table 4: Circuit Assessment of Non-iterative Approximate LMs

Non-iterative LMs	Power (μW)	Area (μm^2)	Delay (ns)	PDP (fJ)	ADP ($\mu m^2 \cdot ns$)
LM	268.9	979.7	1.00	268.9	979.7
ALM-12	196.7	812.1	1.01	198.7	820.2
ALM-10	187.2	762.1	1.05	196.6	800.2
ALM-8	178.0	738.7	0.96	170.9	709.2
ALM-7	174.5	657.3	0.94	164.0	617.9
ALM-6	139.7	603.6	0.93	129.9	561.3
ALM-5	164.2	567.9	0.82	134.6	465.7
ALM-4	124.0	475.1	0.82	101.7	389,6
ALM-3	102.7	405.1	0.66	67.8	267.4
ALM-SOA[13]	175.9	620.0	0.92	161.8	570.4

Table 5: Circuit Assessment of Iterative Approximate LMs

Iterative LMs	Power (μW)	Area (μm^2)	Delay (ns)	PDP (fJ)	ADP ($\mu m^2 \cdot ns$)
ILM	784.6	2397.5	2.25	1765.4	5394.3
IALM-14-14	593.7	2055.9	2.14	**1270.5**	4399.6
IALM-12-12	488.4	1781.7	2.11	**1030.5**	3759.4
IALM-10-10	482.9	1721.8	2.07	999.7	3564.1
IALM-8-8	482.4	1398.4	1.87	902.1	2615.0
IALM-6-6	304.3	1162.4	1.85	563.0	2150.4
IALM-12-10	527.2	1807.2	2.08	1096.6	3759.0
IALM-12-8	535.1	1811.7	2.03	1086.3	3677.8
IALM-12-6	500.1	1740.7	1.93	**965.2**	3359.6
IALM-12-4	411.7	1601.9	1.85	761.6	2963.5
IALM-14-10	570.6	1922.4	2.13	1215.4	40947
IALM-14-8	605.1	1914.9	2.07	1252.6	3963.8
IALM-14-6	539.7	1908.0	1.97	**1063.2**	3758.8
IALM-14-4	418.6	1685.6	2.00	837.2	3371.2
IALM-SL[13]	629.7	1918.9	2.12	1335.0	4068.1

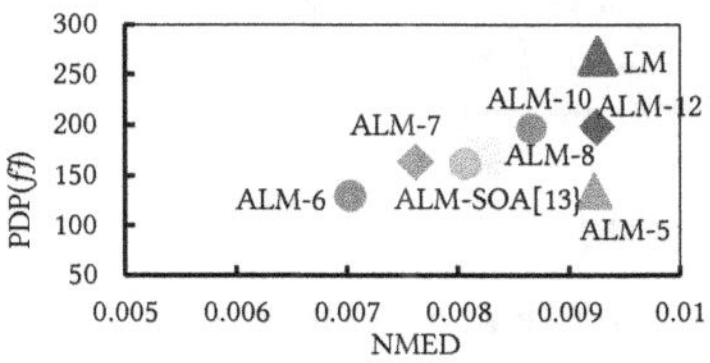

(a) Non-iterative Approximate LMs.

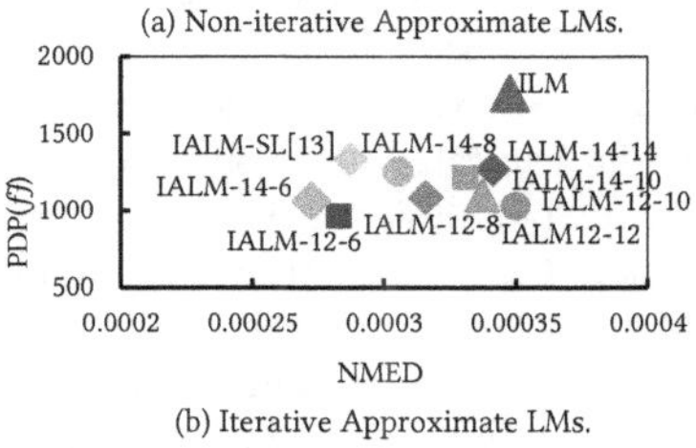

(b) Iterative Approximate LMs.

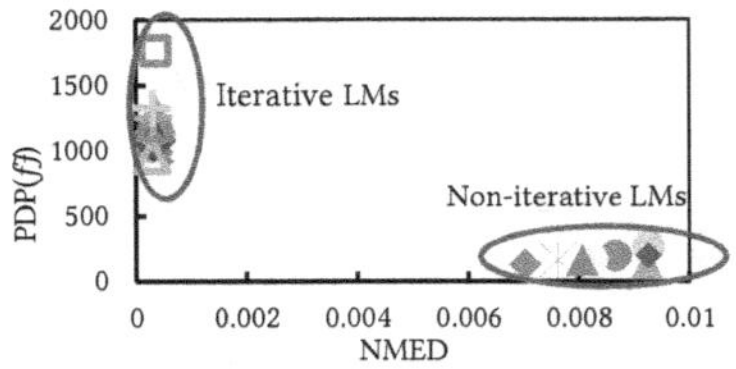

(c) Comparison of Non-iterative and Iterative Approximate LMs.

Fig. 2: NMED and PDP of Non-iterative and Iterative Approximate LMs.

5.1 FIR filter

The FIR filter is designed by the Filter Design and Analysis (FDA) Tool in MATLAB. The pass-band and stop-band frequencies of the filter are 8 *kHz* and 15 *kHz*, respectively. The input of the FIR filter is the sum of three sinusoidal variables $x_1(n)$, $x_2(n)$, and $x_3(\mathrm{n})$ with 1 *kHz*, 15 *kHz*, and 20 *kHz* frequencies respectively, and a White Gaussian Noise $w(n)$ with -30*dBW* power, *i.e.*, $x(n)=x_1(n)+x_2(n)+x_3(\mathrm{n})+w(n)$. White Gaussian noise is used to simulate the random effects found in nature. LMs compute the output of the filter, while adders in these designs are accurate. The simulation results of the FIR filter operation are shown in Table 6. Overall, the non-iterative LMs have more attenuation in $\mathrm{SNR_{out}}$ than the iterative LMs, as corresponding to the NMEDs. The $\mathrm{SNR_{out}}$s for the proposed ALM-6 and IALM-12-6 are both higher than their counterparts (LM and ILM); IALM-12-6 has a similar $\mathrm{SNR_{out}}$ value as the exact multiplier.

5.2 Image processing

In this section, the proposed ALM-6 and IALM-12-6 are applied to image processing. Two images are multiplied on a pixel by pixel basis to blend them into a single output image. The peak signal-to-noise ratio (PSNR) is used to assess the quality of the output image. Image multiplications using an exact multiplier, LM, ALM-6, ILM, and IALM-12-6 are shown in Fig. 3. The PSNRs of the above image are provided in Table 7; the PSNRs of the output image processed by the proposed ALM-6 and IALM-12-6 are both larger than their conventional counterparts LM and ILM. The non-iterative LMs (LM, ALM-6) have smaller PSNR than the iterative LMs (ILM, IALM-12-6). These findings are again consistent with the error analysis previously presented in Section 4.1.

6 CONCLUSION

In this paper, non-iterative and iterative approximate logarithmic multiplier designs have been proposed; the accuracy and designs of ALMs and ILAMs have been assessed by simulation. Simulation results have shown that the non-iterative approximate LM design using 6-bit truncated input operands (ALM-6) and the iterative approximate LM design using 12-bit truncated input operands in iteration 1 and 6-bit truncated input operands in iteration 2 (IALM-12-6) are the most efficient non-iterative and iterative designs with moderate values of NMED and PDP compared with the conventional counterparts and the previous LMs. The best proposed designs have also been applied to image processing and FIR filter to confirm the validity of the proposed approximate LM designs.

Table 6: $\mathrm{SNR_{out}}$ for Exact, Conventional, and Proposed Approximate Multipliers

Multiplier	Exact multiplier	LM	ALM-6	ILM	IALM-12-6
$\mathrm{SNR_{out}}$(*dB*)	34.0117	26.2557	29.0664	32.6197	33.9984

(a) (b) (c) (d) (e)

Fig. 3: Image multiplication using different multipliers: (a) exact multiplier, (b) LM, (c) ALM-6, (d) ILM, (e) IALM-12-6.

Table 7: PSNR of Processed Images Using Conventional and Proposed Approximate Multipliers

Multiplier	LM	ALM-6	ILM	IALM-12-6
PSNR	36.6975	37.8749	42.0440	50.6221

ACKNOWLEDGMENTS

This work is supported by grants from National Natural Science Foundation of China (No. 61401197).

REFERENCES

[1] Venkataramani, S., Chakradhar, S.T., Roy, K., and Raghunathan, A. 2015. Computing approximately, and efficiently. *Design, Automation & Test in Europe Conference & Exhibition*, 748-751.

[2] Kyaw, K.Y., Wang, L.G and Yeo, K.S. 2010. Low-power high-speed multiplier for error tolerant application. *2010 IEEE International Conference of Electron Devices and Solid-State Circuits (EDSSC)*, 1-4.

[3] Narayanamoorthy, S., Moghaddam, H.A., Liu, Z., Park, T. and Kim, N.S. 2015. Energy-efficient approximate multiplication for digital signal processing and classification applications. *IEEE Transcations on Very Large Scale Integration(VLSI) Systems*, 23, 6, 1180-1184.

[4] Soheil, H., Iris, B.R., Sherief, R. 2015. DRUM: A dynamic range unbiased multiplier for approximate applications. *IEEE/ACM International Conference on Computer-Aided Design (ICCAD)*, 418-425.

[5] Mitchell, J.N. 1962. Computer multiplication and division using binary logarithms. *IRE Transactions on Electronic Computers*, EC-11, 4, 512-517.

[6] Nam, B., Kim, H. and Yoo, H. 2008. Power and area-efficient unified computation of vector and elementary functions for handheld 3d graphics systems. *IEEE Transcations on Computers*, 57, 4, 490-504.

[7] Gutierrez, R. and Valls, J. 2011. Low cost hardware implementation of logarithm approximation. *IEEE Transcations on Very Large Scale Integration (VLSI) Systems*, 19, 12, 2326-2330.

[8] Low, J. and Jong, C. 2015. Unified Mitchell-based approximation for efficient logarithmic conversion circuit. *IEEE Transcations on Computers*, 64, 6, 1783-1797.

[9] Brubaker, T.A. and Becker, J.C. 1975. Multiplication using logarithms implemented with read-only memory. *IEEE Transcations on Computers*, C-24, 8, 761–765.

[10] Mclaren, D.J. 2003. Improved mitchell-based logarithmic multiplier for lowpower dsp applications. *IEEE International [Systems-on-Chip] in SOC Conference*, 53–56.

[11] Sullivan, M.B. and Swartzlander, E.E. 2012. Truncated error correction for flexible approximate multiplication. *Proc .Conference Record of the Forty Sixth Asilomar Conference on Signals, Systems and Computers*, 355–359.

[12] Ahmed, S., Kadam, S. and Srinivas, M. 2016. An iterative logarithmic multiplier with improved precision. *Proc. IEEE 23nd Symposium on Computer Arithmetic*, 104-111.

[13] Liu, W., Xu, J., Wang, D. and Lombardi, F. 2017. Design of approximate logarithmic multipliers. *Proc. Great Lakes Symposium on VLSI*, 47-52.

[14] Liang, J., Han, J. and Lombardi, F. 2013. New metrics for the reliability of approximate and probabilistic adders. *IEEE Transcations on Computers*, 63, 9, 1760-1771.

Investigation and Optimization of Pin Multiplexing in High-Level Synthesis

Shuangnan Liu and Francis Lau
The Hong Kong Polytechnic University
Department of Electronic and Information Engineering
shuangnan.liu@connect.polyu.hk,francis-cm.lau@polyu.edu.hk

Benjamin Carrion Schafer
The University of Texas at Dallas
Department of Electrical and Computer Engineering
schaferb@utdallas.edu

ABSTRACT

This paper investigates the effect of pin multiplexing on the resultant micro-architecture of synthesizable behavioral descriptions for High-Level Synthesis (HLS). A method is presented to find the most efficient pin assignments by assigning multiple logic inputs and outputs to the same physical ports such that the performance degradation and area overhead is minimized. The proposed method is a fast heuristic based on the scheduling results of HLS seen as a black box and hence is flexible enough to work with any HLS tool. Experimental results show that our proposed method is very efficient compared to an exhaustive search and a simulated annealing method at a fraction of the time and much better than randomly selecting the pins to be multiplexed.

CCS CONCEPTS

• **Hardware → High-level and register-transfer level synthesis; Datapath optimization;**

KEYWORDS

Pin multiplexing; IOs; High-Level Synthesis; Micro-architecture

ACM Reference Format:

Shuangnan Liu and Francis Lau and Benjamin Carrion Schafer. 2018. Investigation and Optimization of Pin Multiplexing in High-Level Synthesis. In *GLSVLSI '18: 2018 Great Lakes Symposium on VLSI, May 23–25, 2018, Chicago, IL, USA.* ACM, New York, NY, USA, 4 pages. https://doi.org/10.1145/3194554.3194629

1 INTRODUCTION

One paradigm shift which is slowly taken place is the use of higher levels of abstractions to increase the design productivity. This increase in the level of abstraction is based around the use of High-Level Synthesis (HLS). HLS takes as the input a behavioural description and generates a Register-Transfer Level (RTL) description (*e.g.* VHDL or Verilog) which can efficiently execute it. HLS has the additional benefit that the RTL code produced can automatically include test circuitry, low power control circuitry (e.g. clock gating) and also automatically multiplex the input and output pins.

GLSVLSI '18, May 23–25, 2018, Chicago, IL, USA

ACM ISBN 978-1-4503-5724-1/18/05...$15.00
https://doi.org/10.1145/3194554.3194629

Pin multiplexing is extremely important. At the chip-level (inter-chip), it reduces the number of IC pins, which in turn reduces the overall cost of the IC. It is well known that the number of Input/Output (IO) pins is not growing fast enough compared to the increase in logic resources. Thus, one solution that has been adopted is the time-division multiplexing of the IO pins to overcome this issue [7]. This is especially true in Field-Programmable Gate Arrays (FPGAs), which are often used for emulation or prototyping. In general, every pin in a complex system is shared by an average of 30 IO signals [2]. Logic emulation and prototyping enable the functional verification of complex ICs before chip fabrication. However, traditional FPGA-based verification platforms have poor inter-chip communication bandwidth, limiting the gate utilization to less than 20% [1] in the past.

At the component level (intra-chip), pin multiplexing reduces the number of internal interconnects. This reduces the congestion of complex ICs, which facilitates the routability while reducing the wire delay by reducing the size of the interconnect. Congestion can be formally defined as the ratio of routing demand to the available routing resources in each region of a design. Timing closure is still one of the most important issues in state-of-the-art VLSI designs and is getting even harder at sub-micron technologies due to the importance of wire delays.

In traditional VLSI design, during partitioning, the number of logic signals is often greater than that of physical ports. Hence these have to be multiplexed. At the RT-level, this typically involves having to re-write the circuit description to accommodate this pin multiplexing. One of the advantages of C-based VLSI design based on HLS is that pin multiplexing can be automated. This is typically done by specifying as inputs to the HLS process a Port Constraint file (*PCNT*). The *PCNT* file contains the number of ports (the number of physical input and output ports), the type (in, out, or inout), and which logic signals should be mapped to the same physical port. Pin-multiplexing nevertheless affects the way in which HLS synthesizes the micro-architecture as it requires internal logic resources to multiplex the pins. At the same time, the latency of the circuit increases with pin-multiplexing as data is read slower into it.

Thus, it is important to understand how pin multiplexing affects the synthesized design at the behavioural level and find efficient methods to map logic IO signals to physical ports. In particular, the main contributions of this work can be summarized as follows:

- Investigate the effect of pin multiplexing on the area and latency overhead of synthesizable behavioral descriptions.
- Propose a method to efficiently multiplex pins using the scheduling result of HLS as its main port mapping criteria.

- Perform comprehensive experimental results to compare the quality of the proposed method against other methods.

2 RELATED WORK

Pin multiplexing methodologies have been widely studied in multi-FPGA systems, mainly due to their limited number of pins. In [1] the authors studied the dependency of input and output signals in a single FPGA at the RT-level to share a physical wire among several logic signals. The proposed methodology was applied to logic emulation in [13] and [4], where the authors proved that the FPGA utilization improved due to pin multiplexing.

Hauck et al. [6] proposed a pin assignment method for multi-FPGA systems based on a force-directed pin assignment solution and compared it with a random assignment, showing that it can lead to better results. The use of Input and Output Serialization and Deserialization (ISERDES/OSERDES) with Low Voltage Differential Signalling (LVDS) has shown to increase inter-FPGA communication data rate by 10× [12]. However, the complexity of this method is high, and it is only usable on boards which support high-speed serial connections.

Other automatic pin assignment methods at the floor planning level were presented in [10, 11]. In this work, the authors proposed cost function of delay constraint to determine the shape and placement of each cell. In [8], the authors studied pin assignments at PCB level to reduce total wire length.

In all previous work, the designs' architectures did not change as the pin multiplexing is done as a *wrapper* around the original RTL code. This work is different from previous works as it addresses the issue of pin assignment at the behavioural level.

3 PROPOSED METHOD

This section describes in detail the proposed pin multiplexing method. It is based on two phases. The first step, called port allocation, assigns physical ports to the inputs (P_{in}) and outputs (P_{out}), based on the maximum number of available ports (P_{max}). The second phase, called port binding, binds individual input logic signals (LS_{in}) and output logic signals (LS_{out}) to individual physical ports, minimizing the effect of area increase and performance degradation (latency increase).

Fig. 1 shows an overview of the complete flow, divided into the two aforementioned phases.

The inputs to the proposed method are:

(1) C_{in}: the behavioural description of the circuit in C/SystemC.
(2) *Techlib*, f_{target}: the technology library and target frequency for HLS.
(3) P_{max}: the number of total physical ports allowed, which has to be smaller than the sum of logic input and output signals, $P_{max} < LS_{in} + LS_{out}$.
(4) *Cost function*: Cost function weights to determine if the area or latency degradation or any combination of both should be minimized.

The port allocation phase (phase 1) of the method is based on three steps as shown in Fig. 1. Step 1 and 2 *pre-characterize* the area and latency degradation of the inputs and outputs separately for a different number of input and output ports. Based on these results, step 3 allocates the available ports into inputs and outputs, thus $P_{max} = P_{in} + P_{out}$.

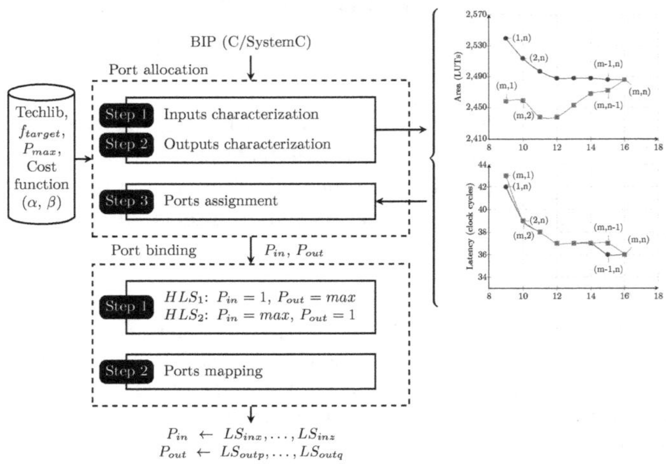

Figure 1: Overview of the proposed method.

Phase 2, in turn, is based on two steps. The first step forces the HLS tool to *reveal* the order in which each input and output is read/written by setting separately the number of inputs ports P_{in}=1 and then $P_{out} = 1$. Based on the scheduling result, step 2 assigns each logic signal to each physical port. As mentioned before, one of the advantages of this method is that it uses the HLS process as a black box. Thus, it has the flexibility to be used with any HLS tool.

The next subsections describe the two phases in detail.

Phase 1: Port Allocation During this work,it was observed that assigning more ports to either inputs or outputs affects the area of the synthesized micro-architecture differently. Because this work relies on the synthesis result of an HLS tool seen as a black box, we cannot determine a priori the synthesis optimization done by this tool in either case. Hence a *pre-characterization* stage is performed to determine the impact of reducing the input and output physical ports on the area and latency of the resultant micro-architecture. The outcome of this stage allocates the maximum number of ports (P_{max}) to inputs and outputs ports (P_{in} and P_{out}). This phase consists of three main steps, which can be summarized as follows:

Step 1: Inputs' Characterization. In order to understand how the port reduction affects the area and latency of the resultant micro-architecture, this first step keeps the number of physical output ports constant to the same as the logic output signals count ($P_{out} = LS_{out}$) and reduces sequentially the number of physical input ports (P_{in}), from their maximum number $P_{in} = LS_{in}$, leading to configurations with different input (m) and output (n) ports $(m, n), (m-1, n), (m-2, n), \dots, (1, n)$, until a single physical input port is allowed, $P_{in} = 1$.

For each unique configuration, the HLS process is called, and the area (A) and latency (L) are extracted from the synthesis report. The outcome of this step leads to a design list:

$$DL_{inputs} = \{(m, n, A_{m\_n}, L_{m\_n}), \dots, (1, n, A_{1\_n}, L_{1\_n})\}$$

where A_{m_n} and L_{m_n} are the area and latency of the synthesized design with m physical input ports and n physical output ports.

Step 2: Outputs' Characterization. The same *pre-characterization* performed in step 1 is repeated in this step for the outputs. This step leads to another design list. Hence, after executing step 1 and step 2 the effect of time-multiplexing the input and output ports on the area and latency degradation is fully made visible.

Step 3: Port Count Assignment. Based on the results of step 1 & 2, the effect on the area and latency of any port combination can be determined by combining the results of both steps. This speeds up the process as it avoids having to re-synthesize any new port combinations. To quantify the combined effect of pin multiplexing the inputs and output

One observation made is that different number of input and output ports affect differently either the area or latency degradation. Thus, one other input required by our method is a cost function with the optimization goal required, either area, latency or a trade-off between area and latency degradation. For this purpose a cost function as follows is used: $C = \alpha A + \beta L$, where A is the area, L is the latency, α and β are the weights to determine if the assignment should minimize the total area or latency. Different weights would lead to different assignments. One option would be to execute the entire assignment process twice: once setting α=1, β=0 and once setting α=0, β=1. This would lead to the best area reduction and best latency reduction assignments, which should be very useful to designers as indicators of upper boundaries.

The result of this assignment is $P_{max} = P_{in} + P_{out}$, where P_{in} are the physical ports assigned to the inputs and P_{out} the physical ports assigned to the outputs. One advantage of using this *pre-characterization*-based method is that the complexity of synthesis iterations is linear $O(m + n)$ with the number of logic input and output signals.

Phase 2: Port Binding Once the maximum number of ports (P_{max}) have been allocated to input (P_{in}) and output (P_{out}) ports, the next step binds each logic signal (LS) to a specific physical port.

The number of possible bindings follows the Stirling numbers of the second kind [5]. The number of possible combinations is a function of ${P_{in}}^{LS_{in}}$ or ${P_{out}}^{LS_{out}}$, which makes an exhaustive search not practical as each new combination has to be synthesized to obtain the area and latency of that particular assignment. Thus, a faster method is required.

The proposed IO to pin assignment method is based on forcing the HLS process to determine the priority of reading and writing data to the IO ports when only having a single physical port. Thus, we call this method **Priority IO Scheduling (PIOS)**. Intuitively, if a signal with lower priority is read first, the area and latency of the circuit will increase as this signal needs to be stored and cannot be used until the rest of the data is available. Moreover, the complexity of finite-state machine (FSM) will increase, further increasing the area and delay of the resultant circuit.

Fig. 2 shows an overview of the method. The method can be decomposed into two main steps as follows.

Step 1: IO Serialization. The first step consists in assigning a single physical port to the inputs, hence P_{in}=1 and as many physical output ports as logic signals, hence $P_{out} = LS_{out}$ and synthesizing (HLS) this configuration. The HLS tool is therefore forced to schedule the inputs sequentially, serializing how data is being read

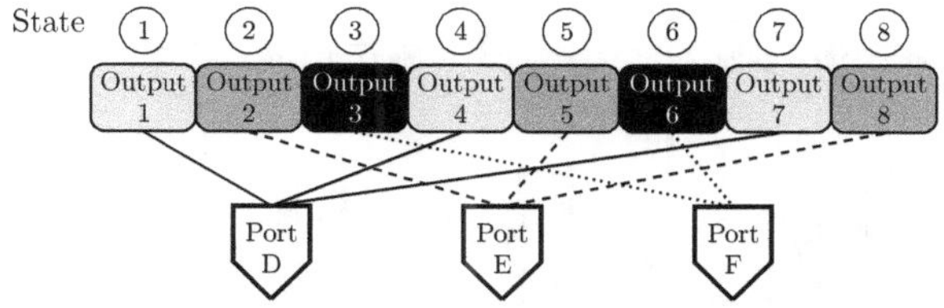

Figure 2: IO scheduling serialization overview.

into the design as there is only a single input port (only one signal can be read in a clock cycle). The key of this method is to rely on the HLS tool to schedule reading the inputs based on their usage priority. As mentioned before this has the additional benefit of making our proposed method HLS tool agnostic. The same operation is repeated for the outputs setting with P_{out}=1 and $P_{in} = LS_{in}$. Thus, the result of this step is two sequences of IO accesses (*IO_schedule*), one for the inputs and one for the outputs. Fig. 2 shows an exemplary access sequence of output signals, where each output is being accessed in a different state (clock cycle).

Step 2: Port Mapping. Based on the results obtained in step 1, the method continues by directly assigning the logic signals sequentially as shown in Fig. 2.

The advantage of this method is that it is extremely fast as it only requires the generation of two configurations independently of the number of signals or ports. Hence the order of complexity is $O(1)$.

4 EXPERIMENTAL RESULTS

This section performs multiple experimental results on the proposed method to study its robustness compared to other methods. We have used five of the benchmarks from the open source benchmark suite (S2CBench [3]) to measure the effectiveness of our proposed method. To study the scalability of our method, two larger complex benchmarks were created by grouping together several of these benchmarks, *e.g.* S1 is composed of idct, kasumi, snow3G and sobe an S2 by combidning interp, snow3G and sobel, instantiated as functions within a top module. Hence, all of the benchmarks are synthesised and optimized together.

The experiments were run on an Intel Pentium 4 running at the 3.20GHz machine with 8 GBytes of RAM running Linux SUSE version 3.0.13-0.27. The HLS tool used in this work is CyberWorkBench v5.5 from NEC [9] and the target HLS frequency set to 100MHz. The target FPGA is a Xilinx XC5VLX330 Virtex 5 FPGA.

To measure the qualitative and quantitative effectiveness of our proposed method, it is compared against an exhaustive search method (*ES*), a random method (*RAND*) and a simulated annealing approach (*SA*). *ES* can guarantee the global optimal result as it explores the entire searching space. *RAND* performs random selections of both port allocation and port binding (most likely method chosen when done manually by a hardware designer). This is obviously the fastest method as it does not require the computation of the assignment effect on the resultant design. Thus, it could be considered the default method.

Because of the conflicting minimizing objectives of reducing area, while also minimise the latency penalty, the experiments were executed twice. Once with the target cost function weights

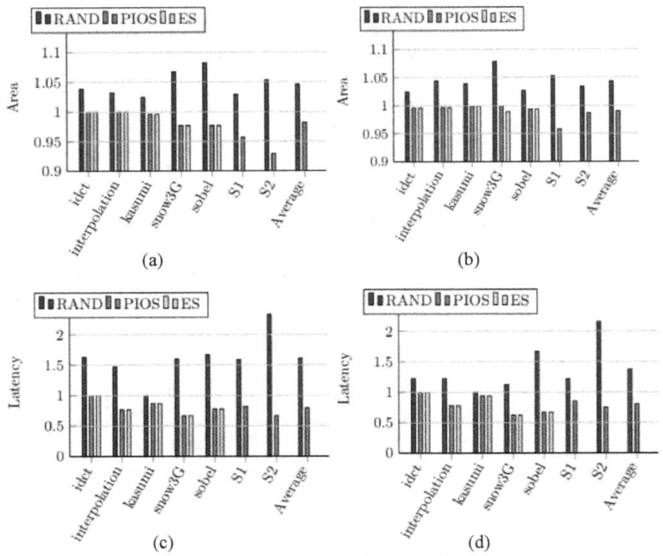

Figure 3: Area and Latency results for different pin multiplexing ratios: (a) area of 25% case; (b) area of 75% case (c) latency of 25% case; (d) latency of 75% case

were set to α=1.0 and β=0 to find the very smallest configuration (optimized for area) and once setting α=0 and β=1.0, optimizing for latency. Two different P_{max} values were used to test our methods. P_{max}=25% and 75% of the total number of logic signals (LS_{in} + LS_{out}).

Fig. 3 show the normalized results of the four methods for the cases which target the optimization of area (α=1.0, β=0) and latency (α=0, β=1.0). In both cases, the 25% and 75% of the original number of ports are used. The vertical axis indicates the normalized area or latency, hence the smaller, the better. Since *SA* is set as a reference, its value is "1" in the figures, and thus only *ES*, *RAND* and *PIOS* are presented. Besides, some of the results of *ES* (*e.g.* S1 in Fig. 3(a)) are not presented since their running time exceeds 7 days. Therefore, the average values of *ES* are not shown either.

For the area driven optimization (Fig.3(a), 3(b), 3(c)), our proposed method (*PIOS*) performs very close to *ES* except for the snow3G case shown in Fig.3(b) and 3(c). In both cases, the results of *PIOS* are about 1% bigger than those of *ES*. When comparing against *SA*, our method is up to 2.3% better and on average 0.5% better for the the five basic benchmarks, but much better for the larger cases due to the increase of the searching space. For these two complex benchmarks our method is up to 7.1% better and on average 4.3% better.

Due to the simplistic nature of the *RAND* method, the results, as expected, are the worst of all the methods. In this respect, our method is up to 15.3% better and on average 6.3% better.

When optimizing for latency (Fig.3(a), 3(b) and 3(c)), the cost function is set to α=0, β=1.0, our method also shows good results. The latency improvements introduced by *PIOS* are up to 45.5% and 71.5%, and on average 22.1% and 41.8% compared with *SA* and *RAND*, respectively. Moreover, our method shows the same behavior as the optimal solution (*ES*), because *PIOS* leverages the scheduling data from the HLS tool to minimize the latency penalty.

Regarding running time efficiency of the 4 methods an average speedup of 20 and 15 is achieved by our method compared with *SA* for the 25% and 75% cases, respectively. Obviously, *RAND* is the fastest among the four methods since only two synthesis iterations are needed, one for I/O data collection and one for the random assignment and the *ES* could not finish within a week for the larger cases (S1 and S2).

It should be noted that because the proposed method is based on a *pre-characterization* stage, this stage only needs to be executed once to fully characterize each behavioral description, and thus, our proposed method can be much more effective when re-using the design in future projects. On average, our proposed method becomes 10× faster, which means that our two-phase approach is very efficient in such practical situations.

Based on the experimental results obtained it is safe to conclude that our method works well, and it is a good compromise between quality of results and running time.

5 CONCLUSION

In this work, we have studied the effect of pin multiplexing on the resultant micro-architectures when synthesized using HLS and presented a method to optimize the port allocation and port binding problems. The proposed method is based on two main phases. The first one performs a *pre-characterization* stage which assigns the optimal number of physical ports to input and output ports. The second one determines which physical port is shared by certain logic signals.

REFERENCES

[1] J. Babb, R. Tessier, M. Dahl, S.Z. Hanono, D.M. Hoki, and A. Agarwal. 1997. Logic emulation with virtual wires. *Computer-Aided Design of Integrated Circuits and Systems, IEEE Transactions on* 16, 6 (Jun 1997), 609–626.

[2] M. Butts. 2014. Logic emulation in the megaLUT era x2014; Moore's Law beats Rent's Rule. In *Field-Programmable Technology (FPT), 2014 International Conference on.* 1–1.

[3] B. Carrion Schafer and A. Mahapatra. 2014. S2CBench: Synthesizable SystemC Benchmark Suite for High-Level Synthesis. *Embedded Systems Letters, IEEE* 6, 3 (Sept 2014), 53–56.

[4] M. Dahl, J. Babb, R. Tessier, S. Hanono, D. Hoki, and A. Agarwal. 1994. Emulation of the Sparcle microprocessor with the MIT Virtual Wires emulation system. In *FPGAs for Custom Computing Machines, 1994. Proceedings. IEEE Workshop on.* 14–22.

[5] H. W. Gould. 1961. The q -Stirling numbers of first and second kinds. *Duke Math. J.* 28, 2 (06 1961), 281–289.

[6] Scott Hauck and Gaetano Borriello. 1997. Pin Assignment for Multi-FPGA Systems. *TCAD* 16, 9 (1997), 956–964.

[7] H. Krupnova. 2004. Mapping Multi-Million Gate SoCs on FPGAs: Industrial Methodology and Experience. In *DATE*. IEEE Computer Society, Washington, DC, USA, 21236–.

[8] T. Meister, J. Lienig, and G. Thomke. 2008. Novel Pin Assignment Algorithms for Components with Very High Pin Counts. In *Design, Automation and Test in Europe, 2008. DATE '08.* 837–842.

[9] NEC. 2015. CyberWorkBench. (Oct. 2015). Retrieved October 10, 215 from http://www.cyberworkbench.com

[10] M. Pedram, K. Chaudhary, and E.S. Kuh. 1991. I/O pad assignment based on the circuit structure. In *ICCD*. 314–318.

[11] M. Pedram, M. Marek-Sadowska, and E.S. Kuh. 1990. Floorplanning with pin assignment. In *Computer-Aided Design, 1990. ICCAD-90. Digest of Technical Papers., 1990 IEEE International Conference on.* 98–101.

[12] Qingshan Tang, H. Mehrez, and M. Tuna. 2014. Multi-FPGA prototyping board issue: the FPGA I/O bottleneck. In *SAMOS*. 207–214.

[13] Russell Tessier, Jonathan Babb, Matthew Dahl, Silvina Hanono, and Anant Agarwal. 1994. The virtual wires emulation system: A gate-efficient ASIC prototyping environment. In *2nd International ACM/SIGDA Workshop on Field-Programmable Gate Arrays*. Citeseer.

Energy Consumption and Lifetime Improvement of Coarse-Grained Reconfigurable Architectures Targeting Low-Power Error-Tolerant Applications

Hassan Afzali-Kusha*, Omid Akbari**, Mehdi Kamal**, and Massoud Pedram*
*Department of Electrical Engineering, University of Southern California, Los Angeles, CA, USA
**School of Electrical and Computer Engineering, College of Engineering, University of Tehran, Tehran, Iran
{afzaliku, pedram}@usc.edu, { akbari.o, mehdikamal}@ut.ac.ir

ABSTRACT
In this work, the application of a voltage over-scaling (VOS) technique for improving the lifetime and reliability of coarse-grained reconfigurable architectures (GCRAs) is presented. The proposed technique, which may be applied to CGRAs used as accelerators for low-power, error-tolerant applications, reduces the (strongly voltage-dependent) wearout effects and the energy consumption of processing elements (PEs) whenever the error impact on the output quality degradation can be tolerated. This provides us with the ability to lessen the wearout and reduce energy consumption of PEs when accuracy requirement for the results is rather low. Multiple degrees of computational accuracy can be achieved by using different overscaled voltage levels for the PEs. The efficacy of the proposed technique is studied by considering the bias temperature instability. The study is performed for two error-resilient applications. The CGRAs are implemented with 15nm FinFET operating at a nominal supply voltage of 0.8V. In addition, supply voltages of 0.75, 0.7, 0.65, and 0.6V are considered as overscaled voltage levels for this technology. Based on the quality constraint requirements of the benchmarks, optimum overscaled voltage levels for various PEs are determined and utilized. The approach may provide considerable lifetime and energy consumption improvements over those of the conventional exact and approximate computation approaches.

KEYWORDS
CGRA, Accuracy Scaling, Aging Effects, NBTI, Energy-Efficiency

1 INTRODUCTION
Accelerators, which are used along with the main processors in digital systems, improve the speed and energy consumption of the computations. Use of reconfigurable architectures such as coarse-grained reconfigurable architectures (CGRAs) provides the flexibility of optimizing the accelerator for each individual application. By eliminating the cost of hardware redesign and re-fabrication processes, rapid yet low cost prototyping of emerging applications may also be achieved through reconfigurable architectures. On the other hand, the industry has continuously scaled the fabrication technology, a trend which is potentially accompanied by the circuit lifetime and reliability degradation due to the increase in the impact of the transistor aging mechanisms.

While decelerating transistor aging and improving device reliability has always been a design challenge, the problem has become worse as the technology scaling has continued, As a result, nowadays there is a lot of renewed interest in device aging and reliability [1]. There are several circuit aging mechanisms where among them Bias Temperature Instability (BTI) and Hot Carrier Injection (HCI) are directly related to the transistor lifetime [2]. Both mechanisms cause an increase in the threshold voltage (V_{th}) of affected transistors causing the on-current (I_{on}) to decrease. A criterion of 20% (10% for automotive applications) performance degradation is a common threshold used to signal a circuit's end of life [3].

The rate of V_{th} change (aging rate) depends on the supply voltage (V_{DD}), die temperature, clock frequency, and activity factor in the circuit. One reason for worsening of the aging effect is that the reduction in device physical dimensions has not been accompanied with the same reduction in supply voltage levels. The connection is that the aging effects are related to the induced electric field (voltage divided by spacing) in the device active region. This fact inspires us to lower the supply voltage in tandem with physical scaling. The supply voltage reduction has also been widely used as a way of reducing both dynamic and static power components of the circuit. Reducing the supply voltage below a critical (nominal) level, however, causes setup time violations at the circuit outputs for input signal values that sensitize the longest timing paths of the circuit. The lower the supply voltage is, the larger is the number of the paths which timing requirements are not satisfied and the higher is the output error rate. Hence, while this voltage reduction improves the lifetime and reliability of the circuit, it can turn the circuit into an inexact (approximate) computation unit which prohibits its use in applications requiring exact computations.

Fortunately, there are applications which do not require computational exactness for several reasons [4]. Examples of these applications include video processing, image recognition, text and data mining, and machine learning. As a matter of fact, approximate computing (AC) in its general sense has emerged as a processing paradigm for lowering the energy consumption, delay, and/or silicon footprint within a technology [5]. Other than lowering the supply voltage below the nominal one which is also called voltage over-scaling (VOS), other approaches have been considered for realizing the AC *e.g.*, [6], [7].

In this work, we present the application of a VOS technique for improving the energy consumption and rate of aging in CGRAs. Here, when the exact computation is required, the nominal supply voltage is applied to the PEs and when some approximation may be tolerated, depending on the required accuracy level, overscaled voltages (i.e., those lower than a nominal voltage level) are applied to the PEs. More explicitly,

ACM Reference Format:
Hassan Afzali-Kusha, Omid Akbari, Mehdi Kamal, and Massoud Pedram. 2018. Energy Consumption and Lifetime Improvement of Coarse-Grained Reconfigurable Architectures Targeting Low-Power Error-Tolerant Applications. In Proceedings of 2018 Great Lakes Symposium on VLSI (GLSVLSI '18). ACM, New York, NY, USA, 4 pages. https://doi.org/10.1145/3194554.3194631

GLSVLSI '18, May 23–25, 2018, Chicago, IL, USA

ACM ISBN 978-1-4503-5724-1/18/05...$15.00
https://doi.org/10.1145/3194554.3194631

overscaled voltages levels are determined and applied to PEs such that the circuit lifetime/reliability is maximized. The unique feature of this approach is the concurrent use of different overscaled voltage levels for different operations of a data flow graph (DFG) while maintaining a required output quality without needing error detection and correction units and without performance penalty.

2 BTI Background

The bias temperature instability (BTI) affects both NMOS and PMOS transistors by generating interface traps at the Si/SiO2 interface [8]. Here, without loss of generality, we only consider NBTI. From [9] and [10], the long-term aging-induced shift of the threshold voltage that incorporates both stress and relaxation phases, is fitted by a power law:

$$\Delta V_{th,NBTI} \cong A e^{-\frac{\kappa}{\theta}} t^{\alpha} E_{OX}^{\gamma} f^{\beta} \qquad (1)$$

where A (= 3.12×10-2), κ (= 50), α (= 0.173), β (= 1/6), and γ (= 3) are technology and power-law fitting parameters, t is the total stress time (s), θ is the temperature in Kelvins (K), f is the duty factor of the stress signal, and $E_{OX} = (V_{DD} - V_{th})/T_{INV}$ is the electric field across the gate oxide (where T_{INV} denotes the thickness of gate inversion layer). This relation indicates the strong voltage dependence of the threshold voltage shift (aging) on the supply voltage.

3 Proposed Architecture and Mapping

In this section, first, details of the proposed CGRA architecture are provided. Next, the accuracy level determination process and mapping the application on the CGRA will be discussed.

3.1 Proposed CGRA Architecture

The overall architecture of the proposed CGRA is depicted in Fig. 1. Compared to the conventional CGRA, the proposed one contains "*Power Switch Box*" units and the PEs have two input voltages, Core Voltage (V_C) and I/O Voltage (V_{IO}). For each row of the CGRA, we suggest using a Power Switch Box unit. The inputs of this unit are the different considered VOS (operating) voltage levels and its outputs are the core voltage of the PEs. This unit consists of large MOSFET switches which connect the input voltage of each PE to the one of the voltage rails based on the considered core voltage level for that PE. Note that we can consider one Power Switch Box unit for all PEs which leads to increasing the size of this unit and the routing complexity of the voltage rails of the PEs. On the other hand, one may consider one small Power Switch Box unit for each PE and place it near each PE which leads to increasing the routing complexity of the considered voltage rails (V_1 to V_n). Hence, we suggest considering one of this boxes for each row. In addition to the core voltage, the I/O voltage of all PEs are connected to the nominal voltage of the system.

In Fig. 2, the internal structure of each PE and the voltage domains are shown. In this work, without loss of generality, the ALU part only consists of a 32-bit Carry Look Ahead adder and a 16-bit Dadda multiplier. The operating voltage of the ALU unit is determined by V_C. The output of the ALU is connected to the 32-bit output level-converter register (consists of level-converter Flip-Flop [11]. The inputs of this register are in the V_C voltage domain while its outputs are in the V_{IO} voltage domain. To connect a PE to its neighbors, two multiplexers and one de-multiplexer are considered for the inputs and output of the PE, respectively. These multiplexers are in the V_{IO} voltage domain. Based on this architecture, all connections between PEs are operated at the nominal voltage while the cores of the PE may have different operating voltage levels. The core voltages are applied by the host processor to the *Power Switch Box* units where the values of these voltages are determined by the approach presented in the next sub-section.

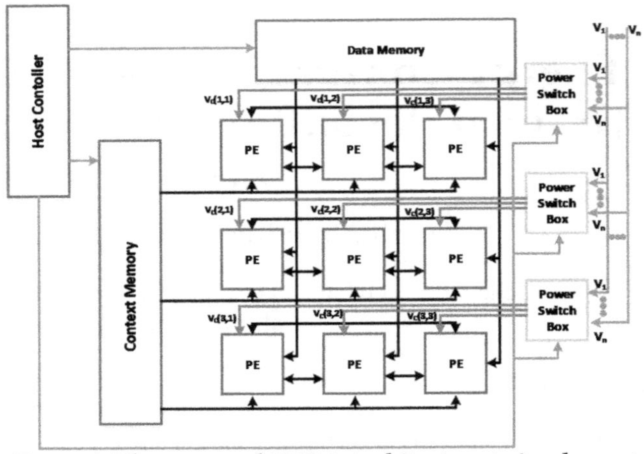

Figure 1: The proposed CGRA Architecture to implement the Voltage Over-Scaling technique.

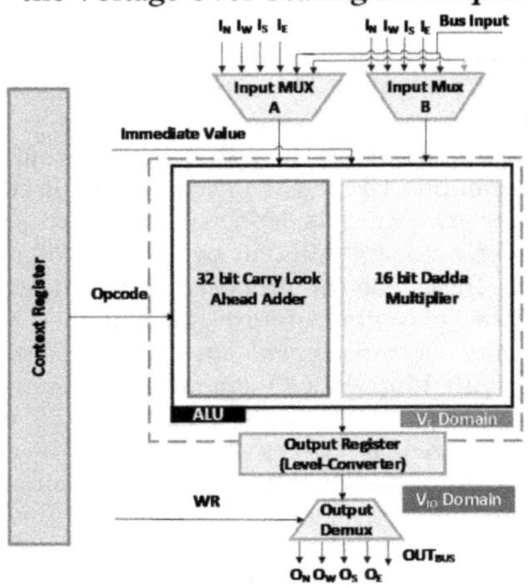

Figure 2: The proposed architecture of each PE.

3.2 Accuracy Determination and Mapping

To map an application onto the proposed CGRA, first the accuracy of the operations should be determined. The output error of a DFG is a linear combination of the operation errors [12]. Hence, the output error is based on the amount of the error that each approximate operation generates and the amount of the generated error by each approximate operation that reaches the output of the DFG. Note that the error distribution of each operation in the DFG is independent of other operations in the DFG unless both operations have the same input data and same hardware implementation.

Error propagations have strong structural correlations which should be used to model the output error [12]. In [12] to obtain the output error, its sensitivity (*ES*) was utilized. The sensitivity indicates the impact of the accuracy of a node on the output when the other nodes are errorless. Let us denote the error sensitivity of the wth node as $ES_{w,o}$ which is defined in [12]. Using this definition, we can formulate the problem of determining the operating voltage level of the DFG nodes for a given predefined expected quality (Q_{EXP}). We propose an ILP formulation which determines the operating voltage levels of the add and multiply operations. The objective of this formulation is reducing the summation of the operating voltage levels of these operations. Hence, this ILP formulation is expressed by

$$\textit{Objective}:$$

$$\textit{Minimize}\left(\sum_{i=1}^{n}\sum_{k=1}^{L}\beta\, V_{DD,k}X_{i,k}+\alpha\sum_{i=1}^{m}\sum_{k=1}^{L}V_{DD,k}Y_{i,k}\right)$$

$$\textit{Subject To}:$$

$$\sum_{\forall w\in AddOperationSet}\sum_{k=1}^{L}ES_{w,o}^{2}\cdot v(\epsilon_{w,k}).X_{w,k}$$

$$+\sum_{\forall w\in MultiplyOperationSet}\sum_{k=1}^{L}ES_{w,o}^{2}\cdot v(\epsilon_{w,k}).Y_{w,k}<Q_{EXP} \quad (2)$$

$$\forall w\in AddOperationSet\left(\sum_{k=1}^{L}X_{w,k}=1\right)$$

$$\forall w\in MultiplyOperationSet\left(\sum_{k=1}^{L}Y_{w,k}=1\right)$$

In this formulation $X_{i,k}$ and $Y_{i,k}$ are binary variables which show the operating voltage index (index k) of the ith add and multiply operation nodes, respectively. Also, $V_{DD,k}$ is the kth operating voltage level where in this work, 1st, 2nd, ..., and 5th operating voltage levels are 800mV, 750mV, ..., and 600mV, respectively. Due to the higher aging effect on the multipliers, we provide parameter α ($0.5<\alpha\leq 1$) and β ($0<\beta\leq 0.5$) to be set by the designer. Using larger value for α leads to more focus on reducing the operating voltage of the multipliers. In (2), the first inequality constraint is used to limit the output quality degradation while the last two constraints are included to force the solver to assign one and only one operating voltage level to each add and multiply operations. Also, $v(\epsilon_{w,k})$ is the error variance of the wth node in the kth operating voltage level and $ES_{w,o}$ is the error sensitivity of the operation w in relation with the output o. Finally, after obtaining the operating voltage level, by using List scheduling and clique partitioning the design is mapped on to the CGRA.

4 Results and Discussion

All the studies have been performed by employing the 15nm FinFET-based Open Cell Library (OCL) technology [13]. To assess the effect of different levels of operating voltage levels, 5 voltage levels have been considered include 800 (nominal voltage), 750, 700, 650, and 600 mV. All the designs have been synthesized by Synopsys Design Compiler under the 15nm technology file in nominal voltage while their design parameters have been extracted by this tool under the technology files which have been characterized in the considered lower voltage levels. For characterizing the technology file, Cadence Encounter Library Characterization (ELC) tool has been employed.

To extract the accuracy, using mean square error abbreviated by MSE (see Lemma in [12]), output of the considered 32-bit CLA adder and 16-bit Dadda multiplier, gate-level post-synthesis simulations under different operating voltage levels have been performed by ModelSim HDL simulator. Note that the timing information of the gates in these simulations for each operating voltage level has been extracted by Synopsys Design Complier. The accuracy of these arithmetic operations was obtained by injecting many randomly generated input operands. Also, in the studied CGRA architecture, we consider one and three cycles for add and multiply operations, and in all the voltage levels the clock frequency was fixed. The clock frequency was obtained in a way that the PEs of the CGRA did not have any output error in 800mV operating voltage level. The aging rate is calculated by (1) that we have assumed all the parameters except for the E_{OX} (voltage dependent) are the same for both conventional and the proposed CGRA.

4.1 Benchmarks

To explore the effectiveness of the proposed method, two benchmarks of an 8-Tap FIR filter (FIR) and a 4th order Polynomial Evaluation (PoE) which have different orders of computations (different sequences of add and multiply operations) were considered. The DFG of these benchmarks are depicted in Fig. 3.

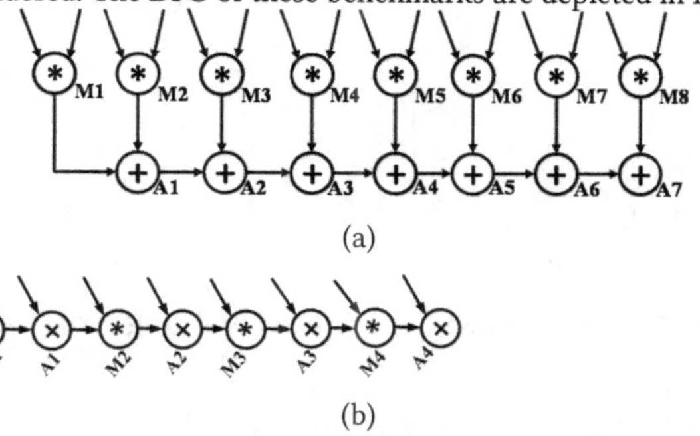

Figure 3: The DFG of the a) FIR, and b) PoE benchmarks.

4.2 8-Tap FIR Filter

The overscaled voltage levels assigned to each PE for performing the nodes of the DFG for different quality levels of 50%, 60%, 70%, 80%, and 90% are presented in Fig. 4(a). The parameter Q_{EXP} which was mentioned previously, is related to quality levels and DFG outputs. For this benchmark, for the quality constraint of 90% (50%), the minimum and maximum voltages were 700mV to 800mV (600mV to 750mV). As expected, the more quality degradation can be tolerated, the lower voltages can be assigned to PEs. For some of the operations, allowing the quality degrading does not lead to the operating voltage level decrease considerably due to their specific feature. For instance, for the add operation A6 (see Fig. 3(a)), all the errors occurred in the previous operations converge to this adder. Therefore, for this adder, its assigned voltage levels are the same and is 750mV which is only one level lower than the full supply voltage.

It should be noted that for the quality of 90%, the operating voltage of some nodes cannot be lowered than 800mV thanks to their criticality from the error perspective. This happens more for the nodes at the middle and the end of the DFG structure or the add operations collecting the errors from the previous nodes. For instance, the A3 operation was assigned to 800mV for 3 consecutive qualities of 90%, 80%, and 70%. The general trend for the FIR benchmark is that the add operations are more critical from the error perspective compared to the multiply operations. For the case of this benchmark, assigning lower voltages to the multiply operations affect the output quality less compared to the add operations. This allows for more VOS improving both the energy efficiency and lifetime/reliability for these PEs.

Generally, voltage reduction provides us with a decrease in aging rates and energy consumptions of the PEs compared to the case of applying the nominal voltage to all PEs. The results for these reductions are presented in Fig. 4(b) and Fig. 4(c), respectively. As was expected, at lower output qualities, there are more opportunity for the voltage, energy consumption (up to 44%), and aging rate reductions (up to 74%). For some qualities, exact operations are required for performing algorithm where the PE must work with the maximum nominal

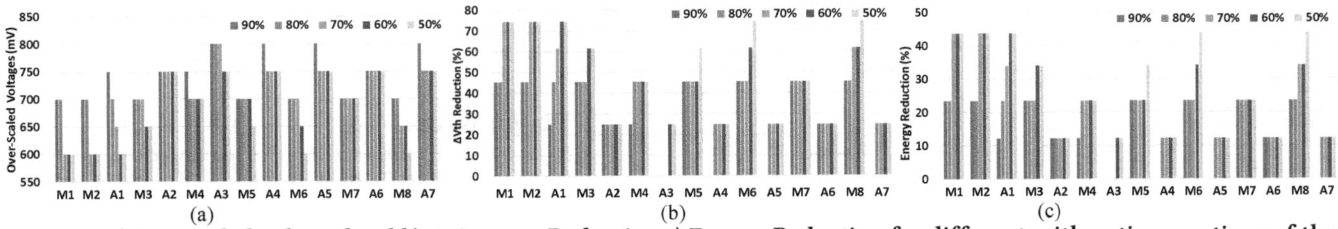

Figure 4: a) Overscaled voltage level b) Aging rate Reduction c) Energy Reduction for different arithmetic operations of the FIR filter benchmark (A: Adder; M: Multiplier)

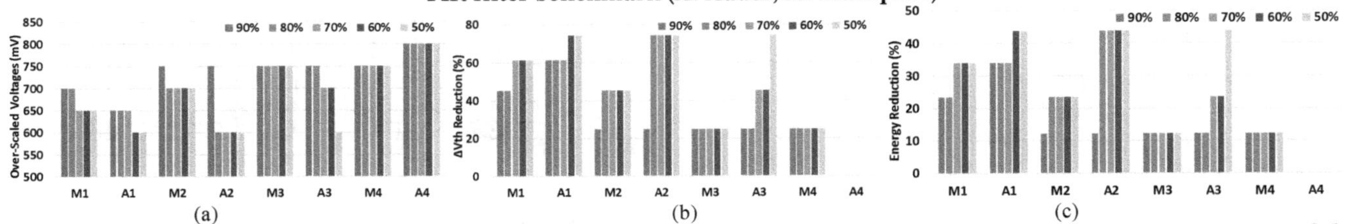

Figure 5: a) Overscaled voltage level b) Aging rate Reduction c) Energy Reduction for different arithmetic operations of the PoE (A: Adder; M: Multiplier)

voltage of 800 mV. Obviously, for these PEs, no decrease in the aging rate or energy consumption is achieved.

4.3 4th Order Polynomial Evaluation

The overscaled voltage levels assigned to each PE used for each DFG node under different quality levels of 50%, 60%, 70%, 80%, and 90% are presented in Fig. 5(a). Again, for some operations, allowing the quality degradation does not lead to considerable operating voltage level decreases due to the specific feature of the benchmark. For instance, for the add operation A4 (see Fig. 3(b)), all the errors occurred in the previous operations somehow add up in this adder. Therefore, this adder may not tolerate any further error and hence the nominal voltage should be used for this adder. The general trend for the PoE benchmark is that the multiply operations are more critical from the error perspective compared to the add operations except for the last add operation (A4). The decrease in aging rate and energy consumption are presented in Fig. 5 (b) and (c). Assigning these voltages to the PEs, the VOS provided us with an average of 29% (47%) of aging rate reduction for the quality constraint of 90% (50%). Also, we achieved an energy reduction of 15% (27%) for the quality constraint of 90% (50%).

4.4 Verifying Extracted Overscaled Voltages

To confirm the trustworthiness of the variance-based model [12] which have been used in this work, the MSE values obtained based on both model and simulation are compared in Table 1. For the implementation, we determined ILP solutions in Verilog HDL for two considered benchmarks. By injecting many random stimuli and performing gate-level simulation (the delays of the gates was based on the chosen operating voltage levels), the values were extracted. Since the MSE values of the simulation were smaller than those of the model which satisfied the quality constraint, one may conclude the variance-based model is credible.

Table 1. The model and simulated MSE of FIR and PoE.

Quality	FIR		PoE	
	MSE		MSE	
	Model	Simulation	Model	Simulation
90%	3.27E+07	8.35E+06	3.50E+05	2.47E+04
80%	1.62E+08	5.89E+07	1.59E+06	5.63E+04
70%	3.58E+08	1.26E+08	3.57E+06	1.01E+06
60%	6.83E+08	1.91E+08	3.69E+06	1.09E+06
50%	1.01E+09	2.53E+08	9.30E+06	1.23E+06

4 CONCLUSION

To improve the lifetime (reliability) and energy efficiency of CGRAs, the use of the VOS technique was proposed. This technique, which was applied to functional units of the PEs, was based on trade-offs between the accuracy and lifetime. For the first time, the use of different overscaled voltage levels for different operations of a DFG of a computational kernel was suggested. The architecture of the CGRA was equipped with power switch boxes for each row of PEs providing the overscaled voltage levels required for each application based on an output quality constraint. The efficiency of the proposed approach was evaluated using two benchmarks. Results indicated considerable improvement in the lifetime and energy consumption. At the end, the VOS results were implemented in Verilog to verify the variance error model for both benchmarks.

ACKNOWLEDGMENT

This work was supported in part by a grant from the Software and Hardware Foundations of the National Science Foundation.

REFERENCES

[1] https://semiengineering.com/transistor-aging-intensifies-10nm/

[2] F. Nakhaee *et al.*, "Lifetime improvement by exploiting aggressive voltage scaling during runtime of error-resilient applications," Integration, The VLSI Journal, 2017.

[3] U. Schlichtmann, "Frontiers of timing," in *Intl. Workshop on System Level Interconnect Prediction,* 2017.

[4] V. K. Chippa *et al.*, "Analysis and characterization of inherent application resilience for approximate computing," in *Proc. DAC*, 2013.

[5] Q. Xu *et al.*, "Approximate computing: A survey", *IEEE Design & Test*, vol. 33, no. 1, pp. 8-22, Feb. 2016.

[6] K. He *et al.*, "Controlled timing-error acceptance for low energy IDCT design," in *Proc. DATE*, 2011.

[7] G. Tziantzioulis *et al.*, "Lazy pipelines: Enhancing quality in approximate computing," in *Proc. DATE*, 2016.

[8] J. W. McPherson, Reliability Physics and Engineering Time-to-Tailure Modeling, 2nd Edition, Springer, 2013.

[9] H. Kukner *et al.* "Scaling of bti reliability in presence of time-zero variability," in *Proc. IRPS,* 2014.

[10] N. Goel *et al.*, "Impact of time-zero and nbti variability on sub-20nm Finnfet based sram at low voltages," in *Proc. IRPS*, 2015.

[11] M. W. Chen *et al.*, "A dual-edged triggered explicit-pulsed level converting flip-flop with a wide operation range," in *Proc. SOCC*, 2013.

[12] C. Li *et al.*, "Joint precision optimization and high level synthesis for approximate computing," in *Proc. DAC*, 2015.

[13] (2017). NanGate—The Standard Cell Library Optimization Company. [Online]. Available: http://www.nangate.com/

MuDBN: An Energy-Efficient and High-Performance Multi-FPGA Accelerator for Deep Belief Networks

Yuming Cheng, Chao Wang, Yangyang Zhao, Xianglan Chen, Xuehai Zhou,Xi Li
University of Science and Technology of China, hefei, 230027, China
{cswang,xlanchen,xhzhou,llxx}@ustc.edu.cn,{yumingc,zhaoyy37}@mail.ustc.edu.cn

ABSTRACT

With the increasing size of neural networks, state-of-the-art deep neural networks (DNNs) have hundreds of millions of parameters. Due to multiple fully-connected layers, DNNs are compute-intensive and memory-intensive, making them hard to deploy on embedded devices with limited power budgets and hardware resources. Therefore, this paper presents a deep belief network accelerator based on multi-FPGA. Two different schemes, the division between layers (DBL) and the division inside layers (DIL), are adopted to map the DBN to the multi-FPGA system. Experimental results demonstrate that the accelerator can achieve 4.24x (DBL) -6.20x (DIL) speedup comparing to the Intel Core i7 CPU and save 119x (DBL) -90x (DIL) power consumption comparing to the Tesla K40C GPU.

KEYWORDS

DBN; multi-FPGA; accelerator

ACM Reference Format:

Yuming Cheng, Chao Wang, Yangyang Zhao, Xianglan Chen, Xuehai Zhou,Xi Li. 2018. MuDBN: An Energy-Efficient and High-Performance Multi-FPGA Accelerator for Deep Belief Networks. In *Proceedings of 2018 Great Lakes Symposium on VLSI (GLSVLSI '18)*. ACM, New York, NY, USA, 4 pages. https://doi.org/10.1145/3194554.3194630

1 INTRODUCTION

With the rapid advancement of machine learning, DNNs have shown significant values of industry and academia and have achieved great success in wide areas, such as Speech Recognition, Image Classification, and Natural Language Processing. At present, the frequently-used processing platform is CPUs and GPUs, but they have disadvantages of low computational efficiency and high energy consumption. As a result, researchers pay more attention to hardware prototypes, like ASIC and FPGA. ASIC has the characteristics of high performance, low power consumption, and small area, but it is difficult to develop and the development cycle is relatively long. FPGA can effectively process complex learning algorithms because of high performance, low power consumption, and reconfigurability. Therefore, this paper presents a DBN accelerator based on multi-FPGA.

GLSVLSI '18, May 23–25, 2018, Chicago, IL, USA

ACM ISBN 978-1-4503-5724-1/18/05…$15.00
https://doi.org/10.1145/3194554.3194630

Contributions are summarized as follows:

1) We analyze intra-layer and inter-layer data dependency of the DBN and explore five fully pipelined processing processes.

2) We adopt various techniques to optimize the performance of our accelerator, such as local storage, data prefetch, tile and approximate substitution, which is proved to improve throughputs and resource utilization.

3) We implement the DBN accelerator based on multi-FPGA using two different division schemes, the division between layers (DBL) and the division inside layers (DIL). Experimental results show the accelerator can gain effective acceleration effects, low energy consumption, and high energy efficiency.

The rest of this paper is organized as follows. Section 2 provides the background information about the DBN and some related work. Section 3 introduces a two-layer-pipeline computation methodology, the architecture of our accelerator, design details and key techniques. The experimental results are shown in Section 4 and Section 5 concludes this paper.

2 BACKGROUND AND RELATED WORK

As for DNNs accelerators based on FPGA, [5] uses a variety of methods to accelerate the inference process of DNNs, achieving average 30x speedup over the Intel Core2 CPU. [3] proposes a large-scale convolutional neural network (CNN) accelerator, which is designed on embedded FPGA. And this accelerator contains a convolver to improve bandwidths and resource utilization and apply the dynamic-precision data quantization method. [6] quantitatively analyzes throughputs and required memory bandwidths, and presents a roofline model in order to achieve better performance and low resource requirements.

For ASIC, DianNao [1], a high-throughput accelerator for machine learning (ML), is based on ASIC with well-organized buffers to reduce memory bandwidths and cache conflicts. And DianNao adopts 16-bit fixed-point arithmetic operators to reduce footprints and computing resources. Besides, they push out a custom multi-chip machine-learning accelerator called DaDianNao [2], which is composed of interconnected nodes with high internal bandwidths and low external communications.

As can be seen from the above research results, research in DNNs accelerator based on FPGA provide many great optimization techniques to improve the performance of accelerators that inspire us. Research in ML accelerator based on ASIC show brilliant design ideas to get high performance, low power consumption, and good scalability. Research in DBN accelerator based on FPGA can get good experimental results, but they mainly explore the parallelism of single-layer RBM calculation and do not take the parallelism

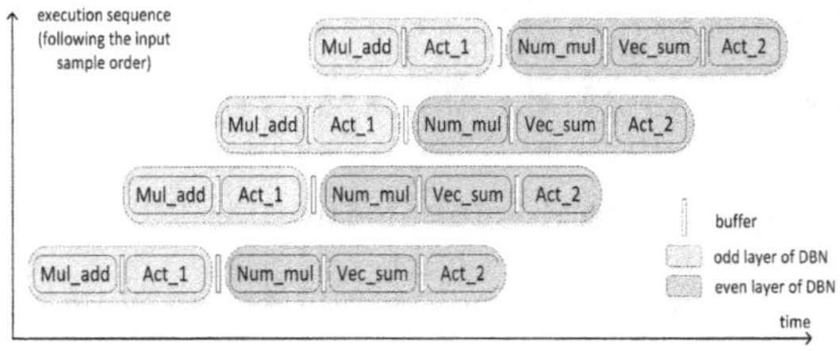

Figure 1: Pipeline sketch

between multi-layer RBM into account. In this paper, the multi-FPGA acceleration system is proposed with full considerations of the parallelism between RBM layers.

3 ACCELERATOR DESIGN EXPLORATION

In this section, we introduce the pipeline between layers firstly. Secondly, we propose the overall architecture of our accelerator. Then, we explain design details of the accelerator. Finally, we introduce various optimizing techniques.

3.1 Pipeline Computations Between Layers

There are two kinds of methods to the matrix multiplication: 1) an input vector and a column of the weight matrix multiply to get an output. Thus, final results are composed of all outputs. 2) an input and a row of the weight matrix multiply to get an intermediate value. Thus, final results are obtained by finite iterative calculations of the result and the last intermediate value. We can combine two different methods to improve system throughput.

As we know, the inference calculation of the DBN consists of many matrix multiplications. Inspired by the EIE [7], an accelerator based on the single FPGA with a two-layer-pipeline computation methodology, we propose a five-stage pipeline to save time and increase throughputs and resource utilization, showing in Figure 1. 1) Mul_add stage: implement the matrix calculation in the form of vector inner product of inputs and weights on the odd RBM layer. 2) Act_1 stage: call activation function to calculate results of the Mul_add stage. 3) Num_mul stage: implement the matrix calculation in the form of scalar multiplication of vectors between inputs and weights on the even RBM layer. 4) Vec_sum stage: add the vector obtained from the Num_add stage and the temporary vector of the previous iteration. 5) Act_2 stage: call activation function to calculate results of the Vec_sum stage.

3.2 Accelerator Architecture Overview

We can see the overall architecture of our accelerator in Figure 2. The acceleration system mainly consists of the hardware accelerator and the host CPU through the PCIe interface. The host CPU takes charge of data transmission and control. The hardware accelerator is mainly composed of a control FPGA and several compute FPGAs. The control FPGA is used to receive and buffer the input data and weights from the host CPU. Data is transferred to the corresponding external memory and buffer of the compute FPGA by the control FPGA. Meanwhile, the compute FPGA gets required data from the corresponding buffer and direct memory access (DMA) and carry out calculations to get results. Each PE represents a compute FPGA, which has its own DMA that is responsible for data transfer between

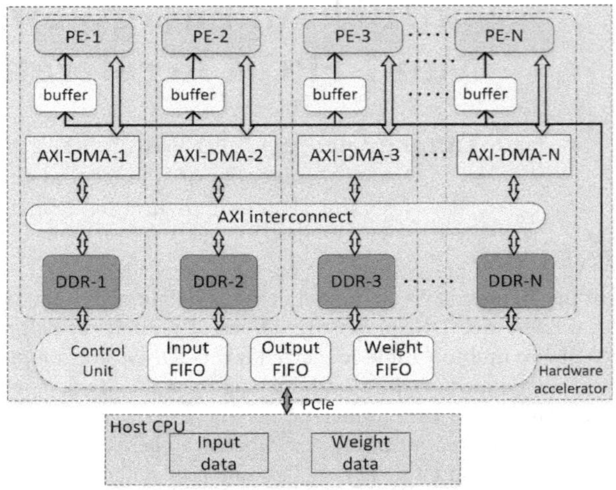

Figure 2: Overall architecture of accelerator

PE and external memory. Calculational results are returned to the host CPU through the control FPGA finally.

3.3 Design Details of the Accelerator

1) Architectures of the control FPGA and the compute FPGA

Division between layers. Firstly, we number the compute FPGAs, starting from 1. We designate the odd FPGA for calculations of the odd-level RBM to complete the matrix calculation in the form of vector inner product. The even FPGA is responsible for calculations for the matrix in the form of scalar multiplication of vectors. Architectures of the odd FPGA and the even FPGA are shown in Figure 3. On the left part of the Figure 3, 1) the communication unit is responsible for receiving data from the buffer and the DMA and then transmit data to the weight buffer and the input buffer. 2) many multipliers and adder trees make up a computational unit for computing. 3) the synchronization unit is in charge of ensuring the accuracy of calculation results. On the right part of the Figure 3, differences between the odd FPGA and the even FPGA are mentioned as follows. 1) The control unit is mainly to accept control signals and control the sequence of execution of the system. 2) The temp buffer is used to buffer intermediate values of matrix multiplication and eliminate data dependency.

Otherwise, the control FPGA is in charge of communicating with the first FPGA and the last FPGA, transmitting data packages to the first compute FPGA and receiving result packages from the last compute FPGA. If we put the adjacent odd FPGA and even FPGA together to form the FPGA group, the single task would be calculated in serial mode between FPGA groups and it is computed in a parallel manner within FPGA groups.

If the depth of the DBN is less than or equal to the number of the compute FPGA, the FPGA group can calculate multiple tasks in the pipeline mode. When the depth of the DBN is more than the number of the compute FPGA, we adopt another method to maintain to calculate multiple tasks in the pipeline mode. Assume that the number of the compute FPGA is N: 1) The system can complete calculations of the first N RBM layer of sample data and

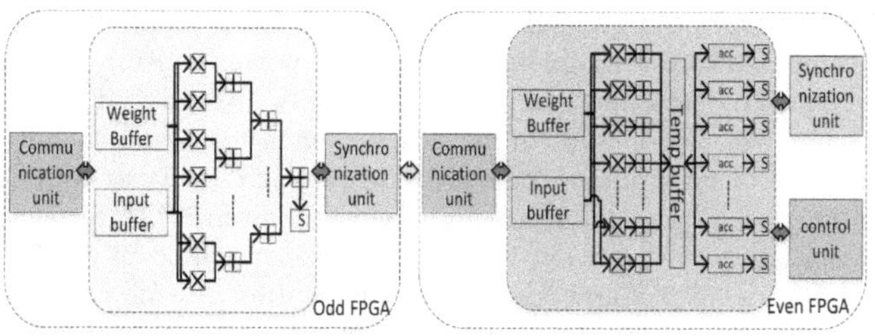

Figure 3: Architecture of DBL

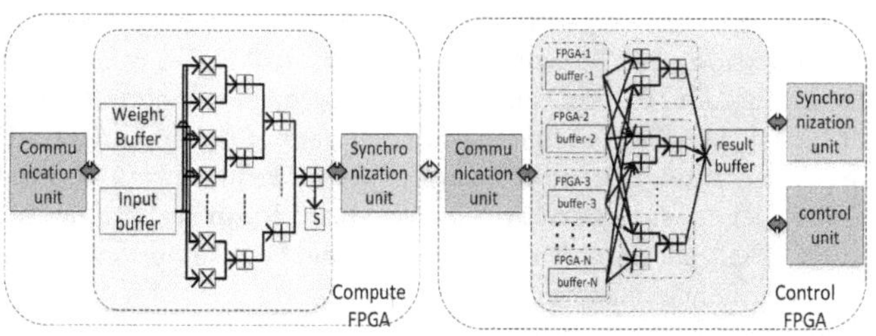

Figure 4: Architecture of DIL

then buffer intermediate results. 2) Then the first compute FPGA get intermediate results and the system starts to calculate the second N RBM layer of sample data and then buffer intermediate results. 3) And so on, until the calculation of all RBM layers of sample data is completed, the final prediction results are obtained. IF the depth of the DBN cannot be divisible by the number of the compute FPGA, redundant compute FPGAs are only responsible for the transmission of data in calculations of the last N RBM layer and do not perform actual calculations. So final calculational results are outputted by the last compute FPGA.

Division inside layers. In Division inside layers, we distribute evenly calculations of the same RBM layer to the compute FPGAs. Each compute FPGA is responsible for calculating part of the same RBM layer. So the architecture of the compute FPGA is like the odd FPGA mentioned above. And the control FPGA takes charge of integrating partial results from the compute FPGAs and communicating with all compute FPGAs. The architecture of DIL is shown in Figure 4. There are numerous buffers to buffer intermediate results from the corresponding FPGA in the control FPGA. Thus, the control FPGA needs to wait for all results from the compute FPGAs and the waiting time depends on the compute FPGA that takes the most time.

2) Communication

As a multi-FPGA accelerator, it is necessary to send control information and data between different FPGAs. Thus, we need to define the data packet format. We can see in Figure 5. 1) The op field is 4 bits to indicate the packet type and the operation type. 2) The size field is 16 bits, specifying the packet size. 3) The saddr field and daddr field are both 4 bits, representing the source address and the destination address. 4) Moreover, the layernum field is also 4 bits, used to indicate that the packet belongs to which layer. 5) The shift field is 32 bits in order to indicate the offset of the data. 6) The data field is the real data, containing required data and control information.

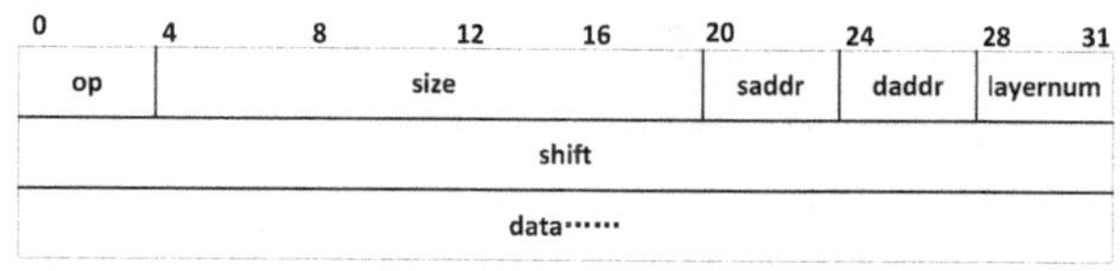

Figure 5: Data package format

3.4 Key Techniques

1) Tile

It is impossible to deploy the whole DNN on the hardware accelerator, such as VGG, GoogLeNet and ResNet. In order to improve scalability, we apply the tiling method to fix scalability problems. For purpose of ensuring high throughputs, the tile size should be equal to the granularity calculated in parallel in the module. When the number of neurons cannot be divisible by the tile size, it is necessary to pad 0 data. Consequently, we can use tile techniques to leverage trade-offs between speedup and hardware cost.

2) Redundant Storage

When we implement the matrix calculation in the form of scalar multiplication of vectors, there is data dependency in the Vec_sum stage. In order to eliminate this data dependency, the space-time method is used to set multiple intermediate buffers, adding the multiplication results with the elements in the corresponding buffers and storing the results in the buffers.

3) Piecewise Linear Interpolation

We adopt this method to implement activation function with negligible accuracy loss. The equation shows the implementation of the sigmoid function. For the cases in x<-8 and x>8, the results are respectively close to the bounds of 0 and 1. For -8<=x<=8, the function is replaced by piecewise linear interpolation. Finally, we divide the sigmoid function into three segments, showing in Equation (1).

$$f = \begin{cases} 0, x \leq -8 \\ a_i x + b_i, -8 < x < 8 \\ 1, x \geq 8 \end{cases} \tag{1}$$

4 EXPERIMENTS AND EVALUATIONS

4.1 Experimental Methodology

In order to compare performances and power consumption of various platforms, we choose the comparison objects, such as the Intel Core i7 CPU with clock at 4GHz and 8G memory, the NVIDIA Tesla K40C GPU with 2880 stream cores working at peak frequency 875MHz and DLAU [4], a deep learning accelerator based on FPGA with 36.1x speedup over the Intel Core2 CPU. For the sake of universality, we demonstrate experimental results on different datasets, like MNIST, Caltech101, and CIFAR-10. In the experiment, we apply the tile size 16 considering the hardware resources. Our accelerater contains one control FPGA (Xilinx Virtex-7 VX690T) and four compute FPGAs (Xilinx Zynq 7Z020). Our accelerator is simulated by System Verilog language with provided Direct Programming Interface to simulate communication between the accelerator and the host CPU. The ModelSim tool can simulate the accelerator execution process and obtain the execution time. Power consumption can be obtained through Xilinx Vivado tool sets for each FPGA.

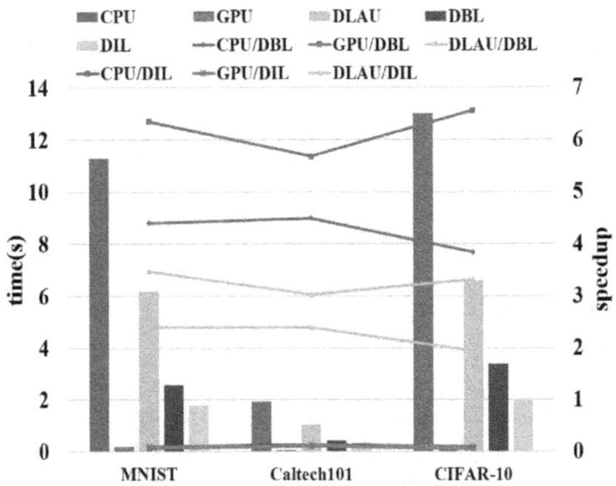

Figure 6: The execution time and speedup between our accelerator and CPU, GPU and CLAU under three different datasets

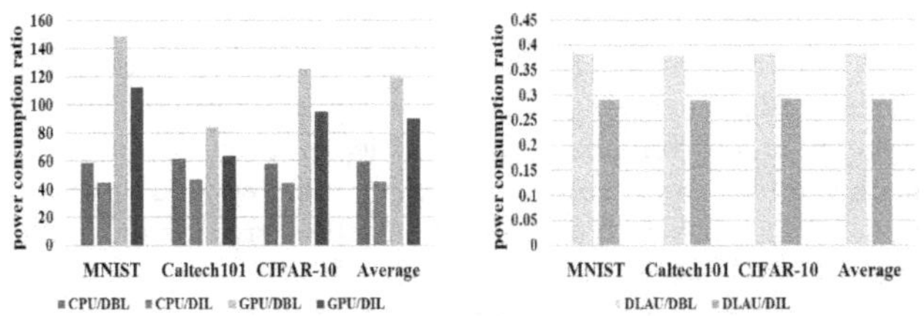

Figure 7: The power consumption ratio between our accelerator and CPU, GPU and DLAU under three different datasets

4.2 Analysis of Experimental Results

1) Speedup

We present the speedup of our accelerator and other platforms in Figure 6. Experimental results demonstrate DBL and DIL are able to achieve average to 4.24x and 6.20x speedup comparing to Core i7 CPU, respectively. The reason why the speedup is not high is limited FPGA working frequency at 100MHz and Core i7 working frequency at 4GHz. The clock frequency of Core i7 is 40 times of that of our accelerator. Comparing with the GPU, DBL, and DIL can achieve only 0.076x and 0.11x speedup. Reasons are organized as follows:1) The GPU work frequency is 875MHz at peak, but FPGA work frequency is only 100MHz. 2) The GPU contains 2880 computational cores, and the parallelism of our accelerator is only 16 64, Which is a huge gap in hardware design. Moreover, our accelerator can achieve 2.2x (DBL) and 3.3x (DIL) speedup comparing to DLAU. Both our accelerator and DLAU are based on the same type of FPGA, so there are no hardware differences between our accelerator and DLAU. Due to the parallelism of multi-FPGA and well-designed architecture, our accelerator can achieve good performance advantages over DLAU.

2) Power Consumption Ratio

Figure 7 illustrate the power consumption ratio between other platforms and our accelerator. Overall, the power consumption of our acceleration system is much lower than that achieved by CPU and GPU, and the power consumption of GPU is the highest. Compared to Core i7 CPU implementation, DBL power consumption is reduced by 59x and DIL power consumption is reduced by 45x. Compared to GPU implementation, DBL power consumption is reduced by 119x and DIL power consumption is reduced by 90x. The power consumption of the DBL system is 0.51W, in which the power consumption of the odd FPGA for each odd layer RBM is 0.125W, and the power consumption of the even FPGA for each even layer RBM is 0.130W. The power consumption of the DIL system is 0.673W and the power consumption of each compute FPGA is 0.125W and the power consumption of the control FPGA is 0.173W. We can sum up two points from the above results. 1) Compared with single FPGA system, the multi-FPGA system can bring significant performance improvements and increase power consumptions. 2) The workload of the control FPGA is larger, so its power consumption is higher. Besides, the power consumption of DLAU is lower than that of our accelerator. Compared to DLAU implementation, DBL power consumption is reduced by 0.38x, and DIL power consumption is reduced by 0.29x. It can be seen that the multi-FPGA accelerator will increase power consumption as well as performance improvement.

5 CONCLUSION

Firstly, we analyze data dependency of the DBN and explore five fully pipelined processing processes. Then we use several techniques to optimize effectively throughputs and resource utilization. Finally, we adopt two diverse division schemes to implement the DBN accelerator based on multi-FPGA. Experimental results demonstrate that the accelerator enjoys commendable speedup, low energy consumption, and high energy efficiency.

ACKNOWLEDGMENTS

This work was supported by the National Science Foundation of China (No.6177050133), Anhui Provincial Natural Science Foundation (No.1608085QF12), Suzhou Research Foundation (No.SYG201625), Youth Innovation Promotion Association CAS (No.2017497), and Fundamental Research Funds for the Central Universities (WK2150110003).

REFERENCES

[1] Tianshi Chen, Zidong Du, Ninghui Sun, Jia Wang, Chengyong Wu, Yunji Chen, and Olivier Temam. 2014. Diannao: A small-footprint high-throughput accelerator for ubiquitous machine-learning. In *ACM Sigplan Notices*, Vol. 49. ACM, 269–284.

[2] Yunji Chen, Tao Luo, Shaoli Liu, Shijin Zhang, Liqiang He, Jia Wang, Ling Li, Tianshi Chen, Zhiwei Xu, Ninghui Sun, et al. 2014. Dadiannao: A machine-learning supercomputer. In *Proceedings of the 47th Annual IEEE/ACM International Symposium on Microarchitecture*. IEEE Computer Society, 609–622.

[3] Jiantao Qiu, Jie Wang, Song Yao, Kaiyuan Guo, Boxun Li, Erjin Zhou, Jincheng Yu, Tianqi Tang, Ningyi Xu, Sen Song, et al. 2016. Going deeper with embedded fpga platform for convolutional neural network. In *Proceedings of the 2016 ACM/SIGDA International Symposium on Field-Programmable Gate Arrays*. ACM, 26–35.

[4] Chao Wang, Lei Gong, Qi Yu, Xi Li, Yuan Xie, and Xuehai Zhou. 2017. DLAU: A scalable deep learning accelerator unit on FPGA. *IEEE Transactions on Computer-Aided Design of Integrated Circuits and Systems* 36, 3 (2017), 513–517.

[5] Qi Yu, Chao Wang, Xiang Ma, Xi Li, and Xuehai Zhou. 2015. A Deep Learning prediction process accelerator based FPGA. In *Cluster, Cloud and Grid Computing (CCGrid), 2015 15th IEEE/ACM International Symposium on*. IEEE, 1159–1162.

[6] Chen Zhang, Peng Li, Guangyu Sun, Yijin Guan, Bingjun Xiao, and Jason Cong. 2015. Optimizing fpga-based accelerator design for deep convolutional neural networks. In *Proceedings of the 2015 ACM/SIGDA International Symposium on Field-Programmable Gate Arrays*. ACM, 161–170.

[7] Yangyang Zhao, Qi Yu, Xuda Zhou, Xuehai Zhou, Xi Li, and Chao Wang. 2016. PIE: A Pipeline Energy-Efficient Accelerator for Inference Process in Deep Neural Networks. In *Parallel and Distributed Systems (ICPADS), 2016 IEEE 22nd International Conference on*. IEEE, 1067–1074.

Performance Impact of Emerging Memory Technologies on Big Data Applications: A Latency-Programmable System Emulation Approach

Mu-Tien Chang, I. Stephen Choi, Dimin Niu, Hongzhong Zheng
Samsung Semiconductor, Inc.

ABSTRACT

This paper presents a performance analysis framework for studying emerging memories. The key component of the framework is a memory-latency programmable emulator, which is based on a FPGA-attached server system. The emulator allows users extend read and/or write latency. In addition, we use regression models to enable system performance studies for memory latencies beyond hardware limitations. Finally, we demonstrate Spark application case studies, analyzing the impact of two key characteristics of emerging memories: extended memory access times and enlarged memory capacities. Results show that the benefit of high capacity memory could outweigh the performance loss due to longer memory latency.

ACM Reference Format:
Mu-Tien Chang, I. Stephen Choi, Dimin Niu, Hongzhong Zheng. 2018. Performance Impact of Emerging Memory Technologies on Big Data Applications: A Latency-Programmable System Emulation Approach. In *Proceedings of Great Lakes Symposium on VLSI 2018 (GLSVLSI'18)*. ACM, New York, NY, USA, 4 pages. https://doi.org/10.1145/3194554.3194633

1 INTRODUCTION

Modern main-memory systems based on DRAM oftentimes cannot meet the capacity need for datacenter applications, such as in-memory computing for Big Data. Past researches have thus considered emerging memory technologies (e.g., PRAM, ReRAM) as DRAM replacement [8, 14]. Unlike DRAM, these new memory technologies have very different characteristics: they have persistency, higher density, and lower standby power, yet have lower bandwidth, longer latency, and higher dynamic energy. In addition, they exhibit asymmetrical read and write, where the time and energy required for write are usually greater than read.

Understanding the system impact of different memory characteristics is a critical step to design and enable new memory technologies. To accomplish that, various approaches were proposed. Mathematical models (e.g., [6]) provide fast and insightful first order evaluations, but are less accurate due to the difficultness of encapsulating complex hardware details. Simulators (e.g., [4]) allow users to conduct detailed microarchitecture analysis, but failed to simulate big workloads due to their 100,000X slowdown compared to native hardware. Emulators (e.g., [9]) provide the speed close to native hardware without neglecting hardware implementation details, but the design exploration space is limited by many hardware constraints.

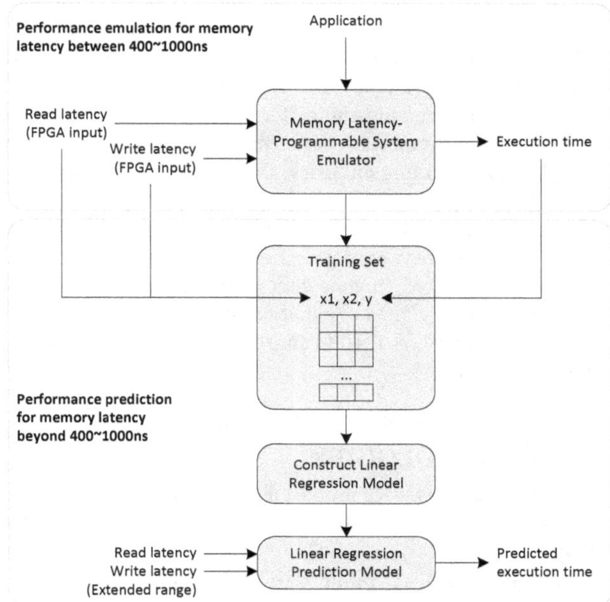

Figure 1: Performance analysis framework.

To overcome the problems described above, we developed a performance analysis framework that is accurate, fast, and extensible. The framework is based on a latency-programmable system emulator, and a linear regression prediction model (Figure 1):

- Latency-programmable system emulator: The system emulator uses FPGA and its DRAM together to represent memory that is latency-extended. This is achieved by implementing delay logic on the FPGA, allowing users to configure the memory access latency. Read latency and write latency can be independently configured, thus enabling users to emulate the effect of asymmetrical read and write performances.
- Linear regression prediction model: Due to the latency limitation inherited from the QPI, FPGA, and DRAM, the extended memory latency range is restricted to 400–1000ns. To overcome this limitation, we use linear regression to predict the system performance with memory latency outside the 400–1000ns range.

GLSVLSI'18, May 23–25, 2018, Chicago, IL, USA

ACM ISBN 978-1-4503-5724-1/18/05...$15.00
https://doi.org/10.1145/3194554.3194633

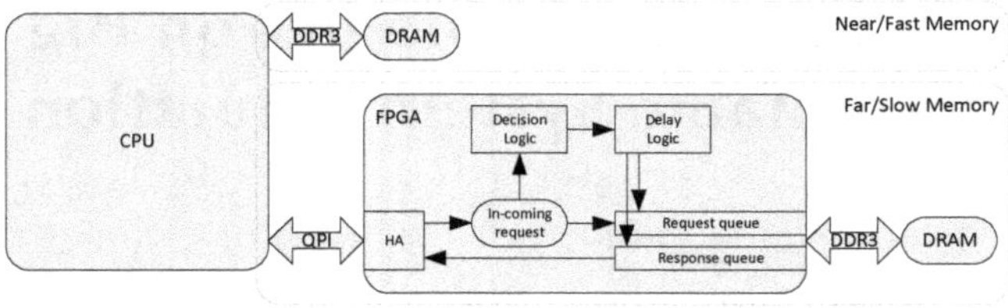

Figure 2: Logical view of the emulator.

Furthermore, we use the proposed framework to analyze the impact of memory latency and capacity on Spark [1], a fast in-memory cluster compute engine for Big Data processing. Prior art [5] has shown the importance of memory performance and capacity to applications running on Spark. Our study shows that both read and write latencies substantially affect the overall performance, with read having more impact. We also show that due to Spark's demand for memory, emerging memories' large capacity could compensate the performance degradation caused by slow access time. For instance, a memory that has 4X longer write latency but 2X higher capacity resulted in shorter application execution time, compared to DRAM.

2 PERFORMANCE ANALYSIS METHODOLOGIES

Various approaches were proposed to evaluate the system impact of new memory technologies. They can be categorized into the following:

- **Mathematical Model.** Mathematical models provide a rapid way to estimate performance. They are fast and extensible, but often overlook hardware implementation details. For instance, [6] presented a model that takes commodity server measurements as input parameters, to estimate the performance impact of memory latency and bandwidth for Big Data workloads. The proposal is useful for providing first-order analysis for memories that have symmetrical access latencies, but not for emerging memories that are read/write asymmetrical.
- **Simulation.** For simulations, one can employ standalone memory simulators (e.g., [11, 12]), and use pre-generated traces as input to obtain the bandwidth and latency of the memory subsystem. To further understand full-system performance, one can integrate memory simulators with full-system simulators (e.g., [4, 10]). The advantages of simulators are that they can be customized easily, providing great flexibility for users to modify microarchitecture details. In some cases, they also provide users an understanding of performance impact at the cycle level. However, they are much slower than native hardware, and oftentimes lack support for running complex workloads such as databases.
- **Emulation.** Memory emulators use modified native hardware to emulate different memories. Because emulators are based on real hardware, they can run applications close to hardware speed. One example is [9], a FPGA-based platform for fast and accurate new memory system exploration. However, [9] is not write latency-configurable, i.e., the emulator always uses non-extended latency for writes. This limits studies for emerging memories that are slower in writes and faster in reads. The emulator also lacks the model support for memory latency beyond hardware limitations.

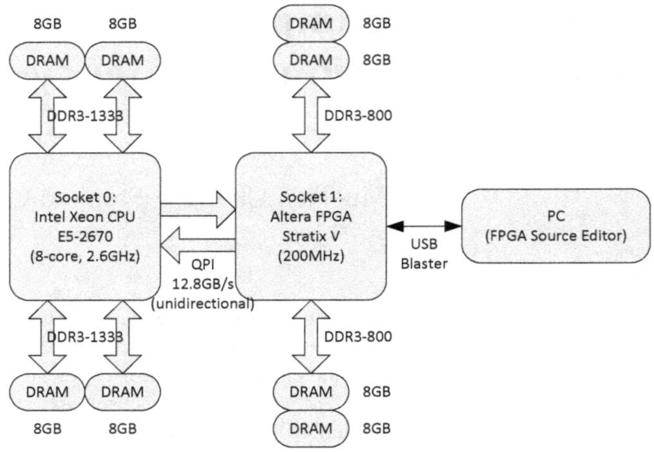

Figure 3: Block diagram of the latency-programmable system emulator.

3 LATENCY-PROGRAMMABLE SYSTEM EMULATOR

3.1 Overview

As shown in Figure 3, the emulator is based on an FPGA-attached server system. There are two sockets in the system, one with an Intel Xeon E5 processor, the other with an Altera Stratix V FPGA [7]. The FPGA is where extended, asymmetric memory latencies are implemented. The processor and the FPGA communicate over the Intel QPI interface [2]. Four DIMMs are connected to the processor, evenly populated on four DDR3 channels. The FPGA has two DDR3 channels attached, each with two DIMMs plugged in.

QPI provides very fast communication between processors in different sockets, maintains cache coherence in the memory spaces. Therefore, unlike PCIe-attached FPGA that have relatively high latency overhead, the low latency of QPI makes it more suitable for new memory system study.

QPI offers communication via two different mechanisms: the Cache Agent (CA) and the Home Agent (HA). With CA, FPGA can access the system memory of the processor; where with HA, the processor can access memory attached to the FPGA as part of the system memory. Our platform is based on HA, where the processor uses FPGA memory as part of its memory. By implementing delay logic in the FPGA, whenever the processor tries to access FPGA memory, extra delay cycles triggered by the FPGA will be added to the memory access path. From the processor's view, the delayed memory access path creates the scenario of extended memory read/write latency.

Figure 2 shows a logical view of the emulator. The FPGA introduces two types of delays: (1) added idle cycles, and (2) queuing delay. When the FPGA receives a memory request from the CPU, the decision logic will first decode the packet type (read or write) and the user-defined read/write delay value. User-defined delays are injected to the data response queue for read requests, and to the request queue if the request is write. The decision logic will also analyze the dependency between the incoming request, and the outstanding requests that are still present in the request queue. If dependency is found, the incoming request will stall in the request queue until all its preceding dependent requests are completed.

Note that due to the latency overhead caused by QPI, HA, etc., even at zero additional FPGA cycle, the round-trip memory access latency (~400ns) is greater than typical DRAM access time (~80ns) [1]. We anticipate memory systems using new memory technologies will adopt new memory interfaces such as Gen-Z, OpenCAPI, or NVDIMM-P. These interfaces offer hand-shaking mechanisms, which allow new memories to have relaxed timings and built-in maintenance capabilities. For instance, future PRAM DIMMs may have on-module controllers that manage wear-leveling, a feature that is critical for PRAM. The latency overhead observed in the emulator can be considered as the interface and controller overhead of future memory interfaces and modules.

3.2 Using the Emulator

In our emulations, we execute unmodified OS and applications. Because in general the OS or application running on the processor will use the processor's locally attached memory, if the memory footprint is small, the FPGA memory is unlikely to be touched. Therefore, in order to explore the impact of extended asymmetric read and write latencies, we must force applications to use FPGA memory. This can be done by reconfiguring the boot loader. For instance, when running a Linux OS, we can modify the GRUB by mapping out most of the CPU memory. As a result, only a small portion of the CPU memory is visible to the OS and application, which will in turn trigger the large FPGA memory capacity that remains visible.

3.3 Regression Model

To analyze the impact of memory access time beyond the emulator's hardware limitation, we use linear regression to construct performance prediction models. For each workload, we execute it on the emulator with different latency values to collect training data. Each execution produces one set of data that consists of a read latency value, a write latency value, and a workload completion time. As shown in Figure 1, the read and write latency values correspond to input data x_1 and x_2, and the completion time corresponds to output value y. We then use these training sets and machine learning modules (sklearn, scipy, scikit-learn, etc.) in Python to obtain the prediction model.

4 CASE STUDY

4.1 Experimental Setup

4.1.1 Spark Framework. We use two sets of cluster systems in this system: HDFS cluster and Spark cluster. The HDFS cluster consists of 8 data nodes and one name node. Each node has two 2.3 GHz hexa-core processors. Each node also comprises 64GB of memory, and 1.25TB of SSD. The Spark cluster consists of one name node and one data node that is capable of performance emulation. The name node has one 3.5GHz hexa-core processor. It also comprises 8GB of memory and 512GB of SSD. The data node, based on our emulator, consists of one 2.6GHz Xeon E5-2670 hexa-processor and a 200MHz Altera Stratix V FPGA. The emulator is configured with 1GB of CPU memory and 32GB of FPGA memory. The 1GB CPU memory acts as near memory, mainly used for the OS. The 32GB FPGA memory acts as far memory, which is mainly used by the application. The emulator also comprises of 360GB of SSD. The experiments use Spark 1.0.1, Tachyon 0.4.1, and Hadoop 1.0.4 for HDFS.

[1]A round-trip memory access starts from CPU load/store instruction, all the way until the request is successfully returned to the CPU.

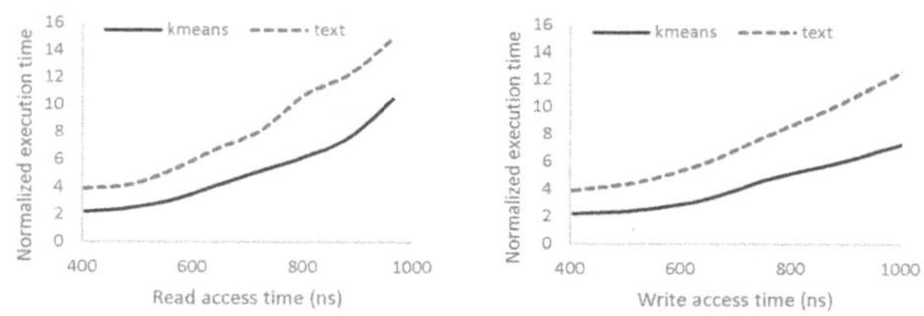

Figure 4: Normalized execution time with respect to various read and write access times. Results are normalized to 32GB CPU DRAM. For read access time sensitivity study, write access time is held constant at 400ns. Similarly, for write access time sensitivity study, read access time is fixed at 400ns.

4.1.2 Workloads and Data Sets. We use two representative Spark applications to evaluate the performance impact of memory technologies on Big Data applications:

- **Kmeans.** K-means is a popular clustering algorithm that clusters data points into a desired number of groups. In this study, we use Spark MLlib [3] implementation of *Kmeans*. We generated 8GB synthetic data that consists of random numbers as input data for *Kmeans*.
- **Text.** In this study, we use Spark's native functions to implement in-memory text search (*Text*). For input data, we use Amazon movie reviews of 9GB with 8 million reviews [13].

4.2 Results and Analysis

4.2.1 Impact of Read and Write Access Times. Figure 4 shows the normalized execution time, with respect to various read and write access times. The results, are normalized to 32GB CPU DRAM (ideal case, not shown). Smaller number means faster completion. We summarize the results as follows:

- **Memory latency, regardless of read or write, has substantial performance impact.** Taking *Text* as an example, when keeping write access time to 400ns, each 100ns read latency addition results in around 2X slowdown on average. Similarly, when keeping read access time to 400ns, each 100ns write latency addition results in around 1.7X slowdown.

  The importance of memory latency can be reasoned by Spark's high memory performance requirement: for *Kmeans*, the read and write usages are 6GB/s and 5GB/s; and for *Text*,

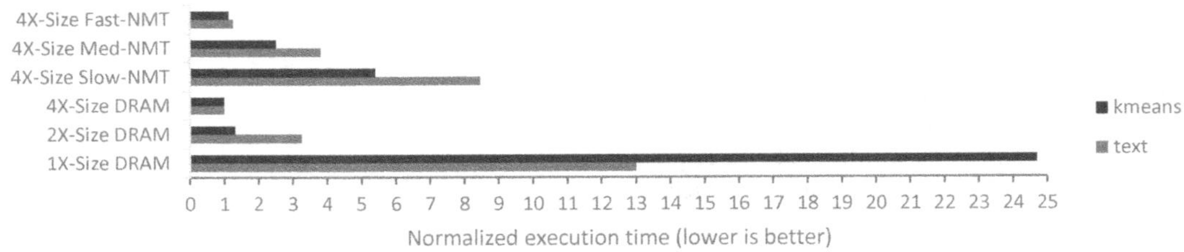

Figure 5: Normalized execution time with respect to various memory types. 1X-Size, 2X-Size, and 4X-Size represent memory capacity for 8GB, 16GB, and 32GB. Slow, Med, and Fast-EMT correspond to read/write access time for 200ns/800ns, 100ns/800ns, and 100ns/400ns. Results show that the benefit of capacity could be greater than the performance loss due to long latency.

the read and write bandwidth usages are around 11GB/s and 9GB/s. These characterizations are based on normal CPU-attached DRAMs.

- **Compared to write, read access time has more performance impact.** Comparing the left chart against the right chart in Figure 4, the slowdown rate appears to be higher when increasing read latency, compared to increasing write latency. Also, for the same execution time, the latency requirement for read is shorter than that of write, meaning that read performance is more critical. Our findings match the workload characteristics, where the demand for read is greater than write.

4.2.2 Impact of Memory Technology. Emerging memory technologies (EMTs) provide higher capacity than DRAM, but have longer latency, especially for write. In this section, we compare several types of memory: 1X-Size DRAM (8GB), 2X-Size DRAM (16GB), 4X-Size DRAM (32GB), 4X-Size Slow-EMT (32GB, 200ns read, 800ns write), 4X-Size Med-EMT (32GB, 100ns read, 800ns read), and 4X-Size Fast-EMT (32GB, 100ns read, 400ns write). We chose these EMT capacity and latency numbers from projection of exiting PRAM parameters.

Results for the DRAM cases are based on real measurements, using different CPU-attached DRAM capacity configurations. For the EMT cases, because the read latencies are made lower than 400ns, we obtain the results based on prediction models constructed from emulation results. Figure 5 shows the comparison. We normalize the results to 4X-Size DRAM (best case). Key observations:

- **Memory capacity matters for Big Data applications.** The working set size for both applications is around 12GB. Therefore, 1X-Size DRAM cannot meet the capacity requirement, resulting in frequent access to the SSD storage, which is more than 2000X slower than DRAM. As a result, though EMT has longer access time, even Slow-EMT outperforms 1X-Size DRAM because of its 4X higher capacity.
- **Obtaining the balance point.** When compared to 2X-Size DRAM, though 4X-Size Med-EMT has higher capacity, it still underperforms due to its 10X longer write time. On the other hand, 4X-Size Fast-EMT resulted in slightly better performance (14% and 71% faster for *Kmeans* and *Text*). For 4X-Size EMT to achieve the same performance as 2X-Size DRAM, its write time should be shorter than 450ns for *Kmeans*, and 700ns for *Text*, respectively.

5 CONCLUSION

To adopt emerging memory technologies as DRAM alternatives in datacenters, it is critical to first understand their impact on system performance. Although existing methodologies have their individual strengths in analyzing different memory choices, they all have limitations when considering datacenter workloads and properties of emerging memories. In this paper, we present a memory-latency programmable emulator, which can be configured with different read and write latencies. Additionally, because the emulator is based on a native server, datacenter workloads can easily be ported and emulated. At the end of this paper, we present a case study using Spark, an in-memory processing framework. Results show that memory access times for both read and write have high impact on Spark performance. Results also show that even with longer access time, emerging memory that has high capacity can potentially speedup Spark.

REFERENCES

[1] Apache Spark. spark.apache.org.
[2] An Introduction to the Intel QuickPath Interconnect. Intel, 2009.
[3] Mllib | apache spark, 2015.
[4] N. Binkert et al. The Gem5 Simulator. *SIGARCH Computer Architecture News*, 39(2):1–7, Aug. 2011.
[5] I. S. Choi et al. Early Experience with Optimizing I/O Performance Using High-Performance SSDs for In-Memory Cluster Computing. In *BigData*, 2015.
[6] R. Clapp et al. Quantifying the Performance Impact of Memory Latency and Bandwidth for Big Data Workloads. In *IISWC*, 2015.
[7] P. Gupta. Xeon+FPGA Platform for the Data Center. CARL, 2015.
[8] B. Lee et al. Architecting Phase Change Memory As a Scalable DRAM Alternative. In *ISCA*, 2009.
[9] K. Malladi et al. FAME: A Fast and Accurate Memory Emulator for New Memory System Architecture Exploration. In *MASCOTS*, 2015.
[10] A. Patel, F. Afram, S. Chen, and K. Ghose. Marss: A full system simulator for multicore x86 cpus. In *DAC*, pages 1050–1055, 2011.
[11] P. Rosenfeld et al. DRAMSim2: A Cycle Accurate Memory System Simulator. *IEEE CAL*, 10(1):16–19, Jan. 2011.
[12] J. Stevens et al. An Integrated Simulation Infrastructure for the Entire Memory Hierarchy: Cache, DRAM, Nonvolatile Memory, and Disk. *Intel Technology Journal*, 17(1):184–200, 2013.
[13] L. Wang et al. BigDataBench: A Big Data Benchmark Suite from Internet Services. In *HPCA*, 2014.
[14] C. Xu et al. Overcoming the Challenges of Crossbar Resistive Memory Architectures. In *HPCA*, 2015.

BiNMAC: Binarized neural Network Manycore ACcelerator

Ali Jafari
Dept. of Computer Science and Electrical Engineering, University of Maryland, Baltimore County
Baltimore, Maryland

Morteza Hosseini
Dept. of Computer Science and Electrical Engineering, University of Maryland, Baltimore County
Baltimore, Maryland

Adwaya Kulkarni
Dept. of Computer Science and Electrical Engineering, University of Maryland, Baltimore County
Baltimore, Maryland

Chintan Patel
Dept. of Computer Science and Electrical Engineering, University of Maryland, Baltimore County
Baltimore, Maryland

Tinoosh Mohsenin
Dept. of Computer Science and Electrical Engineering, University of Maryland, Baltimore County
Baltimore, Maryland

ABSTRACT

This paper presents a low power, domain-specific manycore accelerator referred to as "BiNMAC"- Binarized neural Network Manycore ACcelerator, which effectively maps and executes Binary Deep Neural Networks (BNNs). With only 2.40% and 1.88% area and power overhead, novel instructions such as *Population-Count* and *Patch-Select* are added to the ISA of the BiNMAC, each of which replaces frequently used functions that would have taken 52 and 4 clock cycles respectively with 1 clock cycle. A 64-cluster architecture of the BiNMAC is fully placed and routed in 65 nm TSMC CMOS technology, where a single cluster occupies an area of 0.53 mm^2 with a power of 223 mW at 1 GHz clock frequency. The 64-cluster architecture takes 36.5 mm^2 area and, if fully utilized, consumes a power of 16.4 W. We also propose a multilayer perceptron (MLP) neural network for multimodal time-series data classification. Binarized versions of the 3-layers MLP and ResNet-20 are implemented on BiNMAC. The implementation results show that BiNMAC consumes 0.02 mJ and 3.8 mJ energy which is 13× and 30× lower than implementation of standard non-binarized MLP and ResNet-20 on an equivalent predecessor platform. To compare the performance of the BiNMAC with other off-the-shelf platforms, the two networks are also implemented on the NVIDIA Jetson TX2 SoC (CPU+GPU). BiNMAC achieves 22× and 78× higher throughput and 23× and 41× lower energy consumption compared to TX2 SoC for the binarized MLP and ResNet-20, respectively.

ACM Reference Format:
Ali Jafari, Morteza Hosseini, Adwaya Kulkarni, Chintan Patel, and Tinoosh Mohsenin. 2018. BiNMAC: Binarized neural Network Manycore ACcelerator. In *GLSVLSI '18: 2018 Great Lakes Symposium on VLSI, May 23–25, 2018, Chicago, IL, USA.* ACM, New York, NY, USA, 4 pages. https://doi.org/10.1145/3194554.3194634

GLSVLSI '18, May 23–25, 2018, Chicago, IL, USA

ACM ISBN 978-1-4503-5724-1/18/05...$15.00
https://doi.org/10.1145/3194554.3194634

1 INTRODUCTION

In recent years, Deep Neural Networks (DNNs) have become increasingly popular because of their usability and outstanding results in areas such as computer vision, voice recognition, natural language processing, robotics and time-series data classification. Several methods have been proposed to address efficient training and inference in deep neural networks: Shallow networks, quantizing parameters, network binarization and compressing pre-trained deep networks. Although these methods improve the efficiency of DNNs for implementing on low-power embedded platforms, an off-chip memory is usually required to save large models. Therefore, power consumption is still high due to the need of constantly accessing the off-chip memory. In 2016, [1] proposed Binarized Neural Networks (BNNs) to address the previously mentioned challenges. BNN has a compact representation of network weights and activation values compared to a standard DNN by constraining each weight value to either -1 or +1. During the forward pass BNNs: 1) Drastically reduce the memory requirements. 2) Can eliminate the need of using off-chip memory. 3) Replace multiply and add operations with bit-wise XNOR and population-count operations. Since 2016, different works [1, 8] have shown that BNNs can achieve comparable accuracies to full-precision DNNs for some popular datasets such as MNIST, CIFAR10 and ImageNet. [10, 11] have proposed BNN hardware accelerators on CPU, GPU, FPGA and ASIC. Also, several research work has been carried out in domain specific platforms to implement simple processing cores for kernel-optimization rather than application-centric processors.

In this paper, we propose "BiNMAC"- Binarized neural Network Manycore ACcelerator, a novel energy-efficient programmable cluster-based manycore that is designed specifically for BNNs, implemented on 65 nm technology on chip area of size 36.5 mm^2, with a maximum total power of 16.4 W. The proposed architecture has novel instructions for different layers of BNNs, that reduce computations and consequently execution time. Additionally, a fully-connected BNN topology, is proposed which is designed for multimodal time-series data classification [3, 4]. We evaluate the functionality and performance of BiNMAC using binarazied versions of the fully-connected BNN and fully-convolutional Resnet-20.

2 BINARY DEEP NEURAL NETWORKS

Similar to standard neural networks, binary neural networks consist of convolution and fully-connected layers and activation function.

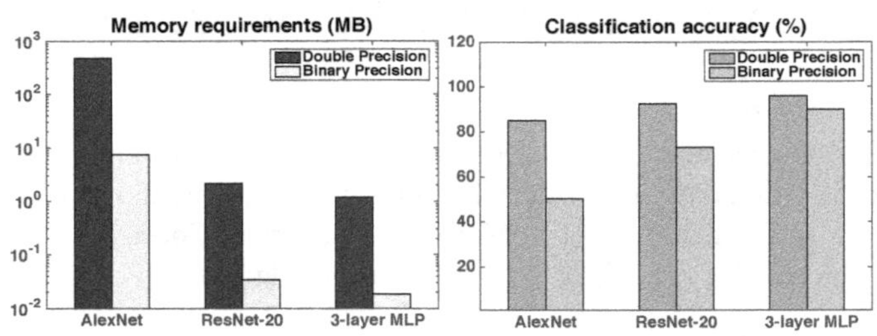

Figure 1: (A) Required memory (B) Classification accuracy for three NNs with double and binary precision weights.

However, these layers are implemented differently in BNNs: For the first layer of BNN, data from each input channel (e.g red, green and blue channels for colored images) are in full-precision values, but model weights of the BNN are constrained to either +1 or -1. Therefore, multiply-accumulate operations are replaced by a series of additions and subtractions. For the next layers, all input features are binarized using binary activation functions, and along with the binarized weights, the multiply-accumulate operations can be performed using only XNOR operations and population-count operation (that will be discussed in Section 3). In order to apply the activation function to the real-valued variables and transform them into either +1 or -1, deterministic or stochastic binarization functions are proposed by [1]. We use deterministic binarization, which is in fact a sign(x) function, since it is more efficient to implement on hardware. In this section, BiNMAC is evaluated using two different case studies including Physical Activity Monitoring and Image Recognition.

2.1 Case study 1: Physical Activity Monitoring

A multi-layer perceptron (MLP) neural network is proposed to classify multimodal time series signals. The proposed network has 3 fully-connected layers. Each layer in the network has a size of 256 nodes, and Sigmoid function is used as the activation function. We used TensorFlow framework to design and evaluate the MLP with a real-world dataset of Physical Activity Monitoring (PAMAP2) [9]. PAMAP2 records 12 physical activities performed by 9 subjects. The physical activities are, for instance: standing, walking, lying and sitting. Three inertial measurement units (IMU) and one heart rate monitor were used to record the data. In total, the dataset includes 40 channels of valid data. The network parameter size, with double precision values, is 1.2 MB. Binarizing the proposed MLP causes the parameter size to reduce by 64x. Also, the average classification accuracy over 8 subjects is 98%.

2.2 Case study 2: Image Recognition

Binarized ResNet-20 for CIFAR-10 image recognition dataset [6] is used to evaluate BiNMAC, without any change in the topology using the Torch implementation provided by [8]. Binarizing ResNet-20 network causes the parameter size to drop by 64x at the expense of 18.1% loss in classification accuracy. Fig. 1-A shows the required memory for three different neural network architectures, AlexNet [5], ResNet-20 [2], and the proposed MLP with binary and double precision weights and Fig. 1-B reflects their classification accuracy.

3 BINMAC MANYCORE ARCHITECTURE

3.1 BiNMAC Overview and Key Features

Fig. 2-A shows the block diagram of a 64 cluster version of the BiNMAC architecture, highlighting the processing cores in a single bus-based cluster. Fig. 2-B shows the post-layout view of a bus-based single cluster. Each processing core, cluster bus, cluster memory and the router was synthesized and fully placed and routed in a 65 nm CMOS technology using Cadence SoC Encounter and the post-layout implementation results for one cluster are summarized in Fig. 2-E. Each cluster comprises of 3 processing cores with 6 pipeline stages, a cluster memory of 3072 words (6KB), and low-latency bus interconnect for communication between cores within the cluster and a hierarchical routing architecture for intra-cluster communication. The processing core operates on a 16-bit data-path.

3.2 BiNMAC Manycore Platform Evaluation

To evaluate the functionality of BiNMAC, we developed a stand-alone simulator and a compiler in Java. This simulator provides cycle accurate results along with task execution and completion time, number of instructions, and memory usage per core. Each task of the neural network application, is first implemented in assembly language on each processing core in a cluster using the simulator. This code is given as an input to the simulator, which reads in the code. It then models the functionality of the processor and calculates the final state of register files and data memories. For execution time and energy consumption analysis of the algorithm, binaries obtained from manycore compiler are mapped on to hardware model of the manycore platform and simulated using Cadence NC-Verilog. The activity factor is then derived and is used by the Cadence SoC Encounter tool for accurate power computation.

3.3 BNN On-chip Memory Processing

In order to avoid use of an external DRAM, binary networks of proper size, whose network parameters and temporary feature map can fit inside the on-chip memory, are chosen. By doing so, not only the hardware overhead is avoided, but also the memory access delay is reduced, therefore the throughput increases. In previous work, filters are stored inside the on-chip memories, but still, the temporary feature map generated in each layer is required to be written to and read from an external DRAM in run-time. In our work, however, both parameters and the temporary feature maps are stored in the on-chip memory.

3.4 Domain Specific Customization of ISA

BiNMAC consists of special instructions for Binary Neural Networks, such as XNOR, PCNT and PCH. All of these instructions require one clock cycle for the execution stage.

3.4.1 XNOR and Popcount Instruction. We added XNOR and PCNT to the ISA of the BiNMAC. XNOR and Population Count are the main operators in BNNs. Population Count operator counts the number of 1s in a data packet (16 bits). With a very small hardware overhead (10 full adders and 6 half adders) for a data packet, PCNT instruction can replace 4 lines of instruction assembly code, and 52 cycles in terms of execution, all fused in one instruction and one clock cycle. XNOR instruction is implemented with an array of 16 XNOR gates that simply performs the bit-wise XNOR operation between two registers or data memory entries.

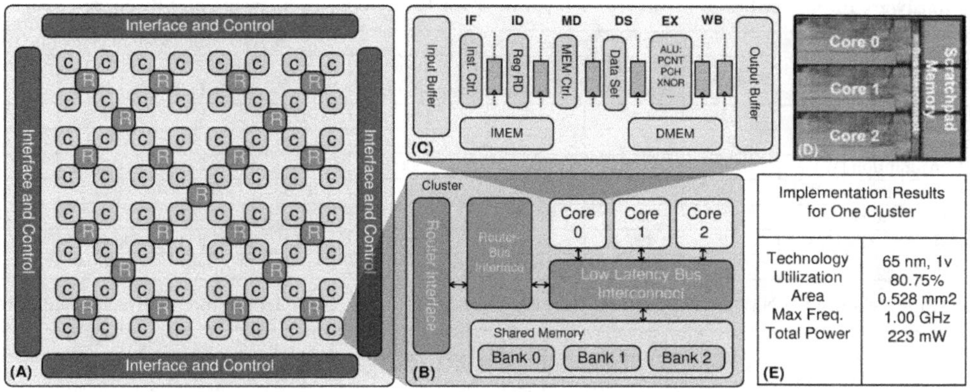

Figure 2: (A) BiNMAC comprising of 64 clusters (B) Cluster Architecture highlighting cluster memory, bus and processing cores (C) Processor architecture consisting of 6 pipeline stages. IF, ID, MD, DS, EX and WB are inst. fetch, inst. decode, memory decode, data set, execution, and write-back stages. IMEM and DMEM are instruction and local data memories. (D) Post-layout view of cluster implemented in 65nm, 1V TSMC CMOS technology (E) Post-layout implementation results of optimized bus-based cluster (consisting of 3 cores + bus + cluster memory).

3.4.2 Patch-select - PCH Instruction. PCH is a new invention to the ISA of BiNMAC which eases the bit packing and bit manipulation. Since coefficients are packed in 16 bit entries, there are times that a patch of a specific size is required to be read from one data entry, and to be shifted and written to another. PCHx is devised to meet this necessity. This optimization saves 4 lines of instruction and 4 clock cycles for the execution. PCHx in BiNMAC has been devised to handle patches of length 1 to 9. Fig. 3 shows an example of a PCH3 instruction, its hardware description language, and its function snippet that is frequently used in the process of a BNN.

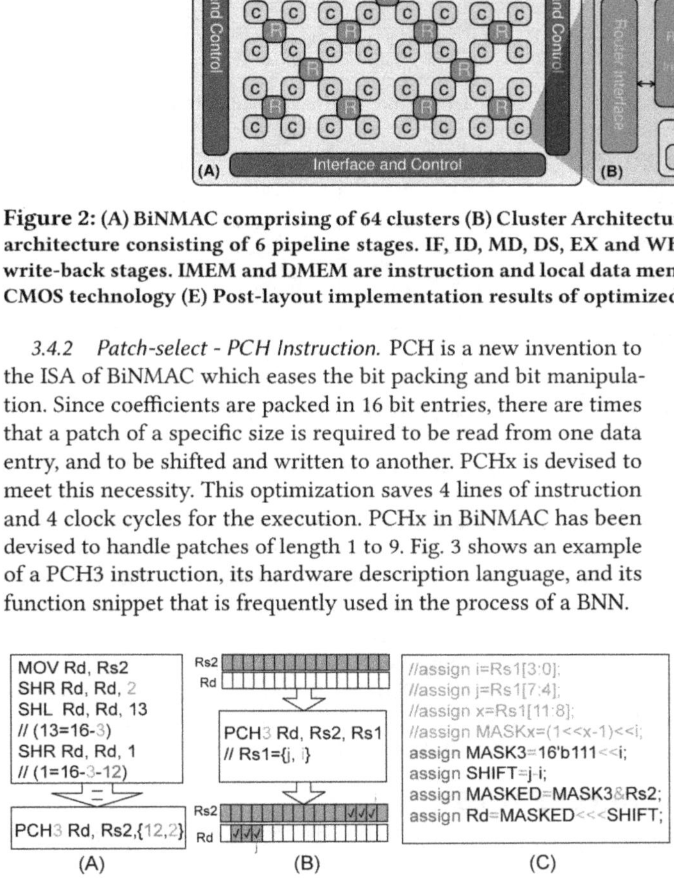

Figure 3: (A) A patch-select snippet and its equivalent instruction that fuses 4 lines of code and 4 execution clock cycles into one. (B) The register transfer illustration of the patch-select example (C) Verilog code that shows implementation of the patch-select instruction using barrel shifters

4 IMPLEMENTATION RESULTS AND PLATFORM COMPARISON

Both binarized 3-layer MLP and ResNet-20 are implemented on BiNMAC and the results are presented in terms of throughput, execution time and energy efficiency for standard and binarized neural networks. To better gauge the performance of BiNMAC, we also implemented the two binarized networks on NVIDIA Jetson TX2 SoC (CPU+GPU) platform. In BiNMAC implementation, all of BNN weights are distributed among the cluster. Due to the architecture scalability of BiNMAC, for different neural networks, different number of clusters are activated to accommodate the network parameters and temporary feature maps, and by means of its Dynamic Frequency Scaling (DFS), one can choose the best frequency given an application. The least number of required clusters, N, for a BNN is derived from equation (1) that guarantees that on-chip memories can always reserve the processing data:

$$N = \frac{NetworkParameterSize}{ClusterMemorySize - BiggestFeatureMapSize} \quad (1)$$

4.1 MLP for Physical Activity Monitoring

The implementation results for the 3-layer MLP are provided in table 1. For this binarized network, at least 4 clusters are required, 98% of their 12K word memory is used to accommodate the network parameters, and the rest accommodate feature map data. In the 3-layer MLP, by means of the DFS, the clock frequency is reduced to 145MHz, which is comparable to 140 MHz of the TX2 GPU. The implementation results for the binarized 3-layer MLP using 4 clusters with 12 cores are obtained in two different scenarios: Without using the PCH instruction It takes 0.085ms (at 145 MHz) to classify one input window of 40 sample whereas it takes 0.077ms if PCH is used at bit-packing phase, resulting in a performance improvement of 1.1× over the latter and 1.8× over the standard version of 3-layer MLP implemented on PENC with 53 clusters.

4.2 Binarized ResNet-20 for CIFAR-10

For the binarized ResNet-20 network, at least 16 clusters are required to be activated for processing and providing a memory of size 48K words, 66% of which is used for network parameters, and the rest is used for the feature map data. Table 1 shows the implementation results in terms of execution time, energy consumption, throughput, and energy efficiency. The implementation results for binarized ResNet-20 using the 16 clusters with 48 cores was done in two different scenarios: with and without PCH instruction. Without a PCH instruction, and only by using its equivalent function as in Fig. 6-A, it takes 1,865,441 clock cycles (1.86ms at 1 GHz) to classify one single image, resulting in a classification throughput of 537.6 label per second, and a power of 3.9 watts when running on 16 clusters at clock frequency of 1 GHz. On the other hand, when taking the PCH instruction into account, due to fusion of 4 instructions into one, which is frequently used in both patch selecting

Table 1: BiNMAC hardware implementation results for 3-layer MLP for the activity monitoring and Binarized ResNet-20 for CIFAR-10

Network/Platfrom	ResNet-20 (System Freq=1GHz)				3-layer MLP (System Freq=145MHz)			
	Standard	BiNMAC w/o PCH	BiNMAC w/ PCH	Improv. over Standard	Standard	BiNMAC w/o PCH	BiNMAC w/ PCH	Improv. over Standard
# of Used Clusters (N)	13	16	16	0.8x	53	4	4	13.2x
Execution Time (ms)	36	1.86	0.98	36x	0.139	0.085	0.077	1.8x
Power Consumption (W)	3.5	3.8	3.9	0.9x	1.9	0.27	0.27	7.3x
Energy Consumption (mJ)	116	7.3	3.8	30x	0.26	0.02	0.02	13x
Throughput (label/s)	27	537.6	1020	36x	7,194	11,765	12,987	1.8x
Throughput/Power (label/s/W)	7.9	137.4	260	30x	3,786	43,574	48,100	13x
EDP (mJs)	4.2	0.01	0.004	1,044x	3.6e-5	1.7e-6	1.54e-6	23x

Table 2: Comparison of BiNMAC w/ PCH results with NVIDIA TX2. For comparison the results are scaled to 28nm.

Network/Platform	ResNet-20				3-layer MLP			
	TX2	BiNMAC Serial	BiNMAC Fully Parallel	Improv. over TX2	TX2	BiNMAC Serial	BiNMAC Fully Parallel	Improv. over TX2
Tech (nm)	28	65	65	–	28	65	65	–
# of Used Clusters (N)	–	16	64	–	–	4	64	–
Frequency (MHz)	1033	1000	1000	–	140	145	145	–
Execution Time (ms)	21.8	0.98	0.28	78x	0.17	0.077	0.0076	22x
Throughput (label/s)	46	1020	3571	78x	5,882	12,987	131,579	22x
Power (W)	3.8	3.9	16.4	0.23x	2.1	0.27	4.84	0.43x
Scaled Power (W)	3.8	1.67	6.9	0.55x	2.1	0.12	2.1	1x
Scaled Energy Consumption (mJ)	83	1.63	1.94	41x	0.37	0.009	0.016	23x
Scaled Throughput/Power (label/s/watt)	12.8	608	512	41x	2800	108,496	63,013	23x

and bit packing phases, the number of clock cycles to classify one single image drops to 981,083 (0.98ms at 1 GHz), thus improving the throughput by almost 1.9×. The latter implementation on BiNMAC has a drastic performance improvement of 36× and an energy consumption per label improvement of 30× over those of a standard ResNet-20 implemented on the precedent version of BiNMAC.

4.3 Implementation Results on TX2 SoC

3-layer MLP and binarized ResNet-20 are implemented on NVIDIA TX2 platform. GPU clock frequency is 140 MHz and 1033 MHz for binarized 3-layer MLP and ResNet-20, respectively. Also, one CPU core is on, running at 345 MHz. Table 2 summarizes the results, and to make a fair comparison, the BiNMAC performance results are scaled to 28nm. Based on the results, BiNMAC achieves 22× and 78× higher throughput and 23× and 41× lower energy consumption compared to GPU for the 3-layer MLP and ResNet-20, respectively.

4.4 Comparison with Existing Work

Table 3 compares the BiNMAC results with state-of-the-art FPGA accelerators for CIFAR-10 dataset. BiNMAC has highest throughput compared to other work. Compared to [7] and [11], BiNMAC achieves 14× and 6× higher throughput. Also, BiNMAC consumes 1.2× lower power compared to [11] but 2× higher than [7].

Table 3: Comparison of BiNMAC with existing work

Design	[7]	[11]	This work
Platform	Artix-7(XC7A200T)	Zynq (7Z020)	Manycore
Latency (ms)	13	6	1
Throughput (img/sec)	72.6	168	1020
Frequency (MHz)	100	143	1000
Power (W)	1.82	4.7	3.9

5 CONCLUSION

We proposed an energy efficient Binarized neural Network Manycore ACcelerator named "BiNMAC" with specialized binary architecture, instructions, and memory access architecture. We also proposed a 3-layer MLP which is a binary neural network designed for multi-modal time-series data classification. Both fully-connected network and convolutional ResNet-20 were binarized and were deployed at BiNMAC. The results show BiNMAC consumes 0.02 mJ and 3.8 mJ energy which is 13× and 30× lower than standard non-binarized MLP and ResNet-20 deployed at an equivalent precedent platform. Furthermore, we implemented the two BNNs on the NVIDIA Jetson TX2 SoC (CPU+GPU), and BiNMAC achieves 22× and 78× higher throughput and 23× and 41× lower energy consumption for binarized 3-layer MLP and ResNet-20, respectively.

REFERENCES

[1] Matthieu Courbariaux et al. 2016. Binarized neural networks: Training deep neural networks with weights and activations constrained to+ 1 or-1. *arXiv preprint arXiv:1602.02830* (2016).

[2] Kaiming He et al. [n. d.]. Deep residual learning for image recognition. In *Proceedings of the IEEE conference on computer vision and pattern recognition.*

[3] Ali Jafari et al. 2017. An embedded FPGA accelerator for a stand-alone dual-mode assistive device. *Memory (Kb)* 101 (2017), 102.

[4] Ali Jafari et al. 2018. A Low-Power Wearable Stand-Alone Tongue Drive System for People With Severe Disabilities. *IEEE transactions on biomedical circuits and systems* 12, 1 (2018), 58–67.

[5] Alex Krizhevsky et al. [n. d.]. Imagenet classification with deep convolutional neural networks. In *Advances in neural information processing systems.*

[6] Alex Krizhevsky and Geoffrey Hinton. 2009. Learning multiple layers of features from tiny images. (2009).

[7] Adam Page et al. 2017. Sparcnet: A hardware accelerator for efficient deployment of sparse convolutional networks. *ACM Journal on Emerging Technologies in Computing Systems (JETC)* 13, 3 (2017), 31.

[8] Mohammad Rastegari et al. 2016. Xnor-net: Imagenet classification using binary convolutional neural networks. In *European Conference on Computer Vision.* Springer, 525–542.

[9] Attila Reiss and Didier Stricker. 2012. Introducing a new benchmarked dataset for activity monitoring. In *Wearable Computers (ISWC), 2012 16th International Symposium on.* IEEE, 108–109.

[10] Yaman Umuroglu et al. 2017. Finn: A framework for fast, scalable binarized neural network inference. In *Proceedings of the SIGDA.* ACM.

[11] Ritchie Zhao et al. 2017. Accelerating Binarized Convolutional Neural Networks with Software-Programmable FPGAs.. In *FPGA.* 15–24.

A Hybrid Approach to Equivalent Fault Identification for Verification Environment Qualification

Chia-Cheng Wu
National Tsing Hua University,
Hsincu, Taiwan, R.O.C.

Tung-Yuan Lee
National Tsing Hua University,
Hsincu, Taiwan, R.O.C.

Yung-An Lai
National Tsing Hua University,
Hsincu, Taiwan, R.O.C.

Hsin-Pei Wang
National Tsing Hua University,
Hsincu, Taiwan, R.O.C.

De-Xuan Ji
National Tsing Hua University,
Hsincu, Taiwan, R.O.C.

Yan-Ping Chang
National Tsing Hua University,
Hsincu, Taiwan, R.O.C.

Teng-Chia Wang
National Tsing Hua University,
Hsincu, Taiwan, R.O.C.

Chin-Heng Liu
National Tsing Hua University,
Hsincu, Taiwan, R.O.C.

Chun-Yao Wang
National Tsing Hua University,
Hsincu, Taiwan, R.O.C.

Yung-Chih Chen
Yuan Ze University,
Chungli, Taiwan, R.O.C.

ABSTRACT

Fault-based verification technique is a method to qualify a verification environment. The better verification environment can detect output differences between the fault-free and fault-injected circuits with a higher probability. Since different injected faults could cause the same output response under all stimuli, which are called equivalent faults, maximally identifying these equivalent faults can improve the efficiency of verification environment qualification without sacrificing its quality. The 2016 CAD Contest at ICCAD posed the problem of identifying equivalent faults in the circuits. This paper presents our work in the Contest with some improvements.

KEYWORDS

Verification environment qualification; fault injection; equivalent fault identification; mandatory assignment (MA)

ACM Reference Format:

Chia-Cheng Wu, Tung-Yuan Lee, Yung-An Lai, Hsin-Pei Wang, De-Xuan Ji, Yan-Ping Chang, Teng-Chia Wang, Chin-Heng Liu, Chun-Yao Wang, and Yung-Chih Chen. 2018. A Hybrid Approach to Equivalent Fault Identification for Verification Environment Qualification . In *Proceedings of Great Lakes Symposium on VLSI 2018 (GLSVLSI'18).* ACM, New York, NY, USA, 4 pages. https://doi.org/10.1145/3194554.3194635

1 INTRODUCTION

Functional verification is a task to confirm the consistency between the implementation and specification. When designs are getting more complex, the process of functional verification takes more time and effort. Simulation-based verification [15] has been a common practice in verification community. However, due to the fact that exhaustive simulation is infeasible for larger designs, *coverage metrics* have been proposed to measure the quality of verification and thus reduced the simulation cost.

Structural coverage metrics [8][13], also known as *code coverage metrics*, are such techniques. However, most structural coverage metrics only focus on activation of the design content from the stimuli, but do not consider the abilities of stimuli to propagate the error effects to observation points or Primary Outputs (POs). Therefore, the higher coverages in these metrics do not always imply the better quality of the verification environments. Thus, *Fault-based verification* technique [7][1][4][2], which is an effective approach for evaluating the quality of the verification environment, has been proposed afterward.

By injecting artificial faults into the original implementation, designers can examine whether the verification environment differentiates the faulty and fault-free designs. If all the injected faults can be detected, it indicates that the verification environment is robust and effective to reveal errors; otherwise, the verification environment contains some weakness points for improvement. Thus, the fault-based verification methodology *does* deal with the error effect propagation issue that the structural coverage metrics do not.

Mutation analysis is a fault-based verification technique originating from the software engineering [17]. Based on two Hypothesis: the *Competent Programmer Hypothesis* and *Coupling Effect Hypothesis*, mutation analysis only targets at a subset of all potential faults and assumes that these faults are sufficient to represent all faults. Competent Programmer Hypothesis states that programmers develop their programs very close to the correct version. Coupling Effect Hypothesis assumes that complex faults can be coupled by simple faults such that a test set detecting all the simple faults in a program will detect a very high percentage of the complex faults [6].

A commercial EDA tool, Certitude^{TM} [12][19], implements the mutation analysis approach, where RT-level designs are usually used for testbench qualification. Recently, *ISO 26262* [16], which is standard for defining functional safety of electrical and/or electronic systems of automobiles, has been deployed. In this standard, artificial faults are injected into gate-level designs [10][9][11][16]

This work is supported in part by the Ministry of Science and Technology of Taiwan under Grant MOST 106-2221-E-007-111-MY3, MOST 106-2221-E-155-056, MOST 103-2221-E-007-125-MY3, and MEDIATEK Research Center Doctoral Talent Fellowship

GLSVLSI'18, May 23–25, 2018, Chicago, IL, USA

ACM ISBN ISBN 978-1-4503-5724-1/18/05...$15.00
https://doi.org/10.1145/3194554.3194635

to see whether the verification environments can detect these faults or not.

Since the injected faults at different locations could cause the same output response under all stimuli, which are called *equivalent faults*, only one of these equivalent faults need to be verified within the verification environment. Thus, maximally identifying these equivalent faults reduces the number of faults to be injected, and improves the efficiency of a verification environment qualification, i.e., the number of verification patterns is reduced without sacrificing its quality. The 2016 CAD Contest at ICCAD [18] posed such problem of identifying equivalent faults, i.e., the faults having the same fault effect, in the circuits. Its formulation is as follows: Given a set of fault models and the original netlist of design consisting of two-input gates, to identify the equivalent faults maximally in the netlist for elevating the verification efficiency under a single fault injection mechanism.

In this paper, we present a hybrid approach to identify the equivalent faults efficiently. The approach consists of four steps, and they are fault collapsing, Mandatory Assignment (MA) calculation, structural matching, and redundant fault identification. To complete the description of the work, we will introduce all the steps in the paper. However, the MA calculation and structural matching steps, which are the main contributions of this work, will be emphasized. Furthermore, from the experimental perspective, these two steps also identify many equivalent faults within a few seconds.

2 PRELIMINARIES

2.1 Fault Model

11 types of fault models in the Contest are divided into three classes.

2.1.1 Stuck-at fault. The faulty wire is set to 0 or 1, and denoted as SA0 and SA1, respectively.

2.1.2 Negated fault. The faulty wire is inverted and denoted as NEG.

2.1.3 Gate-replacement fault. This fault changes the original driver gate type of a faulty wire. The faults in this class are denoted as RDOB_G, where G = { AND, NAND, OR, NOR, XOR, XNOR, NOT, BUFF}.

2.2 Equivalent Fault

With the fault models, a faulty circuit is derived by injecting a single fault into the original circuit. If two faulty circuits have the same output response under all input stimuli, these faults are equivalent faults.

3 EQUIVALENT FAULT IDENTIFICATION

This section presents the proposed algorithm for equivalent fault identification. The algorithm consists of four steps and they are fault collapsing, MA calculation, structural matching, and redundant fault identification.

3.1 Fault Collapsing

The fault collapsing step is only applied to the stuck-at fault model within a fanout-free region. This is because the fault-effect of a single fault in the fanout-free region remains singularly. The idea of fault collapsing is that when the fault-effect of two distinct stuck-at faults are the same, they are equivalent faults. For example, in Fig. 1, the fault-effect at a is 1/0 (fault-free value/faulty value), and b has to be assigned 1 to propagate the fault-effect 1/0 to c. For the output c SA0 fault, the fault-effect at c is also 1/0, and b is also 1. Thus, a SA0 fault and c SA0 fault have the same fault-effect and they are equivalent faults.

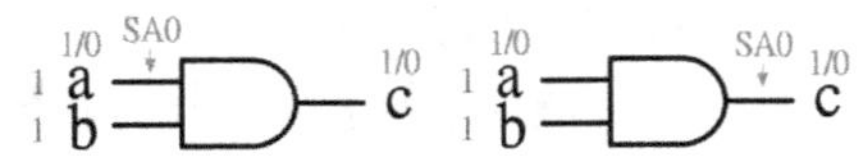

(a) (b)

Figure 1: Equivalent faults for an AND gate.

3.2 MA Calculation

The MA is the unique value assignment to a wire necessary for a test to exist. The *logic implication* is a process of computing MAs for a test. The MAs for a test on a wire w can be computed by setting the fault-activating value or setting the noncontrolling values on the side inputs of w's propagating path. Then, these assignments can be propagated forward or backward to obtain more MAs. Recursive learning [14], can be used to perform logic implications more completely. If the MAs of one fault are inconsistent, the fault is untestable.

To detect the considered fault models, we have to derive their test patterns. Different faults usually have different sets of test patterns. For two distinct but equivalent faults, however, their test pattern sets are identical. To express the test pattern set for a fault, we can explicitly enumerate every test pattern. However, choosing this way might be time-consuming. Thus, to express the test pattern set of a fault compactly, we can use the idea of MA. This is because MAs are the unique value assignments to wires necessary for a test pattern to exist. That is, MAs are the common value assignments to wires among all the test patterns of the fault. Unfortunately, computing all the MAs for detecting a fault, which is equivalent to deriving all the test patterns of a fault, is an NP-hard problem [3]. Thus, we propose another method to determine the equivalent faults based on a partial set of MAs as well as other information, which will be explained in detail in the following paragraphs.

In the process of MA calculation, sometimes we cannot determine a unique value assignment for a fanin node from a known MA at its output. Since these values are not unique for each fanin node, they are not MAs. We name these fanin pairs *active pairs*. For another example, in Fig. 2(a), to activate the fault-effect of $Fault_{g,RDOB\_NAND}$, the fanin nodes (h, i) = {(1, 1), (0, 1), (1, 0), (0, 0)}. This is because these value assignments can differentiate the NAND and AND from their output values. However, to propagate the fault-effect, we have to set (h, i) = (1, 1). As a result, only the active pair (h, i) = (1, 1) is kept, and h = 1, i = 1 are MAs. Furthermore b = 0 is an MA, and (j, k) = {(0, 1), (1, 0), (1, 1)} are active pairs by backward logic implications from h and i, respectively.

To determine the equivalent faults, it is not necessary to derive the test patterns for each fault. Here we propose the idea of *fault-effect influential region*. When injecting a fault into a circuit, certain subcircuit is influenced by the fault. We can construct the fault-effect influential region for representing a fault. This region is constructed in forward and backward directions. In the forward direction, it is from the fault site to the fanout node of the fault-propagating path or POs. In the backward direction, it is from the fault site to the active pairs, the wire with MAs, or PIs. To determine if two faults are equivalent or not, we can construct the fault-effect influential region for each fault first. If the boundaries of these two regions are identical, and the values on the boundaries are the same, these two faults are equivalent faults. This is because the circuit structures surrounding the fault-effect influential regions are exactly identical. Thus, the fault-effects propagation from these regions to the POs are the same. Theorem 1 is used for supporting this equivalent fault identification.

Theorem 1 : Given two faults, if the boundaries of their fault-effect

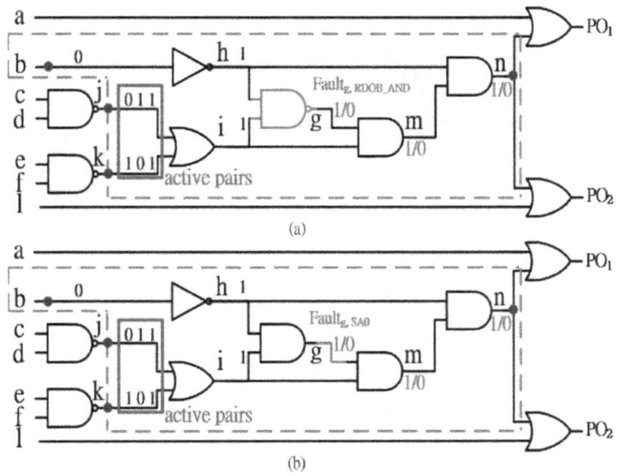

Figure 2: An example of calculating MAs and active pairs of two distinct faults injected into the same circuit. (a) An RDOB_NAND fault occurs at g. (b) A SA0 fault occurs at g.

influential regions are identical, and the values on the boundaries are the same, these two faults are equivalent.

For example, in Fig. 2, consider injecting two distinct faults at g $Fault_{g,RDOB\_NAND}$ and $Fault_{g,SA0}$ in Fig. 2(a) and Fig. 2(b). The dashed regions are their fault-effect influential regions. Since the boundaries of the regions are identical and the values on the boundaries are the same, these two faults are equivalent faults.

3.3 Structural Matching

Since computing all the MAs for a fault is computationally intensive, the MAs derived in the last step might be incomplete for cost and performance tradeoff. Thus, not every equivalent fault pair can be identified. However, we can use structural properties to identify additional equivalent faults. Since XOR and XNOR gates do not have MAs on the side inputs, this step is especially useful for them within fanout-free structures.

Next, we propose some conditions that assert the equivalence of two distinct faults.

Condition 1 : If the structures of two faulty circuits are identical, these two faults are equivalent faults.

Condition 2 : For an XOR or XNOR gate within a fanout-free structure, its input NEG fault and the output NEG fault are equivalent faults.

Definition 1 : A *fanout-free chain* is composed by two gates with a Common Side Input (CSI), and the other two inputs, *a*, *b*, are fanout-free as shown in Fig. 3. If only *b* is fanout-free, the chain is called a *loosened fanout-free chain.*

According to the locations of equivalent faults in a fanout-free chain, we further classify the equivalent faults into two classes and they are summarized in TABLE 1. Here we only discuss one case for class 1 and 2 in Condition 3-1 and Condition 3-2, respectively.

Condition 3-1 : For gate B = XOR and gate C = XOR in the fanout-free chain, a SA1 (SA0) fault at a and a SA1 (SA0) fault at c are equivalent.

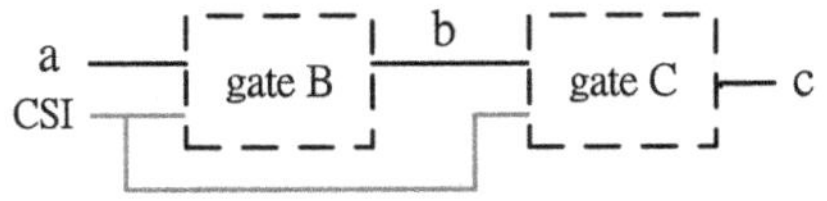

Figure 3: Fanout-free chain.

When an input of an XOR gate is determined, the XOR gate becomes a BUFF or NOT. Hence, we discuss this with a fixed CSI value. In Fig. 3, since a, b are fanout-free, if the CSI is 1, the circuit becomes two connected NOT gates, and the fault-effect at a can be only propagated to c. Similarly, if CSI is 0, the circuit becomes two connected BUFF gates, and the fault-effect at a can be only propagated to c, too. Thus, the fault-effect at c is the same as that at a. That is, $Fault_{a,SA0} = Fault_{c,SA0}$ and $Fault_{a,SA1} = Fault_{c,SA1}$. The other three cases in class 1 can be explained in a similar way.

Condition 3-2 : For gate B = XOR and gate C = XNOR in the loosened fanout-free chain, an RDOB_AND at b and an RDOB_NAND at c are equivalent.

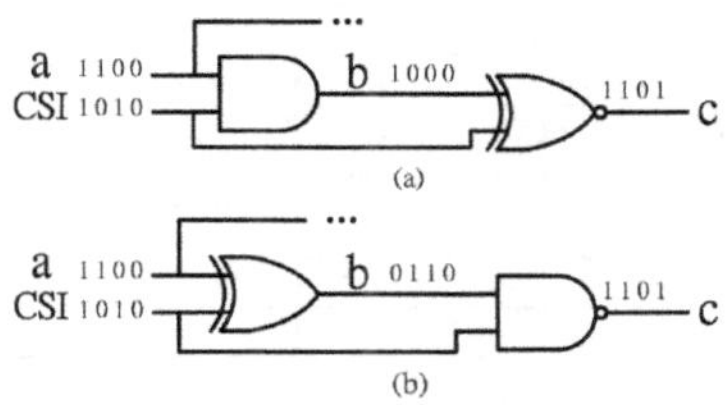

Figure 4: An example for Condition 3-2. (a) RDOB_AND at b. (b) RDOB_NAND at c.

Table 1: Equivalent faults by structural matching.

class	gate B	gate C	equivalent faults
1	**XOR**	**XOR**	**a SA0 = c SA0, a SA1 = c SA1**
	XNOR	XNOR	a SA0 = c SA0, a SA1 = c SA1
	XOR	XNOR	a SA0 = c SA1, a SA1 = c SA0
	XNOR	XOR	a SA0 = c SA1, a SA1 = c SA0
2	**XOR**	**XNOR**	**b RDOB_AND = c RDOB_NAND**
	XNOR	XOR	b RDOB_OR = c RDOB_NOR
	OR	XNOR	b SA0 = c RDOB_NAND
	OR	XOR	b SA0 = c RDOB_AND
	AND	XNOR	b SA1 = c RDOB_OR
	AND	XOR	b SA1 = c RDOB_NOR

3.4 Redundant Fault Identification

After running the first three steps, we group equivalent faults into a fault group. However, there might be groups of faults that are all redundant faults, and should be merged into one group. Next, in this step, we use SAT solvers to merge groups of redundant faults together.

Instead of comparing each fault group with the fault-free circuit exhaustively, we propose a heuristic to elevate the efficiency. We observed that the local functional difference between certain faulty circuit and the fault-free one is very small. This value assignment could be *Satisfiability Don't Cares* (SDCs) of faulty circuit. If this happens, the fault is a redundant fault. For example, when an RDOB_XOR fault replaces an OR gate, the local functional difference between them is only input pair (1, 1). We call this fault a *redundant fault candidate*. Then, we construct a Miter [5] from this faulty circuit and the fault-free circuit and use SAT solvers to verify if this redundant fault candidate is redundant or not. Using this way, only the fault groups containing a redundant fault candidate are considered for checking by SAT solvers, and the efficiency of this step is elevated.

4 EXPERIMENTAL RESULTS

The proposed algorithm was implemented in C++ and the experiments were conducted on the official platform of the Contest. In the experiment, we used the benchmarks which came from the 2016 CAD Contest [18] and compared the results with top three teams in the Contest. The Contest used 4 hidden benchmarks, Case05 to

Table 2: The experimental results on 2016 CAD Contest benchmarks.

Bench.	|PI|	|PO|	|gate|	Init.	Gold.	Team A			Team B			Team C			Ours			100%
						|gp|	CPU	Cov.	|gp|	CPU	Cov.	|gp|	CPU	Cov.	|gp|	CPU	Cov.	CPU
Case05	46	43	401	3098	2029	2044	0.4	98.5	2029	0.6	100	2029	1.0	100	2029	9.2	100	1221
Case06	13	14	648	5008	1020	1620	28.6	84.9	1020	41.6	100	1132	13.1	97.1	1132	4.4	97.1	3808
Case07	17	18	567	4352	1238	1870	14.9	79.7	1770	66.0	82.9	1492	41.2	91.8	1480	15.8	92.3	4011
Avg.	-	-	-	-	-	-	-	87.7	-	-	94.3	-	-	96.3	-	-	96.5	-

Table 3: The experimental results of each step for Case05 to Case07.

Bench.	Case05				Case06				Case07			
	|gp|	Cov.	|gp reduced|	CPU	|gp|	Cov.	|gp reduced|	CPU	|gp|	Cov.	|gp reduced|	CPU
Initial	3098	-	-	-	5008	-	-	-	4352	-	-	-
Fault Collapsing	2810	26.9	288	<0.001	4628	17.1	380	<0.001	3969	12.3	383	<0.001
MA Calculation	2275	77.0	535	0.17	1447	89.3	3181	2.42	1820	81.3	2149	11.83
Structural Matching	2029	100	246	<0.001	1132	97.1	315	0.01	1492	91.8	412	<0.001
Red. Fault Identification	2029	100	0	9	1132	97.1	0	2	1480	92.3	12	4
Total 1	-	-	-	9.17	-	-	-	4.43	-	-	-	15.83
100%	2029	100	0	1211.81	1020	100	112	3803.51	1238	100	170	3995.30
Total 2	-	-	-	1221	-	-	-	3808	-	-	-	4011

Case08, to evaluate the performance of each team. However, for confidentiality reasons, the Case08 benchmark was not publicly released from the Contest such that we cannot get the benchmark for the experiments.

The experimental results of our work and the top three teams in the Contest are summarized in TABLE 2. In TABLE 2, the first four columns show the benchmark information, which are all combinational. Columns 5 and 6 show the numbers of initial fault groups (Init.) and the golden results (Gold.). The golden results represent the maximal grouping of equivalent faults, which were obtained from the Contest. Any two fault groups in the golden result can be distinguished by at least one input vector. The next columns show the announced results of the top three teams, including the number of equivalent fault groups (|gp|), the CPU time measured in second (CPU), and the coverage (Cov.), from the Contest. The Cov. column is calculated by (Init. - |gp|) / (Init. - Gold.). Column Ours shows the corresponding results of our approach. We also show the CPU time of an approach for having 100% coverage in the last column. The approach for having 100% coverage uses SAT solvers to verify if any two fault groups from our results are functionally equivalent after conducting all the steps in Section III.

TABLE 3 also breaks down the results. The Cov. column represents the accumulated coverage from the initial step to the current step. The |gp reduced| column shows the number of fault group reduced in each step, and the CPU column represents the CPU time in each step. The Total 1 row shows the total CPU time used for all the steps in Section III. The Total 2 row shows the amount of CPU time needed for achieving 100% coverage. Our approach cost 9 seconds in the redundant fault identification step without reducing any group number for Case05. For Case07, the redundant fault identification step merges 12 fault groups while cost 4 seconds. However, for achieving 100% coverage, additional 3995 seconds were needed.

According to TABLE 2, our work achieved higher or equal coverages for all the benchmarks than the top three teams. Our average coverage is 96.5%. Furthermore, we can observe from TABLE 3 that the first three steps of our approach can achieve high coverages efficiently for each case. In some cases, we may spend extra time performing the step 4 without getting additional coverages. Nevertheless, with the step 4, we can identify redundant faults in acceptable CPU time.

5 CONCLUSION

Injecting artificial faults can examine whether the verification environment differentiates the faulty and fault-free designs. By maximally identifying equivalent faults, we can improve the efficiency of verification environment qualification. In this work, we propose a hybrid approach to identify equivalent faults in a circuit. In the experiment, the results show that our approach reached the highest average coverage on the hidden benchmarks compared to the winners of the Contest within 20 seconds CPU time.

REFERENCES

[1] A. Benso *et al.* 2007. A functional verification based fault injection environment. In *Proc. Defect and Fault-Tolerance in VLSI Systems.*

[2] A. Fin *et al.* 2000. A VHDL error simulator for functional test generation. In *Proc. Design, Automation and Test in Europe.*

[3] A. Veneris *et al.* 2002. Design rewiring using ATPG. In *IEEE Trans. CAD.*

[4] F. Ferrandi *et al.* 1998. Implicit test generation for behavioral VHDL models. In *Proc. Int. Test Conference.*

[5] F. V. Andrade *et al.* 2008. Improving SAT-based combinational equivalence checking through circuit preprocessing. In *Proc. of Int. Conference on CAD.*

[6] H. Y. Lin *et al.* 2012. A probabilistic analysis method for functional qualification under mutation analysis. In *Proc. Design, Automation and Test in Europe.*

[7] J. Arlat *et al.* 1993. Fault injection and dependability evaluation of fault-tolerant systems. In *IEEE Trans. Computers.*

[8] J. C. Miller *et al.* 1963. Systematic mistake analysis of digital computer programs. In *Commun. ACM.*

[9] L. Pintard *et al.* 2013. Fault injection in the automotive standard ISO 26262: An initial approach. In *Proc. European Workshop on Dependable Computing.*

[10] L. Pintard *et al.* 2014. From safety analyses to experi-mental validation of automotive embedded systems. In *Proc. of Pacific Rim International Symposium on Dependable Computing.*

[11] L. Pintard *et al.* 2015. Using fault injection to verify an AUTOSAR application according to the ISO 26262. In *Society of Automotive Engineers Technical Paper.*

[12] M. Hampton *et al.* 2007. Leveraging a commercial mutation analysis tool for research. In *Proc. Testing: Academic and Industrial Conference Practice and Research Techniques - Mutation.*

[13] S. Tasiran *et al.* 2001. Coverage metrics for functional validation of hardware designs. In *IEEE Design and Test of Computers.*

[14] W. Kunz *et al.* 1994. Recursive learning: A new implication technique for efficient solutions to CAD problems-test, verification, and optimization. In *IEEE Trans. CAD.*

[15] W. Kunz *et al.* 2005. Hardware design verification: Simulation and formal method-based approaches. In *Prentice Hall.*

[16] International Organization for Standardization. [n. d.]. https://www.iso.org/.

[17] R. Hamlet. 1977. Testing programs with the aid of a compiler. In *IEEE Trans. Software Engineering.*

[18] ICCAD. [n. d.]. http://cad-contest-2016.el.cycu.edu.tw/CAD-contest-at-ICCAD2016/.

[19] Synopsys. [n. d.]. https://www.synopsys.com/.

Memristive Crossbar Mapping for Neuromorphic Computing Systems on 3D IC

Qi Xu
EST Department, USTC
xuqi@mail.ustc.edu.cn

Song Chen
EST Department, USTC
songch@ustc.edu.cn

Bei Yu
CSE Department, CUHK
byu@cse.cuhk.edu.hk

Feng Wu
EEIS Department, USTC
fengwu@ustc.edu.cn

ABSTRACT

In recent years, neuromorphic computing systems based on memristive crossbar have provided a promising solution to enable acceleration of neural networks. Meanwhile, most of the neural networks used in realistic applications are often sparse. If such sparse neural network is directly implemented on a single memristive crossbar, it would result in inefficient hardware realizations. In this work, we propose 3D-FNC, a 3D floorplanning framework for neuromorphic computing systems in consideration of both crossbar utilization and design cost. 3D-FNC groups neurons that connect more common neurons into one cluster, where the optimal number of clusters is determined by L-method. As a result, the connections of a neural network can be effectively mapped to memristive crossbars or discrete synapses. Finally, a 3D floorplanning for memristive crossbars and neurons is developed to reduce area and wirelength cost. Experimental results show that 3D-FNC can achieve highly hardware-efficient designs, compared to state-of-the-art.

ACM Reference Format:
Qi Xu, Song Chen, Bei Yu, and Feng Wu. 2018. Memristive Crossbar Mapping for Neuromorphic Computing Systems on 3D IC . In *Proceedings of Great Lakes Symposium on VLSI (GLSVLSI'18)*. ACM, New York, NY, USA, Article 4, 4 pages. https://doi.org/10.1145/3194554.3194636

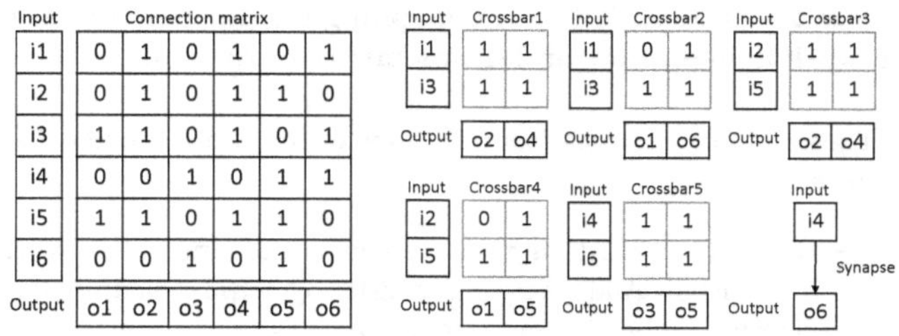

(a) (b)

Figure 1: (a) Connection matrix of a feed-forward neural network with six pre-synaptic neurons $\{i_1, \ldots, i_6\}$ and six post-synaptic neurons $\{o_1, \ldots, o_6\}$; (b) The connections are mapped to five memristive crossbars with high utilizations and one discrete synapse.

1 INTRODUCTION

Neuromorphic computing systems (NCS) based on hardware designs are intended to mimic neuro-biological architectures [1]. However, the CMOS technology implementation has been shown to suffer from mismatch between NCS building blocks (neuron and synapse) and CMOS primitives (Boolean logic) [2]. Moreover, based on the conventional CMOS technology, a large number of transistors are required to mimic a single synapse [3]. To address this problem, many neuromorphic designs on device and architecture level have been explored. The emerging memristor device inspires the approaches of using memristors to implement synapse circuit due to the similarity between the memristive and synaptic behaviors [4]. In order to achieve area efficient design, a memristive crossbar structure that connects all its **pre-synaptic** (i.e. input) neurons to all its **post-synaptic** (i.e. output) neurons is developed [5]. In addition, NCS with high complexity and high connectivity is required to implement increasingly demanding computational tasks. Traditional two-dimensional (2D) integration may be hard to meet these requirements, as longer signal transmission distances are introduced due to a large number of connections in 2D integration. On the other hand, three-dimensional integrated circuits (3D ICs) involve vertically stacking multiple dies connected by through silicon vias (TSVs), providing a promising way to enable high density and high computation speed in NCS [6]. Besides, 3D design in NCS can emulate real biophysical processing in human brain [7].

Many works for NCS implementation on memristive crossbars have been investigated. Wen *et al.* [8] proposed a design automation framework for large scale hybrid neuromorphic computing systems. Wu *et al.* [9] developed a thermal optimization for memristor-based hybrid neuromorphic computing systems. In [8, 9], an iterative spectral clustering is repeatedly performed to group the connections into memristive crossbars. However, since the spectral clustering is executed in every iteration, the methods could be time consuming when the neural network is large. Cui *et al.* [10] proposed a sparse matrix reordering method, which uses both row and column permutation matrices to group the connections into crossbars. However, crossbar utilization is not considered, thus the generated memristive crossbars with low utilization may result in highly area-inefficient designs. In addition, so far all previous works are based on 2D integration, thus some insurmountable obstacles are inevitably introduced by 2D circuits like larger chip area and longer wirelength etc.

To overcome the above issues, in this paper we propose 3D-FNC, a 3D floorplanning framework for neuromorphic computing systems in consideration of both crossbar utilization and design cost. Figure 1 illustrates an example how the proposed framework can effectively map the connections into crossbars with high utilizations. To represent a neural network, in this paper we use connection matrix, which is (0, 1)-matrix that "1" indicates a connection exists between two corresponding neurons and "0" means two corresponding neurons have no connection. As shown in Figure 1(a), if the sparse connection matrix is directly mapped to a crossbar, the utilization of the crossbar is low. However, through several techniques in our framework (e.g. hierarchical clustering), the mapped crossbars with high utilizations are shown in Figure 1(b). The corresponding 3D floorplan is shown

GLSVLSI'18, May 23–25, 2018, Chicago, IL USA

ACM ISBN 978-1-4503-5724-1/18/05...$15.00
https://doi.org/10.1145/3194554.3194636

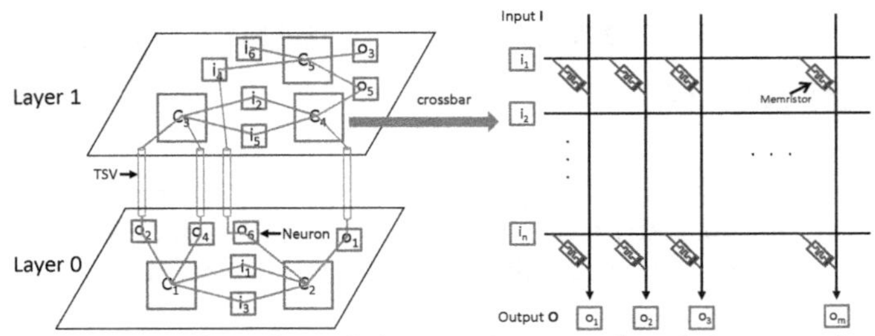

Figure 2: 3D floorplan of the mapping results of the neural network in Figure 1(a) and the memristive crossbar.

in Figure 2. Key technical contributions of this work are listed as follows.

- Hierarchical clustering groups neurons of a neural network into clusters. And the proposed distance metric can ensure that neurons connecting more common neurons are grouped into one cluster.
- An L-method is developed to determine the optimal number of clusters.
- A 3D floorplanning is implemented to minimize the hardware cost.

The remainder of this paper is organized as follows. Section 2 presents preliminaries of NCS. Section 3 is to describe the proposed 3D-FNC framework in details. Section 4 lists experimental results, followed by conclusion in Section 5.

2 PRELIMINARIES

In a neural network, the pre-synaptic neurons send signals into the network and the post-synaptic neurons receive information from the pre-synaptic neurons through the synapses [11]. The synapses apply different weights on the information during the transmission, which can be expressed as $\boldsymbol{O} = \boldsymbol{IC}$. An element c_{ij} in the connection matrix $\boldsymbol{C}$ represents the weight of a synapse between the pre-synaptic neuron i in $\boldsymbol{I}$ and the post-synaptic neuron j in $\boldsymbol{O}$. Since the resistance of memristor is programmed by applying current or voltage, the memristor can be used to implement the weight of the synapse [5]. A memristive crossbar example is shown in Figure 2.

In realistic applications, the size of neural networks is often very large. For instance, AlexNet proposed by Krizhevsky *et al.* [12] in 2012 contains $650K$ neurons and $60M$ synapses. In addition, most of large neural networks are sparse. If a sparse neural network is directly implemented on a memristive crossbar, the crossbar utilization can be low, resulting in highly area-inefficient designs. In this paper, we define the utilization of a memristive crossbar as the ratio between the utilized number of connections and the total available connections in the crossbar. In order to enable energy and area efficient design, the large neural network with high sparsity should be implemented by using smaller size crossbars or discrete synapses.

We define the problem of 3D floorplanning for neuromorphic computing systems (3D-FNC) as follows.

Problem 1 (3D-FNC). Given a sparse neural network with n neurons, we map the connections into memristive crossbars with high utilization or discrete synapses. Then we implement the 3D floorplanning of memristive crossbars and neurons to minimize chip area, wirelength, and TSV numbers.

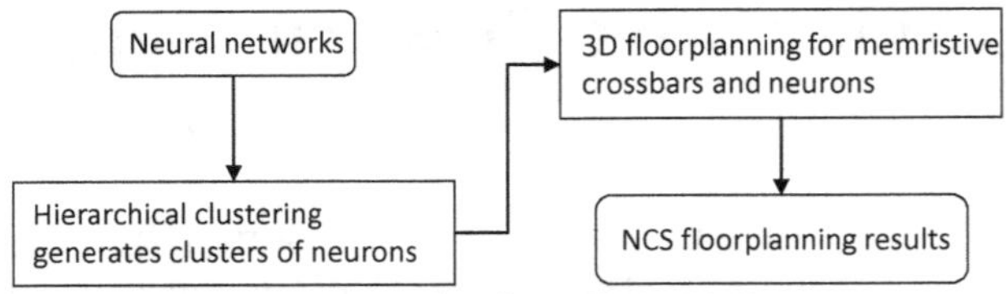

Figure 3: The flow of 3D-FNC.

Algorithm 1 Hierarchical clustering to cluster neurons

Input: Connection matrix C.
Output: A dendrogram of neurons.

Assign each neuron to a cluster;
Calculate distances among clusters; ▷ Equation (1)
for $i \leftarrow 1$ to $n-1$ **do**
  Merge two clusters $\{r\}$ and $\{s\}$ with the shortest distance;
  ▷ Update distances between $\{r,s\}$ and other clusters $\{k\}$
  $d_{\{k\},\{r,s\}} \leftarrow \min[d_{\{k\},\{r\}}, d_{\{k\},\{s\}}]$;
end for
All neurons are clustered into one cluster;

3 3D-FNC FRAMEWORK

Given a sparse neural network, the proposed hierarchical clustering partitions all the neurons into clusters, so that the connections can be easily mapped to set of crossbars with high utilization. Based on the cluster results, we implement a 3D floorplanning of neuromorphic computing systems to achieve a minimum chip area, wirelength, and TSV numbers under fixed-outline and no-overlapping constraints [13]. In this work, the memristive crossbars and the neurons are considered as blocks. The partitioned sequence pair (P-SP) [14] is used to represent 3D floorplans. The chip area is evaluated by the method in [15], which takes the fixed-outline constraint into account. To evaluate the wirelength, we adopt the calculation model in [16] to decompose the nets spanning multiple device layers into sub-nets, one on each device layer, by introducing dummy pins corresponding to TSVs. Besides, the number of TSVs of a net is $|j-i|$ if the net spans layer i to layer j. The flow of 3D-FNC is shown in Figure 3.

3.1 Hierarchical Clustering

Hierarchical clustering is used to generate clusters in a bottom-up iterative manner [17]. In every iteration, two clusters with the shortest distance are merged. Implication of "distance" varies with specific applications in practice. The iterative merging is repeated until all data points are formed into one cluster.

In our proposed framework, we aim to generate clusters that can be mapped to memristive crossbars with high utilization. Therefore, the neurons that connect more common neurons should be grouped into one cluster. In this work, the hierarchical clustering is adopted to cluster neurons. We redefine the distance between two neurons, i_p and i_q ($1 \le p, q \le n$), as follows:

$$\text{dist}(i_p, i_q) = \sqrt{\sum_{j=1}^{n} (c_{pj} \,\&\, c_{qj} - 1)^2}, \tag{1}$$

where c_{pj} represents the connection between neuron i_p and neuron o_j (same for c_{qj}). Since two clusters with the shortest distance are merged in every iteration, the distance metric in Equation (1) can ensure the neurons connecting more common neurons are grouped into cluster.

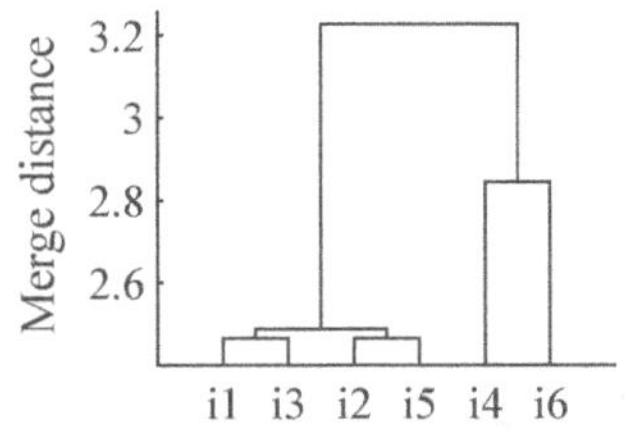

Figure 4: A hierarchical clustering dendrogram.

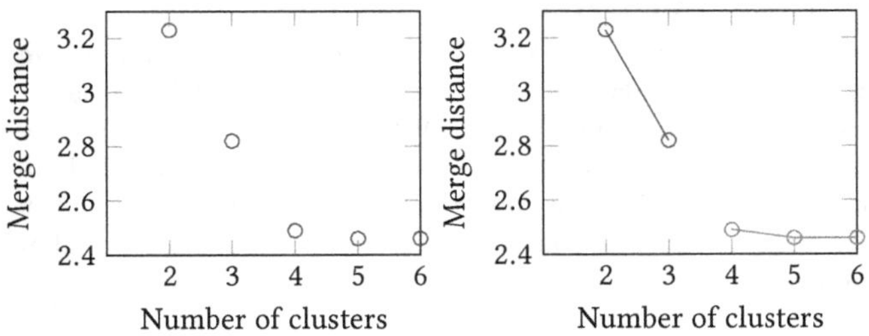

(a) (b)

Figure 5: (a) The evaluation graph of the connection matrix shown in Fig. 1(a). (b) Two best-fit lines are obtained at the transition point x=3 by the L-method.

The flow of hierarchical clustering is shown in Algorithm 1. Starting from n data points, hierarchical clustering first treats each point as a single cluster (line 1). Then the iterative merging steps are performed n-1 times and eventually build a dendrogram (cluster tree) (lines 3–8). Therefore, the data points that are close will be merged first, and far away clusters will not be merged until the late iterations [18]. Figure 4 is used to illustrate the process of hierarchical clustering. For the connection matrix of one layer in a feed-forward neural network shown in Figure 1(a), it contains six pre-synaptic neurons and six post-synaptic neurons. During the first iteration, pre-synaptic neurons i_1 and i_3 are merged into a cluster since the distance between them is the smallest (connect three common post-synaptic neurons o_2, o_4, and o_6). Next, i_2 and i_5 are merged to form a cluster. Finally, two clusters $\{i_1, i_2, i_3, i_5\}$ and $\{i_4, i_6\}$ are merged into one cluster. The generated dendrogram is shown in Figure 4.

3.2 Optimal Number of Clusters

Although the hierarchical clustering can generate a cluster tree, however, if the number of clusters is not given, the hierarchical clustering cannot build the final clustering result. In this work, the L-method is proposed to find the optimal number of clusters. We summarize the major steps of the L-method for selection of the number of clusters in Algorithm 2. The L-method is based on an evaluation graph where the x-axis is the number of clusters and the y-axis is the evaluation metric used by the clustering algorithm. For the hierarchical clustering, the y-axis values are the merge distance between the last two merged clusters at x clusters. Since the hierarchical clustering merges a pair of clusters in every iteration, the evaluation graph can be produced by running the clustering algorithm only once (line 1). Note that the sharp transition point on the evaluation graph is considered to be the optimal number of clusters [19].

To illustrate how the L-method works, we use the connection matrix shown in Figure 1(a) as an example. Based on the dendrogram generated by hierarchical clustering, we plot the evaluation graph in Figure 5(a), where x-axis shows the number of clusters and y-axis represents the merge distance d. The L-method tries to determine the optimal number by searching for two lines that can best-fit the evaluation graph, and the intersection of these two lines represent the transition point of the graph. In Figure 5(b), the two lines can accurately fit the graph where one line fits the data in the interval $x \in [2, 3]$ and the other line fits the data in the interval $x \in [4, 6]$. It can be noticed that the sharp transition point is located at x=3, meaning that the neurons should be grouped into 3 clusters.

Algorithm 2 L-method for selection of cluster numbers

Input: A cluster tree generated by the hierarchical clustering.
Output: The optimal number of clusters $\hat{t}$.

```
1: Construct the evaluation graph based on the cluster tree;
2: for each point t ← 3 to n − 2 do
3:     Solve the regression problem at t;          ▷ Equation (2)
4:     Calculate RMSE_t at t;                      ▷ Equation (3)
5: end for
6: Determine t̂;                                   ▷ Equation (4)
```

Mathematically, the L-method can be formulated as the regression problem [18] (lines 2–5). Considering the evaluation graph where the number of clusters varies from 2 to n (n-1 data points in the graph), and the data points are partitioned into a left region and a right region at transition point x=t. The left region has points with $x \in [2, t]$, and the right region has points with $x \in [t+1, n]$. To ensure each region contains at least two points, the value of t ranges from 3 to n-2. Then the regression problem is solved respectively to achieve two best-fit lines for the left and the right regions as follows:

$$\begin{aligned} \mathrm{RMSE}_l &= \min_{s_l, b_l} \|\boldsymbol{d}_l - s_l \cdot \boldsymbol{x}_l - \boldsymbol{b}_l\|_2, \\ \mathrm{RMSE}_r &= \min_{s_r, b_r} \|\boldsymbol{d}_r - s_r \cdot \boldsymbol{x}_r - \boldsymbol{b}_r\|_2, \end{aligned} \tag{2}$$

where $\boldsymbol{d}_l$ and $\boldsymbol{d}_r$ are the merge distance values for left region $\boldsymbol{x}_l \in [2, t]^\top$ and right region $\boldsymbol{x}_r \in [t+1, n]^\top$, respectively. ($s_l$, b_l) and (s_r, b_r) represent the slope and bias for left-fit and right-fit lines. RMSE_l and RMSE_r are the root mean square error of the two best-fit lines. Then the total root mean square error (RMSE_t) is defines as follows:

$$\mathrm{RMSE}_t = \frac{t-1}{n-1} \cdot \mathrm{RMSE}_l + \frac{n-t}{n-1} \cdot \mathrm{RMSE}_r. \tag{3}$$

We solve the regression problems for all values of t, and the transition point that achieves the minimum RMSE_t is assumed as the optimal number of clusters (line 6):

$$\hat{t} = \operatorname*{argmin}_{t \in [3, n-2]} \ \mathrm{RMSE}_t. \tag{4}$$

After solving the regression problem for the evaluation graph in Figure 4, the transition point x=3 can achieve minimum total root mean square error for the two lines. The three clusters are $\{i_1, i_3\}$, $\{i_2, i_5\}$, and $\{i_4, i_6\}$, respectively.

4 EXPERIMENTAL RESULTS

We implement the hierarchical clustering and the L-method in MATLAB on a 2.20 GHZ 64 bit Windows 7 machine with 4 GB RAM. 3D floorplanning is implemented in C++ language on a 12-core 2.0 GHz Linux server with 64 GB RAM.

4.1 Impact of L-Method

In this work, based on the evaluation graph generated by hierarchical clustering, the L-method can find the optimal number of clusters. In

Table 1: Effectiveness of the proposed 3D-FNC.

Bench	Sparsity	AutoNCS [8]					3D-FNC w/o. LM					3D-FNC				
		Area (um^2)	Wire (um)	#TSV	util	RT(s)	Area (um^2)	Wire (um)	#TSV	util	RT(s)	Area (um^2)	Wire (um)	#TSV	util	RT(s)
n300	94.47%	3925.17	93398.64	353	0.65	20.37	4058.70	96424.28	349	0.45	6.46	3814.78	94389.73	358	0.67	5.21
n400	93.59%	7318.64	269163.17	427	0.76	35.28	7381.36	276821.31	420	0.57	13.23	7153.36	272542.70	426	0.77	11.17
n500	94.39%	10521.18	407018.25	491	0.70	69.43	10994.21	429515.68	477	0.47	32.14	10502.32	411046.51	485	0.68	29.62
avg.	94.15%	7255.00	256526.69	424	0.70	41.69	7478.09	267587.09	416	0.50	17.28	7156.82	259326.31	423	0.71	15.33
ratio	–	1.01	0.99	1.00	0.99	2.72	1.04	1.03	0.98	0.70	1.13	1.00	1.00	1.00	1.00	1.00

order to see the effect of the L-method, we compare the floorplanning results on the clustering results with and without the L-method. Since the size of crossbar, $s \times s$, is limited by the memristive technology, the maximum size of crossbars is set to 64×64 in this work [8]. Without the L-method, the number of clusters is determined by the way, in which iteratively increasing the number of clusters by one in hierarchical clustering until the size of the largest crossbar is below the size limitation. Then we run the 3D floorplanning on the clustering results of the case with and without L-method, respectively. The layer number is set to 2. The area of the neuron in 45nm technology is 2500um^2 [20]. Besides each memristor and memristive crossbar use $4f^2$ and $s^2 \cdot 40f^2$ circuit area (f=feature size), respectively [11]. The experiment is tested on three Hopfield networks in [8] with the size of 300, 400, and 500. In Table 1, "3D-FNC w/o. LM" and "3D-FNC" list the average results. Column "util" gives the average utilization of all mapped crossbars. Columns "Area", "Wire" and "#TSV" represent chip area, total half-perimeter wirelength overhead, and the number of TSVs, respectively. We can see that in the case without L-method, the utilization of mapped crossbars are reduced by nearly 30%. In addition, area and wirelength are increased by around 4% and 3%, which demonstrates that the hierarchical clustering with L-method can result in highly hardware-efficient designs.

4.2 Comparison with Previous Work

We compare 3D-FNC with AutoNCS [8] on the hardware cost. In AutoNCS, the iterative spectral clustering is used for grouping the connections into the memristive crossbars. Since AutoNCS only generates 2D floorplanning output, to provide a fair comparison, we also implement a 3D floorplanning based on the iterative spectral clustering results of AutoNCS. The experiment is also tested on three Hopfield networks in [8] with the size of 300, 400, and 500. Table 1 lists the average statistic results. Column "RT" reports the total computational time in seconds. As shown in Table 1, compared with AutoNCS, 3D-FNC can achieve comparable area, wirelength cost and crossbar utilization, while the runtime of 3D-FNC is far less than AutoNCS. That is because in AutoNCS, the spectral clustering is executed in every iteration, thus the clustering method could be time consuming when the neural network is large.

5 CONCLUSION

In this paper, we have proposed an effective memristive crossbar mapping for neuromorphic computing systems on 3D IC, where both crossbar utilization and design cost are considered. Experimental results show that, compared with state-of-the-art, the proposed 3D-FNC can achieve highly hardware-efficient designs. Memristive crossbar gives hope for the anticipated efficient implementation of artificial neuromorphic networks, thus we expect to see a lot of researches to provide more efficient physical synthesis solutions.

ACKNOWLEDGMENTS

This work was supported in part by the National Natural Science Foundation of China (NSFC) under grant No. 61732020 and The Research Grants Council of Hong Kong SAR (Project No. CUHK24209017). The authors would like to thank the Information Science Laboratory Center of USTC for hardware and software services, as well as Prof. Tsung-Yi Ho from National Tsing Hua University for providing test benches.

REFERENCES

[1] Y. Chen, H. H. Li, C. Wu, C. Song, S. Li, C. Min, H.-P. Cheng, W. Wen, and X. Liu, "Neuromorphic computing's yesterday, today, and tomorrow–an evolutional view," *Integration, the VLSI Journal*, 2017.

[2] A. Ankit, A. Sengupta, and K. Roy, "Trannsformer: Neural network transformation for memristive crossbar based neuromorphic system design," *arXiv preprint arXiv:1708.07949*, 2017.

[3] F. Akopyan, J. Sawada, A. Cassidy, and et.al, "Truenorth: Design and tool flow of a 65 mw 1 million neuron programmable neurosynaptic chip," *IEEE TCAD*, vol. 34, no. 10, pp. 1537–1557, 2015.

[4] S. Acciarito, A. Cristini, G. Susi, and et.al, "Hardware design of lif with latency neuron model with memristive stdp synapses," *Integration, the VLSI Journal*, 2017.

[5] M. Hu, H. Li, Q. Wu, and G. S. Rose, "Hardware realization of bsb recall function using memristor crossbar arrays," in *Proc. DAC*, 2012, pp. 498–503.

[6] M. A. Ehsan, Z. Zhou, and Y. Yi, "Neuromorphic 3D integrated circuit: A hybrid, reliable and energy efficient approach for next generation computing," in *Proc. GLSVLSI*, 2017, pp. 221–226.

[7] H. An, M. A. Ehsan, Z. Zhou, F. Shen, and Y. Yi, "Monolithic 3D neuromorphic computing system with hybrid CMOS and memristor-based synapses and neurons," *Integration, the VLSI Journal*, 2017.

[8] W. Wen, C.-R. Wu, X. Hu, B. Liu, T.-Y. Ho, X. Li, and Y. Chen, "An eda framework for large scale hybrid neuromorphic computing systems," in *Proc. DAC*, 2015, pp. 1–6.

[9] C.-R. Wu, W. Wen, T.-Y. Ho, and Y. Chen, "Thermal optimization for memristor-based hybrid neuromorphic computing systems," in *Proc. ASPDAC*, 2016, pp. 274–279.

[10] J. Cui and Q. Qiu, "Towards memristor based accelerator for sparse matrix vector multiplication," in *Proc. ISCAS*, 2016, pp. 121–124.

[11] B. Liu, Y. Chen, B. Wysocki, and T. Huang, "The circuit realization of a neuromorphic computing system with memristor-based synapse design," in *Neural Information Processing*, 2012, pp. 357–365.

[12] A. Krizhevsky, I. Sutskever, and G. E. Hinton, "Imagenet classification with deep convolutional neural networks," in *Proc. NIPS*, 2012, pp. 1097–1105.

[13] Q. Xu and S. Chen, "Fast thermal analysis for fixed-outline 3D floorplanning," *Integration, the VLSI Journal*, vol. 59, pp. 157–167, 2017.

[14] P. H. Shiu, R. Ravichandran, S. Easwar, and S. K. Lim, "Multi-layer floorplanning for reliable system-on-package," in *Proc. ISCAS*, vol. 5, 2004, pp. V–69.

[15] S. Chen and T. Yoshimura, "Fixed-outline floorplanning: Enumerating block positions and a new objective function for calculating area costs," *IEEE TCAD*, vol. 27, no. 5, pp. 858–871, 2008.

[16] S. Chen, L. GE, M.-F. Chiang, and T. Yoshimura, "Lagrangian relaxation based inter-layer signal via assignment for 3-D ICs," *IEICE Transactions on Fundamentals of Electronics, Communications and Computer Sciences*, vol. 92, no. 4, pp. 1080–1087, 2009.

[17] R. C. Dubes and A. K. Jain, *Algorithms for clustering data*. New Jersey: Prentice Hall Englewood Cliffs, 1988.

[18] M. B. Alawieh, F. Wang, and X. Li, "Identifying wafer-level systematic failure patterns via unsupervised learning," *IEEE TCAD*, 2017.

[19] S. Salvador and P. Chan, "Determining the number of clusters/segments in hierarchical clustering/segmentation algorithms," in *Proc. ICTAI*, 2004, pp. 576–584.

[20] J.-s. Seo, B. Brezzo, Y. Liu, and et.al, "A 45nm CMOS neuromorphic chip with a scalable architecture for learning in networks of spiking neurons," in *Proc. CICC*, 2011, pp. 1–4.

Impact of Aging on Template Attacks

Naghmeh Karimi
CSEE Department
University of Maryland Baltimore County
nkarimi@umbc.edu

Sylvain Guilley
Secure-IC S.A.S.
LTCI, Télécom ParisTech & ENS
sylvain.guilley@secure-ic.com

Jean-Luc Danger
LTCI, Télécom ParisTech
Secure-IC S.A.S.
danger@telecom-paristech.fr

ABSTRACT

Template attack is the most powerful side-channel attack from an information theoretic point of view. This attack is launched in two phases. In the first phase (training) the attacker uses a training device to estimate leakage models for targeted intermediate computations, which are then exploited in the second phase (matching) to extract secret information from the target device. Process variation and discrepancy of operating conditions (e.g., temperature) between training and matching phases adversely affect the success probability of the attack. Attack-success degradation is exacerbated when device aging comes into account. Due to aging, electrical specifications of transistors change over time. Thereby, if the training and target devices have experienced different usage time, the attack will be more difficult. Aging alignment between training and target devices is difficult as aging degradation is highly affected by operating conditions and technological variations. This paper investigates the effect of aging on the success rate of template attacks. In particular, we focus on NBTI and HCI aging mechanisms. We mount several attacks on the PRESENT cipher at different temperatures and aging times. Our results show that the attack is more difficult if there is an aging-duration mismatch between the training and target devices.

ACM Reference Format:
Naghmeh Karimi, Sylvain Guilley, and Jean-Luc Danger. 2018. Impact of Aging on Template Attacks. In *GLSVLSI '18: 2018 Great Lakes Symposium on VLSI, May 23–25, 2018, Chicago, IL, USA.* ACM, New York, NY, USA, 4 pages. https://doi.org/10.1145/3194554.3194638

1 INTRODUCTION

With the aggressive scaling of VLSI technology, various design robustness concerns continue to arise. Among them, aging effects in CMOS devices are one of the major challenges in nanotechnologies. Due to aging, electrical behavior of transistors deviates from its original behavior. This deviation degrades performance; and consequently, the chip fails to meet some of the required specifications [1]. Among aging mechanisms, due to their critical role in urging circuits malfunctions, Negative-Bias Temperature-Instability (NBTI), Hot-Carrier Injection (HCI), and gate Oxide Breakdown (OB) have received the lion's share of attention [2]. Guard-banding, gate-sizing, and voltage tuning are among the methods used in industry to reduce the aging effects. However, these schemes are either insufficient or otherwise over-pessimistic as the rate of aging degradation depends on operating conditions including temperature, voltage bias, and workload [3]. Thereby, aging effects cannot be thoroughly prevented.

GLSVLSI '18, May 23–25, 2018, Chicago, IL, USA

ACM ISBN 978-1-4503-5724-1/18/05...$15.00
https://doi.org/10.1145/3194554.3194638

Aging mitigation is critical not only from device reliability point of view but also regarding device security perspectives. With the increasingly reliance on integrated circuits, it is essential to assure the security of the sensitive tasks performed by these circuits and to guarantee the security of information stored within these devices. In practice, any device that contains a secret data such as a cryptographic key can be targeted by an adversary. Cryptographic cores are used to protect various devices but their physical implementation can be compromised by adversaries via observing dynamic circuit emanations in order to extract the secrets they conceal [4].

Breaking cryptographic secrets by exploiting physical information while a device is processing sensitive data is known as side-channel attack [4]. In this attack, the adversary analyzes the physical leakage (e.g., running time, power consumption, electromagnetic radiation) emitted during cryptographic operations in the device and retrieves the secret information by considering the dependency of this leakage and the secret data. In particular, power analysis attacks analyze the device power consumption to extract the secret information.

Differential power analysis (DPA), correlation power analysis (CPA), mutual information analysis (MIA), and template attacks are the most common power analysis attacks [4–7]. The first three are categorized as non-profiling attacks, as they do not need device characterization before launching the attack, while template attack is a profiling attack that includes a characterization step in which the templates are computed on a training device, and an attack step in which the templates are used to extract the secret data of the target device.

Due to the strength of template attacks in leaking information, in this paper we focus on these attacks and investigate the effect of device aging on their success. As mentioned, due to the aging, electrical specifications of transistors such as their threshold voltage deviate from their original one and thereby power traces change accordingly. If the power traces deployed in the profiling phase of the template attack have been extracted from a new (non-aged) device while the attacker tries to retrieve the secret key of a used device, the aging-related deviation of device parameters may result in modeling mismatch. A similar scenario occurs when the profiled and attack devices experience different usage time (aging). Accordingly, for the first time in the scientific literature, we investigate the effect of aging on the success of template attacks launched on cryptographic devices. The contributions of this paper are as follows:

- A simulation framework which integrates device aging and its security evaluation against template attacks;
- Detailed HSpice MOSRA simulations to evaluate the effect of NBTI and HCI degradations on the success rate of template attacks launched on the PRESENT cipher.

The rest of this paper is organized as follows. Section 2 presents the backgrounds on aging mechanisms and template attacks. Section 3 motivates this research and argues how the template attack is affected by various mismatch of training and attack devices. Experimental results are presented in Section 4. Conclusions are drawn in Section 5.

2 PRELIMINARIES

Background on Aging Mechanisms: Device aging results in performance degradation and eventual failure of digital circuits over time. Among other aging mechanisms, NBTI and HCI are two leading factors in performance degradation of digital circuits. Both mechanisms result in increasing switching and path delays in the circuit under stress, and eventually lead to faster wearout of the system.

NBTI occurs in PMOS transistors. A PMOS transistor experiences two phases of NBTI depending on its operating condition. The first phase (*stress*) occurs when the transistor is "on". In this phase, positive interface traps are generated at the Si-SiO_2 interface which lead to an increase of the threshold-voltage (V_{th}) of the transistor. The second phase (*recovery*) occurs when the transistor is "off". In this phase, the V_{th} drift that occurred during the stress phase will partially recover. Physical parameters of a transistor, supply voltage, temperature, and stress time all affect the magnitude of its threshold voltage drift [3]. Figure 1 shows the V_{th} drift of a PMOS transistor that is continuously under stress for 6 months and a transistor that alternates stress/recovery phases every other month. The values on Y axis are not shown to make the graph generic for different technologies.

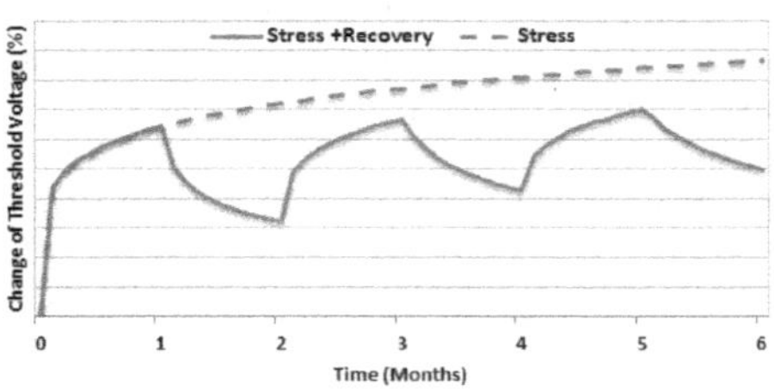

Figure 1: The effect of NBTI aging on a PMOS Transistor.

HCI mainly occurs in NMOS transistors when hot carriers are injected into the gate dielectric during transistor switching and remain there. HCI is a function of switching activity, and degrades the circuit by shifting the threshold-voltage and drain current of transistors under stress. HCI-induced threshold-voltage drift is sensitive to the number of transitions occurring in the gate input of the transistor under stress. HCI effects also depend on the operating temperature [8].

Background on PRESENT Cipher: PRESENT is a lightweight block cipher with 64-bit blocks and a bit oriented permutation layer [9]. It includes 31 rounds and supports two key lengths of 80 and 128 bits. Each encryption round consists of a bitwise XOR operation, a non-linear substitution layer and a linear permutation layer. The non-linear layer uses a single 4-bit S-box which is applied 16 times in parallel in each round [9].

Background on Template Attacks: Side-Channel Attacks (SCA) are mainly launched by adversaries to obtain secret information of a device, e.g., a cryptographic key. These attacks retrieve the secret key by analyzing the physical leakage emitted during operation of a device (e.g., its running time, and power consumption), as this leakage is statistically dependent on the secret key [4]. Profiled SCAs (e.g., template attacks) are the most powerful type of SCAs in which an attacker is able to characterize the leakage of an additional similar device and use the extracted information to break the targeted device.

Template attacks are launched in two phases: training and attack. During training, the attacker has a full control on another copy of the device, and records a large number of traces of the cloned device, corresponding to random values of inputs (plaintexts and keys). These traces are utilized to build a template y_k from the device, using key k. Then, in the attack phase, the recorded traces are classified according to the value of the key and template matching is performed to derive the key value of the target device [7].

In this paper, we aim at studying template attacks in terms of success rate, by analyzing how factors such as aging, temperature and process variation affect them. We consider an ideal setup (for the attacker) where training and attacked devices are otherwise equal, but different in terms of aging, process variations, and temperature. In practice, the actual discrepancy results from a combination of those three (or even more) mismatch factors. We will quantify how these factors contribute in decreasing the success rate of template attacks.

3 AGING-RELATED MISMATCH BETWEEN TEMPLATE AND ATTACK DATA

In side-channel attacks to retrieve the secret data, key-dependent leakage models are compared with actual measurements of the target chip. Thereby, the accuracy of the utilized models highly affects the success of the attack. Although profiling attacks, include an offline learning phase to estimate the leakage model, the profiling method is based on some assumptions (such as Gaussian noise models) or even model estimation can be bounded by the number of measurements during the characterization. Thereby, one of the main challenges in these attacks is to avoid being biased by an incorrect model [10]. In practice, it is hard to reproduce an exact similar operating condition (e.g., temperature) in both profiling and matching phases. Process variations occurring during the manufacturing process also result in discrepancies between profiling and matching chips.

In this research, we focus on a discrepancy that cannot be avoided, i.e., device aging. In practice, it is difficult (if not impossible) to align the age of the profiling and the target devices. One option could be to "accelerate aging" in the younger device (whether it is the profiling or the target one) by artificial aging (e.g., placing the chip in a climate chamber to accelerate aging). However, as aging degradation rate changes exponentially with the drift of operating conditions [3], a slight deviation in the input parameters strongly impacts the acceleration rate. Thereby, it is interesting to quantify how much the security is impacted by the unavoidable effect of aging. In this paper, we study the impact of aging on the success of the template attack.

4 RESULTS AND DISCUSSIONS

4.1 Experimental Setup

We implemented the add-round-key and S-box operations in the first round of the PRESENT cipher with 80-bit keys. Our implementation represents the most compact S-box architecture presented in [11, §3].

The circuit has been implemented in the transistor level using 45-nm NANGATE technology [12]. We used Synopsys HSpice for the transistor-level simulations and deployed the HSpice built-in MOSRA Level 3 model to assess the effect of NBTI and HCI aging [13]. Power traces were extracted for a new device as well as aged devices. The effect of aging was evaluated for 20 weeks of device operation in time steps of one week, in different operating temperatures. As each S-box module in the PRESENT cipher has $n = 4$ input bits, we have a total of $2^{2n} = 256$ input transitions in the S-box. All of these transitions were considered in the profiling phase of the template attacks. The simulated traces contain two parts: the results of key addition and S-box outputs for each initial n-bit value as well as its following n-bit value. For the attack, we considered only the second clock cycle, when the cryptographic circuit transitions from *initial* to *final* value. Cryptographic functions, by essence, randomize the data they manipulate. Therefore, it is natural that in "steady cruising

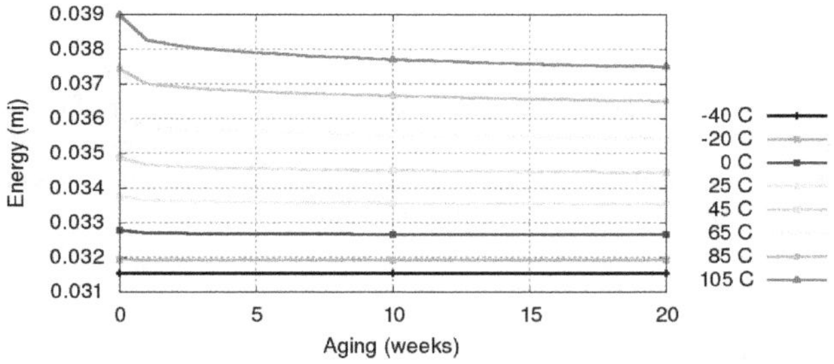

Figure 2: Average energy of S-box for different temperatures and aging.

speed" all possible transitions are considered with equal probability of 2^{-2n} (1/256 when $n=4$). The actual order of the transitions has no real impact as long as all transitions are asymptotically equiprobable.

4.2 Experimental Results

4.2.1 Impact of aging on the average energy consumption in S-box. The first set of results deals with the effect of aging on the energy consumed to compute S-box outputs. In this experiment, we first performed HSpice simulations using all 256 input transitions and recorded the instantaneous power consumption related to each input transition over time. We repeated the simulations for different temperatures and aging times. Then, we evaluated the average energy consumption of S-box using the recorded values. Fig. 2 depicts the distribution of average energy consumption in S-box for different temperatures. As expected, the average energy consumption decreases over time. This is because aging results in the increase of the threshold-voltage of transistors under stress and thus in the decrease of the drain current through them. The degradation is more visible in the first few weeks of device operation. Moreover, the increase of temperature results in more energy consumption. The take away points of this observation is that due to the aging the power traces change over time and accordingly, profiling attacks such as template attacks need to consider aging effects while profiling/matching is conducted.

4.2.2 Impact of aging on the attack success rate. This set of results investigates the effect of aging on the success of the template attack. In this experiment, profiling and attack temperatures were equal. However, the training traces were gathered from a fresh device (i.e., 0 week aging shown as 0w in Fig. 3), while attack was mounted on an aged device. We extracted the results for the devices that experienced aging in the range of 0 and 20 weeks (shown as 0w to 20w in the figure). As our HSpice simulations with MOSRA do not consider any noise, to realize the experiments, we added some level of noise in our analysis.

Figure 3 shows the Success Rate (SR) of attacks when the temperature is 105°C and $\sigma = 0.032$ where σ denotes the standard deviation of the noise considered in our analysis. Note that we considered a large amount of noise compared to the signals (with standard deviation ≈ 150 μW), resulting in signal-to-noise ratio of ≈ 0.005 (typical value, see [14, Fig. 8 in App. A]). As Fig. 3 shows, the success rate slightly decays with aging, as the attacked circuit becomes older and older with respect to the clone used to build the templates. A zoom around 80% of success rate is shown in Fig. 4(a). As depicted, SR drops fast after one week, and then continues to decrease, albeit at a slower rate.

The value of SR in Fig. 4(a) seems noisy as simulating success rates are prone to estimation errors (though we resorted to 1000 attacks). One common practice in side-channel analysis is to *smooth* the SR curve. However, for more sensible approximation, we consider that empirical SR (Fig. 4(a)) can be fitted by the exponential law shown in Eqn. (1), where q is the number of traces (X-axis in Fig. 3 and 4) and the

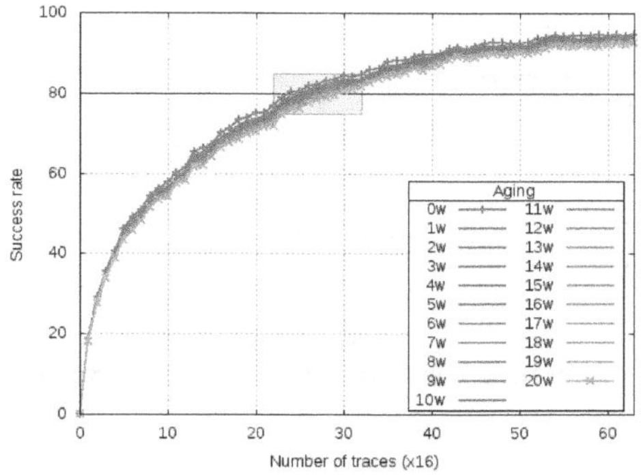

Figure 3: SR after 1000 attacks (Temperature=105°C, $\sigma = 0.032$).

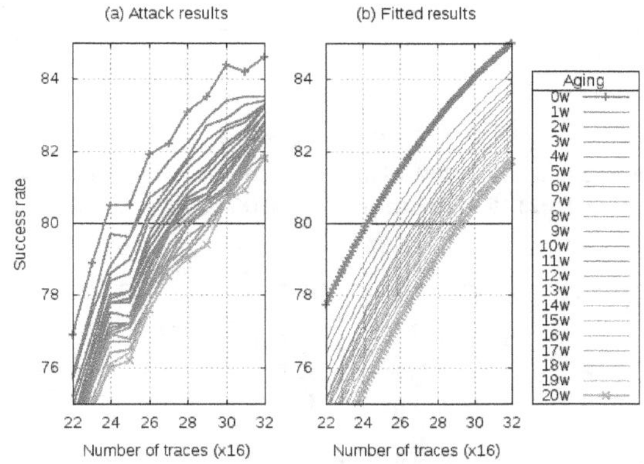

Figure 4: Zoom on the window around SR=80% displayed in Fig. 3, (a) raw data, and (b) fitted data on Eqn. (1).

constant e is the *first order success rate exponent* [15] whose theoretical value can be expressed as a linear function of the signal-to-noise ratio and algorithmic confusion coefficient [16]. In practice, the value of $e \in \mathbb{R}^+$ is extracted by fitting Eqn. (1) to the experimental data.

$$\text{SR} = 1 - \exp(-e \times q) \qquad (1)$$

The law (1) can be interpreted as follows: to increase the success rate of an attack from 90% to 99% (resp. from 99.0% to 99.9%), twice number of traces is needed. Fig. 4(b) shows the result of fitting to Eqn. (1), using linear regression.

Fig. 5 compares the number of traces needed to reach the success rate of 80% for the attacks launched in 65°C and 105°C. In both cases the number of traces to attain 80% success is increasing fast in the first week of aging, and then it grows with a slower rate. The results depict that temperature increase makes the attack more difficult. In particular, **the number of traces required to break the key with probability of 80% in 105°C will increase $\approx 25\%$ after 20 weeks.** Note that in each case, the number of traces is 16 times of the Y-ordinate. To highlight the effect of aging and avoid mismatches caused by process variation, we do not consider process variation in this figure.

To mitigate deviations between profiling and matching phases, template normalization has been proposed in literature [17] where both 2^n templates $\hat{p}$ (for all the values of the key) and 2^n online distributions p are transformed by homothety such that they have the same *zero mean* and *unit variance*. The next set of results shows how normalization affects the success of template attack when there is an aging mismatch between profiling and matching devices. In Fig. 6 the template device is new while the target device is 20 week old. As shown, normalization slightly helps to improve the attack via reducing the number of traces, but does not impact our conclusions.

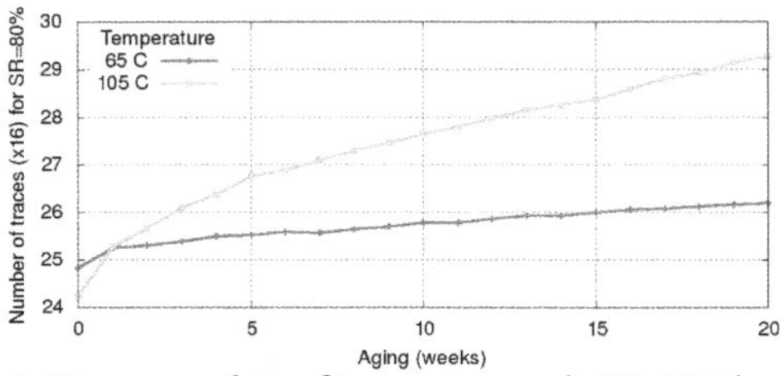

Figure 5: Mean number of traces to reach SR=80% ($\sigma = 0.032$).

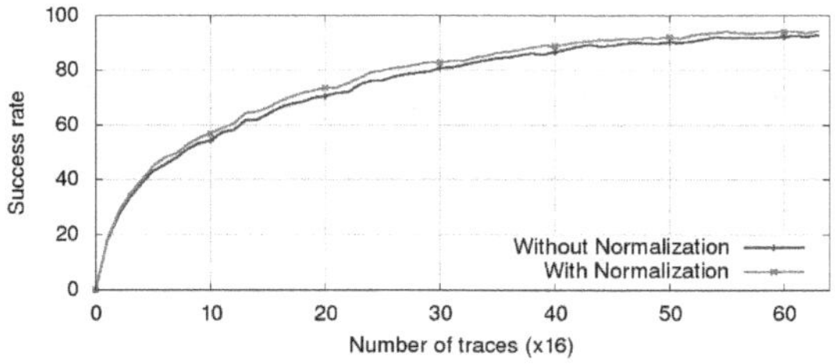

Figure 6: SR after 1000 attacks with and without applying normalization [17] (Temperature=105°C, $\sigma = 0.032$).

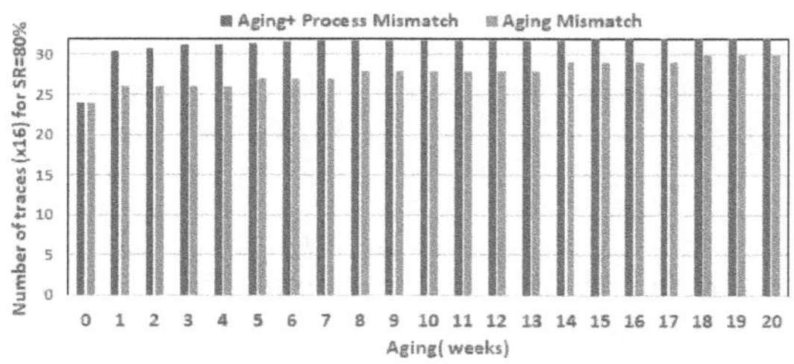

Figure 7: Mean number of traces to reach SR=80% with and without process variations (temperature: 105°C, $\sigma = 0.032$).

In particular, **via normalization, the number of traces required to break the key with probability of 80% decreases ≈ 16% when there is a 20 week aging mismatch and temperature is 105°C.**

4.2.3 Impact of process mismatch. Figure 7 compares the number of traces required to attain 80% success when both aging and process variations are considered with the case when only aging is considered. Simulations were carried out using a Gaussian distribution: transistor gate length L: $3\sigma = 10\%$; threshold voltage V_{TH}: $3\sigma = 30\%$, and gate-oxide thickness t_{OX}: $3\sigma = 3\%$. As expected, the attack is more difficult when both aging and process variation mismatches occur. As shown in Fig. 7, **process plus aging mismatch results in 11% increase of the number of traces after 20 weeks on top of the aging mismatch increase of 25% to attain 80% success.**

4.2.4 Impact of temperature mismatch. Figure 8 depicts the effect of temperature mismatch. In this experiment, profiling was conducted in 0°C and attack was performed in different temperatures. Both profiling and attack were conducted on new devices. As shown, the number of traces for attacks in −40°C, −20°C and 0°C are approximately similar. (Minor deviations are due to the estimation error of the experiments.) By increasing the number of samples in our experiments, we expect to see a global minimum in this graph at 0°C (profiling temperature). As depicted, the attack is more difficult when there is a temperature mismatch between profiling and attack process. **The impact of temperature is to increase the number of traces required to attain 80% success by ≈ 166%, considering the corners −40°C & +105°C required in commercial applications.**

The difficulty of the attack (in terms of number of traces) is exacerbated when both temperature and aging time are not aligned between the profiling and target device. The take away point of the results shown in Fig. 5 and Fig. 8 is that to decrease the number of traces, first, the temperature must be the same for the training and matching devices. Then, ideally, aging should be balanced. However, this is not always possible as activity of trainee and attacker are not similar.

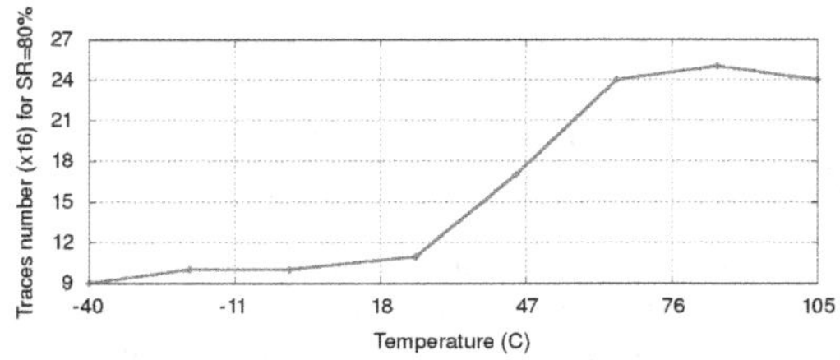

Figure 8: Mean number of traces to reach SR=80% in different attack temperatures (profiling temperature=0°C, $\sigma = 0.032$).

5 CONCLUSION

In this paper we showed the outcome of mounting the template attack on the PRESENT cipher in different temperatures and aging duration mismatches. The results show that the impact of aging on the attack is in the order of 10% after 5 weeks of usage in 105°C. As the impact of temperature mismatch is also highly significant (about 166% change in number of traces to recover the key with probability 80%, between -40°C and 105°C cases), to increase the success rate of the attack, the temperature (in general, the operational environment, including supply voltage, clock signal shape, etc.) must be the same for the training and matching devices. Then, as the secondary factor, aging should be balanced to fine-tune the attack. The technological dispersion (when training and matching devices are not the same) accounts for 11% more traces needed to break the device in 20 weeks on top of 25% more traces needed due to aging mismatches. Those quantitative results are of interest to designers, who can apply simple **derating factors** when estimating the practical strength of cryptographic designs against side-channel attacks.

REFERENCES

[1] O. Sinanoglu, N. Karimi, J. Rajendran, and R. Karri et al., "Reconciling the IC test and security dichotomy," in *ETS*, 2013, pp. 1–6.

[2] Y. Lu et al., "Statistical reliability analysis under process variation and aging effects," in *DAC*, 2009, pp. 514–519.

[3] S. Wang, J. Chen, and M. Tehranipoor, "Representative critical reliability paths for low-cost and accurate on-chip aging evaluation," in *ICCAD*, 2012, pp. 736–741.

[4] P. C. Kocher, J. Jaffe, and B. Jun, "Differential power analysis," in *Int'l Conf. on Advances in Cryptology (CRYPTO)*, 1999, pp. 789–789.

[5] E. Brier, C. Clavier, and F. Olivier, "Correlation power analysis with a leakage model," in *CHES*, 2004, pp. 16–29.

[6] B. Gierlichs, L. Batina, P. Tuyls, and B. Preneel, "Mutual information analysis," in *CHES*, 2008, pp. 426–442.

[7] S. Chari, J. R. Rao, and P. Rohatgi, "Template attacks," in *CHES*, 2002, pp. 13–28.

[8] F. Oboril and M. B. Tahoori, "Extratime: Modeling and analysis of wearout due to transistor aging at microarchitecture-level," in *DSN*, 2012, pp. 1–12.

[9] A. Bogdanov et al., "Present: An ultra-lightweight block cipher," in *CHES*, 2007, pp. 450–466.

[10] F. Durvaux, F.-X. Standaert, and N. Veyrat-Charvillon, "How to certify the leakage of a chip?" in *EUROCRYPT*, 2014, pp. 459–476.

[11] N. Courtois, D. Hulme, and T. Mourouzis, "Solving circuit optimisation problems in cryptography and cryptanalysis," *IACR Cryptology ePrint Archive*, p. 475, 2011.

[12] "Nangate 45nm open cell library," "http://www.nangate.com" (accessed May 2016).

[13] Synopsys, "HSPICE User Guide: Basic Simulation and Analysis," 2016.

[14] C. Carlet et al., "Achieving side-channel high-order correlation immunity with leakage squeezing," *J. Cryptographic Engineering*, vol. 4, no. 2, pp. 107–121, 2014.

[15] S. Guilley et al., "A key to success - success exponents for side-channel distinguishers," in *INDOCRYPT*, 2015, pp. 270–290.

[16] S. Bhasin et al., "Side-channel leakage and trace compression using normalized inter-class variance," in *HASP*, 2014, pp. 7:1–7:9.

[17] M. A. Elaabid and S. Guilley, "Portability of templates," *J. Cryptographic Engineering*, vol. 2, no. 1, pp. 63–74, 2012.

MUCH-SWIFT: A High-Throughput Multi-Core HW/SW Co-design K-means Clustering Architecture

Hadi Mardani Kamali
Department of Electrical and Computer Engineering
George Mason University
hmardani@gmu.edu

Avesta Sasan
Department of Electrical and Computer Engineering
George Mason University
asasan@gmu.edu

ABSTRACT

K-mean clustering is an essential tool for many big data applications including data mining, predictive analysis, forecasting studies, and machine learning. However, due to large size (volume) of Big-Data, and large dimensionality of its data points, even the application of a simple k-mean clustering may become extremely time and resource demanding. In this paper, we propose a two-level filtering algorithm based on binary kd-tree structure, which considerably decreases the time of convergence in K-means algorithm for large datasets. The proposed modification to the classification algorithm, evolves the SW to naturally divide the classification into smaller data sets, based on the number of available cores and size of logic available in an FPGA. The empirical results show that on a multi-core FPGA, provides 330× speed-up compared to a conventional SW-only solution.

KEYWORDS

Clustering, FPGA, K-means, Filtering, kd-tree

ACM Reference Format:
Hadi Mardani Kamali and Avesta Sasan. 2018. MUCH-SWIFT: A High-Throughput Multi-Core HW/SW Co-design K-means Clustering Architecture. In *GLSVLSI '18: 2018 Great Lakes Symposium on VLSI, May 23–25, 2018, Chicago, IL, USA.* https://doi.org/10.1145/3194554.3194648

1 INTRODUCTION

Many current applications of cloud computing, especially when combined with the Internet of Things, are of predictive, data mining, machine learning, or forecasting nature [1, 2, 6]. Such applications are in need of categorizing and clustering very large and high-dimensional input data-sets as a part of their larger computational flow. The ability to classify and cluster a desired set of data is an essential part of building knowledge from data. However, as the size and dimensionality of data increases, the execution time of clustering algorithms grows superlinearly, making it a big challenge when dealing with Big-Data.

The goal of clustering is to classify the data according to a specific metric such that objects within a cluster/group, in terms of having a feature are similar. A clustering algorithm may be supervised (hierarchical) or unsupervised (un-nested), exclusive or fuzzy, and could be complete or partial. Depending on the type of clustering algorithms used, the resulting clusters may be well separated, prototype-based (centroid-based), graph-based, or density-based [4].

GLSVLSI '18, May 23–25, 2018, Chicago, IL, USA

ACM ISBN 978-1-4503-5724-1/18/05...$15.00
https://doi.org/10.1145/3194554.3194648

K-means is one of the simplest and yet most used [4, 5] centroid-based unsupervised clustering algorithms. However, its applicability to Big-Data depends on the scalability of its software (SW) implementation with respect to the available hardware (HW). One of the most promising HW platforms that is leveraged for achieving considerable speedup in big data applications is FPGAs. FPGA solutions enable higher parallelism than clusters of CPUs or GPUs at a much lower cost, at the expense of greater mapping overhead. In order to improve the usability of FPGA solutions when dealing with semi-parallel applications, the FPGAs are equipped with mid to high-performance multi-core processors (e.g. ARM Cortex A9, A12, A15). The existence of multiple mid to high-performance cores on the same die as FPGA, as well as hundreds of thousands of fine-grained logics and coarse-grained communications within FPGA [18, 19], improves the efficiency of HW/SW co-design and provides greater flexibility and wider applicability for use of FPGAs accelerated solutions.

The execution time of k-clustering algorithms could be improved by means of both SW and HW. For example, on the SW side, one could use (1) binary kd-tree structure for dividing search space members into "boxes" [7], and (2) triangle inequality for avoiding redundant distant calculation [8]. On the HW side, more capable or additional computing resources reduce the computational time. In this paper, we present *MUCH-SWIFT*: a HW/SW partitioning architecture that considerably reduces the execution time of kd-tree clustering algorithm compared to the state of the art FPGA mapped solutions. For this purpose, we have implemented a mapping and an aggregation function on top of the kd-tree clustering algorithm. This approach allows us to divide the work across logic and multiple cores in an FPGA to gain the maximum achievable speedup by utilizing all available resources. Additionally, we implemented a custom high-performance DMA in order to transmit data between host and FPGA via PCI Express (PCIe) interface, which considerably reduces the execution time overhead related to data transfer time, and helps us achieve considerable speedup in comparison with a conventional software-based solution.

The rest of the paper is organized as follows. The k-means theory and algorithm are described in Section 2. Section 3 briefly illustrates the structure of binary kd-tree for filtering algorithm. The architecture of MUCH-SWIFT and its parallel structure is elaborated in Section 4. Experimental results are shown in Section 5. Section 6 covers the related work. And finally, Section 7 concludes the paper.

2 K-MEANS CLUSTERING ALGORITHM

K-means is one of the simplest and fastest partitioning algorithms which is widely used for unsupervised centroid-based clustering. It divides the input dataset into "k" groups, called *clusters*, where all members in a cluster are similar. The k-means clustering is a centroid-based algorithm meaning each cluster has a prototype which is the indicator of that cluster. Hence, during the clustering, each data point is assigned to a cluster whose centroid is the closest. In k-means clustering algorithms, In order to calculate the distance between each point and the cluster centroids, three conventional distance metrics have been used: *Manhattan*, *Max*, and *Euclidean* [6]. For instance, if we suppose that each data point is a vector $\overrightarrow{dp} = (p_1, p_2, ..., p_m)$, the Euclidean distance can be defined as follow:

$$EuclidDist(\overrightarrow{dp}, \overrightarrow{cent}) = \Big(\sum_{i=1}^{m}(dp_i - cent_i)^2\Big)^{\frac{1}{2}} \quad (1)$$

The k-means algorithm first initiates k centroids. Then it enters an iterative process where each iteration consists of two steps: (1) *Assignment Step*: where each point will be assigned to a cluster whose centroid is the closest. (2) *Update Step*: where a new centroid is found by re-calculating the mean of new assigned points to each cluster. When the centroids stop changing, the clustering of datasets to k clusters is successfully accomplished.

3 BINARY KD-TREE FOR FILTERING SEARCH SPACE

The Binary kd-Tree filtering algorithm is developed based on binary kd-tree for the purpose of reducing the required time for search queries [7]. In this algorithm, all data points are recursively divided into several *axis-aligned bounding boxes*. This recursive process generates a multi-dimensional binary search tree, whose root is the bounding box of all data points, each level of the tree consists of two meaningful subsets of data points, and each leaf represents at most one data point. Each node stores some essential information, such as the corresponding bounding box members (*cell*), the number of data points in the box (*count*), the weighted centroid (*wgtCent*) which represent the sum of all data points in a box, and potential candidates for the centroid (Z).

Algorithm 1 Filtering algorithm by using binary kd-Tree [7]

```
function FILTER(kdNode u, CandidateSet Z)
    C ← u.cell;
    if u is a leaf then
        z* ← the closest point in Z to u.point;
        z*.WgtCent ← z*.WgtCent + u.point;
        z*.count ← z*.count + 1;
    else
        z* ← the closest point in Z to C's midpoint;
        for all z ∈ Z \ {z*} do
            if z.isFather(z*, C) then
                Z ← Z \ {z*};
        if |Z| == 1 then
            z*.WgtCent ← z*.WgtCent + u.wgtCent;
            z*.count ← z*.count + u.count;
        else
            Filter(u.left, Z);
            Filter(u.right, Z);
end function
```

Alg. 1 depicts the kd-tree filtering algorithm. In each node, Z determines a subset of candidate centroids. If we suppose that we have k clusters, the candidate centroids for the root node are all k centroids, and the candidates for each internal node are a subset of k clusters. Additionally, the candidates of each node are the nearest neighbors for some points. For each node, the distance between $z^* \in Z$ and the midpoint of *cell* is calculated and compared with $z \in Z \setminus z^*$. Then, the sub-tree at the larger distance is pruned.

4 MUCH-SWIFT ARCHITECTURE

MUCH-SWIFT is a HW/SW co-design architecture for accelerating the k-means algorithm. It benefits from utilizing multiple hard-core processors and plenty of resources in a single FPGA that are available in the same chip. For the implementation of MUCH-SWIFT, we have utilized the ZYNQ Ultrascale+ FPGA board. The ZYNQ

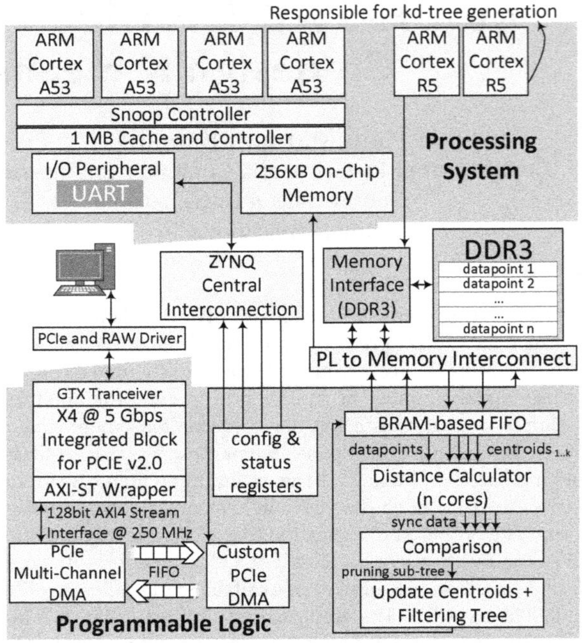

Figure 1. Overall MUCH-SWIFT System-Level Architecture.

Ultrascale+ architecture has four Cortex-A53 with maximum clock frequency of 1.5 GHz, and two Cortex-R5 with max frequency of 600 MHz. It is equipped with 1 GB DDR3 off-chip DDR3 memory, and ZU9EG FPGA chip with around 600K logic cells. In our implementation, the MUCH-SWIFT SW is distributed on Processor System (PS) (the Quad Cortex-A53 processor and the dual Cortex-R5 co-processor). On the HW side, the parallel arithmetic cores that are required for Manhattan distance calculations, comparators, and updaters are mapped to the Programmable Logic (PL) on ZU9EG. Fig. 1 illustrates the overall architecture of MUCH-SWIFT in ZCU102. Our proposed two-level algorithm maximizes the utilization of cores; Each Cortex-A53 core is responsible for evaluating and analyzing one quarter of data points independently. Additionally, in order to reduce the search time, we employ a binary kd-tree structure to filter (prune) some nodes and their children, which their candidates are not the nearest centroid. Then, in order to maximize the utilization of all four Cortex-A53 cores, we build N parallel clusters (N being the number of available cores, which is 4 in our experimental board) by dividing the original data-set into N smaller data-sets at the top of the kd-tree. After clustering the sub-datasets, they are merged together and the filtering algorithm is invoked on top of the merged clusters. Using this two-layer clustering approach increases convergence, which decreases the required number of iterations for the clustering. Furthermore, MUCH-SWIFT is able to process large datasets by using a DMA-based PCIe interface and DDR3 memory in ZCU102 without any significant throughput degradation. In our implementation, one of Cortex-R5 is made responsible for handling custom DMA access between PCIe and DDR3 memory, while another Cortex-R5 generates the initial states of each quarter of data points as well as initial values of centroids. In addition, the second Cortex-R5 is made responsible for controlling the update procedure after pruning in kd-tree structures.

4.1 Parallelism in kd-tree Traversal

To speed up the kd-tree clustering process, we implement a two-layer clustering mechanism. For the first level of clustering, we randomly divide the input data into four independent subsets, and each Cortex-A53 core is made responsible for processing a quarter of data as an independent kd-tree structure into k clusters. From this process, we obtain $4k$ centroids, and a cluster associated with each centroid. Then we combine the clustering result of four divided subsets into one. To achieve this, we combine a cluster in each subset with its three nearest clusters in other subsets. The final step in this process is to run the second level of clustering to update the centroids and cluster members. Considering that we are working on very large datasets and the initial assignment of data to the four subsets was random, the clustering results of the 4 subsets are expected to be very close to one another. Hence, the merged centroids and their associated members are expected to be very close to the final result. In the result, it is expected that the number of iterations for the second level of k-clustering to be very small.

Algorithm 2 Two-level k-clustering Algorithm by Using 4 parallel Binary kd-Tree Structures

```
1: function ParallelClustering(DataPoint_Set DP)
2:     for i = 0 to 3 do
3:         DataPoint_Set QDP[i] ← Quarter(DP, i);
4:         kdNode *kdu[i] ← Gen_KdTree(QDP[i]);
5:         CandidateSet Z_Update[i] ← Lloyd[QDP[i]];
6:         CandidateSet Z_Current[i] ← Z_Update[i];
7:     for i = 0 to 3 do                                  ▷ parallel in PL
8:         Filter(kdu[i], Z_Update[i]);
9:         while Z_Update[i] ≠ Z_Current[i] do
10:            Z_Current[i] ← Z_Update[i];
11:            Filter(kdu[i], Z_Update[i]);
12:    kdNode kdu_top ← Combine(kdu[0 : 3]);
13:    while Z is updated do
14:        Filter(kdu_top, Z);
15: end function
```

Alg. 2 illustrates the pseudo-code of our proposed two-layer partitioning flow. During the initialization state, the dataset is divided into four separate subsets via *Quarter* function. then A kd-tree is generated for each sub-dataset, and the Lloyd function is employed for choosing initial centroids [3]. Then, parallel tree traversal is accomplished (*Line* 8-14), where each Cortex-A53 core is made responsible for transceiving data to/from PL in order to calculate and update its corresponding kd-tree characteristics (i.e. centroids and clusters) in parallel.

4.2 No Limit for Dataset Size via High Throughput DDR3 Memory

We employ DDR3 off-chip memory in ZYNQ Ultrascale+ to maximize the feasible size of data. ZYNQ Ultrascale+ provides an efficient and fast DDR3 memory, which is accessible from both PS and PL, illustrated in Fig. 1. The capacity of this memory is 1 GB, and it has a 128 bits data-bus for read/write access. Also, as it can be seen in Fig. 1), we implement a BRAM-based bridge (*BRAM-based FIFO*) between DDR3 and PL in order to transfer data from PL to DDR3 and vice versa. In order to minimize the required BRAM-based bridge size between DDR3 and PL, we evaluate the data size for each level of tree traversal separately. Similar to [13], hierarchical access allows us to release and reuse the memory at each level (depth) before starting the next level (depth) of tree. In addition, all data is permanently kept in DDR3; hence, overwriting the data can be accomplished without any throughput degradation. As a result, the large size of DDR3 enables us to maximize the dataset size as required. For instance, suppose that MUCH-SWIFT is configured to classify $N = 100000$ data into $K = 1024$ clusters. In the worst case, the structure of kd-tree is like a *degenerate* tree. In this case, we need $(N-1) \times (K) \times (log_2 K) \simeq 122$ MB, which is much less than the DDR3 memory, i.e. 1GB.

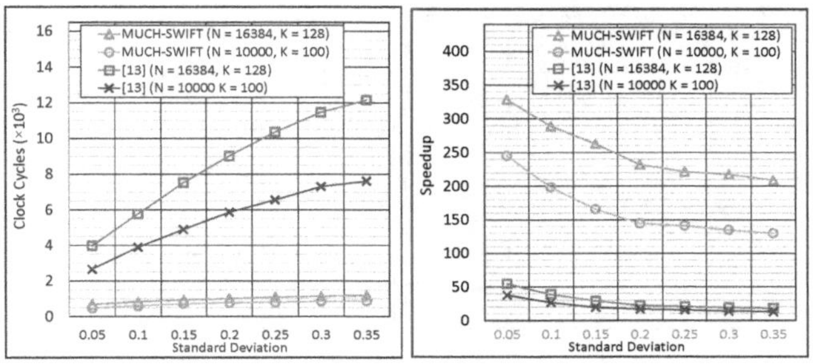

(a) (b)

Figure 2. (a) Average Clock Cycles in each iteration (b) Speedup Against Conventional FPGA-based Single Core

5 IMPLEMENTATION RESULTS

We targeted a large Xilinx ZYNQ-based SoC architecture (ZCU102 evaluation board) to evaluate our proposed architecture. The **PS** consists of a quad Cortex-A53 core and a dual Cortex-R5 core. A53 cores are made responsible for transceiving data to/from each core (Cortex-A53) from/to PL. In this architecture, one of Cortex-R5 handles the custom DMA for transmitting data to DDR3 from PCIe interface, and the other Cortex-R5 controls the updating stage of the filtering algorithm. All floating point arithmetic operations, i.e. Manhattan distance, compare, and update centroids have been done in **PL**. As illustrated in Fig. 1, the **UART** interface was employed to determine the number of clusters as a configurable parameter. The number of clusters is used to determine the number of parallel modules in PL; For instance, if the number of clusters was set to $K = 5$, since we have four sub-datasets, and each sub-dataset should implement a $(K = 5)$-clustering, there will be $20(5 \times 4)$ parallel modules, including Manhattan Distances, compares, and updates, to accomplish the required computation. The **PCIe** interface is employed for transmitting datasets from the host to PL. Note that all interconnections between top modules in our proposed architecture are implemented based-on AXI4. We also employed a 128-bit AXI4 between PL and PS as well as between DDR3 and PS/PL in order to guarantee our required throughput. Additionally, we implemented a 64-bit AXI4-based data-bus to make our custom DMA between PCIe and DDR3 more efficient. Similar to [13], our test case is generated with the normal distribution with varying standard deviation, and all centroids are distributed between data points uniformly.

Fig. 2a illustrates the average number of needed clock cycles for each iteration in MUCH-SWIFT against an FPGA-based kd-tree implementation [13]. As illustrated, the MUCH-SWIFT architecture provides around 8.5× speedup on average. Additionally, as reported in Fig. 2b, MUCH-SWIFT is able to provide up to 330× speed-up compared to an FPGA-based architecture without optimization. Also, it achieves more than 210× acceleration on average compared to an FPGA-based architecture without optimization. Note that all data communications (interaction) between the host and FPGA, which is accomplished via PCIe interface, are counted for timing evaluation. The MUCH-SWIFT's robust and scalable data transfer and DMA management contribute to the reported speedup. In fact, this is why the MUCH-SWIFT achieves 8.5× speedup, compared with a single core filtering algorithm [13] when only utilizing 4 parallel cores as the computation is no longer memory bound.

In order to illustrate the efficiency of our filtering algorithm, we compare the MUCH-SWIFT with the proposed architecture in [17], which is a multi-core implementation of k-clustering. As it can be seen in Fig. 3(a), increasing the number of clusters increases the gap between MUCH-SWIFT and [17] due to parallel arithmetic cores in our proposed architecture. In fact, since the number of

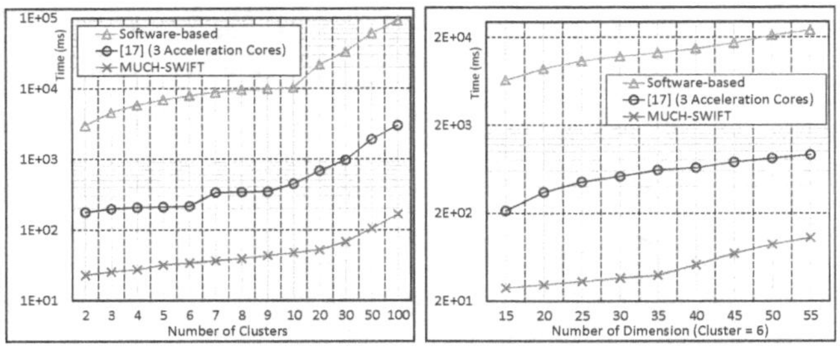

(a) (b)

Figure 3. (a) Execution Time for 10^6 Data Points (a) with Different Clusters (15 Dimensions) (b) with Different Dimensions (6 Clusters)

Table 1: Resource Utilization with Different Cluster Sizes

Cluster Size	LUTs	Registers	BRAMs	DSPs
2	32,985	44,226	37	86
3	51,858	61,928	59	184
4	64,608	74,204	78	257
5	76,852	88,927	99	344
10	134,915	157,712	208	674
20	226,454	287,951	388	1426
Total Available	274,000	548,000	914	2520

parallel arithmetic cores in MUCH-SWIFT depends on the number of clusters, and we use maximum feasible resources on FPGA, we encountered less throughput degradation. Fig. 3(b) focuses on data dimensionality, which shows 12× speedup compared with [17].

Table 1 reports MUCH-SWIFT's resource utilization with the different number of clusters. When increasing the number of clusters, we need more resources for parallelism, and the available resources on FPGA are limited. So, there is a limit for the number of clusters on FPGA for fully parallel architecture. As reported in Table 1, the maximum number of clusters (for fully parallel architecture) is 20, and for the applications with more clusters, we have to share the parallel modules between clusters uniformly. Note that, 20 clusters means that we can implement $20 \times 4 = 80$ parallel modules on ZU9EG, which is significantly large. Also, our implementation employs the highest proportion of BRAMs and DSPs in order to maximize the number of parallel arithmetic cores.

6 RELATED WORK

A HW/SW co-design architecture is implemented in [9] based on NIOS 1.1. But, the HW/SW interface is Peripheral Bus Module (PBM), whose serial infrastructure considerably limits the throughput. Unlike a HW/SW architecture, pure FPGA-based designs [10, 11] provide significant speed-up against HW/SW co-designs by using fixed-point arithmetic. But, on-chip FPGA memories (like BRAMs) is a big restriction for storing large datasets.

In order to avoid redundant distance calculations, triangle inequality [8] has been implemented successfully in [12]. However, the size of data points is truncated to 8 bits, which is small. A filtering algorithm by using a kd-tree structure is implemented in [13]. Due to using on-chip memories for storing data, it is only able to store 64K data simultaneously. Also, the size of data points is limited to 16, and all computations are based on fixed-point arithmetic.

Another pure FPGA-based k-means clustering architecture is implemented in [14]. The number of clusters is fixed in this architecture, and changing it needs re-synthesis and re-implementation. A computer cluster which consists of multiple FPGA-CPU pairs is implemented in [15]. In this architecture, map-reduce programming is designed to allow easy scaling and parallelization across the distributed computer system, Although this evaluation on multiple FPGA-CPU pairs shows considerable throughput against baseline software implementation, it needs evaluating the case for utilizing multiple FPGAs in processing larger datasets.

A specific FPGA accelerator for the Intel QuickAssist FPGA platform is implemented in [16], which provides an integration between threads in a CPU and an Accelerated Function Unit (AFU) in QuickAssist FPGA. But, it is applicable only for this specific type of FPGA platform, i.e. IntelAssist.

7 CONCLUSION

In this paper, we proposed *MUCH-SWIFT*, an FPGA-based architecture for parallelization of the k-clustering algorithm and a modified two-layer filtering optimization. The MUCH-SWIFT employs all processing cores in the ZYNQ Ultrascale+ SoC to reduce the computation time and a two-layer filtering algorithm designed for parallel processing of binary kd-tree structures. Furthermore, by employing ZYNQ Ultrascale+ and utilizing its DDR3 memory, MUCH-SWIFT increases the feasible size of its input datasets. Additionally, MUCH-SWIFT benefits from our proposed HW/SW co-design architecture, which provides a high-throughput DMA-based PCIe channel for transceiving datasets between the host and ZYNQ SoC. By using this HW/SW co-design architecture, the MUCH-SWIFT achieves around 330× speedup compared to a software-only solution.

REFERENCES

[1] Anil K. Jain, "Data Clustering: 50 Years beyond K-means," in *Pattern Recognition Letters (PRL)*, Vol. 31, no. 8, pp. 651-666, 2009.
[2] J. P. Theiler and G. Gisler, "Contiguity-Enhanced K-Means Clustering Algorithm for Unsupervised Multispectral Image Segmentation," in *Proc. Optical Sci., Eng. and Instrumentation (SPIE)*, pp. 108-118, 1997.
[3] S. Lloyd, "Least Squares Quantization in PCM," in *IEEE Transactions on Information Theory*, vol. 28, no. 2, pp. 129-137, 1982.
[4] P.-N. Tan, M. Steinbach and V. Kumar, "Introduction to Data Mining: Pearson New International Edition," *Pearson Education Limited*, 2013.
[5] J. Wu, "Advances in K-Means Clustering," *Springer-Verlag Berlin Heidelberg*, 2012.
[6] M. Estlick, M. Leeser, J. Theiler, and J. J. Szymanski, "Algorithmic Transformations in the Implementation of K-means Clustering on Reconfigurable Hardware," in *Proc. ACM/SIGDA Ninth International Symposium on Field Programmable Gate Array (FPGA)*, pp.103-110, 2001.
[7] T. Kanungo, D. M. Mount, N. S. Netanyahu, C. D. Piatko, R. Silverman, and A. Y. Wu, "An Efficient K-Means Clustering Algorithm: Analysis and Implementation," in *IEEE Transactions on Pattern Analysis and Machine Intelligence (TPAMI)*, vol. 24, no. 7, pp. 881-892, 2002.
[8] C. Elkan, "Using the Triangle Inequality to Accelerate K-Means," in *Proc. Int'l Conference on Machine Learning (ICML)*, pp. 147-153, 2003.
[9] M. Gokhale, J. Frigo, K. Mccabe, J. Theiler, C. Wolinski, and D. Lavenier, "Experience with a Hybrid Processor: K-means Clustering," in *Journal of Supercomputing*, vol. 26, no. 2, pp. 131-148, 2003.
[10] H. M. Hussain, K. Benkrid, H. Seker, and A. T. Erdogan, "FPGA Implementation of K-means Algorithm for Bioinformatics Application: An Accelerated Approach to Clustering Microarray Data," in *NASA/ESA Conf. on Adaptive Hardware and Systems (AHS)*, pp. 248-255, 2011.
[11] H. M. Hussain, K. Benkrid, A. T. Erdogan, and H. Seker, "Highly Parameterized K-means Clustering on FPGAs: Comparative Results with GPPs and GPUs," in *Int'l Conference on Reconfigurable Computing and FPGAs (ReConFig)*, pp. 475-480, 2011.
[12] Z. Lin, C. Lo, and P. Chow, "K-Means Implementation on FPGA for High-Dimensional Data using Triangle Inequality," in *Int'l Conference on Field Programmable Logic and Applications (FPL)*, pp. 437-442, 2012.
[13] F. Winterstein, S. Bayliss, and G. A. Constantinides, "FPGA-based K-Means Clustering using Tree-based Data Structures," in *Int'l Conf. on Field Programmable Logic and Applications (FPL)*, pp. 1-6, 2013.
[14] J. S. S. Kutty, F. Boussaid, and A. Amira,, "High Speed Configurable FPGA Architecture for K-Mean Clustering," in *Proc. Int'l Symposium on Circuits and Systems (ISCAS)*, pp. 1801-1804, 2013.
[15] Y. M. Choi and H. K. H. So, "Map-Reduce Processing of K-Means Algorithm with FPGA-Accelerated Computer Cluster," in *Proc. IEEE Int'l Conf. on ASAP*, pp. 9-16, 2014.
[16] T. S. Abdelrahman, "Accelerating K-Means Clustering on a Tightly-Coupled Processor-FPGA Heterogeneous System," in *Proc. IEEE Int'l Conference on Application-Specific Systems, Architectures and Processors (ASAP)*, pp.176-181, 2016.
[17] J. Canilho, M. Vestias, and H. Neto, "Multi-Core for K-Means Clustering on FPGA," in *Int'l Conference on Field Programmable Logic and Applications (FPL)*, pp. 1-4, 2016.
[18] H. M. Kamali, K. Z. Azar and S. Hessabi, "DuCNoC: A High-Throughput FPGA-Based NoC Simulator using Dual-Clock Lightweight Router Micro-Architecture," in IEEE Transactions on Computers, vol. 67, no. 2, pp. 208-221, 2018.
[19] Xilinx Inc., "Zynq-7000 All Programmable SoC, Technical Reference Manual (UG585)," [Online]. Available: https://www.xilinx.com/support/documentation/user_guides/ug585-Zynq-7000-TRM.pdf, 2016.

An Efficient Cache Management Scheme for Capacitor Equipped Solid State Drives*

Congming Gao⋆, Liang Shi⋆, Yejia Di⋆, Qiao Li†, Chun Jason Xue† and Edwin H.-M. Sha‡
⋆College of Computer Science, Chongqing University
†Department of Computer Science, City University of Hong Kong
‡Department of Computer Science, East China Normal University

ABSTRACT

Within SSDs, random access memory (RAM) has been adopted as cache inside controller for achieving better performance. However, due to the volatility characteristic of RAM, data loss may happen when sudden power interrupts. To solve this issue, capacitor has been equipped inside emerging SSDs as interim supplier. However, the aging issue of capacitor will result in capacitance decreases over time. Once the remaining capacitance is not able to write all dirty pages in the cache back to flash memory, data loss may happen. In order to solve the above issue, an efficient cache management scheme for capacitor equipped SSDs is proposed in this work. The basic idea of the scheme is to bound the number of dirty pages in cache within the capability of the capacitor. Simulation results show that the proposed scheme achieves encourage improvement on lifetime and performance while power interruption induced data loss is avoided.

ACM Reference Format:
Congming Gao⋆, Liang Shi⋆, Yejia Di⋆, Qiao Li†, Chun Jason Xue† and Edwin H.-M. Sha‡. 2018. An Efficient Cache Management Scheme for Capacitor Equipped Solid State Drives. In *Proceedings of 2018 Great Lakes Symposium on VLSI (GLSVLSI'18)*. ACM, Chicago, IL, USA, Article 4, 4 pages. https://doi.org/10.1145/3194554.3194639

1 INTRODUCTION

Solid State Drives (SSDs) have been widely used in embedded systems, personal computer and data centers due to its well identified advantages. Within SSDs, random access memory (RAM) has been widely adopted for achieving better performance. However, due to the volatility characteristic of RAM, there is a risk of data loss when sudden power supply interruption happens, leading to the degradation of robustness of SSDs. In order to solve this issue, capacitor is suggested to be equipped within emerging SSDs as interim power supplier to avoid the data loss [1][2]. However, one of the key issues for the capacitor is the aging problem, which introduces decreased capacitance, especially due to the impact of temperature [3]. With capacitor aging, once the remaining capacitance of capacitor is not able to write all dirty pages back to flash memory, data loss happens. In this work, approaches are proposed to indirectly detect the capacitance of capacitor and then solve the capacitor aging issue with achieving performance and lifetime improvement.

From our investigation, there are few works focusing on capacitor aging induced data loss issue in SSDs. One of the reasons is that traditional SSDs do not equip capacitor within SSDs. The other one is that most of the recent products provide enough capacitance to make sure the dirty pages can be successfully written back to flash memory in normal case [4]. However, for some extreme environment, SSDs are going to suffer from high or low temperature so that the interim capacitor will be highly aged, leading the decrease of the integrity of resided data. In order to solve this issue, Guo et al. [5] proposed to use emerging non-volatile memory as cache to store dirty pages. However, these memories are always expensive and these non-volatile memories generally have lifetime issue. In addition, Huang et al. [4] proposed a smartbackup strategy, which aims at writing dirty pages back to SSDs with faster program speed [6]. But once resided capacitor is highly aged and the number of dirty pages exceeds the capability of remaining capacitance, data loss still occurs.

In this paper, a cache management scheme is proposed to solve the above issue. The basic idea of the scheme is to bound the number of dirty pages in the cache. The proposed scheme is realized in two steps: First, a periodical dirty page budget detection scheme is proposed. Second, with the dirty page budget, a smart dirty page synchronizing scheme is proposed. This scheme can reduce the impact from synchronizing dirty pages through carefully selecting the synchronization timing. To our best acknowledge, this is the first work in designing a cache management scheme without adding other components to combat the capacitor aging issue inside SSDs. With applying this approach, the data loss issue can be avoided and the performance impact also can be minimized. The major contributions of this work are as follows: 1) Proposed a dirty page budget detection, which acquires the number of dirty pages within the capability of capacitor; 2) Proposed a smart dirty page synchronizing scheme, which can achieve the performance and lifetime improvement of SSDs; 3) Implemented the proposed work

*Corresponding author: Liang Shi. Email: shi.liang.hk@gmail.com.
This work is supported by the NSFC 61772092 and 61572411.

GLSVLSI'18, May 23–25, 2018, Chicago, IL, USA

ACM ISBN 978-1-4503-5724-1/18/05... $15.00
https://doi.org/10.1145/3194554.3194639

in an SSD simulator for validating the effectiveness of the proposed cache management scheme.

The rest of the paper is organized as follows. Section 2 presents the background. Section 3 presents the motivation of this work. In Section 4, an efficient cache management is presented. Experiments are presented in Section 5. Finally, Section 6 summarizes the paper.

2 BACKGROUND

Currently, two types of capacitors, super-capacitor [5] and Tantalum capacitor [2], have been widely adopted in advanced SSDs. For super-capacitor, its lifetime is quite sensitivity to temperature. Based on Arrhenius law lifetime model [3], the lifetime of super-capacitor is reduced by half when the temperature is increased by 10°C. For example, previous work [5] presented that the capacitance degradation of super-capacitors under 60°C can be as high as 30% within five years. For Tantalum capacitor, although it can operate with a larger temperature range[1], if the temperature falls out of the range, capacitance will be significantly decreased as well. For example, previous work [7] presented that with a low temperature (e.g., -55°C), the capacitance of Tantalum capacitor will drop by at least 20%. Currently, advanced SSDs are widely equipped with capacitors to avoid the data loss. However, from the above discussion on the aging issue of capacitors, it is still a key problem when the capacitors are aged with a significant capacitance decrease.

Capacitor aging is able to introduce data loss while the number of dirty pages exceeds the remaining capability of capacitor. In order to avoid this issue, emerging non-volatile memory is adopted as a part of cache inside SSD controller, which can be used to store dirty pages for preventing data loss issue [5][8]. In previous works, Guo et al. [5] proposed that when sudden power supply interruption occurs, dirty pages can be moved to phase change random access memory (PRAM) instead of NAND flash memory with less energy demanding. Similarly, Kim et al. [8] proposed to use non-volatile memory for storing these dirty pages exceeding the capability of capacitor. In addition, similar issue also exists in main memory. Kateja et al. [9] proposed to decouple the capacitor requirement and size of main memory through bounding the volume of dirty data in the main memory.

3 MOTIVATION

3.1 Capacitor aging may induce data loss

In work [10], authors show that the maximum energy supplied by capacitor is proportional to the current capacitance of capacitor. For the energy supplied by capacitor, it is in charge of writing dirty pages back to flash memory when power interruption occurs, which is proportional to the energy supplied by capacitor as well [5]. Based on these two works, we can find that the maximum number of dirty pages within the capability of capacitor is proportional to the current capacitance of capacitor.

However, the capacitance will be decreased with capacitor aging. Figure 1(a) presents the capacitance degradation of super-capacitor over time [3]. As shown in this figure, the

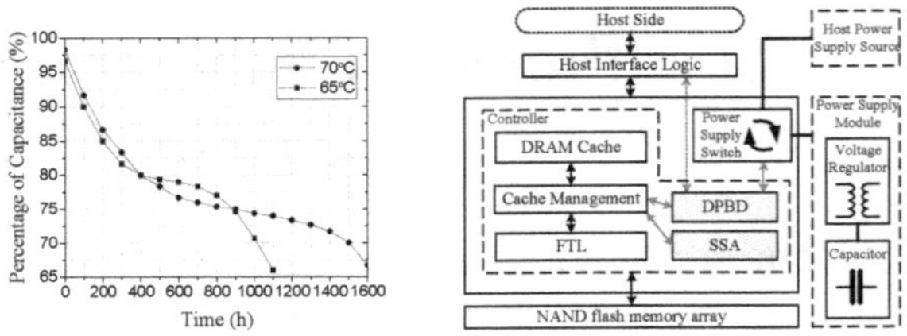

(a) Relative capacitance change with 65°C and 70°C [3]. (b) The framework of proposed approach.

Figure 1: The characteristic of capacitor aging and the architecture of proposed scheme.

Table 1: Normalized latency and write amplification.

	Baseline	Method 1	Method 2
Read Lat.	1	0.8531	0.7607
Write Lat.	1	1.9927	0.1386
Write Amp.	1	1.6136	15.093

capacitance is constantly decreasing during its whole lifetime. In addition, we also find that temperature has a significant influence on the lifetime [3]. That is, at extreme environment, the capacitance of capacitor will decreases sharply. Based on above descriptions, once the capacitance of the equipped capacitor inside SSDs is not able to synchronize all dirty pages back to SSDs, data loss happens.

3.2 Impact of dirty page synchronization

The straightforward method to avoid the capacitor aging induced data loss is to bound the number of dirty pages in the cache. There exist two related methods can be used. The first method (Method 1) is to synchronize dirty pages back to SSD once the number of dirty pages reaches the capability of the capacitor [9]. The second method (Method 2) is to synchronize dirty pages during idle time of SSDs to avoid the performance impact from above method, which has been widely adopted in SSDs for achieving performance improvement [11], especially for garbage collections [12].

In preliminary experiment, STG_0 trace is selected as an example and three schemes are implemented in SSDsim[11]. In the experiment, the dirty page capability is set to 70%, which means that current capacitance of capacitor only can support to write 70% cache capacity of dirty pages. More details are presented at Section 5. Baseline represents the case that there are no capacitor aging problem inside SSDs.

Table 1 presents the normalized access latency and write amplification. From the results, we have following observations: First, Method 1 has smaller write amplification, but introduces a high write access latency. This is because that frequently synchronization operations will block latter coming host requests. Second, Method 2 has a much better access performance, but induces a high write amplification due to synchronizing more dirty pages back to SSD.

From the observations, we can find that although synchronization can avoid data loss issue, the timing of synchronizing dirty pages should be carefully selected to reduce the impact on both performance and lifetime.

4 PROPOSED APPROACH

In the framework, DPBD module is designed to acquire the dirty page budget; SSA module is designed to smartly manage the dirty page synchronization.

4.1 Dirty Page Budget Detection

The basic idea of DPBD is to periodically synchronize the pages in the cache back to SSDs via interim power supplier. The process of the detection module is as follows: during the process of periodically synchronizing pages back to SSDs, dirty pages are synchronized first, and then clean pages are synchronized repeatedly until the capacitor is exhausted. For obtaining dirty page budget, a page counter is used to record the number of synchronized pages, which determines dirty page budget.

In addition, another important issue is the detection period, which indicates the period between two continuous DPBD processes. In this work, we propose to use a fixed threshold, 20 days, as the detection period, which can be set based on the user's demand. After detection period reaches 19 days, idle time should be found for activating detection process in the last day. Otherwise, detection process is activated with highest priority.

In order to minimize the impact of capacitance degradation during two continual DPBD process, a redundant space from the acquired number of pages to the dirty page budget is added. In this work, five discrete budgets are used to maintain the redundancy, 100%, 90%, 80%, 70% and 0%, respectively. Since the lifetime of capacitor reaches the end of life when capacitance drops to 70% of rated capacitance, the last budget is set to 0% after the fourth one (70%). Note that, if the dirty page budget is 0%, write through policy should be adopted in cache management.

4.2 Smart Synchronizing Activation

The basic idea of the scheme is to synchronize dirty pages based on the dirty page budget. If the number of dirty pages in the cache is approaching the budget, they should be synchronized as soon as possible. Otherwise, they are delayed to avoid immature synchronization. In the following, the above scheme is presented in two cases: idle time synchronization and busy time synchronization.

Idle time synchronization: In order to avoid immature synchronization induced severe write amplification in Method 2, two new synchronization timings are selected. The first one is that a new budget threshold is used to determine the activation of the synchronization process. If the number of dirty pages approaches the budget and the distance between them is smaller than the defined threshold, dirty pages are synchronized. Otherwise, no synchronization is activated. The second one is that if there are cold dirty pages in the cache, the synchronization process can be activated even the distance between number of dirty pages in the cache and the budget is smaller than the defined threshold. In this case, these cold dirty pages are synchronized back to SSDs in advance during idle time for minimizing the impact on performance. In this setting, another threshold is added to indicate the coldness. With above approaches, the immature synchronization can be avoided and the number of dirty pages in the cache can be minimized. Figure 2 shows an example for the above two thresholds. Figure 2(a) shows the first case. Assuming dirty page budget is 8, the number of dirty pages is 6, and budget threshold is 6. That is, the number of current dirty pages reaches budget threshold so that page 9 should be synchronized back. Figure 2(b) shows the second case. In this case, assuming coldness threshold is 9, which indicates that pages after the 9th page are identified as cold pages. In this figure, page 9 belonging to cold pages is synchronized back. Note that, in this work, budget and coldness thresholds are set as 5% of dirty page budget and capacity of cache, respectively.

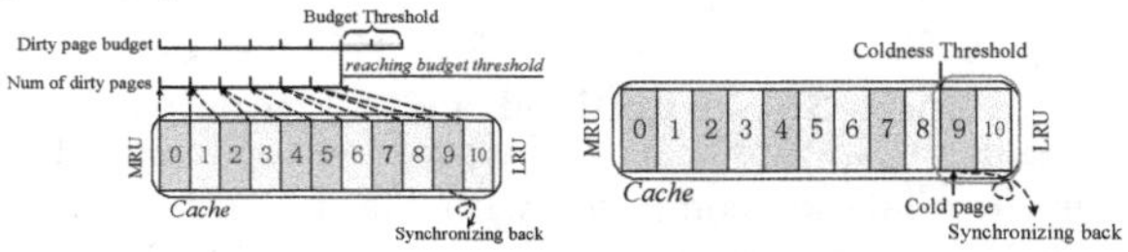

(a) Budget threshold. (b) Coldness threshold.

Figure 2: Two new synchronization timings.

Busy time synchronization: When there are no idle time, we propose to evict pages based on original LRU policy if the number of dirty pages does not approach the budget. Otherwise, dirty pages are synchronized in a higher priority.

Based on the proposed scheme, not only the number of dirty pages can be bounded below the dirty page budget, but also the synchronization induced performance and lifetime degradation can be minimized. During synchronizing dirty pages back to SSDs, these dirty pages are synchronized with write protection for avoiding losing data consistency [9].

5 EXPERIMENT

5.1 Experiment Setup

In this paper, we use a trace driven simulator, SSDsim [11], to evaluate the proposed framework. For the experiment, an 128GB SSD, which is configured with 4 channels with each channel equipped with 4 chips, is modeled. Each flash page size is set to 4KB. The cache capacity is set to 128MB. The workloads include a set of MSR Cambridge traces [13], two Financial traces [14], and one personal computer traces collected via DiskMon [15]. In the experiment part, four schemes, Baseline, Method 1, Method 2, and the proposed scheme, are implemented. Each scheme excepting Baseline contains three cases, 90%, 80% and 70%, which present the dirty page budgets. If dirty page budget is smaller than 70%, the budget is set as 0%. When dirty page budget is set as 0%, all schemes synchronize dirty pages back to SSDs immediately so that all three schemes will achieve same results.

5.2 Results and Analysis

In the following figures, results of Method 1, Method 2 and proposed scheme are normalized to the result of Baseline.

Write Latency: Figure 3 presents the write latency evaluations among four schemes, where dirty page budgets are set as 90%, 80% and 70%, respectively. In this results, we can find that Method 1 commonly introduces a high write latency, Method 2 achieves the minimal write latency. First, Method 1 only synchronizes dirty pages back to SSDs when the number of dirty pages approaches the budget. Hence, there exist more conflicts between synchronized dirty pages and host I/O requests. That is, the poor write performance of Method 1 directly comes from the synchronization induced conflict on host requests. Second, the reason why Method 2 achieves the best write performance is that dirty pages are usually synchronized back in idle time so that host I/O requests can be cached.

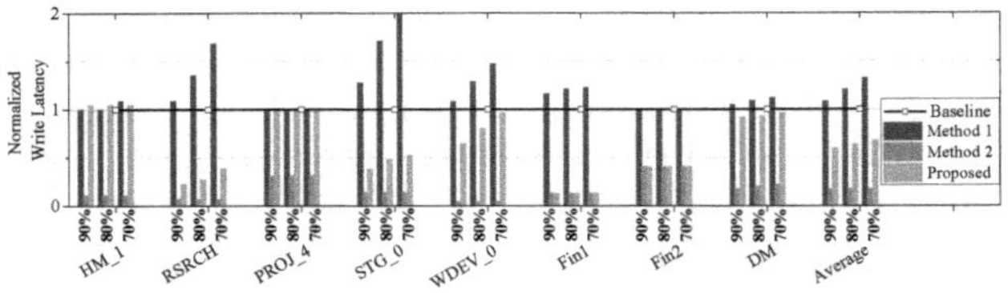

Figure 3: Normalized write latencies.

In addition, in most cases, the proposed scheme achieves better write latency compared with Method 1 and Baseline with little degradation compared with Method 2. The reason comes from that the proposed scheme only synchronizes dirty pages when the number of dirty pages approaches the dirty page budget. In this case, compared with Method 1, the proposed scheme is able to cache more host write requests due to synchronizing dirty pages in advance.

Read Latency: Figure 4 presents the normalized read latency. In this figure, we find that read latency is significantly reduced compared with Baseline. The reason comes from that if dirty pages are synchronized, there will be fewer dirty pages supposed to be evicted when read miss occurs. Two observations can be found from the results: First, in most cases, Method 2 achieves the best read performance among these four schemes. This is because Method 2 achieves better write latency, which reduces the impact of read/write interference [16][17].

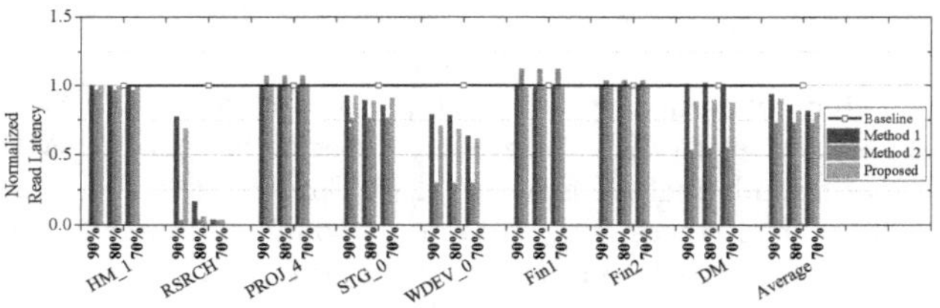

Figure 4: Normalized read latencies.

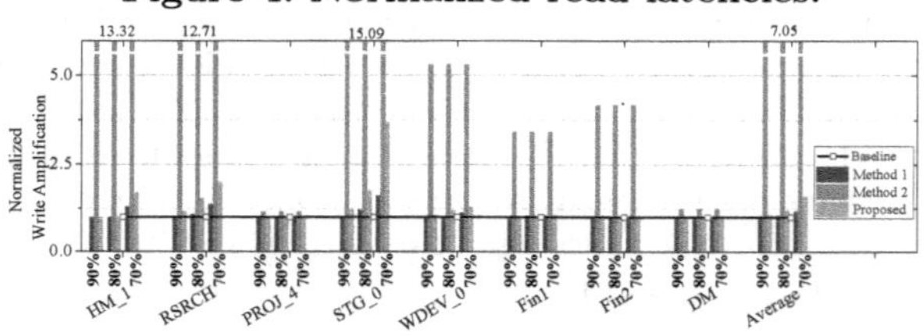

Figure 5: Normalized write amplifications.

Second, when the budget is smaller, read latency is smaller in some cases. This is because more pages in cache are clean. However, there also exist some exceptions, such as PROJ_4 of Method 2. This is because frequently synchronization delays incoming read requests [16][17].

Write Amplification: Figure 5 presents the normalized write amplification. In this figure, we find that Method 1 achieves similar write amplification to Baseline. But Method 2 has the worst write amplification. Different from these two schemes, the proposed scheme achieves similar write amplification to Method 1. This is because that the number of additional write requests is significantly reduced through smartly activating synchronization. In addition, some cases, such as DM2 of Method 2, achieve close results to the Baseline as well. The reason comes from that there exist burst of accessing requests so that less idle time can be used to synchronize dirty pages.

Based on the above results, we can find that the proposed scheme is efficient in improving both performance and lifetime for capacitor equipped SSDs.

6 CONCLUSION

In this paper, first, a dirty page budget detection scheme is proposed. Then, a smart synchronizing scheme is proposed to reduce the synchronizing dirty pages induced passive impacts on SSDs. Experiments show that the proposed scheme improves both performance and lifetime while the capacitor aging induced data loss issue is being avoided.

REFERENCES

[1] Power Loss Imminent (PLI) Technology. In *Intel Corporation*, 2014.

[2] Woon Hak Kang, Sang Won Lee, Bongki Moon, Yang Suk Kee, and Moonwook Oh. Durable write cache in flash memory ssd for relational and nosql databases. In *SIGMOD*, 2014.

[3] G. Alcicek, H. Gualous, P. Venet, R. Gallay, and A. Miraoui. Experimental study of temperature effect on ultracapacitor ageing. In *EPE*, 2007.

[4] Min Huang, Yi Wang, Liyan Qiao, Duo Liu, and Zili Shao. S-martbackup: An efficient and reliable backup strategy for solid state drives with backup capacitors. In *HPCC*, 2015.

[5] Jie Guo, Jun Yang, Youtao Zhang, and Yiran Chen. Low cost power failure protection for mlc nand flash storage systems with pram/dram hybrid buffer. In *DATE*, 2013.

[6] Yuming Chang, Yuanhao Chang, Teiwei Kuo, Yungchun Li, and Hsiangpang Li. Achieving slc performance with mlc flash memory. In *DAC*, 2015.

[7] Chris Reynolds. Tantalum capacitor technology : Options for high-temperature and harsh-environment applications. *Power Electronics Magazine*, 2017.

[8] Dongwook Kim and Sooyong Kang. Dual region write buffering: making large-scale nonvolatile buffer using small capacitor in ssd. In *SAC*, 2015.

[9] Rajat Kateja, Anirudh Badam, and Sriram Govindan. Viyojit: Decoupling battery and dram capacities for battery-backed dram. In *ISCA*, 2017.

[10] Woojin. Choi, Prasad. Enjeti, and J. W. Howze. Fuel cell powered ups systems: design considerations. In *PESC*, 2003.

[11] Yang Hu, Hong Jiang, Dan Feng, Lei Tian, Hao Luo, and Shuping Zhang. Performance impact and interplay of ssd parallelism through advanced commands, allocation strategy and data granularity. In *ICS*, 2011.

[12] Mingchang Yang, Yuming Chang, Chewei Tsao, Pochun Huang, Yuanhao Chang, and Teiwei Kuo. Garbage collection and wear leveling for flash memory: Past and future. In *SMARTCOMP*, 2014.

[13] Dushyanth Narayanan, Eno Thereska, Austin Donnelly, Sameh Elnikety, and Antony Rowstron. Migrating server storage to ssds: analysis of tradeoffs. In *EuroSys*, 2009.

[14] UMassTraceRepository. OLTP Application I/O Traces. http://www.memblaze.com/en/index.php?c=ajax&a=test1.

[15] Microsoft. DiskMon. https://docs.microsoft.com/zh-cn/sysinternals/downloads/diskmon.

[16] Congming Gao, Liang Shi, Mengying Zhao, Chun Jason Xue, Kaijie Wu, and Edwin H. M. Sha. Exploiting parallelism in i/o scheduling for access conflict minimization in flash-based solid state drives. In *MSST*, 2014.

[17] Congming Gao, Liang Shi, Cheng Ji, Yejia Di, Kaijie Wu, Jason Chun Xue, and Edwin Sha. Exploiting parallelism for access conflict minimization in flash-based solid state drives. In *TCAD*, 2018.

Evaluation of the Complexity of Automated Trace Alignment using Novel Power Obfuscation Methods

Bozhi Liu, Kemeng Chen, Minjun Seo, Janet Wang, Roman Lysecky
University of Arizona, Tucson, AZ, USA
bozhiliu@email.arizona.edu, kemengchen@email.arizona.edu, mjseo@email.arizona.edu, meilingw@email.arizona.edu, rlysecky@ece.arizona.edu

ABSTRACT

This paper presents a methodology for evaluating power obfuscation approaches that seek to obfuscate the location of sensitive operations in the power trace, thereby increasing the complexity of automated trace alignment. The paper presents a new adversary model and proposes a new metric, mean trials to success (MTTS), to evaluate power obfuscation methods in the context of automated trace alignment. We evaluate two common obfuscation methods, namely instruction shuffling and random instruction insertion, and we present a new obfuscation method using power shaping to intentionally mislead the attacker.

CCS CONCEPTS

• **Security and privacy ~ Side-channel analysis and countermeasures** • Security and privacy ~ Embedded systems security

KEYWORDS

Power obfuscation, power shaping, automated trace alignment, side channel attacks, embedded systems

ACM Reference format:

B. Liu, K. Chen, M. Seo, J. Roveda, and R. Lysecky. 2018. Evaluation of the Complexity of Automated Trace Alignment using Novel Power Obfuscation Methods In *2018 Great Lakes Symposium on VLSI, Chicago, IL USA, May 2018 (GLSVLSI'18)*, 4 pages. https://doi.org/10.1145/ 3194554.3194640

1 INTRODUCTION

Embedded systems are being widely used in critical systems across a broad range of applications, and they are often more susceptible to attacks by adversaries trying to gain access to or extract sensitive information from the system. Side channel attacks (SCAs) have been proved to be effective across a broad range of systems in extracting sensitive information. Various kinds of side channels exist, including power, electromagnetic radiation, sound, etc.

Automated trace alignment methods are essential for a practical SCA. An attack requires three key steps: 1) automatically determining the information leakage location in each trace, 2) aligning all collected traces, and 3) performing the SCA. SCAs assume the location of sensitive operations in each raw power trace has been determined and that all power traces have been properly aligned. Limited research has addressed the challenge of obfuscating the location of sensitive operations and increasing the complexity of automatic trace alignment to improve the resilience to SCAs.

In this paper, we develop a new adversary model and mean trials to success (MTTS) metric to evaluate the difficulty of automatically identifying sensitive operations within each power trace for a target system. We present a framework for evaluating the effectiveness of existing power obfuscation methods, namely instruction shuffling and random instruction insertion. We further introduce a novel power obfuscation technique called Power Re-Shaping and Mimicry (PReSM) that hides sensitive operations and intentionally mislead attackers to incorrect locations in a power trace. We evaluate the effectiveness of different power obfuscation methods for hiding the location of the sensitive operations and different correlation methods to calculate the MTTS.

2 RELATED WORK

SCAs can be categorized as profiled and non-profiled attacks. In non-profiled attacks, including differential power analysis (DPA) [1], correlation power analysis (CPA) [3], or mutual information analysis (MIA) [4], attackers build power model for each key and use a distinguisher to find the best guess. On the other hand, a profiled attack [2] builds power templates for different keys from power traces on a duplicate device and use the templates to guess the key for new power trace.

SCA countermeasures can be summarized in three categories. The first category decreases the signal to noise ratio of the physical implementation. The second category changes the timing profile of the power traces, such as shuffling [5] and instruction reordering [1], these can be mitigated by preprocessing techniques such as signal integration [6] or better statistical methods to differentiate the traces [7]. The third category, masking [8], adds random masks to vulnerable intermediate operations to change its power profile and reduce

GLSVLSI '18, May 16–18, 2018, Chicago, IL, USA

ACM ISBN 978-1-4503-5724-1/18/05...$15.00
https://doi.org/10.1145/3194554.3194640

information leakage. These methods focus primarily on the obfuscated power trace given the assumption that trace alignment can be performed ideally. Misaligned traces make SCAs more difficult and less effective [9]. Different from the above works, this paper focuses on evaluating the effectiveness of power obfuscation methods to hide the location of sensitive operations, which makes aligning power traces significantly more difficult.

Existing frameworks [6] for evaluating SCA attacks and countermeasures can be utilized, and researchers have proposed using different statistical tools like mutual information [10] and QMS [7] combined with success rate analysis [11]. Different from described metrics above, this paper proposes a novel Mean Trials to Success (MTTS) metric to indicate the difficulty of locating sensitive operations in power traces with an attacker model using different correlation based methods.

3 THREAT MODEL

We assume the adversary has sufficient knowledge of the target device, including the software executing on device, execution sequences, and knowledge of the targeted sensitive operations. With physical access to the device, the adversary has sufficient information to collect power traces within a few thousand cycles of the sensitive operation. However, for a successful SCA, the power traces must be more precisely aligned, typically within a few cycles [9]. To more precisely align the trace, the adversary may construct a pattern of the sensitive operation and use correlation methods to identify the location of the sensitive operations with each collected power traces. Correlation methods may include cross-correlation, Pearson correlation, and mutual information. Additionally, the adversary is expected to know that power obfuscation is being utilized.

4 SENSITIVE OPERATION IDENTIFICATION

The power consumed by the software instruction can be modeled as two parts: the base instruction power and the data-dependent switching power. Base instruction power is the power consumed without data-dependent switching activity. The data-dependent switching power is caused by the switching of gates and registers within the processor. Minimally, the data-dependent switching power is proportional to the number of different bits between the instruction's operands and results.

The first step to perform power analysis is to identify the location of the operation where the sensitive information is present. Since the power consumption of the sensitive operations is a distinguishable pattern, the power consumption profile of the pattern can be used as a power pattern to identify when and where sensitive operations start within the power trace.

Using the base instruction power consumption, a pattern of the power trace for the targeted execution sequence can be constructed. The correlation between the trace pattern and power trace is constructed, which indicates how likely each location of the power trace matches the trace pattern. Three correlation methods are considered to identify the location of the targeted sensitive operation: cross-correlation, Pearson correlation, and mutual information.

4.1 Cross-correlation

The cross-correlation correlates the trace pattern with the entire power trace to find the location of the targeted sensitive operations. Cross-correlation is defined as:

$$(x \star y)[n] = \sum_{m=-\infty}^{\infty} x^*[m] y[m+n] \quad (1)$$

where x is the power trace containing the sensitive operations and y is the trace of interest. Since the trace pattern and power traces are digitized time series, we use discrete cross-correlation. The cross-correlation's amplitude indicates the correlation level between the trace pattern and power trace.

4.2 Pearson Correlation

Pearson correlation detects a general linear dependency between time series, calculated as:

$$\rho_{X,Y} = \frac{cov(X,Y)}{\sigma_X \sigma_Y} \quad (2)$$

$cov(X, Y)$ calculates the covariance between X and Y. σ_X is the variance of X. Pearson correlation is calculated between the trace pattern and power trace at every possible location.

4.3 Mutual Information

Mutual information measures the information overlap between two sets of data. Given time series X and Y, the mutual information between X and Y is calculated as:

$$I(X,Y) = \sum_{y \in Y} \sum_{x \in X} p(x,y) \log\left(\frac{p(x,y)}{p(x)p(y)}\right) \quad (3)$$

$p(x,y)$ is the joint probability of variable x and y. $p(x)$ and $p(y)$ are the marginal probability. The joint probability divided by product of the marginal probability of x and y reflects the dependency between x and y.

5 POWER TRACE OBFUSCATION

The goal of power obfuscation is to obfuscate the power trace such that automatically identifying the sensitive operations' location using state-of-the-art correlation methods is hindered. We evaluate three power obfuscation methods: instruction shuffling (IS), random instruction insertion (RII), and Power Re-Shaping and Mimicry (PReSM). For each obfuscation method, an obfuscation level is defined to control the amount of obfuscation applied. Fig. 1 presents an example of a single original trace and obfuscated traces applying each power obfuscation method.

5.1 Instruction Shuffling

Instruction shuffling (IS) reorders the instruction execution, changing both the timing and power profile of the target system. We implement instruction shuffling stochastically by randomly swapping instructions if no dependencies between those instructions exist. Each instruction in the execution sequence is analyzed to identify data and control dependencies on other instructions. For each pair of instructions with no dependency,

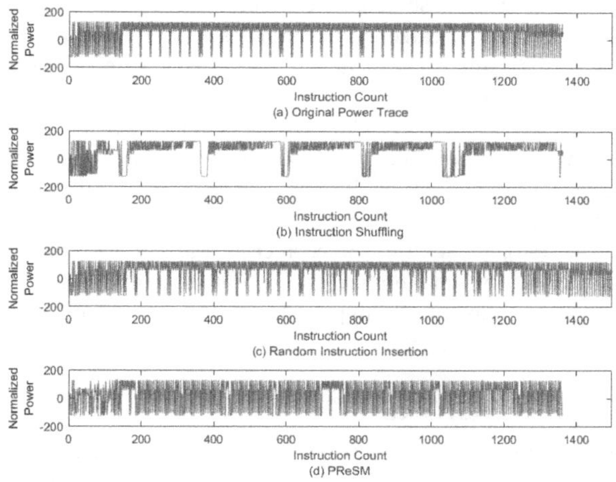

Figure 1: Example actual power traces for target device.

we decide if instructions are shuffled using a shuffling level *L*, which ranges from 0 to 100. A shuffling level *L* means that for each possible pair the probability they are swapped is *L%*.

5.2 Random Instruction Insertion

Random instruction insertion (RII) inserts randomly selected instructions with randomly selected operands at random locations in the software execution sequence. The only restriction on the inserted instructions is that the destination register/memory must not overwrite live data. The insertion level defines the percentage, *P*, of new instructions within an instruction sequence to randomly insert.

5.3 Power Re-Shaping and Mimicry

Power reshaping and mimicry (PReSM) tries to first reshape the power trace of the sensitive operation so that it appears to be unrelated, and then reshapes the power trace of other operations to mimic the sensitive operation, thereby both hiding the sensitive operation and potentially misleading attackers. For a given raw power trace, the first step is to add additional power to reshape the sensitive operations into a random sequence, which will hide the correct location of sensitive operations from correlation analysis. To mislead the attacker, the next step is to add additional power in several random locations that mimic the sensitive operation (i.e., have a high correlation with the target trace pattern), which will mislead an attacker's automated trace alignment. Finally, to compensate for power trace segments without any additional power, a constant power noise is added.

6 MEAN TRIALS TO SUCCESS

MTTS defines the average number of trials an attacker needs before successfully locating the target sensitive operation in a single trace. This metric quantitatively measures the obfuscation effect of different countermeasures for the sensitive operations. Fig. 3 presents an overview of our evaluation methodology for calculating the MTTS for a specific power obfuscation method using a specific correlation method. Given an obfuscated plain trace (*PT*), the selected power obfuscation method is applied to produce the obfuscated trace (*OT*). Using the trace pattern (*P*) for the target operation and the selected correlation method, the correlation trace (*CT*) is calculated. The correlation trace is the input to the MTTS calculation algorithm.

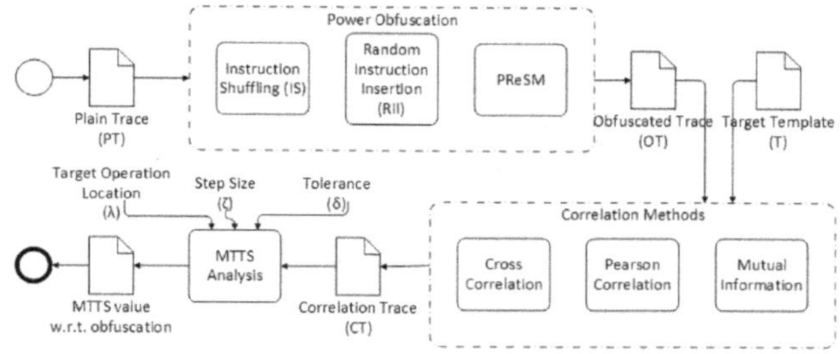

Figure 3: Methodology for calculating the MTTS given a power obfuscation method and correlation method.

ALGORITHM 1: Mean trials to success (MTTS) analysis

Inputs: Correlation Trace (*CT*), Sensitive Operation Location (λ), Step Size (ζ), Tolerance (δ)
Output: Mean Trials to Success (*MTTS*)

```
CTS = sort(CT)
Bins = DivideIntoBins(CTS, ζ);
MTTS = 0;
for each bin in Bins do
  for i = 0 to bin.size do
    if bin[i].location ≥ (λ - δ) and bin.location ≤ (λ + δ) then
      MTTS += bin.size * 0.5
      return MTTS
  MTTS += bin.size
return MTTS
```

Algorithm 1 presents the MTTS analysis algorithm, which assumes an attacker knows which power obfuscation is used. Rather than simply selecting the location with the highest correlation, the attacker would select a set of ζ highest correlated locations and analyze those locations in no particular order before looking at the next set of ζ highest correlated locations. In the MTTS analysis algorithm, ζ is the step size used to divide a sorted correlation trace (*CTS*) into bins. Bins are analyzed in descending order, but the locations within each bin can be analyzed in random. The MTTS analysis algorithm additionally has an input for the tolerance (δ), which defines how close, in cycles, an attacker' guess to the real correct location has to be for a successful attack.

7 EXPERIMENTAL RESULTS

MTTS evaluates both the effectiveness of the power obfuscation methods to hide the sensitive operation's location and the effectiveness of the correlation methods as a countermeasure for automated trace alignment. Our target system consists of an ARM processor-based embedded system executing the ARM-Embed AES implementation compiled using arm-linux-gnueabi-5. We use a simulation-based approach that combines a cycle accurate gem5 simulation [12] with an instrumented version of McPAT [13] to create cycle-by-cycle power traces of the

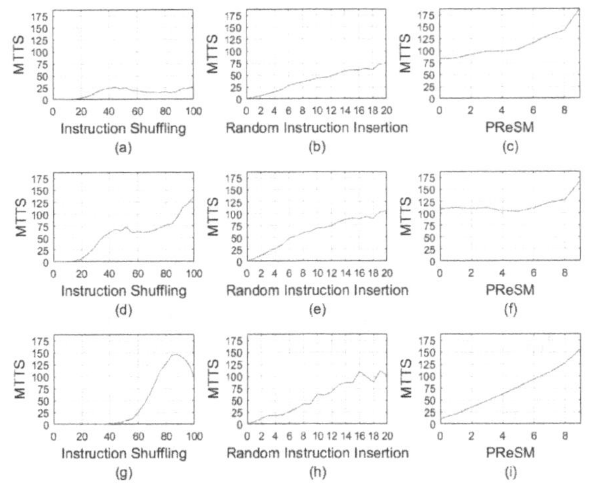

Figure. 4: MTTS using a single obfuscation method for varying obfuscation levels. X-axis represents the obfuscation level for each obfuscation method.

software execution. The first-round AES encryption is the targeted sensitive operation, whereas the entire AES power trace corresponds to the entire process. For performing the MTTS analysis we use a step size ζ = 1% and a tolerance δ = 5.

Fig. 4 shows the MTTS for each power obfuscation method with increasing obfuscation levels and for each correlation method. Rows represent the correlation method used, namely cross-correlation (*top*), Pearson correlation (*middle*), and mutual information (*bottom*). Columns represent the power obfuscation used, namely instruction shuffling (*left*), random instruction insertion (*middle*), and PReSM (*right*). For each combination of power obfuscation and correlation, we present the average MTTS across 500 executions of the software. Because the experimental power trace corresponds to the AES encryption, which is already isolated from the full system power trace, the presented MTTS values are a conservative estimate of the effectiveness of the obfuscation methods.

IS achieves a best-case MTTS of 25, which is significantly lower than other power obfuscation methods. Notably, the performance of IS saturates, and the best MTTS is not at the highest shuffling level. With a high shuffling level, previous shuffled instructions may be shuffled back closer to their original location, thus counteracting the goal of obfuscation. In contrast, RII exhibits a linearly increase in MTTS with an increase in the obfuscation level, achieving a maximum MTTS of 74. The linear increase is achieved irrespective of the correlation method used. PReSM achieves the best MTTS of 168, which is a 6.7X and 2.3X increase compared to IS and RII, respectively. Furthermore, PReSM achieves an MTTS equal to the highest MTTS for IS and RII at obfuscation levels of 1 and 5, respectively.

For attackers, knowing the correlation method that yields the lowest MTTS for a specific power obfuscation method provides an advantage for aligning trace. For IS, mutual information is the best correlation method for low obfuscation levels, but cross-correlation is better when the shuffling level exceeds 60. For a shuffling level of 80, cross-correlation yields an 84% lower MTTS. For RII, Pearson correlation and mutual information provide the same performance, but cross-correlation is better at countering this obfuscation method with a maximum decrease in MTTS of 33%. For PReSM, mutual information is the best correlation method across all obfuscation levels, although at highest obfuscation level Pearson correlation's performance is similar (MTTS of 168 for Pearson correlation and 157 for mutual information). To identify the correct locations, cross-correlation and mutual information are the overall best options. Pearson correlation only has comparable performance for RII, but exhibits worse performance in all other cases.

8 CONSLUSIONS

We presented a new metric to analyze the difficulty of an attacker to systematically identify the location of sensitive operations in a power trace. The MTTS metric provides designers a new perspective to analyze the effectiveness of power obfuscation method. We further presented a novel power obfuscation approach that reshapes the power trace to intentionally mislead attackers to incorrect locations while hiding the real location. PReSM performs best across the considered power obfuscating methods, with a 2.3X increase in MTTS compared to the next best obfuscation method.

ACKNOWLEDGMENTS

This research was supported by the Army Research Office under Grant W911NF-16-1-0130.

REFERENCES

[1] R. Mayer-Sommer. "Smartly analysing the simplicity and the power of simple power analysis on smartcards." Cryptographic Hardware and Embedded Systems, pp. 78-92, 2000.

[2] S. Chari, J.R. Rao, P. Rohatgi. "Template attacks." International Workshop on Cryptographic Hardware and Embedded Systems, pp. 13-28. Berlin, Heidelberg, 2002

[3] E. Brier, C. Clavier, F. Olivier. "Correlation power analysis with a leakage model." Cryptographic Hardware and Embedded Systems, pp. 16-29, 2004.

[4] B. Gierlichs, L. Batina, P. Tuyls, B. Preneel. "Mutual information analysis." Cryptographic Hardware and Embedded Systems, pp. 426-442. 2008.

[5] C. Herbst, E. Oswald, S. Mangard. "An AES smart card implementation resistant to power analysis attack." International Conference on Applied Cryptography and Network Security, pp. 239-252. 2006.

[6] T.S. Messerges. "Using second-order power analysis to attack DPA resistant software." Cryptographic Hardware and Embedded Systems, pp. 238-251, 2000.

[7] J. Demme, R. Martin, A. Waksman, S. Sethumadhavan. "A Quantitative, Experimental Approach to Measuring Processor Side-Channel Security." IEEE Micro, vol. 33, no. 3, pp. 68-77, May-June 2013.

[8] C. H. Gebotys. "A table masking countermeasure for low-energy secure embedded systems." IEEE Transactions on Very Large Scale Integration (VLSI) Systems, vol. 14, no. 7, pp. 740-753, July 2006.

[9] J.G. Van Woudenberg, M.F. Witteman, B. Bakker. "Improving differential power analysis by elastic alignment." RSA Conference, pp. 104-119, 2011.

[10] L. Batina, B. Gierlichs, E. Prouff, M. Rivain, F.X. Standaert, N. Veyrat-Charvillon. "Mutual information analysis: a comprehensive study." Journal of Cryptology 24, no. 2, pp 269-291, 2011.

[11] S. Tillich and C. Herbst. "Attacking State-of-the-Art Software Countermeasures—A Case Study for AES," Cryptographic Hardware and Embedded Systems, pp. 228–243. 2008.

[12] N. Binkert et al. "The gem5 simulator." ACM SIGARCH Computer Architecture News 39, no. 2, pp 1-7, 2011.

[13] S. Li et al. "McPAT: an integrated power, area, and timing modeling framework for multicore and manycore architectures." International Symposium on Microarchitecture, pp. 469-480, 2009.

A CMOS Low Power 4th-Order Delta-Sigma Modulator with One Reconfigurable Amplifier

Jae-hyeon Sung
Inha Univ., Korea
sungjaehyeon@naver.com

Kwang-sub Yoon
Inha Univ., Korea
ksyoon@inha.ac.kr

Abstract

This paper describes the 4th-order feedback delta-sigma modulator with only one reconfigurable amplifier. The modulator is designed with 180nm CMOS standard process. The measurement results demonstrate the power dissipation of 352uW, peak SNDR of 82.41dB and the ENOB of 13.4bits with an input signal frequency of 250Hz, a sampling frequency of 128 kHz, an input signal bandwidth of 1kHz, and an oversampling rate of 64.

Keywords:

CMOS; Delta-Sigma Modulator; Low power; reconfigurable amplifier

ACM Reference format:

Jae-hyeon Sung and Kwang-sub Yoon. 2018. A CMOS Low Power 4th-Order Delta-Sigma Modulator with One Reconfigurable Amplifier In 2018 Great Lakes Symposium on VLSI, Chicago, IL USA, May 2018 (GLSVLSI'18), 4 pages. https://doi.org/10.1145/3194554.3194641

1. INTRODUCTION

Recently, the demand for a low power and high resolution ADC(Analog to Digital Converter) has been increasing with the development of bio signal system. A single block that consumes most of power in DSM is op-amp (operational amplifier). The design technique is to employ an only one amplifier using time-interleaving technique for 4th-order DSM[1]. Normally a 4th-order DSM requires four op-amps. But using time-interleaving technique, 4th-order DSM can be implemented using only one amp. In this proposal, a 4th-order DSM with only one operational amplifier is described. This design is proposed to achieve a low power dissipation with reduced the number of op-amp and high resolution with 4th-order architecture. Second idea of the proposed design is variable-stage operational amplifier. Conventional delta-sigma modulator [2-6] suffers from kT/C noise and the noise is critical for the input-side only. Hence the input capacitance is designed to be large for kT/C noise and the rest of the capacitance is designed to be small for chip size. Using only one amplifier generates a problem of phase margin. To solve the problem variable-stage amplifier is used.

ACM ISBN 978-1-4503-5724-1/18/05...$15.00
https://doi.org/10.1145/3194554.3194641

This paper is organized as follows. In section II, the design technique of the fourth order modulator with a reconfigurable op-amp is described. The simulation results are discussed in section III. Conclusions are drawn in section IV.

2. THE PROPOSED ARCHITECTURE

The block diagram of the proposed architecture is presented in Fig. 1. It employs the fully differential fourth order feedback architecture with only one amplifier. The conventional fourth order feedback delta-sigma modulator requires four op-amps, but the proposed modulator requires only one reconfigurable op-amp. It reduces power dissipation to one-quarter.

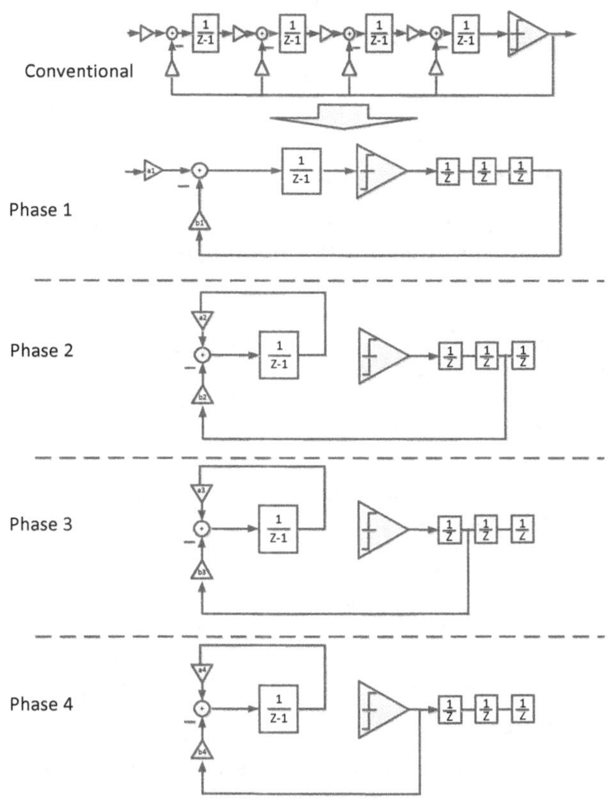

Fig. 1. Block diagram of the proposed fourth order feedback DSM with only one amplifier.

Fig. 1 shows four phases of the proposed fourth order DSM. In each phase, the DSM operates as each stage of a conventional DSM. Therefore it requires four times faster than a conventional

DSM in sampling frequency. This architecture employs a reconfigurable circuit topology with time interleaving technique. During the first phase(Phase 1) in Fig. 1, the modulator performs the sample mode and integration mode. In the second phase(Phase 2), the modulator performs the sample and integration with respect to the output signal of the op-amp in Phase 1. During the third phase(Phase 3), the modulator performs the sample and integration with respect to the output signal of the op-amp in Phase 2. Finally during the fourth phase(Phase 4), the modulator performs the sample and integration with respect to the output signal of the op-amp in Phase 3. Circuit schematic of the proposed low power 4th order ΣΔ modulator with only one amplifier is presented in Fig. 2. The DAC signals such as dacp (dacp3, dacp4, dacp5, dacp6) and dacn (dacn3, dacn4, dacn5, dacn6) are presented in Fig. 3. And those coefficients of the loop factor are illustrated in Table 1. The value of all the capacitors associated with those coefficients is illustrated in Fig. 2.

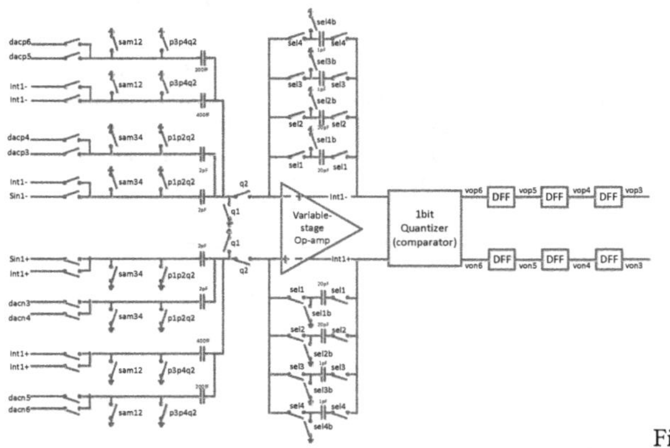

Fig. 2. **Circuit diagram of the proposed low power 4th order modulator with a reconfigurable op-amp.**

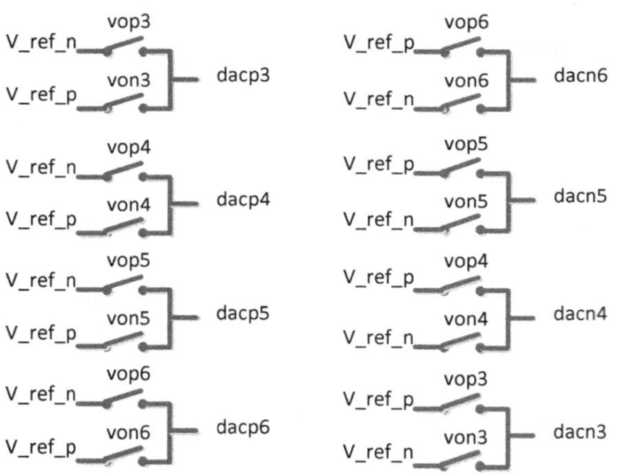

Fig. 3. Circuit diagram to generate dacps and dacns.

Table 1. Coefficients of the loop factor

Coefficient	Value	Coefficient	Value
a_1	0.10	b_1	0.10
a_2	0.10	b_2	0.10
a_3	0.25	b_3	0.20
a_4	0.50	b_4	0.40

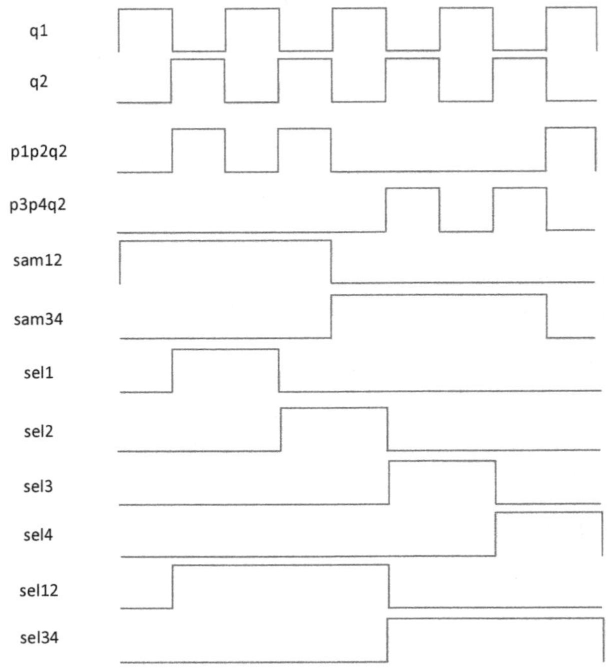

Fig. 4. Phase diagram of the clock signals to control both sample mode and integration mode.

The phase diagram of the clock signals is demonstrated in Fig. 4. All of the clock signals are non-overlapping clock. The q1 clock is the sampling mode and the q2 clock is the integration mode.

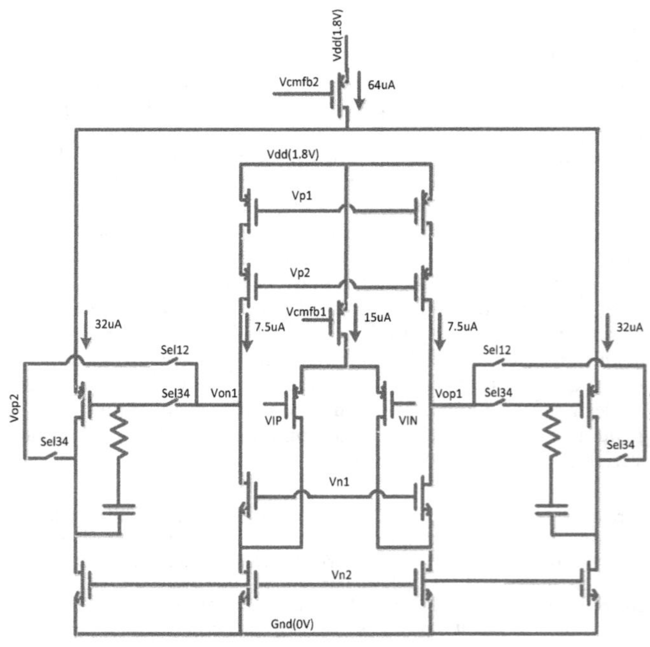

Fig. 5. Circuit schematic of the used Stage-variable Operational Amplifier.

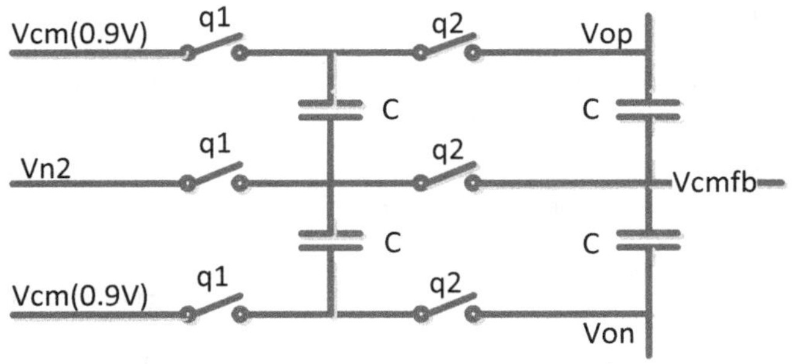

Fig. 6. Circuit schematic of the CMFB circuit.

The Circuit schematic of the reconfigurable op-amp is presented in Fig. 5. And Fig. 6 shows the CMFB circuit for the fully differential op-amp. Conventional delta-sigma modulator suffers from kT/C noise and the noise is critical for the input-side only. Hence the input capacitance is designed to be large and the rest of the capacitance is designed to be small. The designed sampling capacitance of the first and second phase is 2pF. The designed integration capacitance of the first and second phase is 20pF. And the designed sampling capacitance of the third and fourth phase is 400fF. The designed integration capacitance of the third and fourth phase is 1pF. Employment of one reconfigurable amplifier for 4th order delta-sigma modulator generates a problem of phase margin because of the load capacitance difference. In order for the modulator to operate properly, the phase margin of the modulator should remain within 60 to 90 degrees [4].

To solve the problem, a reconfigurable op-amp is employed with reconfigurable switches. In the first and second Phase, the amplifier operates with two stage architecture. In the third and fourth Phase, the amplifier operates as single stage folded-cascode architecture. Based on folded cascade structure, the open loop gain of the op-amp in the first and second phase is 125dB, phase margin is 68 degree and unity gain frequency is 17MHz. The open loop gain of the op-amp in the third and fourth phase is 75dB, phase margin is 86 degree and unity gain frequency is 19MHz. Therefore the op-amp operates properly in all four phases. The spice simulations verify the adequate functionality of the op-amp for all four phases, as shown in Fig. 7.

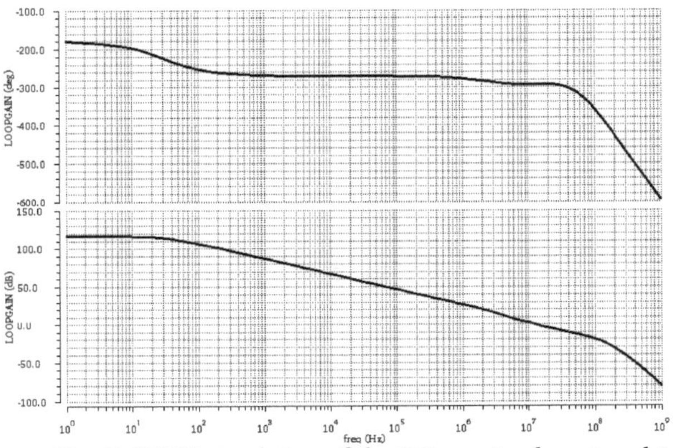

Fig. 7. SPICE simulation of the OP-amp in phase 1 and 2.

The proposed DSM is designed with a 0.18um CMOS process and the microchip photograph of the proposed circuit is represented in Fig. 8. It occupies a core area of 800um x 900um. The power supply voltage is 1.8V. Fig. 9 shows the measurement results of the input (0.9V peak to peak at 250Hz) and output waveform. The FFT measurement result of the proposed DSM is presented in Fig. 10. It demonstrates SNR of 72.8 dB, ENOB of 11.8 bits, and power dissipation of 352uW at sampling frequency of 128kHz, input signal frequency of 250Hz, and the magnitude of the input signal, Vdd/2.

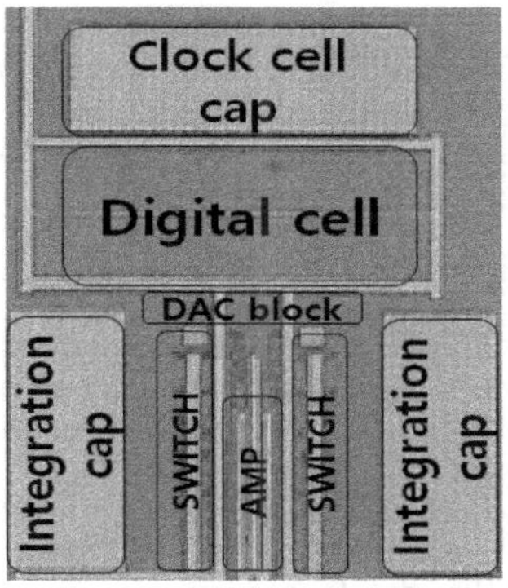

Fig. 8. The microchip photograph of the proposed DSM.

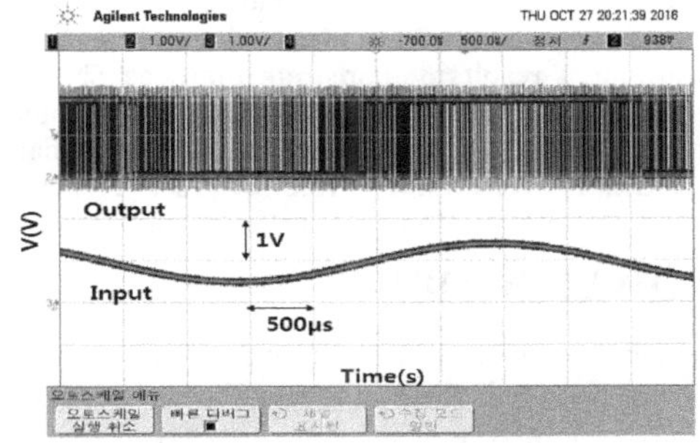

Fig. 9. Measurement of the input and output waveform.

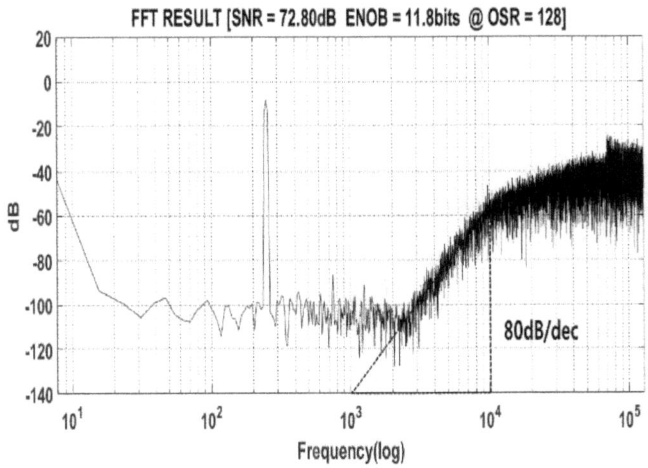

Fig. 10. FFT spectrum measurement result of the proposed modulator.

The power consumption and FOM(Walden) of the proposed work become half, compared with those of [1] which describes the fourth order DSM based upon two OPAMPs. The FOM (Schreier) of the proposed work is more than 12 dB with respect to that of [1]. Compared with the inverter-based DSM [2], the power consumption, SNDR, and DR of the proposed one are greater. The third order DSM with only one two stage OPAMP was implemented with SNDR of 84 dB, DR of 88 dB, and power consumption of 140 μW [4]. Compared to the other inverter-based circuit [7], SNDR and ENOB of the proposed one is superior to [7], but the power consumption and FOM (Walden) of the proposed one is inferior. is increased by 10dB and it can be seen that power consumption is greatly reduced.

3. CONCLUSION

The 4th-order feedback delta-sigma modulator with only one operational amplifier is proposed for the application of bio signal processing. The single reconfigurable fully differential amplifier, which can be either two stage OPAMP (the first and second integrator) or folded-cascode OPAMP (the third and fourth integrator), was employed not only to provide enough phase margin of OPAMPs, but to reduce power consumption of the proposed DSM. This methodology enforces the proposed DSM to increase clock frequency four times with respect to that of the conventional ones. The proposed modulator is designed and implemented with CMOS 0.18um n-well 1 poly 6 metal process. The measurement results demonstrate the peak SNDR of 72.8dB and the ENOB of 11.8bits with an input signal frequency of 250 Hz, a sampling frequency of 256 kHz, an input signal bandwidth of 1 kHz, and an oversampling rate of 128. The total power dissipation was measured to be 356 μW at a supply voltage of 1.8V.

ACKNOWLEDGMENT

This research was supported by Basic Science Research Program through the National Research Foundation of Korea (NRF) funded by the Ministry of Education (2010-0020163).

REFERENCES

[1] S. H. Yang, J. H. Choi and G. S. Yoon, "A Design of Reconfigurable 4th Order delta-sigma Modulator Using Two Op-amps," Journal of The Institute of Electronics and Information Engineers, vol. 52, No. 5, pp. 875-881, May. 2015.

[2] Y. Chae and G. Han, "Low voltage, low power, inverter-based switched-capacitor delta-sigma modulator," IEEE J. Solid-State circuits, vol. 44, no. 2, pp. 458-472, Feb. 2009.

[3] J. Choi and K. Yoon, "A CMOS Third Order ΔΣ Modulator with Inverter-Based Integrators," IEEE System on a chip Conference, September 2017.

[4] A.P.Perez, E. Bonzzoni, and F. Maloberti, "A 88-dB DR, 84-dB SNDR very low-power single op-amp third-order ΣΔ modulator, " IEEE Journal of Solid-State Circuits, Vol. 47, No. 9, pp. 2017-2118, Sep. 2012.

[5] A.Pugliese; F.A.Amoroso; G.Cappuccino; G.Cocorullo, "Analysis of op-amp phase margin on SC delta-sigma modulator performances," Microelectronics Journal. Vol. 41. No. 7, pp. 440-446, July. 2010.

[6] Ali Agah; Katelijin Vleugels; Peter B.Griffin, Mostafa Ronaghi; James D.Plummer; Bruce A. Wooley, "A High-Resolution Low-Power Incremental sigma-delta ADC With Extended Range for Biosensor Arrays", IEEE Journal of Solid-State Circuits, vol.45, no.6, pp. 1099-1110, June. 2010.

[7] F.Michel and M.S.J.Steyaert, "A 250mV 7.5uW 61dB SNDR SC delta-sigma modulator using near-threshold-voltage-biased inverter amplifiers in 130nm CMOS," IEEE Journal of Solid-State Circuits, vol. 47, no. 3, pp. 709-721, Mar. 2012.

[8] Yamamoto, K. and Carusone, A.C. "A 1-1-1-1 MASH Delta-Sigma Modulator With Dynamic Comparator-Based OTAs," IEEE Journal of Solid-State Circuits, vol. 47, no. 1, pp. 1866-1883, Aug. 2012.

[9] A. Ismail and I. Mostafa, "A Process-Tolerant, Low-Voltage, Inverter-Based OTA for Continuous-Time Delta-Sigma ADC", IEEE Transactions on Very Large Scale Integration Systems, vol. 24, pp. 2911-2917, 2016.

[10] S. Richards and G. C. Temes, Understanding Delta Sigma data converters, Wiley Interscience, 2005

[11] S. Richards and J. Silva and J. Streensgaard and G. C. Temes, "Design-Oriented Estimation of Thermal Noise in Switched-Capacitor Circuits," IEEE Transactions On Circuits And Systems. Vol. 52, No. 11, pp. 2358-2368, Nov.2005.

On the Design of Reliable Heterogeneous Systems via Checkpoint Placement and Core Assignment

Edwin Sha[†], Hailiang Dong[‡], Weiwen Jiang[§], Qingfeng Zhuge[†], Xianzhang Chen[‡], Lei Yang[♯]

[†] School of Computer Science and Software Engineering, East China Normal University, Shanghai 200062, China
[‡] College of Computer Science, Chongqing University, Chongqing, 400044, China
[§] Department of Electrical and Computer Engineering, University of Pittsburgh, Pittsburgh, PA 15261, USA
[♯] Department of Computer Science, University of California, Irvine, CA 92697-3435, USA
{edwinsha, leondong1993, jiang.wwen, qfzhuge, xzchen109, yanglary}@gmail.com

ABSTRACT

This paper studies two basic problems in the design of high-performance and high-reliability heterogeneous systems: (1) what type of core to execute each task, and (2) where to place checkpoints in the execution of tasks. The implementation of checkpointing techniques on the novel persistent memory (e.g., 3D Xpoint memory) based heterogeneous systems faces a bundle of new problems. First, the assignments of tasks may greatly influence the execution time of the whole application. Therefore, with the same time constraint, the reliability of the resultant system can be significantly affected. Second, creating checkpoints will incur heavy writes on persistent memories and reduce the lifetime of devices. In this paper, we optimally construct reliable systems by assigning tasks to the most suitable cores and placing minimum number of checkpoints in the application, such that the resultant system can satisfy the time constraint in the presence of faults. We devise an efficient dynamic programming algorithm to obtain the optimal assignment and checkpoint placement. Experimental results demonstrate that, compared with existing approaches, our technique can achieve 44% reductions on the number of checkpoints on average.

ACM Reference Format:
Edwin Sha[†], Hailiang Dong[‡], Weiwen Jiang[‡§], Qingfeng Zhuge[†], Xianzhang Chen[‡], Lei Yang[‡♯]. 2018. On the Design of Reliable Heterogeneous Systems via Checkpoint Placement and Core Assignment. In *Proceedings of Great Lakes Symposium on VLSI 2018 (GLSVLSI'18)*. ACM, New York, NY, USA, 4 pages. https://doi.org/10.1145/3194554.3194642

1 INTRODUCTION

With the increasing demand for high-performance and low-cost design, pipeline techniques have been employed to improve performance and heterogeneous architectures such as heterogeneous Multiprocessor System-on-Chip (MPSoC) have become de facto standard to reduce costs. This promotes the emergence of a new kind of MPSoC, called pipelined MPSoCs [4, 6]. In a pipelined MPSoC, cores are connected in a pipelined configuration and execute different sub-tasks of an application in a pipelined fashion. While pipelining can provide high performance, the fail of a single pipeline stage will lead to the pipeline stall that affects the performance of whole system. Checkpointing techniques are widely employed to guarantee the correctness of system behaviors, in which the system can tolerate a given number of faults [10].

Different from placing checkpoints on single-core systems, conducting the checkpointing technique on the pipelined heterogeneous MPSoC faces a lot of challenges. *First*, due to limited computational resources, tasks in the application need to be partitioned into different pipeline stages. *Second*, due to the heterogeneity in the MPSoC, the execution time of tasks varies on different cores. *Third*, high-reliability requirements and real-time constraints need to be satisfied simultaneously. In order to ensure the system can meet the time constraint even when faults occur, we need to carefully determine three coupled functions: **(1)** the partition of tasks into pipeline stages (called *Partition*), **(2)** the assignment of pipeline stages to heterogeneous cores (called *Assignment*), and **(3)** the number and position of checkpoints (called *Checkpoint Placement*).

Given a task graph of an application, our objective is to minimize the number of checkpoints used to construct a reliable pipelined system that can satisfy a given time constraint even in the presence of faults. Besides the consideration of degradation on performance, we would like to minimize the number of checkpoints since state-of-the-art MPSoCs commonly employ FLASH or non-volatile memory (NVM) as the main memory, which has limited write-endurance.

Our contributions are two-fold. (1) We formally define the problem of Partition and Assignment under Faults (PAF). (2) We present an efficient algorithm that can obtain the optimal solution for PAF problem in seconds. To evaluate the efficiency and effectiveness of the proposed algorithm, we conduct comprehensive experiments based on benchmarks in StreamIT [15]. Experimental results show that, compared with existing approaches, our algorithm can achieve 44% reductions on average in terms of the number of checkpoints.

GLSVLSI'18, May 23–25, 2018, Chicago, IL, USA

ACM ISBN 978-1-4503-5724-1/18/05...$15.00
https://doi.org/10.1145/3194554.3194642

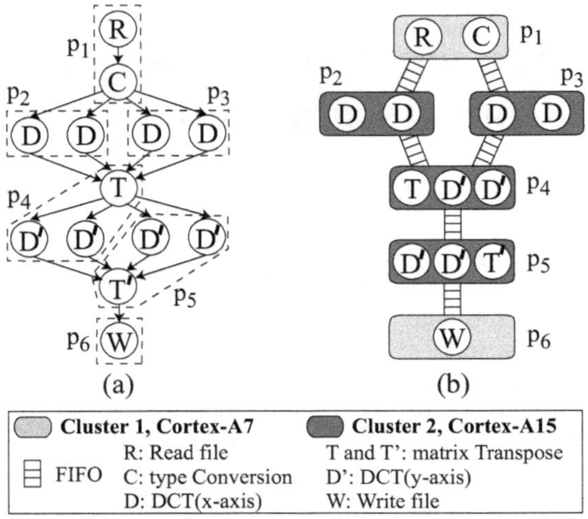

Figure 1: System models: (a) task graph of DCT with partitions; (b) pipelined MPSoC with assignments.

2 SYSTEM MODEL AND PROBLEM

Application Model. In this paper, we consider applications that are iteratively executed on a set of input data (e.g. streaming applications or neural networks). An application is modeled by a task graph $G = \langle V, E\rangle$ where V is a set of nodes representing tasks and $E \subseteq V \times V$ is a set of edges representing data dependencies between tasks. For instance, Figure 1(a) shows the task graph of two dimensional DCT application selected from StreamIT [15].

Architecture Model. This paper targets systems equipped with the heterogeneous MPSoC and persistent memory such as FLASH and NVM (e.g. 3D Xpoint memory [1]). As the increase of the number of cores in an MPSoC, cores are grouped into clusters due to the hardware cost and area requirement. For cores in the same cluster, they usually have identical architectures [14, 18]. An example of commercial heterogeneous cluster MPSoC is ARM big.LITTLE [3], which is widely employed by modern MPSoCs.

A heterogeneous MPSoC is defined as $H = \langle C, m\rangle$, where C is a set of clusters and m is a attribute function. For $c_i \in C$, the attribute $m(c_i)$ represents the number of cores in c_i. Note that when $m(c_i) = 1$ for any c_i, *it indicates all cores in an MPSoC have different architectures.* Hence, algorithms proposed in this paper can also handle the general cases.

Task Assignment. Due to limited computational resources, we need to partition task graph into different groups. Define the partition of task graph G as $P(G) = \{p_i \mid i = 1..s\}$, where p_i is the ith pipeline stage and s is the number of pipeline stages. In this paper, we aims at constructing pipelined MPSoCs where each core corresponds to a pipeline stage [4, 6]. Figure 1 shows the partition of application DCT and the corresponding pipelined MPSoC.

Given a heterogeneous MPSoC H, we define the assignment of task graph G as a function A from domain $P(G)$ to H. $A(p_i) = c_j$ means that pipeline stage p_i will be executed by a core in cluster c_j. For instance, in Figure 1(b), p_3 is assigned to a core in cluster c_2. In next sections, we will use notation $A(G)$ to represent the assignment of task graph G.

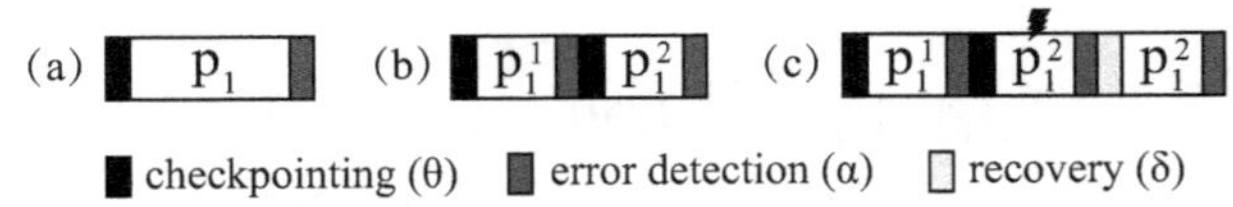

Figure 2: Checkpointing with rollback recovery.

Checkpoint Placement. Fault-tolerant techniques can be divided into two categories: the probabilistic approach that try to maximize the probability of meeting deadlines at a given failure rate and the deterministic approach that can tolerate a given number of faults while preserving deadlines. In this paper, we employ the checkpointing with rollback recovery technique [9–12, 17] to tolerate K transient errors.

Figure 2(a) and (b) illustrates the situation when we place one and two checkpoints at pipeline stage p_1. Note that we call the part of a pipeline stage between two checkpoints as an execution segment and we will use notation p_i^j to represent the jth execution segment of pipeline stage p_i. Figure 2(c) depicts the situation that an error occurs in the execution of p_1^2. We can simply rollback to the correct status by loading the information saved at the second checkpoint, which can considerably reduce the time overhead for recovery. In this paper, the costs of error detecting, checkpointing and recovery are represented by α, θ, δ, respectively.

Given a task graph G, we define the checkpoint placement T as a function from domain $P \times N$ to Z. For pipeline stage $p_i \in P$, $T(p_i, j) = t$ means the jth checkpoint of p_i is placed at the time t. Note that when $T(p_i, j) < 0$, it indicates that p_i do not have the jth checkpoint, i.e., the number of checkpoints in p_i must be less than j. For ease of presentation, we will use notation $T(G)$ to represent the checkpoint placement for all pipeline stages in P.

Iteration Period. The iteration period (the reciprocal of the throughput) of a pipeline system is defined as the maximum latency of all pipeline stages. The latency of pipeline stage p_i is the total execution time that all tasks in p_i have correctly executed once. Given an MPSoC H, a task graph G, We use notation $IP_{P,A,T}(H, G)$ to represent the iteration period under partition $P(G)$, assignment $A(G)$ and checkpoint placement $T(G)$. And we have the following equation.

$$IP_{P,A,T}(H,G) = \max_{\forall p_i \in P(G)} \left\{ RC_i + (\alpha + \theta) \times CN_i + \sum_{\forall v_j \in p_i} et_{j,A(p_i)} \right\}$$

Note that RC_i stands for the recovery cost. When no faults occur in a certain iteration, we have $RC_i = 0$. Otherwise, assume a fault occurs at p_i^k, then we have $RC_i = \alpha + \delta + d_i^k$, where d_i^k is the length of execution segment p_i^k. If there are multiple errors occur in a pipeline stage, we just need to sum the recovery cost of each error.

System Cost. We define the system cost as the summation of the number of checkpoints in all pipeline stages. Given an MPSoC H and a task graph G, We use notation $SC_{P,T}(H, G)$ to represent the system cost under checkpoint placement $T(G)$ and partition $P(G)$, i.e., $SC_{P,T}(H, G) = \sum_{p_i \in P} CN_i = \sum_{p_i \in P} \max\{j | T(p_i, j) \geq 0\}$, where CN_i is the number of checkpoints in p_i.

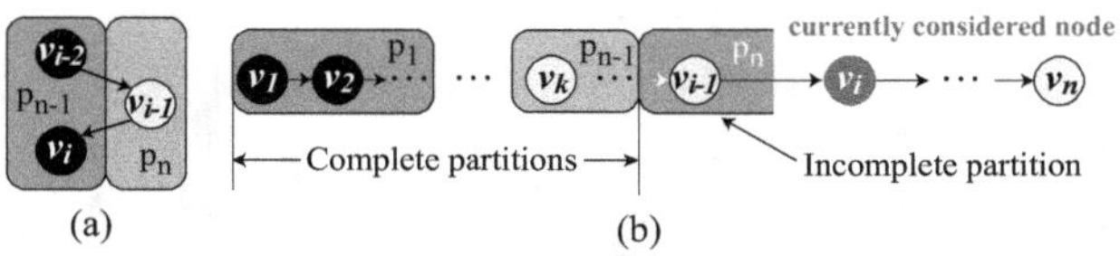

Figure 3: Examples: (a) An invalid partition; (b) Partitions in the consideration of node v_i.

Problem Definition. We define the problem of *Partition and Assignment under Faults (PAF)* as follows. Given an MPSoC H, a task graph G, a required iteration period R and an integer K, the problem is to determine,

P: the partition of task graph G

A: the assignment of pipeline stages in G

T: the checkpoint placement for pipeline stages in G

such that the resultant pipeline has the minimum system cost. In the meantime, its iteration period is less than R even when K faults occur in each pipeline stage.

3 OPTIMAL ALGORITHM

Theorem. Before presenting our algorithm, we introduce an important theorem first.

THEOREM 1. *Execution segments of any pipeline stage p_i in optimal solution must have same length, denoted as L_i.*

The theorem can be proved by contradictory, due to space limitations, detailed proofs are omitted. Based on Theorem 1, instead of determining the position of each checkpoint for pipeline stages, we determine the distance between two consecutive checkpoints, called *checkpoint distance.*

We claim that given the ETWF of a pipeline stage, we can obtain the optimal checkpoint placement in polynomial time. Assume the ETWF of pipeline stage p_i is ET_i, the required iteration period is R and we need to tolerate K faults. Suppose the checkpoint distance is d, thus, the WLUF of pipeline stage p_i should be smaller than R, i.e.,

$$K \cdot (d + \alpha + \delta) + ET_i + (\alpha + \theta) \cdot ET_i/d \leq R \qquad (1)$$

By multiplying d in both sides of the inequality, we can turn it into a quadratic inequality. We can easily obtain the maximum feasible value d_{max}, and the corresponding cost can be calculated as $\lceil ET_i/d_{max} \rceil$. In next sections, we assume we have a general function $CKC(t)$ to obtain the number of checkpoints given the ETWF of a pipeline stage.

Algorithm. Now we are going to introduce the optimal algorithm. Let the topological order of a task graph be $v_1 \rightarrow v_2 \rightarrow \cdots \rightarrow v_N$. In our dynamic programming algorithm, we consider these nodes one by one. In our algorithm, for simplicity, we consider the platform with two clusters. We will construct the dynamic programming table D_{i,j,k,t,m_1,m_2}. Each entry records *the minimum cost* from node v_1 to v_i under the following conditions: (1) node v_i is assigned to a core in cluster c_j; (2) node v_i is partitioned into the kth pipeline stage; (3) the ETWF of last pipeline stage is exactly t; (4) the numbers of assigned cores in clusters c_1 and c_2 are m_1 and m_2, respectively. Note that if there are no solutions satisfy the above conditions, we set $D_{i,j,k,t,m_1,m_2} = \infty$.

Now we introduce how to construct the dynamic programming table D_{i,j,k,t,m_1,m_2}. As shown in Figure 3(b), when considering node v_i, we can either incorporate v_i into a previous partition or create a new partition that only contains node v_i. Note that node v_i can only be absorbed into the last partition p_n, called incomplete partition. Otherwise, the resultant system will not be pipelined, as shown in Figure 3(a). The recursive function (assume $j = 1$) is given as follows.

$$D_{i,j,k,t,m_1,m_2} = \begin{cases} D_{i-1,j,k,\mathbf{t-et_{i,j}},m_1,m_2} + CKC(t) - CKC(t - et_{i,j}) & if\ t > et_{i,j} \\ \min\limits_{j^* \in C, t^* \in [1,R]} \{D_{i-1,j^*,k-1,t^*,\mathbf{m_1-1},m_2}\} + CKC(t) & if\ t = et_{i,j} \\ \infty & if\ t < et_{i,j} \end{cases}$$

It consists of three cases. Case one means that *node v_i is absorbed into the incomplete partition.* In this case, before node v_i has been absorbed, the latency of incomplete partition is $t - et_{i,j}$. Hence, we consider the sub problem $D_{i-1,j,k,\mathbf{t-et_{i,j}},m_1,m_2}$. Since the latency of incomplete stage is updated from $t - et_{i,j}$ to t, we add the extra cost $CKC(t) - CKC(t - et_{i,j})$ in equation (3). For case two, it indicates that *node v_i forms a new partition.* Note that when $j = 2$, we should consider sub problem $D_{i-1,j^*,\mathbf{k-1},t^*,m_1,\mathbf{m_2-1}}$. For case three, since the latency of the incomplete stage cannot be less than the execution time of task v_i on cluster c_j, there is no feasible solutions and we record ∞ in the cell.

The time complexity of the algorithm is $O(|V| \cdot |C|^3 \cdot R^2 \cdot B \cdot B^{|C|})$, where B is the maximum number of cores incorporated in a single cluster. Since the number of clusters in existing platforms is small (2 or 3 clusters)[3, 16], our algorithm is efficient in practice.

4 EVALUATION RESULTS

Experimental setup. We base our experiments on eight benchmarks in StreamIT [15], i.e., `des`, `deskey`, `jpeg`, `serpent`, `matmul`, `vocoder`, `mp3` and `mpeg2`. The execution times of tasks in these benchmarks are obtained by executing the benchmark on the real-world mobile platform Odroid-XU3 [2]. We compare our optimal algorithm with two existing approaches: (1) the combination of the particle swarm algorithm [13] and our checkpoint placement technique (called `PSO`); (2) a greedy algorithm that always use high-performance cores first and tries to equalize the ETWF between clusters and cores (called `Greedy`), it also employs the checkpoint placement technique proposed in this paper. Since the performance of PSO algorithm is closely related to initial solutions, we run `PSO` five times and select the best result in the following experiments for fairness.

Comparisons with existing techniques. Figure 4 reports the detailed results for different reliability requirements. From the results, there are several observations. (1) `Greedy` cannot find any feasible solutions in many cases. The reason is that `Greedy` separately considers the assignment, partition and checkpoint placement. (2) In some cases, `PSO` also fails to obtain feasible solutions. This is because that `PSO` cannot

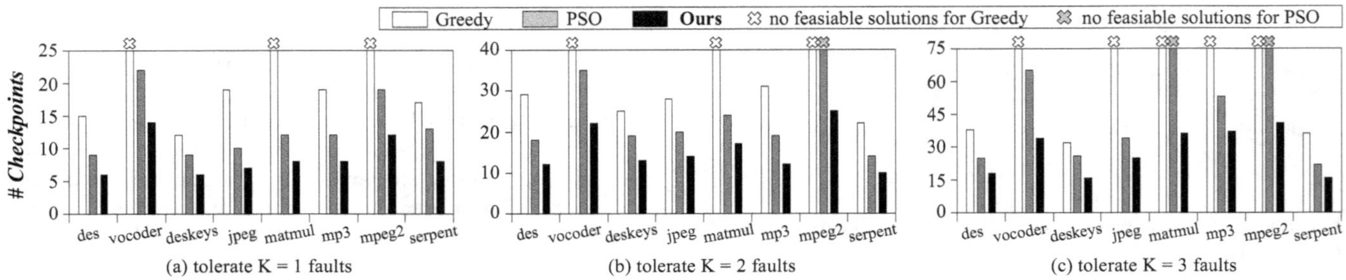

Figure 4: Comparisons on the number of checkpoints under different reliability requirements. Compared with `Greedy` and `PSO`, our algorithm can achieve 54.7% and 33.2% reductions on average, respectively.

fully explore the design space and the quality of initial solutions has a significant influence on the final solution. (3) For those cases that other approaches can find feasible solutions, our algorithm can achieve significant reductions on the number of checkpoints. Specifically, compared to **Greedy**, we can achieve 56.8%, 54.5% and 52.7% reductions on average in terms of the number of checkpoints when the system needs to tolerate one, two and three faults. When compared to **PSO**, those figures are 34.4%, 32.4% and 33.6%, respectively. The evaluation results demonstrate the effectiveness and practicality of our algorithm in real-world benchmarks.

5 RELATED WORK

Many research efforts have proposed assignment and partition methods in the design of pipeline systems. Kuang et al. [8] present ILP formulations to find the optimal partition and pipelined scheduling of embedded multimedia systems.

Recently, more and more studies focus on optimizing systems on heterogeneous architectures under a given time constraint. Javaid et al. [4] aim to optimize the area of a pipelined MPSoC under a given latency or a throughput constraint. Jiang et al. [5, 7] target on minimizing the system cost in the synthesis of special-purpose pipelined architectures. Yang et al. [19, 20] present scheduling and mapping algorithms for NoC based MPSoCs. However, none of these works considers faults in the system. Therefore, solutions generated by those approaches may fail to meet the time constraint and lead to serious consequence.

Checkpointing techniques are widely employed to tolerate transient faults. Salehi et al. [12] propose a two-state checkpointing scheme to achieve low-energy fault tolerance for hard real-time systems. Xie et al. [17] propose an inconsistency-aware checkpointing scheme for energy harvesting powered non-volatile processors.

6 CONCLUSION

In this work, we studied the problem of Partition and Assignment under Faults (PAF) to optimally construct fault-tolerant pipelined MPSoCs using minimum number of checkpoints. We proposed an efficient algorithm that can obtain optimal partition, assignment and checkpoint placement in seconds. Experimental results show that, compared with existing approaches, our algorithm can achieve 44% reductions on average in terms of the number of checkpoints.

ACKNOWLEDGMENT

This work is partially supported by National 863 Program [Grant No. 2015AA015304], National Natural Science Foundation of China [Grant No. 61472052], China Scholarship Council [No. 201706050116, 201706050117].

REFERENCES

[1] 3d xpoint storage memory. http://www.intel.com.
[2] Odroid-xu3. http://goo.gl/Nn6z3O.
[3] Samsung exynos 5422. http://www.samsung.com.
[4] Haris Javaid et al. Optimal synthesis of latency and throughput constrained pipelined mpsocs targeting streaming applications. In *CODES+ISSS*, pages 75–84. IEEE, 2010.
[5] Weiwen Jiang et al. Optimal functional-unit assignment and buffer placement for probabilistic pipelines. In *CODES+ISSS*, page 13, 2016.
[6] Weiwen Jiang et al. Optimal functional unit assignment and voltage selection for pipelined mpsoc with guaranteed probability on time performance. In *LCTES'17*, pages 41–50. ACM, 2017.
[7] Weiwen Jiang et al. On the design of minimal-cost pipeline systems satisfying hard/soft real-time constraints. *IEEE Transactions on Emerging Topics in Computing*, 2018.
[8] Shiann Rong Kuang et al. Partitioning and pipelined scheduling of embedded system using integer linear programming. In *ICPADS - Workshops*, pages 37–41, 2005.
[9] Chen Pan et al. A lightweight progress maximization scheduler for non-volatile processor under unstable energy harvesting. In *LCTES'17*, pages 101–110. ACM, 2017.
[10] Paul Pop et al. Design optimization of time and cost-constrained fault-tolerant embedded systems with checkpointing and replication. *Transactions on VLSI Systems*, 17(3):389–402, 2009.
[11] Sasikumar Punnekkat et al. Analysis of checkpointing for real-time systems. *Real-Time Systems*, 20(1):83–102, 2001.
[12] Mohammad Salehi et al. Two-state checkpointing for energy-efficient fault tolerance in hard real-time systems. *IEEE Transactions on VLSI*, 24(7):2426–2437, 2016.
[13] Ayed Salman et al. Particle swarm optimization for task assignment problem. *Microprocessors and Microsystems*, 26(8):363–371, 2002.
[14] Jelena Spasic et al. Energy-efficient mapping of real-time applications on heterogeneous mpsocs using task replication. In *CODES+ISSS*, page 28. ACM, 2016.
[15] William Thies et al. Streamit: A language for streaming applications. In *Compiler Construction*, pages 179–196, 2002.
[16] SMP Variable. A multi-core cpu architecture for low power and high performance. *Whitepaper-http://www.nvidia.com*, 2011.
[17] Mimi Xie et al. Fixing the broken time machine: Consistency-aware checkpointing for energy harvesting powered non-volatile processor. In *DAC*, pages 1–6, 2015.
[18] Lei Yang et al. Application mapping and scheduling for network-on-chip-based multiprocessor system-on-chip with fine-grain communication optimization. *IEEE Transactions on VLSI Systems*, 24(10):3027–3040, 2016.
[19] Lei Yang et al. Fotonoc: A hierarchical management strategy based on folded torus-like network-on-chip for dark silicon many-core systems. In *ASP-DAC'16*, pages 725–730. IEEE, 2016.
[20] Lei Yang et al. Task mapping on smart noc: Contention matters, not the distance. In *DAC'17*, pages 1–6. IEEE, 2017.

SAT-Lancer: A Hardware SAT-Solver for Self-Verification

Buse Ustaoglu, Sebastian Huhn, Daniel Große, Rolf Drechsler
Cyber Physical Systems, DFKI GmbH, Bremen, Germany
Group of Computer Architecture, University of Bremen, Germany
buse.ustaoglu@dfki.de,{huhn,grosse,drechsle}@cs.uni-bremen.de

ABSTRACT

To close the ever widening verification gap, new powerful solutions are strictly required. One such promising approach aims in continuing verification tasks after production of a chip during its lifetime. This approach is called self-verification. However, for realizing self-verification tasks on-chip, verification packages have to be developed. In this paper, we propose the verification package SAT-Lancer. SAT-Lancer is a compact Boolean Satisfiability (SAT) solver and has been implemented entirely on HW with the capability of solving any arbitrary SAT-instance. At the heart of SAT-Lancer is a scalable memory model, which can be adjusted to given memory constraints and allows to store the SAT-instance most effectively. In comparison to previous HW SAT-solvers, SAT-Lancer utilizes significant less area and can handle order of magnitude larger SAT-instances.

ACM Reference Format:
Buse Ustaoglu, Sebastian Huhn, Daniel Große, Rolf Drechsler. 2018. SAT-Lancer: A Hardware SAT-Solver for Self-Verification. In *Proceedings of 2018 Great Lakes Symposium on VLSI (GLSVLSI '18).* ACM, New York, NY, USA, 4 pages. https://doi.org/10.1145/3194554.3194643

1 INTRODUCTION

Electronic systems are used in various application domains ranging from cars to mobiles, from industrial control to IoT devices. In these domains very different design goals with respect to functionality, performance and power requirement have to be considered. However, the process of verification is fundamental for all electronic systems and it ensures that a design implementation meets its specification. To keep pace with the enormous dimension of freedom in producing chips, a variety of verification methods are available today. Essentially, three main directions can be distinguished: simulation, formal verification and emulation. A strong verification platform spanning from abstract high-level models down to the *Register-Transfer-Level* (RTL) implementation is formed by orchestrating these techniques in a clever way. Simultaneously, on the design side, *Intellectual Property* (IP) re-use has become an integral part of all design flows today. Unfortunately, despite all these advancements, the verification complexity continues to increase at approx. 4 times more than the rate of design creation [11]. To attack this widening verification gap, the new promising and complementary approach of *self-verification* has been recently proposed in [5, 6, 10]. Self-verification allows an electronic system to continue open verification tasks after fabrication. However, to bring self-verification to life, as major components verification packages are needed. The verification packages execute the remaining verification tasks directly on the chip.

In this paper, we target small to mid-sized electronic systems (e.g. from the IoT domain), and hence present a compact verification package for self-verification, which allows to heavily orchestrate SAT-based verification techniques like *Bounded Model Checking* (BMC) [1] directly on-chip. More precisely, we propose **SAT-Lancer: a complete HW SAT-solver IP-component** which can solve any arbitrary SAT-instance that has been generated on-chip. Such a SAT-instance represents a Boolean formula (coming from a verification task) and raises the question whether an assignment to all Boolean variables exists such that the overall formula is *satisfied* (SAT) or remains *unsatisfied* (UNSAT), respectively. Other existing approaches for SAT-solving either focus on accelerating a SW-based SAT-solver by outsourcing the solving process partially to HW [2, 8, 13, 14] or by introducing even for small SAT-instance sizes a large HW-overhead [9, 12]. In contrast to this, the proposed HW SAT-solver is very compact and can be easily integrated as an IP-component into an existing design. At the heart of our HW SAT-solver is a *scalable memory model.* Essentially, the memory model defines how to utilize the memory most effectively for storing the investigated SAT-instance as well as meta information of the SAT-solving process itself.

In an extensive experimental evaluation we demonstrate the advantages of our proposed HW SAT-solver. It shows that SAT-Lancer can handle much larger instances in comparison to existing HW-based approaches and outperform a SW-based SAT-solver, which adheres to area constraints for the underlying HW.

2 SCALABLE MEMORY MODEL

In this section we present the heart of SAT-Lancer, i.e., the scalable memory model. Please note that we assume that the reader is familiar with SAT-solving and the basic DPLL algorithm.

In general, to realize a HW SAT-solver the *Conjunctive Normal Form* (CNF) instance has to be stored in a HW memory. This memory is then accessed by the core of the HW SAT-solver for solving the instance, i.e., to determine a satisfying assignment for the clauses or to prove that no such assignment exists.

The basic idea of our proposed memory model is to store a literal of the current clause as well as meta information about the SAT-solving process itself in a memory word. Thereby, scalability is achieved by identifying, which information is essential and which information can be reduced to adhere given memory constraints (e.g. in terms of word size). Moreover, by following the principle of locality, the actual HW implementation of SAT-Lancer and in particular the interface between the SAT-solver core and the memory can be optimized. This allows to process even large SAT-instances.

2.1 Principle Memory Layout

he principle memory layout is shown in the middle of Fig. 1. As can be seen it is inspired by the DIMACs encoding. More precisely,

GLSVLSI '18, May 23–25, 2018, Chicago, IL, USA

ACM ISBN 978-1-4503-5724-1/18/05...$15.00
https://doi.org/10.1145/3194554.3194643

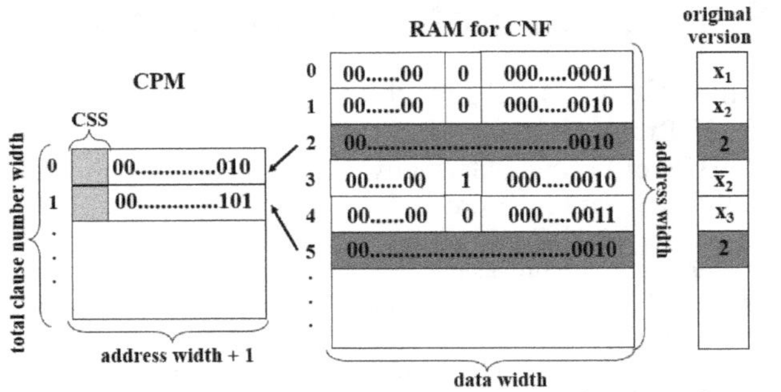

Figure 1: Example of principle memory layout for example CNF $f = (x_1 + x_2) \cdot (\overline{x}_2 + x_3)$

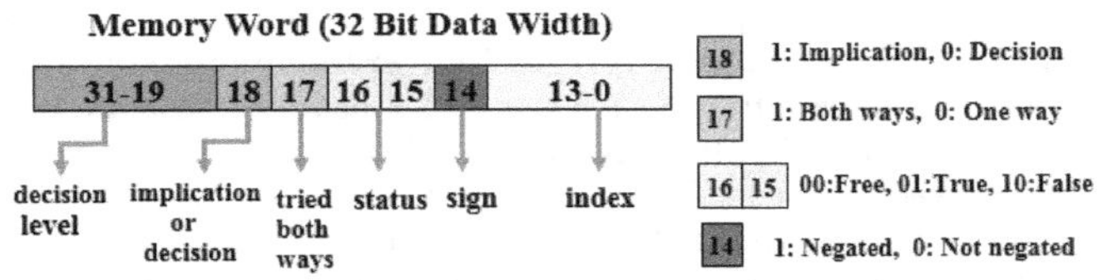

Figure 2: Meta Information and Literal Encoding

we utilize the lower bits of each memory word to store the index and add one further bit to store the sign. When assuming a 32 bit memory, obviously, many bits remain unused and, consequently, should be used to save HW resources. Due to this fact, we identify which information of the SAT-solving process can be stored in the upper bits of a memory word to effectively use the memory.

On the left of Fig. 1 an additional memory is shown which stores the address where a clause ends. We refer to this memory as *Clause Position Memory* (CPM). The CPM allows a fast and direct access to a specific clause. With this knowledge, instead of storing a "0" to mark the end of a clause, we can now use this memory location to store the number of free literals of the clause under the current assignment. Moreover CPM holds the decision level of a literal that has maximum value of the clause.

Finally, the most-significant bit of each CPM entry represents the *Clause SAT Status* (CSS), i.e., whether the current clause is already SAT or not (cf. Subsection 2.2).

2.2 Encoding of Meta Information

Staying with the assumption of a 32 bit memory, we performed a careful analysis of information to be stored in a memory word supplementary to the pure literal encoding. Fig. 2 shows the outcome: For a 32 bit memory word, the lower 14 bits encode the variable index, the 14th bit the sign, bit-15,16 define the status of the literal which can be free, assigned to "0" or assigned to "1", bit-17 defines whether the variable has been assigned to both values ("0" and "1") for conflict resolution at same decision level, bit-18 indicates whether the assignment to the current literal results from a decision of the SAT-solver or an implication and the upper 13 bits (19 to 31) represent the decision level, i.e., the number of decisions, which have so far been done during the solving process.

Based on the general presentation of our memory model, we want to emphasize that the scalability is a major challenge: This is due to the application-specific resource constraints, particularly, constraints concerning the memory size as well as memory width, i.e., the size of a (single) word. As becoming evident from the introduced SAT-instance encoding, our scheme is scalable: the bit width of a memory word can be varied and we can reflect this by adapting the number of bits to represent the index as well as the decision level while the other bits are kept (essential information).

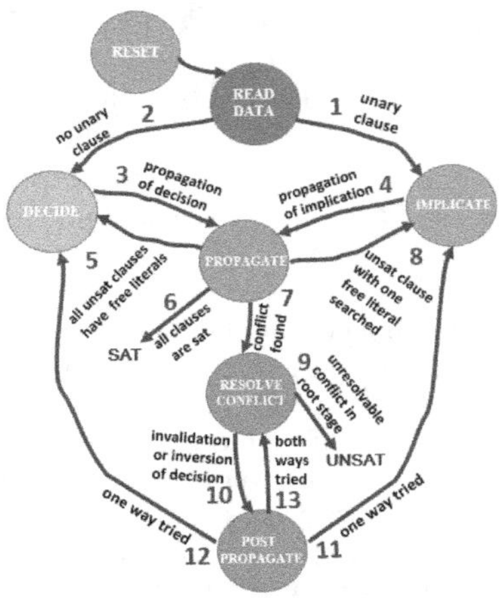

Figure 3: State Machine

3 DESIGN OF SAT-LANCER

This section describes the principle design of SAT-Lancer from a HW point of view and presents an exemplary application of the complete SAT-solving procedure on basis of a comprehensible SAT-instance.

3.1 Main Finite State Machine

In Fig. 3, the *Finite State Machine* (FSM) is represented, which is inspired by the well-known *DPLL*-algorithm [3, 4]. In the following we describe each state in detail by assuming an arbitrary CNF is represented according to the introduced memory model of Section 2.

Reset: This state initializes the complete SAT-solver and, thus, introduces a well-defined state to SAT-Lancer.

Read data: The complete SAT-instance is transferred to the device implementing SAT-Lancer and stored in the main memory. After the transfer is completed, the number of literals in every clause is determined and stored in the memory location (cf. Fig. 2). In the case that the processed CNF contains any unary clause, i.e., a clause hold just one positive or negative literal, the next state to continue is set to "implicate" (cf. Edge 1), and to "decide" (cf. Edge 2) otherwise.

Decide: In this state an assignment to a variable, which has not already been assigned, is determined. A particular clause which has not been yet satisfied and has free variables is identified by the relevant states. If such a literal is determined, an assignment to "0" or "1" to the corresponding variable is derived such that the literal evaluates to true. Furthermore, information concerning the index and the determined decision (assignment) is stored in a dedicated register and the decision level is increased by one. The determined assignment is then propagated to all clauses by entering the "propagate" state (cf. Edge 3).

Implicate: Here, all clauses are further investigated, which are not yet satisfied and which hold just one single unassigned literal. In particular, this literal has to be necessarily assigned in the way that it evaluates to true. These clauses can be easily detected by taking advantage of the collected information concerning the CSS and the remaining number of free variables. If such a variable is identified, this variable is introduced as an implication (set implication status bit) and stored in a separate register. Analogously, the assignment is propagated by entering the "propagate" state (cf. Edge 4).

Propagate: In this state, every (positive as well as negative) literal of the complete SAT-instance holding the specific Boolean variable, which should be assigned, is identified by taking advantage of the determined index information. If a clause is already satisfied, the clause is skipped. Otherwise, for the case that the current assignment satisfies the clause, the SAT counter is increased and the decided bit for the CSS (cf. Fig. 2) is set. Furthermore, the number of free variables of this clause is decreased by one. During the evaluation procedure, the implication address is stored and the implication flag is set for all clauses which are not yet satisfied and which have just one remaining unassigned literal. If the SAT counter equals the total number of clauses, the overall instance becomes SAT (cf. Edge 6). If a clause, which is not yet satisfied, has no more free variables, i.e., every literal evaluates to false under the current assignment, a conflict occurs. This causes an immediate state transition to "resolve conflict" (cf. Edge 7). Otherwise, the state is changed to "implicate" (cf. Edge 8). If there is no conflict and the implication flag is set, the state is changed to "implicate" (cf. Edge 8). Otherwise the state returns to "decide" to assign a further literal (cf. Edge 5).

Resolve conflict: To resolve the conflict, the decision level is decreased by one, i.e., the last assignment to the decision variable is withdrawn and all derived implications are invalidated which are marked by the *implication status bit*. Hence, all previously affected clauses are reevaluated. This step also includes that the counter of free variables is updated for the effected clauses as well unsetting the implication status bit if necessary (cf. Edge 10). In case the conflict occurred at decision level 0 (root level) and it is not possible to flip any variable since all have been already tried in both ways ("0" or "1"), the SAT-instance is UNSAT (cf. Edge 9).

Post propagate: Mainly, this state is invoked by the conflict resolution to check whether a decision variable has already been tried in both ways, i.e., by an assignment with "0" as well as "1", to resolve the conflict. If this is not the case, this not yet tried assignment will be propagated towards "implication" or "decision" state based on the free variable numbers which is same procedure as in "propagate" state (cf. Edges 11 and 12). Otherwise, the status bit *tried both way* of the investigated variable is set and the procedure continues in state "resolve conflict" to further decrease the decision level (cf. Edge 13).

3.2 Example of Solving Process

To demonstrate the solving process of SAT-Lancer we use the following example.

EXAMPLE 1. *Given the SAT-instance*

$$g = (\overline{x}_1 + x_4 + x_5) \cdot (x_1 + \overline{x}_2 + x_3) \cdot (x_1 + \overline{x}_2 + \overline{x}_3) \cdot (x_1 + x_2 + \overline{x}_3) \cdot (x_1 + x_2 + x_3)$$

As it can be seen, g consists of 5 *clauses,* 5 *variables and* 15 *literals. Table 1 lists the steps for solving g with SAT-Lancer. The first column gives the number of the current step. The second column shows the current state of SAT-Lancer (the used abbreviations can be found below the table). The column* Variable Status *shows the assignment to a variable in the form* $x_i = a@d$, *i.e.* x_i *is assigned to a in decision level d; note that during backtracking a variable may be unassigned and the decision level is reset to* 0 *and we denote this as* $x_i = U@0$. *The next column gives the status of the clause after the assignment,*

Table 1: Example of SAT-Lancer's solving process

Step	State	Variable Status	Clause Status	Free Literals	SC
1	D	$x_1 = 0@1$	(T, F, F, F, F)	[-, 2, 2, 2, 2]	1
2	D	$x_2 = 0@2$	(T, T, T, F, F)	[-, -, -, 1, 1]	3
	I	$x_3 = 0@2$	(T, T, T, T, C)	[-, -, -, -, 0]	4
3	R	$x_3 = U@0$	(T, T, T, F, F)	[-, -, -, 1, 1]	3
4	PP	$x_2 = 1@2$	(T, F, F, T, T)	[-, 1, 1, -, -]	3
	I	$x_3 = 1@2$	(T, T, C, T, T)	[-, -, 0, -, -]	4
5	R	$x_3 = U@0$	(T, F, F, T, T)	[-, 1, 1, -, -]	3
	PP	$x_2 = U@0$	(T, F, F, F, F)	[-, 2, 2, 2, 2]	1
6	PP	$x_1 = 1@1$	(F, T, T, T, T)	[2, -, -, -, -]	4
7	D	$x_4 = 1@3$	(T, T, T, T, T)	[-, -, -, -, -]	5

State: Decide, Implicate, Resolve Conflict, Post Propagate, Propagate
Variable Status: $x_i = a@d$ means x_i is assigned to a in decision level d. If $a = U$, x_i is unassigned (decision level is reset to 0)
Clause Status: True, False or Conflict in the respective clause
Free Literals: - means not relevant since the clause is satisfied, otherwise i in the respective clause
SC: SAT Count, i.e., total number of satisfied clauses

i.e., if the clause became True, False *or* Conflicting *(for instance, the assignment* $x_1 = 0@1$ *makes the first clause* $(\overline{x}_1 + x_4 + x_5)$ *true and, hence, the first entry in the vector* (T, F, F, F, F) *becomes* T. *The column* Free literals *reports the number of free literals in the clauses (using the same assignment* $x_1 = 0@1$, *the first clause becomes true, so we mark this one with '-' and for all the other clauses the first literal evaluates to false, so in each of them only 2 free literals are left and, finally, leading to* $[-, 2, 2, 2, 2]$*). The last column* SC *shows the SAT count, i.e., the total number of satisfied clauses. We now describe the solving process for g:*

Step 1 *SAT-Lancer starts by assigning* 0 *to* x_1 *at decision level* 1 *as described above when introducing the notations.*

Step 2 *With the assignment* 0 *to* x_2 *Clauses 2 and 3 become true while the Clauses 4 and 5 still remain false but have only one free literal left. As a consequence an implication is performed on Clause 4 by assigning* x_3 0, *which leads to a conflict on Clause 5 because of the assignments* $x_1 = 0$, $x_2 = 0$ *and* $x_3 = 0$ *and, hence, this clause is false.*

Step 3 *Due to this conflict, we enter the* Resolve Conflict *state and, hence,* x_3 *is unassigned and the number of free literals for Clause 4 increases again to 2.*

Step 4 *Now the decision value for* x_2 *is converted to the inverted value which makes last two clauses true. This leads to an implication for Clause 2 but also to a conflict occurring in Clause 3.*

Step 5 *Since* x_2 *has been already tried in both ways, we need to backtrack to* x_1. *Hence, the implication on* x_3 *and then the decision on* x_2 *are undone. By this the number of free variables are increased.*

Step 6 *By flipping the assignment to* x_1 *from* 0 *to* 1, *Clause 1 becomes false and the others are true.*

Step 7 *After the decision on* x_4 *to* 1, *all clauses are true and, thus, SAT-Lancer returns SAT.*

4 EXPERIMENTAL RESULTS

This section describes the setup used as an implementation basis. Furthermore we present and discuss the conducted experimental results out of several benchmark runs.

SAT-Lancer has been written in Verilog. At first, the claimed compact character of SAT-Lancer is investigated by comparing the occupied HW-resources of our design against the implementation of [12]. Consequently, we implement our design on a *Xilinx Virtex-II Pro* FPGA as used in [12]. Our design implementation just occupies

Table 2: Results from SATLIB

Instance	#Var	#Cls	Status	Leon3[s]	SAT-Lancer [s]
hole6	42	133	UNSAT	5.98	0.06
hole7	56	204	UNSAT	200.30	0.61
hole8	72	297	UNSAT	739.21	7.02
uuf75-1	75	325	UNSAT	0.54	0.34
uuf75-2	75	325	UNSAT	0.55	0.16
uf100-7	100	430	SAT	0.38	0.03
uf100-10	100	430	SAT	0.59	2.80
cbs100-1	100	403	SAT	0.66	6.71
cbs100-10	100	403	SAT	0.55	0.07
ii8e2	870	6121	SAT	0.44	0.25
ii8b4	1068	8214	SAT	0.47	0.40
ii16e2	532	7825	SAT	26.87	6.10
ii32e1	222	1186	SAT	0.39	0.02

Table 3: Results from verification instances

Instance	#Var	#Cls	Status	Leon3[s]	SAT-Lancer [s]
alu8_and	345	839	UNSAT	0.01	0.42
alu8_or	349	851	UNSAT	0.01	0.34
alu8_orf	349	847	SAT	0.01	0.02
fifo_full	2120	4762	UNSAT	0.05	0.04
b3-26	1850	5236	SAT	0.04	0.47
b12-53	2425	14046	UNSAT	0.04	0.01
s38584-90	5999	15402	UNSAT	0.04	1.34

4% of the Slice LUTs. In contrast to this, [12] requires 20 times more resources compared to SAT-Lancer, i.e., it occupies 80% of the overall Slice LUTs. These results clearly show that the proposed design is suitable for environments with limited HW-resources.

In the actual setup, the whole design of SAT-Lancer has been synthesized on a *Xilinx ZedBoard Zynq* with an embedded *xc7z020clg484* FPGA core. This device consists of two components: a dual-core ARM Cortex-A9 microprocessor as well as a Programmable Logic unit - the FPGA as above mentioned. The SAT-instances are emitted by the host system (PetaLinux) running on the ARM microprocessor, which offers a suitable interface to the FPGA. More precisely, the state-of-the-art *Advanced eXtensible Interface* (AXI) is utilized in connection with some self-written middleware to realize all data communications. The current implementation of SAT-Lancer allows to process instances, which hold up to 65536 clauses and up to 32768 variables in the well-established *3-CNF* format, while occupying 1430 Slice LUTs and 136 BRAM Tiles. In fact, these boundaries can be even enhanced by increasing defined implementation parameters, however, further memory has to be allocated. The chosen parameters lead to an occupation of 2.69% Slice LUTs and 96.79% BRAM Tiles of the overall FPGA's resources, respectively.

To evaluate the actual SAT-solving capability of SAT-Lancer, different benchmark sets are considered and the results are shown in Table 2. In particular, the selected SAT-instances represent a wide variety of different problem classes including Pigeon Hole *(hole)*, Uniform Random-3-SAT *(uu)*, Random-3-SAT with Controlled Backbone Size *(cbs)* and Inductive Interference *(ii)*. Besides this, more application-specific SAT-instances (with respect to the intended domain of self-verification) are also investigated and shown in Table 3. These SAT-instances cover the field of sequential circuit problems containing a relevant high number of variables (clauses) up to approx. 6500 (18000). In particular, the unrolling of sequential circuits is covered, i.e., to determine a certain criteria spread over two (or more) time frames. In fact, unrolling is one elementary step in the most of the verification techniques.

To ensure the correctness of the result, all runs have been validated by the software-based SAT-solver *MiniSAT* [7] off-chip on a separate workstation. Besides this, the well-known microprocessor *LEON3* has also been implemented on the FPGA core of the ZedBoard for comparison. This processor executes a cross-compiled version of MiniSAT[1] to determine the resulting solving-time. In fact, this exhaustive microprocessor implementation allocates 7 times more HW-area in terms of Slice LUTs (SAT-Lancer with 2.69% and LEON3 with 16.93%) than the proposed SAT-Lancer and, furthermore, it takes benefit of the well-engineered MiniSAT solver.

Tables 2 and 3 include the instance name (1st col.) for the individual benchmark as sketched above, the total number of variables and clauses (2nd & 3rd col.) and, finally, the result in sense of {SAT,UNSAT} (4th col.) and the solving-time (5th col.) for LEON3 as well as for SAT-Lancer (6th col.) in seconds. It can be noted that the arbitrary SAT-instances of Table 2 are much harder to solve compared to the application-specific ones in Table 3. SAT-Lancer mostly finishes within seconds which is, in fact, negligible from a self-verification point of view.

5 CONCLUSIONS

This paper proposes SAT-Lancer, a complete HW SAT-solver which allows to solve arbitrary SAT-instances on-chip while occupying only moderate hardware resources. Furthermore, it utilizes an scalable memory model such that even on-chip generated SAT-instances can be processed in a dynamic fashion. Moreover, we have shown that SAT-Lancer is capable to process arbitrary benchmark in reasonable run-time. In summary, SAT-Lancer facilitates completely new application scenarios for functional self-verification, particularly, in systems with strictly limited resources like e.g. the rapidly spreading IoT devices.

Acknowledgments: This work was supported by the German Federal Ministry of Education and Research (BMBF) within the project SELFIE under grant no. 01IW16001, by the German Research Foundation (DFG) as part of Collaborative Research Center SFB1320 *EASE – Everyday Activity Science and Engineering* in subproject P04 and by the Collaborative Research Center SFB1232 *High Throughput Exploration for Evolutionary Structural Materials* in subproject P01 *Predictive function*.

REFERENCES

[1] A. Biere, A. Cimatti, E. M. Clarke, and Y. Zhu. 1999. Symbolic model checking without BDDs. In *TACAS*. 193–207.
[2] John D. Davis, Zhangxi Tan, Fang Yu, and Lintao Zhang. 2008. A Practical Reconfigurable Hardware Accelerator for Boolean Satisfiability Solvers. In *DAC*. 780–785.
[3] M. Davis, G. Logeman, and D. Loveland. 1962. A Machine Program for Theorem Proving. *Comm. of the ACM* 5 (1962), 394–397.
[4] M. Davis and H. Putnam. 1960. A computing procedure for quantification theory. *J. ACM* 7 (1960), 506–521.
[5] R. Drechsler, M. Fränzle, and R. Wille. 2015. Envisioning self-verification of electronic systems. In *ReCoSoC*.
[6] R. Drechsler, H. M. Le, and M. Soeken. 2014. Self-verification as the key technology for next generation electronic systems. In *SBCCI*. 1–4.
[7] N. Eén and N. Sörensson. 2004. An extensible SAT solver. In *Theory and Applications of Satisfiability Testing (LNCS)*, Vol. 2919. 502–518.
[8] K. Gulati, M. Waghmode, S. P. Khatri, and W. Shi. 2008. Efficient, scalable hardware engine for Boolean satisfiability and unsatisfiable core extraction. *IET Computers Digital Techniques* 2, 3 (2008), 214–229.
[9] T. Ivan and E. M. Aboulhamid. 2013. An Efficient Hardware Implementation of a SAT Problem Solver on FPGA. In *DSD*. 209–216.
[10] Christoph Lüth, Martin Ring, and Rolf Drechsler. 2017. Towards a Methodology for Self-Verification. In *ICRITO*.
[11] Walden C. Rhines. 2016. Design Verification Challenges: Past, Present and Future. In *DVCon US Keynote Address*.
[12] M. Safar, M. W. El-Kharashi, M. Shalan, and A. Salem. 2011. A reconfigurable, pipelined, conflict directed jumping search SAT solver. In *DATE*. 1–6.
[13] J. Thong and N. Nicolici. 2013. FPGA acceleration of enhanced boolean constraint propagation for SAT solvers. In *ICCAD*. 234–241.
[14] J. Thong and N. Nicolici. 2015. SAT solving using FPGA-based heterogeneous computing. In *ICCAD*. 232–239.

[1] Please note that the learning capability of MiniSAT has been disabled for a fair setup.

FLexiTASK: A Flexible FPGA Overlay for Efficient Multitasking

Joel Mandebi Mbongue
University of Arkansas
Fayetteville, Arkansas
jmmandeb@uark.edu

Danielle Tchuinkou Kwadjo
University of Arkansas
Fayetteville, Arkansas
dtchuink@uark.edu

Christophe Bobda
University of Arkansas
Fayetteville, Arkansas
cbobda@uark.edu

ABSTRACT

One of the major obstacles to the adoption of FPGAs in high-performance computing is their programmability. It requires hardware design skills and long compilation times. Overlays have been proposed as a way to abstract FPGA resources. Unfortunately, most of the time, the topologies they use to connect computing cores impose restrictions on where tasks are placed and how they communicate. In this paper, we propose an overlay architecture designed for efficiency and flexibility. It features a novel Network-on-Chip (NoC) infrastructure making flexible, with no limitation, the placement of hardware tasks. The presented architecture allows tasks to communicate with a low latency and eases the reconfiguration of desired areas on the fabric at runtime. After prototyping the proposed architecture on an Altera Cyclone V FPGA, a maximum frequency of *282 MHz* has been reached and a speedup ranging from 4× to 195× has been observed in some applications compared to the native execution.

KEYWORDS

FPGA; Overlay; Multitasking

ACM Reference Format:

Joel Mandebi Mbongue, Danielle Tchuinkou Kwadjo, and Christophe Bobda. 2018. FLexiTASK: A Flexible FPGA Overlay for Efficient Multitasking. In *GLSVLSI '18: 2018 Great Lakes Symposium on VLSI, May 23–25, 2018, Chicago, IL, USA.* ACM, New York, NY, USA, 4 pages. https://doi.org/10.1145/3194554.3194644

1 INTRODUCTION

The insatiable demand for innovative, faster, and efficient technologies has led from high-clocked single processors to the use of multicores. In multicores with customized components, computing resources can be tailored to applications' needs, resulting in better system throughput and power consumption compared to homogeneous multicores. Devices like FPGAs can play a big role in such platforms because of their reconfigurable nature and low power consumption compared to general purpose cores [6]. For such an integration to be viable, it must be possible to place, execute and replace tasks on the FPGA fabric at runtime. However, using FPGAs at the raw level raises some hurdles. As a prelude to accelerating a task, a corresponding circuit must be synthesized to specify the functionality on the FPGA. Unfortunately, the process of synthesizing hardware designs from hardware description languages or high-level synthesis is time consuming. Secondly, for upcoming tasks, new circuits will have to be synthesized. These problems make this approach unviable. On the other hand, an abstraction layer offering a hardware virtualization of the FPGA resources could help to tackle those obstacles. This will remove the need for synthesizing hardware circuits and reduce the configuration overhead. In addition, it will provide more flexibility to dynamically place and replace threads on specific regions of the FPGA when needed [3]. The problem addressed in this work is hardware multitasking on coarse-grained reconfigurable architectures (CGRAs). The improvement and development of CGRAs arise from the huge variety of research and industry needs for flexible high performance computing. Our main contribution is to propose a novel virtualization architecture which makes flexible and unrestricted the placement, and communication of hardware tasks at runtime.

Recent works in CGRAs and FPGA overlays mostly present dataflow machine architectures [4, 5, 7]. They are usually added into systems as co-processors for accelerating tasks. They have the advantage to exhibit FPGA's flexibility and break the FPGA-ASIC performance gap. Communications among functional units embedded in these architectures are usually based on direct interconnections among neighbor or distant units. Because of that, those architectures do not address the problem of accessibility and flexibility of communication between computational resources. Bus-based communications (see Figure 1a) present a potential alternative but the overhead of hundreds or thousands of processing elements (PE) trying to communicate using a single bus will drastically reduce system performances, and ultimately obfuscate any parallelism and multitasking gain. A Network-on-Chip architecture (NoC) [1] implemented as an abstraction layer to connect all the cores can be a solution to this communication bottleneck. NoCs use messages for communications between cores, memories and peripherals, all of them connected to the network infrastructure instead of using dedicated wires. Their advantages have been deeply studied and discussed in the literature [9]. Despite their great assets, NoCs present some drawbacks. NoCs are usually provided as a 2-dimensional mesh with PEs or routers at the intersection between lines and columns. There are few problems nevertheless raised:

1) Architectures with PEs at the intersection of lines and columns like in Figure 1b only provide communication links between neighbor PEs [4, 5, 7]. Though they allow a high throughput between adjacent PEs, they impose a restricted task placement and fixed communication exchanges. They are not best optimized for multitasking in which communication between distant tasks is needed. 2) In architectures with routers at the intersection of lines and columns (see Figure 1c), each PE is attached to a router [2]. This makes unrestricted the communication between distant cores, but

GLSVLSI '18, May 23–25, 2018, Chicago, IL, USA

ACM ISBN 978-1-4503-5724-1/18/05...$15.00
https://doi.org/10.1145/3194554.3194644

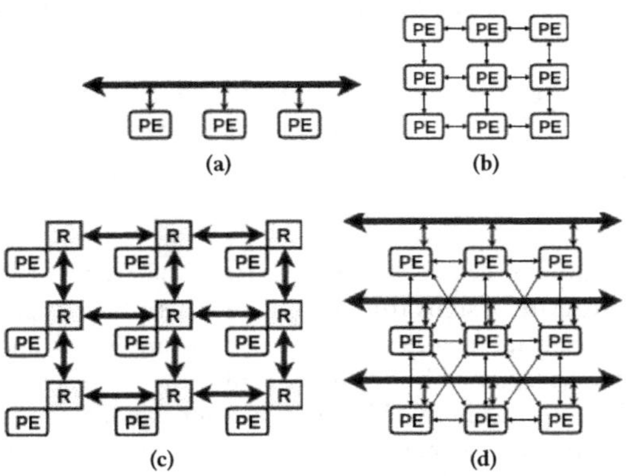

Figure 1: Bus-based Interconnection (1a). PEs at the Intersection of Lines and Columns of the 2-D Mesh (1b). Routers at the Intersection of Lines and Columns (1c), each PE attached to one Router. The Zippy architecture (1d) uses buses for distant communication between PEs belonging to the same row.

introduce a high communication overhead because the number of routers to get packets to their destinations is usually more than what is really needed: more hops between the source and destination of a packet imposes more communication latencies and message blocking probability.

In order to make flexible communications between distant PEs while maintaining direct links between neighbor ones, [8] proposes the Zippy architecture (see Figure 1d). It does not use routers, rather, it features PEs at the intersection of lines and columns of the grid. It employs direct interconnections between adjacent PEs and uses a bus to connect PEs belonging to the same row. The issue with this architecture is the overhead generated by the bus management if the number of PEs is drastically increased. In addition to that, transfers between distant PEs is limited to the same lines.

In this work, we introduce a novel architecture that uses routers for communications between distant cores and direct links between adjacent PEs. It differs from other architectures relying on routers as it decreases the number of routers by increasing the number of PEs attached to each of them.

2 PROPOSED ARCHITECTURE

2.1 General Organization

We propose the general organization of Figure 2. It is a Torus interconnect consisting of a two-dimensional array of routers (R in Figure 2) and programmable processing elements (PE in Figure 2). PEs communicate through a flexible and scalable NoC architecture providing a high path diversity and minimal routes. They are gathered in groups around routers to form a *subnetwork*. The overlay uses data packets for communications. This is beneficial because it makes the overlay scalable, and resources can directly be reused when they complete message transmissions. The Torus topology is implemented to shorten distances between PEs and increase the connectivity: routers at the left edge of the first and last lines are connected to those at the opposite edge, PEs which are all over the edges of the overlay are connected to PEs at their opposite edges.

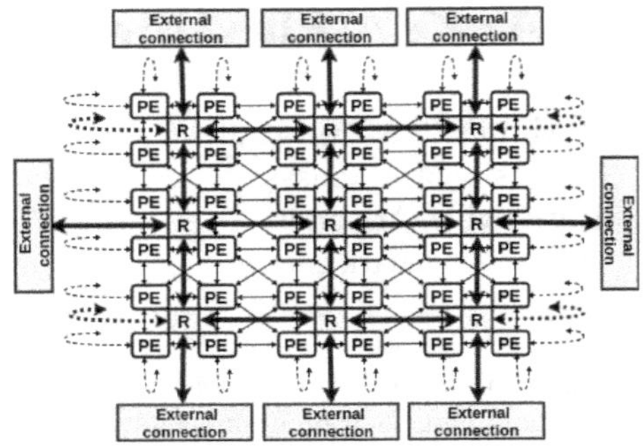

Figure 2: Overlay Architecture

To make it possible to send packets simultaneously to different subnetworks, each router at the edge of the overlay has an external connection. Figure 2 presents an instance of the overlay using 3×3 routers, each surrounded by four PEs. The number of PEs attached to each router, and how many routers to use can be modified according to the needs and available resources on the chip. To be operational, PEs are configured to implement specific operations and send results of their computations to specific targets. There are two configuration modes:**(1) The online mode:** in which configuration packets containing operands are sent. In this case, the next use of the PE will require a new configuration packet. **(2) The offline mode:** configuration packets are sent first, and operands will arrive later from neighbor PEs or through the router of the subnetwork. This mode is interesting for vector processing since configurations can be kept as long as needed.

2.2 Routing and Processing Elements

Routers (see Figure 3a) control paths taken by data to make sure that each packet reaches its destination. Each router features four channels for communicating with adjacent routers and direct links with PEs. The *scheduler* uses the *First Come First Serve* scheduling algorithm, with the highest priority given to communications coming from PEs, to brings packets to the crossbar matrix. FIFOs store packets waiting to be scheduled. Communications from PEs are first considered to have them available for new computations as soon as possible. The *crossbar matrix* transfers packets to the next direction. A PE is directly connected to at most eight other adjacent PEs. The Broadcast unit (see Figure 3b) forwards channels activated by the configuration to input multiplexers. Input Multiplexers select the origin of operands sent to the Functional Unit (FU), while the Demultiplexer chooses where to send results of computations . The Output Register always contains a copy of the latest result computed in the FU. The Configuration Register stores configuration packets received by the PE. This allows to fix the source of operands, the operation to be performed and the destination where to send results. The FU runs computations on one or two 32 bits operands.

2.3 Programming Flow

Overlays have the advantage that application kernels can be mapped with a programmability similar to software executed into processors. The design, implementation and synthesis of the overlay itself is done off-line using vendor tools. Our custom mapping tool is a

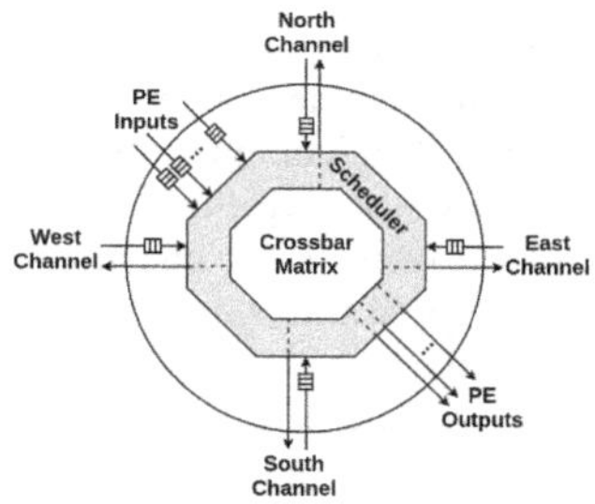

(a)

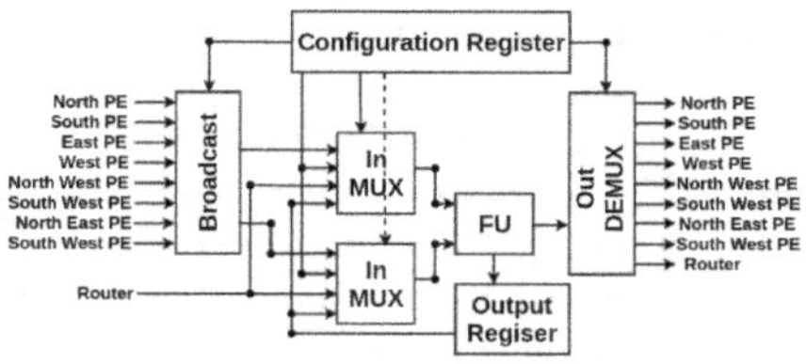

(b)

Figure 3: Router Architecture (Figure 3a). Processing Element (Figure 3b).

C/C++ library providing high level functions to access the overlay resources. In its current version, kernels and where computations will take place on the overlay are specified manually. This because the attention of the paper is on the hardware architecture. Future works will focus on having automatic placements. In order to use some hardware acceleration from the overlay, a C/C++ application just needs to call functions from our library. The code can then be compiled using a regular C/C++ compiler like the GNU Compiler Collection (GCC).

3 EVALUATION

Evaluation Infrastructure: the Terasic DE1-SoC board with an Altera Cyclone V FPGA was chosen to verify the operation of the prototyped architecture. To edit and synthesize the overlay, we used Quartus Prime Standard Edition 16.0. In addition, ModelSim-Intel FPGA Edition allowed to run RTL simulations and observe latencies. Throughout our experimental evaluations, we used an instance of the overlay featuring 5×5 routers, each router surrounded by 4 PEs. **Evaluation Metrics:** we look at speedups compared to the native execution. For that purpose, a sytem-on-chip is designed to evaluate execution times on the Dual-Core ARM Cortex A9 Hard Processor burned into the FPGA, as opposed to the same Hard Processor coupled with our overlay. We also consider the f_{MAX} observed at the level of routers under various conditions. Given that the number of PEs around routers is scalable, we trace routing latencies and also study the impact of increasing the number of PEs on FPGA resources. Finally, we discuss some issues arising when comparing our architecture to existing works. **Evaluation Benchmarks:** we tested three image processing operations on 800×600 input images. Afterwards, we ran some matrix/vector operations with matrices of size 100×100, and vectors of 100 entries. For each application, we manually configured a parallelized placement of operations onto the overlay and a sequential one. The parallelized placement provides an idea on how our overlay performs on multithreaded applications, while the sequential placement demonstrates that our architecture also fits pipelined executions. For evaluation purposes, we examine how much acceleration is achieved on multithreaded and sequential environments. **Observations:** table 1 summarizes execution times observed when running all test applications on our three testing infrastructures. It demonstrates that the overlay excels when tasks are executed in parallel. Figure 4 depicts speed up statistics: the parallel placement of the *Outer product* executed 195× faster than the native execution, and 25× faster compared to the sequential execution on the overlay. While the overlay best performs on multithreaded applications, sequential placements still outperform native executions. The *Matrix multiplication* in the parallel placement on the overlay only executes about 5× faster. This is due to the dependencies between operations, and to the size of the overlay. Using 100 PEs to run computation on matrices of size 100x100 restricts the number of tasks that could be run in parallel. Figure 5 studies the resource usage incurred by the scaling of PEs around routers. Everytime we double the number of PEs in a sub-network, the new circuit synthesized employs about 12 more ALMs and 4 more registers on the FPGA. It demonstrates that PEs are not resource intensive. This observation is particularly interesting as it could pave the way to more PEs for more speed up. However, if increasing the number of PEs provides more computing power, it also influences routing latencies. Figure 6 studies average wait-

Table 1: Execution Times

Applications	Cortex A9	Cortex A9 + Overlay (Sequential Mapping)	Cortex A9 + Overlay (Parallel Mapping)
Roberts Cross	763.69 ms	67 ms	5.15 ms
Corner Detection	488.70 ms	161.77 ms	53.92 ms
Smoothing	116.28 ms	104.98 ms	8.075 ms
Matrix Multiplication	48.77 ms	42 ms	11.4 ms
Outer Product	0.39 ms	0.05 ms	0.002 ms
Dot Product	0.008 ms	0.008 ms	0.001 ms

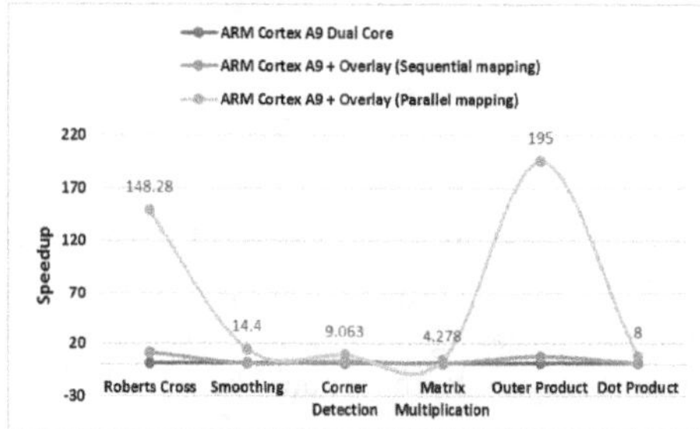

Figure 4: Execution Speedups

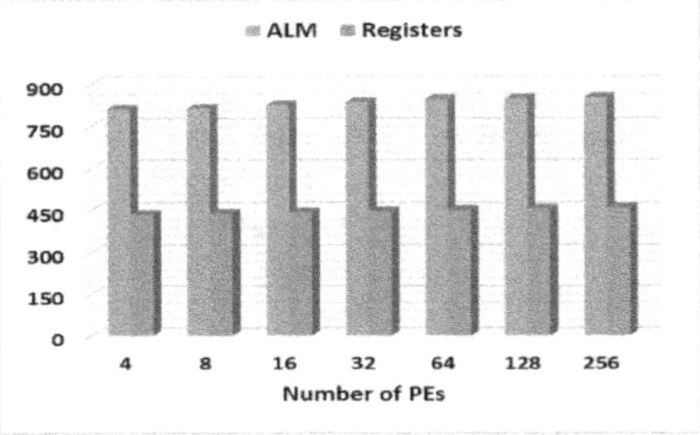

Figure 5: Resource Usage for PE Scaling

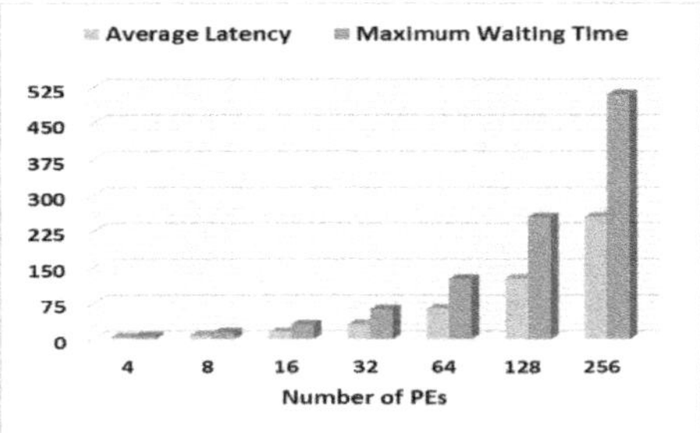

Figure 6: Routing Latencies for PE Scaling

ing times and maximum waiting times for packets simultaneously reaching a router, targeting each PE in the subnetwork. Having 4 PEs, the average routing latency would be 3 clocks cycles and the last packet will wait at most 6 clock cyles. By increasing the number of PEs to 16, the average waiting time could easily increase up to 15 clock cycles and the last packet transferred by the router could wait up to 30 clock cycles. Using more than 32 PEs around a router would become unviable as it will cause an average waiting time of at least 31 clock cycles. The average latency is approximately equal to number of PEs while the maximum waiting time is almost the double. These results indicate that: 1) Though using more PEs looks attractive and not resource hungry, keeping a relative small amount of PEs could drastically decrease the communication overhead, especially when routers are to be crossed. And 2) to best benefit from the architecture, the placement of hardware tasks should avoid saturating routers with communication requests. The f_{MAX} of the overlay is derived from the Quartus Prime Timing Analysis tool. For instance, we observed a maximum frequency of $282MHz$ for 4 PEs around a router and $270MHz$ when having 256 PEs.

In [4], authors propose an architecture for speeding up data flow graph executions using an Altera Stratix III platform. They achieved a maximum frequency of $172MHz$ and a speed up of 9× compared to an execution on a NIOS II soft processor. Sen Ma and al [7] designed an overlay for accelerating custom instructions built on a Xilinx Kintex-7 FPGA for testing purposes. They claimed a speedup of 25× on a 3x3 matrix multiplication. [5] proposes an architecture for pipelined execution of data flow graphs. After prototyping their overlay on an Altera Stratix IV FPGA, they reported a f_{MAX} reaching up to $355MHz$ and throughputs obtained in GFLOPS. It could be tempting to claim that our architecture outperforms results presented in [4] as we obtain a greater speedup and higher maximum frequency. Following the same logic, it might also appear like the architecture described in [5] is more efficient than ours since authors claim to achieve a better maximum frequency. We could even speculate which of our architecture or the one portrayed in [7] offers a better speedup. But this form of comparison is misleading since it lacks context. For instance, [4], [7], and [5] do not use similar testing applications (i.e. lack shared benchmarks). Even when they try to, the size of the dataset is generally different and sometimes not even disclosed. This is on top of the fact that evaluation platforms generally rely on FPGAs from different manufacturers with completely different hardware structures. Finally, even when FPGAs from the same brand are used, using various series produce different results. To illustrate that point, when testing our architecture on an Altera Stratix IV FPGA, we observe a maximum frequency rising up to $359MHz$ compared to the $282MHz$ on the Cyclone V. This new frequency observed even surpasses the one pointed out in [5]. Those three factors make it difficult to fairly provide performance comparisons between architectures as it is particularly challenging to reproduce the exact same testing environment.

4 CONCLUSION

We presented a novel virtualization architecture for FPGAs which is suitable for multithreaded applications but also for sequential execution. The architecture allows to modify the functionality of any region of the layout at runtime. Our evaluation showed that adding our overlay as a co-processor allowed significantly decreased execution time compared to the native execution. Future researches will focus on automatically identifying kernels from application specified with high-level programming languages.

ACKNOWLEDGMENTS

This work was supported in part by the NSF under Grant CNS-1618606 & 1302596.

REFERENCES

[1] Luca Benini and Giovanni De Micheli. 2002. Network on chips: A new soc paradigm. *computer* 35, 1 (Aug. 2002), 70–78. https://doi.org/10.1109/2.976921

[2] Tobias Bjerregaard and Shankar Mahadevan. 2006. A survey of research and practices of network-on-chip. *ACM Computing Surveys (CSUR)* 38, 1 (June 2006), 1. https://doi.org/10.1145/1132952.1132953

[3] Christophe Bobda. 2007. *Introduction to reconfigurable computing architectures, algorithms and applications.* Springer Science & Business Media.

[4] Davor Capalija and T Abdelrahman. 2012. A coarse-grain fpga overlay for executing data flow graphs. *The Second Workshop on the Intersections of Computer Architecture and Reconfigurable Logic (CARL 2012)* (2012).

[5] Davor Capalija and Tarek S Abdelrahman. 2013. A high-performance overlay architecture for pipelined execution of data flow graphs. *Field Programmable Logic and Applications (FPL), 2013 23rd International Conference on* (2013), 1–8. https://doi.org/10.1109/FPL.2013.6645515

[6] Jeremy Fowers, Greg Brown, Patrick Cooke, and Greg Stitt. 2012. A Performance and Energy Comparison of FPGAs, GPUs, and Multicores for Sliding-window Applications. In *Proceedings of the ACM/SIGDA International Symposium on Field Programmable Gate Arrays (FPGA '12).* ACM, New York, NY, USA, 47–56. https://doi.org/10.1145/2145694.2145704

[7] Sen Ma, Zeyad Aklah, and David Andrews. 2015. A run time interpretation approach for creating custom accelerators. *Field Programmable Logic and Applications (FPL), 2015 25th International Conference on* (2015), 1–4. https://doi.org/10.1109/FPL.2015.7293996

[8] Christian Plessl and Marco Platzner. 2011. Hardware virtualization on dynamically reconfigurable processors. (2011).

[9] Muhammad Athar Javed Sethi, Fawnizu Azmadi Hussin, and Nor Hisham Hamid. 2015. Survey of network on chip architectures. *Sci. Int.(Lahore)* 5, 27 (2015), 4133–4144.

An Architectural Support for Reduction of In-rush Current in Systems with Instruction Controlled Power Gating

Sumanta Pyne
Deparment of Computer Science and Engineering
National Institute of Technology, Rourkela
Odisha - 769008, INDIA
pynes@nitrkl.ac.in

ABSTRACT

The present work introduces a hardware based technique for reduction of in-rush current in processors with power gating (*PG*) facility. A *PG* instruction has been introduced which is responsible in turning on multiple components from sleep to active mode at overlapped time intervals. The supporting hardware for the proposed *PG* instruction allows overlapped wake-up as long as the resultant in-rush current is tolerable by the system. The efficacy of the proposed method is evaluated on **MiBench** and **MediaBench** benchmark programs. The proposed method reduces in-rush current by an average of 35% with average performance loss of 5%.

KEYWORDS

Leakage power; power gating; wakeup; in-rush current; architectural support

ACM Reference Format:

Sumanta Pyne. 2018. An Architectural Support for Reduction of In-rush Current in Systems with Instruction Controlled Power Gating. In *Proceedings of 2018 Great Lakes Symposium on VLSI (GLSVLSI '18)*. ACM, New York, NY, USA, 4 pages. https://doi.org/10.1145/3194554.3194645

1 INTRODUCTION

The emergence of deep submicron process technology with the decrease in dimensions of the transistor has increased the transistor count and speed of operation at the cost of greater device leakage currents. Power gating (*PG*) is a technique used to reduce power consumption of VLSI chips, by shutting off the blocks that are not in use, thus reducing stand-by or leakage power. When a power gated block is switched on from sleep mode to active mode it draws a huge amount of in-rush current due to simultaneous charging of its internal capacitors. In-rush current is several times higher than the actual current required by the block to function in active mode. The flow of in-rush current may cause permanent damage to the circuit and also lead to higher power consumption. It can reduce the battery life for battery-operated systems due to rise in load current. The present work proposes a hardware support for *PG* instructions that simultaneously activates multiple components. It allows overlapped wake-up with guaranteed tolerable in-rush current. The existing works on management of in-rush current in *PG* systems are discussed in Sec. 2. The proposed method is explained in Sec. 3. Section 4 covers explaination of the experimental setup with analysis of the results. Finally, Sec. 5 concludes the present work with future directions.

GLSVLSI '18, May 23–25, 2018, Chicago, IL, USA

ACM ISBN 978-1-4503-5724-1/18/05...$15.00
https://doi.org/10.1145/3194554.3194645

2 RELATED WORK

This section discusses the existing research and developmen works on reduction of in-rush current in systems with *PG*. In [1] the authors proposed *PG* structures in which sleep transistors are turned on in a non-uniform stepwise manner to reduce the magnitude of peak current. Such a long daisy chain can cause long propagation delay and the slowly rising voltage can introduce other problems such as hot electron effects [2]. In [4] at wake-up the weak transistors are turned on first so as to slowly turn on the rush currents. When the design is discharged (charged) to a voltage close to zero (V_{dd}), the strong transistor pass is turned on ready for normal operation. A tool named CoolTime [2] guides the designer in setting power switch structure and sequence for controlling in-rush current and wake-up time. An in-rush current limiter circuit in [3] can sense the increased load current and produces sense current having a load current - sense current ratio of 1000:1, hence reducing the in-rush current. Kiong et al. introduced the in-rush current optimization power up flow analysis with PFET removal algorithm [5] to improve the in-rush current. In [6] the wake-up procedure the *PG* scheme implements a small transistor to control the sleep transistor in two stages to limit in-rush current and reduce wake-up time. In [7] the authors proposed model memory access power gating (*MAPG*), a low-overhead technique to enable power gating of an active core when it stalls during a long memory access. A novel framework for generating a proper power-up sequence of the switches to control the in-rush current of a power-gated domain has been introduced in [8]. The authors in [9] explain in-rush current reduction techniques like soft-start with the help of voltage regulators to increase rise time. In [10] Kim et al. discussed the reduction of in-rush current by turning on each switch cell at different times. They showed that in-rush current can be reduced even more if signal transition time to switch each cell is adjusted.

At present there is a scope for architecture level in-rush current management in systems with instruction controlled *PG*.

3 PRESENT WORK

An arrangement for instruction controlled *PG* is shown in Fig. 1. It has n *PG* components $C_0, C_1, \cdots, C_{n-1}$. *PG* is done with the help of the header p-MOS transistors having higher threshold voltage (V_T). The header switches are controlled by an n-bit power gating control register (PGCR) placed in the power gating controller (PGC).

The bits $0, 1, \cdots, n-1$ are the *PG* bits of $C_0, C_1, \cdots, C_{n-1}$, respectively. If any of these bits $\alpha \in \{0, 1 \cdots, n-1\}$ is '0', then the component C_α is in active mode, otherwise C_α is in sleep mode. Let there be two *PG* instructions *switch_off* and *switch_on* each consuming three clock cycles - one cycle in each of instruction fetch (*IF*), instruction decode (*ID*) and execution (*EX*) stages of the instruction pipeline. To put C_α in sleep (or power gated) mode the instruction *switch_off*(C_α) is used to set the value of αth bit of PGCR. C_α in sleep mode can be put to active mode with the help of the instruction *switch_on*(C_α) which resets the value of αth bit of PGCR. Hence, a program can use this *PG* facility.

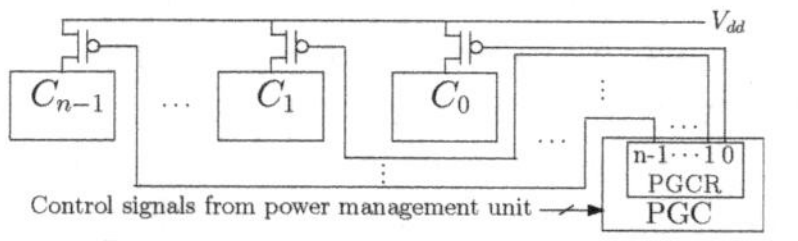

Figure 1: Instruction controlled *PG* system

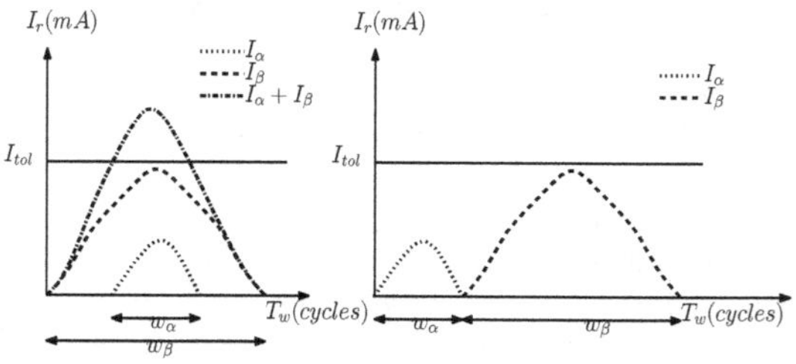

(a) Overlapped wake-up (b) Non-overlapped wake-up

Figure 2: In-rush current for different wake-up

When C_α in sleep mode is switched on using *switch_on*(C_α) it draws in-rush current $I_\alpha \in \mathbb{Z}_{\geq 0}$ for a period of w_α cycles where w_α is the wake-up time (T_w) of C_α. It is considered that $I_\alpha \leq I_{tol}$ for wake-up of any individual *PG* component C_α, where I_{tol} is the maximum tolerable in-rush current for a given system. The problem of intolerable in-rush current may arise during wake-up of multiple components during an overlapped time interval. Fig. 2(a) shows in-rush current (I_r) in milliampere (mA) for overlapped wake-up of two components C_α and C_β where $\beta \in \{0, 1, \cdots, n-1\}$ and $\beta \neq \alpha$. w_β and I_β are the wake-up time and in-rush current of C_β, respectively. The resultant in-rush current is $I_\alpha + I_\beta$. Simultaneous overlapped wake-up of several components can lead to higher flow of in-rush current resulting higher peak power dissipation and reduction of chip reliability. Hence, it is better to have non-overlapped wake-up as shown in Fig. 2(b).

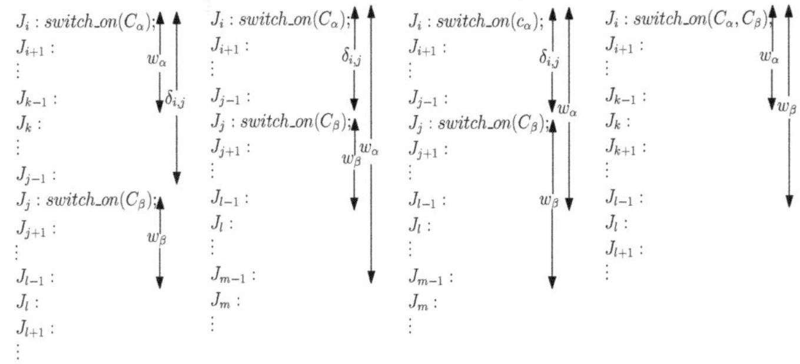

(a) $w_\alpha \leq \delta_{i,j}$, non-overlapped wake-up (b) Overlapped wake-up, $(\delta_{i,j} + w_\beta) < w_\alpha$ (c) Overlapped wake-up, $(\delta_{i,j} + w_\beta) \geq w_\alpha$ (d) Overlapped wake-up, $\delta_{i,j} = 0$ and $w_\beta \geq w_\alpha$

Figure 3: Overlapped wake-up

A program with *switch_on* instructions may cause overlapped wake-up of *PG* components. Considering an assembly language program consuming $N \in \mathbb{N}$ clock cycles. The instructions J_i and J_j are in *EX* stage at i^{th} and j^{th} cycles, respectively. Where J_i is *switch_on*(C_α), J_j is *switch_on*(C_β) and $1 < i \leq j < N$. J_j is executed after $\delta_{i,j} = j - i$ cycles of J_i. J_i and J_j will result non-overlapped wake-up of C_α and C_β if $i < j$ and $w_\alpha \leq \delta_{i,j}$ as shown in Fig. 3(a). Overlapped wake-up occurs if $w_\alpha > \delta_{i,j}$ as shown in figures 3(b), 3(c) and 3(d) where $1 < i \leq j \leq k \leq l \leq m < N$. The total in-rush current due to overlapped wake-up may exceed I_{tol}. To prevent this a hardware arrangement for *switch_on* is proposed that allows overlapped wake-up with guaranteed tolerable in-rush current.

3.1 In-rush aware switch_on instruction

Let *switch_on*(*#components*, *component_list*) be the format of *switch_on* instruction for the proposed approach, where *#components* $\in \{1, 2, \cdots, n\}$ is the number of *PG* components to be activated and *component_list* is the list of *PG* components where the pth element *component_list*$[p] \in \{0, 1, \cdots, n-1\}$ and $p \in \{0, 1, \cdots, \#components - 1\}$. The hardware support for the proposed *switch_on* instruction is shown in Fig. 4 where for each *PG* component C_α an in-rush current table (IT_α) is maintained. The tuple $t \in \{1, 2, \cdots, w_\alpha\}$ of IT_α denoted by $IT_\alpha[t]$ stores I^t_α where I^t_α is the value of I_α during t^{th} cycle of wake-up of C_α. I_α is minimum during cycles 1 and w_α. $I_\alpha = I^{pk}_\alpha$ during cycle $\lceil \frac{w_\alpha}{2} \rceil$ where I^{pk}_α is the maximum or peak value of I_α.

Let $b = \lceil \mathbf{log_2 max}\{I^{pk}_0, I^{pk}_1, \cdots, I^{pk}_{n-1}\} \rceil$ be the number of bits required to represent $IT_\alpha[t]$. I_{tot} is a table having w_{max} tuples, where $w_{max} = \mathbf{max}\{w_0, w_1, \cdots, w_{n-1}\}$. $I_{tot}[t] \in \mathbb{Z}_{\geq 0}$ is the total in-rush current due to overlapped wake-up during cycle $i + t - 1$ where $i \in \{1, 2, \cdots, N\}$ and $t \in \{1, 2, \cdots, w_{max}\}$. $I_{tot}[t] \leq I_{tol} \forall t : t \in \{1, 2, \cdots, w_{max}\}$. $\lceil \mathbf{log_2} I_{tol} \rceil + 1$ bits are used to represent $I_{tot}[t]$. There are w_{max} ($\lceil \mathbf{log_2} I_{tol} \rceil + 1$)-bit adder-subtractors for performing $I_{tot}[t] \leftarrow I_{tot}[t] + IT_\alpha[t]$ and $I_{tot}[t] \leftarrow I_{tot}[t] - IT_\alpha[t]$ operations $\forall t : t \in \{1, 2, \cdots w_{max}\}$ whenever their corresponding control lines ADD and SUB are high. An $\mathcal{O}(w_{max} \times b)$

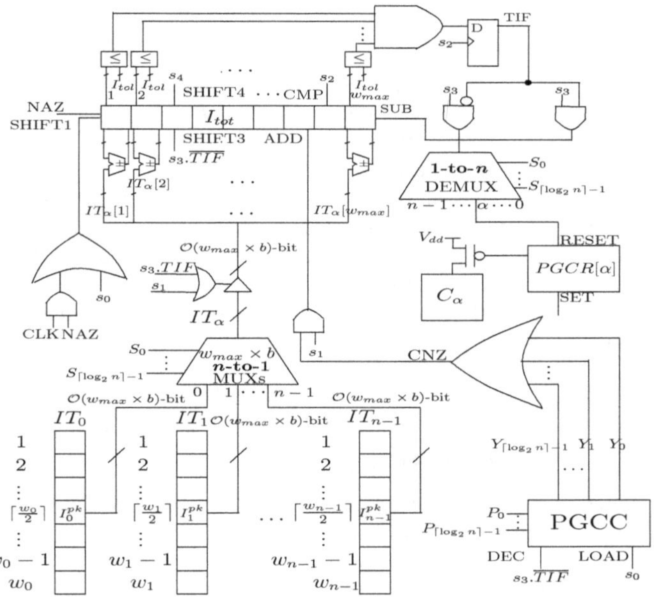

Figure 4: Hardware for in-rush aware *switch_on*

bit bus to carry IT_α. This helps in performing $I_{tot}[t] \leftarrow I_{tot}[t] \pm I_\alpha[t] \forall t : t \in \{1, 2, \cdots, w_{max}\}$ parallely within one clock cycle. $w_{max} \times b$ **n-to-1** bus multiplexers are used to select IT_α, where $S_0, S_1, \cdots, S_{\lceil \log_2 n \rceil - 1}$ are select lines representing α in binary form. Each bit of $IT_\alpha[t]$ is connected to the input line α of the corresponding multiplexer. There are w_{max} ($\lceil \log_2 I_{tol} \rceil + 1$)-bit comparators. They help to compare the values of I_{tot} with I_{tol} when the control line CMP is high. The **tolerable in-rush flag** (TIF) is set if $I_{tot}[t] \leq I_{tol} \forall t : t \in \{1, 2, \cdots, w_{max}\}$. The control lines SHIFT1, SHIFT3 and SHIFT4 shifts the contents of I_{tot} by one, three and four positions, respectively. The **not all zero flag** (NAZ) indicates the requirement of SHIFT1 operation after completion of a *switch_on* instruction. For NAZ=1 a SHIFT1 operation is performed in every cycle until NAZ=0 when all the elements of I_{tot} are zero. In Fig. 4 the output line α of the **1-to-n** demultiplexer is connected to the RESET line of αth bit of PGCR (PGCR[α]). If RESET=1 then PGCR[α]$\leftarrow$ 0. This arrangement helps to turn on the p-MOS transistor that acts as header switch of the *PG* component C_α. The $\lceil \log_2 n \rceil$-bit **power gating component counter** (PGCC) stores the number of *PG* components to be turned on. It is loaded with *#components* field of a *switch_on* instruction through the input lines $P_0, P_1, \cdots, P_{\lceil \log_2 n \rceil - 1}$. The control line LOAD is high during this operation. The content of PGCR is decreased by one after reset of each PGCR[α]. The control line DEC is high during this operation. The output line **count not zero** (CNZ) is low when PGCC reaches zero. This indicates the completion of *switch_on*.

The micro-operations for the proposed *switch_on* are shown in Fig. 5. They are initiated when a *switch_on* enters the *EX* stage and performed in five sequences s_0, s_1, s_2, s_3 and s_4 each consuming a clock cycle. The micro-operations belonging to a particular sequence are performed in parallel. A control signal s_σ in the proposed hardware needs to be high to carry

s_0:
  LOAD: $PGCC \leftarrow \#components$
  SHIFT1: $I_{tot}[t] \leftarrow I_{tot}[t+1], \ \forall t : t \in \{1, 2, \cdots, w_{max} - 1\}$
    $I_{tot}[w_{max}] \leftarrow 0$
$s_1 : \alpha \leftarrow$ *component_list*[*#components* $- PGCC$]
  ADD: $I_{tot}[t] \leftarrow I_{tot}[t] + IT_\alpha[t], \ \forall t : t \in \{1, 2, \cdots, w_\alpha\}$
s_2 :
  CMP: **if** $I_{tot}[t] \leq I_{tol} \forall t : t \in \{1, 2, \cdots, w_{max}\}$ **then** $TIF \leftarrow 1$ **else** $TIF \leftarrow 0$
s_3 : **if** $TIF = 1$ **then**
    RESET: $PGCR[\alpha] \leftarrow 0$
    SHIFT3: $I_{tot}[t] \leftarrow I_{tot}[t+3], \ \forall t : t \in \{1, 2, \cdots, w_{max} - 3\}$
      $I_{tot}[t] \leftarrow 0, \ \forall t : t \in \{w_{max} - 2, w_{max} - 1, w_{max}\}$
    DEC: $PGCC \leftarrow PGCC - 1$
    if $CNZ = 1$ **then** Goto s_1 **else** Goto s_0 and Stop
  else
    SUB: $I_{tot}[t] \leftarrow I_{tot}[t] - IT_\alpha[t], \ \forall t : t \in \{1, 2, \cdots, w_{max}\}$
s_4 :
  SHIFT4: $I_{tot}[t] \leftarrow I_{tot}[t+4], \ \forall t : t \in \{1, 2, \cdots, w_{max} - 4\}$
    $I_{tot}[t] \leftarrow 0, \ \forall t : t \in \{w_{max} - 3, w_{max} - 2, w_{max} - 1, w_{max}\}$
  Goto s_1

Figure 5: Micro-operations for proposed *switch_on*

out micro-operations belonging to the sequence s_σ, where $\sigma \in \{0, 1, 2, 3, 4\}$.

Initially at s_0, PGCC is loaded with *#components* and SHIFT1 is performed on I_{tot} followed by a transition from s_0 to s_1 ($s_0 \rightarrow s_1$). In s_1, α is obtained from *component_list*. The corresponding elements of I_{tot} and IT_α are added. The sums are stored in I_{tot} followed by $s_1 \rightarrow s_2$. In s_2, the elements of I_{tot} are compared with I_{tol}. TIF is set if none of the elements in I_{tot} exceed I_{tol}, otherwise it is reset. This is followed by $s_2 \rightarrow s_3$. In s_3, if TIF=1, then PGCR[α] is reset followed by SHIFT3 and DEC operations on I_{tot} and PGCC, respectively. If CNZ=1, then $s_3 \rightarrow s_1$ takes place. Otherwise, $s_3 \rightarrow s_0$ occurs, indicating the completion of *switch_on*. In s_3 if TIF=0, then IT_α is subtracted from I_{tot} to restore I_{tot} prior to the most recent addition. After the completion of SUB $s_3 \rightarrow s_4$ occurs. In s_4, a SHIFT4 operation is performed on I_{tot} followed by $s_4 \rightarrow s_1$.

4 EXPERIMENT AND RESULTS

To establish the efficacy of the proposed approach, simulations are carried out on **gem5** [13] architecture simulator. McPAT [15] is used for obtaining power values. **gem5** is configured with the instruction set and functional units (FUs) of the ARM Cortex-M4F processor [14]. The processor has seven FUs. Integer ALU (*ialu*) is not power gated because it is used in majority of the instructions. The bits 0, 1, 2, 3, 4 and 5 of PGCR are the *PG* bits of Floating Point Divider (*fpdiv*), Floating Point Multiplier (*fpmul*), Floating Point Adder (*fpadd*), Integer Divider (*idiv*), Integer Multiplier (*imul*), and Barrel Shifter (*bshf*), respectively as shown in Fig. 6. The size of the instruction cache is considered to be 32 KB. The architectural support for the in-rush current aware *switch_on* is incorporated within the simulation environment.

McPAT is configured with the power model of ARM Cortex-M4F based on 32nm process technology, where the leakage power dissipation is almost 70% of the total power consumption. Here, the processor clock frequency $f_{clk} = 1.0$ GHz, and power supply voltage $V_{dd} = 0.9$ V. V_T of processor's n-MOS and p-MOS transistors are $V_{tn} = 0.18$ V and $V_{tp} = -0.18$ V, respectively. V_T of p-MOS transistors which act as header switches are -0.45 V. $I_{tol} = 200$ mA. Table 1 show the values of load capacitance ($c_l^{(\alpha)}$), maximum operating current ($I_{op}^{(\alpha)}$), w_α and peak I_α (I_α^{pk}) for each C_α belonging to ARM Cortex-M4F with *PG*.

Table 1: Values of $c_l^{(\alpha)}, I_{op}^{(\alpha)}, w_\alpha$ and I_α^{pk}

C_α	*fpdiv*	*fpmul*	*fpadd*	*idiv*	*imul*	*bshf*
$c_l^{(\alpha)}$ (in nF)	6.58	5.9	3.89	2.24	1.81	0.8
$I_{op}^{(\alpha)}$ (in mA)	17.24	15.47	12.84	9.63	8.12	4.72
w_α (in *cycles*)	32	30	24	18	16	10
I_α^{pk} (in mA)	185	177	146	112	102	72

The features leading to generation of naive *PG* (using [11, 12]) and in-rush current aware *PG* (*IAPG*) codes are also added to the GCC compiler for ARM Cortex-M4F.

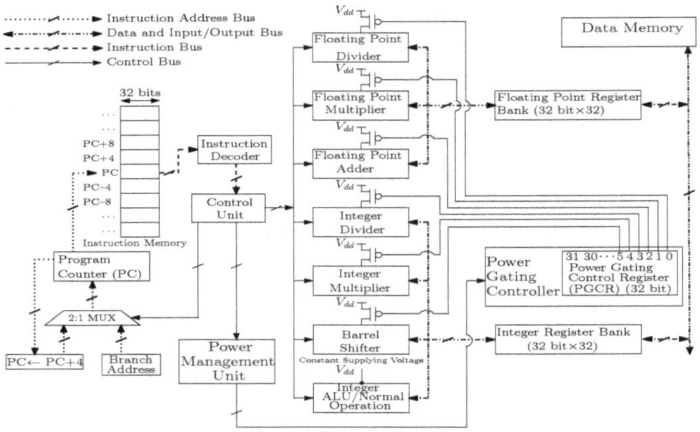

Figure 6: A machine architecture model with *PG*

Table 2: Benchmark description

Program	*fft*	*ffti*	*rsynth*	*mpeg2*	*jpeg*	*epic*	*gsm*	*pgp*
Bench	MiBench	MiBench	MiBench	Media	Media	Media	Media	Media
Category	Telecomm	Telecomm	Office	Video	Image	Image	Speech	Crypto
#cfow	15	8	15	18	14	7	23	9

The proposed technique is tested on MiBench [17] and MediaBench [18] benchmark programs as shown in Table 2, where #cfow is the number of code fragments with overlapped wake-up. The benchmark programs are compiled using updated GCC compiler. The generated target code is executed on gem5 behaving as ARM Cortex-M4F processor. The performance values are generated by gem5 which is used by McPAT to produce values of peak, average, dynamic and leakage power. The value of in-rush current is obtained from the peak power values. The experimental results are shown in Fig. 7. *PG* and *IAPG* are compared with respect to the normalized values of power and delay. Leakage power savings achieved by *IAPG* is similar to that of *PG*. Peak power dissipation $\propto$ in-rush current $\propto$ number of overlapped wake-up (*#overlapped_wake_up*). For *IAPG #overlapped_wake_up* is lesser than that of *PG*. Hence, peak power and in-rush current for *IAPG* are lesser than *PG*. Reduction of in-rush current and peak power dissipation experienced by *IAPG* lie within 16-47% and 18-45%, respectively. This enables *IAPG* to achieve 4-14% savings in total average power consumption. Delay $\propto$ number of *switch_on* instructions $\propto$ $\#cfow$. The proposed *switch_on* consumes $\Omega(\#components)$ cycles whereas the naive *switch_on* takes $\Omega(1)$ cycles. The loss in performance experienced by *IAPG* lies within 0.7-10%.

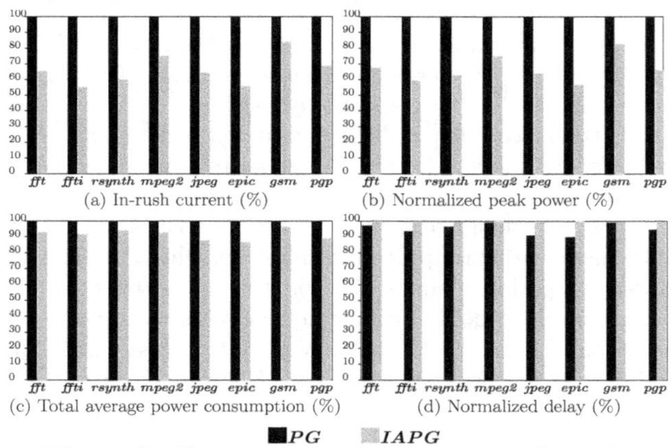

(a) In-rush current (%) (b) Normalized peak power (%) (c) Total average power consumption (%) (d) Normalized delay (%)

Figure 7: Comparison of experimental results

5 CONCLUSION

The present work introduces a hardware based technique for reduction of in-rush current in *PG* sytems. The proposed method *IAPG* reduces in-rush current by allowing ovelapped wake-up within the limitations of tolerable in-rush current. *IAPG* is evaluated on standard benchmark programs. *IAPG* reduces considerable amount of in-rush at the cost of increase in delay, design space and design cost. The future work will investigate to address these issues. Thus making them fit for real-time and safety-critical embedded systems.

REFERENCES

[1] S. Kim, S. V. Kosonocky and D. R. Knebel. Understanding and minimizing ground bounce during mode transition of power gating structures. In *Proc. of Int. Symp. on Low Power Electronics and Design (ISLPED '03)*, August 2003, 22-25.

[2] K. Choi and J. Frenkil. An Analysis Methodology for Dynamic Power Gating. *Sequence Design Inc.*

[3] A. Ball. Integrated in-rush current limiter circuit and method. *US patent US20040090726 A1*, May 2004.

[4] P. Royannez, H. Mair, F. Dahan and U. Ko. 90nm Low Leakage SoC Design Techniques for Wireless Applications. In *Proc. of IEEE Int. Solid-State Circuits Conf.*, February 2005, 138 - 139.

[5] T. S. Kiong and U. C. Kong. Power Gate Optimization Method for In-Rush Current and Power Up Time. *Intel Corporation.*

[6] K. He, R. Luo and Y. Wang. A power gating scheme for ground bounce reduction during mode transition. In *Proc. of 25th Int. Conf. on Computer Design (ICCD 2007)*, October 2007, 388-394.

[7] K. Jeong, A. B. Kahng, S. Kang, T. S. Rosing and R. D. Strong. MAPG: Memory access power gating. In *Proc. of Design, Automation, Test & Exhibition in Europe Conf. (DATE 2012)*, March 2012, 1054-1059.

[8] S. H. Chen, Y. L. Lin and M. C. T. Chao. Power-Up Sequence Control for MTCMOS Designs. *IEEE Trans. on Very Large Scale Integration (VLSI) Syst.* 21,3 (March 2013), 413-423.

[9] A. Kaknevicius and A. Hoover. Managing Inrush Current. *Application Report SLVA670A, Texas Instruments*, May 2015. www.ti.com/lit/an/slva670a/slva670a.pdf

[10] S. Kim, S. Paik, S. Kang and Y. Shin. Wake-up scheduling and its buffered tree synthesis for power gating circuits. *Integration, the VLSI journal, Elsevier* 53 (March 2016), 157-170.

[11] Y. P. You, C. Lee and J. K. Lee. Compilers for Leakage Power Reduction. *ACM Trans. on Design Automation of Elect. Syst. (TODAES)*, 11, 1 (January 2006), 147-164.

[12] S. Roy, S. Katkoori and N. Ranganathan. A Framework for Power-Gating Functional Units in Embedded Microprocessors. *IEEE Trans. on Very Large Scale Integration (VLSI) Syst.* 17, 11 (November 2009), 1640-1649.

[13] http://gem5.org/Main_Page

[14] http://infocenter.arm.com

[15] http://www.hpl.hp.com/research/mcpat/

[16] https://developer.arm.com/open-source/gnu-toolchain/gnu-rm

[17] http://vhosts.eecs.umich.edu/mibench/

[18] http://mathstat.slu.edu/~fritts/mediabench/

Optimal Topology-Aware PV Panel Floorplanning with Hybrid Orientation

Sara Vinco
Politecnico di Torino
Torino, Italy 10129
sara.vinco@polito.it

Enrico Macii
Politecnico di Torino
Torino, Italy 10129
enrico.macii@polito.it

Massimo Poncino
Politecnico di Torino
Torino, Italy 10129
massimo.poncino@polito.it

ABSTRACT

Despite of being one of the most widespread green energy sources, the efficiency of PV rooftop installations is still repressed by shading and by the absence of a rigorous irradiance-aware placement approach. The goal of this work is to reach optimal energy production via an irregular placement of PV modules, by considering two degrees of freedom: *orientation* of each PV module and *topology*. Experimental results will prove the effectiveness of the proposed solution onto two real world case studies, with an increase of power production of up to 40%.

KEYWORDS

Power Optimization; Renewable Energies; PV panels

ACM Reference format:
Sara Vinco, Enrico Macii, and Massimo Poncino. 2018. Optimal Topology-Aware PV Panel Floorplanning with Hybrid Orientation. In *Proceedings of 2018 Great Lakes Symposium on VLSI, Chicago, IL, USA, May 23--25, 2018 (GLSVLSI '18)*, 4 pages.
https://doi.org/10.1145/3194554.3194646

1 INTRODUCTION

The placement of a PV installation is a critical step in its deployment: in order to maximize the return on investment, it is essential to find locations with maximum solar irradiance and minimal or zero shading. For an optimal placement, meteorological information are therefore essential. The literature on the placement of PV installations mostly deals with the positioning of the PV array *as a whole*, while the modules composing the array are all laid out using the same orientation (portrait, more typically, or landscape) without any apparent reason other than ease of connection.

Moreover, topological information is typically not exploited by traditional placements, despite of its impact on the final power production, as it could help matching the variance in irradiance on the surface and minimize the effects of shading. Therefore, thinking in terms of the PV panel as a whole, without any freedom in the orientation and the interconnection of the individual modules, may result in a sub-optimal power production.

GLSVLSI '18, May 23--25, 2018, Chicago, IL, USA

ACM ISBN 978-1-4503-5724-1/18/05...$15.00
https://doi.org/10.1145/3194554.3194646

Clearly, in order to constructively build such a topology-aware placement allowing also hybrid orientation, we need *fine-grain environmental data*, in terms of both spatial and time resolution. Although many Geographic Information Systems (GIS)-based tools are available [2, 5, 7, 9], the only one with the desired spatial and temporal resolution is the one described in [1], which we will adopt as the underlying source of environmental data.

Concerning related approaches, some works leverage finer-grain GIS solar data to drive PV installations at a smaller scale, but in most cases they are just used to identify suitable surfaces (roofs) for the installation. Only few works (e.g. [15]) use fine-grain solar data to identify the best position of PV panels on rooftops; however, they provide only qualitative feedback.

In this work, we specifically address the issue of the *optimal placement of a solar panel on a rooftop based on fine-grain GIS data.* Our method, given a set of irradiance data, a target area for the placement and the topological information of the panel, determines a tiling of the entire surface with a number of PV modules that maximizes the total extracted power. Results show that the determined placement can extract 12-42% more energy than a traditional placement, depending on the target roof, the placement used as a reference, and the adopted PV model.

2 BACKGROUND AND MOTIVATION

2.1 Background

A photovoltaic cell is described by a voltage-current (I-V) characteristic curve, which plots, at a given temperature, the variation of I as a function of the irradiance G [11]. As G increases, the open-circuit voltage V_{oc} increases logarithmically and the short-circuit current I_{sc} increases proportionally. At a given irradiance G, a temperature increase yields a slight increase of the short-circuit current I_{sc}, which determines a decrease of V_{oc}.

In order to increase the output power, cells are connected together according to a series/parallel organization into a PV *module*. PV modules can be further interconnected together. Given n parallel strings each of m modules in series, the total power is obtained as $P_{panel} = V_{panel} \cdot I_{panel}$, where:

$$\begin{cases} V_{panel} & = & \min_{j=1,\ldots,n}(\sum_{i=1,\ldots,m} V_{module,ij}) \\ I_{panel} & = & \sum_{j=1,\ldots,n}(\min_{i=1,\ldots,m} I_{module,ij}) \end{cases} \quad (1)$$

and $V_{module,ij}$ and $I_{module,ij}$ are the voltage and the current extracted from the i-th module in the j-th string. The above formulas show that the total power extracted by the panel P_{panel} depends on its topology and is generally different from the sum of the power of the individual modules, since a non uniform irradiance, e.g., as an effect of shading, heavily affects the total output power of the PV array.

2.2 Motivation

Rooftop PV panels are typically placed by avoiding as much as possible visible or potential shadings and by packing them together tightly using either a "portrait-only" or a "landscape-only" placement style. There is however no technical impediment in using a mix of the two styles: relaxing the constraint of a portrait/landscape only placement could improve the overall extracted power by a better match of irradiance values with respect to the topology.
Orientation of the panels, however, is not the only available degree of freedom. A possibly more powerful option is offered by allowing the connection of non-adjacent modules. Equations 1 highlight indeed that it is convenient to connect modules with similar irradiance (and therefore similar current/voltage levels), in order to minimize the effect of the min() operators.

2.3 Related work

The literature on strategies for the floorplanning of a PV array is quite limited. Some works leverage GIS solar data to drive PV installations, but they generally limit themselves to the identification of suitable surfaces (roofs) for the installation at the urban level.
Only two works use fine-grain solar data to identify the best position of PV panels on rooftops. In [15], the authors provide a qualitative feedback on the portions of a surface that are most suitable for the placement, but they do do not suggest an actual placement. In [12], the authors provide a GIS-based algorithm to place a set of PV modules in such a way that the best match between solar irradiance and modules positions is obtained. In that work, however, it is assumed that the area of the target surface is much larger than the total array surface; the area slack is thus used to generate an irregular (i.e., non rectangular) floorplan. Moreover, the orientation of the modules is kept fixed (specifically, portrait-only).
Our method can be seen as a variant of [12] in which no area slack is provided and both portrait and landscape orientations are allowed.

3 METHOD AND ALGORITHMS

3.1 Problem Definition

The problem we address in this work amounts to the "tiling" of a target surface of area A with a number of N rectangular elements (the PV modules), while maximizing an objective function corresponding to the total extracted power. We assume that the area of the surface has also a rectangular size that can exactly contain the N tiles, i.e., $A \equiv N \cdot A_p$, where A_p is the area of a tile.
This problem can generally be reduced to a particular instance of the well-known binning problem called "domino tiling" [6, 8], once observed that PV panels de-facto have a 2x1 aspect ratio [4].
We assume the target surface has rectangular size $H \times W$, $H = n \cdot d$, $W = m \cdot d$, where d is the grid squares ($d = \sqrt{A_p/2}$). There are therefore $n \times m$ grid elements (Figure 1-(a)). Each panel of area $A_p = d^2$ covers then two grid squares.
From the grid we generate a bipartite graph $G(V, E, W)$ that is a representation of *possible tiling solutions* (Figure 1-(b)). Each vertex $v \in V$ corresponds to a grid element. Grid nodes are shown with alternating "colors" in a checkerboard fashion to denote the partitioning of the set of vertices in two sets. An edge $e_{ij} \in E$ between two vertices V_i and V_j exists if they are adjacent in the checkerboard, i.e, they could be covered by a tile.

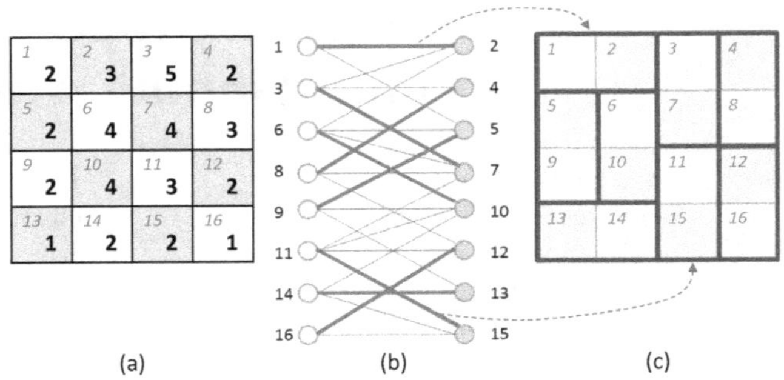

Figure 1: An example 4x4 grid with the relative values (a); the equivalent bipartite graph of the grid (b); an example matching and the corresponding tiling using 2x1 tiles (c).

A *perfect matching* in this bipartite graph represents a tiling of the surface with 2x1 tiles. Figure 1 shows one (randomly chosen) perfect matching (the red edges in Figure 1-(b)) and the corresponding layout of the tiles on the surface (Figure 1-(c)).

3.2 Optimal Tiling Algorithm

This section describes how to derive the weights associated to each grid position and to each edge.
The value assigned to each grid point is a function of the *temporal distribution of irradiance G*, assuming that it is possible to obtain irradiance values at the granularity of our grid cell size d. The average would not be a representative value, since the typical distribution is strongly skewed towards smaller values. As a more aggregate indicator, we therefore use the *75-th percentile of the distribution*, i.e. the value below which 75% of the samples fall (p_{75}). Larger values of the percentile identify distributions that are more skewed towards the upper range of the values; therefore, the suitability metric should combine the percentiles of G, favoring larger values since larger G values are beneficial.
A PV module (tile) covers two grid points, and its cells are typically connected in series. Given that the grid point with the least irradiance will determine the operating point of the whole module, *edge weights* $w_{i,j}$ are simply obtained as $w_{i,j} = \min(p_{75,i}, p_{75,j})$, thus representing the effective irradiance to which the module placed to cover positions i and j will be subject to.
The *maximum matching on the bipartite graph* aims at maximizing these edge weights. We adopted the well-known Hungarian algorithm [10], which in its traditional implementation has a $O(V^4)$ complexity. This is computationally feasible in our case where $|V|$ is in the order of a few tens. The algorithm returns a matching M, which is a subset of the edges (i.e., the red edged is Figure 1.b) and represents the optimal placement of modules (i.e., Figure 1.c).
The next step is to determine the interconnection of the modules according to the specified $s \times p$ topology. This is achieved by using a greedy assignment: we pick edges of M in decreasing order of weight, and assign them in groups of s at a time (a series string). The rationale for this assignment is that it will group modules by guaranteeing a minimal variance of weights w_{ij}, i.e., minimal variance in equivalent irradiance. In this way, the impact of the min() function on the string current (Equation 1) is minimized.

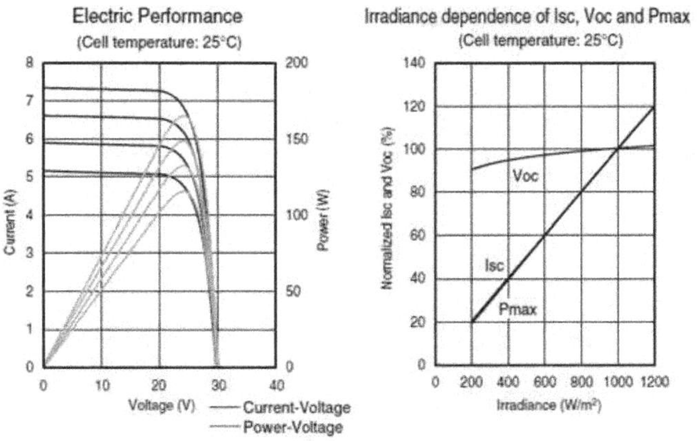

Figure 2: Datasheet of Mitsubishi PV-MF165EB3.

4 EXPERIMENTAL RESULTS

4.1 PV Panel Power Model

In our setup, we consider a PV-MF165EB3 module by Mitsubishi [3]. We adopted a simple PV module model that expresses V_{module} and I_{module} as a function of irradiance G, and we assume that each module extracts the maximum power ($P_{module} \equiv P_{max}$). The model is derived from the plots provided by the datasheet (Figure 2) [13, 14]:

- using the rightmost plot of Figure 2, we first derive the dependence of V_{oc} and P_{max} with respect to irradiance G. The plots are normalized with respect to the reference values at standard condition (25°C, 1000W/cm^2) of $V_{oc,ref}$ = 30.4V and $P_{max,ref}$ = 165W, as reported in the datasheet;
- we derive V_{module} from V_{oc} by exploiting the fact that the maximum power voltage of the module is roughly independent of the irradiance and is $\approx$ 80% of V_{oc} (leftmost plot of Figure 2). This allows to express V_{module} as a function of G;
- I_{module} is then derived as the ratio of P_{max} and V_{module}.

This process results in the following equations:

$$V_{oc}(G) = V_{oc,ref} \cdot (0.006105 \cdot G^2 + 1.169 \cdot G + 0.01108)/100$$
$$V_{module}(G) = 0.8 \cdot V_{oc}$$
$$P_{module}(G) = P_{max,ref} \cdot (0.09002 \cdot G - 0.2857)/100$$
$$I_{module}(G) = P_{module}(G)/V_{module}(G)$$

Using then the interconnection rules described in Equations 1, we can derive the voltage V_{panel} and the current I_{panel} of the panel consisting of a $m \times n$ series-parallel interconnection.
Even if the proposed model is relatively simple, the placement algorithm is independent from the adopted PV model, and it thus can be easily extended to more accurate models.

4.2 Irradiance data generation

Solar data are obtained using the GIS-based infrastructure of [1]. Input GIS data are expressed through a *Digital Surface Model* (DSM), which is a high-resolution raster image representing terrain elevation of the building of interest. The DSM allows to recognize obstacles over the surface (e.g. chimneys) and to estimate the evolution of shadows over time, with 15-minute temporal resolution. The overall trace over time is then obtained by combining weather data, retrieved from weather stations, along with the shadow model.

4.3 Experimental setup

We applied the proposed PV module placement algorithm to the lean-to roofs of two industrial buildings. The roofs face S-S/W with inclination of 26°; the first is of 4m×6m, and the second is of 4m×12m. The key features of each roof are reported in Table 1. Simulations cover one year, from March 2010 to February 2011. Figure 3 shows the 75th percentile of irradiance distribution of the two roofs (brighter colors represent higher irradiance). Irradiance is quite non uniform, as an effect of both roof orientation and of the presence of surrounding encumbrances.

4.4 Simulation results

4.4.1 Execution time. We implemented all algorithms in MATLAB (R2017a). The execution time of the placement is proportional to the number of cells, and it required less than 1.5s for each roof on an Intel 8-core i7 server with 15.4GB of RAM. On average, 16% of the execution time is devoted to the application of the Hungarian algorithm, while about 66% of CPU time is used for the topology construction. This proves the feasibility of the tiling problem, despite of its theoretical complexity.

4.4.2 Generated layout. Figure 3 compares the traditional portrait and landscape placements with the irradiance-driven tiling returned by our algorithm. Colored rectangles represent panels, with panels of the same color belonging to the same series string. The portrait and landscape configurations follow the typical topology: all panels positioned with the same orientation, and nearby panels connected in series. Vice versa, the proposed algorithm places the panels so that irradiance distribution over time is maximized. As a result, both the orientation of the PV modules and their topology reflect the irradiance distributions on the roofs: in the first roof, the least irradiated area is covered by panels connected in series (in blue). Vice versa, in the second roof, the most irradiated area is covered with panels in series, oriented by following the irradiance distribution pattern (purple and green).

4.4.3 Generated power. Table 1 reports the corresponding power production of the two roofs for all configurations. The table shows that the proposed solution can significantly improve energy production on a yearly basis, with improvements that range from 12% to 42%. Obviously, the magnitude of benefit is constrained by the available space, as all solutions occupy the entire roof. However, the numbers show that a more careful orientation and connection of panels can lead to sensible improvements.
Both roofs clearly prove the effectiveness of the adopted irradiance-based topology: the traditional placements have similar topologies, as they put in series the same areas of the roof. The more irregular topology applied by the proposed algorithm (and highlighted by Figure 3) increases the power production by better matching the variance in irradiance on the surface.
Additionally, roof 1 highlights also the advantage of the proposed hybrid orientation, that explains the huge difference in terms of power production between the traditional placements. Roof 1 is indeed characterized by a very heterogeneous distribution of irradiance (Figure 3-(a)): thus, an irradiance-agnostic orientation might place a PV module across two cells that are mismatched in terms of irradiance, thus reducing the possible power production.

Table 1: Characteristics of each roof and power production of the configurations in Figure 3.

Roof	W×H	Panels		PV SYSTEM PRODUCTION						
				PV panel	Portrait	Landscape	Proposed algorithm			
		(#)	Series	model	MWh	MWh	MWh	w.r.t. portrait	w.r.t. landscape	Time (s)
1	8×12	48	12	Proposed	5.811	4.614	6.575	+13.15%	+42.51%	0.664
				[12]	5.917	4.743	6.678	+12.85%	+40.81%	0.801
2	8×24	96	16	Proposed	17.107	17.118	20.391	+19.20%	+19.12%	1.438
				[12]	18.044	18.056	21.526	+19.30%	+19.22%	1.595

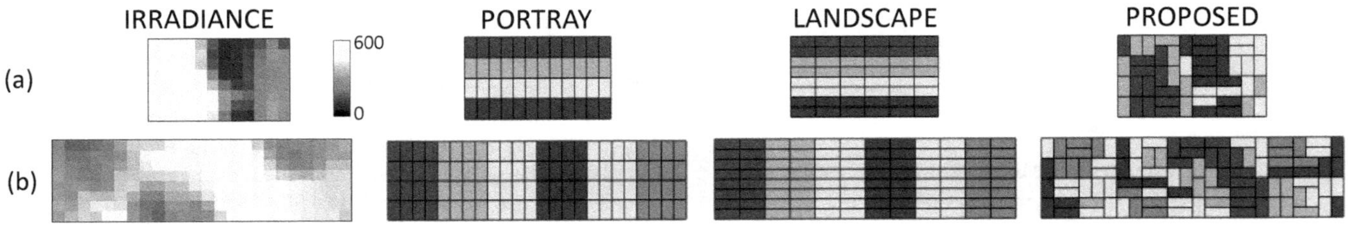

Figure 3: Irradiance distribution over the roofs $[W/cm^2]$ and comparison of three placements: traditional portrait and landscape orientation and result of the proposed algorithm. Rectangles with the same color represent panels connected in series.

4.4.4 Extensibility to other PV module models. To confirm the extensibility of the proposed approach, we applied the placement algorithm to a more complex model built for the same PV module. The model, presented in [12], considers also the effect of temperature on power production, thus gaining a more accurate estimation. Table 1 reports the corresponding power production for the same roof configurations: the results prove that the placement algorithm can be applied also to this more complex model, at the expense of slightly longer simulation times (that are still below 1.6s in all configurations). The difference in terms of power production (in average 3.61%) lies in the different power model. However, the proportion between the configurations is almost identical across the two models.

4.4.5 Wiring costs. The proposed irregular placement will slightly increase the wiring resources, and therefore cost and possibly power. However, a quick analysis of the latter shows that these penalties are marginal. Firstly, since the surface area is a constant, the difference between the total cable length is moderate; Figure 3 shows that an individual series string can indeed be distributed over the entire surface, but some spatial vicinity between blocks of the string is still maintained.
Concerning cost, a typical AWG 10 cable has an approximate cost of $1\$/m$, so, even with 10-20 meters of extra cables the cost overhead would be negligible compared to the cost of the energy increase (avg. 20.14GW). Power overhead is also minimal: the AWG 10 resistive loss is $\approx 7m\Omega/m$; assuming a 4A current in a series string (corresponding to an irradiance of $600W/cm^2$), the power loss is $RI^2 \approx 0.11W/m$, i.e., $\approx 0.5kW/m$ of energy per string in one year (assuming 50% of the time at zero current for dark periods). Multiplying by the number of strings and comparing to the numbers of Table 1, the overhead is below 0.1%.

5 CONCLUSIONS

This work proposed an irradiance-based placement algorithm for PV panels, that sensibly increases power production over a roof tiled with PV modules. The proposed solution exploits two degrees of freedom, namely, PV module orientation and the topology of the overall panel, to match the variance in irradiance on the surface and minimize the effects of shading. We demonstrated the application of the method to two real world case studies, showing an energy increase as much as 12-42% larger than traditional PV installations.

REFERENCES

[1] L. Bottaccioli, E. Patti, E. Macii, and A. Acquaviva. GIS-based software infrastructure to model PV generation in fine-grained spatio-temporal domain. *IEEE Systems Journal*, pages 1--10, 2017.
[2] L. de Sousa, C. Eykamp, U. Leopold, O. Baume, and C. Braun. iGUESS - a web based system integrating urban energy planning and assessment modelling for multi-scale spatial decision making. In *iEMSs 2012*, pages 1--8, 2012.
[3] M. Electric. PV-MF165EB3 datasheet. https://www.mitsubishielectricsolar.com/images/uploads/documents/specs/L-175-4-B6504-A_MF165EB3.pdf.
[4] energysage. What is the average solar panel size and weight? http://news.energysage.com/average-solar-panel-size-weight.
[5] S. Freitas, C. Catita, P. Redweik, and M. Brito. Modelling solar potential in the urban environment: State-of-the-art review. *Renew. Sustainable Energy Rev.*, 41:915--931, 2015.
[6] D. Klarner and J. Pollack. Domino tilings of rectangles with fixed width. *Discrete Mathematics*, 32(1):45--52, 1980.
[7] Mapdwell Solar System. http://www.mapdwell.com.
[8] C. Radin. Space tilings and substitutions. *Geometriae Dedicata*, 55(3):257--264, 1995.
[9] B. Resch, G. Sagl, T. Törnros, A. Bachmaier, J.-B. Eggers, S. Herkel, S. Narmsara, and H. Gündra. GIS-based planning and modeling for renewable energy: Challenges and future research avenues. *ISPRS IJGI*, 3(2):662--692, 2014.
[10] S. Suri. *Bipartite matching & the Hungarian method.*
[11] Y. Tsuno, Y. Hishikawa, and K. Kurokawa. Temperature and irradiance dependence of the I-V curves of various kinds of solar cells. *Proc. of PVSEC*, pages 422--423, 2005.
[12] S. Vinco, L. Bottaccioli, E. Patti, A. Acquaviva, E. Macii, and M. Poncino. GIS-based optimal photovoltaic panel floorplanning for residential installations. *Proc. of IEEE Design, Automation and Test in Europe (DATE)*, pages 1--6, 2018.
[13] S. Vinco, Y. Chen, E. Macii, and M. Poncino. A unified model of power sources for the simulation of electrical energy systems. In *Proc. of ACM/IEEE GLSVLSI*, pages 281--286, 2016.
[14] S. Vinco, A. Sassone, M. Poncino, E. Macii, G. Gangemi, and R. Canegallo. *Modeling and Simulation of the Power Flow in Smart Systems.* Springer, 2016.
[15] T. Voegtle, E. Steinle, and D. Tovari. Airborne laserscanning data for determination of suitable areas for photovoltaics. *ISPRS LS*, pages 215--220, 2005.

ADDHard: Arrhythmia Detection with Digital Hardware by Learning ECG Signal

Sai Manoj Pudukotai Dinakarrao
George Mason University
Fairfax, USA
spudukot@gmu.edu

Axel Jantsch
TU Wien, Institute for Computer Technology
Vienna, Austria
axel.jantsch@tuwien.ac.at

ABSTRACT

Anomaly detection in Electrocardiogram (ECG) signals facilitates the diagnosis of cardiovascular diseases i.e., arrhythmias. Existing methods, although fairly accurate, demand a large number of computational resources. Based on the pre-processing of ECG signal, we present a low-complex digital hardware implementation (*ADDHard*) for arrhythmia detection. *ADDHard* has the advantages of low-power consumption and a small foot print. *ADDHard* is suitable especially for resource constrained systems such as body wearable devices. Its implementation was tested with the MIT-BIH arrhythmia database and achieved an accuracy of 97.28% with a specificity of 98.25% on average.

CCS CONCEPTS

• **Hardware → Full-custom circuits**; On-chip sensors;

KEYWORDS

Arrhythmia detection; FPGA Design; ECG analysis; Digital design

ACM Reference Format:

Sai Manoj Pudukotai Dinakarrao and Axel Jantsch. 2018. ADDHard: Arrhythmia Detection with Digital Hardware by Learning ECG Signal. In *GLSVLSI '18: 2018 Great Lakes Symposium on VLSI, May 23–25, 2018, Chicago, IL, USA.* ACM, New York, NY, USA, 4 pages. https://doi.org/10.1145/3194554.3194647

1 INTRODUCTION

According to World Health Organization (WHO) cardiovascular disease (CVD) statistics 2015 [1], CVDs are the major cause of death globally. Hence, arrhythmia detection (anomaly in Electrocardiogram signal (ECG) acquired from heart) have gained interest among researchers and practitioners.

To perform arrhythmia detection, the structure and characteristics of an ECG signal have to be understood. An ECG signal obtained from each sensing lead reflects the behavior of corresponding part such as arteries, ventricles [6]. An ECG signal is a time series with few millivolts amplitude with a frequency of 0.01-250 Hz [20]. Figure 1 shows a pseudo ECG signal and highlights the five major components P, Q, R, S and T. Spatial and temporal properties such as time intervals, width of these components individually or when combined are used for arrhythmia detection, like variation in T component morphology, ST segment duration, and the R-R interval [6]. The terminology used in this paper to refer to ECG signal properties is defined below:

Component: The components of the ECG signal are the P, Q, R, S and T peaks.

Feature: Features of a component refer to its inherent characteristics such as time period, amplitude, width. For instance, R-R interval can be seen as a feature, similarly the width of the QRS complex, or the amplitude of the R peak.

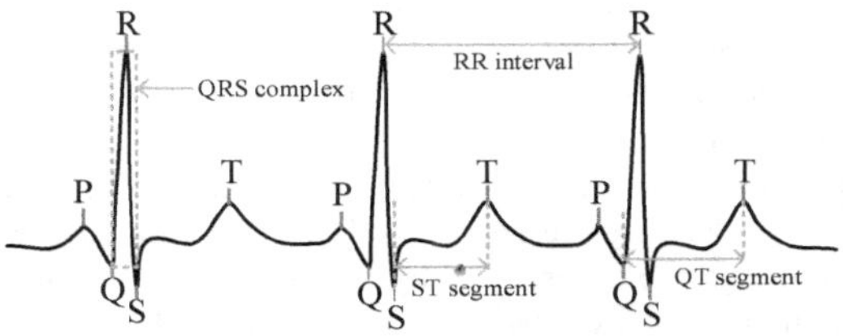

Figure 1: A pseudo ECG signal and its components

Despite of the progress achieved in component detection and feature extraction of ECG signal, Arrhythmia detection with low-complexity and area overheads remain unanswered.

1.1 Challenges in Arrhythmia Detection

Some of the challenges in the arrhythmia detection are: Symptoms of arrhythmia do not show-up all the time; Artifacts and noise from the mechanical components influence the accuracy of anomaly detection; and the characteristics of ECG signal vary among different persons and even vary for same person with time. Thus, there exists no standard rule(s) that can effectively fit everyone. Hence, arrhythmia detection needs to be carried out based on the ECG signal features (time period, amplitude and so on).

1.2 Contributions

We propose *ADDHard* (**A**rrhythmia **D**etection with **D**igital **Hard**ware) to perform arrhythmia detection and address the above mentioned challenges. The proposed method achieves an accuracy of 97.28% on average [12] and has a form factor that fits to be a body wearable device. The contributions of *ADDHard* are:

- A lightweight extracted features dependent analysis of ECG signal is carried out for arrhythmia detection. *ADDHard* circumvents the need for training phase or assumptions required to process ECG signal.
- *ADDHard* effectively detects sinus arrhythmias such as sinus bradycardia, sinus tachycardia, and atrial-ventricular fibrillations. Note, that the aim of this work is to detect the arrhythmia, rather than classification.

ACM ISBN 978-1-4503-5724-1/18/05...$15.00
https://doi.org/10.1145/3194554.3194647

2 RELATED WORK

A vast amount of research is carried out in arrhythmia detection, and a few relevant works are reviewed here.

For detecting arrhythmias, especially ventricular, R-R interval based techniques [13] are popular because of the large amplitude of the R peak. Based on the variations in R-R intervals, statistical parameters such as mean, variance are derived for R-R intervals and the presence of arrhythmia can be determined based on statistical parameter values. Additionally, techniques employing correlation [2], outlier detection [13] and other variants are proposed. Advanced predictors and regression techniques with high efficiency [8], such as auto-regressive integrated moving average (ARIMA) techniques are also used to detect the arrhythmia. These methods are prone to noises as they impact the outcome of regression.

Advancements in machine learning (ML) led to its use for arrhythmia detection. A three-layer feedforward neural network is proposed for arrhythmia detection in [3]. A generalized feedforward neural network trained with static back propagation to detect arrhythmia is proposed in [15]. For the ease of implementation on FPGAs, a block-based neural network (BbNN) structure is often chosen. In general, the BbNNs are trained using evolutionary algorithms such as genetic algorithms (GA). Hermite basis function is one of the efficient feature extraction methods for ECG signals [9]. A BbNN with Hermite expansion coefficients along with R-R intervals as inputs is proposed for ECG arrhythmia classification in [16]. Similarly, arrhythmia detection using different variants of neural networks have been proposed [11, 19]. Neural networks are efficient to detect and classify arrhythmias. However, most of them are computationally expensive due to floating point operations, and complex activation functions. Other ML techniques such as Support Vector Machines (SVM) have been employed for arrhythmia detection [17]. Irrespective of the ML technique used, in addition to the involved complex computations, the system needs to be trained every time a test needs to be carried out on a different person.

Compared to the existing works, *ADDHard* does not need to have an explicit training or specific assumptions about ECG signal or the patient, instead it extracts the features from components and uses them for Arrhythmia detection. In terms of complexity, *ADDHard* makes use of standard hardware blocks such as adders, and comparators; a smaller hardware foot print is sufficient.

3 PROBLEM AND SYSTEM DESCRIPTION

3.1 Problem Formulation

The problem of arrhythmia detection in an ECG signal can be divided into two sub-problems. To have an optimal usage of utilized resources, it is important to find the components of interest, extract and analyze their features for arrhythmia detection. As such, the first sub-problem is defined as:

Sub-problem 1: Detection of a set of components in the ECG signal efficiently, and extract the features of the components.

$$D \subset I(x_1, x_2, ..., x_n)$$
$$C(D) = features. \tag{1}$$

Here, $I(x_1, x_2, ..., x_n)$ represents the input ECG signal, with x_i representing the ECG sample at i-th time instant. Detected components are given by D with extracted features as $C(D)$. .

Once the incoming ECG signal's features are extracted, the system needs to learn the behavior of the signal based on which it could analyze the ECG signal to detect the arrhythmia, which is the second subproblem.

Sub-problem 2: Differentiate the normal and abnormal patterns of ECG signal based on the previously extracted features and the features of ECG signal under test.

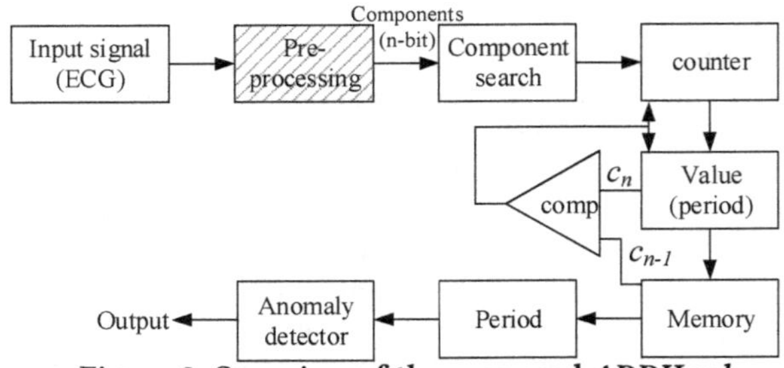

Figure 2: Overview of the proposed *ADDHard*

3.2 System Overview

The block diagram of the proposed *ADDHard* system is presented in Figure 2. The ECG signal is provided as input to the pre-processing block for noise removal and component detection. Functional description of pre-processing stage is presented in Section 4.1. Once the components are detected, they are digitally represented in the form of n-bits. It uses a simple look-up-table to represent the detected components. The component search block receives the digitally represented components from the pre-processing block and searches for a particular component (R component here). Once the component is found in the sequence, it activates the counter. The frequency of the component is found out using simple counters. This frequency or the time interval (c_n) between the components is transferred into the memory. Using the previously analyzed and stored features (c_{n-1}) and the extracted components of the ECG signal (c_n), the variations in features of the ECG and the presence of arrhythmia is signalled. This feature storing, comparing with previously analyzed features are carried out with the aid of standard comparators and registers. Further, this stored period or frequency keeps updating with the input. For better understanding, clock and reset are not shown in Figure 2.

4 PROPOSED ADDHard

Arrhythmia detection using *ADDHard* is performed in three steps, namely: pre-processing and component detection, feature extraction and updation, and signalling arrhythmia.

4.1 Pre-processing and Component Detection

To avoid processing and memory overheads, it is vital to find the components of interest, before extracting the features from a signal. Hence, we perform removal of noises such as baseline wandering, and component detection using *Discrete Wavelet Transform (DWT)* (on software). As wavelet analysis provides a good estimation of time-frequency localization, this method is considered for pre-processing and component (QRS) detection, based on implementation in [18]. Some of the major obstacles to accurate ECG analysis are the baseline wandering and 60Hz interference noise. These are initially filtered using the bandpass filters.

Wavelet transform is a convolution of the signal $f(t)$ with the wavelet function $\psi(t)$, given by

$$X_{j,j} = \int_{-\infty}^{\infty} f(t) \cdot \psi_{j,k}(t)dt \tag{2}$$

here, $(j, k) \in Z^2$. We use Daubechies wavelet (db6) as the mother wavelet and further perform QRS localization and detection using different coefficients. Daubechies wavelets have similar physical properties as QRS complex, hence can detect the QRS effectively. For pre-processing and component detection, the signal is decomposed into 8 levels ($d1$ to $d8$). Coefficients $d3$, $d4$, and $d5$ are used to identify the QRS complex and R components as the maximum points.

4.2 Feature Extraction and Update

Once the components are detected, it is essential to determine the features of detected components for further processing. In this work, the major features of interest are the amplitude, time interval, and period of the detected components. This extraction is performed using simple counters in Figure 2. A sample feature set will be like:

$$C(D) = \{t_{PP}, t_{QQ}, t_{RR}, \ldots, t_{QRS}\} \tag{3}$$

Here $C(D)$ represents the extracted features of the components; t_{RR} indicates the R-R interval in the ECG signal, and the same goes for Q-Q, P-P and QRS components. As such, the features are extracted without any assumptions or explicit training.

Once these features are extracted from the ECG signal, they are compared with the previously stored values and if they are similar i.e., have smaller difference, then it is stored in the memory for reference. We use t_{RR} as the feature in this work. To address the challenge of robustness and being prone to noises, the system monitors features for four consecutive cycles, and if there is no large deviation, an average is considered as the feature that will be used for reference. The rationale to consider four continuous cycles is, in ECG signals most of the irregular heartbeats (arrhythmia) can be detected by observing four consecutive cycles [6].

The characteristics of an ECG signal changes with time and hence needs to be monitored and updated. Update of these characteristics happens gradually in *ADDHard*. For every heartbeat, the features of incoming signal is analyzed and if it is similar to the stored features, an averaging operation is performed and the stored feature value is updated with this new average. Significant variations in the width or any distortion in morphology of an individual component is dealt in pre-processing stage and leads to different digital representation by the component detector. Thus, the *subproblem 1* of feature learning and updation is performed.

4.3 Signaling Arrhythmia

To perform the arrhythmia detection, *ADDHard* makes use of the extracted features from the signal. The arrhythmia detection block validates the features of incoming signal with the features that are stored in the memory. Unlike machine generated signals, biosignals will have some variances in the period, amplitudes. For instance, a peak can occur at 0.70s, followed by peaks after 0.69s and 0.72s. Hence, a tolerance is incorporated into this validation mechanism. When the time interval of a component is similar to the value stored in the memory, i.e., previously extracted feature, system does not signal anomaly and updates the stored value, i.e., feature update (as in Line 11 of Algorithm 1). However, when the stored feature value and the analyzed feature value of the incoming ECG signal differ significantly, i.e., more than tolerance, *ADDHard* signals anomaly.

For R-R feature, for example, the anomaly detection output can be mathematically given as

$$anomaly = \begin{cases} 0, & |St_{RR} - t_{RR}| < \varepsilon \\ 1, & |St_{RR} - t_{RR}| > \varepsilon \end{cases} \tag{4}$$

where St_{RR} represents the R-R time interval stored in memory and t_{RR} indicates the R-R interval of the beat under analysis. The tolerance is given by ε. The assumption of this process is that the anomalies do not occur at the beginning of the process. In case of anomalies in the first few samples, i.e., at the beginning of the setup, the intervals post anomaly will be used as the stored feature values are reset, i.e., there will be a slight delay in learning the features.

Thus, the *Subproblem 2* for ECG arrhythmia detection is solved using extracted and updated features from the ECG signal and circumvents the need for explicit training. Arrhythmia detection with *ADDHard* is summarized in Algorithm 1.

Algorithm 1 *ADDHard* for arrhythmia detection in ECG Signal

Require: ECG signal from sensor ($I(x_1, x_2, \ldots, x_n)$)
Ensure: Arrhythmia detected or not signal $anomaly$

1: **Component Detection:** $DWT(I)$ as given in (2) using Daubechies wavelet
2: Obtain QRS complex, as in Section 4.1
3: **Feature Extraction** using counters, as in Section 4.2
4: For next cycles, extract the features, $C(DD)$
5: **if** $|C(DD) - C(D)| < \varepsilon$ **then**
6:     anomaly ← '0'
7:     **update();**
8: **else**
9:     anomaly ← '1'
10: **end if**
11: **update()**{
12:     $St_{RR} \leftarrow (St_{RR} + t_{RR})/2$ }

5 SIMULATION RESULTS

5.1 Simulation Setup

The simulations and synthesis are performed in Xilinx Vivado. MIT-BIH Arrhythmia database from PhysioNet [12] is used for periodicity detection simulations. Each ECG record is of 30 minutes duration and the pre-processing, i.e., component detection using discrete wavelet transform is performed in Matlab, and digitized to 8-bit data. A 10-bit counter is used in simulations. The tolerance for validation, i.e., ε is set to 15% of the corresponding feature. This value is chosen based on different evaluations to yield best accuracy.

We extracted the power and area information from Design compiler tool for Global Foundry (GF) 65 nm node. *ADDHard* occupies an area of nearly 158.04 μm^2 and consumes nearly 18.69 μW dynamic power. The above mentioned area and power does not include the component detection in Matlab. However, some of the ASIC implementation for pre-processing and component detection algorithms like Pan-Tompkins is presented in [5]. It is reported to have an area of nearly 74,000 μm^2 (0.07 mm^2) for 65 nm CMOS technology for pre-processing. This makes the whole system's are i.e., pre-processing and *ADDHard* less than 0.1 mm^2, which is an ideal fit for body wearable device.

Hardening AES Hardware Implementations Against Fault and Error Inject Attacks

Lake Bu and Michel A. Kinsy
Adaptive and Secure Computing Systems (ASCS) Laboratory
Department of Electrical and Computer Engineering
Boston University
{bulake, mkinsy}@bu.edu

ABSTRACT

The Advanced Encryption Standard (AES) enables secure transmission of confidential messages. Since its invention, there have been many proposed attacks against the scheme. For example, one can inject errors or faults to acquire the encryption keys. It has been shown that the AES algorithm itself does not provide a protection against these types of attacks. Therefore, additional techniques like error control codes (ECCs) have been proposed to detect active attacks. However, not all the proposed solutions show the adequate efficacy. For instance, linear ECCs have some critical limitations, especially when the injected errors are beyond their fault detection or tolerance capabilities. In this paper, we propose a new method based on a non-linear code to protect all four internal stages of the AES hardware implementation. With this method, the protected AES system is able to (a) detect all multiplicity of errors with a high probability and (b) correct them if the errors follow certain patterns or frequencies. Results shows that the proposed method provides much higher security and reliability to the AES hardware implementation with minimal overhead.

KEYWORDS

AES, Error detection, Error correction, Robust codes, Non-linearity.

ACM Reference Format:

Lake Bu and Michel A. Kinsy. 2018. Hardening AES Hardware Implementations Against Fault and Error Inject Attacks. In *Proceedings of Great Lakes Symposium on VLSI 2018 (GLSVLSI'18).* ACM, New York, NY, USA, 4 pages. https://doi.org/10.1145/3194554.3194649

1 INTRODUCTION

In cryptography, the Advanced Encryption Standard (AES) [2] is widely used as a block cipher algorithm. It ensures the confidentiality of a plaintext message through encryption. The computational complexity of the AES algorithm makes it intractable to recover the plaintext message without the appropriate secret key. Since its introduction, there have been numerous proposed attacks against the AES algorithm, especially attacks exploiting potential hardware implementation vulnerabilities. Passive attacks, such as the Differential Power Analysis (DPA) [9], aim to steal the algorithm secret keys by analyzing the AES system runtime power behaviors.

For active attacks, a fault or an error is injected [10] during one or more stages of AES algorithm execution. These attacks infer important information (e.g., key length) about the AES system by observing and analyzing the erroneous output ciphers caused by the injected errors. Our work in this paper focuses on this class of attacks. Beyond attacks, an AES system is also vulnerable to random errors caused by the instability or aging of the cryptographic circuit. This can lead to errors propagating to the outputs of the AES system or its internal stages. Therefore, error detection and error tolerance capabilities are a critical design consideration in these systems. Hardware defense techniques have been explored for both injected and random errors [5]. Another approach is to use error control codes (ECCs) as a built-in self test (BIST) mechanism. ECC-based approaches tend to be more attractive because they (a) can be analyzed using precise mathematical models and (b) offer more cost efficient solutions [8].

Although these approaches have provided a certain level of reliability and security to AES systems, they are often limited in their error detection capabilities. If injected faults are beyond their detection or correction capability, then those errors could be (i) invisible to the detector and (ii) exploited by attackers. Therefore, in this paper, we propose a new method that protects each stage of the AES system with a non-linear code. The proposed approach (a) overcomes the weaknesses seen in linear error detection codes and (b) extends beyond the error correction capability range of previously established non-linear techniques. The key capabilities of the proposed method are:

1. *Conditional All Error Detection:* all errors will be detected with a high probability in a multiplicity of settings;
2. *Conditional All Error Correction:* the method is able to correct all errors under a variety of scenarios with a probability of 1 if the injected error is "lazy", i.e., an error that repeatedly appears in 3 or more cycles or rounds;
3. *Customized Functionality:* the method can be efficiently customized for the four different stages of the AES algorithm/system.

Thus, we characterize the proposed method as "conditional all error detecting and all error correcting" (C-AED-AEC). The rest of the paper is organized as follows. Section 2 has a brief introduction of the four stages of the AES system. In Section 3, we present a widely used error control coding approach for AES systems and highlight some of its vulnerabilities. Section 4 contains the proposed method (C-AED-AEC). Section 5 has the hardware cost and performance results. Section 6 concludes the paper.

GLSVLSI'18, May 23–25, 2018, Chicago, IL, USA

ACM ISBN 978-1-4503-5724-1/18/05...$15.00
https://doi.org/10.1145/3194554.3194649

4 THE CONDITIONAL ALL ERROR DETECTING AND ALL ERROR CORRECTION (C-AED-AEC) SCHEME

In this section, we introduce a new secure and reliable scheme to protect the AES stages from any errors, including ones invisible to the linear SCC. This scheme utilizes a non-linear ECC so [Eq. 6] will not always stand. The advantages of this proposed scheme are:

(1) It detects all errors with a probability close to 1;
(2) There are no errors non-detectable, i.e., invisible, to the decoder;
(3) If the injected error is lazy (i.e., the same error remains for three or more rounds or cycles of AES), it will be corrected with a probability of 1.

Based on the properties above, we name the new scheme *Conditional All Error Detecting and All Error Correction* (C-AED-AEC). The SCC diagram is given below.

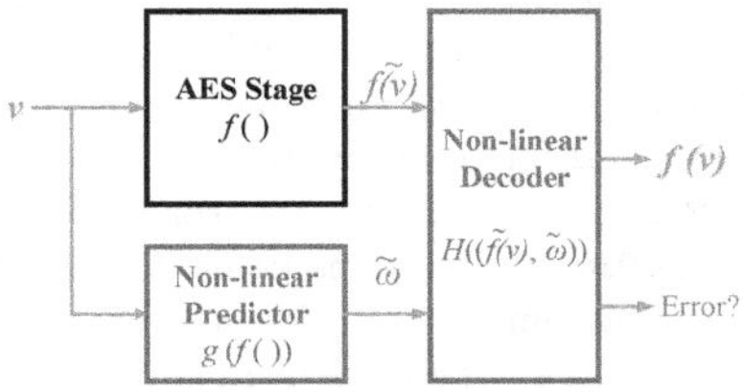

Figure 1: With the non-linear Robust SCC, there is no more $H(e) = 0 \rightarrow H(b \oplus e) = 0 \ \forall b$.

4.1 The Non-linear Robust Code

Before introducing the non-linear ECC code, we will first discuss the concept of Kernel of codes. This will help in understanding why linear ECC protections in AES implementations are vulnerable to certain injected errors.

Definition 4.1 Let $C \subseteq GF(2^N)$ be the set of N-bit codewords and M is an $(R \times N)$ matrix. C is defined by $C = \{c | M \cdot c = 0\}$. Set K_d is called the Kernel of C if:

$$K_d = \{e | e \oplus c \in C, \ \ \forall c \in C\}.$$

If C is linear, then $K_d = C$, and these errors can mask themselves in all verification by $H()$. As discussed at the end of Section 3, a linear ECC has a large invisible error set K_d, namely its legal codeword set. Therefore, it will be ideal to adopt a non-linear code [12] whose Kernel is $K_d = 0$. Thus, there will be no error capable of masking itself in all states under the check of $H()$. In this work, we use the Robust codes for their high error detection capability [3]. Although, the generalized form of the Robust codes has a very complicated construction and proof [7], we introduce a simplified version specially tailored to the four stages of AES.

Construction 4.1 For a vector x that can be equally partitioned into N pieces of b-bit symbols $\{x_0, x_1, \cdots, x_i, \cdots, x_{N-1}\}$, its corresponding b-bit signature symbol ω can be computed as:

$$\omega = \begin{cases} \bigoplus_{i=0}^{(N-2)/2} \ (x_{2i} \otimes x_{2i+1}), & N \text{ is even;} \\ \\ x_0^3 \oplus \left[\bigoplus_{i=0}^{(N-3)/2} \ (x_{2i+1} \otimes x_{2i+2}) \right], & N \text{ is odd.} \end{cases} \tag{7}$$

Note: all computations are carried out over $GF(2^b)$ finite field.

$c_R = (x, \omega) \in C_R$ is a Robust codeword of the Robust code C_R, where x is the information part, and ω the redundant part. ■

4.2 Conditional All Error Detection

A Robust code built by Construction 4.1 has $K_d = 0$. There exists no e which always makes $e \oplus c_R$ a legal Robust codeword $\forall c_R \in C_R$. In other words, any error can be detected with some probability by Robust codes. The lower bound of their error detection probability can be calculated by the error masking equation (EME).

For an error $e = \{e_x, e_\omega\}$ (that $\tilde{x}_i = x_i \oplus e_{x_i}$, $\tilde{\omega} = \omega \oplus e_\omega$) to be invisible to a given Robust codeword, it has to satisfy the EME, which is the equality of [Eq. 7] under $(\tilde{x}, \tilde{\omega})$, where $\tilde{x} = x \oplus e_x$, $\tilde{\omega} = \omega \oplus e_\omega$. Denoting the upper bound of the error masking probability as $\overline{P_{mask}}$, then the error detection probability of the Robust codes is $P_{det} \geq 1 - \overline{P_{mask}}$ for any given $e = \{e_x, e_\omega\}$ (proof in [6]):

$$P_{det} \geq 1 - \overline{P_{mask}} = \begin{cases} 1 - \frac{1}{2^b}, & N \text{ is even;} \\ \\ 1 - \frac{2}{2^b}, & N \text{ is odd.} \end{cases} \tag{8}$$

Larger is b, higher error detection probability: $P_{det} \approx 1$. Furthermore, there are no errors completely invisible to the decoder.

4.3 Conditional All Error Correction

In the proposed approach, we also correct lazy inject errors. A lazy error will remain in place for several cycles or rounds. Here, we introduce two specific algorithms for lazy error correction for the Robust code tailored to the AES stages.

4.3.1 Lazy Error Correction when $N = 1$. Among the four stages of AES, the AddRoundKey and SubBytes operate over single bytes of the state. Therefore, for a Robust code predictor using [Eq. 7], we have the case of $N = 1$, which is an odd number. At this special case there is only one cubic term and [Eq. 7] becomes:

$$\omega = x^3 \tag{9}$$

A legal Robust codeword is $c = (x, x^3)$.

If we assume to have a lazy error $e = (e_x, e_\omega)$ that lasts for at least three different messages $(\tilde{x_0}, \tilde{\omega_0}), (\tilde{x_1}, \tilde{\omega_1}), (\tilde{x_2}, \tilde{\omega_2})$, then by substituting these terms in [Eq. 9], we can solve:

$$x_0 = \left[(\tilde{x_1}^2 \oplus \tilde{x_2}^2) \oplus \frac{\tilde{\omega_0} \oplus \tilde{\omega_2}}{\tilde{x_0} \oplus \tilde{x_2}} \oplus \frac{\tilde{\omega_0} \oplus \tilde{\omega_1}}{\tilde{x_0} \oplus \tilde{x_1}} \right] \Big/ (\tilde{x_1} \oplus \tilde{x_2}) \tag{10}$$

In a similar way, we can solve x_1 and x_2.

4.3.2 Lazy Error Correction when $N = 2$. Among the four stages of AES, the MixColumns and ShiftRows both operate over 4 bytes (a row or a column) of the state, which can be encoded as two Robust codewords with 2 bytes each. [Eq. 7] becomes:

$$\omega = x_0 \otimes x_1 \tag{11}$$

and a legal Robust codeword is $c = (x_0, x_1, x_0 \otimes x_1)$.

If we assume a lazy error $e = (e_{x_0}, e_{x_1}, e_\omega)$ which lasts for at least three different messages $(\tilde{x_{00}}, \tilde{x_{01}}, \tilde{\omega_0}), (\tilde{x_{10}}, \tilde{x_{11}}, \tilde{\omega_1}), (\tilde{x_{20}}, \tilde{x_{21}}, \tilde{\omega_2})$, then by substituting these terms in [Eq. 11], we can calculate each x, e.g.:

$$x_{00} = \tilde{x_{00}} \oplus \left[\tilde{\omega}_1 \oplus \tilde{\omega}_2 \oplus \tilde{x_{20}} \otimes \tilde{x_{21}} \oplus \tilde{x_{10}} \otimes \tilde{x_{11}} \oplus \frac{(\tilde{\omega}_0 \oplus \tilde{\omega}_2 \oplus \tilde{x_{00}} \otimes \tilde{x_{01}} \oplus \tilde{x_{10}} \otimes \tilde{x_{11}}) \otimes (\tilde{x_{20}} \oplus \tilde{x_{10}})}{\tilde{x_{00}} \oplus \tilde{x_{10}}} \right] \Big/ \left[\tilde{x_{11}} \oplus \tilde{x_{21}} \oplus \frac{(\tilde{x_{01}} \oplus \tilde{x_{11}}) \otimes (\tilde{x_{20}} \oplus \tilde{x_{10}})}{\tilde{x_{00}} \oplus \tilde{x_{10}}} \right] \tag{12}$$

Since all errors lasting for a few cycles can be corrected by the formulated SCC, we call this property *Conditional All-Error-Correction* (C-AEC).

4.4 The SCCs Functions for the Four Stages

By [Eq. 9, 11] and the four AES stages' functions [Eq. 1, 2, 3, 4], we have the SCC predictor functions as:

- AddRoundKey ($P_{det} \geq 1 - \frac{2}{2^8} = 99.2\%$):

$$\omega_{\text{AddRoundKey}} = (a_{i,j} \oplus k_{i,j})^3. \tag{13}$$

- SubBytes ($P_{det} \geq 1 - \frac{2}{2^8} = 99.2\%$):

$$\omega_{\text{SubByte}} = (M_{inv} \otimes a_{i,j} \oplus M_{aff})^3. \tag{14}$$

  with $P_{det} \geq 1 - \frac{2}{2^8} = 99.2\%$.
- ShiftRows ($P_{det} \geq 1 - \frac{1}{2^8} = 99.6\%$), each row with two SCCs denoted by α, β:

$$\begin{aligned} \omega_{\text{ShiftRows0-}\alpha} &= (a_{0,0} \otimes a_{0,1}), & \omega_{\text{ShiftRows0-}\beta} &= (a_{0,2} \otimes a_{0,3}); \\ \omega_{\text{ShiftRows1-}\alpha} &= (a_{1,1} \otimes a_{1,2}), & \omega_{\text{ShiftRows1-}\beta} &= (a_{1,3} \otimes a_{1,0}); \\ \omega_{\text{ShiftRows2-}\alpha} &= (a_{2,2} \otimes a_{2,3}), & \omega_{\text{ShiftRows2-}\beta} &= (a_{2,0} \otimes a_{2,1}); \\ \omega_{\text{ShiftRows3-}\alpha} &= (a_{3,3} \otimes a_{3,0}), & \omega_{\text{ShiftRows3-}\beta} &= (a_{3,1} \otimes a_{3,2}). \end{aligned} \tag{15}$$

- MixColumns ($P_{det} \geq 1 - \frac{1}{2^8} = 99.6\%$), each column with two SCCs denoted by α, β:

$$\begin{aligned} \omega_{\text{MixColumns-}\alpha} =& (2a_{0,j} \oplus 3a_{1,j} \oplus a_{2,j} \oplus a_{3,j}) \\ & \otimes (a_{0,j} \oplus 2a_{1,j} \oplus 3a_{2,j} \oplus a_{3,j}); \\ \omega_{\text{MixColumns-}\beta} =& (a_{0,j} \oplus a_{1,j} \oplus 2a_{2,j} \oplus 3a_{3,j}) \\ & \otimes (3a_{0,j} \oplus a_{1,j} \oplus a_{2,j} \oplus 2a_{3,j}). \end{aligned} \tag{16}$$

The decoders are to verify [Eq. 13, 14, 15, 16] under the existence of errors. The error correction probability for lazy errors (lasts for at least 3 rounds) is 100%.

5 EVALUATION

We expanded and optimized the four predictor functions [Eq. 13, 14, 15, 16] over finite field $GF(2^8)$, as well as the decoder functions. Thus the overlay of $g(f())$ functions in the Robust predictors can be precomputed into a simpler function instead of applying $f()$ and $g()$ successively and separately. In our experimentation, we injected 4,019,798 errors of various complexities in the computation stages and measure the error detection rates. To test the lazy error correction capability, the errors are made to last for at least 3 rounds in a given stage, such that [Eq. 10 & 12] can be computed. We used the Xilinx Vertex 7 XC7VX330T FPGA board for our implementations and testing.

Table 1: Hardware and Timing Overhead

Stages	P_{det}	Overhead (C-AED)	Overhead (C-AED-AEC)
AddRoundKey	99.4%	56.3%	92.7%
SubBytes	99.3%	63.7%	101.3%
ShiftRows	99.6%	80.3%	144.0%
MixColumns	99.6%	77.9%	132.9%

[1] Hardware Overhead = $\frac{\text{Stage + Predictor + Decoder}}{\text{Stage}} - 1$.

The P_{det} for the AddRoundKey and SubBytes stages is below $(1 - P_{mask} = 99.6\%)$, because there exists no error satisfying their EMEs in cubic forms. In contrast, there is always a solution satisfying the EMEs equations for the ShiftRows and MixColumns stages. The implementation overhead associated with the error detection plus the error correction (C-AED-AEC) is larger than that of the error detection alone (C-AED). This increase is due to the fact that questions [Eq. 10 & 12] are more complex when compared to the error detection decoders. Altogether, the additional cost is justified since the implementation supports a stronger error tolerance capability.

6 CONCLUSION

In this paper, we have proposed a new technique to harden the reliability and security of AES hardware implementations using a non-linear code self-checking checkers. The proposed method shows key advantages over conventional linear approaches. Unlike the linear ECC approaches, the non-linear technique can (a) detect any injected error with a high probability and (b) guarantee the correction of all lazy errors, which commonly appear in high speed AES hardware implementations. In addition, since the new scheme is built upon error control codes, its performance and capability can be analyzed and estimated using mathematical models. The strong theoretical modeling foundation makes it possible for designers to evaluate and determine the cost/performance trade-off with high accuracy.

7 ACKNOWLEDGMENTS

This research is partially supported by the NSF grant (No. CNS-1745808).

REFERENCES

[1] Luca Breveglieri, Israel Koren, and Paolo Maistri. 2005. Incorporating error detection and online reconfiguration into a regular architecture for the advanced encryption standard. *Defect and Fault Tolerance in VLSI Systems, 2005. DFT 2005. 20th IEEE International Symposium on. IEEE* (2005).

[2] Joan Daemen and Vincent Rijmen. 2013. The design of Rijndael: AES-the advanced encryption standard. *Springer Science and Business Media* (2013).

[3] G. Gaubatz, B. Sunar, and M. G. Karpovsky. 2006. Non-linear residue codes for robust public-key arithme. *Fault Diagnosis and Tolerance in Cryptography* (2006).

[4] Marc Joye and Amir Moradi. 2015. Smart Card Research and Advanced Applications. *Springer International Publishing* (2015).

[5] Ramesh Karri, Kaijie Wu, Piyush Mishra, and Yongkook Kim. 2001. Fault-Based Side-Channel Cryptanalysis Tolerant Rijndael Symmetric Block Cipher Architecture. *Defect and Fault Tolerance in VLSI Systems, 2001. Proceedings. 2001 IEEE International Symposium on. IEEE* (2001).

[6] Konrad Kulikowski, Mark Karpovsky, and Alexander Taubin. 2005. Robust codes for fault attack resistant cryptographic hardware. *Fault Diagnosis and Tolerance in Cryptography, 2nd International Workshop* (2005).

[7] K. Kulikowski, Z. Wang, and M. G. Karpovsky. 2008. Comparative analysis of robust fault attack resistant architectures for public and private cryptosystems. *IEEE 5th Workshop on Fault Diagnosis and Tolerance in Cryptography* (2008).

[8] Nachiketh R. Potlapally, Srivaths Ravi, Anand Raghunathan, and Niraj K. Jha. 2003. Analyzing the energy consumption of security protocols. *Proceedings of the 2003 international symposium on Low power electronics and design. ACM* (2003).

[9] Emmanuel Prouff. 2005. DPA attacks and S-boxes. *nternational Workshop on Fast Software Encryption* (2005).

[10] Cyril Roscian, Jean-Max Dutertre, and Assia Tria. 2013. Frontside laser fault injection on cryptosystems-Application to the AES last round. *Hardware-Oriented Security and Trust (HOST), 2013 IEEE International Symposium on. IEEE* (2013).

[11] Chih-Hsu Yen and Bing-Fei Wu. 2006. Simple error detection methods for hardware implementation of advanced encryption standard. *IEEE transactions on computers* (2006).

[12] W. Zhen, M. Karpovsky, and K. J. Kulikowski. 2009. Replacing linear hamming codes by robust nonlinear codes results in a reliability improvement of memories. *IEEE/IFIP International Conference on Dependable Systems and Networks* (2009).

SimTRaX: Simulation Infrastructure for Exploring Thousands of Cores

Konstantin Shkurko
University of Utah
kshkurko@cs.utah.edu

Tim Grant
University of Utah
tgrant@cs.utah.edu

Erik Brunvand
University of Utah
elb@cs.utah.edu

Daniel Kopta
University of Utah
dkopta@cs.utah.edu

Josef Spjut
NVIDIA
josef.spjut@gmail.com

Elena Vasiou
University of Utah
elvasiou@cs.utah.edu

Ian Mallett
University of Utah
imallett@cs.utah.edu

Cem Yuksel
University of Utah
cem@cemyuksel.com

ABSTRACT

SimTRaX is a simulation infrastructure for simultaneous exploration of highly parallel accelerator architectures and how applications map to them. The infrastructure targets both cycle-accurate and functional simulation of architectures with thousands of simple cores that may share expensive computation and memory resources. A modified LLVM backend used to compile C++ programs for the simulated architecture allows the user to create custom instructions that access proposed special-purpose hardware and to debug and profile the applications being executed. The simulator models a full memory hierarchy including registers, local scratchpad RAM, shared caches, external memory channels, and DRAM main memory, leveraging the USIMM DRAM simulator to provide accurate dynamic latencies and power usage. SimTRaX provides a powerful and flexible infrastructure for exploring a class of extremely parallel architectures for parallel applications that are not easily simulated using existing simulators.

CCS CONCEPTS

• **Computing methodologies** → **Simulation tools**; *Graphics processors*; • **Computer systems organization** → *Multiple instruction, multiple data*;

KEYWORDS

Architecture simulation; single program multiple data; LLVM

ACM Reference Format:

Konstantin Shkurko, Tim Grant, Erik Brunvand, Daniel Kopta, Josef Spjut, Elena Vasiou, Ian Mallett, and Cem Yuksel. 2018. SimTRaX: Simulation Infrastructure for Exploring Thousands of Cores. In *Proceedings of 2018 Great Lakes Symposium on VLSI (GLSVLSI '18)*. ACM, New York, NY, USA, 4 pages. https://doi.org/10.1145/3194554.3194650

GLSVLSI '18, May 23–25, 2018, Chicago, IL, USA

ACM ISBN 978-1-4503-5724-1/18/05...$15.00
https://doi.org/10.1145/3194554.3194650

1 INTRODUCTION

When designing application-specific accelerator architectures, cycle-accurate simulators are indispensable for rapid exploration of the potential design space. Unlike trace-based simulators that can quickly evaluate particular sub-systems under specific work-loads, cycle-accurate simulators capture the precise inner-workings of the entire system. Thus, they provide a testbed for software modifications to make the target application more suitable for the custom accelerator architecture.

This paper describes SimTRaX: a set of tools that resulted from exploring the design space of massively parallel accelerator architectures made up of simple in-order cores combined with shared compute and memory resources. Unlike most other simulators, SimTRaX is designed to simulate thousands of concurrent hardware threads with cycle-accuracy without introducing high-level approximations. SimTRaX provides ample performance to run applications to completion. We support the LLVM compiler [13] to provide simple software access to custom hardware features. We can use source-level debugging symbols provided by LLVM to debug and profile simulated architectures and applications on a wide variety of metrics. Furthermore, accurate simulation of the DRAM behavior produces reliable results especially for applications that process a large amount of data with unpredictable access patterns.

2 BACKGROUND

Although existing simulators enable experimentation within their own expected parameters, we have found that exploring a design space that is more massively parallel can benefit from a new simulation infrastructure. We find that these architectures, and the applications that map well to them, can often be categorized as single-program multiple-data (SPMD) processing. In this case all hardware processors execute the same program, but because they have their own PCs, can be at different points in that program depending on their own data and control flow[1]. This can leverage data

[1]Note that single-instruction multiple-thread (SIMT) processing as defined by NVIDIA [15] is often considered similar to single-program multiple-data (SPMD). However, SIMT support for divergent thread execution only tracks the divergence and

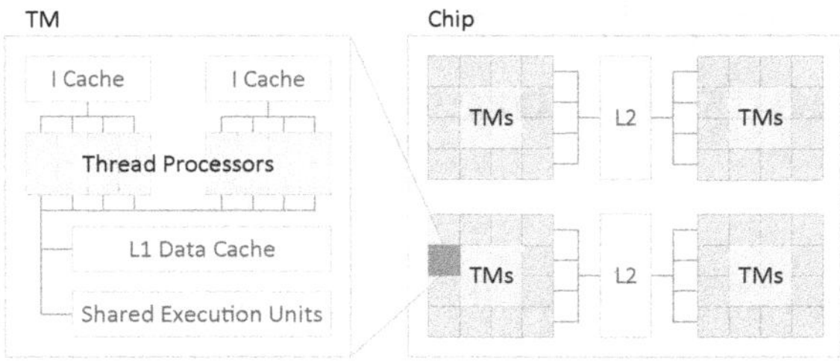

Figure 1: An example of a hierarchically organized parallel architecture [12] supported by SimTRaX.

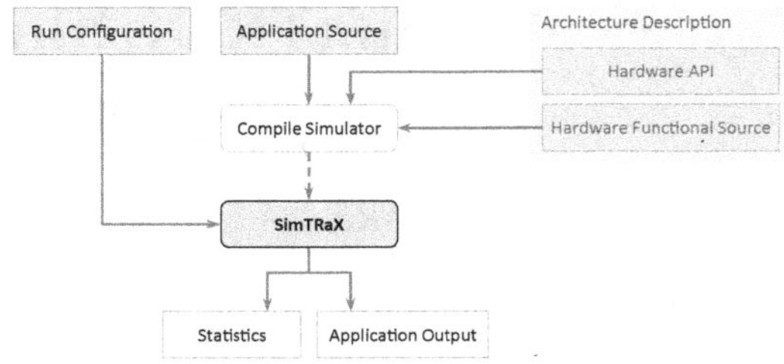

Figure 2: Functional mode work flow. *Application source* and *architecture description* are compiled into SimTRaX executable specific to application. Blue color highlights inputs.

parallelism and simultaneously sharing of large and complex functional units. Examples of such tiled architectures include TRaX [19], Rigel [10], Copernicus [8], STRaTA [11], and SGRT [14].

There are, of course, many existing simulators for exploring new computer architectures. CPU and multi-core simulators such as SimpleScalar [3], Simics [16], and gem5 [2] are designed to simulate up to tens of complex, typically out of order, thread processors with advanced features to accelerate individual thread latency. Simulators for massively parallel architectures like GPUs typically target the single-instruction multiple-data execution model. GPGPU-Sim [1] executes unmodified CUDA and OpenCL workloads on a simulated NVIDIA-like GPU architecture. However, keeping the simulator up to date presents an ongoing challenge.

Tiled architectures generally achieve their performance through massive parallelism via thousands of simple hardware threads. Simulators such as PriME [7], Zsim [18], Graphite [17], and Sniper [4] are focused on increasing simulated parallelism with varying degrees of cycle-accuracy. Rigel [10] is probably the most similar to SimTRaX. Rigel simulates thousands of execution threads, allows configuration of the interconnect and the memory system, and includes development tools based on LLVM. Rigel applications are developed using a simple task-based bulk synchronous parallel programming model to be executed in a SPMD paradigm. While Rigel development seems to have stopped in 2012, it demonstrates that simulation infrastructures that support massive parallelism and compiler integrations are interesting in a variety of domains.

3 SIMULATOR ARCHITECTURE

SimTRaX was designed to help explore application-specific accelerator architectures, modeled as a tiled, hierarchical, parallel architecture with a few thousand processing units. An example is shown in Figure 1. The lowest level is composed of simple in-order Thread Processors (TPs) with limited execution resources. At the middle level, Thread Multiprocessors (TMs) tile a number of TPs alongside units they share access to. At the highest level, a chip can consist of many TMs which share access to chip-wide resources, such as L2 data caches. Such hardware representation offers the ability to simulate a range of architectures, some of which would not map easily to other simulation platforms.

The simulator is designed to keep overhead low when modeling the execution flow for each TP. During each clock, first we simulate all TM-wide units that can enqueue requests into globally-shared units, then global units and finally dynamic random access memory (DRAM).

SimTRaX is accelerated via multiple software simulation threads, each in charge of several TMs. Although access to TM-wide resources requires no simulator synchronization, SimTRaX must serialize access to chip-wide units. Thus simulation times depend in part on the architecture design and the frequency of accesses to globally-shared units. All simulation threads must also synchronize after each simulated cycle. Although relaxing this synchronization requirement increases simulator speed [17], it introduces errors in predicted hardware performance.

4 IMPORTANCE OF ACCURATE DRAM MODELING

The main memory of a simulated architecture typically consists of DRAM. It must be modeled accurately because it can be a primary consumer of both energy and time in data-bound applications. Due to the internal structure and makeup of DRAM circuits, its operation and performance is far more complex than SRAM. In addition to being dynamic, and thus needing periodic refresh operations, the latency and energy consumption of individual accesses can vary widely based on the patterns and addresses of recent accesses.

When simulating memory-bound applications, particularly with thousands of threads, the accuracy of the memory model can drastically impact the results. SimTRaX relies on a modified version of the Utah Simulated Memory Module (USIMM) simulator [5] to accurately model DRAM behavior. SimTRaX reports detailed memory access statistics to help the user tune and evaluate their algorithmic/architectural innovations.

5 LLVM INTEGRATION

SimTRaX incorporates the LLVM toolchain [13] to facilitate developing applications used to benchmark new hardware units and architecture design. The use of LLVM allows extending the instruction set architecture (ISA) with relative ease. Applications are written in a high-level language, such as C++, and then compiled to the modified ISA. In addition, we also include debugging and profiling features within the simulator.

Each custom hardware unit may be supported by an API to expose it to the application. When compiling as the standalone functional simulator, each API call translates into a function call to

still must mask off the results from diverged threads within a SIMT group. SPMD in our model allows threads to make individual progress while diverging.

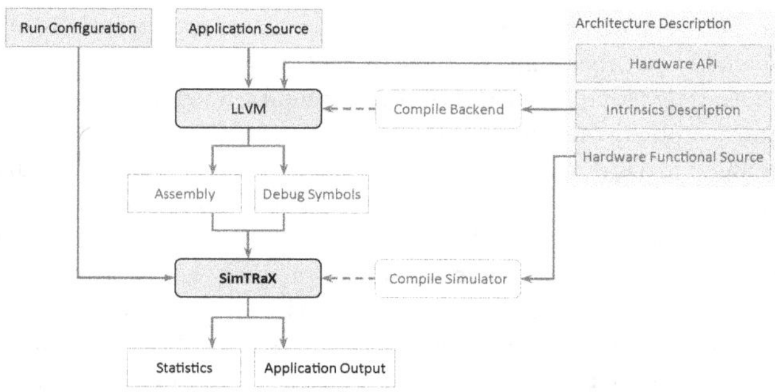

Figure 3: Cycle-accurate mode work flow. The following rely on *architecture description* during compilation: LLVM backend, application assembly which relies on this backend, and SimTRaX executable. Blue color highlights inputs.

```
Time Profile                              FPU Energy Profile
Main                         100.00%      Main                          100.00%
| Shade                       47.57%      | Shade                        51.10%
| | BVH::Intersect            31.16%      | | RandomReflection           15.61%
| | | Tri::Intersect          13.80%      | | | Vec::Normal              11.48%
| | | | Vec::Cross             2.15%      | | | | Vec::Length             7.40%
| | | | Vec::operator-         1.38%      | | | | | sqrt                  7.27%
...                                       ...
```

Figure 4: An example profiler output showing the computation time (left) and energy use (right).

(a) Mandelbrot (b) Path tracing the "Crytek Sponza" scene (c) Path tracing the "San Miguel" scene

Figure 5: Representative output images generated using Mandelbrot and path tracing benchmark applications.

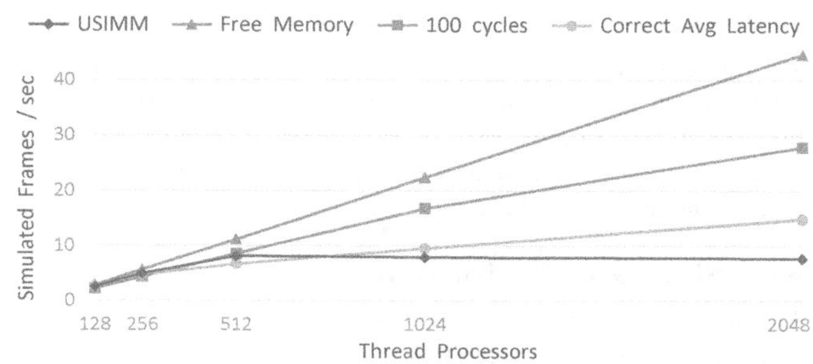

Figure 6: Effect of DRAM accuracy on simulated performance of path tracing on TRaX for San Miguel scene.

the appropriate implementation of the "instruction." Figure 2 shows the work flow for the functional operation.

When the application source is compiled for the cycle-accurate simulator, an assembly file is produced for input into the simulator. Custom instructions exposed by the API calls invoke compiler intrinsics that generate the appropriate assembly instructions. Figure 3 shows the work flow for the cycle-accurate operation.

The LLVM toolchain can embed debug symbols within the assembly of the compiled application. SimTRaX parses and interprets DWARF [6] debugging symbols, and includes a built-in debugger and profiler that operate on the full cycle-accurate state of the simulated machine rather than sampling. Fig. 4 shows an example of the profiler's output with two metrics: a profile for time (left) and the energy spent in floating point arithmetic units (right). The profiler can expose, at the application source code level, the exact source of various behaviors on the chip. As a result, SimTRaX can provide a more complete understanding of the impact aspects of the hardware have on performance when evaluating new architectures.

6 EVALUATION

We evaluate SimTRaX performance when simulating a typical tiled massively parallel architecture targeted at accelerating computer graphics: the TRaX architecture [19]. Selected graphics benchmarks, shown in Figure 5, evaluate the effects of accessing memory on simulator performance. The Mandelbrot benchmark includes a large percentage of computation, where the memory subsystem is accessed only for initial parameters and image output. Path tracing, an algorithm that generates photo-realistic images [9], relies on iterating over tree data structures per pixel and thus can access memory rather incoherently. Smaller scenes, like Crytek Sponza (262,000 triangles), generate more coherent accesses and thus higher cache hit rates than larger scenes like San Miguel (10.5 million triangles).

The output image resolution is 1024×1024, and path tracing benchmark uses maximum ray depth of three. Benchmarked TRaX configuration combines 32-wide TMs into a chip with 128 to 2048 total TPs running at 1GHz. Each TM contains shared execution units and a 32KB L1 data cache. The L1 data cache from each TM is assigned to one of four global 512KB L2 data caches. They connect to the DRAM memory controller set up as 8 channel GDDR5 for a maximum of 512GB/s bandwidth. The performance of the simulated architecture is measured in frames per second (FPS). The simulator is evaluated on a hexa-core Intel i7-5820K CPU running at 3.3GHz and 32GB of DDR4 memory.

6.1 DRAM

To compare the effects of simulating DRAM accurately, consider simulated performance executing path tracing on a TRaX architecture with varying number of TPs, shown in Figure 6. This test includes four different models for DRAM accesses. *USIMM* simulates DRAM behavior correctly. The other modes use a constant access latency: one cycle for *Free Memory*, 100 cycles for *100 cycles*, and 60 – 470 cycles for *Correct Avg Latency* which matches latencies from USIMM simulations. The simulated performance plateaus for the San Miguel scene at 512 TPs when simulating DRAM accurately because the configuration is DRAM bandwidth-limited. However,

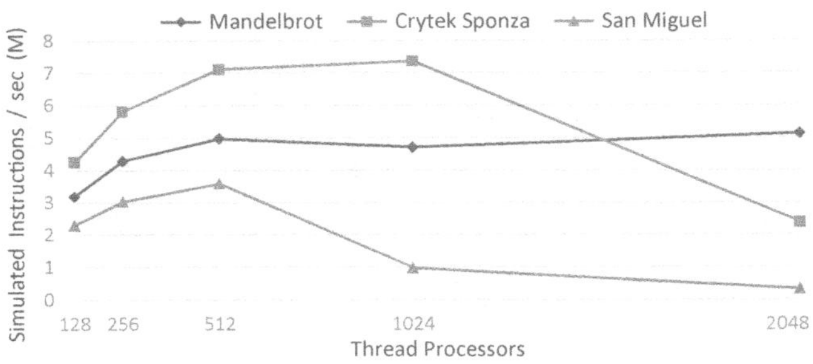

Figure 7: SimTRaX performance measured in millions of simulated instructions per second.

without accurate DRAM simulation, this behavior cannot be accurately captured, and the simulated performance results scale almost linearly with the number of TPs. It is clear that the accuracy of simulating the DRAM dynamic behavior can have a profound effect on reported results of the simulator.

6.2 Simulator Performance

Although cycle-accurate simulators enable highly accurate and detailed evaluation of proposed architectures, they are typically considered slow. However, the combination of architectural choices, using multi-threading and general improvements in processor performance help make cycle-accurate simulations feasible. Figure 7 shows SimTRaX performance measured in millions of simulated instructions per second (MSIPS) as a function of number of TPs while using four simulator threads. SimTRaX simulates at a rate of 0.33 to 7.38 MSIPS depending on how frequently the workload and hardware communicate with chip-wide units. This performance is good enough to enable co-processors with thousands of threads and new hardware units, and benchmark applications running to completion. The performance dips for both Crytek Sponza and San Miguel scenes around 1024 TPs because those configurations become DRAM bandwidth-limited. This results in higher DRAM latencies and more simultaneous requests to the DRAM simulation component, requiring heavy utilization of software locks.

7 CONCLUSION AND FUTURE WORK

We have described SimTRaX, a simulator designed to explore highly parallel co-processor architectures with thousands of simple threads sharing access to expensive computation and memory resources. The simulation infrastructure provides several components essential for quick exploration of possible architecture designs concurrently with targeted software modifications: combined cycle-accurate and functional simulation capability, flexibility in how functional units are connected, a highly accurate DRAM model, and integration of the LLVM toolchain for easy ISA extensions and compiling applications written in a high-level language.

The combination of LLVM debugging information and cycle-accurate system state can be used to generate a highly detailed profile with information beyond just execution time. For example, a user could generate a profile of energy spent in the various chip components during execution. This focus on massively parallel architecture, integration with LLVM, and the resulting ability to profile simulated code in detail on the simulated architecture is not available on other simulator platforms that we are aware of.

An interesting future direction is extending SimTRaX to support more sophisticated memory sharing mechanisms, which would enable SimTRaX to simulate more general architectures. It would also be interesting to explore how we can enable simulations to rely on task-based parallelism while relaxing how often simulation threads need to synchronize. To aid in evaluating radically different architectures faster, SimTRaX's modularity should extend further and enable a node-based graphical interface to configure how functional units are connected and shared. Finally, an automatic system can be used to find optimal architecture configurations by using gradient-descent-like algorithms to optimize a metric produced by the simulator (like energy or performance).

ACKNOWLEDGMENTS

This material is supported in part by the National Science Foundation under Grant No. 1409129. The authors thank Solomon Boulos, Al Davis, Spencer Kellis, Andrew Kensler, Steve Parker, Paymon Saebi, Pete Shirley, and Utah Architecture group for discussions and simulator contributions. Crytek Sponza is from Frank Meinl at Crytek and Marko Dabrovic and San Miguel is from Guillermo Leal Laguno.

REFERENCES

[1] A. Bakhoda, G. L. Yuan, W. W. L. Fung, H. Wong, and T. M. Aamodt. 2009. Analyzing CUDA workloads using a detailed GPU simulator. In *ISPASS*. 163–174.

[2] N. Binkert, B. Beckmann, G. Black, S. K. Reinhardt, A. Saidi, A. Basu, J. Hestness, D. R. Hower, T. Krishna, S. Sardashti, R. Sen, K. Sewell, M. Shoaib, N. Vaish, M. D. Hill, and D. A. Wood. 2011. The Gem5 Simulator. *SIGARCH Comput. Arch. News* 39, 2 (Aug. 2011).

[3] D. Burger and T. Austin. 1997. *The Simplescalar Toolset, Version 2.0.* Technical Report TR-97-1342. University of Wisconsin-Madison.

[4] T. E. Carlson, W. Heirman, and L. Eeckhout. 2011. Sniper: Exploring the Level of Abstraction for Scalable and Accurate Parallel Multi-core Simulation. In *SC*.

[5] N. Chatterjee, R. Balasubramonian, M. Shevgoor, S. Pugsley, A. Udipi, A. Shafiee, K. Sudan, M. Awasthi, and Z. Chishti. 2012. *USIMM: the Utah SImulated Memory Module.* Technical Report UUCS-12-02. Univ. of Utah.

[6] DWARF Debugging Information Format Committee. 2010. DWARF Debugging Information Format V. 4. http://www.dwarfstd.org/doc/DWARF4.pdf. (2010).

[7] Y. Fu and D. Wentzlaff. 2014. PriME: A parallel and distributed simulator for thousand-core chips. In *ISPASS*. IEEE, 116–125.

[8] V. Govindaraju, P. Djeu, K. Sankaralingam, M. Vernon, and W. R. Mark. 2008. Toward A Multicore Architecture for Real-time Ray-tracing. In *IEEE/ACM Micro*.

[9] J. T. Kajiya. 1986. The Rendering Equation. In *Proceedings of SIGGRAPH*. 143–150.

[10] J. H. Kelm, D. R. Johnson, M. R. Johnson, N. C. Crago, W. Tuohy, A. Mahesri, S. S. Lumetta, M. I. Frank, and S. J. Patel. 2009. Rigel: an architecture and scalable programming interface for a 1000-core accelerator. In *ISCA*.

[11] D. Kopta, K. Shkurko, J. Spjut, E. Brunvand, and A. Davis. 2013. An energy and bandwidth efficient ray tracing architecture. In *Proc. HPG*. 121–128.

[12] D. Kopta, K. Shkurko, J. Spjut, E. Brunvand, and A. Davis. 2015. Memory Considerations for Low Energy Ray Tracing. *Comp. Gr. Forum* 34, 1 (2015), 47–59.

[13] C. Lattner. 2008. LLVM and Clang: Next generation compiler technology. In *The BSD Conference*. 1–2.

[14] W. Lee, Y. Shin, J. Lee, J. Kim, J. Nah, S. Jung, S. Lee, H. Park, and T. Han. 2013. SGRT: A mobile GPU architecture for real-time ray tracing. In *Proc. HPG*.

[15] E. Lindholm, J. Nickolls, S. Oberman, and J. Montrym. 2008. NVIDIA Tesla: A Unified Graphics and Computing Architecture. *Micro, IEEE* 28, 2 (2008), 39–55.

[16] P. S Magnusson, M. Christensson, J. Eskilson, D. Forsgren, G. Hallberg, J. Hogberg, F. Larsson, A. Moestedt, and B. Werner. 2002. Simics: A full system simulation platform. *Computer* 35, 2 (2002), 50–58.

[17] J. E. Miller, H. Kasture, G. Kurian, C. Gruenwald, N. Beckmann, C. Celio, J. Eastep, and A. Agarwal. 2010. Graphite: A distributed parallel simulator for multicores. In *HPCA*. IEEE, 1–12.

[18] D. Sanchez and C. Kozyrakis. 2013. ZSim: Fast and Accurate Microarchitectural Simulation of Thousand-core Systems. In *ISCA*.

[19] J. Spjut, A. Kensler, D. Kopta, and E. Brunvand. 2009. TRaX: A Multicore Hardware Architecture for Real-Time Ray Tracing. *IEEE Trans on CAD* 28, 12 (2009).

Static Design of Spin Transfer Torques Magnetic Look Up Tables for ASIC Designs

Aliyar Attaran
School of Engineering, San Francisco State University, San Francisco, CA
aattaran@mail.sfsu.edu

Tyler David Sheaves
School of Engineering, San Francisco State University, San Francisco, CA
tsheaves@mail.sfsu.edu

Praveen Kumar Mugula
School of Engineering, San Francisco State University, San Francisco, CA
pmugula@mail.sfsu.edu

Hamid Mahmoodi
School of Engineering, San Francisco State University, San Francisco, CA
mahmoodi@sfsu.edu

ABSTRACT

In this paper, we propose a static approach to the design of Spin Transfer Torque Look Up Tables (STT-LUT) for integration in ASIC and investigate the sensing reliability in the proposed design in detail. The proposed design style utilizes STT-Latches that their sensing reliability is key in determining the overall reliability of the proposed static STT-LUT. The simulation results in a 10nm FinFET CMOS technology shows that the proposed static STT-LUT design exhibits up to 26% read delay reduction compared to the best dynamic STT-LUT design, and more than 2.5X reduction in sensing failure rate.

CCS CONCEPTS

• **Hardware** → Integrated circuits; **Hardware** → Logic circuits; **Hardware** → Very large scale integration design; **Hardware** → Full-custom circuits; **Hardware** → Reconfigurable logic and FPGAs; **Hardware** → Application-specific VLSI designs; **Hardware** → Standard cell libraries

KEYWORDS

Look up the table, low power, a magnetic tunnel junction, reconfigurable logic, spin transfer torque

1 INTRODUCTION

Spin Transfer Torque Magnetic Memory (STT-MRAM) is a promising technology for non-volatile storage in which the information is stored in the form of magnetic orientation of a Magnetic Tunnel Junction (MTJ) rather than electric charge.

GLSVLSI '18, May 16–18, 2018, Chicago, IL, USA
© 2018 Association for Computing Machinery.
ACM ISBN 978-1-4503-5724-1/18/05...$15.00
https://doi.org/10.1145/3194554.319465

Besides memory applications, this technology is promising for CMOS compatible non-volatile reconfigurable logic design. Given the relatively high power and long delay associated with changing the magnetic state of an MTJ [1], the most efficient method of designing reconfigurable logic using MTJs is the Look-Up-Table (LUT) based approach. In such STT-LUTs, the write to MTJs occurs only during the configuration phase, while for the normal mode of the operation, the MTJs are only read from. Most existing STT-LUT designs are dynamic because of using a shared precharge sense amplifier to read the state of the selected MTJ. Dynamic STT-LUTs are challenging to use along with static combinational logic circuits and are not supported by automated design flow tools. Hence, we propose a static LUT design, in which MTJ-based precharge sense amplifier (PCSA) latches are used as storage cells. The basic programmable logic element is a look-up table that utilizes MTJs for storage (STT-LUT) [2] [3].

Existing designs of STT-LUTs utilize a shared dynamic precharge sense amplifier to read the state of the MTJ selected by the inputs. The dynamic design of the shared sense amplifier makes the entire STT-LUT a dynamic design. While dynamic designs have the advantage of less area using a shared sense amplifier, they suffer from long read delay, less reliability, and difficulty in integration with static logic and lack of support by automated design flow tools. The remainder of the paper is organized as follows. Section 2 offers a background on STT-LUT design and an overview of existing STT-LUT designs. Section 3 presents the proposed static approach to the design of STT-LUTs. Section 4 presents power, performance, and robustness comparisons of the proposed and conventional STT-LUTs. Section 5 described the integration of the proposed STT-LUT in ASIC designs. Finally, conclusions are drawn in Section 6.

2 EXISTING STT-LUT DESIGNS: DYNAMIC

In the existing dynamic approach, in n-input STT-LUT requires 2^n MTJs that store the binary states. A CMOS selection tree (i.e. multiplexer) select a unique MTJ to be biased for reading and a CMOS sense amplifier for producing full swing output voltage. In the write mode, the data input is written to a unique MTJ. The challenging aspect of STT-LUT design is reliable and power and performance efficient sensing of the MTJ resistive state and converting it to a binary voltage.

All existing STT-LUT designs use a variety of dynamic sensing schemes to update the sense amplifier output on a cycle by cycle basis. The SRAM based sensing scheme proposed in [3] uses an SRAM cell that is biased in the metastable condition in the initialization phase and then switches to the full-swing direction according to the resistance difference between the selected MTJ and a reference resistor. This design cannot be cascade because of the initial output voltage level being at around half the supply level (VDD) and hence distorting the sensing of the next stage. The other existing STT-LUT design is the Dynamic Current Mode (DCM) logic-based design [2]. This design uses the concept of the dynamic current mode logic [4], by utilizing a dynamic current source to reduce the current of the selection tree above it and hence to reduce the power consumption. However, by doing so, the read delay becomes very long. The value of the capacitance of the dynamic current source creates a trade-off between power and delay and if the capacitance is to be increased to achieve a competitive delay with other styles, its power consumption will become too high [4]. The Precharge Sense Amplifier (PCSA) STT-LUTs presented in [5] use MTJs in an array with single access transistors per MTJ, and hence relying on a separate decoder to provide the decoded MTJ select signals from primary LUT inputs. Separated Precharge Sensing Amplifier (SPCSA) is also presented in [5] as a more reliable style owing to higher voltage bias on the MTJs and a pre-amplification stage before the sense amplifier. However, the results in [6] show that the SPCSA adds too much area overhead in exchange for a faster operation. The Dynamic Dual Rail (DDR) STT-LUT style is presented in [6] and shown to be the most reliable and high-performance dynamic style for STT-LUTs. The DDR STT-LUT style shown in Fig. 1 is chosen as the representative of the state of the art dynamic STT-LUT style.

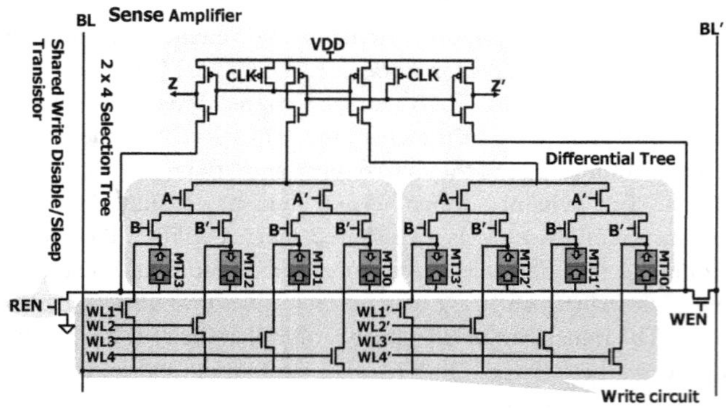

Figure 1. 2-input Dynamic Dual Rail (DDR) STT-LUT [6]

3 PROPOSED STATIC STT-LUT DESIGN

Fig. 2 shows the proposed Static STT-LUT style. By moving the multiplexer stage after the dynamic sense amplifier and using a static implementation of the multiplexer, the STT-LUT logic from input to output becomes static. In this scheme, each MTJ cell requires a unique dynamic latched sense amplifier. The sense amplifiers need to be enabled once at the beginning to have their outputs to be initialized according to the state of their MTJs. This needs to be done once on every power-on. The MTJs retain the content of the LUT in a non-volatile form. In this configuration, the MTJs are read only once and for the rest of the time in the active mode, the LUT read power and delay is determined by the static multiplexer. Moreover, by not reading from the MTJs repetitively as in the dynamic STT-LUT style, the stress is removed from the MTJs enhancing their life-time.

In fig. 3, The MTJ latch uses a pair of differentially programmed MTJs for non-volatile storage, a precharge sense amplifier for sensing the state of the MTJs, and three write driver scheme for parallel write to both MTJs simultaneously with each MTJ receiving full voltage swing, offering more write current. The Sense Enable (SE) signal must be low during the write operation, and the Write Enable (WE) signal must be low during the sensing operation. To avoid conflict of state between the precharge state of the sense amplifier (when SE=0) and the state of the write driver outputs in the write mode, the precharge path to VDD is disconnected via the PMOS driven by the WE signal.

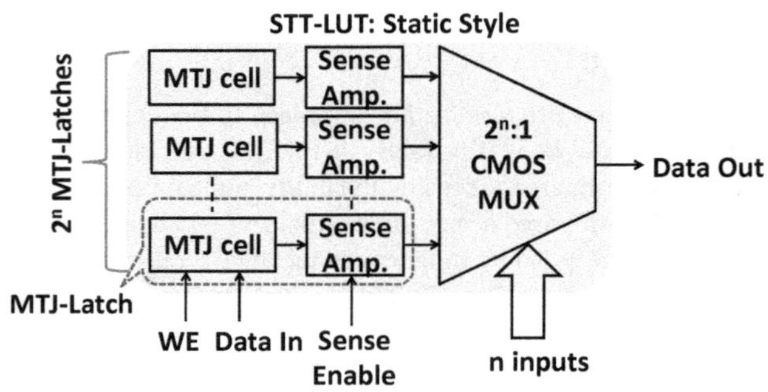

Figure 2. STT-LUT design concept: Proposed static style

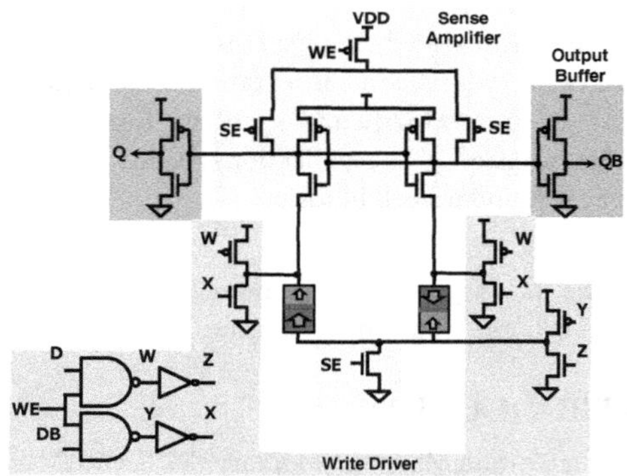

Figure 3. MTJ-Latch

The multiplexer of the LUT is a 2^n to 1 (2^n:1) CMOS multiplexer (MUX) implemented in a static style. The power and performance of the proposed STT-LUT are determined by the multiplexer, but the reliability of its configuration is determined by the sensing reliability of the STT-latch itself.

4 COMPARISONS

4.1 Simulation Setup

The designs are simulated in a predictive 10nm FinFET process [7] with a nominal supply voltage of 0.75V. To achieve a fair comparison, using the embedded Hspice optimizer, transistor sizes in both designs are optimized to minimize the Power-Delay-Product (PDP) under an equal constraint on the area which is 50% larger than the area of the bigger design when all transistors are minimum sized. Since the critical operation in programmable logic applications, where these LUTs are used, is the read mode, we simulated these designs in the read mode, where MTJs can be modeled as resistors. The MTJ resistance depends on the MTJ physical geometries and specifically the thickness of the insulator and the 2D cross-section area of the MTJ, and the voltage bias [8, 9]. The parallel state resistance (R_P) can be modeled as [8, 9]:

$$R_P = \frac{t_{ox}}{F\sqrt{\varphi}A} e^{(1.025 t_{ox}\sqrt{\varphi})} \quad (1)$$

where, F and φ are the tunneling conductivity and potential barrier height of the insulator, respectively. Considering a circular shape 2D area of radius r, area A is expressed as $A=\pi r^2$. The MTJ parallel resistance is estimated for the 16nm process.

The resistance difference between the two MTJ states is quantified by the Tunneling Magneto Resistance (TMR) parameter [10]:

$$TMR = \frac{R_{AP} - R_P}{R_P} \quad (2)$$

A higher difference between R_P and R_{AP} results in better read performance and reliability. Hence, for the STT-LUTs used in the reconfigurable logic application, higher TMR even if it is at the cost of higher written power and delay is desirable. Using crystalline MgO as the insulator, TMR up to 6 is reported [10]. In this study, we choose a TMR value of 4.

4.2 Results and Comparisons

4.2.1 Power, performance, and area comparisons

In this section, the proposed static STT-LUTs from 2 to 6 fan-ins are characterized in terms of delay, active power, leakage power, PDP, area and sensing failure rate; and compared with the DDR STT-LUT. Unlike DDR, in static STT-LUT, the active power consumption is dependent on the switching activities. Therefore, for obtaining a more realistic evaluation of power comparison, the power of the STT-LUT designs was measured at 100%, 50% and 25% output switching activities. Fig. 4(a) shows the active power comparison which is dependent on output switching activity and Fig. 4(b) shows the leakage power which is measured in idle condition. From LUT2 to LUT6, 50% to 43% of the total power is the leakage power and the rest is the switching power. The static LUTs show higher power consumption due to extra sense amplifies and hence more area. As shown in Fig. 4(a), the static LUTs active power in LUT2 is decreased by 25% and depending on fan-in and switching activity, the active power is increased by 1.5X to 10.9X from LUT3 or LUT6, as compared to the DDR LUTs. The Fig. 4(c) shows the delay comparison between static and DDR LUTs. The switching activity does not affect the delay of the circuit, and hence a single bar for static LUT is shown in Fig. 4(c). Compared to DDR, the delay of static LUT is improved by 14%, 17%, 26%, 15%, and 19% for LUT2, LUT3, LUT4, LUT5, and LUT6, respectively. The reduction in delay is because in the static LUT the MTJ sensing delay is not in the critical path. The delay in the normal mode of operation is through a static multiplexer on the path from the select input to the output (Fig. 4). The MTJ sensing delay is not critical as in the proposed design, the MTJ sensing occurs only once at the system power up. After the initial MTJ sensing on power-up, the MTJ states are held by the latched outputs of the sense amplifiers.

It is also noticeable that in the proposed design, the stress on MTJs is removed in run-time because once the sense amplifier has finished sensing, the bias one the MTJs is reduced to zero volts, and hence eliminating any stress on the MTJs and resulting in longer life for the thin insulators of the MTJs. Low delay overhead and its static path from select inputs to output, makes the proposed LUT ideal for integration with static CMOS logic gates in hybrid custom/programmable hardware applications, where a design is implemented partially in LUTs and in custom static CMOS. Fig. 4(d) shows the total area of the static and DDR LUT designs. Except in low fan-in LUTS (LUT2 and LUT3), the area of the DDR LUT is lower due to the sharing of the sense amplifier. Using multiplexer (MUX) in static LUT and dedicated sense-amplifiers, makes the area of high fan-in LUTs larger compared to the DDR design. Fig. 4(d) shows that for LUT2, the static LUT shows a decrease in the area of 8%. The area of the static LUT is increased by 36% and 19%, 24% and 14% in LUT3, LUT4, LUT5, and LUT6, respectively. Fig. 4(e) shows the measurement of PDP of static and DDR LUT styles. For static LUT with 25% switching activity, the PDP is decreased by 2X in LUT2 but increased by 1.64X, 2.31X, 4.90X, and 8.33X from LUT3 to LUT6.

4.2.2 Robustness Comparisons

There are two possible failures in the read mode: read sensing failure and read disturbance failure.

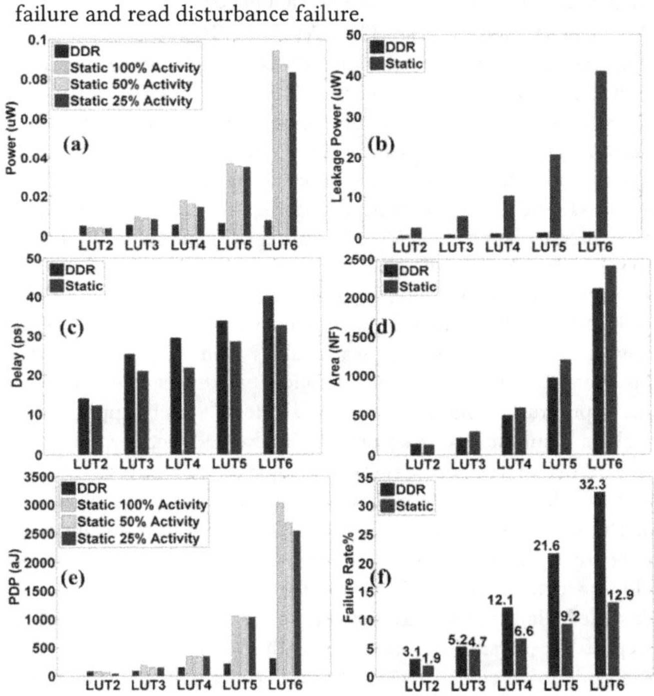

Figure 4. Performance comparisons: (a) Active Power (b) Leakage Power (c) Delay (d) Area (e) PDP (f) Failure rate

The read sensing failure is related to the incorrect sensing by the sense amplifier due to the presence of mismatch caused by CMOS and MTJ variations resulting in low sensing margin. The read disturbance failure is a sensing operation in which the sensing current passing through the MTJ exceeds the critical write current resulting in the flipping of the state of the MTJ (i.e. write operation). In STT-LUTs the read sensing failure is the dominant type because of the stack of transistors in the sensing path limits the read current. Hence, we focus on the read sensing failures. Random statistical variations are applied to MTJ parameters (t_{ox} and r) and threshold voltage (dvt) and read sensing failure rates of the STT-LUTs are measured. The standard deviations of t_{ox} and r variations are set at 10% of their nominal values. From Fig. 4(f), it is very noticeable that the failure rate of static LUT is much lower than the DDR style. The low failure rate in static LUTs is due to lower number of transistors in the MTJ selection paths, which leads to increase in current differentials between the two differential MTJs in the latches and hence increase in the sensing margin in the sense amplifier. The failure rate reductions by static LUTs range from 1.6X to more than 2.5X depending on fan-in. As expected, the failure rate generally increases by fan-in for both LUT styles. However, the failures rates of the proposed design are dramatically lower even for high fan-in LUTs. For hardware reconfigurable applications, near zero failure rate is expected of LUTs. The conventional DDR design is not acceptable for such applications due to its very high failure rates. The proposed design offers very low failure rates and with the proper area, optimization can achieve zero failure rate, which of critical importance for programmable logic applications.

5 INTEGRATION IN ASIC DESIGN

For ASIC applications where an STT-LUT might be needed, it is desirable to be able to specify the STT-LUT at the RTL level and have the supporting models and libraries necessary for the ASIC automated design flow tools be able to insert the STT-LUT in the synthesized netlist and in the physical design stage. The proposed static STT-LUT has a multiplexer part which can be expressed in a synthesizable format at RTL. The other component is MTJ-Latch that is an analog mixed signal circuit that needs to be designed in a full custom fashion and delivered as a hard macro type standard cell. Offering MTJ latch as new standard cell and STT-LUTs as new macros for ASIC flows enables and improves design productivity for a range of new applications that can benefit from such programmable non-volatile elements. Such applications include automotive, security, hardware acceleration of computing, and field programmable logic, to name a few.

The MTJ latch is an analog mixed signal circuit as shown in Fig. 5. Therefore, for introducing it as a cell to the ASIC flow, it needs to be treated as a hard macro cell. Hard macros are typically larger blocks such as memory blocks for which custom layout is designed. Hard macros are typically placed in the floor planning step of the physical design along with other layout blocks that each might have been separately produced using the ASIC flow. A single bit MTJ latch is too small to be defined as a hard macro, and it is desired to be able to use it within a block at the RTL synthesis step. Hence, we propose to design the MTJ latch as a standard cell following the rules of standard cell design in terms of the layout width and height, placement of VDD and VSS layers, and the boundary layer. Fig. 5 shows the layout of the MTJ latch in the standard cell format. The MTJs are fabricated above the cell and Metal 2 pins are placed for connection to the MTJ layers. This layout is done after optimizing the MTJ latch for write and sense operations in the Synopsys 32/28nm PDK for which layout technology files are available.

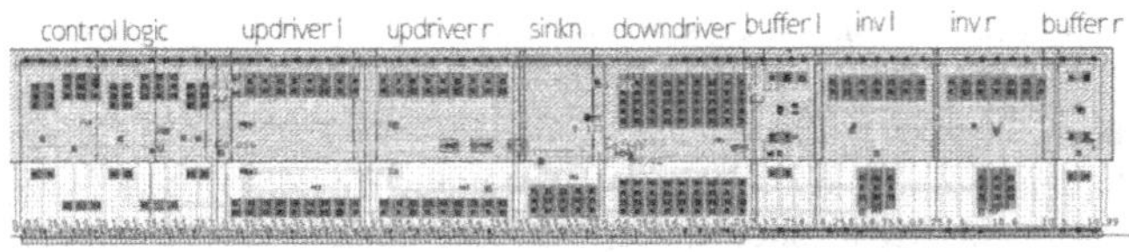

Figure 5. The layout of MTJ latch in standard cell format

6 CONCLUSION

In this paper, a static STT-LUT style is presented and compared with the state of the art dynamic counterpart. The existing STT-LUTs that are dynamic cannot be used in ASIC designs that utilize static logic style gates (standard cells) due to the static to dynamic logic interface issue. The proposed design offers lower MTJ sensing failure rate and better speed. Moreover, dues to its static operation, the proposed design is much easier to integrate with the static CMOS logic and automated ASIC design flows. The comprehensive analysis of the proposed design and its comparison against the DDR LUT design shows that the proposed design superior in all aspects, except area and power at high fan-in LUTs. Its low failure rate even at high fan-ins makes the proposed design a reliable candidate for commercial hardware reconfiguration applications, in which near zero failure rate is expected of LUTs. An approach to integrating the proposed STT-LUT to the ASIC flow is also presented in which the MTJ latch is introduced as a hard macro standard cell, and the multiplexer portion of the STT-LUT is represented in high-level synthesizable RTL code.

ACKNOWLEDGMENTS

This research is funded by the Defense Advanced Research Projects Agency (DARPA-AirForce, FA8650-15-C-7569).

REFERENCES

[1] M. Rasquinha, et al., "An energy efficient cache design using Spin Torque Transfer (STT) RAM," in *Low-Power Electronics and Design (ISLPED), ACM/IEEE International Symposium on*, 2010, pp. 389-394.

[2] D. Suzuki, *et al.*, "Fabrication of a nonvolatile lookup-table circuit chip using magneto/semiconductor-hybrid structure for an immediate-power-up field programmable gate array," *Symposium on VLSI Circuits*, 2009, pp. 80-81.

[3] W. Zhao, et al. "Spin-transfer torque (STT)-MRAM--based runtime reconfiguration FPGA circuit," *ACM Trans. Embed. Comput. Syst.*, vol. 9, pp. 1-16, 2009.

[4] M. W. Allam and M. I. Elmasry, "Dynamic current mode logic (DyCML): a new low-power high-performance logic style," *IEEE Journal of Solid-State Circuits*, vol. 36, pp. 550-558, 2001.

[5] E. Deng, et al. "Design Optimization and Analysis of Multicontext STT-MTJ-based; CMOS Logic Circuits," *IEEE Transactions on Nanotechnology*, vol. 14, pp. 169-177, 2015.

[6] Ali Attaran, et al. "Dynamic Single and Dual Rail Spin Transfer Torque Look Up Tables with Enhanced Robustness under CMOS and MTJ Process Variations," *ICCD*, 2016.

[7] PTM. (2016). Available: http://www.eas.asu.edu/~ptm

[8] Y. Zhang, *et al.*, "Compact Model of Subvolume MTJ and Its Design Application at Nanoscale Technology Nodes," *IEEE Transactions on Electron Devices*, vol. 62, pp. 2048-2055, 2015.

[9] Z. Xu, et al. "Compact modeling of STT-MTJ devices," *Solid-State Electronics*, vol. 102, pp. 76-81, 12// 2014.

[10] S. Ikeda, *et al.*, "A perpendicular-anisotropy CoFeB–MgO magnetic tunnel junction," *Nat Mater*, vol. 9, pp. 721-724, 09//print 2010.

Innovating at Cloud Speed for IoT, AI, and Semiconductor Design

David B. Pellerin
Amazon Web Services
Seattle, WA
dpelleri@amazon.com

ABSTRACT

Rapid adoption and production deployments of connected devices, coupled with AI-driven methods of advanced analytics, have led to an explosion in demand for non-traditional, more scalable computing and data management platforms. This increasing demand is being seen in the public cloud as well as in cloud-connected IoT edge devices.

AI is at the heart of many the newest, most advanced analytics and IoT applications, ranging from robotics and autonomous vehicles, to cloud-connected products such as Amazon Alexa, to smart factories and consumer-facing services in the financial and healthcare sectors.

This talk presents examples of such use-cases within Amazon, as well examples of how Amazon customers increasingly rely on AI coupled with IoT hardware and software stacks, and use cloud-based EDA to innovate faster, and at cloud scales.

CCS Concepts/ACM Classifiers

• Computer systems organization → Cloud computing
• Hardware → Methodologies for EDA

Author Keywords

Cloud; IoT; Electronic Design Automation; Artificial Intelligence

BIOGRAPHY

David Pellerin serves as Head of Worldwide Business Development for Infotech/Semiconductor at Amazon Web Services. Prior to joining AWS, Mr. Pellerin had a career in electronic design automation and hardware-accelerated reconfigurable computing. He has experience with digital logic simulation and optimization, high-level synthesis, grid and cluster computing, FPGA design, and embedded systems. He has published five Prentice Hall technical books including "Practical Design Using Programmable Logic", "VHDL Made Easy", and "Practical FPGA Programming in C".

REFERENCE

1. Amazon Web Services http://aws.amazon.com

GLSVLSI'18, May 23-25, 2018, Chicago, IL, USA.

ACM ISBN 978-1-4503-5724-1/18/05.
DOI: https://doi.org/10.1145/3194554.3200205

Mixed-Signal POp/J Computing with Nonvolatile Memories

Mohammad Reza Mahmoodi and Dmitri B. Strukov
ECE Department, UC Santa Barbara
Santa Barbara, CA 93106-5630 USA
{mrmahmoodi,dimastrukov}@ucsb.edu

ABSTRACT

The present-day revolution in deep learning was triggered not by any significant algorithm breakthrough, but by the use of more powerful GPU hardware [1]. Though this revolution has stimulated the development of even more powerful dedicated digital systems [2, 3], their speed and energy efficiency are still insufficient for ultrafast pattern classification and more ambitious cognitive tasks. The main reason is that the use of digital operations for the implementation of neuromorphic networks, with their high redundancy and noise/variability tolerance, is inherently unnatural. On the other hand, the network performance may be dramatically improved using mixed-signal integrated circuits, where the key inference-stage operation, the vector-by-matrix multiplication, is implemented on the physical level by utilization of the fundamental Ohm and Kirchhoff laws [4,5,6].

In our talk, we will discuss the recent progress of such analog and mixed-signal neuromorphic networks based on floating-gate memories and metal-oxide memristors. In our earlier work we have shown that a minor modification of a highly optimized embedded NOR flash memory [7-9] enabled a successful demonstration of the first medium-scale network for pattern classification [10, 11]. Remarkably for such a first attempt, still using the older, 180-nm technology, the experimentally measured time delay and energy dissipation (per one pattern classification) were below, respectively, 1 µs and 20 nJ [10], i.e. at least three orders of magnitude better than those reported for the best digital implementation of the same task, with a similar fidelity, using the 28-nm IBM's TrueNorth chip [12]. Experimental results for the chip-to-chip statistics, long-term drift, and temperature sensitivity showed no evident showstoppers on the way toward practical deep neuromorphic networks with unprecedented performance [11].

Another way to further scaling down the mixed-signal neuromorphic networks is provided by novel nonvolatile two-terminal devices - "memristors" [13], whose conductance G may be continuously adjusted by the application of short voltage pulses of higher (~1 V) amplitude. These devices have a very low chip footprint, which is determined only by the overlap area of the metallic electrodes, and may be scaled down below 10 nm without sacrificing their endurance, retention, and tuning accuracy. Our group has developed [13, 14] and then improved [15] a new technology of fabrication of these devices (so far, with the ~200 x 200 nm^2 area), sufficiently reproducible to demonstrate the first simple neuromorphic network providing pattern classification based on the most prospective, passive (0T1R) crossbar circuits. The passive memristive technology is also naturally suitable for the 3D integration, e.g. for monolithical back-end ntegration with CMOS circuits, and we have already made the first steps toward such 3D circuits [17, 18].

Our more recent work [19, 20] shows that the performance for vector-matrix multiplier based on nonvolatile memories may be further improved, potentially exceeding the Pop/J computing regime, using a better peripheral circuitry design and a more advanced memory technology. This, in turn, enables more than 100x advantage in speed and an almost 10,000x advantage in energy efficiency over the state-of-the-art purely digital circuits for classification of large, complex patterns (Table 1).

GLSVLSI '18, May 23–25, 2018, Chicago, IL, USA

ACM ISBN 978-1-4503-5724-1/18/05.https://doi.org/10.1145/3194554.3194612

KEYWORDS

Mixed-signal circuits, nonvolatile memories, floating-gate memories, artificial neural networks, metal-oxide memristor, vector-by-matrix multiplier

ACM Reference format:

M. Mahmoodi and D. B. Strukov. 2018. Mixed-signal POp/J Computing with Nonvolatile Memories. In *Proceedings of ACM Great Lake Symposium on VLSI (GLSVLSI), Chicago, Illinois, May 2018 (GLSVLSI'18)*, ACM, New York, NY, 2 pages. https://doi.org/10.1145/3194554.3194612

REFERENCES

[1] Alex Krizhevsky, Ilya Sutskever, and Geoffrey E. Hinton. 2017. ImageNet classification with deep convolutional neural networks. Commun. ACM 60, 6 (May 2017), 84-90. DOI: https://doi.org/10.1145/3065386

[2] Yu Hsin Chen, T. Krishna, J. Emer, and V. Sze. 2016. Eyeriss: An energy-efficient reconfigurable accelerator for deep convolutional neural networks. *IEEE International Solid-State Circuits Conference (ISSCC)*, San Francisco, CA, 262-263. DOI: 10.1109/ISSCC.2016.7418007

[3] Bert Moons, R. Uytterhoeven, W. Dehaene, and M. Verhelst, 2017. Envision: A 0.26-to-10 TOps/W subword-parallel dynamic-voltage-accuracy-frequency-scalable convolutional neural network processor in 28 nm FDSOI. *IEEE International Solid-State Circuits Conference (ISSCC)*, San Francisco, CA, 246-247. DOI: 10.1109/ISSCC.2017.7870353

AlexNet [1] single pattern classification:	Digital [2, 3]			Analog [10, 11, 16]					Visual cortex (estimates)
	GPU 28 nm (16 bit)	ASIC 65 nm (16 bit)	ASIC 28 nm (4 bit)	NOR ESF-1 180 nm (~6 bit)	NOR ESF-3 55 nm (~6 bit)	2D (1T1R) 55/200 nm memristor (~5 bit)	2D memristor 200 nm (~5 bit)	3D memristor 10 nm (~5 bit)	
time (s)	1.5×10^{-2}	2.9×10^{-2}	$\sim0.6\times10^{-2}$	$\sim1\times10^{-4}$	$\sim6\times10^{-5}$	$\sim3\times10^{-5}$	$\sim5\times10^{-6}$	$\sim10^{-6}$	$\sim3\times10^{-2}$
energy (J)	1.5×10^{-1}	0.8×10^{-2}	1×10^{-3}	$\sim3\times10^{-7}$	$\sim2\times10^{-7}$	$\sim2\times10^{-7}$	$\sim2\times10^{-8}$	$\sim10^{-8}$	$\sim5\times10^{-8}$

Table I. Time delay and energy consumption of the signal propagation through the convolutional (dominating) part of a large deep network [1], with $\sim0.65\times10^6$ neurons, at its various 2D implementations. The mixed-signal network estimates are based on the 55×55 = 3,025-step time-division multiplexing (TDM), natural for this particular network, the measured performance of our image classifier prototype [10], and the experimentally measured parameters of the ESF1 and ESF3 cells [7-9] and metal-oxide memristors [16].

[4] Carver A. Mead. 1989. *Analog VLSI and Neural Systems.* Addison Wesley.

[5] Dmitri Strukov, F. Merrikh-Bayat, M. Prezioso, X. Guo, B. Hoskins and K. Likharev. 2015. Memory technologies for neural networks. *IEEE International Memory Workshop (IMW),* Monterey, CA, 1-4. DOI: 10.1109/IMW.2015.7150295

[6] L. Ceze *et al.* 2016. Nanoelectronic neurocomputing: Status and prospects.*2016 74th Annual Device Research Conference (DRC),* Newark, DE, 1-2. DOI: 10.1109/DRC.2016.7548506

[7] Farnood Bayat, X. Guo, H. A. Om'mani, N. Do, K. K. Likharev and D. B. Strukov. 2015. Redesigning commercial floating-gate memory for analog computing applications. *IEEE International Symposium on Circuits and Systems (ISCAS),* Lisbon, 1921-1924. DOI: 10.1109/ISCAS.2015.7169048

[8] Farnood Bayat, X. Guo, M. Klachko, N. Do, K. Likharev and D. Strukov. 2016. Model-based high-precision tuning of NOR flash memory cells for analog computing applications. *74th Annual Device Research Conference (DRC),* Newark, DE, 1-2. DOI: 10.1109/DRC.2016.7548449

[9] Xinjie Guo *et al.* 2017. Temperature-insensitive analog vector-by-matrix multiplier based on 55-nm NOR flash memory cells. *IEEE Custom Integrated Circuits Conference (CICC),* Austin, TX, 1-4. DOI: 10.1109/CICC.2017.7993628

[10] Farnood Merrikh Bayat et al. 2018. High-performance mixed-signal neurocomputing with nanoscale floating-gate memory cells. *IEEE Transactions on Neural Networks and Learning Systems.* DOI: 10.1109/TNNLS.2017.2778940

[11] Xinjie Guo *et al.* 2017. Fast, energy-efficient, robust, and reproducible mixed-signal neuromorphic classifier based on embedded NOR flash memory technology. *IEEE International Electron Devices Meeting (IEDM),* San Francisco, CA, 6.5.1-6.5.4. DOI: 10.1109/IEDM.2017.8268341

[12] S. K. Esser, R. Appuswamy, P. Merolla, J. V. Arthur, and D. S. Modha, 2015. Backpropagation for energy-efficient neuromorphic computing. *Proc. NIPS'15,* Montreal, Canada, 1117-1125.

[13] Mirko Prezioso *et al.* 2015. Training and operation of an integrated neuromorphic network based on metal-oxide memristors. *Nature,* 521, (2015) pp.61-64.

[14] Miko Prezioso *et al.* 2015. Modeling and implementation of firing rate neuromorphic-network classifiers with bilayer Pt/Al_2O3/TiO_{2-x} /Pt memristors. *IEEE International Electron Devices Meeting (IEDM),* Washington, DC, 17.4.1-17.4.4. DOI: 10.1109/IEDM.2015.7409719.

[15] Farnood Merrikh Bayat, M. Prezioso, B. Chakrabarti, I. Kataeva, and D. Strukov. 2017. Memristor-based perceptron classifier: Increasing complexity and coping with imperfect hardware. *IEEE/ACM International Conference on Computer-Aided Design (ICCAD),* Irvine, CA, 549-554. DOI: 10.1109/ICCAD.2017.8203825

[16] Farnood Merrikh Bayat, M. Prezioso, B. Chakrabarti, I. Kataeva, and D. B. Strukov. 2017. Implementation of multilayer perceptron network with highly uniform passive memristive crossbar circuits. ArXiv:1611.04465, submitted to *Nature Comm.*, Nov. 2017.

[17] Gina Adam *et al.* 2017. 3-D memristor crossbars for analog and neuromorphic computing applications. *IEEE Transactions on Electron Devices,* vol. 64 (2017), 312-318.

[18] Bhaswar Chakrabarti *et al.* 2017. A multiply-add engine with monolithically integrated 3D memristor crossbar/CMOS hybrid circuit. *Nature Scientific Reports,* vol. 7 (2017). art. 42429.

[19] Mohammad Reza Mahmoodi and D.B. Strukov. 2018. An ultra-low energy internally analog, externally digital vector-matrix multiplier circuit based on NOR flash memory technology. *Proc. DAC'18,* San Francisco, C,A 1-6.

[20] Mohammad Bavandpour, M. R. Mahmoodi, and D. B. Strukov. 2017. Energy-efficient time-domain vector-by-matrix multiplier for neurocomputing and beyond. *ArXiv:1711.10673.*

Low Power and Trusted Machine Learning

Organizer:
Avesta Sasan
George Mason University
4400 University Dr. Fairfax, VA 22130
+1-703-993-1375 asasan@gmu.edu

Qi Zhu, Northwestern University
Yanzhi Wang, Syracuse University
Jae-Sun Soe, Arizona State University
Tinoosh Mohsenin, University of Maryland

Panel Summary or Overview

In this special discussion session on machine learning, the panel members discuss various issues related to building secure and low power neuromorphic systems. The security of neuromorphic systems may be discussed in term of the reliability of the model, trust in the model, and security of the underlying hardware. The low power aspect of neuromorphic computing systems may be discussed in terms of adaptation of new devices and technologies, the adaptation of new computational models, development of heterogeneous computing frameworks, or dedicated engines for processing neuromorphic models. This session may include discussion on the design space of such supporting hardware, exploring tradeoffs between power/energy, security, scalability, hardware area, performance, and accuracy.

Keywords: Machine learning, low power Neuromorphic Computing, Neuromorphic hardware acceleration, Neuromorphic hardware security.

CCS Concepts/ACM Classifiers

- Security and privacy~Trusted computing
- Computing methodologies~Neural networks
- Hardware~Hardware accelerators

GLSVLSI'18, May 23-25, 2018, Chicago, IL, USA..

ACM ISBN 978-1-4503-5724-1/18/05.
https://doi.org/10.1145/3194554.3216321

Securing the Systems of the Future - Techniques for a Shifting Attack Space

Organizer & Chair:
Ioannis Savidis
Drexel University
Philadelphia, PA 19104
+1-215-571-4584 isavidis@coe.drexel.edu

Swarup Bhunia
University of Florida

Gang Qu
University of Maryland

Matthew Casto
Air Force Research Lab.

Jeremy Muldavin
Office of the Deputy Assistant Secretary of Defense

Panel Overview

Known security vulnerabilities across the computing stack have caused significant concern, even requiring extensive countermeasures and system patches to address. As an example, the Meltdown and Spectre attacks, which were disclosed in January 2018, exploit architectural and circuit vulnerabilities to allow a malicious process access to secrets stored in the memory of another running program. Although software-based patches were distributed, true hardware solutions are only available through replacement.

With such high costs to protect data and patch systems after the fact, the question of securing against an unknown attack space becomes even more critical. The panel aims to address this critical issue, while introducing related considerations including 1) protecting resource constrained systems, 2) countermeasures against multifaceted attacks in the context of an unknown future vulnerability, and 3) trade-offs in circuit and system design to protect critical data and functions.

Keywords: hardware attacks and countermeasures; future attack vectors; countering unknown attacks.

CCS Concepts/ACM Classifiers

• Security in Hardware

GLSVLSI'18, May 23-25, 2018, Chicago, IL, USA.

ACM ISBN 978-1-4503-5724-1/18/05.
https://doi.org/10.1145/3194554.3216322

Author Index

NOTES

www.ingramcontent.com/pod-product-compliance
Lightning Source LLC
LaVergne TN
LVHW082020200926
848481LV00010B/2893
9781450361491